International Trade Law

International Trade Law

A Comprehensive Textbook

Volume Three:
Remedies

FIFTH EDITION

Raj Bhala

BRENNEISEN DISTINGUISHED PROFESSOR
THE UNIVERSITY OF KANSAS, SCHOOL OF LAW
LAWRENCE, KANSAS

SENIOR ADVISOR
DENTONS U.S. LL.P.
KANSAS CITY, MISSOURI

"ON POINT" COLUMNIST
BLOOMBERGQUINT
MUMBAI, INDIA

CAROLINA ACADEMIC PRESS
Durham, North Carolina

ISBN   978-1-5310-1436-0
eISBN 978-1-5310-1437-7
LCCN 2019937679

Carolina Academic Press
700 Kent Street
Durham, North Carolina 27701
Telephone (919) 489-7486
Fax (919) 493-5668
www.cap-press.com

Printed in the United States of America

For Shera and Her Generation,
That They Are Not Scourged by Poverty, Extremism, or a Clash of Civilizations,
But Rather Blessed by Peace through Sustainable Trade and Development.

And for the Glory of God.

Summary of Contents

Part and Chapter titles are for all four Volumes of *International Trade Law, Fifth Edition*. Please see individual Volumes for detailed Table of Contents.

Contents

About the Author

Raj is the inaugural Leo. S. Brenneisen Distinguished Professor (2017–present) at the University of Kansas School of Law, before which he held the inaugural Rice Distinguished Professorship (2003–2017). Both are university-level chairs, the highest accolade for scholarship and research in Kansas. He served as KU's Associate Dean for International and Comparative Law (2011–2017).

Raj is Senior Advisor to Dentons U.S. LLP, the world's largest law firm, focusing on international and comparative legal matters. He practiced law at the Federal Reserve Bank of New York, where he twice won the President's Award for Excellence, thanks to his service as a delegate to the United Nations Conference on International Trade Law, and to the world class New York Fed lawyers who mentored him.

A Harvard Law School (J.D.) graduate, *cum laude*, Raj completed Master's degrees at the London School of Economics, in Economics, and Oxford (Trinity College), in Management-Industrial Relations, as a Marshall Scholar. His undergraduate degree (in Economics), *summa cum laude*, is from Duke, where he was an Angier B. Duke Scholar and inducted into *Phi Beta Kappa*. He graduated from the University School-Milwaukee. At each institution, he was blessed with great teachers.

Raj is author of one of the world's leading textbooks, *International Trade Law: A Comprehensive Textbook*, the 1st edition of which was published in 1996, and which has been used at over 100 law schools around the world. He wrote the first treatise on GATT in nearly 50 years, *Modern GATT Law*, and the first major book on the *Trans Pacific Partnership*, *TPP Objectively*. His book *Trade, Development, and Social Justice* applies Catholic social teaching to GATT special and differential treatment rules.

Raj is the first non-Muslim American scholar to write a textbook on Islamic Law, *Understanding Islamic Law (Sharī'a)*, which is used for courses in law schools and for U.S. Special Operations Forces. His new book projects are *Business Law of Modern India* and *Principles of Law, Literature, and Rhetoric*. "On Point" is his column, which Bloomberg Quint (India) publishes (www.bloombergquint.com).

He has been privileged to live, work, and/or explore about 50 countries across six continents, including India and Pakistan, Israel and most of the Gulf Arab countries, and China and (the separate customs territory of) Taiwan. His abiding professional goal is to educate for peace, that is, to enhance human capital and legal capacity for economic development, political stability, and international understanding.

He is an avid distance runner and has completed three of the "World's Major Marathons" (Boston twice, Chicago, and New York), and is a (rather poor) student of Shakespeare and Hindi. His Wikipedia entry is https://en.wikipedia.org/wiki/Raj_Bhala.

Table of Abbreviations

AANZFTA	ASEAN-Australia-New Zealand Free Trade Agreement
AB	WTO Appellate Body
ABA	American Bar Association
ABI	Automated Broker Interface
ACDB	WTO Accession Commitments Data Base
ACFTU	All China Federation of Trade Unions
ACP	African, Caribbean, and Pacific
ACS	Automated Commercial System
ACTRAV	Bureau for Workers' Activities (ILO)
ACWL	Advisory Center on WTO Law
AD	Antidumping
AD Agreement	WTO Antidumping Agreement (Agreement on Implementation of Article VI of the General Agreement on Tariffs and Trade 1994)
ADB	Asian Development Bank
ADP	Automatic data processing
ADVANCE Democracy Act	2007 Advance Democratic Values, Address Non-democratic Countries and Enhance Democracy Act
AECA	Arms Export Control Act of 1976
AEO	Authorized Economic Operator
AFA	Adverse Facts Available
AfDB	African Development Bank
AFIP	*Administración Federal de Ingresos Públicos* (Argentina, Federal Public Revenue Administration)
AFL-CIO	American Federation of Labor-Congress of Industrial Organizations
AFTA	ASEAN Free Trade Area
Ag	Agriculture
AGOA	2000 African Growth and Opportunity Act

AGOA II	(included in 2002 Trade Act)
AGOA III	2004 African Growth and Opportunity Acceleration Act
Agriculture Agreement	WTO Agreement on Agriculture
AI (1st meaning)	Artificial Intelligence
AI (2nd meaning)	Avian Influenza
AID	U.S. Agency for International Development
AIG	American Insurance Group
AIIS	American Institute for International Steel
AIPAC	American Israel Public Affairs Committee
AIOC	Anglo Iranian Oil Company
ALBA	Bolivarian Alliance for the Peoples of our America
ALJ	Administrative Law Judge
ALOP	Appropriate Level Of Protection
ALT	Alternate (alternate proposed text)
AMA	American Medical Association
AmCham	American Chamber of Commerce
AMPS	Acrylamido tertiary butyl sulfonic acid
AMS (1st meaning)	Aggregate Measure of Support
AMS (2nd meaning)	Agriculture Marketing Services (USDA)
ANAD	National Association of Democratic Lawyers (Mexico)
ANZCERTA	Australia-New Zealand Closer Economic Relations Trade Agreement (CER)
AoA	WTO Agreement on Agriculture
AOG	All Other Goods
AOR	All Others Rate
APEC	Asia Pacific Economic Cooperation (forum)
APOC	Anglo Persian Oil Company
AR	Administrative Review
ARI	Additional (United States) Rules of Interpretation
ARP Act of 2000	2000 Agricultural Risk Protection Act
ARRA	2009 American Recovery and Reinvestment Act
ARS	Advance Ruling System
ASA	American Sugar Alliance

ASCM	WTO Agreement on Subsidies and Countervailing Measures (SCM Agreement)
ASEAN	Association of South East Asian Nations
ASP	American Selling Price
ATAP	1996 Agreement Concerning Certain Aspects of Trade in Agricultural Products (1985 U.S.-Israel FTA)
ATC	WTO Agreement on Textiles and Clothing
ATPA	1991 Andean Trade Preferences Act
ATPDEA	2002 Andean Trade Promotion and Drug Eradication Act
ATT	2014 U.N. Arms Trade Treaty
AU$	Australian Dollar
AUD	Australian Dollar
AUV	Average Unit Value
AV	Audio-Visual
AVE	*Ad Valorem* Equivalent
B&H	Brokerage and handling (costs)
B&O	Washington State Business and Occupation Tax Rate Reduction
BA	Bankers Acceptance
BBS	Bangladesh Bureau of Statistics
B.C.	British Columbia
BCI	Business Confidential Information
BCR	Blue Corner Rebate (Thailand)
BDC	Beneficiary Developing Country
BDS	Boycott, Divestment, and Sanctions
Berne Convention	1886 (1971) Berne Convention for the Protection of Literary and Artistic Works
BFA	Banana Framework Agreement
BIA	Best Information Available (Pre-Uruguay Round U.S. term for Facts Available)
BILA (ILAB)	Bureau of International Labor Affairs (U.S. DOL OTLA)
BIS (1st meaning)	Bank for International Settlements
BIS (2nd meaning)	Bureau of Industry and Security (U.S. DOC)
bis (3rd meaning)	second version (of a text), again, repeat
B.I.S.D.	Basic Instruments and Selected Documents

BIT	Bilateral Investment Treaty
BJP	Bharatiya Janata Party (India)
BNA	Bureau of National Affairs (International Trade Reporter and International Trade Daily)
BOJ	Bank of Japan
BOK	Bank of Korea
Bolero	Bills of Lading for Europe
BOP	Balance Of Payments
BOT	Balance Of Trade
BP	British Petroleum
bpd	barrels per day
Brexit	Withdrawal of the U.K. from EU
BRICS	Brazil, Russia, India, China, and South Africa
BSE (1st meaning)	Bombay Stock Exchange
BSE (2nd meaning)	Bovine Spongiform Encephalopathy (Mad Cow Disease)
BSSAC	Beneficiary Sub-Saharan African Country
BTA (1st meaning)	Bilateral Trade Agreement
BTA (2nd meaning)	2002 Bio-Terrorism Act (Public Health Security and Bioterrorism Preparedness and Response Act of 2000)
BTA (3rd meaning)	Border Tax Adjustment
BTD	May 2007 Bipartisan Trade Deal
C&F	cost and freight
CAA	1979 Clean Air Act
CA$	Canadian Dollar
CAD	Canadian Dollar
CAPES	*Centre d'Analyse des Politiques, Economiques et Sociales* (Burkina Faso)
CAFTA-DR	*Central American Free Trade Agreement—Dominican Republic*
CAN	Community of Andean Nations
CANACAR	*Camara Nacional del Autotransporte de Carga*
CAP (1st meaning)	Common Agricultural Policy (EU)
CAP (2nd meaning)	Carolina Academic Press
CASA	*Construcciones Aeronáuticas SA* (Spain)
CB	citizens band (radio)

CBD	U.N. Convention on Biological Diversity
CBE	Commander of the Most Excellent Order of the British Empire
CBERA	1983 Caribbean Basin Economic Recovery Act
CBI (1st meaning)	Caribbean Basin Initiative
CBI (2nd meaning)	Central Bank of Iran
CBO	Congressional Budget Office
CBOT	Chicago Board Of Trade
CBP	U.S. Customs and Border Protection ("U.S. Customs Service" until 1 March 2003)
CBSA	Canadian Border Services Agency
CC	Cooperative Country (Argentina)
CCB	U.S. Conference of Catholic Bishops
CCC (1st meaning)	U.S. Commodity Credit Corporation (USDA)
CCC (2nd meaning)	Customs Cooperation Council (renamed WCO in 1994)
CCC (3rd meaning)	Commerce Country Chart
CCFRS	Certain cold flat-rolled steel
CCI	Countervailing Currency Intervention
CCL	Commerce Control List
CCP	Chinese Communist Party (or CPC, Communist Party of China)
CCPA	U.S. Court of Customs and Patent Appeals (abolished 1982; transfer to Federal Circuit)
CCS	Carbon Capture and Storage
CDC (1st meaning)	U.S. Centers for Disease Control
CDC (2nd meaning)	Canadian Dairy Commission
CDC (3rd meaning)	Chilean Distortions Commission
CDM	Clean Development Mechanism
CDSOA	2000 Continued Dumping and Subsidy Offset Act (Byrd Amendment)
CEC	Commission for Environmental Cooperation (*NAFTA*)
CEMAC	*Communauté Économique et Monétaire de l'Afrique Centrale*
CEP	Constructed Export Price
CEPR	Center for Economic and Policy Research
CER	Australia-New Zealand Closer Economic Relations Trade Agreement (ANZCERTA)

CET	Common External Tariff
CETA	Comprehensive Economic and Trade Agreement
CFC	Controlled Foreign Corporation
CFIUS	Committee on Foreign Investment in the United States
C.F.R. (1st meaning)	Code of Federal Regulations
CFR (2nd meaning)	Council on Foreign Relations
CGE	Computable General Equilibrium
CH	Order of the Companions of Honor
CHIPS	Clearing House Interbank Payment System
CIA	U.S. Central Intelligence Agency
CIC	Citizenship and Immigration Service for Canada
CIF (c.i.f)	Cost, Insurance, and Freight
CIP	Chhattisgarh Industrial Program (India)
CISADA	2010 Comprehensive Iran Sanctions, Accountability, and Divestment Act
CISG	Convention on Contracts for the International Sale of Goods (U.N.)
CIT	U.S. Court of International Trade (New York, N.Y.)
CITA	U.S. Committee for Implementation of Textile Agreements
CITES	1973 Convention on International Trade in Endangered Species of Wild Fauna and Flora
CITT	Canadian International Trade Tribunal
CJ	Commodity Jurisdiction
CKD	Complete knock down
CME	Chicago Mercantile Exchange
CMI	*Comité Maritime International* (IMO)
CMM	Conservation Management Measures
CMO	Common Market Organization (EU)
CNCE	*Commission Nacional de Comercio Exterior* (Argentina)
CNL	Competitive Need Limitation
CNY	Chinese Yuan
COBRA	Consolidated Omnibus Budget and Reconciliation Act (multiple years)
COCOM	Coordinating Committee on Multilateral Export Controls
COGS	Cost of Goods Sold

COMESA	Common Market for Eastern and Southern Africa
CONNUM	Control Number
COP	Cost of Production
COS	Circumstances of Sale (dumping margin calculation adjustment)
COSCO	Chinese Ocean Shipping Company
CPA	Certified Public Accountant
CPC	U.N. Central Product Classification list
CPSC	U.S. Consumer Product Safety Commission
CPTPP	Comprehensive and Progressive Agreement for Trans Pacific Partnership (entered into force 30 December 2018, informally called TPP 11)
CQE	Certificate of Quota Eligibility
Crop Year 2001 Act	Crop Year 2001 Agricultural Economic Assistance Act
CRS	Congressional Research Service
CRTC	Canadian Radio-Television and Telecommunications Commission
CSCL	China Shipping Container Lines
CSI	Container Security Initiative
CSP (1st meaning)	Conferences of States Parties
CSP (2nd meaning)	Certificate of Supplementary Protection (CETA)
CSPV	Crystalline Silicon Photovoltaic cells, modules, laminates, and panels (solar panels)
CTC	Change in Tariff Classification
CTD	WTO Committee on Trade and Development
CTESS	WTO Committee on Trade and Environment in Special Session
CTH	Change in Tariff Heading
CTHA	WTO Chemical Tariff Harmonization Agreement
CTPA	United States — Colombia Trade Promotion Agreement
C-TPAT	Customs — Trade Partnership Against Terrorism
CTSH	Change in Tariff Sub-Heading
CU	Customs Union
Customs Valuation Agreement	WTO Agreement on Customs Valuation (Agreement on Implementation of Article VII of the General Agreement on Tariffs and Trade 1994)

CUFTA (CUSFTA)	Canada—United States FTA
CV	Constructed Value
CVA	Canadian Value Added
CVD (1st meaning)	Countervailing Duty
CVD (2nd meaning)	Chronic Venous Disorder
CVI	Chronic Venous Insufficiency
CVID	Complete, Verifiable, Irreversible Disarmament
CWP	Circular Welded carbon quality steel Pipe
CY	Calendar Year
DAHD	Department of Animal Husbandry, Dairying, and Fisheries (India)
DARPA	U.S. Defense Advance Research Project Agency
DCR	Domestic Content Requirement
DCS	Destination Control Statement
DDA	Doha Development Agenda
DDTC	U.S. Directorate of Defense Trade Controls (Department of State)
DeitY	Department of Electronics and Information Technology (MCIT, India)
DFQF	Duty Free, Quota Free
DGFT	Director General of Foreign Trade (part of Ministry of Commerce, India)
DHS	U.S. Department of Homeland Security
DJAI	*Declaración Jurada Anticipada de Importación* (Argentina, Advance Sworn Import Declaration)
DIEM	*Derechos de Importación Específicos Mínimos* (Argentina, Minimum Specific Import Duties)
DIFMER	Difference in Merchandise (dumping margin calculation adjustment)
DIY	Do It Yourself
DM (1st meaning)	Dumping Margin
DM (2nd meaning)	*Deutsche Marks*
DMA	Domestic Marketing Assessment
DMZ	De-Militarized Zone
DOC	U.S. Department of Commerce
DOD	U.S. Department of Defense

DOE	U.S. Department of Energy
DOJ	U.S. Department of Justice
DOL	U.S. Department of Labor
DOT	U.S. Department of Transportation
DP (DPW)	Dubai Ports
	Dubai Ports World
DPA	Deferred Prosecution Agreement
DPCIA	1990 Dolphin Protection Consumer Information Act
DPRK	Democratic People's Republic of Korea (North Korea)
DRAM	Dynamic Random-Access Memory
DRAMS	Dynamic Random-Access Memory Semiconductor
DSB	WTO Dispute Settlement Body
DSM	Dispute Settlement Mechanism
DSU	WTO Dispute Settlement Understanding (Understanding on Rules and Procedures Governing the Settlement of Disputes)
DVD	Digital Video Recording
EA	Environmental Assessment
EAA	1979 Export Administration Act
EAC (1st meaning)	East African Community
EAC (2nd meaning)	East Asian Community
EAC (3rd meaning)	Environmental Affairs Council (CAFTA-DR, KORUS)
EADS	European Aeronautic Defense and Space Company NV
EAR	Export Administration Regulations
EBA	Everything But Arms
EBOR	Electronic On Board Recorder
EC (1st meaning)	European Commission
EC (2nd meaning)	European Communities
ECA (1st meaning)	Economic Cooperation Agreement
ECA (2nd meaning)	Agreement between the Government of the United States of America and the Government of the Republic of Korea on Environmental Cooperation (KORUS)
ECA (3rd meaning)	Export Controls Act of 2018 (part of 2018 NDAA)
ECAT	Emergency Committee for Foreign Trade
ECB	European Central Bank

ECC (1st meaning)	Environmental Cooperation Commission (CAFTA-DR)
ECC (2nd meaning)	Extraordinary Challenge Committee (NAFTA)
ECCAS	Economic Community of Central African States
ECCN	Export Control Classification Number
ECE	Evaluation Committee of Experts (NAFTA)
ECFA	Economic Cooperation Framework Agreement
ECHR	European Court of Human Rights
ECJ	European Court of Justice
ECLAC	Economic Commission for Latin America and the Caribbean
E-Commerce	Electronic Commerce
ECU	European Currency Unit
ED	Economic Development Administration (of DOC)
EDBI	Export Development Bank of Iran
EDC	Export Development Corporation (Canada)
EDI	Electronic Data Interchange
EEC	European Economic Community
EEZ	Exclusive Economic Zone
EFSA	European Food Safety Authority
EFTA	European Free Trade Association
EGA	WTO Environmental Goods Agreement
EIB	European Investment Bank
EIF	Enhanced Integrated Framework (formerly "IF," or "Integrated Framework")
EIG	*équipement d'intérêt general* (France)
ELLIE	Electronic Licensing Entry System
ELS	Extra Long Staple (cotton)
EN	Explanatory Note
ENFORCE Act (TFTEA, TEA)	2015 Trade Facilitation and Trade Enforcement Act
EOBR	Electronic On Board Recorder
EP	Export Price
EPA (1st meaning)	Economic Partnership Agreement
EPA (2nd meaning)	U.S. Environmental Protection Agency
EPI	Economic Policy Institute
EPZ	Export Processing Zone

ERP	Effective Rate of Protection
E-SIGN	2000 Electronic Signatures in Global and National Commerce Act
ESCS	European Steel and Coal Community
ESL	English as a Second Language
ESP	Exporter's Sales Price (Pre-Uruguay Round U.S. term for Constructed Export Price)
ERP	Effective Rate of Protection
ET (EST)	Eastern Time (Eastern Standard Time)
ETA	Employment and Training Administration (of DOL)
ETI Act	2000 Extraterritorial Income Exclusion Act (U.S.)
ETP	Eastern Tropical Pacific (Ocean)
ETS	Emission Trading Scheme
EU	European Union
EV	Electric Vehicle
Ex-Im Bank	U.S. Export-Import Bank
FACT Act of 1990 (1990 Farm Bill)	1990 Food, Agriculture, Conservation and Trade Act
FAIR Act of 1996 (1996 Farm Bill)	1996 Federal Agricultural Improvement and Reform Act
FAO	Food and Agricultural Organization
FAS	Foreign Agricultural Service (of USDA)
FAST	Free And Secure Trade
FATA	Federally Administered Tribal Areas (Pakistan)
FATF	Financial Action Task Force
FBI	U.S. Federal Bureau of Investigation
FCIC	U.S. Federal Crop Insurance Corporation (USDA)
FCPA	1977 Foreign Corrupt Practices Act
FDI	Foreign Direct Investment
Federal Circuit	U.S. Court of Appeals for the Federal Circuit (Washington, D.C.)
Fed. Reg.	Federal Register
FERC	U.S. Federal Energy Regulatory Commission
FF	*French Francs*
FFTJ	Fittings, flanges, and tool joints

FICCI	Federation of Indian Chambers of Commerce and Industry
FIFA	*Fédération Internationale de Football Association*
FINCEN	U.S. Financial Crimes Enforcement Network (Department of the Treasury)
FIRRMA	Foreign Investment Risk Review Modernization Act of 2018 (part of 2018 NDAA)
FIT	Feed-in tariff
FMCSA	Federal Motor Carrier Safety Administration
FMSA	2011 Food Safety Modernization Act
FMV (1st meaning)	Foreign Market Value (Pre-Uruguay Round U.S. term for Normal Value)
FMV (2nd meaning)	Fair Market Value
FMVSS	Federal Motor Vehicle Safety Standards
FOA	Facts Otherwise Available
FOB (f.o.b.)	Free On Board
FOP	Factors of Production
FOREX	Foreign Exchange
FPA	Foreign Partnership Agreement
FPC	U.S. Federal Power Commission (predecessor of DOE)
FRAND	Fair, Reasonable, and Non-Discriminatory (terms)
FRCP	U.S. Federal Rules of Civil Procedure
FRCrimP	U.S. Federal Rules of Criminal Procedure
FRE	U.S. Federal Rules of Evidence
FRS	Fellowship of the Royal Society
FRSA	Fellowship of the Royal Society for the Encouragement of Arts, Manufactures, and Commerce
FSA (1st meaning)	U.S. Farm Services Agency
FSA (2nd meaning)	Food Safety Agency (EU)
FSC	Foreign Sales Corporation
FSRI Act of 2002 (2002 Farm Bill)	2002 Farm Security and Rural Investment Act
FTA	Free Trade Agreement
FTAA	Free Trade Area of the Americas
FTAAP	Free Trade Agreement of the Asia Pacific Region
FTC	Free Trade Commission (NAFTA)

FTZ (1st meaning)	Foreign Trade Zone
FTZ (2nd meaning)	Free Trade Zone
FY	Fiscal Year
FX	Foreign Exchange
G7	Group of Seven Industrialized Nations
G8	Group of Eight Industrialized Nations
G20	Group of Twenty Developed Nations
G33 (or G-33)	Group of 33 Developing Countries
G&A	General and Administrative expenses
GAAP	Generally Accepted Accounting Principles
GAIN	USDA FAS Global Agricultural Information Network
GAO	U.S. Government Accountability Office
GATB	General Agreement on Trade in Bananas (15 December 2009)
GATS	General Agreement on Trade in Services
GATT	General Agreement on Tariffs and Trade (GATT 1947 and/ or GATT 1994)
GATT 1947	General Agreement on Tariffs and Trade 1947 and all pertinent legal instruments (Protocols, Certifications, Accession Protocols, and Decisions) entered into under it before entry into force of the WTO Agreement (1 January 1995)
GATT 1994	GATT 1947 plus all pertinent legal instruments (1994 Uruguay Round Understandings and Marrakesh Protocol) effective with the WTO Agreement (1 January 1995)
GCC	Gulf Cooperation Council
GDP	Gross Domestic Product
GE	General Electric
GI	Geographical Indication
GILTI	Global Intangible Low-Taxed Income
GL	General License
GM	Genetically Modified, Genetic Modification
GMO	Genetically Modified Organism
GNH	Gross National Happiness
GNI	Gross National Income
GNP	Gross National Product
GOI	Government of India

GPA	Government Procurement Agreement (WTO Agreement on Government Procurement)
GPO	Government Pharmaceutical Organization (Thailand)
GPS	Global Positioning System
GPT	General Preferential Tariff
GRI	General Rules of Interpretation (of the HS)
GSM	General Sales Manager
GSP	Generalized System of Preferences (U.S.)
GSP+	Generalized System of Preferences Plus (EU)
GTA	Global Trade Atlas
GW	gigawatt
H5N1	Avian Flu (virus)
HCTC	Health Care Tax Credit
HDC	Holder in Due Course
HDI	U.N. Human Development Index
Helms-Burton Act	1996 Cuban Liberty and Democracy Solidarity (*Libertad*) Act
HFCS	High Fructose Corn Syrup
HHS	U.S. Department of Health and Human Services
HIPC	Highly Indebted Poor Country
HKMA	Hong Kong Monetary Authority
HM	Her (His) Majesty
HMG	Her (His) Majesty's Government
HNW	High Net Worth
HOEP	Hourly Ontario Energy Price
Homeland Security Act	2002 Homeland Security Act
HPAE	High Performing Asian Economy
HPAI	High Pathogenic Avian Influenza
HPC	High Performance Computer
HPNAI	High Pathogenic Notifiable Avian Influenza
HQ	Headquarters
HS	Harmonized System
HSBC	Hong Kong Shanghai Banking Corporation
HSBI	Highly Sensitive Business Information

HTS	Harmonized Tariff Schedule
HTSUS	Harmonized Tariff Schedule of the U.S.
HVAC	Heating, Ventilation, and Air Conditioning
IA (1st meaning)	Import Administration (U.S. DOC)
IA (2nd meaning)	Information Available
IA (3rd meaning)	Internal Advice
IADB	Inter-American Development Bank
IAEA	International Atomic Energy Agency
IBRD	International Bank for Reconstruction and Development (The World Bank)
IBT (1st meaning)	International Brotherhood of Teamsters
IBT (2nd meaning)	International Business Transactions
IC (1st meaning)	Indifference Curve
ICs	Indigenous Communities (Inuit and other indigenous communities)
ICAC	International Cotton Advisory Committee
ICC	International Chamber of Commerce
ICE	U.S. Immigration and Customs Enforcement
ICFTU	International Confederation of Free Trade Unions
ICJ	International Court of Justice
ICOR	Incremental Capital Output Ratio
ICS	Investment Court System
ICSID	International Center for the Settlement of Investment Disputes
ICTSD	International Center for Trade and Sustainable Development
IDB	Integrated Database
IDF	Israeli Defense Forces
IEC	Importer-Exporter Code (India)
IEEPA	1977 International Emergency Economic Powers Act
IFPRI	International Food Policy Research Institute
IFSA	2006 Iran Freedom Support Act
IFTA	1985 United States-Israel Free Trade Implementation Act
IGBA	1970 Illegal Gambling Business Act
IGG	*itinéraire à grand gabarit* (France)
IIPA	International Intellectual Property Alliance

ILAB (BILA)	Bureau of International Labor Affairs (U.S. DOL OTLA)
ILC	International Law Commission
ILO	International Labor Organization
ILRF	International Labor Rights Forum
ILSA	1996 Iran and Libya Sanctions Act (called ISA after IFSA)
IMC	Industrial Metal and Commodities
IMF	International Monetary Fund
IMF Articles	Articles of Agreement of the International Monetary Fund
IMO	International Maritime Organization (CMI)
IMTDC	iron mechanical transfer drive component
Incoterms	International Commercial Terms (ICC)
INR (1st meaning)	Initial Negotiating Right
INR (2nd meaning)	Indian *Rupee*
INS	U.S. Immigration and Naturalization Service (reorganized partly into ICE in March 2003)
IO	International Organization
IP	Intellectual Property
IPCC	Intergovernmental Panel on Climate Change
IPIC Treaty (Washington Treaty)	1989 Intellectual Property in Respect of Integrated Circuits
IPOA	International Plan Of Action
IPOA-IUU	International Plan Of Action to Prevent, Deter, and Eliminate Illegal, Unreported, and Unregulated Fishing (FAO)
IPPC	1952 International Plant Protection Convention
IPR (1st meaning)	Intellectual Property Right
IPR (2nd meaning)	International Priority Right
IRC	U.S. Internal Revenue Code
IRG (IRGC)	Iranian Revolutionary Guard Corps (Islamic Revolutionary Guard Corps)
IRISL	Islamic Republic of Iran Shipping Lines
IRQ	Individual Reference Quantity
IRS	U.S. Internal Revenue Service
ISA	Iran Sanctions Act of 1996, as amended, *i.e.*, Iran Sanctions Act of 2012 (formerly ILSA)
ISDS	Investor-State Dispute Settlement

ISIL	Islamic State in the Levant (ISIS)
ISIS	Islamic State in Shams (ISIL)
ISO	International Organization for Standardization
ISTC	International Sugar Trade Coalition
IT	Information Technology
ITA (1st meaning)	WTO Information Technology Agreement (1996)
ITA (2nd meaning)	U.S. International Trade Administration (DOC)
ITA II	Information Technology Agreement (2015)
ITAR	International Traffic in Arms Regulations
ITC	U.S. International Trade Commission
ITDS	International Trade Data System (electronic single window for import-export data)
ITO	International Trade Organization
ITO Charter (Havana Charter)	Charter for an International Trade Organization
ITRD	International Trade Reporter Decisions
ITSR	Iranian Transactions and Sanctions Regulations (31 C.F.R. Part 560)
ITT	ITT Corporation
ITT NV	ITT Night Vision
ITU	International Telecommunications Union
IUU	illegal, unreported and unregulated
JADE Act	2008 Tom Lantos Block Burmese JADE (Junta's Anti-Democratic Efforts) Act
J&K	Jammu and Kashmir (Indian-Administered Kashmir)
JFTC	Japan Fair Trade Commission
JIA	Japanese Investigative Authority
JNPT	Jawaharlal Nehru Port Terminals (Mumbai, India)
JPC	Joint Planning Committee (India)
JV	Joint Venture
KCBT	Kansas City Board of Trade
KDB	Korea Development Bank
KEXIM	Export-Import Bank of Korea
KFC	Kentucky Fried Chicken
KfW	*Kreditanstalt für Wiederaufbau* (Germany, Credit Agency for Reconstruction)

kg	kilogram
KMA	Kubota Manufacturing of America
KMT	*Kuomintang*
KORUS	Korea — United States Free Trade Agreement
KPPI	*Komite Pengamanan Perdagangan Indonesia* (competent international trade authority)
KSA	Kingdom of Saudi Arabia
KU	University of Kansas
kWh	Kilowatt hour
L/C	Letter of Credit
LAN	Local Area Network
LAP	Labor Action Plan (Colombia TPA)
LCA	Large Civil Aircraft
LCD	Liquid Crystal Display
LDBDC	Least Developed Beneficiary Developing Country
LDC (1st meaning)	Least Developed Country
LDC (2nd meaning)	Less Developed Country (includes developing and least developed countries)
LDC (3rd meaning)	Local distribution company
LGBTQ+	Lesbian, Gay, Bisexual, Transgender, Queer (or Questioning), and others
LLDC	Landlocked Developing Country
LNG	Liquefied Natural Gas
LNPP	Large Newspaper Printing Press
LOC	Line of Control (Kashmir)
LPAI	Low Pathogenic Avian Influenza
LPMO	Livestock Products Marketing Organization (Korea)
LOT	Level of Trade (dumping margin calculation adjustment)
LPNAI	Low Pathogenic Notifiable Avian Influenza
LPMO	Livestock Product Marketing Organization (Korea)
LRW	Large Residential Washer
LTFV	Less Than Fair Value
LWR	Light-Walled Rectangular pipe and tube
LWS	Laminated Woven Sacks
MAD	Mutually Assured Destruction

MAFF	Ministry of Agriculture, Forestry, and Fisheries (Korea)
MAI	Multilateral Agreement on Investment
MAP	Monitoring and Action Plan
Marrakesh Protocol	Marrakesh Protocol to GATT 1994
MAS	Monetary Authority of Singapore
MBB	*Messerschmitt-Bölkow-Blohm GmbH* (Germany)
MCIT	Ministry of Communications and Information Technology (India)
MCL	Munitions Control List
MCTL	Military Critical Technologies List
MDG	Millennium Development Goal
MDL	Military Demarcation Line (DMZ)
MEA	Multilateral Environmental Agreement
MEFTA	Middle East Free Trade Agreement
MENA	Middle East North Africa
METI	Ministry of Economy, Trade, and Industry (Japan, formerly MITI)
MFA	Multi-Fiber Arrangement (1974-2004)
MFN	Most Favored Nation
MHI	Mitsubishi Heavy Industries, Ltd.
MHT	*Matra Hautes Technologies* (France)
MIIT	Ministry of Industry and Information Technology (China)
MITI	Ministry of International Trade and Industry (Japan)
MMA	Minimum Market Access (quota)
MMBtu	Million British Thermal Unit
MMPA	1972 Marine Mammal Protection Act
MNC	Multinational Corporation
MNE	Multinational Enterprise
MOCI	Ministry of Commerce and Industry (India, Saudi Arabia)
MOCIE	Ministry of Commerce, Industry, and Energy (Korea)
MOFAT	Ministry of Foreign Affairs and Trade (Korea)
MOFCOM	Ministry of Commerce (China)
MOI (MOI Test)	Market Oriented Industry
MOTIE	Ministry of Trade, Industry, and Energy (Korea)
MOU	Memorandum of Understanding

MP	Member of Parliament
MPC	Marginal Propensity to Consume
MPF	Merchandise Processing Fee
MPS	Marginal Propensity to Save
MRA	Mutual Recognition Agreement
MRE	Meals Ready to Eat
MRL	Maximum Residue Level
MRM	Marine Resource Management
MRS	Marginal Rate of Substitution
MRT	Marginal Rate of Transformation
MSF	*Médecins Sans Frontières*
MSME	Micro, Small, and Medium Sized Enterprise
MSP	Ministry of Social Protection (Colombia)
MST	Minimum Standard of Treatment
mt	metric ton
MTA (1st meaning)	Multilateral Trade Agreement
MTA (2nd meaning)	Metropolitan Transit Authority (New York City)
MTB	Miscellaneous Trade Bill (multiple years)
MTN	Multilateral Trade Negotiation
MTO	Multilateral Trade Organization
MTOP	Millions of Theoretical Operations per Second
MVTO	Motor Vehicles Tariff Order (Canada)
MY	Marketing Year
NAD Bank	North American Development Bank (NAFTA)
NAAEC	North American Agreement on Environmental Cooperation (NAFTA Environmental Side Agreement)
NAALC	North American Agreement on Labor Cooperation (NAFTA Labor Side Agreement)
NAFTA	North American Free Trade Agreement (NAFTA 1.0 and/or NAFTA 2.0)
NAFTA 1.0	North American Free Trade Agreement (original FTA that entered into force 1 January 1994)
NAFTA 2.0	North American Free Trade Agreement (revised FTA based on August 2017-September 2018 renegotiations, formally entitled USMCA, signed 30 November 2018)
NAI	Notifiable Avian Influenza

NAM (1st meaning)	U.S. National Association of Manufacturers
NAM (2nd meaning)	Non-Aligned Movement
NAMA	Non-Agricultural Market Access
NAO	National Administrative Office (NAFTA)
NATO	North Atlantic Treaty Organization
NASA	U.S. National Aeronautics and Space Administration
NBP	National Bank of Pakistan
NCC (1st meaning)	National Chicken Council
NCC (2nd meaning)	Non-Cooperative Country (Argentina)
NCM	Non-Conforming Measure
N.C.M.	*Nomenclatura Común MERCOSUR* (*MERCOSUR* Common Nomenclature)
NCTO	National Council of Textile Organizations
NDA	National Democratic Alliance (India)
NDAA	U.S. National Defense Authorization Act (annual policy bill for DOD and national security since 1962)
NDRC	National Development and Reform Commission (China)
NEI	National Export Initiative
NEP	New Economic Policy (Malaysia)
NFIDC	Net Food Importing Developing Country
NFTC	National Foreign Trade Council
NG	Natural Gas
NGR	Negotiating Group on Rules (WTO Doha Round)
NHI	National Health Insurance (Korea)
NHT	National Hand Tools Corporation
NIC	Newly Industrialized Country
NICO	Naftiran Intertrade Company
NIEO	New International Economic Order
NIOC	National Iranian Oil Company
NITC	National Iranian Tanker Company
NJPA	National Juice Products Association
NLC	National Labor Committee (U.S.)
NLCF	National Livestock Cooperatives Federation
NLD	National League for Democracy (Burma)
NMDC	National Minerals Development Corporation (India)

NME	Non-Market Economy
NMFS	U.S. National Marine Fisheries Service (DOC)
NNSA	U.S. National Nuclear Security Administration (DOE)
NOAA	U.S. National Oceanic and Atmospheric Administration (DOC)
NO_x	Nitrogen oxides
NPA	Non-Prosecution Agreement
NPC	National People's Congress (China)
NPF	Non-Privileged Foreign status
NPL	Non-Performing Loan
NPT	1968 Nuclear Non-Proliferation Treaty
NRA	National Rifle Association
NRC	U.S. Nuclear Regulatory Commission
NRI	Non-Resident Indian
NRL	Nuclear Referral List
NSA	U.S. National Security Agency
NSC	National Securities Commission (Argentina)
NSG	Nuclear Suppliers Group
NSIBR	National Security Industrial Base Regulations
NSM	Jawaharlal Nehru National Solar Mission (India)
NSPD	National Security Presidential Directive
NSS	WTO SPS National Notification System
NTA	National Textile Association (U.S.)
NTB	Non-Tariff Barrier
NTC	National Trade Council (United States)
NTE (1st meaning)	National Trade Estimate Report on Foreign Trade Barriers (USTR)
NTE (NTE sector) (2nd meaning)	Non-Traditional Export (sector)
NTM	Non-Tariff Measure
NTR	Normal Trade Relations
NV	Normal Value
NVOCC	Non-Vessel Operating Common Carrier
NWFP	North West Frontier Province (Pakistan) (Khyber Pakhtunkhwa)

N.Y. Fed (FRBNY)	Federal Reserve Bank of New York
NYU	New York University
NZ$	New Zealand Dollar
NZD	New Zealand Dollar
OAS	Organization of American States
OBE	Officer of the Most Excellent Order of the British Empire
OBRA	Omnibus Budget and Reconciliation Act (multiple years)
OCD	Ordinary Customs Duties
OCR	Out of Cycle Review
OCTG	Oil Country Tubular Goods
ODA	Official Development Assistance
ODC	Other Duties and Charges
OECD	Organization for Economic Cooperation and Development
OED	Oxford English Dictionary
OEE	U.S. Office of Export Enforcement (BIS)
OEM	Original Equipment Manufacturer
OFAC	U.S. Office of Foreign Assets Control (Department of the Treasury)
OIC	Organization of Islamic Conference
OIE	World Organization for Animal Health (*Office International des Epizooties*)
OMA	Orderly Marketing Arrangement
OMO	Open Market Operation
OOIDA	Owner-Operator Independent Drivers Association
OPA	Ontario Power Authority (Canada)
OPEC	Organization of Petroleum Exporting Countries
OPIC	U.S. Overseas Private Investment Association (U.S. International Development Finance Corporation)
OPZ	Outward Processing Zone (KORUS)
OTC	Over the Counter
OTCA	1988 Omnibus Trade and Competitiveness Act
OTCG	Oil Country Tubular Good
OTDS	Overall Trade distorting Domestic Support
OTEXA	Office of Textiles and Apparel (U.S. DOC)
OTLA	Office of Trade and Labor Affairs (in DOL)

OTR	Off-The-Road
PAP	People's Action Party (Singapore)
PAPS	Pre-Arrival Processing System
Paris Agreement	December 2015 Paris Climate Accord, or Paris Climate Agreement, under UNFCCC
Paris Convention	1883 Paris Convention for the Protection of Industrial Property
PASA	Pre-Authorization Safety Audit
PBC (PBOC)	People's Bank of China
PBS	Price Band System
PBUH	Peace Be Upon Him
PC	Personal Computer
PCA	Post-Clearance Audit
PCAST	President's Council of Advisors on Science and Technology (United States)
PCB	Printed Circuit Board
PCG (PCG fibers)	Polyvinyl alcohol (PVA), cellulose, and glass fibers
PDV	Present Discounted Value
PEO	Permanent Exclusion Order
PF	Privileged Foreign status
PFC	Priority Foreign Country
PhRMA	Pharmaceutical Manufacturers of America
PLO	Palestine Liberation Organization
PM	Prime Minister
PNTR	Permanent Normal Trade Relations
PNW	Pine wood nematode
POI	Period of Investigation
POR	Period of Review
POW-MIA	Prisoner of War — Missing in Action
PP	Purchase Price (Pre-Uruguay Round U.S. term for Export Price)
PPA	Power Purchase Agreement
PPF	Production Possibilities Frontier
PPM (1st meaning)	Parts Per Million
PPM (2nd meaning)	Process and Production Method

PPP	Purchasing Power Parity
PPS	Probability-Proportional to Size
PRC	People's Republic of China
PROEX	*Programa de Financiamento às Exportações* (Brazil)
PRO-IP Act	2008 Prioritizing Resources and Organization for Intellectual Property Act
PRS	Price Range System
PSA	Port of Singapore Authority
PSH	Public Stock Holding
PSI	Pre-Shipment Inspection
PSI Agreement	WTO Agreement on Pre-Shipment Inspection
PSRO	Product Specific Rule of Origin
PTA (1st meaning)	Preferential Trade Agreement, or Preferential Trading Arrangement
PTA (2nd meaning)	Payable through account
PTO	U.S. Patent and Trademark Office
PV	Photovoltaic
PVA (PVA fibers)	Polyvinyl alcohol fibers
PVC	Polyvinyl chloride
QE	Quantitative Easing
QIZ	Qualified Industrial Zone
QR	Quantitative Restriction
R&D	Research and Development
R&TD	Research and Technological Development measures
RAM	Recently Acceded Member (of WTO)
RBI	Reserve Bank of India
RCC	United States—Canada Regulatory Cooperation Council
RCEP	Regional Comprehensive Economic Partnership
RCMC	Registration-cum-Membership Certificate (India)
rDNA	recombinant deoxyribonucleic acid
REER	Real Effective Exchange Rate
RFMO	Regional Fisheries Management Organization
RMA (1st meaning)	Risk Management Association (U.S.)
RMA (2nd meaning)	Risk Management Authorization
RMB	*Ren min bi* ("people's money," the Chinese currency)

RMG	Ready Made Garment
RMI (DRM)	Rights Management Information (Digital Rights Management)
ROA	Return on Assets
Rome Convention	1964 Rome Convention for the Protection of Performer, Producers of Phonograms and Broadcasting Organizations
ROO	Rule Of Origin
ROW	Rest Of World
ROZ	Reconstruction Opportunity Zone
RPG	Rocket-propelled grenade
RPL	Relative Price Line
RPT	Reasonable Period of Time
Rs.	*Rupee*
RTA	Regional Trade Agreement
RTAA	Re-employment Trade Adjustment Assistance
RVC	Regional Value Content
S&D	Special and Differential
SAA	Statement of Administrative Action
SAARC	South Asia Association for Regional Cooperation
SACU	Southern African Customs Union
SADC	Southern African Development Community
SAFE Port Act	2006 Security and Accountability for Every Port Act
SAFTA	South Asia Free Trade Agreement
SAGIA	Saudi Arabian General Investment Authority
SAMA	Saudi Arabian Monetary Authority
SAPTA	South Asia Preferential Trading Arrangement
SAR	Special Administrative Region
SARS	Sudden Acute Respiratory Syndrome
SCGP	Supplier Credit Guarantee Program
SCM	Subsidies and Countervailing Measures
SCM Agreement	WTO Agreement on Subsidies and Countervailing Measures (ASCM)
SCP	Sugar Containing Product
SDF	Steel Development Fund (India)
SDG	United Nations Sustainable Development Goal

SDN	Specially Designated National
SE	*Secretaría de Economía* (Secretariat of Economy, Mexico, formerly *SECOFI*)
SEBI	Securities and Exchange Bureau of India
SEC	U.S. Securities and Exchange Commission
SECOFI	Secretary of Commerce and Industrial Development (*Secretario de Comercio y Fomento Industrial*), *i.e.*, Ministry of Commerce and Industrial Development (Mexico, renamed SE in December 2000)
SEI	Strategic Emerging Industry (SEI Catalogue — China)
SEIU	Service Employees International Union
SENTRI	Secure Electronic Network for Travelers Rapid Inspection
SEP	Standard Essential Patent
SEZ	Special Economic Zone
SFO	Serious Fraud Office
SG&A	Selling, General, and Administrative expenses
SG$	Singapore Dollar
SGD	Singapore Dollar
SCI	*Secretaría de Comercio Interior* (Argentina, Secretary of Domestic Trade)
SIE	State Invested Enterprise
SIFI	Systemically Important Financial Institution
SIFMA	Securities Industry and Financial Markets Association
SIL	Special Import License (India)
SIM	*Sistema Informático MARIA* (Argentina, AFIP electronic portal information system)
SIMA	Special Import Measures Act (Canada)
SKD	Semi-knock down
SMART	Secondary Materials and Recycled Textiles Association
SME (1st meaning)	Small and Medium Sized Enterprise
SME (2nd meaning)	Square Meter Equivalent
SMS	Supply Management System (Canada)
SNAP	Supplemental Nutritional Assistance Program
SNAP-R	Simplified Network Application Process — Redesign
S.O.	Statutory Order (India)

SOCB	State Owned Commercial Bank (China)
SOE	State Owned Enterprise
SOF	Special Operations Forces
SOGI	Sexual Orientation and Gender Identity
SPD	Solar Power Developer
SPI (1st meaning)	Seven Pillars Institute for Global Finance and Ethics
SPI (2nd meaning)	Special Program Indicator
SPS (1st meaning)	Sanitary and Phytosanitary
SPS (2nd meaning)	Single Payment Scheme
SPS Agreement	WTO Agreement on Sanitary and Phytosanitary Measures
SPV	Special Purpose Vehicle
SRAM	Static Random Access Memory (chip)
SRO	Special Remission Order (Canada)
SSA	Sub-Saharan Africa
SSAC	Sub-Saharan African Country
SSF Guidelines	Voluntary Guidelines for Securing Sustainable Small-Scale Fisheries in the Context of Food Security and Poverty Eradication (FAO)
SSG	Special Safeguard
SSM	Special Safeguard Mechanism
SSN	Resolutions of the National Insurance Supervisory Authority (Argentina)
STDF	WTO Standards and Trade Development Facility
STE	State Trading Enterprise
STO	Special Trade Obligation
SUV	Sport utility vehicle
SVE	Small, Vulnerable Economy
SWAT	Strategic Worker Assistance and Training Initiative
SWIFT	Society for Worldwide Interbank Financial Telecommunications
T&A	Textiles and Apparel
TAA (1st meaning)	Trade Adjustment Assistance
TAA (2nd meaning)	Trade Agreements Act of 1974, as amended
TAAEA	2011 Trade Adjustment Assistance Extension Act
TAA Reform Act	2002 Trade Adjustment Assistance Reform Act

TABC (TBC)	Trans-Atlantic Business Council (also abbreviated TBC)
TABD	Trans-Atlantic Business Dialogue
TAC	Total Allowable Catch
TB	tuberculosis
TBT	Technical Barriers to Trade
TBT Agreement	WTO Agreement on Technical Barriers to Trade
TCOM	Total Cost of Manufacturing
TCP (1st meaning)	Third Country Price
TCP (2nd meaning)	*El Tratado de Comercio entre los Pueblos*, ("Trade Treaty for the Peoples")
TCS	Tata Consulting Services
TDA	2000 Trade and Development Act
TDEA	1983 Trade and Development Enhancement Act
TDI	Trade Defense Instrument
TDIC	Tourism Development and Investment Company (Abu Dhabi, UAE)
TEA (1st meaning)	Trade Expansion Act of 1962, as amended
TEA (2nd meaning)	Trade Enforcement Act of 2015, as amended (same as TFTEA)
TED	Turtle Excluder Device
TEO	Temporary Exclusion Order
ter	third version (of a text)
TEU	Twenty Foot Equivalent Unit
TFA	WTO Agreement on Trade Facilitation (Trade Facilitation Agreement)
TFAF	Trade Facilitation Agreement Facility
TFP	Total Factor Productivity
TFR	Total Fertility Rate
TGAAA	2009 Trade and Globalization Adjustment Assistance Act
TIEA	Tax Information Exchange Agreement
TIFA	Trade and Investment Framework Agreement
TIPI	Trade and Investment Partnership Initiative
TIPT	Trade and Investment Partnership Initiative
TISA (TiSA, TSA)	WTO Trade in Services Agreement
TN	NAFTA business visa

TNC	WTO Trade Negotiations Committee
TOT	Terms of Trade
TPA (1st meaning)	Trade Promotion Agreement
TPA (2nd meaning)	Trade Promotion Authority (Fast Track)
TPBI	Thai Plastic Bags Industries
TPC	Technology Partnerships Canada
TPEA	2015 Trade Preferences Extension Act
TPF	United States—India Trade Policy Forum
TPL	Tariff Preference Level
TPM (1st meaning)	Trigger Price Mechanism
TPM (2nd meaning)	Technological Protection Measure
TPP	Trans Pacific Partnership
TPP 11	CPTPP (entered into force 30 December 2018)
TRA	Trade Readjustment Allowance
TRB	Tapered roller bearing
TRIMs	Trade Related Investment Measures
TRIMs Agreement	WTO Agreement on Trade Related Investment Measures
TRIPs	Trade Related Aspects of Intellectual Property Rights
TRIPs Agreement	WTO Agreement on Trade Related Aspects of Intellectual Property Rights
TRO	Temporary Restraining Order
TRQ	Tariff Rate Quota
TSA	U.S. Transportation Security Administration
TSUS	Tariff Schedule of the United States (predecessor to HTSUS)
T-TIP	Trans-Atlantic Trade and Investment Partnership
TV	Television
TVE	Town and Village Enterprise
TVPA	2000 Trafficking Victims Protection Act
TWEA	1917 Trading With the Enemy Act
TWN	Third World Network
UAW	United Auto Workers
UBC	University of British Columbia
U.C.C.	Uniform Commercial Code
UCLA	University of California at Los Angeles

UCP (1st meaning)	Uniform Customs and Practices
UCP (2nd meaning)	Unified Cargo Processing
UE	United Electrical, Radio and Machine Workers of America
UES	United Engineering Steel (U.K.)
UETA	1999 Uniform Electronic Transactions Act
UF	Ultra-filtered (milk)
UF_6	Uranium Hexafluoride
UI	Unemployment Insurance
UIEGA	2006 Unlawful Internet Gambling Enforcement Act
U.K.	United Kingdom
U.K.CGC	U.K. Carbon & Graphite Company
UMR	Usual Marketing Requirement (FAO)
UMTS	Universal Mobile Telecommunications System
UN	United Nations
UNCAC	United Nations Convention Against Corruption
UNCITRAL	United Nations Commission on International Trade Law
UNCLOS	United Nations Conference on the Law of the Sea Treaty
UNCTAD	United Nations Commission on Trade and Development
UNEP	United Nations Environmental Program
UNFCCC	United Nations Framework Convention on Climate Change
UNICA	Brazilian Sugarcane Industry Association
UNITA	National Union for the Total Independence of Angola
UNODA	United Nations Office of Disarmament Affairs
UPA	United Progressive Alliance (India)
UPOV	International Union for the Protection of New Varieties of Plants, referring to 1961 International Convention for the Protection of New Varieties of Plants (revised 1972, 1978, 1991)
UPS	United Parcel Service
UPU	Universal Postal Union
URAA	1994 Uruguay Round Agreements Act
U.S.	United States
USAPEEC	USA Poultry and Egg Export Council
U.S.C.	United States Code
USCCAN	United States Code Congressional and Administrative News

USMCA	United States-Mexico-Canada Agreement (revised FTA based on August 2017-September 2018 renegotiations, informally called NAFTA 2.0, signed 30 November 2018)
USML	United States Munitions List
USP	United States Price (Pre-Uruguay Round U.S. term encompassing both Purchase Price and Exporter's Sales Price)
U.S.S.R.	Union of Soviet Socialist Republics
USTR	U.S. Trade Representative
USW (1st meaning)	United Steel, Paper and Forestry, Rubber, Manufacturing, Energy, Allied Industrial and Service Workers International Union
USW (2nd meaning)	United Steel Workers of America
VAT	Value Added Tax
VC	Venture Capital
VCR	Video Cassette Recorder
VEO	Violent Extremist Organization
VER	Voluntary Export Restraint
VEU	Validated End User
Vienna Convention	1969 Vienna Convention on the Law of Treaties
VOC	Volatile organic compound
VRA	Voluntary Restraint Agreement
VW	Volkswagen AG
W120	WTO services classification list (based on CPC)
WA	1995 Wassenaar Arrangement
WAML	Wassenaar Arrangement Munitions List
WCO	World Customs Organization (formerly CCC until 1994)
WHO	World Health Organization
WIPO	World Intellectual Property Organization
WMD	Weapon of Mass Destruction
WMO	World Meteorological Association
WTO	World Trade Organization
WTO Agreement	Agreement Establishing the World Trade Organization (including all 4 Annexes)
WWF	World Wildlife Fund
XITIC	Xiamen International Trade and Industrial Company

ZAC	*zone d'aménagemement concertée* (France)
ZTE	Zhongxing Telecommunications Corp.
1916 Act	Antidumping Act of 1916, as amended (repealed)
1930 Act	Tariff Act of 1930, as amended
1934 Act	Reciprocal Trade Agreements Act of 1934
1934 FTZ Act	Foreign Trade Zones Act of 1934, as amended
1974 Act	Trade Act of 1974, as amended
1978 Act	Customs Procedural Reform and Implementation Act
1979 Act	Trade Agreements Act of 1979
1984 Act	International Trade and Investment Act of 1984 (Trade and Tariff Act of 1984)
1988 Act	United States—Canada Free Trade Implementation Act
1990 Act	Customs and Trade Act of 1990
1993 NAFTA Implementation Act	North American Free Trade Implementation Act of 1993
2002 Act	Trade Act of 2002
2003 Act	Burmese Freedom and Democracy Act of 2003
2007 Act	Implementing Recommendations of the 9/11 Commission Act of 2007
2010 Act	Omnibus Trade Act of 2010
3D	Three dimensional
3PLs	Third Party Logistics Providers
3Ts (3T Issues)	Taiwan, Tiananmen, and Tibet
4Ts (4T Issues)	Taiwan, Tiananmen, Tibet, and The Party (CCP)

Part One

Remedies against "Unfair" Trade: Antidumping Law

Chapter 1

Political Economy of Dumping and AD Duties[1]

I. Summary Table of Trade Remedy Criteria

Of several remedies in International Trade Law, one is AD duties imposed on subject merchandise that is dumped and causes injury or threat thereof. Overall, remedies are divided into two broad categories: remedies against unfair foreign competition; and remedies against fair foreign competition. The remedies in these categories are mutually exclusive. That is, it is not permissible to impose simultaneously an unfair trade and a fair trade remedy against the same subject merchandise. That is logical enough, because either that merchandise is, or is not, fairly traded.

There is no theoretical definition of what constitutes "unfairness" in international trade. Rather, there is a list, which developed historically, with concomitant remedies to protect producers in an importing country of a like domestic product (that is, one like the subject merchandise). On that list is dumping, the receipt of certain types of subsidies, and the infringement of valid IPRs. Thus, to combat dumping, AD duties may be imposed. To offset illegal subsidies, CVDs may be imposed. And, to combat IP piracy of patents, trademarks, copyrights, and semi-conductor mask works, exclusion orders and seizures may be used.

"Fair" competition from foreign imports exists when a foreign producer-exporter does nothing wrong. It does not dump its merchandise in an importing country. Its merchandise does not receive or benefit from an unlawful subsidy. Its merchandise respects all relevant IPRs. Rather, the foreign producer-exporter performs well in making and shipping its product overseas, so well its merchandise surges into an importing country. That surge causes or threatens injury to domestic producers of a like or directly competitive product. To protect these producers, a general safeguard remedy, or Escape Clause, exists. Further, depending on the country from which the subject merchandise is shipped, or the nature of that merchandise, a special safeguard remedy may be applicable.

---

1. Documents References:
    (1) *Havana (ITO) Charter* Article 34
    (2) GATT Article VI
    (3) WTO *Antidumping Agreement*

In this and the next several Chapters, all these remedies are explored. Their historical, economic, and political justifications are reviewed and debated, and their legal criteria explained and analyzed. Grasping similarities and differences in those criteria matters. Table 1-1 provides a synopsis. Note the following points about the Table:

(1) Importance of CBP

With respect to the involvement of U.S. Federal department or administrative agencies, for all remedies, the CBP, which is housed in the DHS, is responsible for enforcing a remedy. Accordingly, if the DOC determines an AD or CVD remedy is justified, then it issues an order to CBP. If the President accepts a recommendation of the ITC to impose a safeguard, or the recommendation of the USTR to pursue a unilateral trade remedy, then the President instructs the CBP as to the order.

In all instances, the order will identify precisely the imports against which the remedy is being taken, using the 4-, 6-. or 8-digit product classification codes in the HTSUS. The order also will specify what penalty is to be imposed, such as a tariff, quota, TRQ, or ban. Any such penalty is in addition to, not in lieu of, the normal MFN rate applied to the imports.

(2) Term "Subject Merchandise"

Note also the term "subject merchandise," which is used in the context of AD-CVD investigations, may also be used for any trade remedy. This term, called in the American statutes the "class or kind of merchandise subject to investigation" in the pre-Uruguay Round era, refers to the imported products that are alleged to violate a particular trade rule, and against which a remedy is imposed if the allegation is proven.

Finally, note that subject merchandise is grown (if it is an agricultural commodity), mined (if it is a raw material), or manufactured (if it is an industrial good) by a producer-exporter in a foreign country, and imported by an importer in the U.S. In the Documentary Sale, these parties are called the Seller-Exporter and Buyer-Importer, respectively. They are the respondents in a trade remedy case. Conversely, in most investigations, the petitioner is a producer in the U.S. That producer may be an American firm or group of workers, or a foreign firm operating in the U.S. (*e.g.*, via a subsidiary). That is, trade remedies are available regardless of the ultimate nationality of the firm, as long as that firm operates in the importing country.

Any trade remedy order issued by CBP is against subject merchandise of the respondents. But, it is typically the buyer-importer that has assets in the U.S. Consequently, it is likely to be held liable for the remedy. Whether it can pass the cost of the remedy up the commercial chain to its producer-exporter depends on the nature of their business relationship.

(3) TAA

TAA is not technically a trade remedy. No action is taken against foreign imports. Rather, imports continue to enter the U.S. under normal MFN duties. However, from the perspective of workers, firms, or communities that qualify and receive it, TAA is a remedy.

TAA is included in the Table for this reason, and also for comparative purposes. It is useful to compare and contrast how "easy" or "hard" TAA is to obtain vis-à-vis conventional trade remedies.

(4) Continuum of Injury Standards

"Material" injury, used in AD-CVD and Section 406 cases, is an easier standard to meet than "serious" injury, used in Section 201 cases. The higher injury test for the latter remedy is justified by the fact that this remedy is against fairly traded import competition. In contrast, AD-CVD actions are against dumped or illegally subsidized merchandise, respectively, and such behavior is deemed unfair. Query what justifies the Section 406 standard?

(5) Continuum of Causation Standards

The easiest causation standard to meet is "by reason of," which applies in AD-CVD cases. The hardest is "substantial" cause, which applies in Section 201 cases. Again, that makes sense, because of the distinction between fair and unfair foreign competition. A Section 201 action is against fairly traded imports, so it ought to be harder to take action against them than against dumped or illegally subsidized products. "Significant" cause, the standard in Section 406, is in between these two standards. Towards the "easy" end of the spectrum, and easier than "significant," is "contributes importantly," which is used for TAA.

This Table should be consulted frequently in conjunction with the study of trade remedies, and ultimately, its contents should become second nature.

II. GATT Article VI and Definition of "Dumping"

Article VI:1 of GATT states dumping occurs when a producer-exporter sells its product in a foreign market at less than normal value. In general, this practice occurs when the price at which the company exports its product is lower than the price it charges in its home country. The difference between the foreign and domestic market prices is commonly referred to as the "dumping margin." Thus, a generic formula for calculation of the dumping margin is:

Table 1-1. Summary of Trade Remedy Criteria

Trade Remedy Criteria	Trade Adjustment Assistance (TAA)	Antidumping (AD)	Countervailing Duties (CVD)	General Safeguard	Special Safeguard: §406 against Communist Countries	Special Safeguard: §421 against China	Unilateral Retaliation: §301	National Security: §232	IPRs: §337
GATT-WTO Reference	None.	GATT Article VI, WTO Antidumping Agreement	GATT Articles VI, XVI, WTO SCM Agreement	GATT Article XIX, WTO Agreement on Safeguards	None	December 2001 WTO Accession Protocol of China	None	GATT Article XXI	WTO TRIPs Agreement
Key U.S. Law	Trade Expansion Act of 1962, as amended	Tariff Act of 1930, as amended	Tariff Act of 1930, as amended	Trade Act of 1974, as amended	Trade Act of 1974, as amended	Trade Act of 1974, as amended	Trade Act of 1974, as amended	Trade Expansion Act of 1962, as amended	Tariff Act of 1930, as amended
Statutory Citation (19 U.S.C. §§)		1673 et seq.	1671 et seq.	2252 et seq.	2436	2451, 2451a, and 2451b		1862	
Bifurcated Procedure? (1 or 2 U.S. Government Agencies Involved?)	No, 1. DOL for Certification of Eligibility. But, relevant State-level Department for distribution of benefits	Yes, 2. DOC for Dumping Margin Determination, and ITC for Injury Determination	Yes, 2. DOC for Subsidization Determination. ITC for Injury determination	No, 1. ITC	No, 1. ITC	No, 1. ITC and USTR	No, 1. USTR	No, 1. Secretary of Commerce, in consultation with Secretary of Defense	No, 1. ITC
Bifurcated Determinations? (Preliminary and Final, or just Final Determination?)	No, 1. DOL conducts single inquiry concerning Certification for Eligibility	Yes, 2. DOC conducts Preliminary and Final Dumping Margin Determinations	Yes, 2. DOC conducts Preliminary and Final Dumping Margin Determinations	No, 1. ITC conducts single inquiry	No, 1. ITC conducts single inquiry.	No, 1. ITC conducts single inquiry (except in "critical circumstances")	No, 1. USTR conducts single inquiry	No, 1. Secretary of Commerce conducts a single inquiry	Yes, 2 are possible, with TEO and PEO

		ITC does Preliminary and Final Injury Determinations	ITC does Preliminary and Final Injury Determinations	ITC does Preliminary and Final Injury Determinations	USTR opines on relief			
Presidential Discretion? (*Presidential Involvement in Determining whether to Impose Remedy, and Fashioning Remedy?*)	None — TAA is automatic if criteria are met	None — AD duties are imposed automatically if criteria are met.	None — CVDs are imposed automatically if criteria are met.	Yes — President can accept, reject, or modify affirmative ITC decision. President cannot overturn negative decision	Yes — President can accept, reject, or modify affirmative ITC decision. President cannot overturn negative decision	Yes — President can accept, reject, or modify affirmative ITC decision. President cannot overturn negative decision.	Yes	Yes	
Judicial Review of Substantive Results? (*As distinct from procedural due process issues, possibility of appeal of substantive determinations and remedies to CIT, Federal Circuit, and Supreme Court?*)	Yes	Yes	Yes	No, Political Question Doctrine bars review	No, Political Question Doctrine bars review	No. Political Question Doctrine bars review	No, Political Question Doctrine bars review	No, Political Question Doctrine bars review	Yes

(continued)

Table 1-1. Summary of Trade Remedy Criteria (*continued*)

Trade Remedy → Criteria	Trade Adjustment Assistance (TAA)	Antidumping (AD)	Countervailing Duties (CVD)	General Safeguard	Special Safeguard: §406 against Communist Countries	Special Safeguard: §421 against China	Unilateral Retaliation: §301	National Security: §232	IPRs: §337
Scope[2] (Type of Domestic Product that May Be Protected by Remedy Imposed on Subject Merchandise?)	Like domestic product	Like domestic product	Like domestic product	Like or directly competitive product	Like or directly competitive product	Like or directly competitive product	Depends on case	Not relevant Rather, issue is imports of a particular product and its derivatives	Imports infringing on valid U.S. patent, trademark, or copyright
Quantitative Standing Test for Filing Petition?	No	Yes 25% and 50% Tests	Yes Same as AD	No Petitioner may be a firm, group of workers, union, or trade association that is "representative of an industry"	No Same as §201	No Same as §201	No	No	No
Typical POI?		Preferably not less than 1 year for dumping margin Preferably not less than 3 years for injury	Preferably not less than 1 year for dumping margin Preferably not less than 3 years for injury	Preferably 3 years	Preferably 3 years	No set POI	No set POI	No set POI	No set POI

	Dumping, that is, non-*de minimis* difference between Normal Value (or one of its proxies) and Export Price (or Constructed Export Price)	Receipt of Prohibited (Export or Import Substitution) Subsidy or Actionable Subsidy	Surge of fairly competing imports.	"Rapid" increase of fairly competing imports from a Communist country	Same as §406	Unfair foreign government act, policy, or practice	Threat to national security from imports	Infringing on valid U.S. patent, trademark, or copyright
Key Criteria Causing Injury? (Key Independent Variable?)								
Injury Standard?	"Material" injury or threat thereof ch. 10	"Material" injury or threat thereof Note WTO subsidies cases use Adverse Effects Test (Injury, Serious Prejudice, or Nullification or Impairment)	"Serious" injury or threat thereof	"Material" injury or threat thereof	Same as §406		None Issue is whether imports threaten or impair national security by virtue of quantities of, or circumstances in which, they enter U.S.	

2. Observe that under U.S. International Trade Law, the scope of no trade remedy is as broad as the formulation in GATT Article III:2, second sentence, and *Ad Article III*, which is "like, directly competitive, or substitutable products."

Table 1-1. Summary of Trade Remedy Criteria (*continued*)

Trade Remedy Criteria	Trade Adjustment Assistance (TAA)	Antidumping (AD)	Countervailing Duties (CVD)	General Safeguard	Special Safeguard: §406 against Communist Countries	Special Safeguard: §421 against China	Unilateral Retaliation: §301	National Security: §232	IPRs: §337
Factors to Determine Injury?		(1) Volume of dumped merchandise, (2) Price effects of dumping (price suppression or price depression), and (3) Any Other Relevant Economic Factors (*e.g.*, idling of productive facilities, inability to operate at a reasonable level of profit, job losses, inability to generate financing to modernize, declines in sales,	Same as AD		(1) Volume of subject merchandise, (2) Price effects of subject merchandise on price of domestic like product, (3) Impact of subject merchandise on domestic producers of like product, and (4) Disruptive pricing practices or efforts to manage trade patterns unfairly Factors for (3) include Other Relevant	Same as §406		(1) Domestic production for projected national defense needs, (2) Capacity of domestic industry to meet projected national defense needs, (3) Existing and expected availability of resources to essential to national defense, (4) Growth demands of domestic industry, (5) Quantity, availability, character, and	

production, wages, or increases in inventories)	Economic Factors (*e.g.,* idling of productive facilities, inability to operate at a reasonable level of profit, job losses, inability to generate financing to modernize, declines in sales, production, wages, or increases in inventories)	use of imports in relation to domestic industry supplying national defense needs, (6) Impact of foreign competition on economic welfare of domestic industry, (7) Displacing of domestic products by excessive imports, resulting in serious effects (*e.g.,* substantial job loss, revenue decline, loss of skills, or decrease in investment).

(*continued*)

Table 1-1. Summary of Trade Remedy Criteria (*continued*)

Trade Remedy → Criteria	Trade Adjustment Assistance (TAA)	Antidumping (AD)	Countervailing Duties (CVD)	General Safeguard	Special Safeguard: §406 against Communist Countries	Special Safeguard: §421 against China	Unilateral Retaliation: §301	National Security: §232	IPRs: §337
Causation Standard?	"Contribute importantly"	"By reason of," meaning a plausible direct causal link, subject to identification of other causes and non-attribution (*i.e.*, effect of causes other than subject merchandise is not wrongly attributed to that merchandise), and subject to *Bratsk* Replacement-Benefit Test in commodity product cases	"By reason of," meaning a plausible direct causal link, subject to identification of other causes and non-attribution (*i.e.*, effect of causes other than subject merchandise is not wrongly attributed to that merchandise)	"Substantial," meaning a direct causal link between subject merchandise and material injury, and such no cause is more important than such cause.	"Significant," meaning a direct causal link between subject merchandise and material injury, *i.e.*, at least an important cause, but need not be greater than or equal to another cause or other causes	Same as §406		Whether imports are in such quantities or under such circumstances "as to" impair or threaten national security	
Additional Relevant Criteria?		Unlike EU and many other WTO Members, no Public Interest Test	Unlike EU and many other WTO Members, no Public Interest Test	Must have a credible plan for positive adjustment if relief is granted	No adjustment plan necessary	No adjustment plan necessary			
Particular Remedy?	Income support, expenses for retraining,	AD duty equal to dumping margin	CVD equal to net subsidization rate	Depends on case	Depends on case	Same as §406, but must try consulting for 60 days with China	Depends on case	Adjustment of level of imports, such as by	TEO, PEO, seizure, and/or destruction of

ch.
18-20

		Unlike EU and many other WTO Members, no Lesser Duty Rule (Under its December 2016 tightening of its TDIs, the EU agreed this Rule is waived, so AD duties apply to the entire dumping margin, if distortions in raw material and energy prices are at least 27% of the COP of the final product (e.g., steel), and the distortion in at least 1 raw material price is 7%.)	Unlike EU and many other WTO Members, no Lesser Duty Rule (The same December 2016 EU restriction on the Lesser Duty Rule for AD duties applies to CVDs. In both contexts, imposition of a full remedial duty depends on the Public Interest Test, which includes an account of the interests of importers.)	Could be tariff, QR (e.g., quota, import licensing), TRQ, entry into international negotiations, or some combination thereof, but not VRA with respect to a WTO Member, because of WTO *Agreement on Safeguards* Article 11:1(b)	Could be tariff, QR (e.g., quota, import licensing), TRQ, or VRA, entry into international negotiations, or some combination thereof	Note §422 Trade Diversion Remedy, for cases in which a safeguard applied by a third country causes or threatens to cause significant diversions of trade into domestic market of U.S.		imposition of fees, quotas, or ban	infringing goods
	jobs search, and relocating, health care insurance credit.								
Duration of Remedy?		5 years, renewable following an affirmative Sunset Review	5 years, renewable following an affirmative Sunset Review	4 years, renewable for one 4-year period	5 years, renewable for one 3-year period	Depends on case	Depends on case	Depends on case	Depends on case
Statutory Remedy Still Operative? (Has Remedy Sunset in U.S.C.?)	Yes	Yes	Yes	Yes	Yes	No, Sunset as of 31 December 2013	Yes	Yes	Yes

Dumping Margin   =   Normal Value – Export Price

where:

Normal Value   =   domestic price, *i.e.*, the price the exporter charges in its home market.

Export Price   =   foreign price, *i.e.*, the price the exporter charges in the importing country in which dumping is alleged.

If the Dumping Margin is: positive, then dumping occurs, if zero or negative, then no dumping occurs.

In certain instances, Constructed Export Price is used as a proxy for Export Price. Often, dumping margins are expressed in percentage terms, namely, as a percentage of the Export Price. The formula then becomes:

$$\text{Dumping Margin} = \frac{\text{Normal Value} - \text{Export Price}}{\text{Export Price}} \times 100$$

Expressing a dumping margin in percentage terms is useful, because it facilitates comparison among different cases. How is it known, for example, whether Jordan is more egregious in its alleged dumping of hummus than Turkey? If the margin for Turkey is 138.6%, and Jordan 68.2%, then the question is answerable. The percentage expression also is useful for a rule of thumb it furnishes. Generally, the DOC is unlikely to be interested in pursuing a case unless the percentage dumping margin is at least in the high double digits. Exactly how high is hard to say, but an 18.9% as opposed to 88.9% margin signals a weaker case.

Dumping is primarily a matter of cross-border price discrimination. Consumers of allegedly dumped merchandise in the importing country are segregated from consumers of the like product in the exporter's home country. There is no leakage of dumped goods back to the home market. Consequently, the exporter is able to reap high profits from home market sales. Such profits may subsidize lower profits earned, or losses incurred, from selling the product at a cheap price in the importing country.

Why does GATT Article VI condemn dumping as a harmful unfair trade practice? If one likes hummus (as does your Textbook author!), then why not enjoy it at cheaper dumped prices? The answer is dumping is not viewed with consumers of dumped goods in mind. Domestic producers of a like product are the group whose interests are exalted:

Firms [that dump their products in an overseas market] are unfairly able to obtain or hold market share which they otherwise would not enjoy by selling their products at below fair market value. This can occur either because of the lack of a competitive market in the domestic market of the dumping industry (for example due to restrictive business practices) or the firm is simply structurally able to absorb losses. Domestic firms in the importing country must either lower their prices to match the dumped price, or attempt to maintain their prices while conceding market share to imports. The results of dumping in the U.S. have been serious. There has been wholesale withdrawal of U.S. companies from industries experiencing dumping, such as the semiconductor and steel industries. This has resulted in a concomitant loss of tens of thousands of jobs.[3]

However, not all dumping is evil. Article VI condemns only injurious dumping.

That is, dumping is actionable only if it causes material injury to an industry in the importing country. More technically, if dumping causes, or threatens to cause, material injury to an established industry in the importing country that competes with the exporter, or if it materially retards the establishment of an industry in the importing country that would compete with the exporter, then it is actionable. Pursuant to Articles VI:1(a) and VI:2, an AD duty may be imposed by authorities in the domestic market. The amount of the duty is calibrated to offset the dumping margin. The result is—supposedly—a leveling of the competitive playing field.

III. Early GATT Cases

Are the foundations of AD law incongruous with economic theory? Generally, international trade negotiators have not questioned whether dumping should be actionable. During the *Havana Charter* negotiations, no delegates challenged the right of a government to impose AD duties. Indeed, until the Kennedy Round, negotiators paid little attention to AD law.

Before the Kennedy Round there was only one AD case—in 1955, involving Sweden's imposition of AD duties on Italian exports of nylon stockings—that resulted in a GATT Panel Report. (*See Swedish Anti-dumping Duties*, GATT B.I.S.D. (3rd Supp.) at 81 (1955) (adopted 26 February 1955).) The Panel found Sweden's AD regulations did not violate Article VI, and in any event the dispute was resolved when Sweden revoked the regulations. The Report failed to yield any clear-cut interpretations of Article VI. However, the Report is significant in two respects.

First, it establishes a clear rule on the determination of "normal value." The Report authorized a fixed price system whereby the price in the importing country of an allegedly dumped good is compared not to the actual price of that good in the exporter's home country, but rather some minimum price. Under the system, that minimum price must be equal to or lower than the price in the home market of the lowest cost producer of the good. No relationship between the minimum price and either costs of production or actual sales prices is required. Second, the Report

---

3. Michael H. Stein, *The Uruguay Round and the Trade Laws: Antidumping, Countervailing Duties, Common Provisions,* I THE COMMERCE DEPARTMENT SPEAKS ON INTERNATIONAL TRADE AND INVESTMENT 881 (1994).

indicates administration of AD law must not lead to delays and uncertainties. For example, a decision on the status of allegedly dumped goods must be made in a matter of days of the arrival of the goods in an importing country, otherwise the regime may discriminate against low-cost producers.

Another early GATT Panel Report on AD law provided important guidance on Article VI. In a 1962 case involving exports of potatoes to Canada, a Panel ruled absent a showing of cross-border price discrimination, an AD claim must fail. (*See Exports of Potatoes to Canada*, GATT B.I.S.D. (11th Supp.) at 88 (1963) (adopted 16 November 1962).) Canada could not prove a difference existed between the price of potatoes consumed in the U.S. and price of potatoes exported to Canada. That is, in respect of the dumping margin calculation, Canada did not appreciate the language in Article VI:1(a) concerning "the comparable price . . . for consumption in the exporting country" imposes an affirmative duty on the petitioner to prove price discrimination and, therefore, determine two prices. A sale cannot be at less than Normal Value (*i.e.*, there is no dumping margin) unless the price of (1) allegedly dumped merchandise in the importing country is less than (2) the like product destined for the exporter's home market.

Since these early GATT Panel Reports, the volume of AD cases has exploded. Today, AD cases are a mainstay of International Trade Law practice. Many result in significant, if highly technical, rulings. Global and regional economic conditions can affect the volume of AD investigations. They are especially likely during recessionary conditions, when Export Prices (or Constructed Export Prices) may be low relative to Normal Values. They also are likely when the currency of an importing country has depreciated relative to that of the producer-exporter country. Then, Normal Value, which must be translated into the currency of the importing country that launches the AD investigation (unless invoicing is in that currency), is high in comparison with Export Price (or Constructed Export Price), which already is denominated in the currency of the importing country.

IV. 1967 Kennedy Round and 1979 Tokyo Round *Antidumping Codes*

The WTO *Antidumping Agreement* was not the first effort at a multilateral accord on AD law. Kennedy Round negotiators produced an *Antidumping Code* in 1967, which entered into force on 1 July 1968. The *Code* sought to ensure AD actions would not be abused. U.S. negotiators were the impetus for putting AD issues on the Kennedy Round agenda. They feared American exports might face discrimination under the guise of AD proceedings. Indeed, an increasing number of GATT contracting parties worried AD law was being or could be used as an NTB. Ironically, the American Congress rejected the *Code*, essentially because AD matters strayed beyond authority Congress had delegated to the Administration of Lyndon B. Johnson (1908–1973, President, 1963–1969).

Tokyo Round negotiators also produced an *Antidumping Code*. Like its predecessor, the Tokyo Round *Code* contained rules about the conduct of AD investigations in an attempt to ensure they were not used as unjustifiable impediments to trade. Unlike its predecessor, the Tokyo Round *AD Code*, which took effect on 1 January 1980 and succeeded its predecessor, was implemented into U.S. law. (Congress did so through Section 2(a) of the *Trade Agreements Act of 1979*.) However, this *Code* was not part of a single undertaking. Rather, it was a plurilateral accord.

V. 1994 WTO *Antidumping Agreement*

- **Overview**

Major changes in AD law, accepted by all GATT contracting parties as part of the Uruguay Round single undertaking, resulted from the WTO *Antidumping Agreement*—formally entitled the *Agreement on the Implementation of Article VI of the General Agreement on Tariffs and Trade 1994*. This *Agreement*, which entered into force on 1 January 1995 when the WTO was born, contains far more specific rules than the Tokyo Round AD *Code* in areas such as calculation of the dumping margin (Article 2), determination of injury (Article 3), evidence (Article 6), and duration of AD duties (Article 11). Sections 201–234 of the *1994 Act* implement the *AD Agreement* in U.S. law. This legislation represents the most significant changes since the *1979 Act*.

True, substantive standards for the ITC to make an injury determination— namely, material injury, threat of material injury, or material retardation of the establishment of an injury—remain the same. But, how the DOC calculates a dumping margin dramatically changed. For cases arising after 1 January 1995, when the *Act* took effect, pre-Uruguay Round jurisprudence on injury may be relevant, but pre- Uruguay Round case law on dumping margin calculations is of less value. *NAFTA*, and associated implementing legislation, the *1993 North American Free Trade Implementation Act*, also ushered in key changes in American AD law. In particular, Chapter 19 of *NAFTA* established a binational panel review process for cases involving U.S., Canadian, or Mexican parties. This process applies both to AD and CVD cases.

- **Standard of Review**

One significant effect of the WTO *AD Agreement* pertains to resolution of AD disputes. What standard of review should a WTO dispute settlement panel apply when examining the decision rendered by the DOC or ITC (or, for that matter, any official responsible for administering AD laws in a particular Member)? This issue is important for exporters that may be accused of dumping in a Member that does not provide respondents in AD actions full participation or appeal rights. It also helps avoid infringements on a Member's sovereignty by ensuring WTO panels do not routinely overturn decisions rendered by national authorities. On this matter, a 1990 GATT Panel Report, which was not adopted, raised serious concerns.

In *Seamless Stainless Steel Hollow Products from Sweden* (ADP/47, decided 20 August 1990), the Panel held the DOC's practice of assuming an American industry supports an AD petition is inconsistent with the Tokyo Round *AD Code*. American Courts had found the relevant statutory language ambiguous and, therefore, deferred to the DOC interpretation. In contrast, the GATT Panel not only substituted its reading for that of the DOC, but also recommended the DOC revoke its AD order. Further, it said the scope of panel reviews might not be limited to facts and issues raised before a domestic body like the DOC or ITC. Rather, Panels might engage in *de novo* review. American negotiators were troubled by this holding and wanted to ensure WTO panels could not "second guess" factual determinations and legal interpretations of the DOC or ITC.

Article 17:6 of the WTO *AD Agreement*, which was finalized after extensive negotiations, indicates WTO Panels must apply a standard of review that discourages the reversal of reasonable decisions rendered by authorities in a Member country. A Panel cannot overturn a factual determination of a national authority, such as the DOC, if that authority's establishment of the facts was "proper" and its evaluation "unbiased and objective," even if the panel might have reached a different conclusion. A Panel cannot overturn a legal determination of a national authority if the relevant provision of the *Agreement* allows for more than one permissible interpretation and the authority's determination rests on one of those interpretations. This Article did not necessitate a change in American AD law. Indeed, it appears similar to the famous *Chevron* standard of review in American administrative law.

Interestingly, this standard of review applies only to AD disputes. Uruguay Round negotiators from many countries preferred a stronger standard of review and, therefore, were unwilling to incorporate Article 17:6 into the WTO *SCM Agreement*. As a result, negotiators could agree only on a declaration AD and CVD cases should be resolved in a consistent manner. Most notably, many American critics of the WTO fault Panels and the Appellate Body for exceeding their authority under Article 17:6. Unsurprisingly, they point to cases in which the U.S. lost.

• **Remedies in Theory and Practice**

What remedies should the WTO Appellate Body (or a Panel) recommend if it disagrees with a DOC or ITC decision? The same question may be asked with respect to an FTA, if it has a dispute resolution mechanism distinct from the DOC-ITC process. Unfortunately, the WTO *AD Agreement* does not resolve this issue. Given this void, consider 4 classes of possible remedies: retroactive, specific, exclusive, and prospective. The WTO *DSU* plainly condones only the last class.

First, a retroactive remedy, which punishes a violator through monetary compensation to the victim for past economic loss the violator caused, is disfavored:

> Traditionally, GATT dispute settlement has been remedial and prospective in nature, the object being to end a situation in which one government is violating the obligations owed to another. GATT dispute settlement has not

operated to punish a government for past behavior, nor has it sought to compensate private parties.[4]

Second, a specific remedy is one that calls for a particular course of action, such as revocation of an AD order. On the one hand, specific remedies are disfavored because they are seen as an encroachment on the sovereignty of WTO Members. The relevant authority within a Member should have discretion to decide the best manner to conform its factual determination or legal interpretation to an adverse panel (or Appellate Body) report. A WTO panel (or the Appellate Body) should focus on systemic flaws in a Member's AD regime. On the other hand, the absence of a specific remedy may make WTO dispute resolution less attractive to an aggrieved Member. Moreover, neither the *DSU* nor the *AD Agreement* bars a panel from recommending a specific remedy.

Third, an exclusive remedy is one that indicates it is the only way for a losing Member to comply with an adverse decision. This remedy is disfavored because a panel (or the Appellate Body) may lack expertise in the domestic law of the losing Member. That law may provide for more suitable remedies than the exclusive remedy recommended by the panel (or Appellate Body). Arguably, a panel (or Appellate Body) should confine itself to determining whether a violation occurs, and then give discretion to the losing Member to determine curative measures. Article 19:1 of the *DSU* seems to look askance at exclusive remedies. It indicates the panel "may" suggest a remedy that the losing Member "could" implement.

Finally, a prospective remedy is designed to obtain relief in the future by alleviating the offending act. *DSU* Article 3:7 calls for prospective remedies, explaining the "first objective" of dispute resolution is "to secure the withdrawal of the measures concerned . . . ." *DSU* Article 19:1 instructs a panel to recommend the losing Member in a dispute bring its measure into conformity with the legal provision in question.

VI. Dumping and Protectionism

· Risk of Protectionist Abuse

The central challenge facing AD law is its articulation to prevent abuse by an industry or workers in an importing country to obtain protection from relatively more efficient foreign companies. If reduction of tariffs and NTBs is not to be offset by protectionist abuse of trade remedies, then these remedies must not operate as NTBs. Because of the Byzantine complexity of dumping margin calculations and

---

4. William D. Hunter, *WTO Dispute Settlement in Antidumping and Countervailing Duty Cases*, *in* I THE COMMERCE DEPARTMENT SPEAKS ON INTERNATIONAL TRADE AND INVESTMENT 557–585, at 579 (Practising Law Institute ed., 1994).

injury determinations, and common procedural delays, there is ample opportunity for abuse. That risk is a source of uncertainty for traders. Traders hate uncertainty.

All trade remedies—when imposed—afford protection to a domestic producer of a product that is like the merchandise subject to the remedy. However, "protectionist abuse" suggests a producer has lost its international competitive advantage, *i.e.*, it is no longer cost-competitive in the global marketplace. The petitioner is unwilling or unable to reduce its cost structure to meet global competitive pressures, fails to incorporate technological innovations in its manufacturing process and product design, or is insensitive to changes in consumer tastes. Its strategy for survival is to restore the *status quo ante* by raising the cost of imported merchandise through an AD duty.

Indeed, the *in terrorem* effect on a respondent of a preliminary affirmative dumping margin determination is real. That determination triggers suspension of liquidation of entries and collection of estimated duties. The respondent may react by raising prices quickly, and settling with a suspension agreement. That may be the whole point, for petitioner, of filing the action, *i.e.*, to coerce the respondent to join a price cartel. Evidence suggests AD law is a tool for producers in an importing country to maintain a price agreement (which, of course, may be a tacit one).

In such instances, imposition of a trade remedy is at odds with free trade theory. For three reasons, differentiating legitimate dumping cases from cases motivated by protectionism has remained the central challenge since the Kennedy Round.

(1) In the 1940s and 1950s only a few contracting parties—most notably the U.S. and Canada—had active AD enforcement programs. Today, every WTO Member has an AD law and attendant enforcement scheme. Yet, AD law across Members is not seamlessly harmonious, nor is implementation always consistent.

(2) As a result of several successful GATT negotiating rounds, tariffs have fallen dramatically. With respect to many products, they are not capable of serving as the principal means of protection, and other means must be sought.

(3) Also following successful rounds, it is increasingly difficult to impose NTBs. Indeed, many NTBs have fallen. AD law is an increasingly attractive vehicle to achieve protectionist aims. Domestic industries that have lost their international comparative advantage (*e.g.*, major American steel companies, as distinct from mini-mills) lobby governmental authorities to uphold their dumping petitions.

Thus, the GATT-WTO regime, translated into domestic AD laws, must balance two competing interests. On the one hand, it must acknowledge the legitimacy of AD actions in some instances. On the other hand, it must strike out attempts to use the remedy as a non-tariff barrier to protect companies whose misfortunes are due largely to grand changes in the global economy, the stupidity of its senior management and directors, or some combination thereof.

For four reasons, a complaint brought by New Zealand that is the subject of a 1985 GATT Panel Report exemplifies the use of AD law for protectionist purposes.[5] First, a New Zealand company on whose behalf the complaint was brought was upset its bid to supply transformers to the New Zealand government was rejected in favor of a bid submitted by a Finnish company. The Finnish company appears to have been a lower-cost producer than the New Zealand company. The Finnish company contended its winning bid was adequate to cover production costs, overheads, and profits. The Finnish company noted that, in contrast, during the period of alleged dumping, the New Zealand company simultaneously experienced increased sales and losses.

Second, the complainant, New Zealand, attempted to manipulate the definition of "industry." It sought to divide the transformer market into four segments in a way not necessarily used by other countries. Its purpose was to increase the likelihood of finding injury caused by dumped imports and obtaining relief for specific lines of production.

Third, it was implausible to argue the New Zealand transformer industry was materially injured by competition from Finland. The relevant company accounted for 92% of the share of the New Zealand transformer market (measured in terms of total 1983 domestic production). In contrast, Finnish imports accounted for only 2.4% of the market (measured in terms of total sales in the New Zealand transformer industry). In addition, only 2.4% of transformers imported into New Zealand were from Finland. Finally, while imports increased by 250% between 1981–1982 and 1982–1983, Finnish transformers represented only 3.4% of this increase. In sum, plainly Finnish transformers played an insignificant role in the New Zealand market.

Fourth, New Zealand's argument "any given amount of profit lost" amounts to "injury" was patently absurd. So, too, was its argument a threat of material injury existed. The Finnish company had no plans to export additional transformers to New Zealand.

The risk an AD action can be used as a NTB might be reduced if GATT Article VI were not such a generally worded provision. However, it was designed to accommodate American AD law as it existed in 1947. It was not drafted to differentiate abusive from legitimate AD petitions with precision. Perhaps the best example of the ambiguity in Article VI is the term "normal value." As GATT Article VI:1 itself suggests, dumping occurs when products of one country are exported to another country at less than Normal Value. The meaning of that key term hinges on the meaning of other key terms in Article VI:1, such as "comparable price," "ordinary course of trade," "like product," "reasonable addition," "cost of production," and "due allowance." What do they mean? Further, tracking the Article VI:1 language,

---

5. *See New Zealand—Imports of Electrical Transformers from Finland*, GATT B.I.S.D. (32nd Supp.) at 55 (1984–85) (adopted 18 July 1985).

when is a domestic price "absent"? What "third country" should be used to obtain a comparable price? How should cost of production be calculated? Unless such ambiguities are resolved with precision, dumping margin calculations are fated to be inconsistent and imprecise.

Might the risk of protectionist abuse be reduced if GATT Article VI imposed an affirmative obligation on contracting parties to refrain from dumping? Nothing in Article VI requires a WTO Member to ensure its exporters do not dump abroad. To the contrary, Article VI tacitly assumes the practice will occur. In contrast, there are affirmative obligations on WTO Members to refrain from providing certain types of subsidies. Certainly, banning dumping would provide a stricter discipline than offsetting a dumping margin through an AD duty. However, might a duty to abstain from dumping be problematical? An outright ban could result in attempts to equate prices of like products in different countries where genuine differences in market conditions or production efficiencies lead to justified price distinctions. That is, banning cross-border price discrimination could amount to an attempt to repeal the law of comparative advantage.

- **Batting Averages**

Generally (based on statistics from the 1980s and 1990s), the DOC renders an affirmative dumping margin determination in about 90% of cases. The ITC renders an affirmative injury determination in about 50% of cases. With these kinds of batting averages, it is not surprising AD law is a preferred bat by petitioners with which to hit at foreign imports. Many respondents do not bother to expend time and money battling a dumping margin determination, simply because of the poor odds. Rather, they choose to concentrate on the injury determination. Notably, petitioners around the world—such as China and India—are picking up the bat and having a go at American imports.

Surely, free traders would have thought, even if the drafters of GATT are forgiven for failing to anticipate the proliferation of AD law as a protectionist device, the ambitious, free trade oriented Uruguay Round negotiators were supposed to dismantle the weapon—or, at least, discipline its use. Fortunately, for protectionists seeking undeserved protection from competitive imports, the AD weapon was not neutralized. Quite the contrary, the WTO *Antidumping Agreement* ensures AD remains a weapon of choice for protectionist purposes. Likewise, Title II, Subtitle A of the *Uruguay Round Agreements Act of 1994* (*1994 Act*) implements the *Agreement* into American law by amending the *Tariff Act of 1930* (*1930 Act*), and similar legislation exists (or is supposed to) in every WTO Member. Protectionist abuse remains possible because of textual ambiguities, and inconsistencies with microeconomic insights, namely, the importance of considering the relationship between pricing strategy and costs of production.

VII. Neo-Classical Economic Analysis of AD Law

- ### International Price Discrimination and Its Conditions

The strengthening of AD law as a trade remedy occurred in the Uruguay Round despite howls from free trade oriented economists. Accordingly, before delving into that law, consider how neo-classical economists view dumping. The legal discussion is then more fruitful, as the incongruity between law and economic theory becomes clear.

Dumping is international price discrimination. It occurs when an exporter sells merchandise in an importing country at a price below that at which it sells like merchandise in its home country (or, if the home market of the exporter is not viable, then in a third country, or if there is no third country, then at below a constructed value):

> Dumping is, in general, a situation of *international price discrimination*, where the price of a product when sold to the importing country is less than the price of the same product when sold in the market of the exporting country. It is generally accepted in the multilateral trading system that if dumping takes place, it might result in *unfair* trade as the domestic industry of the importing country might suffer harm as a result of the dumping.[6]

(Observe "unfairness" is presumed without recourse to a theory of fairness.)

A more restrictive definition of "dumping" is it occurs when an exporter sells merchandise in an importing country at below the cost of production of that exporter. In either event, if dumping causes or threatens to cause material injury to an established industry making a like product in the importing country, or if dumping materially retards the establishment of an industry in that country, then the practice is actionable. The importing country may impose an AD duty on the dumped merchandise in the amount of the dumping margin, *i.e.*, the difference between the prices in the home market of the exporter and importing country.

Authorities in the U.S. and a handful of other countries (*e.g.*, in certain situations, Canada and Mexico), impose AD duties retroactively. That means an exporter (or, typically, the importer) of dumped merchandise must pay an AD duty on all such goods, going backward in time to a relevant date such as the filing date of the AD petition (or, in critical circumstances, even before the filing date) or the date of a preliminary affirmative determination of a dumping margin. Most other countries, and the EU, follow the system Great Britain established, which affords only prospective relief. That means customs authorities in an importing country collect

---

6. Judith Czako, Johann Human & Jorge Miranda, A Handbook on Anti-Dumping Investigations 1 (2003) (emphasis added).

AD duties going forward from a relevant date, such as the date of a final affirmative finding of dumping.

How is it possible for an exporter to pursue a bifurcated, cross-border price strategy? Neo-Classical economists respond with three necessary and sufficient conditions:

First: Market Segregation

The home market of an exporter and the market in the importing country are segregated from one another. Merchandise does not flow between the markets. Tariff and NTBs in the exporter's home market buttress a higher home market price, and consumers face significant costs in traveling to the other market. Consequently, the cross-border price differential persists because of the impracticability of arbitrage, *i.e.*, it is not commercially feasible to buy the product in the cheaper market and sell it in the more expensive market.

The market segregation may result from, or be reinforced by, trade barriers in the home market of the exporter. That is, the government in this market may protect through high tariffs or NTBs the good produced and sold by the exporter. Restrictive business practices in the exporter's home market also may account for, or buttress, the distinctiveness of that market.

Second: Imperfect Competition

An exporter does not face perfect competition in both markets. It has sufficient market power in at least one market to influence prices therein. If it lacked such power, then any price differential for merchandise in the different markets would not be in its control. In an extreme case, the exporter is a monopolist in its home market and perfect competitor in the market of the importing country.

This condition follows logically from the first one. Because of market segregation, there is no leakage of the dumped product to the exporter's home market. The exporter need not contend with the competition arbitrage would provide, and can reap high profits from home market sales. In some instances, the exporter may use super-normal profits to subsidize sales at "unfairly" low prices in the importing country, enabling it to suffer lower profits, or even losses, in that country. The first and second conditions also are related through the fact each may result from, or be reinforced by, trade barriers and restrictive business practices.

Third: Relative Price Elasticities

An exporter faces a relatively more elastic demand curve for merchandise in the market of the importing country, and a relatively less elastic demand curve for like merchandise in its home market. (Elasticity measures the sensitivity of consumer demand to price fluctuations, and arithmetically is the percent change in quantity demanded divided by the percent change

[handwritten margin note: Conditions necessary for dumping to make sense for an exporter]

in price. An elasticity value exceeding one means "elastic," a value less than one means "inelastic.")

Depicted on a Graph, the demand curve in the home market is steeper than the demand curve in the importing country. Again, the differential may result from trade barriers that protect the exporter in its home market and shield it from competition in that market. Absent the differential in the price elasticity of demand, the price charged by the exporter in the importing country would equal or exceed the price charged in its home market. Hence, there would be no dumping.

When all three conditions exist in a market, the environment is conducive to cross-border price discrimination.

- **Harmless?**

Significantly, economists generally agree except for predation, dumping is basically harmless for the importing country. Consumers in that country benefit from the lower price of imported goods. They are beneficiaries of price discrimination because they have access to cheaper merchandise. If they use that merchandise as an input into production of a finished good, then the final product is cheaper than it otherwise would be. Semiconductor chips used in consumer electronics, pasta used in frozen food, steel used in chain link fences, wood used in furniture or homes — all are examples. Why not, save for the exaltation of producer over consumer interests, allow consumers to enjoy the cheaper dumped price?

Producers of a like product in the importing country may be injured by the low-price competition, or may have a legitimate fear of this competition. Still, the net benefit to the importing country may be positive. Indeed, the analysis of imposition of an AD duty is conceptually the same as that of any tariff. (The very same graphical analysis may be used.) Producers gain through increased surplus, and the government of the importing country gains from a tariff revenue, but these gains typically are more than offset by the loss of consumer surplus. The net result is a dead weight loss, consisting of lost consumption opportunities plus inefficient allocation of factors of production to domestic output in the protected sector.

Empirical evidence strongly supports this neo-classical economic theory. It indicates the gain from obtaining dumped merchandise outweighs the cost to producers in the importing country (measured by reduced profits) and their employees (in terms of reduced employment). The policy implication is not to impose an AD duty. Otherwise, the net gain is wiped out. Indeed, one economist conducting a welfare analysis of eight AD proceedings in the U.S. in 1989–1990 concluded:

> such duties are an extremely costly way to improve the profitability of U.S. producers or employment in U.S. industries. In these eight cases, the consumer cost per dollar of increased profits ranged from 2.40 to 25.10 dollars, with an average cost of 8.00. The cost to the U.S. economy per dollar of profit ranges from 0.20 to 10.80 dollars, with an average value of 3.60

dollars. The minimum consumer cost per job created was 113,800 dollars, while the minimum cost to the economy to create an additional job was 14,300 dollars.[7]

No less an authority than the ITC considered the counterfactual question of what the economy-wide welfare effects would be if all outstanding AD and CVD orders in 1991 had been removed. These orders affected $9 billion out of $491 billion, or 1.8%, of all American merchandise imports. The ITC concluded AD and CVD orders imposed a net welfare cost on the American economy of $1.59 billion, or 0.03% of the American GDP ($5.725 trillion). The loss to consumers in the form of higher prices far outweighed the benefit to petitioning industries in the form of increased output and employment.

Certainly, defects plague this kind of neo-classical economic analysis. First, it is static in nature. It may understate—or overstate—effects of AD and CVD orders across time. That is because it amounts to a snapshot of their effects at a moment, or a specified period. Perhaps more damaging is the analysis is narrow.

That is because of a singular focus of the effects of a trade remedy from the perspective of only the importing country imposing an AD order. When both the exporter's and importer's country are considered, it is impossible to show conclusively *a priori* the welfare effects of cross-border price discrimination are, on balance, negative. Consumers in the exporter's home market are harmed by a higher price. But, the source of the evil is not dumping. Rather, it is the exporter's monopoly power. Such power enables the exporter to garner monopoly rents by charging a price above its marginal cost of production. These extra profits do not offset the welfare loss to consumers. The same logic applies to the less extreme situation where the exporter charges a high (but not monopoly) and low (but not perfectly competitive) price in the home and importing countries respectively. Whether the benefits from cheaper prices in the importing country offset the net loss from monopoly prices in the exporter's country is uncertain. Thus, Professor Dam concludes:

> The fact that governments act against dumping only when the low price is charged in their own territory reveals that governments are concerned with the welfare of their own enterprises rather than the protection of their citizens from discriminatorily high prices charged by monopoly sellers. If the problem were really the discrimination itself, then presumably governments would be more concerned to attack high prices than low prices. Where an exporter sold at home at higher prices than he sold abroad, it would be the exporter's government, not the importer's government, that would take coercive action. The General Agreement, like the governments themselves, views the impact in the low-price country as the harmful aspect of dumping . . . .

---

7. Keith B. Anderson, *Antidumping Laws in the United States: Use and Welfare Consequences*, 27 JOURNAL OF WORLD TRADE 99, 115 (April 1993).

. . .

The concern with dumping is therefore a concern with the protection of domestic industry from international competition.[8]

Consider, then, two hypothetical inquiries, each of which illustrates the fallacy of assuming dumping is evil.

First, suppose AD laws are repealed and conditions that facilitate dumping are eliminated. In theory, prices in the home (*i.e.*, exporting) and importing countries converge because of cross-border arbitrage. Consumers in the home country benefit from lower prices. Yet, consumers in the importing country are harmed by higher prices and the exporter's profits decline. Whether the benefits to the winners outweigh the losses of the losers is uncertain. The net welfare effect of the repeal can only be forecast as positive if the exporter's monopoly position in the home country is completely undermined, and it behaves like a perfect competitor in the importing country.

Second, suppose an AD duty is imposed to level the competitive playing field between subject merchandise imports and a domestic like product. The clear losers are consumers. They must pay a higher price for the import, because of the duty. Also, they may have to pay a higher price for the like product, because domestic companies can competitively raise prices to match the price of imports. One observer points out between 1980 and 1989, "almost all foreign companies investigated for alleged dumping [in the U.S.] were found guilty" and concludes:

> While many people consider dumping an arcane subject, dumping penalties have forced Americans to pay more for photo albums, pears, mirrors, ethanol, cement, shock absorbers, roof shingles, codfish, televisions, paint brushes, cookware, motorcycle batteries, bicycles, martial art uniforms, computers and computer disks, telephone systems, forklifts, radios, flowers, aspirin, staplers and staples, paving equipment, and fireplace mesh panels. Dumping laws increasingly prevent American businesses from getting vital foreign supplies and machinery. Commerce Department officials now effectively have direct veto power over the pricing policies of . . . foreign companies. Dumping law constitutes potential political price controls . . . .[9]

In sum, application of AD law makes the playing field less competitive when interests of consumers of dumped merchandise are considered.

• **Predation?**

What about predation, where an exporter tries to drive competitors in an importing country out of business and subsequently raise prices? AD law holds the

---

8. Kenneth W. Dam, The GATT 168 (1970) (emphasis added).

9. James Bovard, The Fair Trade Fraud 108 (1991). *But see* Greg Mastel & Andrew Szamosszegi, Leveling the Playing Field: Antidumping and the U.S. Steel Industry 35–45, 47–51 (February 1999). [Hereinafter, Bovard.]

exporter's conduct unfair, and thus affords protection to its competitors. But, the law is clumsy. Because it neglects the efficiency — specifically, the cost structure — of the exporter, it confuses predatory and non-predatory behavior. As long as the exporter's marginal revenue from sales in the importing country exceed its marginal cost of production, the exporter is behaving in an economically rational fashion.

Further, an exporter selling merchandise in an importing country at a price above its average variable cost of production is not engaging in predatory behavior. Protecting the exporter's competitors from a rational, non-predatory exporter means competitors are not challenged to reduce their cost structures to remain competitive with the exporter. The development of a perfectly or nearly-perfectly competitive market in the importing country is throttled, and consumers are denied the benefit of lower prices:

> [i]n using the predation rationale for AD, purportedly the interests of consumers are being advanced, not those of import-competing firms. Yet in the absence of successful predation, the imposition of AD duties can only harm domestic consumers. As AD actions cause exporters to recoil from the foreign market, competitive pressures are diminished and domestic prices move upward. It is rather paradoxical that vigilant and enthusiastic application of AD by policy officials tends to promote the result that it is supposed to combat under the predation justification: monopoly pricing.[10]

In brief, predation is not a persuasive economic argument in favor of retaining AD laws.

Put differently, AD law ought to be grounded on microeconomic theory. It ought to draw on the theory of the cost structure of a firm, and isolate and sanction predation cases. GATT Article VI, the WTO *Antidumping Agreement*, and American implementing legislation fail this criterion. Hence, the 1983 statement of the Federal Circuit in *Smith-Corona Group v. United States* remains true:

> Antidumping duties are imposed on the basis of differences in value, *not* differences in cost. The importation of foreign merchandise can occur at a price greater than cost, yet *still generate liability* for an antidumping duty. The language of the statute would impose a duty on a foreign producer who "eats" either costs or profits in the American market relative to the home market. Thus, cost criteria alone will not redress the full margin of dumping to which Congress sought to attach an antidumping duty. Value must be considered under the statute.

> . . .

---

10. Bernard M. Hoekman & Michael P. Leidy, *Antidumping and Market Disruption: The Incentive Effects of Antidumping Laws, in* THE MULTILATERAL TRADING SYSTEM: ANALYSIS AND OPTIONS FOR CHANGE 155, 162 (Robert M. Stern ed., 1993).

Congress sought to afford the domestic manufacturer strong protection against dumping, seeming to indicate that the Secretary [of Commerce] *should err in favor of protectionism.*[11]

Of course, whether this kind of reform—or revolution—in AD law will occur is dubious.

- **Repeal?**

Even though AD measures affect only about 2% of American trade (as of July 2011), skepticism about the economic effects of AD law prompts tenacious arguments for the repeal of AD law. This skepticism exists despite compelling arguments from users (petitioners) of AD law. They point out some countries, like China, have a government policy to promote strategic industries, such as steel.

Under that policy, the government artificially controls the prices of key raw materials and inputs (keeping them low), and is heavily involved in directing and managing companies in the strategic industries. Indeed, some of the companies are wholly or partially SOEs. The government also ensures their favored companies have access to cheap credit, typically from state-owned banks. The end result is a formidable program in which the production capacity of the companies expands to the extent the industry has over-capacity. The consequence is predictable: the companies over-produce, and dump their surplus production on world markets. The government insulates the companies from world market signals, such as falls in prices, in part to keep workers employed, through bailouts of one sort or another. The CCP fears widespread, violent civil unrest stoked by an admixture of unemployment, ethnic rivalries, and religious tension—unrest that, ironically, is exacerbated by its own iron-fisted clampdowns, which suppress symptoms but fail to address causes. In this context, for industries in other countries producing like products, such as American or European steel companies, AD law is an indispensable practical private remedy. They fiercely oppose scrapping or weakening the remedy.

Nevertheless, economists use six lines of attack against AD law. First, AD law is redundant. The *Robinson-Patman Act* proscribes price discrimination. Section 2 of the *Sherman Act* outlaws predatory pricing. This redundancy violates the national treatment clause of GATT Article III. AD law does not apply to the domestic context, *i.e.*, a domestic company engaged in price discrimination or predatory pricing only in its home country may run afoul of antitrust, but not AD, law. Of course, a rebuttal is AD law is deliberately designed as an alternative to antitrust laws governing price discrimination and, for that matter, predation:

> [o]ver time, antidumping policy and antitrust policy have diverged strikingly. Antidumping law and policy have evolved along a path of ever-increasing protection for U.S. firms from imports and decreasing concern for consumers and the economy as a whole. Antitrust law relating to predatory

---

11. 713 F.2d 1568, 1575–76 (Fed. Cir. 1983), *cert. denied*, 465 U.S. 1022 (1984) (emphasis added).

pricing, at least in recent decades, has taken a path of increasing concern for consumers and the economy as a whole and decreasing concern for firms suffering intense competition.

Antidumping law no longer acts primarily against predatory pricing. It acts against international price discrimination (sales at a lower price in the United States than in the home country of the exporter) and sales below cost, regardless of whether the sales are predatory or not. Yet, the relevant provisions of the antitrust laws prohibit only predatory pricing; they do not prohibit selling below cost or price discrimination analogous to that prohibited by the antidumping laws except in cases where it is predatory.

This difference is important. Predatory pricing is detrimental to economic welfare because it leads to monopolies, which cause economic inefficiency and raise concerns about social equity. It seldom occurs, however, because it is rarely a profitable strategy and is usually not possible. By contrast, non-predatory price discrimination and sales below cost generally provide net benefits to the country receiving the lower price, and both are relatively common. Moreover, seldom do cases of price discrimination or selling below cost have anything to do with predatory pricing.[12]

Curiously, on the subject of below costs sales, a 1961 GATT *Report of Group of Exports* concluded selling imported merchandise at a loss to obtain a foothold in an importing country market does not constitute dumping under Article VI.[13] Nonetheless, the point is AD law is a practical and political alternative necessary in a world in which cross-border price discrimination is possible because of protection in home markets.[14]

The second line of economic attack is AD law is unnecessary. Injury to an industry in an importing country caused by imports can be addressed by safeguard actions under GATT Article XIX. They condone assistance to companies and workers who suffer from fair foreign competition. Applying it in the context of dumping is legitimate because dumping is not necessarily unfair. One rebuttal to this line of attack is in practice adjustment assistance is difficult to obtain and meager in amount.

Third, AD law cannot address the source of the problem of alleged unfair pricing. While AD law may serve as a bargaining chip to pry open a closed foreign market,

---

12. Congressional Budget Office Memorandum, A Review of U.S. Antidumping and Countervailing-Duty Law and Policy 2–3 (May 1994).

13. GATT, *Report of Group of Exports, Antidumping and Countervailing Duties* at 11 (1961), *reprinted at* B.I.S.D. (9th Supp.) 194–201, at 199 (1961) (adopted 27 May 1960).

14. *See, e.g., Energy Conversion Devices Liquidation Trust v. Trina Solar Ltd.*, Number 2:13-cv-14241-RHC-RSW (E.D. Mich., 31 October 2014) (dismissing a predatory pricing claim under Sections 1–2 of the *Sherman Act* involving solar panel exports from China and below-cost pricing, where such merchandise was dumped and subsidized, and subject to an AD duty of roughly 30%, following an ITC decision that it caused material injury to U.S. producers); Eleanor Tyler, *Bankrupt Solar Panel Maker Can's Assert Antitrust Claim Against Chinese Price Cutters*, 31 International Trade Reporter 1960 (6 November 2014).

its central aim is not to dismantle the duties and NTBs in an exporter's home market that ensure market segmentation. If these barriers are removed, then 1 of the 3 necessary and sufficient conditions for dumping would not exist, hence dumping would be impossible. But, Section 301 of the *Trade Act of 1974*, not AD law, is the unilateral tool to compel market access. Of course, use of Section 301 is constrained by the GATT-WTO regime.

Fourth, AD law creates one of two perverse incentives for an exporter. To minimize the risk of being named a respondent in an AD action, it may reduce exports and increase home-market sales. In turn, the price of its merchandise in the importing country may rise, thereby reducing competitive pressure on producers in that country, while the price of its merchandise in its home country falls. In this instance, AD law thus distorts marketing decisions. Alternatively, if the importing country represents a significant market, the exporter may relocate its production facilities to that importing country. Here, AD law distorts decisions about FDI. As one skeptic puts it, "[e]conomic xenophobia is the foundation of U.S. antidumping law."[15]

Fifth, AD law impedes exports. That is because many AD measures are imposed on raw materials and intermediate goods. Between 2000 and 2009, four out of every five AD measures imposed in the U.S. were on important inputs used by American manufacturers. An AD duty raises the price of subject merchandise, forcing a domestic producer either to pay the higher price, or source inputs from an inefficient domestic supplier (if one exists). Either way, the price of the finished good rises, because it incorporates a higher-cost input. In turn, when exported, the finished good is less competitive on world markets than before.

Sixth, AD law hurts domestic retailers. More generally, it plays off different business sectors against one another: producer-exporters that do not manufacture overseas at all, or that do so to some degree, versus retailers who sell imported goods. For example, in a major case in 2004 involving imports of bedroom furniture from China, the U.S. imposed AD duties to protect domestic producers in North Carolina—some of which had outsourced their production to China, and which also were acting as middlemen between those producers and American retailers. The retailers learned they could place orders directly with the relevant factory, and so they did, to cut out the middleman and thereby cut the cost. The AD duty raised the cost on the retailers, nixing this strategy. Effectively, the case was about which party—the North Carolina based company with some factories in China, or the American retailers—could control manufacturing in China.

However, this lesson is akin to being told "rain is wet" when what is needed is advice on the nearest umbrella vendor. AD law persists, indeed thrives. The call for repeal is quixotic. For approximately a century—long before GATT entered into force—the international trading community condemned dumping. On 4 major occasions in the 20th century (and countless less heralded opportunities), GATT

---

15. Bovard, 107.

contracting parties had the chance to ban AD law: in 1947 (when GATT was finalized), 1964–1967 (when the Kennedy Round *AD Code* was drafted), 1974–1979 (when the Tokyo Round *AD Code* was reached) and 1986–1994 (when the WTO *Antidumping Agreement* was produced). Each time, they affirmed dumping as unfair, and use of AD duties as a remedy.

That is not surprising, as AD law pre-dates modern multilateral trade law. Canada appears to have enacted the first AD legislation in 1903. (Possibly, the *Wilson Bill of 1894* (extended in 1897) in the U.S. qualifies, as it concerned discriminatory pricing of imports. But, it authorized CVDs, not AD duties, in the event of bounty dumping, which referred to government subsidies.) In 1916, the U.S. enacted an *Antidumping Act* (which, roughly 90 years later, the WTO ruled illegal). In the 1920s, the League of Nations gave some attention to AD law, but hardly took steps to curtail or eliminate it. In its proposal for an *ITO Charter*, the U.S. offered a draft text, which, with modification, became GATT Article VI.

Manifestly, AD law has a long history, little of which is characterized by serious, widespread efforts to abolish it. Whether AD law is economically justified is irrelevant. The practical inquiry is whether meaningful circumscribing of that law, to minimize the risk of protectionist abuse, is possible. Trade negotiators generally dodge that question. They permit ambiguities in applicable texts, which petitioners exploit to use AD law as an NTB. Decades ago, this situation was anticipated. In the 1946 London Preparatory Conference, GATT drafters, including the delegate from the U.K., articulated concern the AD remedy would become a NTB to trade. Periodically thereafter, such worries have been expressed but not assuaged.

VIII. China's April 2017 Doha Round Proposal on SMEs in AD-CVD Cases

While MNCs attract media headlines, SMEs account for significant activity as producer-exporters and importers. SMEs create jobs and generate economic growth. Yet, "SMEs face many difficulties and bear a heavy burden in responding to" AD and CVD cases. The problems include:

> difficulty in obtaining qualified professional assistance from lawyers or experts due to high costs. Because of their lack of experience and expertise, these proceedings often lead to unfavourable or even excessively high duty rates for SMEs, resulting in a worse-off situation for them in international trade.[16]

To be sure, Articles 6:13 of the *AD Agreement* and 12:11 of the *SCM Agreement* recognize the special needs of SMEs, saying:

---

16. World Trade Organization, *China Seeks Special Consideration for SMEs in Anti-Dumping, Countervailing Probes*, 11 October 2017, www.wto.org/english/news_e/news17_e/rule_16oct17_e .htm. [Hereinafter, *China Seeks.*]

[t]he authorities shall take due account of any difficulties experienced by interested parties, in particular small companies, in supplying information requested, and shall provide any assistance practicable.

But, China argues this language is insufficient to address the problems SMEs face.

China explained:

SMEs face multifarious difficulties and bear heavy burden in responding to trade remedy proceedings in practice, which may involve several procedural aspects such as access to information, questionnaire, extension, sampling, and price undertaking. For instance, they may have difficulty in obtaining qualified professional assistance from lawyers or experts due to high financial expenses. Because of lack of experience and expertise, even when SMEs have already done their best in cooperating, their questionnaires may still be less than ideal or even incomplete, which could often lead to unfavorable or even excessively highest rates for them. Their applications for price undertaking are also easily disregarded due to their small percentage of industrial representativeness. The above has, in turn, contributed to SMEs' reluctance in responding to other AD and CVD proceedings, resulting in a worse-off situation for SMEs in international trade.[17]

So, in April 2017, China said:

special provisions need to be written into the *Agreements* to help SMEs further, including better access to information on trade remedy investigations, granting SMEs reasonable extensions to deadlines for submitting information to investigating authorities, providing assistance to SMEs in responding to requests for information, and ensuring that results of an investigation are not less favourable to an SME if the information for an investigation is provided to the SME's "best abilities."[18]

China's specific draft—submitted to the Negotiating Group on Rules, as part of the Doha Round negotiations, in the run up to the December 2017 WTO Ministerial Conference in Buenos Aires, was to amend both the *AD* and *SCM Agreements* with a new provision:

Article X

Special Consideration and Treatment of SMEs

The authorities shall, when appropriate or requested, make positive efforts to identify Small and Medium-sized Enterprises (SMEs), take due account of the unique or disproportionate difficulties experienced by them in the

---

17. World Trade Organization, *Follow-Up Paper on Special Consideration and Treatment of Small and Medium-Sized Enterprises in Anti-Dumping and Countervailing Proceedings, Communication from China*, TN/RL/GEN/194 (2 August 2017), Annex 1, www.wto.org/english/news_e /news17_e/rule_16oct17_e.htm. [Hereinafter, *Follow-Up Paper.*]

18. *China Seeks, supra.*

process of investigations and provide them with any practicable assistance. Assistance to SMEs may include but not limited to:

a. The authorities shall take due account of difficulties of SMEs in gaining access to information and take appropriate measures to ensure their easier access to relevant information including initiation, questionnaire, disclosure and public notice etc.

b. The authorities shall give full consideration to SMEs' comments and opinions when sampling for limited examination. If SMEs have genuine difficulties in providing full cooperation and present justifiable explanation therefor, the authorities may decide not to select them for limited examination.

c. If SMEs are unable to submit questionnaires on time with good cause, the authorities shall grant them reasonable extension upon request unless such extension will significantly impede the investigation.

d. The authorities shall provide any assistance practicable to SMEs when they supply information requested by the authorities, including responding in a timely manner to requests for clarification of questionnaires and permitting SMEs to submit questionnaires in less burdensome ways.

e. The authorities shall take due account of price undertakings offered by SMEs where appropriate.

f. Even when information provided by SMEs may not be ideal in all respects, this situation shall not lead to a result which is less favorable to SMEs if they have provided cooperation to the best of their abilities.[19]

The proposal seemed innocuous enough. As China said, its aim was to: "encourage[] the investigating authorities to make positive efforts to identify small and medium-sized enterprises when appropriate, take due account of the unique or disproportionate difficulties confronted by them in responding to proceedings, and provide them with any practicable assistance or help to reduce their burden thereof."[20] Who could be against helping small business, especially given that women and minorities start and operate many SMEs, so assisting them in trade remedy matters can contribute to long-term socioeconomic development? Besides, a careful read of the language indicated many obligations were "Soft Law."

Yet no consensus emerged. Rather six objections emerged. First, should the GATT-WTO regime contain different legal obligations for business associations of different sizes? International Banking Law does, with special rules for "SIFIs"— Systemically Important Financial Institutions. But, that is a line International Trade Law has not crossed. Second, how should an "SME" be defined? Should the qualification criteria be based on the number of employees (several hundred? several

19. *Follow-Up Paper.* The proposal is TN/RL/GEN/185.
20. *Follow-Up Paper, supra.*

thousand?), and/or asset value (several million? book value? market value?)? Third, how much discretion should AD-CVD investigating authorities have to define an entity as an "SME" and thereby accord it special consideration? Fourth, should that consideration be limited to AD-CVD investigations in which an SME is a respondent producer-exporter (and its importer)? Or, should SMEs in the role of petitioner (part of the domestic industry seeking relief) get special treatment, too? After all, SMEs are both targets of trade remedies, and victims of unfair trade behaviour. Fifth, why create new rules, rather than focus efforts on fixing defects in Article 6:13 of the *AD Agreement* and Article 12:11 of the *SCM Agreement*? Sixth, should S&D treatment be given to developing countries and LDCs in respect of their SMEs? If so, then what "breaks" would be appropriate? Perhaps ones focusing on women and minorities?

Chapter 2

Procedures: Original Investigations through Final Determinations[1]

I. Overview of Steps in AD or CVD Case

The principal American statute covering AD-CVD law is the *Tariff Act of 1930*, as amended. Clearly, the statute predates GATT. Many of the amendments made to the *1930 Act* have helped conform U.S. law to GATT-WTO obligations. Conversely, many American negotiating positions in multilateral trade talks have been an effort to legislate, *i.e.*, export, provisions of the *1930 Act* overseas, and thereby ensure new WTO accords are as close as possible to extant American law.

The CVD provisions are set forth in 19 U.S.C. §§ 1671 *et seq*. The AD provisions are in 19 U.S.C. §§ 1673 *et seq*. The considerable statutory overlap intimates commonality between AD and CVD law. Procedures for filing a petition and standing, as well as by preliminary and final determinations, evidence the correctness of that intimation.

By way of synopsis, the *1930 Act* mandates assessment, imposition, and collection of AD or CVD duties after two final administrative determinations. Observe:

(1) "Assessment" refers to a determination of liability, in effect, the estimation of an AD duty or CVD.

(2) "Imposition," as used in 19 U.S.C. § 1677a(c)(1(C), refers to calculation of the amount of the liability, *i.e.*, of the duty that is or will be levied because the DOC issued an AD or CVD order. Thus, "imposition" presumes issuance of an order, and estimation of the duties.[2]

(3) "Collection" refers to garnering the duty.

The conceptually distinct steps this terminology embodies should not imply a large time gap between issuance and imposition.

---

1. Documents References:
   (1) *Havana (ITO) Charter* Article 34
   (2) GATT Article VI
   (3) WTO *Antidumping Agreement* Articles 3, 5, 14, 17
   (4) *NAFTA* Chapter 19
   (5) Relevant provisions in other FTAs
2. *See, e.g., Dupont Teijin Films U.S.A. v. United States*, 407 F.3d 1211, 1217 (Fed. Cir. 2005).

As the CIT said in the 2005 *Dupont Teijin Films* case, "it is reasonable for the Department [of Commerce] to consider a countervailing duty to be *'imposed'* upon *the issuance* of the countervailing duty order."[3] This ruling is in the context of an adjustment to Export Price in a dumping margin calculation. The Court of Appeals upheld the CIT's interpretation that "imposed" requires issuance of a CVD before the CVD can be used to offset (*i.e.*, deducted from) Export Price in a dumping margin calculation.

Obviously, final determinations occur after preliminary determinations. That means in an American AD or CVD investigation, the procedure is bifurcated into preliminary and final stages. Bifurcation also is true in another sense, namely, there are two federal authorities involved: the DOC and ITC. The DOC sits within the Executive Branch, and the Secretary of Commerce is a member of the President's Cabinet. Within the DOC, a division called the "International Trade Administration" (ITA) — and, specifically, a unit within ITA known as "Enforcement and Compliance" — handles AD and CVD investigations.[4]

The ITC is an independent agency within the Executive Branch. It consists of six Commissioners, appointed by the President, with no more than three from one political party. In the event of a tie vote among Commissioners, the determination is deemed to be in favor of petitioners — a result injecting a pro-petitioner bias in AD and CVD injury determinations (and, for that matter, Section 201 Escape Clause cases, as the ITC also is responsible for them). What happens if three Commissioners vote against a finding of injury or threat, while the other three split? For example, suppose one Commissioner votes for an affirmative finding of material injury, and two others vote in favor of an affirmative determination of threat of material injury?

Precisely this pattern happened in the 2015 Federal Circuit case of *Siemens Energy, Inc. v. United States*.[5] The Federal Circuit upheld the decision of the CIT that the pertinent statute (19 U.S.C. Section 1677(11)) unambiguously calls for combining votes on material injury or threat thereof. Hence, Siemens (the respondent) lost its challenge against AD duties (from 44.99% to 70.63%) and CVDs (from 21.86% to 34.81%) on utility-scale wind tower imports from China, and AD duties (from 51.5% to 58.49%) on imports of the towers from Vietnam. Siemens interpreted the pattern as four votes against the presence of material injury. Not so, said both

---

3. *Dupont Teijin Films U.S.A. v. United States*, 297 F.Supp.2d 1367, 1373 (CIT 2003) (emphasis added), *affirmed Dupont Teijin Films U.S.A. v. United States*, 407 F.3d 1211, 1219 (Fed. Cir. 2005).

4. Until 1 October 2013, the Enforcement and Compliance unit of ITA was known as "Import Administration" (or IA). Effective that day, the DOC announced a new flexible organizational structure for ITA, including two other units in ITA: Global Markets, which helps American businesses with market access abroad for exports and investments, and Industry and Analysis, which provides economic studies on specific industries and topics concerning trade and investment.

5. *See* Federal Circuit Number 2014-1725 (25 November 2015); Rossella Brevetti, *Appeals Court Rejects Challenge to Duties on Wind Towers*, 32 International Trade Reporter (BNA) (3 December 2015).

Courts: the fragmented ITC decision amounted to an affirmative injury determination. Even though the Commissioners reached divergent conclusions, there still was substantial evidence in favor of an affirmative finding. The statute says an affirmative vote on (1) material injury, (2) threat of material injury, or (3) material retardation of the establishment of a domestic industry must be treated as an affirmative determination. Put simply, the disjunctive "or" makes all the difference.

In both senses, bifurcation is not universal. Some WTO Members require preliminary and final determinations. Others use a unified procedure. In some WTO Members, there are two central governmental authorities involved in AD and CVD cases. In others, there is only one unit. Almost invariably, the ministry responsible for commerce or international trade (which, typically, is the same ministry) is involved. Whether bifurcated or unified, and whether one authority or two, investigations are almost sure to be complex and contentious. What are the pros and cons of bifurcation?

In an AD case, the responsibility of the DOC is to determine whether the allegedly dumped imports, known as "subject merchandise" (*i.e.*, the "class or kind of merchandise subject to investigation," as they were called under pre-Uruguay Round law) is sold in the U.S. at less than fair value (LTFV). That is, the DOC makes preliminary and final determinations as to the magnitude of the dumping margin—the extent (if any) of cross-border price discrimination. In a CVD case, the DOC is charged with deciding whether a foreign exporter or producer is receiving (or received) an unlawful subsidy and, if so, the amount of that subsidy. The term "subject merchandise" in the CVD context also refers to imports under investigation, though the inquiry focuses on subsidization by the government of the home country of the exporter or producer, not dumping. As in an AD case, a CVD case renders a preliminary and final determination. In either kind of case, prior to a preliminary determination of dumping or subsidization, the DOC may be called upon to assess whether so-called "critical circumstances" (discussed later) exist.

In AD and CVD investigations, the job of the ITC is to consider injury or threat thereof to a domestic (*i.e.*, American) industry posed by subject merchandise. In rare instances, the ITC examines whether establishment of a domestic industry is materially retarded because of dumped or illegally subsidized merchandise. The ITC makes preliminary and final determinations as to whether subject merchandise materially injures or threatens to injure an industry in the U.S., or materially retards its establishment.

Only if both the dumping margin or subsidization determination by the DOC and the injury determination by the ITC are affirmative is an AD or CVD order issued. The DOC is responsible for issuing the order, which it does to CBP (known in the pre-9/11 era as the "Customs Service"). The DOC issues an AD or CVD order to the CBP calling for the collection of a duty equal to the dumping margin or illegal subsidization rate. The CBP collects the duty on a company-specific basis on imports of subject merchandise.

Under pre-Uruguay Round law, an AD or CVD order remained in place, and duties were collected by the Customs Service, for an indefinite period. In the U.S., the average length tended to be a little over eight years. Because of mandatory "Sunset Reviews," instigated under Article 11 of the WTO *Antidumping Agreement*, an order is presumed to terminate no later than five years of the date of its imposition. Other kinds of reviews, specifically "Administrative Reviews" and "Changed Circumstances Reviews," can lead to modification or termination of an AD or CVD order.

Overall, then, an AD or CVD case may be dissected into 10 procedural steps:

Step 1:   Filing an AD or CVD Petition.

Step 2:   Standing and Sufficiency Determination.

Step 3:   Preliminary ITC Injury Determination.

Step 4:   Preliminary DOC Dumping Margin or Subsidization Determination. (Possible "critical circumstances" allegation.)

Step 5:   Final DOC Dumping Margin or Subsidization Determination.

Step 6:   Final ITC Injury Determination.

Step 7:   Issuance of AD or CVD Order.

Step 8:   Reviews of AD or CVD Order.

Step 9:   Appeals (if any).

Step 10:   WTO Adjudication (if any).

Steps 1 through 7 are discussed in turn in detail below. The kinds of Reviews involved in Step 8 (Sunset, Administrative, and Changed Circumstances), and WTO controversies (especially about Sunset Reviews) are discussed briefly below. Steps 9 and 10 involve possibilities of:

(1) Appeal to the CIT, and, thereafter, the Federal Circuit. In rare instances, AD or CVD cases are appealed to the Supreme Court, which hardly ever accepts such appeals.

(2) Appeal to a tribunal associated with an RTA, such as a *NAFTA* Chapter 19 Panel (*i.e.*, a three-member panel created pursuant to *NAFTA* Chapter 19).

(3) An action arising under the *DSU*.

The last two Steps are discussed briefly below.

Note that *de minimis* and negligibility criteria apply, which if satisfied mean a case cannot be launched or if proven is terminated immediately. Article 5:8 of the WTO *AD Agreement* defines 2% (as a percentage of Export or Constructed Price) as a *de minimis* dumping margin, and 3% (of the total volume of imports of the like product into the importing country, unless countries that individually account for less than 3% collectively sum to over 7% of that total) as a negligible volume. For CVD cases, Article 11:9 of the *SCM Agreement* fixes the *de minimis* subsidization rate at 1%. It does not set a volume negligibility figure. These thresholds are in U.S. law (which applies the same volume thresholds in CVD as AD cases).[6]

---

6. For example, 19 U.S.C. § 1677(24) states, "imports from a country of merchandise corresponding to a domestic like product identified by the Commission are 'negligible' if such imports account for less than 3 percent of the volume of all such merchandise imported into the United States" during the most recent 12-month period for which data exist prior to the petition filing date or initiation of investigation. Note that S&D treatment is afforded to developing countries in CVD cases thanks to Article 27:10 of the *SCM Agreement* (with the *de minimis* subsidization rate raised from 1% to 2%, and negligible import thresholds raised from 3% and 7% to 4% and 9%).

Cases where subject merchandise production is multi-jurisdictional can raise disputes about applying the thresholds. In *Kyocera Solar, Inc., v. United States International Trade Commission*, Number 2016-1348 (15 December 2016), the Federal Circuit considered subject merchandise from Taiwan, namely:

> solar modules (*i.e.*, solar panels) that incorporate crystalline silicon photovoltaic ("CSPV") cells from Taiwan. CSPV cells convert sunlight into electricity using mono- or multi-crystalline silicon cells. The CSPV cells are strung together, sealed, laminated, and framed to make solar modules, also known as CSPV modules. CSPV cells are the main electricity-generating component of solar modules.
>
> Kyocera produces and manufactures solar modules abroad and imports them for sale in the United States. The solar modules at issue in this case are ultimately assembled in and imported from Mexico but incorporate Taiwanese CSPV cells.
>
>   . . .
>
> . . . Commerce defined the investigation's scope to include cells and modules produced in Taiwan and certain modules "completed or partially manufactured" in other countries.
>
>   . . .
>
> Kyocera later challenged Commerce's scope determination and requested that it exclude solar modules produced in Mexico from the investigation's scope, including modules produced in Mexico using CSPV cells manufactured in Taiwan. Commerce declined Kyocera's request. It determined that the investigation would include solar modules produced in Mexico that incorporated Taiwanese CSPV cells. Commerce explained that "[m]odules, laminates, and panels produced in a third-country from cells produced in Taiwan are covered by this investigation."
>
>   . . .
>
> Using Commerce's scope determination, the Commission determined that an industry within the United States had been materially injured by imports of CSPV products from Taiwan. The Commission explained that it "must defer to Commerce's determination of the scope of the merchandise subject to these investigations, and Commerce has determined that U.S. imports of CSPV modules assembled in third countries such as Mexico from CSPV cells made in Taiwan are U.S. imports of subject merchandise from Taiwan."
>
>   . . .
>
> Kyocera nevertheless argued that the Commission had to conduct a separate negligibility analysis regarding Mexican solar panels incorporating Taiwanese CSPV cells.

Based on the plain meaning of § 1677(24), the Federal Circuit ruled against Kyocera. The scope of the AD investigation encompassed solar cells from Taiwan, including panels made in Taiwan, but wholly or partially manufactured in Mexico. The solar panels assembled and finished in Mexico still were made in Taiwan, because they had CSPV cells, so no separate negligibility analysis was

II. Steps 1 and 2: Filing Petition, Standing, and Sufficiency

- **Self-Initiation**

Technically, the DOC may initiate an AD or CVD investigation. That is rare. Until October 2017, the DOC did so only three times, and never since 1991. However, in November 2017, the DOC self-initiated an AD-CVD case against aluminum. The subject merchandise was common alloy sheet from China (or from China processed in a third country), specifically, flat-rolled aluminum with a thickness of 6.3 mm or less, but greater than 0.2 mm, in coils or cut-to-length, regardless of width.[7] Excluded from the scope of investigation was aluminum can stock, which is used in beverage cans, lids, and tabs.

Self-initiation occurs under Sections 702(a) [for CVD cases, 19 U.S.C. Section 1671a(a)] and 732(a) [for AD cases, 19 U.S.C. Section 1673a(a)(1)] of the *Tariff Act of 1930*, as amended, which specify that AD and/or CVD investigations "shall be initiated whenever the administering authority determines, from information available to it, that a formal investigation is warranted into the question of whether the elements necessary for the imposition of a duty under [Sections 701 (CVD) or 731 (AD)] exist." So, in the aluminum case, the DOC observed:

> we have information warranting an investigation into whether (1) the United States price [*i.e.*, Export or Constructed Export Price] of common alloy sheet from China may be less than the normal value of such or similar merchandise, (2) imports of common alloy sheet from China may be benefitting from countervailable subsidies , and (3) imports of common alloy sheet from China may be materially injuring, or threatening material injury to, the domestic industry producing common alloy sheet in the United States.[8]

Depending on the subject merchandise, American MNCs can benefit from self-initiation. For instance, upon the DOC announcement of the aluminum investigation, the stock prices of Alcoa Corp. and Century Aluminium Co. rose. Self-initiation also can help SMEs, which may lack the resources to marshal the data for an AD or CVD petition. And, self-initiation is useful if a prospective petitioner fears retaliation

---

needed for them. *See also* Brian Flood, *Duties Remain on Solar Panels Made from Taiwanese Cells*, 33 International Trade Reporter (BNA) 1811 (22 December 2016) (reporting on the case).

7. The DOC announcement provided the HTSUS Sub-Headings at the 8-digit level, for example: 7606.11.3060, 7606.11.6000, 7606.12.3090, 7606.12.6000, 7606.91.3090, 7606.91.6080, 7606.92.3090, 7606.92.6080, 7606.11.3030, 7606.12.3030, 7606.91.3060, 7606.91.6040, 7606.92.3060, 7606.92.6040, and 7607.11.9090. *See* United States Department of Commerce, International Trade Administration, Fact Sheet, *Commerce Self-Initiates Antidumping Duty and Countervailing Duty Investigations of Imports of Common Alloy Aluminum Sheet from the People's Republic of China*, 28 November 2017, www.commerce.gov/sites/commerce.gov/files/fact_sheet_commerce_self-initiates_antidumping _duty_and_countervailing_duty_investigations_of_imports_of_common_alloy_aluminum _sheet_from_the_peoples_republic_of_china.pdf. [Hereinafter, Fact Sheet.]

8. Fact Sheet.

by a foreign government, for example, when an American MNC believes it would be the target of a tit-for-tat AD or CVD action by China (on merchandise it exports to China) if that MNC were to initiate such an action in the U.S. against Chinese producer-exporters (that ship products like those the MNC makes in the U.S.).

- **Persistent Pattern of Dumping from Additional Supplier Countries**

Interestingly, in instances in which more than 1 AD duty order already is in place, Section 609 of the *Trade and Tariff Act of 1984* (codified at 19 U.S.C. § 1673a(2)) empowers the DOC to monitor imports from additional supplier countries for up to one year to determine whether "an extraordinary pattern of persistent injurious dumping" that "caus[es] a serious commercial for the domestic industry" occurs with respect to a particular product and, in turn, whether it should self-initiate an AD investigation of that product from the additional supplier countries. There is no analogous provision for "persistent subsidization" in CVD cases.

- **Petitioner Initiation**

In almost every AD-CVD investigation, it is an "interested party" that files a petition. An "interested party" is one that acts "on behalf of" the allegedly affected U.S. industry and is defined in terms of the following categories of petitioners:

(1) A manufacturer, producer, or wholesaler in the U.S. of a like product.

(2) A certified or recognized union or group of workers that is representative of the affected industry.

(3) A trade or business association with a majority of members producing a like product.

(4) A coalition of firms, unions, or trade associations in which a majority of the individual members have standing.

(5) A coalition or trade association representative of processors, or processor and growers, in cases involving processed agricultural products.

An AD or CVD petition is filed simultaneously with the DOC and ITC. Within 20 days after filing, the DOC must determine whether the petition is legally sufficient to commence an investigation. For SMEs, the DOC is required to give technical assistance in preparing and filing a petition. As a practical matter, counsel for petitioners is well-advised to meet informally with the DOC on a possible draft petition. At that juncture, the DOC cannot render a formal decision about the legal sufficiency of a draft, it may be able to provide useful tips as to how it might view certain aspects of that petition.

While the universe of "interested parties" is large, it is bounded. Individuals or groups not involved in producing a like product are excluded. For example, suppose the subject merchandise is personal computers. Producers of upstream components, such as semi-conductors (*i.e.*, chips), would not be "interested parties." Similarly, producers of downstream products, such as USB hubs, would not have standing as petitioners.

The filing of a petition by a U.S. industry against a foreign exporter or manufacturer, targeting the goods of that foreign company, can have serious adverse effects for the company. At a minimum, it has an *in terrorem* effect. It can lead to the company agreeing quickly to raise its prices in the U.S. Indeed, an ulterior motive for filing a petition may be to coerce a foreign exporter or manufacturer into a tacit price cartel, the members of which are the petitioners (and, possibly, other foreign companies).

To provide some safety that an AD or CVD petition is a *bona fide* representation of the sentiments of a domestic industry, Article 5:4 of the WTO *Antidumping Agreement* contains two quantitative metrics to determine whether a petition is filed "by or on behalf of" that industry, or whether the petition would amount to protectionist abuse. They are called the "25% Test" and the "50% Test." Each Test must be satisfied for a petitioner to have standing. Both tests ensure the support of a critical mass of domestic producers in the importing country.

The DOC is responsible for administering these tests as part of its initial determination as to the legal sufficiency of a petition. Significantly, once standing is decided, it may not be challenged before the DOC (or ITC) as the case proceeds through the preliminary and final review steps. However, standing may be challenged in a subsequent court action.

Do the 25% and 50% Tests, which are designed to ensure a petition is supported by a domestic industry, gauge the common good, *i.e.*, the broad public interest? The answer is a clear "no." They measure industry interest, not the public interest. Might there be overlap between industry and public interest? That depends on the case, and the extent to which "industry" is defined to include at least some of the consumers of the subject merchandise.

The 25% Test focuses on the absolute size, measured in terms of output of the domestic like product, of producers or workers supporting an AD or CVD petition. Under this Test, more than 25% of the total industry output — whether in support of the petition, in opposition to the petition, or abstaining (no view) — must be in favor of the petition. That is, producers expressing support for the petition must account for at least 25% of the total domestic production of the like domestic product, regardless of whether the output is made by a producer supporting or opposing the petition.

As for the 50% Test, it focuses on the relative size of domestic producers (or workers) supporting versus opposing an AD or CVD petition. Under this Test, more than 50% of the output of the domestic like product made by producers (or workers) that have a view (have taken a position) on the petition — whether in support of or in opposition to the petition — must be in favor of the petition. Producers who support the petition must account for more than 50% of the total output of the product made by those producers who either support or oppose the petition. Succinctly put, of the producers expressing a position on the petition, more producers must support than oppose it, otherwise the petition does not represent the industry.

Observe the 50% Test measures support and opposition in terms of output of producers that "yes" or "no" to a petition. The total of supporters and opponents, in terms of output, may not equal the total output of the industry, because several producers may have no view on the petition (in effect, they abstain). Suppose the management of a particular company and the workers employed there take oppositional positions on a petition? Under the *Statement of Administrative Action* accompanying the WTO *Antidumping Agreement*, the DOC treats output of that firm as neither support for nor opposition to the petition. Moreover, if the 50% Test is not satisfied (and assuming the 25% Test is met), then DOC must poll the industry. In the event of such polling, the DOC has 40 days to determine whether to initiate an investigation.

As an example, suppose a petition alleges dumping or illegal subsidization of sugar from the EU. American sugar cane plantation owners in Florida file the petition, as do some Louisiana plantation owners. There is one plantation in Mississippi, on which field workers support the petition, but the owners do not. No sugar beet producer, from which sugar also is derived, agrees with the action. They are located in western states such as Wyoming. Assume American sugar (whether from cane or beet) is considered "like" the EU import, and total domestic (*i.e.*, American) output in the relevant period is 1 million tons. Output of producers supporting the petition is 400,000 tons. But, of this figure, 50,000 tons are from the Mississippi plantation. Output of producers opposing the petition is 200,000 tons. Do the petitioners have standing?

The answer is "yes." The petitioners pass both Tests. Output from the Mississippi plantation does not count in favor of the petition, because of the split views between owners and management. By inference, 400,000 tons of output abstains, expressing no view on the petition. Accordingly, calculation of the 25% Test is as follows:

$$= \frac{\text{Output of Petition Supporters}}{\text{Total Output of Domestic Industry}}$$

$$= \frac{350,000}{1,000,000}$$

$$= 35\%$$

The first Test is met, as the benchmark is at least 25%. As for the 50% Test, it is checked as follows:

$$= \frac{\text{Output of Petition Supporters}}{\text{Output of Petition Supporters} + \text{Output of Petition Opponents}}$$

$$= \frac{350,000}{350,000 + 200,000}$$

$$= 63.6\%$$

This figure is more than 50%, the relevant threshold, hence the 50% Test is passed. As both Tests are met, the petitioners have standing.

Observe from this example the location of the plantations is irrelevant, as is the interests of American sugar consumers. What matters is the vote in favor or against the petition, weighted by quantity of output. However, suppose owners of several Florida plantations are citizens of, or reside in, Brazil. Should their output be counted in favor of the petition, or might they be biased by virtue of their link to Brazil? Would the answer matter if Brazil, as part of *MERCOSUR*, had a FTA with the EU?

In at least one respect, the 25% and 50% Tests are welcome innovations. There were no such harmonized standing requirements in pre-Uruguay Round law. In the U.S., a petitioner was assumed to have standing to file a petition on behalf of an industry, unless another member of the relevant industry challenged that standing. That regime was legally ambiguous, and outcomes depended on circumstances. The Tests offer bright-line rules, with the attendant features such rules provide— certainty and predictability.

Yet, are there conceptual shortcomings associated with the Tests? Do the Tests afford enhanced possibilities for protectionist abuse, especially because they rely on an antediluvian distinction between "foreign" and "domestic" production? To be sure, Articles 4 and 5 of the WTO *Antidumping Agreement* do not require a domestic industry on behalf of which a petition is filed to be owned or controlled by a party in the importing country. But, the Tests depend on an underlying assumption that manufacturing operations are neatly divided along territorial lines between a petitioner in the importing country and respondent in a foreign country. In reality, many finished products are the result of a global chain of raw materials, factor inputs, and intermediate goods. That is, in many industries, it is erroneous to think of 100% American producers facing wholly foreign competitors. Such industries are, in effect, demographically mixed.

Furthermore, do practical flaws bedevil the 25% and 50% Tests, with the result being it is easier to file an AD or CVD petition? Consider the fact that Article 5:4 of the WTO *Antidumping Agreement* broadens the universe of potential petitioners. Footnote 14 to Article 5:4 states "Members are aware that in the territory of certain Members, *employees* of domestic producers of the like product or *representatives* of those employees, may make or support an application for an investigation . . . ." Read literally, the footnote means not only labor unions or other worker associations, but also individual employees or *ad hoc* groups of workers, can file a petition. In the U.S., the effect of this language is to place management and workers on an equal footing with respect to supporting or opposing a petition. There are reasons to favor giving *ad hoc* groups of workers standing. But, those reasons presume (1) the prospect of more AD and CVD cases filed against foreign competitors is positive, and (2) *ad hoc* groups of workers can be trusted to file meritorious claims.

There may be doubts as to whether an industry that has lost its comparative advantage can avoid grasping at protective measures.

Moreover, all such reasons in favor of expanding the universe of petitioner to include *ad hoc* worker groups would have to remember that successful American firms could be the targets of (*i.e.,* respondents in) AD or CVD cases brought by *ad hoc* groups of workers in foreign countries. In the U.S., there is a historical tendency to think of trade remedy cases in a one-way direction, usually offensively from a petitioner perspective. Under the pre-Uruguay Round law of some GATT contracting parties, unions (much less individual employees) may not have had standing to file a petition. Under the *Antidumping Agreement*, both organized and *ad hoc* groups have standing. Consequently, successful U.S. exporters could be vulnerable to attack in such actions.

As another possible practical flaw, query what entities may express an opinion on an AD or CVD petition. Under Article 4:1(i) of the *Antidumping Agreement*, domestic producers related to a respondent are conditionally disenfranchised from expressing an opinion on a petition. There is a perverse burden of proof for a determination of industry support for a petition. To appreciate this point, consider the following example.

Suppose Nippon Steel Corporation (NSC) has an American subsidiary, Nippon U.S.A., to which it exports steel. Nippon U.S.A., which as a subsidiary of NSC obviously is related to NSC, manufactures both steel and steel-based products like tubing, ball bearings and chain-linked fences. Nippon U.S.A. opposes an AD (or CVD) petition filed by Bethlehem Steel, a U.S. producer, filed against NSC. Bethlehem Steel is a competitor of Nippon U.S.A. The Salina Steel Company, a Kansas-based company, is unrelated to the exporter. Salina imports and uses steel directly from NSC. Salina purchases steel and steel-based products from NSC Japan directly, and from Bethlehem Steel. Salina opposes the petition. The Diagram depicts these facts. At issue is whether the DOC considers the opposition of Nippon U.S.A. and SSC when determining industry support for the petition.

In this situation, the DOC can exclude both Nippon U.S.A. and Salina Steel Company from both the 25% and 50% Tests. Indeed, the DOC must exclude Nippon U.S.A., because this entity is considered an opposing domestic producer related to the exporter. As for Salina Steel, the DOC has the discretion to exclude it. That is, the DOC is empowered to exclude from application of both Tests an unrelated importer of subject merchandise. These exclusions make it easier for the petitioner to meet these tests.

The only instance in which a related producer and unrelated importer can be included is if they show an AD or CVD order would adversely affect their interests. (Pre-Uruguay Round law contained no such rule or exception.) Plainly, the presumption of exclusion conditionally disenfranchises an affiliate of an exporter, and unaffiliated importer. It is an inherent pro-petitioner bias. In the example, to

Diagram 2-1. Hypothetical Case on Standing

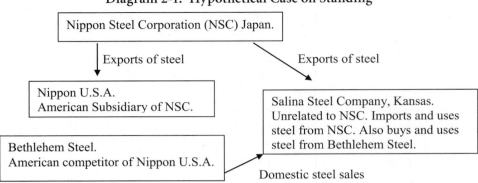

overcome the presumption, Nippon U.S.A., an affiliate of the exporter (NSC), must prove to the DOC:

(1) it uses steel from NSC in the production of steel-based products,

(2) it would be harmed by an increase in the price of steel caused by an AD duty, and

(3) no reliable domestic substitutable steel exists (or it is prohibitively expensive).

Otherwise, Nippon USA will have no voice in the 25% and 50% Tests. Salina Steel Company, an unaffiliated importer, must make the same showing, if it wants a voice.

What is the rationale for putting this burden on affiliates of an exporter and on an unaffiliated importer? One answer is to ensure that foreign producers like NSC, which would not normally be expected to support a petition, are not allowed to prevent investigations from going forward simply by directing or encouraging (implicitly or explicitly) their affiliates in the U.S. to oppose a petition. Is this rationale unfair?

Arguably, it is. First, it is unclear how a related domestic producer that imports subject merchandise can meet the burden of proof. How, for example, can Nippon U.S.A. show its interests as a domestic producer would be adversely affected by imposing an AD or CVD order? Must Nippon U.S.A. demonstrate that it would have to close down production because of the increased cost of imported materials resulting from an AD duty or CVD? Or, would a modest decline in the profits of Nippon U.S.A. be a sufficient adverse effect? These ambiguities mean Bethlehem Steel has ample room to argue a remedial action would have no adverse effect on Nippon U.S.A. Bethlehem Steel could try arguing Nippon U.S.A. cannot possibly be hurt by an AD order, because Nippon USA always can get its steel from its Japanese parent at a non-arm's length price.

Second, the burden of proof operates in a discriminatory manner. The burden is on a related domestic producer, and unrelated importer, to show harm from an AD order. But, no burden is placed on an unrelated domestic producer (or, for that matter, a related importer). Suppose, for example, the Patriot Steel Corporation, a

U.S. company unrelated to NSC, manufactures steel and steel products. To register its opposition to Bethlehem Steel's petition with the DOC, Patriot Steel need not prove it would be injured by an AD or CVD order. Placing the burden on Nippon U.S.A., but not Patriot Steel, assumes corporate affiliation alone determines the position a company takes in an AD action and essentially treats a foreign-owned company as guilty until proven innocent.

It may be countered an American subsidiary is unlikely to challenge its foreign parent. Would that improbability justify the discrimination? To minimize the risk of protectionist abuse, would it be wise to reverse the burden of proof? That would mean the presumption is Patriot Steel (as well as Nippon U.S.A. and Salina Steel) is enfranchised. The petitioner would have to prove these entities should be excluded on the ground that, with respect to Nippon U.S.A., it assesses its interests not from the viewpoint of its American operations, but instead from that of its Japanese parent. Reversing the burden might compel the DOC to consider expressly the possible positive effects of steel imports at allegedly dumped prices, rather than on the claims of Bethlehem Steel.

III. Steps 3 and 4: Preliminary Determinations and Their Effects

Assuming an AD or CVD investigation is commenced, what is the target? Technically, the answer is imports of a particular product from a particular exporting country, called "subject merchandise." Not surprisingly, companies responsible for making and bringing into the importing country the subject merchandise regard themselves as the targets. They are the respondents in the investigation. Petitioners tend to name as many possible respondents as they can—*i.e.*, the exporters, producers, and importers of the merchandise on which they seek to have an AD duty or CVD imposed.

The first preliminary determination is made by the ITC as to whether there is a "reasonable indication" of material injury, or threat thereof, to a domestic producer of a like product. That this determination occurs first is logical enough. If there is no "harm," then there is no "foul." The ITC must make the finding within 45 days of the day a petition is filed. Its decision is based on information available (IA) to it at that time. If the ITC determination is negative, then the petition is dismissed and the case ends.

Only with an affirmative preliminary injury determination does the investigation shift back to the DOC. In an AD case, that Department must make a preliminary dumping margin determination. Specifically, the DOC considers whether there is a "reasonable basis to believe or suspect" subject merchandise is, or is likely to be, sold at LTFV, *i.e.*, whether it is dumped. Accordingly, the DOC must ascertain Normal Value and Export Price (or Constructed Export Price), and consider adjustments to these figures to provide a fair comparison. In a CVD case, the DOC decides whether there is a "reasonable basis to believe or suspect that a counter-vailable subsidy is being provided," *i.e.*, whether subject merchandise benefits (or benefited) from an unlawful subsidy provided by a foreign government (*i.e.*, the government of an exporting country).

The DOC must make its preliminary dumping decision within 140 days after an investigation is initiated, and its preliminary subsidy determination within 65 days after initiation. But, it cannot do so before the ITC makes a preliminary affirmative determination of injury. As with the ITC determination, the DOC uses IA at the time. In two instances, expedited consideration is possible.

First, the DOC may make a preliminary finding within 90 days of initiation, based on IA from the first 60 days. To do so, the information must be sufficient, and the petitioner and respondent must agree to the expedited procedure and waive the need for verification of the evidence available. In a CVD case, an expedited determination is possible under the same conditions, using IA from the first 50 days. Second, in an AD case, a preliminary determination may be made for short-life cycle merchandise (*e.g.*, perishable products), if the foreign producer has been subject to a prior affirmative dumping determination on a similar product.

Conversely, postponements are possible. A preliminary dumping margin determination can be delayed until 190 days after initiation, at the request of the petitioner or if the DOC finds the circumstance are extraordinarily complicated. In a CVD case, either at the petitioner's request or if the DOC finds the issues extraordinarily complicated, extension is possible for 130 days after initiation. Also, in a CVD case, the preliminary subsidy determination can be extended for 250 days if an upstream subsidy is at issue. (An "upstream subsidy" is a financial contribution or benefit, other than an export subsidy, paid by a governmental authority on an input product used in the same country as the authority to manufacture subject merchandise. Under U.S. CVD law, an upstream subsidy is countervailable if it bestows a "competitive benefit" on the merchandise, and has a "significant effect" on the cost of production.)

If the DOC makes a preliminary affirmative dumping margin or subsidy determination by the DOC, then 3 important effects follow.

First Effect: Estimation

The DOC calculates an estimate of the average amount by which NV exceeds EP (or CEP), *i.e.*, of the average dumping margin. In a CVD case, the DOC estimates the net countervailable subsidy, that is, the amount of the unlawful subsidy provided by the government of the exporting country. The figure becomes the estimated duty rate.

Second Effect: Suspension

The DOC directs the CBP to suspend liquidation of all entries of merchandise subject to the affirmative preliminary determination. The suspension applies to shipments of foreign merchandise covered by the investigation from the date the

DOC publishes its preliminary decision (which appears in the *Federal Register*). "Liquidation" means completion of all documentation associated with an entry of a shipment of merchandise, and requires final computation of the duties and fees due on an entry.[9] Thus, suspension of liquidation means the CBP defers calculation of the amount and rate of tariff duty applicable to each individual entry until later. The merchandise may enter the U.S. (or be entered into a warehouse, FTZ, or put in temporary importation in bond). But, as that entry is not liquidated, liability remains for final payment of duties (if any).

Third Effect: Security

For each entry, and subsequent entries, of subject merchandise, the respondent must post with the CBP a cash deposit equal to the estimated dumping margin or estimated net countervailable subsidy the DOC calculates in its preliminary determination. The "coughing up" of funds must occur at the time the merchandise is imported. The obligation to post security is not a mere down payment. It is collateral for (and typically equal to) the full amount in question. This security is required to assure payment of remedial duties, in the event of final affirmative dumping or subsidy and injury determinations and issuance of an AD or CVD order. Until November 2011, the respondent could post a bond or other appropriate security, instead of cash. To ensure the CBP collects the full amount of AD or CVD duties owed should an investigation lead to final liability for them, the DOC amended its regulations to permit only cash deposits (though in "rare and unusual circumstances," determined on a case-by-case basis, the DOC has the discretion to accept a bond).[10] In an era of perpetual budget crises, the change was unsurprising.

The third effect is dramatic. Posting security for estimated duties is costly for the respondent—the importer, producer, and/or exporter of subject merchandise. The respondent also is faced with price uncertainty in its business operations. Should the cost of depositing the estimated duties be passed on to the consumers of the merchandise, assuming they can bear this cost? What if no final AD or CVD duty order is issued, or, what if a final order is issued, but it assesses a duty rate different from the estimated duty rate? The respondent must make important price decisions in a legally uncertain environment. It also must consider whether, in an AD case, the motivation of the petitioner is to compel it to raise its prices. Is the petitioner trying to force it to join a cartel? If so, then is a price cartel unlawful?

Clearly, then, the process is designed to allow the CBP to start collecting security for AD duties or CVDs as soon as the ITC and DOC have preliminarily determined, respectively, that imports are causing or threatening to cause injury, and are being sold at LTFV. The estimated dumping margin or net countervailable subsidy is the relevant figure for collecting the requisite cash deposit or bond following the

---

9. If the DOC fails to liquidate or suspend liquidation of entries within a designated period of time, then the entries of merchandise in question must be entered at the duty rate claimed by the importer.

10. *See* 19 C.F.R. Section 351.205(a).

preliminary determination, and also following final DOC and ITC determinations (if both are affirmative). This figure, or rate, applies to existing entries of subject merchandise, and prospectively to subsequent entries. The estimate may be recalculated during an Administrative Review, otherwise the liability of the importer of record of the merchandise is fixed at the estimated rate.

Furthermore, following an affirmative preliminary dumping margin or subsidy determination from the DOC, the ITC begins a final injury determination. The DOC must provide the ITC with IA relevant to an injury or threat determination. In the meantime, the DOC proceeds directly to a final determination.

Suppose the DOC's preliminary determination is negative. The above 3 effects do not occur, and the ITC does not start a final injury determination. Rather, the DOC proceeds to a final determination, and the ITC awaits the outcome. The ITC never commences or completes a final determination based only on a negative preliminary determination by the DOC. The ITC begins a final determination only after an affirmative preliminary or final determination from the DOC.

Finally, another dramatic event that can occur during a preliminary AD investigation involves "critical circumstances." Petitioners may allege these exist, and if successful, obtain retroactive relief: imposition of the AD duty on subject merchandise entered up to 90 days before the date of the preliminary dumping margin determination. It is for the DOC to find whether "critical circumstances" exist, which it does if: (1) there is an import surge of subject merchandise before issuance of an AD order; and (2) the importer of subject merchandise knew or should have known the subject merchandise was being dumped and dumping would cause material injury. The DOC imputes that knowledge to the importer whenever the dumping margin equals or exceeds 25% as calculated for the POI.[11]

IV. Steps 5 and 6: Final Determinations

Regardless of the outcome of a preliminary dumping margin or subsidy determination, the DOC proceeds to render a final determination. Essentially, its job is to look again at whether LTFV sales are occurring, and check the magnitude (if any) of the dumping margin. Thus, in an AD case, it scrutinizes the calculation of Normal Value and Export Price (or Constructed Export Price), considers adjustments needed to these price figures to ensure a fair comparison, and establishes a figure for

---

11. For an AD investigation involving a "critical circumstances," see the 1994 *Chinese Honey* case. The DOC found them to exist, and in 2003 the CIT agreed. Following multiple remands and appeals, the 2005 Federal Circuit overturned that finding. Following yet another remand, the CIT upheld a DOC determination that no critical circumstances existed. *See Zhejiang Native Produce & Animal By-Products Import & Export Corporation v. United States*, Federal Circuit Number 2013-1574 (10 October 2014); Brian Flood, *Federal Circuit OKs AD Duties on Honey, Despite Suspension Agreement with China*, 31 International Trade Reporter (BNA) 1837 (16 October 2014).

Normal Value and Export Price. In a CVD case, the DOC studies the alleged illegal subsidy and its magnitude, and decides upon the net countervailable subsidy.

If the DOC's final dumping margin or subsidy determination is affirmative, then it comes up with a final estimated dumping margin or final estimated net countervailable subsidy. Further, the DOC orders the CBP to suspend liquidation of entries, and to post a cash deposit, bond, or other security (assuming these actions were not already taken — they would not have been if the preliminary determination had been negative). Further, with an affirmative final determination, the ITC completes its final injury determination, and the DOC awaits notice of this result.

If the DOC's final determination is negative, then the ITC ends its final injury inquiry. An AD duty or CVD follows only after final DOC and ITC determinations. A negative final dumping margin or subsidy determination terminates the investigation and ends a case, as does a negative final injury determination. Any suspension of liquidation of entries ends, *i.e.*, subject merchandise is liquidated. All estimated duties are refunded, and all bonds or other security released.

The DOC must issue a final dumping margin or subsidy determination within 75 days of its preliminary decision.[12] In an AD case, upon acceptance of a timely request, this period can be extended to up to 135 days from the prior determination. In a CVD case involving upstream subsidies, there are special extended time limits. In a case of both AD and CVD claims about the same subject merchandise, the petitioner can request the DOC postpone its final subsidy determination until the date of the final AD determination.

How much time does the ITC have to complete its final injury determination? The answer depends on the outcome of the DOC's dumping or subsidy investigation. If the preliminary determination by the DOC is negative, but is followed by an affirmative determination, then the ITC has 75 days after that final affirmative determination. If the preliminary determination by the DOC is affirmative, then the ITC must make its final determination within the longer of (1) 120 days from an affirmative preliminary determination by the DOC, or (2) 45 days from an affirmative final determination by the DOC. If the ITC's final injury determination is negative, then the case is terminated, and estimated duty deposits are refunded. But, if the ITC's final injury determination is affirmative, then the DOC issues an AD order within 7 days of the ITC's determination.

---

12. Absent the extenuating instances mentioned above, if the DOC delays for longer than 120 days from the date of its preliminary dumping margin or subsidization determination to make a final determination, and it has been collecting estimated AD duties or CVDs, then (under both U.S. law and WTO rules), the DOC cannot collect further duties until a final determination. This rule can create a gap during which allegedly dumped or subsidized merchandise is not "hit" with AD duties or CVD (*e.g.*, if the DOC had been levying estimated duties, but then delays a final decision, as occurred in a *Softwood Lumber* dispute with Canada in August 2017), but it also assures respondents they are not liable interminably for a penalty following a preliminary determination they lost. The DOC has to act — fish or cut bait, as it were.

The legal criteria applied in final injury determinations are set forth in the Article 3 of the WTO *Antidumping Agreement*, Articles 5–6 of the *SCM Agreement*, and U.S. law. In brief, the ITC looks to see whether a domestic producer of a like product (*i.e.*, like the subject merchandise) is, by reason of dumped imports, materially injured, or threatened with material injury, or (in rare instances), whether the establishment of an industry in the U.S. is materially retarded. In an *SCM Agreement* case brought by one WTO Member against another Member under the *DSU*, the grounds for injury are broader, including not only (1) injury to the domestic industry of another member, but also (2) nullification or impairment of benefits accruing to another Member, or (3) serious prejudice to the interests of another Member. Collectively, these grounds are called "adverse effects."

V. Suspension Agreements, Subsequent Dumping, and 2014 China Honey Case

- **Overview**

At any point in an AD or CVD case, settlement may occur. If the petitioner withdraws its petition, then either the DOC or ITC may terminate the investigation. If the investigation was self-initiated, then the DOC has the discretion to terminate. Or, an investigation may be suspended because of settlement. Article 8 of the WTO *Antidumping Agreement* countenances undertakings to suspend investigations. Under what conditions does suspension occur?

In an AD case (pursuant to 19 U.S.C. § 1673c), the DOC may suspend an investigation if it reaches one of three kinds of agreement with exporters accounting for substantially all subject merchandise.

(1) An agreement to cease exports of subject merchandise within six months of suspending the investigation. Essentially, the exporters exit the U.S. market.

(2) An agreement to revise prices to eliminate completely all LTFV sales. In effect, exporters commit to change their pricing strategy in the U.S., which means raising the price of subject merchandise through a price undertaking.

(3) An agreement to revise prices to eliminate completely the injurious effects of exports of subject merchandise on American producers.[13] Again, the undertaking concerns boosting the price of subject merchandise.

---

13. For a case in which the DOC failed to prove a *Suspension Agreement* would protect the petitioning U.S. industry from the "injurious effects," see *Florida Tomato Exchange v. United States*, CIT Number 13-00148 (25 August 2017). The subject merchandise, fresh tomatoes, was dumped from Mexico, which had been covered by *Suspension Agreements* since 1996. A 2013 *Agreement* fixed minimum prices for four categories of Mexican tomatoes during the summer and winter months. The CIT agreed that *Agreement* would restrict dumping into the U.S., but ruled the DOC failed to show the *Agreement* would ensure Mexican tomatoes would not suppress or depress prices in the U.S. Empirical data from the USDA reinforced the decision: in the early 1990s, one-fifth of

Unless the country of exportation is an NME, a promise to impose a quantitative restriction (*e.g.*, to limit exports of subject merchandise via a quota) would not suffice as a basis for suspension. In all instances, the DOC must be sure termination or suspension of an investigation is in the public interest and it is practicable to be monitored.

In a CVD case (pursuant to 19 U.S.C. § 1671c), the DOC may suspend an investigation based on one of three types of agreements with a foreign government, or with exporters accounting for substantially all imports of subject merchandise:

(1) An agreement to eliminate the subsidy completely, or offset it completely within six months of suspension of the investigation.

(2) An agreement to cease exportation of the subject merchandise within six months of suspension of the investigation.

(3) An agreement to eliminate completely the injurious effects of subsidized exports (*e.g.*, through a QR, a possibility not available under AD law unless the country of exportation is an NME).

In both the AD and CVD contexts, the agreement to suspend an investigation is called a "*Suspension Agreement*." In effect, the *Agreement* is a contract involving the petitioner, respondent or respondent's home-country government, and DOC. The DOC promises to end an AD or CVD investigation, in exchange for changed behavior by the other side.

The DOC cannot enter into a *Suspension Agreement* without publishing notice of its intent to suspend an investigation and giving interested parties an opportunity to comment. The DOC can decide not to accept a proposed *Agreement*, but then must explain why to the exporters involved and give them the chance (if practicable) to comment. If the DOC chooses to proceed with an *Agreement*, it must first issue an affirmative preliminary dumping margin or subsidy determination, and publish notice of the suspension. Even if the DOC elects to accept an *Agreement*, both sides—a domestic interested party, and exporters accounting for a significant proportion of exports of the subject merchandise—have 20 days after publication of the notice of the *Agreement* to call for continuation of the investigation. The DOC and ITC must honor this request.

The effect of a *Suspension Agreement* goes beyond termination of an investigation by the DOC into dumping or subsidization. The ITC, too, suspends its injury investigation. Moreover, the suspension of liquidation of entries of subject merchandise (which, as explained below, follows an affirmative preliminary dumping or subsidy determination) terminates. Any deposits of estimated AD duties or CVDs are

---

all tomatoes consumed in America were imported, but by 2016, the figure was 1/3. So, American tomato growers had lost market share to foreign competitors, and Mexico was the single largest foreign source. *See* Brian Flood, *Trade Court Rejects U.S.-Mexico Tomato Deal*, 34 International Trade Reporter (BNA) 1194 (7 September 2017).

refunded, and any cash deposits posted as security for these duties are released. The DOC is responsible for monitoring compliance with any *Suspension Agreement*, and an intentional violation of an *Agreement* is a civil offence punishable by fines.

- **Later Dumping Finding and October 2014 *Chinese Honey* Case**

Can goods covered by a *Suspension Agreement* later be found to be dumped? Ostensibly not: the object of an *Agreement* is to prevent dumping, so a foreign producer-exporter and/or importer raise prices of the goods to eliminate the possibility of a dumping margin. However, the answer is yes, if the purpose of the *Agreement* is not to eliminate dumping. Indeed, the pertinent statute does not mandate an *Agreement* have as its aim the elimination of dumping.

In the infamous *Chinese Honey* AD case, launched in 1994, a *Suspension Agreement* was reached that established annual export limits and reference prices determined by the weighted average import values of honey from countries other than China. The purpose of this *Agreement* was to prevent undercutting of domestic prices. The reference prices were not designed for computation of an LTFV margin. So, in October 2014, when the DOC declared Chinese honey imports under the Agreement subject to AD duties, the Federal Circuit—in *Zhejiang Native Produce & Animal By-Products Import & Export Corporation v. United States*—agreed.[14]

VI. Suspension Agreements, Managed Trade, and 2017 *Mexican Sugar* Case

- **Managed Trade in Sugar under *NAFTA***

NAFTA did not create free trade in sugar.[15] To the contrary, under the originally negotiated terms, Mexican sugar exports to the U.S. were subject to a TRQ. Regarding the quota thresholds of the TRQ:

---

14. *See* Number 2013-1574 (10 October 2014); Brian Flood, *Federal Circuit OKs AD Duties on Honey, Despite Suspension Agreement with China*, 31 International Trade Reporter (BNA) 1837 (16 October 2014).

15. *NAFTA* is hardly the only example of an FTA not freeing up trade in sugar. *CAFTA-DR*, along with America's bilateral FTAs with Chile, Morocco, Panama, and Peru are further examples. Under them, each CY the USTR sets an annual allowance of sugar, sugar-containing goods, and syrup goods from those countries that may enter the U.S. duty-free, which appear in HTSUS Chapter 98 or 99. The allowance depends on whether the FTA party had a trade surplus in sugar products during a recent previous year. For example, in CY 2016, Colombia, Costa Rica, El Salvador, Guatemala, Honduras, and Nicaragua had overall trade surpluses in those products. So, the USTR granted them duty-free access for CY 2018. However, the volume granted is tightly restricted. It is capped at the prior trade surplus, or for *CAFTA-DR* countries, it is the of lesser of the (1) country's trade surplus or (2) specific quantity set out in the *CAFTA-DR* Note for that country and CY. Thus, while Costa Rica had a CY 2016 trade surplus of 122,509 metric tons, the Note sets a 2018 quantity of 13,640 metric tons, so the USTR granted only this amount duty-free access for CY 2018.

In contrast, in CY 2016, Chile, Dominican Republic, Morocco, Panama, and Peru did not export more sugar products than they imported; rather, they had trade deficit in those goods.

The original draft of the *Agreement* between Mexico and the United States regarding sugar permitted Mexico to increase duty-free exports of sugar to the United States from its level of 7,258 metric tons of raw sugar to a maximum of 25,000 metric tons. However, duty-free shipments in excess of the original 7,258 metric ton level was limited to Mexico's net sugar production surplus (domestic sugar production minus domestic sugar consumption).

[The original deal defined "net surplus production" in Mexico as simply as "projected production minus projected domestic consumption."[16] If the difference was a positive number, then Mexico was a "net surplus producer." The *Side Letters*, discussed below, changed the definition to include both sugar and HFCS consumption, as favored by American sugar producers, making it harder for Mexico to qualify as a "net surplus producer."]

In the seventh year of the *Agreement* (2001), Mexico's maximum duty-free access level for sugar exports to the United States would increase to 150,000 metric tons under the same net sugar production surplus provisions specified for the first six years. Moreover, Mexico was permitted to have unlimited access to the U.S. sugar market if Mexico became a net exporter for two successive years following the sixth year of the *Agreement*.[17]

As for the tariff feature of the TRQ:

The United States has a two-tiered tariff system that permitted Mexican sugar to enter the U.S. duty free within their sugar quotas. However, Mexico could export sugar to the United States beyond its quota by paying the second-tier tariff of approximately 17 cents per pound, raw value. Under *NAFTA*, this second-tier tariff was scheduled to decline 15 percent (total) over the first six years and then to zero by year 15 (2008). By the end of the sixth year of the *Agreement* (2000), Mexico would also install a tariff rate quota system, with a second-tier tariff applicable to other countries that is equal to the U.S. second-tariff. In effect, both countries would have

---

For instance, Chile had a trade deficit of 593,524 metric tons. So, the USTR denied for CY 2018 those goods a preference under the Chile and other pertinent FTAs. *See* Office of the United States Trade Representative, *Determination of Trade Surplus in Certain Sugar and Syrup Goods and Sugar-Containing Products of Chile, Morocco, Costa Rica, the Dominican Republic, El Salvador, Guatemala, Honduras, Nicaragua, Peru, Colombia, and Panama*, 82 Federal Register number 248, 61654-61657 (28 December 2017).

The logic of this managed trade scheme appears to be three-fold. First, if an FTA party does not have a trade surplus in sugar products, then there is no need for it to obtain duty-free access for them. Second, granting such access, despite being in a recent trade deficit position, might encourage that party to export more sugar and syrup goods, thereby posing a competitive threat to American producers. Third, granting preferential access to a trade surplus country, without a cap, also would pose a threat to them.

16. American Sugarbeet Growers Association, *North American Free Trade Agreement (U.S./Mexico Trade in Sweeteners)* (2015), https://americansugarbeet.org/north-american-free-trade-agreement-nafta/. [Hereinafter, American Sugarbeet Growers Association.]

17. American Sugarbeet Growers Association.

reduced their second-tier tariffs between themselves to zero by the fifteenth year of the *Agreement*.

The Mexican tariff on HFCS from the United States was 15 percent. It was expected to decline to zero over the next 10 years under *NAFTA*. Mexican barriers to sugar-containing products would be converted to tariffs and then decline to zero over the 10-year period.[18]

However, during the Congressional debate about *NAFTA*, the original sugar deal did not seem so sweet, for three reasons:

(1) If Mexico did in fact achieve unlimited duty-free access to the U.S. sugar market, would there be any access to the U.S. sugar market for the other 39 foreign countries with U.S. sugar quotas?

(2) What would be the status and effectiveness of the U.S. sugar program if Mexico dumped huge quantities of sugar onto the U.S. market?

(3) How much high fructose corn syrup (HFCS) would be substituted for sugar in Mexico's soft drink industry to permit Mexico to achieve net exporter status in sugar?

American sugar interests — a small number of growers and a few large companies — objected to the increased access their Mexican competitors would get under the original terms. Those producers are centered in Florida, Hawaii, Louisiana, and Texas, and they are led by politically powerful families, such as "[t]he sugar barons of Florida, Alfonso and José Fanjul, [who] have been equal-opportunity political donors for decades, showering largess on the campaigns of Democrats and Republicans alike to ensure that lawmakers will protect the American sugar industry."[19]

---

18. American Sugarbeet Growers Association.

19. Elisabeth Malkin, *Sugar Talks May Hint at Trump Approach to U.S.-Mexico Trade*, NEW YORK TIMES, 4 June 2017, https://www.nytimes.com/2017/06/04/world/americas/mexico-nafta-north-american-free-trade-agreement-sugar-subsidies.html. "When Donald J. Trump was preparing to take office as president, the Fanjul brothers wrote another check. Among the contributors to Mr. Trump's inaugural festivities in January was Florida Crystals, a Fanjul-owned company that contributed half a million dollars." *Id.*

Led by its patriarch, Alfonso Fanjul Sr., the Fanjul family arrived in Florida in 1960, fleeing the Castro takeover in Cuba. *See* Justin Villamil, *Sugar Barons Amass $8.2 Billion Fortune by Inflating U.S. Prices*, 34 International Trade Reporter (BNA) (17 August 2017). The Communists seized their business interests and private property, including homes and fine art. Yet even before Castro took power, Alfonso Sr. was "one of the world's most prosperous sugar barons," and had by 1962, had "acquired new refining plants and begun to recreate the Fanjul empire in exile." *Id.* His two eldest sons, Alfonso ("Alfy") and Jose ("Pepe"), aged 80 and 73, respectively (as of August 2017), succeeded him, and control the Florida Crystal Corporation. The Chairman and CEO, Alfy, is a Democrat and has given $1.3 million to the Democratic Party since 1989. *See id.* Pepe, the Vice Chairman and President, is a Republican, and has donated about the same figure to the Republican Party. *See id.* Their campaign contributions are well known, and they, too, admit them:

> The pair have shared so much of their money with politicians over the years that it could be that "sugar, dollar for dollar, is the most influential commodity in the U.S.," said Gary Hufbauer, a Senior Fellow at the Peterson Institute for International Economics

Point (1) concerned the sugar TRQs America had in place since the 1948 Sugar Act. Point (2) raised both AD and CVD concerns. Point (3) was a subtle but vital one, arising from the substitutability of sugar and HFCS. American sugar producers worried that Mexico's soft drink industry might substitute HFCS for sugar:

> the promise of access [for Mexican sugar exporters] to the U.S. market could encourage investment and expansion in Mexico [of sugar production] and change Mexico's demand for imports [away from sugar, and toward HFCS]. Mexico could, for example, shift to HFCS in its soft drink industry. Based on 1990 marketing year data, shifting to HFCS sweeteners in Mexico could free up as much as 1.3 million metric tons of sugar for other uses and would account for nearly all of Mexico's imports.[20]

So, under strong lobbying pressure from American sugar interests, in August 1993, the U.S. pushed Mexico to agree to a side agreement, in the form of "Side Letters," *i.e.*, exchanges of correspondence that did not technically alter the text of *NAFTA*,

---

and former Deputy Assistant Secretary in the Treasury Department. As long as the brothers are around, "I would fall out of my chair at any approach that leads to a free market in sugar."

History ... taught the family some lessons. "One of the reasons why we get involved in American politics is because of what happened to us in Cuba, Alfy Fanjul told *Vanity Fair* in 2011 in a rare interview. "We do not want what happened in Cuba to happen to us again."

. . .

"They give money to everybody who has got a shot," said Carl Hiaasen, a novelist and columnist at the *Miami Herald*. "They'll give money to people they like, but they're too smart not to give money to everybody."

. . .

Among the world's sugar refiners, the Fanjuls are No. 1 . . . . The family owns sugarcane fields in Florida, Louisiana, and the Dominican Republic.

[In 2016–2017,] the Fanjuls' lobbying focus ... [was] ... [NAFTA]. The plan when it was signed in 1992 was for Mexican sugar sales to the U.S. to be liberalized by 2008, but the Fanjuls and other producers and refiners successfully challenged that in anti-dumping complaints . . . .

. . .

In another victory, the two countries . . . [as explained above] closed a loophole Mexican producers had exploited by refining sugar just enough to be considered raw, but sufficiently processed to sell to consumers. Mexico agreed to restrictions on refined sugar sales north of the border, and a new definition of raw sugar that gives U.S. processors like the Fanjuls a leg up, by lowering the quality of what can be considered refined. President Donald Trump said in a Tweet that the deal was "a very good one" for both countries.

. . .

The [Fanjuls' luxury resort in the Dominican Republic, Casa de Camp] sits on 7,000 acres of prime coastline, and includes three golf courses, polo grounds, and an international airport. Political celebrities who've vacationed there include three former Presidents, George H.W. Bush, George W. Bush, and Bill Clinton, and Hilary Clinton.

Id.

20. American Sugarbeet Growers Association.

but merely "clarified" it, on sugar. In effect, the "clarifications" cut back on the access for Mexican sugar into the U.S. market.

In particular, under the *Side Letters*:

> [T]he formula for determining Mexico's net surplus production was amended to include HFCS on the consumption side only. Thus, Mexican sugar production would have to exceed Mexican consumption of both sugar and HFCS for Mexico to be considered a net surplus producer. It was believed that this aspect of the "side" agreement would severely diminish Mexico's chances for becoming a major sugar supplier to the United States.

> For Phase One [following the 1 January 1994 implementation of *NAFTA*] (years 1 through 6, or 1994–99), Mexico would have duty-free access for sugar exports to the United States for the amount of its net surplus production, up to a maximum of 25,000 metric tons, raw value. If Mexico was not a net surplus producer, it would still have duty-free access for 7,258 tons, or the minimum "boat-load" amount authorized under the U.S. tariff rate quota. For comparison purposes, Mexico exported an average of 12,667 metric tons in the four years prior to *NAFTA*.

> In Phase Two (years 7 through 14, or 2000–09), Mexico would have duty-free sugar access to the U.S. sugar market for the amount of its surplus as measured by the formula, up to a maximum of 250,000 metric tons, with minimum duty-free access still at the minimum "boat-load" amount.

> The "side" agreement [*Side Letters*] eliminated the unlimited sugar access provision that was contained in the original *NAFTA* language. That original provision would have allowed Mexico, after the seventh year (2001), to have duty-free access for its total net production surplus, without limit, provided that it had previously achieved a net production surplus for two successive years.[21]

It so happened that notwithstanding the revised definition in the *Side Letters* of "net surplus production," "in 2008, Mexico became the only country in the world with unrestricted access to the American sugar market."[22] In 2013, Mexico experienced a "bumper" sugar crop, hence its exports to the U.S. "soared."[23]

- **July 2017 Mexican Sugar *Suspension Agreement***

American sugar producers fought to protect their home market against the surging Mexican imports with trade remedy cases, and in 2014 the DOC was poised to impose AD duties and CVDs. However, the DOC held off doing so under a December 2014 *Suspension Agreement*, which established quotas and floor prices for

21. American Sugarbeet Growers Association.
22. *Sugar Talks May Hint.*
23. *Sugar Talks May Hint.*

Mexican sugar.[24] Why did Mexico opt not to appeal its loss to a *NAFTA* Chapter 19 Panel? The *Wall Street Journal* furnished the answer:

> [Mexico's] sugar lobby also likes high prices. So instead it agreed to comply with a U.S.-stipulated minimum price and quota, and to restrict the amount of refined sugar it ships. In other words, both sides conspired to run a sugar cartel.[25]

But, in November 2016, the DOC revisited the *Suspension Agreement*, citing concerns some Mexican sugar shipments were in breach of its terms: United States sugar refiners, such as AmCane Sugar LLC and Louis Dreyfus Co.'s Imperial Sugar Co., alleged Mexico shipped too much refined sugar, thus putting downward pressure on refined sugar prices, and not enough raw sugar (so-called "shorting" of the American market), thus hurting American sugar refiners:[26]

> "Our industry is suffering tremendously," said Phillip Hayes, a spokesman for the American Sugar Alliance, which represents sugar farmers and refiners, including Florida Crystals [a company owned by the Fanjul family]. "A refinery needs raw sugar in order to operate," he said. "Mexico has been sending in far too much refined sugar and starving the refineries of raw sugar."[27]

Mexico Economy Ministry responded thusly:

> . . . large American refineries are using the negotiations to lock in their own supply of Mexican raw sugar and eliminate all competition [in the U.S. market] from Mexican refined sugar.[28]

In Mexico, as in the U.S., the sugar industry is heard:

> Mexican sugar cane is grown by 190,000 small farmers scattered across some of Mexico's poorest regions, and at harvest time, the labor-intensive work employs 450,000, making the industry a potent political force.[29]

After tough negotiations, in June 2017 the U.S. and Mexico reached a draft deal. The DOC summarized the terms of the new *Suspension Agreement* as follows:

> The draft amendments, if finalized [which they were, in July 2017, with minor refinements], would update certain provisions, such as, in the *CVD Agreement*, the ratio between the quantities of Refined and Other Sugar [*e.g.*, Raw Sugar] that Mexico may export to the United States during a

---

24. *See* Marvin G. Perez, *Mexico, U.S. Close to Agreement on Sugar, Mexican Chamber Says*, International Trade Daily (BNA) (5 June 2017).

25. *Trump's New Sugar High*, THE WALL STREET JOURNAL, 13 June 2017, at A16. [Hereinafter, *Trump's New Sugar High*.]

26. *See* Rossella Brevetti, *Sugar Industry Rep Warns About NAFTA Talks*, 34 International Trade Reporter (BNA) 921 (22 June 2017).

27. *Sugar Talks May Hint.*

28. *Sugar Talks May Hint.*

29. *Sugar Talks May Hint.*

given export limit period, and the polarity [purity] division between the two types of sugar.

Further, in the *AD Agreement*, the minimum prices of Other Sugar and Refined Sugar would be higher to ensure that Mexican sugar imports do not suppress or undercut domestic price levels, in accordance with statutory requirements.

Finally, each agreement would contain enhanced monitoring and enforcement provisions such as a requirement for polarity testing and stiff penalties for non-compliance.

Each of these elements of the draft amendments, if finalized, would ensure that the agreements provide an adequate remedy to the U.S. domestic sugar industry against the dumping and unfair subsidization determined in the investigations.

In addition, the amendments will ensure that the sugar suspension agreements continue to promote stability in the U.S sugar market, in coordination with USDA's sugar program.

. . .

The *AD* and *CVD [Suspension] Agreements* signed by the Department and the GOM [Government of Mexico] in December 2014 differentiated between "Refined Sugar" at a polarity of 99.5 degrees and above, and "Other Sugar" at a polarity less than 99.5 degrees, and provided that no more than 53 percent of Mexican exports could be of Refined Sugar.

By contrast, the draft amendments define "Refined Sugar" as sugar at a polarity of 99.2 degrees and above, and "Other Sugar" as sugar at a polarity less than 99.2 degrees and shipped in bulk, freely flowing [not solid packed]. [Therefore, large quantities of "Other Sugar" cannot bypass U.S. sugar cane refiners and be consumed directly for end uses.]

These changes, which move the dividing line between Refined and Other Sugar down to 99.2 from 99.5 degrees, and add shipping conditions for Other Sugar, address concerns regarding ensuring an adequate supply of sugar in the U.S. market, and concerns that a large portion of Other Sugar is bypassing cane refiners for direct consumption or end use. [The changes also mandate that Mexico can account for no more than 30 percent of all Refined Sugar, from all sources, entering the U.S. market under the American TRQ measures.[30]]

Specifically, the petitioners have asserted that the sale of Mexican semi-refined sugar subject (to which the lower reference price of Other Sugar set in the *AD Agreement* applies) hinders the competitiveness of U.S. cane

---

30. *See* Nacha Cattan, Andrew Mayeda & Brian Flood, *U.S. Advances Sugar Deal with Mexico as Final Pact Nears*, 34 International Trade Reporter (BNA) 920 (22 June 2017).

refiners by substantively diminishing the supply of [Raw] Mexican sugar for their processing operations, and suppressing U.S. prices for refined sugar [by otherwise increasing the overall supply of Refined Sugar].

Because these changes substantially decrease the proportion of Sugar from Mexico that may be Refined Sugar and mean that a higher reference price applies to semi-refined sugar, there is a greater likelihood that sufficient sugar for further processing would be available in the U.S. market.

For post-April 1 Additional Needs Sugar (over the expected fiscal year U.S. needs [that is, the excess of domestic demand for sugar over what the USDA predicted the domestic industry could supply]) granted to Mexico, USDA will specify whether Raw or Refined Sugar is needed but at a polarity divide of 99.5 and without regard to the pre-April 1 70/30 split. [The "70/30 split" refers to the cap on Mexican shipments of Raw/Refined Sugar to the U.S., namely, a limit of 30% of the total TRQ shipments of Refined Sugar, as explained above.] Importantly, when Additional Needs Sugar is granted to Mexico prior to April 1, such sugar shall be subject to the pre-April 1 70/30 split and the 99.2 polarity divide, added protections for U.S. domestic refiners. Further, USDA retains the flexibility to specify the polarity of post-April 1 Additional Needs sugar specifically needed to rectify certain extraordinary and unforeseen circumstances that seriously threaten the economic viability of the U.S. sugar refining industry.

[In the final deal, the date was changed to 1 May:

"[W]ith respect to additional needs sugar (over the expected fiscal year U.S. needs) granted to Mexico, the date on which the polarity division changes from 99.2 to 99.5 has moved from April 1 to May 1. Thus, when Additional Needs Sugar is granted to Mexico *prior to May 1*, except in cases where an extraordinary or unusual circumstance is declared, such sugar shall be subject to the pre-May 1 99.2 polarity divide. For *post-May 1 Additional Needs Sugar*, USDA will specify whether raw or refined sugar is needed but at a polarity divide of 99.5. Further, at any time during a given fiscal year, USDA retains the flexibility to specify the polarity of additional needs sugar specifically needed to rectify certain extraordinary and unforeseen circumstances."[31]]

Further, the reference price for Other Sugar is being raised from 22.25 cents/pound to 23 cents/pound, while the Refined Sugar price is being raised from 26 cents/pound to 28 cents/pound.

---

31. U.S. Department of Commerce, *Final Amendments to Mexican Sugar Suspension Agreements: Fact Sheet*, 3 July 2017, www.commerce.gov/news/fact-sheets/2017/07/final-amendments-mexican-sugar-suspension-agreements-fact-sheet. The final deal was announced on 3 July. *See* U.S. Department of Commerce, *U.S., Mexico Sign Final Amendments to Sugar Suspension Agreements*, www.commerce.gov/news/press-releases/2017/07/us-mexico-sign-final-amendments-sugar-suspension-agreements.

In addition, the spread between the two prices has increased. This enhanced pricing structure serves to ensure that U.S. producers' prices are not suppressed or undercut by imports of Mexican sugar, thereby ensuring that the agreements provide an adequate remedy to the U.S. domestic industry found to have been injured.[32]

Note the following key inferences from the details, all of which evince the high degree of managed trade in favor of plutocratic interests.

First, with a polarity of 99.2 instead of 99.5, a gap covering so-called "Semi-Refined Sugar," more Mexican sugar is re-defined as "Refined" instead of "Raw." Mexican sugar with a 99.2–99.5 polarity, which had counted as "Raw," is re-categorized as "Refined." Any Mexican sugar considered "Refined" cannot easily enter the American market to compete with U.S. refined sugar—the cap drops from 53% to 30%, meaning Mexico can supply no more than 30% of the total amount of Refined Sugar entering the U.S. from all sources under the American TRQ scheme. With more Mexican sugar counted as "Refined," and a lower cap on Mexican shipments to the U.S. of "Refined Sugar," supply in the American market is further constricted. In turn, that construction means the price of Refined Sugar in the U.S. is kept artificially elevated, indeed at the higher price of 28 cents/pound. That's the point: redefining the polarity dividing line, and lowering the cap, protects American sugar refiners and the high prices they can charge for their output.

Second, that re-definition also helps American sugar refiners by ensuring the newly categorized "Raw" Sugar (that below 99.2 polarity) is available to them, for them to refine and sell in the U.S. The re-definition complements the changed cap. The 30% cap on Refined Sugar means Mexico can ship to the U.S. up to 70% of total TRQ shipments of Raw Sugar, an increase from the previous amount of 47% under the old 47/53 cap.

---

32. U.S. Department of Commerce, Fact Sheet, *Draft Amendments to Mexican Sugar Suspension Agreements*, 6 June 2017, www.commerce.gov/news/fact-sheets/2017/06/draft-amendments-mexican-sugar-suspension-agreements.

Under U.S. agricultural legislation, specifically, the *Farm Bill*, the USDA sets sugar TRQs each year as of 1 October (coinciding with the start of the FY) for a six-month period (so, the first period lasts until 1 April). The TRQs apply to raw cane sugar and refined sugar, plus specialty sugars, sugar syrups, and sugar-containing products. The USDA is barred from admitting any sugar into the American market in excess of the minimum amounts set under commitments the U.S. made during the Uruguay Round under WTO *Agriculture Agreement*, and under other pertinent agreements, *i.e.*, any sugar in excess of the TRQ threshold can enter as over- (above-) quota sugar, but faces a stiff tariff under the TRQ. The date 1 April thus matters, as by then it is apparent whether additional needs exist. After that date, USDA can open the market to additional sugar, which Mexico can supply under the first-refusal right in the *Suspension Agreement* discussed above. *See* Rossella Brevetti, Len Bracken & Andrew Wallender, *U.S. Sugar Producers, Refiners Sour on Mexico Deal*, 34 International Trade Reporter (BNA) 885 (15 June 2017) [hereinafter, *U.S. Sugar Producers*]; Rossella Brevetti, *Sugar Deal Draws Bitter Attention*, 34 International Trade Reporter (BNA) 886 (15 June 2017) (hereinafter, *Sugar Deal*).

Third, American Raw Sugar producers also benefit from protection. Because of the minimum reference price increase from 22.25 to 23 cents per pound, they can raise their prices, too.

Fourth, the use of the old polarity divide of 99.5 for post-May 1 Additional Needs Sugar, and the use of the re-defined divide of 99.2 for pre-May 1 Additional Needs Sugar and for non-Additional Needs Sugar, suggests the arbitrariness of the divide. The number is not based on science, but rather manipulated to suit American sugar growers and refiners, as is the use of the cut-off date of May Day for the so-called "Export Limit Period." The flexibility of the USDA to adjust the number reinforces the scheme.

Fifth, the widened spread in reference prices, from 3.75 cents to 5 cents per pound (the difference of 26–22.25, and 28–23, respectively), further protects American sugar interests. The gap, euphemistically characterized as "enhanced," simply means American refiners can profit from adding more value in the refining process — 5 cents instead of 3.75 cents — a value that is utterly artificial. That said, Mexico retains a privileged position in supplying the U.S. sugar market, getting first priority to supply Additional Needs sugar.

A final point serving plutocratic managed trade interests concerns transportation. "All raw sugar imported into the U.S. from Mexico must arrive freely flowing in bulk in the hold of an oceangoing vessel."[33] Rail and road carriage is forbidden — despite the excellent network, from which Kansas City and other *NAFTA* crossroads centers benefit.

These terms prompted the *Wall Street Journal* to observe:

> No industry has enjoyed as much protection under . . . *NAFTA* as sugar producers and refiners.
>
> . . .
>
> The deal suggests the strategy is to use government power to enforce cartels that protect politically powerful producers . . . .[34]

The Coalition for Sugar Reform, a group of consumer food and beverage manufacturers, labeled the terms of the *Agreement* as "the worst form of crony capitalism."[35]

To see the logic behind these characterizations, consider the specific terms of the June 2017 *Suspension Agreement* in relation to the vested interests of two American sugar constituencies. First, with respect to U.S. sugar refineries, the *Agreement*:

---

33. *See* Nacha Cattan, Andrew Mayeda & Brian Flood, *U.S. Advances Sugar Deal with Mexico as Final Pact Nears*, 34 International Trade Reporter (BNA) 920 (22 June 2017).

34. *Trump's New Sugar High*.

35. Andrew Mayeda, Nacha Cattan, Marvin G. Perez & Rossella Brevetti, *U.S., Mexico Ink Preliminary Sugar Deal as Industry Balks*, International Trade Daily (BNA) (7 June 2017). [Hereinafter, *U.S., Mexico Ink*.]

cuts the amount of refined sugar that Mexico can send the U.S. to 30 percent of the total quota, from 53 percent previously. It increases the proportion of raw sugar to 70 percent.

U.S. refiners wanted to limit the amount of refined sugar that's imported into America from Mexico as part of the quota, which remains unchanged. They would prefer to see more raw sweetener instead, as they would then be able to process it.

The U.S. refining industry was also seeking a lower sucrose content, or level of purity, in the raw sugar that arrives from Mexico. That's because the quality of current shipments, at 99.5 percent sucrose, is high enough for human consumption, which means that it can also bypass refining. With the accord, the maximum purity for raw-sugar imports will now be 99.2 percent, ensuring that the product will head to U.S. refineries for further processing.[36]

Indeed, because the *Agreement* lowered the delineation between refined and raw sugar from 99.5 to 99.2 degree polarity:

> "estandar"—a common variety of sugar from Mexico—will count against the 30 percent limit on refined sugar, according to Commerce.

> With a minimum sucrose content of 99.4 percent, estandar can replace refined sugar in many food and beverage applications.[37]

Likewise, the stiffer penalties against Mexican sugar shipped in violation of the *Agreement* help refiners: cutting sugar that can be imported by an amount that is double (or possibly triple at the discretion of the DOC) the amount of the violating sugar shipments is an incentive for Mexico not to dump sugar.

Second, with respect to raw sugar producers in the U.S.:

> [T]he reference price for raw sugar will be raised from 22.25 cents/pound to 23 cents/pound, while the refined sugar price will be raised from 26 cents/pound to 28 cents/pound. The change in the pricing structure ensures that U.S. producers' prices are not suppressed or undercut by Mexican sugar imports . . . .[38]

Still another constituency that favored the *Agreement* was the American HFCS producers.

> John Bode, president and chief executive officer of the Corn Refiners Association, said that U.S. sugar interests have stronger protections than the previous agreements without threatening the $500 million in U.S. corn sweetener exports to Mexico that support 4,000 U.S. jobs.[39]

---

36. *U.S., Mexico Ink.*
37. *U.S. Sugar Producers.*
38. *U.S., Mexico Ink.*
39. *U.S., Mexico Ink.*

In other words, had the *Agreement* not been reached, then Mexico might have retaliated against American HFCS exports, which would have hurt corn farmers, and perhaps even erected barriers against other U.S. farm and livestock exports:

> The prospect of a trade war is not an idle threat to producers of corn syrup, who have sold more than $3 billion of the sweetener to Mexico over the past five years. Mexico shut off corn syrup in the 1990s in an earlier dispute.

> "If it is an exchange of retaliatory blows, they are quite capable," said John Bode, president of the Corn Refiners Association.[40]

Mexico is not only the largest export source of sugar to America, but also one of the largest American HFCS customers.[41]

What did Mexico get in return? First, the DOC held off imposing AD duties and CVDs as high as 80% on its sugar.[42] Second, as per the DOC summary quoted above, each April the USDA decides whether the U.S. needs additional sugar. Mexico has a first refusal right, in that if the USDA decides in the affirmative, then Mexico can supply 100% of the gap. Mexico would have had this right under *NAFTA*, yet, American sugar lobbyists objected to the right:

> Phillip Hayes, a spokesman for the American Sugar Alliance, said this creates a major loophole that Mexico could exploit to continue to dump subsidized sugar into the U.S. market and short U.S. refineries of raw sugar inputs. The loophole takes away the existing power of the U.S. government

---

40. *Sugar Talks May Hint.*
    One such "earlier dispute" was a case arising in which Mexico said the U.S. was dumping HFCS. Mexico became a "net surplus producer" in sugar a few years after *NAFTA* took effect, but alleged American dumping of HFCS threatened that status. So, on 1 January 2002:
    > the Mexican government imposed a 20 percent "soda tax" on all beverages sold in Mexico that were not sweetened with its own cane sugar. This effectively eliminated the use of U.S. HFCS in the Mexican beverage industry.
    > The U.S. registered strong complaints over the tax, which hurt sales of HFCS to Mexico, lowered corn exports used to produce HFCS, and threatened U.S. beverage exports to Mexico. The U.S. filed a case against the tax through the WTO dispute settlement process. Following the WTO ruling on August 8, 2005, that Mexico's "soda tax" was illegal, Mexico filed an appeal. The WTO Appellate Body overturned the appeal in March 2006, and a bilateral agreement was reached and submitted to the WTO that Mexico would eliminate the tax no later than January 31, 2007.
    > Longstanding differences over the level of market access for Mexican sugar to the U.S. market and over Mexican barriers on imports of U.S. HFCS were resolved in a bilateral agreement reached by both governments in late July 2006.
    American Sugarbeet Growers Association.
    That settlement applied until 1 January 2008, after which the original NAFTA terms governed HFCS trade.
    41. *See* Nacha Cattan & Andrew Mayeda, *U.S., Mexico Rush to End Sugar Standoff Amid Tit-For-Tat Threats*, International Trade Daily (BNA) (2 June 2017).
    42. *See* Len Bracken, Rossella Brevetti, Brian Flood & Jeremy Hainsworth, *Sweet Outcome for Sugar Talks Uncertain, Risking NAFTA*, International Trade Daily (BNA) (5 June 2017).

to determine the type and polarity of any additional sugar that needs to be imported and cedes that power to the Mexican government, he said.

Low sugar prices in the U.S. did not seem to be much of a risk. In reality, Americans pay roughly 1/3 above world market prices for sugar. (The world market price as of June 2017 was 14 cents/pound.) The June 2017 *Suspension Agreement* raised sugar prices in America, costing consumers an estimated $1 billion annually according to the Coalition for Sugar Reform, a group of consumer food and beverage manufacturers.[43]

Consumers were not the only losers from the *Suspension Agreement*: American workers and third countries lost, too. The jobs of workers in sugar-consuming industries in the U.S. were offshored.[44] For instance, it was cheaper to make candy and baked goods overseas, given the lower sugar prices abroad, and ship the candy and baked goods back to America (where it faces a low or zero duty), than to make those items in America (thanks to high sugar input prices in the U.S.).

Third countries shipping sugar under U.S. TRQs also were injured from the deal.[45] America's other *NAFTA* partner, Canada, sought elimination of tariffs the U.S. imposed on Canadian sugar. No such luck, as American sugar refiners bitterly resisted any increase in shipments of refined sugar, and pointed to 20 years of AD duties Canada imposed on American sugar and sweeteners that effectively keep those products out of the Canadian market.

As for non-*NAFTA* countries, annually, on 1 October, the USTR sets country-specific TRQs. Represented by the International Sugar Trade Coalition (ISTC), the likes of the Dominican Republic and Panama complained of erosion of their market share in the U.S., thanks to the provision that gave Mexico the first refusal right to plug the entirety of any Additional Needs. ISTC countries account for about one-half of raw sugar imports (by TRQ volume) into the U.S. Only if Mexico could not fill the Additional Needs would they be allowed to supply at in-quota rates; otherwise, they were stuck with the high above-quota duties. So, from the perspective of third country shippers, the deal had the effect of divide-and-conquer: the rules set by America and Mexico, Latin America's second largest economy, pitted them against each other.

VII. Different Trade Remedies and 2005 *Nucor* Case

What happens if, during the POI in an AD or CVD investigation, a different trade remedy is applied, such as a safeguard action under the Escape Clause (Section 201 of the *Trade Act of 1974*, as amended)? The *Nucor* case deals with this issue.

---

43. *U.S., Mexico Ink.*
44. *Sugar Talks May Hint.*
45. *See Sugar Deal Draws Bitter Attention.*

Nucor Corporation v. United States,

United States Court of Appeals for the Federal Circuit,
414 F.3d 1331, 1334–1342 (2005)

BRYSON, CIRCUIT JUDGE:

The appellants, United States Steel Corporation and Nucor Corporation, are domestic steel producers. Along with other domestic producers, they petitioned the International Trade Commission to investigate imports of cold-rolled steel products to determine if those imports were causing material injury to the domestic steel industry. *See* 19 U.S.C. §§ 1671d(b)(1), 1673d(b)(1). Upon completion of its investigations, the Commission issued final determinations that the domestic steel industry was not materially injured by reason of the imports. The appellants and other domestic producers filed an action in the Court of International Trade challenging the Commission's negative material injury determinations. The Court of International Trade sustained the Commission's determinations. *Nucor Corp. v. United States,* 318 F. Supp. 2d 1207 (Ct. Int'l Trade 2004). U.S. Steel and Nucor appeal. We affirm.

I

Section 201 of the *Trade Act of 1974*, 19 U.S.C. § 2251(a), authorizes the President to take appropriate action to protect domestic industries from substantial injury due to increased quantities of imports. In June 2001, the President requested that the Commission conduct a *Section 201* investigation of steel products imported between January 1997 and June 2001. Following its investigation, the Commission determined that cold-rolled steel products "were being imported into the U.S. in such increased quantities as to be a substantial cause of serious injury to the domestic industry" and recommended that safeguard tariffs be imposed on steel products. Consequently, in March 2002 the President imposed safeguard tariffs on steel products, including cold-rolled steel products, of 30% for the first year, 24% for the second year, and 18% for the third year.

In September 2001, a number of domestic steel producers petitioned the Commission to conduct the antidumping and countervailing duty investigations that gave rise to this case. The Commission's antidumping and countervailing duty investigations, which were directed to certain cold-rolled steel products, overlapped the *Section 201* investigation and the subsequent imposition of tariffs on cold-rolled steel products.

. . .

The Commission issued final determinations on all of the subject investigations in September and November 2002. In those determinations, the Commission found that the "*Section 201* investigation and the President's remedy fundamentally altered the U.S. market for many steel products, including cold-rolled steel." The Commission found that imports of those products declined sharply and that domestic prices increased significantly in the period after the imposition of the *Section 201* tariffs.

The Commission further reported that, according to purchasers, the reduction in imports due to the *Section 201* tariffs had led to "higher prices, supply shortages, and some broken or renegotiated contracts." Based on the results of its investigation, the Commission concluded that the *Section 201* relief was the principal reason for the sharp decline in imports near the end of the investigation period. The Commission further found that, as of the conclusion of the antidumping and countervailing duty proceedings, "the domestic cold-rolled steel products industry is neither materially injured nor threatened with material injury by reason of subject imports." Because the Commission determined that the domestic industry was not suffering present material injury or a threat of material injury as a result of the subject imports, no antidumping or countervailing duties were imposed.

In the Court of International Trade, the domestic producers argued that the Commission's negative material injury determinations were flawed because, among other reasons, the Commission failed to consider the effects of imports in the early portion of the investigation period; it failed to make a determination regarding the significance of importers' underselling on domestic producers; and it erred in its determinations regarding the volume of imports and their impact on domestic prices. . . . [T]he trial court sustained the Commission's determinations.

[Omitted are the portions of the Federal Circuit's decision on the (1) significance of underselling by importers, (2) volume of imports, and (3) impact of volume on prices. On these issues, the Federal Circuit upheld the CIT.]

II

U.S. Steel and Nucor argue that the Commission erred by failing to consider the effects of products imported prior to the imposition of *Section 201* tariffs when it determined that the domestic industry was not suffering current material injury because of imports. In particular, they contend that the requirement in 19 U.S.C. §§ 1671d(b)(1) and 1673d(b)(1) that the Commission determine whether the domestic industry is suffering material injury "by reason of imports" mandated that the Commission consider the effects of imports throughout the period of investigation and not confine its consideration to the effects of current imports. Because, in the appellants' view, the Commission based its material injury determinations solely on current imports, the appellants argue that the Commission's material injury determination was legally flawed.

The trial court held that the Commission had reasonably construed the phrase "by reason of imports" in 19 U.S.C. §§ 1671d(b)(1) and 1673d(b)(1) to allow it to focus its investigation on the most recent import data. The court explained that the Commission had investigated imports for the entire period of investigation. Although the Commission had focused mainly on current imports, it had also considered imports during the early portion of that period in assessing the volume of imports, their effects on price, and the overall impact of imports on the domestic industry. The Commission's particular focus on current imports, according to the trial court, was "in accord with the remedial purpose of duties which are intended merely to prevent future harm to the domestic industry by reason of unfair imports that are presently causing material injury." The court also found that although the Commission did not state explicitly that past imports were not causing present material injury, it implicitly made that determination. According to the court, the Commission properly assessed the effects of imports early in the investigation period in light of the evidence that there was a steep decline in imports near the end of the investigation period.

Sections 1671d(b)(1) and 1673d(b)(1) state that the Commission must determine whether a domestic industry "is materially injured . . . by reason of imports." They do not specify how the Commission should weigh imports early in the period of investigation as compared to imports closer to the date of decision, nor do they provide any guidance as to the considerations that should influence the weight the Commission assigns to data from different portions of the investigation period. Because the statutes are silent on those issues, and because the Commission, together with the Commerce Department, is charged with the responsibility of administering the antidumping and countervailing duty statutes, the Commission's construction of those statutes is entitled to deference under the principles of *Chevron U.S.A. Inc. v. Natural Res. Def. Council, Inc.,* 467 U.S. 837, 81 L. Ed. 2d 694, 104 S. Ct. 2778 (1984). . . .

We agree with the trial court that it was reasonable for the Commission to interpret the statutory language to permit it to accord different weight to imports during different portions of the period of investigation depending on the facts of each case. In particular, the Commission acted reasonably in construing the statutory language to permit it to focus on the most recent imports and pricing data. That construction is reasonable for several reasons. First, the purpose of antidumping and countervailing duty laws is remedial, not punitive or retaliatory, see *Chaparral Steel Co. v. United States,* 901 F.2d 1097, 1103–04 (Fed. Cir. 1990), and current data typically is the most pertinent in determining whether remedial measures are necessary, *see Chr. Bjelland Seafoods A/S v. United States,* 19 Ct. Int'l Trade 35, 44 n. 22 (1995). Second, Section 1677(7)(B)(i) provides that, in making the material injury determination required by Sections 1671d(b)(1) and 1673d(b)(1), the Commission shall consider, *inter alia,* the effects of the subject imports on domestic producers. Section 1677(7)(C)(iii) in turn requires the Commission, in determining the impact of the subject imports on domestic producers, to "evaluate all relevant economic factors which have a bearing on the state of the industry in the United States." As the trial court explained, in most cases the most recent imports will have the greatest relevance to the current state of the domestic industry. Third, the Commission has broad discretion with respect to the period of investigation that it selects for purposes of making a material injury determination. As the Court of International Trade has explained, because the statute "does not expressly command the Commission to examine a particular period of time . . . the Commission has discretion to examine a period that most reasonably allows it to determine whether a domestic industry is injured by [less than fair value] imports." *Kenda Rubber Indus. Co. v.*

United States, 10 C.I.T. 120, 630 F. Supp. 354, 359 (Ct. Int'l Trade 1986). Since the Commission has broad discretion to choose the most appropriate period of time for its investigation, it would be nonsensical to hold that once the Commission has chosen an investigation period, it is required to give equal weight to imports throughout the period it has selected. For these reasons, both this court and the Court of International Trade have typically upheld the Commission's exercise of its discretion to focus on imports during particular portions of the investigation period, especially imports during the most recent portion of that period. *See Chaparral Steel,* 901 F.2d at 1103; *Taiwan Semiconductor Indus. Ass'n v. United States,* 93 F. Supp. 2d 1283, 1294 n. 13, 105 F. Supp. 2d 1363, 24 Ct. Int'l Trade 220 (Ct. Int'l Trade 2000), *aff'd,* 266 F.3d 1339 (Fed. Cir. 2001); *Angus Chem. Co. v. United States,* 20 C.I.T. 1255, 944 F. Supp. 943, 947–48 (Ct. Int'l Trade 1996), *aff'd,* 140 F.3d 1478 (Fed. Cir. 1998).

In this case, the fact that *Section 201* tariffs were imposed during the period of investigation made the recent data far more probative than earlier data as to whether the industry was suffering present material injury as a result of imports. The Commission found that the *Section 201* relief "was having a major impact in the U.S. market for cold-rolled steel and was the overwhelming factor in the sharp decline in subject imports during the most recent period examined." Substantial evidence in the record supports that finding, and the appellants do not challenge the trial court's determination in that regard. Because the imposition of *Section 201* tariffs had such a dramatic impact on the industry, it was reasonable for the Commission to conclude that the most recent data was the most reliable indicator of whether the industry was suffering material injury as a result of the subject imports and whether the imposition of additional duties would be consistent with the remedial purposes of the antidumping and countervailing duty laws.

The appellants argue that the Commission did not simply assign greater weight to current imports, but that it improperly focused exclusively on current imports and failed to give any consideration to whether the domestic industry was suffering material injury by reason of past imports. They contend that the record does not support the trial court's conclusion that the Commission examined imports over the entire investigation period in making its determination that the subject imports were not causing present material injury.

In making the statutory determination that the domestic cold-rolled steel industry was not suffering material injury by reason of the subject imports, the Commission explained that it focused principally on "the current volume of subject imports and the increase in domestic prices in 2002." The Commission concluded that the present condition of the domestic industry was not "attributable in any material respect to the current subject imports" and that "subject imports are not adversely affecting domestic prices to a significant degree." Its ultimate finding was that there was no "material injury currently being experienced by the domestic industry ... by reason of the subject imports," *i.e.,* the imports during the period of investigation. The Commission thus explained that its material injury determination, although focusing mainly on current imports, was not restricted solely to current imports but encompassed all "subject imports" during the investigation period.

The appellants do not argue that past imports continued to cause material injury at the end of the investigation period because of accumulated inventories. Nor could they, as the evidence showed that by the end of that period there were widespread supply shortages in the industry, and many producers had been placed on allocation. Instead, the appellants argue that the Commission ignored the continuing price effects of earlier imports resulting from the fact that the prices set in contracts made earlier in the period of investigation were generally "locked in" at the time of contract formation and continued in effect throughout the later portions of the investigation period. Contrary to the appellants' contention, however, the Commission took those facts into consideration; it simply did not find that they were sufficiently important to alter the ultimate material injury determination. Thus, the Commission noted that past imports "continue[d] to have an effect on the industry's contract prices negotiated before the *Section 201* relief was effective," but it nonetheless concluded that imports were not adversely affecting domestic prices to a significant degree "based on the current volume of subject imports and the increase in domestic prices in 2002." In light of that statement and other portions of the Commission's opinion, the trial court ruled that although the Commission did not explicitly state that earlier imports were not causing present material injury, it was reasonable to infer that the Commission so concluded. In particular, the trial court rested its conclusion with respect to that issue on what it referred to as the Commission's "continued discussion of the effects that subject imports entered earlier in the [period of investigation] had on the domestic industry and its ultimate conclusion that the domestic industry was not suffering present material injury."

We concur in the trial court's analysis. The Commission may not have stated explicitly that earlier imports were not causing material injury, but that conclusion was implicit in its analysis. The clear implication of the Commission's findings on that issue is that the prices fixed by contracts that were negotiated earlier in the investigation period may have suppressed the overall average price of domestic products throughout the period, but in light of the decrease in the current volume of imports and the increase in domestic prices in 2002, the effect of those past imports was not significant. We therefore uphold the trial court's decision with regard to the adequacy of the Commission's treatment of the subject imports from early in the investigation period.

Chapter 3

Procedures (Continued): After Final Determinations[1]

I. Step 7: Remedial Orders and Limits

Following an affirmative final dumping margin or subsidy determination by the ITC, and a final injury determination by the ITC, the DOC must issue an AD or CVD order. It must do so within seven days of notice of the final injury determination by the ITC. Significantly, issuance of an AD or CVD order is automatic after the requisite determinations. Neither the Secretary of Commerce nor the President is authorized to block issuance of the order. Put differently, political influences do not (or, at least, are not supposed to) enter into a case at this stage.

An AD or CVD order is issued to the CBP. Either kind of order describes the goods to which it applies, namely, the subject merchandise and future entries of merchandise. In an AD order, the DOC:

(1) directs the CBP to assess an AD duty equal to the amount Normal Value exceeds Export Price (or Constructed Export Price), *i.e.*, equal to the dumping margin,

(2) requires deposit of estimated AD duties until the entries of merchandise to which the order applies are liquidated, and

(3) requires deposit of normal customs duties (*e.g.*, the MFN tariff).

The final determination by the DOC of the dumping margin not only is the basis for assessing an AD duty on previous entries of subject merchandise, but also for deposits of estimated duties on future entries of merchandise covered by the order.

Similarly, in a CVD order, the DOC:

(1) directs the CBP to assess a CVD equal to the net countervailable subsidy amount,

---

1. Documents References:
   (1) *Havana (ITO) Charter* Article 34
   (2) GATT Article VI
   (3) WTO *Antidumping Agreement* Articles 3, 5, 14, 17
   (4) *NAFTA* Chapter 19
   (5) Relevant provisions in other FTAs

(2) requires deposit of estimated CVDs until the entries of merchandise to which the order applies are liquidated, and

(3) requires deposit of normal customs duties (*e.g.*, the MFN tariff).

The final determination by the DOC of the net countervailable subsidy not only is the basis for assessing a CVD on previous entries of subject merchandise, but also for deposits of estimated duties on future entries of merchandise covered by the order.

In both AD and CVD cases, the importer of record technically is liable for the deposits. This party is the entity importing the dumped or unlawfully subsidized product. This party is not necessarily a respondent in a case. When might it not be, and what legal steps should such an importer take to protect itself from "holding the bag"?

Also in both cases, with respect to previous entries of subject merchandise, there is the possibility of a difference between estimated and final duties. Suppose after an affirmative preliminary or final dumping margin or subsidy determination, the cash deposit or bond posted as security for the estimated AD duty or CVD, respectively, is greater than the amount of the duty assessed in the AD or CVD order. The difference between the (1) deposit (or bond) and (2) amount of the final duty is refunded. Does the refund come with interest, too? The answer depends on when merchandise was entered. For merchandise entered before notice of the final injury decision, no interest accrues on an overpayment. For entries of merchandise after this notice, the difference between estimated and final duties is refunded with interest on the amount of the overpayment.

What if the estimated AD duty or CVD is less than the final amount in the order? Must the deficiency in the cash deposit or bond posted be covered? Must interest be paid on the underpayment? Again, the answer depends on the timing of the entries. For merchandise entered before notice of the final injury determination, the difference between estimated and final duties is disregarded, and no interest accrues. In effect, the underpayment is excused. But, for entries after notice of the final injury determination, the difference between lower estimated duties and higher final duties is collected, along with interest on the underpayment. Why is notice of the final injury determination the key point for determining how to handle differences between estimated and final duties?

II. Reselling Subject Merchandise in Transit

An important but often overlooked practical question is what to do with subject merchandise in transit once an AD or CVD order is issued, be it preliminary or final. One answer is a re-sale of the merchandise to third parties in a third country. That happened in April 2018, when China's MOFCOM levied 178.6% preliminary AD duties on U.S. sorghum. A fascinating tale of five shipments of that subject merchandise followed:

all headed for China when they were loaded at Texas Gulf Coast export terminals owned by grain merchants Cargill Inc. . . . or Archer Daniels Midland Co. [ADM]. . . . Cargill and ADM likely sold most of the grain in the cargoes that are on the water.

. . .

The Panamanian-flagged ship called the *N Bonanza*, was churning its way northeast across the Indian Ocean earlier this week, carrying more than 67,000 tons of sorghum from ADM's elevator in Corpus Christi, Texas. . . .

Eleven hours after the anti-dumping deposits were announced, the ship stopped and then slowly tracked northwest.

The *RB Eden*, a vessel carrying 70,223 tons of sorghum loaded at the same ADM terminal, was headed east-northeast through the Indian Ocean off the coast of South Africa. It turned around.

Hours later, the *Stamford Eagle*—hauling sorghum from Cargill's elevator in Houston—turned around off the western coast of Mexico.

At least two other vessels have also suddenly changed course: the *Ocean Belt* and *Xing Xi Hai*, both loaded at Cargill's terminal.[2]

However, to what extent are re-sales feasible? Factors include the liquidity of the market for subject merchandise, and the nature of the original sales contracts (including terms on events of default and breach).

III. Problems of Scope and Circumvention, and 2013 *Appleton Papers,* 2013 *U.K. Carbon,* 2013 *Diamond Sawblades,* 2014 *Peer Bearing,* and 2016 *Deacero* Cases

What is the scope of an AD or CVD order? The short answer is "prophylactic." It applies to all entries of subject merchandise, past, present, and future, commencing from a specific date indicated in the order. Moreover, an order applies countrywide. It includes all exporters, whether or not investigated, unless the DOC determines a specific exporter is selling its product at a non-dumped price, or is not benefiting from an illegal subsidy. For instance, generally in an LTFV investigation, the DOC attempts to include exporters accounting for 60% of American imports of subject merchandise. Hence, the 40% not investigated still are subject to an AD

---

2. Karl Plume & P.J. Huffstutter, *Exclusive: U.S. Sorghum Armada U-Turns at Sea After China Tariffs,* Reuters, 19 April 2018, www.reuters.com/article/us-usa-trade-china-sorghum-exclusive /exclusive-u-s-sorghum-armada-u-turns-at-sea-after-china-tariffs-idUSKBN1HR03Z; *China Hits $957 Million U.S. Sorghum Trade with Fresh Duty,* 35 International Trade Reporter (BNA) 584 (26 April 2018).

order. Finally, an AD or CVD order also covers merchandise from a new shipper, *i.e.*, an exporter that did not ship merchandise at the time the original order was issued but, thereafter, began exportation.

That said, what happens if merchandise does not fall within the literal wording of an AD or CVD order? What if a producer-exporter of merchandise that is within the literal terms of an order makes minor alterations to it so as to take it outside those terms? What if a producer-exporter routes merchandise from its home country to the U.S. through a 3rd country in which minor processing occurs?[3] These questions concern the scope of an order.

That scope cannot be unlimited. Arguments over whether merchandise is exempt from an order are a zero-sum game. The DOC (and petitioner in the underlying case) argue for the widest imaginable scope. The importer (and respondents in the underlying case) argue for the narrowest possible scope. The DOC, which may conduct a circumvention proceeding to check whether remedial duties should be imposed on merchandise outside the literal terms of an order. The DOC must offer a "clear and coherent rationale" for any scope ruling it issues.[4] Under the AD-CVD statute, the DOC applies a Five Factor Test:

---

3. Precisely this fact pattern was alleged in September 2016 by U.S. steel firms (AK Steel Corp., ArcelorMittal USA LLC, Nucor Corp., California Steel Industries, Steel Dynamics Inc., and United States Steel Corp.) against Chinese competitors. Cold-rolled steel is used in appliances, cars, containers, and construction, and imports of it into the U.S. from Vietnam more than trebled in two years following July 2016 AD-CVD orders against Chinese cold-rolled steel. Cold-rolled steel flat products are made from cold-rolled steel, and from hot-rolled steel that is processed into cold-rolled steel. Vietnam lacked capacity to make hot-rolled steel. It appeared Vietnam was importing hot-rolled steel from China, changing it to cold-rolled steel, and then shipping the flat products to the U.S. If true, then were Chinese producer-exporters circumventing the AD-CVD orders on cold-rolled steel (by sending hot-rolled steel to Vietnam and having it processed there into cold-rolled steel)?

4. *Rubbermaid Commercial Products LLC. V. United States*, CIT Number 11-00463 (Slip Opinion 14-113, 23 September 2014); Brian Flood, *Trade Court Orders Commerce to Re-evaluate Antidumping Duties Assigned to Rubbermaid*, 31 International Trade Reporter (BNA) 1764 (2 October 2014).

In this case, various cleaning products Rubbermaid imported were the subject merchandise under an AD-CVD order on aluminum extrusions. Rubbermaid argued against a DOC ruling that (1) mop frames, (2) mop handles, (3) mopping kits, and (4) squeegee blade replacements were within that scope. The order included parts for final finished products assembled after importation. The order excluded "finished merchandise" and "finished goods kits." Rubbermaid argued those articles (1), (2), and (4) were exempt from the order as "finished merchandise." That is, Rubbermaid said it mop frames and handles were entered into the United States as fully assembled merchandise, so they should benefit from the "finished merchandise" exception. The DOC disagreed, saying they were not "finished merchandise," because they did not have "all necessary parts" with them at the time of importation.

As to article (3), the mopping kits, Rubbermaid did not enter them into the United States as fully assembled merchandise. So, Rubbermaid did not argue they were "finished merchandise." Rather, Rubbermaid said they qualified for the "finished goods kits exception." But, the DOC said a complete mopping kit would require inclusion of a mop head. Because Rubbermaid's kits lacked the interchangeable, disposable mop head when they were imported, they were not "finished goods kits." In turn, they were within the scope of the orders.

Section 781(b)(1) of the *Act* [*i.e.*, the *Tariff Act of 1930*, as amended] provides that the Department may find circumvention of an AD or CVD order when merchandise of the same class or kind subject to the order is completed or assembled in a foreign country other than the country to which

---

The CIT held the DOC erred: the requirement of "all necessary parts" was associated with the "finished goods kits" exception, not the "finished merchandise" exception, *i.e.*, the DOC confused the requirements in the exceptions. The CIT faulted the DOC rationale, namely, that the articles did not qualify for the "finished merchandise" exception, because they worked with other parts not included with them at importation. In fact, those articles, particularly the mop frames and handles, were interchangeable, so that any frame and handle could be matched. The CIT remanded the case to the DOC to justify its distinction between merchandise within and outside the scope of the order.

The DOC did so, clarifying how it interpreted the "finished merchandise" and "finished goods kits" exclusions from the AD-CVD order on aluminum extrusions. The DOC found 13 Rubbermaid products made in China—such as mop frames, mop handles, and mopping kits, including the frames and handles with interchangeable designs so they could be used with any Rubbermaid cleaning system—were beyond the scope of the order. Essentially, on remand the DOC conceded its initial position (that an article could not qualify for the "finished merchandise" exclusion from the order if that article consisted of parts of a larger whole designed to function collaboratively with other components to make a completed product) could lead to absurd results. As long as the article was fully and permanently assembled and completed at the time of entry, then it should not matter whether it is later incorporated with other products into a larger, downstream product. DOC agreed exclusion of mop heads from kits did not mean the kits were not "finished." The CIT upheld the DOC's remand order, against a challenge by domestic aluminum extrusion producers grouped under the banner of the Aluminum Extrusions Fair Trade Committee. *See Rubbermaid Commercial Products LLC v. United States*, Number 11-00463 (Slip Opinion 15-79, 22 July 2015).

For another case on the "finished good" exception in AD-CVD orders, see *Meridian Products, LLC v. United States*, CIT Number 13-00018 (Slip Opinion 16-5, 20 January 2016). In *Meridian*, the CIT affirmed a DOC decision (which the DOC made under protest) that imports of trim kits for refrigerators and freezers were outside the scope of the orders. The kits (which attach to kitchen cabinets enveloping a refrigerator or freezer for a "built-in" look) were packaged combinations of all parts needed to assemble a finished good without further processing or fabrication. DOC initially ruled the kits were not finished, because they consisted only of aluminum extrusion and fasteners (*e.g.*, bolts and screws). The Federal Circuit reversed the CIT decision, defining aluminum extrusions broadly as parts (*e.g.*, kitchen appliance accessories, like trim kits that make up the aesthetic frame around refrigerators and freezers) incorporated into various merchandise (e.g., the fridges and freezers). So, the trim kits were within the scope of the orders, and AD duties of up to 85.94%, and CVD of up to 195.69%, were re-imposed. The DOC orders granted an exception from their scope for "finished goods kits," but also had an exception-to-this-exception, namely, for kits made up of aluminum extrusions along with fasteners such as bolts and screws. Even though the kits had additional items like a wrench, hinge covers, and instructions, those items could be disregarded as extraneous, hence they did not remove the kits from the scope. *See Meridian Products, LLC v. United States*, Federal Circuit Number 2016-1730 (28 March 2017); Brian Flood, *U.S. Wins Duties on Chinese Appliance Trim Kits*, 34 International Trade Reporter (BNA) 498 (30 March 2017).

Conversely, in the 2016 CIT case of *Aluminum Extrusions Fair Trade Committee v. United States*, Number 14-00206 (Slip Opinion 16-31, 31 March 2016), the CIT held aluminum frames with an attached polyester mesh screen that were used for screen printing designs onto fabrics were outside the scope of AD or CVD orders. Those orders covered aluminum extrusions (*i.e.*, objects or parts made by pushing material through a shaped opening), but not frames, which were "assemblies" made of welded extrusions and a screen. Moreover, even if the orders encompassed assemblies," they explicitly excluded "finished merchandise," and the frames at issue were imported in a fully

the order applies. In conducting an anti-circumvention inquiry, under section 781(b)(1) of the *Act*, the Department relies on the following criteria: (A) merchandise imported into the United States is of the same class or kind as any merchandise produced in a foreign country that is the subject of an antidumping or countervailing duty order or finding; (B) before importation into the United States, such imported merchandise is completed or assembled in another foreign country from merchandise which is subject to the order or merchandise which is produced in the foreign country that is subject to the order; (C) the process of assembly or completion in the foreign country referred to in section (B) is minor or insignificant; (D) the value of the merchandise produced in the foreign country to which the AD or CVD order applies is a significant portion of the total value of the merchandise exported to the United States; and (E) the administering authority determines that action is appropriate to prevent evasion of such order or finding.[5]

Factor (A) can be shown from HTSUS tariff classification, *i.e.*, the subject merchandise and goods suspected of circumvention are in the same category. Factor (B)

---

assembled state. *See* Brian Flood, *Chinese Aluminum Extrusions Escape Duties*, 33 International Trade Reporter (BNA) 493 (7 April 2016).

Likewise, in *Whirlpool Corporation v. United States*, Number 14-00199 (Slip Opinion 16-81, 26 August 2016), the CIT sustained a remand determination by the DOC (which the DOC issued under protest) that certain multi-piece kitchen appliance door handles (*e.g.*, for dishwashers, ovens, ranges, refrigerators), and were outside the scope of AD-CVD orders on Chinese aluminum extrusions. Whirlpool is a Fortune 500 MNC headquartered in Benton Harbor Michigan, yet Whirlpool made the subject merchandise in China. Two categories of handles were at issue: single- and multi-piece. The CIT agreed with DOC that single-piece handles were within the scope of the AD-CVD orders, but not the multi-piece ones, because those orders covered only single-piece aluminum components. Whirlpool's multi-piece handles consisted of a basic handle, plastic end caps, and screws to attach the caps to the handles. The only kind of multi-piece handle that could fit within the scope of the orders was a "sub-assembly," meaning partially assembled merchandise. But, once imported from China to the U.S., Whirlpool's multi-piece handles could be used immediately, without any more processing or assembly. *See* Brian Flood, *Whirlpool Scrubs Duties on Chinese Appliance Handles*, 33 International Trade Reporter (BNA) 1257 (8 September 2016).

Unfortunately for Whirlpool, the Federal Circuit reversed in part the CIT decision. It held that door handles for Whirlpool refrigerators might be within the scope of the AD-CVD orders on Chinese aluminum extrusions, and remanded to the DOC for consideration the question of whether those handles fall within the "finished goods" exception. *See Whirlpool Corp. v. United States*, Number 17-01117, 890 F.3d 1302 (23 May 2018) ("*Whirlpool III*"); Brian Flood, *Whirlpool Loses on Fridge Handle Duties Appeal*, 35 International Trade Reporter 725 (BNA) (31 May 2018). So, in light of the Federal Circuit's *Whirlpool III* decision about the scope of the "finished merchandise" exclusion from AD-CVD orders, in January 2019, the CIT issued two rulings ordering DOC to reconsider its scope determinations in the *Meridian* and *Whirlpool* cases. *See Meridian Products v. United States*, CIT Number 13-00246 (Slip Opinion 19-5, 14 January 2019); *Whirlpool Corporation v. United States*, CIT Number 14-00199 (Slip Opinion 19-6, 14 January 2019).

5. Department of Commerce, *Certain Cold-Rolled Steel Flat Products from the People's Republic of China: Initiation of Anti-Circumvention Inquiries on the Antidumping Duty and Countervailing Duty Orders*, Federal Register (November 2016), http://src.bna.com.www2.lib.ku.edu/jUV.

requires an examination of what occurs in the pertinent foreign countries. Whether the process of assembly or completion is "minor or insignificant" under Factor (C) depends on five more factors (specified in Section 781(b)(2) of the 1930 *Act*): (1) level of investment to construct the processing factory, (2) R&D associated with the processing, (3) nature (*i.e.*, complexity) of the production process, (4) extent of production facilities overseas (*e.g.*, in a third country vis-à-vis the exporter's home country), and (5) value of processing (*e.g.*, in a third country).

It is the DOC, not CBP, which has the authority to interpret the scope of an AD or CVD order.[6] In rendering an interpretation, the DOC looks *in seriatim* to (1) the text of the order itself, (2) the language of the duty order petition, the findings of the DOC and ITC in the original investigation and any previous scope determination (so-called "(k)(1) factors"), and (3) physical characteristics of the product, expectations of consumers, and the way the product is advertised and displayed ("(k)(2) factors").[7]

Consider the 2013 CIT case of *Appleton Papers Inc. v. United States*.[8] The dispute, brought by Appvion Inc. (formerly called Appleton Papers), a paper company in Appleton, Wisconsin, raised issues of both the scope and circumvention of an AD-CVD order on lightweight thermal paper produced in China. Interestingly, the respondent company, Paper Resources LLC, was American, too, based in Norwalk, Connecticut.

First, was paper produced in a third country, but converted in China, within the scope of the order? Lightweight thermal paper is made in three steps: (1) jumbo rolls of paper are made, (2) thermal coating is applied to the rolls; and (3) the rolls are converted, meaning they are slit and repackaged. For rolls in which the first two steps occur in a country not covered by the DOC order, but the third step occurs in China, the CIT agreed with the DOC: they are not covered by the order. That is because conversion fails the Substantial Transformation Test for conferring country

---

6. *See LDA Incorporado v. United States*, Number 12-00349 (CIT, Slip Opinion 15-64, 19 June 2015); Brian Flood, *Electrical Conduits Avoid Duties Covering Chinese Pipe, Court Rules*, 32 International Trade Reporter (BNA) 1153 (25 June 2015). In the *LDA* case, a Puerto Rican importer, LDA Incorporado, of steel electrical conduits successfully argued CBP was wrong to find these imports were subject to AD-CVD orders on circular welded carbon quality steel pipe form China. Those orders had an exception for finished electrical conduit. LDA Incorporado said its conduit qualified for the exception, because the interior of the conduit was galvanized with zinc. The CBP countered with its own laboratory tests and decided the imports did not qualify. The CBP claimed the phrase "finished electrical conduit" in the orders was ambiguous. The CIT disagreed, saying the phrase was clear, but even if it was not, the CBP did not have the authority to make decisions about the scope of an AD or CVD order. Scope interpretations were up to the DOC, which after all issues AD-CVD orders. In the *LDA* case, the DOC ultimately decided the imports at issue were excluded from the scope.

7. *See Ethan Allen Operations, Inc. v. United States*, CIT Number 14-00147 (Slip Opinion 16-19, 29 February 2016).

8. *See* Number 12-00116 (Slip Opinion 13-87, 11 July 2013).

of origin status on China. If all that happens in China is conversion, then the rolls are not substantially transformed there. They remain the product of a third country that is not covered by the AD-CVD order.

Second, might such rolls circumvent the order? "Circumvention" can occur with subject merchandise made in a country covered by an AD-CVD order is modified in a minor way in a downstream country, such as through processing or assembly. So, in a circumvention proceeding, the DOC considers whether a good that is technically outside the literal scope of an extant order should be included within that scope and, therefore, treated as subject merchandise on which AD or CVD duties are imposed.

In the *Appleton* case, there was no risk of circumvention, because the merchandise was made in a 3rd country, and the minor downstream operation—processing— occurred in China, which was covered by the order. In *Appleton*, the DOC used the Customs Law test of "Substantial Transformation" to determine the country of origin of a product, *i.e.*, to see if it is from the same country as subject merchandise subject to an AD-CVD order.

In contrast, in the 2013 case of *U.K. Carbon & Graphite v. United States*, the CIT agreed with the DOC that a British company participated in a scheme to circumvent an AD duty order.[9] Small diameter graphite electrodes from China were the subject merchandise, and the DOC contended artificial graphite rods made by the U.K. Carbon & Graphite Company (UKCG) were covered by the pertinent order. UKCG unsuccessfully argued its artificial graphite was classified properly in HTSUS Sub-Heading 3801.10. DOC failed to include that Sub-heading in its initial order, but only added it later. The CIT rejected this argument, saying it is "well settled" that HTSUS classification is not dispositive as to the scope of an AD order. To be sure, both CBP and the EU distinguished between (1) "artificial graphite rods" and (2) "small diameter graphite electrodes." But, the DOC was not bound by their classification determinations. Its decision that artificial graphite rods were classifiable as small diameter graphite electrodes, and thus within the scope of the order, was reasonable.

The DOC rightly buttressed its position, concluded the CIT, by pointing out three key facts about the production process of the subject merchandise. First, the finishing operation in which UKCG engaged in the U.K. were a minor, insignificant step in the overall manufacturing of the subject merchandise. Second, in the U.K., finishing took 5 minutes, but in China, production took days. And, in the U.K., the value of labor and energy inputs was markedly less than that in China. Third, the most significant portion of the value of the final merchandise, as exported to the U.S. came from China. (Interestingly, as China was a NME, that valuation was based on

---

9. *See* Number 12-00242 (Slip Opinion 13-144, 29 August 2013); Brian Flood, *Court Affirms U.K. Company Circumvented AD Order on Graphite Electrodes from China*, 30 International Trade Reporter (BNA) 1351 (5 September 2013).

surrogate data from Ukraine.) These facts indicated UKCG was trying to circumvent the AD order.

Similarly, in the 2013 case of *Diamond Sawblades Mfrs. Coal v. United States*, the CIT agreed with the Substantial Transformation analysis of the DOC.[10] The subject merchandise was diamond saw blades (which are used in the construction industry to cut concrete, stone, and other strong materials) made in Korea by Korean and Chinese firms. The DOC said joining a segment and core is a substantial transformation, because attaching these 2 components results in a functional product, and gives a saw blade its essential quality. So, the country in which that joining occurs is the country of origin of a finished diamond saw blade, and that blade is subject merchandise. If the joining occurs somewhere else, then the blade is outside the scope of the order.

The aforementioned cases beg this question: exactly what factors does the DOC apply under the Substantial Transformation Test? The CIT identified them in the 2014 case, *Peer Bearing Co.—Changshan v. United States*.[11] The subject merchandise was tapered roller bearings (TRBs) the DOC said were made in China. During an Administrative Review of an AD order on TRBs from China, the DOC found that some of the TRBs had been processed—namely, ground, honed, and partly assembled—in Thailand, but using parts from China. So, the DOC said those TRBs should be deemed to be "made in China" under the Substantial Transformation Test, and included as subject merchandise within the extant AD order.

The CIT held the DOC failed to support its country of origin determination with substantial evidence. The DOC applied six criteria to determine whether Chinese components were "substantially transformed" in Thailand, namely:

(1) The "class or kind" of subject merchandise.

(2) Physical and chemical properties and essential character.

---

10. *See* Number 06-00248 (11 October 2013); Brian Flood, *Court Remands Dispute on AD Investigation Into Diamond Sawblade Imports from Korea*, 30 International Trade Reporter (BNA) 1676 (31 October 2013). In separate CIT proceedings, the coalition of domestic manufacturers that supported the imposition of AD duties (1) challenged the effective date of the AD order, and (2) disputed the commencement of a 5-year Sunset Review pending its appeal of the case. *See Diamond Sawblades Manufacturers' Coalition v. DOC*, Number 13-00391 (Slip Opinion 14-41, 14 April 2014); Brian Flood, *Judge Denies Manufacturers' Request to Maintain Order Against Chinese Sawblades*, 31 International Trade Reporter (BNA) 729 (17 April 2014). Also in separate proceedings, the CIT upheld a country wide AD duty rates of 82.12%, and rejected an allegation of targeted dumping against 1 respondent (thereby allowing a 0% duty for it). *See Diamond Sawblades Manufacturers' Coalition v. United States*, Number 13-00241 (Slip Opinion, 15-116, 21 October 2015); Brian Flood, *Court Upholds Chinese Diamond Sawblade Duty Rates*, 32 International Trade Reporter (BNA) 1871 (29 October 2015).

11. *See* Number 11-00022 (Slip Opinion 14-62, 10 June 2014); Number 10-00013 (13 February 2014); Brian Flood, *Trade Court Remands AD Calculations For Chinese Tapered Roller Bearings*, 31 International Trade Reporter (BNA) 111 (19 June 2014); Brian Flood, *Court Grants Clarification, Additional Time In Roller Bearing Country of Origin Case*, 31 International Trade Reporter (BNA) 344 (20 February 2014).

(3) Nature and sophistication of processing.

(4) Level of investment.

(5) Ultimate use.

(6) Third country cost of manufacturing as a percentage of total cost of manufacturing.

Using these criteria, the DOC said "no," *i.e.*, the TRBs still were of Chinese origin. Obviously, the DOC wanted to include the TRBs within the scope of the order, and thereby block any circumvention of the order by processing certain TRBs in Thailand and thereby falsely giving them a "Made in Thailand" country of origin label.

The CIT disagreed: "no part exported to Thailand from China was an 'unfinished or incomplete'" TRB; rather, the items became TRBs in Thailand, not China. What occurred in Thailand was not minor or insignificant. So, when the DOC said the TRBs were "Made in China" and put them within the scope of the AD order, it circumvented the anti-circumvention rules: the DOC should have done a proper anti-circumvention determination to see if the operations in Thailand truly were minor or insignificant.

The CIT objected to how the DOC applied the first, second, and fifth criteria. On the first one, the DOC thought that because the AD order included unfinished and finished items, it could infer TRBs were not substantially transformed in Thailand. So, the DOC concluded "the processing performed in Thailand on the two major components of the TRBs (cups and cones) imparted no substantial changes to the physical and mechanical properties of the subject merchandise." The Court countered: "the hypothetical issue of whether 'the Chinese-origin parts would have been considered subject merchandise had they been exported to the United States' has no apparent relevance to that question [of substantial transformation in Thailand]." The DOC conclusion was unsupported by substantial evidence.

On the second criterion, the DOC also said processing in Thailand did not substantially alter the essential character of the merchandise. But, the CIT said the DOC neglected to deal with evidence showing no single component made in China imparted the essential character to finished TRBs.

As to the fifth criterion, the DOC inferred from the fact the AD order covered unfinished and finished items that they have the same end use. Not so, said the CIT. Incomplete and completed articles may have different end uses. Thus, the Court remanded the origin determination back to the DOC. It did not require the DOC to designate the TRBs as Thai, instead of Chinese. It wanted the DOC to perform a robust country of origin determination in line with record evidence.[12]

---

12. In December 2015, the CIT upheld the DOC decision to exclude certain bearings—ones that were processed in part in Thailand—from the dumping margin calculation. The results were AD duty rates of 6.24% (instead of 7.37%), 21.65% (instead of 22.82%), and 19.45% (instead of 22.12%) for respondents Peer Bearing Company-Changshan, PBCD LLD, and AB SKF (which the first respondent acquired in 2008), respectively. *See Peer Bearing Co.-Changshan v. United States,*

In *Deacero S.A. de C.V. v. United States*, in September 2013 the CIT took the position a Mexican producer-exporter, Deacero, of subject merchandise was not trying to circumvent an AD order.[13] Here the issue was not country of origin, which was Mexico, so the Substantial Transformation was irrelevant. Rather, in controversy was the nature of the product itself. The order was imposed on steel wire rod with diameters of 5.00 to 19.00 millimeters. The DOC conducted a minor alterations analysis, to see if insignificant changes to the product were made so as to avoid the AD duty. The DOC treated imports of 4.75 millimeter wire rod as within the scope of the order, and demanded AD duties on the smaller wire rod, too. Deacero (and its U.S. affiliate) successfully protested.

Deacero pointed out that 4.75 millimeter wire rod had been commercially available before the AD order, and the plain language of that order covered only wire rod between 5 and 19 millimeters in diameter. The CIT, though stating that the pre-existence of a product is not necessarily a dispositive factor in deciding whether that product is non-subject merchandise, agreed. Where an item is sold commercially before an order, and where the AD order specifically excludes it, it is outside the scope of the order. The petitioning domestic producers—Arcelor Mittal, Gerdau Ameristeel, Evraz Rocky Mountain Steel, and Nucor Corp.—knew of the existence of 4.75 millimeter wire rod, and could have sought an order that included it, not just 5.00–19.00 millimeter rod. The CIT said "[t]he minor alterations provision does not apply to goods that Commerce knew existed commercially when writing an order, yet excluded from the order anyway." In other words, when it crafted the order, DOC knew wire rod of 4.75 millimeters in diameter existed, so it could have covered such wire rod if it intended to.

So, left with no choice, on remand in January 2014, DOC reversed its affirmative circumvention finding. In December 2014, the CIT affirmed the DOC's negative circumvention re-determination.[14]

Number 10-00013 (Slip Opinion 15-142, 21 December 2015); *Peer Bearing Co.-Changshan v. United States*, Number 11-00022 (Slip Opinion 15-143, 21 December 2015); Brian Flood, *Trade Court Upholds Chinese Bearing Duties*, 32 International Trade Reporter (BNA) 2222 (24 December 2015). So, the dumping margin and thus the AD duty rate narrowed in all instances once DOC took them out of the computation, which explains its motivation for not wanting to do so in the first place.

13. *See* 942 F. Supp. 2d 1321 (30 September 2013); Brian Flood, *Trade Court Rejects Circumvention Finding For Imports of Wire Rod From Mexico*, 30 International Trade Reporter (BNA) 1675 (31 October 2013).

14. *See Deacero S.A.P.I. de C.V. v. United States*, CIT Number 12-00345 (22 December 2014).

As intimated above, that reversal did not end the case. The petitioners persisted, and in August 2014 persuaded the CIT to hold that the DOC could reconsider its circumvention decision, if it chose to do so, essentially on procedural standing grounds. However, the CIT scolded the petitioners: they were "sophisticated companies that could have proposed to define the Wire Rod Order in broader terms or without reference to diameter. But, instead petitioners selected diameter as a central physical characteristic and risked the clearly foreseeable possibility that small diameter wire rod either was or might soon be in commercial production." *Deacero S.A.P.I. de C.V. v. United States*, Number 12-00345 (Slip Opinion 14-99, 28 August 2014). Is it possible a pre-existing product could be used in an unforeseen manner to circumvent an AD or CVD order? Yes, said the CIT, yet

Yet, the Federal Circuit overturned the CIT decision, thus allowing DOC to re-impose AD duties on wire rod with diameters between 4.75 and 5 millimeters.[15] In its April 2016 *Deacero* ruling, the Federal Circuit said the CIT misapplied precedent, particularly the 1998 decision in *Wheatland Tube Co. v. United States*.[16] The Deacero Court wrote:

> In order to effectively combat circumvention of antidumping duty orders, Commerce may determine that certain types of articles are within the scope of a duty order, even when the articles do not fall within the order's literal scope. *See Target Corp. v. United States*, 609 F.3d 1352, 1355 (Fed. Cir. 2010) (*quoting Wheatland*, 161 F.3d at 1370). The *Tariff Act* [*of 1930, as amended*] identifies four articles that may fall within the scope of a duty order without unlawfully expanding the order's reach: (1) merchandise completed or assembled in the United States with components produced in a foreign country subject to the duty order (19 U.S.C. § 1677j(a)); (2) merchandise completed or assembled in foreign countries using merchandise subject to a duty order (*id.*, § 1677j(b)); (3) merchandise "altered in form or appearance in minor respects . . . whether or not included in the same tariff classification" (*id.*, § 1677j(c)(1)); and (4) later-developed merchandise that would have been included in the order (*id.*, § 1677j(d)).

> The Trade Court erred in interpreting *Wheatland* to mean that if an article is not expressly included within the literal terms of the scope of the duty order, that article cannot be subject to an anti-circumvention inquiry. In *Wheatland*, we held that minor alteration inquiries are inappropriate when the antidumping duty order expressly excludes the allegedly altered product. *Wheatland*, 161 F.3d at 1369-70. In that case, the final determination of less-than-fair-value sales contained an express exclusion that made clear what merchandise was not covered:

>> The scope is not limited to standard pipe and fence tubing, or those types of mechanical and structural pipe that are used in standard pipe applications. All carbon steel pipes and tubes within the physical description outlined above are included within the scope of this investigation, *except line pipe*, oil country tubular goods, boiler tubing, cold-drawn or cold-rolled mechanical tubing, pipe and tube hollows for redraws, finished scaffolding, and finished rigid conduit. *Standard pipe that is dual or triple*

---

that did not occur here. *See* Brian Flood, *Trade Court Gives Commerce Opportunity To Reconsider Wire Circumvention Finding*, 31 International Trade Reporter (BNA) 1554 (4 September 2014).

15. *See Deacero S.A. de C.V. v. United States*, Federal Circuit Number 2015-1362 (5 April 2016); Brian Flood, *Appeals Panel Reimposes Duties on Mexican Wire Rod*, 33 International Trade Reporter (BNA) 492 (7 April 2016).

16. *See* 161 F.3d 1365 (Fed. Cir. 1998).

> *certified/ stenciled that enters the U.S. as line pipe of a kind used for oil or*
> *gas pipelines is also not included in this investigation.*

Id. at 1367 (emphases in *Wheatland* opinion) (citation omitted). We reasoned in *Wheatland* that including the excluded standard pipe products would "frustrate the purpose of the antidumping laws because it would allow Commerce to assess antidumping duties on products intentionally omitted from the ITC's injury investigation." *Id.* at 1371.

> . . .

> Unlike *Wheatland*, the duty order at issue contains no explicit exclusion of small-diameter steel wire rod. Although the scope of the duty order sets a cross-sectional range (5.00 mm to 19.00 mm), that cannot be read to expressly exclude for purposes of anti-circumvention inquiries all products outside that range. . . . The purpose of minor alteration anti-circumvention inquiries is to determine whether articles not expressly within the literal scope of a duty order may nonetheless be found within its scope as a result of a minor alteration to merchandise covered in the investigation. To conclude otherwise would render meaningless Congress's intent to address circumvention concerns. Here, the duty order explicitly excludes certain metallic compositions of steel wire rod, but goes no further. Thus, while the duty order provides a cross-sectional range, it does not provide that steel wire rod less than 5.00 mm diameter should necessarily be excluded from its scope.

In sum, in *Wheatland*, the Federal Circuit held DOC cannot use a minor alterations analysis to expand the scope of an order to cover merchandise, if the order explicitly excludes that merchandise. But, the *Deacero* order did not explicitly exclude wire rod less than 5 millimeters in diameter. So, DOC could broaden this order. Moreover, if the CIT holding stood, then domestic producers would be barred from questioning whether imported products slightly outside the scope of an order ought to be brought within that scope, unless those products were newly created after DOC wrote the order (and thus unbeknownst to DOC when it tailored the order).

Commentators welcomed the Federal Circuit decision as returning circumvention law on minor alterations to the pre-*Deacero status quo*. However, is that *status quo* too biased against producer-exporters, as it encourages DOC not to exclude explicitly any goods from an order?

Note the relevance of the principle of proportionality, and other disciplines, which constrain AD and CVD orders. GATT Article VI, and the WTO *Antidumping* and *SCM Agreements*, state that an AD duty is limited to the margin of dumping, and a CVD is supposed to offset the amount of a subsidy. Moreover, these specifications effectively pre-empt other kinds of remedies. For instance, the WTO Appellate Body ruled against the U.S. *Antidumping Act of 1916*, and against the *Byrd*

Amendment—both of which created remedies beyond the scope of the GATT-WTO regime.[17]

IV. Circumvention, Substantial Transformation, and 2018 *Bell Supply* Case

Bell Supply Company v. United States,

United States Court of Appeals for the Federal Circuit,
Numbers 2017-1492, 2017-1495, 2017-1504 (26 April 2018)

Hughes, Circuit Judge:

Boomerang Tube LLC, TMK IPSCO Tubulars, V & M Star L.P., Wheatland Tube Company, Maverick Tube Corporation, and United States Steel Corporation (collectively, Domestic Steel Companies) appeal the U.S. Court of International Trade's final judgment in favor of Bell Supply Company, LLC. The Trade Court affirmed the U.S. Department of Commerce's determination that certain imported oil country tubular goods (OCTG), fabricated as unfinished OCTG in the People's Republic of China and finished in other countries, were not subject to the antidumping and countervailing duty orders covering OCTG imported from China. The Trade Court also affirmed Commerce's determination that OCTG finished in third countries do not meet the requirements for circumvention under 19 U.S.C. § 1677j. Because we conclude that the Trade Court improperly proscribed Commerce from using the substantial transformation analysis to determine the country of origin for imported OCTG, we vacate the Trade Court's decision and remand for further proceedings.

I.

. . .

After Commerce issues an AD or CVD order, questions may arise about the scope of the order. To resolve these questions, Commerce conducts scope inquiries to clarify which goods are subject to its AD and CVD orders. 19 C.F.R. § 351.225(a). Commerce has established factors under 19 C.F.R. § 351.225(k) for determining whether specific articles fall within the scope of an existing order.

This appeal involves Commerce's scope inquiry regarding AD and CVD orders covering OCTG from China. OCTG are steel pipes and tubes used in oil drilling. To make OCTG, steel is first made into "green tube," which is a steel tube that must be finished before it can meet specifications for oil and gas well applications. The finishing process for green tubes typically includes heat treatment, threading, coating, and other processes.

---

17. *See* Appellate Body Report, *United States—Anti-Dumping Act of 1916*, WT/DS136/AB/R (adopted 26 September 2000), and Appellate Body Report, *United States—Continued Dumping and Offset Act of 2000*, WT/DS217/AB/R (adopted 8 January 2003).

In 2010, Commerce issued AD and CVD orders (the Orders) on OCTG from China. The scope of the Orders is defined as follows:

> The scope of this order consists of certain OCTG . . . whether finished (including limited service OCTG products) or unfinished (including green tubes and limited service OCTG products), whether or not thread protectors are attached. The scope of the order also covers OCTG coupling stock. Excluded from the scope of the order are casing or tubing containing 10.5 percent or more by weight of chromium; drill pipe; unattached couplings; and unattached thread protectors.

Certain Oil Country Tubular Goods from the People's Republic of China: Amended Final Determination of Sales at Less Than Fair Value and Antidumping Duty Order, 75 Fed. Reg. 28,551–54 (May 21, 2010).

Subsequently, U.S. Customs and Border Protection (Customs) determined that OCTG made with unfinished OCTG from China, but finished in Korea or Japan, had a country of origin of Korea or Japan. In particular, Customs noted that "heat treating has been held to substantially transform green tubes into oil well tubing." . . . This decision prompted several domestic steel companies to ask Commerce to clarify whether the scope of the Orders cover finished OCTG made from "green tubes" produced in China, but finished in another country.

In response to this request, Commerce issued a Final Scope Ruling in February 2014 (the 2014 Scope Ruling), which found that OCTG finished in third countries are still within the scope of the Orders. . . . Commerce applied the substantial transformation analysis. But contrary to Customs' decision, Commerce determined that green tubes are not substantially transformed during the finishing process, even if that process includes heat treatment. Accordingly, Commerce ruled that OCTG finished in third countries from Chinese green tubes are still subject to the Orders.

Bell Supply is a U.S. steel importer that purchases green tubes from China and arranges for them to be heat treated and finished in Indonesia. It challenged Commerce's 2014 Scope Ruling at the Trade Court and argued that the scope of the Orders should not extend to OCTG imported from third countries like Indonesia, even if they are made from green tubes produced in China. Bell Supply noted that the language of the Orders does not include OCTG imported from Indonesia, and argued that Commerce cannot use the substantial transformation analysis to sweep in OCTG from Indonesia. Instead, Bell Supply argued that Commerce must conduct a circumvention inquiry under 19 U.S.C. § 1677j before it can impose AD or CVD on products imported from countries not specifically identified in the Orders.

The Trade Court agreed with Bell Supply and found that Commerce failed to properly interpret the Orders in its 2014 Scope Ruling. The Trade Court emphasized that, because "the words of an order must serve as a basis for the inclusion of merchandise within the scope of the order," merchandise is outside an order unless the words of the order support its inclusion.

The Trade Court also held that Commerce should not have applied the substantial transformation analysis to evaluate whether OCTG imported from Indonesia was within the scope of the Orders. The Court noted that the circumvention inquiry under § 1677j provides a specific standard for determining whether foreign producers are trying to evade AD or CVD orders by completing or assembling merchandise in third countries. Thus, if Commerce believed that importers were circumventing the Orders by finishing green tubes in third countries like Indonesia, then "Commerce must apply the statute Congress enacted for that purpose and must satisfy the enumerated requirements within the statute." . . . Accordingly, the Trade Court issued a remand to Commerce to "identify actual language from the scope of the Orders that could be reasonably interpreted to include OCTG finished in third countries."

On remand, Commerce again found the Orders cover OCTG made from Chinese green tubes, even if they are finished in a third country. But this time, Commerce sought to rely on the language of the Orders instead of the substantial transformation analysis. Its decision reasoned that

> Both unfinished OCTG and finished OCTG are in-scope merchandise; that is, they are both "OCTG" within the plain meaning of the scope language. Therefore, contrary to Bell Supply's arguments, the plain language of the scope of the Orders expressly covers unfinished Chinese OCTG, and that language can reasonably be interpreted to include unfinished OCTG, even when finished in a third country. The process of finishing does not remove the product from the plain language of the scope, which includes both unfinished and finished OCTG.

. . . Bell Supply again appealed Commerce's Redetermination Pursuant to Remand to the Trade Court.

On appeal, the Trade Court found that Commerce still erred in its interpretation of the Orders. The Court observed that "[t]he scope language makes no mention of whether green tubes manufactured in China remain subject to the Orders even if the green tubes undergo further processing in a third country. Commerce has not identified any specific language from the Orders that supports such a broad reading of the scope." . . . Because the Orders do not address third country processing, "Commerce cannot use its failure to expressly include third country processing in writing the scope of the Orders and rely upon its own silence to further support its current interpretation." . . . The Trade Court remanded to Commerce for a second redetermination.

In the Final Results of Second Redetermination Pursuant to Remand, Commerce concluded that OCTG finished in third countries are not subject to the Orders. In doing so, Commerce relied on the factors under 19 C.F.R. § 351.225(k). Applying these factors, Commerce found "no information under a . . . § 351.225(k)(1) analysis to indicate that OCTG finished in third countries is subject to the scope of the . . . Orders." . . . Nor did the factors under 19 C.F.R. § 351.225(k)(2) "indicate whether OCTG finished in third countries falls within the Orders." J.A. 3348. Thus,

Commerce found that the language of the Orders does not cover OCTG finished in third countries.

Commerce also concluded that OCTG made with green tubes from China do not meet the standards for circumvention under § 1677j. Commerce determined that "the process of assembly or completion performed . . . in Indonesia is neither minor nor insignificant." . . . Instead, the finishing process adds significant value to the final value of the finished OCTG. Accordingly, Commerce found that OCTG imported from Indonesia cannot meet the requirements for circumvention.

The Domestic Steel Companies appealed Commerce's scope ruling to the Trade Court, which sustained the results of Commerce's Second Redetermination. Applying the same reasoning from its earlier decisions, the Court concluded that the language of the Orders does not include OCTG finished in third countries. The Court also found that Commerce properly concluded that OCTG finished in third countries do not meet the requirements for circumvention under § 1677j.

The Domestic Steel Companies appeal the Trade Court's decision affirming Commerce's Final Results of Second Redetermination Pursuant to Remand. . . .

II.

. . .

A.

We start by addressing the Domestic Steel Companies' argument that the imported OCTG can be considered unfinished OCTG from China. Domestic Steel companies contend that "[f]rom the time the green tubes left the factory gates in China to the time the processed products entered the United States, they were [covered] OCTG." . . . We disagree. The imported merchandise is indisputably *finished* OCTG, and cannot be categorized as unfinished OCTG.

AD and CVD orders only encompass merchandise identified in the language of the Order. *Duferco Steel*, [*Inc. v. United States*,] 296 F.3d [1087,] at 1097 [(Fed. Cir. 2002)]. In *Duferco Steel*, we held that Commerce can only include an imported article within the scope of an AD or CVD order based on the actual language of the order, not on the absence of exclusionary language. *Id.* In that case, the Trade Court had found that AD and CVD orders covered an imported article because "no language in the . . . final orders explicitly excluded the article." Id. at 1089. We reversed, and explained that "Commerce cannot find authority in an order based on the theory that the order does not deny the authority." *Id.* at 1096.

In this case, the imported merchandise cannot be categorized as unfinished OCTG under the Orders because they are brought into the United States as finished OCTG. Domestic Steel Companies argue the merchandise can still be categorized as unfinished OCTG because that is how it left China, and the Orders do not require the unfinished OCTG to be "directly imported." But the absence of a direct importation requirement does not expand the scope of the Orders. The merchandise at issue is unquestionably finished OCTG, and the language from the Orders directed to unfinished OCTG from China cannot be read to include a different product altogether.

B.

We next consider whether the merchandise can be considered *finished* OCTG *from China*. There is no dispute that the products are finished in Indonesia before being imported to the United States, and the Orders do not include OCTG from Indonesia. The parties disagree on the framework for determining whether AD or CVD orders include products finished in a country that is not identified in the orders. Domestic Steel Companies argue that Commerce is entitled to rely on the substantial transformation analysis to determine country of origin for imported articles during scope inquiries. Conversely, Bell Supply contends the substantial transformation analysis would improperly expand the scope of the Orders. Instead, Bell Supply argues that products finished in third countries are only subject to AD or CVD orders if Commerce finds circumvention under § 1677j.

Both the substantial transformation analysis and the circumvention inquiry can apply to imported products that are made in one country, but finished or assembled in a different country. In general, the substantial transformation analysis is used to determine country of origin for an imported article. *E.I. Du Pont de Nemours & Co. v. United States*, 8 F. Supp. 2d 854, 859 (Ct. Int'l Trade 1998). A substantial transformation occurs where, "as a result of manufacturing or processing steps . . . [,] the [product] loses its identity and is transformed into a new product having a new name, character and use." *Bestfoods v. United States*, 165 F.3d 1371, 1373 (Fed. Cir. 1999). To determine whether there has been a substantial transformation, Commerce looks to factors such as (1) the class or kind of merchandise; (2) the nature and sophistication of processing in the country of exportation; (3) the product properties, essential component of the merchandise, and intended end-use; (4) the cost of production/value added; and (5) level of investment.

Separate from the substantial transformation analysis, § 1677j provides an anti-circumvention provision that prevents importers from avoiding AD or CVD orders by routing their merchandise through a third country. Section1677j(b) applies to "merchandise imported into the United States [that] is of the same class or kind as any merchandise produced in a foreign country that is the subject of" an AD or CVD order, but is assembled or completed in a third country not subject to the order. To include such merchandise within the scope of an order, Commerce must determine that (1) "the process of assembly or completion in the foreign country . . . is minor or insignificant," (2) the value added in the country subject to the AD and CVD order is a significant portion of the total value of the merchandise, and (3) "action is appropriate under this paragraph to prevent evasion of such order or finding." § 1677j(b)(1)(C)-(E).

We conclude that Commerce is entitled to use the substantial transformation analysis to determine country of origin before resorting to the circumvention inquiry. Where an imported article is "from" can be an inherently ambiguous question. Because a single article can be assembled from various components and undergo multiple finishing steps, Commerce must have some way to determine the country of origin during scope inquiries. To that end, "[t]he 'substantial transformation' rule provides a yardstick for determining whether the processes performed on merchandise in a country are of such significance as to require that the resulting merchandise be considered the product of the country in which the transformation occurred." *E.I. Du Pont*, 8 F. Supp. 2d at 858. Accordingly, even though the imported OCTG was finished in Indonesia, it can still be considered "from China" if the finishing process in Indonesia did not substantially transform the product. This inquiry into where imported articles are "from" necessarily precedes the circumvention inquiry. Circumvention can only occur if the articles are from a country not covered by the relevant AD or CVD orders.

We have noted that "the substantial transformation test is recognized and well-established in cases involving country of origin determinations." *Target Sportswear, Inc. v. United States*, 70 F.3d 604, 605 (Fed. Cir. 1995). Our conclusion is consistent with the reasoning of the Trade Court's prior decisions, which have approved of Commerce's reliance on the substantial transformation analysis for merchandise finished in countries identified by the AD or CVD order, but produced with components from a third country. *See, e.g., Appleton Papers Inc. v. United States*, 929 F. Supp. 2d 1329, 1335–36 (Ct. Int'l Trade 2013); *Advanced Tech. & Materials Co. v. United States*, No. 09-00511 . . . (Ct. Int'l Trade Oct. 12, 2011). In *Appleton*, the Trade Court explained that "Commerce's decision to conduct a country of origin analysis was reasonable," and upheld "the substantial transformation analysis as a means of determining the country of origin of merchandise produced in multiple countries." 929 F. Supp. 2d at 1335–36. Likewise, the Trade Court also sustained Commerce's substantial transformation analysis in *Advanced Technology & Materials*, where the court emphasized that "the determination of where the merchandise is produced or manufactured is a fundamental step in the administration of the anti- dumping laws." . . .

In this case, however, the Trade Court concluded that "[a] country of origin analysis utilizing the substantial transformation test could only be applicable, if at all, where the circumvention test of § 1677j(b) could not apply." . . . According to the Trade Court, § 1677j was inapplicable in cases like *Appleton* because the statute does not address a situation where merchandise is completed in the country subject to AD or CVD orders. By contrast, the Trade Court held that "[t]he circumvention analysis under § 1677j(b) is the required statutory framework for analyzing the scope of an order when the merchandise is completed or assembled in third countries from subject merchandise or components produced in the subject country." . . . Here, because the imported OCTG was finished in a third country, the Trade Court concluded that § 1677j forecloses Commerce from relying on the substantial transformation analysis.

We disagree with the Trade Court's distinction between products finished in countries subject to AD or CVD orders, and products finished in third countries. In either scenario, Commerce is entitled to use the substantial transformation analysis to determine whether an imported article is covered by AD or CVD orders in the first instance. If the article originates from a country identified in the order, then Commerce need not go any further. *See Peer Bearing Co.-Changshan v. United States*, 986 F. Supp. 2d 1389, 1399 (Ct. Int'l Trade 2014) (explaining that Commerce's authority was limited to two sources: "the scope language of the Order itself . . . and 19 U.S.C. § 1677j(b)"). On the other hand, if Commerce applies the substantial transformation test and concludes that the imported article has a country of origin different from the country identified in an AD or CVD order, then Commerce can include such merchandise within the scope of an AD or CVD order only if it finds circumvention under § 1677j.

The Trade Court also found that allowing Commerce to rely on the substantial transformation analysis "would render § 1677j superfluous" because the substantial transformation test is "an agency-created device to achieve the same purpose." . . . Echoing the court's reasoning, Bell Supply contends that if Commerce were allowed to apply the substantial transformation analysis, then it would be "impossible to envision" a circumstance where Commerce could determine that third country processing results in a substantial transformation, but nevertheless meets the requirements for a finding of circumvention under § 1677j.

Contrary to the Trade Court's reasoning, allowing Commerce to apply the substantial transformation analysis for scope inquiries would not render § 1677j superfluous. Although the substantial transformation and circumvention inquiries are similar, they are not identical. The substantial transformation test asks whether, as a result of manufacturing or processing, the product "loses its identity and is transformed into a new product having 'a new name, character and use.'" *Bestfoods*, 165 F.3d at 1373 (*quoting United States v. Gibson-Thomsen Co.*, 27 C.C.P.A. 267, 273 (1940)). However, even if a product assumes a new identity, the process of "assembly or completion" may still be minor or insignificant, and undertaken for the purpose of evading an AD or CVD order. For example, in its notice of supplemental authority, Appellant Maverick Tube Corporation notes that hot-rolled steel or cold-rolled steel from China can be "substantially transformed" when it is processed into corrosion-resistant steel in Vietnam. *See, e.g., Bell Supply Co. LLC v. United States*, No. 2017-1492, Dkt. 103 (Fed. Cir. Dec. 11, 2017). Nevertheless, Commerce applied § 1677j to preliminarily determine that imported corrosion-resistant steel products from Vietnam circumvented AD and CVD orders directed to steel products from China. *Id.* at 24–33. Thus, even where an article is substantially transformed, Commerce can still find that it is subject to an AD or CVD order after conducting a circumvention inquiry.

Nor do we believe that Congress enacted § 1677j to preclude Commerce from making a country of origin determination in scope inquiries. Bell Supply contends that Congressional "intent would be frustrated if Commerce is permitted to include within an order merchandise completed or assembled in a third country that does not meet the criteria established in section 1677j." . . . The legislative history of

§ 1677j, however, says nothing about limiting Commerce's ability to determine the country of origin for imported products.

To the contrary, legislative history indicates that § 1677j can capture merchandise that is substantially transformed in third countries, which further implies that § 1677j and the substantial transformation analysis are not coextensive. In the Conference Report accompanying the *Omnibus Trade and Competitiveness Act of 1988*, Pub. L. No. 100-418, 102 Stat. 1107 (1988), Congress explained that § 1677j addresses situations where "parts and components . . . are sent from the country subject to the order to the third country for assembly or completion." H.R. Rep. No. 100-576, at 600 (1988). Likewise, the *Statement of Administrative Action Accompanying the Uruguay Round Agreements Act*, Pub. L. No. 103-465, 108 Stat. 4809 (1994), describes how foreign exporters will attempt to "circumvent an antidumping duty order by . . . [p]urchasing as many parts as possible from a third country" and assembling them in the United States. H.R. Doc. No. 103-316, at 893 (1994). Assembling off-the-shelf electronic components may very well create a new product that is "from the U.S." or a third country, but such assembly could still be relatively minor and undertaken with the intention of evading AD or CVD orders. We believe that § 1677j is meant to address these attempts at circumvention, not preclude Commerce from making a country of origin determination in the first instance.

III.

. . . [W]e conclude that Commerce may rely on the substantial transformation analysis to determine whether the imported OCTG can be considered from China. . . . [W]e vacate the Court of International Trade's Decision to Sustain Commerce's Second Remand Results. We remand the case to the Trade Court to determine whether Commerce properly applied the substantial transformation analysis.

[Consider the observation of one international trade practitioner as to why the Bell Supply case is so important:

> George Thompson, founder of the international trade law firm Thompson and Associates PLLC in Washington, D.C., and a former attorney with the International Trade Commission, . . . [said] the . . . decision clarifies in two ways how Commerce interprets the scope of duty orders.

> First, it confirms that whether a good is "finished" or "unfinished" for the purpose of duty orders depends on its condition when it enters the U.S., not when it leaves the subject country for a third country. If the court had taken the opposite view, Thompson said, duties on unfinished goods would be applied to downstream products no matter how much processing they undergo in third countries.

> Such a standard "would be impossible to administer, since it would require monitoring of downstream products from multiple countries," Thompson said. "The Federal Circuit's decision bars such an approach and thus provides guidance for how similar language in other orders should be interpreted.

Second, Thompson said, it confirmed that Commerce has the authority to use the "substantial transformation" test when an article undergoes third country processing.[18]

Do you agree?]

V. Step 8: Reviews, Critical Circumstances, and Termination

There are three kinds of reviews of AD or CVD orders: Sunset Reviews, Changed Circumstances Reviews, and Administrative Reviews. (New shippers also are subject to review, as discussed below.) The criteria for, and application of, Sunset Reviews have generated WTO adjudication. What constraints do Article VI of GATT and Article 11:3 of the WTO *Antidumping Agreement* impose on Sunset Reviews?[19]

In brief, under Article 11 of the WTO *Antidumping Agreement*, an AD or CVD order presumptively terminates (*i.e.*, sunsets) after 5 years from the date of its imposition. The exception is if, through a Sunset Review, a WTO Member finds expiry of an AD or CVD order likely would lead to continuation or recurrence of dumping or subsidization, respectively, and material injury. To rebut the presumption of a sunset, there must be evidence dumping or unlawful subsidization has not ceased, or a reasonable indication dumping or unlawful subsidization likely would occur again. The point of a Sunset Review is to ensure orders do not take on a lengthy, perhaps interminable, life of their own, as they did in some GATT contracting parties before the Uruguay Round.

The DOC publishes notice of initiation of a Sunset Review no later than 30 days of the fifth anniversary of an AD or CVD order (or Suspension Agreement). Any party interested in maintaining the order (or Agreement) must respond by giving the DOC and ITC evidence about the likely effects of revocation. The DOC has 240 days from the date of initiation to complete the Review, and the ITC has 360 days. Extensions are possible if the case is extraordinarily complicated.

In a Sunset Review of an AD order (or Suspension Agreement), the DOC's charge is to decide whether revoking the order (or terminating the Agreement) would be likely to lead to continued or recurred dumping. The DOC examines:

---

18. *Quoted in* Brian Flood, *Federal Circuit Reignites Oil Drilling Equipment Case (1)*, 35 International Trade Reporter (BNA) 604 (3 May 2018).

19. *See* WTO Appellate Body Report, *United States — Sunset Reviews of Anti-Dumping Measures on Oil Country Tubular Goods from Argentina*, WT/DS268/AB/R (adopted 29 November 2004).

The American statutory provision on Sunset Reviews is 19 U.S.C. Section 1675. Section 1675(c) authorizes the DOC and ITC to perform such a Review after five years pass from the "date of publication" of the relevant order. For a case in which the DOC and ITC prematurely launched a Sunset Review, see *Diamond Sawblades Manufacturers Coalition v. DOC*, CIT, Number 13-00391 (23 September 2014).

(1) the weighted average dumping margin calculated in the original investigation, and in any subsequent Administrative or Changed Circumstances Review,

(2) the volume of imports of subject merchandise before and after the order was issued (or Agreement accepted), and

(3) with good cause, a list of other factors.

The DOC then informs the ITC of its estimated dumping margin likely to exist if the AD order is revoked (or Agreement terminated). Similarly, in a CVD case, the DOC considers whether revoking an order (or terminating a Suspension Agreement) likely would lead to continued or recurred unlawful subsidization. The DOC checks:

(1) the net countervailable subsidy calculated in the original investigation, and in any subsequent Administrative or Changed Circumstances Review,

(2) any change in the subsidy program of the foreign government involved, and whether such change is relevant, and

(3) with good cause, a list of other factors.

The DOC then provides the ITC with a re-calculated net countervailable subsidy figure the DOC prognosticates on the assumption the CVD order is revoked (or Agreement terminated).

For its part, the ITC considers whether revoking an AD or CVD order (or terminating a Suspension Agreement) likely would lead to continued or recurred material injury within a reasonably foreseeable period. The ITC studies:

(1) the likely volume, price effect, and impact of subject merchandise on the industry from revocation of the order (or termination of the Agreement),

(2) its earlier injury determinations,

(3) whether the state of the domestic industry has improved,

(4) whether that industry is vulnerable to material injury,

(5) in an AD Sunset Review, the magnitude of the dumping margin, and

(6) in a CVD Sunset Review, the magnitude of the net countervailable subsidy rate and the nature of the subsidy (namely, whether the subsidy is prohibited as a "Red Light" under Article 3 of the *SCM Agreement*, or is a "Dark Amber" subsidy actionable under Article 6:1 of this *Agreement*).

May the ITC assess cumulatively the volume and effects of imports of subject merchandise from all countries subject to a Sunset Review to determine if these imports likely would compete with each other, and with domestic like products in the U.S.? The answer is yes, unless there is no discernible adverse impact on the affected American industry. Cumulation is significant. Imports from any one country might not justify continuation of an AD or CVD order. By aggregating imports from multiple countries, it may be possible to show a likelihood of continued or recurred material injury.

Unlike Sunset Reviews, Changed Circumstances Reviews are not mandatory. They apply to an affirmative final determination resulting in an AD or CVD order (or to a Suspension Agreement). They occur only if the DOC or ITC receives information, or a request from an interested party, showing (in the language of 19 U.S.C. § 1675(b)(1)) "changed circumstances sufficient to warrant a review of" the final determination (or Agreement). Without good cause, a Changed Circumstances Review cannot be done within 24 months of the notice of a final determination (or Suspension Agreement). It is the party seeking revocation of an AD or CVD order that bears the burden of persuasion to show circumstances exist to warrant the Review and, ultimately, revocation of the order. What kinds of circumstances might justify the Review? In an AD case, would changes in market prices — *e.g.*, lower Normal Values, or higher Export Prices — suffice? In a CVD case, would changes in subsidization policy in the exporter's home country be persuasive? Or, in both kinds of cases, would it be necessary to show the petitioner in the original investigation no longer is injured or threatened with injury?

Though not mandatory, Administrative Reviews are of great practical significance during the life of an AD or CVD order. (These Reviews also apply to Suspension Agreements.) Each year, in the anniversary month in which the DOC issued an order, either party may ask it to review whether the estimated duty rate (the cash deposit rate) is accurate or should be adjusted to yield a new amount applicable to the prior 12 months of imports. In the first year following the order, the estimated duty rate is derived from the dumping margin or net countervailable subsidy calculated by the DOC in the preliminary and final determinations, *i.e.*, from the original AD or CVD investigation. These estimates yield the final AD duty or CVD liability for the previous year, Year 1. At the end of Year 1, the petitioner and respondent can decide whether to seek re-calculation through an Administrative Review.

If neither party requests a Review, then the same estimates remain the basis for estimated duty liability in Year 2. That is, the cash deposit rate becomes the "duty assessment rate" or "final liquidation rate."[20] At the end of Year 2, if no Review is requested, then these estimates are finalized — and, these estimates are used as the estimated AD duty or CVD duty for Year 3, the "going forward cash deposit rate."

Upon request of either side, the DOC conducts an Administrative Review. In an AD case, the DOC re-calculates the dumping margin, *i.e.*, Normal Value, Export Price (or Constructed Export Price). In a CVD case it re-computes the net countervailable subsidy. Suppose this Review occurs after Year 1, and it results in a different AD duty or CVD rate than estimated in the preliminary and final determinations.

---

20. Technically, under the pertinent statute, Customs and Border Protection (CBP) is required to liquidate entries of subject merchandise within 6 months of the publication of the final results of an Administrative Review. *See SKF USA Inc. v. United States*, CIT, Number 10-00284 (Slip Opinion 13-131, 25 October 2013), *SKF USA Inc. v. United States*, CIT, Number 07-00393 (14 October 2011).

The new amount—the duty assessment or final liquidation rate, not the previously estimated cash deposit rate—serves as the final figure for the previous 12 months (Year 1), *i.e.*, for assessment of duties on all entries of merchandise subject to the Review. The new amount also serves as the basis for deposit of estimated duties for all entries subsequent to the period of the Review (*e.g.*, Year 2), *i.e.*, the going forward cash deposit rate.

Once again, there may be a difference between estimated deposits and final assessed duties. If the DOC determines in an Administrative Review a higher amount is appropriate, then the respondent is liable for the difference between the old estimated and new final amounts, plus interest. If a lower amount is right, then the respondent receives a refund for the difference, with interest. In either event, the new final AD or CVD rate stays in effect until the next Administrative Review, *i.e.*, the new rate is the deposit rate until completion of the next Review.

Thus, a new calculation of the dumping margin or net countervailable subsidy serves two purposes. First, it is the final AD duty or CVD rate for subject merchandise covered by the order in the previous 12 months. Second, it is the estimated amount for the deposit of an AD duty or CVD in the next year. The dual purposes are why U.S. AD and CVD remedies are dubbed both "retrospective" and "prospective." The remedy extends backward in time, to the moment of importation of subject merchandise, and forward for as long as the dumping or illegal subsidization occurs. Note the significance of the preliminary dumping margin or subsidization determination: if it is affirmative, then it triggers the suspension of liquidation of entries of subject merchandise and the requirement to post the estimated cash deposit rate. In contrast, in all other WTO Members, the remedies are only prospective. In cases under the *DSU*, remedies are prospective. Does a retrospective dimension raise concerns under Article 10 of the WTO *Antidumping Agreement*?[21]

---

21. Another question prompted by a retrospective AD-CVD duty collection scheme is whether it leads to unpaid duties. In a July 2016 study, the GAO said yes, echoing a March 2008 study. GAO reported CBP is handicapped collecting full duties in a timely manner, because:

> (1) The U.S. system for determining such duties involves the setting of an initial estimated duty rate upon the entry of goods, followed by the retrospective assessment of a final duty rate; (2) the amount of AD/CV duties for which an importer may be ultimately billed can significantly exceed what the importer pays when the goods enter the country; and (3) the assessment of final AD/CV duties can occur up to several years after an importer enters goods into the United States, during which time the importer may cease operations or become unable to pay additional duties.

GOVERNMENT ACCOUNTABILITY OFFICE, ANTIDUMPING AND COUNTERVAILING DUTIES: CBP ACTION NEEDED TO REDUCE DUTY PROCESSING ERRORS AND MITIGATE NONPAYMENT RISK, GAO-16-542 (July 2016), at 2, www.gao.gov/assets/680/678419.pdf. The uncollected duty figure was huge: $2.3 billion (as of mid-May 2015, based on duty bills for FYs 2001–2014):

> We estimate the amount of uncollected duties on entries from fiscal year 2001 through 2014 to be $2.3 billion. While CBP collects on most [about 90% of] AD/CV duty bills it issues, it only collects, on average, about 31 percent of the dollar amount owed. The large amount of uncollected duties is due in part to the long lag time between entry and

Consider this question where a petitioner alleges "critical circumstances." In an AD case, the DOC applies (based on IA at the time) a three-pronged test so see if these circumstances exist:

(1) there is a history of dumping and material injury, in the U.S. or elsewhere, of the subject merchandise,

(2) the importer knew or should have known (a) the merchandise was being sold at LTFV, and (b) there was likely to be material injury because of such sales, and

(3) massive imports of subject merchandise occurred over a relatively short period.

In a CVD case, the DOC (again, using IA) applies a slightly different three-pronged test:

(1) subject merchandise originates in a "country under the Agreement" (*i.e.*, a WTO Member country, or a country with which the U.S. has an agreement for unconditional MFN treatment but does not expressly allow for trade remedy actions under the GATT-WTO accords or import restrictions to counter unfair practices),

(2) the alleged subsidy violates the WTO *SCM Agreement*, and

(3) massive imports of subject merchandise occurred over a relatively short period.

If all three prongs are satisfied, then the DOC deems the circumstances "critical." It may make this determination before a preliminary dumping margin decision or injury ruling.

If the DOC finds critical circumstances, the remedial implication is dramatic. Any suspension of liquidation of entries the DOC orders applies retroactively to un-liquidated entries of merchandise entered up to 90 days before the date on which the DOC ordered the suspension. That is, the respondent must post security for estimated AD or CVD duties on merchandise technically not subject to the investigation, but which was imported "close enough" to the time of the investigation, where "close enough" is defined as entry within 90 days of the DOC preliminary

---

billing in the U.S. retrospective AD/CV duty collection system, with an average of about 2-and-a-half years between the time goods enter the United States and the date a bill may be issued. Large differences between the initial estimated duty rate and the final duty rate assessed also contribute to unpaid bills, as importers receiving a large bill long after an entry is made may be unwilling or unable to pay.

Id., 13, 56.

In its earlier study, GAO reported a duty collection shortfall of over $600 million (as of September 2007, since 2001). *See* Government Accountability Office, Congress and Agencies Should Take Additional Steps to Reduce Substantial Shortfalls in Duty Collection, GAO-08-391 (March 2008), www.gao.gov/products/GAO-08-391.

affirmative determination of dumping or subsidization and its suspension order applying to subject merchandise.

The logic behind retroactivity of up to 90 days is to ensure that if a final AD or CVD is issued, it will not have been rendered inutile, or undermined, by a large volume of illegally dumped or subsidized merchandise that entered the U.S. after the investigation commenced. Suppose cleverly calculating respondents rushed a massive amount of merchandise they had planned to dump, or for which they received subsidies, into the American market as soon as the case against them was initiated. The petitioner would not be protected from injury by this merchandise if its remedy was deferred until conclusion of the case, or a phase thereof, and was only prospective. The 90-day critical circumstance period allows a petitioner to reach further back in time, and thereby make any subsequent final order meaningful—because the petitioner has not been buried by unfair imports during the investigation.

What about revocation of an extant AD or CVD order, or termination of a Suspension Agreement? That is, how does a case end assuming an order was issued or an investigation was suspended? For the DOC to revoke an AD or CVD order, or terminate a Suspension Agreement, "substantially all" of the domestic producers of the like product at issue must express a lack of interest in the Agreement or order. The DOC interprets the statutory term "substantially all" (set out in Sections 734 and 782(h)(2) of the *Tariff Act of 1930*, as amended, and 19 C.F.R. Section 351.222(g)(1)(i)) as producers accounting for at least 85% of the domestic like product.

VI. New Shippers and 2013 *Qingdao Maycarrier* and 2014 *Xinjiamei Furniture* Cases

As their name suggests, New Shipper Reviews deal with producer-exporters that contend their merchandise should not be covered by an extant AD or CVD order, because they did not begin shipping merchandise until after that order was issued. A key point is whether a purported new shipper really is "new," or just an imposter mimicking a respondent producer exporter. In the 2013 case of *Qingdao Maycarrier Import & Export Company v. United States*, the CIT said the DOC acted correctly in rescinding a New Shipper Review. The CIT held the DOC has this authority in cases where a producer-exporter tries to obscure its sales of subject merchandise that occurred during a relevant period of review, in effect fraudulently claiming it is a new shipper.

The subject merchandise, exported by Weifang Naike Foodstuffs Company, was garlic from China. Maycarrier argued its garlic should not be subject to the AD order covering the garlic from Weifang, because it was a different entity from Weifang, and, in contrast to Weifang, exported garlic after the relevant period of Administrative Review for the Weifang garlic. Substantial evidence showed otherwise, including information the DOC gleaned from over two dozen websites:

(1) The same telephone number for the sales departments appeared for Wei-fang and Maycarrier.

(2) Both companies were listed as part of the "Weifang Naike Group."

(3) Employees of Weifang were listed as contacts for Maycarrier, with those employees directing potential customers to Maycarrier.

(4) Weifang employees posted sales information for Maycarrier profiles.

In addition:

(5) The General Manager of Maycarrier managed internet sales for Maycarrier and Weifang, and had the same mobile phone number as the Chairman of Weifang.

(6) There were no tax records for Maycarrier in the online database of the Shangdong Province National taxation Bureau.

(7) The business registration form in China for Maycarrier listed it as "connected to another entity."

Simply put, Weifang and Maycarrier were the same entity, shipping subject merchandise during the entire relevant period. The CIT agreed, thus upholding the DOC decision to revoke treatment of Maycarrier as a new shipper, and to impose a China-wide AD rate of $4.71 per kilogram on Maycarrier's garlic.

Once items from a new shipper have been included in the scope of subject merchandise of an extent trade remedy order, subsequent New Shipper Reviews can raise many of the same issues as other types of Reviews. For example, identifying whether items exported by a new shipper come within the scope of an existing AD or CVD order sometimes requires use by the DOC of the Best Information Available (BIA), or to use the post-Uruguay Round term based on Article 6:6 of the *WTO Antidumping Agreement*, "Facts Available." If that shipper is from an NME, then surrogate values may be needed to get a supposedly accurate estimate of Normal Value by computing Constructed Value.[22] (To be sure, applicable statutory rules and case law thereunder oblige the DOC to select BIA for surrogate values for respondents

---

22. In a different garlic bulb dispute, the 2014 case of *Qingdao Sea-Line Trading Company v. United States*, the Federal Circuit upheld a 155.53% New Shipper AD rate the DOC assigned to Chinese fresh whole garlic bulbs. *See* Number 2013-1581 (10 September 2014); Brian Flood, *Federal Circuit Affirms AD Rate For Chinese Garlic Bulb Exporter*, 31 International Trade Reporter (BNA) 1666 (18 September 2014). The DOC based that rate on a data set of "Grade Super A" garlic bulb prices that pre-dated the period of review. The DOC showed customers care about size, and pay a premium for large bulbs, so size is more important than contemporaneity of sales. The DOC also proved it was right to use financial statements from an Indian company, Tata Tea Ltd., to compute surrogate financial ratios, because the tea Tata made during the POR closely simulated garlic production processes. In earlier Administrative Reviews, the DOC had rejected that data. The Federal Circuit upheld as neither arbitrary nor unreasonable the decision of the DOC, based on new information and arguments, to use Tata Tea data in this instance.

in original investigations and Administrative Reviews.[23] They also require the DOC to use common sense.[24])

Consider the case of *Xinjiamei Furniture (Zhangzhou) v. United States*.[25] In its original New Shipper Review, the DOC assigned a weighted average dumping margin of 2.78% for metal folding chairs and tables produced and exported by a Chinese firm, Xinjiamei Furniture. This rate applied from 1 June 2009 through 31 May 2010. The exporter complained, saying the DOC provided no rational basis for using import data from India, published in the Global Trade Atlas. The DOC did so as a surrogate value for cold-rolled steel coil, which was an input into the subject merchandise. The CIT agreed, and remanded the case to the DOC. On remand the DOC stayed with the same data, but explained those Indian values and volumes were comfortably in the range in other surrogate countries. That was a sufficient explanation for basing the AD duty rate on Indian data from the GTA.

VII. Steps 9 and 10: Appeals and WTO Adjudication?

Frequently, an interested party is unhappy with the outcome of an AD or CVD investigation. Judicial review of a final AD or CVD determination may be obtained by filing a summons and complaint, within 30 days of publication of the determination, with the CIT. That Court, which is organized under Article III of the U.S. Constitution and has national jurisdiction, is statutorily bound to apply to the administrative action the following standard of review: whether "substantial

---

23. *See, e.g., Xiamen International Trade & Industrial Company v. United States*, CIT Number 11-0041 (Slip Opinion 14-100, 28 August 2014) (upholding remand results in an Administrative Review of an AD order imposing a 5.76% rate on Chinese preserved mushrooms from one mandatory respondent, Xiamen International Trade and Industrial Company (XITIC), where the DOC on remand used the same Global Trade Atlas data from its original investigation for white button mushroom spawn, even though those data included other spawn varieties, because the respondent could not show those data were artificially inflated, and thus a reasonable mind could agree the DOC selected BIA on mushroom spawn); Brian Flood, *Court Upholds Revised AD Rates On Chinese Preserved Mushrooms*, 31 International Trade Reporter (BNA) 1669 (18 September 2014).

24. *See, e.g., DuPont Teijin Films China Ltd. v. United States*, CIT Number 13-00229 (11 September 2014) (remanding for recalculation by the DOC a 12.8% dumping margin from an Administrative Review of Chinese polyethylene terephthalate film, sheet, and strip (PET film), because the DOC wrongly assumed brokerage and handling (B&H) costs, *i.e.*, the time and expense to complete export procedures in China, like document preparation, customs formalities, and port and terminal technicalities, were less for shipments with lower weights; the DOC converted surrogate values for B&H costs into a per kilogram amount when computing the dumping margin, but it did so based on container weight, not the shipment as a whole, so agreeing with the Chinese PET exporter, the CIT said: "Common sense indicates that a half-full, twenty-foot container would incur the same document preparation and customs clearance costs as a full twenty-foot container of a single type of good.")

25. *See* Number 11-00456 (Slip Opinion 14-17, 18 February 2014); Brian Flood, *Chinese Metal Folding Chair Exporter Loses New Shipper Review Challenge*, 31 International Trade Reporter (BNA) 344 (20 February 2014).

evidence on the record" supports the determination, or whether the determination is "otherwise not in accordance with law."

In so doing, it respects what in Administrative Law is known as *"Chevron"* deference. Technically, the CIT has its own procedural rules, which are modeled after the *Federal Rules of Civil Procedure*. Trials are extraordinarily rare, and much of the litigation is via motion. The CIT may *accept amicus* briefs, but not if they blur the distinction between being an intervenor and a friend of the Court.[26] An important part of CIT practice is to know the limited subject matter jurisdiction of the Court, which put simply is to AD/CVD, customs classification, and TAA cases.

An interested party may appeal a DOC decision not to initiate an investigation, or a negative preliminary injury determination by the ITC. In that appeal, the CIT considers whether the action is "arbitrary, capricious, [or] an abuse of discretion, or [is] otherwise not in accordance with law." It also is possible to appeal the result of a Sunset, Changed Circumstances, or Administrative Review of an AD or CVD order. If a litigant is unsatisfied with a CIT decision, then it may appeal to the Federal Circuit. From there, appeal is to the Supreme Court, though review at that level is improbable. Is an affirmative preliminary injury determination, or a preliminary dumping margin or subsidy determination, reviewable by the CIT?

Certain RTAs provide for review of domestic AD or CVD orders. *NAFTA* Chapter 19 is a quintessential example. This Chapter dates to the 1989: Canada wanted a neutral arbitration for AD-CVD cases. It got this mechanism in *CUSFTA* as negotiations on *NAFTA's* predecessor neared an end. A *NAFTA* Chapter 19 Panel may review a final AD or CVD decision if subject merchandise originates in *NAFTA* Parties. A *NAFTA* Panel must apply the law and standard of review of the country in which the AD or CVD case occurred. Thus, in reviewing a DOC or ITC determination, a Panel must apply U.S. law and judicial review standards.[27] Once appeal is

---

26. *See Changzhou Hawd Flooring Co. v. United States*, Number 12-00020, Slip Opinion 14-93 (11 August 2014); Brian Flood, *In AD Dispute, Court Blocks Amicus Brief By Chinese Flooring Importers, Exporters*, 31 International Trade Reporter (BNA) 1466 (14 August 2014). The subject merchandise was multi-layered wood flooring from China. The CIT refused to accept the *amicus* from a group of hardwood floor exporters and importers, because they had too significant an interest in the outcome. Many of them had participated in the DOC dumping margin investigation, some as separate rate respondents, so they had a financial stake in any AD duties imposed. Rather than helping the CIT with facts and arguments not in the briefs of the parties, these companies merely repeated arguments already presented by the respondents.

27. For example, in June 2014 a *NAFTA* Panel rejected a challenge to a DOC determination by Canadian producer-exporters of certain alloy steel wire rod. The complainants argued DOC should not have used zeroing in the 2006–2007 Administrative Review of their subject merchandise, which led to a 2.33% dumping margin. The complainants pointed out DOC stopped zeroing in original investigations in 2006 to comply with adverse WTO Appellate Body decisions, so it should not have continued to employ zeroing in Administrative Reviews for several years thereafter. The *NAFTA* Panel applied the precedent of *Union Steel v. United States*, 713 F.3d 1101 (Fed. Cir. 2013): DOC could zero in Administrative Reviews, but not original investigations, because of differences in how prices are compared in the two contexts.

made to a Chapter 19 Panel, it is not possible to return to a domestic court system (*e.g.*, the CIT or Federal Circuit). The only exception, set forth in *NAFTA* Article 1905:1(d), is if a constitutional issue is at stake.

Private parties are involved directly in *NAFTA* Chapter 19 cases. The Panels have produced a large and growing body of jurisprudence, and a considerable literature of commentary and analysis on it exists. Sometimes the litigation is bitter, as in the *Softwood Lumber* CVD case, while other times it centers on technical matters such as the use of information available. One common concern is the extent to which Panelists are skillful in applying law that is not there one. For instance, how well can an American or Canadian Panelist apply pertinent Mexican law?

Observe that not every RTA creates special tribunals for AD and CVD cases. For instance, there are no such provisions in the U.S. FTAs with Australia, Bahrain, Chile, Singapore, Jordon, Israel, Morocco, or Oman—in other words, *NAFTA* Chapter 19 is unusual in the American array of FTAs. Somewhat unique are RTAs that ban the use of AD rules. One example is the 1983 *Australia—New Zealand Closer Economic Relations Trade Agreement* (the *ANZCERTA*, or *CER* for short). Article 15 of the 1983 *CER* permits AD actions. However, in 1988, Australia and New Zealand agreed to a *Protocol* to the *CER*. Article 4 of the *Protocol* bans the use of the AD remedy. Another instance is the FTA between Singapore and the *EFTA* countries, signed in 2002 and effective in 2003. Article 16 forbids AD actions between Singapore and the *EFTA* members. A 3rd instance is *EFTA* itself—Article 36 proscribes AD actions among the *EFTA* members.

Some AD or CVD cases generate a dispute between WTO Members. There are two basic sources of conflict. First, one Member may challenge an AD or CVD law maintained by another Member as inconsistent with one or more GATT-WTO obligations. Second, one Member may argue the process or outcome of a particular AD or CVD investigation violates one or more GATT-WTO obligations. Whether the dispute is a "statutory" or "investigation" challenge, it is handled according to *DSU* procedures. AD and CVD disputes take up a sizeable percentage of the docket of WTO tribunals. The jurisprudence is both considerable and evolving. Must all remedies under local law be exhausted before an AD or CVD matter can be brought under the *DSU*?

What happens not if, but when, a WTO Panel or the Appellate Body finds an action by the DOC or ITC is inconsistent with America's obligations in the GATT-WTO regime? Section 129(a) of the 1994 *URAA* provides the answer.[28] For a DOC action, the USTR, after consulting with Congress, may request the DOC to issue a determination that would not be inconsistent with the WTO Panel or Appellate Body findings. The USTR also may direct DOC to implement its revised determination, effective for liquidated entries of subject merchandise on or after the date of this direction.

---

28. *See* 19 U.S.C. § 3538.

As for the ITC, the USTR may ask it to issue an advisory report as to whether the relevant statute permits it to take steps to render its determination not inconsistent with the WTO panel or Appellate Body findings. If the ITC provides an affirmative report, then the USTR may ask it to make a new determination. If the result is an AD or CVD order no longer is justified, then the USTR—after checking with Congress—may direct the ITC to revoke the order, effective for liquidated entries of subject merchandise entered on or after this direction. Interestingly, the President, after consulting with Congress, may reduce, modify, or terminate an ITC action.

A critical, unresolved set of issues concerns interaction among various levels of review. To what extent, if any, must a *NAFTA* Chapter 19 panel pay attention to a ruling by a WTO Panel or the Appellate Body? To what extent, if any, must the CIT or Federal Circuit Court take into account a Chapter 19 Panel, WTO Panel, or Appellate Body decision? Consider the same questions, but change the verb from "must" to "should."

VIII. Third Country Dumping

Suppose there is fierce competition in Brazil between rice exports from India and Thailand. The Thai rice farmers accuse their Indian competitors of dumping rice in Brazil. They do not, however, allege the Indians are dumping rice in Thailand. What recourse, if any, do the Thai rice farmers have against dumping in Brazil?

The hypothetical example illustrates "third country dumping," where the third country is Thailand, the importing country is Brazil, and India is the alleged dumper. Article 14 of the WTO *Antidumping Agreement* creates a claim for AD action on behalf of a third country. Under it, Thai government authorities are entitled to apply to the Brazilian AD authority and request Brazil take action against the Indian rice. Article 14:2 requires the Thai action be supported by price information showing the Indian rice is, in fact, being dumped in Brazil, and the dumping causes injury to Thai rice farmers.

It is the third country producers (Thai rice farmers), not domestic producers in the importing country (*e.g.*, rice farmers in Brazil) alleging injury. Article 14:4 makes clear the importing country has sole discretion on proceeding with the case. Why might Brazil choose to bring the action, especially if it has no domestic sector claiming injury? One answer is good citizenship. If Brazil expects serious consideration when it approaches other countries to take up AD claims on its behalf, then it had better take the claims of other countries seriously. Brazil might (indeed, should) anticipate being a "repeat player" in third country AD cases, sometimes as the importing country, and sometimes as the complainant third country. However, might Brazil also have to weigh its trade, investment, and financial relations with the respondent, India?

The standard requirements in a conventional AD case must be met in a third country case. Proof is needed of a positive dumping margin, as well as injury caused by dumping. The threshold test of comparability of products—namely, the third country product (*e.g.*, Thai rice) is like the allegedly dumped product (*e.g.*, Indian rice)—must be passed.

In the U.S., a domestic industry exporting goods to another country alleging injury from dumping in that other country must petition the USTR. (For instance, California rice farmers exporting to Brazil might petition the USTR for relief from Indian rice dumped in Brazil.) If the USTR agrees a reasonable basis for the claim exists, then it applies to the appropriate authority in the importing country requesting action be taken on behalf of the U.S. The DOC and ITC assist the USTR in preparing the application (*e.g.*, to provide price and injury data). Here, the U.S. is the third country seeking relief. Suppose authorities in the importing country reject the American application. Then, the USTR must consult with the petitioning industry on whether other action could be taken. What remedy might there be? Would unilateral trade retaliation under Section 301 work?

Conversely, the USTR has discretion to initiate an AD investigation upon request by a third country. It consults with the DOC and ITC about the merits of the petition, and obtains approval from the WTO Council for Trade in Goods before commencing the action. Consider the second sentence of Article 14:4 of the *Antidumping Agreement*. Does this sentence mean Council approval is mandatory, or simply best practice?

Chapter 4

Data Issues in AD Cases[1]

I. POI and May 2000 WTO *Recommendation*

French President Charles de Gaulle (1890–1970, President, 1959–1969) once remarked: "We are not here to laugh."[2] His comment might well apply to procedures used in AD and CVD cases. For lawyers like your *Textbook* author who despised Civil Procedure as a law student, it does apply! Yet, understanding how AD and CVD cases "work" is important, if for no other reason than the practical one: legal practitioners and scholars ought to understand how AD and CVD investigations and adjudications proceed, because they will encounter them. But, there is an additional reason: embedded in certain procedural details (such as the effects of a preliminary affirmative dumping margin determination under U.S. law) are grand issues of protectionism. As a consolation to the unconvinced, it so happens that many of the procedures are the same in both AD and CVD cases, so to learn how cases in one context work largely is to learn how they work in both contexts.

To begin, what is the POI in an AD or CVD case? Neither Article VI of GATT nor Article 5:2 of the WTO *Antidumping Agreement* specifies the POI. Yet, in every case, the POI is critical. Data on alleged dumping, subsidization, and injury or threat of injury are collected relating to a POI.[3] Selection of the starting and ending dates in the POI can strengthen, or destroy, a claim. If the claim is successful, then the POI also is the basis for a remedial duty, both in the sense of the timing of assessment of the duty and scope of merchandise on which the duty is imposed.

In May 2000, the WTO adopted a *Recommendation Concerning the Periods of Data Collection for Anti-Dumping Investigations*. The *Recommendation* sets 12 months as

---

1. Documents References:
   (1) *Havana (ITO) Charter* Article 34
   (2) GATT Article VI
   (3) WTO *Antidumping Agreement* Articles 3, 5, 14, 17
   (4) *NAFTA* Chapter 19
   (5) Relevant provisions in other FTAs

2. *Quoted in* the *Independent* (London), 21 April 1990.

3. *See, e.g., Yantai Xinke Steel Structure Co. v. United States*, Number 10-00240 (Slip Opinion 14-38, 9 April 2014), in which the CIT upheld a remand determination by the DOC, leading to a downward revision of the AD duty rate on subject merchandise, steel grating from China (an NME), from 145.18% to 38.16% for two out of three producer-exporters. The CIT did so in part because the DOC on remand used surrogate value data from India on hot-rolled steel coil that was more contemporaneous with the POI than data it used in its original investigation.

the normal POI in a dumping margin investigation, but in no instance less than six months. What should the POI be when investigating alleged unlawful subsidization? For injury or threat investigations, the *Recommendation* calls for a POI of at least three years, and an overlap between this period and the POI in a dumping margin investigation. Thus, the most recent 12-month, and three-year, period from which reliable data are attainable are, in practice, the POIs in most dumping margin and injury or threat investigations. Why is a longer period needed in an injury or threat investigation? The answer is more economic variables are studied in it than in a dumping margin inquiry, which involves prices.

The *Recommendation* explains a WTO Member is not supposed to collect data on dumping relating to the time after initiating a dumping margin investigation. Some Members collect post-initiation data on injury or threat. Why? Might the answer lie in a time lag between dumping as a cause of injury or threat and the manifestation of deleterious effects of dumping? If an investigation takes 12–18 months, then limiting injury or threat data to the pre-initiation period might understate the true effects of dumping. However, might post-initiation data be distorted by the effect of the investigation itself in the market for subject merchandise or a foreign like product?

II. Positive Evidence, Selecting Particular POIs, and 2005 *Mexico Rice* Case

WTP Appellate Body Report,

Mexico — Definitive Anti-Dumping Measures on Beef and Rice,
Complaint with Respect to Rice,
WT/DS295/AB/R (Adopted 20 December 2005)

I. Introduction

. . .

2. The Mexican Rice Council filed an anti-dumping petition on 2 June 2000 with the Ministry of Commerce and Industrial Development ("SECOFI"), Mexico's investigating authority at that time. The investigation was initiated in December 2000 by the Ministry of Economy ("*Economía*"), which succeeded SECOFI as Mexico's investigating authority. The notice of initiation, a copy of the petition and attachments thereto, and the investigation questionnaire were sent to the Government of the United States and to the two exporters that were specifically identified in the petition as the "exporters", Producers Rice Mill, Inc. ("Producers Rice") and Riceland Foods, Inc. ("Riceland"). Two additional exporters, The Rice Company and Farmers Rice Milling Company ("Farmers Rice"), came forward following the initiation of the investigation and before the preliminary determination, and requested copies of the questionnaire.

3. The period of investigation for the purpose of the dumping determination was 1 March to 31 August 1999. For the purpose of the injury determination, *Economía* collected data for the period March 1997 through August 1999, but based its analysis on the data for 1 March to 31 August for the years 1997, 1998, and 1999 and issued its final affirmative determination on 5 June 2002. *Economía* found that Farmers Rice and Riceland had not been dumping during the period of investigation and consequently imposed a zero per cent duty on these exporters. With respect to The Rice Company, *Economía* determined a dumping margin of 3.93 per cent and imposed a duty in that amount. *Economía* also imposed on the remaining United States exporters of the subject merchandise, including Producers Rice, a duty of 10.18 per cent, calculated on the basis of the facts available.

V. *Economía's* Injury Determination

A. The Period of Investigation and the Terms of Reference

147. . . . The investigation [by *Economía*] was initiated on 11 December 2000, 15 months after the end of the period of investigation. Final anti-dumping measures were imposed on 5 June 2002, just less than three years after the end of the period of investigation.

. . .

B. The Use of a Period of Investigation Ending in August 1999 and the Criterion of Positive Evidence

. . .

159. The Panel found that, by choosing to base its determination of injury on a period of investigation that ended more than 15 months before the initiation of the investigation, Mexico failed to comply with the obligation to make a determination of injury based on positive evidence. As a consequence, the Panel found that Mexico acted inconsistently with Articles 3:1, 3:2, 3:4, and 3:5 of the *Anti-Dumping Agreement*. . . .

160. Mexico challenges the Panel's findings regarding *Economía's* use of a period of investigation ending in August 1999. . . . According to Mexico, the Panel erred in finding that there is an "inherent real-time link" between the investigation and the data on which it is based. Mexico alleges that this "real-time link" requirement is inconsistent with the option of using a past period as the period of investigation. Mexico also argues that the Panel contradicts itself because the Panel acknowledged that it is impossible that the period of investigation used for purposes of data collection coincide exactly with the time period in which the investigating authority conducts its investigation. For Mexico, the content of Article 3:1 of the *Anti-Dumping Agreement* does not focus on how remote the investigation period is, but on the applicability of the data used.

. . .

162. The Panel considered that the [May 2000] recommendation adopted by the Committee on Anti-Dumping Practices—the *Recommendation Concerning the*

Periods of Data Collection for Anti-Dumping Investigations (the "*Recommendation*") —
provides useful support for the correct interpretation of the obligations found in the
text of the *Anti-Dumping Agreement*. . . .

. . .

164. The Panel described "positive evidence" as evidence that is relevant and pertinent with respect to the issue to be decided, and that has the characteristics of being
inherently reliable and creditworthy. The Panel was of the view that, under the positive evidence criterion of Article 3:1, the question whether the information at issue
constituted "positive evidence" — that is to say, was relevant, pertinent, reliable, and
creditworthy — had to be assessed with respect to the current situation.

165. We agree with the Panel that evidence that is not relevant or pertinent to the
issue to be decided is not "positive evidence." We also agree with the Panel that
relevance or pertinence must be assessed with respect to the existence of injury
caused by dumping at the time the investigation takes place. Under Article VI of the
GATT 1994 and its "application" in the *Anti-Dumping Agreement*, the conditions
for imposing an anti-dumping duty — injury caused by dumping — should obtain
at that time. Article VI:2 of the GATT 1994 provides that anti-dumping duties are
imposed "to offset or prevent" dumping. The term "offset" suggests that the scheme
established in Article VI of the GATT 1994, and applied through the provisions of
the *Anti-Dumping Agreement*, fulfils a corrective function: Members are permitted
to take corrective measures in order to counter the injurious situation created by
dumping. Under the logic of this corrective scheme, the imposition of anti-dumping
duties is justified to the extent that they respond to injury caused by dumping. To
use the Panel's terminology, anti-dumping duties "counterbalance[]" injury caused
by dumping. Because the conditions to impose an anti-dumping duty are to be
assessed with respect to the current situation, the determination of whether injury
exists should be based on data that provide indications of the situation prevailing
when the investigation takes place.

166. This, of course, does not imply that investigating authorities are not allowed to
establish a period of investigation that covers a past period. . . . [T]he Panel did not
state that the *Anti-Dumping Agreement* requires a coincidence in time between the
investigation and the data used therein. On the contrary, the Panel recognized that
"it is well established that the data on the basis of which [the determination that
dumped imports cause injury] is made may be based on a past period, known as the
period of investigation." In order to determine whether injury caused by dumping
exists when the investigation takes place, "historical data" may be used. We agree
with the Panel, however, that more recent data is likely to provide better indications
about current injury.

167. We agree with Mexico that using a remote investigation period is not *per se* a
violation of Article 3:1. In our view, however, the Panel did not set out such a principle, as its findings relate to the specific circumstances of this case. The Panel was

satisfied that, in this specific case, a *prima facie* case was established that the information used by *Economía* did not provide reliable indications of current injury and, therefore, did not meet the criterion of positive evidence in Article 3:1 of the *Anti-Dumping Agreement*. The Panel arrived at this conclusion on the basis of several factors. The Panel attached importance to the existence of a 15-month gap between the end of the period of investigation and the initiation of the investigation, and a gap of almost three years between the end of the period of investigation and the imposition of final anti-dumping duties. However, these temporal gaps were not the only circumstances that the Panel took into account. The Panel, as trier of the facts, gave weight to other factors: (i) the period of investigation chosen by *Economía* was that proposed by the petitioner; (ii) Mexico did not establish that practical problems necessitated this particular period of investigation; (iii) it was not established that updating the information was not possible; (iv) no attempt was made to update the information; and (v) Mexico did not provide any reason—apart from the allegation that it is Mexico's general practice to accept the period of investigation submitted by the petitioner—why more recent information was not sought. Thus, it is not only the remoteness of the period of investigation, but also these other circumstances that formed the basis for the Panel to conclude that a *prima facie* case was established. In the light of the general assessment of these other circumstances carried out by the Panel as trier of the facts, we accept that a gap of 15 months between the end of the period of investigation and the initiation of the investigation, and another gap of almost three years between the end of the period of investigation and the imposition of the final anti-dumping duties, may raise real doubts about the existence of a sufficiently relevant nexus between the data relating to the period of investigation and current injury. Therefore, we have no reason to disturb the Panel's assessment that a *prima facie* case of violation of Article 3:1 was made out.

. . .

169. Mexico also argues that the Panel erred because it based its finding that the period of investigation used by *Economía* was inconsistent with the *Anti-Dumping Agreement* on the *Recommendation* . . . , a non-binding document adopted by the Committee on Anti-Dumping Practices. The *Recommendation* stipulates, *inter alia*, that the period of data collection should end as close to the date of initiation of the investigation as is practicable. We disagree with Mexico's argument. The Panel took care to recall that this *Recommendation* is a "non-binding guide" that "does not add new obligations, nor detract from the existing obligations of Members under the [*Anti-Dumping Agreement*]." It appears to us that the Panel referred to the *Recommendation*, not as a legal basis for its findings, but simply to show that the *Recommendation*'s content was not inconsistent with its own reasoning. Doing so does not constitute an error of law. In any event, we note that the *Recommendation* was not a decisive factor that led the Panel to conclude that the criterion of "positive evidence" in Article 3:1 was not met.

. . .

171. . . . The Panel had to decide whether the information relating to a period of investigation ending in August 1999 constituted an appropriate basis for making a determination of injury. The issue before the Panel centred on the manner in which *Economía* conducted the injury analysis, not the interpretation of a specific provision of the *Anti-Dumping Agreement*. Furthermore, . . . the Panel expressed the view that the data on the basis of which a determination of injury caused by dumping is made may relate to a past period, to the extent this information is relevant with regard to the current situation. It appears to us that the Panel's view is compatible with Mexico's own reading of the *Anti-Dumping Agreement*, according to which using data relating to a past period does not, *per se*, entail a violation of that Agreement. For these reasons, we are of the view that Mexico's argument regarding Article 17:6(ii) of the *Anti-Dumping Agreement* is without merit.

172. Accordingly, we *uphold* the Panel's finding . . . that *Economía's* use of a period of investigation ending in August 1999 resulted in a failure to make a determination of injury based on "positive evidence" as required by Article 3:1 of the *Anti-Dumping Agreement*. As a result of this finding, we also *uphold* the Panel's finding . . . that by choosing this period of investigation, Mexico acted inconsistently with Articles 3:2, 3:4, and 3:5 of that *Agreement*.

C. The March–August Period

173. We turn now to the issue whether the Panel erred in finding that, in limiting the injury analysis to the March–August period of 1997, 1998, and 1999, *Economía* failed to make a determination of injury that involves an "objective examination" as required by Article 3:1 of the *Anti-Dumping Agreement*.

174. For the purposes of examining the injury to the domestic industry, *Economía* collected data for a continuous period of three years covering 1997, 1998, and 1999. However, *Economía* limited its analysis to data for the months of March to August of these years; data from the period September to February of each of these years were disregarded. In the Panel's view, such an examination, made on the basis of an incomplete set of data and characterized by the selective use of certain data for the injury analysis, could not be "objective" within the meaning of Article 3:1 . . . , unless a proper justification were provided. In this respect, the Panel noted that Mexico's only argument was that it was necessary to examine data relating only to the six months from March to August because this was also the six-month period chosen for the analysis of the existence of dumping. The Panel considered that this did not constitute a proper justification for ignoring half of the data concerning the state of the domestic industry. For the Panel, the *Anti-Dumping Agreement* does not require that "a period of investigation [for] the injury analysis should be chosen to fit the period of investigation for the dumping analysis in case the latter . . . covers a period of less than 12 months."

175. The Panel also underscored that, in the petition submitted in June 2000, the domestic producers suggested that the six-month period of March to August should be used because it reflected the period of highest import penetration. Thus,

according to the Panel, this period would show the most negative side of the state of the domestic industry. . . . The Panel explained that, although *Economía* was discussing the imports of paddy rice — the raw material for the production of the subject long-grain white rice — *Economía* nevertheless "clearly accepted the link made between production of paddy rice and the imports of the final product which the applicant points out is mainly imported in the period March–August." Thus, the Panel noted that the Preliminary Determination referred to the petitioner's claim that the main import activity of the final product takes place within the period March to August, during which period "paddy rice is not harvested and for that reason this period adequately reflects the import activity."

176. The Panel found that the injury analysis of *Economía*, which was based on data covering only six months of each of the three years examined, did not allow for an "objective examination," as required by Article 3:1 . . . , for two reasons: first, whereas the injury analysis was selective and provided only a part of the picture, no proper justification was provided by Mexico in support of this approach; and secondly, *Economía* accepted the "period of investigation proposed by the applicants because it allegedly represented the period of highest import penetration and would thus show the most negative side of the state of the domestic industry." . . .

. . .

180. The Panel expressed the view that, under Article 3:1, an injury analysis can be "objective" only "if it is based on data which provide an accurate and unbiased picture of what it is that one is examining." This view is consistent with the Appellate Body's statement in *US — Hot-Rolled Steel* [Appellate Body Report, *United States — Anti-Dumping Measures on Certain Hot-Rolled Steel Products from Japan*, WT/DS184/AB/R, (adopted 23 August 2001)] regarding the requirement to conduct an "objective examination" under Article 3:1 of the *Anti-Dumping Agreement*:

> [A]n "objective examination" requires that the domestic industry, and the effects of dumped imports, be investigated in an unbiased manner, without favouring the interests of any interested party, or group of interested parties, in the investigation. The duty of the investigating authorities to conduct an "objective examination" recognizes that the determination will be influenced by the objectivity, or any lack thereof, of the investigative process. (footnote omitted)

Therefore, the question to be decided is whether the Panel erred in finding that the data used by *Economía* in the injury analysis, which relate to the same six-month period in 1997, 1998, and 1999, did not provide an "accurate and unbiased picture" of the injury suffered by the domestic industry.

181. We note that the Panel's finding is based not only on *Economía*'s selective use of the information gathered for the purpose of the injury analysis. Indeed, in reaching the conclusion that the data used by *Economía* did not provide an "accurate and unbiased picture," the Panel also relied on another factor: the acceptance by *Economía* of the period of investigation proposed by the petitioner, knowing that

the petitioner proposed that period because it allegedly represented the period of highest import penetration. . . . [T]hese two factors, considered together, were sufficient to make out a *prima facie* case that the data used by *Economía* did not provide an "accurate and unbiased picture."

. . .

183. In *US—Hot-Rolled Steel*, the Appellate Body stated that, from the definition of injury provided in footnote 9 of the *Anti-Dumping Agreement*, "[i]t emerges clearly . . . that the focus of an injury determination is the state of the 'domestic industry.'" We fail to see how, in the present case, the use of data relating to the whole year, as opposed to the March to August period, would have introduced "distortions" of the assessment of the "state of the domestic industry." Rather, . . . examining data relating to the whole year would result in a more accurate picture of the "state of the domestic industry" than an examination limited to a six-month period. Moreover, the explanation put forward by Mexico implies that the dumping determination and the injury determination are integrated. This is not the case; although injury and dumping must be linked by a causal relationship, these determinations are two separate operations relying on distinct data seeking to determine different things. Accordingly, we see no reason to disagree with the Panel that the explanation provided by Mexico with respect to *Economía's* choice of a limited period of investigation for purposes of the injury analysis was not a "proper justification" sufficient to refute the *prima facie* case that the data used by *Economía* did not provide an "accurate and unbiased picture" of the state of the domestic industry. We therefore agree with the Panel that the data used by *Economía* in the injury analysis, relating to the March to August period of 1997, 1998, and 1999, did not provide an "accurate and unbiased picture" of the state of the domestic industry and, thus, did not result in an "objective examination" as required by Article 3:1 . . . .

184. On appeal, Mexico's objections to the Panel's reasoning are not, in substance, different from the arguments it submitted before the Panel. Mexico argues that the proposition that the March to August period is the period of highest import penetration is an unsubstantiated assumption that reflects a "mere opinion." We disagree. In its reasoning, the Panel referred to the petitioner's position that the main import activity of long-grain white rice takes place within the March to August period— during which paddy rice is not harvested in Mexico—and that, for this reason, this period adequately reflects the import activity. Making such a reference is not, in our view, making an unsubstantiated assumption that reflects a "mere opinion."

185. Nor can we accept Mexico's argument that the Panel created a presumption that an injury analysis based on data relating to only parts of years is not objective. We note, first, that the Panel underscored that its "ruling should not be read as to imply that there could never be any convincing and valid reasons for examining only parts of years." Secondly, the Panel's finding is not based exclusively on the fact that *Economía* was selective as regards the data it used in the injury analysis. It is the combination of this factor with another—"the acceptance of a period of investigation proposed by the applicants because it allegedly represented the period of

highest import penetration and would thus show the most negative side of the state of the domestic industry"—that led the Panel to consider that a *prima facie* violation of Article 3:1 had been established. Mexico had an opportunity to refute the *prima facie* case by presenting a "proper justification" for the use of the March to August period; however, it failed to do so.

186. Mexico submits that the methodology used was not flawed because six-month periods with the same structure were compared. We agree with Mexico that it was not improper for *Economía* to make comparisons with previous years. The Panel, however, did not find that *Economía* could not make comparisons with previous periods in the injury analysis. The Panel discussed a different question, namely, whether *Economía's* methodology was flawed because segments of years were compared instead of full years.

187. . . . Mexico also contends that the domestic production of long-grain white rice is independent of the production cycles of paddy rice. . . . Mexico questions what it alleges are the premises on which the Panel based its assertion that the period March to August shows the most negative side of the state of the domestic industry. Mexico's allegations refer to facts concerning import patterns of long-grain white rice and the relationship between the production of long-grain white rice and that of paddy rice. Contrary to what Mexico suggests, the Panel's reasoning was not centred on an assessment of the import patterns of long-grain white rice or the relationship between the production of long-grain white rice and that of paddy rice. On these questions of fact, the Panel did not make any finding, because it considered it was unnecessary to do so. Rather, the Panel's position was based on the findings that *Economía* selected the same period of investigation as that put forward by the petitioner, and that the petitioner proposed this period because the months March to August allegedly represent the period of highest import penetration. . . . [T]he Panel did not err by taking into account this factor in its analysis.

188. For these reasons, we *uphold* the Panel's findings . . . that, in limiting the injury analysis to the March to August period of 1997, 1998, and 1999, Mexico failed to make a determination of injury that involves an "objective examination," as required by Article 3:1 of the *Anti-Dumping Agreement*. Accordingly, we also *uphold* the Panel's findings . . . that, in limiting the injury analysis to the March to August period of 1997, 1998, and 1999, Mexico acted inconsistently with Article 3:5 of that *Agreement*.

III. Filling in Missing Data with 19 U.S.C. Sections 1677e(a)–(b)

- **Practical Problem and Statutory Solution**

An obvious question in any AD or CVD case concerns the sources of information about dumping margins, subsidies, and injury or threat thereof. "BIA," or the terms "IA" (for "Information Available"), "Facts Otherwise Available" ("FOA"), or

"AFA" ("Adverse Facts Available"), and "verification," are pertinent here. Generally, the administering agency—such as the DOC or ITC in the U.S.—obtains data from any reliable source possible. The starting point is the petition, but the problem with data therein is that they almost surely contain pro-petitioner biases. So, the agency sends the respondent a questionnaire. That questionnaire is long and complex, but if the respondent successfully and accurately completes it, the outcome of the case may favor it.

This said, a frequent problem in AD-CVD cases is administering authorities lack the data they need to produce a well-grounded, just determination. When information is missing or not forthcoming, the DOC needs a proxy. It must use substitute sources of data on which to base its calculation of the dumping margin. U.S. law anticipates this problem in 19 U.S.C. Section 1677e(a)–(b), offering two options for data to fill a gap.[4] Under Section 1677e(a), the DOC can use "facts otherwise available." As the term suggests, the DOC looks for the BIA to complete its investigation or review.

· **IA and Cooperative Respondents**

The need to invoke Section 1677e(a) is not that a respondent is uncooperative. Rather, the respondent, a producer-exporter located overseas, often lacks the capacity to fill out the questionnaire in a proper and timely fashion. Legal counsel is required, but depending on the country, legal capacity to handle the case may be limited. Not surprisingly, then, many questionnaires, or portions thereof, go

---

4. *See Mueller Commercial de Mexico v. United States*, Federal Circuit Number 2013-1391 (29 May 2014); Rossella Brevetti, Commerce Must Recalculate Dumping Margin for Mexican Steel Pipe Exporter, 31 International Trade Reporter (BNA) 1027 (5 June 2014).

In *Mueller*, the Federal Circuit dealt with a DOC calculation of a dumping margin in Administrative Review of an AD order against subject merchandise from a Mexican steel exporter, Muller. The DOC based the calculation at issue on facts available. Mueller obtained the subject merchandise, steel pipe, from 2 unaffiliated Mexican suppliers: Tuberia and Ternium. All three were mandatory respondents, and Mueller and Tuberia fully cooperated. The DOC decided Ternium did not cooperate to the best of its ability, so it applied AFA for the cost of production for subject merchandise Ternium sold to Mueller. Consequently, the dumping margin—19.81%—for steel pipe Mueller exported, included facts available for Mueller's production costs, but AFA for Ternium's costs.

Mueller argued successfully the DOC wrongly limited its analysis to an unfavorable subset of Tuberia data, namely, the three least favorable Ternium transactions (though Mueller accepted the DOC's use of Tuberia data as a surrogate for data from Ternium). The DOC failed to persuade the Court that picking those three transactions as facts available yielded the most accurate dumping margin for Mueller. The Federal Circuit remanded to DOC recalculation of the dumping margin to reach a more accurate rate.

Mueller is a noteworthy case in 3 respects. First, it is an instance in which a respondent challenges use of facts available, rather than AFA. Second, the DOC defended its actions partly on the ground it sought to get Mueller to induce cooperation by Ternium: in effect, using facts available from Tuberia that yielded a high dumping margin would push Mueller to pressure Ternium to cooperate, giving better facts available than Tuberia, and obviating the need for AFA. The Court did not opine on whether an inducement rationale was legitimate in the case, but said the overriding goal of the DOC must be accuracy in the margin determination. Third, the Court clearly explains the Section 1677e(a)–(b) framework.

unfilled. In such instances, the DOC is left with no choice but to look to IA, which may well be petitioner data. Nevertheless, the burden of providing reliable information is on the respondent. It is not the job of the DOC to create an accurate record.

- **AFA and Uncooperative Respondents**

In contrast, an uncooperative respondent is the justification for relying on Section 1677e(b). A respondent refusing to provide necessary information to the DOC is a common occurrence. That is true notwithstanding the reality that AFA "acts 'like a sword hanging over' companies, pushing them to answer Commerce's questions quickly and thoroughly, or risk very expensive duty rates."[5] One reason not to cooperate is a desire not to incur legal expenses to deal with American authorities in a "game" the respondent regards as "fixed" against it. Of course, that reason can be a self-fulfilling prophecy: failure to provide exculpatory information will not help a respondent lower or eliminate a dumping margin or subsidization rate. Another reason is suspicion of American authorities, namely, giving confidential business data to them will lead to leakage of those data, to the benefit of domestic producers in the U.S., or to further trouble with other authorities (*e.g.*, the Internal Revenue Service). A respondent may well view the entire American government as a coordinated monolith that collaborates with American businesses against foreign producer-exporters.

When faced with a problematic respondent, the DOC turns to Section 1677e(b). This provision allows it to use AFA. To be sure, any AD or CVD rate the DOC calculates using AFA must be a reasonable approximation of the "true" margin or subsidization amount for the respondent, and the DOC can increase that rate to deter non-compliance. Here is where the DOC may draw inferences, including ones adverse to a party that fails to cooperate with information queries from the DOC to the best of its ability.[6] But, to draw an adverse inference, the DOC must conclude the respondent failed to cooperate.

IV. Verification, 19 U.S.C. Section 1677e(c), and 2014 *Essar Steel* Case

In many AD-CVD cases, "verification" is necessary. "Verification" (called "on the spot investigation" in Annex I to the WTO *Antidumping Agreement*) means checking to see if data submitted by petitioner, respondent, or both to justify their

---

5. Brian Flood, *German Paper Manufacturer Takes Duty Fight to Supreme Court (1)*, 35 International Trade Reporter (BNA) 1244 (27 September 2018) (*quoting* Leslie Allen Glick, Butzel Long). [Hereinafter, German Paper Manufacturer.]

6. *See* 19 U.S.C. § 1677e(b). This authorization permits DOC to apply adverse inferences even if a respondent producer-exporter cooperates. For instance, failure of a foreign government (China) to provide requested information, despite the respondent (in China) cooperating with the DOC and not having control over that government, is enough for the DOC to draw adverse inferences. *See Fine Furniture (Shanghai) Ltd. v. United States*, U.S. Court of Appeals for the Federal Circuit, Number 2013-1158 (23 April 2014).

respective positions on any aspect of the dumping margin are accurate. The responsible administering authority conducts verification. Section 1677e(c) of title 19 obliges the DOC to corroborate data. When necessary, DOC or ITC officials travel overseas to ascertain the accuracy of data a respondent submits. In practice, verification can play an important role in the outcome of a case, leading to rejection of data presented by one side or the other. Verification can occur at any stage of a case, and in an anti-circumvention proceeding on prevention of future evasion of an existing AD or CVD order.

Subsidies provided in the Indian state of Chhattisgarh, under the Chhattisgarh Industrial Program (CIP), provided an occasion for the DOC to corroborate data in a 2014 CVD case, *Essar Steel, Ltd. v. United States*.[7] Essar Steel denied receiving nine types of countervailable CIP subsidies for hot-rolled carbon steel products it shipped from India to the U.S. It said it had no manufacturing facilities in Chhattisgarh. The DOC said other evidence the producer-exporter put on the record contradicted these claims, and neither the Indian central government nor the Chhattisgarh state government responded to DOC requests for information. So, the DOC applied AFA, resulting in a CVD rate of 54.68%. The CIT remanded the case to the DOC to explain how it corroborated this rate.

On remand, the DOC admitted it had no information about company-specific benefits from the CIP. To cope with the void, the DOC synthesized data on the 9 types of support it had garnered from Essar in this investigation with data from other Indian hot-rolled steel producer-exporters in other investigations. Ultimately, the Federal Circuit approved as reasonable the DOC aggregation of information from various sources and cases, saying its "ability to corroborate the secondary information under § 1677e(c) was limited by Essar's lack of cooperation . . . ."[8]

---

7. *See* Federal Circuit Number 2013-1416 (12 June 2014); Brian Flood, *Federal Circuit Affirms CVD Rate For Steel Products Manufacturer*, 31 International Trade Reporter (BNA) 1110 (19 June 2014).

8. For another CVD case involving AFA, see *POSCO v. United States*, Number 16-00225 (10 September 2018). In POSCO, the CIT upheld a lower CVD rate as calculated by DOC on remand— 42.61% instead of 58.36% on cold-rolled steel flat products imported from Korea. The CIT explained that:

> Commerce's selection of subsidy rates when making an adverse inference is governed by 19 U.S.C. § 1677e(d). . . . Subsection (d)(1) permits Commerce to "use a countervailable subsidy rate applied for the same or similar program in a countervailing duty proceeding involving the same country," or "if there is no same or similar program, use a countervailable subsidy rate for a subsidy program from a proceeding that the administering authority considers reasonable to use." 19 U.S.C. § 1677e(d)(1)(A). Subsection (d)(2) directs Commerce to base its selection of the subsidy rate, which may include the highest rate, on an "evaluation . . . of the situation that resulted in the [agency] using an adverse inference." *Id.*, § 1677e(d)(2).

The problem in the case was:

> In the *Issues and Decision Memorandum* accompanying the *Final Determination*, Commerce explained that "[i]t is the [agency's] *practice* in CVD proceedings to compute an AFA rate for non-cooperating companies using the *highest* calculated program-specific

V. AFA and 2013 *Guangxi Jisheng Foods*, 2013 *Max Fortune*, 2013–2014 *Hubscher Ribbon*, 2015 *Dongtai Peak Honey*, and 2016 *Nan Ya Plastics* Cases

In the 2013 *Guangxi Jisheng Foods* case, the CIT was confronted with substantial errors a Chinese producer-exporter, Guangxi Jisheng Foods, made in response to a DOC questionnaire.[9] The DOC asked about the value of the firm's factors of production in connection with an Administrative Review of an AD order on Chinese preserved mushrooms. The errors were formatting, inconsistent duplicates, and logical impossibilities. On factors of production for eight product types it produced, Guangxi Jisheng Foods gave no information. Even when it later submitted data, it made the same mistakes, re-introducing the same errors. Thus, the DOC used AFA, and drew inferences adverse to Guangxi Jisheng Foods. The CIT easily upheld the DOC action.

Timing is important throughout an AD or CVD case, including during a verification phase and any review. During verification, suppose a party provides data to DOC, but does so at the last hour of the last day on which those data are due. Technically, the data are "in on time," but must the DOC accept it? The CIT faced this question in the 2013 case *Max Fortune Industrial Co. v. United States*, and answered in the negative.[10] The petitioner was Seaman Paper. Max Fortune, the respondent,

---

rates determined for a cooperating respondent in the same investigation, or, if not available, rates calculated in prior CVD cases involving the same country." . . . (emphasis added). The Court remanded Commerce's selection of the highest calculated subsidy rates as lacking the case-specific evaluation required by subsection (d)(2). . . . The Court reasoned that Sub-section (d)(2) contemplates a range of possible rates from among which Commerce may choose based on its "evaluation of the specific situation," and faulted the agency for "fail[ing] to fulfill its statutory duty because it failed to explain why this case justified its selection of the highest rates." . . .

On remand, Commerce explained that by selecting the highest rate within each prong of its adverse facts available hierarchy, it "strikes a balance between [] three necessary variables: inducement, industry relevancy, and program relevancy." . . . Commerce further explained that it interprets 19 U.S.C. § 1677e(d)(2) to constitute:

an exception to the selection of an adverse facts available rate under [§ 1677e(d)(1)]; that is, after "an evaluation of the situation that resulted in the application of an adverse inference," Commerce may decide that given the unique and unusual facts on the record, the use of the highest rate within that step is not appropriate.

. . . Commerce evaluated the situation that resulted in the use of adverse inferences and concluded that no deviation from the highest rates was merited.

The CIT held POSCO failed to articulate any reason for its assertion that the DOC failed to comply with the CIT's remand order.

9. *See* No. 11-00378 (Slip Opinion, 13-112, 23 August 2013); Brian Flood, *Chinese Company's Questionnaire Reponses Lacking in Mushroom AD Review, Court Finds*, 30 International Trade Reporter (BNA) 1522 (3 October 2013).

10. *See* No. 11-00340 (Slip Opinion 13-53, 15 April 2013); Brian Flood, *Commerce Has Discretion to Reject Information Filed at Last Minute, Court Says*, 30 International Trade Reporter (BNA) 751 (23 May 2013).

produced and exported tissue paper products from Vietnam. Pursuant to an extant AD order on such products from China, it was not supposed to use tainted paper, that is, materials originating in China in products for export to the U.S. During its preliminary and final circumvention determinations, the DOC used total AFA. The CIT upheld the DOC reliance on AFA, the DOC determination that Max Fortune circumvented the existing AD order on certain tissue paper from China, and the DOC order to CBP to collect cash deposits for AD duties on Max Fortune merchandise.

Max Fortune did not provide the DOC with verifiable production data, or tie its export sales data to its production data. It also failed to answer fully DOC questionnaires about its activities. So, the record about Max Fortune was incomplete: it did not provide monthly trial balances or detailed accounting records, hence the DOC could not determine when Max Fortune ceased to use materials originating in China to make products for shipment to the U.S. In fact, Max Fortune had not even adhered to basic record keeping requirements under Vietnamese law. At the last hour of the verification phase, Max Fortune offered to provide DOC with documents about Chinese jumbo tissue paper rolls it had in its inventory. The DOC rejected the offer, because it could not possibly check the completeness of those documents within the allotted time.

So, in its preliminary circumvention determination, the DOC relied on AFA. The DOC determined Max Fortune had jumbo tissue paper rolls of Chinese origin in its inventory, plus tissue paper in finished goods and work-in-progress inventory. The DOC said Max Fortune could not link directly any such merchandise to its domestic or export sales. Thus, the DOC decided all tissue paper Max Fortune sent to the U.S. was made from jumbo rolls originating in China, to which the existing AD order applied. In turn, the DOC found Max Fortune circumvented the existing AD order. The DOC ordered CBP to collect cash deposits on all tissue paper Max Fortune produced and exported, to prevent circumvention. Then, in its final circumvention determination, the DOC reaffirmed its reliance on AFA, as Max Fortune did not provide the requisite records.

Max Fortune argued the DOC violated the 2012 precedent of *Fischer S.A. Comercio, Industria and Agricultura and Citrosuco North America, Inc. v. United States*.[11] In that case, the CIT held the DOC abused its discretion by rejecting new data offered during verification. The CIT rejected this argument. The *Fischer* case was distinguishable on the facts. There, the new data clarified and corrected information that already had been submitted properly. Here, Max Fortune had not provided information requested by the DOC, and its last-minute attempt to submit data raised the specter it was trying to manipulate the record. The CIT also rejected the contention of Max Fortune that even if some tainted paper from China found its way into merchandise made in Vietnam and exported to America, the amount

---

11. *See* No. 11-00321 (Slip Opinion 12-1249, 6 December 2012).

of Chinese materials was *de minimis*. There is no *de minimis* exception in a circumvention case.

Unfortunately for Max Fortune, its poor records and non-responsive attitude to the DOC made it impossible to wipe away the AFA-driven result that some Chinese inputs were in the toilet paper it made in Vietnam. To be sure, the DOC must verify all information on which it relies to make a final determination. But, how it does so is a matter to which Courts defer, and they are cognizant of the constraints on the time and resources of the DOC. Here, the DOC did not abuse its discretion to rely on AFA.

The 2013 CIT case of *Hubscher Ribbon Corp. v. United States* illustrates how adverse to a respondent producer-exporter AFA can be.[12] Taiwanese narrow woven ribbons and woven selvedge were the subject merchandise. The respondent, Hubscher Ribbon Corp. of Lachine Quebec, Canada, cooperated in the original AD investigation. In the Administrative Review, it gave the DOC data on the size and quantity of spools it imported during the POR. But, owing to a lack of personnel and financial resources, it informed the DOC it no longer could cooperate. The DOC computed the dumping margin at 137.20%, the highest rate alleged in the original petition for the AD order.

Hubscher argued this whopping rate was unreasonable. It was the only respondent in the Administrative Review, but in the original investigation, in which there were three respondents, all of which cooperated, the DOC computed rates of 0, 0, and 4.37%. The CIT held in favor of the DOC, reasoning that the DOC examined model-specific dumping margin data from the cooperating respondents in the original investigation, along with the size and quantity data Hubscher submitted in the Review before it stopped cooperating. The DOC found many examples from the original investigation of ribbon models that were comparable in size and volume to those of Hubscher with a margin of 137.20% or higher. That was enough corroborative evidence, said the CIT, to justify the high AD rate. Hubscher also argued the DOC could not draw a reliable conclusion about price from data on size and quantity, but the CIT reply was predictable: then Hubscher should have cooperated with the DOC to provide more facts.

In the 2014 *Hubscher Ribbon Corp. v. United States* case, matters were even worse for Hubscher.[13] The subject merchandise was narrow woven ribbons with woven selvedge from China. In the original investigation, the DOC assigned a 0% dumping margin to Yama Ribbons and Bows Company (Yama), and 247.65% to Ningbo Jintian Import & Export Company (Ningbo). That was because Ningbo refused to

---

12. *See* Number 13-00004 (Slip Opinion 13-137, 8 November 2013); Brian Flood, *Court Upholds Commerce's Dumping Rate For Non-Cooperating Taiwan Ribbon Importer*, 30 International Trade Reporter (BNA) 1768 (14 November 2013).

13. *See* Number 13-00071 (Slip Opinion 14-43, 15 April 2014); Brian Flood, *Court Confirms AFA Dumping Rate For Exporter of Chinese Ribbon*, 31 International Trade Reporter (BNA) 800 (1 May 2014).

cooperate with the DOC in the investigation.[14] (The DOC set a rate of 123.83% for separate rate respondents, the average of the two other rates.) In the first Administrative Review, Hubscher, initially cooperated with the DOC, saying all its ribbons came from Yama, but then ceased to do so. The DOC applied the AFA rate of 247.65%, whereupon Hubscher argued that rate was unreasonable.

Not so, held the CIT. During the period of review, several shipments of subject merchandise from Yama were at high dumping margins. Hubscher argued those shipments were only a small percentage of the total volume it imported from Yama. Nevertheless, the DOC inferred the AFA 247.65% applied to Hubscher. By not cooperating, Hubscher failed to prove the high-margin shipments were aberrant or unreflective of its commercial reality. With a limited record, an AD duty rate of 247.65% was a reasonable approximation of Hubscher's actual rate.

How strict the DOC can be on timing issues, yet still be judged reasonable, is clear from the 2015 *Dongtai Peak Honey* case.[15] At issue was an Administrative Review of an AD order on honey exported from China by Dongtai Peak Honey Industry Company. Dongtai responded to the initial questionnaire, but its answers provoked a follow-up inquiry by (*i.e.*, a supplemental questionnaire from) the DOC, which set a deadline of 17 April 2012 for return. On 19 April, Dongtai asked the DOC to extend the deadline, because of (1) logistical difficulties in communicating with its lawyers in the U.S., (2) the need to translate between English and Chinese, (3) a Chinese national holiday, and (4) computer failure. Dongtai asked twice for an extension. The pertinent regulations, 19 C.F.R Section 351.302(b), permit the DOC to extend a time limit for good cause, if the requesting party asks for extension before the deadline expires. Ten days after the deadline, on 27 April, Dongtai answered the follow-up questions.

The DOC rejected the extension request and answers, and found insufficient evidence in the record to calculate a company-specific AD duty rate. The DOC said Dongtai neither showed good cause for an extension nor submitted its request

---

14. In a different case, Ningbo Jiulong Machinery, Co., Ltd. was the only mandatory respondent in a CVD investigation in which DOC studied 11 Chinese government programs to see if they entailed illegal subsidies to production or exportation of steel grating. The DOC found 2 schemes subsidized inputs (hot-rolled steel and steel wire rod) for steel grating. Noticing material discrepancies in mill certificates Ningbo gave the DOC, the DOC said those certificates were unreliable and unverifiable. Ningbo then admitted the certificates were fabricated, at which point DOC drew an adverse inference, as Ningbo had "significantly impeded" the investigation. DOC determined the 2 schemes were countervailable, and set a 62.46% CVD rate based on a previous investigation, which (because Ningbo was the mandatory respondent) the DOC applied to all other respondents, such as Yantai Xinke Steel Structure Co. Ltd. (Yantai). The CIT rejected Yantai's argument that the DOC's inference was unreasonable. *See Yantai Xinke Steel Structure Co., Ltd. v. United States,* No. 10-00239 (Slip Opinion 15-103, 15 September 2015); Brian Flood, *Duty Rate on Chinese Steel Grating Upheld*, 32 International Trade Reporter (BNA) 1595 (17 September 2015).

15. *See* CIT Number 12-00411 (21 March 2014); Brian Flood, *Court Affirms Honey Dumping Rate For Tardy Chinese Respondent*, 31 International Trade Reporter (BNA) 580 (27 March 2014).

before the 17 April deadline. The DOC also said Dongtai's argument that the DOC would have had sufficient time to consider the late submission was incorrect: the DOC would have needed a lot of time to study it with care. So, the DOC slapped Dongtai with the country-wide rate, based on AFA, of $2.63 per kilograms. It was reasonable to impose the country-wide rate on Dongtai. Absent reliable data submitted in a timely fashion, there was insufficient proof that Dongtai was free of *de jure* or *de facto* control by the Chinese government. (Had it been able to prove this point, then it would have qualified for a separate rate analysis.) The CIT upheld the DOC actions, and the Federal Circuit affirmed.[16]

Finally, in setting an AFA rate, is it permissible for the DOC to use the highest transaction-specific margins available in the record of a case? To frame the issue differently, would using the highest margins as a basis for the AFA be unreasonable, because those margins are aberrational? The CIT confronted this issue in the 2014 case of *Nan Ya Plastics Corp. v. United States*.[17] The subject merchandise was polyethylene terephthalate film, sheet, and strip produced in and exported from Taiwan. The DOC assigned an AFA of 74.34% to Nan Ya, using the highest-transaction specific dumping margin from Shinkong Materials Technology Co. That company cooperated with the Administrative Review of the AD order at issue, whereas Nan Ya did not.

Nan Ya complained it was "unlawful" for the DOC to use an "aberrant outlier" for the AFA, as that outlier did not reflect the commercial reality of Nan Ya. To be sure, the purpose of an AFA is to discourage non-compliance. But, any AFA must be an adequate reflection of the commercial reality of the non-compliant respondent. Nan Ya used 3 statistical exams to prove the margins the DOC used were aberrational: standard deviation analysis; a gap test; and an inter-quartile range method employed by the IRS.

Nan Ya lost, even though the DOC did not corroborate the highest transaction-specific margins it used. That margin did not need independent verification, because it was not "secondary information." It was primary data from the Review. Moreover, by analyzing the available prior transaction specific data from Nan Ya, the DOC found the margins were appropriate. Most importantly, the CIT held that just because the DOC picks the highest margins in the record to compute the AFA does not mean those margins are aberrational. In the case, the Shinkong merchandise was not significantly different from that of Nan Ya, Shinkong itself did not protest

---

16. *See Dongtai Peak Honey Industry Company v. United States*, Number 2014-1479 (30 January 2015); Brian Flood, *Federal Circuit Affirms AD Rate For Tardy Chinese Honey Exporter*, 32 International Trade Reporter (BNA) 291 (5 February 2015).

17. *See* Number 11-00535 (Slip Opinion Number 14-94, 14 August 2014); Brian Flood, *Court Upholds Adverse AD Rate For Taiwanese Plastics Producer*, 31 International Trade Reporter (BNA) 1523 (21 August 2014).

the use of the highest margins, and the DOC did not draw those margins from too small a quantity of sales transactions.

In 2016, the Federal Circuit affirmed the CIT ruling, and thereby the 74.34% AD duty rate.[18] Nan Ya had failed to cooperate with DOC, entitling DOC to compute the rate using AFA based on "any other information placed on the record," as 19 U.S.C. Section 1677e(b) puts it. The whole point of assigning a high rate is to deter non-compliance: after all, why would a respondent comply if it could obtain a lower rate by ignoring or disrespecting informational requests from DOC?[19] The Federal Circuit rejected the argument by Nan Ya that such a high rate was neither "accurate" nor reflective of "commercial reality." The Court held a DOC determination is "accurate" if it is mathematically and factually correct (and thus supported by substantial evidence), and reflects "commercial reality" if it is computed via a method provided in the statute. Citing the precedent it set in a 1992 case, *Suramerica de Aleaciones Laminadas, C.A. v. United States*, the Court said: "[o]ur duty is not to weigh the wisdom of, or to resolve any struggle between, competing views of the public interest, but rather to respect legitimate policy choices made by [DOC] in interpreting and applying the statute."[20]

Moreover, the Appellate Court strengthened the DOC position. DOC argued the statutory phrase "any other information in the record" was ambiguous, so under Administrative Law principles of judicial review of administrative agency action, the Court should defer to its (that is, DOC's) interpretation. The Court not only agreed with DOC's construal of the statutory language, thus allowing DOC to nail non-cooperative respondents with high AD duty rates, but also said the language was unambiguous: "any other information in the record" indubitably includes the highest transaction-specific dumping margin in the Administrative Review in question. Lexicographically, "any" means no "restriction or limitation."[21] No corroboration by DOC of that margin is needed; rather, under the statute (19 U.S.C. § 1677e(c)), DOC need only check "secondary information" (*e.g.*, data from the original investigation or an earlier Review).

---

18. *See Nan Ya Plastics Corp. Ltd. v. United States*, Number 2015-1054 (19 January 2016); Brian Flood, *Appeals Court Upholds Duties on Taiwanese Plastic Film*, 33 International Trade Reporter (BNA) 90 (21 January 2016).

19. *See* 19 U.S.C. Section 1677e(b). *See also SAA* to the WTO *AD Agreement* in Uruguay Round Agreements Act, House of Representatives Report Number 103-316, volume 1, at 870, *reprinted in* 1994 USCCAN 4040, 4149 (stating DOC "may employ [such] inferences . . . to ensure that the party does not obtain a more favorable result by failing to cooperate than if it had cooperated fully").

20. *Nan Ya Plastics Corp. Ltd. v. United States*, Number 2015-1054 (19 January 2016), at 17, *quoting Suramerica*, 966 F.2d 650, 665 (Fed Cir. 1992).

21. *Nan Ya Plastics Corp. Ltd. v. United States*, Number 2015-1054 (19 January 2016), at 19–20, *quoting* Webster's *Dictionary*.

VI. Partial versus Total AFA, 2014 *Mukand*, 2015 *Dongguan Sunrise Furniture*, and 2016 *Koehler* Cases

Under CIT jurisprudence, there is a distinction between "partial" and "total" AFA. If a discrete category of information is missing, then the DOC uses partial AFA, covering only the missing data with adverse facts. But, if the missing information is "core, not tangential," as the CIT put it in the 2016 case of *Papierfabrik August Koehler SE v. United States*, then it treats any and all data the respondent provided as unreliable and unusable.[22]

The respondent, Koehler, exported lightweight thermal paper to America. The DOC assigned it a 75.36% AD rate (rather than the 4.33% for which the respondent argued). The petitioning producer of a like product, Appleton Papers (renamed Appvion, Inc.) of Wisconsin, submitted an affidavit from a confidential source alleging Koehler failed to disclose certain home market sales. It sent paper to third countries, knowing the paper would return to and be consumed in Germany. That way, the paper would be excluded from the DOC's Normal Value calculation, presumably resulting in a lower dumping margin.

Koehler said rogue employees whom it later punished were responsible for these trans-shipments, and cooperated with the DOC by filing new home market sales data correcting the omissions. Still, the DOC decided Koehler was uncooperative, and applied total AFA. The CIT agreed, saying senior management of Koehler was responsible for the initial disclosures and accountable for the entire company, and the Federal Circuit affirmed.

The 2014 case of *Mukand, Ltd. v. United States* presented the Federal Circuit with a textbook case on the use of total AFA.[23] The Indian manufacturer of subject merchandise, stainless steel bars, said the DOC ought to have used partial AFA in an Administrative Review that resulted in a 21.02% AD duty. The DOC found size was one of 6 material characteristics that mattered in distinguishing steel bars. So, the DOC asked Mukand for cost of production data for each different size of steel bar, gave Mukand a sample chart to fill out, and offered to help. Still, Mukand failed to explain in its response to the initial DOC questionnaire why size was an

---

22. *See* Number 13-00163 (Slip Opinion 14-102, 3 September 2014); Brian Flood, *German Manufacturer Loses Challenge To AD Duty Rate on Thermal Paper*, 31 International Trade Reporter (BNA) 1617 (11 November 2014). The Federal Circuit decision mentioned above is *Papierfabrik August Koehler SE v. United States, Appvion, Inc.*, Number 2015-1489 (16 December 2016). In September 2018, Papierfabrik appealed to the Supreme Court—a longshot, given that the Court had not taken a trade case since 2009. *See Papierfabrik August Koehler SE v. United States*, U.S. Number 18A42 (*certiorari* petition filed, 21 September 2018); *German Paper Manufacturer*; Brian Flood, *Administration Seeks Delay in Supreme Court Paper Duty Fight (1)*, 35 International Trade Reporter (BNA) 1541 (29 November 2018).

23. *See* Number 2013-1425 (16 September 2014); Brian Flood, *Federal Circuit Upholds AFA Dumping Rate For Imports of Indian Stainless Steel Bars*, 31 International Trade Reporter (BNA) 1663 (18 September 2014).

insignificant factor. In four subsequent supplemental questionnaires, Mukand asserted without support that size did not affect costs, and so it did not have such data reasonably available.

But, once the DOC issued its preliminary results, Mukand offered data it previously said it did not compile. The DOC found Mukand's submissions so incomplete as to warrant use of total AFA. The CIT agreed. The Federal Circuit affirmed: "Without cost data broken by product size, Commerce was unable to differentiate between different types of steel bar products and could not calculate an accurate Constructed Value for any of Mukand's products." The DOC was right to conclude the deficient information concerned the core of the AD analysis, making use of partial AFA inappropriate.

The use of partial AFA can do more than plug data gaps that arise from a less-than-stellar effort by a respondent to answer DOC queries. A respondent might behave strategically by intentionally withholding data on high dumping margin sales, and offering information only on low margin sales. It might hide home market sales for which Normal Values (or its proxies) are high, to avoid their inclusion in the calculation of a weighted average dumping margin, thereby reducing or eliminating that margin. In the 2014 CIT case of *Dongguan Sunrise Furniture Company v. United States*, American furniture producers accused four individually investigated Chinese furniture companies—Dongguan Sunrise Furniture Co., Ltd., Taicang Sunrise Wood Industry Co., Ltd., Taicang Fairmont Designs Furniture Co., Ltd., and Meizhou Sunrise Furniture Co., Ltd., collectively called "Fairmont"—of concealing unreported sales to obtain a lower duty rate.[24]

The subject merchandise was wooden bedroom furniture, particularly armoires, chairs, dressers, and nightstands. Using partial AFA, the DOC computed a dumping margin of 44.64%. The CIT rejected the partial AFA rate as too high. The CIT said that rate was based on too small a percentage of sales of subject merchandise—no more than 15% of the sales of Fairmont—to be sure it accurately reflected the commercial reality of these Chinese producer-exporters, as the U.S. AD statute mandates.

The American petitioners, which obviously hoped the CIT would uphold the 44.64% rate, tried to get the CIT to reconsider its initial ruling. But, they failed to prove the respondents deliberately concealed sales with high dumping margins. The CIT accepted the DOC view that a partial AFA analysis was justified on the ground that Fairmont did not make a solid effort to produce data requested by the DOC, but not on the ground it intentionally hid sales. The CIT remanded the case to the DOC for re-computation. Indeed, there were 4 iterations of CIT-ordered revisions.

---

24. *See* Number 10-00254 (Slip Opinion Number 14-117, 6 October 2014); Brian Flood, *Trade Court Will Not Reconsider Chinese Furniture Dumping Ruling*, 31 International Trade Reporter (BNA) 1803 (9 October 2014).

In 2015, the CIT affirmed a revised 41.30% AD rate for Fairmont (a drop from the 43.23% the DOC set in the original investigation), and the same rate for the separate rate respondents (Langfang Tiancheng Furniture Co. and Longrange Furniture Co., Ltd.), and the Federal Circuit upheld the CIT decision.[25] The CIT said DOC, at last, based the rate on sufficient evidence: the DOC combined the rates from (1) sales the companies reported with (2) partial AFA for sales the companies inadvertently did not report. For partial AFA, the DOC used 50% of the sales reported for each of the same general product type (armoires, chairs, dressers, and nightstands) with the highest dumping margins, using them to fill the gap of unreported sales. The CIT agreed this methodology was "sufficiently representative of Fairmont's commercial reality in selling those types of products."

VII. Individual Rate versus AOR and Sampling

• **Right to Request Individual Rate**

Some AD and CVD cases have a large number of respondents. It is impractical for the DOC to investigate each individual respondent, and calculate individual dumping margins or net countervailable subsidization rates, for each one of them. That also is true in respect of Administrative Reviews of AD or CVD orders. Typically, DOC typically limits individual investigations to two or three respondents. In such instances, the DOC ascribes an individual dumping margin or subsidization rate to certain respondents, in particular, the ones that have provided reliable, verifiable data in a timely fashion.

These cooperating, individually-investigated respondents are called "mandatory" respondents. For the other respondents, which also are cooperating but are not individually investigated, the DOC may calculate an "All Others Rate," or "AOR." The AOR for non-mandatory respondents is based on the individual determinations for the mandatory respondents. The general rule the DOC uses is to average the weighted dumping margins (or subsidization rates), for the individually-investigated respondents, except ones that get a rate that is *de minimis* or drawn entirely from facts available. The average then becomes the AOR. If because of the exclusion of *de minimis* margins and margins based entirely on facts available there are no qualifying margins left from the individually-investigated respondents, then the DOC (under the pertinent statute) may compute the AOR using "any reasonable method."

---

25. *See Dongguan Sunrise Furniture Company v. United States*, Federal Circuit Number 2015-1450 (12 October 2016); *Duties on Chinese Bedroom Furniture Survive Appeal*, 33 International Trade Reporter (BNA) 1490 (20 October 2016); *Dongguan Sunrise Furniture Company, Ltd. v. United States*, Number 10-00254, (Slip Opinion 15-3, 14 January 2015); Brian Flood, *Trade Court Affirms Revised AD Rate For Chinese Bedroom Furniture Imports*, 32 International Trade Reporter (BNA) 189 (22 January 2015).

Any respondent DOC does not select for an individual determination is entitled to request one. The DOC must oblige, but only if (1) the requesting respondent provides the data for which, and by when, the DOC asks, and (2) it would not be unduly burdensome or inhibit the timely completion of the investigation or Review for the DOC to render an individual calculation for that respondent. Under these criteria, DOC usually denies requests from respondents to participate on a "voluntary" basis.

DOC knows they do so out of self-interest: they think their data will yield a lower net subsidization rate or dumping margin. Moreover, under 19 U.S.C. Section 1677m(a), DOC can reject their request, because the "additional individual examination of such exporters or producers would be *unduly burdensome* to the administering authority and *inhibit the timely completion* of the investigation."[26] Under the *2015 TPEA*, Congress listed factors qualifying as "unduly burdensome," with a broad one stating "[s]uch other factors relating to the timely completion of each such investigation and review as the administering authority considers appropriate." This language allowed DOC to reject a voluntary respondent for a reason CIT jurisprudence had not permitted: DOC's normal workload.[27]

Conversely, suppose DOC selects a respondent for individual investigation, but that later respondent asks to be included in the general pool of respondents to which the AOR would be applied. This problem arose in the 2016 Federal Circuit case of *Viet I-Mei Frozen Foods Company v. United States*.[28] The CIT agreed with Viet I-Mei when it asked for an order to compel DOC to investigate it individually. Once the DOC started to do so, Viet I-Mei tried to flip flop, because it realized its individual rate would exceed the AOR. DOC refused Viet I-Mei's request to stop the individual inquiry, and assigned it an individual AD rate of 25.76%. The rate DOC imposed on most of the non-individually investigated respondents was just 3.92%. The Federal Circuit said DOC was under no statutory obligation to agree to the request, so Viet I-Mei was stuck with the higher duty. If a respondent could cancel an individual inquiry, then it could manipulate outcomes in its favor if, as the case progressed, they projected the AOR would be below its individual rate.

• **Methods for Computing AOR**

Section 1673d(c)(5) of Title 19 relates to the general rule for how to compute an AOR in AD cases.[29] As just suggested, an AOR is the weighted average of estimated

---

26. Emphasis added.

27. *See* Eric Emerson & Henry Cao, *Impact of the Amendments to U.S. Antidumping and Countervailing Duty Law in the Trade Preferences Extension Act of 2015*, 32 International Trade Reporter (BNA) 1518 (27 August 2015). [Hereinafter, *Impact.*]

28. Number 2016-1006 (11 October 2016); Brian Flood, *Vietnamese Shrimp Producer Loses Duty Appeal*, 33 International Trade Reporter (BNA) 1490 (20 October 2016).

29. *See Xiaman International Trade & Industrial Company v. United States*, Ct. Int'l Trade, Number 11-00411, 20 December 2013; Rossella Brevetti, *Court Orders Commerce to Revisit Decisions on Mushrooms from China*, 31 International Trade Reporter (BNA) 30 (2 January 2014). Preserved mushrooms were the subject merchandise, and the CIT remanded an Administrative Review to

weighted average dumping margins calculated for producer-exporter respondents that are individually investigated, excluding any dumping margin that is zero, *de minimis*, or established for an uncooperative respondent (or government of the respondent) from AFA.[30] At the discretion of the DOC, the dumping margin and consequent AD duty rate based on AFA may be the higher of the (1) rate for which the petitioner argues in its filings, or (2) highest rate calculated during the investigation. A similar general rule exists for the net countervailable subsidization rate.

How does the DOC limit its examination to certain respondents and thereby compute individual dumping margins or net countervailable subsidization rates? Under the AD and CVD statutes, it has two options. Either the DOC can:

(1) select a statistically valid sample of respondents (*i.e.*, producers, exporters, or producer-exporters) or product types, based on IA to it, or

---

the DOC. There were three mandatory respondents: Jisheng, with a 266.13% dumping margin; Blue Field, with a 2.17% margin; and Xiamen, with a 13.12% margin. The DOC calculated an AOR for the non-individually investigated producer-exporters, Iceman Group and Golden Banyan, as a weighted average of these three margins. The DOC put up the losing argument that read literally, 19 U.S.C. § 1673d(c)(5) did not obligate it to exclude any of these 3 margins from its weighted average calculation, because none of them was zero, *de minimis*, or determined under a facts available analysis. But, the CIT held it was wrong for the DOC to include the 266.13% dumping margin in the weighted average, because it was dramatically more than the margins, and led to an absurd AOR.

30. Use of AFA applies in CVD cases, too. *See, e.g.*, *Maverick Tube Corp. v. United States*, Federal Circuit Number No. 16-CV-1649 (30 May 2017); Rossella Brevetti, *Federal Circuit Backs Commerce in Subsidies Dispute*, 34 International Trade Reporter (BNA) 816 (1 June 2017). The subject merchandise in the Maverick case was OCTG (hollow steel pipes used to extract oil and natural gas) from Turkey. The respondents—Borusan Mannesmann Boru Sanayi Ve Ticaret A.S. and Borusan Istikbal Ticaret, collectively, "Borusan"—received unfair government subsidies, namely, hot-rolled steel, which is an input into OCTG, from two steel mills. During the original investigation, they failed to provide information to the DOC on the DOC's initial questionnaire about this input, so the DOC used AFA. Borusan had 3 production facilities, at Gemlik, Halkali and Izmit, but offered data only for the first of them, saying that to do so for the other 2 plants would "impose great burdens [for] "no purpose." The DOC did not accept this rationale, and asked again for data from the other two plants. Borusan neither provided such data nor attested that they were unavailable, hence the DOC applied AFA. The Federal Circuit rejected Borusan's argument that it cooperated with DOC to the best of its ability:

Borusan does not dispute that it had access to information relating to the Halkali and Izmit locations, and that it did not provide that information. . . .

Thus, Borusan effectively concedes that it possessed information necessary to Commerce's investigation, that Commerce requested that information, and that Borusan did not provide that information. Such behavior cannot be considered "maximum effort to provide Commerce with full and complete answers." *Nippon Steel Corp. [v. United States]*, 337 F.3d [1373] at 1382 (Fed. Cir. 2003).

Borusan's arguments do not convince us otherwise. First, although Commerce's supplemental request required it only to provide the information or explain why it was unable to do so, Borusan did neither. Borusan admits it did not provide the information, and the explanation of its difficulties does not constitute a statement that it was unable to provide the information.

(2) choose the respondents that account for the largest volume of subject merchandise from the exporting country at issue that the DOC can reasonably examine.

Until November 2013, the DOC openly preferred the second option.[31] But, it realized its practice created an enforcement problem.

The second option means the DOC does not individually examine respondents with small import volumes. In AD cases, once those respondents appreciate they are excluded from individual examination, they may lower their Export Prices. After all, to them the DOC applies an AOR dumping margin. Suppose that margin, and consequent AD duty, is 18%. An unscrupulous respondent might rationally calculate it can pay the duty, yet lower its Export Price so that its true individual margin is 28%. It thus gains sales from its dumped subject merchandise. The respondent knows its AD duty is capped at the AOR rate, so it might as well dump to a greater degree, and thereby obtain market share in the U.S.

• **November 2013 Change to Random Sampling**

In November 2013, the DOC changed its practice: in AD Administrative Reviews, but not original investigations, it would use sampling via random selection.[32] In particular, it would do so if (1) an interested party asked for sampling, (2) the DOC had the resources to sample, (3) the three largest respondents by import volume of subject merchandise over the relevant review period did not account for over 50% of total volume, and (4) IA to the DOC gave it a reasonable basis to suspect that average Export Prices or dumping margins for the largest respondents differ from those for the remaining (smaller) respondents. By preferring random selection, then, small respondents would know they might get "hit" with an individual rate, and thus caught if they lowered their Export Prices.

• **Need for Corroboration, 2000 *Martino* Case, and *2015 TPEA* Amendment**

The discretion of DOC in using AFA is not unbounded. If DOC applies AFA to a respondent producer-exporter because it is non-cooperative, then (under the pertinent statute) DOC must "corroborate" the AFA "to the extent practical." The 2000 Federal Circuit Case of *F.Lli de Cecco di Filippo Fara S. Martino S.p.A. v. United States*, the Federal Circuit held a dumping margin based on AFA "should be reasonable hand have some basis in reality," and also ought to be "a reasonably accurate estimate of the respondent's actual rate."[33]

---

31. *See* Rossella Brevetti, *Commerce to Generally Use Sampling In AD Reviews Respondent Selection*, 30 International Trade Reporter (BNA) 1729 (7 November 2013).

32. The random sampling technique the DOC uses includes stratification by import volumes (to ensure companies with different import volumes are included) and choosing Probability-Proportional to Size (PPS) samples (to ensure the probability a respondent is selected is proportional to its share of subject merchandise imports in the stratum). *See* 78 Federal Register 65,963 (4 November 2013).

33. 216 F.3d 1027 (Fed. Circ. 2000).

However, must DOC modify an AD or CVD rate it computes from AFA based on a supposition about data a respondent producer-exporter would have provided if it had complied with DOC's request for data? The answer, thanks to the *2015 TPEA*, is "no." Even if DOC could make an assumption about data the respondent would have supplied if it done what the DOC asked, the DOC need not make that assumption. It can stick with AFA, and thus with a dumping margin or net countervailable subsidization rate unfavorable to the respondent. Does this statutory change effectively repeal the *Martino* case?[34] Consider the fact DOC need not estimate what the margin or rate would have been if the respondent had complied with its data request.

VIII. Voluntary Respondents, AOR, and 2014 *MacLean-Fogg* Case

In a CVD investigation, suppose DOC must calculate an AOR owing to the large number of respondents. As indicated above, the same may occur in an AD case. In both contexts DOC typically limits individual investigations to two or three respondents. The individually investigated respondents are called "mandatory" respondents. The DOC then calculates a weighted averaged of the net subsidization rates or dumping margins of the mandatory respondents, and applies that weighted average—the AOR—to the respondents it did not choose for individual investigation.

But, suppose in the case, DOC calculates individual duty rates for "voluntary" respondents, that is, ones that volunteered to participate in an individual investigation by turning over to DOC their company-specific data on costs, sales, and other pertinent matters. When the DOC computes the AOR, must it use the individual rates in the computation? The Federal Circuit confronted this issue in the 2014 case of *MacLean-Fogg Co. v. United States*, and answered "yes."[35]

---

34. *See Impact*, in which the authors argue "yes."

35. *See* Number 2013-1187 (3 June 2014); Brian Flood, *Federal Circuit Panel Orders Commerce To Use Voluntary Rates in All-Others Inquiry*, 31 International Trade Reporter (BNA) 1063 (12 June 2014).

In a subsequent action, the CIT ruled as unlawful the 7.42% CVD rate the DOC imposed on aluminum extrusion imports from China. *See MacLean-Fogg Co. v. United States*, Number 11-00209 (Slip Opinion 15-85, 11 August 2015). The problem was the DOC failed to calculate the AOR using weighted average CVD rates: it used the simple average of the AD duty rates from respondents that volunteered for individual investigations, rather than an average based on their respective sales revenues. As is typical in a case involving many respondents, DOC selected for investigation a small sample as "mandatory," slating each of them for an individual rate. Other respondents could petition to be "voluntary," which 2 of them—Zhaoqing New Zongya Aluminum Company and Yongji Guanghai Aluminum Industry Company—did, because they felt they could persuade the DOC their individual rate should be low. The rest would receive the AOR, which the DOC computed originally at 374.15%. Following the 2014 Federal Circuit decision, DOC cut the AOR to 7.42%.

The DOC argued the pertinent statute was ambiguous as to whether it had to include voluntary respondent rates in the calculation of an AOR. It opted not to, resulting in an AOR against subject merchandise—aluminum extrusions (which are metal shapes used in auto, construction, energy, telecom, and other industries) from China—of a whopping 137.65%. As usual, in the original investigation the DOC sampled mandatory respondents. Three mandatory respondents declined to cooperate with the DOC, so they received CVD rates based on AFA.

But, generally, any foreign producer or exporter of the subject merchandise not selected for individual investigation (*i.e.*, not a "mandatory" respondent) can choose to have the DOC do one on it. These "voluntary respondents" give the DOC the data it needs to compute for them an individual rate. All other producer-exporters, *i.e.*, the ones for which the DOC does not assign an individual rate, have the AOR apply to them.

It so happened there were 2 voluntary respondents, and the DOC assigned them individual rates. The controversy was that it did not include those rates in its AOR computation. The DOC stuck to its "Two Track System" whereby (1) it used individual rates computed for mandatory respondents to calculate the AOR, but (2) it did not use individual rates from any voluntary respondent in the AOR. The System made sense: any foreign producer-exporter choosing to be a voluntary respondent would do so only if it thought its individual rate would be low (in particular, lower than the AOR), *i.e.*, it was shrewd enough to foresee it would be better off with a *sui generis* rate than being lumped in with a group of non-individually investigated respondents. So, if the individual rates of voluntary respondents were mixed into the weighted average computation of AOR, then the AOR would be artificially depressed.

Mathematically, the DOC was correct, and two CIT decisions sided with it. But, the Federal Circuit overturned them, saying the law was not on the side of the DOC. The plain meaning of, and legislative history to, the statute was clear that a voluntary respondent is an "individually investigated" producer or exporter. After all, it receives an individual rate. In turn, the individual rates of these "individually

---

The American petitioners—the Aluminum Extrusions Fair Trade Committee—successfully challenged that reduction. The CIT agreed with them that DOC was wrong to calculate the 7.42% AOR from a simple average of the CVD rates of the voluntary respondents, rather than from a weighted average based on their respective sales volumes. *See* Brian Flood, *Court Rejects Revised Aluminum Extrusions CVD Rate*, 32 International Trade Reporter (BNA) 1458 (20 August 2015). After all, said the CIT, there was a "significant disparity" in the sales volumes of 2 voluntary respondents. The DOC's losing argument was it could not compute a weighted averaging of CVD rates, as that would mean disclosing confidential business information of Zhaoqing and Yongji, and they did not submit publicly available alternative data. The CIT held not "expend[ing] minimal effort" to find missing public versions of the data was "unreasonable." After further proceedings, the CIT upheld a revised AOR of 7.39%. *See MacLean-Fogg Co. v. United States*, Number 11-00209 (Slip Opinion 15-119, 23 October 2015); Brian Flood, *Duty Rate Remains on Chinese Aluminum Extrusions*, 32 International Trade Reporter (BNA) 1872 (29 October 2015).

investigated" voluntary respondents must be included in the AOR, unless they and all mandatory respondents get assigned rates of zero, *de minimis* rates, or rates based on AFA. The Federal Circuit also pointed out the logical flaw in the DOC position: a voluntary respondent gets an individual rate, but if it is not considered "individually investigated," then the AOR applies to it. So, the DOC had to recalculate the AOR with the voluntary respondent rates. The nearly certain result was to lower the AOR.

IX. Adverse Facts, AOR, and 2014 *Navneet* Case

Suppose after individually investigating certain respondents, the DOC is left with only *de minimis* margins for those respondents, and an AFA rate for non-cooperative respondents (the ones who refused to respond to the DOC questionnaire).[36] May the DOC use the AFA rate in calculating the AOR for the remaining cooperative respondents? In other words, does the statutory language "any reasonable method" allow the DOC to base the AOR on an AFA rate?

A "yes" answer seems unfair. An AOR applies to respondents that are willing to cooperate with the DOC, but happen not to be selected by the DOC for individual investigation. Why treat them like non-cooperative respondents? Yet, a "yes" answer is what the CIT issued in a 2014 dispute, *Navneet Publications (India) Ltd. v. United States.*[37]

In *Navneet*, the DOC selected two respondents for individual investigation, and found their dumping margins to be *de minimis*. For the five non-cooperative respondents, the DOC calculated an AFA rate of 22.02%. Navneet Publications Ltd. argued the pattern of its pricing and sales of subject merchandise—certain lined paper products—was like that of the individually-investigated respondents. So, said Navneet, if the DOC had investigated it, then it would have received a *de minimis* rate.

Unfortunately for Navneet, the DOC averaged the *de minimis* and AFA rates, resulting in an 11.01% final margin. That figure was aberrationally high compared to other rates cooperating respondents received in earlier proceedings about the AD order.

---

36. Use of AFA is permitted under GATT-WTO rules, but does the DOC's AFA scheme violate those rules? In May 2018, Korea said it thought so, because it fails to evaluate facts "properly and objectively," and launched under the *DSU* a major "as such" challenge against that scheme. The case arose from six AD-CVD cases in which an array of Korean steel exports to the U.S. was the subject merchandise

37. *See* Number 13-00204, Slip Opinion 14-87 (22 July 2014); Brian Flood, *Trade Court Remands All-Others Rate For Indian Paper Antidumping Review*, 31 International Trade Reporter (BNA) 1424 (7 August 2014).

The CIT remanded the case to the DOC to recalculate the rate for Navneet. That was because the DOC defended its methodology by saying it had limited data to confirm whether the two investigated respondents were representative of Navneet (and the other non-individually investigated cooperative respondents). Perhaps that was because the DOC choose only two respondents to investigate. Further, the CIT said the DOC was responsible for verifying whether the rate it assigned to Navneet reflected its economic reality. However, of great note was the CIT's statement that "the all-others rate statute expressly permits the inclusion of facts available rates [*i.e.*, AFAs]." In other words, what the DOC did—using an AFA to compute an AOR—was not per se illegal, but in this instance the DOC did not justify sufficiently its action.

Chapter 5

Dumping Margin Calculation[1]

I. Dumping Margin Formula

"Dumping" refers to the sale or likely sale of imported merchandise at less than fair value (LTFV). What is "fair value," and against what is it gauged? The answer is the standard definition of the term. It is found in Article VI:1 of GATT and Article 2:1 of the WTO *Antidumping Agreement*.

A product is dumped if its "Export Price" (EP) is less than "Normal Value" (NV). Hence, the formula for the absolute dumping margin is:

$$\text{Dumping Margin} = NV - EP$$

Expressed in percentage terms, the formula is:

$$\text{Dumping Margin} = \frac{NV - EP}{EP} \times 100$$

If a positive dumping margin exists, and dumped merchandise causes or threatens to cause material injury to a producer of a like product in the importing country, then that country may impose a duty on the dumped merchandise.

The AD duty is on top of the normal MFN tariff (or otherwise applicable rate), and may be up to the full amount of the dumping margin. The U.S. imposes an AD duty in the full amount of the dumping margin. In contrast, the EU adheres to the "Lesser Duty Rule," imposing an AD duty just high enough to rectify the dumping. The punitive duty is the remedy for the unfairness of selling at below fair value — or, so the justification goes.

Appearances notwithstanding, the study and practice of AD law is not formulaic. The definition and formulas for the dumping margin raise 3 questions:

(1) What is "NV"?

(2) What is "EP"?

(3) What steps are taken to ensure NV and EP are comparable?

---

1. Documents References:
    (1) *Havana Charter* Article 34
    (2) GATT Article VI
    (3) WTO *Antidumping Agreement* Articles 1–2

The answers to these questions, in turn, spawn a myriad of questions that make AD law both intellectually fascinating and technically complex. Further, calculation of the dumping margin is only the first of three phases in an AD case. The second phase is the injury determination, and third phase involves a review of an outstanding AD order.

II. Normal Value

- **Pre- versus Post-Uruguay Round Terminology**

To begin, "Normal Value" is a foreign home market price, specifically, the price of a foreign like product sold in the ordinary course of trade (*i.e.*, not to a related party or below-cost) for consumption in the country of the exporter (or producer). Under pre-Uruguay Round terminology used in the U.S., Normal Value was called "Foreign Market Value," or "FMV." Table 5-1 summarizes pre- and post-Uruguay Round dumping terms.

The exporter (or producer) refers to the entity alleged to be dumping merchandise in an importing country. Thus, if China is the importing country, and the exporter is an American company, then Normal Value is the price of the foreign like product sold in the U.S. This scenario is increasingly common. Decades ago, few countries other than the U.S. and EU brought AD cases. In the decade after the Uruguay Round, China, India, and other developing countries became increasingly aggressive about bringing AD cases.

Table 5-1. Pre- versus Post-Uruguay Round Terminology in AD Law

Pre-Uruguay Round Expression	Post-Uruguay Round Expression
Less Than Fair Value (LTFV)	Less Than Fair Value (LTFV)
Dumping Margin (DM)	Dumping Margin (DM)
Foreign Market Value (FMV)	Normal Value (NV)
United States Price (USP) (referring either to Purchase Price or Exporter's Sales Price)	No equivalent term. Must specify either Export Price or Constructed Export Price
Purchase Price (PP)	Export Price (EP)
Exporter's Sales Price (ESP)	Constructed Export Price (CEP)
Class or kind of merchandise subject to investigation	Subject merchandise
Like product	Domestic like product
Such or similar merchandise	Foreign like product
Best Information Available (BIA)	Facts Available

Reference to a "foreign like product" connotes a threshold likeness issue. Is allegedly dumped imported merchandise, known as the "subject merchandise" (because it is the goods subject to investigation) "like" the product the exporter sells in its home country? That is, in every AD case, there are three categories of goods involved:

(1) The *foreign like product*, which is the good foreign exporter or producer sells in its home country.

(2) The *subject merchandise*, which is the allegedly dumped import.

(3) The *domestic like product*, *i.e.*, the product made in the importing country that is allegedly victimized by dumping.

The foreign like product must be compared to subject merchandise for purposes of calculating Normal Value (based on foreign like product sales) and Export Price (or, as explained below, Constructed Export Price). If the foreign like product and subject merchandise are different, then it is inappropriate to compare prices from their sales. In addition, subject merchandise must be compared with the domestic like product. If these goods differ, then it is inappropriate to base an injury determination relating to the domestic un-like product on dumping of subject merchandise.

For instance, suppose Caterpillar, Inc. is accused of dumping tractors in China. To calculate the dumping margin, sales in the U.S. on which Chinese AD authorities base Normal Value must be of tractors that are like tractors allegedly dumped in China, from which the authorities derive Export Price. To determine whether dumped tractors cause or threaten injury, those dumped tractors must be like Chinese-made tractors.

III. Proxies for Normal Value: Third Country Price and Constructed Value

It cannot be presumed Normal Value exists in every instance. To continue the example, suppose Caterpillar does not sell the same kind of tractors in the U.S. as in China. Rather, it sells those models in third countries, such as Australia, Japan, and Mexico. Or, suppose it sells the same model in the U.S., but in the POI by Chinese AD authorities, the number of American sales is small. As still another possibility, suppose the sales by Caterpillar in the U.S. are sufficient in number, but below the cost of production. In such instances—no home market sales, an insufficient number of home market sales, or below cost sales—price data from the U.S. are unavailable or unreliable. Consequently, a proxy for the exporter's home market—here, a substitute for the U.S.—must be found. Chinese AD authorities might look to Caterpillar tractor sales in a market that resembles, as far as possible, the U.S.—such as Australia.

These instances can be related. Suppose some sales of the foreign like product made in the home country of the exporter or producer are made at below cost of production. Depending on the facts—namely, whether below-cost sales are in the ordinary course of trade, and the volume of below-cost sales—some or all sales may be disregarded as a basis to calculate Normal Value. If all of them are tossed out, then the home country is not a viable market in which to determine Normal Value. It becomes necessary to consider alternatives, *i.e.*, to find a proxy for Normal Value. The opposite situation can arise, namely, where there are a large number of sales in the exporter's home country (or where a large number of adjustments must be made to Normal Value). In that case, averaging or sampling techniques may be used to calculate Normal Value.

When a country other than the exporter's home market is used, then price data from that country may be used as the basis for a proxy for Normal Value. In other words, third country sales generate the Normal Value proxy, the proxy is known as "Third Country Price," and the dumping margin formula becomes:

$$\text{Dumping Margin} = \text{Third Country Price} - \text{Export Price}$$

Essentially, Third Country Price is the price of the foreign like product in a third country.

In some instances, there is no viable third country market from which to derive a price, *i.e.*, there is no third country in which sales of a foreign like product exist to form an adequate basis for comparison against sales of the allegedly dumped merchandise. Then, the proxy for Normal Value is Constructed Value, and formula becomes:

$$\text{Dumping Margin} = \text{Constructed Value} - \text{Export Price}$$

When either proxy is used, the dumping margin still may be expressed as a percentage, by dividing the difference by Export Price and multiplying the result by 100.

In contrast to Normal Value and Third Country Price, which are market-observed prices, Constructed Value is a bottom-up calculation of the foreign like product price. It is the sum of the cost of production (*e.g.*, factor inputs and materials that go into the product), plus figures for selling, general, and administrative (SG&A) expenses, and for profits. Article 2:2:2 of the WTO *Antidumping Agreement* mandates that SG&A expenses be actual production and sales data in the ordinary course of trade, But, if they are unavailable, the Article allows for the use of surrogates.

Article 2:2:2 permits three alternative sources from which to derive data are permissible. First, data may come from sales of merchandise in the domestic market of the country of origin, where the merchandise is in the same general category of products as the like product. Second, it is possible to use a weighted average for actual amounts incurred and realized of SG&A expenses, and profits, respectively, by other exporters or producers with respect to the like product as sold by them in the domestic market of the country of origin. Third, any other reasonable method may be used, as long as the amount adjusted for profit does not exceed the profit normally realized by other exporters or producers on sales of products in the same general category in the home market.

There is a clear order of preference, with Normal Value the first choice. Only if NV is unavailable or unreliable is recourse made to TCP. In turn, only if that Price is unavailable is CV used as a last resort proxy for NV. Whenever NV or TCP is used, observe it is a single value expressed in U.S. dollars. Moreover, this value is a weighted average of prices in the exporter's home country, or a third country, during the POI.

IV. Export Price and Constructed Export Price

What is "EP"? It is the price at which subject merchandise is purchased (or agreed to be purchased) before the date of importation into the country in which this merchandise is allegedly dumped. Critically, EP must be an arm's length price between unrelated parties. Those parties are the purchaser (*e.g.*, importer) in the importing country and exporter (or producer). Thus, EP sometimes is defined simply as the price of subject merchandise between an exporter and unrelated buyer.

If the buyer and seller are related, then a substitute figure, CEP, must be used. CEP is the price at which subject merchandise is sold (or agreed to be sold) in the importing country before or after importation, where the sale is by or for the account of the exporter (or producer) to the first unrelated purchaser. That is, Constructed Export Price is sometimes defined as the first sale to an unrelated party in the importing country.

In a world populated by multinational corporations, intra-corporate trade is significant. Hence, related party pricing issues are common. An exporter might sell subject merchandise to a related party (*e.g.*, an importer that is an agency, branch, or subsidiary of the exporter) at a below-market price. The motive of the exporter could be to maximize profits of the affiliate, because applicable tax rates are lower in the importing country than exporting country. If tax rates are higher in the importing country, the exporter might charge its affiliated importer an above-market price, and thereby drain profits from the affiliate. Related-party pricing may have important tax consequences. From the perspective of AD law, if a price between an exporter and related party importer is off-market, then it cannot be used as a basis for a fair comparison to NV. That is because NV (or its proxy) is derived from open market transactions.

V. 2015 *Peer Bearing* Case

As one of many interesting examples of the use of Constructed Export Price, consider the 2015 CIT case of *Peer Bearing Co.–Changshan v. United States*.[2] Tapered

---

2. *See* Number 09-00052 (Slip Opinion, 15-61, 16 June 2015); Brian Flood, *Trade Court Reinstates Higher AD Rate On Roller Bearing Imports from China*, 32 International Trade Reporter

roller bearings from China were the subject merchandise, and Diagram 5-1 depicts the commercial sale chain. On first remand from the CIT, the DOC calculated the dumping margin using Constructed Export Price starting prices, namely, the prices at which Peer Bearing sold subject merchandise to unaffiliated customers, and then devised its own method to adjust those starting prices to reach final adjusted values—in effect, a final CEP. The CIT said the DOC violated the CEP

Diagram 5-1. Facts in 2013 *Peer Bearing* Case

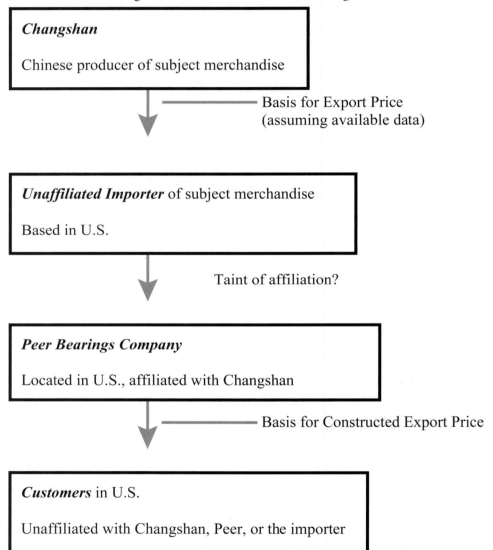

Changshan

Chinese producer of subject merchandise

Basis for Export Price
(assuming available data)

Unaffiliated Importer of subject merchandise

Based in U.S.

Taint of affiliation?

Peer Bearings Company

Located in U.S., affiliated with Changshan

Basis for Constructed Export Price

Customers in U.S.

Unaffiliated with Changshan, Peer, or the importer

(BNA) 1154 (25 June 2015); Number 09-00052 (Slip Opinion 13-116, 30 August 2013); Brian Flood, *Court Upholds Remand Results Of Chinese Roller Bearing AD Order*, 30 International Trade Reporter (BNA) 1350 (5 September 2013).

statute (Section 751(a)(2)(A) of the *Tariff Act of 1930*) by applying its own method of adjusting CEP data.

Ideally, what the DOC should have done was calculate the dumping margin for Peer Bearing-Changshan using Export Price data from the U.S., that is, price data from sales by Changshan in China to the unaffiliated importer in the U.S. Yet, such data were insufficient to calculate Export Price. So, said the CIT, if the DOC had to use CEP, it could not concoct its own methodology for doing so.

On second remand from the CIT, the DOC recalculated the dumping margin, using CEP data from the U.S. The result was a 6.52% margin, a rate not based on AFA. In contrast, after first remand, the DOC used AFA and computed the rate as 60.95%. Following second remand, the CIT upheld the 6.52% rate. But, the Federal Circuit reversed the CIT, ordering the CIT to reinstate the dumping margin from first remand using AFA, namely 60.95%.

The *Peer Bearing* case raises many questions. For instance, are there instances in which an exporter and importer are related, yet EP rather than CEP may be used? The answer is "yes."

Suppose the purchaser of subject merchandise is a processor of sales-related documentation, but plays no role in setting the price to the first unrelated buyer. Here, the relationship between purchaser and exporter does not affect the price charged to an unaffiliated customer. The purchaser is a pass-through entity. The price is set by arm's length bargaining between exporter and customer. Then, that price is acceptable as a basis for Export Price.

VI. Comparing Apples to Apples

• **Importance of Adjustments**

On the third question posed at the outset about the dumping margin calculation, a variety of steps are needed to ensure what practitioners call an "apples-to-apples" comparison between NV and EP (or CEP). In seeking fairness, it is essential to inquire whether any term in the dumping margin formula requires one or more adjustments to ensure comparability. In principle, adjustments ought to lead to scientific-like precision of comparability. In practice, arguing about adjustments is common, with *post hoc* rationalization of an addition or subtraction to serve the interest of the petitioner or respondent.

Thus, as GATT Article VI:1 and Article 2:4 of the WTO *Antidumping Agreement* indicate, adjustments are made to NV account for differences in

(1) Merchandise.

(2) Quantities sold.

(3) Circumstances of sale (COS).

(4) Levels of trade (LOT) at which sales occur.

Adjustments to EP (or CEP) help obtain an *ex-factory* price (*i.e.*, the price of subject merchandise when it leaves the factory door in the home country of the exporter or producer). These adjustments include subtractions for:

(1) Delivery expenses.

(2) Import duties.

Some adjustments are made uniquely to CEP. They include deductions for

(1) Selling commissions.

(2) Indirect selling expenses.

(3) Expenses and profit for further manufacturing (if any) in the importing country.

(4) Related-party profit (if any) earned from the sale of subject merchandise through a related distributor to an end-use in the importing country.

(The last deduction is linked to the LOT adjustment to NV.)

In theory and practice, adjustments are a zero-sum game. Any adjustment either widens a dumping margin, which benefits petitioners, or narrows the margin, which pleases respondents. Each side tends to employ a formidable team of accountants and economists to run computer-based dumping margin calculations with different hypothetical adjustments. The simulation best suited to interests of a side — maximizing the margin for petitioners, or minimizing (or eliminating it entirely) for respondents — is sure to be favored by that side. To the extent there is supporting evidence, the adjustments in the "winning" simulation may be justified — *post hoc* — as appropriate.

Observe the LOT adjustment can prove especially tricky. The *Uruguay Round Agreements Act of 1994* (codified at 19 U.S.C. §§ 3501-3624, and amending several other Title 19 provisions) and the accompanying Clinton Administration *Statement of Administrative Action* changed LOT adjustment methodology. The DOC should deduct from NV any price difference between two levels of trade, if it is proven sales occur at different levels. Ostensibly, this adjustment ensures both NV and EP (or CEP) are derived from wholesale prices, or from retail prices, and eschews comparing wholesale prices in one market (*e.g.*, the exporter's home country) and retail prices in the other market (*e.g.*, the importing country). However, the intent behind the change is to provide a NV counterpart to a CEP adjustment. The relevant adjustment to CEP is a deduction for related party profits (*i.e.*, profits earned by a party affiliated with the exporter). Supposedly, the effect is comparison of a sale in the exporter's home market with one in the U.S. at the same point in the commercial chain.

- **Reminder about Best Information and *De Minimis* Thresholds**

Two problems, in addition to the issues outlined above, at the outset of a dumping margin calculation concern the choice of information about price data and the need to check whether *de minimis* thresholds are crossed. The first issue is epistemological: how does an investigating authority know the information about NV and

EP (or CEP) is reliable? Ultimately, the authority may have to conduct a "verification" visit in the home country of a respondent to check data from which Normal Value is derived. Likewise, some kind of verification of data about sales transactions in the importing country may be needed.

Generally, an investigating authority seeks to use the best information available, or "BIA." It asks a respondent to complete a lengthy questionnaire, which calls (*inter alia*) for information about pricing. If the respondent fails to fill it out, or if the responses are incomplete or untimely, then the BIA may be data the petitioner provides. Many disputes arise from whether a respondent failed to comply with requirements of the questionnaire, and thus whether reliance on the petitioner's data was reasonable.[3]

One revision to U.S. AD law made by the *1994 Act*, pursuant to the WTO *Antidumping Agreement*, is a change in terminology. "Facts otherwise available"—or, simply "facts available"—replaced "BIA."[4] The concept remained the same. The *Statement of Administrative Action* for the *Agreement* observes that neither the DOC nor ITC "must prove that the facts available are the best alternative information. Rather, the facts available are information or inferences which are reasonable to use under the circumstances." The administering agencies are supposed to balance all evidence in a record, and from it draw reasonable inferences. They cannot possibly be expected to demonstrate their inferences are the same as those they would have made if they had perfect information.

De minimis thresholds are another issue arising at the outset. Article 5:8 of the WTO *Antidumping Agreement* establishes a two-part *de minimis* inquiry.

(1) Is there a volume of imports of subject merchandise below which authorities should ignore alleged dumping? The answer is "yes, 3%." (Under pre-Uruguay Round law, there was no *de minimis* volume test.)

(2) Is there a value, *i.e.,* a level below which a dumping margin should be ignored? The answer is "yes, 2% *ad valorem*." (Under pre-Uruguay Round, the *de minimis* margin threshold was 0.5%.)

If either the volume or margin is *de minimis*, then an AD investigation is terminated.

The 3% *de minimis* volume test means an investigation starts if the volume subject merchandise is less than 3% of total imports of like merchandise from all countries. There is a built-in exception for cases in which more than one country exports subject merchandise. If the total volume of exports from such countries collectively exceeds 7%, then an investigation may start, even though no one exporting country's share exceeds 3% and is, therefore, negligible. The 2% *de minimis* margin test means a dumping margin of 2% or less is too small to bother about, and no

---

3. For a *NAFTA* Chapter 19 Panel Report on BIA, see *Fresh Cut Flowers from Mexico, Final Results of Antidumping Administrative Review*, USA-95-1904-05 (16 December 1996).

4. *See* 19 U.S.C. § 1677e.

investigation ensues. Are these *de minimis* thresholds sufficiently high to help mitigate the risk of protectionist abuse of AD law? Would 10% be better?

VII. Three Comparison Methodologies

What methodologies are used to compare Normal Value with Export Price (or Constructed Export Price)? That is, what kind of comparison should be made between sales transactions of the foreign like product in the home market of an exporter or producer (*i.e.*, Normal Value data) and sales transactions of the subject merchandise in the importing country (*i.e.*, Export Price, or Constructed Export Price)? The answer is a comparison between a weighted average of Normal Value data and Export Price (or Constructed Export Price) data, or between individual transactions.

The *Tariff Act of 1930*, as amended, authorizes the DOC to use any of the following three comparison methodologies when considering Normal Values to Export (or Constructed Export) Prices:[5]

(1) *Average-to-Average* comparisons, *i.e.*, comparing the weighted average of Normal Values during the POI to the weighted average of Export Prices

---

5. *See* 19 U.S.C. Section 1677f-1(d).

Comparison methodologies and the application of this statute raise a topic known as "zeroing," whereby the DOC sets to 0 any comparison involving a negative dumping margin. The *Dictionary of International Trade Law* contains an extensive entry on "Zeroing."

In brief, zeroing disallows non-dumped sales from offsetting dumped sales, and thus artificially inflates the dumping margin. The U.S. defended the DOC practice of zeroing, not only in original investigations, but also in other contexts, such as Administrative Reviews, against many lawsuits at the WTO. The WTO case law on zeroing began with a landmark 2001 Appellate Body Report, EC Bed Linens, in which India successfully challenged the EC's practice of zeroing. In ruling in India's favor, the Appellate Body found that zeroing does not entail a "fair" comparison of "all" available data, as required by Article 2:4 of the WTO Antidumping Agreement. That is because the artificial setting of positive dumping margins (i.e., non-dumped sales) means the data associated with those transactions are disregarded.

Despite the *EC Bed Linens* precedent (and the discontinuation of zeroing by European authorities), the U.S. continued with the practice, and castigated the Appellate Body for judicial activism — namely, interpreting words like "fair" and "all" in such a way as to weaken trade remedies, which (said the U.S.) was a matter only the WTO Membership was empowered to deal with through the General Council and Ministerial Conference.

Many other Members thus lined up to sue the U.S. for its zeroing, and with Congress unable and/or unwilling to amend U.S. AD law, the USTR defended the suits, one by one, across much of the the 2000s and beyond. The U.S. lost every WTO case.

Nevertheless, the CIT and Federal Circuit sustained the methodology, as Panel and Appellate Body Reports are not a source of authority to cause a change in U.S. law. And, Congress did not change the statute.

But, by administrative fiat, the DOC abandoned zeroing in all except targeted dumping cases. in December 2006, the DOC dropped the use of "Model Zeroing" in original investigations, and ceased to use "Simple Zeroing" in February 2012. It continued until February 2012 to use both Model and Simple Zeroing in Administrative Reviews, and other Reviews. By February 2013, the

during the POI (also called the "Weighted Average-to-Weighted Average" approach);

(2) *Average-to-Transaction* comparisons, *i.e.*, comparing the weighted average of Normal Values from the POI to Export Prices of individual transactions during the POI (also called the "Average-to-Individual" approach); and

(3) *Transaction-to-Transaction* comparisons, *i.e.*, comparing Normal Values and Export Prices from individual transactions during the POI (also called the "Individual-to-Individual" approach).

The DOC may use these methods in an Administrative Review, too.

Note, then, an Average-to-Average comparison in an Administrative Review allows for non-dumped sales to offset dumped sales. That is because the POR is 12 months. The DOC computes a dumping margin for each month, and aggregates them into a final weighted average. But, if the DOC uses the Average-to-Transaction method, and aggregates the weighted average of Normal Values for 12 months with individual Export Price transactions, then it may—under U.S. law—disregard negative dumping margins. That is, it might engage in "zeroing" in targeted dumping cases.

Article 2:4:2 of the WTO *Antidumping Agreement* indicates the comparison should be between weighted average price data on both sides, or between individual transactions. So, under the WTO *Antidumping Agreement*, as a general rule, comparing a weighted average with an individual transaction—method (2) under U.S. law—is not permitted. The reason is obvious. There is a bias in favor of finding a positive dumping margin if the Normal Value figure is an average of many sales transactions, and compared with an Export Price (or Constructed Export Price) figure from a sole transaction. (By analogy, imagine comparing body weight from a 1-month average with body weight from a scale reading the day after Thanksgiving.) The rule seeks to avoid this pro-petitioner bias. Usually, the most reliable comparison is between weighted averages, as individual sales transactions may be unrepresentative of a market.

VIII. Targeted Dumping and 2010 *Nails* and 2014 *Apex* Cases

- **2010 *Nails* Case and Three Step Test**

Article 2:4:2 of the WTO *Antidumping Agreement* is not entirely successful in eliminating the pro-petitioner bias associated with Average-to-Transaction comparisons. In one instance, it permits comparison between (1) Normal Value, from

---

DOC announced it was ceasing zeroing in all future cases in both original investigations and Reviews. The DOC has yet to declare it will eschew zeroing in respect of petitioner complaints about targeted dumping.

a weighted average of prices, with (2) Export Price (or Constructed Export Price), from an individual transaction. That instance is where an investigating authority finds evidence of a "pattern" that Export Prices "differ significantly among purchasers, regions or time periods." Accordingly, Section 229 of the 1994 *Uruguay Round Agreements Act* preserves the ability of the DOC to make Average-to-Individual comparisons.[6]

As explained earlier, the *Tariff Act of 1930*, as amended, authorizes the DOC to compute a dumping margin using the Average-to-Average or Individual-to-Individual approach.[7] They are the standard methodologies. Only if the DOC suspects targeted dumping does it resort to the Average-to-Individual approach.[8] "Targeted" (or "masked") dumping occurs if dumping is directed at a specific geographic area or time period, or at some but not other customers. The DOC must find Export Prices differ significantly among producer-exporters, across regions, or depending on time periods or importers, such that it cannot account for those variations using the first 2 standard methods. So, in practice, the DOC uses the Average-to-Individual method if neither an Average-to-Average nor an Individual-to-Individual comparison will identify targeted dumping.[9]

How does the DOC determine whether targeted dumping occurs in the first place? Inevitably, terms such as "pattern" and "differ significantly" are ambiguous. Fortunately, under the 2010 CIT decision in *Mid Continent Nail Corp. v. U.S.*, helps answer the question.[10] The DOC applies the so-called "*Nails*" test, which involves 3 Steps.

---

6. *See* 19 U.S.C. § 1677f-1(d)(1)(A)(ii).

7. The latter methodology also is called the Transaction-to-Transaction approach.

8. This methodology also is called the Average-to-Transaction approach.

9. When the DOC invokes the Average-to-Individual method, it must do more than assert more than that "the pattern of price differences identified cannot be taken into account using the standard A-to-A [average-to-average] methodology, because the A-to-A methodology conceals differences in price patterns between the targeted and non-targeted groups by averaging low-priced sales to the targeted group with high-priced sales to the non-targeted group." When the DOC offered precisely that assertion, without more, in the 2014 CIT case of *Beijing Tianhai Industrial Company v. United States*, the CIT responded:

> The Department's purported explanation says nothing more than that Commerce has found a pattern of differing prices and invokes the mathematical truism that, when you average a set of numbers, the differences among the individual numbers averaged cease to be apparent. Thus, it is the case that any time a pattern of disparate pricing exists, the prices will "mask" the differences in the individual prices.

Number 12-00203 (9 September 2014). The CIT thus remanded the case to the DOC for recalculation of the 6.62% AD rate the DOC had assigned to high-pressure steel cylinders from China. *See also* Brian Flood, *Targeted Dumping Analysis Was Inadequate In Steel Cylinders Inquiry, Says Trade Court*, 31 International Trade Reporter (BNA) 1668 (18 September 2014) (discussing this case).

10. *See* 712 F. Supp 2d 1370 (2010); Brian Flood, *Court Upholds Targeted Dumping Inquiry, But Needs Explanation for De Minimis Test*, 31 International Trade Reporter (BNA) 856 (8 May 2014).

Certain steel nails produced and exported from the UAE by Dubai Wire FTZ and Precision Fasteners, LLC were the subject merchandise. After various proceedings, the DOC calculated AD duty rates of 6.09% and 2.51%, respectively, which it later revised to 2.68% and zero, and which the CIT approved. *See Mid Continent Nail Corporation v. United States*, Number 12-00133 (Slip

First, the DOC asks whether at least one-third of the sales of subject merchandise of an alleged targeted dumper are at prices notably below the average price of all sales. If the answer is "no," then the DOC decides against a finding of targeted dumping.

If the answer is "yes," then the DOC proceeds to Step Two: it measures the difference between the (1) average sales price of subject merchandise by the alleged targeted dumper and (2) next higher average sales price of a non-targeted dumper.

In Step Three, the DOC compares this price differential to the average difference among prices by a non-targeted dumper. The result is a gap (or not) between the first price differential (between (1) and (2)) and the average non-targeted dumping prices. If this gap is more than 5% of the volume of sales by the respondent-producer exporter to the target (*i.e.*, the purchaser, region, or time period), then the DOC says targeted dumping has occurred. In the 2014 *CP Kelco Oy v. United States* decision, the CIT summarized the *Nails* Test as follows:

> . . . The method, widely known as the "*Nails* test," proceeds as follows. In the first step, called the "standard deviation test," Commerce determines "the volume of the allegedly targeted group's (*i.e.*, purchaser, region, or time period) sales of subject merchandise that are at prices more than one standard deviation below the weighted-average price of all sales under review, targeted and non-targeted." Standard deviations are calculated on a product-specific basis by control number ("CONNUM"). If more than thirty-three percent of allegedly targeted sales are at least one standard deviation below the average price of all reviewed sales in a given CONNUM, Commerce moves to step two.
>
> In step two, the "gap test," the agency considers by CONNUM the sales that passed the standard deviation test. Commerce first calculates the difference between the weighted-average price of allegedly targeted sales and the next higher weighted-average price of sales to a non-targeted group (the "target gap"). Next, Commerce calculates the average difference, weighted by sales volume, between prices to non-targeted groups (the "non-target gap"). Finally, the agency compares the target gap to the non-target gap. If the target gap exceeds the non-target gap for more than five percent of the exporter's sales to the alleged target by volume, Commerce finds that targeted dumping occurred. The agency may then use A-T [Average to Transaction] to calculate the exporter's margins, but only if Commerce cannot account for observed price differences using A-A [Average to Average].[11]

Opinion 15-122, 3 November 2015); Brian Flood, *Antidumping Duty Rates for Steel Nails Upheld*, 32 International Trade Reporter (BNA) 1912 (5 November 2015). *See also Mid Continent Nail Corp. v. United States*, Federal Circuit Number 2016-1426 (27 January 2017) (concerning *Administrative Procedure Act* issues, and upholding the revised rates).

11. *CP Kelco Oy v. United States*, Number 13-00079 (Slip Opinion 14-42, 15 April 2014) (footnotes omitted).

Simply put, the *Nails* test asks how far away allegedly targeted dumped sales are from the average of sales: the further away, the more likely the respondent is targeting.

What prevents an investigating authority from disregarding prices above Normal Value when choosing an individual Export Price (or Constructed Export Price) transaction? That is, what rule bars the authority from ignoring non-dumped sales when doing an Average-to-Individual comparison? For example, suppose a producer sells a foreign like product in its home market at $9, $10 and $11. It would be found to have dumped subject merchandise if there are three sales transactions made at the same prices in the U.S. market. The average Normal Value would be $10 ($30 divided by 3). The result is a $1 dumping margin when compared individually with the $9 U.S. sale. That comparison would mean disregarding the non-dumped sales made at $10 and $11.

As a practical matter, query whether an exporter exercising reasonable care and judgment can determine, at the time it sets its prices for overseas shipments to markets like the U.S., that it risks a dumping charge. For example, suppose a foreign exporter makes its first U.S. sale in January. At that juncture, how can it ascertain what its weighted-average home market prices for the next six months, or year, will be? The repercussion of an answer "it cannot" is the exporter is unable to determine *a priori* what prices may lead to an accusation of dumping.

- **Explanations, the 0.5% Threshold, and 2014 *Apex* Case**

Must the DOC account for seasonal changes in product demand when deciding whether to use the Average-to-Transaction method? The answer is "no," as producer-exporters of warm water shrimp from India found out in the 2014 CIT case of *Apex Frozen Foods Private Ltd. v. United States.*[12] The producer-exporters denied intentional targeted dumping, arguing changes in demand may have accounted for sales price fluctuations during the 12 month POR covering the Administrative Review of an AD order against their merchandise. The CIT held that the U.S. statute does not require the DOC to determine why some sales are targeted, and some are not, before it opts to use the Average-to-Transaction method.

For another CIT case involving the differential pricing methodology, see *The Stanley Works (Langfang) Fastening Systems Co., Ltd.v. United States,* Number 17-00071 (13 August 2018). The importer of steel nails from China, Stanley, argued the subject merchandise should not be subject to a 5.78% AD duty, which had been in place since 2008, but rather enter the U.S. duty free. The CIT expressly rejected the importer's argument that the Appellate Body, in the 2016 *Korea Washers* case (*i.e., United States—Antidumping and Countervailing Measures on Large Residential Washers from Korea,* WT/DS464/AB/R (adopted 7 September 2016) had held the methodology was illegal under the WTO *Antidumping Agreement.* Said the Court: "WTO decisions are irrelevant to the interpretation of domestic U.S. law." *Id.,* 50.

12. *See* Number 13-00283 (Slip Opinion 14-138, 1 December 2014); Brian Flood, *Trade Court Sustains AD Duty Rate On Imports of Shrimp from India,* 31 International Trade Reporter (BNA) 2130 (11 December 2014). Producer-exporters failed to convince the CIT to overturn the ruling. *See Apex Frozen Foods Private Ltd. v. United States,* Number 13-00283 (27 July 2015).

A different 2015 *Apex* case, concerning deduction from Export Price for AD duties, is discussed in a separate Chapter.

All the DOC needed to do was explain why its default approach, the Average-to-Average methodology, could not work in accounting for targeted dumping. The DOC did so, namely, it used a 0.5% threshold: if the difference in the dumping margin between the Average-to-Average and Average-to-Transaction methods was more than 0.5%, then that difference was not *de minimis*. In that instance, the DOC would apply the Average-to-Individual methodology. In *Apex*, the DOC found no dumping margin with the Average-to-Average approach, but a 3.49% margin with the Average-to-Individual approach on subject merchandise entered between February 2011 and January 2012. That difference was non-*de minimis*, so the DOC stuck with the latter approach. That was reasonable, said the CIT, and in July 2017, the Federal Circuit affirmed.[13]

Still, the Indians were lucky. A 3.49% dumping margin is nearly *de minimis*.

---

13. *See Apex Frozen Foods Private Ltd. v. United States*, Federal Circuit Number 2015-2085 (12 July 2017); *Apex Frozen Foods Private Ltd. v. United States*, Federal Circuit Number 2016-1789 (12 July 2017). The Federal Circuit also upheld duty rates of 1.97% to 3.01% on subject merchandise entries between February 2012 and January 2013.

Chapter 6

Dumping Margin Calculation Issues: Viability, Below-Cost Sales, and Merchandise Comparisons[1]

I. Home Market Viability, Normal Value, and 5% Test

Suppose the number, or nature, of sales of a foreign like product in the home market of an exporter or producer is insufficient to ascertain NV. By "number," the implication is the volume of sales may be low, or even zero. By "nature," the suggestion is sales may be — to use the language of Article 2:2 of the WTO *Antidumping Agreement* — outside of "the ordinary course of trade in the domestic market of the exporting country." In either instance, one of two proxies for NV must be used — a TCP or CV.

However, the supposition about sufficiency of number and nature presumes a legal test for "insufficiency." How does an administering authority ascertain whether home market sales are, in fact, deficient in some way? The technical term for this issue is "home market viability." This rubric evinces the matter concerns capability of price data from the home market to germinate NV. A footnote to Article 2:2 of the WTO *Antidumping Agreement* addresses the topic by providing a home market viability test.

Briefly, if sale transactions in the home market of an exporter (or producer) are less than 5% of its sales to the importing country (*i.e.*, the one in which dumping is alleged), then "normally" the quantity of those sales is deemed too small to render the home market viable. Then, export prices to a third country are used in lieu of the home market price. Failing an acceptable TCP, CV is used. So, the formula for home market viability is:

$$\text{Home Market viability} = \frac{\substack{\text{Quantity of sales by Exporter} \\ \text{in its Home Market}}}{\substack{\text{Quantity of sales by Exporter} \\ \text{in the Importing Country}}} \times 100$$

---

1. Documents References:
   (1) *Havana (ITO) Charter* Article 34
   (2) GATT Article VI
   (3) WTO *Antidumping Agreement* Articles 1–2

If this ratio exceeds 5%, then the home market is viable.

In the U.S., until the Uruguay Round, the formula used bore the same numerator, but a different denominator. The pre-Uruguay Round formula was

$$\text{Home Market viability} = \frac{\text{Quantity of sales by Exporter in its Home Market}}{\text{Quantity of sales by Exporter in All Countries Except the Importing Country}} \times 100$$

The pre- vs. post-Uruguay Round denominator change was from sales excluding the rest of the world to sales excluding the importing country (*e.g.*, the U.S.), *i.e.*, from measuring the home market against the market in the importing country to measuring the home market against markets in the rest of the world (except the U.S.).

The rationale for an ostensibly minor technical change was to prevent reliance on price data to calculate Normal Value from "thin" (*i.e.*, a small volume of) home market sales. If the DOC uses sales figures from countries other than the U.S. in which the volume of sales is low, then the size of the denominator is reduced. In turn, the probability of satisfying the benchmark for viability, and thus using a Normal Value based on thin home market sales, increases. By preventing this outcome, calculation of the dumping margin is said to be less susceptible to manipulation by petitioners.

II. Viability, Product Parts, and 1991 *NMB Singapore* Case

NMB Singapore Ltd. v. United States,
United States Court of International Trade,
780 F. Supp. 823 (1991)

TSOUCALAS, JUDGE:

Plaintiffs, NMB Singapore, Ltd., Pelmec Singapore, Ltd. and NMB Corporation (collectively, "NMB") ... contest the final determinations of the Department of Commerce, International Trade Administration ("Commerce" or "ITA") in *Final Determination of Sales at Less Than Fair Value: Ball Bearings and Parts Thereof From Singapore*, 54 Fed. Reg. 19,112 (1989).... [P]laintiffs contend that the ITA erred in including ball bearing parts in its calculation of the viability of the Singapore home market for NMB's ball bearings. Plaintiffs also assert that the ITA improperly included related party transfers of parts in the viability calculations when there were no comparable sales of parts to unrelated parties.

Background

Defendant-intervenor The Torrington Company ("Torrington") filed a petition ... requesting that the ITA impose antidumping duties on all imports of antifriction bearings and parts thereof, except for tapered roller bearings, from a number of countries, including Singapore. In the course of the ensuing investigation, the ITA determined that NMB's home market for ball bearings in Singapore was not an appropriate market to compare to the United States market for purposes of calculating the dumping margin. Thus, the ITA resorted to using NMB's sales in a third country, Japan, to determine the margin. . . . [T]he ITA published an antidumping duty order for ball bearings and parts thereof from Singapore, setting an estimated weighted average margin of 25.08% on NMB's merchandise.

Discussion

. . .

I. Inclusion of Parts in Viability Calculations

. . .

Home market sales generally are considered too small if they constitute less than five percent of the quantity sold in countries other than the United States. In that case, since the home market is not "viable," FMV [Foreign Market Value, *i.e.*, Normal Value] must be calculated by alternative means, that is, by using either third country sales or constructed value.

Plaintiffs' complaint is that the ITA wrongly included parts of bearings in its calculation of the viability of NMB's home market for ball bearings; that is, the ITA considered ball bearing parts to be merchandise which is "such or similar" to finished ball bearings, and that this caused NMB's home market sales to fall below the regulatory benchmark of 5% of its non-U.S. sales.

The government's response is that it tested viability based on the five classes or kinds of bearings under investigation (ball bearings, spherical roller bearings, cylindrical roller bearings, needle roller bearings and spherical plain bearings) rather than on the such or similar merchandise [*i.e.*, foreign like product] categories normally compared. The reason was that the variations in characteristics of the such or similar merchandise selected by Commerce would have made it "necessary to conduct several hundred viability tests."

Consequently, all sales of antifriction bearings fitting within one of the five classes of bearings, as well as all sales of parts of those bearings, were compared together. Thus, sales of ball bearings and parts of ball bearings in Singapore were divided by sales of ball bearings and parts of ball bearings in all non-U.S. markets, and the resulting percentage was less than 5%.

NMB claims this was unfair and improper because almost all of its sales of ball bearing parts were to its Thai sister company, NMB/Pelmec Thailand, and NMB did not sell parts in the home market. Since each part was treated as if it was equal to each finished bearing, dividing home market sales by non-U.S. sales yielded a figure of less than 5%. The government asserts that it tested parts with finished bearings under each of the five classes of bearings because it would have been wrong to recognize the distinction between finished bearings and parts, and not recognize the hundreds of permutations among bearings based on other characteristics such as outside diameter.

. . . The Court concurs that, given the large number of variations in merchandise and the unique complexity of the bearings investigations, testing viability based on the five classes was appropriate. However, within each class or kind, the ITA should have tested parts separately from finished bearings, where there was no uniform indication of how many parts comprise a bearing, and where the sale of each part was treated the same as the sale of each bearing. The distinction between a finished product and its component parts is fundamental and it would not have sabotaged the class distinctions favored by Commerce for the ITA to have tested parts and finished bearings separately.

. . .

While the "complex facts" of this case permit Commerce to test viability based on the five classes of bearings, they do not justify the decision not to test parts separately from finished bearings. The result would have been just five more viability tests, not "several hundred," and a more accurate determination of the status of the home market would have ensued. Given the lack of data as to how many parts comprise an average bearing, and the consequent equation of one part to one bearing, the decision to treat parts and completed bearings as such or similar merchandise was not reasonable and was not in accordance with either the letter or the spirit of 19 U.S.C. § 1677b(a)(1)(A).

However, during the investigations, Commerce did in fact respond to the complaints of the few importers whose home markets of finished bearings and parts thereof were found to be non-viable, by testing the viability of finished bearings alone. NMB was such an importer, and the results of the re-testing were that NMB's home market sales of *finished* ball bearings constituted more than 5% of its total non-U.S. sales of finished ball bearings.

Nonetheless, the ITA decided to disregard these results and use NMB's third country data in the price comparisons. The first reason given was that NMB's "submissions on value and volume of sales data were inconsistent with respect to which parts were reported and on what basis (*i.e.*, date of shipment vs. date of purchase order) they were reported." . . . Second, the ITA stated that the increase in the home market's percentage of total non-U.S. sales was not significant, even though the percentage went from under the 5% benchmark to over it. The ITA explained that, because of these reasons, it could not be confident of the viability of the home market and thus third country data from Japan was used instead.

. . . The fact that the increase in the home market's share of total sales was only slight is not a compelling reason [for departing from the U.S. AD statute, the *Tariff Act of 1930*, as amended, and DOC regulations], where the percentage [of 5%] did surpass the regulatory benchmark.

The other reason, that the home market data was ambiguous and inconsistent, is a more potent argument. However, the *Final Determination* indicates that the "inconsistent" reporting was only with regard to the sales of parts. . . . Once parts are removed from the equation, this inconsistency will dissipate. Therefore, this reason is inapplicable to the viability of the home market for finished ball bearings . . . .

. . . [T]he Court remands this case to the ITA with instructions that it use NMB's home market sales data for finished ball bearings from Singapore in the price comparisons for purposes of the less than fair value determination. The ITA shall also determine the viability of NMB's home market for ball bearing parts in a separate calculation. . . .

II. Related Party Transfers

NMB also asserts that the ITA improperly used related party transfers in the viability calculations . . . .

All of plaintiffs' sales of parts were to a related party. Thus, plaintiffs assert that these sales should be disregarded since there were no sales to unrelated parties which could serve to determine if the related party transfers were at arm's length.

The *Tariff Act* makes no mention of related party transfers in the context of the viability analysis. . . . Related party transfers *must* be excluded only from actual price comparisons, not from the home market viability tests. This is because the viability test seeks only to determine the level of market activity in a given country, not whether that activity was at arm's length. The arm's length determination is relevant only to the LTFV comparisons. Hence, the ITA's decision to include related party transfers in the viability computations was in accordance with law and is affirmed.

III. Sample, Sporadic, and Related Party Sales, and 1999 *NSK* Case

NSK LTD. v. United States,

United States Court of Appeals for the Federal Circuit,
190 F.3d 1321–35 (1999)

MICHEL, CIRCUIT JUDGE:

This consolidated appeal concerns the Department of Commerce, International Trade Administration's ("Commerce's") fourth annual administrative review of the antidumping order on certain antifriction bearings and parts thereof (the "antifriction bearings"). *See Antifriction Bearings (Other Than Tapered Roller Bearings) and Parts Thereof From France, et al.; Final Results of Antidumping Duty Administrative Reviews, Partial Termination of Administrative Reviews, and Revocation in Part of Antidumping Duty Orders*, 60 Fed. Reg. 10,900 (Dep't Commerce, 1995) ("*Final Results*"). On appeal, the Court of International Trade granted in part and denied in part various parties' motions for judgment on the agency record and remanded to Commerce for various re-determinations in accordance with its opinion. *See NSK*

Ltd. v. United States, 969 F. Supp. 34 (Ct. Int'l Trade 1997) ("*NSK I*"). Commerce made the re-determinations as ordered on remand. See *Final Results of Redetermination Pursuant to Court Remand, NSK Ltd., et al. v. United States, 969 F. Supp. 34,* slip op. 97-74 (1997), (Dep't Commerce Apr. 28, 1998) ("*Remand Results*"). The Remand Results were subsequently affirmed by the Court of International Trade in their entirety. *See NSK Ltd. v. United States, 4 F. Supp. 2d 1264,* slip op. 98-77 (Ct. Int'l Trade 1998) ("*NSK II*").

Plaintiffs-Appellants Koyo Seiko Co., Ltd. and Koyo Corporation of U.S.A. (together "Koyo Seiko"), Plaintiffs-Appellants NTN Bearing Corporation of America, American NTN Bearing Manufacturing Corp., NTN Corporation, NTN Driveshaft, Inc., and NTN-Bower Corporation (collectively "NTN"), and Defendant-Cross Appellant The Torrington Company ("Torrington") now appeal and cross appeal to this court from various aspects of *NSK I* and *NSK II*. We affirm the judgment of the Court of International Trade with respect to NTN's appeal because we find no error, legal or factual, with regard to (i) Commerce's inclusion of certain sample sales and sales with a sporadic sales history as home market sales in its calculation of foreign market value ("FMV") [*i.e.*, Normal Value (NV)]; (ii) Commerce's exclusion of related party sales from the home market sales used in its calculation of FMV; (iii) Commerce's refusal to adjust FMV to take account of NTN's reported home market discounts; and (iv) Commerce's comparison of sales across different levels of trade in its calculation of FMV. However, with respect to the Court of International Trade's rejection of the home market warranty expense factor reported by Koyo Seiko and accepted by Commerce as a "circumstances of sale" adjustment to FMV, we reverse on the grounds that Commerce's acceptance of the adjustment was based upon a reasonable interpretation of the governing statute, accorded with applicable precedent, and its rejection by the court was therefore error. Finally, we affirm with respect to Torrington's cross appeal of the determination of the United States price of the antifriction bearings bought and resold by Defendants-Appellees Honda Motor Co., Ltd., American Honda Motor Co., Inc., Honda of America Mfg., Inc. and Honda Power Equipment Mfg., Inc (collectively, "Honda"). Like the Court of International Trade, we hold that Commerce reasonably interpreted the term "reseller" in the governing antidumping statute and that substantial evidence supports Commerce's determination that Honda constitutes such a "reseller" with regard to its sales of subject antifriction bearings.

[Omitted is the Court's discussion of NTN's appeal of issues (iii) and (iv). Omitted, too, is the Court's discussion of the appeal by Koyo Seiko concerning the circumstances of sale adjustment (COS) to Foreign Market Value.]

Background

The fourth annual administrative review of the antidumping order at issue covered antifriction bearings entered during the period May 1, 1992, through April 30, 1993. Although the review concerned imports from eight countries, the judgments on appeal here concern only imports from Japan. Because the review was initiated prior to January 1, 1995, the applicable antidumping law and regulations are those that were in effect prior to the changes made by the Uruguay Round Amendments [*sic*—the correct word is "Agreements"] Act, Pub. L. No. 103-465, 108 Stat. 4809 (1994) (the "*URAA*"). See *URAA* § 291(a)(2), (b); *Cemex, S.A. v. United States*, 133 F.3d 897, 899 n.1 (Fed. Cir. 1998).

. . .

. . . NTN argues (i) that substantial evidence does not support Commerce's inclusion in its FMV [Foreign Market Value, *i.e.*, Normal Value] calculation of certain sales identified by NTN as sample sales and sporadic sales; [and] (ii) that Commerce unreasonably excluded from its calculation of FMV certain of NTN's home market sales to related parties . . . .

. . .

Discussion

. . .

II. NTN's Appeal

A. The Alleged Sample and Sporadic Sales

Under 19 U.S.C. § 1677b(a)(1)(A) (1988), FMV is the price "at which such or similar merchandise [*i.e.*, foreign like product] is sold or, in the absence of sales, offered for sale in the principal markets of the country from which exported, . . . in the ordinary course of trade for home consumption" (emphasis added). As defined by statute:

> The term "ordinary course of trade" means the conditions and practices which, for a reasonable time prior to the exportation of the merchandise which is the subject of an investigation, have been normal in the trade under consideration with respect to merchandise of the same class or kind.

19 U.S.C. § 1677(15) (1988).

In the *Final Results*, Commerce included as home market sales in the ordinary course of trade certain sales identified by NTN as sample sales and sales with sporadic sales histories. Commerce reasoned that NTN's mere designation of certain sales as sample sales did not satisfy its burden of proving that the sales were made outside of the ordinary course of trade. . . . Similarly, Commerce rejected NTN's claim that certain sales of small quantities of products with sporadic sales histories were outside of the ordinary course of trade, explaining that "such sales histories are typical of certain types of products." . . .

In *NSK I*, the Court of International Trade remanded to Commerce for a redetermination in light of this court's ruling in *NSK, Ltd. v. United States*, 115 F.3d 965, 973–75 (Fed. Cir. 1997), that samples given without consideration do not constitute sales under the antidumping statute. In its *Remand Results*, Commerce explained that certain of the transactions labeled by NTN as "sample and other similar transfers" were, in fact, transfers in which monetary consideration was paid for the bearings. Consequently, the Court of International Trade amended its prior ruling in *NSK I* to order Commerce only to exclude those transactions for which NTN received no consideration. Commerce complied with this instruction on remand and its determinations were sustained by *NSK II*.

We are not persuaded that substantial evidence does not support Commerce's determination that NTN failed to meet its burden to prove that the alleged sample and sporadic sales were sales outside of the ordinary course of trade. The evidence submitted by NTN consisted of its records indicating sales of samples under the term "SAMPLEH" and sporadic sales under the term "NORDCH." The sales designated by NTN as sporadic were simply those in which there were seven or less transactions in the total review period with three or less units per transaction. No evidence was submitted that the process of ordering or shipping these alleged sample or sporadic sales differed from "ordinary" sales. Nor was evidence submitted that any of these sales required, for example, unique engineering specifications. Moreover, no evidence was submitted that the alleged sample sales for which monetary consideration was paid, differed in any material respect, other than by their designation as "SAMPLEH", from "ordinary" sales of the same merchandise for monetary consideration. Thus, given our deferential standard of review, we cannot say that Commerce's finding of a failure of proof was unsupported by substantial evidence.

B. The Related Party Sales

Under 19 U.S.C. § 1677b(a)(3) (1988), Commerce may base FMV on related party transactions. To implement this statute, Commerce promulgated a regulation requiring importers to demonstrate that their sales to related parties are comparable in price to unrelated party transactions. Specifically, the regulation provides:

> If a producer or reseller sold such or similar merchandise to a person related as described in section 771(13) of the *Act*, the Secretary ordinarily will calculate foreign market value based on that sale only if satisfied that the price is comparable to the price at which the producer or reseller sold such or similar merchandise to a person not related to the seller. 19 C.F.R. § 353.45(a) (1993).

In the fourth annual administrative review, NTN responded to Section C of Commerce's questionnaire by listing its sales and annotating them with a "1" or a "2" to indicate whether they were, respectively, related or unrelated party sales. After conducting an "arm's-length test" using weighted average prices for each class of merchandise to determine whether the prices that NTN charged related parties were representative of market prices, Commerce excluded the reported related party sales of ball and cylindrical roller bearings due to the related party prices being lower than the corresponding unrelated party prices. . . . However, Commerce included the reported related party sales of spherical roller bearings due to the reported prices not being less than the corresponding prices to unrelated parties. . . . In *NSK I*, the

Court of International Trade affirmed, reasoning that NTN had presented no evidence that Commerce's test was unreasonable. . . .

On appeal, NTN argues that Commerce's use of weighted averages to compare related and unrelated party sales unreasonably distorted the comparison. To illustrate, NTN provides a hypothetical example in which the actual per unit price to both the related and unrelated parties is the same but, because different quantities are sold to the related and unrelated parties, the weighted average price for the goods sold to the unrelated party is higher.

In light of "the substantial discretion accorded Commerce when interpreting and applying its own regulations," *Torrington Co. v. United States*, 156 F.3d 1361, 1363 (Fed. Cir. 1998), we are unpersuaded that Commerce's use of weighted averages was unreasonable. . . . Commerce's methodology was reasonable because, without the use of weighting, small sales that might be "outliers" could be given undue weight in the calculation. Without employing such a weighting, Commerce's approach would be susceptible to the "perceived danger that a foreign manufacturer will sell to related companies in the home market at artificially low prices, thereby camouflaging true FMV and achieving a lower antidumping duty margin." *NEC Home Elecs., Inc. v. United States*, 54 F.3d 736, 739 (Fed. Cir. 1995). Moreover, although NTN's hypothetical suggests a potential anomaly of using a weighted average test, NTN has not provided evidence, nor even suggested, that such an anomalous result occurred here. Thus, NTN's hypothetical does not demonstrate that Commerce's test was unreasonable as applied to NTN's actual situation, only, at the very most, to circumstances not here present.

IV. Below-Cost Sales and 1984 *Southwest Florida Winter Vegetable* Case

What happens if home market sales of a foreign like product by a respondent producer-exporter are made at below the cost of production? Including them in the Normal Value calculation would distort the dumping margin, possibly even eliminating it. Such sales result in a lower Normal Value than otherwise would be the case if the product were sold on (at least) a cost-recovery basis. Not surprisingly, the U.S. AD statute contains a Cost Recovery Test: the DOC may disregard in its Normal Value computation sales made at less than the cost of production of the foreign like product, but must include in that computation sales made at prices that "permit recovery of all costs within a reasonable period of time."[2]

What if those sale prices are below the cost of production at the time the sales are made, but above the average cost of production for the entire POI or POR? Then,

---

2. 19 U.S.C. § 1677b(b)(2)(D).

those prices are considered cost-recoverable, and the DOC must include them in computing Normal Value.[3]

Southwest Florida Winter Vegetable Growers Association v. United States,

United States Court of International Trade,
584 F. Supp. 10 (1984)

CARMAN, JUDGE:

This case presents a novel issue of whether Commerce may disregard a substantial number of below cost sales, reflecting the perishable nature of produce, in determining whether sales were made at less than fair value under our antidumping laws. It is an important determination not only to the parties to this action but to the domestic and Mexican produce industries as a whole. . . .

Plaintiffs filed a petition with the United States Treasury Department (Treasury) . . . alleging certain fresh winter vegetables—tomatoes, squash, eggplant, bell peppers and cucumbers—were imported from Mexico . . . and were being sold in the United States at less than fair value. [At the time of filing, Treasury was an administering authority.] The petition of plaintiffs alleged that Southern Florida and the State of Sinaloa, Mexico, provided the source of virtually all fresh winter vegetables for markets in the United States and that Nogales, Arizona, was the point of importation for over 95 percent of all winter vegetables from Mexico.

. . . Treasury issued . . . a *Tentative Determination of Sales at Not Less Than Fair Value.* . . . Subsequently, the antidumping investigation was transferred to Commerce. . . . Treasury's preliminary negative determination was treated as though it had been issued by Commerce. . . .

. . . Commerce issued a *Final Determination of Sales at Not Less Than Fair Value.*

. . .

. . . Plaintiffs' contentions in essence are: (1) Commerce erred in using the third country sales methodology rather than the constructed value methodology in determining foreign market value because a substantial number of third country sales at below cost existed making the valuation inaccurate; [and] (2) Commerce improperly refused to disregard a substantial amount of below cost sales . . . . [Omitted are the Plaintiffs' contentions regarding the DOC's adjustments and use of regression analysis.]

Defendant has responded to plaintiffs' arguments, noting: (1) the *1979 Act* [*i.e.,* the *Trade Agreements Act of 1979,* which implemented the Tokyo Round agreements] establishes a general preference for the use of third country sales over constructed

---

3. For a CIT case discussing and applying this Cost Recovery Test, resulting in a reduction of the AD duty rate from 7.64% to 5.38%, see *Dongbu Steel Co., Ltd. v. United States*, Number 14-0098 (Slip Opinion 15-99, 31 August 2015, and Slip Opinion 15-43, 5 May 2015).

value; [and] (2) the decision to include up to 50 percent below cost sales is supported by uncontroverted evidence and is authorized by statute. . . .

. . .

I. Methodology Employed

To determine whether sales at less than fair value occurred, Commerce had to calculate the "fair value" of the subject merchandise pursuant to the procedures specified for determining foreign market value. Three methods are available for this calculation: (1) the sales price of the merchandise in the country of export (home market sales), (2) the sales price of the merchandise in a country other than the United States (third country sales), or, (3) the "constructed value" of the merchandise (sum of costs for material, fabrication, general expenses and profit).

Before 1979, the third country sales methodology instead of constructed value methodology was required by statute where the home market sales methodology was not available. . . . Although the mandatory preference for third country sales is no longer required, the legislative history and relevant regulations indicate, nevertheless, a preference for third country sales where there is adequate confirmation subject to timely verification. . . . The criteria employed in selecting the third country sales methodology are in order of significance: similarity of product, volume of sales, and similarity of market from an organizational and development point of view. . . .

If Commerce is unable to establish foreign market value based on home market prices (*e.g.*, where there is no home market) or upon third country sales (*e.g.*, where there is inadequate information that can be verified within the time required), then the constructed value methodology may be employed.

In this case, the home market sales methodology was not employed because an insufficient domestic Mexican market existed for fresh winter vegetables. Commerce utilized the third country (Canada) sales method of comparison instead of the constructed value method noting the general preference for third country sales and its greater accuracy in the case at hand. Furthermore, as noted by Commerce, use of constructed value would be wholly unsuitable to the economic realities presented in this case. A principal characteristic of the fresh winter vegetable market is wide price fluctuations, both within a day and over the season. As the Commerce determination reflects, it is a necessary practice for many individual sales to be below the average cost of production. Profitability depends on sales over the course of a season. The use of a price arrived at by constructed value would necessarily give the appearance of dumping even though sellers would be acting in a normal, indeed in a necessary, manner in light of industry demands. Thus, the constructed value methodology is inappropriate because it would require finding that an economically necessary business practice is unfair. As the Senate Report noted: "[T]hird country prices will normally be preferred over constructed value if presented in a timely manner and if adequate to establish foreign market value." . . .

Plaintiffs argue that third country price data in this case is inadequate for the fair value comparison because of the presence of price volatility and the existence of a significant number of sales below the cost of production. This court cannot agree.

First, the proportion of Canadian sales to United States sales (*i.e.*, Canadian sales are approximately 20 percent of United States sales) affords an adequate basis for comparison in using third country sales and is within established administrative guidelines. Second, plaintiffs conceded in their administrative petition that the two markets are almost identical. And third, the record reflects substantial evidence to support the conclusion of price equality.

Furthermore, plaintiffs' contention that constructed value should have been utilized because (1) some growers had too few or no Canadian sales; (2) on some days, growers had sales to the United States, but none to Canada; and, (3) some growers had insufficient above-cost sales to Canada, is without merit. There is no support for the proposition that Commerce was required to utilize constructed value for those transactions that could not be matched with United States transactions for the same grower's product, size and day.

Based on the general preference for the use of third country sales over constructed value, and the existence of adequate data for third country sales, this court cannot find Commerce erred in its use of this methodology.

II. Treatment of Below Cost Sales

. . . Commerce concluded that "it would be appropriate to disregard below-cost Canadian sales only if such sales constituted 50 percent or more of a grower's total sales to Canada of the type of produce under consideration." . . . Plaintiffs argue this 50 percent benchmark resulted in the erroneous consideration of a significant number of below cost sales in the determination by Commerce of foreign market value. Neither the statute nor its legislative history, however, supports this contention by plaintiffs.

. . . Commerce is required to disregard below cost sales only when they have been made in substantial quantities over an extended period of time, and are not at prices that permit recovery of all costs within a reasonable period of time in the normal course of trade. As legislative history reflects, "[s]tandards would not require the disregarding of below-cost sales in every instance, for under normal business in both foreign countries and the United States, it is frequently necessary to sell obsolete or end-of-model year merchandise at less than cost . . . . [I]nfrequent sales at less than cost, or sales prices which will permit recovery of all costs based upon anticipated sales volume over a reasonable period of time would not be disregarded." . . .

Commerce found that the fresh winter vegetable markets, in contrast to markets for industrial products or agricultural products with a relatively longer shelf life, normally experience below cost sales, and such sales are common and expected.

Commerce determined that Mexican producers do not have the ability to control their short-term output and cannot store their products. They look to make profits over the season as a whole, and do not expect to recover full costs on individual sales. The record reflects that it is not uncommon for some sales by foreign and domestic producers of fresh winter vegetables to be as much as 50 percent below the cost of production.

In short, the statute permits the consideration of below cost sales made in the normal course of trade at prices that permit full cost recovery within a reasonable period of time, and there is substantial evidence in the administrative record to support Commerce's determination that below cost sales in this case up to 50 percent were made in the normal course of trade and at prices that permit full cost recovery within a reasonable period of time. Commerce, therefore, properly regarded the below cost sales in its determination of foreign market value.

V. Comparing Merchandise and 1997 *NTN Bearing* Case

NTN Bearing Corporation of America v. United States,

United States Court of Appeals for the Federal Circuit,
127 F.3d 1061–65 (1997)

RADER, CIRCUIT JUDGE:

. . . NTN Bearing Corporation of America, American NTN Bearing Manufacturing Corporation, and NTN Corporation (collectively, NTN) dispute [the Department of] Commerce's calculation of the fair market value for TRBs [tapered roller bearings]. Because substantial evidence supports Commerce's actions, this court affirms.

I

. . . TRBs are a type of antifriction bearing made up of an inner ring (cone) and an outer ring (cup). Cups and cones sell either individually or as a preassembled "set."

Commerce's fundamental task in an antidumping investigation is to compare the United States price of imported merchandise with the value of "such or similar merchandise" [*i.e.*, foreign like product] in the [exporter's] home market, 19 U.S.C. § 1677 (16) (1988), and assess a duty, known as a dumping margin, for any deficiency. [As the Court explained in a footnote: "This section was amended on December 8, 1994. As both Commerce's administrative review and the Court of International Trade's adjudicatory proceeding were conducted under the statute as written prior to the 1994 amendment, we will refer to the statute in its pre-amended form. The amendment does not affect the outcome in this case."] When Commerce identifies "such" or identical home market merchandise, the comparison between matched goods is easy and accurate. Without identical goods for value comparison, Commerce must find "similar" home market merchandise to make a proper comparison with the imports.

Commerce has established methods to determine the constructed value of "similar" merchandise in the home market. . . . First, Commerce "splits" sales of TRB sets sold in Japan into their component cups and cones. Next, Commerce compares the cups and cones with their imported counterparts using five physical criteria: (1) inner ring bore (inside diameter); (2) outer ring diameter; (3) width; (4) load rating; and (5) "Y", factor (measure of thrust load capability). Finally, Commerce uses a "sum of deviations" method, coupled with a twenty percent difference-in-merchandise test, to find the best matching TRB model.

After assessment of duties, NTN appealed to the Court of International Trade challenging eleven actions by Commerce . . . . In April 1996, the trial court denied in all respects NTN's motion for judgment on the agency record. *NTN Bearing Corp. of Am. v. United States*, 924 F. Supp. 200 (Ct. Int'l Trade 1996). Specifically, the Court of International Trade held that Commerce's set-splitting method prevents an importer from manipulating home market calculations.

Conceding that Commerce may split sets to calculate fair market value, NTN raises only one issue on appeal, namely, the judgment upholding Commerce's splitting of certain "unsplittable" TRB sets. NTN claims that because it never separately sells the cups and cones of certain bearing models—TRB units, TRB double row models, TRB thrust bearings, TRB flanged bearings, and TRB high precision models—Commerce cannot calculate fair market value based on the constituent parts of these bearings. NTN contends that Commerce exceeded its discretion by applying its setsplitting methodology to these unsplittable sets.

II

. . .

. . . [T]he relevant inquiry is whether the trial Court properly sustained Commerce's use of its set-splitting method to split "unsplittable" sets in arriving at a value for similar merchandise." The *Tariff Act of 1930*, as amended . . . broadly defines the phrase "such or similar" as applied to goods for comparison under the antidumping test. Because it does not specify a method for matching a U.S. product with a suitable home-market product, the *Act* has implicitly authorized Commerce to choose a way to identify "such or similar" merchandise. . . .

. . .

This Court has previously upheld Commerce's set-splitting and sum of deviations methods to identify "such or similar" goods for the antidumping comparison. *See, e.g.,* id. at 1204 [*i.e., Koyo Seiko Co. v. United States*, 66 F.3d 1204 (Fed. Cir. 1995)]. These earlier decisions have stressed that Commerce possesses discretion to calculate the fair market value based upon a "close-as-possible" matching of physical characteristics of separate cups and cones. This method does not require an identical match of home market and imported cups and cones. Rather, Commerce remains within its discretion when it strives to find price data for closely analogous bearing components.

The five unsplittable sets at issue always sell as sets in the Japanese market. However, as part of its efforts to match imported components with similar goods sold in the home market, Commerce split the Japanese market sets into their component cups and cones. Commerce then performed a critical physical analysis on each cup and cone, placing the Japanese components into a "pool" of potential "such or similar" home market TRB cups and cones. Commerce used this pool in its "sum of the deviations" methodology and twenty percent difference-in-merchandise test to determine the best matching TRB model components in Japan to compare with the imported cups and cones.

Because it was unable to identify "such" or identical home market goods after a reasonable search for a match to the imported parts, Commerce reasonably applied its splitting methodology to unsplittable sets sold in the home market to identify "similar" goods for a value comparison. This reasonable method was, therefore, in accord with the statute. . . . The antidumping act simply does not require the sale of "similar" merchandise in the same manner in both the United States and home markets. Likewise, the act does not prohibit the separation of unsplittable sets. (In fact, unsplittable sets is a bit of a misnomer. This term includes sets sold in Japan that are easily, but not currently, split, and sets that are assembled into housings that make physical splitting into components difficult.) Acceptance of NTN's argument that Commerce may not split into components products sold only as sets in the home market would allow importers to circumvent the law. An importer could manipulate Commerce's determinations by depriving it of a pool of similar products sold in the home market with which it could compare the imported goods. In the absence of a statutory prohibition against splitting these sets, Commerce's actions are reasonable.

Thus, the Court of International Trade properly upheld Commerce's actions as supported by substantial evidence and in accordance with law.

Chapter 7

Dumping Margin Calculation Issues (Continued): Proxies for Normal Value[1]

I. Choice of Proxy between Third Country Price and Constructed Value, and 1995 *Floral Trade Council* Case

Floral Trade Council v. the United States,

United States Court of Appeals for the Federal Circuit,
74 F.3d 1200–04 (1995)

NIES, CIRCUIT JUDGE:

. . .

Background

This court action commenced with FTC's [*i.e.*, plaintiff-petitioner Floral Trade Council] and Asocolflores's [*i.e.*, defendant-respondent *Asociacion Colombiana De Exportadores de Flores* (*Asocolflores*)] challenge to the final results of an International Trade Administration (ITA) antidumping duty review respecting certain fresh cut flowers from Colombia. 55 Fed. Reg. 20,491 (1990). FTC contested, *inter alia*, ITA's use of constructed value for the foreign market value (*i.e.*, Normal Value) as opposed to using third country prices. *Asocolflores* objected, *inter alia*, to ITA's selection of monthly instead of annual average U.S. prices.

The trial court upheld ITA's use of constructed value, finding reasonable ITA's interpretation of its governing statute that third country prices may be abandoned if there is an adequate factual basis in the record for doing so. Further, that court credited the factors underlying the ITA conclusion that using constructed value was proper because reliance on European prices for third country prices would produce misleading results due to differences between the floral markets in Europe and the United States. The trial court was also persuaded that monthly averaging of U.S. prices was an appropriate compromise, whereas annual averaging would

---

1. Documents References:
   (1) *Havana (ITO) Charter* Article 34
   (2) GATT Article VI
   (3) WTO *Antidumping Agreement* Articles 1–2

mask dumping. *Floral Trade Council v. United States*, 15 C.I.T. 497, 775 F. Supp. 1492, 1497, 1500 (Ct. Int'l Trade 1991). After remand on grounds not pertinent to this appeal, judgment was entered upholding ITA's review and the parties appealed to this Court. . . .

Analysis

The ITA determinations under review must be upheld unless the determinations are "unsupported by substantial evidence on the record, or otherwise not in accordance with law." *Tariff Act of 1930*, § 516A, 19 U.S.C. § 1516a(b)(1)(B) (1988); *Rhone Poulenc, Inc. v. United States*, 899 F.2d 1185, 1189, 8 Fed. Cir. (T) 61, 65 (Fed. Cir. 1990). Substantial evidence "means such relevant evidence as a reasonable mind might accept as adequate to support a conclusion." *Matsushita Elec. Indus. v. United States*, 750 F.2d 927, 933 (Fed. Cir. 1984) (citing *Universal Camera Corp. v. NLRB*, 340 U.S. 474, 477 . . . (1951)). Moreover, under traditional principles of judicial deference to agency interpretation of statutes the agency administers, our review questions whether the agency's interpretation is reasonable. *Chevron U.S.A. v. Natural Resources Defense Council*, 467 U.S. 837, 844 . . . (1984) . . . .

I

Constructed Value

On appeal, FTC argues that ITA unlawfully abandoned third-country prices as the basis for foreign market value. Citing statutes and regulations expressing a preference for third-country prices, FTC contends that ITA could not depart from that preference in this case. FTC asserts that verified third country prices were available and that no unusual facts justified ITA's rejection of them.

The *Tariff Act of 1930*, as amended in 1979, directs ITA to determine the foreign market value based on (1) the price at which similar merchandise is sold in the country from which exported (here Colombia); or (2) if the exporter's home market consumption is low or nonexistent, then the price at which the merchandise is sold for exportation to a third country. 19 U.S.C. § 1677b(a)(1). ITA's own regulations announce a clear preference for third country prices if adequate and verifiable information is available. . . . However, the statute also gives ITA the discretion to construct a value when home market prices cannot be determined. . . .

. . . ITA determined that it could not determine the price under the first statutory directive and, due to extraordinary circumstances, it chose to use a constructed value rather than third country prices. ITA reasoned that the United States and European markets are not positively correlated and that this negative correlation could mask dumping in certain instances or exaggerate it in others. First, ITA determined that the European market for flowers is mature with a constant demand, whereas the United States market exhibits extreme volatility due to sporadic gift-giving. Second, Colombian growers are not a constant participant in the European flower auction houses and, therefore, Colombian growers sell flowers in Europe only occasionally. Third, European and United States holidays often do not coincide, resulting in different peak periods in the two markets. Last, Colombians plan their production cycles on the U.S. market and, therefore, sell excess flowers in markets where they did not necessarily plan to sell, which adds an element of chance to prices obtained for those flowers.

FTC takes issue with ITA's exercise of discretion in choosing to use a constructed value rather than using third country prices. We are unpersuaded of factual or legal error in ITA's selection of constructed value or of an abuse of discretion. We find no restriction either in the statute or the regulations limiting use of constructed value to situations where verified information is not available for third country prices. Further, ITA's explanation for rejecting such prices was reasonable.

FTC also attacks the evidence underlying the factors on which ITA relied. Both *Asocolflores* and the government amply demonstrate that substantial evidence exists to support ITA's findings. More than ten years ago, we faced a similar evidentiary challenge and stated:

> That [FTC] can point to evidence which detracts from the evidence which supports the [ITA's] decision and can hypothesize a reasonable basis for a contrary determination is neither surprising nor persuasive. It is not the function of a court to decide that, were it the [ITA], it would have made the same decision on the basis of the evidence. Our role is limited to deciding whether the [ITA's] decision is "unsupported by substantial evidence on the record, or otherwise not in accordance with law."

Matsushita Elec., 750 F.2d at 936. "The possibility of drawing two inconsistent conclusions from the evidence does not prevent an administrative agency's finding from being supported by substantial evidence." *Id.* at 933 (quoting *Consolo v. Federal Maritime Comm'n*, 383 U.S. 607, 619–20 . . . (1966)). Here, FTC asks us to accept its view of the facts, which we decline to do.

. . . [W]e affirm ITA's use of constructed value on the facts of this case.

II

Monthly Averaging

Asocolflores's appeal challenges ITA's selection of monthly, instead of annual, average U.S. prices as unsupported by substantial evidence. Asserting that ITA's reasoning for selecting a monthly average is merely speculative, *Asocolflores* states that ITA's choice is not based on any evidence and is inadequate as a matter of law. *Asocolflores* notes that ITA's internal analyses all support an annual averaging. Further, *Asocolflores* claims that the constructed value for foreign market value is based on an annual average, so that comparing monthly U.S. prices to a constructed annual value will necessarily establish dumping anytime the Colombian grower does not meet its average annual profit. With perishable flowers, growers must occasionally sell at a loss, but at other times the growers sell at a great profit, so that their annual profit balances the peaks and valleys of selling. Last, *Asocolflores* notes that ITA's reasoning for rejecting an annual average for U.S. prices directly contradicts its reasoning for rejecting third country prices for foreign market value.

The *Tariff Act* empowers ITA to use averaging in determining United States price. 19 U.S.C. § 1677f-1(b). The determination to select averages *rests exclusively* with the ITA if the averages are "representative of the transactions under investigation." *Id.* Because ITA has discretion to use averages, *Asocolflores's* challenge must be directed to whether the averages are "representative" of the transactions under investigation.

In its preliminary determination, ITA found averaging was necessary to account for perishability. Growers do not control when flowers will be sold nor the price at which they will be sold. With flowers having such a limited life span, growers cannot await a better market by warehousing nor may growers regulate production in the short term. Growers must sell what their plants produce when the plants produce. In its final determination rejecting economic reports submitted by the growers, ITA stated that annual averaging would mask dumping by balancing high prices in peak months with low prices in other months. ITA also rejected FTC's proposal to use a daily or weekly averaging because ITA wanted a long enough period to account for both distress and non-distress sale prices. Reasoning that flowers can last more than one week and that perishability is a function of variables other than merely time, ITA selected a monthly period for averaging.

The trial court noted: "No period accounts for the legitimate concerns of all parties. Monthly averaging is one acceptable compromise. ITA averaged over what it considered the shortest period possible to ensure that dumping was not obscured entirely, and at the same time, to account for as many perishability factors as possible." *Floral Trade Council*, 775 F. Supp. at 1500. The government argues in its brief that 19 U.S.C. § 1675(a)(2)(A) directs ITA to compare each entry of merchandise subject to the antidumping order, whereas *Asocolflores's* annual averaging would violate that mandate by masking individual instances of dumping. Under an annual averaging, dumping would only be found if the annual aggregate sales of a foreign seller were at less than fair value.

. . . [W]e agree with the government that an annual average would mask dumping related to individual sales. Although some dumping would also be masked under a monthly average, Commerce chose to use a monthly average as representative of the U.S. price to account for perishability of the flowers. Even *Asocolflores* admits that "in general, shorter averaging periods are preferable to longer averaging periods." Basing the U.S. price on an annual average in this market would completely eviscerate determining dumping on the statutorily mandated "each entry of merchandise." Yearly averaging is clearly not more "representative" of the U.S. price than monthly averaging in the circumstances of this case.

In sum, Asocolflores has not persuaded us that ITA abused its discretion, committed an error of law or made its determination of the amount of dumping unsupported by substantial evidence.

II. Taxes, Interest Expenses, and 1998
AIMCOR Case

Aimcor v. the United States,
United States Court of Appeals for the Federal Circuit,
141 F.3d 1098 (1998)

SCHALL, CIRCUIT JUDGE:

This antidumping action stems from the investigation of ferrosilicon imported from Brazil. [As the Court explains in a footnote, "[f]errosilicon is a ferroalloy produced by combining silicon and iron through smelting in a submerged-arc furnace." Its primary use is as an alloying agent in the production of steel and cast iron. Also, in the steel industry, it is used as a deoxidizer and a reducing agent, cast iron producers use it as an inoculant.] Plaintiffs/Cross-Appellants, AIMCOR, Alabama Silicon, Inc., American Alloys, Inc., Globe Metallurgical, Inc., and American Silicon Technologies (collectively "AIMCOR"), are United States ferrosilicon producers, manufacturers, or resellers. Defendant/Appellant, *Companhia Ferroligas Minas Gerais-Minasligas* ("*Minasligas*"), is a Brazilian producer and exporter of ferrosilicon. *Minasligas* appeals the decision of the United States Court of International Trade sustaining the determination of the International Trade Administration, United States Department of Commerce ("Commerce"), that *Minasligas* had sold ferrosilicon at less than fair value and imposing an antidumping order. See *AIMCOR v. United States*, 1996 Ct. Intl. Trade LEXIS 88, No. 94-03-00182, 1996 WL 276955, at *2 (Ct. Int'l Trade May 21, 1996). Specifically, *Minasligas* challenges the inclusion of Brazilian value-added taxes as part of the cost of materials in determining constructed value pursuant to 19 U.S.C.§ 1677b(e)(1)(A) (1988). See *AIMCOR, 1996 Ct. Intl. Trade LEXIS 88, 1996 WL 276955,* at *1. AIMCOR cross-appeals, challenging the interest rate used by Commerce to calculate *Minasligas*' imputed negative, United States credit expenses. We affirm.

[In a footnote, the Court observed the AD statutes were amended by the *1994 Act*, and this *Act* does not apply to investigations initiated before 1 January 1995. The investigation here commenced was initiated before that date, and all citations are to the 1988 edition of the U.S. Code.]

. . .

II

. . . [O]n January 12, 1993, AIMCOR; Silicon Metaltech Inc.; United Autoworkers of America Local 523; United Steelworkers of America Locals 12646, 2528, 5171, and 3081; and Oil, Chemical & Atomic Workers Local 389 (collectively "petitioners") petitioned Commerce, alleging that ferrosilicon from Brazil was being sold or was likely to be sold in the United States at less than fair value. . . . The petitions were filed on behalf of the United States industry and the employees producing, manufacturing, and reselling material like the product at issue. . . . The period of inquiry was from July 1 through December 31, 1992.... On August 16, 1993, Commerce issued its preliminary determination, finding dumping and suspending liquidation of ferrosilicon from Brazil. *Preliminary Determination of Sales at Less Than Fair Value: Ferrosilicon From Brazil*, 58 Fed. Reg. 43,323, 43,327 (Aug. 16, 1993) ("*Preliminary Determination*"). On January 6, 1994, Commerce issued its final determination, finding that *Minasligas* had not sold ferrosilicon at less than fair value. *Final Determination of Sales at Less Than Fair Value: Ferrosilicon From Brazil*, 59 Fed. Reg. 732, 739–40 (Jan. 6, 1994) ("*Final Determination*").

In making its *Final Determination*, Commerce based *Minasligas*' United States price on purchase price [*i.e.*, Export Price] because its ferrosilicon was sold to unrelated purchasers in the United States prior to importation and other circumstances did not indicate the exporter's sales price.... As far as foreign market value [*i.e.*, Normal Value] was concerned, since petitioners had alleged that *CBCC's* [*i.e.*, *Cia Brasileira Carbureto de Calcio*, a Brazilian exporter of ferrosilicon] and *Minasligas*' home market sales were made at less than the cost of production ("COP") and that foreign market value should be based on constructed value, Commerce initiated COP investigations of *CBCC* and *Minasligas* prior to making its Final Determination.... In a COP investigation, Commerce compares the cost of production of the goods at issue to home market sales.... [I]f Commerce determines that a sufficient quantity of home market sales were made at prices below the cost of production, Commerce bases foreign market value on constructed value. In making its Final Determination, Commerce determined that *CBCC's* and *Minasligas*' home market sales were viable bases for calculating foreign market value. In its *Final Determination*, it therefore did not base foreign market value upon constructed value....

[As the Court explains in footnotes, first, "[c]ost of production consists of the cost of materials and fabrication; selling, general, and administrative expenses; and inventory carrying costs." Second, "[g]enerally, if more than ninety percent of domestic sales are made at prices below the cost of production, Commerce will use constructed value as the basis for determining foreign market value. Third, Commerce used Constructed Value to set Foreign Market Value for one of *CBCC's* sales because data were insufficient to base foreign market value on home market sales in this instance."]

In conducting the COP investigations of *CBCC* and *Minasligas* and in arriving at its *Final Determination* that home market sales were viable bases for calculating foreign market value, Commerce determined that Brazil's economy was hyperinflationary during the period of inquiry. [In a footnote, the Court states "Commerce generally defines a hyperinflationary economy as one in which the annual inflation rate exceeds fifty percent, causing the value of the relevant currency to rapidly decline in relatively short periods of time."] ... Consequently, Commerce calculated monthly values for foreign market value, cost of production, and constructed value to eliminate the distortive effects of inflation.... In the COP investigations, Commerce included Brazilian value-added taxes as a cost of materials in the cost of production, for purposes of determining whether home market sales were made at prices above the cost of production. Commerce also included these taxes in calculating constructed value. . . . This decision to include the value-added taxes for purposes of the COP investigations was relevant to *CBCC* and *Minasligas* to the extent that it determined whether Commerce would base foreign market value on home market sales or constructed value.

However, in determining whether value-added taxes should be included in determining constructed value, if this method eventually was used to determine foreign market value, Commerce stated:

> When using [constructed value] as a surrogate for home market prices we must determine if in fact the entity under investigation is able to recover all of the taxes paid on inputs (raw materials) from its domestic sales of subject merchandise. If domestic sales of subject merchandise fully recover all of the domestic taxes paid on inputs, then these taxes would appropriately be excluded from the margin analysis. However, if the producer is not able to recover all input taxes from its sales of subject merchandise, then these actual costs must be reflected in the [Constructed Value].

Final Determination, 59 Fed. Reg. at 737 (citing *Camargo Correa Metais, S.A. v. United States*, 17 C.I.T. 897, 911 (1993)). This meant that value-added taxes would only be included in constructed value if the taxes paid on input materials were not fully recovered through the taxes collected on domestic sales. Since Commerce concluded in the *Final Determination* that *Minasligas'* home market sales were made at prices above the cost of production, the decision to include value-added taxes as a cost of materials in the COP investigations did not directly affect *Minasligas*. Since the foreign market value of *Minasligas'* goods was being based on home market sales, and not constructed value, the possibility of including the taxes in constructed value did not affect *Minasligas*. The possibility of including these taxes in determining constructed value was directly pertinent to *CBCC*, though, because Commerce was basing a portion of its foreign market value on constructed value. However, Commerce excluded the value-added taxes paid by *CBCC* on input materials from the cost of materials, and therefore constructed value, the reason being that these taxes were fully offset by taxes collected by *CBCC* on domestic sales of the subject merchandise. . . .

In determining foreign market value for *Minasligas*, Commerce made circumstances of sale adjustments for differences in *Minasligas'* credit expenses pursuant to 19 U.S.C. §1677b(a)(4)(B) and 19 C.F.R. §353.56(a) (1997). . . . Commerce made such adjustments for finance charges, warehousing, and quality control expenses. . . . Commerce also imputed negative credit expenses to offset the interest revenue *Minasligas* could earn on advance payments received by *Minasligas* prior to shipping export orders, as more fully explained below. . . .

In response to comments alleging errors in connection with the *Final Determination*, Commerce issued an amended final determination on February 23, 1994. *Notice of Amended Final Determination of Sales at Less Than Fair Value: Ferrosilicon*

From Brazil, 59 Fed. Reg. 8598 (Feb. 23, 1994) ("*Amended Final Determination*"). Commerce determined that it had erred in its COP investigations and revised its analysis, using constructed value as the measure of foreign market value for *CBCC's* and *Minasligas'* ferrosilicon. . . . At this time, Commerce's previous decision to include value-added taxes paid on input materials as a cost of materials in determining constructed value, if not fully offset by taxes collected on domestic sales, became directly applicable to *Minasligas* because the foreign market value of its ferrosilicon was now being calculated using constructed value, rather than home market sales. However, as with *CBCC*, Commerce determined that *Minasligas* had fully recovered the value-added taxes paid on input materials through taxes collected on domestic sales. . . . Therefore, Commerce did not include these value-added taxes in the cost of materials in calculating constructed value. . . . Correcting its errors, Commerce determined that *Minasligas* had sold ferrosilicon at less than fair value. . . .

Two Brazilian value-added taxes are at issue in this appeal: (1) the *imposto sobre produtos industrializados* ("*IPI*"), and (2) the *imposto sobre circulacao de mercadorias e servicos* ("*ICMS*"). The *IPI* is a value-added *ad valorem* excise tax, levied at varying rates on manufactured products. The *ICMS* is a value-added sales and service tax levied on sales or the physical movement of goods, freight, transportation and communications services, and electric energy. Most products exported from Brazil are exempt from both taxes. For each tax, a manufacturer offsets taxes paid by it on monthly purchases of raw materials or component parts against taxes collected by it from domestic sales of manufactured products.

Minasligas documents taxes paid on raw materials used in its production process and taxes collected from its sales of finished products in separate accounting ledgers. These ledgers are balanced each month to determine the amount of tax owed to the Brazilian government. If taxes collected from domestic sales exceed the taxes paid on raw materials, *Minasligas* forwards the excess to the Brazilian government. If taxes paid on raw materials exceed the taxes collected from domestic sales, *Minasligas* carries a tax credit forward to the following month and makes no payment to the Brazilian government.

In making its determination that *Minasligas* had made sales at less than fair value, Commerce nevertheless rejected the petitioners' claims that it had erroneously imputed negative credit expenses to *Minasligas* and had incorrectly used a *cruzeiro*-denominated interest rate to calculate those credits. [The *cruzeiro* is a Brazilian currency unit.] . . . The petitioners had sought to eliminate the imputed negative credit expenses, which had the effect of lowering foreign market value, and therefore, the dumping margin. The petitioners had also challenged the use of a *cruzeiro*-denominated interest rate in calculating imputed negative credit expenses, their underlying rationale being that an alternative interest rate would lower the negative credit expenses, thereby increasing foreign market value and the dumping margin.

Negative credit expenses are explained as follows: *Minasligas* financed United States sales of ferrosilicon through the use of United States advance exchange contracts ("AECs"). Under the AECs, which were between *Minasligas* and a bank, the bank would advance *Minasligas* a portion of the value of new export contracts, prior to actual execution of the contract. Commerce determined that *Minasligas* was earning "negative credit expenses" by receiving these advance payments before shipping the subject ferrosilicon.

Commerce's established practice is to calculate credit expenses from the date of shipment to the date payment is received from the customer. . . . *Minasligas* incurred negative credit expenses (or earned credit revenue) from the United States AECs because the advances were received prior to shipment of the ferrosilicon by *Minasligas* and prior to actual payment by the customer. This allowed *Minasligas* to use the money prior to shipment of the ferrosilicon or payment by the customer. *Id.* Commerce determined that the date *Minasligas* received advanced funds was equivalent to receipt of payment from the customer. . . . Commerce computed the imputed negative credit expenses by multiplying the time between receipt of the AEC advances by *Minasligas* and the actual shipment of the ferrosilicon by *Minasligas* by a *cruzeiro*-denominated interest rate.

[In footnotes, the Court explains, first:

> A company effectively extends credit to purchasers when it ships merchandise prior to payment, *i.e.*, "during this period, the seller incurs additional expenses through the process of borrowing funds pending receipt of payment or through the fact that funds are tied up due to the existence of accounts receivable." ANTIDUMPING MANUAL, ch. 8, at 18. Commerce uses credit expenses to account for these extensions of credit. Since *Minasligas* received payment prior to shipment, in computing foreign market value, Commerce imputed a negative credit expense, as part of a circumstances of sale adjustment, to account for the interest *Minasligas* could earn on this money between receiving the advance and the actual shipment of the ferrosilicon. See id. at 19. As the Court of International Trade explained, "payment received prior to shipment provides an additional transactional benefit to the seller." *AIMCOR*, 19 C.I.T. 966, 1995 WL 431186, at *6.

Second, "Commerce adds . . . credit expenses to constructed value, thus leading to a higher foreign market value that accounts for the cost of extending credit to purchasers and carrying accounts receivable. This higher foreign market value increases the possibility of a dumping determination and the size of any dumping margin." Third, "[w]hen Commerce adds imputed negative credit expenses to constructed value, a lower foreign market value results, thus reducing the possibility of a dumping determination and the size of any dumping margin."]

III

AIMCOR and *Minasligas* appealed to the Court of International Trade . . . challenging various aspects of the *Final Determination* and the *Amended Final Determination* and seeking judgment upon the agency record . . . . AIMCOR asserted that Commerce had erred in excluding Brazilian value-added taxes from the cost of materials in determining constructed value because these taxes were not remitted or refunded upon exportation of the merchandise within the meaning of 19 U.S.C.§ 1677b(e)(1)(A). . . . *Minasligas* conceded that the *IPI* and *ICMS* value-added taxes were not remitted or refunded upon exportation of the subject ferrosilicon. . . . Noting that the statute requires that constructed value include the cost of materials "at a time preceding the date of exportation of the merchandise," 19 U.S.C. § 1677b(e)(1)(A), the court held that *Minasligas* might be able to show that the value-added taxes paid on input materials did not in fact constitute a cost of materials because these taxes were fully offset by taxes collected on domestic sales prior to exportation of the subject merchandise. . . . The court remanded for Commerce to determine if *Minasligas* had fully recovered value-added taxes paid on inputs prior to exportation of the subject ferrosilicon. . . .

At the same time, the court upheld Commerce's COP analysis. . . . The court also upheld Commerce's analysis of negative credit expenses, resulting from the AECs, but remanded with instructions that Commerce apply a United States dollar-denominated interest rate to the amounts at issue, rather than a Brazilian *cruzeiro*-denominated interest rate. . . .

Commerce issued its final remand determination on January 17, 1996, after comment from the parties. *Final Redetermination of Remand in Ferrosilicon from Brazil*, at 1 ("*Final Remand Determination*"). In the *Final Remand Determination*, Commerce included value-added taxes, the *IPI* and *ICMS*, as a cost of production in calculating constructed value because *Minasligas* could not show that the taxes were fully recovered prior to exportation. . . . Commerce required a sale-specific correlation between taxes paid on input materials and taxes recovered on the products produced from those materials:

> During the remand proceeding, [Commerce] requested that *Minasligas* and *CBCC* provide, for each U.S. sale, the date and amount of the *ICMS* and *IPI* taxes paid on the material inputs used in the production of merchandise sold to the United States, and evidence that these specific taxes were completely recovered prior to exportation for each U.S. sale. However, because each U.S. sale was exported on a unique date, the only way to determine, on a sale-specific basis, whether the taxes paid on the inputs used to produce the merchandise were recovered prior to exportation is to track the specific taxes paid for each input and measure whether these taxes were fully recouped by domestic sales revenue. The parties failed to submit this data. Indeed, they said they were unable to provide this data. The only information they did provide was monthly totals of taxes paid and collected. It is not possible to determine from this data whether the taxes paid on inputs were fully recovered. Accordingly, we find insufficient evidence to conclude that these taxes were fully recovered.

. . . In the *Final Remand Determination*, Commerce also announced that it was revising its general policy concerning Brazilian value-added taxes, stating that it should have included those taxes in its earlier determinations because the taxes were not remitted or refunded prior to exportation, as required by 19 U.S.C. § 1677b(e) (1)(A). . . . Under its revised policy, Commerce assumes that the taxes paid on input materials are recouped by being included in the price of the exported products. Commerce stated its intention to include Brazilian value-added taxes as a cost of materials in constructed value in future investigations unless these taxes are remitted or refunded upon exportation. . . .

In the *Final Remand Determination*, Commerce rejected the use of United States dollar-denominated interest rates from the AECs as evidence of the rate at which *Minasligas* could borrow money. . . . Commerce refused to use these interest rates in computing the negative credit expenses because *Minasligas* received the advances, pursuant to the AECs, in *cruzeiros*. [In a footnote, the Court explained "Commerce normally uses United States interest rates for calculating imputed credit expenses when a respondent has actual United States dollar borrowings. . . . Since *Minasligas* received *cruzeiros* pursuant to the AECs, Commerce determined that the AECs did not constitute United States dollar borrowings."] . . . Instead, Commerce used an aircraft lease with an interest rate denominated in United States dollars to determine the interest rate for calculating the negative credit expenses because this was *Minasligas*' only evidence of United States dollar borrowings and it reflected the credit terms *Minasligas* would encounter when borrowing United States dollars. [The Court observed in a footnote "the actual transaction referred to was the financing of an aircraft purchase," "[t]he interest rate in this 'lease' was the interest rate associated with the loan to finance the aircraft purchase," and "[f]or consistency, we refer to the financing agreement as the 'aircraft lease.'"] . . .

On May 21, 1996, the Court of International Trade ruled on the *Final Remand Determination*. In so doing, the court sustained Commerce's treatment of the value-added taxes. *AIMCOR, 1996 Ct. Intl. Trade LEXIS 88, 1996 WL 276955*, at *1. The court held that *Minasligas* had failed to carry its burden of proving that its pre-exportation cost of materials did not include value-added taxes. . . . The court also held that Commerce's decision to use the aircraft lease as evidence of *Minasligas*' United States dollar-denominated interest rate for purposes of recalculating the negative credit expenses was rational and well within Commerce's discretion. . . . The court rejected AIMCOR's contention that the interest rate in the aircraft lease was not short-term. [In a footnote, the Court explains "[a] short-term borrowing rate is generally used as the interest rate for imputed credit expenses because this rate is most suited for the short-term extension of credit between a buyer and a purchaser."] . . . Since AIMCOR failed to raise before Commerce the issue of whether the chosen interest rate was annual or monthly, the court refused to address this contention by AIMCOR. . . .

Minasligas appeals to us challenging the inclusion of value-added taxes as a cost of materials in calculating constructed value. AIMCOR cross appeals challenging Commerce's use of the aircraft lease to determine the United States dollar-denominated interest rate applicable to the negative credit expenses. . . .

Discussion

. . .

III

Commerce included the *IPI* and *ICMS* value-added taxes, paid by *Minasligas* on input materials, as a cost of materials in calculating constructed value. . . . *Minasligas* argues that this was error because these taxes were fully recovered through taxes collected on domestic sales. AIMCOR and the government support Commerce's decision, claiming that the taxes were not remitted or refunded prior to exportation, as required by 19 U.S.C. § 1677b(e)(1)(A), and arguing alternatively that *Minasligas* failed to show that taxes paid on inputs were fully recovered prior to exportation.

Under 19 U.S.C. § 1677b(e)(1)(A), in determining constructed value, "any internal tax applicable in the country of exportation directly to such materials or their disposition, but remitted or refunded upon the exportation of the article in the production of which such materials are used" is excluded from the "cost of materials" component of constructed value. Words in a statute are deemed to have their ordinary meaning. . . . "Refund" means "to give or put back . . . to return (money) in restitution, repayment, or balancing of accounts," and "remit" means "to let go back, send back." WEBSTER'S THIRD NEW INTERNATIONAL DICTIONARY 1910, 1920 (1986). It is undisputed that the *IPI* and *ICMS* taxes are not remitted or refunded upon exportation within the meaning of the statute. . . . In other words, these taxes are not paid back to *Minasligas* upon exportation of the ferrosilicon produced from the raw materials on which *Minasligas* paid taxes. Instead, as discussed above, *Minasligas* maintains ledgers in which it records on a running basis taxes it pays and collects. Then, each month, it "settles up" with the Brazilian government.

Commerce's position in the *Final Determination* was that "if in fact the entity under investigation is able to recover all of the taxes paid on inputs (raw materials) from its domestic sales of subject merchandise . . . then these taxes would appropriately be excluded from the margin analysis." . . . The Court of International Trade concurred, stating, "[A] respondent that has fully recovered value-added taxes upon input costs prior to exportation, has not in fact incurred the value-added tax as a 'cost of materials.'" . . .

Using this interpretation, Commerce gave *Minasligas* the opportunity, during the remand proceedings, to provide evidence that the taxes paid on inputs were recovered prior to exportation through taxes collected on domestic sales of the merchandise produced from those inputs. . . . This was consistent with *Camargo*, in which Commerce was to develop a method to account for the economic reality that taxes paid on inputs are not a cost of materials if fully recovered through taxes collected on domestic sales. . . . In this case, Commerce sought from *Minasligas* a sale-specific correspondence between the taxes paid on input materials (raw materials) and the taxes collected on the sale of the product (ferrosilicon) produced from those inputs. . . .

The only evidence *Minasligas* produced on remand consisted of monthly totals of value-added taxes collected and paid. . . . While *Minasligas'* evidence, two tax ledgers containing taxes paid and taxes collected, is regularly inspected by the Brazilian government and conforms to Brazil's generally accepted accounting principles, this evidence is insufficient to show that *Minasligas* fully recovered the value-added taxes prior to exportation. *Minasligas* admitted that it was unable to provide the type of sale-specific correspondence between taxes paid on inputs and taxes collected on domestic sales of the products produced from those inputs that Commerce sought. . . . Even the monthly totals of taxes paid on input materials and taxes collected on domestic sales of finished products did not show that the value-added taxes were fully recovered. We agree with the Court of International Trade that *Minasligas* failed to meet its burden of proving that value-added taxes were fully recovered and that its pre-exportation cost of materials did not include value-added taxes. . . .

Minasligas argues that Commerce effectively denied it the opportunity to prove that the value-added taxes were fully recovered prior to exportation. In the *Final Remand Determination*, Commerce announced that, in future investigations, it would include Brazilian value-added taxes as a cost of materials in calculating constructed value unless the taxes were "remitted or refunded upon exportation," as expressly stated in 19 U.S.C. § 1677b(e)(1)(A). . . . *Minasligas* argues that Commerce, in effect, applied this construction of the statute to it. It claims that because ferrosilicon is produced through a continuous process where raw materials are continuously loaded into electric furnaces to produce a liquid product it is not possible to provide the sale-specific correspondence Commerce sought. We reject this argument. Commerce gave *Minasligas* the opportunity to show that value-added taxes were fully recovered prior to exportation. Even in a continuous process, such as the production of ferrosilicon, we believe it is possible to maintain records that show to some degree that taxes paid on input materials are offset by taxes collected from the domestic sale of products produced from those materials. Essentially, *Minasligas* is arguing that since generally accepted accounting principles in Brazil do not require these sale-specific records, it should not be faulted for not having the records. We cannot agree. The failure to track the taxes on input materials and the taxes recovered from the sale of the merchandise produced from those materials rests solely with *Minasligas*. *Minasligas* had a meaningful opportunity to present evidence, and the evidence it presented was insufficient.

We decline to address whether we would accept the interpretation of 19 U.S.C. § 1677b(e)(1)(A) announced by Commerce in its final remand determination. This interpretation was not applied to *Minasligas* in this case and is not properly before this court. Any statement on this future methodology would constitute an advisory opinion, which we decline to provide. We simply hold that, in this case, the Court of International Trade correctly sustained Commerce's methodology and inclusion of the *IPI* and *ICMS* value-added taxes in the cost of materials in calculating constructed value.

IV

. . . Commerce imputed negative, United States credit expenses to *Minasligas* to account for its receiving payment, prior to shipment of the subject ferrosilicon, pursuant to the AECs. . . . These negative credit expenses account for the additional benefits the seller receives from obtaining payment prior to shipment. . . . In this case, the negative credit expenses were used to offset credit expenses in determining foreign market value. [In a footnote, the Court states "[c]redit expenses are the costs associated with carrying accounts receivable on the books and the expenses related to extending credit to purchasers for the interim between shipment and payment," and "Commerce accounts for these credit expenses by making circumstances of sale adjustments to foreign market value."] . . . Commerce originally used a *cruzeiro*-denominated interest rate to calculate the negative credit expenses, but switched to a United States dollar-denominated rate in the *Final Remand Determination*, as instructed by the Court of International Trade. . . . Commerce rejected the interest rates stated in the AECs and based its calculations on the interest rate in an aircraft lease submitted by *Minasligas*. . . . In its cross-appeal, AIMCOR argues that Commerce incorrectly used this aircraft lease in determining *Minasligas'* imputed negative credit expenses. AIMCOR argues that the AECs principal amounts and interest rates were expressed in United States dollars and that the Court of International Trade erred in concluding that the AEC advances were not United States dollar borrowings because *Minasligas* converted them to *cruzeiros*.

Commerce's stated policy is to use an interest rate tied to the currency in which future payments are expected:

> When sales are made in, and future payments are expected in, a given currency, the measure of the company's extension of credit should be based on an interest rate tied to the currency in which its receivables are denominated. Only then does establishing a measure of imputed credit recognize both the time value of money and the effect of currency fluctuations on repatriating value.

Final Determination of Sales at Less Than Fair Value: Oil Country Tubular Goods From Austria, 60 Fed. Reg. at 33,555 . . . . Commerce requires evidence of actual United States dollar borrowings to support a proffered United States dollar-denominated interest rate. . . . Commerce uses a short-term borrowing rate to calculate imputed credit expenses.

Commerce refused to apply the AEC interest rates, which were expressed in United States dollars, in calculating negative credit expenses because *Minasligas* actually received the AEC advances in *cruzeiros*. . . . Consistent with its stated policy of using the interest rate in which receivables are denominated, Commerce sought a United States dollar-denominated interest rate to apply to the negative credit expenses because *Minasligas'* receivables were denominated in United States dollars, i.e., *Minasligas'* customers were to pay for the ferrosilicon in United States dollars.

Given that Brazil's economy was hyperinflationary during this period, . . . and the *cruzeiro* was declining at a rate of 25 to 30 percent per month, Commerce did not err in rejecting the AEC interest rates which were tied to advances received in *cruzeiros*. Commerce's decision to reject the AEC interest rates because *Minasligas* was paid in *cruzeiros* and its receivables were denominated in United States dollars is supported by substantial evidence on the record.

The only other evidence of United States dollar-denominated borrowings that *Minasligas* submitted was an aircraft lease. . . . Commerce relied on this lease to determine the interest rate for the imputed negative credit expenses. Commerce did not err in using this rate because it was the only evidence of record of *Minasligas*' United States dollar borrowings. The Court of International Trade rejected AIMCOR's objection that the interest rate in the aircraft lease was not a short-term interest rate. . . . Given that Commerce's first priority is to match the denomination of the interest rate to that of receivables, we uphold the court's decision sustaining Commerce's choice of interest rate. We reject AIMCOR's argument that the AECs were United States dollar borrowings, the reason being that *Minasligas* borrowed, and was paid in, *cruzeiros*.

. . .

Conclusion

The Court of International Trade did not err in sustaining the *Final Remand Determination* of Commerce that included Brazilian value-added taxes paid on input materials as a cost of materials in calculating the constructed value of ferrosilicon, because *Minasligas* failed to show that the taxes were fully recovered prior to exportation of the ferrosilicon that was produced from the taxed raw materials. The court also did not err in sustaining Commerce's choice of interest rate for determining imputed negative, United States credit expenses. . . .

III. Cost of Production, Major Input Rule, and 2004 *NTN Bearing* Case

Suppose production of merchandise involves a transaction in a "major" input between two affiliated entities. Those affiliates might be a producer-exporter parent and its subsidiary, or two subsidiaries of that same parent. Suppose, further, they undervalue that input. For instance, between two affiliates in China, assume one sells an input to another for $600,000, when in fact the input is worth $1 million. The second affiliate benefits because (*inter alia*) in any AD investigation, Normal Value of the foreign like product it produces using that input is artificially low by $400,000. So (*ceteris paribus*), any dumping margin (the difference between (1) that Normal Value for the foreign like product, or a proxy for Normal Value, like Constructed Value, and (2) Export Price or Constructed Export Price for subject merchandise) is artificially low by that amount.

If the DOC has reasonable grounds to believe the value of the input is below its cost of production, then it may disregard the input valuation between the affiliates. The DOC may value the input using any other information available to it. But, to do so, the input has to be a "major" one—that is, significant relative to the total costs of production of subject merchandise.[2]

NTN Bearing Corporation of America v. United States,

United States Court of Appeals for the Federal Circuit,
368 F.3d 1369–78 (2004)

Linn, Circuit Judge:

NTN Bearing Corporation of America, American NTN Bearing Manufacturing Corporation, and NTN Corporation (collectively "NTN"), and NSK, Limited and NSK Corporation (collectively "NSK") appeal from a judgment of the United States Court of International Trade, in which the court reviewed the final determination of the Department of Commerce ("Commerce") relating to antidumping duties on the import of tapered roller bearings from Japan and China. *NTN Bearing Corp. of Am. v. United States,* 186 F. Supp. 2d 1257 (Ct. Int'l Trade 2002) ("*NTN Bearing I*"). The Timken Company ("Timken") cross-appeals . . . . [W]e affirm.

Background

Commerce initiated an antidumping duty administrative review of several manufacturers and exporters of tapered roller bearings from Japan in 1996. . . . Commerce issued questionnaires to the affected parties, including both NTN and NSK, and based its preliminary determination in part on their responses. . . .

Commerce gave the interested parties an opportunity to comment on the preliminary results and then issued final results that took those comments into account. See *Tapered Roller Bearings and Parts Thereof, Finished and Unfinished, From Japan, and Tapered Roller Bearings, Four Inches or Less in Outside Diameter, and Components Thereof, From Japan,* 63 Fed. Reg. 2558 (Dep't Commerce January 15, 1998) (final admin. review) ("*Final Results*"). In these results, . . . Commerce: (1) employed affiliated-party cost data in (a) determining whether "foreign like products" were merchandise similar to U.S. tapered roller bearing models, (b) calculating the difference in merchandise ("difmer") adjustment for non-identical U.S. and home-market matches, and (c) recalculating NSK's reported U.S. inventory carrying costs . . . ; (2) relied on facts available to adjust NTN's reported home market billing adjustments . . . : (3) relied on its own sampling of affiliated-party inputs to adjust NTN's reported cost of production ("COP") and constructed value ("CV") for those inputs . . . ; (4) rejected Timken's argument that NTN's warehousing expenses

---

2. *See Diamond Sawblades Manufacturers Coalition v. United States*, CIT Number 06-00248 (Slip Opinion 14-127, 29 October 2014); Brian Flood, *Trade Court Upholds Revised AD Rates On Chinese Diamond Sawblade Imports*, 31 International Trade Reporter (BNA) 1964 (6 November 2014).

were incorrectly allocated . . . ; and (5) rejected NTN's argument that zero-priced transactions should be excluded from the margin calculations, ...

   . . .

[Omitted are three portions of the appellate court opinion, which concern facts available, inclusion of transactions adjusted to a zero price, and warehousing expenses. Note the usual practice of DOC is to deduct from Normal Value only warehousing expenses associated with a foreign like product after that product has left the facility in which it was manufactured. *See CC Metals and Alloys, LLC v. United States*, CIT Number 14-00202 (Slip Opinion 16-3, 12 January 2016) (where the subject merchandise was ferrosilicon imports from Russia). What might be examples of such expenses incurred while the product still is in the manufacturing plant?]

Analysis

   . . .

B. Use of Affiliated Supplier Cost Data and 19 U.S.C. § 1677b(f)

In the course of its administrative review, Commerce requested that NSK provide cost data for major inputs received from affiliated parties and used to produce the tapered roller bearings that were the subject of the review. NSK duly provided the data, but protested Commerce's request on the ground that 19 U.S.C. § 1677b(f)(3) permits Commerce to request such data only where it "has reasonable grounds to believe or suspect that an amount represented as the value of [a major] input is less than the cost of production of such input," 19 U.S.C. § 1677b(f)(3) (2000), and Commerce had no such reasonable grounds. Commerce noted that it "had found home market sales below the cost of production (COP) in [its] most recently completed final results for NSK," and conducted a cost test to determine if any of NSK's home market sales in this review were similarly below COP. Based on the result of this test, Commerce used NSK's affiliated supplier cost data to recalculate NSK's total cost of manufacturing ("TCOM"), which the agency then used to recalculate NSK's inventory carrying costs in the United States. Commerce also employed the recalculated TCOM data in determining the difmer adjustment. The agency used this value, which represents differences in physical characteristics between merchandise sold in the United States and that sold abroad, . . . to control which U.S. and home market tapered roller bearings would be compared: Commerce "used a 20 percent [difmer] cost deviation cap as the maximum difference in cost allowable for similar merchandise." . . .

NSK challenges Commerce's use of the affiliated supplier cost data to calculate these variables. In particular, NSK argues that Commerce violated 19 U.S.C. § 1677b(f), which permits the use of these data for "purposes of *subsections (b)* and *(e)*." Those provisions relate to the calculation of COP and CV, respectively. . . . Citing *FAG Italia, S.p.A. v. United States*, 291 F.3d 806 (Fed. Cir. 2002), NSK argues that the grant of authority to Commerce to use these data for COP and CV calculations implies that Commerce does not have the authority to use the data for other purposes. We disagree.

Section 1677b(f) is entitled "special rules for calculation of cost of production and for calculation of constructed value." NSK sees in this, together with the reference to "purposes of *subsections (b) and (e)*" in the statutory text, confirmation that Congress intended the use of affiliated supplier cost data to be limited to these two purposes. The statute does not, however, contain words of restriction limiting the data's use solely to the calculation of COP and CV. NSK thus relies in essence on the maxim *expressio unius est exclusio alterius* ["the expression of one thing is the exclusion of another"] arguing that the expression of subsections (b) and (e) in Section 1677b(f) permits an inference that Congress intended to preclude use of affiliated supplier cost data for any other purpose.

In focusing exclusively on Section 1677b(f) to the exclusion of the other statutory provisions governing Commerce's actions, NSK stretches this well-worn maxim too far. The maxim is not applied where, *inter alia*, "its application would thwart the legislative intent made apparent by the entire act." NORMAN J. SINGER, SUTHERLAND STATUTES AND STATUTORY CONSTRUCTION § 47:25 (6th ed. 2000). We believe that such is the case here.

Commerce's calculation of the adjustments at issue in this case is governed only secondarily by Section 1677b(f); the agency's authority derives directly from other statutory provisions. Similar merchandise, or "foreign like products" in the terms of the statute, is defined by 19 U.S.C. § 1677(16)(B)(ii) as merchandise "like [the subject] merchandise in component material or materials and in the purposes for which used." Commerce is required to determine what merchandise is a "foreign like product" for purposes of, *inter alia*, determining normal value. . . . Similarly, Commerce derives its authority to calculate a difmer adjustment from 19 U.S.C. § 1677b(a)(6), and derives its authority to account for inventory carrying costs from 19 U.S.C. § 1677a(d). Because these statutes provide authority to Commerce to calculate the values in question, we look to the text of these statutes in the first instance for Congress' intent as to how the values are to be calculated. None of these provisions preclude Commerce's use of affiliated supplier cost data in the calculation of these values. NSK's reliance on a maxim of dubious applicability to interpolate restrictions on the use of affiliated supplier cost data into statutes that are silent on the question is unconvincing.

Nor is *FAG Italia* dispositive in this situation. That case involved a statutory grant of authority to Commerce to conduct duty absorption inquiries "during any review . . . initiated 2 years or 4 years after the publication of an antidumping duty order." 19 U.S.C. § 1675(a)(4) (2000). Commerce claimed that this provision did not preclude it from conducting a duty absorption inquiry in the second year after the January 1, 1995 "deemed issuance date" of a transition order (*i.e.*, an antidumping order originally issued before the date that the *Uruguay Round Agreements Act* amendments came into force), which was seven years after the publication of the antidumping duty order in question. . . . We rejected the agency's argument on the grounds that "the absence of a statutory provision cannot be the source of agency authority," . . . and that "statutory provisions governing annual reviews for

Commerce do not confer general authority that might include the power to consider duty absorption," . . . . However, we recognized that other more general statutory provisions might provide such authority, but we declined to "reach the question whether Commerce might have been authorized to conduct duty absorption inquiries as part of" another provision. . . .

In this case, . . . authority to calculate the values at issue does not derive from Section 1677b(f), but rather from other statutory provisions. Commerce noted that it "does not rely on a respondent's reported costs solely for the calculation of COP and CV," . . . and concluded that it would be distortive to adjust those costs only for those calculations, but not for others in which they were used. . . . We concur with Commerce's analysis and hold that it did not err in interpreting these provisions to permit it to employ affiliated supplier cost data to calculate cost deviations to limit the definition of similar merchandise, the difmer adjustment, and inventory carrying costs.

C. Validity of 19 C.F.R. § 351.407(b)

NTN challenges Commerce's use of available record information to increase the transfer prices of "major inputs" from affiliated suppliers that NTN used to calculate COP and CV, in order to reflect market value. The statutory scheme that governs calculation of cost of production and constructed value is set forth in 19 U.S.C. § 1677b(f):

(2) Transactions disregarded

A transaction directly or indirectly between affiliated persons may be disregarded if, in the case of any element of value required to be considered, the amount representing that element does not fairly reflect the amount usually reflected in sales of merchandise under consideration in the market under consideration. If a transaction is disregarded under the preceding sentence and no other transactions are available for consideration, the determination of the amount shall be based on the information available as to what the amount would have been if the transaction had occurred between persons who are not affiliated.

(3) Major input rule

If, in the case of a transaction between affiliated persons involving the production by one of such persons of a major input to the merchandise, the administering authority has reasonable grounds to believe or suspect that an amount represented as the value of such input is less than the cost of production of such input, then the administering authority may determine the value of the major input on the basis of the information available regarding such cost of production, if such cost is greater than the amount that would be determined for such input under paragraph (2).

[Following the example at the outset, suppose the production of subject merchandise entails a transaction in a major input between affiliated parties, and the DOC reasonably suspects the value reported by a respondent for that input is below its cost of production. Then, the DOC can use information available as to its cost and thereby assign a value to that input.[3]]

Under its authority to administer this statutory scheme, . . . Commerce has formulated a regulatory interpretation under which it uses the highest of transfer price, market value and the affiliated supplier's cost of production:

> For purposes of Section 773(f)(3) of the *Act*, the Secretary normally will determine the value of a major input purchased from an affiliated person based on the higher of:
>
> (1) The price paid by the exporter or producer to the affiliated person for the major input;
>
> (2) The amount usually reflected in sales of the major input in the market under consideration; or
>
> (3) The cost to the affiliated person of producing the major input.

19 C.F.R. § 351.407(b) (1998).

NTN maintains that it provided Commerce with both COP and transfer price information and argues that under the "major input rule" set forth in Section 1677b(f)(3), Commerce can only resort to information available regarding the COP of an element if Commerce has reason to suspect that the transfer price is less than the affiliated supplier's COP. In NTN's view, "subsection (2) does not . . . apply specifically in the case of an affiliated party transaction in which one of the parties has produced a major input for the merchandise under consideration," and therefore is inapplicable to the valuation of major inputs, which is governed solely by subsection (3). NTN states that on the basis of the COP and transfer price information it supplied, Commerce had no basis for a belief that the transfer price was below the COP for many of the inputs, and alternative valuation methods should not have been used for those inputs, in accordance with Section 1677b(f)(3).

. . .

The statutory scheme is not a model of clarity, particularly with respect to the question of the applicability of subsection (2) to the valuation of major inputs. We must therefore determine whether Commerce's interpretation of the statute is permissible. . . . NTN seeks to persuade us that it is not; according to NTN, subsection (2) is simply inapplicable here, and if the transfer price is greater than the cost of production, that transfer price must be accepted as the valuation for the major input. The statute does not compel the construction that NTN forces upon it. Section 1677b(f)(3) itself references subsection (2). *See* 19 U.S.C. § 1677b(f)(3) (mandating the use of COP for the valuation of major inputs "if such cost is greater than the amount that would be determined for such input under paragraph (2)"). This

---

3. *See Diamond Sawblades Mfrs. Coal v. United States*, CIT, Number 06-00248 (11 October 2013); Brian Flood, *Court Remands Dispute on AD Investigation Into Diamond Sawblade Imports from Korea*, 30 International Trade Reporter (BNA) 1676 (31 October 2013).

suggests subsection (2) is of no applicability in considering the valuation of major inputs. Rather, it is reasonable to conclude that where the transfer price is less than market value, per subsection (2), or the cost of production, per subsection (3), the transfer price is abandoned in favor of the higher of those two values. Commerce's interpretation of the statute, under which it simply uses the highest value among the transfer price, market value, and cost of production, is neither arbitrary, capricious, nor manifestly contrary to the statute, see *Chevron* [*U.S.A., Inc. v. Natural Resources Defense Council, Inc.*, 467 U.S. 837 (1984)], 467 U.S. at 844, and we accordingly affirm that interpretation.

IV. Constructed Value, Profit Cap, Exclusion of Below-Market Surrogate Sales, and 2013 *Atar* Case

In the 2013 case of *Atar S.R.L. v. United States*, the Federal Circuit reviewed a decision by the CIT in which the CIT ordered the DOC to recalculate the profit cap applicable to an Italian exporter.[4] The context was the ninth Administrative Review of an AD order on pasta from Italy. The Federal Circuit reversed, upholding the DOC original calculation methodology as reasonable.

The DOC could not calculate NV based on data from Italy, the home market of Atar, nor could it obtain data on Third Country sales by Atar. So, it used CV to compare against EP. Constructed Value must include profits that a non-dumping exporter could expect to receive for its goods in the home market of the dumping exporter. (Those goods technically would not be the "foreign like product." They are sold by the non-dumping exporter, which—because it is not dumping—is not being investigated. But, surely they would be pretty close to the subject merchandise, to make the comparison between CV and EP realistic.) Otherwise, if profits were excluded, then CV would be artificially low. But, what if such profit data are unavailable?

The pertinent statute identifies three alternatives to derive substitute profits values to build into CV:[5]

(1) Actual Profits from Same General Category—

The DOC can use the actual profits of the dumping exporter from foreign sales of the same general category of merchandise as subject merchandise.

(2) Weighted Average of Ordinary Course Sales—

The DOC can look to the weighted average of profits that other dumping exporters, also subject to the investigation or Administrative Review, obtain

---

4. *See* No. 2013-1001 (11 September 2013); Brian Flood, *Federal Circuit Sides With Commerce On Valuation of Pasta in Dumping Review*, 30 International Trade Reporter (BNA) 1440 (19 September 2013).

5. *See* 19 U.S.C. § 1677b(e)(2)(B)(i)-(iii).

from selling the foreign like product in the ordinary course of trade. (These goods are the "foreign like product," because respondents sell them.)

(3) Backstop Method (Profit Cap) —

The DOC can employ some other reasonable method. Using the third method, the DOC must not estimate an amount for profit in excess of the amount exporters normally received in connection with sales for consumption in the foreign country of merchandise that is in the same general category as the subject merchandise. This limitation is called the "profit cap." Its purpose is to ensure the DOC does not artificially inflate Constructed Value by over-estimating profits.

In the case, the DOC used the backstop method, and computed the profit cap for Atar using data from sales by respondents in the eighth Administrative Review of the order.

But, the DOC excluded data from sales those respondents made outside the ordinary course of trade. In particular, four of the six respondents made sales at below cost, and the DOC excluded them. Obviously, sales below cost are unprofitable, so by excluding them, the DOC arrived at a higher profit cap, and thus a higher CV, than it would have had it included them. In turn, with a higher CV, the dumping margin was larger than it otherwise would have been — a pro-petitioner result. The CIT rejected the DOC profit cap. It said including all sales, whether below or above cost, gives a more accurate picture of the profits conditions in the home market of the respondents.

The Federal Circuit disagreed with the lower Court. Nothing in the statute suggested excluding below-cost sales when calculating the profit cap to CV was unreasonable. Indeed, the substitute profit values option required focusing on sales made in the ordinary course of trade. And, there was a good reason for excluding below cost sales. If they are included, then the respondent exporter benefits from its own unfair pricing. By selling at below cost, the respondent may undercut the market in its home country, compelling its competitors there to sell at unprofitable prices. In the AD case, that exporter benefits from a lower CV, and thereby a reduced dumping margin (if any).

V. Constructed Value, Financial Expense Ratio, and 2014 *Fischer* Case

Calculating CV can be nightmarishly technical, giving rise to heated argumentation. Keeping the incentives of the players in mind helps cut through the thicket. Consider the 2014 case of *Fischer S.A. Comercio, Industria & Agricultura v. United States*. The CIT upheld the DOC decision to assign in an Administrative Review an 8.73% AD duty rate on orange juice concentrate produced and exported by the

Brazilian company, Fischer, between 1 March 2010 and 28 February 2011.[6] In so doing, the CIT agreed with how the DOC calculated a financial expense ratio for the respondent.

The case required use of CV, because all home market sales by Fischer were made at less than the COP. To calculate CV, the DOCV examined audited financial statements for a time period close, but not identical to, the POR. From those statements, the DOC computed a financial expense ratio, namely:

$$\text{Financial Expense Ratio} = \frac{\text{Net Financial Expenses}}{\text{Cost of Goods Sold (COGS)}}$$

Both numerator and denominator represent the full year expenses and COGS, respectively, for the respondent.

For 2 reasons, Fischer said the DOC behaved arbitrarily in calculating the ratio: The DOC treated long-term interest expenses differently from long-term interest income. The DOC excluded long-term interest income from the numerator. That is, the DOC offset short- and long-term interest expenses against interest Fisher earned on short-term assets. But, the DOC did not offset interest expenses against interest earned on long-term interest-bearing assets.

The CIT rejected both reasons, finding the DOC acted reasonably.[7] The CIT said offsetting short- and long-term interest expenses against interest earned on short-term assets made sense, because Fischer could use those assets to cover its current operations. By definition, those assets were liquid: they were short-term, interest bearing instruments, so Fischer could sell them to raise cash quickly. Likewise, not offsetting long-term interest expenses against long-term interest earnings was sensible. Those assets were illiquid, so Fischer could not convert them to cash easily, *i.e.*, it could not use them to defray daily operating costs. The CIT explained that "[w]hile long-term interest income undoubtedly benefits a company's bottom line, Commerce need not deduct that income if the interest-generating investment is unrelated to production during the review period."

Why did Fisher make the argument it did? The answer is that it sought as low a figure for CV as possible, which in turn would reduce or even eliminate any dumping margin once the low CV were compared to EP. So, Fisher wanted its Financial Expense Ratio to be as small as possible, meaning it wanted to minimize the numerator and maximize the denominator. Ideally from Fischer's perspective, the

---

6. *See* Number 12-00340 (Slip Opinion, 27 May 2014); Brian Flood, *Trade Court Affirms Dumping Rate For Brazilian Orange Juice Producer*, 31 International Trade Reporter (BNA) 1153 (26 June 2014).

7. Fisher also objected to inclusion by the DOC in net financial expenses of Fisher's unrealized hedging losses in net financial expenses. The CIT rejected this argument, too, saying the DOC had no practice of excluding such losses, and in any event, there was no detriment in what the DOC did to Fisher.

DOC would have subtracted long-term interest income from its long-term interest expenses, just as the DOC offset short-term interest income with short- and long-term interest expenses. Had the DOC done so, then the Net Financial Expenses numerator would have been smaller, thus reducing the Ratio, and ultimately the dumping margin and associated AD duty.

Chapter 8

Dumping Margin Adjustments: Adjustments to Normal Value[1]

I. Currency Conversion

Normal Value is based on price data from sales of a foreign like product in the home market of the producer-exporter. Those data are likely to be denominated in a currency other than the U.S. dollar, because the official currency of that home market is unlikely to be the dollar. If it is India, then the currency is the *rupee*. In contrast, Export (or Constructed Export) Price is based on price data from sales of subject merchandise in the importing country in which the AD case is based. So, if that country is the U.S., then those prices will be denominated in dollars. Obviously, matching Normal Value in *rupees* with Export Price in dollars would not be an apples-to-apples comparison. The *rupee*-denominated price data need to be converted to dollars.

It also is possible that subject merchandise is invoiced in a currency other than the dollar. That is especially true if the currency of the home country of the producer-exporter is a hard one, *i.e.*, widely accepted as a means of payment, and for which there is a highly liquid market. (A "soft" currency is not so widely accepted, and the market is less liquid.) For example, a producer-exporter in the U.K. may prefer payment from a U.S. buyer-importer in pound sterling. Likewise, a producer-exporter in Japan may want payment from its American customer in *yen*. In such cases, the Export (or Constructed Export) Price will need to be translated into dollars, as will price data on Normal Value from the sales of the foreign like product in the U.K. and Japan, respectively.

The problem of currency conversion also occurs in the context of proxies for Normal Value, *i.e.*, Third Country Price or Constructed Value, or in NME cases when surrogate values are used for costs or inputs. In the 2014 CIT case of *Timken Co. v. United States*, the underlying facts of which involved targeted dumping (discussed later), the DOC had to recalculate the dumping margin for imports of

---

1. Documents References:
   (1) *Havana (ITO) Charter* Article 34
   (2) GATT Article VI
   (3) WTO *Antidumping Agreement* Articles 1–2

Chinese tapered roller bearings made by Changshan and Peer Bearing.[2] The DOC initially misread Chongshan's manufacturing costs as denominated in U.S. dollars when, in truth, they were in Thai *baht*—hence, the remand order from the CIT to recalculate, resulting in lowering the dumping margin from 14.91% to zero.

As the *Timken* case suggests, dumping margins can be affected greatly by selection of the FX rate for these conversions. What exactly are those effects? As general rules, *ceteris paribus* (all other factors remaining constant):

(1) "Foreign Currency Weakens against Dollar Means Normal Value Falls, Thus Dumping Margin Narrows"

If the currency of the home country of the producer-exporter depreciates relative to the U.S. dollar, then prices of the foreign like product denominated in that currency will decrease in dollar terms. Therefore, the dollar-denominated equivalent of Normal Value will fall. In turn, the dumping margin will decrease.

(2) "Foreign Currency Strengthens against Dollar Means Normal Value Rises, Thus Dumping Margin Widens"

If the currency of the home country of a producer-exporter appreciates relative to the U.S. dollar, then prices of the foreign like product denominated in that currency will increase in dollar terms. Therefore, the dollar-denominated equivalent of Normal Value will rise. In turn, the dumping margin will increase.

In brief, dumping cases are harder to bring in an importing country the currency of which is strengthening during the POI, but easier to bring if the currency is weakening during that POI. (Be sure to try an example of each rule.)

Each rule assumes the price of the foreign like product denominated in the home country currency remains the same. For instance, suppose the foreign like product is 1,000 *rupees*, as sold in India. That price remains the same regardless of whether the *rupee* depreciates from 60 *rupees* per dollar to 80 *rupees* per dollar, and regardless of whether the rupee appreciates (moving in the opposite direction, as from 80 to 60 *rupees* per dollar). What changes is not the home market price in the foreign currency, but rather the price of subject merchandise sold in the U.S. as denominated in dollars.

Intuitively, these rules make sense. If the dollar strengthens against a foreign currency, then Americans find goods from the country of that currency more attractive, because those goods are cheaper in dollar terms. Americans do not need to convert so many dollars into that foreign currency to buy those goods. The opposite is true if the dollar weakens: foreign goods are more expensive to Americans, as

---

2. *See* CIT Number 13-00069 (19 August 2014); Brian Flood, *Trade Court Upholds AD Rate For Chinese Roller Bearings*, 31 International Trade Reporter (BNA) 1522 (21 August 2014).

they have to sell more dollars to buy the foreign currency they need to purchase foreign goods denominated in that currency.

Obviously, selecting the POI is important if there have been significant trend movements in the foreign currency of producer-exporter's home market relative to the dollar. But, notwithstanding the POI, exactly what rate is used for Normal Value and Export (or Constructed Export) Price conversions? Who decides that rate? Neither GATT Article VI nor the WTO *Antidumping Agreement* precisely answers. Save for certain exchange-traded FX derivatives (*e.g.*, futures and options), the FX market is over-the-counter (OTC), with different rates — such as spot and forward — quoted on a 24/7 basis. Respondent producer-exporters prefer a rate that minimizes a dumping margin, while petitioning domestic producers of a like product seek a rate to maximize the margin.

U.S. AD law gives a clear answer to both questions: the Federal Reserve Bank of New York identifies the "Noon buying rate."[3] Everyday at 12 Noon Eastern Time (ET), the New York Fed certifies to CBP the exchange rate of the U.S. dollar against each foreign currency. In an AD case, that rate must be used for Normal Value and Export (or Constructed Export) Price conversions. Section 1677b-1(a) of 19 U.S.C. states:

> In an antidumping proceeding . . . , the administering authority [*i.e.*, the DOC] shall convert foreign currencies into United States dollars *using the exchange rate in effect on the date of sale of the subject merchandise*, except that, if it is established that a currency transaction on forward markets is directly related to an export sale under consideration, the exchange rate specified with respect to such currency in the forward sale agreement shall be used to convert the foreign currency. Fluctuations in exchange rates shall be ignored.[4]

The "exchange rate in effect" is the New York Fed-certified 12 noon ET buying rate.

What happens if the subject merchandise was sold into the U.S. based on a forward foreign exchange contract? The statute calls for use of that forward rate. The 1998 Federal Circuit case of *Thyssen Stahl v. United States* involved currency hedging through a forward contract.[5] The facts arose in 1992, so the case involved pre-Uruguay Round law, and involved an adjustment to Constructed Export Price (then called Exporter's Sales Price) for currency hedging gains associated with U.S. sales of subject merchandise.[6] What would happen if the hedging instrument is different, such as a currency swap? Would the rate in that instrument be used?

---

3. *See* 19 U.S.C. § 5151 (concerning certification by the Federal Reserve Bank of New York of the Noon Buying Rate).

4. Emphasis added.

5. *See* 1998 U.S.App. LEXIS 17064 (1998).

6. The Federal Circuit over-turned the DOC adjustment, saying:

   . . . Commerce adjusted U.S. Price upward to account for Thyssen's currency hedging gains associated with its U.S. sales [of cold-rolled and corrosion-resistant carbon steel

II. Overview of Adjustments and Zero-Sum Game

No more complicated aspect of AD law exists than adjustments in a dumping margin calculation. How nice it would be if the price of an allegedly dumped product—subject merchandise—as sold in the importing country could be compared straight away with the price of the foreign like product as sold in the home market. The difficulty is the two prices are not necessarily comparable.

Perhaps the price in one market is wholesale, while the price in the other market is retail. Perhaps the price in one market contains the cost of containers, as well as freight charges, while the price in the other market does not have them. Perhaps in one or both markets there are expenses directly and indirectly related to selling the product, items like warranties or guarantees, rebates, advertising, and commissions. Perhaps the allegedly dumped product is not identical to the foreign like product, *i.e.*, there are distinguishing physical features. Perhaps there are differences in the way in which subject merchandise and the foreign like product are taxed. Perhaps there are differences in the normal volume sold of the allegedly dumped product and the foreign like product. And so on.

Each possibility shows the naïveté of a straightforward comparison of home and importing country market prices. To ensure an "apples-to-apples" analysis, adjustments are made to observed prices to account for differences in packaging and freight, levels of trade, circumstances of sale, physical features of the merchandise, taxation, volume, and a number of other factors. Indeed, GATT Article VI:1 and Article 2:4 of the WTO *Antidumping Agreement*, plus U.S. AD law (19 U.S.C. §§ 1673 *et seq.*), demand due allowance be taken for differences affecting price comparability.

Once all adjustments are done, it is safe—or, at least, safer—to say "apples" in the home market are being compared to "apples" in the importing country. That is,

---

products]. The statute states: "For purposes of this section, the exporter's sales price [*i.e.*, Constructed Export Price] shall also be adjusted by being *reduced* by the amount, if any, of . . . (2) expenses generally incurred by or for the account of the exporter in the United States in selling identical or substantially identical merchandise . . . ." 19 U.S.C. § 1677a(e) (1988) (emphasis added).

The statute clearly contemplates only reductions in U.S. Price to account for expenses, and not increases to account for gains, associated with selling the merchandise. Commerce, however, increased the U.S. Price through linguistic artistry by deeming the gains received by Thyssen on its currency hedging activities "negative expenses." Commerce's interpretation of the statutory section, which would bring both increases and reductions of U.S. Price within the section's reach, contradicts the statute's unambiguous expression of congressional intent, and we therefore owe it no deference. See *Chevron U.S.A. Inc. v. Natural Resources Defense Council, Inc.*, 467 U.S. 837, 842–43 . . . (1984). Commerce's decision to increase U.S. Price for Thyssen's gains received in its currency hedging activity was not in accordance with law, and the Court of International Trade was correct in reversing it. [The Court added in a footnote that is expresses "no view on whether the facts of this case relating to the currency hedging activity would warrant an adjustment under 19 U.S.C. § 1677b(a)(4)(B) (1988) for "other differences in circumstances of sales."]
Thyssen, 1998 U.S.App. LEXIS 17064 (1998).

Zero sum game (handwritten annotation)

Table 8-1. Summary of Motivations of Petitioner and Respondent in Dumping Margin Calculation

Item	Petitioner's Motivation	Respondent's Motivation
Dumping Margin = Normal Value − Export (or Constructed Export) Price	Maximize the Dumping Margin	Minimize the Dumping Margin
Value of Normal Value	Maximize Normal Value	Minimize Normal Value
Adjustments to Normal Value	Maximize Normal Value by adding to it as many adjustments as possible. Avoid adjustments that are deductions from Normal Value.	Minimize Normal Value by avoiding adjustments that increase Normal Value. Seek as many adjustments as possible that are deductions from Normal Value.
Value of Export (or Constructed Export) Price	Minimize Export (or Constructed Export) Price	Maximize Export (or Constructed Export) Price)
Adjustments to Export (or Constructed Export) Price	Minimize Export (or Constructed Export) Price by advocating adjustments that are deductions. Avoid adjustments that are additions.	Maximize Export (or Constructed Export) Price by advocating adjustments that are additions. Avoid adjustments that are deductions.

the comparison is more likely to be a "fair" one only if adjustments are made. "Fairness" is the standard Article 2:4 of the WTO *Antidumping Agreement* and U.S. law (19 U.S.C. § 1677b(a)) set. Thus, Normal Value and Export (or Constructed Export) Price are not based solely on raw data on observed prices in two markets. Those data are adjusted to arrive at figures that assure a better degree of comparability.

Only a Textbook dedicated solely to AD law could convey the details of all possible adjustments in a dumping margin calculation. (The book would be of dubious popularity!) After all, only seasoned AD lawyers are conversant with the gamut of adjustments. But, it is possible here to introduce the key adjustments. Before that, it is critical to understand the motivations of the players, petitioner and respondent. Table 8-1 summarizes them. They are diametrically opposed. The players are locked in a zero-sum game. In theory, at least, an administering agency, such as the DOC, is the impartial referee standing between them to assure fairness.

Adjustments to Normal Value and Export (or Constructed Export) Price are made for a variety of reasons, but they take only two forms: an addition or a deduction. That is, some adjustments to Normal Value are additions to the raw data value (or starting point) for Normal Value, while others take the form of deductions. When all the additions and subtractions to the starting point are completed, the result is a final figure for Normal Value. Likewise, some adjustments to Export (or Constructed Export) Price are additions to the raw data value, while others are deductions from that starting point. When all the additions and subtractions are made, the result is a final amount for Export (or Constructed Export) Price. Then, the dumping margin is simply the difference between Normal Value and Export (or Constructed Export) Price. As a percent, the margin is the difference divided by Export (or Constructed Export) Price.

As the Table indicates, a petitioner wants to maximize the dumping margin by maximizing the size of Normal Value and minimizing the size of Export (or Constructed Export) Price. The respondent wants just the opposite. Better yet, for the respondent, is no dumping margin at all. How does the petitioner play the game? It argues for adjustments to Normal Value that are additions, and against any adjustments that are deductions. The petitioner also argues in favor of adjustments that lower Export (or Constructed Export) Price, *i.e.*, in favor of deductions from Export (or Constructed Export) Price. The petition opposes additions to Export (or Constructed Export) Price.

The respondent engages in strategic behavior that is a mirror image of what the petitioner does. The respondent seeks to prove adjustments to Normal Value that decrease Normal Value are appropriate, and that adjustments to Export (or Constructed Export) Price that increase Export (or Constructed Export) Price are proper. Thus, the respondent tries to fit the facts of the case into deductions from Normal Value and additions to Export (or Constructed Export) Price. The respondent endeavors to rebut facts that call for additions to Normal Value or deductions from Export (or Constructed Export) Price.

III. Tabular Summaries of Major Adjustments

What, then, are the major adjustments commonly found in practice? The Tables below summarize them, organized according to the price variable and whether the potential change is an addition to, or subtraction from that variable. Table 8-2 lists additions to Export (or Constructed Export) Price. Table 8-3 lists deductions from Export (or Constructed Export) Price. Table 8-4 lists deductions unique to Constructed Export Price. Tables 8-5 and 8-6 list additions to, and deductions from, Normal Value, respectively. Table 8-7 lists adjustments to Normal Value that may be additions to, or deductions from, that variable, depending on the facts of the case. No adjustment need be made if it already is included in the starting point for Normal Value or Export (or Constructed Export) Price. For example, if data already include overseas packing costs, then there is no need to add them to a variable.

All of the Tables list analogous adjustments (if any). That is, the Tables concerning adjustments to Export Price and Constructed Export Price present any corresponding adjustments to Normal Value. Likewise, the Tables concerning adjustments to Normal Value set out any corresponding adjustments to Export Price and Constructed Export Price.

Table 8-2. Additions to Export Price or Constructed Export Price

Addition to Export Price or Constructed Export Price	Statutory Reference in 19 U.S.C.	Analogous Adjustment to Normal Value?	Rationale?
Overseas packing costs Containers, coverings, and all other costs incident to packing subject merchandise for shipment to U.S.	§ 1677a(c)(1)(A)	Addition to Normal Value for overseas packing costs § 1677b(a)(6)(A)	Helps ensure an "apples-to-apples" comparison with Normal Value Also, a similar addition is made to Normal Value
Rebated or uncollected import duties Any import duties imposed by exporting country rebated or not collected because subject merchandise is exported to U.S. (*e.g.*, drawback).[7]	§ 1677a(c)(1)(B)	None. Because foreign like product is not exported, no analogous adjustment expected	Helps ensure an "apples-to-apples" comparison with Normal Value. Drawback is not available for a foreign like product sold in the home market (it is offered only upon export). It is properly part of the price of the foreign like product.
CVDs imposed on subject merchandise	§ 1677a(c)(1)(C)	None No analogous adjustment expected, because CVDs are not imposed on foreign like product	Helps achieve a more accurate price for subject merchandise, based on what a buyer pays for it

---

7. For a case in which the DOC rejected a request to reduce EP through a drawback adjustment, see *Maverick Tube Corp. v. United States*, Fed. Cir. Number 2016-2330 (3 July 2017); Brian Flood, *Turkish Oil Drilling Equipment Makers Lose Antidumping Appeal*, 34 International Trade Reporter (BNA) 960 (6 July 2017). The Federal Circuit held DOC is not legally obligated to make a drawback adjustment to EP, contrary to the contention of a Turkish petitioner, Çayirova Boru Sanayi Ve Ticaret A.S. Çayirova sought a reduction from a 13.59% AD rate on its subject merchandise, OCTG, based on drawback granted by the Turkish government to Çayirova for its imports of steel (from overseas into Turkey) to make OCTG—even though that imported steel was not the type of steel Çayirova used to make the OCTG it exported to the U.S. Turkey offered drawback for imported inputs used in exported goods, but also for equivalent inputs. Çayirova said it used equivalent material, namely, Turkish-made steel, in the OCTG it shipped to the U.S. But, DOC said it was inappropriate to adjust the dumping margin for equivalent drawback, because that drawback was for an input (Turkish-produced steel) that could not be used in the subject merchandise.

Table 8-3. Deductions from Export Price or Constructed Export Price

Deduction from Export Price or Constructed Export Price	Statutory Reference in 19 U.S.C.	Analogous Adjustment to Normal Value?	Rationale?
U.S. import duties The statute mandates a deduction for "costs, charges, or expenses, and United States import duties, which are incident to bringing the subject merchandise" from the exporting country to the U.S.	§ 1677a(c)(2)	Not applicable	Such duties would not be paid on the foreign like product, because it is sold in the home market of the producer-exporter, not imported into the U.S.
Overseas freight charges Any additional costs incident to bringing subject merchandise from place of shipment in exporting country to place of delivery in U.S. Port charges also would be deducted	§ 1677a(c)(2)(A)	Deduction from Normal Value for internal freight charges § 1677b(a)(6)(B)(ii)	Helps achieve an *ex-factory* price for subject merchandise Also, a similar deduction is made from Normal Value
Export taxes Any tax imposed by exporting country upon exportation of subject merchandise to U.S.	§ 1677a(c)(2)(B)	None	Helps ensure an "apples-to-apples" comparison with Normal Value, and ex-factory price for subject merchandise Export taxes would not be included in price of foreign like product sold in the home market. Because that product is not exported, it bears no export tax

**Table 8-4. Further Deductions from (and Unique to)
Constructed Export Price**

Deduction from Constructed Export Price	Statutory Reference in 19 U.S.C.	Analogous Adjustment to Normal Value?	Rationale?
Selling commissions Commissions for selling subject merchandise in U.S.	§ 1677a(d)(1)(A)	None	Helps achieve an *ex-factory* price for subject merchandise
Direct selling expenses Examples include credit expenses, guarantees, and warrantees	§ 1677a(d)(1)(B)	None	Helps achieve an *ex-factory* price for subject merchandise
Selling expenses paid by seller on behalf of purchaser	§ 1677a(d)(1)(C)	None	Helps achieve an *ex-factory* price for subject merchandise
Indirect selling expenses Any other selling expenses not included above The amount of such other expenses establishes the "Constructed Export Price offset cap"	§ 1677a(d)(1)(D)	"Constructed Export Price offset," by which indirect selling expenses are deducted from Normal Value, but capped at the amount deducted from Constructed Exported Price § 1677b(a)(7)(B)	Helps achieve an *ex-factory* price for subject merchandise The CEP offset accounts for at least some indirect selling expenses incurred in home market, up to the amount of such expenses incurred in U.S.
Cost of further manufacture or assembly Labor and additional material, in effect, value added in U.S. to subject merchandise	§ 1677a(d)(2)	None.	Helps achieve an *ex-factory* price for subject merchandise
Profits allocated to any of the above expenses	§ 1677a(d)(3)	None	Helps achieve an *ex-factory* price for subject merchandise

Table 8-5. Additions to Normal Value

Addition to Normal Value	Statutory Reference in 19 U.S.C.	Analogous Adjustment to Export Price or Constructed Export Price?	Rationale?
Overseas packing costs Cost of all containers, coverings, and expenses to place subject merchandise in condition for shipment to U.S.	§ 1677b(a)(6)(A)	Addition to Export Price or Constructed Export Price for overseas packing charges § 1677a(c)(1)(A)	Helps ensure an "apples-to-apples" comparison with Export Price or Constructed Export Price The price of subject merchandise, because it has been imported into U.S, would entail an overseas packing charge If none is included, then an addition is made to Export Price or Constructed Export Price

Table 8-6. Deductions from Normal Value

Deduction from Normal Value	Statutory Reference in 19 U.S.C.	Analogous Adjustment to Export Price Or Constructed Export Price?	Rationale?
Internal packing charges Cost of all containers and coverings, and all other costs, to place foreign like product in condition ready for shipment to place of delivery to purchaser	§ 1677b(a)(6)(B)(i)	None	Helps achieve an *ex-factory* price for foreign like product
Internal freight charges Any costs associated with bringing the foreign like product from the original place of shipment to place of delivery to purchaser	§ 1677b(a)(6)(B)(ii)	Deduction from Export Price or Constructed Export Price) for overseas freight charge § 1677a(c)(2)(A)	Helps achieve an *ex-factory* price for foreign like product. Similar adjustment made to Export Price or Constructed Export Price
Rebated or uncollected taxes Any taxes imposed directly on foreign like product that is rebated, or not collected, on subject merchandise, to the extent such tax is included in the price of foreign like product	§ 1677b(a)(6)(B)(iii)	None Under pre-Uruguay Round law, this adjustment took the form of an addition to Export Price or Constructed Export Price	Helps achieve an *ex-factory* price for foreign like product

Deduction from Normal Value	Statutory Reference in 19 U.S.C.	Analogous Adjustment to Export Price Or Constructed Export Price?	Rationale?
Constructed Export Price Offset Deduction for indirect selling expenses incurred in the home market based on sales of foreign like product Applied only under certain conditions, namely, Normal Value is based on a more advanced stage of distribution than the Level of Trade (LOT) of Constructed Export Price, but available data do not permit a LOT adjustment to Normal Value Capped at the amount of indirect selling expenses incurred in U.S.	§ 1677b(a)(7)(B)	Constructed Export Price offset to CEP for indirect selling expenses incurred in U.S. associated with subject merchandise § 1677a(d)(1)(D)	Helps achieve an *ex-factory* price for foreign like product Accounts, up to the amount of the cap, for indirect selling expenses incurred in home market

Table 8-7. Additions to or Deductions from Normal Value (Depending on Facts of Case)

Addition to or Deduction from Normal Value	Statutory Reference in 19 U.S.C.	Analogous Adjustment to Export Price or Constructed Export Price?	Rationale?
Quantity Adjustment for differences in the quantity sold between foreign like product in home market, and subject merchandise in U.S.	§ 1677b(a)(6)(C)(i)	None	Helps explain some of the difference between Normal Value and Export Price or Constructed Export Price
Quality (DIFMER) Adjustment for differences in the quality of foreign like product and subject merchandise. This "difference in merchandise" (DIFMER) adjustment is made when foreign	§§ 1677b(a)(6)(C)(ii) and 1677(16)(B)-(C)	None	Helps explain some of the difference between Normal Value and Export Price or Constructed Export Price

(continued)

Table 8-7. Additions to or Deductions from Normal Value
(Depending on Facts of Case) (*continued*)

Addition to or Deduction from Normal Value	Statutory Reference in 19 U.S.C.	Analogous Adjustment to Export Price or Constructed Export Price?	Rationale?
like product used to determine Normal Value is not identical in physical characteristics with, and produced in the same country by the same person, as subject merchandise			
Circumstance of Sale (COS) *Encompasses a variety of circumstances*	§ 1677b(a)(6)(C)(iii)	None	Helps explain some of the difference between Normal Value and Export Price or Constructed Export Price
Level of Trade (LOT) *Made when there is a difference in the level of trade between Normal Value and Export Price or Constructed Export Price, which involves (1) different selling activities, and (2) demonstrably affects price comparability based on a consistent pattern of price differences*	§ 1677b(a)(7)(A)	None	Helps explain some of the difference between Normal Value and Export Price or Constructed Export Price

IV. Four Points

The adjustments listed in the Tables are self-explanatory only to a limited degree. It is necessary to read the statutory provisions, and case law elaborations, for a fuller understanding of a particular adjustment. For now, four points are worth observing.

- **Applicability to Proxies**

First, The adjustments potentially available in calculating Normal Value also exist when using a proxy for Normal Value. That is, generally speaking, they apply in Third Country Price or Constructed Value scenarios. However, exceptions exist — for instance, in respect of DIFMER and Constructed Value.

- **Unifying Theme**

Second, to the extent there is any common theme unifying all of the adjustments, any common policy logic, it is this: the adjustments are designed to ensure the comparison between Normal Value and Export (or Constructed Export) Price is fair, a "fair" comparison means an "apples-to-apples" one, and "apples-to-apples" generally is defined in terms of *ex-factory* prices. In other words, for the most part, the adjustments are designed to ensure the figures are prices prevailing when merchandise leaves the factory in which it is made. Indeed, Article 2:4 of the WTO *Antidumping Agreement* makes the point that the comparison between Normal Value and Export (or Constructed Export) Price normally is to be at the *ex-factory* level.

- **Offsets**

Third, do what extent is the mandate of Article 2:4 of the *Antidumping Agreement* not followed universally? In particular, do non-dumped sales offset dumped sales? Notwithstanding the plethora of Appellate Body holdings against zeroing, should this type of offset be permitted, at least not in certain contexts? Is that kind of systematic bias remains in favor of a petitioner acceptable? Consider the imperfect analogy that it is not an acceptable defense to a charge of speeding that on an earlier occasion the driver drove under the speed limit, nor is it an acceptable defense to a charge of homicide that on previous occasions the defendant was nice to some people. In other words, there are areas of law in which violations (akin to dumped sales) are not offset by non-violations (akin to non-dumped sales).

Suppose a respondent sells merchandise in Tulsa, Oklahoma, and Wichita, Kansas. The sales in Tulsa are at dumped prices, *i.e.*, the dumping margin is positive. Sales in Wichita are at prices above Normal Value. Ideally, the respondent would like to use the negative dumping margins from Wichita sales to offset the positive margins from the Tulsa sales. That is not possible. To be sure, in calculating Normal Value and Export (or Constructed Export) Price, large volumes of data on home market and U.S. prices, respectively, are averaged. In this sense, the Wichita sales are included in the overall computation. But, there is no specific "rubbing out" of a dumped sale in Tulsa by a non-dumped sale in Wichita.

- **Ingenuity in Argumentation and 2014 *Apex Exports* Case**

The ingenuity of petitioners and respondents to argue for or against a particular adjustment that widens or collapses, respectively, the dumping margin is boundless. It also can be quite intricate. Consider the 2014 CIT decision in *Apex Exports v. United States*.[8] The subject merchandise was frozen warm water shrimp shipped to the U.S. by 2 Indian exporters, Apex Exports and Falcon Marine Exports Ltd., to which the DOC assigned dumping margins of 2.31% and 1.36%, respectively. In an Administrative Review, DOC refunded certain AD duties they had paid, which they subsequently invested. They earned interest income on these investments.

Normal Value incorporates costs of production, such as administrative and financial expenses. Typically, the DOC deducts from those expenses any interest

---

8. *See* Number 11-00291 (Slip Opinion 13-158, 9 January 2014); Brian Flood, *Court Affirms Final Dumping Margins For Exporters of Frozen Indian Shrimp*, 31 International Trade Reporter (BNA) 106 (16 January 2014).

accruing to a respondent on its short-investments associated with subject merchandise. So, Apex Exports and Falcon Marine argued the DOC was wrong to deny their request to subtract from Normal Value the interest they obtained on their investment of AD duty refunds from the prior Administrative Review.

The CIT disagreed, upholding the DOC denial. Said the CIT: "The hallmark of a short-term deposit is whether it 'constitutes liquid working capital reserves which would be readily available for the companies to meet their daily cash requirements.'" How could an AD duty refund qualify as a short-term deposit, when it is mandated by statute, and not a working capital reserve, and may be unavailable to met daily cash needs even after entries of subject merchandise are liquidated? How indeed, but this distinction did not deter the Indian exporters from trying out the argument on the CIT.

Conversely, the petitioners, the Ad Hoc Shrimp Trade Action Committee and American Shrimp Processors Association, argued for a deduction from Export Price that would have increased the dumping margin. They said the DOC erred by not deducting assessed AD duties from Export Price under statutory language as "United States import duties" and "costs, charges or expenses." Again, the CIT sided with the DOC: AD duties are not normal customs duties, nor are they a selling expense. Moreover, what the petitioners wanted would lead to a circular result involving double counting: the DOC would have to (1) calculate an initial dumping margin and assess an AD duty based on it, (2) then revise the dumping margin, boosting it by the amount of the assessed AD duty via a deduction from Export Price, (3) then assess the new, higher duty, and (4) then deduct again from Export Price the AD duty as a selling expense. That would be absurd. Nonetheless, the petitioners tried out the creative argument.

V. Dignity and Truth of Adjustments

As technical as dumping margin adjustments are, perhaps they raise a deep jurisprudential issue: do these adjustments, motivated as they are by diametrically opposed interests of the players, undermine the dignity of AD law? It could be argued the whole affair is a game in which "truth"—a comparison of the true prices in the home and importing country markets—is not really the object, or at least not the result. Indeed, the arbitrariness of certain adjustments—both conceptually, in the abstract, and in particular contexts—is a complaint often heard from AD lawyers.

The fact is a petitioner and respondent fight intensely for or against an adjustment simply based on what mathematical effect that adjustment has on the calculation. They attempt to cloak their arguments in technical terms, and try to fit the facts within the parameters of established adjustment categories. Sometimes, the fit is a Procrustean one. The argument for or against an adjustment then crosses the line between a good faith effort to push or circumscribe the boundaries of the category, on the one hand, and a rather ridiculous effort to ignore those boundaries, on the other hand.

The question that ought not to be ducked is: what does the great game of adjustments do to the dignity of international trade law? Armies of lawyers, reinforced by legions of accountants, spend an enormous amount of time and effort calculating the effects of every possible addition and subtraction to the dumping margin. This process hardly is what most people have in mind when they think of the grandeur or majesty of the legal system. Yet, that is exactly what happens every day in the "trenches" of AD law. The stakes of battle are very high. Whether a dumping margin exists, and thus whether a case goes forward, may depend centrally on whether a particular adjustment is made or not made. Small wonder, then, why legal and accounting firms that work on AD cases have sophisticated computer programs to "run the numbers" and check the effects of one adjustment versus another.

In these "trenches," query whether truth and justice are the casualties. Do they wind up as far-off, romantic concepts? Often the outcome of "running the numbers" leads to a claim for (or against) a particular adjustment. A vision of the law as something noble means argumentation ought not be crassly consequential in nature. What is "right," not what works out best in terms of the dumping margin formula, ought to motivate an argument, and ought to carry the day.

VI. Direct Selling Expenses and 1999 *SKF* Case

SKF U.S.A., Inc. v. INA Walzlager Schaeffler KG,

United States Court of Appeals for the Federal Circuit,
180 F.3d 1370 (1999)

EDWARD S. SMITH, SENIOR CIRCUIT JUDGE:

. . . SKF GmbH is a manufacturer and exporter of AFBs [antifriction bearings] in Germany, and SKF USA, Inc. is a United States importer of German AFBs (collectively "SKF"). SKF appeals from two decisions of the United States Court of International Trade, which sustained [the Department of] Commerce's denial of SKF's billing adjustment two and cash discounts. We agree that Commerce properly disallowed SKF's billing adjustment two and cash discounts because the claimed adjustments were not limited to merchandise within the scope of the antidumping order. We therefore affirm.

Background

. . .

. . . SKF participated as a respondent in Commerce's review of AFB imports . . . . SKF submitted information on its sales of AFBs in the German home market during the period of review, including its sales prices and adjustments to those prices . . . Commerce disallowed two adjustments known as billing adjustment two and cash discounts, that SKF claimed in calculating its FMV [Foreign Market Value, *i.e.*, Normal Value]. . . .

In rejecting SKF's adjustments, Commerce relied upon *Torrington Co. v. United States*, 818 F. Supp. 1563 (Ct. Int'l Trade 1993) ("*Torrington CIT*"), wherein the Court of International Trade held Commerce cannot calculate the FMV of merchandise that is within the scope of an antidumping review ("in-scope" merchandise) using a methodology that includes discounts, rebates, and price adjustments on merchandise outside the scope of the antidumping review ("out-of-scope" merchandise). . . . Commerce denied SKF the requested adjustments because they were not reported in a transaction-specific manner and therefore were not limited to merchandise within the scope of the antidumping review. . . .

SKF filed a complaint with the Court of International Trade alleging among other things that Commerce erred in its calculation of the FMV by disallowing adjustments for SKF's billing adjustment two and cash discounts. . . . SKF claimed that all of the adjustments should be treated as "direct" and allowed as adjustments to the FMV. . . . Commerce had rejected that contention, however, because SKF failed to show that the allocated price adjustments at issue were calculated solely on the basis of merchandise under review. . . .

. . .

We affirm the decision[] of the Court of International Trade on the basis of the in-scope/out-of-scope rule articulated in *Torrington CIT*, and applied by Commerce in disallowing SKF's billing adjustments in this case.

. . .

Analysis

. . .

In determining whether goods are being sold at less than fair value, Commerce may allow adjustments to the FMV for direct selling expenses based on three criteria: (1) differences between quantities sold in the foreign and domestic markets; (2) differences in the circumstances of sales; and (3) differences in physical characteristics of the product. . . . [The Court points out in two important footnotes, #6 and #7, that direct selling expenses "are expenses which vary with the quantity sold," *Zenith Electronics Corp., v. United States*, 77 F.3d 426, 431 (Fed. Cir. 1996), or that are "related to a particular sale." *Torrington v. United States*, 68 F.3d 1347, 1353 (Fed. Cir. 1995). In contrast, indirect selling expenses "'are those that do not vary with the quantity sold.'" *Zenith Elecs.*, 77 F.3d at 431 . . . or that are "not related to a particular sale," *Torrington*, 68 F.3d at 1353. Commerce may deduct indirect selling expenses from Normal Value under the Constructed Export Price offset rule.] . . .

When this procedure was followed in the instant case, Commerce found that SKF's billing adjustment number two and cash discounts were in the nature of direct expenses because they were allocated adjustments that were not granted as a fixed and constant percentage of sale. SKF's adjustments were granted after sale, apparently to correct billing errors (billing adjustment number two) or to lower the price for a particular customer (cash discounts). Commerce disallowed SKF's billing adjustment number two and cash discounts because they were not reported in a transaction-specific manner and therefore were not limited to merchandise within the scope of the antidumping review. . . .

The Court of International Trade agreed with Commerce's characterization of SKF's billing adjustment number two and cash discounts as being in the nature of direct expenses, and agreed that SKF's failure to report them on a transaction-specific basis precluded treatment of the adjustments as direct expenses. . . .

The In-Scope/Out-of-Scope Rule

The in-scope/out-of-scope rule relied on by Commerce in this case was clearly articulated by the Court of International Trade in *Torrington CIT*. . . . In that case, the foreign manufacturer claimed adjustments to FMV for certain post-sale price adjustments ("PSPAs") and rebates that were granted as an ordinary part of its business but which were not tracked on a product-specific basis. The adjustments at issue were not allocated on a product-specific basis and "no effort was made to eliminate PSPAs and rebates paid on out of scope merchandise." . . . Thus, PSPAs and rebates that had been granted on out-of-scope merchandise had been included in calculating the claimed adjustments.

Commerce allowed the claimed adjustments, treating them as indirect expenses. . . . The Court of International Trade reversed, on the basis that "[m]erchandise which is outside the scope of an antidumping duty order cannot be used in the calculation of antidumping duties." . . .

We agree with the *Torrington CIT* court that antidumping duties must be calculated based solely on merchandise within the scope of the antidumping duty order. This requirement is mandated by statute: "If . . . a class or kind of *foreign merchandise* [called "subject merchandise" in post-Uruguay Round AD law] *is being . . . sold in the United States at less than its fair value*, and [a domestic industry is injured by the dumping], then there shall be imposed upon such merchandise an antidumping duty . . . in an amount equal to the amount by which the foreign market value exceeds the United States price *for the merchandise*." 19 U.S.C. § 1673 . . . . The statutory language thus requires that the antidumping duty be calculated on the basis of the difference between the FMV and the USP for "the merchandise"; *i.e.*, the "foreign merchandise [which] is being . . . sold in the United States at less than its fair value." . . . Price adjustments granted on goods *outside the scope* of the antidumping duty order are irrelevant to calculating the FMV of goods *within the scope* of the antidumping duty order; they simply play no part in determining the FMV of the in-scope goods themselves. The statutory language therefore precludes the use of price adjustments granted on sales of goods outside the scope of the antidumping duty order in calculating the FMV of goods within the scope of the antidumping duty order.

. . .

In addition, a rule requiring direct price adjustments to relate exclusively to in-scope merchandise is necessary in order to allow Commerce to calculate the FMV as accurately as possible to determine whether dumping has indeed occurred. To allow adjustments to FMV for direct price adjustments encompassing both in-scope and out-of-scope goods would have the effect of averaging prices, diluting some and inflating others, and thereby reduce the accuracy of Commerce's dumping determinations.

. . .

Application of the Rule

In this case, SKF requested an adjustment to FMV for its billing adjustment two and cash discounts. SKF reported to Commerce that these post-sale price adjustments generally related to multiple invoices and therefore could not be reported in a transaction-specific manner. . . . Commerce denied the adjustments because "SKF did not demonstrate that [either] adjustment[ ] pertained to subject merchandise only," . . . in that "SKF provided no means of identifying and segregating billing adjustments paid on non-scope merchandise." . . .

The party seeking a direct price adjustment bears the burden of proving entitlement to such an adjustment. . . . Commerce determined in this case that SKF had not carried its burden . . . .

We agree with Commerce and the Court of International Trade that the law requires price adjustments to be calculated solely on the basis of merchandise within the scope of an antidumping duty order. . . . Commerce applied the correct legal standard in requiring SKF to show that the claimed adjustments pertained to subject merchandise only. SKF did not do so, and Commerce appropriately denied the requested adjustments.

VII. Circumstances of Sale and 1998 *Torrington* Case

The Torrington Company v. United States,

United States Court of Appeals for the Federal Circuit,
156 F.3d 1361–66 (1998)

MICHEL, CIRCUIT JUDGE:

This appeal continues the enduring saga of the efforts of this American ball bearing manufacturer to obtain relief from certain foreign competitors under the trade laws. Here, The Torrington Company ("Torrington") appeals the judgment of the United States Court of International Trade upholding the final determination of the United States Department of Commerce ("Commerce") in its fourth administrative review [in 1995] of the importation of antifriction bearings from various countries. . . . Defendants-Appellees NMB Thai Ltd., Pelmec Thai Ltd., NMB Hi-Tech Bearings Ltd., and NMB Corp. (collectively, "NMB Thai") were interested party-respondents in the underlying antidumping administrative review and were defendants-intervenors at the Court of International Trade. In this appeal, Torrington contends only that the Court of International Trade erred by upholding the determination of Commerce to adjust the foreign (home) market value [*i.e.*, Normal Value] of the subject antifriction bearings to take account of certain international freight expenses. Because Commerce's decision to allow an adjustment for such freight expenses was based upon a reasonable interpretation of its own regulations and thus was entitled to deference, we affirm.

Background

NMB Thai is a producer of antifriction ball bearings in Thailand. These bearings are both sold in Thailand and exported to the United States. The antidumping review encompassed importations of such bearings entered between May 1, 1992, and April 30, 1993. During this period, NMB Thai sold its ball bearings in the Thai market through two distinct channels. "Route A" sales were shipped directly to the customer in Thailand via a domestic route. "Route B" sales, however, were first shipped abroad to a warehouse operated by a related company in Singapore and then back to Thailand. The purpose of this circuitous Route B was to obtain certain favorable tax and duty treatment from the Thai government and, in particular, to avoid government restrictions on sales to Thai customers who were certified by the Thailand Board of Investment but did not have a bonded warehouse.

On May 15, 1989, Commerce published antidumping duty orders on antifriction bearings from Thailand. . . . The Commerce decision at issue in the Court of International Trade was rendered in the fourth administrative review of the antidumping duty order.

In the antidumping review, Commerce determined the "United States price" [*i.e.*, Export Price or Constructed Export Price] and the "foreign market value" ("FMV") of the subject merchandise and used this data to calculate antidumping margins in accordance with 19 U.S.C. § 1675. These margins were then used by Commerce to assess antidumping duties on the entries of merchandise covered by the review as well as to calculate estimates of antidumping duties for future entries. . . .

In determining FMV, Commerce is permitted to make adjustments for certain "circumstances of sale" ("COS") . . . . Such COS adjustments are made when the seller incurs certain costs in its home market sales that it does not incur when selling to the United States market. Such adjustments may be made if "the amount of any price differential is wholly or partly due to such difference [in circumstances of sale]" and "those circumstances . . . bear a direct relationship to the sales compared." 19 C.F.R. § 353.56(a)(1). In addition, adjustments to FMV may also be made for indirect selling expenses "incurred in selling such or similar merchandise up to the amount of expenses . . . incurred in selling the merchandise." 19 C.F.R. § 353.56(b)(2). In the antidumping review, Commerce deducted from FMV the pre-sale freight costs for shipping merchandise from Thailand to Singapore as indirect selling expenses pursuant to 19 C.F.R. § 353.56(b)(2). Commerce also deducted from FMV the post-sale freight expenses of shipping the merchandise from Singapore back to Thailand as direct selling costs pursuant to 19 C.F.R. § 353.56(a)(1).

Before the Court of International Trade, Torrington argued, *inter alia*, that NMB Thai's Route B freight expenses were not "selling expenses" for purposes of 19 C.F.R. § 353.56, but rather were general costs incurred for the purpose of receiving government benefits. The Court of International Trade, however, rejected this contention, explaining that this court had previously held both that the "Route B sales were properly classified as home market sales" and that "Commerce may deduct indirect home market transportation expenses from FMV [subject] to the exporter's sales price . . . offset cap [*i.e.*, the Constructed Export Price offset]." . . .

On appeal to this Court, Torrington argues that the plain meaning of the governing statute and regulation both indicate that the Route B freight expenses are not selling costs that may be accepted as downward COS adjustments to FMV and, moreover, that permitting such adjustments would defeat the purpose of the COS provisions because the freight costs were offset by savings in NMB Thai's taxes and duties.

Discussion

Our analysis must begin with the controlling statutory language. Under 19 U.S.C. § 1677b(a)(4), "due allowance shall be made" for "the amount of any difference between the United States price and the foreign market value . . . wholly or partly due to . . . other differences in circumstances of sale." This court has previously explained that "the statute does not define the term 'circumstances of sale' nor does it prescribe any method for determining allowances. Congress has deferred to the Secretary's expertise in this matter." *Smith-Corona Group v. United States*, 713 F.2d 1568, 1575, . . . (Fed. Cir. 1983). Accordingly, under the authority of this statute, Commerce promulgated 19 C.F.R. § 353.56, which sets forth the criteria required for the allowance of COS adjustments to FMV. . . . [S]uch adjustments are permitted to take account both of circumstances bearing "a direct relationship to the sales compared," . . . and indirect expenses "incurred in selling such or similar merchandise" ("selling expenses"), . . .

In light of the substantial deference accorded to Commerce when interpreting and applying its own regulations, we find no error in the Court of International Trade upholding Commerce's decision to make a COS adjustment to FMV to take account of NMB Thai's Route B freight costs. The parties do not dispute that Commerce's regulation, which permits adjustments for, *inter alia*, "selling expenses," is an authorized and reasonable administrative interpretation of the governing statute. Moreover, there is no dispute that such selling expenses may properly include freight costs. See, e.g., *Torrington Co. v. United States*, 68 F.3d 1347, 1356 (Fed. Cir. 1995); *Sharp Corp. v. United States*, 63 F.3d 1092, 1097 (Fed. Cir. 1995). In determining that the two Route B freight costs at issue in this case were selling expenses properly the subject of a COS adjustment, Commerce was simply interpreting its own regulations. We give substantial deference to that interpretation. . . .

Commerce's interpretation of its regulation is not "plainly erroneous or inconsistent with the regulation." *Thomas Jefferson Univ. v. Shalala*, 512 U.S. [504,] at 512 [1994]. Rather, its interpretation is a reasonable one in a complex field in which it has special and unique expertise. To interpret the regulation, as Torrington apparently suggests, to require Commerce to parse all freight costs to determine the intent behind such costs would, moreover, be administratively impracticable. Indeed, it is difficult to comprehend the method by which Commerce could be expected to divine the subjective intent behind the decision to transport merchandise by a particular method or along a particular route. For example, a decision to transport certain goods within the country of manufacture by rail rather than road might be due to government rail subsidies, high gasoline taxes, delivery timing requirements, or a combination of such factors. To expect Commerce to determine the specific business strategy behind the decision to use rail transport under such a scenario would be to expect the unattainable. Thus, under circumstances akin to the instant case, where the freight expenses are found directly or indirectly to support the relevant sales, it is appropriate for Commerce to avoid inquiring into the subjective intent behind the incurring of those expenses. Accordingly, we do not regard Commerce's interpretation of its regulation to be unreasonable when the alternative interpretation proffered by Torrington is utterly unworkable.

We also do not agree with Torrington's assertion that allowing NMB Thai a COS adjustment from FMV for the Route B freight expenses somehow vitiates the statutory and regulatory scheme or its policy goals. In support of this proposition, Torrington contends that by permitting NMB Thai this adjustment, Commerce is permitting an adjustment for an expenditure that does not affect price. However, Torrington does not point to any finding in the record substantiating its factual claim that these Route B freight expenses do not affect price. Indeed, notwithstanding any tax, customs, or bonding benefits, Torrington has not brought forward any evidence suggesting that the Thai customers of NMB Thai do not ultimately pay for the circuitous Route B freight costs. Or, to put it differently, Torrington has not produced any evidence that the Route B shipping route provides a net cost saving to Thai customers, only that the Route B costs are incurred to avoid expending the presumably greater costs associated with the Thai tax penalty, customs, and bonding requirements. Accordingly, it is far from apparent that NMB Thai's customers in Thailand do not bear the expense of the roundabout Route B shipping arrangement and we, therefore, do not regard allowing this adjustment to be inconsistent with the overall statutory and regulatory scheme or its policy goals.

. . .

Dissent

Archer, Senior Judge, Dissenting:

The decision of the Court of International Trade sustaining Commerce's deduction from foreign market value (FMV) of the Route B freight costs as home market selling expenses should in my view be reversed. Torrington is correct in arguing that under the governing statute and regulation Route B freight costs are not normal expenses related to home market sales but rather are additional costs incurred to obtain general benefits for the company, *i.e.*, to preserve favorable VAT tax and export duty exemptions.

In general the antidumping statute and regulations seek to produce a fair, "apples-to-apples" comparison between FMV and United States price (USP). To achieve that end, adjustments are made to the base value of both FMV and USP to permit comparison of the two prices at a similar point in the chain of commerce.... The USP is adjusted by deducting expenses incurred in selling the merchandise in the United States.... FMV is adjusted by deducting direct selling expenses under the circumstances of sale (COS) provision,... Moreover, when the USP is based on the exporter's sales price (ESP), the FMV is reduced by the indirect selling expenses to the extent of the deduction for indirect selling expenses from USP....

Home market transportation costs have been considered by Commerce to be sales related and have been treated as selling expenses.... As a result, post-sale transportation costs have been allowed as a COS adjustment. Pre-sale transportation costs (not related to any particular sale) have been allowed as indirect selling expenses when the USP is based on ESP [Exporter's Sales Price, *i.e.*, Constructed Export Price]....

Deductions for transportation costs have previously been made for in-country transportation costs—transportation within the country in the normal course of home market sales. See *Cemex, S.A. v. United States*, 133 F.3d 897, 901 (Fed. Cir. 1998) (in-country transportation for home market sales).... There is no evidence that Commerce has previously made an adjustment for transportation costs to and from a point outside the country in which home market sales occurred.

... In this case,... Commerce's own verification clearly shows that the Route B transportation costs were not incurred in the process of selling, but were incurred in order to obtain import duty and VAT tax benefits for NMB Thai. To this end, the verification shows that these Route B transportation costs were incurred because bearings produced in their bonded factories "continue to carry duty-free status when they are exported" and when shipped back to related or unrelated Board of Investment (BOI) companies in Thailand they are treated as "duty-free" imported raw materials. The verification states that NMB Thai found it much simpler to import raw materials in this way. Because the verification establishes the reasons why NMB Thai used the circuitous transportation route, it was not necessary for Commerce to delve into the "subjective intent behind the decision to transport merchandise by a particular method or along a particular route," which is one of the principal concerns of the majority. In this case, the reasons are clear in the verification record and establish that the added transportation costs cannot properly be classified as a form of selling expense.

It is evident in this case that Commerce did not make an "apples to apples" comparison. By allowing an adjustment for a transportation diversion of the nature and magnitude as here involved, Commerce has not made an adjustment in arriving at

FMV which reaches the similar point in the chain of commerce to make a proper comparison with the USP. Torrington correctly argues that the excess transportation costs were in the nature of general and administrative overhead costs "related to the company's overall corporate strategy to reduce costs generally and reduce its tax and duty burdens specifically." Selling expenses are commonly understood to be expenses made to support and promote sales. See *NSK v. United States*, 115 F.3d 965, 974 (Fed. Cir. 1997) (when terms not explicitly defined should be given their "ordinary meaning"). [The Dissent points out in a footnote that "Torrington concedes that an adjustment for some transportation costs might be appropriate if NMB Thai can show what it would have cost to ship directly to Route B customers."] The commonly understood definition of selling expenses was not applied here.

I would, therefore, reverse the decision below and remand the case to Commerce to make a transportation adjustment in an amount that reflects what would be a normal transportation cost to Route B customers of NMB Thai.

VIII. Differences in Merchandise and 2001 *Mitsubishi* Case

Mitsubishi Heavy Industries, Ltd. v. United States,

United States Court of Appeals for the Federal Circuit,
275 F.3d 1056–66 (2001)

CLEVENGER, CIRCUIT JUDGE:

. . .

I

Background

This case involves large newspaper printing presses exported to the United States from Japan. Although all LNPPs [Large Newspaper Printing Press] have similar design and function, individual LNPPs are custom-made per the customer's specification. The companies provide their customers with a menu of various components that can be built into the machine, and the customer decides what components to order. As a result, individual orders for LNPPs can vary to a greater or lesser extent, depending on what components the customer chooses. Because Japanese and United States newspapers have somewhat different characteristics in terms of size, use of color, etc., the LNPPs used to produce them also have somewhat different components. Thus, every contract for sale of an LNPP contains different terms — including price terms — because the LNPPs themselves have different components from contract to contract.

Upon a petition by Rockwell Graphics Systems, Inc., a U.S. competitor now known as Goss Graphics Systems, Inc. ("Goss"), the Department of Commerce ("Commerce") launched an antidumping investigation of two manufacturers, MHI

[Mitsubishi Heavy Industries] and TKS [Tokyo Kikai Seisakusho]. In due course [in 1996], Commerce issued its final antidumping determination finding sales at less than fair value and announcing a dumping margin of 56.28 percent for TKS, the appellant here.... .... Commerce used constructed value ("CV") to calculate the dumping margin, ... and it used home market (*i.e.*, Japanese) LNPPs as the foreign like product in its determination of profit, which is one component of CV, see 19 U.S.C. § 1677b(e)(2) (1994), despite having earlier found that direct price-to-price comparisons with home market LNPPs were impracticable as a basis for normal value—a finding that led to its original decision to use CV as a basis for normal value....

TKS and MHI appealed numerous aspects of Commerce's determination in Japan Final, including its foreign like product determination.... TKS, in particular, argued that Commerce's reliance upon 19 U.S.C. § 1677b(e)(2)(A) to calculate profit was inappropriate because "the findings that led Commerce to rely on CV rather than home-market sales in calculating normal value constituted evidence that no foreign like product existed in the home market." ... The profit calculation under § 1677b(e)(2)(A) relies upon sales of "a foreign like product." ... Because Commerce did not describe adequately its profit calculation so as to permit judicial review, the Court of International Trade remanded the case to Commerce to explain upon which of the three statutory definitions of foreign like product it relied to make its profit calculation.... In its remand determination, Commerce explained that it had relied upon the definition of foreign like product in 19 U.S.C. § 1677(16) (C), which requires, *inter alia*, that the foreign like product be merchandise that "the administering authority determines may reasonably be compared with" the exported merchandise subject to the investigation....

TKS and MHI appealed the remand determination, and the Court of International Trade remanded again, this time because Commerce failed to explain the factual basis for its determination that the LNPPs sold in Japan and the United States could "reasonably be compared" as required by 19 U.S.C. § 1677(16)(c)(iii).... The Court of International Trade was troubled because in its first remand determination, Commerce made statements that made it appear that it had previously conducted a difmer analysis and concluded that the home market and export LNPPs could not reasonably be compared.... In its second remand determination, Commerce clarified that it had not conducted a difmer analysis.... In addition, Commerce explained the factual basis for its finding that the home-market LNPPs could "reasonably be compared" with their United States counterparts, which included the common use to which the products are put (*i.e.*, printing newspapers) and TKS's and MHI's responses to detailed questionnaires showing that the Japanese and United States LNPPs share the same set of detailed press characteristics....

[In a footnote, the Court explained DIFMER adjustments as follows:

When the foreign merchandise is not identical to the exported goods, Commerce may conduct a "difmer" analysis, which "adjusts normal value for the 'difference in cost attributable to the difference in physical characteristics'—the difference in merchandise ('difmer') adjustment." *Mitsubishi Heavy Indus., Ltd. v. United States*, 97 F. Supp. 2d 1203, 1206 n.4 (Ct. Int'l Trade 2000). If the "difmer" exceeds 20 percent, Commerce will make a finding that the merchandise cannot be reasonably compared, unless it can otherwise justify the comparison. In other words, a >20% difmer finding creates a presumption of non-comparability. *Id.* Obviously the difmer analysis is conducted—if at all—prior to a decision to use CV, because the difmer adjustment is made to normal value, not CV.

Query why DIFMER adjustments do not apply to Constructed Value?]

Based on Commerce's explanation of the factual basis underlying its comparability determination, the Court of International Trade affirmed the dumping determination. . . . The court denied TKS's motion for reconsideration, . . . and this appeal by TKS followed. . . .

II

A

. . .

On appeal, TKS primarily argues that Commerce's determination that home and United States market LNPPs may reasonably be compared is not supported by substantial evidence. We note that in pursuing this argument, TKS has chosen a course with a high barrier to reversal. The Supreme Court has defined substantial evidence as "such relevant evidence as a reasonable mind might accept as adequate to support a conclusion." *Universal Camera Corp. v. NLRB*, 340 U.S. 474, 477, 95 L. Ed. 456, 71 S. Ct. 456 (1951) (quoting *Consol. Edison Co. v. NLRB*, 305 U.S. 197, 229, 83 L. Ed. 126, 59 S. Ct. 206 (1938)). The conclusion reached by Commerce need not be the only one possible from the record, for "even if it is possible to draw two inconsistent conclusions from evidence in the record, such a possibility does not prevent Commerce's determination from being supported by substantial evidence." *Am. Silicon Techs. v. United States*, 261 F.3d 1371, 1376 (Fed. Cir. 2001) . . . . After reviewing the record, we conclude that substantial evidence supports Commerce's determination that home-market LNPPs are a foreign like product.

In its second remand decision, Commerce clarified the evidence underlying its decision to use home-market LNPPs as the foreign like product, explaining that "TKS's home market LNPP may reasonably be compared to its sales of LNPP in the United States based on evidence that LNPP in both markets share detailed product characteristics." . . . Commerce noted that its conclusion was further "supported by the common use—to produce newspapers—to which both home market and U.S. LNPP are employed." . . . During the investigation, both TKS and MHI responded to a questionnaire sent by Commerce asking them to identify both United States and home-market LNPPs using the same set of detailed press characteristics. . . . TKS's and MHI's responses to this questionnaire, which indicated that their United States and home-market LNPPs do in fact share a majority of the same—or highly similar—characteristics, provide the principal factual predicate for Commerce's finding. TKS argues that this evidence is "self-serving" because Commerce prepared the questionnaire itself, forcing TKS and MHI to describe their Japanese and United States products using the same characteristics. To the extent that TKS accuses Commerce of stacking the deck against them, its argument is not well taken. As the agency to which Congress delegated the authority to determine antidumping duties, Commerce is responsible for gathering information to make dumping determinations. Commerce uses the information it collects in order to reach its decision—in this case that the home-market and United States LNPPs are reasonably comparable. Although Commerce is an agent of the United States government, it nevertheless makes its dumping determination based on an impartial analysis of the evidence. Furthermore, administrative acts by Commerce enjoy a presumption of regularity that includes, in this case, impartiality in its decision-making process, and one seeking to rebut that presumption carries a heavy burden. . . . There is no evidence to suggest that Commerce made up its mind in advance and cunningly planned its questionnaire to support its position.

MHI's and TKS's responses to Commerce's information-gathering request provide ample support for Commerce's finding. First, the questionnaire responses confirm "that the LNPP sold in Japan and the LNPP sold in the United States share the detailed press characteristics that [Commerce] set out in its questionnaire." . . . And within each characteristic, the responses indicated that the individual specifications for each press characteristic were also similar. Obviously, because the LNPPs are custom-made, each individual LNPP may contain a different mix of these common characteristics. However, it is apparent that they all reflect a choice from among similar characteristics. Based on the long list of shared features, Commerce could reasonably conclude that Japanese and United States LNPPs could reasonably be compared for calculating CV profit.

TKS retorts that whatever the value of the questionnaire, Commerce did not consider the whole record when making its comparability determination, because the weight of evidence points the other way. First, TKS notes that United States LNPPs often contained significantly more individual components than did their Japanese counterparts. However, because profit is calculated as a percentage of the sale price, the fact that Japanese LNPPs may have fewer components (and thus, perhaps, a lower overall price) is immaterial. The individual differences between the United States and Japanese models that TKS cites are significant (for example, the United States units use "tower printing units" instead of the "satellite printing units" and "spot color units" more prevalent in Japan). However, such differences are unavoidable in customized equipment. That a United States buyer chooses a somewhat different mix of components than does a Japanese one may preclude price-matching the two contracts, but it does not mean that the machines themselves may not reasonably be compared.

TKS also takes umbrage at Commerce's reference to the English-language and Japanese-language Spectrum product brochures that TKS submitted in response to Commerce's demand to provide all brochures relating to the merchandise under investigation. Commerce cited the brochures as an example of an LNPP model—the Spectrum model—marketed in both the United States and Japan, and noted that the Japanese and English versions of the brochure were identical. TKS argues that this brochure does not show that all United States Spectrums have identical characteristics as their Japanese counterparts, and that Commerce erred in citing the brochures as evidence of comparability. But this is simply another way of saying that the Spectrums, like all LNPPs, are custom-made. The critical point is, given that individual differences exist from order to order, can the custom-made merchandise from Japan and the United States be reasonably compared? Commerce, looking at a brochure offering identical menus of features to Japanese and United States purchasers, could reasonably conclude that one Spectrum LNPP described in the brochure would be reasonably—not perfectly, not identically, but reasonably—comparable to any other Spectrum model.

In short, TKS does not provide any compelling evidence to suggest that Commerce neglected its duty to base its decision on the whole record. To the extent that TKS urges that the evidence before Commerce could be open to multiple interpretations, its argument does not require, or even allow, reversal. . . . Obviously, TKS draws a different conclusion from the evidence of the variations between individual product specifications than did Commerce, but that cannot—and does not—mean that Commerce's interpretation should be overturned. Accordingly, we hold that substantial evidence supported Commerce's decision to treat Japanese market LNPPs as the foreign like product for its determination in this case.

Chapter 9

Dumping Margin Adjustments (Continued): Adjustments to Export Price or Constructed Export Price[1]

I. One Off Transactions, Export Price for SG&A, and 2014 *Thai Plastic Bags* Case

One of several potential adjustments made by administering authorities when computing a dumping margin is for Selling, General, and Administrative (SG&A) expenses, or simply for General and Administrative (G&A) expenses. When comparing Export Price to Normal Value, an authority like the DOC must account for the fact Export Price is based costs associated with sales of subject merchandise a respondent producer-exporter makes. Such costs include G&A expenses.

The higher G&A expenses, the lower Export Price, and thus the larger the dumping margin (the difference between NV and EP). But, what if a respondent earns revenues by selling equipment or capital goods? Should the DOC include those revenues in Export Price, thus increasing Export Price and reducing the dumping margin?

The DOC says "yes." Under its "One Off" policy, it distinguishes between sales of equipment that are routine parts of the process of manufacturing subject merchandise from sales that are one off transactions. If those sales are routine, then the DOC allows the revenues from them to offset G&A expenses. Such an offset helps respondents by limiting the extent to which G&A expenses reduce Export Price, and thus limiting the increase in the dumping margin.

In the 2013 case before the CIT, *Thai Plastic Bags Industries Co. v. United States*, the DOC argued that sale by the respondent—Thai Plastic Bags—of an office building and its land was a one off transaction, not part of the normal process of making plastic bags.[2] So, the DOC declined to allow revenues from the sale to offset

---

1. Documents References:
    (1) *Havana (ITO) Charter* Article 34
    (2) GATT Article VI
    (3) WTO *Antidumping Agreement* Articles 1–2

2. *See* Number 11-00408, Slip Opinion 13-139 (13 November 2013); Brian Flood, *Court Sustains Commerce AD Rates For Thai Retail Carrier Bag Exporters*, 30 International Trade Reporter (BNA) 1808 (21 November 2013).

G&A expenses. The DOC said the size of the sale, and its circumstances, indicated it was not a routine part of production. The CIT agreed with the DOC. So, the revised AD duty rate for the Administrative Review period (POR, namely, entries from 1 August 2009 to 31 July 2010) rose form 35.71 to 35.79%.

A related issue in the case was whether the DOC acted properly by denying Thai Plastic Bags, Co., Ltd., Master Packaging, Inc., and Inteplast Group, Ltd. (collectively, TPBI), an adjustment to Cost of Production (COP) for a Thai rebate program called the "Blue Corner Rebate" (BCR) scheme.[3] Under the BCR, the Thai government gave a rebate to any domestic manufacturer making and exporting goods from raw materials a domestic supplier to that manufacturer imports. TPBI made its plastic bags from polyethylene resin, and got that resin from Thai suppliers. Those suppliers imported raw materials they needed to make the resin. When TPBI exported finished plastic bags, the Thai government gave TPBI a rebate. The rebate was based on presentation by TPBI of a tax certificate the Thai resin suppliers gave to TPBI in exchange for a compensation fee.

TPBI argued (unsuccessfully) that its BCR revenue should be deducted from its COP, specifically G&A expenses, because the compensation fees it paid to its resin suppliers (and which were offset by the BCR revenues), were part of its G&A expenses to make plastic bags. The DOC refused to offset rebates from TPBI's COP of the plastic bags, and disregarded home market sales in Thailand that TPBI made at below COP. The DOC said the BCR scheme was not related to COP, but rather tied to TPBI export sales, hence reducing the G&A element in COP by them would be inappropriate. The CIT agreed, and so did the Federal Circuit.

Note the important technical incentive TPBI had to make its argument: DOC excludes home market sales made at below COP from its calculation of Normal Value (or a proxy for it, namely, Constructed Value). So, the lower the figure for COP, the larger the number of sales DOC includes (because they are above this lower threshold). In turn, the dumping margin (and the AD duty rate) is lower, on account of the lower Normal (or Constructed) Value measured against Export Price.

II. No Deduction for AD Duties and 2015 *Apex* Case

At issue in the 2015 Federal Circuit case of *Apex Exports v. United States* was whether the DOC correctly interpreted 19 U.S.C. Section 1677a(c)(2) in denying a deduction for previously assigned AD duties on subject merchandise.[4] This Section

---

3. *See Thai Plastic Bags Industry Co. v. United States*, Federal Circuit Number 2014-1237 (24 December 2014); Brian Flood, *Federal Circuit Affirms AD Rates On Plastic Bag Imports from Thailand*, 32 International Trade Reporter (BNA) 23 (1 January 2015).

4. *See* Number 2014-1234 (5 February 2015); Brian Flood, *Federal Circuit Upholds Shrimp AD Rates, Commerce's Calculation of Export Prices*, 32 International Trade Reporter (BNA) 345 (12 February 2015). The 2014 *Apex* case, concerning targeted dumping, is discussed in a separate Chapter.

mandates DOC deduct from Export (or Constructed Export) Price "costs, charges, or expenses, and United States import duties, which are incident to bringing the subject merchandise" from the exporting country into America. The DOC relies on it to deduct freight costs, port charges, and U.S. customs duties (*i.e.*, MFN tariffs).

The logic is such expenses are not incurred with respect to foreign like product sales in the home market of the producer-exporter, so they would not be in Normal Value (or its proxy, Third Country Price or Constructed Export Price). If they are included in Export (or Constructed) Export Price, then that Price is artificially high, so the dumping margin is artificially low. This logic can be explained in the converse: bringing subject merchandise into the U.S. is the cause of these expenses. So, the producer-exporter, and/or importer, inevitably raises the price it charges in the U.S. market, to recoup these expenses. The expenses themselves do not affect the underlying fair value of subject merchandise, so they can and should be deducted. By ensuring these expenses are included neither in Normal Value or Export Price, the comparison between the prices of foreign like product sales and subject merchandise sales is "apples-to-apples."

The subject merchandise was frozen warm water shrimp from India. The DOC assigned to the importers, Apex Exports and Falcon Marine Exports Ltd., AD rates of 2.31% and 1.36%, respectively. Representing the petitioning U.S. shrimp industry, the Ad Hoc Shrimp Trade Action Committee called on DOC to deduct from Export Price these AD duties. The Committee invoked 19 U.S.C. Section 1677a(c)(2). Precedent was against it, as in the 2007 case of *Wheatland Tube Co. v. United States*, the Federal Circuit ruled the DOC acted reasonably in deciding AD duties do not fall within the statutory phrase "United States import duties." In *Apex*, the Committee argued AD duties fit within the phrase "costs, charges, or expenses." The Committee lost.

The Federal Circuit agreed Section 1677a(c)(2) was unclear on the issue of whether AD duties are costs that relate (1) solely to importation, or (2) decisions about pricing made by the producer-exporter. The Federal Circuit deferred to the DOC interpretation of the statute, finding it reasonable: no deduction for AD duties is required by any of the statutory language. Moreover, said the Court, the DOC interpretation was consistent with statutory purpose:

> to prevent dumping by effectively raising the price of subject merchandise in the U.S. to the fair value. The importer has less incentive to charge an unfairly low price, because it will have to make up the difference through a duty payment.

Simply put, the Indian shrimp importers already raised their U.S. prices to account for the AD duties, and to cover the risk of such duties.

The Federal Circuit offered an astute consequentialist rationale: "following Ad Hoc's suggestion [to deduct the AD duties from Export Price] would in fact result in double counting that amount." For example, for Apex Exports it would reduce Export Price by the assigned AD duty rate the DOC assigned to it of 2.31%, and thereby enlarge the dumping margin by that amount. Then the DOC would impose and AD duty rate that is 2.31% higher than it otherwise would have been. That scenario intimates another adverse consequence: the cycles of enlargement could go on *ad infinitum*.

III. Using Constructed Export Price, Affiliates, and 2000 *AK Steel* Case

AK Steel Corporation v. United States,

United States Court of Appeals for the Federal Circuit,
226 F.3d 1361, 1363–76 (2000, Revised Opinion)

MICHEL, CIRCUIT JUDGE:

AK Steel Corporation, Inland Steel Industries, Inc., Bethlehem Steel Corporation, LTV Steel Company, Inc., National Steel Corporation, and U.S. Steel Group (collectively "domestic producers" or "appellants") appealed to this court the judgment of the United States Court of International Trade in this anti-dumping duties case. The International Trade Administration, United States Department of Commerce ("Commerce") issued a decision: (1) using a three-part test it adopted informally in 1987 to determine whether certain sales to U.S. buyers of Korean steel by U.S. affiliates of the Korean producers were properly classified as Export Price ("EP") sales rather than Constructed Export Price ("CEP") sales, as defined in 19 U.S.C. § 1677a(a)-(b) (1994) and (2) declining to apply the "fair-value" and "major-input" provisions of 19 U.S.C. § 1677b(f)(2)-(3) (1994) to transfers among affiliated steel producers in Korea that it had treated as one entity for purposes of the anti-dumping determination. [Omitted is the portion o the opinion concerning the fair value and major input provisions. The Court uses short-hand for Korean producer names: "Dongbu" for Dongbu Steel Co., Ltd., "Union" for Union Steel Manufacturing Co., Ltd. ("Union"), "POSCO" for Pohang Iron & Steel Co., Ltd., "POCOS" for Pohang Coated Steel Co., Ltd. ("POCOS"), and "PSI" for Pohang Steel Industries Co., Ltd. ("PSI"). Collectively, they are the "Korean producers" or "Korean manufacturers."] As a consequence of these methods and their application, the duty rates were minimal. The domestic producers then filed suit challenging these methods as contrary to the anti-dumping statute. The trial court, however, upheld Commerce's decision and its methods as consistent with the statute. . . . This court, in an opinion issued February 23, 2000, held that the three-part test employed by Commerce is contrary to the express terms defining EP and CEP in the anti-dumping statute as amended in 1994 and therefore reversed-in-part and remanded for a redetermination of the anti-dumping duties. . . . As to the fair-value and major-input provisions we held that Commerce's decision not to apply those provisions to the transactions in suit was reasonable and within its discretion, and its method consistent with the statute, and therefore we affirmed-in-part. . . . The Korean producers then filed a petition for rehearing and suggestion for rehearing *en banc*. Because the Korean producers raised statutory questions that were not raised in the briefs or at oral argument, the panel took the case on reconsideration to address the statutory arguments. This opinion addresses the Korean producers' statutory arguments; however, the outcome of the case is unchanged.

Background

In 1993 Commerce issued an order imposing anti-dumping duties on certain steel products from Korea. *See Certain Cold Rolled Steel Flat Products from Korea*, 58 Fed. Reg. 44,159 (Dep't of Commerce 1993) (hereinafter *"Certain Steel Products from Korea"*). . . . [Administrative Reviews occurred in 1995 and 1997, the latter resulting in *Certain Cold-Rolled and Corrosion-Resistant Carbon Steel Flat Products from Korea*, 62 Fed. Reg. 18,404, 18,434 (Dep't of Commerce 1997) (hereinafter *"Final Results"*).]

I

. . . In general, Commerce applies the EP methodology to a sale when the foreign producer or exporter sells merchandise directly to an unrelated purchaser located in the United States. Commerce applies the CEP methodology when the foreign producer's or exporter's steel is sold to an unaffiliated U.S. buyer by a producer-affiliated company located in the United States. If the sale is classified as a CEP sale, additional deductions are taken from the sales price to arrive at the U.S. Price. . . .

[In a footnote, the Court observes "[t]he classification of the sales impacts the determination of the dumping margin because the statute provides for certain deductions from CEP that are not deducted from EP. Specifically, commissions for selling, any expenses from the sale (such as credit expenses), the cost of further manufacture, and the profit allocated to those costs and expenses must be deducted from CEP sales. *See* 19 U.S.C. § 1677a(d). Therefore, use of CEP is more likely to result in a determination of dumping." Also in a footnote, the Court states: "[t]he administrative review at issue in this appeal was initiated after the effective date of the 1994 amendments to the anti-dumping laws contained in the *Uruguay Round Agreements Act* ('*URAA*'). Thus, the statute as amended by the *URAA* applies to this case."]

For the sales of steel produced by each of the appellees challenged here, Commerce calculated the U.S. Price based on an EP classification. In determining whether to classify the sales here as EP or CEP, Commerce applied a three-part test (the "*PQ Test*") that it developed on a remand from an unrelated 1987 case, *PQ Corp. v. United States*, 11 C.I.T. 53, 652 F. Supp. 724, 733–35 (Ct. Int'l Trade 1987). An agency interpretation of 19 U.S.C. § 1677a(a)-(b), the test has been applied when a foreign manufacturer's affiliated entity in the United States makes a sale to an unaffiliated U.S. purchaser prior to import, as in the case of the sales at issue here. Using the *PQ Test*, Commerce classifies sales made by U.S. affiliates as EP sales if the following criteria are met:

(1) the subject merchandise was shipped directly from the manufacturer to the unrelated buyer, without being introduced into the inventory of the related shipping agent;

(2) direct shipment from the manufacturer to the unrelated buyer was the customary channel for sales of this merchandise between the parties involved; and

(3) the related selling agent in the United States acted only as a processor of sales-related documentation and a communication link with the unrelated U.S. buyer.

. . .

All of the sales at issue in the present case were "back-to-back" sales: the Korean producer sold the steel to an affiliated Korean exporter; the exporter sold it to its U.S. affiliate; and finally, the U.S. affiliate sold it to the unaffiliated U.S. purchaser. In most cases, however, the steel was shipped directly to the unaffiliated purchaser without entering the inventory of the U.S. affiliate. In the second administrative review, whether the sales of steel manufactured by the Korean producers satisfied the third prong of the *PQ Test* was one of the principal factual issues in dispute. In classifying the sales at issue, Commerce rejected the domestic producers' argument that the activities of the Korean exporter's U.S. affiliates failed the third prong of the test because they "exceeded those of a mere communications link or processor of documents." . . .

II

Commerce "collapsed" POSCO and its related companies, POCOS and PSI, into one entity for purposes of the anti-dumping analysis and then levied a single anti-dumping duty on the entity. In the second administrative review, Commerce determined that "a decision to treat affiliated parties as a single entity necessitates that transactions among the parties also be valued based on the group as a whole . . . . [Thus] among collapsed entities, the fair-value and major-input provisions are not controlling." . . . Therefore, in its 1995 review, Commerce declined to treat the transfers between the related companies as sales between affiliates, but rather treated them as transfers between divisions of the same company and did not apply the fair-value and major-input provisions of 19 U.S.C. § 1677b(f)(2)-(3).

The domestic producers challenged the *Final Results* by filing suit in the Court of International Trade, calling illegal the *PQ Test* and its application to appellees, the decision to collapse the POSCO affiliates, and the determination that the fair-value and major-input provisions did not apply to transfers among the collapsed companies. The Court of International Trade sustained Commerce's *Final Results*, holding the *PQ Test* to be a reasonable interpretation of the statute and the application in this case to be sustainable. In addition the court held that the decisions to collapse the affiliated producers and not apply the fair-value and major-input provisions were within the agency's discretion. . . . The domestic producers timely appealed to this court those portions of the judgment based on statutory interpretation, challenging the legality of the PQ Test and the decision not to apply the fair-value and major-input provisions, assuming the affiliates were properly collapsed. This court issued an opinion on February 23, 2000 reversing the trial court's decision upholding the *PQ Test* and affirming its decision upholding Commerce's decision to collapse the Korean producers and their affiliates. . . .

The Korean producers filed a timely petition for rehearing and suggestion for reconsideration *en banc* with this court. In that petition the Korean producers argued, for the first time, that language in the URAA implementing act rendered the *Statement of Administrative Action* ("*SAA*") submitted to Congress with the *URAA* a judicially binding interpretation of the agreement and the implementing statute. The panel granted the motion for reconsideration to more fully address the *SAA*.

. . .

Discussion

. . .

II *PQ Test*

The Court of International Trade held that the *PQ Test* did not contradict the statute as amended. The court found that the test was "simply a means to determine whether the sale at issue for anti-dumping duty purposes is in essence between the exporter/producer and the unaffiliated buyer, in which case the EP rules apply." . . . The domestic producers argue that Commerce's *PQ Test* conflicts with the unambiguously expressed intent of Congress because the statute and legislative history make clear that a sale by any producer-affiliated seller in the United States to an unrelated U.S. buyer must be classified as CEP. The appellees argue, however, that the statute is ambiguous about how to classify those sales that occur before importation but that are made by producer-affiliated entities in the United States. Therefore, according to appellees, the *PQ Test* is an appropriate methodology for determining whether EP or CEP classification is applied to those sales.

The language of the statute must be viewed in context. The U.S. Price [*i.e.*, EP or CEP] used in making anti-dumping determinations is meant to be the sales price of an arm's-length transaction between the foreign producer and an unaffiliated U.S. purchaser. The U.S. Price is derived from either EP or CEP sales. To isolate an arm's-length transaction under the current statute, Commerce looks to the first sale to a purchaser that is not affiliated with the producer or exporter. If the producer or exporter sells directly to the U.S. purchaser, that sale is used because it is considered an arm's-length transaction. In that situation the sale is classified as EP. [In a footnote, the Court observes "the statute appears to allow for a sale made by the foreign exporter or producer to be classified as a CEP sale, if such a sale is made 'in the United States.' 19 U.S.C. 1677a(a). No such transaction is at issue in this appeal."] If, however, the first sale to an unaffiliated purchaser occurs in the United States, then that sale must be used to determine the U.S. Price. Such a sale will be classified as a CEP sale and have additional deductions made to account for certain expenses of the seller in the United States. The purpose of these additional deductions in the

CEP methodology is to prevent foreign producers from competing unfairly in the United States market by inflating the U.S. Price with amounts spent by the U.S. affiliate on marketing and selling the products in the United States. In the administrative review process, the foreign producers submit to Commerce the information about sales to unaffiliated purchasers. Those sales must be classified as either: (1) between an unaffiliated U.S. purchaser and the producer or exporter, and thus EP; or (2) between the unaffiliated U.S. purchaser and another entity in the United States that must, by definition, be related to the producer, and thus CEP. Sales in the United States between unaffiliated purchasers and unaffiliated sellers are never at issue; such a sale could never be the first sale to an unaffiliated purchaser.

The question at the root of this appeal is whether a sale to a U.S. purchaser can be properly classified as a sale by the producer/exporter, and thus an EP sale, even if the sales contract is between the U.S. purchaser and a U.S. affiliate of the producer/exporter and is executed in the United States. Appellees argue that it can, if the role of the U.S. affiliate is sufficiently minor that the sale passes the *PQ Test*. The domestic producers argue that the plain language of the statute prevents such a classification. We agree with the domestic producers.

Commerce's three-part *PQ Test* and much of the Court of International Trade case law reviewing it were created before the enactment of the *URAA* in 1994. Prior to the *URAA*, "purchase price" (now EP) was described as:

> the price at which merchandise is purchased, or agreed to be purchased, prior to the date of importation, from a reseller or the manufacturer or producer of the merchandise for exportation to the United States.

19 U.S.C. § 1677a(b) (1988). The "exporter's sales price" (now CEP) was defined as:

> the price at which merchandise is sold or agreed to be sold in the United States, before or after the time of importation, by or for the account of the exporter.

19 U.S.C. § 1677a(c) (1988). The amendments to the statute most relevant to this issue are the addition of the phrase "outside the United States" to the definition of EP, and "by a seller affiliated with the producer" to the definition of CEP. Thus, the 1994 statute reads:

> (a) Export Price
>
> The term "export price" means the price at which the subject merchandise is first sold (or agreed to be sold) before the date of importation by the producer or exporter of the subject merchandise outside of the United States to an unaffiliated purchaser in the United States or to an unaffiliated purchaser for exportation to the United States . . . .
>
> (b) Constructed Export Price
>
> The term "constructed export price" means the price at which the subject merchandise is first sold (or agreed to be sold) in the United States before

or after the date of importation by or for the account of the producer or exporter of such merchandise or by a seller affiliated with the producer or exporter, to a purchaser not affiliated with the producer or exporter . . . .

19 U.S.C. § 1677a(a)-(b).

Despite these changes to the definitions of EP and CEP, the *SAA* submitted to Congress with the *URAA* states that the statutory changes did not alter the "circumstances under which export price (formerly purchase price) versus constructed export price (formerly exporter's sales price) are used." H.R. REP. No. 103-316, vol. 1 at 822 (1994), reprinted in 1994 U.S.C.C.A.N. 3773, 4163. This panel was aware of the *SAA* when it prepared its original opinion, now withdrawn. Prior to a petition for panel rehearing none of the parties brought to the court's attention, however, that in the statute itself, Congress declared that the *SAA* is to be considered

> an authoritative expression by the United States concerning the interpretation and application of the Uruguay Round Agreements and this Act in any judicial proceeding in which a question arises concerning such interpretation or application.

19 U.S.C. § 3512(d). When confronted with a change in statutory language, we would normally assume Congress intended to effect some change in the meaning of the statute. . . . Here, however, the *SAA* prevents us from making such an assumption and we have revised our opinion primarily to address the authoritative weight given the SAA in the statute.

The *PQ Test* arises from Commerce's interpretation of the pre-1994 statutory language. In interpreting the pre-1994 statute, the Court of International Trade in *PQ Corporation* focused on whether there was an affiliate relationship between the foreign producer and the U.S. importer as the primary factor enabling Commerce to differentiate between the two sales classifications. In response to Commerce's argument that there was no statutory requirement that "the importer must be an independent party in order to apply [EP]," the court held that:

> while the statute does not state in so many words that [purchase price] and [exporter's sales price] are to be distinguished by the relationship of the foreign producer to the U.S. importer, the statutory definitions of [purchase price] and [exporters sales price] have been distinguished upon this basis from their inception . . . . The express terms of the statute make it clear that a U.S. importer's relationship to a foreign producer will affect the determination of whether [purchase price] or [exporter's sales price] will apply.

PQ Corp., 652 F. Supp. at 732–33 (emphasis added). Despite the Court of International Trade's emphasis on the relationship between the importer and the foreign producer, however, the test developed by Commerce after the remand in *PQ Corporation* actually does not directly examine the legal relationship between the producer and the importer, but rather seeks to determine the role played by the importer in the transaction. The agency continued to apply the test after the statute was amended in 1994.

We are confronted here with a complex statutory interpretation task. The language of the old and new statutes is not identical, yet it is apparently intended to be applied to the same effect in the same "circumstances." The court opinion in *PQ Corporation* interpreting the old version of the statute relies on the legal relationship between an exporter and importer, while the test developed by the agency in response to that interpretation examines the role the importer plays in the transaction. Confronted with these potential contradictions, we start by examining the current statute, as it is the clearest and most current expression of congressional intent.

A. 1994 Statute

Read without reference to the old statutory language, the plain meaning of the language enacted by Congress in 1994 focuses on where the sale takes place and whether the foreign producer or exporter and the U.S. importer are affiliated, making these two factors dispositive of the choice between the two classifications.

The text of the 1994 definition of CEP states that CEP is the "price at which the subject merchandise is first sold in the United States." 19 U.S.C. § 1677a(a) (emphasis added). In contrast, EP is defined as the price at which the merchandise is first sold "outside the United States." 19 U.S.C. § 1677a(b). Thus, the location of the sale appears to be critical to the distinction between the two categories. Appellees, however, point to a decision of the Court of International Trade holding that the words "outside the United States" were ambiguous, finding that it was unclear whether they described the location of the sale or the location of the producer/exporter. *See Mitsubishi Heavy Indus., Ltd. v. United States*, 15 F. Supp. 2d 807, 812 (Ct. Int'l Trade 1998). We do not perceive the same ambiguity. In any event, the trial court's decision is not binding on us.

When the EP definition is read in conjunction with the CEP definition, the alleged ambiguity in the EP definition disappears. The language of the CEP definition leaves no doubt that the modifier "in the United States" relates to "first sold." The term "outside the United States," read in the context of both the CEP and the EP definitions, as it must be, applies to the locus of the transaction at issue, not the location of the company. Therefore, the critical differences between EP and CEP sales are whether the sale or transaction takes place inside or outside the United States and whether it is made by an affiliate. A sales contract executed in the United States between two entities domiciled in the United States cannot generate a sale "outside the United States." Thus, if "outside the United States" refers to the sale, as the appellees argues in this appeal, one of the parties to the sale or the execution of the contract must also be "outside the United States" for an EP classification to be proper. [In a footnote, the Court adds "[w]hile we can hypothesize a sales contract between two U.S. domiciled entities that is entirely executed outside the United States, we make no determination regarding whether such a sale would be classified as an EP or CEP sale."] Accordingly, the conclusion of the *Mitsubishi* court, that the phrase "outside the United States" ambiguously modifies either the sale or the producer/exporter, is incorrect. In general, a producer/exporter in a dumping investigation will always be located outside the United States. Thus, it must be the locus of the transaction that is modified by "outside the United States" in the EP definition for otherwise the description of the producer/exporter would be pure surplusage. Of course, whether a sale is "outside the United States" depends, in part, on whether the parties are or are not located in the United States. A transaction, such as those here, in which both parties are located in the United States and the contract is executed in the United States cannot be said to be "outside the United States." Thus, such a transaction cannot be classified as an EP transaction. Rather, classification as an EP sale requires that one of the parties to the sale be located "outside the United States," for if both parties to the transaction were in the territory of the United States and the transfer of ownership was executed in the United States, it is not possible for the transaction to be outside the United States.

In the *Final Results*, Commerce attempted to circumvent this geographic restriction on the use of EP sales by stating that when the *PQ Test* was satisfied it "considered the exporter's selling functions to have been relocated geographically from the country of exportation to the United States, where the [U.S. affiliate] performs them." The trial judge's holding that the *PQ Test* does not contradict the statute because it is a means of defining whether a sale is "in essence" between a producer/exporter and the unaffiliated buyer suggests the same point. But it is not a valid point because it departs from the factors Congress put in the statute. As discussed above, the plain language of the EP definition precludes classification of a sale between two U.S. entities (*i.e.*, a U.S. affiliate of the producer and a U.S. purchaser) as an EP sale. Thus, the "relocation" concept produces a result that is contrary to the plain language of the statute.

In addition, the Court of International Trade decision in *PQ Corporation* precludes "relocation" of selling activity by holding that the "statute provides no mechanism for imputing actual sales by an importer to that importer's related 'foreign manufacturer or producer of the merchandise' so that [purchase price (now EP)] will apply." *PQ Corp.*, 652 F. Supp. at 733. Thus, Commerce's decision to redefine the activities occurring inside the United States as occurring outside the United States makes an impermissible end-run around both the plain meaning of the statutory language and the mandate of the Court of International Trade in *PQ Corporation*. Congress has made a clear distinction between the two categories based on the geographic location of the transaction; the agency may not circumvent this geographic distinction by "relocating" the activities of the producer/exporter.

Similarly, the statute also distinguishes the categories based on the participation of an affiliate as the seller. The definition of CEP includes sales made by either the producer/exporter or "by a seller affiliated with the producer or exporter." 19 U.S.C. § 1677a(b). EP sales, on the other hand can only be made by the producer or exporter of the merchandise. *See* 19 U.S.C.§ 1677a(a). Consequently, while a sale made by a producer or exporter could be either EP or CEP, one made by a U.S. affiliate can only be CEP. Limiting affiliate sales to CEP flows logically from the geographical restriction of the EP definition, as a sale executed in the United States by a U.S. affiliate of the producer or exporter to a U.S. purchaser could not be a sale "outside the United States." The location of the sale and the identity of the seller are critical to distinguishing between the two categories.

Congress provided for only two mutually exclusive categories: EP or CEP sales. In distinguishing the two, Congress opted for what can be seen as a structural approach to defining EP and CEP sales, not the function-driven approach of the *PQ Test*. Congress chose clear and unambiguous words such as "affiliated," "sold," and "in" or "outside" the United States. In no sense did it leave the distinguishing factor to the agency to identify. When, as here, there are contracts showing that the sales at issue took place in the United States between two entities with United States addresses, one of which was an affiliate of the producer/exporter, it is contrary to the plain meaning of the statute for Commerce to nevertheless use the *PQ Test* to define the sales as effectively occurring outside of the United States, and thus EP sales rather than CEP sales.

The sales contracts in evidence plainly prove that the sales to the unaffiliated U.S. purchasers were made by affiliates of the foreign producers or exporters that are located in the United States. If the importer and the producer/exporter are affiliated, then the first sale to an unaffiliated party is necessarily the sale between the affiliated importer and the unaffiliated purchaser (unless there is another intermediate U.S. affiliate involved, which would have no effect on the analysis). Thus, the sales at issue fall squarely within the definition of CEP as articulated in the 1994 version of the statute.

. . .

The Korean producers argue that it is the question of who is the seller that is left unresolved by the statute. Because the terms "seller" and "sold" are undefined in the statute, they are therefore ambiguous, assert the Korean producers [and deference under the Chevron doctrine should be accorded to the *PQ Test*]. . . . We, however, are not persuaded that this language in the statute is ambiguous.

When a word is undefined in a statute, the agency and the reviewing court normally give the undefined term its ordinary meaning. . . . *Black's Law Dictionary* (6th ed. 1990) defines "seller" as "one who has contracted to sell property . . . the party who transfers property in the contract of sale." As to "sold," this court previously addressed the meaning of that term in the definition of the Exporter's Sales Price (now CEP). *See NSK Ltd. v. United States*, 115 F.3d 965, 973 (Fed. Cir. 1997). In that case we defined "sold" to require both a "transfer of ownership to an unrelated party and consideration." . . . We see no reason to depart from those definitions, and therefore hold that the "seller" referred to in the CEP definition is simply one who contracts to sell, and "sold" refers to the transfer of ownership or title. . . . .

Rather than impliedly delegating the task of distinguishing between the two types of sales to the agency, Congress did so right in the statute.

The sales activities of the U.S. affiliates of the Korean producers or exporters clearly meet these definitions, as evidenced by the contracts for sales between the U.S. affiliates and the U.S. purchasers. The record in this appeal is not disputed; it was the U.S. affiliates of the Korean producers that contracted for sale with the unaffiliated U.S. purchasers. The title or ownership passed from the U.S. affiliate to the unaffiliated U.S. purchaser. There were no contracts between the Korean producers and the unaffiliated U.S. purchasers. Thus, the U.S. affiliates were the "sellers," as indicated by the plain language of the statute. Commerce does not require a cumbersome test, examining the activities of the affiliate, to determine whether or not the U.S. affiliate is a seller, when the answer to that question is plain from the face of the contracts governing the sales in question. If Congress had intended the EP versus CEP distinction to be made based on which party set the terms of the deal or on the relative importance of each party's role, it would not have written the statute to distinguish between the two categories based on the location where the sale was made and the affiliation of the party that made the sale.

. . .

When Congress makes such a clear statement as to how categories are to be defined and distinguished, neither the agency nor the courts are permitted to substitute their own definition for that of Congress, regardless of how close the substitute definition may come to achieving the same result as the statutory definition, or perhaps a result that is arguably better. Normally, having determined that the agency's test employs terms that are contrary to those in the statute, our analysis would stop. In this case, however, we are confronted with the *SAA*, which Congress has stated provides a guide to authoritative interpretation of the statute.

B. The *Statement of Administrative Action*

Here, despite the plain meaning of the amended language of the statute, the *SAA* that accompanied the *URAA* declares that the "new section 772 retains the distinction in existing law between 'purchase price' (now called the 'export price') and 'exporters sales price' (now called the 'constructed export price')." The *SAA* goes on to state that "notwithstanding the change in terminology, no change is intended in the circumstances under which export price . . . versus constructed export price . . . are used." H.R. REP. No. 103-316, vol. 1 at 822 (1994), *reprinted in* 1994 U.S.C.C.A.N. 3773, 4163. Appellees cite to the *SAA* as evidence of congressional intent to endorse the *PQ Test* as a proper interpretation of the new statutory language. We, however, do not so interpret the *SAA*.

First, the *PQ Test* is hardly consistent with the pre-1994 statute, read as a whole. Prior to the 1994 amendments, the statute required only that "purchase price" sales be made "prior to the date of importation" without any explicit reference to where the sales had occurred. 19 U.S.C. § 1677a(b) (1988). The "exporters sales price" (now CEP), however, was defined, as it is today, as the "price at which merchandise is sold or agreed to be sold in the United States." 19 U.S.C. § 1677a(c) (1988). Thus, the distinction based on the location of the sale was already present, although less complete, in the prior version of the statute. Use of the *PQ Test* to "relocate" the sales activity from the producer/exporter to the U.S. affiliate therefore appears inconsistent with the pre-1994 statutory language for the same reasons it is inconsistent with the language of today's statute. In addition, the legislative history of the earliest versions of the anti-dumping statute also indicates that Congress traditionally distinguished between EP and CEP based on the presence of an affiliate in the United States. For example, in hearings before the Senate Committee on Finance discussing Sections 203 and 204 of the *Antidumping Act of 1921*, the equivalent of an EP classification was said to apply if "the merchandise is sold by the foreign seller to an American purchaser having no interest in the business of the foreign seller." EMERGENCY TARIFF AND ANTIDUMPING: HEARINGS ON H.R. 2435. BEFORE THE SENATE COMM. ON FINANCE, 67TH CONG. at 11 (1921). In the same hearings, the Exporters Sales Price (or CEP) was said to apply if "the merchandise is sold, by a foreign seller having an interest in the American purchasing agency." . . .

Second, this Court has never endorsed the *PQ Test* as a proper interpretation of the pre-1994 statute. Prior to this case, this court has never considered the legality of the test, much less held that the test is a reasonable interpretation of an ambiguous statute. In fact, when describing the EP/CEP distinction, this court has repeatedly relied on the affiliate relationship between the producer/exporter and the importer. . . . In cases heard prior to the amendments, however, the Court of International Trade did approve application of the test that resulted in a purchase price (now EP) classification despite the fact that a U.S. affiliate processed the orders. . . . Nevertheless, in light of this court's earlier statements on the EP/CEP distinctions and Congress's clarification of the statute in 1994, we do not find the Court of International Trade's endorsement of the *PQ Test* to reflect an accurate interpretation of the pre-1994 statute.

Furthermore, in situations where the Court of International Trade has reviewed the application of the *PQ Test* after the 1994 amendments, it has only upheld applications that resulted in the sales in question being classified as CEP sales, rather than as EP sales. . . . Until this case, the Court of International Trade was not confronted with EP classification of a sale in the United States by an affiliate. In addition, the Court of International Trade itself has expressed reservations about the test, admonishing "this is not an easily administrable test and the court suggests that Commerce attempt to draw some sharper lines." *U.S. Steel Group*, 15 F. Supp. 2d at 903.

Finally, there is no indication in the legislative history that Congress intended to retain the *PQ Test* upon amending the statute because the test is nowhere mentioned. The Korean producers correctly argue that Congress is presumed to know the administrative or judicial interpretation given a statute when it adopts a new law incorporating the prior law. *See Lorillard v. Pons*, 434 U.S. 575, 580–81 . . . (1978). *Lorillard*, however, is limited to those situations where Congress "enacts a statute without change." . . . Here we cannot ignore the fact that Congress indeed changed the language of the statute, particularly because the changes are directly at odds with the *PQ Test*. If Congress had intended to endorse the *PQ Test* it would not have undercut the test by adding the clarifying language to the statute in 1994.

Our review of the pre-1994 statute and the 1994 amendments reveals language that is consistent, although clearer in the amended version. Since the amendment, recent court interpretations of the statute and review of the *PQ Test* have also been consistent in interpreting the statute to require CEP classification when a U.S. affiliate is doing the selling. Indeed, the addition of the word "affiliated" to the CEP sales definition in the 1994 amendments is entirely consistent with the relationship-based distinction first articulated by the Court of International Trade in *PQ Corporation* and repeatedly stated by this court. Similarly, the logical interpretation of Congress's addition in 1994 of the words "outside the United States" to the definition of an EP sale is that Congress intended to codify the traditional distinction between the EP and CEP. The addition of these terms merely echoed the interpretation given by the Court of International Trade in *PQ Corporation* and reinforced the language in the statute prior to the 1994 amendment by emphasizing that the critical question was not the role of the affiliate in the sale but the legal relationship between the seller and the producer/exporter, *i.e.*, whether the U.S. importer is an affiliate of the foreign producer. Since the amendments in 1994, there has been no judicial endorsement of the use of the *PQ Test* to "relocate" the sales activities of the exporters to their U.S. affiliates. Despite earlier endorsement of the test by the Court of International Trade, we find nothing in the pre-1994 statute or the *SAA* to indicate that Congress intended that the distinction between EP and CEP to be based on the activities of the importer rather than the legal relationship between the importer and the producer/exporter. Thus, we will not now hold the *SAA* to be an endorsement of an agency interpretation that is inconsistent with the plain language of the current statute, particularly where it is clear to us that the test was never consistent with the statute or congressional intent.

Accordingly, we hold that if the contract for sale was between a U.S. affiliate of a foreign producer or exporter and an unaffiliated U.S. purchaser, then the sale must be classified as a CEP sale. Stated in terms of the EP definition: if the sales contract is between two entities in the United States, and executed in the United States and title will pass in the United States, it cannot be said to have been a sale "outside the United States"; therefore the sale cannot be an EP sale. Similarly, a sale made by a U.S. affiliate or another party other than the producer or exporter cannot be an EP sale. Thus, we reverse the decision of the Court of International Trade and remand to that court (for remand, if necessary, to the Department of Commerce) for a re-determination of anti-dumping duties that is consistent with this holding.

[What is the definition of "affiliate" under U.S. AD law? *See* 19 U.S.C. § 1677(33).]

IV. Profit Adjustment to Constructed Export Price and 2005 *SNR Roulements* Case

SNR Roulements v. United States,

United States Court of Appeals for the Federal Circuit,
402 F.3d 1358–63 (2005)

CLEVENGER, CIRCUIT JUDGE:

The United States and The Torrington Company ("Torrington") appeal the decision of the United States Court of International Trade that the Department of Commerce ("Commerce") is statutorily required to include imputed credit and inventory carrying costs in "total expenses" when those costs are included in "total United States expenses" for the purpose of calculating constructed export price profit. . . . Because the Court of International Trade erroneously interpreted 19 U.S.C. § 1677a as not permitting Commerce to use actual expenses instead of imputed expenses to account for credit and inventory carrying costs when determining "total expenses," we reverse its decision and remand the case with the instruction that Plaintiffs [*i.e.,* Torrington] be provided an opportunity to make a showing that their dumping margins were wrongly determined because Commerce's use of actual expenses did not account for U.S. credit and inventory carrying costs in the calculation of total expenses.

I

"Dumping" refers to the sale or likely sale of goods at less than fair value. 19 U.S.C. § 1677 (2000). When reviewing or determining antidumping duties, the administering authority is required to determine "(i) the normal value and export price (or constructed export price) of each entry of the subject merchandise, and (ii) the dumping margin for each such entry." 19 U.S.C. § 1675 (2000). Constructed export price ("CEP") refers to the price, as adjusted pursuant to Section 1677a, at which the subject merchandise is sold in the United States to a buyer unaffiliated with the producer or exporter. The "dumping margin" refers to the amount by which the normal value exceeds export price or CEP. § 1677.

Section 1677a authorizes several adjustments to the price that gives rise to CEP. One adjustment involves reducing the price by the profit ("CEP profit") allocated to the "total United States expenses." 19 U.S.C. § 1677a(d)(3) (2000). Total United States expenses include the following:

(1) the amount of any of the following expenses generally incurred by or for the account of the producer or exporter, or the affiliated seller in the United States, in selling the subject merchandise (or subject merchandise to which value has been added) —

(A) commissions for selling the subject merchandise in the United States;

(B) expenses that result from, and bear a direct relationship to, the sale, such as credit expenses, guarantees and warranties;

(C) any selling expenses that the seller pays on behalf of the purchaser; and

(D) any selling expenses not deducted under subparagraph (A), (B), or (C);

(2) the cost of any further manufacture or assembly (including additional material and labor), except in circumstances described in subsection (e) of this section . . . .

§ 1677a(d). CEP profit is calculated by multiplying the "total actual profit" by the "applicable percentage," which is obtained by "dividing the total United States expenses by the total expenses." § 1677a(f). Total expenses

means all expenses in the first of the following categories which applies and which are incurred by or on behalf of the foreign producer and foreign exporter of the subject merchandise and by or on behalf of the United States seller affiliated with the producer or exporter with respect to the production and sale of such merchandise.

§ 1677a(f)(2)(C). The applicable category for purposes of this appeal further defines total expenses as those

incurred with respect to the subject merchandise sold in the United States and the foreign like product sold in the exporting country if such expenses were requested by the administering authority for the purpose of establishing normal value and constructed export price.

§ 1677a(f)(2)(C)(i).

II

In the seventh administrative review [published at 62 Fed. Reg. 61,963 (20 November 1997)] of the antidumping duty order on antifriction bearings, Commerce determined that Plaintiffs had made sales at less than fair value. . . .

Plaintiffs sought judicial review of Commerce's final decision in the Court of International Trade contending, *inter alia*, that Commerce unlawfully calculated CEP profit because Commerce included an imputed amount for credit and inventory carrying costs when calculating total United States expenses, but relied on actual amounts, to the exclusion of an imputed amount, when calculating total expenses. . . . In particular, Plaintiffs contended that 19 U.S.C. § 1677a unambiguously requires that an imputed amount be used in the calculation of total expenses when an imputed amount is used in the calculation of total United States expenses. Relying for support on *Chevron U.S.A. Inc. v. NRDC*, 467 U.S. 837, . . . (1984), the Court of International Trade interpreted Section 1677a as unambiguously establishing that total United States expenses was a subset of total expenses and that therefore: "Commerce must include imputed credit and inventory carrying costs in 'total expenses' when they are included in 'total United States expenses.'" . . .

The Court of International Trade remanded the case to Commerce, ordering that it re-determine Plaintiff's margin in accordance with the court's construction of the statute. . . . On remand, Commerce complied, but objected to the Court of International Trade's understanding of Section 1677a. Commerce explained:

> Since the cost of the U.S. and home-market merchandise includes the actual booked interest expenses, it is not appropriate to include imputed interest amounts as well in total expenses. Doing so double-counts this expense to a certain extent and overstates the cost attributed to sales of this merchandise. This overstatement of cost understates the ratio of U.S. selling expenses to total expenses and consequently understates the amount of actual profit allocated to selling, distribution, and further-manufacturing activities in the United States.

Final Results of Redetermination Pursuant to Court Remand (Oct. 13, 2000) . . . .

The Court of International Trade affirmed the remand results, . . . and the government and Torrington appeal. . . .

III

The issue in this case is whether it is lawful for Commerce to account for credit and inventory carrying costs with an imputed expense when calculating total United States expenses and to account for the same costs with the presumption that they are embedded in a respondent's actual expenses when calculating total expenses. Because Section 1677a does not unambiguously address the issue, we hold that Commerce may account for credit and inventory carrying costs using imputed expenses in one instance and using actual expenses in the other provided that Commerce affords a respondent who so desires the opportunity to make a showing that the amount of imputed expenses is not accurately reflected or embedded in its actual expenses.

The parties contend that the analysis set forth in *Chevron* controls the outcome of this case. Under that analysis, when a court reviews an agency's interpretation of a statute the agency administers it applies a two-step analytical paradigm. 467 U.S. at 842–43. First, a court considers whether Congress has directly spoken to the precise question at issue. If so, all that remains is for a court to ensure that the agency gives effect to the unambiguously expressed intent of Congress. Second, however, if Congress has not directly spoken to the precise question at issue, making the statute silent or ambiguous with respect to the specific issue, a court considers whether the agency's interpretation is a permissible construction of the statue. *Id*. The parties here divide on whether this case resolves at step one of the *Chevron* analysis.

Appellants [*i.e.*, Commerce] assert that the language of Section 1677a does not show that Congress directly addressed the issue of the manner in which Commerce may account for credit and inventory carrying costs. Therefore, they argue, the question for this court is whether Commerce's election to use imputed expenses when calculating total United States expenses and actual expenses when calculating total expenses reflects a permissible construction of Section 1677a. According to the government, this construction is permissible because (1) it avoids double counting of interest expenses and (2) Commerce interprets the statute to require that actual expenses be used to calculate total expenses.

Appellees [*i.e.*, Torrington] deny that we have authority to consider whether Commerce's interpretation is permissible because, they argue, when Congress drafted Section 1677a it made crystal clear that all expenses "incurred with respect to the subject merchandise sold in the United States" are to be included in the calculation of total expenses. Thus, Appellees contend, because U.S. credit and inventory carrying costs are literally "expenses," if an imputed number is used to account for these expenses when calculating total United States expenses, Congress has unambiguously stated that Commerce must add that number to the calculation of total expenses even if some or all U.S. credit and inventory carrying costs are already accounted for in a respondent's actual expenses.

Appellees' contention that in Section 1677a Congress has unambiguously and directly spoken to the precise issue in this case is implausible. The statute describes CEP profit as the product of total actual profit multiplied by the applicable percentage. § 1677a(f)(1). The applicable percentage is calculated by "dividing the total United States expenses by the total expenses." § 1677a(f)(2)(A). Total United States expenses are defined as those expenses enumerated in Section 1677a(d)(1) and (2). § 1677a(f)(2)(B). Finally, total expenses in this case include "expenses incurred with respect to the subject merchandise sold in the United States." § 1677a(f)(2)(C)(i). These statutory subsections contain no mention of what manner or form of accounting Commerce is required to use when calculating total United States expenses and total expenses. They also do not state or clearly indicate that Commerce may or may not impute expenses in some calculations and rely on actual expenses in others. Because nothing in the language addresses the question of whether Commerce must use an imputed value when calculating total expenses if it has used an imputed value in calculating total United States expenses, there is no basis to conclude that Congress has provided clear instructions on the issue. . . . [T]he remaining question is whether the agency's interpretation of the section is permissible.

Beyond their arguments directed to the first step of the *Chevron* analysis, Appellees do not seriously dispute that the government's interpretation of Section 1677a is permissible. Our precedent indicates that in antidumping cases, we accord substantial deference to Commerce's statutory interpretation, . . . and this record does not show that Commerce's interpretation is unlawful. In this case, we do not understand the government to argue that Commerce views expenses pertaining to U.S. credit and inventory carrying costs as outside the category of expenses incurred with respect to the subject merchandise sold in the United States. In addition, there is no indication that Commerce interprets Section 1677a to permit the exclusion of expenses pertaining to U.S. credit and inventory carrying costs from its calculation of total expenses. Instead, according to the government and Torrington, when Commerce calculates total expenses it does so under the presumption that using actual expenses in the calculation produces a result that takes into account U.S. credit and inventory carrying costs that were imputed to total United States expenses.

We note, however, that neither the government nor Torrington is unequivocal in this assertion. For instance, the government's brief asserts that "the respondent's interest expenses are included in its actual booked expenses, and these interest expenses already largely account for imputed expenses." Torrington's brief asserts that a respondent's audited financial records "presumptively include all financial expenses, including such financial expenses as might be associated with extending credit to U.S. or home market customers, or in maintaining inventory before sale."

Antidumping laws intend to calculate antidumping duties on a fair and equitable basis. . . . Assuming there are cases where actual expenses do not take into account U.S. credit and inventory carrying costs, it is at least possible that in such cases a respondent's dumping margins are not calculated on a fair and equitable basis. The reason is that the additive increase to the numerator of the applicable percentage fraction may not be adequately reflected in the denominator of the fraction. This may impermissibly distort the CEP profit calculation, and accordingly, the dumping margin.

In this case, the question is whether a respondent is entitled to an adjustment where it can show that expenses imputed to U.S. credit and inventory carrying costs are not reflected or embedded in its actual expenses. We understand the government to concede that an adjustment may be appropriate under normal accounting principles when a respondent can show that CEP profit is unfairly distorted by Commerce's practice of relying on actual amounts for total expenses. In this case, there is no dispute that Plaintiffs-Appellees were not afforded an opportunity to make a showing that Commerce's use of actual expenses did not account for U.S. credit and inventory carrying costs for which imputed values were used in the total United States expenses calculation. Because in appropriate circumstances such a showing may support an adjustment to CEP profit, we remand the case with the instruction that Plaintiffs be provided an opportunity to make a showing that their dumping margins were wrongly determined because Commerce's use of actual expenses did not account for U.S. credit and inventory carrying costs in the calculation of total expenses.

IV

For the reasons stated above, we reverse the Court of International Trade's interpretation of Section 1677a and remand the case with the instruction that Plaintiffs be provided an opportunity to make a showing that their dumping margins were wrongly determined because Commerce's use of actual expenses did not account for U.S. credit and inventory carrying costs in the calculation of total expenses.

V. Further Manufacturing, Indirect Selling Expenses, CEP Offset, and 1998 *Mitsubishi* Case

Mitsubishi Heavy Industries, Ltd. v. United States,

United States Court of International Trade,
15 F. Supp.2d 807–824 (1998)

POGUE, JUDGE:

Plaintiffs Mitsubishi Heavy Industries, Ltd. ("MHI") and Tokyo Kikai Sei-sakusho, Ltd. ("TKS"), respondents in the underlying investigation, and Plaintiff Goss Graphic Systems, Inc. ("Goss"), petitioner in the underlying investigation, filed separate motions challenging various aspects of the [1996] final determination of the International Trade Administration of the United States Department of Commerce ("Commerce" or "ITA") regarding imports of large newspaper printing presses ("LNPPs") from Japan. . . . The motions were consolidated.

The antidumping investigation of LNPPs from Japan was conducted simultaneously with Commerce's [1996] investigation of sales of LNPPs from Germany. . . .

Discussion

I. Constructed Export Price

. . .

For each of the relevant LNPP sales by MHI and TKS to the United States, Commerce calculated U.S. price based on a CEP methodology. TKS had reported its sales as CEP sales and therefore does not object to Commerce's methodology. However, MHI reported its sales as EP sales. MHI objects to Commerce's decision to reclassify all of its sales as CEP sales. [MHI lost on this argument. Omitted is this portion of the opinion, because the court applies the *PQ Test* for distinguishing EP from CEP—the very Test overturned subsequently in the *AK Steel* case, excerpted above.] MHI also objects to Commerce's decision to treat its installation costs as further manufacturing, Commerce's methodology for allocating general and administrative ("G&A") expenses for MHI's U.S. subsidiary, and Commerce's decision to deduct from U.S. price, indirect selling expenses incurred in Japan. Both TKS and MHI object to Commerce's refusal to grant a level-of-trade ("LOT") adjustment or CEP offset.

. . .

2. Further Manufacturing by MHI

In calculating MHI's U.S. price, Commerce treated MHI's installation of the subject merchandise as part of further manufacturing "because the U.S. installation process involves extensive technical activities on the part of engineers and installation supervisors and the integration of subject and integral, non-subject merchandise necessary for the operation of LNPPs." . . . According to the statute, CEP is to be reduced by, "the cost of any further manufacture or assembly (including additional material and labor) . . . ." 19 U.S.C. § 1677a(d)(2).

MHI maintains that installation expenses should have been treated as movement-related expenses, pursuant to 19 U.S.C. § 1677a(c)(2)(A), which requires Commerce to reduce EP and CEP by "the amount, if any, included in such price, attributable to any additional costs, charges, or expenses . . . which are incident to bringing the subject merchandise from the original place of shipment in the exporting country to the place of delivery in the United States . . . ."

The distinction is significant because Commerce calculates movement-related expenses without imputed profit. Further manufacturing costs, on the other hand, include an imputed profit attributable to the value added by the further manufacturing activities.

. . .

MHI argues that prior to the *URAA* [*i.e.*, the 1994 *Uruguay Round Agreements Act*], the statute only permitted Commerce to deduct "any increased value, including additional material and labor, resulting from a process of manufacture or assembly performed on the imported merchandise *after the importation of the merchandise and before its sale* . . . ." . . . The current statute does not specify a time period within which the further manufacture or assembly must take place. However, MHI argues, "Congress made it clear . . . that the new provision 'is not intended to effect any substantive change in the deduction made under the current statute for value added from processing or assembly in the United States' . . . ." . . . Because the assembly activities at issue here took place after the sale, MHI argues, they cannot be deducted as further manufacturing.

The Court does not agree. As MHI recognizes, the statute governing the instant investigation does not include any temporal restriction in the definition of further manufacturing. Furthermore, even before the *URAA* took effect, Commerce treated activities occurring after the relevant sales as further manufacturing in certain cases. For example, in *Certain Small Business Telephone Systems and Subassemblies Thereof from Korea,* 54 Fed. Reg. 53,141, 53,151 (Dep't. Commerce 1989) (final det.) ("*SBTS*") the respondent argued specifically that installation occurred after the sale and therefore, could not be considered as value added. Commerce disagreed, explaining, "[w]hether this value is added before or after the sale is irrelevant because, for this product, [respondent's] customers expect the installed system to have the characteristics added by the non-subject merchandise." . . . The physical further manufacturing may have occurred after the sale, but the value added by that further manufacturing was reflected in the sale price of the merchandise. For this reason, *SBTS* was in accordance with the prior statute.

Commerce relied on the same reasoning in this case. "'Whether value is added before or after the sale is irrelevant because, . . . customers expect the installed system to have the characteristics added by the non-subject merchandise.'" . . . Commerce's explanation is reasonable. LNPPs are custom made to order. Therefore,

MHI's installation activities, including the addition of non-subject merchandise would all be included in the sales price of the LNPP agreed upon prior to importation. Furthermore, Commerce's interpretation of the statute has not changed from its pre-*URAA* interpretation. Therefore, Commerce's actions were consistent with the interpretation of the statute articulated in the *SAA* [*i.e.*, the *Statement of Administrative Action* for the *WTO Antidumping Agreement* accompanying the *URAA*].

. . .

Commerce's decision was consistent with the statute and did not violate any longstanding agency policy. Therefore, the court finds Commerce's action to be in accordance with law.

. . .

4. Indirect Selling Expenses Incurred in Japan for MHI

The CEP provision requires that Commerce reduce the price of the first sale to an unaffiliated customer in the United States by the amount of selling expenses "incurred by or for the account of the producer or exporter, or the affiliated seller in the United States, in selling the subject merchandise . . . ." 19 U.S.C. § 1677a(d) (1). Indirect selling expenses are a component of selling expenses. *See* 19 U.S.C. § 1677a(d)(1)(D) (requiring that Commerce deduct from CEP any selling expenses not deducted as commissions or direct selling expenses). As part of indirect selling expenses, Commerce included expenses incurred in Japan to support U.S. sales. MHI argues that Commerce should have deducted only those indirect selling expenses incurred by MLP in the United States.

The CEP methodology is intended to determine a U.S. price "calculated to be, as closely as possible, a price corresponding to an export price between non-affiliated exporters and importers." . . . "Accordingly, when ITA makes its CEP adjustments to U.S. price, its objective is to identify indirect selling expenses that would not exist in an EP sale and deduct those expenses . . . ." . . . MHI contends that Commerce should not have deducted expenses incurred by MHI in Japan "for . . . activities that were fully consistent with an EP transaction." . . .

However, once Commerce has decided to rely on CEP, the statute does not require that Commerce examine every potential CEP deduction to determine whether the activity generating the expense would be inconsistent with an EP transaction. The statute contains a list of mandatory deductions, which includes selling expenses incurred in selling the subject merchandise. The statute does not specify as to the location of the activities generating these expenses. Here, Commerce deducted all indirect selling expenses related to respondents' United States sales. This decision was consistent with the statutory CEP provision.

MHI makes a second argument, that the *SAA* specifically limits CEP deductions to "expenses (and profit) associated with economic activities occurring in the United States." . . . MHI interprets this provision to require that the activities generating the deducted costs must occur in the United States. However, MHI's reading is too narrow. Expenses incurred outside of the United States could still be "associated with" economic activities occurring in the United States. Commerce's approach limited the deductions to those indirect selling expenses "directly associated" with U.S. economic activity.... Thus, Commerce's application of the statute was limited enough to be consistent with the interpretation of the statute articulated in the *SAA*.

The petitioner, Goss, objects to Commerce's allocation of respondents' indirect selling expenses incurred in Japan and Germany, arguing that "Commerce undervalued these expenses by deducting only that portion of the indirect selling expenses attributable to U.S. sales when calculating the CEP." ...

The Court will not address Goss' argument at this time, because in reviewing its allocation of indirect selling expenses to U.S. sales, Commerce came to the conclusion that its methodology overstated the amount of indirect selling expenses to be deducted from CEP. Specifically, Commerce explained that the pool of indirect selling expenses incurred in the home market and allocated to MHI's U.S. sales included "various office and planning expenses ... [that] are not the type of expenses that ordinarily would be associated with United States economic activity." ...

. . .

... [I]ndirect selling expenses must be associated with economic activity occurring in the United States. Commerce erred by deducting certain expenses that were not so associated. Therefore, the Court will remand this issue, pursuant to Commerce's request, in order that Commerce may correct its error. Upon remand, Commerce will evaluate whether its allocation methodology either understates or overstates respondent's indirect selling costs. ...

5. The CEP Offset for MHI and TKS

MHI and TKS both contend that they were entitled to a CEP offset, pursuant to 19 U.S.C. §1677b(a)(7)(B):

> When normal value is established at a level of trade which constitutes a more advanced stage of distribution than the level of trade of the constructed export price, but the data available do not provide an appropriate basis to determine ... a level of trade adjustment, normal value shall be reduced by the amount of indirect selling expenses incurred in the country in which normal value is determined on sales of the foreign like product ....

Commerce declined to grant the adjustment because, "[i]n this instant investigation, the respondents failed to provide the Department with the necessary data for the Department to consider a LOT [level-of-trade] adjustment.... Absent this information, the Department cannot determine whether an LOT adjustment is warranted, nor whether the level of trade in the home market is in fact further removed than the level of trade in the United States."

As the *SAA* makes clear, "if a respondent claims an adjustment to decrease normal value, as with all adjustments which benefit a responding firm, the respondent must demonstrate the appropriateness of such adjustment." ... In this case, Commerce concluded that neither TKS nor MHI had provided sufficient information to demonstrate the appropriateness of the CEP offset. Specifically, Commerce said, "[r]espondents now contend that there is one home market level of trade to which CEP is being compared, but this claim is not well substantiated. The information we have on the record for sales in the home market does not support this conclusion. . . . For neither TKS nor MHI can we ascertain which selling functions are performed by them and which are provided by leasing companies, trading companies or other entities for each type of home market sale. Thus the minimal amount of information provided does not support the conclusions reached by respondents." . . .

Commerce's conclusion was based upon substantial evidence. . . . In the absence of sufficient information, Commerce's refusal to grant either an adjustment or a CEP offset was appropriate.

VI. Repacking Expenses, Level of Trade, CEP Offset, and 2004 *NSK* Case

NSK Ltd. v. United States,

United States Court of Appeals for the Federal Circuit,
390 F.3d 1352–61 (2004)

Linn, Circuit Judge:

NSK Ltd. and NSK Corp. (collectively "NSK") appeal from the judgment of the Court of International Trade affirming the determinations of the Department of Commerce ("Commerce") holding that NSK's repacking expenses were correctly classified as a selling expense under 19 U.S.C. § 1677a(d)(1)(B) and refusing to grant NSK a partial level of trade adjustment for certain sales comparisons to normal value. . . . Because Commerce's classification of NSK's repacking expenses as selling expenses, and not movement expenses under 19 U.S.C. § 1677a(c)(2)(A), was arbitrary, we vacate and remand that determination. Because Commerce correctly refused to grant NSK a partial level of trade adjustment, we affirm that decision.

I. Background

This is an antidumping appeal, pertaining to antidumping duty orders on ball bearings and cylindrical roller bearings imported into the United States from May 1, 1996, through April 30, 1997. . . . NSK Ltd. manufactured and sold the bearings in Japan during the review period; and NSK Corp., a related U.S. corporation, imported them into the United States.

NSK Corp. made deliveries to unaffiliated customers in the United States from various U.S. warehouses it owned and operated. NSK submitted to Commerce a list of expenses incurred in bringing the bearings from Japan to its U.S. customers. These expenses included costs for, *inter alia*, Japanese inland freight, Japanese warehousing, international freight, marine insurance, U.S. inland freight (from port to warehouse, and from warehouse to U.S. unaffiliated customers), U.S. customs duties, U.S. pre-sale warehousing, and U.S. repacking. Commerce allowed deductions for all the expenses as movement expenses under 19 U.S.C. § 1677a(c)(2)(A), except U.S. repacking expenses, which it treated as direct selling expenses under 19 U.S.C. § 1677a(d)(1)(B). According to NSK, its repacking expenses were incurred when it unpacked merchandise in its warehouse from the international shipping packets into individual or small quantity boxes prior to shipment to unaffiliated U.S. customers.

NSK also submitted to Commerce data about its home market sales. Commerce determined that there were two home market levels of trade: original equipment manufacturers and aftermarket customers. Commerce also found that constructed export price sales constituted a third, distinct level of trade. NSK requested that Commerce calculate a level of trade adjustment measured by price differences between the level of trade found in the home market aftermarket and original equipment manufacturers' levels of trade. Commerce rejected the request, and instead used a "constructed export price offset."

NSK appealed Commerce's classification of repacking expenses and its adjustment as to the level of trade. The Court of International Trade affirmed both of Commerce's determinations, . . . and . . . dismissed the case. NSK appealed to this court. . . .

II. Discussion

. . .

B. Repacking Expenses

Section 1677a(c)(2)(A) allows the constructed export price to be reduced by movement expenses. It provides that "the price used to establish export price and constructed export price shall be . . . reduced by":

> the amount, if any, included in such price, attributable to any additional costs, charges, or expenses, and United States import duties, which are incident to bringing the subject merchandise from the original place of shipment in the exporting country to the place of delivery in the United States. . . .

19 U.S.C. § 1677a(c)(2)(A) (2000).

A separate provision provides for different treatment of direct selling expenses, which are also used in calculating the constructed export price: "For purposes of this section, the price used to establish constructed export price shall also be reduced by . . . expenses that result from, and bear a direct relationship to, the sale, such as credit expenses, guarantees and warranties . . . ." *Id.* § 1677a(d)(1)(B).

NSK submitted to Commerce a list of expenses, which included its U.S. repacking expenses. Commerce reduced the U.S. price of the merchandise for all expenses that NSK listed except its repacking expenses. Commerce denied NSK an allowance for the repacking expenses under § 1677a(c)(2)(A), instead treating NSK's repacking expenses as direct selling expenses under § 1677a(d)(1)(B). . . . Commerce reasoned that:

> We do not view repacking expenses as movement expenses. The repacking of subject merchandise in the United States bears no relationship to moving the merchandise from one point to another. The fact that repacking is not necessary to move merchandise is borne out by the fact that the merchandise was moved from the exporting country to the United States prior to repacking. Rather, we view repacking expenses as direct selling expenses respondents incur on behalf of certain sales which we deduct pursuant to section 772(d)(1)(B) of the statute [19 U.S.C. § 1677a(d)(1)(B)] . . . .

The Court of International Trade affirmed. . . . [It] reasoned that NSK's repacking expenses were properly classified as selling expenses because § 1677a(d)(1)(B) did not provide an exhaustive list and was not limited simply to credit expenses, guarantees, and warranties. . . . The Court of International Trade concluded that it was reasonable to classify the repacking expenses as selling expenses because the repacking was performed on individual products to facilitate their sale to unaffiliated U.S. customers. . . . Moreover, the Court of International Trade found that NSK's repacking expenses were not incidental to bringing the subject merchandise from the original place of shipment to the place of delivery in the United States, and that Commerce thus acted reasonably in refusing to classify the repacking expenses as movement expenses under § 1677a(c)(2)(A). . . .

1. The Parties' Arguments

NSK argues that Commerce erred in classifying its U.S. repacking expenses as selling expenses rather than movement expenses. First, NSK points out that Commerce permitted the constructed export price to be reduced by several other types of similar expenses that it concluded were movement expenses under § 1677a(c)(2)(A). These included: Japanese inland freight (from plant to warehouse, and from warehouse to exit port), international freight, U.S. inland freight (from entry port to warehouse, and from warehouse to U.S. unaffiliated customers) ("U.S. shipping"), Japanese warehousing, marine insurance, U.S. brokerage, U.S. customs duties, and U.S. pre-sale warehousing. NSK argues that if these categories of expenses were deemed movement expenses under § 1677a(c)(2)(A), then U.S. repacking expenses, which are indistinguishable from other pre-sale warehousing, handling, and insurance expenses, should also be categorized as movement expenses.

. . . NSK [next] contends that whether repacking was required to bring merchandise from Japan to NSK's U.S. warehouse is irrelevant. NSK also argues that the repacking expenses were movement expenses because they were necessary to bring the merchandise to the place of delivery in the United States, e.g., each customer's place of business. . . . [R]epacking was necessary to make the requested quantities of bearings deliverable to U.S. customers. Finally, NSK argues that Commerce's contention that repacking was needed to sell the merchandise to an unaffiliated U.S. customer is inconsistent with its allowance of U.S. inland freight costs as movement expenses, which under Commerce's reasoning also would be "directly related" to specific sales.

Commerce responds that the Court of International Trade properly affirmed its decision that NSK's U.S. repacking expenses were selling expenses. Commerce relies on the following questionnaire response provided by NSK as evidence that its repacking expenses were selling expenses: "Merchandise normally is shipped from the U.S. warehouse in its original containers. In some instances, different pallets were used for shipment to U.S. customers and some repackaging may have occurred to accommodate smaller distributor orders." . . .

Commerce asserts that its rationale is correct that repacking bears no relationship to movement of the merchandise because the merchandise was moved from Japan to the United States prior to any repacking. Commerce further argues that repackaging expenses are distinct from warehousing expenses, because warehousing expenses are associated with storage before or during the movement process. Commerce finally argues that its statutory construction is correct because § 1677a(d)(1)(B) did not limit direct selling expenses to the enumerated credit expenses, guarantees, or warranties.

2. Analysis

. . .

Neither provision [the movement and sale provisions of the AD statute] mentions repacking specifically. On the one hand, repacking [expenses] could be a movement expense because it could arise "incident to bringing the subject merchandise from the original place of shipment . . . to the place of delivery in the United States." 19 U.S.C. § 1677a(c)(2)(A) (2000). Just as warehousing is considered a movement expense, repacking, especially to enable warehousing, could be deemed a movement expense. On the other hand, repacking could be a selling expense because it could be an "expense[] that results from, and bears a direct relationship to, the sale" to particular customers. *Id.* § 1677a(d)(1)(B). Having received an order, the importer could repack the merchandise to accommodate the customer. Because the movement and selling expense statutes do not unambiguously classify repacking expenses in one category or the other, we must consider Commerce's interpretation under step two of *Chevron* (*i.e.*, *Chevron U.S.A. Inc. v. Natural Resources Defense Council, Inc.*, 467 U.S. 837, 843–44, . . . (1984).)

"If the statute is silent or ambiguous with respect to the specific issue, the question for the court is whether the agency's answer is based on a permissible construction of the statute." *Chevron*, 467 U.S. at 843. We conclude that Commerce's determination that NSK's repacking expenses are properly classified as selling expenses under 19 U.S.C. § 1677a(d)(1)(B) is impermissible. Commerce's classification of repacking expenses as selling expenses is internally inconsistent with its classification of U.S. warehousing expenses and U.S. warehouse-to-customer-shipping expenses as movement expenses.

Commerce's first attempt to explain why repacking is not a movement expense is that "the repacking of subject merchandise in the United States bears no relationship to moving the merchandise from one point to another." . . . This point is unpersuasive because it is inconsistent with Commerce's treatment of warehousing. If the test is "bearing [a] relationship to moving the merchandise," then U.S. warehousing (*i.e.*, storing goods while awaiting sale to a customer) should not be a movement expense—goods do not move when they are stored.

Commerce next argues that NSK's successful movement of merchandise from Japan to the United States without repacking is evidence that "repacking is not necessary to move merchandise." . . . This rationale is unpersuasive because it too is inconsistent with Commerce's treatment of the U.S. warehousing expense. Under Commerce's rationale, U.S. warehousing also should be excluded from the scope of § 1677a(c)(2)(A) movement expenses because the merchandise, in theory, could be moved from Japan to a U.S. customer without U.S. warehousing, simply by shipping the merchandise directly from Japan to the U.S. customer. However, Commerce considers U.S. warehousing to be a movement expense.

Finally, Commerce implies that even though the statute might allow it to classify repacking as a movement expense, because repacking occurs to enable a sale—whether to satisfy a customer's request for a different lot size or to accommodate shipping—it is a sales expense under § 1677a(d)(1)(B). . . . Commerce's rationale is internally inconsistent. Treating repacking as a sales expense is inconsistent with treating U.S. shipping as a movement expense. If enabling sales is the test, then U.S. shipping should be a sales expense. Like repacking that enables sales, U.S. shipping occurs after a customer places an order. Indeed, the cost of shipping the merchandise from the U.S. warehouse to the U.S. customer is incurred only because of and in furtherance of the sale. Commerce treats U.S. shipping as a movement expense, however, and fails to explain the inconsistency.

Expenses incurred for U.S. repacking, U.S. warehousing, and U.S. shipping (from the warehouse to particular customers) are analogous. To be consistent, it would appear that Commerce should classify them as the same type of expenses, whether that be as movement expenses or as sales expenses. If Commerce wants to treat these expenses inconsistently, then under *Chevron* we still must defer, but only if Commerce reasonably explains the inconsistency and does not act arbitrarily. . . . Because Commerce did not sufficiently explain the . . . inconsistencies, its determination is arbitrary and impermissible. Commerce's classification of NSK's repacking expenses as selling expenses is vacated and remanded . . . .

On remand, we caution Commerce to be mindful that repacking may have occurred for a number of different reasons. NSK indicated in its questionnaire response . . . that NSK's practice is to bulk ship its merchandise from Japan to U.S. warehouses on pallets used for international shipping. NSK was required to unpack the merchandise from the international shipping pallets, and "in some instances," repack the merchandise into individual or small quantity boxes prior to ship-ment to U.S. customers. . . . On this record, substantial evidence may not support a determination that NSK's repacking expenses were incurred as a direct result of or in furtherance of sales to particular customers. Indeed, NSK's counsel noted at oral argument that repacking is sometimes done for other reasons, *e.g.*, to enable warehousing.

C. Partial Level of Trade Adjustment

Commerce is directed by statute to base normal value upon home market sales at the same level of trade as the export price or the constructed export price. 19 U.S.C. § 1677b(a)(1)(B) (2000); see also *Micron Tech., Inc. v. United States*, 243 F.3d 1301, 1303–04 (Fed. Cir. 2001). The same level of trade means comparable market-ing stages in the foreign market and in the U.S. market. . . . If Commerce cannot find sales in the foreign market at the same level of trade as in the U.S. market, then it will compare sales in the U.S. and foreign markets at different levels of trade. . . . When comparing sales at different levels of trade, Commerce may make a level of trade adjustment ("LOT adjustment") based on the price differences between the two levels of trade:

> The [normal value] shall also be in creased or decreased to make due allowance for any difference (or lack thereof) between the export price or constructed export price . . . that is shown to be wholly or partly due to a difference in level of trade between the export price or constructed export price and normal value . . . .

19 U.S.C. § 1677b(a)(7)(A) (2000) . . . .

In some instances, Commerce will lack sufficient data regarding sales in the two markets to make a LOT adjustment. In those instances, the statutes provide for the application of a constructed export price offset ("CEP offset"), instead of a LOT adjustment. 19 U.S.C. § 1677b(a)(7)(B) (2000) ("When normal value is established at a level of trade which constitutes a more advanced stage of distribution than the level of trade of the constructed export price, but the data available do not provide an appropriate basis to determine under subparagraph (A)(ii) a level of trade adjust-ment, normal value shall be reduced by the amount of indirect selling expenses incurred in the country in which normal value is determined on sales of the foreign like product . . . .") . . . .

Commerce determined that there were two distinct levels of trade for NSK in the Japanese home market—aftermarket sales and original equipment manufac-turer sales—and that these home market levels of trade were at a more advanced stage of distribution than the single constructed export price level of trade in the U.S. market. . . . Commerce found that there was no record evidence to quantify the price difference between the two home market levels of trade and the single U.S. constructed export price level of trade. . . . Thus, Commerce made a CEP off-set to the normal value for all of NSK's CEP transactions. . . . Contrary to NSK's arguments, Commerce concluded that it lacked "explicit authority to make a level-of-trade adjustment between two home-market levels of trade where neither level is equivalent to the level of the U.S. sale." . . .

On appeal, the Court of International Trade affirmed Commerce's use of a CEP offset. . . . The Court of International Trade interpreted 19 U.S.C. § 1677b(a)(7)(A) and concluded that a LOT adjustment was to be made to a price-based normal value only for a difference that is shown to be wholly or partly due to a difference in level of trade between the constructed export price or export price and the normal value. . . . Under 19 U.S.C. § 1677b(a)(7)(B), a CEP offset was required when there was no sufficient data to determine a LOT adjustment under § 1677b(a)(7) (A). . . . The Court of International Trade concluded that Commerce's practice at the time, as provided in 19 C.F.R. § 351.412(d) (1998), was to refuse to calculate a LOT adjustment in those cases where the home market data does not demonstrate that a constructed export price level of trade exists with respect to any transactions. . . . The Court of International Trade concluded that Commerce's conclusion that § 1677b(a)(7)(A) did not provide for a LOT adjustment, other than that based upon price differences in the home market between constructed export price and normal value market levels of trade, was reasonable. . . .

1. The Parties' Arguments

On appeal, NSK does not dispute the manner by which Commerce determined the levels of trade of its constructed export price or normal value transactions. NSK objects to Commerce's decision not to calculate what it terms a "partial" LOT adjustment for constructed export price sales matched to aftermarket normal value sales, based on the price differences between original equipment manufacturer normal value sales and aftermarket normal value sales. NSK relies on language in 19 U.S.C. § 1677b(a)(7)(A) that normal value must be adjusted to reflect any difference "that is shown to be wholly or *partly* due to a difference in level of trade between the export price or constructed export price and normal value." (emphasis added). NSK argues that because the language requires a LOT adjustment if it "partly" adjusts for differences in the levels of trade, a "partial" LOT adjustment is mandated in this case.

. . . Commerce argues that it correctly interpreted 19 U.S.C. § 1677b(a)(7) (and properly concluded that it lacked statutory authority to make a LOT adjustment using two home market levels of trade where neither level is equivalent to the CEP level of trade.

2. Analysis

We agree that Commerce correctly interpreted 19 U.S.C. § 1677b(a)(7) and properly denied NSK's request for a "partial" LOT adjustment. NSK's statutory interpretation is predicated on the presence of the word "partly" in § 1677b(a)(7)(A). Section 1677b(a)(7)(A) provides:

(A) Level of trade

The price described in paragraph (1)(B) shall also be increased or decreased to make due allowance for any difference (or lack thereof) between the export price or constructed export price and the price described in paragraph (1)(B) (other than a difference for which allowance is otherwise made under this section) that is shown to be wholly or partly due to a difference in level of trade between the export price or constructed export price and normal value, if the difference in level of trade—

(i) involves the performance of different selling activities; and

(ii) is demonstrated to affect price comparability, based on a pattern of consistent price differences between sales at different levels of trade in the country in which normal value is determined.

In a case described in the preceding sentence, the amount of the adjustment shall be based on the price differences between the two levels of trade in the country in which normal value is determined.

19 U.S.C. § 1677b(a)(7)(A) (2000) (emphasis added). The word "partly" indicates that a LOT adjustment should be made even when pricing differences between home market levels of trade are only partly attributable to the difference in the level of trade. The partial adjustment must still be between normal value at one level of trade and normal value at the same level of trade as the U.S. sale. Thus, the use of the term "partly" does not mandate a partial LOT adjustment when there are no comparable levels of trade in the home and U.S. markets, and Commerce determines there was insufficient data to make a LOT adjustment. In those instances, 19 U.S.C. § 1677b(a)(7)(B) mandates the use of an alternate adjustment, known as a "CEP offset":

(B) Constructed export price offset

When normal value is established at a level of trade which constitutes a more advanced stage of distribution than the level of trade of the constructed export price, but the data available do not provide an appropriate basis to determine under subparagraph (A)(ii) a level of trade adjustment, normal value shall be reduced by the amount of indirect selling expenses incurred in the country in which normal value is determined on sales of the foreign like product but not more than the amount of such expenses for which a deduction is made under section 772(d)(1)(D) [19 U.S.C. § 1677a(d)(1)(D)] . . . .

19 U.S.C. § 1677b(a)(7)(B) . . . (emphases added). This court noted in *Micron Technologies*:

In some instances, the level of trade in the home market will constitute a more advanced stage of distribution than the level of trade in the United States, yet Commerce will lack sufficient data regarding the sales in the two markets to make a level of trade adjustment, that is, it will be unable to determine how much to reduce the foreign sale price to arrive at a price comparable to the U.S. price. In those cases, the statute provides for the award of a 'constructed export price offset' [("CEP offset")].

243 F.3d at 1305. A CEP offset is designed to cover situations such as these for which the normal value is at a more advanced stage than the constructed export price level

of trade, and for which Commerce determines there is insufficient data to make a LOT adjustment. *See* 19 U.S.C. § 1677b(a)(7)(B) (2000); see also *Koyo Seiko Co. v. United States*, 22 C.I.T. 424, 8 F. Supp. 2d 862, 866 (Ct. Int'l Trade 1998) ("Commerce's interpretation . . . is reasonable, in light of the existence of the CEP offset to cover situations such as those at issue."). Thus, we conclude that Commerce did not err in applying a CEP offset and denying NSK's request for a "partial" LOT adjustment.

III. Conclusion

Because Commerce's classification of NSK's repacking expenses as a selling expense was arbitrary, we vacate that determination and remand . . . . Because Commerce correctly refused to grant NSK a partial level of trade adjustment, we affirm that portion of its decision.

Chapter 10

Injury[1]

I. Overview

An inquiry into injury and causation is an indispensable phase of every AD case. In an AD case, injury may be actual material injury, or threat thereof. Similarly, injury and causation are essential features of every CVD case, save for ones involving a prohibited (Red Light) subsidy. However, in a CVD case, under the WTO *SCM Agreement*, the relevant concept is broader than injury — it is adverse effects, which may be material injury or threat thereof, price depression or suppression, or nullification or impairment of benefits. Moreover, where a Red Light (*i.e.*, export or import substitution) subsidy is proven, there is an irrebuttable presumption that adverse trade effects exist. What rebuttable presumption arises in a case involving a Dark Amber subsidy?

Evidently, understanding and applying the legal criteria for injury and causation, both at national and multilateral levels, are critical in the successful prosecution or defense of an AD or CVD case. The drama of this aspect of the case involves competing stories woven from data. For AD cases, Article 3:1 of the WTO *Antidumping Agreement* demands a determination of injury, to be consistent with Article VI of GATT, must be based on "positive evidence," and "involve an objective examination" of three variables:

(1) *Volume*, that is, the volume of subject merchandise (*i.e.*, the dumped imports).

(2) *Price Effects*, that is, the effect of subject merchandise on suppressing or depressing prices in the importing country of like products (which are domestically-manufactured merchandise that compete with the dumped goods).

(3) *Impacts*, that is, the consequences of subject merchandise for producers in the importing country of like products.

Significantly, Article 3:4 calls for a broad inquiry into "all relevant economic factors and indices having a bearing on the state of the industry." It lists several indicia,

---

1. Documents References:
   (1) *Havana (ITO) Charter* Article 34
   (2) GATT Articles VI, XVI
   (3) WTO *Antidumping Agreement* Articles 1, 3–6, 15

including (1) declines (actual and potential) in sales, profits, output, market share, productivity, return on investments, and capacity utilization, (2) domestic price suppression or depression, (3) the magnitude of the dumping margin, (4) negative effects (actual and potential) on cash flow, inventories, employment, wages, growth, and ability to raise new capital.

As intimated, following a dumping margin or subsidization determination, there is a 2-pronged inquiry—into injury, and into causation. Conceptually, that inquiry indeed is in 2 steps. Are there deleterious repercussions? If so, then are they the result of subject merchandise? In practice, these steps often are conflated. On causation, both WTO and U.S. law are considerably less precise than on injury. Essentially, as long as injury occurs by reason of dumped merchandise, causation is assumed. Small wonder, then, that in practice, causation winds up being confused with correlation. Clever choice of the POI helps ensure the time during which merchandise is dumped corresponds to the time of woe as described by a petitioner.

II. Six Key Technical Points

- **First: Second "Like" Product Determination**

At the outset, a few technical details are important to appreciate. Tripping up on them can affect the outcome of an injury investigation, and thereby an AD or CVD case.

While the DOC renders a decision about like products during the dumping margin or subsidy determination phase of an AD or CVD case, respectively, the ITC typically also must do so in the injury-causation phase.[2] The DOC decision is based on a comparison of subject merchandise to a foreign product, asking whether the allegedly dumped or subsidized merchandise is "like" that sold in the home market of the exporting country. The ITC decision entails comparing allegedly dumped or subsidized merchandise with a product made in the U.S. The inquiry is whether the subject merchandise is "like" a domestic one.

- **Second: Circularity in Definition of "Materiality"**

Do not bother looking to Title 19 of the U.S.C. for a meaningful definition of a key term, namely, "materiality." In an AD or CVD case in the U.S., existence of "material" injury typically is alleged. Alleging threat of "material" injury is not uncommon. Yet, the definition of "materiality" is of little help to petitioner or respondent (unless either side views ambiguity as an asset). That definition is harm that is not inconsequential, immaterial, or unimportant.[3] To say the quantum of "materiality" must be "material" manifestly is circular. Legend has it the definition arose out of

---

2. *See* 19 U.S.C. § 1677(10) (definition of "domestic like product"); *Torrington Company v. United States*, 747 F.Supp. 744 (CIT 1990), *aff'd* 938 F.2d 1278 (Fed. Cir. 1991).
    3. *See* 19 U.S.C. § 1677(7).

Tokyo Round era negotiations involving the USTR in the Carter Administration (1977–1981), Robert Strauss (1918–2014), and the EC.

- **Third: Threats Require Prognostication**

  It is impossible to determine whether a threat of material injury exists without forecasting future outcomes. Inherent in the concept of "threat" is that an injury has not yet occurred—but it might, soon. The same three injury factors are used, price, volume, and all other relevant variables, but with a view to the future.

  For example, in the 2014 CIT case of *Downhole Pipe & Equipment L.P. v. United States*, the ITC looked into projections in the American market for:[4]

  (1) Import penetration, *i.e.*, the share of subject merchandise (which was drill pipes and collars made in China and imported by Downhole Pipe of Sugarland, Texas)?

  (2) Price depression?

  (3) Capacity utilization?

  (4) Inventory of subject merchandise held by importers?

  Initially, the first two factors led the ITC to find (on a 3–3 vote) that subject merchandise posed a threat, especially as the domestic industry (*e.g.*, Rotary Drilling Tools, Texas Steel Conversions, Inc., and U.S. Steel Corp) was vulnerable to injury because of its weakened state. Following challenges by the importer—which had good reason to fight, as the AD duty ranged from 69.32% to 429.95% (plus a CVD of 18.18%)—the ITC emphasized the first, third, and fourth factors. There was no significant increase in subject merchandise inventory, and excess production capacity in China would not lead to greater import penetration. The CIT upheld the revised ITC decision, a negative threat determination, and the Federal Circuit affirmed, hence extant duty orders were revoked.[5]

- **Fourth: Material Retardation**

  Technically, a third basis on which to render an affirmative injury determination under American AD or CVD law is material retardation of the establishment of a domestic industry.[6] However, as a practical matter, that basis is rarely if ever successful. The reason is the extraordinarily low threshold for "establishing" an industry, and thus the truly difficult proposition to prove, namely, that dumped or subsidized merchandise are materially retarding that establishment.

---

4. *See* Number 11-00080 (10 November 2014); Brian Flood, *Court Upholds Decision Against Duties On Imports of Chinese Drill Equipment*, 31 International Trade Reporter (BNA) 2032 (20 November 2014).

5. *See Downhole Pipe & Equipment LP v. U.S. International Trade Commission*, Number 2015-1233 (6 November 2015); Brian Flood, *U.S. Drill Equipment Producers Lose Appeal*, 32 International Trade Reporter (BNA) (12 November 2015).

6. *See* 19 U.S.C. § 1673b(a)(1)(B).

It is an overstatement to say the ITC is likely to conclude a domestic industry is set up if the first few steps of implementing a business plan and holding key meetings (*e.g.*, with bankers) have been taken. Any substantial commitment, by the petitioner, to commence production — even if manufacturing has not started — is enough to "establish" an industry. No machinery or facility need be acquired, put into operation, or even contracted for. What if an existing producer (*e.g.*, of dry, salted codfish) seeks a new source of supply for a raw material (*e.g.*, cod from Alaska), but alleges dumping inhibits it from procuring that source? The ITC response is sure to be a new source of supply for an input would not mean a new industry is established, hence the converse situation — no new input — is not one in which creation of a new industry is thwarted.[7]

- **Fifth: National, Regional, or Multilateral Forums**

Save for a statutory ("as such") challenge, as in the WTO Appellate Body cases on the *1916 Act* and the *Byrd Amendment*, AD and CVD cases typically start — and finish — at the national level. So, they involve private parties arguing before an administrative tribunal (such as the DOC and ITC), and possibly to a formal court (the CIT and Federal Circuit). Only if the case raises issues under an applicable FTA does it escalate into a regional dispute, such as under *NAFTA* Chapter 19. Only if the case raises issues under the WTO *Antidumping* or *SCM Agreement* does it lead to a case between sovereigns, namely, the importing and exporting WTO Member countries, under the *DSU*.

- **Sixth: *2015 TPEA* Amendments**

Thanks to two amendments to the AD-CVD statute wrought by the 2015 *TPEA*, the ITC can render an affirmative injury determination more easily than before.[8] Both concern the profitability of a domestic industry making a product like that of subject merchandise.

First, the ITC is barred from deciding there is no material injury, or no threat of material injury, "merely because that [domestic] industry is profitable, or because the performance of that industry has recently improved." Second, the ITC is authorized to examine different categories of profits, namely, gross profits, net profits, and operating profits. These categories, as well as other factors like Return on Assets (ROA) and ability to service debts, may be metrics of injury to a domestic industry.

---

7. *See Memorandum to the International Trade Commission from the General Counsel, Legal Issues in Certain Dried Salted Codfish from Canada*, Inv. No. 731-TA-199 (preliminary) (22 August 1984).

8. *See* Eric Emerson & Henry Cao, *Impact of the Amendments to U.S. Antidumping and Countervailing Duty Law in the Trade Preferences Extension Act of 2015*, 32 International Trade Reporter 1518 (BNA) (27 August 2015). [Hereinafter, *Impact*.]

III. Defining Domestic Industry, Excluding Related Parties, and 1992 *Torrington* Case

Torrington Company v. United States,

790 F. Supp. 1161, 1168–1169 (CIT 1992), *aff'd* 991 F.2d 809 (Fed. Cir. 1993)

DiCarlo, Chief Judge:

Plaintiff brings this action challenging the negative preliminary determinations of injury by the U.S. International Trade Commission in the antidumping and countervailing duty investigations regarding *Ball Bearings, Mounted or Unmounted, and Parts Thereof, from Argentina, Austria, Brazil, Canada, Hong Kong, Hungary, Mexico, the People's Republic of China, Poland, the Republic of Korea, Spain, Taiwan, Turkey, and Yugoslavia*, 56 Fed. Reg. 14,534 (Int'l Trade Comm'n 1991) (neg. prelim.). . . . The Court affirms the Commission's determinations and holds the Commission did not abuse its discretion . . . by declining to exclude related parties from its consideration of the condition of domestic industry . . . . [The Court also affirmed the ITC's determination that (1) the ITC did not abuse its discretion in relying upon questionnaire data to determine the condition of the industry, (2) there was no reasonable indication of material injury or threat thereof to a domestic industry, and (3) the Commission should not cumulate imports. Omitted are those portions of the opinion.]

. . .

Discussion

. . .

B. The Commission's Decision not to Exclude Related Parties

Plaintiff contends the Commission erred by failing to exclude from its analysis of the domestic industry related parties who import or are related to exporters of the subject merchandise. *See* 19 U.S.C. § 1677(4)(B) . . . . Plaintiff argues financial indicators relevant to the condition of the domestic industry were skewed by inclusion of related parties.

The decision whether to exclude parties who import or are related to exporters of the subject merchandise from consideration of the domestic industry is within the discretion of the Commission. . . . In making this determination, the Commission examines whether there are "appropriate circumstances" for excluding the firm in question from the definition of the domestic industry. . . . The court has upheld the Commission's practice of examining such factors as: 1) the percentage of domestic production attributable to related producers; 2) the reason why importing producers choose to import the subject merchandise (whether to benefit from unfair trade practice or to enable them to continue production and compete in the domestic market), or; 3) the competitive position of the related producer vis-à-vis other domestic producers. . . .

The Commission concluded that appropriate circumstances did not exist to exclude related parties from consideration of the domestic industry. . . . The Commission noted that the ball bearing industry is global in nature and dominated by a small number of multinational companies. . . . Those companies, including plaintiff, operate production facilities in several countries, where production is rationalized to meet the particular needs of each country's market. . . . Since those companies do not find it efficient to produce all ball bearing lines in their U.S. facilities, they import ball bearings or parts from their foreign production operations. . . . The Commission found the related parties' importation was not undertaken principally to benefit from unfair trade practices. . . . The Commission also explained the related parties generally had a longstanding presence as U.S. producers, and that import volume from the subject countries was smaller than U.S. production for each of the related parties and was in most instances quite low. . . . It also noted the related parties collectively account for a substantial proportion of U.S. sales and include some of the largest domestic producers of ball bearings. The Commission determined that exclusion of the related parties could present a distorted view of the industry. . . . The Court finds it was reasonable for the Commission to conclude appropriate circumstances did not exist for exclusion of any of the related parties.

Plaintiff argued the related parties' production rationalization and import practices indicate they shielded their domestic operations from the effects of the imported merchandise. As a result, according to plaintiff, the related parties benefited from unfairly traded ball bearings imported from the subject countries as well as from nine other countries already subject to an antidumping order. Nonetheless, the Commission has the discretion to make a reasonable interpretation of the facts, and the Court will not decide whether it would have made the same decision on the basis of the evidence.

IV. Defining Like Product Market, Captive Production, and 2001 *Japan Hot-Rolled Steel* Case

Making a like product for a downstream article (which could be a finished article, derivative article, or more advanced version of the article) is called "captive production," and by definition it is not for sale in the merchant market. That is, "captive production" refers to internal transfers of a like product from within different parts of a business enterprise. That production does not enter the open—*i.e.*, merchant market—into which a like product is sold to independent buyers. Obviously, vertical integration is a classic instance in which captive production occurs.

Of the three categories of data an administering authority can use to assess material injury, or threat thereof, in an AD or CVD case, namely, (1) volume, (2) price, and (3) all other relevant economic factors, by far the third category is the largest. Within the third category, one important economic statistic used to assess effects of allegedly dumped or subsidized merchandise on a domestic industry is the Import Penetration Ratio. Conceptually, its formula is:

$$\text{Import Penetration Ratio} = \frac{\text{Imports of Subject Merchandise}}{\text{Total U.S. Market}} \times 100$$

The denominator includes both imports of subject merchandise and the domestically-produced like product. The figures in both the numerator and denominator must be from the same POI, and could be in value or volume terms.

But, the market for a domestically-made like product itself consists of two segments:

(1) The merchant market, wherein buyers of the product are independent of the producer-seller.

(2) The captive production market, wherein the producer-seller consumes the product at issue, as an input into a finished or derivative article, or a more advanced version of the product.

In the merchant market, a domestic like product competes directly with subject merchandise. In the captive production market, that is not so. The buyer is affiliated with, and relies for supply on, the producer-seller. The quintessential, common instance of this commercial chain is vertical integration.

The obvious question in an injury determination in which the Import Penetration Ratio is studied and captive production exists is whether it is fair to include in the denominator of the Ratio data from the captive production market. That is, should the ITC focus solely on the merchant market, when a producer-seller transfers a significant amount of its production of the like domestic product? Articles 3–4 of the WTO *Antidumping Agreement* (detailed as they are) do not answer the question, nor does GATT Article VI (as the GATT drafters almost certainly did not contemplate the issue). However, U.S. law treats the question head on.

Under that law, the short answer is "yes, the ITC should focus on the merchant market." Specifically, Section 222(b)(2) of the *1994 Uruguay Round Agreements Act* amended U.S. AD and CVD law in respect of market share and other factors affecting the financial performance of a domestic industry.[9] If the ITC finds a domestic like product that is produced internally and consumed captively in a downstream article:

(1) does not enter the merchant market for that product, *i.e.*, it does not compete with subject merchandise imports, and conversely the domestic like product sold in the merchant market is not generally used to make the downstream article, and

(2) is the predominant material input in making the downstream article,

---

9. *See* 19 U.S.C. § 1677(7)(C)(iv).

then the ITC considers only the merchant market. The ITC must exclude captive production from the denominator of the Import Penetration Ratio.

Excluding captive production sales from the denominator will decrease the size of the denominator, thereby boosting the Ratio and strengthening the case for the petitioner. (A higher Ratio suggests subject merchandise has a greater deleterious effect on domestic producers.) Small wonder, then, why Japan sued the U.S. in the WTO, arguing the American statute was inconsistent with the *Antidumping Agreement*, both as such and as applied.[10] In the underlying American proceeding, the ITC based an affirmative injury determination on just 30% of domestic sales by American steel producers. Because of the statute, the ITC ignored the larger, more profitable, segment of the American steel market, wherein producers consumed hot-rolled steel internally to make other products. Surely the statute precludes a balanced assessment of the economic health of the overall industry. It neglects the plain fact American steel companies do very well for themselves in the captive production market, which is shielded entirely from import competition. To put bluntly the Japanese argument, an injury determination that segments a market in this way, dwelling on the segment affected by imports, is biased in in favor of the petitioner.

Both sides scored a partial victory. Japan failed to prove the statute was a *prima facie* violation of GATT-WTO obligations, particularly Articles 3:1 and 3:4 of the *Antidumping Agreement*. That was because the American statute directs the ITC to "focus primarily" on the merchant market. Neither it nor the *SAA* orders the ITC to focus "exclusively" on that market. But, the U.S. failed to defend the use of the statute by the ITC in the case at bar, because an exclusive focus is precisely what the ITC gave to the merchant market.

In a case such as *Japan Hot-Rolled Steel*, to what extent does the Appellate Body render an interpretation of American trade remedy law, as well as provide an opinion on how the relevant statute is applied by American authorities? Is the interpretation ineluctable? Is it an infringement on sovereignty?

---

10. *See United States — Anti-Dumping Measures on Certain Hot-Rolled Steel Products from Japan*, WT/DS184/AB/R (adopted 23 August 2001).

For an argument that the *2015 TPEA* amendment to Section 771(7) of the 1930 *Tariff Act* was pro-respondent, see *Impact*. The authors point out that before the change, the statute directed the ITC to examine 3 criteria as to whether the captive production exception was met, namely: (1) the internally-consumed domestic like product (that is a candidate for captive production) used to make a downstream article does not enter the merchant market; (2) that internally-consumed domestic like product is the "predominant material input" in the downstream article; and (3) the domestic like product sold in the merchant market is not generally used to produce that same downstream product as is the internally-consumed domestic like product. The 2015 change removed the third factor. This removal enabled the ITC to focus on the merchant, not downstream, market more easily than before. Focusing on the merchant markets favors the petitioning U.S. domestic industry. That is because the ITC looks at a smaller market (the merchant one alone, not the merchant and downstream markets together) in which to judge injury. Thus, import penetration ratios and other metrics are more likely to point to injury.

V. Material Injury, Evaluating All Factors, and 2001 *Thailand Steel* Case

WTO and FTA case law on injury and causation continues to evolve. One trend is a lack of tolerance for sloppy injury investigations. Rightly so, the Appellate Body has enforced rules in Article 3 of the *Antidumping Agreement* requiring a careful, reasoned inquiry into the factors that caused injury in an AD case and adverse trade effects in a CVD case. In the 2001 *Thailand Steel* case, Thailand assessed final AD duties of 27.78% on "H beams" from Poland made of iron or non-alloy steel.[11]

A key issue on appeal was Article 3:4 of the WTO *Antidumping Agreement*. Must an administering authority examine all economic variables listed therein when making an injury determination? Thailand argued "no," stressing the adjective in Article 3:4 that all "relevant" factors must be checked. (Thailand also interpreted semi-colons and the disjunctive ("or") in Article 3:4 oddly, to suggest the list of factors in the provision amounted to checking one index in each of the four factor groupings.) Poland emphasized the word "all."

The Appellate Body agreed with the Panel: "all" means "all." It also agreed with the reasoning of the Panel: the application of customary international law on treaty interpretation, plus the precedent of the 2000 *Argentina Footwear* Appellate Body Report in which it interpreted a provision on injury determination factors in the WTO *Agreement on Safeguards*, Article 4:2(a), which is akin to Article 3:3 of the *Antidumping Agreement*.[12] In sum, each index associated with each factor listed in Article 3:4 must be checked. There are 15 variables in Article 3:4, and checking each is mandatory.

VI. Specific Material Injury Factors and 1982 *SCM* Case

SCM Corp. v. United States,
United States Court of International Trade,
544 F. Supp. 194, 195–196, 198–201 (1982)

NEWMAN, JUDGE:

I. Background

This action, brought . . . by SCM Corporation (SCM), a domestic portable typewriter manufacturer, is again before the Court following my remand to, and the responsive Statement of Reasons by, the United States International Trade

---

11. *See* Appellate Body Report, *Thailand — Anti-Dumping Duties on Angles, Shapes and Sections of Iron or Non-Alloy Steel and H-Beams from Poland,* WT/DS122/AB/R (adopted 5 April 2001).

12. *See Argentina — Safeguard Measures on Imports of Footwear,* WT/DS121/AB/R (adopted 12 January 2000).

Commission ("Commission") in *Portable Electric Typewriters From Japan* . . . .
Plaintiff has contested the Commission's negative determination of injury, . . . and
now before the Court is the Commission's new Statement of Reasons . . . .

. . .

. . . [O]n remand, the Commission has reexamined the record before it and provided this Court with a new Statement of Reasons. The central issue is whether
the Commission's negative injury determination is correct in light of the reasons
advanced in its initial and new Statement[s] of Reasons and the record before the
Commission. . . . [T]he Commission's negative injury determination is affirmed.

. . .

II. Opinion

. . .

C. Market Penetration by LTFV Imports

In its original Statement of Reasons, the Commission majority acknowledged
that the LTFV [less than fair value] imports from Japan had obtained a significant share of the domestic market for portable typewriters during the period of . . .
investigation (October 1973 — March 1974), but posited that "[i]mport penetration
alone is not an adequate basis for determining injury." The Commission majority
explained that none of the other tests of injury applied in this case showed injury
to the domestic industry, but to the contrary such tests indicated that the domestic
industry (*viz.*, SCM) had prospered and was likely to continue expanding.

In its new Statement, the Commission has . . . further elaborated upon its view
that market penetration alone is an insufficient basis for an affirmative finding of
injury.

The Commission's new Statement on remand cites the facts that the affected
domestic industry in this case is represented by a single large firm (SCM) that has
no domestic competitors and holds a dominant position in the United States market; that during the period covered by the investigation (1971–74) SCM showed
improved performance in all indices of the health of the industry; and that the
Commission's view respecting market penetration is consistent with prior Commission precedent. Further, the Commission observed:

> In view of the expanding and increasingly profitable business of the sin-
> gle domestic producer, the mere fact of significant import penetration is
> not by itself capable of demonstrating injury. This is even more the case
> since the data show that import penetration dropped sharply in the last
> year for which information was collected.

And apparently recognizing that the market penetration issue posed by the
Court's remand raises essentially a question of law, the Commission stated:

> If increasing penetration alone were adequate to show injury, such a con-
> clusion could be reached by a computer, negating the need for the conceived

scheme of economic analysis, and *weighing of all factors* such as production, shipments, capacity utilization, employment and profitability by a collegial body of human beings. [Emphasis added.]

I fully agree with the Commission's rejection of what in essence amounts to a *per se* injury rule based upon significant market penetration. In *Armstrong Bros. Tool Co., et al v. United States (Daido Corporation, Steelcraft Tools Division, Party-in-Interest)*, 483 F. Supp. 312, *aff'd*, 626 F.2d 168 (1980), . . . this Court emphasized the complex multifaceted economic and financial analysis involved in making an injury determination . . . and the broad discretionary authority vested in the Commission. Hence, although significant market penetration by the LTFV imports is obviously a highly relevant factor, the Commission has the discretion — indeed an obligation — to consider and weigh a number of other pertinent economic and financial criteria, and consider all the facts and circumstances, including the health of the domestic industry. That approach is precisely what the Commission followed in this case, eschewing any *per se* injury rule predicated upon significant market penetration.

In view of *Armstrong*, there is now a judicially approved explanation as to the reason why no single economic or financial factor necessarily constitutes injury . . . . Therefore, quite apart from the Commission's rationale expressed in its new Statement of Reasons, the question of law raised on remand pertaining to significant market penetration has been judicially answered in agreement with the rationale applied by the Commission.

Plaintiff's arguments are directed essentially at the relative weight and significance the majority Commissioners accorded to the various factors considered (including market penetration), and also directed at the weight of the evidence. But fundamentally, the relative weight the Commission chose to accord market penetration vis-à-vis other equally pertinent injury criteria considered was a matter of discretion and expert judgment; and as we have seen, it is not the function of the Court in reviewing an injury determination of the Commission . . . to weigh the evidence or to substitute its judgment for that of the Commission. Here, the Commission in making its injury determination acted well within its discretion in giving more weight to the various indices of the health of the domestic industry (supported by substantial evidence) than to the factor of significant market penetration, which market penetration the Commission noted had dropped precipitously in the last year for which information was collected.

D. Price Suppression

The Commission's original Statement found the evidence of record insufficient to establish price suppression. Plaintiff argued in its original motion for summary judgment that in determining the existence of price suppression, the Commission should have made a comparison between the wholesale price index for portable typewriters and that for office typewriters, rather than between the index for portable typewriters and that for office and store machines and equipment. In the remand order, . . . the Commission was directed "to reconsider and advise this

Court whether there was price suppression, after comparing the wholesale price indexes for portable typewriters and office (electric) typewriters; or to supply this Court with specific reasons why such basis for comparison is inappropriate."

The Commission, in its new Statement, has "upon reevaluation of the record" again found no substantial evidence of price suppression as a result of the LTFV imports of portable electric typewriters. Indeed, on remand the Commission, after comparing the respective wholesale price indexes for portable typewriters and office electric typewriters (the comparison ordered by this Court), found:

> ... prices for both types of typewriters increased at a similar pace through-out the 1971–1974 period. This information strongly tends to show no sup-pression of prices by reason of LTFV imports.

In the course of reconsidering its prior finding relative to the absence of price suppression, as required by this Court, the Commission carefully considered and discussed in its new Statement the problem of using certain base years for making a realistic wholesale price-index comparison between office typewriters and portable typewriters. Given all the facts and circumstances taken into account by the Commission, I find the Commission's approach to be rational and supported by substantial evidence. Plaintiff's discussion in its brief of statistical methodology suggesting the re-basing of indexes and assertion of certain facts to challenge the Commission's findings are unsupported by the record.

E. Lost Sales

The majority's original Statement of Reasons made no explicit finding of lost sales. However, the dissenting Commissioners apparently reasoned that lost sales were implicit or inferable from SCM's loss of a significant share of the market. However, no evidence of record respecting lost sales is referred to by the dissenters.

My order of remand directed the Commission to "make and report to this Court a specific finding of fact respecting whether there were lost sales as a consequence of market penetration by the Japanese LTFV imports." Responding, the Commission's new statement concluded that "[n]o information in the record of this case offers substantial evidence that the domestic industry lost a significant number of sales, or was injured thereby, as a result of imports of portable electric typewriters from Japan."

Plaintiff maintains that the Commission's new Statement is not responsive to the Court's directive. This contention is plainly untenable. In point of fact, the Commission set forth in detail the basis for its conclusion and specifically addressed plaintiff's contentions.

Thus, the Commission rejected the argument that the increased market share obtained by the Japanese imports must necessarily have been achieved at the expense of the domestic industry in the form of lost sales. The information before the Commission showed that while the percentage of the market attained by the Japanese imports increased during the period of 1971–74, *the market share* in that period for all *imports dropped, and consequently, SCM's own sales increased substantially, both relatively to imports and in absolute terms.* Moreover, the Commission points out that the introduction of lower-priced models from Japan

> . . . created a vastly increased market for portable typewriters by stimulating demand. As a result, only at most a small portion of the sales of Japanese imports represented a loss to SCM; instead, many represent sales that likely would never have been made in the absence of the low-end models from the market.

The Commission further considered plaintiff's contention that SCM lost specific sales to customers in the mass-merchandising area. On that score, the Commission found the information presented by SCM was "largely speculative and . . . rebutted in part by other information in the record." Specifically, the Commission rejected SCM's claimed losses to three accounts predicated, not on an actual decline in sales, "but on a projection of the amount of sales that SCM might have made in the absence of LTFV imports." In that connection, the Commission observed:

> SCM compares its actual average sales per store for three accounts in 1970 with its sales per store in 1974, measuring its claimed loss by the difference between the actual 1970 sales and the sales SCM would have made if it had maintained its 1970 ratio of sales per store.

> The assumption that each new store added by the three mass merchandisers handled as many portable typewriters as each store did in 1970 is disputed by other testimony in the record. It was pointed out that new stores opened by K-Mart in 1973 and 1974 were smaller than prior stores and devoted less display space to typewriters. In addition, one of the three mass merchandisers, in a confidential submission, informed the Commission that SCM's sales to it steadily increased between 1971 and 1973, and that it only began purchasing directly from the Japanese respondents in 1974. It also stated that if its purchases of LTFV imports had any effect on its business with SCM, it was because of (1) SCM's inability to provide it with the beginning price point models that were purchased prior to 1974 from Royal, and (2) SCM's failure to provide it with the full quantity of SCM's innovative cartridge ribbon typewriters that it could have sold. Finally, . . . the underlying assumption that there was a one-to-one relationship between sales of Japanese imports and sales lost by SCM . . . is untenable. *Thus, there is no creditable evidence of record demonstrating significant lost sales by the domestic industry by reason of LTFV imports.* [Footnotes omitted.] [Emphasis added.]

I agree with the Commission's determination that there is no basis in the record for finding that SCM lost significant sales by reason of the LTFV imports. To overturn the Commission's conclusion on this aspect of the case would require the Court to engage in speculative second guessing, and judging the credibility and weight of certain evidentiary matters in the administrative record, which would usurp the Commission's discretion.

VII. Underselling, COGS to Net Sales Ratio, Post-Petition Effects, and 2014 *CP Kelco* Case

What metric does the ITC use to gauge whether price suppression or depression is occurring on account of dumped subject merchandise? One answer is the ratio of Cost of Goods Sold to the value of net sales, that is:

$$\frac{COGS}{Net\ Sales\ Value}$$

Suppose during the POI, a domestic producer of a like product shows an increasing COGS/net sales value ratio. That is, over time in the POI, the ratio rises. What inference could the ITC draw from the upward trend in the ratio?

Normally, if production costs rise, then a producer would seek to raise its sale prices to cover those costs with higher revenues. But, if that ratio rises—meaning the producer does not raise its prices—then something is awry: any manufacturer would prefer to have raised its prices to offset (partly if not wholly) higher costs. The ITC may draw the inference this producer cannot do so because of price suppression or depression caused by dumped foreign merchandise.

The ITC used that methodology, but with a different outcome, in the 2014 *CP Kelco* case.[13] The subject merchandise was xanthan gum (used, for example, in the oilfield sector) from Austria and China. In June 2013, using the COGS/Net Sales Value ratio, the ITC rendered a negative injury determination. The ITC found subject merchandise imports were not injuring the domestic industry producing a like product. To be sure, the ratio trend indicated some underselling occurred, affecting some segments of the petitioning industry. But, that underselling did not lead to market-wide injury. The CIT agreed. Fortunately for the petitioner, the ITC rendered an affirmative threat of material injury determination, so the DOC issued an AD order on Chinese xanthan gum with duties of 12.90%–154.07%. (There was no order against Austrian gum.)

The *CP Kelco* case raised a second interesting issue: post-petition effects of dumped subject merchandise on a domestic industry. Once an AD petition is filed,

---

13. *See CP Kelco U.S., Inc. v. United States*, Number 13-00287 (Slip Opinion 14-123, 22 October 2014); Brian Flood, *Court Upholds Trade Commission Decision Against Present Injury From Xanthan Gum*, 31 International Trade Reporter (BNA) 1962 (6 November 2014).

For another interesting CIT case on price depression, see *LG Electronics, Inc. v. International Trade Commission*, Number 13-00100 (Slip Opinion 14-129, 6 November 2014); Brian Flood, *Challenge to Residential Washers Duties Rejected by Court of International Trade*, 31 International Trade Reporter (BNA) 1999 (13 November 2014). The CIT rejected arguments by Indian, Korean, and Mexican producer-exporters of dumped, subsidized large residential washing machines that the subject merchandise did not depress prices of American-made like products. The CIT upheld the ITC conclusion that imports of large-capacity washing machines, even though higher priced than domestically-made washers, undercut the smaller, less expensive U.S. washers. Further, the CIT treated Electrolux as a domestic producer, even though it moved production to Mexico. The CIT noted it did so because the shift to Mexico was unrelated to import competition.

demand for subject merchandise may fall. Importers and ultimate purchasers of that merchandise may hesitate to buy it, as they know it could face suspension of liquidation of entries (upon a preliminary affirmative AD determination) and remedial duties. That diminution in demand may mean reduced severity in the material injury factors affecting the domestic industry. That is, post-petition effects of subject merchandise may be less than pre-petition effects, because of the drop in demand upon filing of the petition.

U.S. AD law mandates the ITC consider post-petition effects: are there changes in the material injury factors after the filing date that distort the injury data? If so, *i.e.*, if the ITC finds post-petition effects exist, then it may give less weight to data from the date after the petition was filed. The domestic industry in C.P. Kelco argued their domestic shipments rose relative to subject merchandise imports following the petition. However, the ITC found no overall post-petition effects. It acknowledged some segments of the domestic industry felt them, but not across the whole industry. Here, too, the CIT agreed.

Note the similarity of the reasoning on the underselling and post-petition effects issues: the ITC refused to let segments-specific results sway its decision; it looked at the petitioning industry in aggregates.

VIII. Threat of Material Injury and 1988 *Goss Graphics* Case

Goss Graphics System, Inc. v. United States,

United States Court of International Trade,
33 F. Supp. 2d 1082, 1085, 1089–1102, 1104 (1998)

POGUE, JUDGE:

Plaintiffs Koenig & Bauer-Albert AG and KBA-Motter Corp. ("KBA"), MAN Roland Druckmaschinen AG and MAN Roland Inc. ("MAN Roland"), Mitsubishi Heavy Industries, Ltd. ("MHI") and Tokyo Kikai Seisakusho, Ltd. ("TKS"), respondents in the underlying investigation, seek review of the final determination of the U.S. International Trade Commission ("ITC" or "Commission"), in *Large Newspaper Printing Presses and Components Thereof, Whether Assembled or Unassembled, From Germany and Japan*, Inv. Nos. 731-TA736 & 737, U.S. ITC Pub. No. 2988 (Aug.1996) ("Final Determination"). Specifically, Plaintiffs challenge the ITC's determination that the industry in the United States producing large newspaper printing presses ("LNPPs") is threatened with material injury by reason of imports from Germany and Japan that are sold at less than fair value ("LTFV") . . . .

Background

LNPPs are presses that are designed to print major daily papers for large metropolitan newspapers. LNPPs are capable of producing tens of thousands of newspapers per hour. They have a long life-expectancy and must be extremely reliable. LNPPs are individually designed to meet each newspaper's requirements and require sophisticated engineering, programming and manufacturing capabilities. Their design, construction and installation generally require long-term contracts covering all aspects of sale, delivery and construction.

. . . [T]he ITC found that there was a single domestic industry, consisting of all LNPP producers of the domestic like product. Included in the domestic industry were Goss, the petitioner in the underlying investigation, as well as three LNPP producers that are owned or controlled by foreign LNPP manufacturers.

. . .

Discussion

. . .

II. The ITC's Threat Determination
A. The ITC's Consideration of Economic Factors

In determining whether an industry in the United States is threatened with material injury by reason of imports, (or sales for importation) of the subject merchandise, the ITC is required to consider, "among other relevant economic factors," the following nine factors:

(I) if a countervailable subsidy is involved, such information as may be presented to it by the administering authority as to the nature of the subsidy . . . .

(II) any existing unused production capacity or imminent, substantial increase in production capacity in the exporting country indicating the likelihood of substantially increased imports of the subject merchandise into the United States, taking into account the availability of other export markets to absorb any additional exports,

(III) a significant rate of increase of the volume or market penetration of imports of the subject merchandise indicating the likelihood of substantially increased imports,

(IV) whether imports of the subject merchandise are entering at prices that are likely to have a significant depressing or suppressing effect on domestic prices, and are likely to increase demand for further imports,

(V) inventories of the subject merchandise,

(VI) the potential for product-shifting if production facilities in the foreign country, which can be used to produce the subject merchandise, are currently being used to produce other products,

(VII) in any investigation under this title which involves imports of both a raw agricultural product . . . and any product processed from such raw agricultural product . . . ,

(VIII) the actual and potential negative effects on the existing development and production efforts of the domestic industry, including efforts to develop a derivative or more advanced version of the domestic like product, and

(IX) any other demonstrable adverse trends that indicate the probability that there is likely to be material injury by reason of imports (or sale for importation) of the subject merchandise (whether or not it is actually being imported at the time).

19 U.S.C. § 1677(7)(F)(i).

Furthermore, the ITC is to "consider the factors set forth [above] as a whole in making a determination of whether further dumped . . . imports are imminent and whether material injury by reason of imports would occur unless an order is issued . . . ." 19 U.S.C. § 1677(7)(F)(ii).

According to the Court of Appeals for the Federal Circuit, "[a]n affirmative injury determination requires both (1) present material injury and (2) a finding that the material injury is 'by reason of' the subject imports." *Gerald Metals, Inc. v. United States*, 132 F.3d 716, 719 (Fed. Cir.1997). The section of the antidumping statute that discusses the threat factors also includes the "by reason of" language. Thus, a positive threat determination also requires a showing of a causal connection between the LTFV goods and the threatened material injury. . . .

Therefore, after considering all relevant economic factors in making a determination of whether further dumped imports are imminent, the Commission must take an analytically distinct step to comply with the "by reason of" standard: the Commission must determine whether these factors as a whole indicate that the LTFV imports made a material contribution to the threat of the material injury. "[E]vidence of *de minimis* (*e.g.*, minimal or tangential) causation of injury does not reach the causation level required under the statute." *Id.* at 722.

Both German and Japanese Plaintiffs oppose the ITC's finding that the domestic industry is threatened with material injury by reason of subject imports. . . . Plaintiffs complain that although the ITC "claimed that it had 'considered, . . . all statutory factors that are relevant to these investigations,'" it never found that further imports were imminent, and never explained "why it was likely, or even possible, that material injury by reason of imports would occur unless an order was issued." . . . The ITC responds that "the Commission was not required to incorporate in its determination language that simply tracked the statutory language . . . ." . . .

While the ITC is correct, in that this court has stated the ITC need not use the precise language of the statute in making its determination, the ITC's statements and analysis must be "sufficient for the Court to infer that the [Commission] found the threat to be real and imminent." *Metallverken Nederland B.V. v. United States*, 728 F.Supp. 730, 747 (1989) . . . .

The Court addresses the parties' challenges according to the factors as considered by the Commission in making its determination.

1. Capacity

Threat factors II and VI both pertain to production capacity. In the underlying administrative proceeding, Plaintiffs argued that they were operating at nearly full capacity and therefore, "they could not make substantial additional sales to the United States." . . .

The Commission rejected this argument, explaining, "although producers may be operating at high capacity utilization rates, they have demonstrated the ability to shift significant future production to the United States from other export markets in the future." . . .

Plaintiffs challenge the Commission's decision, arguing, "[t]he ITC has not provided any cogent rationale why the plaintiffs would expand capacity and divert exports to the United States . . . ." . . . However, Plaintiffs mis-characterize the Commission's position. It is true that the Commission did not find that Plaintiffs *planned* to expand productive capacity or divert exports to the United States. However, it did not claim to have made such a finding. The Commission simply found that Plaintiffs have the ability to compete for and fill U.S. sales orders. . . . Therefore, the Commission concluded, Plaintiffs' high capacity utilization figures did not preclude a threat determination. . . . The Commission never argued that Plaintiffs' capacity data constituted positive evidence that levels of subject imports would increase. The Commission treated Plaintiffs' capacity data as a neutral factor and appropriately attributed less weight to this data than to its other findings. . . .

Plaintiffs also argue, "the ITC took capacity and capacity utilization 'off the table' and presumed that plaintiffs could fill additional orders in the U.S. market despite their reported capacity limitations." . . . However, the commission did not merely presume the Plaintiffs could fill additional orders, the Commission provided substantial evidence demonstrating that "producers are capable of quickly increasing capacity to satisfy new sales," . . . and that "the capacity of the German and Japanese producers appears to vary in correlation with their production figures." . . . These statements are supported by capacity data in the staff report showing that capacity for both German and Japanese Plaintiffs fluctuated widely during the period of investigation. . . .

Based on these data, the Commission reasonably concluded that subject producers' reported capacity figures did not impose strict limits on their ability to increase production and sales. Thus, the ITC's determination that Plaintiffs' high capacity utilization rates did not preclude further imports was supported by substantial evidence.

2. Home-Country and Third-Country Sales Opportunities

In considering the statutory factor of "existing unused production capacity or imminent increase in production capacity," the ITC is required to take into account, "the availability of other export markets to absorb any additional exports . . . ." 19 U.S.C. § 1677(7)(F)(i)(II).

Plaintiffs argue that, "the ITC never made any finding that the [Plaintiffs] lack sales opportunities outside the United States or that adverse market conditions outside the U.S. market will cause them to step up efforts in the United States." . . . Furthermore, Plaintiffs claim to have "introduced unrebutted evidence that demand for LNPPs was increasing in Asia, Eastern Europe and Latin America. The ITC is subject to reversal if it ignores affirmative evidence that its predictions of increased imports are improbable or impossible." . . .

. . .

Because the data provided by Plaintiffs concerning third-country markets was not specific to LNPPs, the Commission's decision to attribute less weight to that data was reasonable. Furthermore, the table relied on by TKS, showing that home market shipments had increased in 1995, and were expected to increase further in 1996 and 1997, also shows that the percentage of shipments going to the United States will be higher in 1997 than in any year during the period of investigation . . . . Thus, the Commission had substantial evidence to support its determination that the third-country and home-market data did not preclude a finding that exports to the United States could increase in the near future.

3. Increased Imports and Market Prevention

Regarding Factor III, Plaintiffs argue, "[t]he *Act* [*i.e.,* the *Tariff Act* of 1930, as amended] requires that the ITC shall consider, in making threat determinations, whether there has been a significant rate of increase of the volume or market penetration of imports of the subject merchandise *indicating the likelihood of substantially increased imports.*" . . . "Although the ITC claimed to have found 'a significant increase' in the value of import sales in 1994 and 1995," Plaintiffs argue, "it could not have found that this increase was indicative of any similar increase in 1996, since its staff projected that the German and Japanese producers would make no sales in that year . . . ."

Plaintiffs are correct. [Their data] . . . show no sales by German or Japanese producers in 1996. However, this by itself is not conclusive. There is other evidence on the record that tends to support the Commission's conclusion. The record shows that the volume and market penetration of subject imports increased significantly in 1994 and 1995. . . . Furthermore, the Commission found that German and Japanese producers were competing with Goss on more than seventy-five percent of the sales that would be made in the twelve months following the final determination. . . . The evidence also demonstrates that in 1996, German producers submitted bids on approximately two thirds of the bids pending in the market as of August 1, 1996. . . . Similarly, the Japanese producers had submitted bids on approximately half of the sales pending as of August 1, 1996. . . . Thus here, the Commission's finding of a high number of pending contracts for which German and/or Japanese producers had submitted bids was supported by substantial evidence.

As the Commission explained, "[b]ecause the number and value of sales fluctuate considerably from year to year, changes in industry performance on a year-to-year basis may be of limited utility . . ." . . . Thus, the Commission's decision to attribute less weight to the 1996 data was reasonable.

Plaintiffs also argue that because the *Washington Post* sale was the only sale of subject merchandise in 1995, the Commission's determination that subject imports are increasing was unjustified. . . .

The Court agrees with plaintiffs that one sale "does not make a 'trend,'" and that it would have been unreasonable for the ITC to base predictions of future import levels on one sale, even one as large as the *Washington Post* sale. However, the Commission's determination regarding the likelihood of increased future imports was not based solely on the 1995 sales data. In fact . . . the Commission acknowledged the "changes in industry performance on a year-to-year basis may be of limited utility." . . .

"The Commissioners have the discretion to determine the weight to be given factors they consider." *Metallverken Nederland*, 728 F. Supp. at 735 . . . . The high number of pending contracts for which German and/or Japanese producers had submitted bids, together with the Commission's findings regarding the subject imports' increasing value and market share in 1994 and 1995, constitute substantial evidence that imports are likely to increase in the near future.

. . .

4. Price Effects of the Subject Merchandise

With respect to the price effects of future imports, Plaintiffs argue that "the proposition that imports had suppressed or depressed prices was contrary to the findings of the ITC's staff." . . . Specifically, Plaintiffs argue,

> [t]he *Staff Report* indicates that "given a particular specification and level of quality, the final installed price to the customer will be a significant deciding factor." . . . However, the Staff recognizes that non-price factors such as technology, quality, service and compatibility with existing presses are more important than price . . . .

. . . Thus, Plaintiffs contend, "[t]he ITC Staff concluded only that price is determinative for *a hypothetical* sale, where technology, quality and other significant non-price factors are assumed to be the same for foreign and domestic bidders." . . . However, Plaintiffs read the ITC *Staff Report* too narrowly. In fact, the ITC Staff found that during the bid process, "the bids are expected to converge," so that by the time of the final bid, "the presses offered by the different makers generally are reasonably similar and meet specifications." . . . This finding supports the Commission's determination that competition during the bid process plays a significant role in determining the sales price of the subject merchandise.

Plaintiffs also argue that a large fraction of the bids were non-competitive and in a significant number of the competitive bids, the bid was not awarded to the lowest bidder. Plaintiffs maintain "[b]oth of these phenomena are inconsistent with a finding that price is the predominant factor driving procurement decisions." . . .

Again, Plaintiffs mischaracterize the Commission's findings. The Commission did not find that price was the *predominant* factor driving procurement decisions. In fact, the Commission stated, "[a]lthough price appears *not* to be the dominant factor in many bid situations, it is nevertheless often an important factor in the purchaser's decision at the final stage of the bid process." . . . Furthermore, the Commission reasonably determined that the fact that bids were not awarded to the lowest bidder in all cases did not necessarily preclude a finding of price suppression or depression by subject imports. As the Commission explained, "purchasers may seek to negotiate more expensive equipment or additional services at the same price level, thereby exacting a higher value product for what appears to be a price similar to that quoted by a different supplier." . . .

In addition, the Court finds, the Commission's findings were supported by substantial evidence. According to the Commission, the "conventional approach to pricing analysis [was] not particularly useful in these investigations," due to, "the nature of the sales process and the relatively unique characteristics of each LNPP or addition sold," as well as, "the fact that price competition occurs primarily during the extensive and highly competitive bid/negotiation process for LNPP sales . . . ." The Court agrees that because each LNPP is made to customer specifications, a more conventional approach, based, for example, on price trends over time, would not have been useful. Thus, the Commission's decision to rely on anecdotal evidence in evaluating price effects of the subject merchandise was reasonable.

. . .

Finally, Plaintiffs argue, the ITC's findings as to the price effects of future imports failed to consider the impact of competition among U.S. producers. . . . "To the extent that this competition would have caused the same price effects in the absence of subject imports, it was improper for the ITC to claim that the price suppression or depression it allegedly observed had been caused by subject imports." . . .

. . . [B]ased on the evidence, the Commission could reasonably have concluded that competition among domestic producers alone could not have caused the price effects attributed by the ITC to the subject imports. Both the Plaintiffs and the Commission agree that price effects of competition, to the extent they exist, occur during the period of negotiation after producers have submitted their bids to the purchaser. . . . [I]n a significant number of the competitive contracts awarded during the period of investigation, Goss faced competition only from foreign producers because no other domestic producers submitted bids. . . . Thus, any price effects caused by competition in these sales could not be the result of other domestic producers. Thus, the Commission could reasonably conclude that at least part of the price effect caused by competition would not have occurred in the absence of the subject merchandise.

There is competing evidence on the record that would tend to support Plaintiffs' view that subject imports did not cause depression or suppression of LNPP prices. For example, the evidence indicates that for many purchasers price is "a threshold factor that competing producers must meet for their initial bids to be competitive." . . . The threshold is set, not by the bids offered by competitors, but by the purchaser's budgetary constraints. . . . Thus, even in the absence of subject merchandise, domestic manufacturers would not be able to charge higher prices at this stage, because prices are limited by the purchaser's budget. . . .

. . .

Nevertheless, the totality of the evidence does not require a single conclusion. "It is not the Court's function to reweigh the evidence, but to decide whether the Commission's determinations are supported by substantial evidence." *Granges Metallverken [AB v. United States]*, 716 F. Supp. [17] at 21 [(1989)]. "[T]he possibility of drawing two inconsistent conclusions from the evidence does not prevent an administrative agency's finding from being supported by substantial evidence." . . . Here, the Court finds substantial evidence supports the Commission's conclusion that the continued participation of producers of merchandise sold at less than fair value in the bidding process is likely to suppress or depress in the imminent future.

5. Pending Sales

In its final determination, the Commission stated that

> [the] small number of pending sales, valued . . . [at more than $125 million], will likely result in intense competition among domestic and foreign suppliers for bid awards. Moreover, this intensified competition for a smaller pool of sales opportunities increases the incentive for suppliers of LTFV imports to compete on the basis of price. . . . This smaller value of pending sales also makes it more likely that purchasers will continue to use the LTFV imports to extract price concessions from domestic producers.

. . .

Plaintiffs contest the Commission's finding that only a small number of LNPP contracts will be awarded in the near future. . . .

The Commission found "the record shows that German and Japanese producers are now in direct competition with domestic producers for bids that are now pending in the LNPP market. While there is evidence of . . . [fewer than twenty] currently pending sales of LNPPs and additions, there is a varying degree of likelihood that contracts will be awarded on these pending sales in the [then near] future." . . . The Commission concluded that only one-third of these sales are likely to occur in the near future-the first half of 1997 or earlier. . . .

In determining which of these pending sales were "imminent," the Commission chose to rely on the expected sales dates reported in its questionnaire responses and confirmed by purchasers.

Plaintiffs challenge the validity of the Commission's process for identifying imminent purchases. . . . Plaintiffs argue that the Commission based its finding on incomplete and unreliable data. . . . Plaintiffs also claim that the Commission did not pursue purchaser information on the status of a small number of pending additions sales on which petitioner was the sole bidder. . . .

To the extent that Plaintiffs' argument rests on the theory that the ITC could have obtained more data, Plaintiffs' argument is irrelevant. The question is not whether the Commission might have obtained additional information, but whether the determination is supported by substantial evidence on the record. . . .

The limits on the ITC's methodology are of a different character. As long as the methodology and procedures are a "reasonable means of effectuating the statutory purpose, and there is substantial evidence in the record supporting the agency's conclusions, the court will not impose its own views as to the sufficiency of the agency's investigation or question the agency's methodology." *Makita Corp. v. United States*, 974 F.Supp. 770, 787 (1997) (*quoting Ceramica Regiomontana, S.A. v. United States*, 636 F.Supp. 961, 966 (1986), *aff'd*, 810 F.2d 1137 (Fed. Cir.1987) . . .) . . . .

The Commission's determination here relied on information from producers, importers and purchasers. The Commission issued several questionnaires requesting data relating to sales pending in the market place. Specifically, the Commission asked the domestic producers and the German and Japanese importers to report all LNPP bid solicitations that were then pending in the marketplace and requested them to submit detailed information describing the status of the bidding process for these bids. Similarly, in its purchaser questionnaire, the Commission asked purchasers to report detailed bid information for sales that had been finalized during the period and for bids that were then pending.

Subsequently, the Commission staff conducted an investigation to determine how many of the bids pending in the market were to be awarded imminently. . . .

Based on this information, the Commission concluded that one-third of these pending sales [*i.e.*, sales of LNPPs that various producers identified as being pending in the market] were more likely to occur in the near future than other pending sales. . . .

Plaintiffs argue that the Commission's finding is contradicted by marketing data presented by them and the petitioner, showing a large number of orders, with a total value of more than $500 million to be awarded in the near future. . . . Plaintiffs misunderstand the nature of the Commission's threat analysis.

The Commission is required to assess whether imports are imminent and material injury would occur in the absence of an order. Because it takes years to complete the bid process, the Commission appropriately concluded that only pending bids, particularly those in which an award was imminent, were relevant to its threat analysis.

Furthermore, the Commission's decision to include among imminent sales only the pending sales that purchasers confirmed were imminent was reasonable. The Commission has the discretion to assess the probative nature of the evidence obtained in its investigation and to determine whether to discount the evidence or to rely on it. . . . Here, the Commission declined to rely on producer estimates of sales dates when it could not obtain confirmations from the purchasers. . . .

. . .

6. Research and Development

Plaintiffs argue that the Commission's findings with respect to the impact of subject imports on domestic producers' research and development (R&D) activities were not supported by the evidence. . . . Specifically, Plaintiffs assert "[b]ased on the ITC's own findings, subject imports were present at what the ITC described as 'a significant level' throughout the POI [period of investigation] . . . . Yet, that did not prevent Goss from spending a relatively constant amount annually on research and development, or from increasing its R & D spending in years that imports increased . . . ." . . . Furthermore, Plaintiffs argue that the ITC's tables show that Goss's sales increased significantly from 1994 to 1995, while its R & D expenditures decreased during the same period.

. . .

The Commission found, "there is a relatively direct correlation between a producer's research and development expenditures and its sales revenues." . . . The Commission concluded, "the continued significant presence of the subject imports in the market will significantly hamper the industry's ability to develop the advanced technologies necessary to stay competitive in this market." . . .

The Commission based its finding in part on the testimony of witnesses for the petitioner noting that the petitioner's ability to commit capital to R & D was directly linked to sales revenues. . . . Consistent with this testimony, the other evidence before the Commission shows that annual expenditures on R & D fluctuated in the same direction as annual sales revenues for 1991–95 each year during the period of investigation. . . .

Plaintiffs' arguments appear to ignore the data regarding the industry's R & D expenditures in 1991, which were more than double those in any other year of the period under investigation. . . . In light of the industry's R & D expenditures for 1991, it was reasonable for the Commission to conclude that there was a relatively direct correlation between a producer's R & D expenses and its sales revenues.

Furthermore, the Commission did not neglect the short-term data relied upon by the Plaintiffs. The Commission simply found that "changes in industry performance on a year-to-year basis" is of limited utility. . . . The Commission relied on the correlation between long-term declines in revenue and research spending, and the inverse relationship of these trends with the long-term increase in import penetration. The Commission has the discretion to make reasonable interpretations of the evidence and to determine the overall significance of any particular factor in its analysis.

. . .

7. The Commission's Vulnerability Finding

Plaintiffs argue that the Commission substituted a finding that the domestic industry was vulnerable for an analysis of the appropriate threat criteria. . . .

While the ITC did state that, "[i]n these investigations, the vulnerability of the domestic industry is an important factor in our consideration of the threat of material injury from subject imports," . . . the Commission did not substitute its finding of vulnerability for consideration of a statutory criteria. As summarized above, the ITC considered each of the statutory criteria relevant to this proceeding.

Furthermore, the ITC's consideration of the current state of the domestic industry was appropriate and relevant to this proceeding. . . .

. . .

8. The Impact of Possible Changes in the ITA's Dumping Margins

[Plaintiffs argued the magnitude of the dumping margins calculated by the DOC ITA heavily influenced the ITC in rendering an affirmative threat determination. Plaintiffs said if the ITC computed a new dumping margin, on account of the Plaintiffs' appeal, then the CIT must remand the case to the ITC for the ITC to revaluate its threat determination in light of the recomputed dumping margins. The Court rejected the Plaintiffs theory that a subsequent change in dumping margins is itself an adequate basis for remand.]

The antidumping statute directs the Commission to consider the "magnitude of the margin of dumping" in its injury analysis in any antidumping proceeding.[14] Specifically, the statute defines the "magnitude of the margin of dumping" in a final injury determination as the margin "most recently published by [the Department of Commerce] prior to the closing of the Commission's official record."[15]

The statute does not contemplate that a change in margins provides an automatic basis for remand to the Commission. In fact, the *Statement of Administrative Action* accompanying the [1994] *Uruguay Round Agreements Act* recognizes that "[t]he finality of injury determinations would be seriously compromised if the Commission was required to amend or revisit its determination each time the administering authority modified its dumping margin." . . . Therefore, a subsequent change in margins does not automatically mandate a remand to the Commission by this Court.

. . .

Conclusion

For the foregoing reasons, the ITC's Final determination . . . is sustained.

---

14. 19 U.S.C. § 1677(7)(c)(iii)(V).
15. 19 U.S.C. § 1677(35)(c)(ii).

IX. Cumulation and 2018 *T.B. Woods* Case

T.B. Woods, Inc. v. United States,

United States Court of International Trade,
Slip Opinion 18-164, Number 17-00022 (29 November 2018)

Stanceu, Judge:

Plaintiff T.B. Wood's Incorporated ("T.B. Wood's") contests final negative injury and threat determinations made by the United States International Trade Commission (the "Commission" or "ITC") in antidumping duty investigations of imports of certain iron mechanical transfer drive components ("IMTDCs") from Canada and China and a parallel countervailing duty investigation of imports of these products from China. The court sustains the contested determinations.

I. Background

. . .

B. The Plaintiff and Defendant-Intervenors

T.B. Wood's, a U.S. manufacturer of iron mechanical transfer drive components, was the petitioner in the investigations culminating in the Final Determinations. T.B. Wood's alleged in its petitions, filed with Commerce and the Commission on October 28, 2015, that imports of certain IMTDCs from Canada and China were being sold in the United States at less than fair value and, in the case of imports from China, were being subsidized by the government of China. . . . The petitioner alleged material injury or threat of material injury to the U.S. industry producing these components. . . .

There are two defendant-intervenors in this litigation: the China Chamber of International Commerce's *ad hoc* Coalition of Producers and Exporters of Certain Iron Mechanical Transfer Drive Components from the People's Republic of China (the "Coalition"), and Powermach Import & Export Co., Ltd. (Sichuan) ("Powermach"). The Coalition was formed by several Chinese respondents, each a producer and exporter of the subject merchandise, that participated in the final phase of the ITC's investigations, including Powermach, Shijiazhuang CAPT Power Transmission Co., Ltd., and Yueqing Bethel Shaft Collar Manufacturing Co., Ltd. . . .

C. The Antidumping Duty and Countervailing Duty Investigations

Upon receiving the petitions from T.B. Wood's, the Commission initiated . . . AD investigations of IMTDCs from Canada and China and a . . . CVD investigation of IMTDCs from China. . . . The . . . POI for each was the beginning of 2013 through the first six months of 2016. The ITC analyzed annual data for 2013, 2014, and 2015 and also compared data for "interim 2015," i.e., the first six months of 2015, with data for "interim 2016," *i.e.*, the first six months of 2016. This allowed the ITC to compare data for a six-month period prior to the filing of the petition (which occurred in late October 2015) with data for a corresponding period in 2016 occurring after the filing of the petition.

Prior to the ITC's final negative determinations, the International Trade Administration of the U.S. Department of Commerce ("Commerce") concluded AD and CVD investigations that resulted in affirmative less-than-fair-value and subsidy determinations on imports of the subject merchandise from China. . . . Commerce also reached an affirmative less-than-fair-value determination on imports of the subject merchandise from Canada. . . .

The Commission issued the Final Determinations on December 16, 2016. . . . The Determinations were unanimous, with all six commissioners voting. . . . As required by the *Tariff Act of 1930, as amended* (the "Tariff Act"), the negative determinations by the ITC resulted in termination of the investigations by Commerce and the ITC without the issuance of antidumping duty or countervailing duty orders. *See* 19 U.S.C. §§ 1671d(c)(2) (termination of countervailing duty investigation), 1673d(c)(2) (termination of antidumping duty investigation).

. . .

II. Discussion

. . .

B. Scope of the Antidumping Duty and Countervailing Duty Investigations

Under the *Tariff Act*, antidumping duties are imposed, in defined circumstances, on "foreign merchandise . . . being, or . . . likely to be, sold in the United States at less than its fair value." 19 U.S.C. § 1673(1). Countervailing duties are imposed, in defined circumstances, on "merchandise imported, or sold (or likely to be sold) for importation, into the United States" for which "the government of a country or any public entity within the territory of a country is providing, directly or indirectly, a countervailable subsidy with respect to the manufacture, production, or export" of that merchandise. *Id.* § 1671(a)(1).

The scope of an antidumping duty or countervailing duty investigation is determined by Commerce. Commerce described the subject IMTDCs as "[i]ron mechanical transfer drive components, whether finished or unfinished (*i.e.*, in blanks or castings)" and as being "in the form of wheels or cylinders" and "often referred to as sheaves, pulleys, flywheels, flat pulleys, idlers, conveyer pulleys, synchronous sheaves, and timing pulleys." . . . In its Report, the Commission gave a general description of IMTDCs, as follows:

> IMTDCs are iron castings in the shape of wheels or cylinders for use in belted drive assemblies in fans, conveyers, compressors, pumps, and mixers. Circular IMTDCs may be referred to as sheaves, pulleys, or flywheels, and cylindrical IMTDCs, which are designed to attach the shaft to the circular IMTDC, may be referred to as bushings. Regardless of size or shape, IMTDCs are connected with belts and used to transfer power from a shaft operated by a motor or engine. IMTDCs may be produced in finished or unfinished (referred to as blanks or castings) form. IMTDCs may be manufactured in a variety of sizes as measured by the outer diameter.

... The Commission added that "IMTDCs have a center bore hole for a shaft to be inserted and an outer circumference, with a variety of teeth or grooves, designed to mesh with a belt." ... IMTDCs are commonly used in belted drive shaft systems, where they function, in conjunction with other components, to transfer, store, and release power. ... They have applications in various industries, including mining, oil extraction, manufacturing, and heating, ventilating, and air conditioning (HVAC). *Id.* at I-28 to I-31. Due to their wide range of end uses, IMTDCs are produced in various shapes and sizes.

. . .

C. The Commission's Role in the Imposition of Antidumping and Countervailing Duties

Before antidumping or countervailing duties may be imposed, the Commission must determine that an industry in the United States is materially injured or is threatened with material injury, or that the establishment of an industry in the United States is materially retarded, by reason of imports, or sales (or the likelihood of sales) for importation, of the merchandise Commerce has found to be unfairly traded, i.e., subsidized or dumped. 19 U.S.C. §§ 1671d(b)(1) (countervailing duties), 1673d(b)(1) (antidumping duties).

1. The Domestic Industry and the Domestic Like Product

Because it must determine whether an "industry in the United States" is materially injured or threatened with material injury, *id.* §§ 1671d(b)(1), 1673d(b)(1), the ITC identifies as part of its investigation the "domestic industry" or "industries" and the "domestic like product" or "products." The statute defines "industry" as "the producers as a whole of a domestic like product, or those producers whose collective output of a domestic like product constitutes a major proportion of the total domestic production of the product." *Id.* § 1677(4)(A). The statute defines "domestic like product" as "a product which is like, or in the absence of like, most similar in characteristics and uses with, the article subject to investigation." *Id.* § 1677(10). The Commission may determine that there is a single domestic like product or that there are multiple like products. A finding of multiple like products requires a finding of corresponding domestic industries. *See id.* § 1677(4)(A).

In identifying the domestic like product or products, the Commission is not confined by the scope of an AD or CVD investigation as determined by Commerce. In the investigations at issue, the ITC found that there was one like product, which it defined more broadly than the scope as defined by Commerce. While Commerce excluded from the scope IMTDCs under 4 inches in nominal outside diameter, the ITC defined the domestic like product as "all forms of finished and unfinished IMTDCs described in the investigations' scope and including small-diameter IMTDCs under 4 inches in maximum nominal outside diameter." ... The Commission defined the domestic industry as "all U.S. producers of the domestic like product, including foundries manufacturing unfinished IMTDCs, firms engaged solely in machining unfinished IMTDCs into finished IMTDCs, and integrated producers of

IMTDCs." . . . Before the court, plaintiff does not contest the ITC's determinations of the domestic like product or the domestic industry.

2. Statutory Factors for the Material Injury Determination

The *Tariff Act* defines "material injury" as "harm which is not inconsequential, immaterial, or unimportant." 19 U.S.C. § 1677(7)(A). Due to the statutory requirement of "causation," the ITC may reach an affirmative determination of material injury or threat of material injury only when the material injury or threat of material injury occurs "by reason of" the subject imports. *Id.* §§ 1671d(b)(1) (countervailing duties), 1673d(b)(1) (antidumping duties). The Commission is directed to consider three basic factors: the volume of imports of the merchandise subject to investigation ("import volume"), the effect of those imports on U.S. prices of the domestic like product or products ("price effects"), and the impact of those imports on domestic producers of the domestic like product or products, but only in the context of production operations in the United States ("impact on the domestic industry"). *Id.* § 1677(7)(B)(i). The statute provides further requirements as to what the Commission must consider for each of the three factors. *Id.* § 1677(7)(C)(i) (volume), (ii) (price effects), (iii) (impact on the domestic industry). Additionally, the Commission "may consider such other economic factors as are relevant." *Id.* § 1677(7)(B)(ii).

3. Cumulation

In making its injury determination, the ITC assesses together ("cumulates") the volume and effect of imports of the subject merchandise from all countries with respect to which petitions were filed on the same day (as occurred here), if such imports compete with each other and with domestic like products in the United States market. *Id.* § 1677(7)(G). The Commission "cross-cumulated" the subsidized and dumped imports from China with the dumped imports from Canada in reaching its negative injury determination. . . .

In determining threat of material injury, the ITC in its discretion may cumulatively assess the volume and effect of imports of the subject merchandise if such imports compete with each other and with domestic like products in the United States market. *See* 19 U.S.C. § 1677(7)(H). The Commission did not cumulate the Chinese and Canadian imports in performing its threat analyses. . . .

D. The Court Sustains the ITC's Determinations that Cumulated Subject Imports from Canada and China Are Not Injuring the Domestic Industry

. . .

2. Plaintiff's "Economic Logic" Argument Misinterprets the Causation Requirement in the *Tariff Act*

T.B. Wood's argues that "the agency's determinations as a whole are tainted by its failure to reconcile its conclusion that there was no correlation between subject imports and domestic industry performance with basic economic logic." . . . According to plaintiff, "[t]he agency found that subject IMTDC's were present in large volumes throughout the POI," "characterized these volumes as significant on multiple bases," and "found that the subject goods pervasively undersold the domestic like product." . . . T.B. Wood's maintains that "[w]ith such a factual predicate, it should not be possible for there to be 'a lack of correlation' between subject imports and the domestic industry's condition." . . . Plaintiff describes the ITC's conclusions as "unexplained and unsupported by reason of this failure to acknowledge fundamental economic principles, or to explain how a decision that ignores such principles can be consistent with law." . . .

The Court rejects plaintiff's "economic logic" argument, which disregards the effect of the causation requirement in the statute. An affirmative injury determination requires a finding that material injury to the domestic industry occurred "by reason of" the subject merchandise. 19 U.S.C. §§ 1671d(b)(1), 1673d(b)(1). Although the *Tariff Act* directs the ITC to "consider" the factors of import volume, price effects, and impact on the domestic industry (all of which the ITC considered in the investigations), the statute does not require the ITC to *presume* that the presence in the U.S. market of competing imports, at significant volumes and at prices that in most comparisons undersold the domestic like product, is itself sufficient to support a finding of causation, regardless of other evidence of record. In this case, according to other record evidence, the volume of the subject imports did not show a sustained pattern of increasing significantly throughout the POI and the share they occupied of the U.S. market remained relatively steady over the POI as a whole. No less significant was the Commission's finding, supported by record evidence consisting of questionnaire responses, that price was not the only factor, and not always even the most important factor, in purchasing decisions. The Commission found that "purchasers cited quality most frequently as the most important factor (7 firms), followed by price (5 firms), whereas price was the most frequently reported second- and third-most important factor (5 firms each)." . . . "Purchasers also reported that 'quality meets industry standards,' 'availability,' 'product consistency,' 'reliability of supply,' and 'delivery time' were important factors in their purchasing decisions." . . .

. . .

6. The ITC Permissibly Reached a Negative Finding on the Impact of Subject Merchandise on the Domestic Industry

The ITC found that "cumulated subject imports from Canada and China did not have a significant impact on the domestic industry during the POI." . . . The Commission acknowledged that "the domestic industry's financial performance was poor throughout the POI," but it found temporal correlations between various indicia of the industry's financial condition and changes in demand (measured by apparent U.S. consumption), including the notable reduction in demand that occurred in 2015, which coincided with an increase in costs (measured by the COGS to net sales ratio). . . . The ITC noted that overall "apparent U.S. consumption fluctuated during the POI; it increased from 2013 to 2014, decreased between 2014 and 2015, and was lower in interim 2016 than in interim 2015." . . . The Commission observed that "[m]any of the domestic industry's performance indicators mirrored these changes in apparent U.S. consumption over the POI *and are not otherwise explained by trends in cumulated subject imports*." . . . All of this occurred, the ITC noted, while the domestic industry's share of apparent U.S. consumption remained relatively unchanged over the course of the POI.

The Commission's negative findings on the impact of subject imports on the domestic industry are supported by substantial record evidence. From the data compiled by the ITC staff, the Commission readily could see that a number of changes in the indicia of the industry's condition, including indicia on overall profitability, correlated temporally with changes in demand (measured by apparent U.S. consumption) but not with changes in the volume of cumulated subject imports. . . . Instead, cumulated subject imports declined with the 2015 reduction in demand. By value, they increased 4.6% from 2013, the first year of the POI, to 2014 but then declined 8.8% from 2014 to 2015, coinciding with the lowered demand occurring at that time. . . . As the Commission found, "[i]n terms of pieces, the domestic industry's production, capacity utilization, U.S. shipments, and net sales all followed a similar trajectory; they increased from 2013 to 2014, decreased from 2014 to 2015, and were lower in interim 2016 than in interim 2015." . . . The record data supported the ITC's conclusions that "[c]umulated subject imports followed similar trends, and the domestic industry's share of apparent U.S. consumption showed little change over the POI." . . .

. . .

T.B. Wood's next argues that the Commission failed to consider evidence detracting from its conclusion that subject imports were not a significant cause of the condition of the U.S. industry. . . . In doing so, plaintiff states that it "does not contest that demand and cost trends influenced domestic performance over the POI," conceding that "such trends are relevant to the performance of any industry at any time." . . . Thus, while not disputing that the reduction in overall demand, and with it increased unit costs, had negative effects, plaintiff insists that neither changes in demand, nor the changes in unit costs that the ITC correlated with them, fully explain the domestic industry's condition and that "[s]omething else is affecting performance." . . . In identifying that "something else," plaintiff points to "the constant pricing pressure of large volumes of subject imports that pervasively undersold the domestic like product." . . . Stated summarily, plaintiff's argument is that the ITC looked at the effects of changes in demand without also looking at what plaintiff terms "supply." . . . According to T.B. Wood's, "in analyzing the health of the domestic industry, the ITC examined demand conditions but failed to provide a meaningful analysis of supply conditions—most particularly the significant volumes of fungible, lower-priced subject IMTDCs." . . . This is essentially a restatement of plaintiff's "economic logic" argument. But as the Court has explained, the *Tariff Act* does not compel the ITC to presume causation solely from the sustained presence in the market of significant volumes of subject imports that pervasively undersold the domestic like product. As the Commission permissibly found, a

factor other than subject imports — reduced demand and concomitant increased
unit cost — correlated temporally with changes in the industry's condition whereas
import volumes did not. The Commission also considered that price was not the
sole determinant in purchasing decisions and that the domestic industry's share of
the market for the domestic like product did not change materially over the course
of the POI.

> . . .

E. The Court Sustains the ITC's Negative Threat Determinations

1. Statutory Factors for the Threat Determination

The *Tariff Act* lists eight specific economic factors that the Commission must
consider in making a threat determination. Summarized briefly, these eight specific factors are: (1) the nature of any countervailable subsidy involved and whether
imports of the subject merchandise are likely to increase; (2) unused production
capacity, or imminent substantial increase in production capacity, in the exporting country; (3) a significant rate of increase of the volume or market penetration of imports of subject merchandise; (4) whether subject imports are entering
at prices likely to have a significant depressing or suppressing effect on domestic
prices, and are likely to increase demand for further imports; (5) inventories of
subject merchandise; (6) potential for product-shifting if production facilities in
the foreign country used to produce other products can be used to produce subject
merchandise; (7) product-shifting for agricultural products (not relevant here); and
(8) actual and potential negative effects on existing development and production
efforts of the domestic industry, including efforts to develop a derivative or more
advanced version of the domestic like product. *Id.* § 1677(7)(F)(i)(I)-(VIII).

The statute adds a ninth, more general, factor that directs the Commission to
consider any other demonstrable adverse trends indicating the probability of material injury by reason of subject imports. *Id.* § 1677(7)(F)(i)(IX). The presence or
absence of any of the named factors "shall not necessarily give decisive guidance
with respect to the determination," which "may not be made on the basis of mere
conjecture or speculation." *Id.* § 1677(7)(F)(ii).

2. Plaintiff's Arguments Challenging the ITC's Negative Threat Determination

T.B. Wood's first challenges the ITC's decision to analyze Canadian and Chinese
imports separately rather than cumulate these imports for purposes of the threat
analysis. . . . Plaintiff also contends that the agency's separate negative threat determinations with respect to the two individual countries must remanded for further
consideration and explanation. As to Canada, plaintiff contends, in support of both
its cumulation argument and its threat argument, that the ITC placed too much
reliance on the 2016 closure of the largest Canadian exporter of subject IMTDCs,
ignoring the prospect that unfinished IMTDCs still could threaten the domestic
industry. Regarding China, T.B. Wood's relies on some of its previous arguments
but also argues that the importance of the United States as an export market to Chinese IMTDC producers indicates a threat of increased subject imports.

3. The ITC Permissibly Declined to Cumulate Subject Imports for its Threat Analysis and Permissibly Reached a Negative Threat Determination on Subject Imports from Canada

Under the statute, the Commission, "[t]o the extent practicable . . . *may* cumulatively assess the volume and price effects of imports of the subject merchandise from all countries with respect to which . . . petitions were filed under section 1671a(b) or 1673a(b) of this title on the same day . . . if such imports compete with each other and with domestic like products in the United States market." 19 U.S.C. § 1677(7) (H) (emphasis added). In deciding whether to cumulate for threat purposes, the Commission considers whether subject imports from the countries involved are likely to compete under similar conditions in the domestic market in the imminent future. In this investigation, the ITC found they would not. . . .

The ITC based its negative cumulation decision, as well as its negative threat determination as to Canada, largely on its finding that "the largest source of subject imports from Canada during the POI (Baldor Canada) closed its St. Claire, Quebec facility on May 27, 2016 and relocated its finishing equipment from Canada to the Baldor facilities in Weaverville and Marion, North Carolina." . . . Plaintiff does not dispute this finding but, noting that Baldor Canada was merely a finisher of IMTDCs, argues that "a significant amount of Canadian castings . . . would suddenly be without a home by reason of Baldor Canada's closure." . . . T.B. Wood's argues that the ITC failed to consider "how Canadian castings would be sold (and where) given Baldor's closure." *Id.* This argument rests entirely on speculation, not record evidence. The ITC was not required to presume, in the absence of any supporting record evidence, that the unfinished castings to which plaintiff refers, or finished IMTDCs made from them, in the imminent future would be subject imports that threaten the domestic industry. As the statute instructs, the Commission's threat determination "may not be made on the basis of mere conjecture or speculation."

19 U.S.C. § 1677(7)(F)(ii). Rather than provide support for plaintiff's speculation, the evidence of record supports, with substantial evidence, the Commission's separate negative threat determination as to Canada. The Commission quite reasonably concluded that "the closure of the largest source subject merchandise from Canada has fundamentally altered how any IMTDC industry will compete in the U.S. market in the imminent future." . . . Based on questionnaire responses from various parties, the ITC concluded, specifically, that "Baldor Canada accounted for nearly all known imports of subject merchandise during the POI, and there is no indication that another firm in Canada will export meaningful volumes of unfinished or finished IMTDCs to the United States in the imminent future." . . . Because they are based on the record information on the closure of the Baldor Canada facility and the questionnaire data the ITC reviewed, the Commission's decision not to cumulate subject Canadian and Chinese IMTDC imports for threat purposes, and its negative threat determination as to the subject Canadian imports, are supported by substantial evidence.

4. The ITC Permissibly Reached a Negative Threat Determination
on Subject Imports from China

. . .

Plaintiff next argues, unconvincingly, that the data on the home market and export shares of Chinese production of IMTDCs detract from the ITC's negative threat finding by signifying the importance of the U.S. market to Chinese producers and by also signifying "greater export pressure" on them. . . . These arguments are speculative at best, particularly in light of the trends the record data showed: over the POI, Chinese subject imports maintained a relatively stable share of the U.S. market while the share of Chinese production exported to the United States declined substantially. . . .

Plaintiff also points to volume and market share of Chinese subject imports in an attempt to make the most of relatively small changes in the reported numbers over the course of the POI. . . . For this argument, plaintiff cites the data in Table C-1 of the confidential version of the Final Staff Report, . . . but the data presented therein on the magnitude and relative market share of the subject imports over the POI do not support T.B. Wood's argument. According to the data, Chinese subject import volumes and market share, as measured by value, did not show a steady upward trend over the course of the POI. . . . The total value of subject imports from China declined, and Chinese imports maintained a relatively steady share of the domestic market, over the POI. . . .

In summary, the ITC permissibly concluded, on the basis of substantial record evidence, that the domestic industry was not threatened with material injury by reason of subject imports of IMTDCs from China.

Part Two

Remedies against "Unfair" Trade (Continued): Countervailing Duty Law

Chapter 11

Political Economy of Subsidies and CVDs[1]

I. Neo-Classical Economic Analysis of Domestic Production Subsidy

For sound economic reasons, the WTO *SCM Agreement* takes a harder line against export subsidies (and import substitution subsidies) than it does against production subsidies. This "line" is drawn between Part II of the *SCM Agreement* (Articles 3–4) and Part III of the *Agreement* (Articles 5–7). Part II defines "Prohibited" or "Red Light Subsidies" as export (and import substitution) subsidies. Part III defines "Actionable" or "Yellow Light" and "Dark Amber" subsidies. There is an irrebuttable presumption a Red Light subsidy causes an adverse effect—namely, (1) material injury or threat of material injury, (2) nullification or impairment of GATT benefits, or (3) serious prejudice to the interests of another WTO Member. Accordingly, a CVD may be imposed without needing to show a Red Light subsidy causes an adverse effect. In contrast, a complainant alleging a measure is Actionable does not benefit from this presumption, and must show an adverse effect to countervail the subsidy. Not surprisingly, a large number of hard-fought battles in CVD cases are over whether a measure is a Red Light subsidy.

Conceptually, why does the *SCM Agreement* take a hard line against Red Light subsidies? The answer is the welfare effects of export subsidies in comparison with domestic production subsidies. In short, export subsidies are more trade-distorting than non-export subsidies. Indeed, export subsidies are the most trade-distorting of any support measure. That is their purpose, *i.e.*, to alter from free trade equilibrium the pattern of exports or imports, or the world market price, in a particular market for goods (or, presumably, services). In this respect, the term "trade distorting" is a positive concept. But, it also has a normative dimension. "Distortions" arise in connection with the welfare effects of a support measure, and the welfare costs of an export subsidy are worse than those from a production subsidy. Graph 11-1 shows the welfare effects of a domestic production subsidy.

---

1. Documents References:
   (1) *Havana (ITO) Charter*, Articles 25–28, 34
   (2) *GATT* Articles VI, XVI
   (3) WTO *SCM Agreement*

To appreciate this and other Graphs, recall the following five economic principles:

(1) *Demand Curve*

The line slopped downward to the right represents total demand for a good, whether that good is manufactured domestically or imported. The line slopped upward and to the right is the supply of that good as manufactured by domestic producers. Thus, the two lines depict a product market in a particular importing country.

The Demand Curve captures various quantities of an imported good and domestic like product that consumers in the country are ready, willing, and able to buy at alternative prices. There is an inverse relationship between quantity demanded, measured on the horizontal or "X" axis, and price, gauged on the vertical or "Y" axis. This inverse link reflects the common sense idea that *ceteris paribus* (all other factors held constant), consumers buy more of a good as the price at which they can purchase it falls.

(2) *Consumer Surplus*

The area underneath the demand line (*i.e.*, to the left and toward the origin of the Graph, "0"), bounded by the equilibrium price of the product, represents "Consumer Surplus." If, for example, that price is P^{WFT}, then Consumer Surplus is the triangular area demarcated by the points M, N, and P^{WFT}, because consumers whose preferences are embodied in the Demand line between points M and N are ready, willing, and able to pay a price for the product higher than P^{WFT}. The fact they need pay only P^{WFT} means they save money, or in economic jargon, obtain a "surplus."

Suppose the price falls from P^{WFT} to some lower level, such as P^1. Then, this surplus would expand accordingly. That would occur because more consumers—reflected in the Demand Curve between points corresponding to P^{WFT} and the new, lower price level—enter the market for the product. These consumers start purchasing (again, either the imported item or the domestic like product) at the lower price, which is less than the price they would be willing to pay (as shown by the higher prices corresponding to the points on the Demand Curve between P^{WFT} and the lower price level). What might cause the price decline from P^{WFT} to P^1? One answer is a subsidy provided by an exporting country's government to companies in manufacturing the product in the foreign country.

(3) *Supply Curve (Domestic, Upward Sloping)*

A Supply Curve illustrates the various quantities of a domestic like product that producers located in the importing country are ready, willing, and able to manufacture at alternative price levels. There is a direct relationship between quantity supplied (also measured on the horizontal axis) and price (again, gauged on the vertical axis). It is based on the common sense idea that *ceteris paribus*, producers will make more of a good as the price at which they can sell the good rises. Significantly, the upward sloping Supply line does not include imported merchandise.

(4) *Supply Curve (World, Horizontal)*

Sometimes, a Supply Curve is depicted as a horizontal line emanating from the vertical (Y) axis. (Graph 11-2 showing welfare effects of export subsidies is an instance.) This line shows supply of imported merchandise. It is horizontal because of an implicit assumption: the importing country is a "price taker." The country cannot affect the world market price of the product. It is not a large enough producer of that product, nor is the product market characterized by monopoly, oligopoly, or other forms of imperfect competition that would translate into an upward sloped world supply line. The product market is a globally competitive one.

(5) *Producer Surplus*

The area above the supply line (*i.e.*, to the left and away from the origin, "0") is "Producer Surplus" for domestic manufacturers. If the price of the output they sell is P^{WFT}, then their Surplus is demarcated by the points P^{WFT}, R, and P^1. The domestic producers whose interests are embodied on the supply line between points P^1 and R are ready, willing, and able to manufacture and sell the good for a price below P^{WFT}. But, in fact, they receive P^{WFT} when they sell the good. The difference between the price they would have accepted, and the price they obtained, is surplus to them.

What happens if the price falls from P^{WFT} to a price between P^{WFT} and P^1? Producer Surplus declines accordingly. Many domestic producers (specifically, the ones embodied on the Supply Curve between point R and a point corresponding to the lower price level) are not ready, willing, or able to manufacture at the lower price. They are knocked out of the market. Why might the price decline? Again, a foreign government might subsidize merchandise that competes with output of domestic producers.

The hypothetical example is the market for rice in Thailand, which Graph 11-1 portrays.

By assumption, the Thai rice market is competitive. Hence, the Supply and Demand Curves slope upward and downward, respectively. An additional assumption in the Neo-Classical Economic analysis of a domestic production subsidy concerns the size of the subsidizing country. Thailand is assumed to be an important producer of rice. Therefore, its exported output could affect the world market price.

The support measure at issue is a payment by the Thai government to rice farmers. It is a production subsidy available only to domestic producers, and excepted from the *GATT* Article III:4 national treatment principle by Article III:8(b). As a practical matter, the Thai subsidy payments could be linked to output, such as 40 *baht* per kilo of rice produced. Alternatively, the government could fund shifting land from the cultivation of other crops to rice paddy, possibly with the amount of

Graph 11-1. Welfare Effects of Domestic Production Subsidy

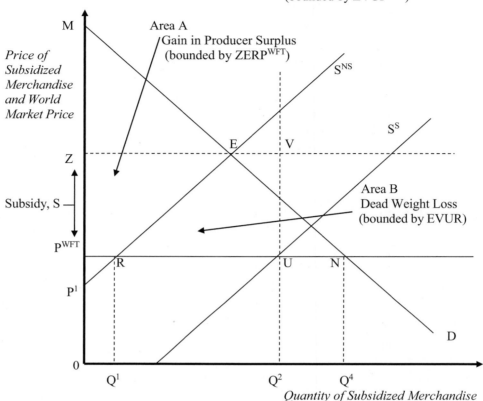

Areas A + B
Cost to Thai Government of Subsidy
(bounded by ZVUP^{WFT})

funds disbursed linked to the amount of land re-allocated to rice production (*e.g.*, 4,000 *baht* per hectare).

Significantly, Thai farmers are eligible for the subsidy whether or not they export their output. (The fact exporters, as well as other beneficiaries, receive a subsidy is enough to qualify the subsidy as export contingent, and thus a Red Light export subsidy under Article 3:1(a) of the *SCM Agreement*. For now, the point is the payments are not, in an economic sense, tied directly to exportation.) Also, the payment is not a "set aside," *i.e.*, it is not a payment to cut rice production or take paddy fields out of cultivation. A production-limiting payment, or support de-coupled from production, would not generate the boost in output shown in the Graph.

Before the government in Bangkok intervenes in the domestic rice market with a production subsidy, the prevailing price for rice is P^{WFT}. It is a world market price ("W" stands for "World," and "FT" for "Free Trade"). Next, the Thai government pays the subsidy, S, to rice farmers. As the Graph shows, provision of the subsidy does not change this price. Because there is no change in the price Thais pay for rice, P^{WFT}, there is no change in consumer surplus (the area beneath the demand curve down to the price level, which signifies the positive difference between the amount a family is willing and able to pay for rice versus what it actually has to pay).

Predictably, Thai farmers respond by increasing their output of rice, from Q^1 to Q^2. That is the goal of a production subsidy. In effect, the domestic supply of rice shifts outward (to the right) from Supply NS (where "NS" stands for "No Subsidy") to Supply S (where "S" stands for "Subsidy"). The vertical distance between S^{NS} and S^S is the amount of the subsidy. That distance is the gap between P^{WFT} and Z, or equivalently, between U and V. Intuitively, the Supply Curve shifts because the subsidy reduces the average and marginal costs of production. (This response depends on the *ceteris paribus* assumption, *i.e.*, all other relevant variables are unchanged.) There are two obvious welfare consequences:

(1) *Producer Surplus*

Producer Surplus (the area above a Supply Curve up to the price suppliers receive, which denotes the revenue producers obtain above and beyond what they require in order to produce) increases by the Area A. S^{NS} remains the Curve to gauge this surplus.

Would it be acceptable to use S^S as the Curve to gauge this surplus? That would mean the gain in Producer Surplus would be defined by Areas A + B, *i.e.*, by the points $ZVUP^{WFT}$. Intuitively, that would connote the gain in Surplus is a full transfer of government funds to the producers, plus gain from higher volume. If that were the case, then it would mean there is no net welfare loss from the subsidy, because (as explained below), Area B is Dead Weight Loss. That would be overly optimistic. Put differently, using S^S as the basis for evaluating the effects of a domestic production subsidy would be inappropriate, because that Supply Curve embodies those effects. The more accurate gauge of the effects of a subsidy is the Supply Curve that is market-based, undistorted by the subsidy, which is S^{NS}.

(2) *Government Expenditures*

Government spending equals the amount of the subsidy, S, multiplied by the output subsidized, which is the difference between Q^2 and the origin, 0. The Area A + B (specifically bounded by P^{WFT}, U, V, and Z) shows this transfer to Thai rice farmers.

The net welfare effect is a cost to Thailand, Area B. Whereas Area A is a transfer of Thai taxpayer funds to farmers, Area B is a Dead Weight Loss from production inefficiency. The subsidy artificially alters the incentives farmers have to deploy land, physical capital, technology, as well as their own labor and human capital, tipping them toward rice production and away from other pursuits.

In a legal dispute, the fact the price of a good is unaffected by a subsidy measure could be critical. It would mean the subsidy does not suppress or depress the world market price, either of which is an adverse effect, namely, serious prejudice, under Article 6 of the WTO *SCM Agreement*. Accordingly, some other adverse effect would have to be proven in order to countervail the subsidy.

Finally, the Graph—when juxtaposed with the welfare effects of a tariff—shows why mainstream economists counsel in favor of an output subsidy over a tariff as a form of government intervention. If there has to be government intervention to help domestic producers, then it ought not to be a tariff. A subsidy does not affect equilibrium domestic consumer prices or consumption levels, but a tariff raises prices, leading to reduced consumption opportunities. A subsidy is a less inefficient means of boosting output than a tariff, because it intervenes only on the supply side of a market. A tariff has repercussions for both supply and demand sides.

Why, then, do governments resort to tariffs—and, for that matter, quotas? One answer is tariffs (but not quotas) raise money for governments. (Quotas raise no funds for the government, but lead to rents for quota license holders, and consumers tend to view a quota as costless.) Some governments, especially in poor countries with inchoate or corrupt tax systems, rely for a large proportion of their revenue on tariffs. These facts lead to a second answer. A subsidy is a cost to a government. A third reason concerns a potential benefit of a subsidy. Depending on the nature and amount of a production subsidy, it could lead to lower domestic prices. However, consumers do not necessarily understand this benefit, or if they do, they might not champion it over the expenditure it entails. Finally, a domestic industry might feel politically uncomfortable about receiving a subsidy from the government, especially if the handout is subject to transparent scrutiny through the process of formulating the government's budget. A tariff may be a relatively quieter way of getting the competitive boost sought.

II. Neo-Classical Economic Analysis of Export Subsidy

Graph 11-2 depicts the effects of an export subsidy. To continue the example of the Thai rice market, with the assumptions this market is competitive, and Thailand is big enough to affect the world price for rice—suppose the government in Bangkok decides to pay a subsidy of 40 *baht* per kilo of rice. This subsidy is paid only for rice grown in and exported from Thailand, not for Thai rice sold domestically. This kind of subsidy is a crude cash payment. There are many kinds of subtle, indirect, or *de facto* export subsidies, some of which central governments provide, and others of which provincial or local authorities dole out.

The critical point to unlock Graph 11-2 is to appreciate the incentive created for Thai rice farmers by an export subsidy. Because these farmers get paid the 40 *baht* per kilo only if they export rice, they divert some of their output from sales to domestic consumers, and toward foreign customers. That is, paddy they would have dedicated to Thai sales they re-allocate, for example, to American consumers. The

Graph 11-2. Welfare Effects of Export Subsidy

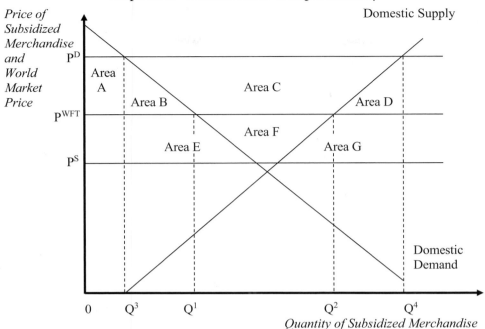

Price of Subsidized Merchandise and World Market Price

P^D

Area A

Area B

Area C

P^{WFT}

Area D

Area F

P^S

Area E

Area G

Domestic Supply

Domestic Demand

0 Q^3 Q^1 Q^2 Q^4

Quantity of Subsidized Merchandise

farmers even expand total output, by dedicating more land to paddy fields, or cultivating existing fields more intensively. They sell this extra output overseas. (Observe this response depends on the *ceteris paribus* assumption, *i.e.*, all other relevant variables are unchanged.)

Consequently, Thailand exports more rice than it did before implementing the export subsidy. In turn, rice prices in Thailand drift (or shoot) upward, because of the diversion of rice production from the domestic to overseas markets. But, rice prices overseas—the world market price—could fall. There could be (in the terms of the *SCM Agreement*) price depression. This adverse effect, a form of serious prejudice, would occur if Thailand is a big enough player in the world rice market that its extra rice exports have an appreciable impact on prices. (In fact, Thailand, Vietnam, and California are the world's largest rice producers.) Used in the non-technical sense, the export subsidy could lead to "dumping" of rice by Thailand on the world market. Even if Thailand is not so large a player, there could be price suppression, as the *SCM Agreement* puts it, which is another form of adverse effect. It means prices cannot rise owing to the subsidy.

The Graph shows these price movements. The initial world market rice price with free trade is P^{WFT} (where "W" is for "World" and "FT" is for "Free Trade"). This price prevails with no government intervention. At this price, Thai farmers produce Q^2 kilos of rice, and Thai families buy Q^1 kilos. The farmers export their surplus production, which is the difference between Q^2 and Q^1. When the administration in Bangkok promulgates the subsidy, Thai rice farmers respond to the incentive as described. The domestic price of rice, P^D (where "D" stands for "Domestic") rises, and the price on the world market, P^S (where "S" stands for "Subsidy"), falls. The difference between P^D and P^S is the amount of the subsidy, 40 *baht* per kilo. The rise in the domestic rice price, P^D, is less than the full subsidy amount, because the fall in the rice price in foreign markets is to P^S.

Thai farmers get paid P^D — if they export rice, then they earn P^S from foreign buyers, plus the government subsidy amount. (That is, Thai farmers are willing to accept the lower export price, P^S, because their government makes up the difference between it and the higher domestic price, P^D.) If they sell rice domestically, then they get paid P^D from Thai customers, because the rice price in Thailand is elevated due to the constriction of domestic supply caused by diversion of output to foreign markets. Accordingly, with price P^D, Thai rice farmers expand output to Q^4. But, fewer Thai families can afford the higher rice price associated with the export subsidy regime. So, they curtail consumption to Q^3. The gap $Q^1 - Q^3$ is sales diverted abroad. In brief, the increase in Thai rice production from Q^2 to Q^4, coupled with the decrease in Thai rice consumption from Q^1 to Q^2, generate a larger exportable surplus than existed without the subsidy.

The large areas denoted by capital letters on the Graph symbolize the welfare effects of an export subsidy.

(1) *Consumer Surplus*

Consumer surplus in Thailand falls by the amount A + B. Some Thai families are less well off than before. As represented by points on the Demand Curve, fewer families benefit from the gap between P^D and what they are willing and able, as represented by points on the Demand Curve, than the gap between P^{WFT} and that Curve.

(2) *Producer Surplus*

Producer surplus rises by the amount A + B + C. At P^D, there are more Thai farmers earning above the minimum amount at which they would be willing and able to cultivate rice, as depicted by points on the Supply Curve.

(3) *Government Expenditures*

The Thai government must pay the subsidy on the amount of rice exported. The amount it transfers to farmers is B + C + D + G + E + F, which equals the amount of the subsidy ($P^D - P^S$) multiplied by the quantity exported ($Q^4 - Q^3$).

(4) *New Welfare Effect*

The net welfare effect is the difference between producer gain and losses to consumers and Thai government, *i.e.*, the area B + D + E + F + G. It is a net loss reflecting:

(5) *Production and Consumption Distortions*

Area B + D is the distortion to consumption and production patterns the export subsidy causes. Area B signifies the diminution in consumption opportunities. But for the subsidy, Thai families would not have to decrease rice consumption from Q^1 to Q^3. Area D bespeaks the rising marginal cost of Thai rice production. That marginal cost exceeds what consumers in other countries pay for Thai rice. Area D shows the inefficient allocation of Thai factors of production to rice paddy. But for the subsidy, the labor, land, human capital, physical capital, and technology Thailand dedicates to expanding rice production from Q^2 to Q^4 would be used in some other endeavor. The consumption and production distortions Areas B + D represent are akin to the losses resulting from a tariff.

(6) *Terms of Trade (TOT) Effect*

This effect is different from the instance of a tariff (except in the rare case of an "optimal tariff"). Area E + F + G shows the effect of the export subsidy on TOT. Insofar as the export subsidy depresses the world market price for rice, from P^{WFT} to P^S, Thailand's TOT (the ratio of its export to import prices) worsen.

One question is whether a depression of the world market price, from P^{WFT} to P^S, is inevitable. That is, must there be a TOT effect in every instance of an export subsidy? The answer is "no." It depends on the significance of the export subsidizing country in the world market: if it is a big player in the market, then when it ships more of the subsidized good overseas, a fall in P^{WFT} is likely. But, if that country does not account for a large percentage of global exports of the merchandise it is subsidizing, then P^{WFT} may be unaffected. Yet, even if that occurs, the export subsidy would still cause a net welfare loss: it would be Areas B + D, the production and consumption distortions, but not Aras E + F + G, the TOT effect.

Observe even if there is no TOT effect, *i.e.*, no price depression to PS, there still could be price suppression. That is, PWFT might not rise, because of the extra supply of subsidized rice on the world market. Both of these possibilities, price depression and price suppression, constitute adverse effects under Articles 5(c) and 6:3(c) of the *SCM Agreement* in respect of Yellow Light (Actionable) subsidies.

To be sure, foreign consumers benefit from a world market price decline — unless their governments impose a CVD. Still, for the exporting country, an export subsidy unequivocally yields costs over benefits. Also, the world price drop hurts rice producers in countries other than Thailand. Therein is an adverse effect under the *SCM Agreement*.

III. Neo-Classical Economic Analysis of CVD

What are the welfare effects of offsetting a foreign government subsidy with a CVD? From a Neo-Classical Economic perspective, the short answer is they are no different from imposing a tariff. More precisely, a CVD is simply a duty on top of the MFN (or otherwise applicable) tariff. Hence, the welfare analysis is the same as increasing a tariff rate. In turn, it is not difficult to appreciate why economists look askance at CVDs. Graph 59-3 demonstrates the analysis.

The critical point to appreciate about Graph 11-3 is it portrays the market in the importing country—the country imposing the CVD—for the good (or service) subsidized by a foreign government. It does not depict the effect of the CVD on foreign producers or exporters. Suppose America is the importing country, and it decides to countervail a Thai rice subsidy. The Graph shows the effect of the CVD on American consumers of rice, American rice farmers (in California, in particular, which itself is one of the largest rice producing regions in the world), and the American government.

The welfare effects of a tariff and CVD are the same. Like a tariff, a CVD lifts the price of subsidized imported goods (subject merchandise) up to its pre-subsidized price. The lift to this level assumes the CVD fully offsets the subsidy, and is not a partial offset in accordance with an EU-style "Lesser Duty Rule" to impose just enough of a CVD to counteract a subsidy. The CVD causes a loss of Consumer Surplus that outweighs the gain in producer surplus and CVD revenue accrued by the importing country government. Table 11-1 summarizes these results.

The price P^{UNS} is an unsubsidized price (with "UNS" meaning "unsubsidized"), while P^S is a subsidized price (with "S" for "Subsidized"). If a foreign government pays a subsidy, directly or indirectly, to farmers or processors of a commodity, or manufacturers of a product located in the territory over which the government has jurisdiction, then those farmers, processors, or manufacturers can sell their output—both in their home market and in overseas markets—at a lower price than they are able to without the subsidy. That certainly could be the case with a Thai rice export subsidy.

Hence, P^S and its corresponding supply line are beneath P^{UNS} and its corresponding supply line. As a result of the subsidy, Consumer Surplus expands by the area $P^{UNS}BCP^S$, i.e., from P^SCQ^30 (at the unsubsidized price P^{US}) to $P^{US}BCQ^30$ (at the subsidized price P^S). However, Producer Surplus falls by the area $P^{UNS}AFP^S$, i.e., from $P^{UNS}AG$ (at the unsubsidized price P^{UNS}) to P^SFG.

What is the net welfare effect on the importing country of the foreign government subsidy? For context, assume the U.S. is the importing country. The gain in Consumer Surplus of $P^{UNS}BCP^S$ outweighs the loss in Producer Surplus of $P^{UNS}AFP^S$. Points A, B, C, and F, i.e., Area ABCF, mark off the difference. American rice consumers are better off by the increase in their surplus, which more than offsets the damage done to producer interests in that country.

The story might not end here. Producers may lobby American politicians for protection, and file a CVD petition. Assume the petition is successful, and CVD relief to offset exactly the subsidy is granted. On the Graph, the result is an upward shift in the import supply line, and thus a rise in the price of imported merchandise back

Graph 11-3. Welfare Effects of CVD

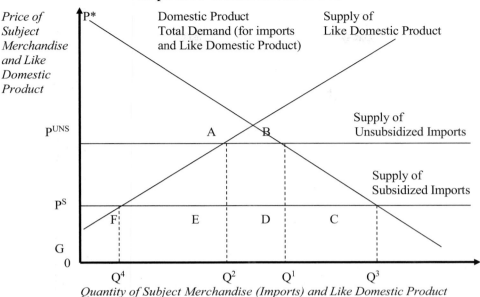

Quantity of Subject Merchandise (Imports) and Like Domestic Product

to P^{UNS}. What is the net welfare effect of the CVD? It is redolent of the net welfare effect of a tariff. If domestic producers of the like product (*e.g.*, California rice farmers) take advantage of the protection by raising the price of their product to (or near to) the level of P^{UNS}, then there are three effects:

Table 11-1. Summary of Welfare Effects of CVD

	Consumer Surplus	Producer Surplus	Tariff Revenue	Net Welfare Effect
Unsubsidized Merchandise Sold at P^{UNS}	P*BP^{UNS}	P^{UNS}AG	None	Not applicable
Subsidized Merchandise Sold at P^S	Expands by P^{UNS}BCP^S	Declines by P^{UNS}AFP^S	None	Increase in Consumer Surplus outweighs decrease in Producer Surplus by ABCF
Subject Merchandise Sold with CVD Imposed at P^{UNS}	Declines by P^{UNS}BCP^S	Expands by P^{UNS}AFP^S	ABDE	BCD (lost consumption opportunities) plus AEF (inefficient allocation of productive resources)

(1) *Consumer and Producer Surplus*

The gain in Consumer Surplus from the subsidy of P^{UNS}BCP^S is wiped out, as is the loss in Producer Surplus from the subsidy of P^{UNS}AFP^S. That is, Consumer Surplus declines by P^{UNS}BCP^S, and Producer Surplus expands by P^{UNS}AFP^S.

(2) *Government Revenue*

The U.S. government earns revenue from the CVD imposed on the amount of merchandise subject to the remedy order, which is the difference between Q^1 and Q^2. (Without the order, imports are higher, the difference between Q^3 and Q^4, because domestic production of the like product is lower, at Q^4 rather than Q^2.) In particular, tariff revenue is ABDE (the amount of the CVD, which is P^{UNS} minus P^S, multiplied by the level of imports, Q^1 minus Q^2).

(3) *Net Welfare Loss*

The net welfare loss consists of two triangles, BCD and AEF, which combined are Dead Weight Loss. The triangle BCD reflects lost consumption opportunities ("lost" in that consumers no longer get low subsidized merchandise prices). The triangle AEF is the allocation of productive resources in the importing country to an inefficient activity, namely, production of the like product. It is "inefficient" when compared with subsidized foreign production.

This Neo-Classical Economic Analysis proves a CVD damages the welfare of an importing country imposing it. If a foreign government willingly expends resources on a subsidy scheme, and consumers in the importing country benefit (along with producers and exporters of the subsidized good), then why take remedial action?

Even within the paradigm of economics, there are responses focusing on analytical shortcomings. First, the analysis is narrow in scope. It considers welfare effects only in an importing country. An analysis of the effects of the program on the exporting and importing countries, third countries, or the entire trading system, might be insightful.

Second, the analysis is narrow because it is static. A dynamic analysis, *i.e.*, one assessing effects of a subsidy over time, might reveal other implications. For example, a CVD imposed by one country may cause a foreign exporter of subsidized merchandise to re-direct exports to countries with no penalty. The result is elimination of some or most of the revenue previously accruing to the CVD-imposing government, *i.e.*, depicting ABDE as tariff revenue on the Graph is an overstatement.

Third, a number of questionable implicit assumptions underlie the Neo-Classical critique of CVDs. For instance:

(1) *Perfect Competition?*

Product and import markets in the importing country are perfectly competitive. In truth, these markets may be characterized by monopoly, oligopoly, or monopsony. They may not adjust quickly to a dis-equilibrating influence.

(2) *Perfect Substitutes?*

Subsidized imported merchandise and a domestic like product are perfect substitutes. Often, foreign and domestic firms compete through brand names, and slightly differentiating their products. That is, competition may be imperfect, as firms seek some monopoly power by defining a market niche.

(3) *Specific Deterrence?*

Imposition of a CVD is an ineffective tool to deter subsidization. However, the goal of the duty may be not only to remove the offending subsidy, but also to deter future subsidies, *i.e.*, general, not just specific, deterrence. The latter goal helps exporters in the importing country that must compete with producers of subsidized merchandise in third countries.

(4) *TOT Enhancement?*

Imposition of a CVD will not improve the TOT of the importing country. Albeit rarely, an importing country might account for a sizeable percentage of world consumption of the product in question. (That is, consumers in an importing country might have monopsony power.) Levying a CVD on subject merchandise causes the price of that merchandise in the importing country to rise. Therefore, demand for it in that country falls. This decrease also implies a noticeable drop in world demand for the subsidized merchandise. That occurs because of the importance of consumption by the importing country to world consumption. In turn, with the drop in world demand, the world market price of the subsidized merchandise declines. That drop means the TOT of the importing country improves. If this phenomenon occurs, then Neo-Classical Theory suggests a CVD can increase the net welfare of the importing country.

Intuitively, the reason is that where a CVD shifts the TOT to the importing country, making imports less expensive than before the duty, part of the tariff revenue accruing to the government of the importing country comes out of the Producer Surplus of foreign exporters. Foreign exporters capture less Surplus, because the price of their merchandise falls. In contrast, where the TOT are unaffected by the duty, all of the revenue comes from domestic consumer surplus. Certainly, instances of improved TOT through CVD imposition are unusual, and it is unlikely government officials can carefully calibrate the CVD amount to achieve the desired TOT improvement. Officials risk setting the duty too high, so subsidized merchandise imports are choked off, or too low, so domestic demand for them is not materially affected.

If any assumption is, in fact, incorrect, then the bottom-line conclusions are in doubt.

IV. Level Playing Field Argument

Whether to impose a CVD is not merely an economic matter. For instance, a pragmatic response to the question "Why impose a CVD?" is "because some domestic producers can." This answer relates to the politics of trade remedies, and implicates a body of analysis known as Public Choice Theory. A CVD may be imposed simply because a petitioning industry can obtain an order. In turn, it is likely to be able to marshal itself into a legal force if it is not too diffuse, and has common interests.

More generally, as with the economic critique of AD law, is there an air of unreality about the Neo-Classical Analysis of CVD law? If the critique sufficed, then CVD law might be abolished for lack of a strong economic foundation. Yet, it persists. It was re-organized and strengthened by the WTO *SCM Agreement*. Governments have legitimate reasons to bestow a subsidy, such as developing a poor region, encouraging research and development, or promoting environmentally-friendly production methods. CVD law has continuing vitality because of widespread perception that some subsidies are a form of unfair competition against which domestic producers must have a remedy. That perception begs a foundational question, namely, what is "fairness" in international trade law?

Leveling the international competitive playing field may be a matter of fairness. A subsidy provided by a foreign government may distort international trade patterns, and that is unfair. Consider China. In *Subsidies to Chinese Industry: State Capitalism, Business Strategy and Trade Policy* (2013), Professor Usha Haley of West Virginia University and George Haley of the University of New Haven estimated that each year since 2001, when China acceded to the WTO, China subsidized over 20% of the industrial expansion of both SOEs and private enterprises. And, China subsidized over 30% of all of its industrial output (measured in U.S. dollar terms). Non-Chinese unsubsidized manufacturers of a like product in an importing country cannot possibly compete. They are forced to cut wages or lay off workers. Those actions have ill effects on families and communities. A CVD rectifies the unfairness. Implicit in this response is use of a free, unsubsidized market price as the indicator of "fairness," and a correlative implicit assumption that there is such a thing as a normal trade pattern.

The problem with the defense that a CVD levels the playing field is three fold. First, it exalts property rights and interests of the minority over the majority. Domestic producers, the output of which a CVD protects, gain. But, their gain is the loss of the public, which pays higher prices. Second, a CVD is an artificial interference with property rights. As Professor Robert McGee says in *A Trade Policy for Free Societies* (1994), "fairness" can be defined as non-coercive exchange. So long as an export-import deal is voluntary, with no official tariff, quota, or remedy (which would make trade coercive), then it is "fair."[2] Third, underlying CVD law is a philosophically flawed assumption—trade is a zero sum game. It is, or is supposed to be, a win-win game with mutually beneficial results.

---

2. *See* ROBERT W. MCGEE, A TRADE POLICY FOR FREE SOCIETIES 6, 15–17 (1994).

Chapter 12

Definition of "Subsidy," First Element: "Financial Contribution"[1]

I. Problem of Scope

U.S. law allows the DOC to impose a CVD on merchandise made with the benefit of a "subsidy."[2] That begs a threshold problem: defining the term "subsidy." As a theoretical matter, the starting point is the economic concept of a subsidy, which is a "benefit conferred on a firm or product by action of a government."[3] The difficulty with this definition is its potential scope. Read literally, the definition includes activities typically provided by virtually every government in the world: police and fire protection; infrastructure development (*e.g.*, roads, power plants); technological development (*e.g.*, telecommunications), and primary and secondary educational instruction.

These activities confer a benefit on a foreign exporter (or producer) because they reduce its costs. The exporter need not pay (or not pay as much) for its own security and fire officials, basic infrastructure and technology, and training of workers (though it pays for these benefits indirectly through taxes, some of which may be used to fund the subsidy). The same difficulty exists under a different economic approach to defining a subsidy: any cost incurred by or imposed on the granting government. Focusing on cost to define "subsidy" still is overly broad. It includes routine activities every government performs. Also, this focus is misplaced: what should matter is not whether the subsidizing government incurs a cost, but whether the subsidized exporter benefits.

Economic approaches to the definition of "subsidy" are of little practical use in CVD law. If that law incorporates a broad economic conception of a subsidy, then an enormous array of foreign government programs will be countervailable. In turn, foreign governments might retaliate by imposing CVDs of their own on central or sub-central government programs. After all, no government wants—or should be

---

1. Documents References:
    (1) *Havana (ITO) Charter*, Articles 25–28, 34
    (2) *GATT* Articles VI, XVI
    (3) WTO *SCM Agreement*
2. *See* 19 U.S.C. § 1671(a).
3. John H. Jackson, The World Trading System 261 (1989) (citation omitted). *See also id.*, at 262–264.

required to—give up its ability to support police and fire protection, infrastructural and technological development, and educational services.

So, the result of defining "subsidy" in a broad manner that conforms with economic theory would be a deadlock created by (1) exporting countries that use subsidies to further legitimate public policy goals, and (2) importing countries that retaliate against these subsidies with CVDs designed to level the playing field on which domestic producers of a like product must compete with subsidized imports. Virtually every country would fall into both camps: it would retain its subsidy programs, and it would countervail foreign subsidy programs. The multilateral trading system would be highly contentious, and the deadlock might undermine efforts at trade liberalization.

Unfortunately, GATT provides no help in defining the term "subsidy." The term is used blithely in several provisions of Articles VI and XVI. Nowhere in Article VI or XVI (or any other GATT provision) does a definition of "subsidy" or "subsidization" appear. Equally troublesome is the fact Articles VI and XVI are rather generic and to some extent hortatory. Thus, they impose no meaningful discipline on subsidies.

II. Four Government Practices

Given the definitional void in GATT, Article 1 of the WTO *Agreement on Subsidies and Countervailing Measures (SCM Agreement)* is a welcome development. The definition contains two critical concepts, namely, "financial contribution" and "benefit," that help determine what governmental activities are subsidies. Moreover, the Article 1:1 definition leads to two devices that help delineate subsidies against which CVD action may be taken from subsidies that are non-actionable. These devices are a Specificity Test, and a scheme for categorizing subsidies known as the "Traffic Light System." These devices, along with the definition of a "subsidy" as a "financial contribution" that "confers a benefit" are implemented into American CVD law via the *1994 Uruguay Round Agreements Act*.[4]

The definition of "subsidy" in Article 1:1 of the *SCM Agreement* indicates a government program is not a subsidy and, therefore, is not countervailable, unless the government is providing a "financial contribution" to an exporter, producer, group of exporters or producers, industry, group of industries, or to private economic agents in general. Critically, the contribution may be made by "a government or any public body" within that government's territory. Whether the government provides the contribution directly or through an intermediary, including a private body, is irrelevant.

---

4. *See* 19 U.S.C. § 1677(5A) (concerning specificity, export subsidies, import substitution subsidies, and domestic subsidies), (5B) (concerning non-countervailable subsidies).

In this respect, the language "entrusts or directs" in the Article 1:1 definition, and implemented into American law, is noteworthy. As legislative history to the *1994 Act* makes clear, this language is to be "interpreted broadly to prevent the 'indirect' provision of a subsidy from becoming a harmful loophole to effective enforcement of the countervailing duty law."[5] Accordingly, the DOC expectedly continues its pre-Uruguay Round practices, evident in famous cases like *Certain Softwood Lumber Products from Canada*, of countervailing alleged foreign government subsidy programs provided through private parties.[6]

What, then, is a "financial contribution"? The Article 1:1 definition of "subsidy" specifies four government practices that constitute a "financial contribution":

(1) A direct transfer of funds, such as an equity infusion, loan, or grant, from the government to a firm. This practice is the most obvious type of "financial contribution." But, a potential direct transfer of funds from the government, such as a loan guarantee or assumption of liabilities, also is a "financial contribution."

(2) Foregone or uncollected government revenue, such as a tax credit or tax abatement. For example, the practice of many states and localities to lure business by offering these sorts of tax incentives are clearly "financial contributions." Indeed, it is rather curious why this practice has not caused greater controversy. One reason may be that foreign companies investing in the U.S. often are the beneficiaries of these "financial contributions," and thus foreign governments are hesitant to complain as long as all of the companies from their country have equal access to them along with American competitors. Another likely reason is until a subsidized product is exported, there is no occasion to initiate a CVD proceeding, because no injury from imports yet exists.

(3) Government provision of goods or services other than general infrastructure may be a "financial contribution." Suppose a government provides components at a below-market price that are used to manufacture a finished product. The manufacturer is receiving a "financial contribution" (measured by the reduction from the market price).

(4) Purchase of goods by a government from a firm may be a "financial contribution." Suppose a government buys a finished product from the manufacturer at an above-market price. Plainly, the government is providing the

5. SENATE COMMITTEE ON FINANCE, SENATE COMMITTEE ON AGRICULTURE, NUTRITION, AND FORESTRY, AND SENATE COMMITTEE ON GOVERNMENTAL AFFAIRS, URUGUAY ROUND AGREEMENTS ACT, SENATE REPORT NUMBER 412, 103d Congress, 2d Sess. 88, at 91 (1994).

6. *See* SENATE COMMITTEE ON FINANCE, SENATE COMMITTEE ON AGRICULTURE, NUTRITION, AND FORESTRY, AND SENATE COMMITTEE ON GOVERNMENTAL AFFAIRS, URUGUAY ROUND AGREEMENTS ACT, SENATE REPORT NUMBER 412, 103d Congress, 2d Sess. 88, at 91 (1994); HOUSE COMMITTEE ON WAYS AND MEANS, URUGUAY ROUND AGREEMENTS ACT, HOUSE OF REPRESENTATIVES REPORT NUMBER 826, 103d Congress, 2d Session 107-127, at 108–109 (1994).

manufacturer with a "financial contribution" (measured by the excess over market price). Likewise, a government scheme to support the income of a firm, or the price of a firm's output, which has the effect of stimulating exports or reducing imports, is a "financial contribution."

Of course, to impose a CVD, it is not enough that a foreign government provide a "financial contribution." Were it sufficient, then any subsidy could be countervailed. To make a CVD lawful, the contribution must confer a benefit on a specific recipient.

As intimated above, the definition of "financial contribution" in Article 1:1(a)(1) consistently refers to "government." More generally, the whole idea of an unlawful subsidy presumes the party providing the subsidy is a governmental body, or somehow connected to one. That is, it must be a governmental body that provides the "financial contribution." Support from a purely private sector group cannot quality as an illicit subsidy: its source, being the private sector, takes it out of the definition of "financial contribution." The fourth of the four types of financial contribution in this provision, that is, Article 1:1(a)(1)(iv), ensures a "government" does not undermine disciplines against subsidies by funneling support through a proxy, such as a funding mechanism, or a private body that the government "entrusts or directs."

III. Case Law on First Element, "Government": 2005 *Korea DRAMs*, 2011 *U.S. AD-CVD*, and 2014 *India Carbon Steel*

• 2005 *Korea DRAMS*[7]

A year after *Softwood Lumber*, the Appellate Body addressed the meaning of "financial contribution" for the second time. The Korea *DRAMS* dispute arose following a

---

7. *See* Appellate Body Report, *United States—Countervailing Duty Investigation on Dynamic Random Access Memory Semiconductors (DRAMS) from Korea*, WT/DS296/AB/R (adopted 20 July 2005).

See also Appellate Body Report, *Japan—Countervailing Duties on Dynamic Random Access Memories (DRAMS) from Korea*, WT/DS336/AB/R (adopted 28 November 2007). In this 2007 *Japan DRAMS (Korea)* case, the Appellate Body again addressed Article 1:1(a)(1)(iv) of the *SCM Agreement* in the 2007 *Japan DRAMS (Korea)*, related to the 2005 *Korea DRAMS* case. Japan investigated DRAMS manufactured in and imported from Korea, and imposed a CVD order on them. The subsidies occurred through financial transactions entered into by Hynix Semiconductor, Inc. Japanese investigative authority concluded the Korean Government entrusted or directed four of the private creditors of Hynix to participate in debt-restructuring programs. The relevant appellate issue was whether the investigating authority used the proper evidentiary standard to determine entrustment or direction. Siding with Japan, the Appellate Body held the Panel erred in failing to consider the evidence in its totality, whereas the Japanese investigating authority rightly looked at all of the evidence before finding the Korea provided a subsidy via entrustment or direction.

This case is not useful in interpreting Article 1:1(a)(1), in that it does not add to the jurisprudence on "entrustment" or "direction." As it relates to "financial contribution," this case is

final CVD order by the U.S. on importation from Korea of dynamic random-access memory semiconductors (DRAMS) and memory modules containing DRAMS. In this case, the Appellate Body discussed Article 1:1(a)(1)(iv) of the *SCM Agreement*.

Facts and Issue:

In response to a petition filed by Micron Technology, Inc., the DOC investigated the subsidy rate for Hynix Semiconductor, Inc. (Hynix) and Samsung Electronics Co., Ltd. (Samsung). The DOC found numerous Korean financial institutions participated in financial transactions related to Hynix. In its final injury determination, the ITC concluded the U.S. DRAMS industry was materially injured by reason of imports of subsidized DRAMS from Korea. So, the DOC issued a CVD order imposing CVDs of 44.29% on Hynix, paid as cash deposits by importers.[8]

Following the Korean action under the *DSU*, a WTO Panel found the DOC and ITC determinations to be inconsistent with Articles 1, 2, and 15:5 of the *SCM Agreement*. In the appeal by the U.S., it was clear the problematic financial institution was the Korea Development Bank, which was founded in 1954 and is a 100% state owned policy bank. The KDB administered a Fast Track Debenture Program, through which selected companies redeemed 20% of their bonds maturing in 2001, paying the holders of those bonds their full face value. As to the remaining 80% of the maturing bonds, KDB purchased them, and the selected companies issued new bonds that essentially replaced those that KDB purchased.

Who bought the newly issued bonds from the selected companies? KDB held 10% of the new bonds. Creditors of the selected companies purchased 20% of them, and got permission from the Government of Korea to exceed their loan exposure limits. The remaining 70% of new bonds were bundled and sold as Collateralized Bond Obligations or Collateralized Loan Obligations, which the Korean Government guaranteed.

At play was Article 1:1(a)(1) of the *SCM Agreement*, which sets forth the situations in which a government or public body makes a "financial contribution." Recall Sub-Paragraphs (i)–(iii) refer to a "financial contribution" provided directly by the government through the direct transfer of funds, foregoing of revenue otherwise due, provision of goods or services, or purchase of goods. In contrast, Sub-Paragraph (iv) says a "financial contribution" also is present when a government "entrusts or directs a private body to carry out one or more of the type of functions illustrate in (i) to (iii) . . . which would normally be vested in the government and

---

about evidentiary standards, and stands for little else than the proposition that if an investigating authority makes a determination in a CVD case based on the totality of the evidence, then a WTO Panel also must look to the totality of the evidence. It may not dispose of a determination by that authority simply because some of the evidence lacks support. A Panel should consider whether, in light of the remaining evidence, the investigating body nevertheless could have reached its finding.

8. The DOC found the subsidy rate for Samsung was 0.04%, thus below the *de minimis* threshold of 1% for developed country merchandise under Article 11:9 of the *SCM Agreement*.

the practice, in no real sense, differs from practices normally followed by governments." As the Panel stated in 2001 *Export Restraints*, Sub-Paragraph (iv) focuses on the identity of the actor, while Sub-Paragraphs (i)–(iii) deal with the nature of the action.[9] Additionally, said the *DRAMS* Appellate Body, for Article 1:1(a)(1) to be satisfied, there must be a demonstrable link between the government and the conduct of the private body.[10]

At the time of the *DRAMS* case, the Appellate Body had not yet interpreted the terms "entrusts" and "directs." As a result, at issue was whether the terms should be read narrowly as "delegation" and "command," or could encompass a broader meaning. The Appellate Body opted for an expansive interpretation, thereby reversing the Panel and upholding the American arguments supporting the DOC and ITC CVD determinations.

Losing Argument:

Korea argued the interpretation of the Panel of "entrusts or directs" was appropriate. The Panel took the ordinary meaning of the terms as "delegate" and "command," respectively. But, the Panel failed to define or clarify further these terms.

Holding:

Overturning the Panel holding, the Appellate Body ruled "entrusts" and "directs" in Article 1:1(a)(1)(iv) of the *SCM Agreement* were not limited to "delegation" and "command," respectively. That definition was too narrow. The Appellate Body said there could be other means by which a government could give responsibility to or exercise authority over a private body.

Rationale:

Similar to its approach in *Softwood Lumber IV*, the Appellate Body interpreted the contested terms using dictionary definitions and foreign language comparisons. First, in interpreting "entrusts," the Appellate Body acknowledged the American assertion that *The New Shorter Oxford English Dictionary* definition included "[i]nvest with a trust; give (a person, etc.) the responsibility for a task . . . [c]ommit the . . . execution of (a task) to a person."[11] Additionally, the Appellate Body looked to the Spanish and French versions of the *SCM Agreement*, and determined "entrusts" connotes the action of giving responsibility to someone for a task or an object. As a result, the Appellate Body found limiting the interpretation of the term "entrusts" to "delegation" was too narrow, because there may be other means that governments could employ.

Second, the *OED* definition of "direct" includes "[c]ause to move in or take a specified direction; turn towards a specified destination or target"; "[g]ive authoritative

---

9. *See* Panel Report, *United States—Measures Treating Export Restraints as Subsidies*, WT/DS194/R (adopted 29 June 2001), ¶ 8.53.

10. *Korea DRAMS* Appellate Body Report, ¶ 112.

11. *Korea DRAMS* Appellate Body Report, ¶ 109.

instructions to; to ordain, order (a person) *to do,* (a thing) *to be done*; order the performance of"; and "[r]egulate the course of; guide with advice."[12] The Appellate body distinguished among some definitions of "directs." It said those which imply authority over a person (*e.g.,* "give authoritative instructions to" and "order (a person) *to do*") fit better with the language "to carry out" found in Article 1:1(a)(1)(iv). Additionally, the Spanish and French versions of the *SCM Agreement* supported the view that implicit in the meaning of "direct" is authority. However, limiting the interpretation of "direct" to "command" is too narrow, thought the Appellate Body. That is because a "command" is one of multiple ways a government can and does exercise authority. Every government has more subtle means at its disposal.

Conclusion:

Though the 2005 *DRAMS* case dealt only with Article 1:1(a)(1)(iv) of the *SCM Agreement,* it showed for the second time the Appellate Body favors broad interpretations of the terms relating to "financial contribution." To circumscribe those terms too narrowly would be to emasculate the disciplines on subsidies, because governments could behave in ways (such as non-command type directions, if "direct" meant only "command") to provide support to beneficiaries.

However, the Appellate Body said a balance must be borne in mind. Article 1:1(a)(1)(iv) should not be interpreted so broadly as to allow a WTO Member to apply CVD measures to imported merchandise whenever the government of the exporting Member merely exercises its general regulatory powers.

- **2011 *U.S. AD-CVD***[13]

Facts and Issue:

In *United States AD-CVD,* China disputed AD and CVD measures imposed concurrently by the U.S. against the same subject merchandise from China. On appeal, the Appellate Body addressed the meaning of "public body" under *SCM Agreement* Article 1:1(a)(1). The dispute arose after the DOC ordered AD and CVD duties against Chinese circular welded carbon quality steel pipe (CWP), light-walled rectangular pipe and tube (LWR), laminated woven sacks (LWS), and certain new pneumatic off-the-road tires (OTR). Like the DOC, the WTO Panel based its findings on the fact that the Chinese Government held majority ownership stakes in state owned enterprises (SOEs, the manufactures of the previously mentioned products), and state owned commercial banks (SOCBs, which financed the SOEs). The Panel held a "public body" as used in Article 1:1(a)(1) of the *SCM Agreement* is "any entity controlled by a government."

China appealed two Panel determinations relating to the interpretation and application of the term "public body." First, in regard to all four CVD investigations,

---

12. *Korea DRAMS* Appellate Body Report, ¶ 109.

13. *See* Appellate Body Report, *United States — Definitive Anti-Dumping and Countervailing Duties on Certain Products from China,* WT/DS379/AB/R (adopted 25 March 2011). [Hereinafter, *U.S. AD-CVD* Appellate Body Report.]

China took issue with the determination that a SOE is a "public body." Second, as to the OTR CVD investigation, China argued a SOCB is not a "public body."

Holding:

Reversing the Panel interpretation of the term "public body" under Article 1:1(a)(1) of the *SCM Agreement*, the Appellate Body agreed with China, and outraged many in the U.S. Congress. The Appellate Body determined a public body is an entity that possesses, exercises, or is vested with, government authority. In other words, whereas the Panel essentially said "control is enough" to constitute a "public body," the Appellate Body said "control is not enough." Rather, a body is "public" only if the government gives it government-like authority.

However, regarding the application of the term "public body" to the facts, the Appellate Body handed China only a half-victory. It found China had established the SOEs did not constitute public bodies, but also found China failed to establish the DOC was wrong to determine that SOCBs constituted public bodies.

Losing Argument:

The Panel, like the DOC before it, accepted the American argument that the test for "public body" is both simple and broad: government ownership is not only highly relevant, but also possibly dispositive, in deciding whether a body is "public." The Appellate Body rejected that test as missing the key ingredient of what it is to be a government, namely, to hold governmental authority.

Rationale:

As required by Article 31 of the *Vienna Convention*, the Appellate Body turned first to the definitions of "public" and "body" in the *Shorter Oxford English Dictionary*. That led nowhere, because the *OED* definitions of "public" and "body" could accommodate both the Chinese and American definitions.[14]

Next, the Appellate Body examined the use of the term "government" in Article 1:1(a)(1)(iv) of the *SCM Agreement*, which therein is juxtaposed with the term "private body," that is, where a "government" entrusts or directs a "private body" to conduct the previously enumerated functions in (i)–(iii) of that Article (*i.e.*, transferring funds, collecting revenue, or providing goods and services, respectively). The Appellate Body also considered the term "government" in the narrow sense, that a "public body" is functionally equivalent to "government," which it had indicated was correct in its 1999 *Canada—Dairy* decision.[15] The term "government" was not, contrary to the finding of the Panel, merely a device to facilitate the drafting of the *Agreement*, nor was it an entirely distinct concept from the term "pubic body." Each term had real meaning, and each is related to the other.

---

14. *See U.S. AD-CVD* Appellate Body Report, ¶ 285.

15. *See* Appellate Body Report, *Canada—Measures Affecting the Importation of Milk and the Exportation of Dairy Products*, WT/DS103/AB/R, WT/DS113/AB/R (adopted 27 October 1999).

Hence, the Appellate Body posed the key question: what are the essential characteristics an entity must share with a government to be considered a "public body" in the narrow sense, and thus part of that government in the collective sense? It cited its 1999 *Canada—Dairy* precedent. After wasting a sentence defining the word "government" and footnoting the *OED* for that definition, the Appellate Body invoked its precedent and said:

> the essence of government is that it enjoys the effective power to regulate, control, or supervise individuals, or otherwise restrain their conduct, through the exercise of lawful authority.[16]

Again referencing *Canada—Dairy*, the Appellate Body said these essential characteristics derive from the functions a government performs, and the power and authority a government has to perform those functions. So, for an entity to be considered a "public body," it must possess these essential characteristics: it must be vested with, and exercise, lawful power or authority to regulate, control, supervise, and restrain conduct.[17] Belaboring the point, the Appellate Body distinguished a "public" from "private" in terms of the subject exercising authority, *i.e.*, a public official versus a private individual.[18]

Applying these essential characteristics to the context of Article 1:1(a)(1)(iv) of the *SCM Agreement* meant that if a government "directs" a private party, then the government itself must have the requisite authority to compel or command that private party, and if it "entrusts" a private party with responsibility, it must be vested with that responsibility, too.[19] What kind of authority or responsibility must an entity exercise or be vested with in order to be classified as a "public body"?

The items enumerated in the preceding provisions of Article 1:1(a)(1) are helpful to answer this question, but not dispositive. Article 1:1(a)(1)(i) speaks of loans and loan guarantees, which in reality are provided by the government or private parties. Article 1:1(a)(1)(iii) discusses the provision of goods or services, and likewise government or private parties offer them. In contrast, Article 1:1(a)(1)(ii) concerns the foregoing of the collection of government revenue otherwise due. Those functions (collecting revenue and the decision not to do so) are inherently sovereign matters.[20]

Following its lexicographic analysis of the term "public body," the Appellate Body examined this term in light of the object and purpose of the *SCM Agreement*. The Panel took the view "public body" should not be defined narrowly, as that would exempt entities that actually are government-controlled or directed, or entrusted by the government with responsibility, from the disciplines of the *Agreement*, and

---

16. *U.S. AD-CVD* Appellate Body Report, ¶ 290.
17. *See U.S. AD-CVD* Appellate Body Report, ¶ 290.
18. *See U.S. AD-CVD* Appellate Body Report, ¶ 291.
19. *See U.S. AD-CVD* Appellate Body Report, ¶ 295.
20. *See U.S. AD-CVD* Appellate Body Report, ¶ 296.

thereby circumvent those disciplines. The Appellate Body demurred, finding the object and purpose of the *Agreement* unhelpful in interpreting "public body."[21]

Ultimately, the Appellate Body said a "public body," to be one, shares attributes with the "government." But, whether such sharing exists depends on a case-by-case examination of the facts. If an entity is vested with authority to exercise governmental functions, or if it exercises authority on behalf of the government, then it is a "public body." But, formal links, like majority share ownership, between an entity and government are probably insufficient to prove the entity possesses governmental authority. Consequently, the Panel was wrong to hold that control of an entity by a government is, in itself, enough to prove the entity is a "public body." The term "public body" as used in Article 1:1(a)(1) of the *SCM Agreement* does not mean "any entity controlled by a government."[22]

Conclusion:

It is important to understand the differences between the American arguments accepted by the Panel, and the Chinese arguments accepted by the Appellate Body. They were not mutually exclusive. The American view that "public body" means government ownership or control certainly includes the possibility an entity performs governmental functions. Conversely, the Chinese approach that the term requires an examination of authority does not exclude the possibility of government ownership or control.

From a practical standpoint, arguably, the Appellate Body precedent creates unnecessary barriers for complaining parties. Though it is possible for an entity to be government owned or controlled, but not vested with the power to perform any government functions, why does the burden fall on the complainant to prove otherwise? Thanks to the Appellate Body, a WTO Member must do more than what the U.S. did, namely, define a particular SOE, SOCB, or other entity as a "public body" based on the fact it is owned or controlled by a government. The litigant must adduce evidence beyond state ownership or control. Never mind that such evidence is hard to come by, in countries lacking transparency or plagued by corruption, especially countries run by one-party authoritarian regimes like the China of the Communist Party. In sum, the Appellate Body would have done better to find that

---

21. The Appellate Body also expended 11 paragraphs on an inconclusive analysis about a text adopted by the International Law Commission (ILC) in 2001, namely, *Articles on Responsibility of States for Internationally Wrongful Acts. See U.S. AD-CVD* Appellate Body Report, ¶¶ 305–316. The Appellate Body did so, because of Article 31(3)(c) of the 1969 *Vienna Convention on the Law of Treaties*, which (in the hierarchy of techniques for interpreting words of an international agreement) calls for an examination of any relevant rules of international law applicable in the relations between disputing parties. The ILC *Articles* were such rules (particularly if they reflected customary international law, and were not superseded by the *SCM Agreement* as *lex specialis*). *See id.*, ¶ 304. Essentially, the Appellate Body said the ILC *Articles* are not helpful in interpreting the term "public body" under Article 1:1(a)(1) of the *Agreement*, because they do not address whether the Appellate Body can take them into account. *See id.*, ¶ 316.

22. *U.S. AD-CVD* Appellate Body Report, ¶ 359.

when an entity is majority-government owned, there exists at least a rebuttable presumption that the entity is a "public body."

- **2014 *India Carbon Steel*[23]**

Facts and Issues:

India is the 4th largest producer of steel in the world, bested only by China, Japan, and America.[24] Steel is an important export industry for India, and various agencies of the Indian government support the viability of this industry. Indeed, the ties between titans of Indian steel and leaders in the government have been close ever since Indian independence from the British in 1947. At issue in the 2014 India *Carbon Steel* case is support in the form of certain alleged government subsidies. One such alleged subsidy was iron ore and mining rights supplied by the National Minerals Development Corporation (NMDC), a mining company 98% of the stock of which is held by India's Ministry of Steel.[25] Loans extended to steel producers by India's Steel Development Fund (SDF) were another purported subsidy.

American steel producers challenged these subsidies under U.S. CVD law. That law, of course, is designed to be consistent with the requirements of Part V of the WTO *SCM Agreement*. Their case before the DOC and ITC was successful. It resulted in imposition of CVDs on steel imported from India into the U.S. India then challenged the CVDs at the WTO under the *DSU*. Indeed, India challenged not only the CVDs imposed by the U.S. in the course of the original administrative proceeding, but also CVDs the U.S. imposed or continued in five Administrative Reviews and two Sunset Reviews.

Before the WTO Panel, India challenged many aspects of U.S. CVD statutes "as such," contending the provisions on their face were inconsistent with the *SCM Agreement*. India also challenged U.S. CVD laws and regulations "as applied" by the DOC and ITC in their investigations and Reviews were inconsistent with that *Agreement*.[26] In fact, at the Panel stage, India made 22 different claims under the *Agreement*, plus some under GATT Article VI and the *DSU*. India over-argued the case.

On appeal, India and the U.S. sparred over several procedural issues, resulting in yet another Appellate Body report of extraordinary length (268 pages) and complexity. The U.S. challenged several of the Panel's adverse findings. Several of the most important rulings are discussed in this and subsequent chapters. There were three key issues on appeal, all arising under the *SCM Agreement*:[27]

---

23. *See* Appellate Body Report, *United States — Countervailing Measures on Certain Hot-Rolled Carbon Steel Flat Products from India*, WT/DS436/AB/R (adopted 19 December 2014). [Hereinafter, *India Carbon Steel* Appellate Body Report.]

24. World Steel Association, *World Steel in Figures 2014*, 9, www.worldsteel.org.

25. *India Carbon Steel* Appellate Body Report, ¶ 4.3.

26. *India Carbon Steel* Appellate Body Report, ¶ 1.2.

27. A fourth notable issue concerned benchmarking determinations. The Appellate Body consumed almost 50 pages of its Report on this matter, and applied its *U.S. AD-CVD* and *Softwood*

(1) In respect of the definition of "subsidy," what constitutes a "public body" under Article 1:1(a)(1)?

(2) Also in respect of the definition of "subsidy," is the grant of mining rights for iron ore and coal to Indian steel producers by NMDC, and certain loans by SDF, "financial contributions" under Article 1:1(a)(1)?

(3) As for material injury, in a CVD case, is cross-cumulation permitted under Article 15, that is, is it permissible to consider both subsidized subject merchandise and non-subsidized dumped imports in determining whether imports are causing or threatening to cause material injury?

The first two issues are discussed below, and the third is covered in as separate Chapter.

Panel Holding and Rationale on "Public Body" under Article 1:1(a)(1):[28]

Article 1:1(a)(1) of the *SCM Agreement* provides that:

> For the purpose of this *Agreement*, a subsidy shall be deemed to exist if . . . there is a *financial contribution by a government or any public body* within the territory of a Member (referred to in this *Agreement* as "government") . . . .[29]

Thus, if the subsidy is not provided by a government directly, or by a public body, then no actionable subsidy is considered to exist.

The DOC, in determining NMDC was a public body, looked to evidence of control, as well as ownership. The DOC based its conclusion on the fact the Government

---

Lumber IV precedents (both of which are discussed later in this Chapter). *See India Carbon Steel* Appellate Body Report, ¶¶ 140–193.

In essence, the Appellate Body upheld under Article 14 of the *SCM Agreement* the DOC subsidization determinations "as such." Contrary to India's suggestion, the American benchmarking mechanism did not preclude adjustments to reflect delivery charges that approximate the generally applicable delivery charges in the country of provision.

But, the Appellate Body faulted certain details of those determinations, *i.e.*, it disapproved of them "as applied." The Appellate Body criticized the DOC for not including NMDC exports in the DOC's computation of a world market benchmark. (The DOC instead assumed without investigation that those exports were not market-based.) The Appellate Body also looked askance at the manner in which the DOC calculated the cost of subsidized loans the SDF provided, because the DOC added administrative costs of acquiring the loans to the prime lending rate the SDF charged. So, on the "as applied" claim, the Appellate Body rejected the Panel findings, but was unable to complete the analysis. To be sure, the DOC could correct easily these deficiencies by expanding the questionnaires it sends to the GOI, and adjusting its annual Administrative Reviews.

India also appealed the Panel interpretation and application of Article 12:7 of the *SCM Agreement*, again both "as such" and "as applied." *See id.*, ¶¶ 205–234. As regards the "as such" challenge, the Appellate Body found the Panel failed to make an objective assessment of India's claim, because it did not consider certain relevant evidence when making its determination. On the "as applied" claim, the Appellate Body held the Panel did not apply an "unnecessary burden of proof" with respect to the application of an alleged rule on selecting the highest non-*de minimis* subsidy rates.

28. *See India Carbon Steel* Panel Report, ¶¶ 4.1–4.55.

29. Emphasis added.

of India owned 98% of the stock, plus the right to appoint all officers and directors, of NMDC. Hence, said the DOC, NMDC is a public body. In its proceedings, the DOC applied a "simple control" test, and an analysis of the evidence of the nature of the relationship between GOI and NMDC, which suggested that GOI controlled NMDC and could use NMDC resources as its (GOI's) own.

The Panel stated the relationship between GOI and NMDC was "very different from the relationship that would normally prevail between a private body and the government."[30] The Panel concluded the DOC determination that NMDC, based on record evidence, effectively amounted to a finding that the NMDC was under the meaningful control of the Indian government.

However, in its 2011 *U.S. AD-CVD* Report, the Appellate Body had opined that "being vested with governmental authority is the key feature of a public body," so that to meet the requirements of the *SCM Agreement*, a public body "must be an entity that possesses, exercises, or is vested with governmental authority."[31] An entity does not necessarily have to possess the power to regulate in order to be a public body, or to entrust or direct private bodies to carry out the functions identified in Article 1:1(a)(1)(i)-(iii) of the *Agreement*. India relied on the *U.S. AD-CVD* Appellate Body, arguing the DOC should not have focused on the percentage of shares the GOI held in NMDC, and thereby in deciding NMDC was a "public body" under Article 1:1(a)(1). According to India, to be deemed a "public body," an entity must perform a governmental function, and have the power and authority to perform said function.

Interestingly, the Panel tacitly acknowledged the *de facto stare decisis* Panels practice, insomuch as it cited *U.S. — Continued Zeroing* for the idea that although a Panel is required by *DSU* Article 11 to make an objective assessment of the matter before it, it is appropriate, and expected, that the Panel follows conclusions of the Appellate Body from earlier disputes, "especially where the issues are the same."[32] As a result, the Panel relied on the findings of the Appellate Body in *U.S. AD-CVD*. But, the Panel added to India's interpretation of the dispute.

The Panel stated that percentage control of an entity was a meaningful core feature of an entity's powers and authorities, which allow it to perform governmental functions in question. The Panel found it dispositive that India held 98% of the shares of NMDC. It agreed with the approach and considerations of the DOC, and found that in addition to assessing the ownership of NMDC, the DOC had adequately addressed the question of control.

---

30. *India Carbon Steel* Panel Report, ¶ 7.87.

31. *See* Appellate Body Report, *United States—Definitive Anti-Dumping and Countervailing Duties on Certain Products from China*, WT/DS379/AB/R ¶ 317 (adopted 25 March 2011). [Hereinafter, *U.S. AD-CVD* Appellate Body Report.]

32. The Panel quoted Appellate Body Report, *U.S. — Continued Zeroing*, ¶ 362.

Appellate Body Holding and Rationale on "Public Body" under Article 1:1(a)(1):[33]

On appeal, India put forward a standard claim that the Panel erred in its interpretation and application of Article 1:1(a)(1) of the *SCM Agreement*. For the Appellate Body, neither a broad nor a narrow interpretation of the term "public body" was warranted.[34] Whether the conduct of an entity is that of a public body:

> must in each case be determined on its own merits, with due regard being had to the core characteristics and functions of the relevant entity, its relationship with the government, its relationship with the government, and the legal and economic environment prevailing in the country where the investigated entity operates.

That is, citing *U.S. AD-CVD*, the Appellate Body reiterated that a case-by-case approach must be employed.

The Appellate Body added that express statutory delegation of governmental authority is not necessary for a "public body" to exist. However, the factors to consider vary, and evidence an entity exercises governmental functions, or that a government is exercises meaningful control, may substantiate a claim that a public body exists. The key point is that existence of mere formal links between an entity in question and a government is not, in and of itself, enough to establish the necessary possession of governmental authority. In a vital passage, the Appellate Body said:

> the mere ownership or control over an entity by a government, without more, is *not* sufficient to establish that the entity is a public body [under Article 1:1(a)(1) of the *SCM Agreement*].[35]

And, as the Appellate Body also emphasized, investigating authorities should avoid focusing exclusively or unduly on any single characteristic without considering the full context of a relationship.

The Appellate Body noted the DOC made no such inquiry with respect to NMDC. Moreover, the Panel erred in its use of a "meaningful control" substantive standard, where it should have the evidence as a whole. The Panel also erred in its treatment of the evidence on the administrative record of the U.S. DOC investigation. Said the Appellate Body, the Panel gave insufficient consideration to India's assertion that evidence before the DOC showed NMDC, as a *Miniratna* or *Navratna* enterprise, lacked governmental control, and that "government directions or policies have not influenced the transactions or pricing of the products sold by" NMDC. Indeed, the Appellate Body faulted both the DOC and Panel for failing to consider the relationship between the GOI and NMDC within the Indian legal order, and whether the GOI in fact "exercised" meaningful control over NMDC as an entity and in its conduct. Also, the DOC failed to explain certain evidence in its record

---

33. *See India Carbon Steel* Appellate Body Report, ¶¶ 112–128, 261–265.

34. *India Carbon Steel* Appellate Body Report, ¶ 4.28 (*citing U.S.—Antidumping and Countervailing Duties (China),* Appellate Body Report, ¶ 303).

35. *India Carbon Steel* Appellate Body Report, ¶ 4.10 (emphasis added).

that was cited before the Panel. So, the Appellate Body held the Panel erred in rejecting India's claim that the DOC's public body determination was inconsistent with Article 1:1(a)(1) of the *SCM Agreement*.

The Appellate Body considered whether it could complete the legal analysis and decide if NMDC is a public body. The Appellate Body noted the DOC failed to provide "a reasoned and adequate explanation of the basis for its determination that the NMDC is a public body" Under Article 1:1(a)(1). The DOC did not study the core features of NMDC and its relationship with the government, or (again) think about its status within the Indian legal order or the extent to which the GOI exercised "meaningful control" over it and its conduct. The DOC did not look at any factors beyond government shareholding and the power to appoint directors. Rather, the DOC inquiry focused only on "formal indicia of control . . . ." "These factors are certainly relevant, but do not provide a sufficient basis for a determination that an entity is a public body that possesses, exercises or is vested with governmental authority."

Thus, handing India a victory, the Appellate Body found the DOC's public body determination was inconsistent with Article 1:1(a)(1) of the *SCM Agreement*. Analyzing only formal indicators will not do, as it is too simplistic. The inquiry must be more nuanced, and even look at what might be called "Comparative Law" factors. Though the Appellate Body did not use that term, a reasonable inference from its ruling is formal indicia that intimate control in one country might not constitute control in another one.

IV. Case Law on First Element, "Financial Contribution": 2004 *Softwood Lumber IV*, 2012 *Boeing*, 2013 *Canada Renewable Energy*, and 2014 *India Carbon Steel*

The WTO Appellate Body has elaborated on what is and is not a "financial contribution." It has applied the *SCM Agreement* Article 1:1 definition to a diverse array of fact patterns in a several high profile cases.

- **2004 *Softwood Lumber*[36]**

In 2004, the *Softwood Lumber* dispute provided the Appellate Body with its first substantial opportunity to address what constitutes a "financial contribution" within the meaning of Article 1:1 of the *SCM Agreement*.[37] More generally, the case

---

36. *See* WTO Appellate Body Report, *United States—Final Countervailing Duty Determination with Respect to Certain Softwood Lumber from Canada*, WT/DS257/AB/R (adopted 19 January 2004). [Hereinafter, *Softwood Lumber*.] The case also is known as *Softwood Lumber IV*.

37. In 2000, the Panel in *United States—Foreign Sales Corporation* (*FSC*) addressed what constituted a "financial contribution" under Article 1:1(a)(1)(ii) of the *SCM Agreement* when it found American tax exemptions for Foreign Sales Corporations (FSCs) were prohibited export subsidies.

was the fourth of four major battles in a war dating to 1982 between the U.S. and Canada over Canadian subsidies to its lumber industry. (The two countries reached a tentative settlement in April 2006.) *Softwood Lumber* arose following a final affirmative CVD determination by the DOC and final affirmative injury determination by the ITC pertaining to certain softwood lumber imports from Canada.

Facts and Issue:

Through "stumpage programs," provincial governments in Canada, most notably that of British Columbia (B.C.), made standing timber (*i.e.*, a tree that had yet to be cut down, or harvested) available to Canadian harvesters. The stumpage arrangements gave these harvesters (called "tenure holders") the right to enter onto government land and cut standing timber, plus gave them exclusive rights to the timber they harvest.

The U.S. alleged the stumpage arrangements provided a "financial contribution" within Article 1:1(a)(1)(iii) of the *SCM Agreement*. Thus, at issue was whether the Canadian government "provided goods or services" via its stumpage programs within the meaning of this provision.

Losing Argument:

On appeal, Canada unsuccessfully contended "goods" does not refer to tangible or movable personal property other than money.[38] Canada argued for a narrow interpretation of the term "goods" as "tradable items with an actual or potential tariff classification."[39] To be sure, softwood lumber is wood that is harvested. Hence, it has a tariff classification. But, the stumpage programs focused on making standing timber available to harvesters, *i.e.*, getting them access to trees before they have been cut down. Canada pointed out the terms "goods" or "products" are used throughout the Multilateral Agreements on Trade in Goods set forth in Annex 1A to the *WTO Agreement*.[40] There, these terms refer to items that are traded, imported, or exported.

Canada also contended the Panel erred in finding provincial governments "provide" standing timber through stumpage programs. Canada said "provides" does not mean "to make available," in a passive sense. Rather, as used throughout the accords in Annex 1A, "provided" means "supplying" or "giving," in proactive sense. Canada said the governments only provided the intangible right to harvest.

However, the U.S. did not, as a general proposition, challenge this finding on appeal. *See FSC*, ¶ 24. On appeal, the Appellate Body briefly recognized the term "otherwise due" established a "but for" test, but that such a "test must yield in situations where a specific standard exists for determining whether revenue is 'otherwise due.'" *See FSC*, ¶ 24.

38. *See Softwood Lumber*, ¶ 31.

39. *See Softwood Lumber*, ¶ 31.

40. Referring to what is formally known as the *Marrakesh Agreement Establishing the World Trade Organization*. Annex 1A is titled "Multilateral Agreements on Trade in Goods."

Holding:

The Appellate Body upheld the Panel finding, which itself upheld the DOC determination. The Appellate Body found the ordinary meaning of "goods" does not exclude tangible items of property, like trees, which are severable from land. It added the way in which the municipal law of a WTO Member classifies an item cannot in itself be determinative of WTO provisions. Lastly, the Appellate Body upheld the Panel finding that provincial governments do "provide" goods within the meaning of Article 1:1(a)(1)(iii) of the *SCM Agreement*, simply by virtue of making standing timber available to the harvesters. There is no passive-active distinction in the word "provided."

Rationale:

In defining "goods," the Appellate Body first looked to the ordinary definitions in *Black's Law Dictionary*. *Black's* was helpful, because it included in the term "growing crops, and other identified things to be severed from real property." The Appellate Body also found useful a comparison of the English, French, and Spanish versions of the *SCM Agreement*. Article 33(3) of the *Vienna Convention* provides treaty language authenticated in more than one language is presumed to have the same meaning in each authentic text. Here, the ordinary meanings of the French "*biens*," and the Spanish "*bienes*," include immovable property, as did the English definition.

With regard to the definition of "provides," the Appellate Body looked to *The New Shorter Oxford English Dictionary*.[41] There, "provides" is defined as to "supply or furnish for use; [to] make available." Moreover, the *Collins Dictionary of the English Language* defines "provides" as "to put at the disposal of."

In addition to the lexicographic sources confirming that simply "making available" is enough to "provide," the Appellate Body emphasized that consequences of a transaction matter.[42] Evidence in the case suggested that making available timber is the *raison d'être* of the stumpage arrangements.

Conclusion:

Softwood Lumber is the first of several precedents the Appellate Body set that show it will not read key terms in the definition of "financial contribution" narrowly, and thereby not circumscribe the reach of CVD law. To do so would undermine the disciplines on subsidies contained in the *SCM Agreement*. Thus, "goods" includes items that are precursors to merchandise that has a tariff classification in the HS, and is actually shipped across borders, and "provides" can be the mere setting aside of assets for certain enterprises.

---

41. Noting the definition of "provides" was unchanged in the newer *Shorter Oxford English Dictionary*.

42. *See Softwood Lumber*, ¶ 75.

- **2012 *Boeing***[43]

In the tit-for-tat trade war concerning large civil aircraft (LCA), the 2012 *Boeing* case was the European response to the American complaint in the 2011 *Airbus* case.[44] The *Airbus* Panel addressed the issue of a "financial contribution" within Article 1:1(a)(1) of the *SCM Agreement*, but on appeal the EU did not dispute the Panel finding, In contrast, in *Boeing*, the U.S. appealed the Panel findings relating to Article 1:1(a)(1)(i)-(iii) of the *SCM Agreement*.

Facts and Issues:

Numerous measures were at issue in *Boeing*, but just three of them mattered to the "financial contribution" analysis. They were (1) NASA Procurement Contracts, (2) DOD Assistance Instruments, and (3) Washington State Business and Occupation (B&O) Tax Rate Reduction.

First, it was undisputed NASA paid Boeing to conduct research services under the Procurement Contracts. The Appellate Body characterized these payments as composite, in the sense they involved a combination of elements. For example, the Procurement Contracts provided Boeing with access to NASA equipment, facilities, and employees. Additionally, the contracts provided Boeing with NASA-owned tools and hardware. Lastly, in addition to access to some employees, some of the contracts awarded to Boeing provided research teams including NASA employees.

Second, the DOD Assistance Instruments included cooperative agreements, technology investment agreements, and other transactions entered into by the DOD that carried out basic, applied, and advanced research projects. Under the Assistance Instruments, both the DOD and Boeing contributed financial resources to research projects (later equated to as "joint ventures" by the Appellate Body). Even the U.S. admitted the DOD involvement was "substantial," and included collaboration, participation, and intervention. Lastly, similar to the NASA Procurement Contracts, the DOD Assistance Instruments provided Boeing with access to DOD facilities.

Third, the Washington State B&O Tax Rate Reduction was enacted under Washington State House Bill 2294. This Reduction was a tax on the "gross receipts of all businesses operating in Washington State, as a measure of the privilege of engaging in business." House Bill 2294 provided for a decrease in the B&O tax rate, to occur in two stages for manufacturers of commercial airplanes or components of such airplanes.[45] The first stage took place from 1 October 2005 to 30 June 2007, cutting the tax rate from 0.484% to 0.4235%.[46] The second stage lowered the tax rate to 0.2904% as of 1 July 2007, or as of the commencement of final assembly

---

43. *See* Appellate Body Report, *United States—Measures Affecting Trade in Large Civil Aircraft (Second Complaint)*, WR/DS353/AB/R (adopted 12 March 2012). [Hereinafter, *Boeing* Appellate Body Report.]

44. *See* Appellate Body Report, *European Communities—Measures Affecting Trade in Large Civil Aircraft*, WR/DS316/AB/R (adopted 18 May 2011). [Hereinafter, *Airbus* Appellate Body Report.]

45. *See Boeing* Appellate Body Report, ¶ 459.

46. *See Boeing* Appellate Body Report, ¶ 459.

of a "super-efficient" airplane, whichever was later.[47] Lastly, the taxation reduction applied until 2024, unless the final assembly of a super-efficient aircraft had not commenced by 31 December 2007, in which case the tax rate reverted to 0.484% for manufacturing and wholesaling activities, and 0.471% for retailing activities.[48]

NASA Procurement Contracts and DOD Assistance Instruments were similar enough that the Panel and Appellate Body grouped them together for purposes of their financial contribution analysis. The Panel started by saying a "direct transfer of funds" under Article 1:1(a)(1)(i) of the *SCM Agreement* does not include measures "properly characterized" as purchases of services. Then, the Panel proceeded to consider whether the disputed measures qualified as purchases of services. The Appellate Body rightly rejected the Panel inverted logic: the correct first question is "what are the disputed measures, *i.e.*, what is the correct characterization for them?" Once the measures have a factually accurate label attached to them, then the second question is whether that label falls within the definition of a "financial contribution" in Article 1:1(a)(1)(i), or any of the other three Sub-Paragraphs, of the *Agreement*.

So, one question was whether payments made to Boeing under the Procurement Contracts and Assistance Instruments qualified as a "direct transfer of funds." Another question was whether, under those measures, access to facilities, equipment and employees provided to Boeing constituted the "provision of goods or services" within the meaning of Article 1:1(a)(1)(iii) of the *SCM Agreement*.

With regard to the Washington State B&O Tax Rate Reduction, the applicable provision was Article 1:1(a)(1)(ii) of the *SCM Agreement*. Thus, the appellate issue was whether the Tax Rate Reduction constituted a financial contribution in the form of "foregone" "government revenue" that was "otherwise due" to the U.S. This issue translated into whether the Panel used an appropriate normative benchmark for the comparison of tax rates.

Losing Argument:

The first losing argument related to the analytical approach suggested by the U.S. regarding purchases of services and Article 1:1(a)(1)(i) of the *SCM Agreement*. The U.S. asserted the measures were properly characterized as purchases of services, a category of transactions it claimed to be excluded from the scope of Article 1:1(a)(1)(i), which covers only "direct transfers of funds." The Appellate Body criticized this approach as putting the cart-before-the horse: the American argument assumed the measures were purchases of services, rather than considering as an initial matter the proper characterization of the measures. So, once the proper characterization is set, then a Panel should examine whether those measures fall within the scope of Article 1:1(a)(1) of the *Agreement*.

Another relevant losing argument related to the Washington State B&O Tax Rate Reduction. In its appeal, the U.S. challenged the reliance by the Panel on a

---

47. *See Boeing* Appellate Body Report, ¶ 459.
48. *See Boeing* Appellate Body Report, ¶ 459.

benchmark consisting of general manufacturing, wholesaling, and retailing tax rates. The U.S. argued this benchmark failed to account for other important features of the tax system, namely, 36 categories of business activities individually identified in the Washington State tax code. The Appellate Body rejected the American argument, saying a tax system as a whole cannot operate as a benchmark. A tax system is composed of various tax rates for different activity categories. These rates cannot all simultaneously serve as the basis for a comparison with the challenged rate. In brief, the American argument in favor of using as a benchmark an effective average tax rate was too simplistic, as it conflated different categories of taxable activities.

Holding:

Even though the Appellate Body disagreed with the Panel approach regarding Article 1:1(a)(1)(i) of the *SCM Agreement*, it ultimately upheld the Panel ruling, but by different means. The Appellate Body said the NASA Procurement Contracts and the DOD Assistance Instruments were akin to a joint venture (JV), and thus similar enough to equity infusions. In turn, an equity infusion is a "financial contribution" by a government under Article 1:1(a)(1)(i). Additionally, access to NASA and DOD facilities, equipment, and employees given to Boeing constituted the "provision of goods or services" within the meaning of Article 1:1(a)(1)(iii) of the *Agreement*.

The Appellate Body also agreed with the Panel selection of a normative benchmark. It upheld the Panel finding that the Washington State B&O Tax Rate Reduction applicable to commercial aircraft and component manufactures constituted the "foregoing" of "revenue otherwise due." So, the Tax Rate Reduction was a "financial contribution" within the meaning of Article 1:1(a)(1)(ii).

In sum, the U.S. lost its argument that the Contracts and Assistance Instruments were not "financial contributions." To the contrary, they fit within three of the four Sub-Paragraphs of Article 1:1(a)(1).

Rationale:

The Panel did not arrive at a definitive characterization of the NASA and DOD measures; rather it made determinations by exclusion. That is, it rejected the characterizations as "purchases of services," or "grants," but never said what the right descriptions were. That left the Appellate Body with the task of properly analyzing the disputed measures.

As to the proper characterization of the NASA Procurement Contracts, the Appellate Body emphasized the mutual relationship they created. Under the Contracts, NASA provided Boeing with funding and access to NASA facilities, equipment, and employees, while Boeing contributed more labor and the use of its own facilities. Additionally, NASA and Boeing often determined collaboratively the subject of the research, as if they were professors in the same engineering department.

Accordingly, the outcomes of the Contracts were technical information, discoveries, and data. Each party received differing rights to these outcomes. But, Boeing was not required to pay royalties to NASA for any resulting commercial rewards. As a result, the Appellate Body determined the Contracts essentially created a JV.

As to the DOD Assistance Instruments, the Appellate Body again focused on the collaborative relationship they created. A review of the Instruments showed both parties committed financial resources to the projects, but the DOD funded at least 50% of the costs. Moreover, the DOD gave Boeing access to its facilities. Thus, from a funding perspective, the measures involved pooling money with non-monetary resources.[49]

The outputs from the Boeing and DOD transactions were similar to those from the NASA Procurement Contracts. The parties shared the resulting scientific information, and Boeing got royalty-free government use and purpose licenses to the inventions. So, mirroring its findings on the Contracts, the Appellate Body found the DOD Assistance Instruments had the features of a JV arrangement.

Having characterized the disputed measures as JVs, the Appellate Body then compared its characterization to the four categories of "financial contributions" in Article 1:1(a)(1) of the *SCM Agreement*. Its analysis regarding the structure of Article 1:1(a)(1) was important. Sub-Paragraphs (i)–(iv) exhaust the types of government conduct deemed by the Uruguay Round negotiators to constitute a "financial contribution." However, Article 1:1(a)(1)(i) of the *Agreement* contains illustrative examples indicative of the common features a measure constituting a financial contribution may contain. These examples include "grants," "loans," and "equity infusions," but even they do not exhaust the possibilities contemplated by Sub-Paragraph (i).[50] As the Appellate Body stated: "in [the 2007] *Japan—DRAMs (Korea)* [case], the Appellate Body found that transactions that are similar to those expressly listed in subparagraph (i) — in that case, debt forgiveness, the extension of a loan maturity, and debt-to-equity swaps — are also covered by that provision."[51]

Focusing on an "equity infusion," the Appellate Body rightly understood it as a transaction whereby a government provides capital to an enterprise, with the understanding the government is entitled to dividends and capital gains attributable to the investment. The return on investment depends on the success of the recipient enterprise, and the government has no assurance how well or poorly the enterprise will perform.

The Appellate Body also looked to Article 1:1(a)(1)(iii), contemplating the "provision of goods or services" to, or the "purchases of goods" from, an enterprise.[52]

---

49. *See Boeing* Appellate Body Report, ¶ 607.

50. *See Boeing* Appellate Body Report, ¶ 615.

51. *See Boeing* Appellate Body Report, ¶ 615 (*citing* Appellate Body Report, *Japan—DRAMs (Korea)*, ¶¶ 251, 252).

52. In a leap of logic, the Panel said omission of services from the phrase "purchases goods" in Sub-Paragraph (iii) meant the *SCM Agreement* drafters wanted to exclude "purchases of services" from Sub-Paragraph (i). The Appellate Body declined to sort out the matter. *See Boeing* Appellate Body Report, ¶ 620.

The Appellate Body observed Sub-Paragraph (iii) does not specify whether a government provides goods or services gratuitously or in exchange for money or other goods or services. So, it inferred the provision of goods or services may include transactions in which the recipient is not required to make any form of payment. As it reasoned, the difference between Sub-Paragraphs (i) and (iii) is the transfer of financial resources from a government versus the provision of a good or service by a government, respectively.

The final stage of the Appellate Body analysis decided NASA Procurement Contracts and DOD Assistance Instruments fell within the government functions contemplated by Article 1:1(a)(1) of the *SCM Agreement*. NASA and the DOD provided funding (*i.e.*, payments) on terms similar to an equity infusion. In so doing, NASA and the DOD (*i.e.*, the government) expected returns in the form of scientific and technical information, discoveries, and data. And, like equity infusions, at the time they provided funding, NASA and the DOD had no certainty the research would be successful. So, the JV arrangements between NASA and Boeing, and the DOD and Boeing, were analogous to equity infusions. As such, the NASA and DOD funding constituted a direct transfer of funds within the meaning of Article 1:1(a)(1)(i) of the *SCM Agreement*.

Additionally, Boeing accessed NASA facilities, equipment, and employees, and DOD facilities. The Appellate Body said this use constituted a provision of goods or services within the meaning of Article 1:1(a)(1)(iii) of the *Agreement*. But, it failed to articulate its rationale, lumping it together with its Sub-Paragraph (i) JV analogy.

What about the rationale of the Appellate Body as to the Washington State B&O Tax Rate Reduction, that is, whether House Bill 2294 constituted a "financial contribution" under Article 1:1(a)(1)(ii) of the *SCM Agreement*? The Appellate Body synthesized discussions of "foregone revenue otherwise due" in two precedents, its 2000 *Foreign Sales Corporation* Report, and its 2002 *Foreign Sales Corporation (Article 21:5—EC)* Compliance Proceeding Report

> 806. We begin our analysis by recalling the core aspects of the Appellate Body's reasoning in *U.S.—FSC* and *U.S.—FSC (Article 21:5—EC)* as they relate to the interpretation of Article 1.1(a)(1)(ii) of the *SCM Agreement*. The Appellate Body observed that the foregoing of revenue otherwise due implies that less revenue has been raised by the government than would have been raised in a different situation, and that the word "foregone" suggests that the government has given up an entitlement to raise revenue that it could "otherwise" have raised. This purported entitlement, however, cannot exist in the abstract. There must be "some defined, normative benchmark against which a comparison can be made between the revenue actually raised and the revenue that would have been raised 'otherwise.'" Moreover, the basis of comparison must be the "prevailing domestic standard" established by the tax rules applied by the Member in question, because "[w]hat is "otherwise due" . . . depends on the rules of taxation that each Member, by its own choice, establishes for itself."

807. In the compliance proceedings in *U.S.—FSC (Article 21:5—EC)*, the Appellate Body further elaborated its understanding of the standard set out in Article 1:1(a)(1)(ii). The Appellate Body underscored that a financial contribution does not arise under Article 1:1(a)(1)(ii) simply because a government does not raise revenue that it could have raised. Although a government might be said to "forego" revenue when it chooses not to tax certain income, this alone is not determinative of whether the revenue foregone is "otherwise due." In other words, the Appellate Body stated that "the mere fact that revenues are not 'due' from a fiscal perspective does not determine that the revenues are or are not 'otherwise due' within the meaning of Article 1.1(a)(1)(ii)."[53]

The first Paragraph makes sense, but the second manifestly is another illustration of contorted logic that sometimes emanates from the judges of Geneva. In every instance in which a government could tax an enterprise, individual, or transaction, but opts not to, that government is foregoing revenue. Put bluntly, the government leaves money in the hands of the taxpayer, in lieu of collecting that money as revenue.

Nevertheless, the Appellate Body opined an "otherwise due" examination may be difficult. There may be situations in which a disputed measure might be described as an exception to the general rule of taxation, so a "but for" test may be appropriate. It gave no persuasive illustration, thus reinforcing the perception that on this point, indeed it should have tolerated a "but for" test. It concluded with milk toast language that such a test is not the only possible one, and application of actual treaty language should be a priority.[54]

Regardless, the Appellate Body reasoned that in theory, proper application of Article 1:1(a)(1)(ii) of *SCM Agreement* requires examining whether a government uses a tax regime to achieve outcomes equivalent to the results the government would obtain if it provides a direct payment. In practice, how should this examination be done? The Appellate Body said to make a comparison using a defined normative benchmark: "identification of circumstances in which government revenue that is otherwise due is foregone requires a comparison between the tax treatment that applies to the alleged subsidy recipients and the tax treatment of comparable income of comparably situated taxpayers."[55] So, first, identify the tax treatment that applies to the income of the alleged recipients. Second, identify the benchmark tax treatment for comparison by scrutinizing the tax regime of the respondent Member. Last, compare the reasons for the challenged tax treatment with the benchmark tax treatment.

---

53. *See Boeing* Appellate Body Report, ¶¶ 806, 807.
54. *See Boeing* Appellate Body Report, ¶ 810.
55. *See Boeing* Appellate Body Report, ¶ 812.

Applying this three-step test to the facts, the Appellate Body looked to the Panel's factual conclusions about general or normal B&O tax rates. The Panel concluded that manufacturing and wholesaling activities generally were taxed at 0.484%, while retailing activities were taxed at 0.471%. The Panel also concluded there was a lower, exceptional taxation rate for a subset of that business income, consisting of income generated from commercial aircraft and component manufacturing, wholesaling, and retailing activities.

The Appellate Body agreed these levels were the proper comparable rates, not because commercial aircraft manufacturing were previously taxed at the general rate, but because those rates still reflected what would be applied to the commercial aircraft manufacturers if the conditions for the lower rate were not met. It could be misleading to compare the rate for commercial aircraft manufacturing to general and exceptional rates, without considering whether the scope of the exceptions undermines the existence of a general rule. That is, if every industry has a special tax rate, then the general rate never is applied, and thus is a meaningless benchmark.

The U.S. argued 60% of manufacturing industries in Washington State were taxed at a special rate, so the general rate was not a good benchmark. The EU retorted the commercial aircraft industry accounted 40% of that 60% figure. Thus, the exceptional rate does not swallow the general rate, nor undermine the general rate as a benchmark: once the commercial aircraft industry is excluded, only 20% of manufacturers get a special rate. The Appellate Body bought the European argument the general rate was an appropriate benchmark.

Having agreed with the choice by the Panel of a benchmark for comparison with the Washington State B&O Tax Rate Reduction, the Appellate Body needed hardly any analysis to uphold the legal conclusion of the Panel. The lower tax rate of 0.2904% applied to the gross income of commercial aircraft and component manufactures under House Bill 2294 entailed the foregoing of government revenue otherwise due within the meaning of Article 1:1(a)(1)(ii) of the *SCM Agreement*.

Conclusion:

The 2012 *Boeing* case is pedagogically instructive in that it gives the proper framework for analyzing whether a measure is a "financial contribution" under Article 1:1(a)(1)(i)-(iii) of the *SCM Agreement*. Though the Appellate Body provided scant analysis of Sub-Paragraph (iii), it exhaustively discussed Sub-Paragraphs (i) and (ii), providing three insights:

(1) To determine whether a measure is a direct transfer of funds, it is first necessary to characterize the measure, and then examine whether that measure falls within the parameters of the relevant Sub-Paragraph.

(2) JVs count among the list of illustrative examples of "direct transfers of funds" under Sub-Paragraph (i). JVs are an addition to the expressly listed examples ("grants," "loans," and "equity infusions"), and an addition to the 2007 *Japan — DRAMS (Korea)* list of debt forgiveness, extension of loan

maturity, and debt-equity swaps. In sum, there is a long and expanding catalogue of what qualifies as a "direct transfer of funds."

(3) The Appellate Body reaffirmed its 2000 and 2002 *Foreign Sales Corporation* precedents, using a normative benchmark to compare a disputed form of government revenue foregone. It made clear the obvious "but for" test is not the only applicable one, *i.e.*, it is not improper to use it when comparing tax rates, as long as others are acknowledged, too. But, a tax system as a whole cannot act as a normative benchmark.

Unfortunately, these insights come only after the time-consuming, frustrating process of reading through a Report of 599 pages and 2,716 footnotes.

- **2013 *Canada Renewable Energy*[56]**

Issue:

An important substantive issue addressed by the Appellate Body was whether the disputed measures were subsidies within the meaning of Article 1 of the *SCM Agreement*. To be deemed a subsidy under Article 1:1 of the *SCM Agreement*, a measure must be found to consist of a "financial contribution" that confers a "benefit" to the recipient. The pertinent provision states:

Article 1: Definition of a Subsidy

1.1 For the purpose of this *Agreement*, a subsidy shall be deemed to exist if:

(a)(1) there is a financial contribution by a government or any public body within the territory of a Member (referred to in this *Agreement* as "government"), *i.e.*, where:

(i) a government practice involves a direct transfer of funds (*e.g.*, grants, loans, and equity infusion), potential direct transfers of funds or liabilities (*e.g.*, loan guarantees);

(ii) government revenue that is otherwise due is foregone or not collected (*e.g.*, fiscal incentives such as tax credits) [footnote omitted];

(iii) a government provides goods or services other than general infrastructure, or purchases goods;

(iv) a government makes payments to a funding mechanism, or entrusts or directs a private body to carry out one or more of the type of functions illustrated in (i) to (iii) above which

---

56. *See* Appellate Body Report, *Canada—Certain Measures Relating to the Renewable Energy Sector*, WT/DS412/AB/R (24 May 2013); and Appellate Body Report, *Canada—Measures Relating to the Feed-In Tariff Program*, WT/DS426/AB/R (24 May 2013) [hereinafter jointly referred to as *Canada Renewable Energy* Appellate Body Report]. The Appellate Body issued, and the DSB adopted, these Reports on the same days. For most purposes, the Appellate Body treated the two disputes as one, and—unless otherwise noted—such is the treatment herein.

The facts of this case are discussed in an earlier Chapter.

> would normally be vested in the government and the practice, in no real sense, differs from practices normally followed by governments;

or

(a) (2) there is any form of income or price support in the sense of Article XVI of GATT 1994;

and

(b) a benefit is thereby conferred.

On appeal, the presence of a financial contribution was not contested.

However, Japan posed a strategic challenge. It maintained the Panel characterization of the disputed measures as "purchases [of] goods" was incorrect. Japan argued the disputed measures should be, either on their own, or jointly with the Panel determination, characterized as "direct transfer[s] of funds," "potential direct transfers of funds," or "income or price support." The Panel found a disputed measure could be considered only one type of financial contribution, but Japan insisted the Sub-Paragraphs of Article 1:1(a)(1) were not mutually exclusive.

The Appellate Body agreed in part with Japan, finding different aspects of the same measures could apply to different types of financial contributions under Article 1:1(a)(1). However, after upholding the Panel decision that the disputed measures consisted of government "purchases [of] goods," the Appellate Body found Japan failed to establish different aspects of the measures that would warrant characterization under other Sub-Paragraphs of Article 1:1(a)(1).

Japanese Losing Arguments and Appellate Body Holdings:

Japan was the only party to appeal the Panel findings regarding Article 1:1(a) of the *SCM Agreement*. In this regard, the Japanese issues with the Panel findings are interesting. Japan did not allege the disputed measures did not satisfy the requirements of Article 1:1(a) of the *Agreement*. Instead, Japan sought only to have the disputed measures characterized as "direct transfer[s] of funds," "potential direct transfers of funds," or "income or price support," rather than "purchases [of] goods" under the *Agreement*. Thus, the Japanese appeal was strategic, as it considered the outcome relevant to subsequent arguments relating to the market benchmark analysis associated with Article 1:1(b) of the *Agreement*. Arguably, it may be inferred from this strategy that *de facto stare decisis* operates in WTO jurisprudence — otherwise, why care about an adverse "precedent"?

Japan challenged the Panel interpretation and application of Article 1:1(a)(1) of the *SCM Agreement*. With regard to the interpretation of the relevant provision, Japan argued the Panel was incorrect when it said a disputed measure could be characterized at law as both a government "purchase [of] goods" and a "direct transfer of funds" under Articles 1:1(a)(1)(i) and (iii), respectively. Japan cited the 2012 *Boeing* case to support the assertion that a measure may be properly characterized in multiple ways under Article 1:1(a)(1) of the *Agreement*. There, the Appellate

Body found that Article 1:1(a)(1) does not preclude that a measure could fall within the scope of multiple Sub-Paragraphs.

Canada responded the Japanese claim lacked merit. According to Canada, it was correct that Article 1:1(a)(1) does not preclude a measure from being covered by more than one Sub-Paragraph, but asserted from a logical perspective the same aspects of the same measures could not be simultaneously characterized as "purchases [of] goods" and "direct transfer[s] of funds." Under similar reasoning to Canada, the Panel considered that finding in favor of Japan would require infringing upon principles of treaty interpretation. Additionally, the Panel noted the lack of the word "or" between the Sub-Paragraphs suggested the Sub-Paragraphs could not be found to apply simultaneously.

With regard to the mutual exclusivity of Sub-Paragraphs (i) and (iii) of Article 1:1(a)(1) of the *SCM Agreement*, the Appellate Body disagreed with the Panel. Instead, it favored Japan's argument that its 2012 findings in *Boeing* supported the potential simultaneous application of multiple Sub-Paragraphs in Article 1:1(a)(1). In its view, the complex and multifaceted nature of some disputed measures may mean that different aspects of the same transaction may fall under different types of financial contributions, within the meaning of Article 1:1(a). The Appellate Body clarified that, unlike the suggestion by the Panel, the fact a transaction may fall under more than one type of financial contribution does not mean that the types of financial contributions found in Article 1:1(a)(1) are the same, or that the distinct legal concepts set out in the provision would become redundant. As a result, the Appellate Body found the Panel findings in this regard to be moot and of no legal effect.

Having interpreted Article 1:1(a)(1) of the *SCM Agreement*, the Appellate Body next applied its interpretation to the facts of this dispute. Japan challenged the Panel finding that the disputed measures constituted government "purchases [of] goods" within the meaning of Article 1:1(a)(1)(iii), requesting instead that the Appellate Body characterize the disputed measures as "direct transfer[s] of funds," "potential direct transfers of funds," or "income or price support."[57] In the alternative, Japan asked the Appellate Body to find the disputed measures to be government "purchases [of] goods," while concurrently classifying the disputed measures as one of its previously asserted financial contributions under Article 1:1(a).[58]

The Panel characterized the disputed measures as "purchases [of] goods" within the meaning of Article 1:1(a)(1)(i) of the *SCM Agreement*, because it fell within its definition of the term, namely that the purchase of goods occurs when a government or public body obtains possession over a good by making a payment of some kind.[59] Japan attacked the Panel finding in three arguments.

---

57. *See Canada Renewable Energy* Appellate Body Report, ¶ 5.122.
58. *Canada Renewable Energy* Appellate Body Report, ¶ 5.122.
59. *Canada Renewable Energy* Appellate Body Report, ¶ 5.123.

First, Japan focused on the unbundled nature of the Government of Ontario's electricity supply system.[60] In its view, the different functions delegated to separate government entities must be considered individually. For example, Japan asserted it was significant that one government entity, the OPA, paid for electricity in Ontario, while another government entity, Hydro One, received and transmitted the electricity delivered by suppliers. Japan maintained that OPA thus served as a financing entity, rather than a purchasing entity, because it never took possession of the electricity.

The Appellate Body disagreed with Japan as to the significance of the unbundling of functions within Ontario's electricity supply system. Instead, it took a broader view, reasoning that the individual functions of the OPA and Hydro One still were within the umbrella of the Government of Ontario and thus, that Government purchased electricity through the disputed measures. The Appellate Body pointed to the Panel finding that the OPA and Hydro One were "public bodies" within the meaning of Article 1:1(a)(1) of the *SCM Agreement*. The Panel even addressed the separate functions of the government entities, when it used the language "combined actions" of the three public bodies and found that the Government of Ontario purchased electricity under Article 1:1(a)(1).[61]

The second argument asserted by Japan also related to the distinct roles of entities operating in Ontario's electricity system. In this regard, Japan contended the goal of the Government of Ontario of achieving a stable supply of electricity and stimulating renewable energy was not addressed through the purchase of electricity, but instead through the allocation of separate roles by government entities and implementation of government programs. The Appellate body again disagreed with Japan.

In this regard, the Appellate Body said the Japanese argument disregarded the nature of the programs the Government of Ontario uses to implement its policies, insomuch as they involve the purchase of electricity by the government. Again, regardless of the delegated roles of separate government entities, the Government of Ontario purchases the electricity through the disputed measures.

The final Japanese argument focused on the characterization of a measure by the respondent government itself. According to Japan, the Panel assumed that because the disputed measures were purchases of electricity under the relevant domestic law (*i.e.*, the *Electricity Act of 1998*), they were also purchases of electricity under WTO law. But, the Appellate Body pointed out the Panel did not consider the characterization under domestic law to be dispositive, instead considering it simply as circumstantial evidence, along with other evidence for its finding.[62] As a result, the Appellate Body sided with the Panel and upheld the finding that the disputed

60. *Canada Renewable Energy* Appellate Body Report, ¶ 5.124.
61. *Canada Renewable Energy* Appellate Body Report, ¶ 5.124.
62. *Canada Renewable Energy* Appellate Body Report, ¶ 5.124.

measures constituted "purchases [of] goods" within the meaning of Article 1:1(a)
(1)(iii) of the *SCM Agreement*.

The Appellate Body then addressed whether Japan sufficiently demonstrated that,
in the alternative, the disputed measures should also be characterized as "direct
transfer[s] of funds" or "potential direct transfers of funds" within the meaning of
Article 1:1(a) of the *SCM Agreement*.[63] Here, Japan argued the disputed measures
were "direct transfer[s] of funds" under Article 1:1(a) because the OPA distributed
the funds to renewable energy electricity generators from amounts collected from
consumers. Additionally, Japan contended that because the renewable electricity
generators were entitled to guaranteed payments during the contract period, the
contracts constituted "potential direct transfers of funds" under Article 1:1(a). The
Appellate Body did not consider these aspects of the disputed measures to be different from those used to support its finding that the disputed measures constituted
the government "purchase [of] goods."[64] Thus, it found Japan failed to establish a
basis for an additional characterization of the disputed measures. Accordingly, the
Appellate Body rejected Japan's appeal.

- **2014 *India Carbon Steel*[65]**

*GOI Iron Ore and Coal Mineral Rights Grants as "Financial Contributions" under
Article 1:1(a)(1):*[66]

India disagreed that two of its support measures constituted illegal subsidies.
First, India claimed its granting of mining rights did not constitute a "provision
of goods" under Article 1:1(a)(1)(iii) of the *SCM Agreement*. Second, India argued
the DOC attributed the distribution of certain loans to the wrong entity, and thus
the Panel erred in finding that India provided a "direct transfers of funds" under
Article 1:1(a)(1)(i).

The GOI supported the Indian steel industry by granting producers mining
rights for iron ore and coal, allegedly at prices below market-determined rates. The
program brings to mind the practices in the 2004 *Softwood Lumber IV* case.[67] There,
the Canadian or provincial governments provided lumber producers not with the
lumber *per se*, but rights to the lumber, known as "stumpage." India asserted to the
Panel, as Canada had in *Softwood Lumber IV*, that a grant of mining rights was not
a provision of goods under Article 1:1(a)(1)(iii) of the *SCM Agreement*. That was
because, in this case, of "intervening acts of non-government entities" (*i.e.*, private
companies that extracted the minerals). India said those intervening acts resulted

---

63. *Canada Renewable Energy* Appellate Body Report, ¶ 5.131.

64. *Canada Renewable Energy* Appellate Body Report, ¶ 5.131.

65. This case is cited, and its facts summarized, earlier in this Chapter.

66. *India Carbon Steel* Appellate Panel Report, ¶¶ 4.3–4.103; *India Carbon Steel* Appellate Body
Report, ¶¶ 128–140; 261–265.

67. *United States—Final Countervailing Duty Determination with Respect to Certain Softwood
Lumber from Canada*, WT/DS257/AB/R (adopted 17 February 2004).

in a connection that was too remote to meet the "reasonably proximate relationship" standard the Appellate Body set in *Softwood Lumber IV.*

Beyond the intervention from non-governmental entities (*e.g.*, private extraction companies), there was another reason the granting of mining rights for iron ore and coal could not be considered the "provision of goods." It was too uncertain. That is, there is uncertainty attached to mining activities: who knows what, if anything, a mine might yield, and at what price? So, again citing *Softwood Lumber IV* as support, India claimed the link between the granting of mining rights and actual amount of iron ore or coal extracted was too remote to meet the standard of a "reasonably proximate relationship."[68]

India lost this argument. Both the Panel and Appellate Body rejected India's application of *Softwood Lumber IV.* According to the Panel, if such a standard was adopted, then it would lead to too much inconsistency in results, based on the complexity of the processes required to extract the relevant good. To be sure, the Panel followed *Softwood Lumber IV,* noting: "a government may provide goods constituting a final contribution 'by making them available through the grant of extraction rights.'" The Panel concluded that "given the GOI's direct control over the availability of the relevant minerals, the GOI's grant of rights to mine them essentially made those minerals available to, and placed them at the disposal of, the beneficiaries of those rights" making them "reasonably proximate" to the use and enjoyment of the minerals such as to be provision of a good under Article 1:1(a)(1)(iii) of the *SCM Agreement.*

In addition, India contended this Article does not apply to grants that required the beneficiaries, such as the steel producers, to engage in significant intervening acts. This, said India, distinguished the facts from *Softwood Lumber IV,* because stumpage rights were not severable from standing timber. The U.S., of course, disagreed, urging that it made no difference whether (1) ore was mined directly by GOI or (2) mining rights to ore were sold by GOR to another entity that may extract the minerals: "[w]hen a government gives a company the right to take a government-owned good, such as iron ore and coal from government lands, the government is 'providing' the goods within the meaning of Article 1.1(a)(1)(iii) of the *SCM Agreement.*" The Panel agreed with the U.S.

So, too, did the Appellate Body. On appeal, India maintained its arguments and interpretation of *Softwood Lumber IV.* In effect, India's argument was based on a distinction between efforts necessary to harvest timber and mine minerals. In its view, the series of significant actions performed by the beneficiary of the mineral rights, at its own risk and cost, sever the relationship between granting of rights and the actual provision of the mineral (*e.g.*, iron ore and coal). Therefore, as the argument goes, a provision of goods cannot be found to exist under Article 1:1(a)(1)(iii) of the *SCM Agreement.*

---

68. *India Carbon Steel* Panel Report, ¶ 4.61.

Not true, said the Appellate Body. To be sure, it questioned certain aspects of the Panel's reasoning. Nevertheless, it held that the fact the Indian enterprises paid royalties tied to the amount of minerals extracted substantiated the Panel's conclusion that there was "a reasonably proximate relationship between the GOI's grant of mining rights and the final goods consisting of extracted iron ore and steel." Furthermore:

> rights over extracted iron ore and coal follow as a natural and inevitable consequence of the steel companies' exercise of their mining rights, which suggests that making available iron ore and coal is the *raison d'être* of the mining rights. This, in our view, supports the Panel's conclusion that the government's grant of mining rights is reasonably proximate to the use or enjoyment of the minerals by the beneficiaries of those rights.

SDF Loans as "Financial Contributions" under Article 1:1(a)(1):[69]

India also appealed the Panel's conclusion that the DOC's determination that SDF provided direct transfers of funds was not inconsistent with Article 1:1(a)(1)(i) of the *SCM Agreement*. India argued the SDF loans were not provided to borrowers by the SDF Management Committee, which DOC found to be a public body, but by the Joint Planning Committee (JPC), which DOC agreed was not a public body. That is, India claimed that the loans attributed to the SDF Management Committee were, in fact, disbursed by the JPC, which was not a "public body." Hence, the loans could not properly be considered as "direct transfers of funds" under Article 1:1(a)(1)(i).

The Panel observed the Management Committee "handles all decisions regarding the issuance, terms, and waivers of SDF loans, that it considers and grants the ultimate approval on loan proposals put forth by the JPC, and that the JPC handles the day-to-day affairs of the SDF, such as overseeing and administering the SDF loans." The Panel also noted India admitted the Managing Committee was the decision-maker with regard to issuance, terms and waivers of the SDF loans. So, despite the role of the JPC, the Panel considered it was reasonable for the DOC to determine that the SDF Management Committee was directly involved in issuance of loans, and made decisions as to whether the loans would be issued and on what terms. For its part, the Appellate Body observed that the: "Panel reasoned that, even though the SDF Managing Committee may not have taken title over the funds . . . the SDF Managing Committee was instrumental due to its role as decision-maker regarding the issuance, terms, and waivers of SDF loans." The Panel further concluded the Management Committee had "made available" the funds once the loan authorizations were provided. Not surprisingly, then, at the Panel state, India lost the argument about SDF lending.

---

69. *India Carbon Steel* Appellate Panel Report, ¶¶ 4.3–4.103; *India Carbon Steel* Appellate Body Report, ¶¶ 128–140; 261–265.

India lost at the Appellate Body stage, too. On appeal, India argued a direct transfer means there must be an immediate link without involving any intermediary or intervening agency. India focused on the term "direct" in Article 1:1(a)(1)(i) of the *SCM Agreement*, stating that if the Appellate Body were to allow transfers of funds made by an intermediary or intervening agency to constitute a "direct transfer of funds" under Article 1:1(a)(1), then it would render the provision inutile. The argument was weak, as it was conceptually premised on an extreme meaning of "direct." India added that because the JPC formally administered the funds, it was the JPC, not the SDF Management Committee, which transferred the funds. Under such circumstances the SDF funds should not be considered government funds.

In rebuttal, the U.S. contended that the Panel, "by looking to the design, operation, and effects of the SDF loan program" correctly interpreted Article 1:1(a)(1)(i). The Panel was right to emphasize that (1) SDF levies were collected by the JPC, and once collected, remitted to the SDF, and (2) funds held by the SDF were disposed of in according with instructions of the SDF Managing Committee. The JPC itself did not resemble a private body, because it operated under the supervision of the Management Committee, and had no authority to issue loans.

For the Appellate Body, it was significant that under Article 1:1(a)(1)(i) there must be a government practice involving a direct transfer of funds, including not only money, but also financial resources. The term "direct transfer" connotes "something occurring immediately, without intermediaries or interference." But, the provision does not indicate under what circumstances the transfer may be considered to be direct. Significantly:

> The use of the word "involves" [in Article 1:1(a)(1)(i)] thus suggests that the government practice need not consist, or be comprised, solely of the transfer of funds, but may be a broader set of conduct in which such a transfer is implicated or included. The term also appears to introduce an element suggesting a lack of immediacy to the extent that it does not prescribe that a government must necessarily make the direct transfer of funds, but only that there be a "government practice" that "involves" the direct transfer of funds.

Noting the tension between elements of Article 1:1(a)(1)(i) that "alternatively appear to narrow and broaden the scope of coverage," the Appellate Body reasoned this Article:

> does not rigidly prescribe the scope of its coverage. Rather, the provision reflects a balance of different considerations to be taken into account when assessing whether a particular transfer of funds constitutes a financial contribution.

That is, when interpreting Article 1:1(a)(1)(i) of the *SCM Agreement*, the Appellate Body recognized the "direct transfer" language cited by India, but focused on language in the provision that a "financial contribution" exists where a "government practice involves" the "direct transfer of funds." In the Appellate Body view, the words "practice" and "involve" negate the immediacy associated to the term "direct transfer" when considering by itself.

Stated differently, on the one hand, the term "direct" suggests a certain immediacy in the conveyance of funds and a close nexus for the actions relating to the transfer of the funds. On the other hand, the requirement that "a government practice involves" suggests a "more attenuated role for a government public body . . . than what would otherwise have been understood through an examine of the phrase 'direct transfer of funds.'" The Appellate Body decided India over-relied on the word "direct." Once the Appellate Body attributed a broader interpretation to Article 1:1(a)(1)(i) than India preferred, the legal conclusion was inevitable. The Appellate Body upheld the Panel finding, rejected India's contention that the DOC determination that the SDF Managing Committee provided "direct transfers of funds" was inconsistent with Article 1:1(a)(1)(i).

The Appellate Body also confirmed that circumstances under Article 1:1(a)(1)(iv) may exist where an intermediary is "entrusted" or "directed" by a government. In other situations, there may be insufficient entrustment or direction for Article1.1(a)(1)(iv), but there still may be a "financial contribution" under Article 1.1(a)(1)(i). In brief, it is important to assess the role and involvement of any intermediaries to determine which of these two provisions is applicable.

Here, in considering whether SDF loans were a direct transfer of funds under Article 1:1(a)(1)(i), the Appellate Body noted that DOC found the SDF Managing Committee was a public body, but made no similar finding with regard to the JPC. The Panel had determined the Management Committee was directly involved in providing the SDF loans. Given that fact, the Appellate Body said the relationship between SDF and the loan beneficiaries was not "undermined by the nature of the involvement of the JPC." The Appellate Body concluded that "even if the issuance of SDF loans forms only part of an overall SDF loan scheme funded by the eventual loan recipients, it was nevertheless proper for the Panel to focus on the role of the SDF Managing Committee vis-à-vis the JPC in assessing whether it constituted a government practice that involves a direct transfer of funds." The Appellate Body, like the Panel, also rejected India's contention that under this Article the government body (the SDF Management Committee) must have title to the funds. Thus, the Panel had a "credible basis" to conclude the role of the Management Committee supported a finding that its actions involved a direct transfer of funds under Article 1:1(a)(1)(i).

Chapter 13

Definition of "Subsidy," Second Element: "Benefit" Conferred[1]

I. Four Examples

Unfortunately, neither the *SCM Agreement* nor American CVD law defines expressly the concept of "benefit." Individual WTO Members have some discretion in tailoring their law on when a "benefit" results from a financial contribution. However, Article 14 of the *SCM Agreement* provides some useful guidance. It has four examples of when a benefit is conferred:

(1) *Equity Capital Infusions*

Article 14(a) indicates a "benefit" is conferred where a government provides equity or capital to a recipient that is "inconsistent with the usual investment practice . . . of private investors." The degree of inconsistency is a measure of the value of the benefit.

(2) *Loans*

Article 14(b) states a "benefit" is conferred when a government provides a loan on more favorable terms than the recipient-borrower could obtain for a comparable loan from a commercial bank. In particular, there is a "benefit" if there is a difference between the amount a borrower (1) pays on the loan from the government, and (2) would pay on a comparable loan from a commercial bank. The value of the benefit conferred equals the difference between these two amounts.

(3) *Loan Guarantees*

Article 14(c) explains a "benefit" is conferred on the recipient-borrower if a government provides a loan guarantee that allows the borrower to obtain more favorable terms on a loan from a commercial bank that is guaranteed by the government than the borrower would obtain on a comparable loan from the commercial bank without the government guarantee. That is, a benefit exists if there is a difference between the amount (*i.e.*, surely the

---

1. Documents References:
   (1) *Havana (ITO) Charter*, Articles 25–28, 34
   (2) *GATT* Articles VI, XVI
   (3) WTO *SCM Agreement*

total amount, including principal, interest, and fees) the borrower receiving the guarantee (1) pays on the guaranteed loan, and (2) would pay on a comparable loan from a commercial bank absent the guarantee. The benefit conferred equals the difference between these two amounts.

(4) *Provision of Goods or Services*

Article 14(d) explains a "benefit" is conferred if a government provides goods and services to a recipient for less than adequate remuneration, or purchases goods and services from the recipient for more than adequate remuneration. In other words, if a government provides goods or services at a below-market price, a "benefit" is conferred. The value of the "benefit" equals the difference between (1) the price the government charges for the goods or services and (2) the market price for those same goods or services. Similarly, if a government buys goods or services supplied by a company at an inflated price, then the measurement of the "benefit" is the difference between what the government pays and the prevailing market price for those goods or services.

American CVD law tracks these same four examples.[2] In studying the examples, consider the advantages and disadvantages of the methodology or methodologies an administering authority uses, or should use, to measure the amount of benefit conferred. Is the private sector the best benchmark in all instances?

This list does not state it is non-exclusive, but that is a reasonable reading of Article 14. Moreover, the relevant *Statement of Administrative Action* refers to the Article 14 list as a set of "guidelines," and the American CVD statute uses the word "including" before presenting the list. Hence, there may well be other financial contributions that confer a "benefit" that do not fit neatly within these examples.

II. Case Law on Second Element: 1999 *Canada Aircraft*, 2007 *Japan DRAMs*, 2011 *Airbus*, and 2012 *Boeing*

The WTO Appellate Body has elaborated on the meaning of "benefit." It has applied the *SCM Agreement* Article 1:1 definition and Article 14 guidance to a diverse array of fact patterns in a several high profile cases.

• **1999 *Canada Aircraft*[3]**

The 1999 *Canada Aircraft* dispute gave the Appellate Body its first opportunity to develop a means to analyze whether a benefit is conferred under Article 1:1(b) of the *SCM Agreement*. Indeed, along with the 1999 *Brazil Aircraft* dispute, it was the first case dealing with the *Agreement* to reach the Appellate Body, and the DSB adopted

---

2. *See* 19 U.S.C. § 1677(5).

3. *See* Appellate Body Report, *Canada — Measures Affecting the Export of Civilian Aircraft*, WT/DS70/AB/R (adopted 2 August 1999). [Hereinafter, *Canada Aircraft* Appellate Body Report.]

both Reports on the same day (2 August 1999). So, the Appellate Body holding in *Canada Aircraft* on benefit analysis is cited regularly as a seminal precedent.

Facts and Issues:

Brazil made claimed numerous Canadian entities and organizations subsidized the Canadian regional aircraft industry, particularly Bombardier. Brazil alleged the subsidies were Red Light, inconsistent with Articles 3:1(a) and 3:2 of the *SCM Agreement*, in that they were contingent (in law or in fact) on export performance. Specifically, Brazil challenged the following Canadian measures:

(1) Financing and loan guarantees provided by the Export Development Corporation (EDC), including equity infusions into corporations established to facilitate the export of civil aircraft.

(2) Debt financing from the Canada Account to the civil aircraft industry.

(3) Funds from Technology Partnerships Canada (TPC) (and predecessor programs) to the civil aircraft industry.

(4) Sale by the Ontario Aerospace Corporation, an agency or instrumentality of the Government of the Province of Ontario, of a 49% interest in a civil aircraft manufacturer (de Havilland Holdings Inc.) to another civil aircraft manufacturer (Bombardier) on other than commercial terms.

(5) Benefits provided under the Canada-Québec Subsidiary Agreement on Industrial Development.

(6) Benefits provided by the Government of Québec under the *Société de Développement Industriel du Québec.*

As to measures (2) and (3), the Panel agreed with Brazilian complaint, but rejected the challenge to the other measures. That is, the Panel found:

> that Canada Account debt financing since 1 January 1995 for the export of Canadian regional aircraft [and Technology Partnerships Canada] assistance to the Canadian regional aircraft industry constitute[d] prohibited export subsidies inconsistent with [the *SCM Agreement*].[4]

On appeal, Canada argued the Panel erred in its interpretation of Article 1:1(b) of the *SCM Agreement*. The question for the Appellate Body was whether the Panel properly relied on Article 14 of the *Agreement* and ordinary meanings of the terms "benefit" and "conferred" in its interpretation of Article 1:1(b) of the *Agreement*.

Losing Argument:

Canada said the Panel should not have focused on the commercial benchmarks in Article 14 of the *SCM Agreement* "to the exclusion of cost to government." Rather, the Panel should have paid attention to Annex IV of the *Agreement*, which is entitled "Calculation of the Total *Ad Valorem* Subsidization (Paragraph 1(A) of Article 6))."

---

4. *See Canada Aircraft* Appellate Body Report, ¶ 2.

Canada thought Annex IV supports the assertion that "cost to the government" matters in a benefit analysis.

Holding:

The Appellate Body rejected the Canadian position after ascertaining the ordinary meanings of the words "benefit" and "confer," and after studying the relationship between Articles 1 and 14 of the *SCM Agreement*. First, it said the Panel correctly interpreted the word "benefit," as used in Article 1:1(b) of the *SCM Agreement*. That word encompasses some form of an advantage, so the focus of the inquiry should be on the recipient, rather than on any cost to government. Additionally, the marketplace provides an adequate comparison as to whether the recipient was "better off."

Rationale:

In accordance with Article 31 of the 1969 *Vienna Convention on the Law of Treaties*, the Appellate Body started with the ordinary meaning of "benefit" and "confer." Citing the *OED*, it defined "benefit" as an "advantage," "good," "gift," "profit," or, more generally, "a favorable or helpful factor or circumstance." And, "confer" means (*inter alia*) to "give," "grant," or "bestow."

The Appellate Body inferred from these definitions, taken together, that the focus of an Article 1:1(b) inquiry should be on the recipient, not the granting authority. After all, a "benefit" is not a disembodied spirit. It must be connected to a recipient. Moreover, coupled with the word "thereby," the inquiry naturally asks: "what was conferred on the recipient?"[5] Thus, the Canadian assertion that "cost to government" found in Annex IV of the *SCM Agreement* was one way to discern whether a "benefit" exists was at odds with the ordinary meaning under Article 1:1(b).

The Appellate Body next used Article 14 of the *SCM Agreement* to strengthen its position that benefit to the recipient is what matters in this discernment. Article 14 is entitled "Calculation of the Amount of a Subsidy in Terms of the Benefit to the Recipient," and sets four rules for applying CVDs under Articles 10–23. Still, because the *chapeau* of Article 14 expressly refers to "paragraph 1 of Article 1," it is eminently fair to use Article 14 to define "benefit" in Article 1. The clear result is that "benefit" is defined in terms of a gain to a recipient, not via cost to government. In contrast, Annex IV of the *Agreement* references only the serious prejudice provisions in Article 6.

The Appellate Body summarized its sensible interpretation as follows:

> The focus of the first element is on the action of the government in making the "financial contribution." That being so, it seems to us logical that the second element in Article 1:1 is concerned with the "benefit . . . conferred" on the *recipient* by that governmental action. Thus, subparagraphs (a) and

---

5. *See Canada Aircraft* Appellate Body Report, ¶ 154.

(b) of Article 1:1 define a "subsidy" by reference, first, to the action of the granting authority and, second, to what was conferred on the recipient.[6]

Next, the Appellate Body discussed the need for some sort of a comparison, as implied by Article 1:1(b).

The Appellate Body explained "there can be no 'benefit' to the recipient unless the 'financial contribution' makes the recipient 'better off' than it would otherwise have been, absent that contribution."[7] To analyze whether a recipient is "better off," a Panel should look to a pertinent market benchmark. That is, it should compare whether a financial contribution conferred on a recipient is received on terms more favorable than those available to the recipient in the commercial marketplace.

Conclusion:

First, the 1999 *Canada Aircraft* stands for the proposition that the focus of any benefit inquiry under Article 1:1(b) of the *SCM Agreement* should be on the recipient of a financial contribution, not on the cost to the government providing that contribution. Note the contrast with Article 1:1(a): there, the focus is on the provider, namely, whether a governmental authority provides the contribution. Second, *Canada Aircraft* makes clear Article 14, but not Annex IV, of the *Agreement* is useful in interpreting Article 1:1(b). Third, the Appellate Body Report counsels that the marketplace should be used to gauge whether a "benefit" truly makes a recipient better off.

- **2007 *Japan DRAMS*[8]**

The 2007 *Japan DRAMS* dispute was the second opportunity for the Appellate Body to address whether a benefit is conferred.[9]

Facts and Issues:

Briefly, Japan investigated DRAMS manufactured in and imported from Korea, and imposed on them a CVD order. The subsidies occurred through financial transactions entered into by Hynix Semiconductor, Inc. The Japanese Investigative Authority concluded the Korean government entrusted or directed four of the private creditors of Hynix to participate in debt-restructuring programs. Those restructurings occurred in October 2001 and December 2002.

Pertinent to the case was the so-called "Deutsche Bank Report." This Report was a restructuring plan prepared by its namesake and made available to four creditors of Hynix at the time they undertook the December 2002 restructuring.[10] The JIA questioned the credibility of the Report, because of a press release suggesting the

---

6. *See Canada Aircraft* Appellate Body Report, ¶ 156 (emphasis original).

7. *See Canada—Aircraft* Appellate Body Report, ¶ 157.

8. *See* Appellate Body Report, *Japan—Countervailing Duties on Dynamic Random Access Memories (DRAMS) from Korea*, WT/DS336/AB/R (adopted 28 November 2007). [Hereinafter, *Japan DRAMs.*] The case also is known as *Japan DRAMS (Korea)*.

9. The facts of this dispute are briefly discussed in a footnote earlier in a separate Chapter.

10. *See Japan DRAMS* Appellate Body Report, ¶ 125.

Korean government intervened and influenced its substantive findings. The Panel disagreed, saying there was insufficient evidence to undermine the integrity of the Report, and finding the creditors acted in a commercially reasonable manner.

On appeal, the first of two relevant issues was whether the Panel properly found the JIA determination of "benefit" for the December 2002 Restructuring was inconsistent with Articles 1:1(b) and 14 of the *SCM Agreement*. The second issue concerned the October 2001 restructuring. Korea took issue with the Panel analysis of a benefit. In its view, whether a measure is conferred on terms more favorable than the market requires recourse to a market comparison as per the 1999 *Canada Aircraft* precedent. But, the Panel used a commercial reasonableness test to determine whether the terms of the October 2001 restructuring were more favorable than what was available on the market.

Holding:

The Appellate Body upheld both relevant Panel determinations, thus handing Korea a victory on the first issue, and Japan a win on the second issue. First, as to the December 2002 restructuring, the Appellate Body upheld the Panel rejection of the JIA findings. In its view, the Deutsche Bank Report supported the conclusion that the four creditors of Hynix acted with commercial reasonableness. So, no benefit was conferred upon Hynix under Article 1:1(b) of the *SCM Agreement*. Second, the Appellate Body upheld the Panel finding that the October 2001 Restructuring was not based on commercial reasonableness. As a result, the October 2001 Restructuring did confer a benefit upon Hynix within the meaning of Article 1:1(b).

Rationale:

Defending its imposition of CVDs on Korean computer chips on appeal, Japan first attacked the acceptance by the Panel of the Deutsche Bank Report. Japan questioned the independence of the Report, and said the Panel failed to consider the totality of press stories relating to the Report. At least one news account suggested the Korean government intervened with the Report, and, therefore, decisions made by the four creditors of Hynix to enter into the December 2002 restructuring could not have been based on reasonable commercial considerations. In other words, the Japanese logic was this: Suppose decisions by government, or government-directed or -entrusted, creditors of a debtor are not commercially reasonable. From their commercially unreasonable behavior, it can be inferred the creditors conveyed a benefit to the debtor that the debtor would not have obtained on the market. The debtor, then, is the recipient of a benefit.

The Panel saw that rejection by the JIA of the Report was a key factor in the JIA conclusion that the participation of the four Hynix creditors in the December 2002 Restructuring was not commercially reasonable. But, the Panel said this rejection was unjustified, and the Appellate Body agreed. The Appellate Body found the Panel rightly considered the totality of the press reports, but simply did not feel a suggestion in one out of the nine of them about Korean government intervention was sufficient to discredit the Deutsche Bank Report. In brief, the Deutsche Bank Report supported a finding that the four creditors acted on a commercial basis.

Thus, with regard to the December 2002 restructuring, the JIA determinations about alleged Korean subsidies were inconsistent with Article 1:1(b) and Article 14 of the *SCM Agreement*. Note, however, the Appellate Body never expressly rejected the aforementioned logic put forth by Japan. Indeed, both the Panel and Appellate Body accepted this logic: commercially unreasonable behavior gives rise to an inference that a benefit is conferred. The Panel simply reversed the conclusions of the JIA based on the facts of the case, and the Appellate Body agreed.

As to the October 2012 restructuring, the Appellate Body observed that as a general matter, the Panel mirrored the Appellate Body statements in *Canada Aircraft*: a "benefit" within the meaning of Article 1:1(b) exists when a financial contribution is made available on terms more favorable than the recipient could have obtained on the market. However, the Panel added to the comparison test suggested in *Canada Aircraft*.

In the earlier case, the Appellate Body said a Panel should examine the existence of a benefit by gathering available evidence of the terms that would have been offered in the market, and comparing those terms to the financial contribution at issue. The Panel in *Japan DRAMS* acknowledged this comparative approach, but said in some circumstances the evidence might not allow for such a comparison. But, what if there is no obvious market benchmark? Then, a Panel might need to decide whether a financial contribution provides a benefit by considering in a unilateral sense whether that contribution was commercially reasonable. Evidence of non-commercial considerations indicates terms more favorable than those that would have been available from a market, had such a market existed.

Here, the Panel upheld the JIA finding that the October 2001 restructuring was not commercially reasonable, thus the restructuring conferred a benefit on Hynix. That was because (in part) the creditors of Hynix failed to analyze properly the terms of the restructuring, and because two relevant financial reports were not made available to the creditors.[11] The Appellate Body saw no error in the Panel reasoning.

Conclusion:

This *Japan DRAMS* case is useful because of acceptance by the Appellate Body of a second way in which to determine whether a benefit is conferred under Article 1:1(b) of the *SCM Agreement*. With the Report, there are two methods in which to test whether a disputed measure is conferred on terms more favorable than are available on the market, and thus whether a recipient is better off: the Market Benchmark, or Comparison Test, and the Commercial Reasonable Test.

---

11. *See Japan DRAMS* Appellate Body Report, ¶ 224.

First, as per *Canada Aircraft*, a comparison can be made between (1) the terms offered by the financial contribution at issue, and (2) marketplace terms. This method presumes an appropriate market benchmark exists.

Second, a Panel can look at the commercial reasonableness of the measure at issue, and draw an inference as to whether a benefit is conferred. This method is useful when no market metric is available, and hence is a unilateral, not comparative, approach. If a measure is not commercially reasonable, then it must be conferring a benefit upon the recipient, because rational economic actors in a normally-functioning capitalist market would behave in a commercially reasonable manner. Or, so the logic goes.

- **2011 *Airbus*[12]**

The 2011 *Airbus* dispute was the "punch" to the EU "counter-punch" in the 2012 *Boeing* case. The Appellate Body Report here again provides numerous exhaustive discussions of various WTO provisions. As to Article 1:1(b), the Report adds to the analysis of a benefit generally, and addresses an interesting European argument regarding diminished or removed benefits.

When the EU is the respondent in a WTO action, it almost always is true the facts are monstrously complex. Like the 1997 *Bananas* case, the 2011 *Airbus* case is a quintessential example of the byzantine schemes designed in the EU that violate one or more multilateral trade rules. In the *Airbus* case, at issue were a number of transactions involving Airbus companies, railed against by Boeing, but which the EU alleged had the effect of extinguishing and extracting all or part of the subsidies ostensibly provided to these companies by certain EU countries. Additionally, akin to the issue of pre-privatization subsidies, the EU said circumstances surrounding the corporate restructuring and legal reorganization of Airbus companies from a consortium to a single corporate entity required a showing by the U.S. the subsidies continued through the reorganization.

Despite the complexity of the 2011 *Airbus* case, query whether the length of the Panel and Appellate Body Reports is justified. In the *Airbus* case, WTO adjudicators broke their own ignominious record for issuing the longest reports. The *Airbus* Panel report numbers 1,049 pages, and 6,083 footnotes. The Appellate Body cut the fat down to 613 pages and 3,068 footnotes. (Mind you, these figures are with Business Confidential Information deleted from both Reports, and exclude their Annexes.) The previous Panel Report record seems to have been set in the 2006 *Genetically Modified Organisms* case, while the previous Appellate Body Report record appears to have been in the 2005 *Cotton* case. More was coming: the Panel Report in the 2012 *Boeing* case was a hefty 783 pages (again, without BCI and Annexes). The Appellate Body followed up with a ridiculously long report of 576 pages and 2,716 footnotes.

---

12. *See* Appellate Body Report, *European Communities—Measures Affecting Trade in Large Civil Aircraft*, WT/DS316/AB/R (adopted 18 May 2011). [Hereinafter, *Airbus* Appellate Body Report.]

Airbus History:[13]

Airbus Industrie did not exist until 1970. In that year, it was formed as a consortium of aerospace companies from France, Germany, Spain, and the U.K., and operated as such until 2001. The consortium companies as of the 1970 founding included:

(1) From France, *Aérospatiale Société Nationale Industrielle (Aérospatiale)*

(2) From Germany, *Deutsche Airbus GmbH (Deutsche Airbus)*

(3) From Spain, *Construcciones Aeronáuticas SA (CASA)*

In 1979, from Britain, Britain, the British Aerospace Corporation joined the consortium. Many corporate restructurings occurred between 1979 and 2000 affecting *Aérospatiale, Deutsche Airbus*, and British Aerospace. Nonetheless, the shareholdings (discussed below) in the consortium remained the same.

The consortium companies sometimes were referred to as "partners" in the consortium, and the terms *"Airbus Industrie"* and "Airbus consortium" are interchangeable. The consortium operated in a partnership arrangement through a French entity called *Airbus GIE*.[14] So, the terms *"Airbus Industrie"* and "Airbus consortium" refer collectively to the partners in Airbus, and the Airbus GIE entity. As Table 13-1 summarizes, each partner in the Airbus consortium held the following interests in the over-arching partnership, Airbus GIE.

Table 13-1. Shares in Airbus (1979–2000)

Country	Airbus Partner in the Consortium	Percentage of Shares of Airbus GIE Held by the Company
France	*Aérospatiale*	37.9 %
Germany	*Deutsche Airbus*	37.9 %
Spain	*CASA*	4.2 %
U.K.	British Aerospace	20 %

Note Airbus GIE was not itself engaged in production activities. Rather, each Airbus partner produced specific parts of various models of Airbus LCA. Airbus GIE coordinated those manufacturing activities, allocated sales revenues and profits to the partners, and took responsibility for marketing, sales contracts, aircraft delivery, and customer service.

In 2000, the Airbus partners from France, Germany, and Spain merged their activities in the aeronautics, defense, and space activities. The governments took all of their shares in their respective companies (*Aérospatiale, Deutsche Airbus*, and

---

13. *See Airbus* Appellate Body Report, ¶¶ 573–582.

14. "GIE" is the French acronym for *"Groupement d'Intérêt Économique." See Airbus* Appellate Body Report, fn. 1376 at ¶ 577.

CASA), and created under Dutch law a public limited liability company called the "European Aeronautic Defense and Space Company NV," typically referred to as "EADS." The percentage shareholding stake each government received in EADS was in proportion to the relative values of the shares of their respective companies that they put into EADS. British Aerospace continued to hold a 20% interest in Airbus GIE.

In 2001, EADS and British Aerospace put all of their assets and operations related to Airbus, and their shares in Airbus GIE, into a new holding company, Airbus SAS.[15] This new company was organized under French law, and the Airbus assets and operations, and shares in Airbus GIE, were under the common control of Airbus SAS. Thus, for example, the assets related to LCA located in France, Germany, Spain, and the U.K. were transferred to Airbus SAS, specifically, to subsidiaries of Airbus SAS located in those respective countries. The LCA assets of *Aérospatiale* shifted to Airbus France SAS. The LCA assets of *Deutsche Airbus* moved to Airbus Deutschland GmbH. The LCA assets of *CASA* were transferred to *Airbus España*. British Aerospace transferred its LCA-related assets to Airbus SAS, in exchange for a 20% stake in Airbus SAS. Then, Airbus SAS transferred those assets to Airbus U.K.

With these transactions completed, EADS held an 80% stake in Airbus SAS, and thus wielded effective control over Airbus operations. British Aerospace held a 20% stake, with specific minority rights. The last major corporate transaction occurred in 2006, when EADS bought this 20% stake from British Aerospace, making Airbus SAS a wholly owned subsidiary of EADS thereafter.

Synopsis of Key Facts:

The U.S. took aim at over 300 separate instances of alleged subsidies to Airbus SAS (Airbus) across roughly 40 years. These subsidies (as discussed below) were granted by the EU, or in some instances, by governments of 4 EU countries, France, Germany, Spain, and the U.K.

By way of brief summary, the Appellate Body (as well as the Panel) held that the government backers of Airbus, namely, France, Germany, Spain, and the U.K. gave illegal Yellow Light subsidies to Airbus via Launch Aid loans and via certain kinds of infrastructure support. Airbus benefited from the Launch Aid loans, because the interest rate the EU government charged on them was more favorable than the rates private lenders would have charged Airbus. Airbus benefited from the infrastructure, because it otherwise would not have been developed by the private sector, or would have been at a relatively more significant cost to Airbus. The illegal subsidies helped every type of civil aircraft in the Airbus fleet. These Yellow Light subsidies caused serious prejudice to the U.S., in particular, to Boeing, the archrival

---

15. "SAS" is the French acronym for *Société par Actions Simplifiée*. *See Airbus* Appellate Body Report, ¶ 582.

of Airbus. The serious prejudice took the form of displacement of exports, and lost sales, of Boeing aircraft in the EU, and in third countries, particularly Australia, China, and Korea.

Summarized with a bit more particularity, in respect of the vast array of disputed subsidies, the Appellate Body held that under Articles 5(c) and 6 of the *SCM Agreement*, certain support falling in one of five broad categories of subsidy measures were actionable, because they were specific to Airbus, conferred a benefit to Airbus, and caused serious prejudice to the U.S. There were five broad categories of illegal actionable (Yellow Light) or prohibited (Red Light) subsidies. Within each category, there were many measures.

The five categories, and the measures in them the Panel and Appellate Body agreed were legally problematic, are as follows:

(1) Launch Aid Measures (Member State Financing)[16]

Launch Aid (also called Member State Financing) is funding for the design and development of specific models of Airbus aircraft. France, Germany, Spain, and the U.K. gave these subsidies to Airbus for the development of the entire fleet of Large Civil Aircraft made by Airbus. That fleet consists of six LCA models: A300; A310; A320; A330/A340 (including the variants of the A330/A340, namely, A330-200 and A340-500/600); A350; and A380. The A380 is the massive aircraft equivalent to roughly two Boeing 747 jumbo jets, and is capable of carrying roughly 600 passengers.

The U.S. argued all forms of Launch Aid provided to Airbus qualified as a "subsidy" under the definition of that term in the *SCM Agreement*, namely, each form was a "financial contribution" under Article 1:1(a)(1)(i), which conferred a "benefit" on Airbus under Article 1:1(b). Moreover, said the U.S., all Launch Aid was "specific" to Airbus under Article 2.

What were the forms of Launch Aid at issue? The answer is there were many forms. Launch Aid took the form of actual and potential direct transfers of funds, under Article 1:1(a)(1)(i). That is, Launch Aid amounted to Airbus on preferential terms. It also took the form of the assumption or forgiveness of some of the debt incurred by Airbus in connection with launch aid and LCA development and production financing.

Put succinctly, the U.S. said the common features of all Launch Aid were these: unsecured loans to Airbus to develop new aircraft models, at below market interest rates, and on repayment terms that were back-loaded and success-dependent (*i.e.*, dependent on the success of Airbus aircraft sales). Over time, the proportion of development costs funded by such loans declined, from nearly 100% for the early

---

16. *See Airbus* Appellate Body Report, ¶¶ 583–610.

models (A300 and A310), to between 64% and 85% for the A300/A310, to 33% (for the A33-200, A340-500/600, and A380).

With respect to the interest rate, the percentage varied depending on the contractual arrangement (discussed below) for Launch Aid to one model of Airbus aircraft versus another. For some models, Launch Aid was provided free of any interest. For other models, the rate varied, and different formulas were used to calculate the interest depending on the model.

Regarding disbursement, in some instances—again, depending on the contractual arrangement (discussed below)—Airbus received Launch Aid before incurring actual development costs based on projected expenditure by Airbus. In other instances, Airbus received Launch Aid after incurring costs. That is, Aid funds could be provided in 1 of 2 ways: up front, before any actual development costs were incurred, based on projected expenditure; or disbursement up to agreed amounts after actual costs were incurred.

As for repayment, in most cases Airbus was contractually obligated to reimburse all Launch Aid funds, plus interest, exclusively from revenues generated by sales and deliveries of the particular Airbus aircraft model for which it received financing. Airbus was obliged to repay all funding, with interest at a contractually agreed rate, exclusively from revenues it earned by delivering a model of LCA that received financing.

Consequently, the Panel described Launch Aid as "unsecured," as there was no guarantee Airbus could repay the Aid in full if it did not make the number of LCA sales and deliveries needed to generate the requisite funds. Moreover, the Panel observed the scheduled repayments were not collateralized by any lien on Airbus assets, nor guaranteed by a third party. And, all funding was non-recourse, so the lending governments could not make claims on Airbus if Airbus failed to repay its obligations.

The payments tended to take the form of a per-aircraft levy, and followed a pre-established repayment schedule, with the first payment coinciding with delivery of the first aircraft or after delivery of a specified number of deliveries. Once Airbus started repaying the Launch Aid, the amounts graduated on an ascending scale, *i.e.*, repayments on the first aircraft deliveries were lower than repayments on later deliveries. (The exact degree of graduation in the scale varied from one Airbus model to another.) For certain Launch Aid connected to the A340-500/600 from the Spanish government, and Launch Aid from the British, German, and Spanish governments for the A380, accelerated repayment provisions applied. Further, some Launch Aid contracts called for Airbus to pay royalties to the creditor governments if Airbus made deliveries of aircraft in excess of the number Airbus needed to secure repayment. Such royalties were defined either as a specified percentage of the price of aircraft sold on deliveries above a specified threshold, or as gradually increasing sums on aircraft deliveries above a certain level.

Regardless of its form, France, Germany, Spain, and the U.K. provided Launch Aid through one of two types of contractual frameworks: an inter-governmental arrangement plus direct, bilateral arrangements, or just through direct, bilateral arrangements. That is, under the first type, there were two sets of contracts:

First: A general inter-governmental agreement among contracting parties, *i.e.*, general agreements among France, Germany, Spain, and the U.K., which specified the relative commitments of each country to fund the development of a particular model of LCA, along with

Second: Related separate contracts between the government of each country and the Airbus entity in its territory to implement Launch Aid financing at the national level.

The purpose of any inter-governmental arrangement was to specify key terms and conditions of Launch Aid, such as the amounts to be disbursed by, and the modes of repayment, to each government.

Under the second type of contractual framework, there was no inter-governmental agreement. Rather, there was only a set of contracts, namely, individual contracts between each government and the Airbus entity in its territory.

Launch Aid for several Airbus models followed the first contractual framework. For instance, in one arrangement, called the "1969 A300 Agreement," France and Germany agreed to fund the development of the A300 through loans, which Airbus would repay via graduated levies on the sale of each aircraft.

Subsequent arrangements followed the 1969 template, but with some deviations therefrom. For example, the "1981 A310 Agreement" embodied the core principles of the 1969 and 1971 Agreements for the A300, and applied them to the development of the A310. In the 1981 Agreement, France, Germany, Spain, and the U.K. provided A310 funding through loans to be repaid via graduated levies on aircraft sales. It also specified the amount of A310 development costs that Belgium and the Netherlands would bear. Significantly, with respect to the A300 and A310, the Agreements made clear that the costs of production of aircraft were not to be financed by the governments, but rather by the manufacturers (*e.g.*, British Aerospace, *Deutsche Airbus*, etc.) themselves.

The contractual framework for the A320 and A330/340 Airbus models was like that for, but less precise than, the A300 and A310 projects. They — including the 1991 A320 Agreement and 1994 A330/340 Agreement — set out financial contributions expected from the governments of France, Germany, Spain, and the U.K., plus Belgium, and stated that repayments would come from aircraft sales revenues. But, these inter-governmental accords did not specify the form, value, or timing of the payments. Again, production costs were not financed under these accords, but remained the responsibility of the manufacturers. Notably, the 1994 A330/340 Agreement said the British, French, German, and Spanish governments would support export financing (with the Spanish government limiting its export support to purchases of the A330/340 by Spanish airlines).

For various other Airbus models, the second type of contractual framework was used. For example, for the A330-220 and A340-500/600 models, there were no inter-governmental agreements. That also was true for the A380, though in 2003, France, Germany, Spain, and the U.K. reached the "2003 Agreement" with Airbus SAS. It contained general principles and obligations for all Airbus models, especially the A380. For the A330-220, A340-500/600, and A380, governments entered into sepa-rate, national-level contracts with the manufacturers, namely, *Aérospatiale*, *CASA*, Airbus France, *Airbus Deutschland GMbH*, EADS Airbus, and British Aerospace. That is, these models followed the second type of contractual framework.

Neither before the Panel nor on appeal did the EU contest the American argu-ment that Launch Aid satisfied the "financial contribution" test in Article 1:1(a)(i), or that it was "specific" under Article 2. Rather, the EU argued that none of its Launch Aid conferred a "benefit" to Airbus under Article 1:1(b).

(2) Preferential Lending Measures[17]

The European Investment Bank (EIB) provided 12 loans to Airbus on off-market terms between 1998 and 2002 for the design and development of aircraft. In partic-ular, the 12 loans fell into the following categories: (1) a single 2002 loan to EADS for research and development activities for the Airbus A380; (2) three loans to *Aéro-spatiale* to produce *Super Transporteurs* aircraft in 1993, and to pay facilities and equipment in 1988 and 1992 for the A330/A340; (3) four loans to British Aerospace to design, develop and manufacture wing boxes for the A330 and A340 in 1990 and 1991, and to design and develop wings for the A320 in 1988 and 1989; (4) three loans to CASA, one in 1989 and two in 1990, to design and produce various parts for the A320 and A330/340; and (5) a single 1990 loan to Airbus GIE for R&D of the A321.

(3) Corporate Restructuring Measures[18]

France and Germany provided equity infusions and grants to companies that joined in the consortium to form Airbus. They also forgave the debt of Airbus. The French and German central governments did so through government-owned and government-controlled banks.

France provided five equity infusions to *Aérospatiale* in 1987, 1988, and 1994. These transactions were capital investments in *Aérospatiale*, namely, of *French Francs* 1.25 billion in 1987, another *FF* 1.25 billion in 1988, and *FF* 2 billion in 1994. *Crédit Lyonnais* made one such capital contribution in 1992. *Crédit Lyonnais* took a 20% equity interest in *Aérospatiale*, which had been wholly owned by the French government until then, paying *FF* 1.4 billion for a mix of newly issued shares and shares from the government. For the shares held by the government, *Crédit Lyonnais*

---

17. *See Airbus* Appellate Body Report, ¶¶ 1(b), 610.
18. *See Airbus* Appellate Body Report, ¶¶ 1(d), fn. 1382 at 578, 629–632.

paid the government 2% of its own share capital (*i.e.*, a stock-for-stock, rather than stock-for-cash, acquisition).

Further, on 30 December 1998, France transferred its 45.76% equity interest (and all associated voting rights) in *Dassault Aviation* to *Aérospatiale* (*i.e.*, Airbus). The French government had acquired this stake in 1978 from a privately held producer of business, regional, and military jets. With this stake, because of certain double voting shares, the French government had a controlling interest in *Dassault*. With the transfer of the shares to *Aérospatiale*, those double-voting rights were cancelled.

In return, *Aérospatiale* agreed to issue new shares of itself at a later date, once a panel of independent experts agreed on a fixed exchange ratio. The panel gave its report on 19 March 1999, setting an exchange ratio of two *Aérospatiale* shares for each *Dassault Aviation* share. So, the panel agreed with the contribution of *Dassault Aviation* shares to *Aérospatiale* at an amount equal to their net book value of *FF* 2.658 billion. And, on 6 May 1999, *Aérospatiale* issued 9,267,094 new shares to the French government.

This entire transaction was part of a larger French government plan to consolidate the French aeronautical, defense, and space industries by combining *Aérospatiale* with *Matra Hautes Technologies* (*MHT*), a French government corporation. The combination occurred in 1998, and in 1999 France partially privatized the entity, *Aérospatiale-MHT*, resulting in it holding 48% of the shares, with employees, a private company, and the public holding the remaining 2%, 33%, and 17% stakes.

As for Germany, in the late 1980s, the central government restructured *Deutsche Airbus*. That restructuring involved three controversial transactions that the U.S. charged involved subsidization, the first two of which the Appellate Body agreed with the American arguments: the (1) 1989 acquisition by the German government, through its development bank, *Kreditanstalt für Wiederaufbau* (Credit Agency for Reconstruction, or *KfW*), of a 20% equity interest in *Deutsche Airbus*; (2) 1992 sale by *KfW* of that interest to, *Messerschmitt-Bölkow-Blohm GmbH* (*MBB*), which is the parent company of *Deutsche Airbus*; and (3) the 1998 forgiveness of 7.7. billion *Deutsche Marks* of debt owed by *Deutsche Airbus* to the German government.

Also challenged by the U.S. was the 1998 agreement of the German government to accept a payment of *DM* 1.75 billion from *Deutsche Airbus* to settle outstanding claims after the restructuring of that company. The U.S. argued the total accumulated principal amount of the debt that *Deutsche Airbus* owed to its government as at least *DM* 9.4 billion. Hence, said the U.S., the transaction was one of debt forgiveness worth *DM* 7.7 billion.

(4) Infrastructure Measures[19]

From EU countries, Airbus received goods, services, and grants to establish, expand, and upgrade its manufacturing sites, especially so it could develop and

---

19. *See Airbus* Appellate Body Report, ¶¶ 1(c), 622–628.

produce the A380. The German central government provided assistance to Airbus to lease land at an industrial site in Hamburg, Germany, known as the "*Mühlenberger Loch.*"

In 2000 the City of Hamburg decided to turn wetlands in this *Loch* into usable land, *i.e.*, to reclaim land. In February 2001, Hamburg began building new dykes, upgrading the height of extant dykes, around the Airbus facility in the area. The dyke provided flood protection for reclaimed land. Further, Hamburg built special purpose facilities on the reclaimed land, namely, a quay, sluice and pump building, drainage ditch, roll-on-roll-off area, and sternfender. The total cost to Hamburg was € 751 million.

In turn, Hamburg leased the reclaimed land to Airbus Germany through a scheme known as "*Projektierungsgesellschaft Finkenwerder GmbH & Co. KG,*" or "*ProFi.*" The annual lease rate was € 3.60 per square meter (adjusted based on the German Consumer Price Index). Additionally, via *ProFi*, Hamburg and Airbus Germany concluded four lease agreements for the special purpose facilities for 20 years. These leases called for a rental rate to assure Hamburg would get a 6.5% rate of return on its investment in each facility, namely, an annualized sum of € 5,619,200 (adjusted for inflation).

Germany also supported the right of Airbus to exclusive use of an extended runway at the airport in Bremen, Germany, and assisted with noise-reduction measures relating to the lengthening of the runway. The City of Bremen extended the runway in 1989–1990 by 300 meters at either end, from 2,034 to 2,634 meters, to comply with EU requirements for a safety margin (namely, 300 meters at each end of a runway). Bremen bore the cost of both the runway extension and noise-reduction measures, namely, *DM* 40 and 10 million respectively. Significantly, with the exception of emergencies, the Bremen runway is for the exclusive use of flights transporting Airbus wings from Bremen.

Also in Germany, sub-central governmental authorities in Nordenham gave regional grants to Airbus. That is, the German Land of Lower Saxony provided money for Airbus to expand its facility at Nordenham.

In France, the central government provided to Airbus the *Aéroconstellation* industrial site in Toulouse, and improved the road relating to that cite. In particular, in 1999 government officials authorized the development of an industrial site next to the Toulouse-Blagnac Airport for the exclusive purpose of aeronautical activities. The zoned the site a "*zone d'aménagemement concertée*" (*ZAC*), which meant the government buys, improves, and sells the land for economic development.

For the *Aéroconstellation ZAC* industrial site, the French government had to convert agricultural land to land for industrial, hence it had to put in drainage, sewage, and water circulation systems, and equip the property with fencing, fire protection, landscaping, and lighting. The government also established specialized facilities, called "*équipement d'intérêt general*" (*EIG*). The EIG were infrastructure specially designed for aeronautical activities, namely, aircraft parking areas, service areas, taxiways and roads, and underground technical galleries.

Once the French government completed the *Aéroconstellation ZAC* industrial site, it sold all but 11 hectares of the site to different aeronautical companies, including ones involved in the development and production of the Airbus A380. Buyers included Airbus France and Air France Industries. The buyers, all of which paid the same square meter price for differently sized plots, formed an association called *"AFUL,"* (*Association Foncière Urbaine Libre*). Then, the City of Toulouse authorities leased the *EIG* facilities to *AFUL*, the members of which paid rent for the facilities based on their respective usage of them. Only *AFUL* members could use the *EIG* facilities.

Also during the late 1990s and early 2000s, the French government improved several roads around the *Aéroconstellation* site, particularly to link the site to an extra-wide highway (*an itinéraire à grand gabarit*, or *IGG*). The IGG was used by Airbus to transport A380 components produced elsewhere from the French coast to the *Aéroconstellation* site, for use by the *AFUL* members.

Likewise, in Spain, the sub-central governments of Andalucia and Castilla-La Mancha each gave regional grants to Airbus. These grants allowed for the expansion and modernization of Airbus and EADS plants in Sevilla, Illescas, La Rinconada, Puerto Real, Puerto de Santa Maria, and Toledo.

In the U.K., Welsh authorities gave Airbus infrastructure support—again, a grant—for its facility Broughton.

(5) Research and Technological Development (R&TD) Measures[20]

This subsidy involved funding in the form of grants and loans for R&TD from the EU, and from France and Spain at the central and sub-central governmental level, to Airbus, to help Airbus undertake research. In particular, R&TD funding to Airbus took six different forms, chronicled in Table 13-2.

Synopsis of Key Conclusions:

Before the Panel, the U.S. challenged every measure in the above five categories as a specific subsidy that satisfied the tests for "financial contribution," "benefit," and "specificity" under Articles 1 and 2 of the *SCM Agreement*, and alleged the measures caused adverse effects to the U.S. under Articles 5 and 6 of the *Agreement*. In other words, the U.S. contended every measure was an actionable, or Yellow Light, subsidy. The Appellate Body held all of the aforementioned subsidy measures in the 5 categories to be actionable, that is, unlawful Yellow Light support. Further, the U.S. argued certain Launch Aid measures were prohibited under Article 3 of the *Agreement*. That is, the U.S. highlighted a few Launch Aid measures as Red Light subsidies.

---

20. *See Airbus* Appellate Body Report, ¶¶ 1(e), 611–621.

At the same time (as discussed below), the Appellate Body made clear not all subsidies from the EU or EU countries about which the U.S. complained were actionable and caused serious prejudice under Articles 5(c) and 6 of the *SCM Agreement*. The Appellate Body ruled some types of support under these categories did not even satisfy the Specificity Test of Articles 1-2 of the *Agreement*. And, no serious prejudice existed (or was proven to occur by the U.S.) with respect to the following three types of schemes:

First: Certain Corporate Restructuring Measures, namely, the 1998 transfer of a 45.76% equity interest in *Dassault Aviation* by France to *Aérospatiale* (*i.e.*, Airbus).

Second: Certain Infrastructure Measures, namely, the special purpose facilities at the *Mühlenberger Loch* industrial site in Hamburg, Germany, and the *Aéroconstellation* industrial site, and related facilities (such as parking and taxiways), in Toulouse, France.

Third: Various R&TD Measures, that is, loans and grants to support Airbus research and development of LCA, specifically:

(1) loans under the Spanish *PROFIT* Program;

(2) grants under the Second, Third, Fourth, Fifth, and Sixth European Communities (EC) Framework Programs;

(3) grants by France between 1986 and 1993;

(4) grants by Germany under the *LuFo* I, II, and III Programs;

(5) grants by Bavaria, Bremen, and Hamburg; and

(6) civil aircraft research and development (CARAD) and aeronautics research programs (ARP) by the U.K.

In excluding the above-listed schemes from the scope of its Yellow Light findings under Articles 5(c) and 6, the Appellate Body largely agreed with the conclusions of the Panel. But, the Appellate body reached its conclusions for different reasons from those of the Panel. Of course, regardless of the rationale, the net result was a partial victory for the EU, as not all of the subsidy schemes challenged by the U.S. were held illegal. Moreover, (also as discussed more fully below), the Appellate Body reversed the finding of the Panel that Launch Aid to the Airbus A380 was a Red Light subsidy.

Five sections of the *Airbus* Report are relevant to the "conferral of a benefit" analysis under Article 1:1(b) of the *SCM Agreement*. The first concerns an important threshold issue: whether the Panel correctly found that Articles 1, 5, and 6 of the *SCM Agreement* require a complainant to demonstrate the existence of a "present" benefit, or a "benefit that continues," during the reference period. The remaining 4 sections are the application by the Appellate Body of Article 1:1(b) to the disputed measures.

Losing Argument:

The EU hoped to win the entire case on the threshold issue. It argued the text of the *SCM Agreement* shows that it is essential to prove the existence of a "continuing benefit" from an alleged subsidy. First, the EU pointed to the phrase "shall be deemed to exist" in Article 1. It is in the present tense. Surely this tense indicates the *Agreement* is not concerned with subsidies that no longer exist and no longer capable of causing adverse effects. Second, the EU called out the present tense in Articles 5 and 6. That tense in those Articles meant subsidies that have been withdrawn, have ceased to exist, or the effects of which have diminished, cannot currently "cause" present adverse effects.

The EU relied heavily on this argument, because most of the Airbus subsidies alleged by the U.S. had ceased long before it brought the case. The European logic was that if there is no present benefit, then the respondent has no actionable gripe. But, the Appellate Body had none of it.

Table 13-2. Disputed RT&D Measures

Form of RT&D Measure	Summary of Measure
First	Grants under the Second, Third, Fourth, Fifth, and Sixth EC Framework Programs, which covered four-year from 1987 through 2006, and regulated by Decisions from the EU Council. Those Decisions set out the type of research that would be funded (*e.g.*, under the Second Program, pre-competitive research on airplanes and helicopters; under the Third Program, environment-related technologies, aircraft operation, aerodynamics and aerothermodynamics, aeronautical structures and manufacturing, avionic systems, and mechanical, utility, and actuation technologies; under the Fourth Program, transport means plus two other fields; under the Fifth Program, acquisition of critical technologies, technology integration for new-generation aircraft, and operational efficiency and safety; and under the Sixth Program, aeronautics and space research on aircraft safety, emissions, and operational capacity and safety of the air transport system). Those Decisions also stated the fund amounts for identified research areas (called "indicative allocations"). The allocated funds were denominated in European Currency Units (such as ECU 500 million in the Second Program, ECU 663 million in the Third Program, ECU 1.617 billion and ECU 230.5 million, allocated to specific types of research in the Fourth Program, and at least ECU 700 million in the Fifth Program), or in euros (€) (such as € 1.075 billion for aeronautics and space research under the Sixth Program).
Second	French government funding of € 1.2 billion between 1986 and 2005 for civil aeronautics research, split (according to 7 French Senate reports on which the U.S. relied in its pleadings) between € 391 million from 1986–1993, and € 809 million 1994–2005.
Third	German government aid worth € 217 million under its *Luftfahrtforschungsprogramm* (Aviation Research Program, or *LuFo*) I, II, and III, which covered three successive periods between 1995 and 2007.

(*continued*)

Table 13-2. Disputed RT&D Measures (*continued*)

Form of RT&D Measure	Summary of Measure
Fourth	Spanish government loans under the *Plan Tecnológico Aeronáutico* (*PTA*) I and II Programs covering successive periods from 1993 to 1998, and over € 60 million in loans starting in 2000 pursuant to the *Programa de Fomento de la Investigación Técnica* (*PROFIT*, or Funding Program for Technological Research) Program.
Fifth	British government grants from 1992 to 2005 under CARAD, which later became the ARP.
Sixth	Three grant programs run by the sub-central governments of Bavaria (starting in 1990 through at least 2000 for LCA-related R&TD projects), Bremen (valued at € 11 million for Airbus materials and system technologies), and Hamburg.

Holding on Threshold Issue of Existence of Continuing Benefit:

On the threshold issue, the Appellate Body disagreed with the EU. It held a benefit must occur at the time a financial contribution occurs, and adverse effects may occur even if the benefit is not continual. Thus, the *SCM Agreement* does not demand of a complainant that it prove a present or ongoing benefit.

Logically, the Appellate Body was right. Consider an analogy between a subsidy and its benefits, and a criminal or tortious act and its harm. (Note the analogy is not between the adverse effects of a subsidy and the harm of the criminal or tortious act.) Harm caused by a criminal or tortious act typically begins with the act itself, but it could manifest thereafter. Does the harm, once manifest, continue for years to come? It depends on the act (and perhaps also the victim). In some cases, the harm ends fairly soon after the act, while in others, the victim feels the harm from the act for years. But, to focus on when the harm manifests, or on its duration, is to miss the mark. The act is a culpable one (if coupled with any relevant *mens rea* requirement), regardless of when and for how long it is felt. So, too, is it with a subsidy: that there was a subsidy, and that it created a benefit, are what matter. That the benefit persists is not the essential point. (And, as discussed below, adverse effects caused by the subsidy are a separate matter.)

Note the continuance of a benefit is not irrelevant in all contexts. In cases brought against pre-privatization subsidies, wherein a SOE received a benefit from a financial contribution, but was later privatized, it is necessary to show that benefit continued through the change in ownership of the recipient. That is the Appellate Body teaching in the 2000 *British Steel* and 2003 *Certain Products* cases.

Holdings on Application of Article 1:1(b) to Airbus Subsidies:

The Appellate Body proceeded to four holdings, the sum and substance of which was to hand the U.S. an overall—but not complete—victory. First, it upheld the Panel decision, stating Launch Aid Measures conferred a benefit within the meaning of Article 1:1(b) of the *SCM Agreement*.

Second, regarding the Infrastructure Measures, the Appellate Body acknowledged in certain circumstances, the costs incurred by a seller may be relevant, but still rejected the Panel analysis and sought to complete the analysis itself, yielding 2 results:

(1) The lease of the land at the *Mühlenberger Loch* industrial site conferred a benefit on Airbus within the meaning of Article 1.1(b).

(2) The right to exclusive use of the extended runway at the Bremen Airport conferred a benefit on Airbus under that Article.

But, insufficient facts prevented the Appellate Body from completing the analysis in respect of the infrastructure provided to Airbus at the *Aéroconstellation* industrial site.

Third, as to the Corporate Restructuring Measures, the Appellate Body upheld the Panel, finding the four challenged capital investments were inconsistent with the usual investment practice of private investors in France, and thus conferred a benefit on *Aérospatiale* within the meaning of Article 1.1(b).

Fourth, also concerning these Measures, the Appellate Body reversed the Panel finding that the 1998 transfer of shares by the French Government of its interest in Dassault Aviation to *Aérospatiale* conferred a benefit under Article 1.1(b). That was a small victory for the EU amidst losses on the first three Measures.

Rationale:

The Panel acknowledged that because of transactions involving Airbus predecessor companies, Airbus SAS did not currently receive the subsidies of its predecessors. However, it rejected the proposition that a subsidy can cause adverse effects pursuant to Article 5 of the *SCM Agreement* only if it can be shown to confer a benefit presently on a recipient. For a complaining Member to succeed on an adverse effects claim under Article 5 of the *Agreement*, it must first establish existence of a subsidy pursuant to Articles 1 and 2 of the *Agreement*.

The Panel reasoned the use of "thereby" in Article 1:1(b) of the *SCM Agreement* suggests a financial contribution and benefit come into existence at the same time. Relying on the 199 *Canada Aircraft* Appellate Body Report, the Panel reiterated that the focus of the inquiry into the existence of a "benefit" is whether a financial contribution places the recipient in a more advantageous position than would have been the case but for the financial contribution. So, the Panel found it hard to understand how the concept of a "continuing benefit" fit within Article 1 of the *Agreement*.

The Appellate Body reviewed Article 1:1 of the *SCM Agreement*, and compared it to Articles 5 and 6. First, the Appellate Body reviewed the definitions of "financial contribution," and cited *Canada Aircraft* for the proposition a financial contribution and a benefit conferred are two distinct concepts to be analyzed separately. It also cited *Canada Aircraft* when defining a "benefit," and reiterated its acceptance of the use of Article 14 of the *Agreement* to interpret this term. Though much of its discussion was a regurgitation of its previous jurisprudence, the Appellate Body encapsulated its view of the proper "benefit" analysis by stating: "the determination of benefit under Article 1:1(b) of the *SCM Agreement* is an *ex ante* analysis that does *not* depend on how the particular financial contribution *actually performed after* it was granted."[21] As it went on to say:

> 707. The ordinary meaning of Article 1:1, read in the light of Article 14 of the *SCM Agreement*, confirms, therefore, that a benefit analysis under Article 1:1(b) is forward-looking and focuses on future projections. The nature, amount, and projected use of the challenged subsidy may be relevant factors to consider in an assessment of the period over which the benefit from a financial contribution *might be expected* to flow. A panel may consider, for example, as part of its *ex ante* analysis of benefit, whether the subsidy is allocated to purchase inputs or fixed assets; the useful life of these inputs or assets; whether the subsidy is large or small; and the period of time over which the subsidy is expected to be used for future production.[22]

The U.S. and EU agreed on the basic point a subsidy has a life, which may come to an end, either through removal of a financial contribution or expiration of a benefit.

However, importantly, the U.S. and Appellate Body agreed the adverse effects analysis under Article 5 is distinct from the "benefit" analysis under Article 1:1(b). In sum, to decide whether a benefit is conferred, the analysis must look to the benefit at the time of the financial contribution. But, any analysis as to whether adverse effects exist is a separate matter. There is no need to show that a benefit still exists in order to prove that a subsidy causes adverse effects later in time, after the subsidy ceases.

Next, the Appellate Body addressed whether the EU conferred a benefit upon Airbus Launch Aid and Member State Financing. Again, it looked to *Canada Aircraft* for an interpretation of the term "benefit." Citing Article 14 of the *SCM Agreement*, the Appellate Body felt the guideline in Sub-paragraph (b) was relevant to the LA/MSF measures characterized as unsecured loans. This Sub-paragraph states:

> [A] loan by a government shall not be considered as conferring a benefit, unless there is a difference between the amount that the firm receiving the loan pays on the government loan and the amount the firm would pay on a comparable commercial loan which the firm could actually obtain on the market. In this case the benefit shall be the difference between these two amounts[.]

This calculation as to whether a loan confers a benefit is based on the size of the loan, interest rate, duration, and other relevant terms of the transaction. The calculation is as of the moment in time when lender and borrower commit to the transaction, and thus depends on the structure and risks of the loan, not on how the loan

---

21. *See Airbus* Appellate Body Report, ¶ 706 (emphasis added).
22. *See Airbus* Appellate Body Report, ¶ 707.

actually performs over time.[23] In most cases, data for the calculation are imperfect. So, deciding whether the investment was commercially rational is to be ascertained based on the information available to the investor at the time the decision to invest was made.

In the *Airbus* case, the Appellate Body weighed expert testimony the U.S. and EU submitted. The American expert created a three-part formula consisting of (1) government borrowing rate, (2) general corporate risk premium, and (3) project-specific risk premium. When added together, this formula gave the rate of return a market lender would demand. The European expert accepted the American formula, as well as the first two components. But, the experts differed in the calculation of the project-specific risk premium. The Panel and Appellate Body agreed the risk premium proposed by the European expert understated the premium a market operator would have reasonably demanded Airbus to pay for financing.

Ultimately, it did not matter. Having conceded the first two components of the formula, all but two of the European Launch Aid measures provided better rates than the market even without considering the project-specific risk premium. On those two, if risk premiums suggested by the EU were used, then those measures also provided better rates than the market. At oral argument, the EU said its calculations should be applied only to the A380 project. But, it was too late—new assertions of fact or expert opinion cannot be introduced at the appellate stage. The Appellate Body upheld the Panel, stating Launch Aid conferred a benefit within the meaning of Article 1:1(b) of the *SCM Agreement*.

Regarding the Infrastructure measures, the Panel said help from the EU member governments for the *Mühlenberger Loch* industrial site in Hamburg, airport runway in Bremen, and *Aéroconstellation* industrial site in Toulouse, conferred a benefit on Airbus. That was because each governmental investment in that infrastructure exceeded the governmental return on the investment. The EU argued the Panel erred when it assessed the existence of a benefit under Article 1:1(b) of the *SCM Agreement* on the basis of whether costs incurred by the government exceeded the returns to Airbus generated by purchase and lease payments. Supposedly, this "return-to-government" analysis was equivalent to the "cost-to-government" standard rejected in *Canada Aircraft*.

The Appellate Body looked to Sub-paragraph (d) in Article 14 of the *SCM Agreement* for guidance, in accordance with *Canada Aircraft*. It states:

> [T]he provision of goods or services or purchase of goods by a government shall not be considered as conferring a benefit unless the provision is made for less than adequate remuneration, or the purchase is made for more than adequate remuneration. The adequacy of remuneration shall be determined in relation to prevailing market conditions for the good or service in question in the country of provision or purchase (including price,

---

23. *See Airbus* Appellate Body Report, ¶ 836.

quality, availability, marketability, transportation and other conditions of purchase or sale).

Again relying on *Canada Aircraft*, the Appellate Body recalled that a marketplace comparison is the way to see if a benefit is conferred. So, a benefit "is to be determined, not by reference to whether the transaction imposes a net cost on the government, but rather by reference to whether the terms of the financial contribution are more favourable to what is available to the recipient on the market."[24] The Appellate Body also acknowledged its *Korea DRAMs* finding that some situations may not allow for a market comparison, but the underlying rationale still stands— is the recipient better off?

The Panel, in applying its "return-to-government" standard, said the government cost of providing infrastructure exceeded the amount of government return on investment for all three relevant measures. The Appellate Body acknowledged that in certain circumstances, cost to a seller may be relevant, but still rejected the Panel analysis for the reasons expressed by the Appellate Body in *Canada Aircraft*. Having decided in favor of the EU on this point, the Appellate Body considered whether it could complete the Panel analysis. As a general matter, an Appellate Body may complete that analysis "only if the factual findings by the panel, or the undisputed facts in the panel record" provide a sufficient basis for the Appellate Body to do so.[25]

The Appellate Body felt two of the three relevant measures met this standard: the lease of land at the *Mühlenberger Loch* industrial site, and the right to exclusive use of the extended runway at Bremen Airport, conferred a benefit on Airbus under Article 1:1(b) of the *SCM Agreement*. However, as to infrastructure provided to Airbus at the *Aéroconstellation* industrial site, the Appellate Body could not complete the analysis.

Four equity infusions, in the form of capital investments and a share transfer, were the last measures on appeal relevant to Article 1:1(b) of the *SCM Agreement*. Mercifully, the Appellate Body analysis was shorter, as it already had discussed the standard for assessing a "benefit."

First, the Appellate Body looked to Article 14(a) of the *SCM Agreement*, relating to the provision of equity capital:

> [G]overnment provision of equity capital shall not be considered as conferring a benefit, unless the investment decision can be regarded as inconsistent with the *usual* investment *practice* (including for the provision of risk capital) of private investors in the territory of that Member.[26]

---

24. *See Airbus* Appellate Body Report, ¶ 974.
25. *See e.g.*, Appellate Body Report, *United States—Hot-Rolled Steel*, ¶ 235.
26. Article 14(a) of the *SCM Agreement* (emphasis added).

The Appellate Body considered "usual" and "practice" to be the operative terms. In accordance with the *Vienna Convention*, it looked to the *OED* definitions. "Usual" signifies "commonly or customarily observed or practiced," and "practice" means "usual or customary action or performance."[27] Synthesized, the Appellate Body took "usual practice" to mean the common or customary conduct of private investors in respect of equity investment.

So, as with Launch Aid, for equity infusions, the examination should focus on the costs and expected returns at the moment the decision to invest is undertaken. Ultimately, the Appellate Body upheld the Panel, finding the 4 challenged capital investments were inconsistent with the usual investment practice of private investors in France and conferred a benefit on *Aérospatiale* under Article 1:1(b) of the *SCM Agreement*.

Lastly, the Appellate Body addressed the Panel finding that the 1998 transfer by the French Government of its interest in *Dassault* Aviation to *Aérospatiale* conferred a benefit under Article 1:1(b) of the *SCM Agreement*. The Panel simply concluded *Aérospatiale* was not in a strong enough financial position to attract private capital. The Panel ought to have identified a proper "investment decision" against which to compare to the "usual investment practice," but failed to do so. In consequence of the failure to use this market benchmark test, the Appellate Body reserved the Panel finding.

Conclusion — Two Propositions:

The *Airbus* Appellate Body Report, insofar as it relates to Article 1:1(b) of the *SCM Agreement*, stands for two propositions.

First, Article 1:1(b) does not require proof of a "present" or "continuing benefit." The European rationale, which is based on an analogy to an adverse effects analysis under Articles 5 and 6 of the *Agreement*, favoring such proof is flawed. A subsidy and its effects, adverse or not, do not always occur simultaneously. They might not even overlap. Instead, the only temporal aspect of the test about conferral of a benefit test is whether a benefit occurs at the same time as the related financial contribution, *i.e.*, what matters is the simultaneity of (1) conferral of a benefit when (2) the specific financial contribution to which that benefit is tied is made.

Second, *Airbus* reinforces *Canada Aircraft*, through strong reliance on two Appellate Body precedents from the earlier case. As to the first precedent, the *Airbus* Appellate Body cites *Canada Aircraft* repeatedly to use Article 14 to help interpret Article 1:1(b). As to the second, *Airbus* confirms the *ex ante* analysis *Canada Aircraft* used in the conferral of a benefit standard, and makes clear that when comparing a loan or investment decision, the examination should focus on costs and expected returns at the moment a decision to invest is made, not on actual investment performance over time.

---

27. *See Airbus* Appellate Body Report, ¶ 999.

- **2012 *Boeing*[28]**

Boeing is another dispute in which the Appellate Body addressed Article 1:1(b) of the *SCM Agreement*. The Report itself is unconscionably long, with only one measure at issue on appeal pertinent to this Article. The U.S. disputed the Panel finding NASA Procurement Contracts and DOD Assistance Instruments conferred a benefit to Boeing under Article 1:1(b).

Losing Argument:

The EU provided the losing argument, though ultimately it was victorious: upon completing the analysis of the Panel, the Appellate Body upheld the pro-European Panel decision, but for a different reason from the European argument. The EU argued that since the American appeal regarding Article 1:1(a)(1) (definition of a "financial contribution") failed, its appeal on Article 1:1(b) (conferral of a "benefit") also must fail, because it based the latter on the former. The EU said the transactions were principally for the benefit and use of Boeing, and consequently, they conferred a benefit on Boeing.

Holding:

The Appellate Body rejected the reasoning by the EU and Panel, but, following its completion of the analysis, still found a benefit to be conferred upon Boeing because of the predetermined allocation of IPRs under American law. Via this allocation, the NASA Procurement Contracts and DOD Assistance Instruments conferred a benefit on Boeing under Article 1:1(b) of the *SCM Agreement*.

Rationale:

Once again, the Appellate Body began by citing the 1999 *Canada Aircraft* to define "benefit." Then, it looked back to its 2011 *Airbus* decision to support the use of a marketplace comparison, and highlight the important temporal aspect of that comparison. That is, calculation of a benefit depends on the terms and conditions of the challenged transaction at the time it is made, and compares them to terms and conditions that would have been offered in the market at that time.

The Appellate Body also gave important criticisms of the Panel decision. In its attempts to use the "financial contribution" and "benefit" tests from *Canada Aircraft* and *Airbus*, the Panel rightly asked whether a financial contribution is more favorable to the recipient than what the recipient would have been able to obtain in the market. But, in deciding whether a "financial contribution" exists that confers a "benefit," the Panel asked the same questions: whether the measures were purchases of services, and if so, then which party used them, that is, which party to the transaction derives the principal benefit and use from the research?[29] Simply put, the Panel asked the same question in both the "financial contribution" and "benefit" contexts.

---

28. This case is cited, and its facts summarized, earlier in this Chapter.
29. *See Boeing* Appellate Body Report, ¶ 641.

The Appellate Body disagreed with that methodology, because it conflated the two separate elements from the definition of a subsidy in Article 1:1 of the *SCM Agreement*. Said the Appellate Body:

> . . . [A] determination that a transaction is not a purchase of services— because the R&D is principally for the benefit of the commissioned party rather than the commissioning government—makes the determination of benefit almost a foregone conclusion [*i.e.*, finding no purchase of services was made impels the conclusion no benefit was conferred].[30]

The Appellate Body also looked askance at the sloppy use by the Panel of the term "benefit" in the generic sense, rather than carefully using its distinct legal meaning. Still another troubling matter was the Panel examination of the principal user or beneficiary of research: the Panel looked to its own five factors, in disregard of the mandate of Article 1:1(b), which requires consideration of whether a measure is consistent with a market benchmark.

Even when the Panel considered the market benchmark, the Appellate Body said it did a botched job. The Panel stated:

> [N]o commercial entity, *i.e.*, no private entity acting pursuant to commercial considerations, would provide payments (and access to its facilities and personnel) to another commercial entity on the condition that the other entity perform R&D activities principally for the benefit and use of that other entity.[31]

This conclusory statement was based exclusively on the view of the Panel as to how a commercial actor would behave and inferences as to what a rational investor would do. The Appellate Body saw no evidence supporting that view. Perhaps the Panel was using its own common sense, or its own conception of economic rationality, but either was unsatisfactory. Even after the EU suggested the Panel address the evidence, the Panel refused.[32]

Citing two economic texts, the Appellate Body countered the Panel view regarding potential private actors in this situation:

> In addition to the concerns we have expressed above about the Panel's approach, we are not persuaded that, *a priori*, it can be excluded that two market actors would enter into a transaction with each other in circumstances where the returns are unequally distributed between them. Transactions between market actors may take place even when the returns earned by each party are asymmetric, as long as both parties earn a reasonable return on the investment. Thus, it may not always be the case that a market actor would refuse to enter into a R&D project if the fruits of the research

---

30. *See Boeing* Appellate Body Report, ¶ 641.
31. *See Boeing* Appellate Body Report, ¶ 642.
32. *See Boeing* Appellate Body Report, ¶ 644.

(which provide a reasonable return on the investment) are not distributed between the parties in an exact proportion to their contributions to the project. In general, how the costs and revenues are divided between the parties to a transaction will depend on, among other things, the bargaining strength of the parties and the alternatives available to the parties in the event that the transaction were not to proceed. A market actor could accept a situation where it contributes half of the cost but obtains less than half of the returns, because the alternatives available to that actor would be worse. In sum, there is no presumption as to whether the returns on an investment in the market are evenly distributed.[33]

So, rejecting the Panel reasoning, the Appellate Body completed the analysis where sufficient factual findings by the Panel, or undisputed facts on the record, enabled it to.

To complete the analysis, the Appellate Body reviewed the NASA Procurement Contracts and DOD Assistance Instruments and the American legal regime in which they operated. That regime predetermined allocation of IPRs in government contracts. In contrast, in a transaction between two market actors, the party undertaking the research must bargain to obtain ownership of the IPRs. So, in terms of the benefit-to-the-recipient analysis under the *SCM Agreement*, Boeing was better off through the Contracts and Instruments than it would have been in a transaction with private parties, simply because Boeing did not need to negotiate for its IPRs. It got them, without any give-and-take with NASA or the DOD, by operation of American law. For the Appellate Body, that was enough to find the joint venture arrangements by Boeing with NASA and the DOD conferred a benefit on Boeing under Article 1:1(b) of the *SCM Agreement*.

To be sure, depending on its bargaining power, a private actor like Boeing could emerge from a market transaction with a better deal as to its allocation of IPRs than what it got with the government agencies. But, the evidence in the case did not suggest this outcome. (The Appellate Body said American law allocated to Boeing more IPRs, and NASA and the Pentagon fewer, than each would have obtained in a purely private deal.) The key distinction on which the case turned was the need to negotiate for IPRs, and the attendant risks therein. A legal entitlement to IPRs is a fixed outcome that provides certainty and predictability, from which any business benefits.

Conclusion:

The additions to Article 1:1(b) jurisprudence *Boeing* makes are simple. First, the financial contribution and benefit conferred analyses must not be conflated. They must be kept separate, and follow a logical sequence. Second, a Panel may not use its own common sense, or its own conceptions of economic rationale, in these

---

33. *See Boeing* Appellate Body Report, ¶ 646.

determinations. Such determinations must be based on evidence or accepted economic principles.

- **Airbus or Boeing: Who Is the Worst Offender?**

The *Airbus* Appellate Body Report was the first result in a punch—counterpunch sequence between the U.S. and EU. The U.S. complained against European subsidies to Airbus, and Europe hit back with a complaint against American subsidies to Boeing. In terms of the "bottom line," what did the Appellate Body decide in each case, and which respondent was the worst offender of GATT-WTO subsidy disciplines? The answer is:

(1) In the June 2011 *Airbus* Report, the Appellate Body held the EU and France, Germany, Spain, and U.K. provided illegal subsidies to Airbus. These subsidies took three principal forms: (1) Launch Aid Measures; (2) Infrastructure Support; and (3) Corporate Reorganization Measures (specifically, equity infusions).

(2) The adverse trade effects caused by the illegal Airbus subsides to the U.S., *i.e.*, to Boeing, were the loss of sales of 342 aircraft worth $22 billion, and the displacement of Boeing aircraft in many markets, including the EU and China, which are among the largest large civil aircraft (LCA) markets in the world.

(3) In the March 2012 *Boeing* Report, the Appellate Body held the U.S. provided illegal subsidies to Airbus. These subsidies took five major forms: (1) a subsidy worth $2.2 billion from the *Foreign Sales Corporation (FSC)* scheme and *Extraterritorial Income Exclusion (ETI)* Act; (2) subsidies worth $2.6 billion through procurement contracts issued by NASA and use by Boeing of the facilities, equipment, and staff of NASA at no charge to Boeing; (3) subsidies worth between $100 million and $1.2 billion via payments from the DOD and free use of DOD facilities; (4) support from the State of Washington and city of Everett, Washington between 1989–2006 totaling $16 million through the B&O tax reductions and credits; and (5) support from the State of Kansas and city of Wichita, Kansas totaling $476 million through the floatation of IRBs.

(4) The adverse trade effects to the EU, *i.e.*, Airbus, from the illegal subsidies to Boeing were between $3.176–$4.392 billion.

In short, for all the heated rhetoric spouted by the U.S. and EU concerning subsidies to LCA, the fact is that via different subsidy schemes, both ran significantly afoul of multilateral rules on subsidies, but the European violations were more egregious in outright dollar terms. To be sure, both sides overstated their cases, as the Appellate Body determined the number of subsidy schemes and attendant trade damage was considerably less than that alleged by the respective complainants. Still, the damage inflicted by European subsidies to Boeing were on the order of 5 times greater than inflicted by American subsidies to Airbus (roughly $22 versus $4 billion).

III. Market Benchmarks and 2013 *U.S. Steel,* 2013 *Canada Renewable Energy,* and 2015 *China CVD* Cases

Benchmarks obviously are a source of contention in subsidy disputes, as the 1999 *Canada Aircraft,* 2011 *Airbus,* and 2012 *Boeing* cases illustrate. Whether a benchmark gives an accurate picture of what would have happened in a normal-functioning market, but for the alleged subsidy, is the key issue. This issue, however, begs other questions: Is there a normal functioning market? How is the benchmark best constructed? What is comparable to what? The answers lead to a zero-sum game, with petitioners arguing for benchmarks that exacerbate dumping margins or net countervailable subsidization rates, and respondents calling for ones that minimize or even eliminate those margins or rates.

· **2013 *U.S. Steel* Case**

These problems arise in domestic CVD disputes, too. Consider the 2013 *U.S. Steel Corp. v. United States* case.[34] The CIT upheld the DOC decision to use a benchmark interest rate for loans from a Korean government-owned bank, and the DOC computation of that benchmark. The DOC used that benchmark to determine the extent to which sales by a Korean company in the U.S. were impacted by a countervailable subsidy.

Hyundai Hysco Ltd. imported certain corrosion-resistant carbon steel flat products from Korea into the U.S. That subject merchandise was subject to a CVD order, because Hyundai Hysco had received short-term, variable rate loans from the Export-Import Bank of Korea (KEXIM) that the DOC found in the original CVD investigation to be at subsidized interest rates. Hyundai Hysco got all KEXIM loans in 2008, and KEXIM extended their terms into 2009. Hyundai Hysco also took out commercial loans in 2008. During an Administrative Review of the order, U.S. Steel Corporation challenged the benchmark interest rate used by the DOC in the Review.

Initially, the DOC said the right benchmark for the KEXIM loans was the interest rate on all commercial loans Hyundai Hysco obtained in 2008. But, Hyundai Hysco convinced the DOC to change its position: interest rates in 2008 were far higher than in 2009 (given the global financial crisis triggered by the collapse of Lehman Brothers in September 2008), and the KEXIM loans were extended into 2009.

So, in the Administrative Review the DOC agreed to use average annual interest rates in 2009 as a benchmark against which to judge whether the KEXIM loans were subsidized. In constructing the benchmark, the DOC excluded any loans Hysco took out in 2009 from the benchmark, because all KEXIM loans were made in 2008. And, the DOC also focused only on short-term variable interest rate commercial loans, because only they were comparable to the KEXIM loans. The DOC computed a weighted average interest rate based on 2009 monthly base certificate of deposit

---

34. *See* Number 12-00070, Slip Opinion 13-97 (31 July 2013).

(CD) rates, as reported by the Korean Financial Investment Association, plus fees, and interest rate spreads.

In brief, the DOC benchmark was what short-term interest rates would have been in 2009 for commercial loans obtained by Hyundai Hysco in 2008. That is, the benchmark was an estimate of what interest rate Hyundai Hysco would have paid for short-term, commercial loans made in 2008 and extended into 2009, with principal and interest payments due on the same dates as the actual KEXIM loan payments. The result was bad for U.S. Steel: the DOC found the net countervailable subsidization rate was 0.46%, which was *de minimis*, and thus not countervailable.

U.S. Steel complained to the CIT that the DOC benchmark was artificial, and that the DOC should have used a national average interest rate (which, presumably, would have resulted in a non-*de minimis* subsidization rate). The CIT sided with the DOC: in the absence of specific direction, under the governing statute (19 U.S.C. § 1677(5)(E)(ii)) and regulation (19 C.F.R. § 351.505(a)(2)(iv)), the DOC has the discretion to develop any reasonable methodology. The DOC reasonably judged KEXIM loans against commercial loans taken out in the same year, 2008, and focused on short-term, variable interest rates in the market, because the KEXIM loans were of the same type.

- **2013 *Canada Renewable Energy* Case**[35]

Competing Benchmarks:

An interesting issue in the 2013 *Canada Renewable Energy* case relating to the *SCM Agreement* concerned the conferral of a benefit analysis by the Panel and Appellate Body. In ascertaining whether the disputed measures conferred a benefit to its recipients, the Panel and Appellate Body separately considered potential market benchmarks, as Article 1:1(b) of the *SCM Agreement* envisions in the context of Article 14. Unfortunately, the Panel and Appellate Body, though through different means, eventually encountered the same underwhelming outcome.

The Panel rejected numerous proposed benchmarks put forth by the parties, and eventually developed its own market benchmark. Yet, when it attempted to apply its market benchmark, it found there to be insufficient evidence to conclude the analysis. Similarly, rejecting the proposed benchmarks by the parties, and the benchmark developed by the Panel, the Appellate Body also created its own market metric. However, it also found there was insufficient evidence to complete its analysis. Thus, Canada won this portion of the dispute, though effectively by default.

---

35. *See* Appellate Body Report, *Canada—Certain Measures Relating to the Renewable Energy Sector*, WT/DS412/AB/R (24 May 2013); and Appellate Body Report, *Canada—Measures Relating to the Feed-In Tariff Program*, WT/DS426/AB/R (24 May 2013) [hereinafter jointly referred to as *Canada Renewable Energy* Appellate Body Report.] The Appellate Body issued, and the DSB adopted, the Reports on the same days. For most purposes, the Appellate Body treated the disputes as one, and—unless otherwise noted—such is the treatment herein.

The facts of this case are discussed in an earlier Chapter.

Legal Arguments:

Arguably, the most interesting issue in the entire 2013 *Canada Renewables Energy* case was the last substantive one with which the Appellate Body dealt, namely, the Panel findings under Article 1:1(b) of the *SCM Agreement*. The EU and Japan appealed the Panel finding that they, the complainants, failed to establish the challenged measures "confer[red] a benefit" within the meaning of Article 1:1(b). Ultimately, though the Appellate Body rejected the Panel analysis, the result was unchanged.

On appeal, Japan argued two claims and the EU made one. First, Japan contended the Panel erred in its interpretation of Article 1:1(b), because it limited the benefit analysis to the scope of Article 14(d) of the *SCM Agreement*. Second, Japan argued the Panel wrongly rejected the Japanese proposed benchmarks for the market analysis, and that the benchmark obtained by the Panel ignored the demand-side of the market. The EU also took issue with the market analysis by the Panel. The EU said the Panel should have simply recognized the "uncontested fact" that renewable energy electricity generators would not have obtained remuneration from the market in Ontario in absence of the disputed measures.

In response, Canada asserted the approaches of Japan and the EU ignored the Panel findings that the wholesale market administered by the IESO was not a "market" appropriate for a "benefit" analysis, and absent the disputed measures, new entrants into the wind- and solar PV-generated electricity market would likely still negotiate on price.[36] Moreover, Canada said the complainants' criticisms regarding the Panel's benchmark analysis were misplaced. As viewed by Canada, the Panel discussion about an alternative constructed benchmark was not a legal finding by the Panel.

Holdings and Rationale:

To address the first Japanese claim regarding interpretation, the Appellate Body sought guidance from relevant WTO jurisprudence to analyze the meaning of "benefit" within the meaning of Article 1:1(b) of the *SCM Agreement*. Citing the 1999 *Canada Aircraft* case, it recognized the determination of whether a benefit was conferred must include assessing whether the recipient received a financial contribution on terms more favorable than those available to the recipient on the market. Additionally, the Appellate Body observed that in *Canada Aircraft* in 1999, and *Airbus* in 2011, the Appellate Body relied on Article 14 as context for the interpretation of a benefit under Article 1:1(b).

From a purely textual perspective, Article 14 is directly applicable only to benefit calculations in countervailing duties cases. However, the Article does provide guidelines that may be useful during the determination of a benefit analysis, including Subparagraph (d) on whether a recipient is "better off."[37] According to the

---

36. *Canada Renewable Energy* Appellate Body Report, ¶ 5.146.
37. *Canada Renewable Energy* Appellate Body Report, ¶ 5.146.

Appellate Body, logic suggested that there must be a benchmark is necessary if one intends to determine whether a benefit was conferred. Thus, the Appellate Body rejected the Japan's first claim regarding the use of Article 14 of the *SCM Agreement* when analyzing whether a benefit was conferred under Article 1:1(b).

Turning to the application of Article 1:1(b) of the *SCM Agreement*, the Appellate Body quickly disagreed with the Panel approach to its analysis on three fronts. First, a benefit analysis should start with a definition of the relevant market, rather than conclude with it. In its view, any market comparisons undertaken by an adjudicating body must be done in the relevant market, or else no useful information will be gained.

Second, though electricity is physically identical regardless of how it is generated, that does not preclude the possibility that there may be factors that limit the demand-side substitutability of electricity. The Appellate Body said the Panel should have considered factors such as the type of contract, the size of the customer, and the type of electricity generated. Those factors, it said, may differentiate the market. Of particular concern to the Appellate Body were base-load and peak-load electricity needs for larger customers.

Third, the Appellate Body criticized the Panel for failing to analyze supply-side factors in its discussion of the potential relevant market. The Appellate Body pointed to its 2011 *Airbus* Report, in which it the stated evidence a supplier can switch its production from one product to another may show that two products share a market.

The Appellate Body went on to say supply-side factors suggest wind- and solar-PV producers of electricity could not compete with other, traditional, electricity producers due to differences in cost structures and operating costs and characteristics. The noted differences included high capital costs, low operating costs, fewer, if any, economies of scale, intermittent electricity production, and the inability to be used as base-load or peak-load electricity. The evidence showed conventional electricity generation was able to exercise price constraints on wind and solar power, but not *vice versa*. In the view of the Appellate Body, as long as the differences in costs for conventional and renewable electricity remained high, markets for wind- and solar PV-generated electricity would only exist as a matter of government regulation. The Appellate Body added, "the definition of a certain supply-mix by the government cannot in and of itself be considered as conferring a benefit."[38]

Expanding on its attack of the supply-side analysis by the Panel, the Appellate Body acknowledged final retail consumers may not differentiate between forms of electricity generation, but at the wholesale level, the government does differentiate in this regard. The Government of Ontario differentiated between forms of electricity when it defined the supply-side mix based on governmental policy decisions. The Appellate Body considered some policy concerns could include reducing

---

38. *See Canada Renewable Energy* Appellate Body Report, ¶ 5.175.

fossil fuels for the purpose of creating sustainable electricity markets, appeasing environmentally-conscious consumers, and dealing with certain externalities associated to particular types of electricity.

This discussion is worth mentioning because it was vital to the Appellate Body finding regarding the appropriate benchmark. The Appellate Body continued its criticisms of the Panel analysis when it stated that had the Panel thoroughly scrutinized supply-side factors in its analysis, the proper conclusion would have been clear. The Panel would have found "supply side factors suggest that important differences in cost structures and operating costs and characteristics among generating technologies prevent the very existence of wind power and solar PV generation, absent government definition of the energy supply-mix of electricity generation technologies."[39]

Having rejected the market benchmark by the Panel, the Appellate Body turned to identification of its own proper market benchmark. It began by reviewing Article 14(d) of the *SCM Agreement*, which deals with the calculation of a benefit relating to the provision of goods or services by a government, and states:

> [T]he provision of goods or services or purchase of goods by a government shall not be considered as conferring a benefit unless the provision is made for less than adequate remuneration, or the purchase is made for more than adequate remuneration. The adequacy of remuneration shall be determined in relation to prevailing market conditions for the good or service in question in the country of provision or purchase (including price, quality, availability, marketability, transportation and other conditions of purchase or sale).

The Appellate Body focused on two key aspects of Article 14(d).

First, it recognized the importance of the adequacy of remuneration. Second, it noted the significance of the term "prevailing market conditions."[40] Use of Article 14 is not required during the Article 1:1(b) "conferral of a benefit" analysis. Instead, Article 14 normally used once an illegal subsidy is found in order to calculate the benefit conferred. However, previous WTO adjudicators have used Article 14 as context. Here, the Appellate Body said the second of the two key aspects requires comparison to a market benchmark. The Appellate body also recalled that in its 2004 *U.S. Softwood Lumber IV* Report, it found when prices are distorted, an analysis may use an out-of-country benchmark or constructed benchmark, provided adjustments are made to reflect the conditions of the market in question.

Continuing on the topic of distorted markets, the Appellate Body said it did not think situations where governments intervened to create a market excluded the use of a market benchmark during the analysis pertaining to Article 1:1(b) of the *SCM Agreement*. It referred to the Hogan Report, an expert report relied upon by the

---

39. *Canada Renewable Energy* Appellate Body Report, ¶ 5.178.
40. *Canada Renewable Energy* Appellate Body Report, ¶ 5.178.

Panel, which emphasized the need for continuously balanced supply and demand. According to the report, and the view adopted by the Appellate Body, government intervention is required for the proper functioning of large-scale electricity grids, and no relevant market (to be used for comparison) would include unconstrained forces of supply and demand.

The Appellate Body then explained although renewable electricity costs more, from a monetary vantage point, it might have more value than non-renewable energy. Some of its positive externalities include long-term energy sustainability and less impact on the environment. Conversely, non-renewable electricity costs less, but may include negative externalities, such as adverse impacts on human health, fossil fuel energy emissions, and nuclear waste disposal.

And thus, the Appellate Body provided its own market benchmark, stating:

> ... [I]n view of the fact that the government's definition of the energy supply-mix for electricity generation does not *in and of itself* constitute a subsidy, we believe that benefit benchmarks for wind- and solar PV-generated electricity should be found in the markets for wind- and solar PV-generated electricity that result from the supply-mix definition. Thus, where the government has defined an energy supply-mix that includes wind power and solar PV electricity generation technologies, as in the present disputes, a benchmark comparison for purposes of a benefit analysis for wind power and solar PV electricity generation should be with the terms and conditions that would be available under market-based conditions for each of these technologies, taking the supply-mix as a given.[41]

However, before applying its own market benchmark, the Appellate Body reviewed the arguments presented by the EU and Japan.

The EU contended that use of hypothetical market counterfactuals or proxies was unnecessary. It its view, Appellate Body conclusion should have been simple, and relied on the uncontested fact that renewable energy electricity generators "would not have obtained any remuneration from the market in Ontario in view of the 'prevailing market conditions' where the same good (electricity) produced by using other generating technologies was much less remunerated."[42] Japan agreed with a similar assertion made in the dissenting Panel Report. In Japan's view, a benefit was present simply because "the history of the Ontario electricity market and the design, structure, and operation of the [disputed measures] demonstrate that solar PV and wind power generators would not be able to operate in the Ontario market without the [disputed measures]."[43]

The Appellate Body referred to the arguments by the EU, Japan and the dissenting Panel opinion as pleas for the use of a "but for" test. Simply put, but for the

---

41. *Canada Renewable Energy* Appellate Body Report, ¶ 5.190 (emphasis original).
42. *Canada Renewable Energy* Appellate Body Report, ¶ 5.190.
43. *Canada Renewable Energy* Appellate Body Report, ¶ 5.195.

measures in dispute, wind power and solar PV generators would be absent from the Ontario electricity market. The Appellate Body rejected this test. To it, the "but for" counterfactual presented by the EU, Japan and the dissenting Panel opinion pre-supposed that the relevant market is electricity generated from all energy sources. However, under the facts of this dispute, the government defined the energy supply-mix. Therefore, a separate market for wind- and solar PV-generated electricity was created.

Conversely, the Appellate Body agreed in part with Canada's definition of the market. Canada accepted that the HOEP and its derivatives were insufficient to attract investment in new generation technology of any kind but that prospective wind and solar PV generators would likely still negotiate a deal with the Government of Ontario. Even so, the Appellate Body found the markets for wind- and solar PV-generated electricity existed in Ontario only because of government intervention. The relevant question was whether wind power and solar PV electricity suppliers would have entered the wind- and solar PV-generated electricity markets absent the disputed measures, not whether they would have entered the blended wholesale electricity market.

Japan attempted to add support to the argument that the renewable energy electricity generators would not have existed in the market absent the disputed measures by suggesting its own relevant benchmarks based on Article 14(d). Japan introduced evidence regarding the weighted-average wholesale rate and the commodity portion of Ontario retail prices under the Regulated Price Plane (RPP).[44] The RPP retail prices were significantly lower than the rates provided by the disputed measures, and did not depend on the Hourly Ontario Energy Price (HOEP) because they were fixed by contract or regulation. The Panel rejected the benchmarks, saying that they were distorted by government intervention. Japan responded by citing the 2004 *Softwood Lumber* case, where it was argued a market influenced by government intervention still can serve as a relevant benchmark, and does not necessarily result in a circular comparison. The Japanese rationale, taken from *Softwood Lumber*, was that the inquiry at this stage in the analysis concerned the existence of a subsidy, not its size. Thus, though a government-influenced market might skew the prices, it did not always make it impossible to ascertain whether a subsidy existed.

Regardless, just as the Panel had done, though for different reasons, the Appellate Body rejected all of the proposed benchmarks available to it and the out-of-province benchmarks. In reality, the Appellate Body had no choice once it determined its own market benchmark. All of the proposed benchmarks were composed of blended electricity markets, and the Appellate Body found that the relevant benchmark must only include wind- and solar PV-generated electricity in a government regulated market.

---

44. *Canada Renewable Energy* Appellate Body Report, ¶ 5.195.

The Appellate Body then turned to arguments put forth by the EU and Japan, regarding the textual interpretation of Article 1:1(b) of the *SCM Agreement*. Japan and the EU argued that the Panel erred when it chose not to equate the meaning of "advantage" in the *chapeau* of Paragraph 1(a) of the *Illustrative List of the TRIMs Agreement* with the meaning of "benefit" under Article 1:1(b) of the *SCM Agreement*. The Panel said on these facts, it would satisfy the standard for an advantage under the *TRIMs Agreement*, but that the meaning of "benefit" was narrower.

In its 1999 *Canada Aircraft* Report, the Appellate Body, using the *Oxford English Dictionary*, defined "benefit" as an "advantage, good, gift, profit, or more generally, a favorable or helpful factor or circumstance."[45] However, it also, as suggested by the Panel, considered the scope of "advantage" to be larger than "benefit," as it stated "the ordinary meaning of 'benefit' clearly encompasses some form of advantage."[46] The Appellate Body here did not waiver from this earlier jurisprudence.

Lastly, in the Appellate Body's conclusion of its Panel analysis, it clarified the burden of persuasion present in a dispute under Article 1:1(b) of the *SCM Agreement*. As it stated, it is the duty of the complainant to providence evidence and arguments for the panel to objectively assess. But, as the Appellate Body stated in its 1998 *Beef Hormones* and 2003 *Certain Products* cases, Panels are allowed to develop their own legal reasoning to support their own findings and conclusions. Using this support, the Appellate Body criticized the Panel for limiting its analysis to the proposed benefit approach and benchmarks. Applying these principles, Japan and the EU had the burden to identify suitable potential benchmarks for a benefit analysis under Article 1:1(b). Here, in response to the Canadian benchmark suggestion, the EU did present evidence of non-blended markets containing only renewable energy. In the Appellate Body's view, the Panel should have explored those arguments and evidence relating to non-blended electricity markets. This error was enough for the Appellate Body to reverse the Panel finding that the complainants failed to establish the existence of a benefit.

The Appellate Body was left to decide whether sufficient factual findings and undisputed facts existed to allow it to complete the analysis and determinate whether a benefit was conferred under Article 1:1(b) of the *SCM Agreement*. Relying on its previous findings regarding the appropriate relevant market benchmark, the Appellate Body reviewed the evidence to see if it could complete the analysis. Unfortunately, the Appellate Body determined that absent any findings by the Panel regarding the adequacy of the proposed benchmarks for wind- and solar PV-generated electricity (*i.e.*, the RES initiatives), there was insufficient evidence to complete the analysis. Therefore, though it reversed the Panel finding regarding

---

45. *Canada Renewable Energy* Appellate Body Report, ¶ 5.207 (*quoting* Appellate Body Report, *Canada Aircraft*, ¶ 153) (*quoting The New Shorter Oxford English Dictionary*, 4th ed., L. Brown (ed.) (Clarendon Press, 1993)).

46. *Canada Renewable Energy* Appellate Body Report ¶ 5.207, (*quoting* Appellate Body Report, *Canada Aircraft*, ¶ 153).

Article 1:1(b), the result was unchanged. Canada emerged victorious in the battle under the *SCM Agreement*, but still lost the dispute under the previous findings by the Appellate Body under the GATT and the *TRIMs Agreement*.

Practicability of Market Benchmark Test?:

Ultimately, the *Canada — Renewable Energy* dispute amounted to a victory for the EU and Japan. The Appellate Body determined the FIT Program, with the domestic content requirements, was inconsistent with Article 2:1 of the *TRIMs Agreement* and Article III:4 of GATT. However, two interesting aspects of the dispute emerged relating to the benefit analysis under Article 1:1(b) of the *SCM Agreement* and the potential broader implications of the dispute, respectively.

First, though it was not significant to the case outcome, the Panel and Appellate Body analyses under Article 1:1(b) of the *SCM Agreement* were frustrating. The parties, given the jurisprudence using Article 14 in context of Article 1:1(b), were well prepared with evidence supporting their proposed market benchmarks. Yet, the Panel repeatedly rejected all of the benchmarks proposed to it. Then, after creating its own, the Panel was unable to complete its analysis because there was insufficient evidence.

When the Appellate Body examined the proposed benchmarks, and that of the Panel, it also rejected each of them and constructed its own. Again the outcome was unchanged, as the Appellate Body was also unable to complete its analysis. In hindsight, this underwhelming outcome is not surprising. Parties present evidence to the Panel with the view of supporting their arguments. Thus, if the eventual benchmark used is not one they considered, it is unlikely there will be evidence to support an analysis.

Over time, the measures at issue and the supporting evidence in WTO disputes has become increasingly complex. In an attempt to mount persuasive arguments for their claims, and provide relevant evidence to buttress them, countries spend millions of dollars per dispute (some estimates claim parties should expect to spend in the range of $10 million each for disputes that result in an Appellate Body Report). In the end, do the complex economic analyses and evidence of relevant markets really provide much value?

In this dispute, the EU and Japan asserted the conferral of a benefit analysis should have been relatively simple. As they asserted, "but for" the implementation of the FIT Program in Ontario, renewable energy electricity generators would not have had the opportunity to enter the wholesale electricity market. Additionally, from an admittedly simple perspective, does not the fact that renewable energy generators apply and remain in the program provide some evidence of a benefit? There is no requirement they enroll in the program to sell electricity into the grid. If they did not benefit from the program, then the generators of renewable energy would just sell electricity to the Government of Ontario and not be obligated to comply with any requirements of the FIT Program. Was the benefit analysis ever intended to be so complicated?

Broader Implications?:

Second, consider the ramifications of the case for future WTO disputes. An underlying characteristic of the case, understandably not directly addressed by the adjudicators, was the sensitive nature of the subject matter. Historically, WTO Members have not been aggressive in pushing matters relating to energy grids in foreign markets. Energy systems are vital to the economic and national security of countries. Absent reliable, consistent electricity, the digitalized electronic markets and computer systems running countries would be in jeopardy. Renewable energy arguably is not as sensitive, given it is still, for the lack of a better term, a bit of a luxury. That is to say, some argue renewable energy is not yet required with the current state of fossil-fuel based energy.

Nonetheless, the parties seemed careful to maintain that management of the supply mix, and the energy grid in general, fell within the realm of legitimate government policy objectives. In some respects, it appeared the Panel and the Appellate Body were cognizant of the potential sovereignty issues and attempted to ensure their decisions did not open the door to future disputes that could attack more significant aspects of a country's regulatory choices regarding energy.

- **2015 *China CVD* Case**[47]

Facts:[48]

This dispute arose in May 2012, following several initiation decisions, as well as preliminary and final determinations in 17 CVD investigations the DOC conducted between 2007 and 2012. The subject merchandise exported from China included aluminum extrusions, citric acid, drill pipe, kitchen shelving, lawn groomers, line pipe, magnesia bricks, oil country tubular goods, pressure pipe, print graphics, seamless pipe, steel cylinders, steel sinks, solar panels, thermal paper, wind towers, and wire strand.

The wide range of products was due to the scope of the legal questions involved. Between 2006 and 2012, DOC had engaged in 40 CVD investigations of Chinese goods, and applied rules based on the idea the Chinese market was distorted, and the Chinese Government controlled the exporting enterprises. So, in many instances, the DOC determined the provision of inputs was for less than adequate remuneration. China disagreed, and sued the U.S. at the WTO for what it claimed to be over 5 years of WTO-inconsistent treatment by the DOC.

---

47. Appellate Body Report, *United States—Countervailing Duty Measures on Certain Products from China*, WT/DS437/AB/R (adopted 16 January 2015). [Hereinafter, *China CVD* Appellate Body Report.] The Panel Report is *United States—Countervailing Duty Measures on Certain Products from China*, WT/DS437/R (adopted as modified by the Appellate Body, 16 January 2015). [Hereinafter, *China CVD* Panel Report.]

48. *See China CVD* Appellate Body Report, ¶¶ 1:1–1:6.

Determination and Calculation of "Benefit" under SCM Agreement Articles 1:1(b) and Article 14(d):[49]

Four issues were raised on appeal. The Appellate Body could not, or chose not, to complete the legal analysis with respect to some such issues. The key issues on which the Appellate Body was able to complete its legal analysis were the (1) determination and calculation of a "benefit" under Articles 1:1(b) and 14(d) of the *SCM Agreement*, and (2) sequence of analysis within the Specificity Test under Article 2:1 of *SCM Agreement*. (Issue (2) is discussed in a subsequent Chapter.)

The Appellate Body considered in-country private price benchmarks and the determination of a "benefit" under Article 1:1(b) of the *SCM Agreement*, in conjunction with Article 14(d) thereof. Recall Article 1:1 of the *SCM Agreement* defines the term "subsidy" as a "financial contribution" (or "any form of income or price support in the sense of [GATT] Article XVI") where a benefit is thereby conferred. In addition, Article 14 concerns CVD investigations. In particular, this provision concerns the calculation of the amount of a subsidy in terms of the "benefit" to the recipient. Of course, it must be a governmental entity of some sort that confers an alleged benefit.

China's Losing Argument on Relationship between Articles 1 and 14:

On appeal, China contended the legal standard for determining what constitutes "government," and specifically a "public body," in a "financial contribution" analysis under Article 1:1(a)(1)(iii) of the *SCM Agreement* also should apply when determining what constitutes "government" for purposes of the selection of a benefit benchmark under Article 14(d) of the *Agreement*. China was arguing that, based on previous WTO jurisprudence,[50] if government ownership and control are an insufficient basis to deem the provision of goods by an SOE to be "governmental" conduct under Article 1:1(a)(1)(iii), then such factors must be an insufficient basis for finding the provision of goods by an SOE constitutes "governmental" conduct under Article 14(d).

The Appellate Body agreed there is a single legal standard that defines the term "government" under the *SCM Agreement*. That term encompasses the government, both in the "narrow sense," and broadly "any public body within the territory of a Member."[51] But, the Appellate Body said the proper analysis for choosing a benefit benchmark under Article 14(d) does not depend on whether any relevant entities in the market fall within the definition of "government," even if a relevant entity is an SOE that is a a public body.[52]

---

49. *See China CVD* Appellate Body Report, ¶¶ 4:29–4:107.

50. China cited Appellate Body Report, *United States—Final Countervailing Duty Determination with respect to Certain Softwood Lumber from Canada*, WT/DS257/AB/R (adopted 20 December 2005), ¶¶ 93 and 101. [Hereinafter, *Softwood Lumber IV* Appellate Body Report.]

51. *See China CVD* Appellate Body Report, ¶ 4:42 (*citing Softwood Lumber IV* Appellate Body Report, ¶ 286).

52. *See China CVD* Appellate Body Report, ¶ 4:43.

In the view of the Appellate Body, China missed the core issue:[53]

> 4.43 [. . .] China's argument that there is a single standard for defining the term "government" does not answer the question of whether the prices of goods provided by private or government-related entities in the country of provision are to be considered as market determined for purposes of selecting a benefit benchmark. . . . [T]he term "government" appears *only* in the first sentence of Article 14(d), which establishes that "the provision of goods . . . by a *government* shall not be considered as conferring a benefit unless the provision is made for less than adequate remuneration." The first sentence of Article 14(d) thus provides guidance for assessing whether the provision of goods confers a benefit, following a previous affirmative determination that such provision of goods constitutes a financial contribution under Article 1:1(a)(1)(iii) that was carried out by a "government" as defined in Article 1:1(a)(1).

An important aspect of this Paragraph is a footnote omitted from the above quote.

In footnote 509, the Appellate Body stated it used "the term 'government-related entities' to refer to all government bodies, whether national or regional, public bodies, and any other government-owned entities for which there has not been a 'public body' determination."[54] Footnote 509 presents the 1st time WTO adjudicators have used the term "government-related entities." That matters, because it raises the question of whether there are 3 types of entities — "government," "public body," and "government-related" — for purposes of a market benchmark analysis.

The Appellate Body summarized its jurisprudence on the relationship between Article 1:1(b) and Article 14(d) of the *SCM Agreement*. Broadly, the "benefit" analysis under Article 1:1(b), and in turn under Article 14(d), implies a comparison is needed. That is because, as the Appellate Body famously put in 2000 in its *Canada Aircraft* Report,[55] no benefit is conferred to a recipient "unless the 'financial contribution' makes the recipient 'better off' than it would otherwise have been, absent that contribution."[56] So, under Article 14(d), a determination on adequacy of remuneration requires use of a market benchmark in comparison to the price of the government-provided good in question. As the Appellate Body stated in its 2002 *German Carbon Steel* Report regarding an Article 14(d) analysis, adequacy "shall be determined in relation to prevailing market conditions for the good or service in question in the country of provision or purchase."[57]

---

53. Footnotes omitted.

54. *See China CVD* Appellate Body Report, fn. 509.

55. *See* Appellate Body Report, *Canada—Measures Affecting the Export of Civilian Aircraft*, WT/DS70/AB/R (adopted 4 August 2000). [Hereinafter, *Canada Aircraft* Appellate Body Report.]

56. *See China CVD* Appellate Body Report, ¶ 4:44.

57. *See China CVD* Appellate Body Report, ¶ 4:45 (*quoting* WTO Appellate Body Report, *United States—Countervailing Duties on Certain Corrosion-Resistant Carbon Steel Flat Products*

The Appellate Body reiterated the point a determination under Article 14(d) does not hinge on whether the relevant entities constitute "public bodies" within the meaning of Article 1:1(a)(1). Rather, it depends on whether investigating authorities in the importing country correctly reach the conclusion that price distortion in the market, due to governmental intervention, warrants recourse to an alternative benchmark. Put colloquially, the Appellate Body told China: "it does not matter what you call the entities in question; what matters is whether the investigating authority adequately evaluates, on a case-by-case basis, whether the market is distorted given the evidence available."

China's Winning Argument on Facts:

The Appellate Body next applied the law to the facts, ultimately finding in favor of China. Even though the Appellate Body found the Panel correctly understood previous WTO jurisprudence, it held the Panel did not properly apply the standard required by Article 14(d) to the determinations China challenged. The Appellate Body said the Panel failed to conduct a case-by-case analysis of the DOC's work, namely: did the DOC properly examine whether the relevant in-country prices were (1) market determined, or (2) distorted by governmental intervention? Instead, the Panel blithely assumed China failed to establish the DOC acted inconsistently with Article 14(d).[58] Hence, the Appellate Body reversed the relevant Panel findings.

The Appellate Body then completed the legal analysis under Articles 1:1(b) and 14(d) of the *SCM Agreement* pertaining to four CVD investigations, as follows:

(1) *Oil Country Tubular Goods*: The Appellate Body found the DOC did not consider whether the prices of Chinese-owned or -controlled firms "as such" were market determined. Instead, the DOC accepted, without examination, the relevant prices were distorted by government intervention. Contrary to the 2014 *India Carbon Steel* Appellate Body Report, the Panel assumed any entity "owned or controlled" by the Chinese government could be treated as a "public body."[59]

(2) *Solar Panels*: The Appellate Body noted the DOC found 37 out of the 47 producers of polysilicon in China were the entities through which the Chinese Government influenced and distorted the market of polysilicon. But, the DOC failed to explain whether and how the relevant 37 producers

---

from Germany, WT/DS213/AB/R ¶ 157 (adopted 19 December 2002) (hereinafter, *German Carbon Steel* Appellate Body Report)).

58. The Panel made this erroneous assumption based on the Appellate Body facing a similar situation in the 2014 *U.S. China AD-CVD* case. *See* Appellate Body Report, *United States—Countervailing and Anti-Dumping Measures on Certain Products from China*, WT/DS449/AB/R (adopted 22 July 2014).

59. *See China CVD* Appellate Body Report, ¶ 4:92 (*quoting* Appellate Body Report, *United States—Countervailing Measures on Certain Hot-Rolled Carbon Steel Flat Products from India*, WT/DS436/AB/R ¶ 4:10 (adopted 19 December 2014) "mere ownership or control over an entity by a government, without more, is not sufficient to establish that the entity is a public body").

possessed and exerted market power in a manner that distorted other in-country prices.

(3) *Pressure Pipe*: The Appellate Body recalled the Panel found SOEs accounted for approximately 82% of the relevant pressure pipe production in China during the POI. Again, the Appellate Body found the Panel rushed to judgment and, consequently, assumed the prices of government-related entities automatically were distorted due to the relationship with the Chinese Government.

(4) *Line Pipe*: The Appellate Body called to mind the DOC, on the basis of AFA, found prices stemming from private transactions within China could not give rise to an undistorted price. However, the Appellate Body reasoned "the relevant inquiry for purposes of finding a proper benchmark under Article 14(d) . . . is whether or not certain in-country prices are distorted, rather than whether such prices originate from a particular source (*e.g.*, government-owned entities)."[60]

In essence, with respect to determining and calculating a "benefit" under the *SCM Agreement*, China "lost the battle, but won the war."

The Appellate Body was unconvinced by China's legal argument that if an entity is not a "public body" for purposes of Article 1 of the *Agreement*, then it is not "government" for purposes of Article 14. The Appellate Body held that argument to be irrelevant. Instead, the Appellate Body identified the vital inquiry to be whether the prices of goods provided by a private or government-related entity in a subsidizing country are market determined for purposes of selecting a "benefit" benchmark. But, when the Appellate Body engaged in this inquiry with respect to the facts of the case, China emerged victorious. The Appellate Body held the DOC repeatedly assumed, without sufficient evidence, that the market in China was distorted. Therein lay the U.S. violation.

---

60. *See China CVD* Appellate Body Report, ¶ 4:105.

Chapter 14

Definition of "Subsidy,"
Third Element: Specificity Test[1]

I. Purpose

Having identified a "subsidy" in the sense of a governmental financial contribution that "confers a benefit," it becomes necessary to consider whether that "subsidy" is directed specifically to certain beneficiaries. Not every "subsidy" is or should be countervailable, because governments have a legitimate interest in supporting certain activities, like police and fire services, infrastructure development, and educational services. The Specificity Test in Article 2 of the WTO *SCM Agreement* (and American CVD law, in 19 U.S.C. § 1677(5)(A), (5A)) is indispensable in delineating lawful (*i.e.*, non-countervailable) from unlawful (*i.e.*, countervailable) subsidies.

The Specificity Test, which is not new in CVD jurisprudence, checks to ensure whether a subsidy is provided to certain enterprises.

> As the Court of International Trade (CIT) made clear in 1983 in the *Carlisle Tire* case, the basic purpose of the specificity test is to serve as a means for differentiating between government assistance that genuinely is available broadly and used widely throughout an economy and subsidies provided to or used by discrete segments of the economy. Thus, while the specificity test is intended to avoid the imposition of countervailing duties in situations where a subsidy is widely available and used throughout an economy, it must not be allowed to serve as a means for avoiding the imposition of duties in other circumstances. The [Senate Finance] Committee welcomes and supports the intention of the Administration, as set out in the *Statement of Administrative Action* [for the *SCM Agreement*], to apply the specificity test "in light of its original purpose, which is to function as an initial screening mechanism to winnow out only those foreign

---

1. Documents References:
   (1) *Havana (ITO) Charter*, Articles 25–28, 34
   (2) *GATT* Articles VI, XVI
   (3) WTO *SCM Agreement*

subsidies which truly are broadly available and widely used throughout an economy."[2]

The Specificity Test helps mediate the tension between the legitimate interest of exporting countries to subsidize certain projects and the legitimate interest of importing countries to assure a level competitive playing field for their domestic producers.

Accordingly, to be countervailable, a subsidy must be "specific" to an enterprise, industry, or group of enterprises or industries. Conversely, suppose government assistance is both generally available and widely and evenly distributed throughout the jurisdiction of the subsidizing authority. Then, it is not countervailable. Article 2:4 of the *SCM Agreement* requires a specificity determination to be "clearly substantiated on the basis of positive evidence." Thus, contrary to pre-Uruguay Round DOC practice, there is a presumption of non-specificity.

What economic rationale justifies the Specificity Test? In general, a subsidy that is generally available is less likely to create distortions in trade and output patterns than a subsidy that is specific to exporters. Consider, for example, a case where the German government wants to improve economic conditions in the former East Germany. It provides a subsidy to any German company that builds a factory in the former East Germany so long as the factory employs at least 100 workers for five years. The subsidy covers the extra costs associated with building a factory in that location, such as roads, extensions of water, sewage, and natural gas pipes, and additional power generation stations. Because the subsidy is available to a company regardless of the type of merchandise it manufactures and regardless of whether it exports its output, no distortion in the pattern of German output or exports should occur, nor should there be any adverse effects on a foreign country.

In this hypothetical, suppose as a matter of practice the subsidy is used only by exporters of certain merchandise. There still may be trade distortive effects. The German government—or any clever drafter of a subsidy program—could make the subsidy generally available, but attach conditions that make it useful only to some exporters. This supposition intimates the need to recognize—and obliterate—any distinction between *de jure* and *de facto* specificity. Both sorts of specific subsidies ought to be actionable. Fortunately, this distinction is explicit in the *SCM Agreement* (and American CVD law).

The Specificity Test works in tandem with the Traffic Light System, which places subsidies into one of three categories: (1) "Red Light," or prohibited, subsidies, which are countervailable; (2) "Yellow Light" or "Dark Amber" subsidies, which are collectively called "actionable" subsidies, and which may be countervailed; and

---

2. SENATE COMMITTEE ON FINANCE, SENATE COMMITTEE ON AGRICULTURE, NUTRITION, AND FORESTRY, AND SENATE COMMITTEE ON GOVERNMENTAL AFFAIRS, URUGUAY ROUND AGREEMENTS ACT, SENATE REPORT NUMBER 412, 103d Congress, 2d Sess. 88, at 92–93 (1994).

(3) "Green Light," or non-actionable subsidies, which (while the category existed) could not be countervailed.

II. Case Law on Third Element: 2011 *U.S. AD-CVD*, 2011 *Airbus*, 2012 *Boeing*, and 2015 *China CVD*

In several high-profile cases, the WTO Appellate Body distinguished specific from non-specific subsidies.[3] In them, it applied *SCM Agreement* Articles 1:2, 2, and 8:1.

• 2011 *U.S. AD-CVD*[4]

Not until the 2011 *U.S. AD-CVD* dispute did the Appellate Body have its first substantive opportunity to address the Specificity Test of Article 2 of the *SCM Agreement*.[5] In its appeal, China disagreed with the Panel interpretation and application of Article 2:1(a) of the *SCM Agreement* in respect of the DOC determination

---

3. In addition to the cases discussed below, in the 2014 *India Carbon Steel* case, the Appellate Body considered the issue of what "*de facto* specificity" means under Article 2:1(c) of the *SCM Agreement. See India Carbon Steel* Appellate Body Report, ¶¶ 193–205, 261–265. This case is discussed, and its facts summarized, in an earlier Chapter. The Report on this topic, however, is not especially enlightening.

India appealed (*inter alia*) the Panel analysis with respect to the DOC determination that the sale of iron ore by NMDC was "specific" under Article 2:1(c). India's first argument was a 2-pronged attack on the Panel interpretation of this Article. As to the first prong, India interpreted the word "of" between "limited number" and "certain enterprises" in Article 2:1(c). India said this phrasing indicates the beneficiaries of a subsidy program in question must form a subset of the "certain enterprises" being examined. The Appellate Body disagreed, holding the better interpretation was the provision is meant to apply to a group of enterprises whose quantity is limited.

The second prong of the first Indian argument was based on a similar concept of dependence or relate-ability. India argued the first factor under Article 2:1(c) requires a finding of discrimination between certain enterprises and similarly situated enterprises. However, the Appellate Body considered said the relational concept is limited to the third factor of Article 2:1(c), and thus upheld the Panel's findings.

India also claimed the Panel erred by allowed for a finding that a government provision of goods under Article 2:1(c) of the *SCM Agreement* can be "*de facto* specific," based merely on the inherent limitations on use of the goods provided. According to India, if a good is scarce, or the distribution is limited by the government, then a finding of "financial contribution" automatically would force a finding of specificity, a result which would render the Article 2:1(c) inutile. That is, India argued that if the inherent characteristics of a subsidized good limit the possible use of the subsidy to a certain industry, then the subsidy will not be "specific," unless access to this subsidy is further limited to a subset of this industry.

Here, too, the Appellate Body disagreed with India. The Appellate Body said that although such conclusions could be reached in any dispute, they still remain distinct from one another. Therefore, the Appellate Body upheld the Panel.

4. This case is cited, and its facts summarized, earlier in this Chapter.

5. The Appellate Body briefly addressed specificity in *Korea DRAMs*, but the finding was based solely on a previous finding relating to entrustment and direction under Article 1:1(a)(1)(iv) of the *SCM Agreement.*

that the provision of SOCB lending in the OTR investigation was specific to the tire industry.[6]

Holding:

The Appellate Body Report contained 3 general holdings, all in favor of the U.S. First, it upheld the Panel interpretations of "subsidy" and "explicitly," under Article 2:1(a). It found availability of a subsidy could be limited explicitly to the financial contribution or benefit conferred; such access does not need to be restricted both as to financial contribution and benefit in order to meet the Specificity Test. That is, "specificity" refers either to access of an enterprise or industry to a financial contribution, or to a benefit conferred on an enterprise or industry. While "specificity" could cover both, depending on the facts of the case, it need not, meaning there is no need to prove that a financial contribution is specific, and also the attendant benefit is specific, to meet the Specificity Test. That is because the two concepts (financial contribution and benefit) are tied, so if one is specific, the other one will be, too.

Second, the Appellate Body upheld the Panel finding regarding the application by the DOC of Article 2:1(a). The evidence in the record did not support the Chinese appeal.[7] Easily, the first holding, being one of interpretation as opposed to application, was the one of greatest enduring value.

---

6. In its appeal, China also claimed the Panel erred in its interpretation of the term "subsidy" in Article 2:2, when it reviewed the DOC regional specificity determination in the LWS investigation. The Panel found the DOC "acted inconsistently with the obligations of the U.S. under Article 2 of the *SCM Agreement* by determining that government provision of land-use rights, in the LWS investigation, was regionally-specific." *See U.S. AD-CVD* Appellate Body Report, ¶ 402. Interestingly, even though the Panel ruled in favor of China on this issue, China appealed nonetheless, because it was concerned with the systemic implication that could flow from the Panel reasoning.

Moreover, the Chinese appeal was narrow. First, it asked the Appellate Body to find the Panel erred when it said Article 2:2 of the *SCM Agreement* permits a finding of specificity based solely on a showing that financial contributions — rather than the subsidy — is geographically limited. The U.S. responded such a position relies on the erroneous interpretation China already put forth regarding Article 2:1(a), and thus should fail. The Appellate Body agreed, reiterating any limitation on access to a financial contribution also will limit access to any resulting benefit.

Next, China said the Appellate Body should reverse the Panel finding that existence of a "distinct regime" is relevant to a determination of specificity under Article 2:2. China contended the Panel finding suggested a subsidy would be regionally specific if provided as part of a "distinct regime," even if the identical subsidy were also available elsewhere.

In actuality, China was concerned with *dicta* by the Panel, in which it said if it had evidence relevant to whether a "unique regime" existed in a Chinese industrial park, then "it might have resulted in a finding of regional specificity consistent with Article 2:2 of the *SCM Agreement*." *Id.*, ¶ 417. To China, the same subsidy does not become "a different subsidy merely because it is provided under a distinct 'program' or 'regime.'" *Id*, ¶ 418. The Appellate Body rejected the premise of the Chinese appeal, and said it was not necessary to consider further. In the view of the Appellate Body, the language contested by China simply qualified a factual finding, and was case-specific.

7. The appeal against the application of Article 2:1(a) came in 2 parts. First, China argues the Panel failed to apply its own interpretation of the terms "subsidy" and "explicitly" to the facts of this dispute. Second, China contended the Panel erred in finding that policy lending subsidies were limited to "certain enterprises" within the meaning of Article 2:1(a) of the *SCM Agreement*.

Rationale:

The Chinese appeal covered Articles 2:1 and 2:2 of the *SCM Agreement*. China argued against the Panel interpretation and application of Article 2:1(a), and its application of Article 2:2. So, as to Article 2:1(a), China: (1) disagreed with the Panel interpretation of the terms "subsidy" and "explicitly," and (2) alleged the Panel erred in its application of Article 2:1(a) as to the DOC determination of *de jure* specificity in respect of SOCB lending in the OTR investigation.

The Appellate Body recognized this case was one of first impression in respect of its interpretative issues under Article 2 of the *SCM Agreement*. So, it began with the text and a summary of that provision:

> Its first paragraph sets out a number of principles for determining whether a subsidy is specific by virtue of its limitation to an enterprise or industry or group of enterprises or industries ("certain enterprises"). Article 2:2 of the *SCM Agreement* identifies limitations related to the geographical location of beneficiaries that render a subsidy "regionally" specific. Article 2:3 deems all prohibited subsidies within the meaning of Article 3 (export subsidies

---

According to China, even if the Appellate Body accepted the Panel interpretation of specificity under Article 2:1(a), the Panel finding that SOCBs were instructed to provide financing to the "encouraged" projects did not identify an explicit limitation on access to the relevant financial contribution. *Id.*, ¶ 382. In particular, the SOCBs also provided loan to the industries under the "permitted" category, which encompassed the entire range of economic activity in China that did not fall within the encouraged, restricted, and eliminated categories. *Id.*, ¶ 382. The U.S. responded there was no evidence in the record to support the proposition SOCB lending also was available to the "permitted" category.

The Appellate Body found the Chinese understanding of the Panel finding was too broad. The Panel did not find that projects and industries under the "permitted" rubric were eligible to receive the same loans as the "encouraged" projects and industries. Instead, the Panel found projects and industries not falling within the 3 categories were to be regarded as "permitted." There was no evidence on the issue of how financial institutions were to conduct themselves as to projects and industries within that category.

Next, China alleged the Panel erred in finding that the 539 "encouraged" industries were "described in very specific and narrowly-circumscribed terms." *Id.*, ¶ 387. Instead, the industries represented a broad segment of economic activity. Additionally, China contends the Panel erroneously relied on the "restricted" and "eliminated" categories in reaching its conclusion that the "encouraged" industries constituted "certain enterprises." The U.S. countered the "described in very specific and narrowly-circumscribed terms" Panel finding was a factual finding, thus, not subject to review.

In reality, the Appellate Body analysis on this issue concerned itself with the Panel reasoning as compared to that of the DOC. The DOC specificity determination was based on documents at all government levels relating to the measures at issue. However, the Panel analysis focused on the significance of the "restricted," "eliminated," and "permitted" categories of projects and industries. However, upon further analysis, the Appellate Body felt comfortable finding the Panel had considered the DOC examination, and appeared to accept that the documents, taken together, demonstrated a clear lending policy directed to favor the tire industry.

Therefore, the Appellate Body upheld the Panel finding that China did not establish the DOC acted inconsistently with the obligations of the U.S. under Article 2:1(a) of the *SCM Agreement* by determining in the OTR investigation that SOCB lending was specific to the tire industry.

and import substitution subsidies) to be specific. Lastly, Article 2:4 requires that any determination of specificity be "clearly substantiated on the basis of positive evidence."[8]

Focusing on Article 2:1, the Appellate Body looked to the *chapeau* for interpretative guidance as to the scope and meaning of the subsequent Sub-Paragraphs.

Using the *chapeau*, the Appellate Body said the central inquiry is whether a subsidy is specific to "certain enterprises," and the principles in Sub-Paragraphs (a)–(c) apply in that examination. Additionally, the use of the term "principles," rather than "rules," suggests "subparagraphs (a) through (c) are to be considered within an analytical framework that . . . accords appropriate weight to each principle."[9] Thus, no one Sub-Paragraph of Article 2:1 necessarily determines specificity.

Turning to the Sub-Paragraphs, the Appellate Body said:

> . . . [Articles 2:1(a)–(c)] . . . set out indicators as to whether the conduct or instruments of the granting authority discriminate or not: Article 2:1(a) describes limitations on eligibility that favor certain enterprises, whereas Article 2:1(b) describes criteria or conditions that guard against selective eligibility. Finally, Article 2:1(c) sets out that, notwithstanding any appearance of non-specificity resulting from the principles laid down in subparagraphs (a) and (b), other factors may be considered if there are reasons to believe that a subsidy may, in fact, be specific in a particular case.[10]

The critical feature in Sub-Paragraphs (a) and (b) is eligibility. The question is not whether the government grants a subsidy to certain enterprises, but rather whether access to that subsidy is limited. Sub-Paragraphs (a) and (b) are not mutually exclusive. A subsidy might be specific under Article 2:1(a), yet should non-specific under Article 2:1(b). For example, a subsidy is "specific" under Sub-Paragraph (a) if it is explicitly limited to certain enterprises. But, it is non-specific under Sub-Paragraph (b) if the eligibility criteria, manifest in law, are objective, automatic, and scrupulously applied. Where Sub-Paragraphs (a) and (b) are not conclusive, as in this example, it is necessary to apply Sub-Paragraph (c). As a result, absent unequivocal indication of specificity or non-specificity, the principles of Article 2:1 are to be interpreted together. Simply put, all 3 Sub-Paragraphs should be checked.

The Chinese appeal focused on the proper interpretation of "explicitly." As defined by the *OED*, the adverbial form of "explicitly" signifies "[d]istinctly expressing all that is meant; leaving nothing merely implied or suggested; unambiguous; clear."[11] So, rather mechanically, the Appellate Body said specificity under Article 2:1(a) exists when "the limitation on access to the subsidy to certain enterprises is

---

8. *U.S. AD-CVD* Appellate Body Report, ¶ 364.
9. *U.S. AD-CVD* Appellate Body Report, ¶ 366.
10. *U.S. AD-CVD* Appellate Body Report, ¶ 367.
11. *U.S. AD-CVD* Appellate Body Report, ¶ 372.

express, unambiguous, or clear from the content of the relevant instrument, and not merely 'implied' or 'suggested.'"[12]

Turning to the term "certain enterprises," the Appellate Body looked to the *chapeau* of Article 2:1. It refers to "an enterprise or industry or group of enterprises or industries." The *OED* defines "certain" as "[k]nown and particularized but not explicitly identified; (with sing. noun) a particular, (with pl. noun) some particular, some definite."[13] Additionally, it defines the word "group," as "[a] number of people or things regarded as forming a unity or whole on the grounds of some mutual or common relation or purpose, or classed together because of a degree of similarity."[14] Moreover, "enterprise" is a "[a] business firm, a company," whereas "industry" signifies "[a] particular form or branch of productive labor; a trade, a manufacture."[15] Lastly, the Appellate Body looked to *Upland Cotton*, where the Panel said "certain enterprises" requires a case-by-case analysis, but that the term suggests a single enterprise or industry, or a class of enterprises or industries that are known and particularized.[16]

China thought the relevant inquiry under Article 2:1(a) is whether the words of legislation limit access to the financial contribution and its associated benefit. After all, the *chapeau* of Article 2:1 expressly refers to "a subsidy, as defined in paragraph 1 of Article 1 [of the *SCM Agreement*]." The U.S. disagreed: a financial contribution and benefit from it do not have to be set forth explicitly at law to conclude that access is limited to certain enterprises. Rather, access to a subsidy could be limited explicitly to the financial contribution, or benefited conferred, but not both. That is, specificity in respect of one or the other (financial contribution or benefit) is enough to meet the Article 2 Specificity Test. That is because "financial contribution" and "benefit" are sufficiently closely related that specificity as to one surely entails specificity as to the other.

The Appellate Body agreed with the U.S. What matters is whether there is a limitation on access to a subsidy to certain enterprises, regardless of how that explicit limitation is established. The Appellate Body reasoned that financial contribution and benefit are tied. For example:

> [A]n explicit limitation on access to a financial contribution would necessarily entail a limitation on access to the benefit conferred, since only the enterprises or industries eligible for that financial contribution would be eligible to enjoy the benefit resulting therefrom.[17]

So, the Appellate Body upheld the Panel interpretation of *SCM Agreement* Article 2:1(a).

---

12. *U.S. AD-CVD* Appellate Body Report, ¶ 372.
13. *U.S. AD-CVD* Appellate Body Report, ¶ 373.
14. *U.S. AD-CVD* Appellate Body Report, ¶ 373.
15. *U.S. AD-CVD* Appellate Body Report, ¶ 373.
16. *U.S. AD-CVD* Appellate Body Report, ¶ 373.
17. *See U.S. AD-CVD* Appellate Body Report, ¶ 377.

Conclusion:

The value of the 2011 *U.S. AD-CVD* dispute, insofar as it relates to the Specificity Test, is straightforward. To satisfy the specificity requirement of Article 2.1(a), access to a subsidy may be explicitly limited to the financial contribution or the benefited conferred. Financial contribution and benefit conferred are tied, thus access to a subsidy does not need to be explicitly limited to both.

• **2011 *Airbus*[18]**

Not long after penning its 2011 *U.S. AD-CVD* decision, the Appellate Body again addressed specificity in its 2011 *Airbus* Report. In *Airbus*, the EU appealed the Panel finding that certain R&TD grants provided to Airbus were specific under *SCM Agreement* Article 2:1(a).

Losing Argument:

The EU put forth a rather weak argument regarding the aeronautic-related R&TD funding. Under its reading of the EC Framework Program, aeronautic researching funding was not available under the general funding provided by the Program. So, funding provisions designed for aeronautics research was needed to ensure this research had a support scheme comparable to that available under general funding for non-aeronautics research. But, said the European Union — rather incredulously — such provisions did not mean the support was specific to the aeronautics industry.

Holding:

The Appellate Body upheld the Panel finding that the R&TD subsidies granted to Airbus under each of the EC Framework Programs were "specific" under Article 2:1(a) of the *SCM Agreement*.

Rationale:

Not surprisingly, the Appellate Body began by adopting its recent interpretation of Article 2:1 in *U.S. AD-CVD* as to the central inquiry regarding "certain enterprises" and use of the term "principles," rather than "rules," in the *chapeau*. Citing itself, it said: "the application of one of the Sub-Paragraphs of Article 2:1 may not by itself be determinative in arriving at a conclusion that a particular subsidy is or is not specific."[19] Thus, the Appellate Body again cautioned against "examining specificity on the basis of the application of a particular Sub-Paragraph of Article 2:1, when the potential for application of other Sub-Paragraphs is warranted in the light of the nature and content of measures challenged in a particular case."[20]

The EU argued the Panel should have looked at each EC Framework Program as a whole to determine the existence of specificity under Article 2:1(a) of the *SCM Agreement*. Some EC Framework Programs limited access to certain R&TD projects

---

18. This case is cited, and its facts summarized, earlier in this Chapter.
19. *Airbus* Appellate Body Report, ¶ 942.
20. *Airbus* Appellate Body Report, ¶ 945.

to aeronautics, because those aeronautics projects did not have access to funds under the remainder of the EC Framework Program budgets. When viewed holistically, allocation of funding to aeronautics-related research ensured equal access. The U.S. successfully showed the facts did not support the European view.

The Appellate Body quickly rejected the European argument. It accepted the Panel finding that the EC Framework Programs targeted funding to economic activities in both horizontal (for all sectors) and sector-specific ways (for aeronautics only, or for other sectors only). Thus, even without sector-specific aeronautic funding, aeronautics-related R&TD funding was accessible by the general EC Framework Program budgets. There was no need for the EU to create sector-specific funding for aeronautics R&TD projects, because these projects did, in fact, qualify for support under the general (horizontal) schemes. In creating sector-specific funding for aeronautics, the European Union was giving aeronautics, in particular, a boost. Therein lay the specificity.

In accord with its *U.S. AD-CVD* decision, the Appellate Body also considered the need for further analysis under Article 2:1(b) of the *SCM Agreement*. However, neither party advanced arguments concerning the applicability of Article 2:1(b), and the Appellate Body did not consider that the Panel record called for a review of the objective criteria or conditions under Article 2:1(b). The Appellate Body did not feel it was warranted to consider further analysis under Article 2:1(c), because the foregoing analysis did not give rise to an "appearance of non-specificity."[21]

Conclusion:

Airbus added little value as to Specificity Test jurisprudence. The Appellate Body Report simply adopted the interpretation of Article 2:1 of the *SCM Agreement* from *U.S. AD-CVD*. Though Appellate Body Reports technically not binding on non-parties, Reports such as *Airbus* are evidence that, in effect, *stare decisis* is alive in WTO adjudication.

- **2012 *Boeing***[22]

The year after its *Airbus* Report, the Appellate Body again addressed specificity under Article 2 of the *SCM Agreement* in its *Boeing* Report. The Appellate Body examined specificity as it related to three of the disputed measures: the (1) allocation of patent rights by NASA and DOD; (2) Washington State B&O Tax Rate Reduction; and (3) City of Wichita, Kansas IRBs. Ultimately, the Appellate Body upheld the Panel findings regarding each of the relevant measures at issue, favoring the U.S. on the first measure (finding it to be non-specific), and the EU on the second and third measures (finding them to be specific).

---

21. *Airbus* Appellate Body Report, ¶ 951.

22. *See* Appellate Body Report, *United States — Measures Affecting Trade in Large Civil Aircraft — Second Complaint*, WT/DS353/AB/R (adopted 23 March 2012). [Hereinafter, *Boeing* Appellate Body Report.] The facts of this case are summarized in an earlier in this Chapter.

Holdings:

As to the allocation of patent rights, the Appellate Body rendered 3 holdings. First, the term "granting authority" in Article 2:1 could be interpreted broadly (such as referring to an entire government, and not simply an agency or department). Second, the allocation of patent rights was not *de jure* specific, because the NASA and DOD contracts followed the same rules as were available to government contractors generally. Third, the EU failed to adduce evidence sufficient to prove *de facto* specificity.

The Appellate Body was quick in its analysis pertaining to the Washington State B&O Tax Rate Reduction. The Appellate Body rejected the American appeal, and said the Panel correctly examined the evidence when it decided the Washington State B&O Tax Rate Reduction was specific under Article 2:1(a) of the *SCM Agreement*.

Regarding the City of Wichita IRB subsidies, the Appellate Body agreed with the U.S. that perhaps another test would be reasonable when examining why the granting of a subsidy was disproportionate. But, it said the U.S. failed to provide sufficient counterevidence. So, the Appellate Body found the IRB subsidies were specific under Article 2:1(c) of the *SCM Agreement*.

Specificity, Allocation of Patent Rights, and European Union Losing Arguments:

On appeal, the EU disagreed with the Panel finding that even if the NASA Procurement Contracts and DOD Assistant Instruments constituted "subsidies" under Article 1:1 of the *SCM Agreement*, they were not "specific" under Article 2:1 of the *Agreement*. Allocation of patent rights under the relevant Contracts and Instruments, said the EU, was one reason for specificity. The U.S. countered that an item (such as patent rights) that is the product of a subsidy (pursuant to the Contracts and Instruments) cannot itself constitute a subsidy.

The Appellate Body addressed each European argument and Panel finding.[23] First, the EU said the Panel erred in the interpretation of Article 2:1(a) of the *SCM*

---

23. Note the Appellate Body disagreed with the *arguendo* approach to specificity used by the Panel. Under this approach, a Panel skips the first part of an analysis and assumes it to be true (*e.g.,* a "subsidy" exists). Based on this assumption, it moves to the second part of the analysis (*e.g.,* the assumed subsidy is "specific"). The *arguendo* approach essentially is a short cut, whereby a Panel has a view on specificity, and is eager to express that view, without bothering with a subsidy analysis.

The Panel thought its adoption of an *arguendo* approach was consistent with the 2010 *China Audiovisual Products* Appellate Body Report. As such, the Panel chose to assess the issue of specificity before addressing whether the disputed measures were subsidies under Article 1:1 of the *SCM Agreement*. However, the *arguendo* approach "may also be problematic for certain types of legal issues, for example, issues that go to the jurisdiction of a panel or preliminary questions on which the substance of a subsequent analysis depends." *See Boeing* Appellate Body Report, ¶ 739 (*quoting Boeing* Panel Report, fn. 2933 ¶ 7.1294). In this case, the failure to assess first whether a subsidy exists was problematic, because there was potentially overlap in claims put forward by the EU. Additionally, a negative finding on the issue of specificity would leave the Article 1:1 appeal unanswered.

Put simply, the Appellate Body does not like Panels to take an *arguendo* approach because if the Appellate Body disagrees with the outcome of the Panel, then it is difficult or impossible to re-do the analysis. Here, the Panel assumed a "subsidy" exists, and then moved to "specificity." But, if the

Agreement. Second, the EU stated the Panel mistakenly applied Article 2:1(a). Third, the EU alleged the Panel failed to address its claim of *de facto* specificity under Article 2:1(c). The EU lost all 3 arguments.

On the first claim, the EU said the Panel was wrong to consider the American government "as a whole" could be a "granting authority" under Article 2:1, rather than limiting the "granting authority" title to NASA and the DOD. At issue, then, was what entity is granting each subsidy: the entire government, or one agency? In the American view, nothing in the text of Article 2:1(a) prevents a Panel from considering multiple authorities participating in the subsidy granting process to be part of the "granting authority." Thus, the first substantive issue was the definition of "granting authority."

As expected, the Appellate Body began by recalling its own interpretation of Article 2:1 in the 2011 *U.S. AD-CVD* and Airbus Reports. In particular, the Appellate Body focused on language it used in these precedents:

> [T]he reference in subparagraphs (a) and (b) of Article 2:1 to "the granting authority, or the legislation pursuant to which the granting authority operates," is critical because it situates the analysis for assessing any limitations on eligibility in the particular legal instrument or government conduct effecting such limitations. In other words, the source of any limitation is the legislation pursuant to which the granting authority operates, or the granting authority itself.[24]

The Appellate Body coupled these precedents with use of the term "subsidy program" in Article 2:1(c), which the Appellate Body said intimates a potentially large scheme that could implicate numerous organs of a government. So, the Appellate Body held the term "granting authority" does not preclude the possibility of multiple granting authorities. Thus, it rejected the European appeal regarding the interpretation of Article 2:1(a).

Second, the Appellate Body addressed whether the Panel erred in its application of Article 2:1(a). The question before the Appellate Body was whether, assuming the allocation of patent rights under the NASA Procurement Contract and DOD Assistance Instruments was a self-standing subsidy (as distinct from payments and other support), access to this subsidy (the patent rights) was explicitly limited to certain enterprises.

Under general principles of American patent law, an inventor is the initial owner of any rights stemming from the invention of that owner. Those rights include the right to (1) exclude others from manufacturing or using the patented technology, (2) license the technology to others, and (3) assign or transfer the patent. Regarding

---

Appellate Body disagrees with the Panel "specificity" analysis, it cannot re-do the Panel "subsidy" analysis—because there was none. It was merely an assumption.

24. *See Boeing* Appellate Body Report, ¶ 748 (*citing U.S. AD-CVD* Appellate Body Report, ¶ 368 and *Airbus* Appellate Body Report, ¶ 943).

public sector contracts, before 1980, the U.S. government took all rights to patents over inventions produced by contractors under federally funded R&D contracts. In 1980, the U.S. changed its policy. It allowed government contractors to retain ownership of patents over any invention they produced with federal funding under R&D contracts. The EU highlighted the explicit limitations in the types of R&D NASA and the DOD could fund. These restrictions limited the enterprises that could benefit from the patent rights, thereby satisfying the Specificity Test.

That is, the EU claimed the only companies eligible for NASA and DOD funding were aerospace companies. Hence, the patent rights resulting from NASA Procurement Contracts and DOD Assistance Instruments were available only to aerospace companies, and specific under Article 2:1(a). The Appellate Body disagreed. It emphasized the fact that allocation of patent rights by NASA and the DOD were not *sui generis*. Rather, they were consistent with the legislative and regulatory framework applying generally to public sector R&D contracts entered into by all organs of the U.S. government. Eligibility to receive patent rights is not limited to the class of enterprises that conducts aerospace R&D. So, the Appellate Body rejected the EU's second argument on Article 2:1(a).

Third, the Appellate Body addressed the European allegation of *de facto* specificity under Article 2:1(c). This appeal related to NASA and the DOD discretion on allocating patent rights or accepting a contractual arrangement with contractors. Surely, if there is no *de jure* specificity under Article 2:1(a), there could be *de facto* specificity under Article 2:1(c), based on the way in which legislation or policy is implemented.

According to the EU, from 1991 through 2004, Boeing received a disproportionate amount of NASA Procurement Contracts and DOD Assistance Instruments. Boeing received on average 23.4% of all NASA contracts awarded. Moreover, Boeing personnel participated in the NASA Advisory Council. And, Boeing received 12.6% of all DOD deals.

Looking to the specificity analysis of the Panel, the Appellate Body agreed with the EU: the Panel failed to provide a complete Article 2:1 analysis. Citing its 2010 *U.S. AD-CVD* Report, the Appellate Body said specificity under Article 2:1 may arise through concurrent application of Sub-Paragraphs (a) through (c) to the various legal and factual aspects of a subsidy. Here, the Panel acknowledged the *de facto* specificity argument in its summary of arguments, but never actually addressed the European argument in its analysis. The Appellate Body opted to complete the analysis.

That analysis was quick. The EU attempted to support its arguments by referring to the authority of NASA to deny a request for patent waiver, and of the DOD to preclude a contractor from retaining patent rights. However, the EU failed to present sufficient evidence showing actual use of this discretion to steer patent rights to the aerospace industry. To the contrary, as the Panel cited, a study showed all waivers for patent rights regarding NASA contracts "were essentially automatically granted."[25]

---

25. *Boeing* Appellate Body Report, ¶ 798.

(Technically, the contracts gave NASA all patent rights, but a contractor such as Boeing could—and did—apply to NASA to waive those rights, thus transferring them to the contractor. The reason NASA always waived those rights was a 1983 Presidential Memorandum and 1987 Executive Order that all such waiver applications were to be granted. Hence, there was no discretion.) A similar scenario applied to the Pentagon.

Additionally, the Appellate Body felt the European claim regarding the share of contracts and funding to Boeing was unpersuasive. It reviewed the Panel findings under the assumption the allocation of patent rights was a self-standing subsidy, distinct from the payments and other support provided under the NASA Procurement Contracts and DOD Assistance Instruments. An attack on the specificity of those rights would have to point to evidence other than the raw data regarding the share of contracts awarded to Boeing. Instead, the European should have adduced more targeted evidence about the overall value of patent rights originating from government contracts, and the proportion of rights held by Boeing. Thus, the Appellate Body found the allocation of patent rights was not specific under Article 2:1(c).

Specificity, Washington State B&O Tax Rate Reduction, and American Losing Arguments:

The second issue regarding specificity dealt with the Washington State B&O Tax Rate Reduction under House Bill 2294. The U.S. claimed the Panel failed, when applying Article 2:1(a) of the *SCM Agreement*, to consider the entirety of the subsidy the Panel itself found to exist. The U.S. contended the Panel did not look at all of the differential tax rates in Washington, nor did it consider whether access was sufficiently broadly available throughout the economy. Both factors were relevant to determining whether the subsidy was specific to certain enterprises. The EU rebutted this argument by saying the Panel was required only to look at House Bill 2294, though it still did, in fact, evaluate the B&O tax system as a whole, which should have satisfied the U.S.

The Appellate Body wholly rejected the U.S. argument. The Panel indeed had correctly looked to the other differential tax rates in Washington, and properly concluded they were not part of the same subsidy scheme. Only House Bill 2294 was relevant in the final determination. Thus, the Appellate Body upheld the Panel finding: the Washington State B&O Tax Rate Reduction granted under House Bill 2294 was a subsidy that was specific under Article 2:1(a).

Specificity, Wichita IRBs, and American Losing Arguments:

Were municipal bonds floated by the City of Wichita, Kansas, specific to Boeing? Typically, Wichita issued IRBs to the general public on behalf of a qualifying private entity. Then, that entity used the bond sale proceeds to purchase, construct, and improve commercial property for itself. The entity was responsible for timely payment of principal and interest to the bondholders. IRBs were attractive, in part because they carried tax benefits, such as a Kansas sales tax exemption for the entity on whose behalf Wichita issued them.

However, in this case, Boeing (and Spirit Airlines) cleverly purchased the IRBs itself, thereby funding its own property development. The result was Boeing (and Spirit) used the sales tax exemptions associated with the IRBs.

The Panel found the IRB subsidies were not specific under Article 2:1(a), and neither party appealed this finding. Therefore, given the nexus between Sub-Paragraphs (a) and (b) of Article 2:1, the Appellate Body said consideration of Sub-Paragraph (b) was unnecessary. Candidly, the Appellate Body failed to provide a clear explanation of its reasoning here. It ought to have given its explanation in *U.S. AD-CVD* that Sub-Paragraphs (a) and (b) are not mutually exclusive (meaning a subsidy could be specific under one, but not the other, provision), and that specificity under all 3 Sub-Paragraphs should be tested.

In any event, the Appellate Body skipped to Sub-Paragraph (c). The U.S. challenged the Panel finding that Wichita granted the IRB subsidies in disproportionately large amounts under 2:1(c). The U.S. took issue with the Panel decision to use company-specific employment levels relative to total manufacturing employment in Wichita as the benchmark for its disproportionality analysis. In this case, the Panel looked at employment levels at Boeing (and Spirit Airlines) compared to total aircraft and non-aircraft industry jobs in Wichita.

According to the Panel and EU, the logic was this: the proportion of subsidies given to a company should mimic the proportion of employment for which it accounts. For example, suppose a company accounts for about one-third of all industry jobs in Wichita, but gets two-thirds of subsidies via IRBs. Manifestly, the subsidies are flowing disproportionately to that company, which in turn suggests *de facto* specificity. It so happens that these figures were the ones applicable to Boeing and Wichita. Yet, the Appellate Body rejected this kind of proportionality test— upholding the Panel and European Union position, using a different logic.

In explaining Article 2:1(c), the Appellate Body stated the inquiry focuses on:

> ... whether a subsidy, although not apparently limited to certain enterprises ..., is nevertheless allocated in a manner that belies the apparent neutrality of the measure. This inquiry requires a panel to examine the reasons as to why the actual allocation of "amounts of subsidy" differs from an allocation that would be expected to result if the subsidy were administered in accordance with the conditions for eligibility for that subsidy.[26]

Moreover, the reasons to believe a subsidy may in fact be specific relate to factors set out in Sub-Paragraph (c).

Pursuant to the second sentence in Article 2:1(c), four factors should be considered: (1) use of a subsidy program by a limited number of certain enterprises; (2) predominant use by certain enterprises; (3) the granting of disproportionately

---

26. *Boeing* Appellate Body Report, ¶ 877.

large amounts of subsidy to certain enterprises; and (4) the manner in which discretion has been exercised by the granting authority in the decision to grant a subsidy. The third sentence in Article 2:1(c) adds two more factors: (5) account must be
taken of the extent of diversification of economic activities within the jurisdiction
of the granting authority, as well as (6) the length of time the subsidy program has
operated. The Panel checked each factor, but based its specificity finding on the
third one: through the Wichita IRBs, Boeing was a "certain enterprise" that got a
disproportionately large amount of the subsidy.

This logic seemed sensible enough. Yet, the Appellate Body added its own 2-part
test:

> [(1)] where the granting of the subsidy indicates a disparity between the
> expected distribution of that subsidy, as determined by the conditions of
> eligibility, and its actual distribution, [(2)] a panel will be required to exam-
> ine the reasons for that disparity so as ultimately to determine whether
> there has been a granting of disproportionately large amounts of subsidy to
> certain enterprises.[27]

Briefly put, "whether?," and "why?," *i.e.*, first, whether there is an indication of
disparity, and if so, second, why does the disparity exist? Here, the two-part test
required examined the allocation of IRB subsidies granted to Boeing (and Spirit
Airlines) by Wichita, and the reasons why such amounts of subsidy may or may
not have been disproportionately large. The Panel completed the first, but not the
second, part of the test.

The EU gave evidence that from 1979 to 2005, the City of Wichita granted (*i.e.*,
issued on behalf of) Boeing and Spirit Airlines 61% of all IRBs, and 69% of all IRBs
that included property tax abatements. The U.S. argued the evidence failed to consider Boeing was the largest private sector employer in the State of Kansas, so these
proportions were expected and normal. The EU countered that to assess properly
these figures, employment by Boeing as a percentage of local employment should be
considered.

Siding with the EU, the Appellate Body found persuasive the lack of distribution of companies granted IRBs across different sectors of the Wichita economy.
Contrary to the American point, a wider distribution would have been expected,
but instead Wichita granted IRB subsidies in disproportionately large amounts to
certain enterprises. However, the Appellate Body did not agree the share of employment by Boeing (and Spirit Airlines) was relevant to the second prong of its test. The
share of employment in Wichita was evidence only of the disproportionate amount
of subsidies being granted to the aerospace industry (the first part of the test), but
did not explain why the disparity existed (the second part of the test).

---

27. *Boeing* Appellate Body Report, ¶ 879.

Even so, ultimately the Appellate Body upheld the Panel finding. The U.S. argued for a "qualifying investments" standard, looking at the proportion of companies that actually made investments in industrial or commercial property in Wichita. The Appellate Body agreed such a test was reasonable, but saw no evidence in the record relevant to that inquiry. The U.S. was left to make generalized claims that Wichita is known as the "Air Capital of the World," and that the core of the industry in Wichita is aircraft production, so the disproportion is just. Unfortunately, the U.S. was unable to provide concrete evidence to demonstrate two-thirds of the IRB subsidies was the proper ratio. Thus, lacking evidence to find to the contrary, the Appellate Body felt it had no choice but to uphold the Panel, albeit with its own two-part inquiry into not only whether a disparity exists, but also why it does.

Conclusion:

At least as it pertains to a Specificity Test, the *Boeing* Appellate Body Report is technical and unimpressive. It offers two lessons, but potentially muddies the waters.

First, the approach on appropriation of patent rights may be important in future disputes. The parties, Panel, and Appellate Body treated those rights as separate from the payments and other support provided under contractual obligations. That meant a claim that allocated IP rights are specific should not focus on the number of relevant contracts. Rather, evidence of specificity should point to the value of the IP rights granted to an entity, as compared to the total value of IP rights the government allocates elsewhere.

Second, when a party argues *de facto* specificity under Article 2:1(c), it must pay homage to the two-part test the Appellate Body concocted. It may not be enough just to show a disproportionate amount of subsidies goes to one company or industry. Evidence on why this disproportionate amount exists may be needed.

On the one hand, query whether the Appellate Body examination of the specificity of Wichita IRBs was parlous? Arguably, that those IRBs were specific based on the proportionality analysis of the Panel was sufficient. Is there any textual justification in the *SCM Agreement* to create a new two-part test, the second prong of which is "why?" disproportionality exists? Does the *Agreement* care only about disparity, not the reasons therefor? Did the Appellate Body convolute the Specificity Test, calling for an almost *de novo* reexamination of evidence?

On the other hand, consider the ramifications of asking "why?" disproportionality exists. The Appellate Body essentially created a new defense for a subsidizing government: once confronted with a disparity, it can justify handing over the lion's share of subsidies to a narrow subset of firms. That justification might be other non-subsidized firms eligible for support did not apply for it. Put differently, asking "why?" is a way to scrutinize data indicative of disproportionality. At bottom, all the Appellate Body does with its second prong is push parties to think about statistics they fling at each other.

- **2015 *China CVD* Case**[28]

Sequence within Article 2:1 Specificity Test:

In the 2015 *China CVD* case, the Appellate Body considered the Specificity Test under Article 2:1 of the *SCM Agreement*. This provision contains 3 Sub-Paragraphs, of which (a) and (b) apply to instances of *de jure* specificity, and (c) applies to instances of *de facto* specificity.

On appeal, China contended (*inter alia*) the Panel erred in its interpretation and application of Article 2:1 when it found the DOC did not act inconsistently with that provision by analyzing specificity exclusively under Article 2:1(c) of the *SCM Agreement*. As the Appellate Body explained:

> 4.116. China's appeal raises the question of whether, in certain circumstances, it may be permissible for an investigating authority to proceed directly to a specificity analysis under Article 2:1(c), or whether an application of the principles set out in Sub-Paragraphs (a) and (b) is always required before an analysis can be conducted under subparagraph (c). [. . .].

China argued the evaluation of the "other factors" referred to in the first sentence of Article 2:1(c) is conditional on non-specificity following application of Sub-Paragraphs (a) and (b). China rationalized this *in seriatim* approach by stating in normal circumstances, governments administer subsidies pursuant to adopted legislation, so application of the Specificity Test should begin by evaluating the relevant written legal instruments.

The Appellate Body looked to its Report in *U.S. Anti-Dumping and Countervailing Duties (China)*, as well as its 2012 *Boeing* Report. The Appellate Body focused on the portion of its analysis in *U.S. Anti-Dumping and Countervailing Duties (China)* where it discussed the effect of the chapeau of Article 2:1 of the *SCM Agreement*. The *chapeau* of Article 2:1 refers to the "principles" set out in Sub-Paragraphs (a) through (c), as distinguished from the potential alternative of "rules." The Appellate Body found the use of such term (*i.e.*, "principles") "suggests that Sub-Paragraphs (a) through (c) are to be considered within an analytical framework that recognizes and accords appropriate weight to each principle."[29]

Looking to its *Boeing* Report, the Appellate Body highlighted its use of the term "ordinarily" when addressing the same sequencing issue under Article 2:1 of the *SCM Agreement* in that dispute.[30] That is, in *Boeing*, the Appellate Body agreed that normally application of Sub-Paragraph (a) and (b) should precede application of Sub-Paragraph (c), *i.e.*, they should be utilized *in seriatim*. But, investigating authorities are not required to follow a strict sequential order. To buttress the point, the Appellate Body spilled too much ink on its own textual analysis that in mirrored

---

28. *See China CVD* Appellate Body Report, ¶¶ 4:108–4:132. The facts of this case are summarized in an earlier Chapter.

29. *See China CVD* Appellate Body Report, ¶ 4:117.

30. *See China CVD* Appellate Body Report, ¶ 4:118.

its previous Reports. The essential take-away was the Appellate Body confirmed a case-by-case approach is best.

Applying the law to the facts, the Appellate Body turned to China's claim that the Panel erred when it concluded the "unwritten nature" of the alleged input subsidies at issue was a circumstance that allowed the DOC to skip the application of Sub-Paragraphs (a) and (b) Article 2:1 of the *SCM Agreement*, and instead proceed directly to analyze the issue under Sub-Paragraph (c). The Appellate Body found reasonable the Panel approach. Given the implication that a *de jure* analysis normally involves analysis of written measures, the application of Sub-Paragraphs (a) and (b) serves no purpose under the facts of this case. As a result, the Appellate Body upheld the findings of the Panel, concluding the DOC did not act inconsistency with Article 2:1.

Chapter 15

Traffic Light System: Red Light (Prohibited) Subsidies[1]

I. Overview of Traffic Light System

WTO *SCM Agreement* Articles 1–2 define a "subsidy" as a financial contribution from a government that confers a benefit specific to an enterprise, industry, group of enterprises, or group of industries. Not every "subsidy," however, is illegal under the *Agreement*. How does the *Agreement* differentiate lawful from unlawful subsidies?

The answer is the Traffic Light system, established (albeit not by name) in Articles 3–9. It is one of the most conceptually clear and elegant ways of organizing the confusing universe of subsidies yet devised. Briefly, there are three categories of subsidies:

- **Red Light (Prohibited) Category (Articles 3–4)**

There are two Red Light Subsidies:

(1) Export subsidies, *i.e.*, subsidies contingent *de jure* or *de facto* on export performance), and

(2) Import substitution subsidies, *i.e.*, subsidies contingent on the use of domestic over imported goods.

Annex I to the *SCM Agreement* contains an illustrative list of export subsidies. All Red Light Subsidies are *per se* illegal, irrebuttably presumed to be specific, and irrebuttably presumed to cause an adverse effect.

- **Yellow Light and Dark Amber (Actionable) Category (Articles 5–7)**

Subsidies considered actionable may be countervailed. Yellow Light Subsidies are schemes that do not fit into any other category. In effect, the Yellow Light grouping is the default category. A CVD cannot be imposed against a subsidy in this category unless it is proved the subsidy is specific, and causes an adverse trade effect.

Four kinds of support are classified as Dark Amber:

(1) more than 5% of the value of a product is subsidized;

(2) operating losses of an industry is subsidized;

---

1. Documents References:
   (1) *Havana (ITO) Charter* Articles 25–29
   (2) GATT Articles VI, XVI–XVII
   (3) WTO *SCM Agreement*

(3) operating losses of a firm are subsidized (except for a one-time, non-recurring funding to provide time for the firm to reach a long-term solution and avoid an acute social problem); and

(4) direct forgiveness of debt incurred by a firm.

A Dark Amber Subsidy is deemed rebuttably to cause one particular type of adverse trade effect: serious prejudice. But, there is no presumption as to specificity (*i.e.*, specificity must be proven). Under Article 31, this Category lapsed on 31 December 1999 (though in June 2007, in the Doha Round the U.S. called for renewing the latter 3 items in it).

- **Green Light (Non-Actionable) Category (Articles 8–9)**

There are three kinds of Green Light Subsidies:

(1) support for R&D (up to a commercial prototype);

(2) assistance to a disadvantaged region (*i.e.*, a poorer area, in terms of income or employment, within a WTO Member); and

(3) funds for environmental adaptation (that is, to retro-fit production facilities with equipment needed to comply with new environmental regulations).

All Green Light Subsidies are lawful and non-countervailable. But, under Article 31, as of 31 December 1999, this Category lapsed. Why did the WTO Committee on Subsidies not lift the 5-year sunset rule (1 January 1995 through 31 December 1999) on this Category? What does the lack of a Green Light Category say about the views of WTO Members on funding R&D, less developed regions, and environmental retro-fitting?

II. Case Law on Export Contingency Other Than Tax Exemptions: 1999 *Canada Aircraft*, 1999 *Brazil Aircraft*, 2000 *Canada Autos*, 2005 *Cotton*, and 2011 *Airbus*

- **1999 *Canada Aircraft*[2]**

The 1999 *Canada Aircraft* dispute gave the Appellate Body its first opportunity to address "benefit" under Article 1:1(b) of the *SCM Agreement*. The dispute also gave the Appellate Body its first chance to develop a means to analyze whether a subsidy is "contingent . . . in fact . . . upon export performance" under Article 3:1(a) of the *Agreement*.

---

2. *See* Appellate Body Report, *Canada—Measures Affecting the Export of Civilian Aircraft*, WT/DS70/AB/R (adopted 20 August 1999). [Hereinafter, *Canada Aircraft* Appellate Body Report.]

The facts are summarized in an earlier Chapter.

Issue:

Brazil claimed numerous Canadian entities and organizations subsidized the Canadian civil regional aircraft industry, including prominent manufacturers like Bombardier (which competes with Brazil's Embraer in the small passenger aircraft market). Funds from the Technology Partnerships Canada (TPC) program to the industry were particularly controversial. The Panel found TPC assistance to the industry was contingent in fact upon export performance under Article 3:1(a) of the *SCM Agreement*.

Holding:

The Appellate Body found the Panel properly considered the facts as a whole, and agreed with the Panel that criteria for eligibility used in the TPC program created *de facto* export contingency. So, the Appellate Body upheld the Panel finding that this program was a prohibited export subsidy under Article 3:1(a).

Rationale:

The Appellate Body began by interpreting the text of Article 3:1(a). It reads:

> Except as provided in the *Agreement on Agriculture*, the following subsidies, within the meaning of Article 1, shall be prohibited:
>
> (a) subsidies contingent, in law or in fact,[4] whether solely or as one of several other conditions, upon export performance, including those illustrated in Annex I . . .

---

[4] This standard is met when the facts demonstrate that the granting of a subsidy, without having been made legally contingent upon export performance, is in fact tied to actual or anticipated exportation or export earnings. The mere fact that a subsidy is granted to enterprises which export shall not for that reason alone be considered to be an export subsidy within the meaning of this provision.

The Appellate Body identified "contingent" as the key word in Article 3:1(a).

As defined by the *OED*, the ordinary meaning of "contingent" is "conditional" or "dependent for its existence on something else."[3] Moreover, the text of Article 3:1(a) links the terms "contingency" and "conditionality," because it states export contingency can be the sole condition, or one of several other conditions.

The Appellate Body found helpful the footnote, as it highlights the type of evidence sufficient to show *de facto* contingency. With *de jure* contingency, the words of relevant legal texts must be studied. But, for *de facto* contingency, the Appellate Body said:

> the existence of this relationship of contingency, between the subsidy and export performance, must be inferred from the total configuration of the facts constituting and surrounding the granting of the subsidy, none of which on its own is likely to be decisive in any given case.[4]

---

3. *Canada Aircraft* Appellate Body Report, ¶ 166.
4. *Canada Aircraft* Appellate Body Report, ¶ 167.

Footnote 4 makes clear the facts must demonstrate *de facto* export contingency.

Footnote 4 also helps create the test for determining *de facto* export contingency. Three elements must be shown: (1) the "granting of a subsidy"; (2) "is . . . tied to . . ."; and, (3) "actual or anticipated exportation or export earnings."[5]

The Appellate Body eschewed an in-depth analysis of the first element.[6] Canada argued the analysis of contingency on export performance should focus on the reasonable knowledge of the recipient. Not so, said the Appellate Body: the standard relates to the "*granting* of the subsidy."[7] That is, the prohibition is on the granting authority, and the *SCM Agreement* imposes obligations on the granting WTO Member, not the recipient.

Next, the Appellate Body looked to the second substantive element provided by footnote 4: "tied to." There are many meanings of the word "tie." But, in the context of Article 3:1(a), the Appellate Body chose "limit or restrict as to . . . conditions," because "tie" is immediately followed by the word "to."[8] It does not suffice to demonstrate solely that a government granting a subsidy anticipated exports would result. Rather, it must be proven that the subsidy and anticipated exports are tied.

To finish creating the legal standard, the Appellate Body discussed the third element. According to the Appellate Body analysis, the key word in the last element is "anticipated." The *OED* defined "anticipated" as "expected."[9] Here again, the Appellate Body made clear distinguishing whether exports are anticipated or expected is a separate matter from the "tied to" examination. Even so, the second and third substantive elements must be considered together, because whether a subsidy is "tied to" the anticipation of exportation is crucial. The Appellate Body essentially repeated itself, but to be fair, it was difficult for it to avoid some redundancy when discussing these elements.

The key point is this: a government can anticipate that exports will increase following the enactment of a subsidy, but that alone is not enough for a finding of *de facto* contingency. "[T]he heart of the legal standard" is whether or not the anticipated exports are "tied to" (that is, limited or restricted in their eligibility conditions to) the subsidy in question.[10] Put differently, *de facto* contingency requires a

---

5. *Canada Aircraft* Appellate Body Report, ¶ 169.

6. Canada asserted the Panel confused "considerations" with "conditions" based on export performance. This argument related to the first element of *de facto* contingency. In the Canadian view, the eligibility criteria set out in the TPC Handbook were simply considerations, not formal conditions tantamount to *de facto* contingencies. The argument backfired. The Appellate Body accepted the "considerations" label, but nonetheless found those considerations were sufficient to demonstrate *de facto* contingency, when taken together with the other available facts. In effect, the Appellate Body looked past the formality of labels, and onto the underlying substantive links between support and exportation.

7. *Canada Aircraft* Appellate Body Report, ¶ 170.

8. *Canada Aircraft* Appellate Body Report, ¶ 171.

9. *Canada Aircraft* Appellate Body Report, ¶ 172.

10. *Canada Aircraft* Appellate Body Report, ¶ 171.

showing that any anticipated increase in exports is tethered in some way to (but not necessarily solely caused by) the subsidy program.

Next, the Appellate Body applied the 3-pronged Footnote 4 legal standard to the facts. Canada argued the Panel accepted the export orientation of the regional aircraft industry as the "effective test" for *de facto* contingency, *i.e.*, the Canadian industry sold aircraft mainly overseas, hence support to the industry as a whole was, in fact, tied to exportation. The Appellate Body did not agree with Canada that the Panel got the test wrong. The Appellate Body said Footnote 4 explicitly states *de facto* contingency cannot be found solely because a subsidy is granted to enterprises that export. As for the work of the Panel, it examined 16 factual elements that, when considered together, demonstrated the subsidies TPC granted were "tied to" actual or anticipated exports. In so doing, the Panel properly accounted for the facts relating to the TPC program as a whole, so the Appellate Body upheld its legal finding.

Conclusion:

Just as it is the predominant dispute relating to "benefit" analysis in Article 1 of the *SCM Agreement, Canada Aircraft* also is the seminal case on *de facto* export contingency under Article 3:1(a). The Appellate Body accepted and elaborated on the legal standard created by Footnote 4. All three elements must be met, but special care should be given to the second element. It is not enough that a subsidy is granted to enterprises that export, or that the relevant industry is export-oriented. The subsidy in question must be "tied to" anticipated or expected exportation or export earnings.

- **1999 *Brazil Aircraft*[11]**

On the same day the Appellate Body released the *Canada Aircraft* Report, it issued its *Brazil Aircraft* decision. The Appellate Body examined the Brazilian appeal regarding Item (k) on the Illustrative List of Export Subsidies found in Annex I of the *SCM Agreement*.[12]

Facts:

Canada took issue with certain export subsidies granted under the Brazilian *Programa de Financiamento às Exportações* (*PROEX*) on sales of Embraer aircraft to

---

11. This case is cited in an earlier Chapter.

12. The Appellate Body first addressed a procedural burden of proof question relating to "Special and Differential Treatment of Developing Country Members" under Article 27 of the *SCM Agreement*. The discussion relating to Article 27:4 is not pertinent for an understanding of export contingency under Article 3 of the *SCM Agreement*.

Briefly, the Appellate Body concluded the burden of proof is on the complaining party (such as Canada) to demonstrate that a developing country Member (*e.g.*, Brazil) is not in compliance with at least one of the elements found in Article 27:4 before a Panel may analyze whether the prohibition in Article 3:1(a) applies to the relevant developing country Member. Article 27 creates positive obligations on developing countries. So, so logically, the burden is on the complainant to prove a developing country has not met one or more of those obligations. Here, Canada had the burden to prove Brazil did not qualify special and differential treatment under Article 27. Canada met that burden.

foreign purchasers. Under *PROEX*, Brazil provided interest rate equalization subsidies for sales by Brazilian exporters, including Embraer. During each transaction, the lending bank would charge its normal interest rate, but receive its payment from two sources: the purchaser and Brazil. Brazil would pay 3.8 percentage points, and the aircraft purchaser would pay the remainder. (So, for example, suppose the purchaser was liable for an overall interest rate of 10%. The purchaser would be pay only 6.2%, with the government paying the balance.) The result was a reduction in financing costs for the purchaser, and thus a reduction in the overall cost of purchasing each Embraer aircraft.

Issue:

At issue was whether Item (k) of Annex I of the *SCM Agreement* permits the *PROEX* payments, on the ground that (in the language of Item (k)) the payments were not "used to secure a material advantage in the field of export credit terms." The Panel found Item (k) did not justify the *PROEX* payments, thus *PROEX* was a prohibited export subsidy under Article 3:1(a) of the *SCM Agreement*.

Holding:

The Appellate Body upheld the Panel finding. Brazil failed to adduce any evidence allowing for a comparison between *PROEX* and an accepted market benchmark for a non-subsidized export credit. Therefore, *PROEX* was a prohibited export subsidy under Article 3:1(a).

Losing Argument:

Brazil appealed the Panel conclusion that it failed to demonstrate *PROEX* payments were not "used to secure a material advantage in the field of export credit terms." Brazil argued the Panel erred twice: first, in interpreting the ordinary meaning of the word "secure," and second, in determining "advantage" with respect to "the terms that would have been available in the absence of the payment." Brazil also contended the Panel misconstrued the context of the phrase "material advantage." As Brazil clarified during oral argument, *PROEX* subsidies are not "used to secure a material advantage" in the sense of Item (k), because they are designed only to offset "Brazil risk" (*i.e.*, country risk relating to Brazil) and to "match" the subsidies given by Canada to Bombardier.

Rationale:

Annex I of the *SCM Agreement* contains an Illustrative List of Export Subsidies. Subsidies falling within one of the listed Items are deemed *per se* contingent on export performance. Item (k) was relevant, because it prohibits a government from paying all or part of the costs incurred by exporters (such as Embraer) or financial institutions (such as a Brazilian bank) in obtaining export credits, insofar as they are used to secure a material advantage in the field of export credit terms. That is, Item (k) deems as an illegal export subsidy such payments.

In effect, Brazil argued a negative implication from Item (k). If relevant language in Item (k) is considered as a two-part test, then a measure could satisfy the first part of the test, but not be deemed a prohibited export subsidy if it did not also satisfy the second part of that test. Brazil conceded the first part of the test: *PROEX* payments were payments by the government for all or part of the costs incurred by exporters or financial institutions in obtaining credits. But Brazil argued the payments flunked the second part: *PROEX* payments were not used to secure a material advantage in export credit terms. As a result, they did not satisfy Item (k), and should be permitted. The Brazilian argument was interesting, because it effectively admitted if Item (k) were not present in the *SCM Agreement*, then the measures at issue would be prohibited directly under Article 3:1(a).

The Panel did not address the Brazilian interpretation of Item (k). It said Brazil failed to demonstrate the *PROEX* payments were not used to secure a material advantage as to export credit terms. In its view, satisfaction of this element would be met where payment resulted in availability of an export credit on terms more favorable than would otherwise have been available to the purchaser in respect of the transaction in question.

The Appellate Body began its analysis by examining the ordinary meaning of the "material advantage" phrase in Item (k). It agreed with the Panel definition of "advantage" as "a more favorable or improved position" or a "superior position." However, the Appellate Body said the Panel erred by reading out the word "material," which qualifies the word advantage in Item (k). Interestingly, the Appellate Body also criticized the Panel for adopting an interpretation of "material advantage" that was, in effect, the same as the *Canada Aircraft* definition of the term "benefit" in Article 1:1(b) of the *SCM Agreement*. In the Appellate Body view, for "material advantage" to have any meaning, it must mean something different from "benefit" in Article 1:1(b).

In giving the "material advantage" phrase meaning, the Appellate Body found the second paragraph of Item (k) useful. That paragraph applies when a WTO Member is party to an international undertaking on official export credits. Then, an export credit practice that conforms to the provisions of an international undertaking on official export credits shall not be considered an export subsidy barred by the *SCM Agreement*.

The relevant international undertaking here is the *Organization for Economic Cooperation and Development Arrangement*. The *OECD Arrangement* establishes minimum interest rate guidelines for export credits supported by its participants. The Appellate Body cited the *OECD Arrangement* as one example of an appropriate market benchmark by which to assess whether payments by a government are used to secure a material advantage in the field of export credit terms.

Unfortunately, the analysis stopped there. Brazil failed to provide the Panel any information regarding the net interest rates as compared to those under the *OECD Arrangement*. As such, Brazil failed to meet its burden of proof in respect of using Item (k) to justify *PROEX* payments as not being used to secure an unfair advantage, and thus not being *de facto* contingent on exports.

As discussed above, the Appellate Body disagreed with the Panel interpretation of the phrase "used to secure a material advantage in the field of export credit terms." The Panel failed to define "material" as it associated to "advantage." But, ultimately, the Appellate Body upheld the Panel decision, because Brazil failed to demonstrate the *PROEX* payments were not used to secure a material advantage in the field of export credit terms. Therefore, the *PROEX* payments were prohibited export subsidies under Article 3:1(a) of the *SCM Agreement*.

Conclusion:

The case is confusing, in large part because of misplaced and weak arguments by Brazil. In subsequent WTO disputes, such as the 2005 *Cotton* case, Brazil displayed markedly better legal capacity. The Panel and Appellate Body never had to address the negative implication Brazil put forth regarding Item (k), so this argument could be resurrected in the future.

Nonetheless, one aspect of this Report is clear. It is difficult for the Appellate Body to accept an Item in Annex I as an affirmative defense to an allegedly *de facto* export contingent subsidy. After all, Annex I is a non-exclusive proactive list of examples of schemes that are export subsidies.[13] Simply put, Brazil tried to turn that list on its head.

Comment:

The Appellate Body missed completely a crucial international banking point: arguably, Item (k) is not relevant at all. That is because the *PROEX* payments helped the purchasers of Embraer aircraft, by cutting their interest payments. The Brazilian government picked up the tab, as it were, for 3.8 percentage points of the overall interest rate liability to a Brazilian bank. How, then, did *PROEX* payments reduce the costs of Embraer, or of Brazilian banks, in obtaining export credits for the purchasers? Simply put, is the Brazilian analogy of PROEX to an export credit misplaced and weak?

• **2000 *Canada Autos*[14]**

The Appellate Body again addressed whether a measure is a subsidy, which is in the 2000 *Canada Autos* dispute.

Facts:

(1) Basic Bargain

In January 1965, President Lyndon Johnson and Canadian Prime Minister Lester Pearson signed an agreement to liberalize trade in autos and auto parts between the countries. Through this pact — formally known as the "*Agreement Concerning*

---

13. A second clear point from the case is that when lodging a complaint against a developing country, the burden is on the complainant (such as Canada) to show the developing country respondent (here, Brazil) has failed to satisfy at least one of the provisions of Article 27 of the *SCM Agreement*.

14. This case is cited, and its facts summarized, in an earlier Chapter.

Automotive Products Between the Government of Canada and the Government of the United States" (Auto Pact) — Canada sought to "Canadianize" the auto and auto parts market. Canada implemented the *Auto Pact* through the Motor Vehicles Tariff Order of 1965, and Tariff Item 950 Regulations. Both were replaced by the MVTO of 1988, and that was replaced by the MVTO of 1998.

The basic bargain was this: Canada agreed to grant duty-free treatment to vehicles and original equipment manufacturing parts (other than tires and tubes), but only if the importer of the cars or parts met the definition of a motor vehicles "manufacturer" set forth in the *Auto Pact*. The MVTO specified the terms of duty-free entry for imported cars and car parts.

(2) Three Tests

What was that all-important definition of "manufacturer" contained in the *Auto Pact* and given effect in the MVTO?

The definition was really three tests to be met to qualify as a "manufacturer." First, the importer must have produced in Canada during the base year 1963–1964 motor vehicles of the category it was importing. In other words, the importer had to have been established and made cars in Canada since before the *Auto Pact* entered into force. In effect, these importers were also foreign direct investors, such as General Motors of Canada, Ltd., Ford Motor Company of Canada, Ltd., and Chrysler Canada Ltd. — American companies that imported cars into Canada that they made in the U.S. (or elsewhere), and that also made cars in Canada. Not surprisingly, the "Big Three" — General Motors, Ford, and Chrysler — all satisfied this first prong of the definition. So, too, did American Motors (which Chrysler absorbed in 1987).

Second, the importer had to comply with a ratio of (1) the sales value of its locally (*i.e.*, Canadian) produced vehicles of that class of vehicle to (2) the sales it makes in Canada of that type of vehicle. This ratio was called a production-to-sales ratio, because item (1) was the value of the importer's local production, and item (2) was the value of its local sales. Technically, item (1), which was the numerator in the ratio, was the net sales value of the vehicles produced in Canada. Item (2), which was the denominator, was the net sales value of all vehicles of that type sold in Canada. Hence, the production-to-sales ratio was expressed as follows:

$$\text{Production-to-sales ratio} = \frac{\text{Net sales value of vehicles produced in Canada}}{\text{Net sales value of all vehicles of the same class sold in Canada}}$$

This ratio was measured on an annual basis.

Under the *Auto Pact*, to receive duty-free treatment, an importer had to keep the ratio above a certain minimum threshold. Why? Because the ratio was a gauge of the extent to which the importer sold the cars it made in Canada to Canadian consumers, *i.e.*, selling its local production locally, and possibly also selling the cars it made locally to foreign countries. Put succinctly, the ratio was a measure of an importer's commitment to domestic (*i.e.*, Canadian) production. American auto companies pledged to respect a one-to-one, or 100% ratio, meaning the net sales value of cars they produced in Canada at least equaled the net sales value of the vehicles they sold in Canada. That is, they agreed to increase the number of cars they made in Canada so the value of Canadian-produced cars would be no less than the value of cars they sold in Canada.

To see how this ratio helped "Canadianize" the auto industry, observe that an importer that also manufactured in Canada would have two sources (other than inventory) for the vehicles it sold in Canada: imported vehicles (*i.e.*, cars that it makes overseas) and locally-made vehicles. The production-to-sales ratio ensured the importer did not get all of the vehicles it sold in Canada from abroad. Rather, the importer used its local factories to source a sizeable percentage, if not all, of the local sales, and perhaps also to source exports from those factories.

For example, suppose an importer made $6 million worth of cars in Canada, and sold $8 million in Canada. This 75% (6/8) ratio indicates the remaining $2 million of sales would have to have been sourced from imports. Conversely, suppose the manufacturer made $8 million worth of cars in Canada, but sold only $6 million there. Unless the company accumulated the remaining $2 million of local production in inventories, then it must have sold the $2 million overseas. That is, the 133% (8/6) ratio suggests exportation of local product. In sum, the production-to-sales ratio simply is designed to ensure some production occurs locally.

How exactly did the *Auto Pact* specify the production-to-sales ratio? The obvious way would have been to do so along the lines of the above example, namely, a straight percentage like 75% or 133%. However, the *Pact* used a different approach. It called for a comparison between the production-to-sales ratio in the current year with the production-to-sales ratio in a base year. The ratio in the current year had to be equal to or greater than the ratio in the base year.

Moreover, the *Auto Pact* specified the ratio must never be lower than 75/100, *i.e.*, 3/4. The reason for the range was that the precise ratio differed depending on the beneficiary—it all depended on the ratio in the base year. For instance, for Ford, the ratio might be 83%, while for GM it might be 91%. The differences would reflect the individual production-to-sales ratios of the companies in the base year. In the example, GM's ratio presumably was higher than Ford's ratio.

Thus, for example, suppose the base year is defined as 1964, and the production-to-sales ratio in 1964 is 80%. That ratio would mean that in 1964, of the cars the importer sold in Canada, 80% (measured in terms of net sales value) of them were produced in Canada. The *Pact* demanded that for the current year, the ratio be equal to or greater than 80%. Put differently, the importer cannot shift production out of Canada in a way that would cause the ratio to drop below the base year.

Third, the importer had to achieve a minimum amount of Canadian Value Added in its local production of vehicles (and, in certain instances, parts). That is, the importer's Canadian production facilities could not be mere assembly operations (like a *maquiladora* on the U.S.-Mexican border). There had to be significant economic activity going on in Canada. So, included in the CVA were (1) the cost of parts and materials of Canadian origin, (2) Canadian labor costs, (3) manufacturing overhead costs, (4) general and administrative expenses incurred in Canada that were attributable to the production of vehicles, (5) depreciation of machinery and permanent plant equipment located in Canada that was directly attributable to the production of vehicles, and (6) capital costs for land and buildings used in the production of motor vehicles.

The specific CVA requirement was not stated in terms of a simple percentage — for instance, like 35% of the value of the vehicle produced in Canada must be derived from Canadian parts. Rather, it was set forth in terms of a comparison: (1) how much CVA exists in vehicles produced in the current year in comparison with (2) the CVA that existed in vehicles produced in a defined base year? The requirement was that (1) could not fall below (2).

That is, the CVA in the current year had to be at equal to or greater than the CVA in the base year. As with the production-to-sales ratio, the precise CVA threshold differed for each importer that was a beneficiary of the *Auto Pact*. The threshold depended on the CVA level during the base year. That is not to say a simple CVA percentage was unimportant. In general, the American auto companies agreed to use in each car assembled in Canada a large portion of Canadian-made parts, specifically, a 50% Regional Value Content Test (prescribed under the *CUFTA*, which entered into force on 1 January 1988). The companies pledged to increase the Canadian value content of cars and car parts by at least 60% of the growth in their car sales in Canada.

If an importer did not satisfy this 3-pronged definition of "manufacturer," then it was liable for payment of the applicable customs duties on all vehicle imports (of the class in question) for the year in which it failed the tests. The loss of duty-free treatment was only for that year, and the importer did not lose its status as a beneficiary of the *Auto Pact*. (Moreover, the duties were owed only on additional imports, not on vehicles already imported, because calculation of the production-to-sales ratio included only duty-free imports.)

(3) Special Remission Orders

To avoid losing duty-free treatment in any particular year, an importer had one recourse. It could request the Canadian government to grant it an exemption from one or more of the three prongs, and thus get the benefit of duty-free treatment for the cars and car parts it imports. This grant was called a "Special Remission Order."[15] Each SRO set forth a CVA and production-to-sales ratio.

---

15. Under an SRO, Canada offered duty-free treatment through full duty remission, whereas under the three tests discussed above, Canada offered a complete exemption from duties.

Conceptually, these tests were no different from those mentioned above. But, the exact CVA levels and ratio tests varied from one SRO to another, *i.e.*, from one SRO grantee to another. As a general matter, SROs tended to have a CVA threshold of at least 40%, a production-to-sales ratio of 75 to 100, and laid down reporting obligations on the grantee. In other words, they could be reasonably strict.

(4) Protecting Jobs

Why did Canada want to "Canadianize" the auto and auto parts industry? In short, to protect jobs. Before the *Auto Pact*, over 90% of all cars made in Canada were manufactured by subsidiaries of American companies, and Canada imported far more automotive products from the U.S. than it exported to the U.S. Canada's search was motivated partly by concerns about control over a vital economic sector, arguably one of strategic importance, and by a perceived need to develop a national economic identity.

Why did the U.S. accept the idea of an *Auto Pact*? Probably in part out of fear the Canadian government might adopt unilateral measures unfavorable to American auto and auto parts companies. The U.S. also anticipated that while the relative market share of the Canadian market held by American companies might decline, because of economic growth in Canada, absolute sales volumes would not fall.

(5) CUFTA and NAFTA

The *Auto Pact* was retained under the 1988 *CUFTA*, and 1993 *North American Free Trade Agreement* (*NAFTA*, which took effect on 1 January 1994), with a few modifications. *CUFTA* made an important change to the first prong of the three-pronged definition of "manufacturer." The change was to close the list of eligible importers. Eligibility was limited to the *Auto Pact* manufacturers (*i.e.*, those that had qualified already), manufacturers designated by the Canadian government as beneficiaries before the *CUFTA* was signed, and other firms that were expected to be designated as beneficiaries by the Canadian Government before 1989. That is to say, *CUFTA* closed the list of companies entitled to import autos and auto parts duty free into Canada.

Canada's import duty exemption rules were continued in the *NAFTA*. Under *NAFTA*, all American automotive products began entering Canada duty-free as of 1 January 1998, and all Mexican automotive products entered Canada duty-free as of 1 January 2003. Of course, the duty-free *NAFTA* rules apply only if the *NAFTA* rules of origin for autos and automotive products are satisfied.

(6) Not Really Free Trade

The *Auto Pact* was touted, and sometimes still thought of, as a free trade agreement. It was far from that. It is an overstatement to say each country agreed to eliminate its tariffs with respect to autos and auto parts from the other country. To understand precisely what the *Pact* achieved, it is important to understand the *status quo ante*. Before 1965 (when the *Pact* took effect), Canada imposed a 17½% duty on car imports, and a duty of up to 25% on imports of parts. Furthermore, Canada imposed a content requirement on vehicle manufacturers located in Canada: their output had to contain at least 60% Canadian content. At that time, the U.S. had an import duty of 6½% on cars, and 8½% on parts. It did not impose any domestic content requirement.

Under the *Auto Pact*, Canada agreed to abolish its tariffs on imports from the U.S. of certain finished vehicles, and on imports of certain parts for use as original equipment in vehicles to be produced in Canada. Canada agreed auto parts could be imported duty-free not only from the U.S., but also from third countries. However, not everyone could benefit from the duty-free treatment for autos and auto parts—only qualifying persons could. As defined in the *Pact*, the qualifying persons were none other than the major American manufacturers, namely, Ford, General Motors, and Chrysler. Obviously, they liked being relieved of burdensome tariffs when they exported cars and parts to Canada from their plants in the U.S. (Not surprisingly, the importers of such products generally were American car companies or their Canadian subsidiaries.) Canada maintained its tariff on vehicles and parts from all other persons and countries: a 6.7% duty on finished cars, and a 6% duty on auto parts. Thus, a car dealer in North Dakota could not sell vehicles across the border duty free, and a Japanese parts producer could not export components to Canada duty free. (By 1999, Canada's car tariff had fallen to 6.1%.) Finally, Canada dropped its bar against the imports of used autos from the U.S.

What did the U.S. do for Canada in return? Under the *Auto Pact*, the U.S. extinguished its tariffs on imports from Canada of certain vehicles. For imports of cars from all other sources, the U.S. did not drop its tariff. (In 1999, for example, it applied a 2.5% tariff on non-Canadian car imports.) The U.S. also agreed to drop tariffs on imports from Canada of certain auto parts for use as original equipment in the manufacture of those designated vehicles. The fact the abolition of duties on parts applied only to imports going to an automobile manufacturer meant an importer that planned to sell Canadian-made parts to car repair businesses or auto supply stores would have to pay a tariff.

In sum, while the 1965 *Auto Pact* was the first so-called "free trade agreement" to which the U.S. was a party, that appellation is a misnomer. In fact, the deal liberalized trade for a chosen few in a particular industrial sector. Over time, particularly with the *CUFTA* and *NAFTA*, that "liberalization" became even more dubious. Recall under the *CUFTA*, it was agreed the benefits of the *Auto Pact* would continue to be limited to the manufacturers already enjoying its benefits. These qualifying *Auto Pact* companies were the Big Three—Ford, General Motors, and Chrysler—plus CAMI Automotive Inc., a joint venture between GM and Suzuki. Thus, potential Japanese competitors were excluded and could not acquire preferential status. Also in the *CUFTA*, it was also agreed the local content rule would be 50%, and any components made in North America would qualify. (To calculate local content, "factory cost"—also called "direct cost of manufacturing"—that included labor, materials, and processing, but not advertising or overhead, was used.) With

NAFTA, the Regional Value Content (RVC) threshold to qualify as a vehicle originating from within the *NAFTA* region rose to 62.5%.

(7) Results

For the intended beneficiaries, the positive results of the *Auto Pact* were indisputable. Consider Canada. The *Pact* helped increase production and employment. Since the 1960s, aside from periods of recession, Canadian car assembly plants boomed, as did, consequently, employment in that sector. Many American producers set up new production and assembly factories in southern Ontario. By 1999, the auto and auto parts industry accounted for 12% of Canadian manufacturing. For every car Canadians bought, they assembled 1.8 cars, mostly for the North American market. Since the early 1980s, Canada has enjoyed large surpluses in its trade in autos and auto parts with the U.S.

Issue:

The subsidy issue pertained to Article 3:1(a) of the *SCM Agreement*. Though not expressly limited by the text of the MVTO 1998, did the import duty ratio requirements found in the MVTO 1998 create a necessary implication of export contingency in law?

Holding:

The Appellate Body agreed with the Panel. The measures at issue were subsidies "contingent . . . in law . . . upon export performance" under Article 3:1(a) of the *SCM Agreement*. Therefore, Canada violated that provision.

Rationale:

The Appellate Body began by quoting itself its 1999 *Canada Aircraft* decision. As it noted in the earlier dispute, the text of Article 3:1(a) of the *SCM Agreement* "makes an explicit link between 'contingency' and 'conditionality' in stating that export contingency can be the sole or 'one of several other *conditions*.'"[16] Additionally, though *Canada Aircraft* dealt with *de facto* contingency, the Appellate Body restated that the "legal standard expressed by the word 'contingent' is the same for both *de jure* and *de facto* contingency."[17] The difference lies in what evidence may be used to prove export contingency. As the Appellate Body said in *Canada Aircraft*:

> *De jure* export contingency is demonstrated on the basis of the words of the relevant legislation, regulation or other legal instrument. Proving *de facto* export contingency is a much more difficult task. There is no single legal document which will demonstrate, on its face, that a subsidy is "contingent . . . in fact . . . upon export performance." Instead, the existence of this relationship of contingency, between the subsidy and export performance, must be inferred from the total configuration of the facts constituting and

---

16. *Canada Autos* Appellate Body Report, ¶ 98 (*quoting Canada Aircraft* Appellate Body Report, ¶ 166).

17. *Canada Autos* Appellate Body Report, ¶ 99.

surrounding the granting of the subsidy, none of which on its own is likely to be decisive in any given case.[18]

It is uncommon for a condition on exportation to be set out expressly (*i.e.*, on the face of the law, regulation or other legal instrument), as few governments are daft enough to create a "smoking gun." So, the Appellate Body said *de jure* contingency also exists where the condition to export is clearly, though implicitly, in the instrument comprising the measure. Conditionality may be derived by necessary implication from the words actually used in the measure.[19]

Applied to the facts of *Canada Autos*, the relevant legal instrument was the MVTO 1998. The ratio requirements applicable to the MVTO 1998 beneficiaries were, "as a general rule," 95:100 for automobiles, at least 75:100 for specified commercial vehicles (SCVs), and at least 75:100 for buses. The exact ratios applicable to each automobile manufacturer beneficiary were confidential, but the average was approximately 95:100. Additionally, regarding the SROs, almost all had a ratio requirement of 100:100.

The Panel and Appellate Body simplified the analysis by considering the ratios in two parts: cases in which the production-to-sales ratio was (1) 100:100 versus (2) less than 100:100 (such as the Big Three MVTO automobile manufacturer beneficiaries that had, on average, ratio requirements of 95:100).

First, agreeing with the Panel, the Appellate Body failed to see how a manufacturer subject to a production-to-sales ratio of 100:100 could obtain access to the import duty exemption without exporting. With such a ratio, the value of motor vehicles that could be imported duty-free was limited strictly to the value of motor vehicles exported, *i.e.*, a manufacturer could not import into Canada a single vehicle duty-free, even if it met the 100:100 ratio, unless it also exported one or more vehicles from Canada. Thus, the import duty was "clearly conditional, or dependent upon, exportation and, therefore, was contrary to Article 3:1(a) of the *SCM Agreement* [when the ratio requirement is 100:100]."[20]

Simply put, to qualify for duty-free treatment for imported autos or auto parts, a manufacturer had to meet the one-to-one ratio test of production in Canada and sales in Canada, respectively, and also ship cars out of Canada. That was the MVTO 1998 rule: the Canadian government cared about production and sales in Canada, and was willing to grant duty-free treatment on autos and auto parts to a manufacturer only on the condition that manufacture exported cars. This conditionality, of course, helped boost exports from Canada, and sometimes is referred to as a "trade balancing requirement" (though that term is not restricted to the duty-free context, *i.e.*, it can pertain to any rule restricting importation by demanding a value or volume of exportation).

---

18. *Canada Aircraft* Appellate Body Report, ¶ 167.
19. *Canada Autos* Appellate Body Report, ¶ 100.
20. *Canada Autos* Appellate Body Report, ¶ 104.

So, "Canadianization" entailed encouraging both local production and exportation, with a view to protecting Canadian jobs. (A Marxist might seize on the policy to inquire whether the underlying problem in Canada might be over-production in Canada, hence the need of the Canadian government to push manufacturers to search for new markets overseas. But, whether a manufacturer could not sell in Canada everything it made in Canada was unclear from the facts.) But, as the Appellate Body held, tying duty-free treatment to exportation was a *de jure* export subsidy.

Second, the Appellate Body held that even when the ratio requirement was less than 100:100, Canada still violated Article 3:1(a) of the *SCM Agreement*. Though less straightforward, if a manufacturer wished to increase its "allowance" for duty-free treatment, then it had to increase the value of vehicles exported. Thus, the Appellate Body again agreed with the Panel, finding the import duty was sufficiently tied to export performance. As the Appellate Body stated in its conclusion:

> Even where the ratio requirement for a particular manufacturer is set at less than 100:100, in our view, there is contingency "in law" upon export performance because, as a result of the operation of the MVTO 1998 and the SROs themselves, the granting of, or the entitlement to, the import duty exemption *is tied to* the exportation of motor vehicles by the manufacturer beneficiaries. By the very operation of the measure, the more motor vehicles that a manufacturer exports, the more motor vehicles it can import duty-free.[21]

Note carefully the Appellate Body formula for "contingency" under Article 3:1(a): it equals "tied to."

Conclusion:

This dispute is useful precedent for complainants attempting to broaden the *de jure* standard in WTO disputes. The standard the Appellate Body sets does not demand explicit contingency. Rather, it allows for a text that clearly implies export contingency. Succinctly put, *de jure* contingency can be explicit or implicit. However, that step to implicit *de jure* contingency is troublesome.

First, it is judicial lawmaking. The Appellate Body allows for *de jure* export contingency to be implied from a legal document, thus broadening the reach of that document. Second, this allowance gives Article 3:1(a) greater strength than perhaps the *SCM Agreement* drafters intended. If they wanted 3 categories of export contingency — explicit *de jure*, implicit *de jure*, and *de facto* — then would they not have said so? Third, the Appellate Body holding potentially blurs the distinction between *de jure* and *de facto* contingency, possibly in a subjective way. The Appellate Body can find in favor of contingency, short of a fact pattern that would amount to *de facto* contingency, and short of a text that creates explicitly a *de jure* export-contingent subsidy.

---

21. *Canada Autos* Appellate Body Report, ¶ 108 (emphasis added).

To be fair to the Appellate Body, consider its position retrospectively. Around the world, doubts about the effectiveness of IOs, including the WTO, are raised. The *DSU* is a, if not the, crown jewel of the WTO. Why not empower WTO texts via expansive, even activist, judicial interpretation? Why wait for years of trade negotiations, the outcomes—and even success—of which are uncertain?

• **2005 *Cotton***[22]

Issues and Holdings:

As for export subsidies, the Brazilian attack focused on two American programs—Step 2 Payments and Export Credit Guarantees. On appeal, there were three issues of major substantive importance. Technically, the first issue—involving Step 2 Payments to users, as distinct from exporters, is one of import substitution, not export subsidization. However, as Article 3 of the *SCM Agreement* deems both *per se* illegal, properly they were considered together.

First Issue and Holding:
Step 2 Payments to Users as Red Light Import Substitution Subsidies[23]

Were Step 2 Payments to domestic users of American cotton subsidies contingent on the use of domestic over imported goods and, therefore, import substitution subsidies that were *per se* illegal under the Red Light category of Article 3:1(b) of the *SCM Agreement*?

Upholding the Panel finding, the Appellate Body replied "yes."

Second Issue and Holding:
Step 2 Payments to Exporters as Red Light Export Subsidies[24]

Were Step 2 Payments to exporters of American cotton subsidies contingent on export performance under Article 9:1(a) of the *Agreement on Agriculture* and, therefore, not only inconsistent with Articles 3:3 of that *Agreement*, but also *per se* illegal export subsidies under the Red Light category of Article 3:1(a) of the *SCM Agreement*?

Again upholding the Panel finding, the Appellate Body said "yes."

Third Issue and Holding:
Export Credit Guarantees as Red Light Export Subsidies[25]

One issue in the 2005 *Cotton* case was whether Export Credit Guarantees—specifically, the GSM 102, GSM 103, and SCGP measures—illegal Red Light export subsidies under Article 3:1(a) of the *SCM Agreement*?

---

22. This case is cited, and its facts summarized, in an earlier Chapter.
23. *See Cotton* Appellate Body Report, ¶¶ 249(d)(i), 763(d)(i).
24. *See Cotton* Appellate Body Report, ¶¶ 249(d)(ii), 763(d)(ii).
25. *See Cotton* Appellate Body Report, ¶¶ 249(e)(i), (iii)-(iv), 763(e)(i), (iii)-(iv).

Like the Panel, the Appellate Body said "yes." To reach this conclusion, the Appellate Body had to address two specific questions:

(1) Did Article 10:2 of the *Agreement on Agriculture* exempt export credit guarantees from the export subsidy disciplines of Article 10:1?

The Panel replied "no." Two of the 3 Appellate Body members agreed with the Panel. Significantly, one member dissented, saying Article 10:2 does carve out export credit guarantees from the Article 10:1 disciplines.[26]

(2) If Article 10:2 did not provide this exemption, then are Export Credit Guarantees within Item J on the Illustrative List of Export Subsidies annexed to the *SCM Agreement*? That is, did the U.S. provide these Guarantees at premium rates inadequate to cover long-term operating costs and losses, as Item J states?

The Panel and Appellate Body answered "yes."

Rationales for Export Subsidy Holdings:

The Appellate Body Report does not differ significantly in rationale or conclusion on major substantive export subsidy issues from the Panel Report—with one key exception. The distinction is the Dissenting Opinion on the scope of Article 10:2 of the *Agreement on Agriculture*, with the Dissent arguing the Panel and Appellate Body Majority misread this provision by holding it does not exempt export credit guarantees from the Article 10:1 disciplines on export subsidies. Arguably, the Dissent is the stronger of the views.

First: Step 2 Payments to Users as Red Light Import Substitution Subsidies[27]

The argument on which Brazil prevailed at the Panel stage also succeeded on appeal, namely, that Step 2 payments to American cotton users are contingent on the use of American over imported cotton, thus fitting within the Red Light import substitution category of Article 3:1(b) of the *SCM Agreement*. The essence of the contingency is payments are conditional on proof of consumption of domestically produced cotton.

The U.S. did not contest that Step 2 payments were subsidies (*i.e.*, financial contributions conferring a benefit to a specific enterprise or enterprises), nor that a user had to open a bale of domestically produced baled cotton to get a payment. The U.S. also did not essay a Peace Clause defense, as Article 13 of the *Agriculture Agreement* was irrelevant to the Brazilian claim under Article 3:1(b) of the *SCM Agreement*. Rather, the American defense was the Step 2 payments comply with American domestic support reduction commitments under Article 6:3 of the

---

26. The Presiding Member was Merit E. Janow. The other Members were Luiz Olavo Baptista and A.V. Ganesan. By way of speculation, with no supporting evidence other than the familiar American style of writing judicial opinions, which of course may be imitated, and a gut instinct about the rationale of the Dissent—the Dissenter was the Presiding Member.

27. *See Cotton* Appellate Body Report, ¶¶ 249(d)(i), 518–552, 763(d)(i).

Agriculture Agreement. In other words, the U.S. used the *Agriculture Agreement* as a shield against the sword of the *SCM Agreement*—because Step 2 payments to domestic users were permissible under the *Agriculture Agreement*, they did not violate the *SCM Agreement*.

The textual support for the American defense was the introductory clause in the *chapeau* to Article 3:1(b) of the *SCM Agreement*, Article 21 of the *Agriculture Agreement*, and Paragraph 7 of Annex 3 to the *Agriculture Agreement*. Entitled "Prohibition," Article 3 of the *SCM Agreement* provides:

> Except as provided in the *Agreement on Agriculture*, the following subsidies, within the meaning of Article 1, shall be prohibited:
>
> . . .
>
> (b) subsidies contingent, whether solely or as one of several other conditions, upon the use of domestic over imported goods.

Article 21:1 of the *Agriculture Agreement* states:

> The provisions of GATT 1994 and of other Multilateral Trade Agreements in Annex 1A [which includes the *SCM Agreement*] to the *WTO Agreement* [*i.e.*, the *Agreement Establishing the World Trade Organization*] shall apply subject to the provisions of this *Agreement*.

Paragraph 7 of Annex 3 of the *Agriculture Agreement* is as follows:

> The AMS [*i.e.*, Aggregate Measure of Support] shall be calculated as close as practicable to the point of first sale of the basic agricultural product concerned. Measures directed at agricultural processors shall be included to the extent that such measures benefit the producers of the basic agricultural products.[28]

Using the first two texts, the U.S. sought to set up a conflict between the *Agriculture* and *SCM Agreements*, invoke the primacy of the former over the latter *Agreement*, and thereby exonerate Step 2 Payments. The *chapeau* to Article 3:1(b) clearly defers to the *Agriculture Agreement*. Further, as the Panel observed, Article 21:1 both acknowledges the application of GATT and the *SCM Agreement* to agricultural products, and says the *Agriculture Agreement* takes precedence in the event, and to the extent, of any conflict between it and any other Annex 1A accord.

---

28. Article 1(a) of the *Agriculture Agreement* defines "AMS" as:
> the annual level of support, expressed in monetary terms, provided for an agricultural product in favor of the producers of the basic agricultural product or non-product-specific support provided in favor of agricultural producers in general, other than support provided under programs that qualify as exempt from reduction under Annex 2 to this *Agreement* . . . .

For a discussion of how AMS is calculated, including the exemptions from it for Blue Box and *De Minimis* Support, see Raj Bhala, *World Agricultural Trade in Purgatory*, 79 NORTH DAKOTA LAW REVIEW 691–830 (2003).

As for the third text, America read it to create an exception to the Article 3:1(b) prohibition on import substitution subsidies. Unless Paragraph 7 to Annex 3 of the *Agriculture Agreement* is read to carve out from this prohibition payments to agriculture processors, the Paragraph is inutile. That is because if a domestic user, like an American textile mill, could get a Step 2 Payment regardless of the origin of cotton — American or foreign — then the benefit to American cotton producers would evaporate, and the Step 2 Payment scheme would change from a subsidy in favor of agricultural producers to an input subsidy. That is, the scheme would be not a cotton subsidy, but a textile subsidy.

The American defense hinged on two fundamental questions. First, in the *Cotton* case context, did the *Agriculture* and *SCM Agreements* conflict? Second, does Paragraph 7 of Annex 3 to the *Agriculture Agreement* say what the U.S. thinks? "No" was the answer to both questions.

The inference the U.S. drew from the introductory clause of the *chapeau* to Article 3:1(b) of the *SCM Agreement* and Article 21:1 of the *Agriculture Agreement* was a *non sequitur*. Drawing on these textual provisions meant the U.S. was relying on yet another, and key, provision of the *Agriculture Agreement*, Article 6:3, which states:

> A Member shall be considered to be in compliance with its domestic support reduction commitments in any year in which its domestic support in favor of agricultural producers expressed in terms of Current Total AMS does not exceed the corresponding annual or final bound commitment level specified in Part IV of the Member's Schedule.

Article 6:3 does not excuse Red Light subsidies, be they import substitution subsidies or export subsidies. Rather, Article 6:3 caps the amount of domestic agricultural support a WTO Member can provide in keeping with its Uruguay Round commitments to cut progressively this support.

In brief, Article 6:3 does not delineate permissible from forbidden types of support. Rather, it speaks only to permissible support, and addresses whether the volume of that support is excessive. As the Panel explained, just because a subsidy program satisfies the Article 6:3 reduction commitment does not mean the program is lawful under the *SCM Agreement*, nor does it immunize the program from a claim it is illegal under the *SCM Agreement*. The *Agriculture* and *SCM Agreement* obligations — to stay within reduction commitments and to eschew Red Light subsidies, respectively — are parallel obligations. Moreover, as the obligations are coherent and consistent, there is no conflict between the accords, hence Article 21 of the *Agriculture Agreement* was inapplicable.

As for the third textual provision, the U.S. simply read Paragraph 7 to Annex 3 of the Agriculture Agreement wrongly. Nothing in it even intimates an exemption from the ban on Red Light import substitution subsidies, nor is its scope limited to support with an import substitution component. Further, even if Step 2 Payments were made to processors regardless of the origin of the cotton they used, they would still buy at least some American cotton. Consequently, American cotton farmers would get some benefit from the measure. Contrary to the American argument, the Paragraph refers to support for agricultural process that, in turn, benefit producers of a basic agricultural product.

The Appellate Body agreed wholeheartedly with the Panel's analysis. It rejected the American contention the Panel failed to give meaning to the introductory phrase of Article 3:1(b) of the *SCM Agreement*, or that the Panel had rendered Paragraph 7 to Annex 3 of the *Agriculture Agreement* inutile by refusing to limit its scope to import substitution subsidies. In attempting to use Article 6:3 of the *Agriculture Agreement* as a shield against an Article 3:1(b) claim, the U.S. stretched too far the meaning of Article 6:3. Rather, said the Appellate Body, Brazil correctly characterized matters: the obligations of the *Agriculture* and *SCM Agreements* apply cumulatively, unless there is an exception or conflict. But, no inconsistency exists in this case. A WTO Member can—and plenty of them do—grant domestic support to farmers without making them contingent on domestic content.

With no stronger shield on appeal than before, the U.S. itself might have predicted the conclusion the Appellate Body would reach, namely, to uphold the finding of the Panel. Step 2 Payments to users are manifestly contingent on the use of American cotton. The U.S. admitted a domestic user must open a bale of domestically produced cotton in order to qualify for a subsidy. It had no other choice. The Payments are a textbook example of *de jure* import substitution subsidy forbidden by Article 3:1(b) of the *SCM Agreement*, as Section 1207(a) of the *FSRI Act of 2002* states the cotton must be "domestically produced," and "not imported," and expressly establishes use of the American cotton as a prerequisite for receipt of the subsidy.

Second: Step 2 Payments to Exporters as Red Light Export Subsidies[29]

Brazil won at the Panel and appellate stage with the same 2-pronged argument against Step 2 Payments to exporters. They violate the *Agriculture Agreement* and *SCM Agreement*. The Brazilian argument proceeded in accordance with the Appellate Body Compliance Report, *Canada—Dairy (Article 21:5—New Zealand and U.S.)*.[30] In that case, the Appellate Body held the WTO-consistency of an export subsidy for an agricultural product must be examined, first, under the *Agriculture Agreement*, and second, if necessary, under the *SCM Agreement*.

This two-step method, however, does not preclude using the *SCM Agreement* for guidance to interpret the *Agriculture Agreement*. To the contrary, as the Appellate Body observed in the Compliance Report in the *Foreign Sales Corporation* case, the export contingency requirement in Article 3:1(a) of the *SCM Agreement* and Article

---

29. *See Cotton* Appellate Body Report, ¶¶ 249(d)(ii), 553-584, 763(d)(ii).

30. *See* Appellate Body Report, *Canada—Measures Affecting the Importation of Milk and the Exportation of Dairy Products—Recourse to Article 21:5 of the DSU by New Zealand and the United States*, ¶ 123, WT/DS103/AB/RW, WT/DS113/AB/RW (3 December 2001), *Cotton* Appellate Body Report, ¶ 570.

1(e) of the *Agriculture Agreement* and is the same.[31] Likewise, Brazil successfully exploited the nearly identical language in Article 9:1(a) of the *Agriculture Agreement* and Article 3:1(a) of the *SCM Agreement,* namely, ("contingent on export performance"). The already-considerable jurisprudence on export subsidies under Article 3:1(a) was instructive, and there is no reason to interpret the phrase differently in the two *Agreements.* Additionally, Brazil took advantage of an irrebuttable presumption. If a measure fits in one of the two Red Light categories of the *SCM Agreement* (an Article 3:1(a) export subsidy, or an Article 3:1(b) import substitution subsidy), then there is no need to show it has an adverse effect.

First, Step 2 Payments for exporters easily fit on the list of export subsidies in Article 9:1(a) of the *Agriculture Agreement,* because (in the words of that Article), they are "contingent on export performance." Article 9:1(a) speaks of

> the provision by governments or their agencies of direct subsidies, includ-
> ing payments-in-kind, to a firm, to an industry, to producers of an agricul-
> tural product, to a cooperative or other association of such producers, or to
> a marketing board, contingent on export performance . . . .

Article 9:1(a) is relevant, because Article 1(e) of the *Agriculture Agreement* refer-ences it. Article 1(e) defines "export subsidies" as "subsidies contingent upon export performance," including the export subsidies listed in Article 9 of the *Agreement.* What does "contingent" mean?

The ordinary meaning, which the Appellate Body noted in its 1999 Report in the *Canada—Aircraft* case,[32] and its Compliance Report in that case, *Canada—Aircraft (Article 21.5—Brazil),*[33] is "conditional," "dependent," or "tied to." Thus, any relationship of this nature between the granting of a subsidy and export perfor-mance is an export subsidy under Article 3:1(a) of the *SCM Agreement,* and under Article 9:1(a) of the Agriculture Agreement. Without doubt, that relationship exists as regards Step 2 Payments to exporters. The authorizing legislation, Section 1207(a) of the *FSRI Act,* expressly conditions receipt of payment on proof of exportation of American cotton. It says support is available to "exporters" for "sales for export by exporters," and in order to claim a Payment, an exporter must submit an applica-tion and supporting documentation, including proof of export, to the CCC. There could hardly be a closer tie between payment and exportation. Thus, held the Panel

31. *See* Appellate Body Report, *United States — Tax Treatment for "Foreign Sales Corporations" — Recourse to Article 21:5 of the DSU by the European Communities,* ¶ 192, WT/DS108/AB/RW (14 January 2002) [hereinafter *Tax Treatment* Appellate Body Report]; *Cotton* Appellate Body Report, ¶ 571.

32. *See* Appellate Body Report, *Canada—Measures Affecting the Export of Civilian Aircraft,* ¶ 179, WT/DS70/AB/R (2 August 1999); *Cotton* Appellate Body Report, ¶¶ 574, 578, 582.

33. *See* Appellate Body Report, *Canada—Measures Affecting the Export of Civilian Aircraft—Recourse by Brazil to Article 21:5 of the DSU,* ¶ 47, WT/DS70/AB/RW (21 July 2000); *Cotton* Appel-late Body Report, ¶¶ 574, 578, 582.

and Appellate Body, the Payments are inconsistent with Articles 3:3 and 8 of that *Agriculture Agreement*.

The second prong of the Brazilian argument against Step 2 Payments to exporters invoked the *SCM Agreement*. They are *per se* illegal, because they are *de jure* Red Light export subsidies under Article 3:1(a) of the *SCM Agreement*. This provision states:

> Except as provided in the *Agreement on Agriculture*, the following subsidies, within the meaning of Article 1, shall be prohibited:
>
> (a) subsidies contingent, in law or in fact[4], whether solely or as one of several other conditions, upon export performance, including those illustrated in Annex I;[5]

---

[4] This standard is met when the facts demonstrate that the granting of a subsidy, without having been made legally contingent upon export performance, is in fact tied to actual or anticipated exportation or export earnings. The mere fact that a subsidy is granted to enterprises which export shall not for that reason alone be considered to be an export subsidy within the meaning of this provision.

[5] Measures referred to in Annex I as not constituting export subsidies shall not be prohibited under this or any other provision of this *Agreement*.

If Step 2 Payments are contingent on export performance under the *Agriculture Agreement*, then so too are they under the above-quoted provision. "Indeed," replied the Appellate Body—albeit with considerably more words than one.

To the *Cotton* Panel and Appellate Body, the U.S. made the same losing argument: Step 2 Payments are not export subsidies, because they are available not only to exporters, but also to domestic users of American cotton. That this argument, summarized by the phrase "the subsidy is export-neutral because it is available in both circumstances," would be unsuccessful was predictable. That is because it was conceptually no different from the unsuccessful American defense of the *Extraterritorial Income Exclusion Act (ETI Act)* in *U.S.—Foreign Sales Corporation (Article 21:5—EC)*.[34] The *ETI Act* was the effort of the Clinton Administration to comply with the adverse Appellate Body decision in the *Foreign Sales Corporation* case. The EC charged the *ETI Act* (like its predecessor) still provided an export subsidy. The Appellate Body agreed, ruling in the Compliance Report, *U.S.—Foreign Sales Corporation (Article 21:5—EC)*, an expansion of the universe of potential beneficiaries beyond exporters does not negate the reality an export subsidy exists:

> 579. The Appellate Body rejected the United States' contention in *US—FSC (Article 21:5—EC)* because it considered it necessary, under Article 3.1(a) of the *SCM Agreement*, "to examine separately the conditions pertaining to the grant of the subsidy in the two different situations." It then confirmed the Panel's finding that the tax exemption in the first situation, namely for property produced within the United States and held for use

---

34. *See Tax Treatment* Appellate Body Report, ¶¶ 110, 115, 119–120.

outside the United States, is an export-contingent subsidy. In its reasoning, the Appellate Body explained that whether or not the subsidies were export-contingent in both situations envisaged by the measure would not alter the conclusion that the tax exemption in the first situation was contingent upon export:

> Our conclusion that the ETI measure grants subsidies that are export contingent in the first set of circumstances [property produced in the U.S. and held for use outside the U.S.] is not affected by the fact that the subsidy can also be obtained in the second set of circumstances [property produced outside the U.S. and held for use outside the U.S.]. The fact that the subsidies granted in the second set of circumstances *might* not be export contingent does not dissolve the export contingency arising in the first set of circumstances. Conversely, the export contingency arising in these circumstances has no bearing on whether there is an export contingent subsidy in the second set of circumstances.

580. As in *US — FSC (Article 21:5 — EC)*, the Panel in this case found that Step 2 payments are available in two situations, only one of which involves export contingency. The Panel's conclusion, therefore, is consistent with the Appellate Body's holding in *US — FSC (Article 21:5 — EC)* quoted above that "the fact that the subsidies granted in the second set of circumstances *might* not be export contingent does not dissolve the export contingency arising in the first set of circumstances."[35]

In brief, to pass muster as a lawful subsidy, an export contingency must be dissolved entirely, not merely diluted by broadening the beneficiaries to include non-exporters.

Indubitably, the U.S. was aware of the adverse precedent from the *Foreign Sales Corporation* case. It repeated the argument, however, because it said the facts in the *Cotton* case were distinguishable from the facts in *Foreign Sales Corporation*. They were akin to the facts in the 1999 *Canada — Dairy* dispute.[36] Thus, to be fair to the American argument, it followed old-fashioned legal advice of arguing facts when facts are favorable and law is not. The problem for the U.S., however, was the facts were as unfavorable as the law. Further, the lawyers for Brazil — a civil law country — proved every bit as adept, even more so, as their common law counterparts at distinguishing factual and legal situations.

---

35. *Cotton* Appellate Body Report, ¶¶ 579–580.

36. *See* Panel Report, *Canada — Measures Affecting the Importation of Milk and the Exportation of Dairy Products*, ¶¶ 7.41, 7.124 fn. 496, WT/DS103/R, WT/DS113/R (17 May 1999) (modified by the Appellate Body Report, *Canada — Measures Affecting the Importation of Milk and the Exportation of Dairy Products*, WT/DS103/AB/R, WT/DS113/AB/R (13 October 1999); *Cotton* Appellate Body Report, ¶ 581.

In *Canada—Dairy*, the complainants argued providing milk to exporters and processors, though various mechanisms called "special milk classes," was an export-contingent subsidy. The Panel in that case held the special milk classes were not export-contingent, because the milk also was available, often exclusively, to processors, which produce for the Canadian market. However, the relevant Canadian legislation and regulations did not have an explicit condition limiting a segment of the payments of subsidies to exporters. The Step 2 Payments legislation clearly delineated two sets of recipients—eligible domestic users, and eligible exporters. Moreover, the special milk classes were a single regulatory category of milk, and there was one set of conditions, not two, for payment. The Step 2 Payments scheme had two such categories with distinct requirements—support for users who opened a bale of American cotton, and support for exporters who proved they exported American cotton.

Third: Export Credit Guarantees as Red Light Export Subsidies[37]

The last major substantive appellate issue was whether the 3 American Export Credit Guarantee programs—GSM 102, GSM 103, and SCGP—were illegal. This issue, like the matter of the legality of Step 2 Payments, to exporters, is pedagogically useful and technically intriguing. It shows the relationship and interaction of the *SCM* and *Agriculture Agreements*. Agreeing with Brazil, the Panel found they were *per se* unlawful under Article 3:1(a) of the *SCM Agreement*, *i.e.*, they were Red Light export subsidies.

The Panel finding depended on two legal interpretations under the *Agriculture Agreement*. First, Article 10:2 of the *Agriculture Agreement* does not exempt the Export Credit Guarantees from the disciplines of Article 10:1 of that *Agreement*. These provisions state:

1. Export subsidies not listed in paragraph 1 of Article 9 shall not be applied in a manner which results in, or which threatens to lead to, circumvention of export subsidy commitments; nor shall non-commercial transactions be used to circumvent such commitments.

2. Members undertake to work toward the development of internationally agreed disciplines to govern the provision of export credits, export credit guarantees or insurance programs and, after agreement on such disciplines, to provide export credits, export credit guarantees or insurance programs only in conformity therewith.

Brazil also charged the Export Credit Guarantees violate Article 8 of the *Agriculture Agreement*, which states "[e]ach Member undertakes not to provide export subsidies otherwise than in conformity with this *Agreement* and with the commitments as specified in that Member's Schedule." The second legal interpretation concerns

---

37. *See Cotton* Appellate Body Report, ¶¶ 249(e)(i), (iii)-(iv), 585, 590–630, 763(e)(i), (iii)-(iv).

the *Peace Clause*. Because the Guarantees are not exempt from the Article 10 disciplines, and violate Article 8, they are not entitled to immunity under Article 13(c)(ii) of the *Agriculture Agreement*. In turn, without the immunity, the Guarantees are vulnerable to challenge under the *SCM Agreement*.

The Panel's finding also relied on the *SCM Agreement* to classify the Guarantees as an "export subsidy." Neither the *Agriculture Agreement* nor *SCM Agreement* explains precisely what an "export subsidy" is, in the sense of defining when a subsidy is "contingent on export performance." Article 1(e) of the *Agriculture Agreement* has a general definition of "export subsidies," namely, "subsidies contingent upon export performance, *including* the export subsidies listed in Article 9 of this *Agreement*."[38] Brazil argued Article 1(e) encompasses export credit guarantees, and thus places them within the scope of the Article 10:1 disciplines. Brazil said Article 10:2, which establishes 2 obligations, but no exceptions, does not remove them from this scope.

Moreover, as referenced in Article 1(e), Article 9:1 of the *Agriculture Agreement* sets out a non-exhaustive list of export subsidies. Significantly, Brazil and the U.S. stipulated export credit guarantees are not included on the Article 9:1 list. Entitled "Export Subsidy Commitments," Article 9:1 of the *Agriculture Agreement* states in full:

> 1. The following export subsidies are subject to reduction commitments under this *Agreement*:
>
> (a) the provision by governments or their agencies of direct subsidies, including payments-in-kind, to a firm, to an industry, to producers of an agricultural product, to a cooperative or other association of such producers, or to a marketing board, contingent on export performance;
>
> (b) the sale or disposal for export by governments or their agencies of non-commercial stocks of agricultural products at a price lower than the comparable price charged for the like product to buyers in the domestic market;
>
> (c) payments on the export of an agricultural product that are financed by virtue of governmental action, whether or not a charge on the public account is involved, including payments that are financed from the proceeds of a levy imposed on the agricultural product concerned or on an agricultural product from which the exported product is derived;
>
> (d) the provision of subsidies to reduce the costs of marketing exports of agricultural products (other than widely available export promotion and advisory services) including handling, upgrading and other processing costs, and the costs of international transport and freight;

---

38. Emphasis added.

(e) internal transport and freight charges on export shipments, provided or mandated by governments, on terms more favorable than for domestic shipments;

(f) subsidies on agricultural products contingent on their incorporation in exported products.

2. (a) Except as provided in sub-paragraph (b), the export subsidy commitment levels for each year of the implementation period, as specified in a Member's Schedule, represent with respect to the export subsidies listed in paragraph 1 of this Article:

> (i) in the case of budgetary outlay reduction commitments, the maximum level of expenditure for such subsidies that may be allocated or incurred in that year in respect of the agricultural product, or group of products, concerned; and

> (ii) in the case of export quantity reduction commitments, the maximum quantity of an agricultural product, or group of products, in respect of which such export subsidies may be granted in that year.

(b) In any of the second through fifth years of the implementation period, a Member may provide export subsidies listed in paragraph 1 above in a given year in excess of the corresponding annual commitment levels in respect of the products or groups of products specified in Part IV of the Member's Schedule, provided that:

> (i) the cumulative amounts of budgetary outlays for such subsidies, from the beginning of the implementation period through the year in question, does not exceed the cumulative amounts that would have resulted from full compliance with the relevant annual outlay commitment levels specified in the Member's Schedule by more than 3 per cent of the base period level of such budgetary outlays;

> (ii) the cumulative quantities exported with the benefit of such export subsidies, from the beginning of the implementation period through the year in question, does not exceed the cumulative quantities that would have resulted from full compliance with the relevant annual commitment levels specified in the Member's Schedule by more than 1.75 per cent of the base period quantities;

> (iii) the total cumulative amounts of budgetary outlays for such export subsidies and the quantities benefiting from such export subsidies over the entire implementation period are no greater than the totals that would have resulted from full compliance with the relevant annual commitment levels specified in the Member's Schedule; and

> (iv) the Member's budgetary outlays for export subsidies and the quantities benefiting from such subsidies, at the conclusion of the implementation period, are no greater than [64] percent and [79]

percent of the 1986–1990 base period levels, respectively. For developing country Members these percentages shall be [76] and [86] percent,
respectively.

3. Commitments relating to limitations on the extension of the scope of
export subsidization are as specified in Schedules.

4. During the implementation period, developing country Members shall
not be required to undertake commitments in respect of the export subsidies listed in sub-paragraphs (d) and (e) of paragraph 1 above, provided
that these are not applied in a manner that would circumvent reduction
commitments.

However, because the list is not exclusive, would it be too strong an inference to say
"the Article 10:1 disciplines on export subsidies are inapplicable to export credit
guarantees because these guarantees are not on the Article 9:1 list"? For two reasons, the Panel, and two Appellate Body members, thought so.

First, the first clause of Article 10:1 (a maddening double negative) carves out
from its disciplines only one kind of export subsidy—export subsidies listed in
Article 9:1 of the *Agriculture Agreement*. (Stated in the affirmative, if an export subsidy *is* listed in Article 9:1, then it is exempt from the anti-circumvention obligations
of Article 10:1.) Because of the Brazilian-American stipulation, the disputed guarantees were not on the list. Hence, they were not exempted under the first clause.[39]
This plain-meaning logic is the strongest point in favor of the majority view.

Second, the Panel and Appellate Body majority turned to Annex I of the *SCM
Agreement*. This Annex, entitled "Illustrative List of Export Subsidies," offers guidance relevant to the interpretation of the term "export subsidy" as used in Article 10
of the *Agriculture Agreement*. Of particular relevance is Item (j) on the List, which
deals with guarantee provided at premium rates inadequate to cover long-term
operating costs and losses of the guarantee programs. Item (j) states:

> The provision by governments (or special institutions controlled by gov-
> ernments) of export credit guarantee or insurance programs, of insurance
> or guarantee programs against increases in the cost of exported products or
> of exchange risk programs, at premium rates which are inadequate to cover
> the long-term operating costs and losses of the programs.

Brazil urged, and the Panel and two Appellate Body members agreed, the American
Export Credit Guarantees fit within Item (j). Consequently, they believed it was
appropriate to apply Article 10:1 of the *Agriculture Agreement* to these Guarantees.

Manifestly, Article 10:2 mentions export credit guarantees, as well as export credits and insurance programs. The two obligations it creates are to construct disciplines on these measures, and to abide by the disciplines once they are in place. But,

---

39. *See Cotton* Appellate Body Report, ¶¶ 614–615.

Article 10:2 does not expressly exempt these measures from the existing disciplines of Article 10:1 in the *inter regnum*. If the Uruguay Round negotiators intended to carve out these measures from the Article 10:1 duty not to circumvent export subsidy commitments, then they would have explicitly revealed that intention in the text of Article 10:1 or 10:2.

The whole point of Article 10, reasoned the Panel and two-member Appellate Body majority, is to prevent circumvention of export subsidy commitments by establishing specific, binding rules for export competition. The title of the Article is "Prevention of Circumvention of Export Subsidy Commitments." The American position would leave WTO Members free to grant unlimited export subsidies, in the form of export credit guarantees, and thus circumvent those commitments.

Put succinctly, the Americans would have export credit guarantees completely unregulated until a WTO consensus is reached on disciplines. That may be true, but it is a fact of life in many international trade negotiations. The majority's statement—"[w]e find it difficult to believe that the [Uruguay Round] negotiators would not have been aware of and did not seek to address the potential that subsidized export credit guarantees, export credits and insurance programs could be used to circumvent a WTO Member's export subsidy reduction commitments"[40]—suggests the majority substituted its preference for a historical negotiating outcome.

The U.S. offered a powerful rebuttal to the Brazilian argument, and Panel holding. Article 10:2 makes it clear export subsidy disciplines in both the *Agriculture* and *SCM Agreements* are inapplicable to export credit guarantee programs. As a legal matter, the U.S. had the better argument, but it persuaded only one of the Appellate Body members (who filed a Dissent). The essence of the American argument was during the Uruguay Round, negotiators did not agree to put disciplines on agricultural export credits, export credit guarantees, and insurance programs. The negotiators took a deliberate decision not to include export credit guarantees, export credits, and insurance programs in Article 9:1 of the *Agriculture Agreement*. Rather, they opted to continue negotiations, and defer imposition of any obligations until a consensus is reached:

> On appeal, the United States again relies on the drafting history of the *Agreement on Agriculture*, which it considers "reflects that the Members very early specifically included export credits and export credit guarantees as a subject for negotiation and specifically elected *not* to include such practices among export subsidies in the WTO Agreements with respect to those goods within the scope of . . . the *Agreement on Agriculture*." The United States adds that "[b]y deleting an explicit reference to export credit guarantees from the illustrative list of export subsidies in Article 9:1, Members demonstrated that they had not agreed in the case of agricultural products

---

40. *Cotton* Appellate Body Report, ¶ 617.

that export credit guarantees constitute export subsidies that should be subject to export subsidy disciplines."[41]

Thus, until a bargain on export credits is reached, possibly in the Doha Round, the GSM 102 and 103 Programs, and SCGP, are not subject to Article 10:1 scrutiny. Further, by virtue of Article 21:1 of the *Agriculture Agreement*, these Programs also are not subject to the export subsidy disciplines of the *SCM Agreement*.

The American rendition of the history was accurate, as adduced by documents from the Uruguay Round. Further, it would be illogical for the negotiators of that Round to subject Amber Box subsidies to Article 6 reduction commitments, and to include export credits, guarantees, and insurance programs, but not also include them as part of the AMS calculation for the reduction commitments. Why would the negotiators have treated these measures as already disciplined export subsidies, but not permitted them to be included in the reduction commitments? (Brazil's reply to this question was the U.S. took a calculated risk when it steadfastly refused to consider its export credit guarantees as export subsidies, and decided not to include them in its Article 9 reduction commitments.) Moreover, the U.S. observed, the actions of WTO Members speak volumes. No Member had reported export credit guarantees in its schedule of commitments concerning export subsidy cuts.

Nevertheless, the Appellate Body rejected the American version of Uruguay Round history and its implications:

> We agree with the Panel that the meaning of Article 10:2 is clear from the provision's text, in its context and in the light of the object and purpose of the *Agreement on Agriculture*, consistent with Article 31 of the *Vienna Convention*. The Panel did not think it necessary to resort to negotiating history for purposes of its interpretation of Article 10:2. Even if the negotiating history were relevant for our inquiry, we do not find that it supports the United States' position. This is because it does not indicate that the negotiators did not intend to discipline export credit guarantees, export credits and insurance programs *at all*. To the contrary, it shows that negotiators were aware of the need to impose disciplines on export credit guarantees, given their potential as a mechanism for subsidization and for circumvention of the export subsidy commitments under Article 9. Although the negotiating history reveals that the negotiators struggled with this issue, it does not indicate that the disagreement among them related to whether export credit guarantees, export credits and insurance programs were to be disciplined at all. In our view, the negotiating history suggests that the disagreement between the negotiators related to which kinds of specific disciplines were to apply to such measures. The fact that negotiators felt that internationally agreed disciplines were necessary for these three measures also suggests that the disciplines that currently exist in the *Agreement*

---

41. *Cotton* Appellate Report, ¶ 622.

on Agriculture must apply pending new disciplines because, otherwise, it would mean that subsidized export credit guarantees, export credits, and insurance programs could currently be extended without any limit or consequence.

As for why no Member has reported in its schedule export credit guarantees as an export subsidy, the Appellate Body said "[t]here could have been several reasons . . . ."[42] The Appellate Body proceeded to give just one explanation: maybe they thought their particular export credit guarantee, export credit, or insurance program was free of any subsidy component, so the measure was not subject to export subsidy commitments.

Well, maybe. Evidently, the Appellate Body was more comfortable resting on its own speculation than the logic articulated by the U.S. and the practice of the Members. The Appellate Body concluded by holding:

> Accordingly, we do not believe that Article 10:2 of the *Agreement on Agriculture* exempts export credit guarantees, export credits and insurance programs from the export subsidy disciplines in the *Agreement on Agriculture*. This does not mean that export credit guarantees, export credits and insurance programs will necessarily constitute export subsidies for purposes of the *Agreement on Agriculture*. Export credit guarantees are subject to the export subsidy disciplines in the *Agreement on Agriculture* only to the extent that such measures include an export subsidy component. If no such export subsidy component exists, then the export credit guarantees are not subject to the *Agreement's* export subsidy disciplines. Moreover, even when export credit guarantees contain an export subsidy component, such an export credit guarantee would not be inconsistent with Article 10:1 of the *Agreement on Agriculture* unless the complaining party demonstrates that it is "applied in a manner which results in, or which threatens to lead to, circumvention of export subsidy commitments." Thus, under the *Agreement on Agriculture*, the complaining party must first demonstrate that an export credit guarantee program constitutes an export subsidy. If it succeeds, it must then demonstrate that such export credit guarantees are applied in a manner that results in, or threatens to lead to, circumvention of the responding party's export subsidy commitments within the meaning of Article 10.1 of the *Agreement on Agriculture*.[43]

In brief, the Appellate Body drew a far weaker inference than the U.S. from the decision of Uruguay Round negotiators to exclude from the list of export subsidies in Article 9:1 express mention of export credit guarantees, export credits, and insurance programs.

---

42. *Cotton* Appellate Body Report, ¶ 625.
43. *Cotton* Appellate Body Report, ¶ 626.

In so doing, the Appellate Body made matters far more complicated than the text of the *Agriculture Agreement* suggests. At bottom, the regulatory scheme for export subsidies in Article 9 and 10 is not Byzantine. Article 9:2 creates reduction commitments for export subsidies listed in Article 9:1. Article 10:1 deals with export subsidies not listed in Article 9:1. The 2 provisions are mutually exclusive, and taken together, cover the universe of export subsidies—with the major exception of programs covered by Article 10:2. If a particular export subsidy is not listed in Article 9:1, then it must be covered by Article 10:1, or exempt under Article 10:2. The obligation in Article 10:1 is to eschew circumvention of export subsidy commitments in Article 9. (Though it split the infinitive, the Dissent rightly put it: "I see the first part of Article 10:1 as setting out a catch-all provision, designed to potentially cover an export subsidy that is used to circumvent the reduction commitments under Article 9."[44])

In effect, Article 10:1 preserves the integrity of these commitments. It anticipates an unscrupulous or naïve WTO Member might create an export subsidy program not on the Article 9:1 list, and the non-listed program might undermine the Member's Article 9:2 reduction commitments. As for Article 10:2, it proclaims the types of export subsidy programs on which there has been no consensus—either as to reducing their value and volume under Article 9:2, or as to imposing the anti-circumvention rule of Article 10:1.

The Appellate Body would have done the world trading community a service (which, admittedly, is not its express mandate), if it had provided a simple tutorial on how Articles 9–10 work. It might also have saved itself from the Dissent. Put differently, the Appellate Body would have realized the Americans got this one right—Article 10:2 does exempt export credit guarantees like the GSM 102 and 103, and SCGP measures from the discipline of Article 10:1.

The U.S. had a fallback argument. Even if the export subsidy disciplines of the *Agriculture* and *SCM Agreements* cover export credit guarantee programs, Article 3:1(a) of the *SCM Agreement* does not prohibit the particular American measures—GSM 102 and 103, and SCGP—at issue. These measures do not satisfy the criteria for inclusion in Item (j) of Annex I to that *Agreement*. The Appellate Body rather easily, though erroneously, upheld the Panel's contrary finding, and ruled the measures are *per se* illegal Red Light Export subsidies. The Appellate Body offered 2 rationales: the first logical, and the second quantitative.

First, said the Appellate Body, the American argument is premised on the proposition Article 10:2 of the *Agriculture Agreement* exempts export credit guarantees from the export subsidy disciplines of that *Agreement*. Because the Appellate Body found the American proposition meretricious, it rejected the fall back contention.[45] Second, the Appellate Body upheld the Panel analysis that the premiums associated

---

44. *Cotton* Appellate Body Report, ¶ 635.
45. *See Cotton* Appellate Body Report, ¶¶ 629–630, 658–674.

with the disputed American measures are inadequate to cover the long-term operating costs and losses of the American export credit guarantee programs. Thus, the measures fit within Item (j) of the *Illustrative List of Export Subsidies* annexed to the *SCM Agreement*. In 17 rather tedious paragraphs, the Appellate Body explained that regardless of the calculation methodology applied—Net Present Value (favored by the U.S.), Cost (*i.e.*, Cash Basis Accounting, favored by Brazil), or Fiscal Year/Cash Basis (using American data)—the premiums charged by the U.S. could not possibly cover long-term costs and losses.

Food aid was a final, interesting—but, ultimately, unpersuasive—consequentialist argument the American made. The U.S. said international food aid is, and should be, excluded from coverage under the *Agriculture Agreement*. But, under the expansive approach of Brazil and the Panel to Article 10:1 of the *Agreement*, it is subject to the full array of export subsidy disciplines. That is because Article 10:1 does not expressly exclude food aid (as it does not expressly exclude export credit guarantees). Moreover, said the U.S., food aid would be subject to a second set of disciplines, namely, the ones set forth in Article 10:4 of the *Agreement*. Article 10:4 states:

Members donors of international food aid shall ensure:

(a) that the provision of international food aid is not tied directly or indirectly to commercial exports of agricultural products to recipient countries;

(b) that international food aid transactions, including bilateral food aid which is monetized, shall be carried out in accordance with the FAO "Principles of Surplus Disposal and Consultative Obligations," including, where appropriate, the system of Usual Marketing Requirements (UMRs); and

(c) that such aid shall be provided to the extent possible in fully grant form or on terms no less concessional than those provided for in Article IV of the Food Aid Convention 1986.

In turn, urged the U.S., food security in developing countries and LDCs would be adversely affected, and surely the *Agreement* drafters did not intend this consequence.

Well-intentioned as the American argument might have been, the Appellate Body rejected it. It replied Article 10:4 does not exclude international food aid from the scope of Article 10:1. Rather, this aid is covered by the second clause of Article 10:1, at least to the extent the aid is a "non-commercial transaction." Article 10:4, then, ensures food aid is not used to circumvent the commitments a WTO Member makes on export subsidies. In other words, a WTO Member is free to grant as much food aid as it wishes, as long as it does so consistently with Articles 10:1 and 10:4.

Conclusion:

For at least three reasons, the *Cotton* case deserves exhaustive study. First, the dispute is a case study in relations between the North and South, developed and developing countries. The U.S. and Brazil, which had battled in the Uruguay Round over issues of industrial tariff and NTBs, services, and IP protection, continued their fight over agriculture from that Round into the *Cotton* case. Maddeningly to the U.S., Brazil sued it over its cotton subsidies, even though American Congressional officials responsible for writing farm subsidy legislation purportedly checked with Brazilian officials about that legislation. The American side thought it had an "O.K." from the Brazilian side, only to be sued after the Round. In bringing that case, Brazil was a voice for many poor countries, which chafed rather helplessly at a competitive playing field for their farm goods against American ones on world markets skewed by U.S. subsidies. The Cotton Four countries, Benin, Burkina Faso, Chad, and Mali, plus India, were among the poor countries for which the Brazilians spoke.

Second, *Cotton* puts paid the notion that poor countries cannot take on hegemonic trade powers and win. While many such countries still lack legal capacity to mount a challenge against America of the breadth, depth, and sophistication that Brazil did, the fact Brazil did so ought to give them hope. Brazil did not always have that capacity. It visibly increased its legal capacity with earlier disputes such as the 1999 *Canada Aircraft* case, and by meticulously reviewing American Farm Bills searching for potentially illegal subsidies. The complexity of local trade and trade-related laws in foreign countries, written and interpreted in a foreign language, can be overwhelming, even to a developed country with substantial legal capacity. But, *Upland Cotton* is proof that as far back as 2005, a developing country was able to recruit the legal capacity necessary to mount a successful legal attack on the world's most advanced one.

Third, the WTO jurisprudence on subsidies emanating from *Cotton* is critical. It gives key precedents on what constitutes an export subsidy, and why. To be sure, the Appellate Body did not do so in an economical way: its Report spans roughly 311 pages, of which 170 address the main issues. However, within a few years, with the 2011 *Airbus* and 2012 *Boeing* Reports, its written work would get far longer.

October 2014 Settlement:

In October 2014, America and Brazil signed an MOU settling their battle over cotton, putting an end to a case Brazil had launched 12 years earlier. Its key terms were:

The U.S. agreed to—

(1) Pay $300 million to the Brazil Cotton Institute.

(2) Change its GSM 102 export credit guarantee program for cotton to operate within certain parameters, namely, the payback period for financing would decrease from over two years to no more than 18 months.

In exchange, Brazil—

(1) Dropped all claims against the U.S. associated with the *Cotton* case, meaning it gave up its right to retaliate, which the WTO Appellate Body granted in the amount of $830 million, against an array of American companies.

(2) Promised not to sue the U.S. on the modified cotton subsidy programs America included in its 2012 *Farm Bill* until that *Bill* expired, which was 30 September 2019, *i.e.*, there would be no retaliation against cotton subsidy programs under the *Bill* in place at the time of the MOU.

For the U.S., the MOU ended uncertainty about retaliation. In 2010, Brazil opted not to retaliate only because the U.S. agreed to make annual $147 million payments to help its cotton industry compete against the subsidies the Appellate Body had ruled unlawful. Brazil again threatened retaliation in October 2013, when America ceased those payments thanks to cuts in the U.S. budget.

As for Brazil, even more than the lump sum payment, it cared about the reduction in distortions to global cotton prices it anticipated would occur because of the GSM 102 modifications. But, without an end to all American cotton subsidies, how significant would the reduction be?

The MOU set a precedent in American agricultural trade policy. For the first time, the U.S. agreed in the context of GATT-WTO negotiations to singling out a particular crop—cotton—for special treatment from other crops eligible for governmental support.[46]

- **2011 *Airbus*[47]**

Issue:

The key schemes the U.S. targeted were seven types of Launch Aid (also called LA/MSF) contracts for the A330-200, A340-500/600, and A380, granted by the governments of Germany, Spain, and the U.K. The U.S. alleged these Launch Aid measures were, in fact, tied to anticipated exportation of the A380 and, therefore, were contingent in fact on export performance. So, on appeal at issue was whether the Panel was correct that certain subsidies were prohibited export subsidies under Article 3:1(a) and Footnote 4 of the *SCM Agreement*, as *de facto* contingent on anticipated export performance.

Holding:

The Appellate Body reversed the Panel, giving the EU a victory. However, the victory was incomplete. The Appellate Body did not say the EU was correct, nor did it say the controversial subsidies were not contingent on export performance. Instead, it said the facts on the record were insufficient to determine whether the Launch Aid subsides were:

> granted so as to provide an incentive to Airbus to export in a way that is *not simply reflective of the conditions of supply and demand in the domestic and export markets* undistorted by the granting of these subsidies.[48]

---

46. *See* Randy Schnepf, *Status of the WTO Brazil—U.S. Cotton Case*, Congressional Research Service 7-5700, R3336 (1 October 2014), www.crs.gov.

47. This case is cited, and its facts summarized, in an earlier Chapter.

48. *Airbus* Appellate Body Report, ¶ 1104 (emphasis added).

This language is important. It creates a standard for *de facto* export contingency useful in future disputes.

Rationale:

To understand the Appellate Body reversal of the Panel, recall the analysis of the Appellate Body in the 1999 *Canada Aircraft* dispute. Both the Panel and Appellate Body relied heavily on the definition of "contingent." As discussed in *Canada Aircraft*, to make out a case for a *de facto* export subsidy, according to Article 3:1(a) and Footnote 4, a complainant must show (1) a subsidy was granted, and (2) the subsidy is tied to (3) actual or anticipated exportation or export earnings. As the Appellate Body reiterated:

> . . . the Appellate Body emphasized [in *Canada Aircraft*] that, under the second sentence of Footnote 4, "merely knowing that a recipient's sales are export-oriented does not demonstrate, without more, that the granting of a subsidy is tied to actual or anticipated exports." Rather, "the export orientation of a recipient may be taken into account as *a* relevant fact, provided that it is one of several facts which are considered and is not the only fact supporting a finding."[49]

However, in applying the standard of *Canada Aircraft*, the Panel in *Airbus* erroneously created a new standard that conflicted with the prior precedent.

Configuring and analyzing the facts, the Panel found in favor of the U.S.:

> . . . without being decisive, this evidence supports the view that the provision of LA/MSF on sales-dependent repayment terms was, at least in part, "conditional" or "dependent for its existence" upon the EC [European Community] member States' anticipated exportation or export earnings.[50]

On appeal, the EU argued the Panel got the standard under Article 3:1(a) and Footnote 4 wrong. The Panel created a "dependent motivation test," whereby *de facto* export contingency could be shown simply by observing a government anticipated exports, and that because of its anticipation of exports, it granted the subsidy.[51] The EU called this test "dependent motivation," because the Panel looked at dependency on anticipated exportation, and then inquired whether the motivation for the subsidy was because of that anticipation.

Stated differently, this test was backwards reasoning, as it inferred from (1) the anticipation of exports that (2) a government granted a subsidy. But, because of the nature of the LCA market, exports invariably are anticipated, so a subsidy invariably would be inferred. Research, development, and production of LCA are too costly, and no domestic market is sufficiently large and profitable, such that Airbus (or Boeing, for that matter) would operate without exportation. Here, Airbus could

---

49. *Canada Aircraft* Appellate Body Report, ¶ 1039 (emphasis original).
50. *Airbus* Panel Report, ¶ 1032.
51. *Airbus* Appellate Body Report, ¶¶ 1040, 1060.

only repay the Launch Aid loans if it exported LCA. The EU knew this fact when it granted the loan contracts, and thus must have expected that—by virtue of the contracts—Airbus exports would increase.

The Panel said therein lays the *de facto* contingency: anticipation of exports. But, is that truly enough to constitute a tie to exports, or—as *Canada Aircraft* indicates—it is necessary to show the motivation for the subsidy increased exports? The EU countered that mere anticipation of exports does not necessarily mean it granted Launch Aid as an inducement to export, or to alter normal market conditions of supply and demand.

So, when are exports anticipated or expected, and what is the correct standard for *de facto* export contingency? The Appellate Body provided the following insight:

1044. Where a subsidy is alleged to be "in fact tied to . . . anticipated exportation," the relationship of conditionality is, unlike in the case of *de jure* export contingency, not expressly or by necessary implication provided in the terms of the relevant legal instrument granting the subsidy. Under such circumstances, we consider that *the factual equivalent of such conditionality can be established by recourse to the following test: is the granting of the subsidy geared to induce the promotion of future export performance by the recipient?*

1045. In reaching this interpretation of the standard for *de facto* export contingency under Article 3:1(a) and Footnote 4 of the *SCM Agreement*, we do *not* suggest that the standard is met merely because the granting of the subsidy is designed to increase a recipient's production, even if the increased production is exported in whole. We also do *not* suggest that the fact that the granting of the subsidy may, in addition to increasing exports, *also* increase the recipient's domestic sales would prevent a finding of *de facto* export contingency. Rather, *we consider that the standard for de facto export contingency under Article 3:1(a) and Footnote 4 of the SCM Agreement would be met when the subsidy is granted so as to provide an incentive to the recipient to export in a way that is not simply reflective of the conditions of supply and demand in the domestic and export markets undistorted by the granting of the subsidy.*

1046. The existence of *de facto* export contingency, as set out above, "must be *inferred* from the total configuration of the facts constituting and surrounding the granting of the subsidy," which *may include the following factors*: (i) the *design and structure* of the measure granting the subsidy; (ii) the *modalities of operation* set out in such a measure; and (iii) the relevant factual circumstances surrounding the granting of the subsidy that provide the *context* for understanding the measure's design, structure, and modalities of operation.

1047. Moreover, where relevant evidence exists, the assessment could be based on a comparison between, on the one hand, the ratio of *anticipated* export and domestic sales of the subsidized product that would come about in consequence of the granting of the subsidy, and, on the other hand, the situation in the absence of the subsidy. The situation in the absence of the subsidy may be understood on the basis of historical sales of the same product by the recipient in the domestic and export markets before the subsidy was granted. In the event that there are no historical data untainted by the subsidy, or the subsidized product is a new product for which no historical data exists, the comparison could be made with the performance that a profit-maximizing firm would hypothetically be expected to achieve in the export and domestic markets in the absence of the subsidy. *Where the evidence shows, all other things being equal, that the granting of the subsidy provides an incentive to skew anticipated sales towards exports, in comparison with the historical performance of the recipient or the hypothetical performance of a profit-maximizing firm in the absence of the subsidy, this would be an indication that the granting of the subsidy is in fact tied to anticipated exportation within the meaning of Article 3:1(a) and footnote 4 of the SCM Agreement.*[52]

In brief, the test for *de facto* export contingency is a market-based one, akin to the test for "benefit" from a financial contribution: from the total configuration of the facts (or what American lawyers call the "totality of the circumstances"), is the recipient encouraged to alter its pattern of domestic versus foreign sales for reasons other than normal market supply and demand factors?

An important point to remember is that actual effects are irrelevant—whether the subsidy does change the ratio of export sales does not matter. Rather, what matters is whether it is anticipated that it will do so on the basis of information available to the government at the time the government provides the subsidy.[53]

As the Appellate Body later summarized:

> . . . [W]e do not consider that the Panel erred in its interpretation of "anticipated exportation" under Footnote 4 of the *SCM Agreement*. We also do not consider that the Panel's interpretation of the term "anticipated exportation" led to the imposition of an erroneous "dependent motivation" standard. However, *the Panel erroneously interpreted Article 3:1(a) and Footnote 4 of the SCM Agreement by equating the standard for finding that the granting of a subsidy is in fact "tied to" anticipated exportation with a standard based on the reasons for granting a subsidy. . . . [T]o determine whether the granting of a subsidy is in fact tied to anticipated exportation, recourse may be had to the following test: Is the granting of the subsidy geared to induce the promotion of future export performance by the recipient?* The Panel's interpretation

---

52. *Airbus* Appellate Body Report, ¶¶ 1044–1046 (footnotes omitted) (emphasis original; emphasis added on last sentences in ¶¶ 1044–1045, and in ¶¶ 1046–1047).

53. *Airbus* Appellate Body Report, ¶ 1049.

of the term "in fact tied to" under Article 3:1(a) and Footnote 4 of the *SCM Agreement* is not consistent with this interpretation we set out above. We therefore *reverse* the Panel's interpretation that, in order to find that the granting of a subsidy is in fact tied to anticipated exportation, a subsidy must be granted *because* of anticipated export performance.

The Panel should have looked at whether Launch Aid contracts gave Airbus an incentive to export in a way that did not reflect demand and supply forces in domestic and export markets for LCA vis-à-vis those forces in the absence of a subsidy.[54]

Consequently, the Appellate Body reversed the Panel findings that the U.S. successfully demonstrated that Launch Aid contracts for the A380 by the British, German, and Spanish governments were *de facto* Red Light subsidies.[55] They were not. Likewise, it reversed the Panel conclusion that the French A330-200, A340-500/600, and A380 contracts, and the Spanish A340-500/600 contracts were not contingent in fact on export performance. However, because of insufficient facts, the Appellate Body could not complete the analysis, and provide a definitive determination as to whether all such contracts were, or were not, illegal. By invalidating the Panel findings, the Appellate Body handed the Europeans a default victory against the American challenge.

Clarification but Questions:

This dispute is important because it gave the Appellate Body an opportunity to clarify its interpretation of Article 3:1(a) of the *SCM Agreement*. Even though it has been repeated numerous times, the concept behind Footnote 4 can be difficult to understand. It is not enough that a government knows or believes exports likely will increase if a subsidy is granted. Instead, to violate Article 3:1(a), a government must grant a subsidy in order to increase exports. Citing both *Canada Aircraft* and *Airbus* for this proposition provides a cogent synthesis of Appellate Body jurisprudence.

Is such a standard difficult to prove? Should it be difficult? How should the economic fact that Red Light subsidies are the most egregious affect the standard? How should the irrebuttable legal presumption that the Specificity Test is satisfied in a Red Light subsidy case affect the standard? In *Airbus*, did the Appellate Body heighten the criteria needed to satisfy Article 3, or simply maintain the level of scrutiny from *Canada Aircraft* and the language of that Article and its Footnote 4?

Does the Airbus standard create practical problems of proof? Consider that the Appellate Body language easily could be recast as an intent test: *de facto* export contingency requires proof a government intended to boost exports. How would a complainant meet this burden? Adroit governments are unlikely to create a clear record they intended to boost exports with their scheme. A complainant may have to look to legislative history, or circumstantial evidence. But, some legal systems reject reliance on one, the other, or both.

---

54. *Airbus* Appellate Body Report, ¶ 1104.
55. *Airbus* Appellate Body Report, ¶ 1083.

III. 2000 *Foreign Sales Corporations* Case on Export-Contingent Tax Exemptions

- **2000 *U.S. Foreign Sales Corporation*[56]**

Facts:

The Foreign Sales Corporation case lies at the intersection of International Trade Law and Tax Law. That means its facts are complex. Fortunately, in Section II of its Report, the Appellate Body gave an unusually clear, thorough summary of those facts:

A. *Overview of Relevant United States Tax Laws*

6. For United States citizens and residents, the tax laws of the United States generally operate "on a worldwide basis" [also called "unitary taxation"]. This means that, generally, the United States asserts the right to tax all income earned "worldwide" by its citizens and residents. A corporation organized under the laws of one of the fifty American states or the District of Columbia is a "domestic," or United States, corporation, and is "resident" in the United States for purposes of this "worldwide" taxation system. Under United States tax law, "foreign" corporations are defined as all corporations that are *not* incorporated in one of the fifty states or the District of Columbia.

7. The United States generally taxes any income earned by foreign corporations within the territory of the United States. The United States generally does not tax income that is earned by foreign corporations outside the United States. However, such "foreign-source" income of a foreign corporation generally will be subject to United States taxation when such income is "effectively connected with the conduct of a trade or business within the United States." United States tax laws and regulations provide for the tax authorities to conduct a factual inquiry to determine whether a foreign corporation's income is "effectively connected" income.

8. Many foreign corporations are related to United States corporations. Generally, a United States parent corporation is only subject to taxation on income earned by its foreign subsidiary when such income is transferred to the United States parent in the form of a dividend. The period between the earning of such income by the subsidiary and the transfer to the United States parent company of a dividend is called "deferral" under the United States tax system, because the payment of tax on that income is deferred until the income is repatriated to the United States.

---

56. *See* Appellate Body Report, *United States — Tax Treatment for "Foreign Sales Corporations,"* WT/DS108/AB/R (adopted 20 March 2000).

9.   The United States has also adopted a series of "anti-deferral" regimes that depart from the principle of deferral and that, in general, respond to specific policy concerns about potential tax avoidance by United States corporations through foreign affiliates. One of these regimes is Subpart F of the United States Internal Revenue Code (the "IRC"), which limits the availability of deferral for certain types of income earned by certain controlled foreign subsidiaries of United States corporations. Under Subpart F, certain income earned by a foreign subsidiary can be imputed to its United States parent corporation even though it has not yet been repatriated to the parent in the form of a dividend. The effect of Subpart F is that a United States parent corporation is immediately subject to United States taxation on such imputed income even while the income remains with the foreign subsidiary.

10. These generally prevailing United States tax rules are altered for FSCs by the FSC measure.

B.   *The FSC Measure*

11. FSCs are foreign corporations responsible for certain sales-related activities in connection with the sale or lease of goods produced in the United States for export outside the United States. The FSC measure essentially exempts a portion of an FSC's export-related foreign-source income from United States income tax. The relevant tax regime is comprised of three separate elements, which affect the tax liability under United States law of an FSC as well as of the United States corporation that supplies goods for export. . . .

12. A corporation must satisfy several conditions to qualify as an FSC. To qualify, a corporation must be a foreign corporation organized under the laws of a country that shares tax information with the United States, or under the laws of a United States possession other than Puerto Rico. The corporation must satisfy additional requirements relating to its foreign presence, to the keeping of records, and to its shareholders and directors. The corporation must also elect to be an FSC for a given fiscal year. There is no statutory requirement that an FSC be affiliated with or controlled by a United States corporation. The FSC measure is, however, such that the benefit to both FSCs and the United States corporations that supply goods for export will, as a practical matter, often be greater if the United States supplier is related to the FSC. As a result, many FSCs are controlled foreign subsidiaries of United States corporations.

13. The foreign-source income of an FSC may be broadly divided into "foreign trade income" and all other foreign-source income. "Foreign trade income" is essentially the foreign-source income attributable to an FSC from qualifying transactions involving the export of goods from the United States. An FSC's other foreign-source income may include

inter alia "investment income," such as interest, dividends and royalties, and active business income not deriving from qualifying export transactions. This appeal raises a number of issues with respect to the taxation of an FSC's *foreign trade income*. Foreign trade income is in turn divided into *exempt* foreign trade income and *non-exempt* foreign trade income. As explained below, the United States tax treatment of an FSC's *exempt* foreign trade income differs from the United States tax treatment of an FSC's *non-exempt* foreign trade income.

14. An FSC's foreign trade income is its "foreign trading gross receipts" generated in qualifying transactions. Qualifying transactions involve the sale or lease of "export property" or the performance of services "related and subsidiary" to such sale or lease. "Export property" is property manufactured or produced in the United States by a person other than an FSC, sold or leased by or to an FSC for use, consumption or disposition outside the United States, and of which no more than 50 per cent of its fair market value is attributable to imports. In addition, for FSC income to be foreign trade income, certain economic processes relating to qualifying transactions must take place outside the United States, and the FSC must be managed outside the United States.

15. Under the FSC measure, an FSC may, at its option, choose to apply one of three transfer pricing rules in order to calculate its foreign trade income from qualifying transactions. These pricing rules serve two purposes. First, the transfer pricing rules allocate the income from transactions involving United States export property as between an FSC and its United States supplier. The part of this income attributable to the FSC is its foreign trade income (*i.e.*, exempt and non-exempt foreign trade income). The second purpose of the transfer pricing rules is to determine how much of the income from transactions involving United States export property that is allocated to the FSC as foreign trade income is *exempt* foreign trade income, and how much of it is *non-exempt* foreign trade income. The transfer pricing rule applied to determine the amount of the FSC's foreign trade income must also be applied to determine the division of that foreign trade income into exempt and non-exempt foreign trade income.

C. *Exemptions Provided by the FSC Measure*

16. The FSC measure establishes three main exemptions which affect the United States tax liability of the FSC, of its United States supplier and, possibly United States shareholders. The first exemption relates to the United States tax treatment of the foreign-source income of a foreign corporation. Under United States law generally, the foreign-source income of a foreign corporation engaged in trade or business in the United States is taxable only to the extent that it is "effectively connected

with the conduct of a trade or business within the United States." This rule applies whether or not a foreign corporation is controlled by a United States corporation. To determine whether the foreign-source income of a foreign corporation is "effectively connected with the conduct of a trade or business within the United States," a factual inquiry is undertaken by the tax authorities. Under the FSC measure, however, the exempt portion of an FSC's foreign trade income is "treated as foreign source income which is not effectively connected with the conduct of a trade or business within the United States." In other words, the exempt portion of the FSC's foreign trade income is not subject to a factual inquiry to determine if it is "effectively connected with the conduct of a trade or business within the United States." Thus, under this first exemption, a portion of an FSC's foreign-source income is *legislatively determined not to be* "effectively connected" and, therefore, is not taxable in the hands of the FSC—without regard to what conclusion an administrative factual inquiry might come to in the absence of the FSC measure.

17. The second exemption relates to the United States tax treatment of certain income earned by a foreign corporation that is controlled by a United States corporation. Under United States law generally, a United States shareholder in a controlled foreign corporation must include in his gross income each year a *pro rata* share of certain forms of income of the foreign controlled corporation which has not yet been distributed to its United States parent. Such income is known as "Subpart F income." The United States shareholder corporation is immediately subject to United States tax on its Subpart F income, even though it has not yet received the income from its foreign affiliate. Under the FSC measure, however, the foreign trade income of an FSC is generally exempted from Subpart F. Thus, under this second exemption, the parent of an FSC is *not* required to declare its *pro rata* share of the undistributed income of an FSC that is derived from the foreign trade income of the FSC, and is *not* taxed on such income.

18. The third exemption deals with the tax treatment of dividends received by United States corporations from foreign corporations. Under United States law generally, dividends received by a United States corporation which are derived from the foreign-source income of a foreign corporation are taxable, unless such income has already been taxed under the Subpart F rules. Under the FSC measure, however, United States corporate shareholders of an FSC generally may deduct 100 per cent of dividends received from distributions made out of the foreign trade income of an FSC. Thus, under the third exemption, the parent of an FSC is generally not taxed on dividends received that are derived from the foreign trade income of the FSC.

Issue:

The key issue in the *Foreign Sales Corporation* dispute relevant to export subsides was whether the foreign sales credit (FSC) tax benefits provided by the U.S. IRC were subsidies contingent upon export performance, and thus prohibited under Article 3:1(a) of the *SCM Agreement*.

Holding:

The Appellate Body upheld the Panel, thus finding the FSC tax exemptions were subsidies contingent upon export performance prohibited under Article 3:1(a) of the *SCM Agreement*. To do so, the Appellate Body found Item (e), and Footnote 59, of the *Illustrative List of Export Subsidies* in Annex I of the *SCM Agreement* was not applicable to the dispute. Additionally, the 1981 Council action was not binding or helpful authority in this dispute.

Losing Arguments:

According to the U.S., Footnote 59 to the *Illustrative List of Export Subsidies* in Annex I of the *SCM Agreement* justified the FSC tax exemptions. Footnote 59 relates to Item (e) of the List. The pertinent part of Item (e) identifies as an export subsidy "the full or partial exemption, remission, or deferral specifically related to exports, of . . . social welfare charges paid or payable by industrial or commercial enterprises."

Moreover, the U.S. pointed to action taken by the GATT 1947 Council, in adopting 4 Tokyo Round Era GATT Panel Reports, known collectively as the *Tax Legislation Cases*, as interpretive authority regarding this Footnote. For these reasons, the FSC measure should not be classified as a Red Light export subsidy under Article 3:1(a).

Given these arguments, the Appellate Body spent much of its 65-paged Report addressing whether Footnote 59 applied, and the extent to which the 1981 Council action should be used as interpretive authority.

Rationale on Footnote 59:

To address the American argument, the Appellate Body examined footnote 59 sentence by sentence. Footnote 59 reads:

> The Members recognize that deferral need not amount to an export subsidy where, for example, appropriate interest charges are collected. *The Members reaffirm the principle that prices for goods in transactions between exporting enterprises and foreign buyers under their or under the same control should for tax purposes be the prices which would be charged between independent enterprises acting at arm's length.* Any Member may draw the attention of another Member to administrative or other practices which may contravene this principle and which result in a significant saving of direct taxes in export transactions. In such circumstances the Members shall normally attempt to resolve their differences using the facilities of existing bilateral tax treaties or other specific international mechanisms, without prejudice

to the rights and obligations of Members under GATT 1994, including the right of consultation created in the preceding sentence.

> Paragraph (e) is not intended to limit a Member from taking measures to avoid the double taxation of foreign-source income earned by its enterprises or the enterprises of another Member. (emphasis added)

Even a cursory review of this tortured language suggests the American argument was weak, and the Appellate Body analysis bore out that suggestion.

The first sentence did not bear much significance. It qualified a statement in Footnote 59 regarding deferral of direct taxes. However, the FSC measure did not involve the deferral of direct taxes, thus the Appellate Body said the first sentence of Footnote 59 was unhelpful in deciding whether the FSC measure was an export subsidy.

The second sentence of Footnote 59 reaffirmed, for tax purposes, the price of goods between exporting enterprises and controlled foreign buyers had to be determined according to the "arm's length" principle. To analyze the American argument regarding the arm's length requirement, the Appellate Body accepted, for the sake of argument, that WTO Members are not obliged to tax foreign-source income, and that Members may tax such income less than they tax domestic-source income. Moreover, even in the absence of Footnote 59, the Appellate Body made clear Members are not obligated by WTO rules to tax any categories of income, whether foreign or domestic.

These points led the Appellate Body to consider Article 1:1(a)(ii), which identifies as a "subsidy" government revenue that is "otherwise due," but is "foregone." The U.S. argued that absent a requirement to tax export-related foreign-source income, a government has not "foregone" revenue if it elects to tax that income. That is, only if a government is legally obligated to tax foreign-source income, but does not by a lawful exemption, can that government be said to have forewent taxes.

The Appellate Body disagreed. In its view, if the American argument were taken to its logical extreme, then there could never be a foregoing of revenue otherwise due. That is because a government always has the legal authority to tax all of the relevant income, or put conversely, no government ever is forced to tax. A reading of WTO rules that would render this provision inutile would be inappropriate.

The Appellate Body clarified the idea behind the foregoing of revenue otherwise due. As it put:

> the issue in dispute is whether, *having decided to tax a particular category of foreign-source income*, namely foreign-source income that is "effectively connected with a trade or business within the United States," the United States is *permitted to carve out an export contingent exemption from the category of foreign-source income that is taxed under its other rules of taxation.*[57]

---

57. *Foreign Sales Corporation* Appellate Body Report, ¶ 99.

To the Appellate Body, the second sentence of Footnote 59 did not address this question. The arm's length principle operates when a Member chooses not to tax, or to tax less, certain categories of foreign-source income. However, the operation of the arm's length principle is unaffected by the choice a Member makes as to which categories of foreign-source income, if any, it will not tax or will tax less.[58]

The third and fourth sentences of Footnote 59 relate to remedies, and were not relevant. The fifth sentence of Footnote 59 clarifies that Paragraph (e) was not intended to limit a Member from taking measures to avoid the double taxation of foreign-source income. Here, the Appellate Body rejected the American argument on procedural grounds. The Appellate Body found no indication the U.S. asserted the fifth sentence during the Panel stage. Under Article 17:6, the Appellate Body is mandated to address "issues of law covered in the Panel Report and legal interpretations developed by the panel."[59] The Appellate Body found the Panel did not review this substantive issue, thus it would be outside the scope of the Article 17:6 mandate.

Understanding Relationship among Different Provisions:

The Appellate Body did not spell out carefully its chain of logic, but essentially it was this: Item (e) identifies certain tax exemptions, remissions, or deferrals as *per se* unlawful export subsidies. Footnote 59 to Item (e) elaborates on deferral of taxes. Article 1:1(a)(1) of the *SCM Agreement* speaks about revenue otherwise due that is foregone, and such revenue invariably is associated with taxes. Such foregone revenue is not a subsidy.

The U.S. sought to argue the FSC measure was not an export subsidy within the meaning of Item (e). Rather, the FSC measure fell within the language of Footnote 59, namely, a tax exemption that conformed to the arm's length principle. If true, then the U.S. was not obligated to tax export-related foreign-sourced income. So, the FSC exemption was not revenue otherwise due but foregone, *i.e.*, it was not the kind of subsidy Article 1:1(a)(ii).

Put differently, the question is what is the relationship among Articles 1 and 3 of the *SCM Agreement* and the Annex I *List of Export Subsidies*? Conceptually, it is necessary to show a disputed measure is a "subsidy" under Article 1, and is contingent in law or fact on exportation under Article 3. It then is a Red Light export subsidy. The Annex I *List* provides illustrations that may buoy this conclusion if the disputed measure is on the *List*, or rightly analogized to an example on the *List*. But, because the List is non-exclusive, even if the disputed measure is not on the *List*, or not analogous to an item on the *List*, it still is unlawful if it meets the Article 1 and 3 requirements.

Is it permissible in a subsidy analysis to proceed directly to the *List*? There is no hard rule against doing so, and then working backwards. Suppose a disputed measure looks like an item on the *List*. The conclusion that it is an illegal export subsidy then requires satisfaction of the Articles 1 and 3 tests. The U.S. seemed to be taking

---

58. *Foreign Sales Corporation* Appellate Body Report, ¶ 99.
59. *Foreign Sales Corporation* Appellate Body Report, ¶ 103.

the converse of this approach: its FSC exemption was not on the List, and hence it did not qualify as an Article 1 subsidy.

Rationale on 1981 GATT Council Decision:

The second American contention, which also pertained to Footnote 59, was that the 1981 GATT Council action was relevant to the dispute, because that action formed part of GATT 1994. As such, it confirmed the American interpretation of Footnote 59.[60]

The 1981 Council action arose out of 4 disputes, the *Tax Legislation Cases*.[61] They involved France, Belgium, the Netherlands, and the U.S. The GATT Panels in these disputes, composed of the same individual members, found tax measures in each country involved export subsidies under GATT 1947, Article XVI:4. After some controversy and time, the CONTRACTING PARTIES adopted the Panel Reports, as the basis of a decision that became known as the "1981 Council action." It reads:

> The Council adopts these reports on the understanding that with respect to these cases, and in general, economic processes (including transactions involving exported goods) located outside the territorial limits of the exporting country need not be subject to taxation by the exporting country and should not be regarded as export activities in terms of Article XVI:4 of the General Agreement. It is further understood that Article XVI:4 requires that arm's-length pricing be observed, *i.e.*, prices for goods in transactions between exporting enterprises and foreign buyers under their or the same control should for tax purposes be the prices which would be charged between independent enterprises acting at arm's length. Furthermore, Article XVI:4 does not prohibit the adoption of measures to avoid double taxation of foreign source income.[62]

When adopted, the Chairman of the GATT 1947 also made the following Statement:

> Following the adoption of these reports the Chairman noted that the Council's decision and understanding does not mean that the parties adhering to Article XVI:4 are forbidden from taxing the profits on transactions beyond their borders, it only means that they are not required to do so. He noted further that the decision does not modify the existing GATT rules in Article XVI:4 as they relate to the taxation of exported goods. He noted also that this decision does not affect and is not affected by the Agreement on the Interpretation and Application of Articles VI, XVI and XXIII. Finally,

---

60. *See Foreign Sales Corporation* Appellate Body Report, ¶ 103.

61. Panel Reports, *Tax Legislation—United States Tax Legislation (DISC)*, L/4422, adopted 7–8 December 1981, B.I.S.D. (23rd Supp.) at 98; *Tax Legislation—Income Tax Practices Maintained By France*, L/4423, adopted 7–8 December 1981, B.I.S.D. (23rd Supp.) at 114; *Tax Legislation—Income Tax Practices Maintained By Belgium*, L/4424, adopted 7–8 December 1981, B.I.S.D. (23rd Supp.) at 127; *Tax Legislation—Income Tax Practices Maintained By The Netherlands*, L/4425, adopted 7–8 December 1981, B.I.S.D. (23rd Supp.) at 137.

62. *Tax Legislation*, L/5271, 7–8 December 1981, B.I.S.D. (28th Supp.) at 114.

he noted that the adoption of these reports together with the understanding does not affect the rights and obligations of contracting parties under the General Agreement.[63]

So, the first issue relating to the 1981 Council action was whether it formed part of GATT 1994 as an "other decision" under paragraph 1(b)(iv) of the language incorporating GATT 1994 into the *WTO Agreement*.

Though various legal instruments were included in this incorporation, Panel Reports are not typically included. In its 1996 *Japan Alcoholic Beverages* Report, the Appellate Body reasoned that Panel Reports are not binding, except with respect to resolving a particular dispute between the parties to that dispute. Yet, interestingly, the opening sentence of the 1981 Council action included the language "in general" when referring to the manner in which it was to be adopted.

According to the U.S., this language was enough to indicate the 1981 Council action was an authoritative interpretation of Article XVI:4 of GATT 1947, and bound all contracting parties. Neither the Appellate Body nor the Panel agreed with the U.S. They felt the ambiguity of the 1981 Council was insufficient to resolve the conflict, so they looked to the Chairman's Statement made when the 1981 Council action was adopted.

In that Statement, the Chairman said "the adoption of these reports together with the understanding does not affect the rights and obligations of contracting parties under the General Agreement."[64] This particular utterance was sufficient for the Appellate Body to find the 1981 Council action was only binding to the parties of the *Tax Legislation Cases*. Even so, the adopted panel reports in the *Tax Legislation Cases*, together with the 1981 Council action, may provide guidance.

But, using the *Tax Legislation Cases* Panel Reports as guidance was problematical. Those cases dealt with GATT Article XVI:4, whereas *Foreign Sales Corporation* dealt with Article 3:1(a) of the *SCM Agreement*. In previous cases where an Appellate Body examined a GATT Article with a supplementary agreement, that agreement explicitly addressed the relationship between the two relevant provisions.

Those pertinent provisions, the prohibition on export subsidies, and what standards to apply, differed significantly. Article XVI:4 prohibits export subsidies only when they result in the export sale of a product at a price lower than the "comparable price charged for the like product to buyers in the domestic market." In effect, this Article deals with export subsidies that facilitate dumping. In contrast, the *SCM Agreement* sets a much broader prohibition against any subsidy that is "contingent upon export performance."[65] Thus, Article XVI:4 does not provide much guidance regarding what would constitute a subsidy under Article 3:1(a) of the *SCM Agreement*.

---

63. *Tax Legislation*, L/5271, 7–8 December 1981, B.I.S.D. (28th Supp.) at 114.
64. *Foreign Sales Corporation* Appellate Body Report, ¶ 112.
65. *Foreign Sales Corporation* Appellate Body Report, ¶ 117.

In the end, the *Tax Legislation Cases* were of little consequence to the Appellate Body. It stated that even if the U.S. was correct that the 1981 Council action was relevant to Article 3:1(a) of the *SCM Agreement*, the *Tax Legislation Cases* were easily distinguishable on factual grounds:

> . . . [T]he GATT 1947 Council was not addressing the issue of whether, having decided to tax a particular category of foreign-source income, namely foreign-source income that is "effectively connected with a trade or business within the United States," the United States may provide an export contingent exemption from the category of foreign-source income that is taxed under its other rules of taxation.[66]

Thus, the Appellate Body upheld the Panel, finding the FSC tax exemptions involved subsidies contingent upon export performance barred by Article 3:1(a).

Conclusion:

Jurisprudentially, the Appellate Body decision on export subsidies in *Foreign Sales Corporation* is underwhelming. In the end, like a Common Law Court, the Appellate Body distinguished the facts of this case from those in the *Tax Legislation Cases*, and effectively disposed of the export subsidies issues in one paragraph.

But, in *dicta*, the Appellate Body provides some useful guidance for interpreting Item (e) of the Illustrative List of Export Subsidies in Annex I of the *SCM Agreement*. Insofar as it addressed the American arguments about The *List*, Footnote 59, and the Article 1:1(a)(ii) language concerning government revenue otherwise due that is foregone, the Appellate Body Report yields language useful for future disputes. Additionally, the Report contains a helpful review of the conflict between numerous WTO legal instruments, in particular finding that Article XVI:4 of GATT 1947 is not helpful in interpreting Article 3:1(a) of the *SCM Agreement*.

Real Underlying Dispute:

The true conflict between the U.S. and EU in the *Foreign Sales Corporation* case is manifest from the facts as described by the Appellate Body. In brief, the U.S. is alone in the world with its Unitary Taxation scheme, taxing income based not on territorial jurisdiction (the territory in which that income is sourced), but rather on nationality (being American).[67] This scheme puts American entities at a competi-

---

66. *Foreign Sales Corporation* Appellate Body Report, ¶ 120.

67. Under the *Tax Cuts and Jobs Act of 2018*, the U.S. introduced into the IRC the concept of GILTI—Global Intangible Low-Taxed Income. GILTI is a synthetic, formula-based income earned from offshore intangible assets. Essentially, GILTI equals the amount of income of a foreign subsidiary in excess of a 10% deemed rate of return on the depreciable tangible business assets of that subsidiary. GILTI rules allow for a 100% tax exemption on certain dividends from foreign subsidiaries (a "controlled foreign corporation," or "CFC"), so as to encourage parent U.S. companies to repatriate income from intangible, income-producing assets they previously shifted offshore. GILTI represents a partial shift from a worldwide (Unitary) to a territorial tax system. *See* 26 U.S.C. §§ 951A, 957.

tive disadvantage vis-à-vis European and other non-American entities that adhere to the territorial principle. In the EU, that adherence is manifest in a VAT.

As any traveller to the EU knows, items purchased there but carried outside the Union may receive a VAT rebate. So, too, is it with exports: the EU does not impose the VAT on exported merchandise. Adhering to the territorial principle, export revenues are generated outside the EU, namely, from the importers overseas. So, taxation (if any) would be by the importing country. Businesses operating in and exporting from the U.S. have long viewed this difference as unfair: they do not get an exemption from the American world-wide income tax scheme when they export from America, but businesses exporting from Europe do.

The FSC measure was tax relief, in the form of a tax exemption, designed to cure the problem. Supposedly, it would put American producer-exporters on a level playing field with their European counterparts. Moreover, the infamous Footnote 59 was designed to immunize the FSC measure from a lawsuit that the exemption was a subsidy. As per the Appellate Body Report, the sloppily drafted Footnote failed in this respect.

Anticipating the hue and cry its Report would bring, the Appellate Body finished it with two extraordinary paragraphs:

179. We wish to emphasize that our ruling is on the FSC measure only. As always, our responsibility under the *DSU* is to address the legal issues raised in an appeal in a dispute involving a particular measure. Consequently, this ruling is in no way a judgment on the consistency or the inconsistency with WTO obligations of any other tax measure applied by any Member. Also, this is not a ruling that a Member must choose one kind of tax system over another so as to be consistent with that Member's WTO obligations. In particular, this is not a ruling on the relative merits of "worldwide" and "territorial" systems of taxation. A Member of the WTO may choose any kind of tax system it wishes—so long as, in so choosing, that Member applies that system in a way that is consistent with its WTO obligations. Whatever kind of tax system a Member chooses, that Member will not be in compliance with its WTO obligations if it provides, through its tax system, subsidies contingent upon export performance that are not permitted under the covered agreements.

180. By entering into the *WTO Agreement*, each Member of the WTO has imposed on itself an obligation to comply with *all* the terms of that Agreement. This is a ruling that the FSC measure does not comply with *all* those terms. The FSC measure creates a "subsidy" because it creates a "benefit" by means of a "financial contribution," in that government revenue is foregone that is "otherwise due." This "subsidy" is a "prohibited export subsidy" under the *SCM Agreement* because it is contingent upon export performance. . . . Therefore, the FSC measure is not consistent with the WTO obligations of the United States. Beyond this, we do not rule.

In effect, the Appellate Body is saying: "We know America and the EU differ fundamentally in their taxation principles. Please understand we take no position on whether a country should, or should not, follow Unitary or Territorial Taxation. That is not within our authority."

IV. S&D Treatment and Export Competitiveness

Historically and to the present day, export subsidies have been one policy among many in the economic growth strategies of poor countries. Recognizing this fact, Article 27:2 of the *SCM Agreement* affords S&D treatment. It exempts low-income developing countries from the prohibition on export subsidies in Article 3:1(b). That provision, and Annex VII, puts such countries into three categories:

(1) Category 1 (Article 27:3)

  LDCs referenced in Annex VII, Paragraph (a) *i.e.*, the poorest of the poor based on U.N. criteria.

(2) Category 2 (Article 27:2(b))

  Developing countries specifically itemized in Annex VII, Paragraph (b), once their annual *per capita* GNP reaches U.S. $1,000 (at 1990 exchange rates), which are: Bolivia, Cameroon, Congo, Côte d'Ivoire, Dominican Republic, Egypt, Ghana, Guatemala, Guyana, India, Indonesia, Kenya, Morocco, Nicaragua, Nigeria, Pakistan, Philippines, Senegal, Sri Lanka, and Zimbabwe.

(3) Category 3 (Article 27:2(a))

  All other developing countries.

In effect, Category 2 ensures those itemized countries, which are not least developed, would get the benefit of the S&D treatment provided to Category 3 countries, even when they cross the $1,000 annual *per capita* income threshold. There are slightly different, and tricky, rules for these groupings.

Under Article 27:3, the prohibition on Red Light Export Subsidies did not even take effect for LDCs, *i.e.*, those in Category 1, for eight years from the entry into force of the *WTO Agreement* (1 January 1995), or 1 January 2003. In effect, LDCs received an initial eight-year grace period in which they could provide export subsidies (if they could afford them) with impunity. There was no in-built deadline for them phasing out this kind of support, as long as they remained least developed.

Similarly, under Article 27:3, the prohibition against Red Light Export Subsidies was not triggered for developing countries in Categories 2 and 3 until five years after the entry into force of *WTO Agreement*, *i.e.*, its application to them was suspended until 1 January 2000. So, developing countries got an initial five-year grace period to provide export subsidies (again, if they could afford them) without fear of a WTO action being brought against them.

However, in contrast to Category 1 countries, Category 2 and 3 countries did have a set time frame for phasing out export subsidies: a further eight years (following the end of the five year grace period). They were obliged to do so preferably in a "progressive manner." Also, they were forbidden from raising their export subsidies, and compelled to eliminate any such subsidy "inconsistent" with their "development needs."

Category 2 and 3 countries could apply to the WTO Committee on Subsidies and Countervailing Measures for an extension of the eight-year phase out period. Many did so. Before granting an extension, the Committee looked at "all . . . relevant economic, financial, and development needs" of the requesting developing country. If the request were rejected, the country would have "two years from the end of the last authorized period" to phase out its remaining export subsidies.

Also as to Category 2 and 3 countries, the general exemption from the prohibition on export subsidies, and the possibility of obtaining extensions for the period in which to phase them out, was subject to a key limit: export competitiveness. That is, this S&D treatment was contingent on not becoming export competitive in the subsidized product.

If a Category 2 or 3 country achieved export competitiveness in a particular product, then it must cease granting, within eight years, any export subsidy for that product. "Export competitiveness" meant exports of the product from the country exceed 3.25% of total world trade for two straight calendar years.[68] The calculation was made either by the developing country itself, or by the WTO Secretariat upon request of any Member.

In the November 2001 Doha Ministerial *Decision on Implementation-Related Issues and Concerns*, WTO Members directed the Committee on Subsidies and Countervailing Measures to extend the Article 27:4 transition period for certain export subsidies, "after taking into account the relative competitiveness in relation to other developing-country Members who [*sic*] have requested extension of the transition period."[69] They sought to ensure Members at similar stages of development, accounting for a similar magnitude of share in world trade, are not treated differently in respect of (1) obtaining an extension for the same kind of eligible program, or (2) the length of such an extension. So, in 2002, the Committee granted 20 developing countries extensions of the eight-year transition period for certain of their export subsidy programs.

---

68. Disputes can arise as to when export competitiveness is reached. For instance, in an October 2016 WTO SCM Committee meeting, India contested America's assertion that India received export competitiveness in 2007. India said it did not achieve this level until 2010, and urged it could continue until 2018 with its subsidies (*e.g.*, interest on loans, and incentives to export carpets and handicrafts via duty-free imports of inputs), which support 45 million jobs and account for nearly 14% of total Indian exports.

69. WT/MN(01)/17, ¶ 10:6, www.wto.org.

In July 2007, the General Council adopted a *Decision on Procedures for Continuation of Extensions Pursuant to Article 27:4 of the SCM Agreement of the Transition Period under Article 27:2 of the SCM Agreement for Certain Developing Country Members.*[70] Aside from setting a record for the longest title of a GATT-WTO *Decision*, this particular *Decision* barred any transition period extension beyond a 2-year period starting 31 December 2013. So, on 31 December 2015, all extended transition periods ended. As of June 2013, 19 countries benefited from that final extension.

In February 2010, the U.S. made a calculation request. It said India had reached export competitiveness in textile and clothing products under Section XI, Chapters 50–63 of the HS. WTO figures supported the American claim, showing Indian exports accounted for 3.4% and 3.6% ($21 and $23 billion) in 2007 and 2008, respectively, of total world textile and clothing exports. The products (at the 4-digit HS level) included:

(1) Cotton — 14.6% and 14.4% of global market share in 2007 and 2008, respectively.

(2) Home furnishing articles — 30.3% and 28.8%.

(3) Synthetic woven fabrics — 3.4% and 4.8%.

(4) T-shirts — 4.7% and 4.9%.

(5) Women's/girl's blouses and shirts — 10.5% and 11.4%.

(6) Women's/girl's suits, jackets, dresses, skirts, and trousers — 3.3% and 3.6%.

The U.S. asked India to phase out all textile and clothing export subsidies by 2015, by which time it said India certainly had reached export competitiveness. India disagreed, but in March 2017, India pledged to phase out the subsidies by 2018. That development was significant, particularly given the long-standing use in India of subsidies, and noteworthy for a sector that accounts for over 13% of total Indian exports, and employs over 38 million Indians.

Yet, the USTR argued India did not fulfill its pledge, and in March 2018 launched a full-throttle case in the WTO against all of India's export subsidy schemes, namely:

• Merchandise Exports from India Scheme

• Export Oriented Units Scheme and Sector-Specific Schemes

• Electronics Hardware Technology Parks Scheme

• Biotechnology Parks Scheme

• SEZs

• Export Promotion Capital Goods Scheme

• Duty Free Imports for Exporters Program

---

70. *See* WT/L/691 (31 July 2007), www.wto.org.

Via these mechanisms, the USTR alleged India exempts various duties, fees, and taxes, and cuts import liabilities, for the benefit of chemicals, IT, pharmaceuticals, steel, and T&A exporters. Their consequence is to boost Indian exports, and dampen exports of American merchandise.

To be sure, there is more to mounting an Article 27:6 challenge than empirics. First, at what point should a phase out of export subsidies begin? The earliest possibility would be whenever export competitiveness is reached. Competitor nations (such as the U.S. vis-à-vis India) favored this time. But, another possibility is later, when empirical proof was presented that this status had been achieved.

Second, should world trade figures for the product concerned include exports under bilateral and regional FTAs, and PTAs like the GSP? On the one hand, a holistic appraisal suggests "yes." On the other hand, such aggregation might be unfair, penalizing a low-income developing country for being a party to an FTA or a BDC under the GSP.

Third, what happens if a developing country is export competitive in a product, phases out its export subsidy, but subsequently loses its export competitiveness? Can it resume the subsidy scheme? Article 27 provides no safe harbor for such resumption.

Note, finally, Article 27 provides two other types of S&D treatment for poor countries. Article 27:9 limits actions for Yellow Light subsidies to instances in which a complainant can prove adverse effects in the form of (1) nullification or impairment of tariff concessions or other GATT obligations, (2) displacement or impedance of a like product into the market of the subsidizing country, or (3) injury to a domestic industry in the complaining country. In other words, displacement or impedance of imports in a third country market is not ground for an adverse effects showing. And, Articles 27:10–12 establish *de minimis* thresholds below which a CVD investigation against a developing country must be terminated: of 2% (or in some cases 3%) for the subsidization rate; and 4% (or in some cases 9%) for the volume of subsidized imports (as a percentage of total imports of the like product into the importing country).

Article 27:4 was the subject of one Appellate Body Report: the 2000 *Brazil Aircraft* case.[71] The Appellate Body ruled Article 27:4 created positive obligations, not affirmative defenses. The Panel said the overall level of export subsidies was an appropriate measure to gauge compliance with Article 27:4, and the appropriate reference period was the one immediately before the entry into force of the *WTO Agreement*.

---

71. *See* WT/DS46/AB/R (adopted 12 January 2000).

Chapter 16

Traffic Light System: Yellow Light (Actionable) Subsidies[1]

I. Three-Pronged Adverse Effects Test

In a WTO CVD action, injury criteria are not exactly the same as in an AD case in that forum. The CVD injury criteria under the WTO *SCM Agreement* are narrower or broader, depending on the kind of alleged illegal subsidy, than under the *Antidumping Agreement*.

They are narrower in the instance of a prohibited, or Red Light, subsidy. Articles 3–4 of the *SCM Agreement* do not require any showing of injury, if a complainant proves the subsidy at issue falls within the Red Light category. That makes sense, because this category contains the two most trade-distorting subsidies of all—export subsidies and import substitution subsidies. Their purpose is to boost exports of domestically-produced merchandise, and reduce imports of a like product. It is entirely appropriate to deem irrebuttably that injury occurs from such subsidies.

That argument is not as easily made for actionable subsidies, *i.e.*, the Yellow Light and (lapsed) Dark Amber category. Programs in these categories may distort trade, but whether they do cannot be a matter of irrebuttable presumption. Thus, in the Yellow Light category—which, essentially, is a catch-all for any program that is not Red or Dark Amber—a complainant must prove that adverse effects occur as a result of the subsidy in question. Article 5 of the *SCM Agreement* sets out a three-pronged test for what constitutes an "adverse effect" from a Yellow Light subsidy:

(1) Injury to the domestic industry of the complaining WTO Member.

(2) Serious prejudice, or threat of serious prejudice, to the interests of the complaining Member, or to the interests of any other Member, with "serious prejudice" meaning (under Article 6:3) any one or more of the following effects from the subsidy:

---

1. Documents References:
   (1) *Havana (ITO) Charter* Articles 34
   (2) GATT Articles VI, XVI–XVII
   (3) WTO *SCM Agreement* Articles 1, 3–8, 10, 15–16, 27

(a) displacing or impeding imports of a like product into the market of the subsidizing Member (the respondent in the case),

(b) displacing or impeding exports of a like product in a third country market (because the subsidized goods are exported to the third country market, too),

(c) significant price undercutting, price suppression, or price depression in the "same market," or

(d) increasing world market share (on a consistent trend during the subsidization period) of the subsidizing Member in respect of the subsidized product (compared with the average share it had in the previous 3-year period).

(3) Nullification or impairment of benefits accruing directly or indirectly to the complaining Member, or any other Member, under GATT, in particular the benefits of concessions bound under GATT Article II.

The test is phrased in the disjunctive ("or"), hence any single adverse effect will do. Significantly, with a Dark Amber subsidy—defined exclusively as 1 of 4 types, in Article 6:1 of the *SCM Agreement*—a rebuttable presumption arises of serious prejudice.

Here is where the *SCM Agreement* injury criteria are broader than in the *Antidumping Agreement*—serious prejudice or nullification or impairment of benefits never are grounds for showing injury under the latter accord. But, does the *SCM Agreement*, like the *Antidumping Agreement*, allow for threat of material injury? Examine, also, U.S. law as to whether injury criteria in AD and CVD cases are the same.

Finally, the adverse effects scheme of the Traffic Light System creates litigation incentives. Complainants will seek to characterize facts as a Red Light Subsidy, to alleviate any burden of proving adverse effects. If the facts do not honestly fit that category, then Dark Amber is their next best choice, because they benefit from a rebuttable presumption of serious prejudice. (In both instances, respondents have the diametric opposite incentive.) Failing that, the battleground is in the Yellow Light category, and a critical issue is whether adverse effects exist.

II. Serious Prejudice, Price Suppression, and 2005 *Cotton* Case[2]

· **Holding on Relevant Market and Price**

In *Cotton*, the Appellate Body addressed issues on the relevant market and relevant price under Article 6:3(c) of the *SCM Agreement* regarding significant price

---

2. This case is cited, and its facts summarized, in an earlier Chapter.

suppression.[3] The U.S. appealed the Panel finding that the effect of Marketing Loan Program, Step 2, Market Loss Assistance, and Counter-Cyclical payments was significant price suppression within the meaning of Article 6:3(c), and thus constituted to serious prejudice under Article 5(c).[4]

The first question the Appellate Body addressed was which market was relevant to the analysis.[5] According to Article 6:3(c), serious prejudice in the sense of Article 5(c) may arise where:

> the effect of the subsidy is a significant price undercutting by the subsidized product as compared with the price of a like product of another Member in the same market or significant price suppression, price depression or lost sales in the same market[.]

The Panel suggested, and the parties later agreed, that the burden is on the complainant to identify the market in which it alleges the effect of the subsidy is significant price suppression.[6] The Appellate Body recalled that Brazil identified numerous relevant markets before the Panel, including:

(i) the world market for cotton;

(ii) the Brazilian market;

(iii) the American market; and

(iv) 40 third country markets to which Brazil exports its cotton and in which American and Brazilian cotton are found.

The Panel accepted the use of the "world market" as the relevant market for cotton.

The Panel defined the word "market," using the *New Shorter Oxford English Dictionary* and the *Merriam-Webster Dictionary*, as "a place . . . with a demand for a commodity or service," "a geographical area of demand for commodities or services," and "the area of economic activity in which buyers and sellers come together and the forces of supply and demand affect prices."[7] The Panel found the "world market" was the relevant market under Article 6:3(c) of the *SCM Agreement*. The Panel supported this holding with a textual interpretation relative to Articles 6:3(a)-(b) and 15:2 of the *Agreement*. Those provisions contain geographic limitations (*i.e.*, market of the subsidizing Member, a third country market, and reference to imports, respectively). Plus, the Panel found the evidence showed a "world market" for cotton exists.

The Panel also stated that "[w]here price suppression is demonstrated in [the world] market, it may not be necessary to proceed to an examination of each and every other possible market where the products of both the complaining and

---

3. *Cotton* Appellate Body Report, ¶ 395.
4. *Cotton* Appellate Body Report, ¶ 395.
5. *Cotton* Appellate Body Report, ¶ 400.
6. *Cotton* Appellate Body Report, ¶ 400.
7. *Cotton* Appellate Body Report, ¶ 404.

defending Members are found."[8] Indeed, once it found that price suppression occurred in the same world market for cotton, the Panel did not find it necessary to analyze any individual country markets.

The response from the U.S., which became the notable question on appeal, was that under Article 6:3(c) of the *SCM Agreement*, the relevant market must be "a particular domestic market of a Member," and cannot be a "world market."[9]

The Appellate Body agreed with the Panel definitions of "market."[10] Those lexicographic definitions had no effect on the analysis of whether the world market was relevant under Article 6:3(c). The definition of "market" does not impose limits on the geographical scope of a "market." Rather, the geographic scope of a market depends on the product itself and its ability to be traded across distances.

The Appellate Body also agreed with the Panel that the term "same market" in Article 6:3(c) does not impose a geographical limitation on the scope of the relevant "market."[11] Indeed, in addition to the geographical references in Articles 6:3(a)-(b) the Panel cited, Article 6:3(d) uses the term "world market share." Thus, Article 6:3(c), when read in the context of its surrounding Sub-Paragraphs, neither requires nor excludes the possibility of a national market or a world market.

The remaining question thus was "when can two products be considered to be 'in the same market' for the purposes of a claim of significant price suppression under Article 6:3(c) [of the *SCM Agreement*]?"[12] The Appellate Body relied on the definition from the *Merriam-Webster Dictionary*: a market is "the area of economic activity in which buyers and sellers come together and the forces of supply and demand affect prices."[13] Additionally, it said two products could be in the same market if they are engaged in actual or potential competition in that market. It followed, then, that two products may be in the same market, even if they are not necessarily sold at the same time and in the same place or country. The Appellate Body also agreed with the Panel's analytical factors, including the nature of the product, homogeneity of the conditions of competition, and transport costs.[14] As for existence of a world market, that depends on the facts. An adjudicator must see evidence that a world market in the product at issue.

The U.S. countered with the point that such an interpretation allows for too broad of an analysis. To it, under the Panel and Appellate Body definitions, all like products in the world could be considered to be in the same market. The Appellate Body disagreed. It said the burden of proof still is on of the complaining party to

---

8. *Cotton* Panel Report, ¶ 7.1252.
9. *Cotton* Appellate Body Report, ¶ 400.
10. *Cotton* Appellate Body Report, ¶ 405.
11. *Cotton* Appellate Body Report, ¶ 406.
12. *Cotton* Appellate Body Report, ¶ 408.
13. *Cotton* Appellate Body Report, ¶ 408.
14. *Cotton* Appellate Body Report, ¶ 408.

establish that the relevant product is in actual or potential competition in the world market.

When applied to the facts, the Appellate Body upheld the Panel decision, finding a world market for cotton exists. To meet its proof burden, Brazil identified 40 third country markets in which it and the U.S. sell like cotton. Applying the standard set by the Panel, the Appellate Body held that the world market was one in which both Brazilian and American cotton were present and competed against one another for sales.

Next, the Appellate Body addressed arguments regarding the relevant price under Article 6:3(c) of the *SCM Agreement*.[15] To identify the world price in the world market for cotton, the Panel and Appellate Body relied on the so-called "A-Index," which captures world prices. But, the U.S. argued use of a world price index was misplaced. Analysis of the world price was irrelevant to a finding of significant price suppression under Article 6:3(c). Instead, said the U.S., Brazil needed to show the effect of the challenged subsidies was significant suppression of the price of Brazilian cotton in the "world market."[16] That is, the Americans urged that A-Index did not matter, because it is a metric for a generic world market price; rather, Brazil had to show the price of its cotton was suppressed.

The Appellate Body disagreed. Not only are prices for cotton largely determined by the A-Index price, as the Panel found, but also movements in the world price for cotton inevitably affect prices of Brazilian cotton wherever it competes with American cotton. Thus, the American argument was logically flawed.[17] If the world market price for cotton as measured by the A-Index is suppressed, then the price of Brazilian cotton also must be suppressed. So, the Appellate Body upheld the Panel finding: the world price for cotton was the relevant price under *SCM Agreement* Article 6:3(c).

Note the American argument was not as illogical as the Appellate Body (or Brazil) thought. There are plenty of instances when a world market price index moves in one direction, but prices in a particular market move in the opposite direction, or not at all. Consider a world market index for equities that falls in a given year. Does that mean prices on the Bombay Stock Exchange (BSE) fell that year, too? Not necessarily: absent a cross-border financial crisis, local conditions affect stock market movements.

- **Price Suppression Caused by Price-Contingent Subsidies**

On the second of two notable appellate issues, the Appellate Body examined the work of the Panel on actual price suppression as the effect of the price-contingent American subsidies. This portion of the Appellate Body Report matters in that it is the inception for a debate regarding the Unitary versus two-step approaches to the

---

15. *Cotton* Appellate Body Report, ¶ 415.
16. *Cotton* Appellate Body Report, ¶ 415.
17. *Cotton* Appellate Body Report, ¶ 418.

determination of significant price suppression and its cause under Article 6:3(c) of the *SCM Agreement*.

The Appellate Body recognized:

> Article 6:3(c) does not set forth any specific methodology for determining whether the effect of a subsidy is significant price suppression. There may well be different ways to make this determination.[18]

Additionally:

> Article 6:3(c) is silent as to the sequence of steps to be followed in assessing whether the effect of a subsidy is significant price suppression. We note that Article 6:8 indicates that the existence of serious prejudice pursuant to Articles 5(c) and 6:3(c) is to be determined on the basis of information submitted to or obtained by the panel, including information submitted in accordance with *Annex V* of the *SCM Agreement*. *Annex V* provides some limited guidance about the type of information on which a panel might base its assessment under Article 6:3(c). But we find little other guidance on this issue.[19]

As a result, the Appellate Body gave the Panel considerable deference.

The Panel analysis took the following order:

(1) Is there price suppression?

(2) Is it significant price suppression?

(3) What is the effect, if any, of the subsidy?

The U.S. challenged this approach, arguing that the effect, if any, of a subsidy should be addressed first. After all, how could one know that prices were lower than they otherwise would have been without knowing what allegedly caused the prices to be lower?[20]

Unfortunately for the U.S., given the limited guidance Article 6:3(c) provides on the methodology for determining price suppression, the Appellate Body did not feel the Panel was precluded from examining first whether significant price suppression existed and then, if so, whether the significant price suppression was the effect of the subsidy. The Appellate Body understood the Panel considered that in the absence of significant price suppression, there is no need to analyze the effect of the subsidy.[21]

The remaining discussion of the American argument was uninteresting. Again, the *SCM Agreement* did not provide definitive factors that had to be considered. So,

18. *Cotton* Appellate Body Report, ¶ 427.
19. *Cotton* Appellate Body Report, ¶ 431.
20. *Cotton* Appellate Body Report, ¶ 430.
21. *Cotton* Appellate Body Report, ¶ 431.

analysis by a Panel or the Appellate Body depends on the individual facts of each dispute. Here too, the Appellate Body deferred to the Panel. It upheld the Panel findings that significant price suppression occurred within the meaning of Article 6:3(c), that a casual link existed between (1) price-contingent subsidies and (2) significant price suppression, and that other factors (mentioned by the Americans) did not intervene to attenuate this link.

More interesting was whether precise measurement of the degree of price depression matters. The Appellate Body agreed with the Panel—no. When determining whether significant price depression (or suppression) exists, the *Agreement* does not require quantification of the amount of that depression (or suppression). Note, then, the distinction between measuring the precise benefit conferred by subsidies in question, for purposes of determining an appropriate CVD versus the extent of price depression (or suppression) for purposes of determining adverse effects of those subsidies.

- **Unitary versus Two-Step Debate**

What did the future hold for the Unitary versus Two-Step approaches? The Panel took the "Two-Step" approach, to which the Appellate Body deferred. The Panel (1) focused on prices of cotton in the world market when analyzing whether significant price suppression occurred, and then (2) addressed causal factors related to the challenged subsidies. The Appellate Body expressed its preference for what later became known as the "Unitary" approach, saying in *obiter dicta* it is difficult to separate these two analyses in deciding whether significant price suppression happened. Still, it deferred to the Panel approach.

Interestingly, in the compliance proceedings to *Cotton*, the Panel and Appellate Body supported a different approach, based on the Appellate Body suggestion in the original proceedings that the Two Step approach is difficult. The Appellate Body in those proceedings concluded: "it is difficult to separate price suppression from its causes" and the Panel's Unitary analysis "at least in respect of identifying price suppression and its causes, has a sound foundation."[22]

---

22. *Cotton (Article 21.5—Brazil)* Appellate Body Report, ¶ 354.

The last topic the Appellate Body addressed was the Panel finding that, under Article 6:3(d) of the *SCM Agreement*, the phrase "world market share" of a subsidizing WTO Member refers to the share of the world market supplied by that subsidizing Member of the product concerned. Brazil argued the phrase concerns the world market for exports, while the U.S. said it is about the share of consumption of a WTO Member. The Appellate Body result was underwhelming. It found that for the purposes of the case, it did not need to rule on the interpretation of the phrase "world market share" in Article 6:3(d) of the *Agreement*. The Appellate Body was concerned that providing an opinion on this subject, which would not affect the outcome of the dispute, would be *dicta*, and thus not aligned with its object and purpose under the *DSU*. That concern was ironic, and the Appellate Body would have done better simply to invoke judicial economy as the reason for its non-ruling.

III. Serious Prejudice, Price Suppression/Depression, and 2011 *Airbus* Case[23]

- **Unitary versus Two Step Approach Again**

The 2011 *Airbus* dispute is yet another chapter in the debate between the Unitary versus Two-Step approaches when determining whether serious prejudice exists. Recall under a Two-Step approach, a Panel asks first whether serious prejudice (*e.g.*, in the form of displaced and lost sales) occurred as a factual matter. If it did, then in the second step, the Panel considers whether the challenged subsidies actually caused that serious prejudice. Under a Unitary analysis, both questions are considered together — market phenomena and causal relationships. The Appellate Body in *Airbus* described this analysis as a counterfactual one:

> . . . the counterfactual analysis entails comparing the actual market situation that is before the adjudicator with the market situation that would have existed in the absence of the challenged subsidies. This requires the adjudicator to undertake a modelling exercise as to what the market would look like in the absence of the subsidies. Such an exercise is a necessary part of the counterfactual approach.[24]

Going against the Unitary approach taken by the Panel and Appellate Body in *Cotton* compliance proceedings, in the *Airbus* case, the Panel used the Two-Step approach, saying the American arguments about serious prejudice in the form of price suppression rendered that method "entirely appropriate."[25]

Both the U.S. and EU accepted the use by the Panel of this methodology, so it was not a significant issue on appeal. Nonetheless, in its *Airbus* report, the Appellate Body reiterated its preference for the Unitary Approach. It felt the Panel was justified in its use of the 2-Step Approach, but made clear its "view remain[ed] that a Unitary Approach that uses a counterfactual will generally be the more appropriate approach to undertaking the assessment required under Article 6:3 of the *SCM Agreement*."[26]

- **Serious Prejudice**

Turning to the arguments on appeal, the Appellate Body faced the question of whether the Panel correctly held that certain subsidies provided by the EU and governments of some EU countries to Airbus are illegal under Articles 5(c) and 6:3 of the *SCM Agreement*. The issue was one of first impression for the Appellate Body: never before had it examined claims of displacement under Article 6:3 of the *Agreement*. In brief, was the Panel correct that Yellow Light subsidies to Airbus caused

---

23. This case is cited, and its facts summarized, in an earlier Chapter.
24. *Airbus* Appellate Body Report, ¶ 1110.
25. *Airbus* Appellate Body Report, ¶ 1108 (*quoting Airbus* Panel Report).
26. *Airbus* Appellate Body Report, ¶ 1109.

"serious prejudice" to the U.S.? The Appellate Body responded "yes," thus upholding the Panel and handing America an important victory.

What, exactly, was the serious prejudice to the U.S.? There were four untoward effects during the 2001–2006 POI to the interests of Boeing alleged by Boeing, as follows, uncovered by the Panel, as follows. The Appellate Body agreed on some aspects of the Panel rulings, but not others, as also follows. As indicated earlier, in reaching its findings, the Panel applied a Two-Step Test under Articles 5(c) and 6(a)-(b), namely:

Step 1:   Serious Prejudice?

           Did serious prejudice in the form of displacement and/or lost sales, or threat thereof, from the subsidizing country and/or third countries occur?

Step 2:   Causation?

           If serious prejudice (as defined in Step One) occurred, then was it the effect of the subsidies, namely, Launch Aid?

The Appellate Body held both Steps of the Two-Step Test were satisfied: displacement occurred on certain LCA models and in certain markets, and Launch Aid caused the displacement. In reaching this conclusion, the Appellate Body upheld several of the findings of the Panel, though on two particular points it reversed those findings. The Appellate Body recommended the EU remove the adverse effects from the illegal subsidies, so as not to cause serious prejudice to the U.S., or withdraw those subsidies entirely.

• **Displacement of Market Share**

According to the Appellate Body, "displacement" under Article 6:3(a)-(b) of the *SCM Agreement* occurs:

> . . . where a complainant puts forward a case based on the existence of displacement as a directly observable phenomenon and the panel opts to examine it under a two-step approach, as was done in this dispute, *displacement arises under Article 6:3(a) of the SCM Agreement where imports of a like product of the complaining Member are declining in the market of the subsidizing Member, and are being substituted by the subsidized product.* Similarly, *under Article 6.3(b), displacement arises where exports from the like product of the complaining Member are declining in the third country market concerned, and are being substituted by exports of the subsidized product.* . . . [D]isplacement must be discernible. The identification of displacement under this approach should focus on trends in the markets, looking at both volumes and market shares. *The trend has to be clearly identifiable and an assessment based on a static comparison of the situation of the subsidized product and the like product at the beginning and at the end of the reference period would be inadequate.* Where a two-step approach is used under Article 6:3(a) and (b), and displacement has been shown on a preliminary

basis, the complaining Member will have to establish, in addition, that such displacement is the effect of the challenged subsidies.[27]

Obviously, displacement of exports from the market of the subsidizing country (*e.g.,* displacement of Boeing aircraft sales in the EU in favor of Airbus) violates Article 6:3(a) of the *SCM Agreement.* Displacement of exports from the market of another country (*e.g.,* displacement of Boeing aircraft sales in China, in favor of Airbus) violates Article 6:3(b) of the *Agreement.* Applying this meaning to the facts at hand, the Appellate Body agreed with the panel that disputed Airbus subsidies caused displacement of exports from the U.S. of certain models of Boeing aircraft from the EU and third country markets.

In particular, said the Appellate Body, the subsidies caused displacement of exports of single-aisle and twin-aisle Boeing LCA to the EU, China, and Korea during the reference period 2001–2006.[28] They also resulted in displaced exports of single-aisle Boeing aircraft from Australia during this POI. The key pieces of evidence for such displacement were data on market share:

(1) In the EU, the market share of Boeing in twin-aisle LCA declined from 2001 to 2006. In the single-aisle LCA market, its market share was steady between 2001 and 2004, but then declined in 2005 and 2006.

(2) In Australia, the dominant market position held by Boeing in the single-aisle LCA product market eroded during the POI. Its market share increased from 50% to 75% between 2005 and 2006, but those shares were well below the levels Boeing hit between 2001 and 2003. As for twin-aisle aircraft, Boeing made no sales in Australia during the reference period.

(3) In China, the market share of Boeing in single-aisle LCA fell from 67% to 50% between 2001 and 2006, and in twin-aisle aircraft plunged from 100% to 11% during that period.

(4) In Korea, in the single-aisle LCA market, Boeing lost market share throughout the POI. For twin-aisle LCA in 2001 and 2002, there was a split of 2/3 of the market for Boeing and 1/3 for Airbus. That percentage split became 50–50 in 2003, 2004, and 2006 (and 60–40% in 2005).

Obviously, in the EU and third-country markets, Airbus aircraft took the position of the displaced Boeing planes.

---

27. *Airbus* Appellate Body Report, ¶ 1170 (emphasis added).

28. *See Airbus* Appellate Body Report, ¶¶ 1181-1206, 1414(l), (m)(ii)-(iii), (p).

In addition to single- and twin-aisle LCA, the Appellate Body considered a third product market: very large aircraft. However, for such aircraft, Boeing was the sole supplier during the reference period in several of the geographic markets at issue. *See id.*, ¶¶ 1181, 1183, 1185, 1189, 1191, 1193, 1195, 1197.

• **Two Controversies Concerning Displacement**

Certainly, the Appellate Body did not agree wholeheartedly with all of the conclusions of the Panel on displacement. Two in particular were problematic. First, to reach its conclusion that sales of Airbus aircraft displaced those of Boeing in both the EU and third country markets, and thus a form of serious prejudice under Article 5(c) of the *SCM Agreement*, the Panel had to interpret the terms "market" and "like product," as they are used in Article 6:3(a)-(b), which identifies potential types of serious prejudice for purposes of Article 5(c).[29] The Panel took the easy path: it simply defined one single market, and one like product, namely, LCA. That is, the Panel assessed displacement of Boeing aircraft sales on the basis of a single subsidized product encompassing all Airbus models, and a single product market for LCA.

That was too easy, or rather, too simplistic, said the Appellate Body, reversing the "single product market finding" of the Panel.[30] The Panel relied on the American characterization of the "market," "like product," and, therefore, the "subsidized product." The Panel ought to have distinguished among different types of aircraft models, and different LCA product markets. The Panel should have provided its own, independent determination about these terms. Its failure to do so was a violation of *DSU* Article 11.

Had the Panel done so, then it would have realized that the reality about displacement was more complex than it found. Whether Airbus aircraft displaced those of Boeing depended on the aircraft model type and market at issue. That is why (as just explained), the Appellate Body distinguished between single-aisle and twin-aisle LCA, and between the market of the subsidizing countries (*i.e.*, the EU) and third countries (*e.g.*, Australia, China, and Korea).

In particular, the Panel defined "market" and assessed "displacement" on the basis of a single subsidized product, and a single product market for LCA.[31] That is, the Panel said there was a single product market in which all Airbus and Boeing LCA competed. But, the Panel did not make its own independent assessment of the facts. Rather, the Panel accepted the American characterization of the terms "market" and "product."

Yet, the Appellate Body said it was unable to complete the analysis to determine whether there was one, or more than one, LCA product market. The evidence was insufficient. Accordingly, the Appellate Body rejected the EU argument that there were four separate allegedly subsidized families (*i.e.*, product groupings), or five separate products, of Airbus LCA.[32] Significantly, while the EU said that the error of the Panel with respect to the "single product market" undermined the finding of the Panel concerning displacement, the EU did not argue no displacement occurred. To

---

29. *Airbus* Appellate Body Report, ¶ 571(j).
30. *See Airbus* Appellate Body Report, ¶¶ 1124–1147.
31. *See Airbus* Appellate Body Report, ¶¶ 1112–1113.
32. *See Airbus* Appellate Body Report, ¶¶ 1113–1114.

the contrary, the EU admitted that there were uncontested data that under various approaches to the "product market," displacement occurred. Consequently, the quarrel on appeal between the EU and U.S. revolved around the degree of competition across LCA models, especially as between the extremes of the product ranges of Airbus and Boeing.[33]

The Appellate Body did point out that from the text of Article 6:3(a)-(b), it is clear the analysis of displacement or impedance of sales is geographically constrained to the territory of the subsidizing Member, or of any relevant third country. Potentially, this constraint may not be all that limiting, as the market for a product could be the world market. The analysis of products and markets is connected, because the term "market" in Article 6:3 is used along with the term "like product." The latter is defined in footnote 46 of the *SCM Agreement* as:

> Throughout this *Agreement* the term "like product" (*"produit similaire"*) shall be interpreted to mean a product which is identical, *i.e.*, alike in all respects to the product under consideration, or in the absence of such a product, another product which, although not alike in all respects, has characteristics closely resembling those of the product under consideration.

Thus, as the Appellate Body said, identity or close resemblance is one factor to consider when deciding whether products are "like" and, in turn, in the same product market.

The Appellate Body went on to point out that the scope of the "market" to be studied under Article 6:3(a)-(b) may vary from case to case, depending on the facts.[34] That scope may extend beyond "like products" defined according to the familiar GATT criteria of physical characteristics, end uses, and consumer preferences. Such criteria help establish whether two products are in the same market. But, to decide whether two products create competitive constraints on one another, *i.e.*, whether they are substitutes for one another, other factors concerning demand- and supply-side substitutability (that is, whether consumers consider the products to be substitutes, and whether manufacturers can switch production quickly and at low cost from one good to another) may be examined to see if two products are in a single market.

A second area of disagreement between the Appellate Body and Panel, and thus an occasion for reversal by the Appellate Body, concerned the exact markets in which displacement occurred. The Panel ruled the disputed subsidies caused serious prejudice, in the form of displacement, of Boeing aircraft in the market of the subsidizing country, the EU, and in the following third country markets: Australia, Brazil, China, Mexico, Singapore, and Taiwan, and threatened displacement in India.

---

33. *Airbus* Appellate Body Report, ¶ 1148. That said, one Appellate Body member essentially dissented, stating it is logically incorrect to complete the analysis of displacement when it is not possible to complete the analysis of the relevant product market or markets. *See id.*, ¶¶ 1149, 1205.
    34. *See Airbus* Appellate Body Report, ¶¶ 1120–1123.

To reach its conclusion that Boeing LCA were displaced from the EU market, the Panel applied a Two Step Test under Article 6:3(a) of the *SCM Agreement*.[35] The Panel also used the Two Step Test to reach its finding that Boeing LCA were displaced under Article 6:3(b) from the third country markets of Australia, Brazil, China, Korea, Mexico, Singapore, and Taiwan, and that a threat of displacement existed with respect to India.[36] The Appellate Body disagreed with respect of some of these markets, and reversed these rulings. The Appellate Body said the evidence did not establish displacement during the 2001–2006 POI in the third country markets of Brazil, Mexico, Singapore, or Taiwan, nor of a threat of displacement in India.[37]

- **Lost Sales**

The U.S. alleged Boeing lost out on sales of its planes to Airbus, when Airbus launched spirited campaigns on behalf of certain types of aircraft that benefitted from subsidies.[38] Boeing LCA lost out to the Airbus A320 on sales to Air Asia, Air Berlin, Czech Airlines, and EasyJet.[39] Boeing LCA also lost out to the Airbus A340 to Iberia, South African Airways, and Thai Airways. And, Boeing LCA lost out on sales to the Airbus A380 to Emirates, Qantas, and Singapore Airlines. This result (lost sales), urged the U.S., constituted a violation of Article 6:3(c) of the *SCM Agreement.*

Interestingly, evidence presented by the U.S. to support its allegation was anecdotal.[40] It consisted of media reports, press releases, and public disclosures by various airlines. These materials pointed to discounts offered by Airbus in competitive bidding against Boeing as being the reason why Boeing lost out in the sales campaigns. The Panel agreed with America.

The Appellate Body upheld the findings of the Panel.[41] Citing the *New Shorter Oxford English Dictionary*, the Appellate Body defined "lost" (as in "lost sale") as

---

35. *See Airbus* Appellate Body Report, ¶ 571(o)(i), (iv).
36. *See Airbus* Appellate Body Report, ¶ 571(l)-(m), (o)(i), (iv).
37. *See Airbus* Appellate Body Report, ¶ 1414(n).
In particular, the Appellate Body found that market share data did not show a trend of Boeing losing market share to Airbus in 4 other third-country markets, Brazil, Mexico, Singapore, and Taiwan. In Brazil, the Appellate Body said the data were insufficient to show Boeing losing market share to Airbus in either the single- or twin-aisle markets. *See id.,* ¶¶ 1189–1190. It rendered a similar finding with respect to the Mexican, Singaporean, and Taiwanese markets. *See id.,* ¶¶ 1193–1194, 1195–1196, 1197–1198. Generally speaking, in these third country markets, the market share of Boeing in the single- and twin-aisle markets held steady. As for India, the Appellate Body said evidence on market share was insufficient to prove the American contention that Boeing was threatened with displacement. Indeed, Boeing gained market share in 2005 and 2006 in the single-aisle LCA market, and the decline in those years for the twin-aisle market was too sketchy a basis from which to infer a threat (especially given there were no sales of twin-aisle LCA in 2001–2004). *See id.,* ¶¶1199–1202.
38. *See Airbus* Appellate Body Report, ¶¶ 1207–1228.
39. *See Airbus* Appellate Body Report, ¶ 571(o)(ii), (iv).
40. *See Airbus* Appellate Body Report, ¶ 1208.
41. *See Airbus* Appellate Body Report, ¶¶ 571(n), 1414 (o).

a sale "that a supplier failed to obtain," and pointed out that the adjective "significant" in Article 6:3(c) of the *SCM Agreement* modifies all three relevant phrases—lost sales, price suppression, and price depression.[42] Accordingly, the Appellate Body explained how to discern the existence of "lost sales" under the Two Step and Unitary Approaches:

> To summarize, we consider that, under Article 6.3(c), "lost sales" are sales that suppliers of the complaining Member "failed to obtain" and that instead were won by suppliers of the respondent Member. It is a relational concept and its assessment requires consideration of the behaviour of both the subsidized firm(s), which must have won the sales, and the competing firm(s), which allegedly lost the sales. The assessment can focus on a specific sales campaign when such an approach is appropriate given the particular characteristics of the market or it may look more broadly at aggregate sales in the market. The complainant must show that the lost sales are significant to succeed in its claim. Where lost sales are assessed under a two-step approach such as the one adopted by the Panel in this case, the finding of lost sales in the first step is necessarily preliminary and of limited significance in coming to a conclusion under Article 6:3(c). Similarly to the phenomena of displacement under Article 6 (a) and (b), a definitive determination under Article 6:3(c) must await consideration of whether such lost sales are the effect of the challenged subsidy. While a two-step approach to the assessment of lost sales is permissible, in our view, the most appropriate approach to assess whether lost sales are the *effect* of the challenged subsidy is through a unitary counterfactual analysis. This would involve a comparison of the sales actually made by the competing firm(s) of the complaining Member with a counterfactual scenario in which the firm(s) of the respondent Member would not have received the challenged subsidies. There would be lost sales where the counterfactual analysis shows that, in the absence of the challenged subsidy, sales won by the subsidized firm(s) of the respondent Member would have been made instead by the competing firm(s) of the complaining Member.[43]

Like the Panel before it, the Appellate Body rejected the EU contention that Boeing lost sales not because of subsidies to Airbus, but because of non-price factors.[44] Such factors included mismanagement of customer relations, fleet and route structure, political considerations, and technical specifications. This losing EU argument is noteworthy in that it shows the Steps in the Two Step Approach are entirely separate from one another, as the Appellate Body essentially concedes in the above-quoted passage. A discussion of alternative causal factors sometimes arises in the context of the first Step.

---

42. *Airbus* Appellate Body Report, ¶¶ 1214, 1215.
43. *Airbus* Appellate Body Report, ¶ 1220 (emphasis added).
44. *See Airbus* Appellate Body Report, ¶ 1209.

In the appeal, the principal point the EU contested was whether sales by Airbus of the A380 to Emirates Airlines constituted lost sales of Boeing 747 LCA. The Panel said they did, and so, too, held the Appellate Body. The Appellate Body said the Panel was correct in the first Step of the Panel's Two Step approach under Article 6:3(c), and thus in reaching the conclusion sales of the A380 to Emirates Airlines constituted significant "lost sales," even though formal offers might not have been requested or made.[45]

- **Causation as Regards Launch Aid Subsidies**

Agreeing with the Panel, the Appellate Body found a "genuine and substantial" causal link between Launch Aid subsidies, on the one hand, and both displacement and lost sales, on the other hand.[46] This test—"a genuine and substantial relationship of cause and effect"—was the right one to apply under Articles 5(c) and 6:3(c) of the *SCM Agreement*, following the Appellate Body precedent in the 2005 *Cotton* case.[47] And, as set out in the *Cotton* case, establishing a causal relationship means ensuring "the effects of other factors are not improperly attributed to the challenged subsidies," *i.e.*, non-attribution is a key part of proving causation.[48] In proving causation, a "but for" evaluation is helpful, as long as it is accompanied by a non-attribution analysis:

> The Appellate Body has said [in its 2008 *Cotton* compliance decision at Paragraphs 374–375] . . . it may be possible to assess whether the particular market phenomena are the effect of the subsidies by recourse to a "but for" approach. Thus, one possible approach to the assessment of causation is an inquiry that seeks to identify what would have occurred "but for" the subsidies. In some circumstances, a determination that the market phenomena captured by Article 6:3 of the *SCM Agreement* would not have occurred "but for" the challenged subsidies will suffice to establish causation. This is because, in some circumstances, the "but for" analysis will show that the subsidy is both a necessary cause of the market phenomenon *and* a substantial cause. It is not required that the "but for" analysis establish that the challenged subsidies are a sufficient cause of the market phenomenon

---

45. *See Airbus* Appellate Body Report, ¶ 1228.

At the Panel stage, there also were arguments about another form of adverse effects from Launch Aid, namely, impediment and price suppression or depression under Articles 5(c) and 6:3(a)-(c) of the *SCM Agreement*. The U.S. contended that Launch Aid for each Airbus model impeded imports of Boeing LCA into the EU, and also impeded exports of Boeing LCA from third counties. That kind of import and export impediment violated Article 6:3(a)-(b) of the *Agreement*. The Panel disagreed, and the Appellate Body did not deal with the matter. The U.S. also urged that Launch Aid gave Airbus the financial flexibility to lower it prices. The consequence was significant price suppression and depression between 2001 and 2006, a violation of Article 6:3(c). Not so, said the Panel. Here too, the matter was not a principal topic of appeal.

46. *Airbus* Appellate Body Report, ¶ 1300.

47. *Airbus* Appellate Body Report, ¶ 1232 (*quoting Cotton* Appellate Body Report, ¶ 438).

48. *Airbus* Appellate Body Report, ¶ 1232 (*citing Cotton* Appellate Body Report, ¶ 437).

provided that it shows a genuine and substantial relationship of cause and effect. However, there are circumstances in which a "but for" approach does not suffice. For example, where a necessary cause is too remote and other intervening causes substantially account for the market phenomenon. This example underscores the importance of carrying out a proper non-attribution analysis.

The U.S. advanced a "product theory" of causation, under which it said Launch Aid impacted the ability of Airbus to create and market LCA that it otherwise could not have.[49] In other words, the U.S. used a "but for" test: the adverse effects to Boeing would not have occurred but for the subsidies to Airbus. Referring frequently to the "but for" causation test, and examining competing reports submitted by the U.S. (the "Dorman Report") and EU (the "Wachtel Report"), the Panel essentially did, too.[50] The Panel also addressed non-attribution, examining alleged mismanagement of customer relations by Boeing, geopolitics, and the role of engine manufacturers in various sales campaigns.[51]

The essence of the EU argument about causation was that most of the contested Launch Aid subsidies were decades old and, therefore, could not be the cause of present serious injury to Boeing. Indeed:

> . . . [T]he A300 and A310 were launched more than 30 years ago, that is, in 1969 and 1978 respectively. The first delivery of an A300 to a customer took place in 1974, while the A310 was first delivered to a customer and put in service in 1985. According to the European Union, German LA/MSF [Launch Aid] for these LCA models was fully disbursed by the end of 1988; LA/MSF provided by France was disbursed by 1986; and Spanish LA/MSF for the A300 and A310 was fully provided to CASA by the end of 1992.[52]

Moreover, pushing a counterfactual analysis, the EU argued that even without Launch Aid, Airbus could have built and sold the single-aisle A320 LCA with 100–200 seats and the twin-aisle A330 with 200–300 seats in 1987 and 1991, respectively, three or four years after Airbus actually produced and sold these LCA models.[53] The Aid might have accelerated the time frame in which these models came to market, but did not change the outcome. That was because, said the EU, Airbus had gained technological experience, there was growing demand for these models, and Boeing had outdated products.

The EU argument was unsuccessful. The Appellate Body repeated its findings under Article 5 of the *SCM Agreement*, namely, that subsidies do have a life, that they may be amortized over time and eventually may be removed, and that their

---

49. *See Airbus* Appellate Body Report, ¶ 1243.

50. *See Airbus* Appellate Body Report, ¶¶ 1234, 1244–1257.

51. *See Airbus* Appellate Body Report, ¶¶ 1259–1300.

52. *Airbus* Appellate Body Report, ¶ 1239.

53. *See Airbus* Appellate Body Report, ¶¶ 1274–1298. The EU conceded that without subsidies, Airbus would not have launched the A300 and A310 in 1969 and 1978, respectively.

effects generally diminish over time and eventually come to an end with the passage of time.[54] The Appellate Body accepted the conclusions of the Panel, namely, that without subsidies, Airbus would not have achieved the market presence it did in the 2001–2006 POI, that Airbus would have been a much weaker aircraft manufacturer and produced an inferior product at less competitive prices without the subsidies, and that sales of Airbus LCA would have been much lower than they were without the subsidies.[55] Thus, said the Appellate Body, the Panel was correct in the second Step of the Two Step Test: the effect of Launch Aid was displacement of market share of Boeing in favor of Airbus, and lost sales of Boeing in favor of Airbus to Air Asia, Air Berlin, Czech Airlines, EasyJet, and Emirates, Qantas, and Singapore Airlines.[56]

The Appellate Body also upheld, with some criticism, the finding of the Panel that but for Launch Aid, Airbus could not in 2000 have developed and introduced into the LCA market the A380:

> . . . we do not find that the Panel acted inconsistently with Article 11 of the *DSU* [which requires the Panel conduct an objective assessment of the facts] in finding that "either directly or indirectly, LA/MSF [Launch Aid] was a necessary precondition for Airbus' launch in 2000 of the A380." Although we consider the Panel to have fallen into error in speculating about an alleged "economic incentive" to overstate sales and in referring to *ex post* events in its assessment of the Airbus A380 business case, we do not consider that these deficiencies invalidate the Panel's conclusions in relation to Airbus' ability to launch the A380 in 2000 in the absence of LA/MSF. The Panel's ultimate conclusion that LA/MSF was a "necessary precondition" for Airbus' launch of the A380 in 2000 was based on multiple considerations, such as the A380 business case itself, evidence on Airbus' ability to fund the A380 in the absence of LA/MSF, and the financial and technological impact of LA/MSF provided in relation to previous models of Airbus LCA. . . . . . . [B]ased on these multiple considerations, the Panel had a sufficiently objective basis for its ultimate finding that LA/MSF was a "necessary precondition" for the launch of the A380 in 2000. Accordingly, we uphold the Panel's finding that "either directly or indirectly, LA/MSF was a necessary precondition for the launch of the A380 in 2000."[57]

- **Causation as Regards Subsidies Other than Launch Aid**

The Panel held subsidies other than Launch Aid caused displacement of Boeing LCA from the EU and various third country markets.[58] That was a violation of Article 6:3(a)-(b) of the *SCM Agreement*. And, decided the Panel, those subsidies

---

54. *See Airbus* Appellate Body Report, ¶¶ 1236–1238.
55. *See Airbus* Appellate Body Report, ¶¶ 1270–1272.
56. *See Airbus* Appellate Body Report, ¶ 1414(p).
57. *Airbus* Appellate Body Report, ¶ 1356.
58. *See Airbus* Appellate Body Report, ¶¶ 1358–1380.

caused lost sales in contravention of Article 6:3(c). The Panel focused on Corporate Restructuring (especially equity infusions), Infrastructure Development (namely, the *Mühlenberger Loch* and *Aéroconstellation* industrial sites, Bremen Airport runway extension, and regional grants by German and Spanish authorities), and R&TD Support (that is, the Second, Third, Fourth, Fifth, and Sixth EC Framework Programs, the Spanish PROFIT and PTA program loans, and grants to Airbus from the British, French, and German central governments and German sub-central governments). These measures complemented and supplemented the product effect of Launch Aid. They contributed to the ability of Airbus to develop and sell LCA models, thereby displacing Boeing in market share, and gaining sales at the expense of Boeing. To reach these conclusions, the Panel aggregated the effects of the various subsidy schemes, declaring their structure, design, and operation did not preclude consideration of their combined effects.

On appeal, the EU objected. It argued the Panel should have linked each specific subsidy scheme to the launch of a particular Airbus model. The Appellate Body checked over the work of the Panel, and upheld it. That is, in applying Step Two of the Two Step Test, the Appellate Body examined whether the Panel properly distinguished between the effects of Launch Aid in causing serious prejudice, on the one hand, from the effects of the other types of subsidies in causing serious prejudice, on the other hand.[59] It did, said the Appellate Body, agreeing with the Panel that the effects of Launch Aid in causing serious prejudice were complemented and supplemented by the Infrastructure Measures that were specific to Airbus, and by the Equity Confusions that met the Specificity Test. But, the Appellate Body reversed the finding of the Panel that the product effect of Launch Aid was complemented and supplemented by R&TD subsidies.

So, the Appellate Body affirmed that the equity infusions and infrastructure measures that were specific subsidies under Articles 1–2 of the *SCM Agreement* indeed did complement and supplement the product effect of Launch Aid, and thus caused serious prejudice to American interests under Articles 5(c), and 6:3(a)-(c) of the *SCM Agreement*.[60] Simply put, with respect to the subsidies the Appellate Body agreed were specific to Airbus, there was a genuine causal link between them and the success of Airbus vis-à-vis Boeing. Without these measures, Airbus would have been unable to develop LCA models and features thereof on the schedule that it did.[61]

---

59. *See Airbus* Appellate Body Report, ¶¶ 571(p), 1414 (q)-(s).

60. *See Airbus* Appellate Body Report, ¶¶ 1381–1391 (concerning equity infusions), 1392–1400 (infrastructure measures), and 1410–1412 (summarizing the findings).

61. The U.S. also argued the Launch Aid, Corporate Restructuring, and Infrastructure Measures allowed Airbus to undercut the pricing of Boeing aircraft. Such price undercutting violated Article 6:3(c) of the *SCM Agreement*. *See Airbus* Appellate Body Report, ¶ 4. However, neither the Panel nor the Appellate Body reached a definitive conclusion on price undercutting.

Only on causation of displaced and lost sales by R&TD subsidies did the Appellate Body overturn the Panel holding.[62] The Appellate Body did not opine the R&TD support had no such causal effect. Rather, it said the facts reviewed by the Panel showed only that such support helped Airbus with pre-competitive LCA development, but did not speak to the question of giving Airbus a competitive advantage against Boeing in sales. More evidence was needed to prove that the R&TD support led to technologies incorporated into Airbus LCA models that made production of them more efficient, or otherwise aided Airbus relative to Boeing.

In sum, the victory for the U.S. on Yellow Light subsidies was a solid, albeit not total, one. For several models of Airbus aircraft, Launch Aid, and certain Corporate Restructuring and Infrastructure Support measures that were specific to Airbus, caused adverse effects. Those effects were serious prejudice, namely, displacement and lost sales. This victory was more than enough. Technically, the Americans needed to show only one kind of serious prejudice, not the full panoply of possibilities, and prove causation by only one or a few subsidies. In actuality, they showed the EU schemes for Airbus were riddled with illegalities.[63]

IV. Serious Prejudice, Price Suppression/Depression, and 2012 *Boeing* Case[64]

- **Subsidies at Issue**

In *Boeing*, the Appellate Body again addressed "adverse effects" within the meaning of Articles 5 and 6 of the *SCM Agreement*. As opposed to addressing each measure on its own, the Panel felt it best to separate the subsidies into three groups (each with a relevant product market), and identified three relevant product markets. Additionally, the Panel considered 2 mechanisms through which the subsidies allegedly caused serious prejudice. Those mechanisms included the effects on (1) prices of Boeing LCA, *i.e.*, Price Effects, and (2) technological development for new Boeing LCA models, *i.e.*, Technological Effects.

The three groups of subsidies created by the Panel were:

(1) "Aeronautics R&D Subsidies";

(2) "Tied tax Subsidies"; and

(3) "Remaining Subsidies."[65]

---

62. *See Airbus* Appellate Body Report, ¶¶ 1401–1409, 1411–1413

63. The U.S. also failed to prove, at the Panel stage, that the challenged subsidies caused injury to the American LCA industry, in violation of Article 5(a) of the *SCM Agreement*. Because the U.S. showed serious prejudice, its defeat on showing injury did not alter the outcome of the case, as under Article 5 of the *Agreement*, the test for adverse effects is a 3 pronged one (injury, nullification or impairment, or serious prejudice), with the prongs understood to be connected by the disjunctive ("or," *i.e.*, it is not necessary to prove all three prongs, just one).

64. This case is cited, and its facts summarized, in an earlier Chapter.

65. *See Boeing* Appellate Body Report, ¶ 892.

The Aeronautics R&D Subsidies included:

(1) Payments made to Boeing, plus the access for Boeing to NASA facilities, equipment, and employees pursuant NASA procurement contracts; and

(2) Payments made to Boeing, plus the access for Boeing to USDOD facilities pursuant to the USDOD assistance instruments.

The Panel found these subsidies amounted to at least $2.6 billion. The Panel evaluated these subsidies on the basis of their alleged Technology Effects.[66]

The Tied Tax Subsidies included:

(1) Tax exemptions and exclusions from the FSC/ETI legislation;

(2) The Washington State B&O tax rate reduction; and

(3) The City of Everett, Washington, B&O tax rate reduction.

The Panel found these subsidies amounted to approximately $2.2 billion. The Panel assessed them according to their alleged Price Effects.[67]

The 8 Remaining Subsidies included:

(1) Property and sales tax abatements issued by the City of Wichita, Kansas;

(2) Washington State B&O tax credits for preproduction development, computer software and hardware, and property taxes;

(3) Washington State sales and use tax exemptions for computer hardware, peripherals, and software;

(4) Washington State workforce development program and Employment Resource Center;

(5) Reimbursement by the State of Illinois of a portion of the relocation expenses of Boeing;

(6) The 15-year Economic Development for a Growing Economy ("EDGE") tax credits provided by the State of Illinois;

(7) The abatement or refund by the State of Illinois of a portion of the property taxes paid by Boeing; and

(8) The payment to retire the lease of the previous tenant of the new headquarters building of Boeing in Chicago, Illinois.

The Panel found these subsidies amounted to approximately $550 million.[68] As it had with the Tied Tax subsidies, the Panel examined these subsidies according to their alleged Price Effects.

---

66. *See Boeing* Appellate Body Report, ¶ 896.
67. *See Boeing* Appellate Body Report, ¶ 896.
68. *See Boeing* Appellate Body Report, ¶ 895.

• **Appellate Body and Causation-Non-Attribution Analysis**

As the Appellate Body said, a plain reading of the language of Articles 5, 6:2, and 6:3 makes clear a complainant must demonstrate not only the existence of the relevant subsidies and adverse effects to its interests, but also that the subsidies at issue have caused such effects. In the 2005 *Cotton* and 2011 *Airbus* disputes, the Appellate Body articulated the causal link required as "a genuine and substantial relationship of cause and effect."[69] Further, "the mere presence of other causes that contribute to a particular market effect does not, in itself, preclude the subsidy from being found to be a 'genuine and substantial' cause of the effect."[70] Thus, a proper analysis must ensure the effects of those other causal factors are not attributed to the subsidies at issue. In practice, this non-attribution analysis can be difficult. Often, a Panel has to consider other factors, and their varying degrees of contribution.

• **Issues on Causation of Adverse Effects**

The Appellate Body addressed three general topics. First, it considered the American appeal of the findings of the Panel with respect to the Technology Effects of the Aeronautics R&D Subsidies. Second, it addressed the U.S. view of the Price Effects of the Tied Tax Subsidies. Third, on the Remaining Subsidies, the Appellate Body addressed the European appeal of the decisions of the Panel not to undertake a collective assessment of these Subsidies and their effects when examining their alleged seriousness.

• **Technology Effects**

With regard to the Technology Effects, the U.S. put forth 3 arguments. First, the U.S. sought reversal of the Panel's legal finding that the aeronautics R&D subsidies caused adverse effects to the interests of the EC.[71] Second, the American appeal said the Panel erred in finding, "absent the aeronautics R&D subsidies, Boeing would not have been able to launch an aircraft incorporating all of the technologies that are incorporated on the 787 in 2004, with promised deliveries commencing in 2008."[72] Third, the U.S. challenged each of the Panel findings relating to significant lost sales, threat of displacement and impedance, and significant price suppression.[73]

First: 5 Specific Grounds for American Appeal

The U.S. took issue with the conclusion of the Panel at the close of the first stage of its analysis. There, the Panel found the Aeronautics R&D Subsidies:

> contributed in a genuine and substantial way to Boeing's development of technologies for the 787 and that, in the light of the conditions of competition

---

69. *Boeing* Appellate Body Report, ¶ 913.
70. *Boeing* Appellate Body Report, ¶ 914.
71. *See Boeing* Appellate Body Report, ¶ 1012.
72. *See Boeing* Appellate Body Report, ¶ 1013.
73. *See Boeing* Appellate Body Report, ¶ 1051.

in the LCA industry, these subsidies conferred a competitive advantage on Boeing.[74]

The Panel reached this conclusion by considering 4 factors: the (1) objectives of the aeronautics R&D subsidies; (2) structure and design of the aeronautics R&D subsidies; (3) operation of the aeronautics R&D subsidies; and (4) conditions of competition in the LCA industry.[75]

On appeal, the U.S. pointed to five Panel factual findings, which it argued the Panel failed to take into account. Those were:

(1) Much of the work NASA funded bore a weak relationship to the 787, as it was not directed toward the six critical 787 technologies identified by the Panel.

(2) Even NASA research most directly on the development pathway toward the 787 was far removed from the ultimate technologies used on that aircraft.

(3) NASA funding was only one of many sources available to Boeing for technology development, and was unavailable for later stages of the research.

(4) Non-Subsidy sources were responsible for most of the technology eventually used to make the 787 and for ability of Boeing to apply that technology to the 787;

(5) Magnitude of the subsidies was small in relation to the cost of developing the 787.

The Americans contended when the above findings were considered in their totality, they demonstrated no possible cause and effect relationship existed between support for Boeing and adverse effects visited on the EU (*i.e.*, Airbus).[76]

The Appellate Body was puzzled by the standard the U.S. intended to apply. To the Appellate Body, the American argument raised numerous questions. What if it felt the Panel only failed to consider properly one or more (but not all 5) of the findings? Does it matter that the five findings only apply to the third step in the Panel's analysis? More importantly, is this not a question of the weight given to factual findings and, therefore, an issue under Article 11 of the *DSU*? (That certainly was the argument of the EU, *i.e.*, that all five points were factual matters contestable properly under *DSU* Article 11, not in terms of causation under the *SCM Agreement*.)

Ultimately, the Appellate Body accepted some of the American arguments as legal, while it took others to be questions of fact the U.S. should have appealed under Article 11 of the *DSU*. No matter. The Appellate Body went one-by-one through the five above-mentioned American arguments, and rejected every one of them. To be candid, the entire discussion of the Appellate Body was largely a waste of time. The Appellate Body analysis could have been summarized thusly: "Our [the Appellate Body's] review of the record of the case indicates the Panel did examine properly

74. *See Boeing* Appellate Body Report, ¶ 934 (*citing Boeing* Panel Report, ¶ 7.1783).
75. *See Boeing* Appellate Body Report, ¶ 934.
76. *See Boeing* Appellate Body Report, ¶ 951.

the five contentions raised by the U.S. Therefore, we find the Panel was correct in identifying the *SCM Agreement* causation standard, namely, that there be a genuine and substantial relationship between the unlawful subsidy of the respondent and adverse effects of complainant, and that such a relationship existed here."

Second: American Appeal of Panel Counterfactual Analysis

The second American appellate argument on causation of adverse effects contended the Panel erred in finding that absent the Aeronautics R&D subsidies, Boeing would not have been able to launch in 2004 an aircraft incorporating all of the technologies found in the 787, with promised deliveries commencing in 2008.[77] The Panel found these Aeronautics R&D subsidies caused adverse effects to the EU. In the first and second stages of the Panel assessment of the technology effects, the Panel analyzed the effect of the Aeronautics R&D subsidies on Boeing and Airbus, respectively. The U.S. argued the counterfactual analysis at both stages was insufficient.

With regard to the first stage, the U.S. argued the Panel failed to take fully into account the research priorities and activities of Boeing, as well as its available resources when it found Boeing would not have launched the 787 when it did absent the Aeronautics R&D subsidies.[78] The main American argument the Appellate Body considered, put simply, was that the fierce competition between Boeing and Airbus created strong incentives for Boeing to invest in R&D, regardless of whether it obtained assistance from other entities. The Appellate Body rejected this argument. The Appellate Body reasoned that such an incentive does not show whether or not Boeing necessarily would have undertaken investment.[79]

Another American argument the Appellate Body reviewed was that the Aeronautics R&D subsidies were inconsequential. The U.S. said the $16 billion spent by Boeing repurchasing stock from 1986–2006, compared to the amount spent on Aeronautics R&D subsidies, showed how relatively little the subsidies meant to Boeing. However again, the Appellate Body sided with the Panel in rejecting the American argument.[80] The Appellate Body said the value of Aeronautics R&D subsidies to Boeing were not directly comparable to the cash amounts paid to shareholders, and the effects of the subsidies were not reducible to their cash value. Instead, the Appellate Body accepted the Panel finding that Aeronautics R&D subsidies were meant to have multiplier effects.

With regard to the second stage of the Panel analysis, the U.S. argued the Panel should have explored further a counterfactual scenario involving Boeing aircraft it deemed "most likely" to have occurred in the absence of subsidies.[81] The Panel considered two scenarios most likely to occur if Boeing did not receive the Aeronautics

---

77. *See Boeing* Appellate Body Report, ¶ 1013.
78. *See Boeing* Appellate Body Report, ¶ 1014.
79. *See Boeing* Appellate Body Report, ¶ 1032.
80. *See Boeing* Appellate Body Report, ¶ 1035.
81. *See Boeing* Appellate Body Report, ¶ 1015.

R&D subsidies.[82] Boeing added the Panel should have also considered a counterfactual scenario involving a "767-plus."[83] The 767-plus is the LCA Boeing would have likely developed had it not chosen to develop the 787.

Ultimately, the Appellate Body rejected the scenario proposed by the U.S. At the Panel stage, neither Party advanced that scenario. But, the larger point concerned discretion available to a Panel.[84] As long as the scenarios a Panel considers are reasonable, the Panel does not need to explore every hypothetical possibility.

The U.S.-proposed counterfactual analysis broke down to three parts. First, the Panel should have made findings as to how a Boeing 767-plus would have competed against the older Airbus A330, or whether the Original A350 would have been launched at all, given that the A350 was a response to the 787. Second, the Americans contended the Panel only looked at the price suppressive impact of the 787 on the A330 and Original A350 prices, when it should have considered the price impact from a 767-plus. Third, in its assessment of lost sales and threat of displacement or impedance, the Panel should have considered whether airlines that ordered the 787 would have bought the 767-plus in its place, had the 787 not been available.

The Appellate Body easily rejected the American argument. It said the adequacy of a counterfactual analysis must be determined according to (*inter alia*) the scenarios, arguments, and evidence on record of a particular dispute. In the *Boeing* appeal, the American arguments were derived from the counterfactual analysis of the Panel, but not based on any counterfactual arguments of the parties.

Third: American Appeal Relating to Second Stage of Panel Analysis

The U.S. also appealed Panel findings in the second stage of its analysis, where it examined the effects of the Aeronautics R&D subsidies on the prices and sales of Airbus LCA. The Panel analysis of the EU claims of serious prejudice examined allegations of significant lost sales, threat of displacement or impedance, and significant price suppression. The Panel first examined EU allegations of significant lost sales.

On that matter, the Panel determined:

> the performance characteristics of the 787 and/or its scheduled entry into service in 2008 appear to have been the decisive factors in the outcomes of the Qantas, Ethiopian Airlines, and Icelandair campaigns in 2005 and the Kenya Airways campaign in 2006.[85]

Therefore, the Panel found but for the effects of the Aeronautics R&D subsides, Airbus would not have suffered significant lost sales within the meaning of Article 6:3(c) of the *SCM Agreement*.

---

82. *See Boeing* Appellate Body Report, ¶ 1017.
83. *See Boeing* Appellate Body Report, ¶ 1037.
84. *See Boeing* Appellate Body Report, ¶ 1020.
85. *Boeing* Appellate Body Report, ¶ 1043.

Additionally, the Panel concluded there was a threat of displacement and imped-ance within the meaning of Article 6:3(b) of the *Agreement* on EU exports in the third-country markets of Australia, Ethiopia, Kenya, and Iceland. It did so based on market share data from those relevant third-country markets in which it found lost sales. Here, the Panel used actual delivery data and projected future delivery data to support its findings. So, the Panel also found that but for the effects of the Aeronau-tics R&D subsidies, Airbus would have obtained additional orders for its A330 or Original A350 LCA from customers in third-country markets, and would not have suffered the threat of displacement or impedance of its exports from third-country markets, within the meaning of Article 6:3(b) of the *Agreement*.

Lastly, the Panel considered the EU allegations regarding significant price sup-pression suffered by Airbus in the 200–300 seat LCA market. The Panel deter-mined the launch of technologically-advanced aircraft forced competing aircraft with older technology to be offered at lower prices. The Panel was satisfied with this explanation relating to the A330 and the launch of the Boeing 787 in 2004. The Panel supported its finding that the Aeronautics R&D subsidies contributed in a genuine and substantial way to the development by Boeing of technologies for the 787 with evidence of pricing trends on the A330 and market share data. Therefore, the Panel concluded that but for the effect of the Aeronautics R&D subsidies, Airbus would not have suffered significant price suppression within the meaning of Article 6:3(c) of the *SCM Agreement*.[86]

In sum, the allegations the Panel examined resulted in a violation of Article 6:3 of the *SCM Agreement*, and each violation constituted serious prejudice to the inter-ests of the EU within the meaning of Article 5(c) of the *Agreement*.[87]

Thus, on appeal, the U.S. challenged each of the three Panel findings relating to significant lost sales, threat of displacement and impedance, and significant price suppression. Ultimately, the U.S. was successful in having the Panel finding of threat of displacement and impedance reversed. However, the Appellate Body upheld the remaining Panel findings.[88]

First: Significant Lost Sales

The U.S. first challenged the Panel finding that the effects of the Aeronautics R&D subsidies were significant lost sales by Airbus within the meaning of Article 6:3(c) of the *SCM Agreement*. The U.S. first asserted the Panel "double-counted" lost sales, because it treated each sale won by the 787 as a lost sale for both the Original A350 and A330.[89] Next, the U.S. argued the Panel erred by failing to consider other factors.

The Appellate Body began by looking to its own decision in the 2011 *Airbus* and 2005 *Cotton* cases. In *Airbus*, the Appellate Body defined a "lost sale" as one that a

---

86. *See Boeing* Appellate Body Report, ¶ 1049.
87. *See Boeing* Appellate Body Report, ¶ 1049.
88. *See Boeing* Appellate Body Report, ¶ 1126.
89. *Boeing* Appellate Body Report, ¶ 1056.

supplied "failed to obtain."[90] Additionally, the concept of a lost sale is "relational," entailing consideration of the subsidized firm, which must have won sales, and the competing firm that allegedly lost sales due to the effect of the subsidy.[91] Moreover, in *Cotton*, the Appellate Body noted the term "significant" means "important, notable or consequential."[92]

The first argument by the U.S. contended the Panel "double-counted" lost sales because it treated each sale won by Boeing as two lost sales for Airbus. The U.S. said for the lost sales found by the Panel, Airbus either did not submit a bid or offered the Original 350 against the 787. However, in reviewing the Panel findings, the Appellate Body observed no statement or implication by the Panel that it considered two sales had been lost by Airbus for each 787 ordered. In particular, the Appellate Body noted the repeated use of "or" by the Panel when referring to airlines' considerations of the Original 350 or the A330.[93]

Second, the U.S. argued the Panel erred in finding lost sales to certain airlines because it failed to account for other factors, namely, "customer-specific situations."[94] America pointed to customer-specific situations including relationships of Boeing with relevant airlines, and the failure of Airbus to submit a formal offer within the time limit specified by an airline.

In the American view, had the Panel considered properly the relationships of Boeing with other airlines, the Panel would have considered the Boeing relationships with the relevant airlines here, namely, Ethiopian Airlines, Icelandair, and Kenya Airways. The EU countered with the assertion that such a consideration was impossible due to the Highly Sensitive Business Information (HSBI) nature of those sales campaigns. Moreover, the EU argued the American arguments implicated weight of evidence considerations, and should have been raised under *DSU* Article 11.

The Appellate Body sided with the EU. In the Appellate Body view, it had no reason to doubt the Panel assessment, but was concerned such an assessment was not evident. However, even with this concern, a challenge to the Panel finding should have been brought under Article 11 of the *DSU*. Additionally, the same could be said with regard to the U.S. claim Airbus lost the Icelandair sales campaign because of a failure to submit a formal offer within a specified time limit. Therefore, the Appellate Body found the Panel did not err in applying Article 6:3(c) of the *SCM Agreement* in its consideration of the sales campaigns involving Ethiopian Airlines, Icelandair, and Kenya Airways with regard to the lost sales finding.[95]

---

90. *Boeing* Appellate Body Report, ¶ 1052 (*citing Airbus* Appellate Body Report, ¶ 1214).
91. *Boeing* Appellate Body Report, ¶ 1052 (*citing Airbus* Appellate Body Report, ¶ 1214).
92. *Boeing* Appellate Body Report, ¶ 1052 (*citing Cotton*, Appellate Body Report, ¶ 426).
93. *Boeing* Appellate Body Report, ¶¶ 1059–1061.
94. *Boeing* Appellate Body Report, ¶ 1064.
95. *See Boeing* Appellate Body Report, ¶ 1068.

Second: Threat of Displacement and Impedance

Next, the U.S. put forth three arguments challenging the Panel finding that the Aeronautics R&D subsidies caused a threat of displacement and impedance of exports of Airbus aircraft in the "third-country markets" of Ethiopia, Kenya, and Iceland. First, the U.S. alleged the Panel failed to establish that Ethiopia, Kenya and Iceland constitute "third-country markets" within the meaning of Article 6:3(b) of the *SCM Agreement*.[96] Second, the U.S. asserted the Panel finding of threat of displacement and impedance in Ethiopia, Kenya and Iceland contradicted its legal finding that treating a single sales campaign as a "market" nullifies the meaning of that term. Third, the U.S. argued the low volume of orders in the relevant sales campaigns demonstrated no trend of Airbus exports being threatened with displacement and impedance.

The Appellate Body first took the opportunity to recall the meaning of displacement and impedance. As explained in the 2011 *Airbus* decision, "displacement" refers to an economic mechanism in which exports of a like product are replaced by the sales of a subsidized product. In the context of Article 6:3(b) of the *SCM Agreement*, "displacement arises where exports of the like product of the complaining Member are substituted in a third country market by exports of the subsidized product."[97] An analysis of displacement should examine trends in data relating to export volumes and market shares over an appropriately relative period.[98] Additionally, "impedance" involves a broader range of situations than displacement and while there may be some overlap between the concepts, they are not interchangeable.

The Appellate Body looked to its consideration of impedance in *Airbus*:

> . . . impedance arises in "situations where the exports or imports of the like product of the complaining Member would have expanded had they not been 'obstructed' or 'hindered' by the subsidized product," as well as when such exports or imports "did not materialize at all because production was held back by the subsidized product."[99]

The U.S. first took issue with the meaning the Panel attributed to the term "market" in Article 6:3(b) of the *SCM Agreement*.[100] Using *Airbus* as guidance, the Appellate Body said there was both a geographic and product market component to the assessment of displacement and impedance. The determination of a geographic market is determined on a number of factors. In part, a particular market may exceed national boundaries or encompass a world market. However, using a plain reading of Article 6:3(b) the *Agreement*, the Appellate Body in *Airbus* explained

---

96. *Boeing* Appellate Body Report, ¶ 1069.

97. *Boeing* Appellate Body Report, ¶ 1071 (*quoting Airbus*, Appellate Body Report, ¶ 1160).

98. *See Boeing* Appellate Body Report, ¶ 1071 (*citing Airbus* Appellate Body Report, ¶¶ 1165–1166, 1170).

99. *Boeing* Appellate Body Report, ¶ 1071, *quoting Airbus* Appellate Body Report, ¶ 1161).

100. *Boeing* Appellate Body Report, ¶ 1075.

that even in cases where the geographic dimension of a particular market exceeds national boundaries, a claim under Article 6:3(b) of the *Agreement* should focus on displacement and impedance in the territory of the third countries involved.[101]

The Panel recognized Article 6:3(b) of the *SCM Agreement* expressly requires examination of displacement and impedance based on a third country market. Thus, the Panel felt it was irrelevant whether or not a complaining party established the existence of a third country market. The Appellate Body saw no error in such an approach.[102]

In Appellate Body view, the evidence relied on by the EU, coupled with the failure by the U.S. to point to differences in the competitive condition within the relevant countries, supported the Panel finding. Additionally, the Appellate Body said a secondary argument by the U.S. — that the Panel finding of threat of displacement and impedance in Ethiopia, Kenya and Iceland contradicted its legal finding that treating a single sales campaign as a "market" nullifies the meaning of that term — confused definitions of "market" under Articles 6:3(b) and (c), respectively.[103]

The last American argument was that the volume of orders involved in the relevant third country markets campaigns were too low to be capable of demonstrating a threat of displacement and impedance, and that there were insufficient trends of Airbus exports. The Appellate Body first assessed the Panel finding of displacement, then considered its finding of impedance.

Recalling its guidance from *Airbus* with regard to displacement, the Appellate Body recognized the assessment of a claim of displacement must check if trends are discernible.[104] Additionally, the identification of a trend is more accurate the larger the data set used in the analysis.[105] Thus, two characteristics normally are necessary to reach a finding of displacement under Article 6:3(b) of the *SCM Agreement*.[106]

First, at least a portion of the market share of the exports of the like product of the complaining Member must have been taken over or substituted by the subsidized product. Second, it must be possible to discern trends in volume and market share.

On appeal, the U.S. challenged the Panel finding that there was a threat of displacement in Ethiopia, Kenya, and Iceland. Though the U.S. did not appeal the Panel finding with regard to Australian market, the Appellate Body considered the Australian market a useful tool. In the Australian market, Boeing had no deliveries in 2006, but progressed to 50% of deliveries by 2008, and 100% of deliveries

---

101. *See Boeing* Appellate Body Report, ¶ 1076 (*quoting Airbus* Appellate Body Report, ¶ 1117 (quotations omitted)).

102. *See Boeing* Appellate Body Report, ¶ 1078.

103. *Boeing* Appellate Body Report, ¶ 1079.

104. *See Boeing* Appellate Body Report, ¶ 1081 (*citing Airbus* Appellate Body Report, ¶ 1166).

105. *See Boeing* Appellate Body Report, ¶ 1081 (*citing Airbus* Appellate Body Report, ¶ 1167).

106. *See Boeing* Appellate Body Report, ¶ 1082.

by 2011. To contrast, in the other three third country markets at issue (Ethiopia, Kenya, and Iceland), Boeing was the sole supplier in all years for which data was provided. On this basis alone (namely, the complete absence of Airbus in the Ethiopian, Kenyan, and Icelandic markets), there was no way the Appellate Body could sustain the affirmative finding of the Panel that Boeing threated to displace Airbus in those third country markets. Simply put, it is impossible to displace a product (Airbus LCA) from a market (the other three third country markets) if that product never was in that market in the first place.

Though the Panel never distinguished between displacement and impedance, it did refer to both jointly throughout its findings. Thus, the Appellate Body felt it appropriate to consider also the Panel finding of threat of impedance. The Appellate Body again looked to its decision in *Airbus* as guidance in defining and analysis threat of impedance. As explained in *Airbus*, impedance refers to a situation in which (1) exports or imports of the like product of the complaining Member would have expanded more, had they not been obstructed or hindered by the subsidized product, or (2) exports or imports of the like product did not materialize at all, because production was held back by the subsidized product.[107] Additionally, changes in the relative market share in favor of the subsidized product need to occur over a sufficiently representative period to demonstrate "clear trends" in the development of the market concerned.

In *Boeing*, the Appellate Body looked at data provided for Ethiopia, Kenya, and Iceland.[108] The Appellate Body disposed quickly of any possibility of a clear trend of impedance in Iceland and Kenya. In Iceland, the market share of Boeing market share remained at 100%. In Kenya, the delivery numbers did not vary enough to constitute an unequivocal trend. In Ethiopia, the data were more mixed, but even still, fluctuation was minimal and did not convince the Appellate Body of a clear trend.

Consequently, the Appellate Body rejected the American appeal that the Panel erred by failing to identify and establish third-country "markets" in Iceland, Kenya, and Ethiopia within the meaning of Article 6:3(b) of the *SCM Agreement*. However, it did reverse Panel finding that there was a threat of displacement and impedance in those same third-country markets. That was a modest victory for the U.S. in the case.

Third: Significant Price Suppression

The U.S. pushed 3 arguments in favor of reversal of the Panel finding of significant price suppression.[109] First, the Panel improperly relied on a perceived coincidence between the launch of the 787 in 2004, and a decline in A330 prices during the reference period. Second, price suppression could not be found, because of insufficient

---

107. *See Boeing* Appellate Body Report, ¶ 1086 (*citing Airbus* Appellate Body Report, ¶ 1161).
108. *See Boeing* Appellate Body Report, ¶ 1087.
109. *See Boeing* Appellate Body Report, ¶ 1091.

evidence provided by Airbus. Third, the Panel was required, but failed, to determine the existence of significant price suppression for the product as a whole.

The Americans first argued the Panel improperly relied on a perceived coincidence between the launch of the Boeing 787 and a drop in A330 prices.[110] The U.S. asserted the Panel failed to look rigorously at the evolution of relevant trends showing no discernible correlation between the presence of 787 LCA in the market and the prices of the Airbus A330.

The Appellate Body took the American argument as a suggestion the Panel should have looked at specific figures during the reference period.[111] However, the Appellate Body was satisfied with the consideration by the Panel of overall trends demonstrating erosion of the market share of Airbus.[112] As explained by the Panel, and accepted by the Appellate Body:

> the combination of the superior technology and lower operating costs of the 787 clearly affected the comparative value of Airbus' A330 . . . leaving Airbus no other option but to reduce the prices of its aircraft in order to compete.[113]

Additionally, the Appellate Body saw no reason to require the Panel to attach decisive weight to specific data points, in light of the economic reasoning and broad data considerations by the Panel.

Second, the U.S. asserted the Panel finding of price suppression for the Original A350 should be reversed, because it was not supported by pricing data and used anecdotal evidence covering barely 30% (exactly 30.4%) of sales of the Original A350 in the 200–300 seat LCA market. The Appellate Body dispatched of that assertion quickly. It simply disagreed with the American contention that insufficient data and evidence were provided. In its view, 1/3 of sales campaigns for the Original A350 constituted direct and sufficiently representative evidence.[114] Accordingly, the Appellate Body upheld the Panel finding that the Aeronautics R&D subsidies caused significant price suppression in the 200–300 seat LCA market: the pricing data concerning the Original A350, albeit covering just 30% of the market, were sufficient.[115] Notwithstanding the Appellate Body holding, arguably the Americans had the better argument: drawing a conclusion about price suppression from data for 30% of the sales in a market seems rather parlous.

The last U.S. argument was the Panel was required, but failed, to determine the existence of significant price suppression for the product as a whole.[116] Using the

---

110. *See Boeing* Appellate Body Report, ¶ 1104.
111. *See Boeing* Appellate Body Report, ¶ 1106.
112. *See Boeing* Appellate Body Report, ¶ 1107.
113. *Boeing* Appellate Body Report, ¶ 1109 (*quoting Boeing* Panel Report, ¶ 7.1792).
114. *See Boeing* Appellate Body Report, ¶ 1116.
115. *See Boeing* Appellate Body Report, ¶ 1119.
116. *See Boeing* Appellate Body Report, ¶ 1120.

2005 *Korea—Commercial Vessels* Panel Report as support, the U.S. argued a finding in favor of the EU would be valid only if the effect of the subsidy was significant price suppression for all three of the 200–300 seat Airbus models. The EU contended the Panel properly found price suppression based on pricing information for the A330 and the Original A350, but that any data on the A350XWB-800 would be of limited relevance, because there was only one data point.

The Appellate Body questioned the American reliance on the *Korea—Commercial Vessels* case. But, it said even if it assumed a finding of price suppression should have been made for the Airbus product as a whole in the 200–300 seat LCA market, the U.S. failed to provide sufficient evidence of its allegation. In particular, the Appellate Body said the U.S. failed to show that if sales or price levels of the A350XWB-8000 been taken into account, then they would been sufficiently significant to prevent the Panel from reaching its finding.[117]

Additionally, the Appellate Body looked to the EU submission of price trend data in respect of all sales of the A330 during the reference period. Those data showed sales of the A330 accounted for 65.7% of total Airbus sales during the reference period. Taken as a whole, *i.e.*, coupled with pricing data for the Original A350, the Panel considered roughly three-quarters of Airbus sales in the 200–300 seat LCA market during the reference period.[118] That was sufficient for the Appellate Body to agree with the Panel. Therefore, the Appellate Body upheld the Panel finding relating to the treatment of evidence and concluded overall that the effect of Aeronautics R&D subsidies was significant price suppression in the 200–300 seat LCA product market.[119]

• **Price Effects**

The next aspect of the American appeal concerned the analysis by the Panel of the price effects of the Tied Tax Subsidies. As explained earlier, this appeal concerned the FSC/ETI subsidies, Washington State B&O tax rate reductions, and City of Everett B&O tax rate reductions.[120] Moreover, the appeal was limited to the 100–200 seat and 300–400 seat LCA markets.

The Appellate Body assessed the causation analysis of the Panel in three steps. First, it addressed the general aspects of that analysis. Second, the Appellate Body addressed the American contention the Panel committed specific errors in reaching

---

117. *See Boeing* Appellate Body Report, ¶ 1123.

118. *See Boeing* Appellate Body Report, ¶ 1124. Note the apparent odd mathematical discrepancy. The data for the Original A350 purportedly covered 30% of sales in the 200–300 seat LCA market. Thus, the sum should be roughly 90%. However, to go from 65.7% to roughly ¾ of the market would entail only 10% of the sales. But, there was no discrepancy in fact: the 30% figure referred to sales to three different companies of A350 aircraft, but as a whole, A350 sales accounted for 10% of total Airbus LCA sales. So, as a percentage of total Airbus sales, the A350 (10%) plus the A330 (65.7%), sums to about 75%.

119. *See Boeing* Appellate Body Report, ¶ 1125.

120. *See Boeing* Appellate Body Report, ¶ 1149.

its affirmative finding of significant price suppression, significant lost sales, and displacement and impedance. Third, the Appellate Body considered the elements together to provide an overall assessment of the causation analysis by the Panel.

Step 1: Proper Causation Analysis?

So, first, did the Panel conduct a proper causation analysis? The Appellate Body checked the American allegations concerning (1) reliance by the Panel on an impermissible presumption, (2) magnitude of the Tied Tax Subsidies, (3) counterfactual analysis by the Panel, and (4) consideration of other factors advanced by the U.S. to explain market effects (*i.e.*, prices and sales of LCA by Boeing and Airbus).

First: Reliance on Impermissible Presumption?

The U.S. contended the Panel erred in relying on a presumption that subsidies found to be prohibited under Part II of the *SCM Agreement* cause adverse effects within the meaning of Part III of the *Agreement*.[121] Though not stated in the Appellate Body Report, the U.S. seemed to be alleging the Panel had characterized the American subsidies as Red Light under the Traffic Light system. In response, the EU did not even address whether such a presumption existed. Instead, the EU contended the Panel only referred to the FSC/ETI subsidies as export subsidies to support its characterization of the nature of those subsidies. As a general matter, the Appellate Body agreed with the EU.

In the view of the Appellate Body, when the reasoning of the Panel is considered in its totality, it does not indicate the Panel applied any presumption. The Appellate Body distinguished the findings of the Panel, because in the view of the Panel, the legal status of subsidies under Article 3:1(a) of the *SCM Agreement* (the provision on Red Light, or Prohibited, subsidies) does not determine the characterization of those effects for purposes of Article 6:3 of the *Agreement*. Instead, the Panel simply stated export subsidies are "*more likely* to cause adverse trade effects."[122] Thus, the Appellate Body considered the statement of the Panel as giving considerable weight in its analysis to whether there was serious prejudice.

Further support for this finding came from the Panel's reliance on various other factors. In addition to its characterization of the subsidies as export subsidies, the Panel the FSC/ETI subsidies and B&O tax rate reductions increased the profitability of LCA sales because they were tied to sales of individual LCA. The Panel also considered the amount and duration of the FSC/ETI subsidies. Furthermore, the Panel referred to statements by Airbus and Boeing executives and the USTR indicating the FSC/ETI subsidies "were essential to enhancing the international competitiveness of Boeing versus its foreign competitors."[123] None of these aspects were challenged by the U.S., and when considered together they support the Panel's findings.[124]

---

121. *See Boeing* Appellate Body Report, ¶ 1184.
122. *Boeing* Appellate Body Report, ¶ 1185.
123. *See Boeing* Appellate Body Report, ¶ 1183.
124. *See Boeing* Appellate Body Report, ¶ 1186.

Second: Magnitude of Tied Tax Subsidies?

The aspect of the causation analysis of the Panel was the magnitude of the Tied Tax Subsides. The Panel concluded the evidence showing FSC/ETI benefits amounted to less than 1% of the value of Boeing's sales was not informative or illustrative as to the capacity of the subsidies to affect LCA prices and sales.[125] The U.S. contended this conclusion fails to account for the small magnitude of the FSC/ETI subsidies in relation to LCA values. The EU contended the Panel's qualitative assessment did account for important contextual factors relating to the nature and duration of the subsidies, as well as the conditions of competition. To state plainly, the Panel decided that in a highly competitive market, including one characterized by duopoly, even a 1% benefit could have a substantial effect on prices and sales throughout the market.

The Appellate Body recalled its own decision in the 2005 *Cotton* case. There, the Appellate Body rejected the American contention that Article 6:3(c) of the *SCM Agreement* requires a Panel to quantify precisely the amount of the challenged subsidy benefiting the product at issue.[126] The Appellate Body went on to quote what it considered the significant language from *Cotton*:

> ... in analyzing a claim of significant price suppression, "a panel will need to consider the effects of the subsidy on prices" and that, in doing so, "it may be difficult to decide" whether the effect of a subsidy is significant price suppression without having regard to "the magnitude of the challenged subsidy and its relationship to prices of the product in the relevant market." Moreover, although "[t]he magnitude of the subsidy is an important factor," a panel needs to take into account "all relevant factors" in determining the effects of subsidies on prices.[127]

Here, the Appellate Body explained "an assessment of whether subsidy amounts are significant should not necessarily be limited to a mere inquiry into what those amounts are, either in absolute or per-unit terms."[128]

The Appellate Body listed examples of factors that could be considered for a larger, more relative (*i.e.*, comparative) inquiry. Examples included:

> the size of the market as a whole, the size of the subsidy recipient, the per-unit price of the subsidized product, the price elasticity of demand, and, depending on the market structure, the extent to which a subsidy recipient is able to set its own prices in the market, and the extent to which rivals are able or prompted to react to each other's pricing within that market structure.[129]

---

125. *See Boeing* Appellate Body Report, ¶ 1187.
126. *See Boeing* Appellate Body Report, ¶ 1192.
127. *Boeing* Appellate Body Report, ¶ 1192 (citations omitted).
128. *Boeing* Appellate Body Report, ¶ 1193.
129. *Boeing* Appellate Body Report, ¶ 1193.

As it did throughout the *Boeing* Report, the Appellate Body here did not pass up an opportunity to critique the decision of the Panel. The Appellate Body felt the Panel should have explained why it dismissed evidence advanced by the parties with regard to the magnitude of the subsidies before it went on to discuss the significance of the FSC/ETI subsidies.[130] Yet, the discussion by the Panel, and the Appellate Body critique of it, were confusing. The "takeaway" appears to be that both the absolute and relative value of a subsidy is likely to be relevant and, therefore, should be considered.

Third: Counterfactual Analysis of Panel?

The U.S. argued the Panel should have engaged in a proper counterfactual analysis. Specifically, the Panel should have established, absent the Tied Tax Subsidies, Boeing LCA prices would have been higher.[131] The EU contended that absent subsidies, Boeing would not have had the resources to act on commercial incentives. The EU also stated the U.S. agreed Tied Tax Subsidies have an impact on output and prices.

The Appellate Body noted the Panel stated its intent to conduct a counterfactual analysis at the outset of its adverse effect analysis, but never expressly referred to it during its discussion.[132] So, the Appellate Body criticized the conclusion of the Panel that that the Tied Tax Subsidies "enabled Boeing to lower its prices beyond the level that would otherwise have been economically justifiable."[133] This conclusion lacked a sufficient explanation.[134]

Further, the Appellate Body saw the counterfactual analysis of the Panel was internally inconsistent. The U.S. pointed to the Panel discussion of how it was unconvinced Boeing needed the subsidies to price the LCA as it did. The Panel found the total subsidies amounted only to $5.3 billion, so it was "untenable" that Boeing could not have engaged in the pricing and product development behavior it did without subsidies. This finding conflicted with the eventual conclusion of the Panel (that adverse effects occurred), and "underscore[s]" the Appellate Body's concern with the Panel's conclusion.[135]

Fourth: Effects of Other Factors?

The last American argument on general aspects of the causation analysis of the Panel was a catch-all of other factors related to the FSC/ETI subsidies the U.S. alleged the Panel failed to consider. As a general matter, the Appellate Body made clear:

---

130. *See Boeing* Appellate Body Report, ¶ 1194.
131. *See Boeing* Appellate Body Report, ¶ 1196.
132. *See Boeing* Appellate Body Report, ¶ 1198.
133. *Boeing* Panel Report, ¶ 7.1818.
134. *See Boeing* Appellate Body Report, ¶¶ 1200–1201.
135. *Boeing* Appellate Body Report, ¶ 1204.

. . . when confronted with multiple factors that may have contributed to the alleged adverse effects, a panel must seek to understand the interactions between the subsidies at issue and the various other factors, and make some assessment of their connection to, as well as the relative contribution of the subsidies and the other factors in bringing about, the relevant effect.[136]

Thus, an adjudicator need not determine that a subsidy is the sole, or even substantial, cause. That would be an insurmountable test for any complainant, and in any event would not be justified by the GATT-WTO texts. But, an adjudicator must ensure other factors do not dilute the causal link between the subsidy, on the one hand, and adverse effects, on the other hand.

On this matter of attribution, the Panel said it would take "potential non-attribution factors into account simultaneously with the effect of the subsidies and in the context of conditions of competition affecting the market."[137] But, the actual discussion by the Panel of other factors was limited to a brief recognition that the U.S. had identified other factors. The Panel opted not to pursue these factors further, because the FSC/ETI program was in effect before the reference period (2001–2003). Thus, it was impossible to determine the effects of the subsidies through direct observation of market share and price trend data.

The Appellate Body did not like the work of the Panel. The Appellate Body stated though mere correlation between payment of subsidies and significantly suppressed prices is insufficient, it still is a relevant inquiry.[138] The U.S. pointed to: (1) Airbus undercutting the prices of Boeing in the 100–200 seat and 300–400 seat LCA markets, and (2) Boeing changing its LCA pricing policy in 2004 and 2005 because of the prices of Airbus.[139] The EU maintained it was Boeing that undercut prices first, yet even if that were not so, the FSC/ETI subsidies gave Boeing an additional pricing advantage.

The Appellate Body did not consider relevant either of the factors the U.S. highlighted. The pertinent question was not why Boeing lowered its LCA prices. Instead, the Appellate Body felt the salient question was whether Boeing lowered its prices using the Tied Tax (*i.e.*, FSC/ETI) subsidies.[140] As the Appellate Body reasoned, the bidding and negotiation process for LCA orders consisted of a series of successively lower bids. Thus, the identity of the party that first submitted a lower bid price would have had little bearing on the end result as to which party won the bid. Instead, the relevant consideration is what cost factors allowed one party or the other to submit a lower bid.

---

136. *Boeing* Appellate Body Report, ¶ 1206.
137. *See Boeing* Appellate Body Report, ¶ 1207 (*citing Boeing* Panel Report, ¶ 7.1660).
138. *See Boeing* Appellate Body Report, ¶ 1209.
139. *See Boeing* Appellate Body Report, ¶ 1210.
140. *See Boeing* Appellate Body Report, ¶ 1212.

Yet, even though the Appellate Body rejected these other factors, it did agree there could be other factors that the Panel ought to have considered. For example, perhaps fuel efficiency on disputed aircraft models, or which LCA producer was the incumbent supplier to certain airlines, were factors worthy of analysis. Moreover, the Appellate Body found it strange the Panel was able to consider properly other factors with respect to the Aeronautics R&D subsidies, but not with respect to the Tied Tax subsidies. Regardless, the Appellate Body held the Panel erred by not considering other causal factors (some of which the U.S. advanced).[141]

Step 2: *Proper Analysis of Significant Price Suppression, Significant Lost Sales, and Displacement and Impedance?*

The Panel concluded the Tied Tax subsidies enabled Boeing to lower its prices below what was "economically justifiable." However, it also found it impossible to ascertain the effects of the FSC/ETI subsidies during the 2000–2006, because the program was in operation prior to 2000.[142] The Panel felt it had only two options:

(1) to "decline to make a serious prejudice finding because of the difficulty of calculating with mathematical certitude the precise degree to which Boeing's pricing of [2 families of aircraft were] affected";

(2) to "deduce" the effects of those subsidies on Airbus' sales and prices during the reference period "based on commonsense reasoning and the drawing of inferences" from its conclusions regarding the nature of the subsidies, the duration of the FSC/ETI subsidies, and the nature of competition between Airbus and Boeing.[143]

The Appellate Body was "puzzled" by the view of the Panel that it was limited to "two diametrically opposed alternatives."[144]

The Appellate Body did not see the need for "mathematical certitude," nor did it feel the drawing of common sense and inferences to be an exceptional option.[145] Instead, it felt drawing inferences and from conclusions reached was a typical and acceptable method when supported by clear identification of those conclusions. Though, here, it seems the Panel failed to adequately support its findings.[146]

First: *Significant Price Suppression*

The U.S. asserted the Panel failed to consider the effects of other relevant factors on LCA prices, and did not assess the degree of price suppression to determine whether it constitute significant price suppression.[147] The EU argued the Panel did not need to examine price trend data because of its analysis of "various qualitative

---

141. *See Boeing* Appellate Body Report, ¶ 1216.
142. *See Boeing* Appellate Body Report, ¶ 1218.
143. *Boeing* Appellate Body Report, ¶ 1219 (quoting *Boeing* Panel Report, ¶¶ 7.1820–7.1822).
144. *See Boeing* Appellate Body Report, ¶ 1220.
145. *Boeing* Appellate Body Report, ¶ 1220.
146. *See Boeing* Appellate Body Report, ¶ 1222.
147. *See Boeing* Appellate Body Report, ¶ 1223.

factors."[148] However, the Appellate Body did not agree that no analysis could be done, even though there were no data before 2000 on which to compare the data from the reference period.[149] There still was sufficient evidence that should have triggered an analysis of the price trend data: in particular, there was the fact prices of subsidized products were lower even during periods of lower subsidization. As such, the Panel analysis was incomplete.

Second: Significant Lost Sales

Next, the Americans alleged the Panel should have considered specific lost sales from sales campaigns, as was done in the 2011 sister case, *Airbus*.[150] The EU argued the global sales approach used by the Panel was sufficient, because in *Airbus*, the Appellate Body concluded that approach might be permissible if keyed to the nature of the claim.

Here, the Appellate Body recognized a global sales approach might be permissible, but did not feel the Panel had properly articulated which sales campaigns it was using in its analysis.[151] Moreover, it did not state whether it was even taking such a broad approach in finding lost sales. Again, the Appellate Body noted it was strange the Panel properly concluded its analysis with regards to the technology effects of the aeronautics R&D, yet failed to do so with the FSC/ETI subsidies. In sum, the lack of clear support for the findings of the Panel rendered its findings yet again unreliable.

Third: Displacement and Impedance

Last, the U.S. contended the Panel failed to determine whether any of the countries in which the EU alleged displacement or impedance occurred constituted a "market" within the meaning of Article 6:3(b) of the *SCM Agreement*.[152] The U.S. argued though the Panel identified the third countries relevant to the 200–300 seat LCA market, it failed to do so with regard to the 100–200 seat and 300–400 seat LCA markets. The EU contended it was not necessary for the Panel to identify or address individual third-country markets in order to reach its finding.

The Appellate Body analysis focused on two distinctions. The first distinction was between displacement and impedance and significant lost sales.[153] The second was between establishing a particular third-country market and determining whether displacement or impedance occurred in a particular third-country market.

First, the Appellate Body did not agree with the Panel reasoning that the phenomena of displacement and impedance follow from a finding of significant lost sales. The Appellate Body looked to its recent decision in the 2011 *Airbus* case, where it

---

148. *Boeing* Appellate Body Report, ¶ 1224.
149. *See Boeing* Appellate Body Report, ¶¶ 1225–1226.
150. *See Boeing* Appellate Body Report, ¶ 1228.
151. *See Boeing* Appellate Body Report, ¶ 1232.
152. *See Boeing* Appellate Body Report, ¶ 1237.
153. *See Boeing* Appellate Body Report, ¶ 1241.

acknowledged the potential overlap of lost sales, and displacement and impedance, because both relate to sales of a firm.[154] In *Airbus*, the Appellate Body observed the assessment of displacement or impedance had "a well-defined geographic focus," whereas a geographic market for lost sales may extend further, even to the world market.[155] Additionally, the Appellate Body in *Airbus* noted the assessment of "significant" lost sales must have both quantitative and qualitative dimensions, whereas displacement and impedance require only a quantitative analysis. Though these phenomena may overlap, they are not interchangeable concepts.

Prior to the displacement or impedance analysis, the Panel found it reasonable to infer the effects of the subsidies are significant in terms of lost sales and price suppression, and thus concluded such effects constituted significant lost sales and significant price suppression. However, the Panel felt this was sufficient to conclude such effects also constituted displacement and impedance of exports from third-country markets.[156] The Appellate Body did not agree with the Panel dependence upon the relationship between lost sales and displacement and impedance. The Appellate Body said the Panel failed to address the relationship between these phenomena.

The second distinction discussed by the Appellate Body dealt with when naming particular third-country markets was necessary. The Appellate Body agreed with the EU contention that the Panel did not need to establish the existence of a particular third-country market because the LCA market is a world market. However, the Appellate Body stated it was still necessary to identify or discuss particular third countries in which displacement or impedance occurred.

At the onset of the serious prejudice analysis by the Panel, it correctly recognized it was required to determine, "based on evidence occurring in those countries," whether there had been displacement and impedance "in the particular country market."[157] However, even with particular data submitted by the EU, the Panel only referred in general terms to displacement and impedance in third country markets. The Appellate Body said that was inappropriate give the "well-defined geographic focus" of Article 6:3(b).[158] Moreover, the Appellate Body noted the Panel is entirely capable of conducting a proper analysis, because it did so with regards to the Aeronautics R&D subsidies in the 200–300 seat LCA market.

The Appellate found that taken together, the deficiencies in the Panel's reasoning amounted to a legal error in its analysis of serious prejudice in the 100–200 seat and 300–400 seat LCA markets.[159] The Panel did not provide a proper legal basis for

---

154. *Boeing* Appellate Body Report, ¶ 1241 (*citing Airbus* Appellate Body Report, ¶ 1218).

155. *Airbus* Appellate Body Report, ¶ 1218.

156. *Boeing* Appellate Body Report, ¶ 1240 (*quoting Boeing* Panel Report, ¶ 7.1822 (quotations omitted)).

157. *Boeing* Appellate Body Report, ¶ 1242 (*quoting Boeing* Panel Report, ¶ 7.1674).

158. *Boeing* Appellate Body Report, ¶¶ 1218, 1242.

159. *See Boeing* Appellate Body Report, ¶ 1249.

its generalized findings that significant price suppression, significant lost sales, and displacement and impedance, within the meaning of Article 6:3(b) and (c) of the *SCM Agreement* were the effects of: (1) the FSC/ETI subsidies and the Washington State B&O tax rate reduction in the 100–200 seat LCA market; and (2) the FSC/ETI subsidies and the Washington State and the City of Everett B&O tax rate reductions in the 300–400 seat LCA market. Accordingly, the Appellate Body reversed the Panel findings.

Step 3: *Appellate Body Completion of Analysis*

Having found the Panel legal analysis to be insufficient, the Appellate Body took it upon itself to complete and rule on the EU's claim that the Tied Tax Subsidies caused serious prejudice within the meaning of Article 5(c) and 6.3(b) and (c) of the *SCM Agreement*. Quoting itself in the 2001 *U.S. Hot-Rolled Steel* case, but citing numerous previous cases, the Appellate Body emphasized it may complete the analysis "only if the factual findings of the panel, or the undisputed facts in the panel record" provided a sufficient basis for it to complete an analysis.[160]

The Appellate body began its analysis by recalling findings and uncontested facts on the Panel record and then made some logical determinations and conclusions. First, it said Tied Tax Subsidies are directly tied to the sale of each LCA because they lower the taxes Boeing paid with respect to each sale.[161] Additionally, the Appellate Body said FSC/ETI subsidies are more likely to produce adverse trade effects in the market. As the Appellate Body reasoned, subsidies contingent on export modify a domestic producer's incentives and reward discrimination in favor of production for export markets over the domestic market, thereby reducing export prices.

Next, the Appellate Body considered the magnitude of the Tied Tax subsidies. The Appellate Body said the dollar amounts appeared to be substantial in absolute terms.[162] However, as discussed previously, the relative magnitude of subsidies may also be relevant to the effects of subsidies on prices. Some considerations the Appellate Body felt relevant were the nature of the Tied Tax subsidies, the dynamics of price competition between Boeing and Airbus in a duopolistic market, and whether the benefits of the tied tax subsidies Boeing received applied to prices in all sales or whether the benefits were disproportionately applied to lower prices of only certain sales.

Having already considered the nature of the Tied Tax subsidies, the Appellate Body turned to the dynamics of price competition between Boeing and Airbus in a duopolistic market. The Appellate Body recalled that Airbus and Boeing each possessed market power and that each manufacturer may influence the other's pricing

---

160. *Boeing* Appellate Body Report, ¶ 1250 (*quoting* Appellate Body Report, *US — Hot-Rolled Steel*, ¶ 235).

161. *See Boeing* Appellate Body Report, ¶ 1252.

162. Recall Boeing received $435 million in FSC/ETI subsidies, $13.8 million from B&O tax rate reduction in the State of Washington, and $2.2 million from the B&O tax rate reduction in the City of Everett. *See Boeing* Appellate Body Report, ¶ 1254.

through its own supply and pricing decisions.[163] The most significant factors are differences in price, capacity, and direct operating cost of competing LCA. But, both parties agreed that since performance characteristics are fixed at the initiation of a sales campaign, the principles variables modified during a sales campaign are price and other price-related concessions.

After summarizing the economics of the competitive relationship between Airbus and Boeing's relationship, the Appellate Body stated:

> . . . where it can be established that Boeing was under particular pressure to reduce its prices in order to secure LCA sales in particular sales campaigns, and there are no other non-price factors that explain Boeing's success in obtaining the sale or suppressing Airbus' pricing, we can conclude that the subsidies contributed in a genuine and substantial way to the lowering of Boeing's prices. We are moreover satisfied that the effect of such price reductions in the markets at issue was that Boeing either won the sale from Airbus, or that Airbus was forced to suppress its own price in order to secure the sale.[164]

However, unlike the Panel assessment of the effects on a generalized basis, the Appellate Body said a proper analysis demands identification of uncontested facts showing the pricing dynamic described above occurred in particular LCA sales campaigns.

The parties presented evidence regarding 11 sales campaigns in the 100–200 seat LCA market and four sales campaigns in the 300–400 seat LCA market.[165] In respect of the campaigns submitted as evidence of lost sales and displacement and impedance, the EU argued the magnitude of the Tied Tax subsides was larger than the difference between the final prices offered by Boeing and Airbus. The U.S. rebutted by submitting evidence of what it identified as "other factors" which undermined the causal link between the Tied Tax subsidies and the market effects.[166] Because the Panel failed to consider these "other factors," the Appellate Body had to consider the facts in dispute. Therefore, it was not able to complete the analysis in all four sales campaigns in the 300–400 seat LCA market and 9 of the 11 sales campaigns in the 100–200 seat LCA market.

The U.S. failed to specifically identify "other factors" contributing to the effects of two sales campaigns in the 100–200 seat LCA market, specifically on orders for Boeing's 737NG. Those sales campaigns were a 2005 order from Japan Airlines, and a 2005 order from Singapore Aircraft Leasing Enterprise.[167] The evidence showed these two sales campaigns were particularly price-sensitive. Considering the

---

163. *See Boeing* Appellate Body Report, ¶ 1257.
164. *Boeing* Appellate Body Report, ¶ 1260.
165. *See Boeing* Appellate Body Report, ¶1262.
166. *Boeing* Appellate Body Report, ¶ 1264.
167. *See Boeing* Appellate Body Report, ¶ 1271.

Appellate Body's previous finding that where price was the only factor, Boeing was substantially likely to use the tied tax subsidies to lower prices, it found the subsidies contributed in a genuine and substantial way to the lowering of Boeing's prices.

In accordance with Article 6:3(c) of the *SCM Agreement*, the lost sales campaigns must also be "significant." In *Cotton*, the Appellate Body understood "significant" to mean "something that can be characterized as important, notable or consequential."[168] Additionally, whether or not a lost sale is significant can have quantitative and qualitative dimensions. Here, the Singapore Aircraft Leasing Enterprise order involved 20 firm orders and 20 purchase rights. The Japan Airlines order had 30 firm orders and 10 options. In addition to this quantitative consideration, the Appellate Body said the sale had qualitative significance, because of the importance of securing a sale from a particular customer.

In sum, after completing the analysis where the uncontested facts allowed, the Appellate Body concluded only two sales campaigns included a genuine and substantial causal relationship between the FSC/ETI subsidies and the Washington State B&O tax rate reduction, through their effects on Boeing's prices, and the significant lost sales experienced by Airbus.[169]

• **Collective Assessment of Subsidies and Their Effects**

The last appeal considered by the Appellate Body was the EU challenge of two decisions taken by the Panel to assess separately the alleged effects of different groups of subsidies. The EU asserted the Panel erred in its interpretation and application of Articles 5(c) and 6:3 of the *SCM Agreement* by failing to conduct an integrated assessment of the effects of relevant subsidies. Specifically: (1) the refusal of the Panel to assess collectively the effects of the B&O tax rate reductions and the effects of the aeronautics subsidies; and (2) the Panel failure to assess collectively the effects of the Tied Tax subsidies and the effects of the eight other remaining subsidies.

The Appellate Body discussion of this matter may well prove to be one of the most important and oft-cited features of the 2012 *Boeing* case. Simply stated, with the *Boeing* decision, the Appellate Body made clear that when multiple controversial subsidies are challenged, there are two approaches in respect of causation, that is, to analyze whether those subsidies cause adverse effects (such as serious prejudice). One comes from the 2005 *Cotton* case, and the other from the 2011 *Airbus* case. As the Appellate Body itself said in *Boeing*, there are "two distinct means of undertaking a collective assessment of the effects of multiple subsidies."[170] Manifestly in so declaring, the Appellate Body was making law and establishing, in a *de facto* sense, a precedent.

---

168. *Cotton* Appellate Body Report, ¶ 426 (referring to *Cotton* Panel Report, ¶ 7.1326).
169. *See Boeing* Appellate Body Report, ¶ 1273.
170. *See Boeing* Appellate Body Report, ¶ 1282.

In particular, in the *Boeing* case, the Appellate Body found it important to start with different approaches Panels took in the 2005 *Cotton* and 2011 *Airbus* cases, with respect to the collective assessment of the effects of multiple subsidy measures. The approach in *Cotton*, referred to as the "aggregate" approach was defined as:

> ... an *ex ante* decision taken by a panel to undertake a single analysis of the effects of multiple subsidies whose structure, design, and operation are similar and thereby to assess in an integrated causation analysis the collective effects of such subsidy measures.[171]

Whereas, the second approach, used in *Airbus*, is referred to as the "cumulation" approach and defined as:

> ... an examination undertaken by a panel *after* it has found that at least one subsidy has caused adverse effects as to whether the effects of other subsidies complement and supplement those adverse effects.[172]

The structure chosen by a panel may vary by case, but some considerations of the appropriateness of the approach include design, structure, and operation of the subsidies at issue; the alleged market phenomena; and the extent to which the subsidies are provided in relation to a particular product or product.

First: Should Effects of Aeronautics R&D Subsidies and B&O Tax Rate Reductions Have Been Assessed Collectively?

In examining the price effects of the subsidies within the 200–300 seat LCA market, the Panel declined to consider the effects of the R&D subsidies together with the effects of the B&O tax rate reductions on the grounds that "the two groups of subsidies operate through entirely distinct causal mechanisms."[173] In the EU view, because the Panel found the Aeronautics R&D subsidies were a genuine and substantial cause of significant price suppression in the 200–300 seat LCA market, and the B&O tax rate reductions had a genuine (though not substantial) causal relationship with the same kind of adverse effect, the Panel was required to consider how the B&O tax rate reductions complemented or supplemented the Aeronautics R&D subsidies. Further, the EU argued cumulation was appropriate, because the Aeronautics R&D subsidies and the B&O tax rate reductions allegedly had the same effects on Airbus' pricing and sales, even if they were produced pursuant to different causal mechanisms.

The U.S. counter-argued the Panel was correct in focusing on whether the various subsidies operate through the same casual mechanism to cause adverse effects, and such a decision was within the Panel's discretion.[174] Here, the Aeronautics R&D subsidies were alleged to enhance Boeing ability to launch the 787, whereas the B&O

---

171. *Boeing* Appellate Body Report, ¶ 1282.
172. *Boeing* Appellate Body Report, ¶ 1282.
173. *Boeing* Appellate Body Report, ¶ 1302 (*quoting Boeing* Panel Report, ¶ 1824).
174. *See Boeing* Appellate Body Report, ¶¶ 1306–1307.

tax rate reductions were alleged to affect Boeing's prices. In the American view, the EU's position would wrongly require a cumulative assessment in all cases.[175]

The Appellate Body favored the EU position. As it stated:

> . . . We do not see any *a priori* reason—such as, that different subsidies operate through distinct causal mechanisms—why cumulation would be precluded outright. We are particularly hesitant to set out a rigid benchmark against which panels should test whether or not cumulation is appropriate based on the facts of this dispute or of [*Airbus*].[176]

The Appellate Body then said there might be cases, especially ones not involving duopolies, where the "product" or "technology" effects of subsidies can be examined separately from their "price" effects.[177] In the Appellate Body view, the Panel should have considered whether it would have been appropriate to cumulate the effects of the B&O tax rate reduction and the Aeronautics R&D subsidies.

Thus, the Appellate Body rejected a narrow approach by the Panel, to consider only distinct casual mechanisms, and found the Panel erred in failing to consider whether the price effects of the B&O tax rate reductions complement and supplement the technology effects of the aeronautics R&D subsidies in causing significant lost sales and significant price suppression, and a threat of displacement and impedance, in the 200–300 seat LCA market.[178] However, perhaps by mistake during appellate arguments, the EU did not request for the Appellate Body to complete the analysis.

Second: Should Effects of Tied Tax subsidies and Remaining Subsidies Have Been Assessed Collectively?

The EU contended the Panel erred by declining to undertake a collective assessment of the remaining subsidies and the Tied Tax subsidies. According to the EU, both subsidies had a nexus with the subsidized LCA and with Boeing prices. The U.S. contended there was virtually no evidence as to how the remaining subsidies were used, so it would not be possible to establish a sufficient nexus.[179]

The Appellate Body was unsure of whether the Panel declined to collectively assess the two groups of subsidies because it felt they operated through distinct causal mechanisms or for some other reason.[180] However, it concluded the Panel did not act outside its scope of discretion, as far as it relates to the aggregated analysis. The Appellate Body found the Panel discussions of the Tied Tax and remaining subsidies "strongly suggest[ed]" it considered them to be different in nature.[181]

---

175. *See Boeing* Appellate Body Report, ¶ 1308.
176. *Boeing* Appellate Body Report, ¶ 1319.
177. *Boeing* Appellate Body Report, ¶ 1319.
178. *See Boeing* Appellate Body Report, ¶ 1321.
179. *See Boeing* Appellate Body Report, ¶ 1324.
180. *See Boeing* Appellate Body Report, ¶ 1325.
181. *See Boeing* Appellate Body Report, ¶ 1326.

Additionally, the Appellate Body felt the arguments put forth by the EU supported this conclusion.

But, the Appellate Body felt the Panel erred in failing to make a cumulative assessment of whether the remaining subsidies affected Boeing's prices in a way similar to the tied tax subsidies. According to the Appellate Body, the "cursory analysis" by the Panel of the alleged effects of the remaining subsidies should not have been limited to whether these subsidies constituted a genuine and substantial cause of serious prejudice "*on their own.*"[182]

Third: Appellate Body Completion of Analysis

Having found the Appellate Body erred with regard to the remaining subsidies and the Tied Tax subsidies, the EU requested the Appellate Body to complete the analysis and find the subsidies caused adverse effects when assessed collectively. The Appellate Body opted not to conduct an aggregated assessment, because it previously found the Panel did not err in failing to conduct such an analysis. Instead, it addressed the EU alternative request: a cumulation assessment. The U.S. contended the EU failed to identify facts that would enable such an analysis, nor were there any present, but the Appellate Body still moved forward with the analysis.[183]

The Appellate Body already had found the FSC/ETI subsidies and the State of Washington B&O tax rate reduction were a genuine and substantial cause of significant lost sales in the 100–200 seat LCA market. Accordingly, the sole question remaining before the Appellate Body was whether the effects of the remaining subsidies complemented and supplemented the FSC/ETI subsidies and the State of Washington B&O tax rate reductions.

Recall the relevant test developed in the 2011 *Airbus* case asks whether the effects of one group of subsidies is shown to have a genuine causal connection with the relevant effects and market phenomena cause by the second group of subsidies.[184]

In *Boeing*, it was undisputed that none of the remaining subsidies were contingent upon the production or sale of particular LCA. However, as the U.S. and EU both accepted, receipt of such subsidies "may still affect the behavior of the recipient of the subsidy in a manner that causes serious prejudice, depending upon the context in which it is used."[185] Moreover, the Appellate Body accepted several factors that also affected the affirmative serious prejudice finding with regard to the Tied Tax subsidies. Those factors were equally relevant to the analysis of whether the remaining subsidies had a genuine casual link to the prices of Boeing 737NG aircraft in its 2005 Japan Airlines and 2005 Singapore Aircraft Leasing Enterprise sales campaigns.

---

182. *Boeing* Appellate Body Report, ¶ 1328 (emphasis added).
183. *See Boeing* Appellate Body Report, ¶¶ 1332, 1334–1335.
184. *See Boeing* Appellate Body Report, ¶ 1335 (*citing Airbus* Appellate Body Report, ¶¶ 1378–1379).
185. *Boeing* Appellate Body Report, ¶ 1336 (*quoting Boeing* Panel Report, ¶ 7.1828).

The eight remaining subsidies were categorized as benefiting the 787 only, multiple aircraft families (including the 737NG at issue here), or benefiting Boeing LCA business in general. Of those categories, only the second potentially could be linked to production of the 737NG.[186] Those subsidies and their amounts were:

(1) the Washington State B&O tax credits for preproduction development, and for computer software and hardware ($41.3 million);

(2) the Washington State sales and use tax exemptions for computer hardware, peripherals, and software ($8.3 million);

(3) the property and sales tax abatements provided to Boeing pursuant to IRBs issued by the City of Wichita ($475.8 million)[187]

There was no indication in the record that Washington State B&O tax credits were received in connection with expenditures related to the 737NG.[188] Additionally, there was no indication the Washington State sales and use tax exemptions were received or expected to be received in connection with expenditures related to the 737NG.

In other words, the B&O tax credits, and the sales and use tax exemptions, were not specifically linked to the 737NG. Absent such a link, these subsidies cannot be added to other subsidies (like the FSC/ETI support) that do cause serious prejudice in respect of this LCA model. Doing so would overstate the serious prejudice done to Airbus in trying to compete with the 737NG, and would be unfair to Boeing. Put bluntly, there should be no commingling of subsidies that do not cause serious prejudice with those that do. Here, the B&O tax credits and sales and use tax exemptions from Washington State did not exacerbate the serious prejudice caused by other subsidies, and so should not be included in the causation analysis with those other subsidies.

That was not true of the City of Wichita IRBs. The Wichita IRBs, issued to Boeing, were used for the purpose of enhancing Boeing facilities in Wichita, in which parts for the 737NG were produced.[189] This last point was critical: because 737NG parts were made in those plants, there was a nexus between the IRBs and the 737NG model. Indeed, Boeing's own website stated that 75% of the airframe for the 737 was produced in Wichita. In the view of the Appellate Body, this fact revealed a close connection between the IRBs and production of the Boeing 737NG.

Accordingly, the Appellate Body found the effects of the City of Wichita IRBs complemented and supplemented the price effects of the FSC/ETI subsidies and the State of Washington B&O tax rate reduction (but not Washington State B&O tax credits, nor sales and use tax exemptions), thereby causing serious prejudice, in the

---

186. *See Boeing* Appellate Body Report, ¶¶ 1341–1342.
187. *See Boeing* Appellate Body Report, ¶ 1343.
188. *See Boeing* Appellate Body Report, ¶ 1344.
189. *See Boeing* Appellate Body Report, ¶ 1347.

form of significant lost sales, within the meaning of Articles 5(c) and 6:3(c) of the *SCM Agreement*, in the 100–200 seat LCA market.[190]

In sum, through a painstaking analysis, the Appellate Body looked at 3 broad categories of Tied Tax subsidies: (1) FSC/ETI, (2) the Washington State B&O tax rate reductions, and (3) the eight so-called "remaining subsidies." Following the standard analysis for adverse effects, namely, serious prejudice, in a Yellow Light (Actionable) subsidy case, the Appellate Body asked whether any of these subsidies caused serious prejudice to Airbus. It held that the first two categories of Tired Tax subsidies (FSC/ETI and Washington State B&O tax rate reductions) did cause serious prejudice to Airbus. As for the eight remaining subsidies, the Appellate Body eliminated five, because the category into which the EU put them could in no way have a causal nexus to serious prejudice. Of the remaining three, only one—the Wichita IRBs—had the requisite nexus. In coming to this conclusion, the Appellate Body offered an important innovation: it blessed two tests for causation of serious prejudice, aggregate (from the 2005 *Cotton* case), and cumulation (from the 2011 *Airbus* case), in a multiple-subsidies examination.

Might there be yet more such tests? The Appellate Body did not rule out this possibility.

---

190. *See Boeing* Appellate Body Report, ¶ 1348.

Chapter 17

CVDs against Pre-Privatization Subsidies[1]

I. Issue Posed by Pre-Privatization Subsidies

So important to so many countries is transition from communism or socialism to market capitalism that it is difficult to imagine a WTO trade remedy case more relevant to these countries than the 2000 *British Steel* Appellate Body Report.[2] The issue in it is simple to state: when a SOE or STE is privatized, to what extent, if any, do benefits from subsidies the firm previously received while in state hands continue on after the privatization?

That is, the issue is whether subsidies continue into the after-life: does the subsidy from the firm's life as an SOE (or STE) carry over into its life as a private business? At bottom, it is a problem of causation over time. At what point, and under what circumstances, is a cause such as the benefit of a subsidy no longer felt by the recipient, or erstwhile recipient?

In *British Steel*, and in progeny cases, there is no dispute the SOE — *qua* SOE — received state subsides. Nor is there any dispute about what happened next: those subsidies were cut off after privatization. The dispute is whether it right for a country importing goods from the newly-privatized entity to impose a CVD on these goods, on the theory these goods still receive a benefit from the subsidies of yesteryear?

If the answer is "yes," imagine how many CVD actions can be brought against imports from transition-economy WTO Members (not to mention Brazil, Mexico, and India). Imagine the possible CVD actions against new Members (*e.g.*, China, Saudi Arabia, and Vietnam), and likely future Members (*e.g.*, Iran, Laos, Syria). If the answer is "no," then imagine the relief among the governments of all these countries — and the consternation in major developed trading countries fighting to retain their industrial base.

---

1. Documents References:
   (1) *Havana (ITO) Charter* Articles 25–29
   (2) GATT Articles VI, XVI–XVII
   (3) WTO *SCM Agreement*
2. *See United States—Imposition of Countervailing Duties on Certain Hot-Rolled Lead and Bismuth Carbon Steel Products Originating in the United Kingdom*, WT/DS138/AB/R (adopted 7 June 2000).

II. Change in Ownership Methodology
and 2000 *British Steel* Case

· **Facts**

Ostensibly, it is ironic this 2000 case involves British Steel plc, and not a company from a more evidently socialist economy than that of England. ("Plc" stands for "public limited company." While in state hands, British Steel plc was the "British Steel Corporation"). But, the irony ends when it is remembered that Thatcherism and Blair-ism are relatively recent in Britain. For most of Britain's post-Second World War history, the pre-Blair Labor Party ideals of a large and visible state hand guiding the economy prevailed, and British Steel was a public-sector company. Prime Minister Margaret Thatcher privatized British Steel in December 1988 through a sale of shares. This sale was at an arm's length, and the purchasers paid fair market value for the shares. The Prime Minister also privatized United Engineering Steel (UES) at the same time.

In March 1995, British Steel bought UES, making it a wholly owned subsidiary of British Steel (and, for simplicity, "British Steel" refers to the pre-and post-privatization entity, including the subsidiary). In October 1999, British Steel merged with a Dutch company, *Koninklijke Hoogvens* NV. The combined Anglo-Dutch entity is called the "Corus Group."

The U.S. alleged Her Majesty's Government provided over $11.2 billion in subsidies to British Steel when it owned the company. These subsidies took the form of equity infusions by the British Government to British Steel between fiscal years 1977–78 and 1985–86. The DOC categorized them as "non-recurring," and spread the presumed benefit from them out over 18 years. That is, the DOC calculated the benefit of the pre-privatization subsidies as of the year in which they were granted. Then, it allocated their benefit over a lengthy period. The DOC said 18 years was the useful life of productive assets in the steel industry. Most importantly, the DOC concluded the benefits of the subsidies during 1977–1986 passed through the change in ownership, and thus continued on into the enterprise's new life as a private company.

In March 1993—clearly after the privatization—the DOC imposed CVDs on imports of certain steel products made by British Steel. This imposition followed a final determination by the DOC of a subsidy rate of 12.69%, and a final affirmative injury determination by the ITC. The DOC maintained the CVDs through subsequent administrative reviews in 1995, 1996, and 1997, though the subsidy rates fell with these reviews. (The reviews in other years were not at issue in the case.) The subject merchandise was hot-rolled lead and bismuth carbon steel, commonly known as leaded steel bars, produced by British Steel.

In rendering its decision, the DOC used what is known as the "change-in-ownership" methodology. Under it, the change in ownership effected by privatization does not matter. The benefits of the pre-privatization subsidies continue, or carry over, through to the new corporate incarnation of the former SOE. In effect, the change-in-ownership methodology is a legal presumption—an automatic conclusion about the endurance of benefits that is dreadful for any respondent in a CVD case.

Thus, two extreme and not easily reconcilable perspectives were raised: that all subsidies received from HMG carried over after privatization, and that none of them did. Emboldened by Senator Orrin G. Hatch (Republican-Utah) and other politicians, the U.S. urged a mere change in ownership does not affect the application of the CVD remedy. A former SOE can benefit from a carry-over effect of a subsidy received before privatization. After all, the WTO *SCM Agreement* condones imposition of a CVD if a benefit to a recipient is shown. In brief, who owns the recipient is immaterial. What matters is the benefit to the recipient.

In fact, the U.S. argued the premise of CVD law is calculation of a benefit received from a subsidy as of the year of bestowal of the subsidy. This premise is explicit in Article 1:1 of the *SCM Agreement*, which does not speak of examining the continued existence of a benefit. Rather, urged the U.S., Article 1:1 calls for a determination of benefit as of bestowal. It would be neither conceptually correct nor practicable to re-evaluate the benefit conferred by a subsidy every year, year-after-year, and years long after the subsidy initially was granted. Once a benefit at the time of bestowal is shown, the original determination is not to be re-opened. How could it be? CVD law would be nightmarishly difficult to administer if a WTO Member had to demonstrate continually that the benefit originally conferred remained an advantage to the recipient.

The EU position was diametrically opposite. Challenging the CVD order, the EU argued the DOC acted contrary to the *SCM Agreement* by failing to consider whether the pre-privatization subsidy provides a benefit after privatization. That is, a pre-privatization subsidy cannot be allocated over time, unless a continued benefit to the recipient is shown. (Interestingly, in February 1995, the U.S. CIT agreed with this argument, made to it by British Steel.) But, in October 1997, the Court of Appeals for the Federal Circuit partly reversed the CIT decision.[3] The particular provisions under which the EU complained were Articles 10 and 19:4 of the *SCM Agreement*. Article 10 allows imposition of a CVD only after an investigation conducted in accordance with the *SCM Agreement*. Absent proof the targeted imports received the benefit of a subsidy, a CVD may not be imposed. Article 19:4 bars imposition of a CVD in excess of the amount of the subsidy revealed by the investigation. The EU also argued the DOC methodology used by the DOC to calculate the amount of the subsidy lacked any rational basis.

• **Lessons**

America lost the case. Like the WTO Panel before it, the Appellate Body found the DOC was wrong to conclude pre-privatization subsidies received by British Steel

---

3. *See British Steel PLC v. U.S.*, 127 F.3d 1471 (Fed. Cir. 1997).

were transmitted through the privatization and onto the successor private company. Change in ownership does matter, said the Appellate Body, hence ruling against the change-in-ownership methodology under which pre-privatization subsidies are deemed automatically to yield benefits to a former SOE. The Appellate Body found no validity to a doctrine of automatic pass through, or continuation of benefits, after privatization.

Quite the contrary, said the Appellate Body. What must be shown is the subject merchandise has received, directly or indirectly, a subsidy. Failing to link the pre-privatization subsidies with the imports in question was a violation of Article 10. Given the violation of this provision, the Appellate Body (like the panel) applied the principle of judicial economy and declined to decide the Article 19:4 issue. Significantly, the Appellate Body recommend the Commerce Department regulations and practices be changed in accordance with its ruling.

The Appellate Body rejected the American interpretation of Article 1:1 of the *SCM Agreement*. The U.S. relied on the present tense of the verb in Article 1:1—"is conferred," inferring from this tense a necessity to show a benefit only at the time a subsidy is granted. The Appellate Body found no basis for this inference. Nothing in Article 1:1 speaks to the question of when a financial contribution or benefit conferred must be shown to exist. It is simply wrong to draw out of the verb tense in Article 1:1 a benefit from a subsidy is to be shown as of the time a subsidy is bestowed, but no other time thereafter. Lest there be any doubt about this reading of Article 1:1, said the Appellate Body, surely Article 21:1-2 clear up that doubt. These provisions make it quite obvious a renewed inquiry into subsidization—whether or not the subsidy continues to exist—is essential, and if no subsidy is found, then there is no need for a CVD.

Article 21:1 says a CVD is to remain in place for only so long as necessary to counteract effects of subsidization. Article 21:2 calls for establishment of an administrative review mechanism to ensure compliance with Article 21:1. During a review, the DOC (or relevant authority in other Members) is supposed to examine all evidence placed before it by a petitioner and respondent, and that it has obtained. The whole point of an Article 21:2 review is to see whether this evidence constitutes positive information that (1) the subsidizing government has withdrawn its financial contribution, (2) the recipient has repaid the subsidy, or (3) the benefit of the subsidy no longer accrues to the recipient. Thus, the language of Article 21:2 states plainly "[t]he authorities shall review the need for the continued imposition of the duty" and are to "examine whether the continued imposition of the duty is necessary to offset subsidization."

The Appellate Body was every bit as firm in rejecting the American argument the benefits of pre-privatization subsidies passed through to the privatized British Steel firm as it was in rejecting the Article 1:1 contention. There could never be anything more than a rebuttable presumption of a carry over of benefits after privatization; but the presumption must never be an irrebuttable one, as it was under the DOC's change-in-ownership methodology. The U.S. premised its argument in support of this methodology on an interpretation of the text of Article 10 (specifically, footnote 36 thereto) of the *SCM Agreement* and Article VI:3 of GATT, namely, the phrase concerning a subsidy bestowed "upon the manufacture, production or export of any merchandise." The U.S. urged these provisions mean what matters is whether a company's productive operations get the "benefit" of a subsidy. The recipient of interest is not the legal or natural person owning the company, but rather the productive assets of the company. Accordingly, change-of-ownership through privatization is irrelevant—the assets still may be said to receive the benefit of the previously-bestowed subsidies.

Not so, ruled the Appellate Body. First, it cited its own 1999 report from the *Canada—Measures Affecting the Export of Civilian Aircraft* case to support its conclusion a benefit implies a recipient, and a recipient must be a natural or legal person. Second, what matters in deciding whether a "financial contribution" confers a "benefit" is whether a recipient gets that contribution on terms more favorable than those available in the market. In a privatization scenario, it is necessary to consider the value paid for the productive assets and goodwill of the SOE. Was it a fair market value?

Why is this question so important? The underlying rationale of the Appellate Body seems to be as follows. As long as the shares of an SOE are sold to a private company (or the public at large) at a market price, and not an artificially low one, then the privatization is a *bona fide* arm's length one. In turn, it can be inferred no subsidy—no financial contribution to the new owners of the former state-owned productive assets and goodwill—is involved. The new owners are putting the assets and goodwill to work to produce the subject merchandise, but they are not benefiting from any help from the former state owner. In particular, the new owners cannot be deemed to continue to reap the benefits of the pre-privatization subsidy. Consider a contrasting scenario: the new owners buy the SOE at a below-market price from the government. Then, they could be said to receive a benefit. They purchased assets and goodwill at a discount. That discount is the vehicle through which the pre-privatization subsidy passes.

The Appellate Body would have done well to elaborate on the link between Wall Street and receipt of benefits from a pre-privatization subsidy. It reasoned—correctly—the share price (assuming it is a fair market value) of an SOE being privatized incorporates the expected future earnings stream of the company. In turn, that stream reflects the benefit of a subsidy previously received. That is, the stock market accounts for the benefit of a subsidy when it establishes a price for the shares. Presumably, that benefit increases the expected revenue stream and, therefore, increases the share price. If new owners pay this higher price, then they are—in effect—buying, or paying for, the subsidy (or the remaining benefits there from).

For example, suppose the aggregate share price for an SOE that received pre-privatization subsidies is $1 billion. If the share purchasers pay $1 billion, then they are paying back to the government seller that subsidy (or at least the remaining benefits therefrom), and thus buying any lingering benefits from that subsidy. To countervail the products from that privatized entity would be to penalize the new owners twice—the first time was when they paid a share price that included the subsidy benefits, and the second time would be when they pay the CVD. Conversely, suppose the share purchasers pay just $750 million for their shares. Then, they are not paying for the continued benefit of the subsidy (here assumed to be $250 million). Rather, they are receiving that benefit.

In the *British Steel* case, the WTO Panel pointed out the privatization of British Steel occurred at a fair market price, and the U.S. accepted this fact. So, too, did the Appellate Body. Thus, the Appellate Body essentially said a fair market privatization was reincarnation—a new life, not a continuation of an existing life—for an enterprise. If a company purchases an SOE at fair market value, then the SOE is fully reincarnated, and the new owners cannot be subject to duties designed to countervail subsidies bestowed in the last life. Only if they do not pay fair market value is it right to conclude the benefits of pre-privatization subsidies automatically carry over to the new company.

The only point on which the Appellate Body reversed the Panel concerned the nature of an Article 21:2 Administrative Review. Should such a Review of a CVD order be conducted in the same manner as an original subsidy investigation? The Panel said "yes." The Appellate Body said "no." In the investigation, the goal is to determine the existence and extent of a benefit from a subsidy, and all prerequisites in the *SCM Agreement* for imposition of a CVD must be checked. In the Review, only issues an interested party or the administering agency raise need addressing. Quite logically, an investigation is broader in scope than a review.

III. Modified Change in Ownership Methodology and 2003 *Certain Products* Case

• Facts

In 2003, the U.S. fought another case on CVDs and pre-privatization subsidies.[4] As in *British Steel*, in *Certain Products* the Appellate Body was presented with CVD orders from the DOC orders against subject merchandise from foreign producers that had received government subsidies. In both cases, subsidies were paid while the producers were SOEs. But, the subsidies ceased on or before privatization. Privatization meant a change in the ownership of the entities. Thus, in both cases, controversy raged over technical tests of ownership change, with large policy implications.

---

4. *See United States—Countervailing Measures Concerning Certain Products from the European Communities*, WT/DS212/AB/R (adopted 8 January 2003).

The tests were used by the DOC in CVD investigations to determine whether the benefit of a pre-privatization subsidy carries through to a newly privatized entity. Only if the benefit survives the change in ownership could the U.S. lawfully impose a CVD. In particular, according to the change in ownership methodology, the DOC presumed non-recurring subsidies granted to a former producer of a good, before the ownership of this producer changed (*i.e.*, granted while it was an SOE) pass through to the current producer of the good after the change of ownership (*i.e.*, after privatization). Put succinctly, the presumption in the methodology is benefits from a pre-privatization subsidy continue after privatization, even though the subsidy itself terminated by the time of privatization, hence it is appropriate to levy a CVD against imports from the privatized entity.

The statute pursuant to which the DOC engaged in the change in ownership methodology is Section 771(5)(F) of the *Tariff Act of 1930*, as amended.[5] It says:

> A change in ownership of all or part of a foreign enterprise or the productive assets of a foreign enterprise does not by itself require a determination by the administering authority that a past countervailable subsidy received by the enterprise no longer continues to be countervailable, even if the change in ownership is accomplished through an arm's-length transaction.

In June 2003, the DOC modified its change-in-ownership methodology. It developed a rebuttable presumption, which it described in its regulations:

> The [new] methodology is based on certain rebuttable presumptions. . . . *The "baseline presumption" is that non-recurring subsidies can benefit the recipient over a period of time . . . normally corresponding to the average useful life of the recipient's assets.* However, an interested party may *rebut this baseline presumption* by demonstrating that, during the allocation period, a *privatization occurred* in which the *government sold* its ownership of *all or substantially all of a company or its assets, retaining no control* of the company or its assets, and that the *sale was an arm's-length transaction for fair market value.*[6]

In effect, the DOC revised methodology was a Two Step Test:

---

5. *See* 19 U.S.C. § 1677(5)(F).

6. *Notice of Final Modification of Agency Practice Under Section 123 of the Uruguay Round Agreements Act*, 68 Federal Register 37,125 (23 June 2003) (emphasis added).

Before this innovation, the DOC used a different test, combining the change in ownership methodology with another inquiry, called the "same person" method, thereby creating a Two-Step test. The DOC developed this "same person change in ownership" methodology following a major decision by the Federal Circuit, *Delverde SrL. v. United States*, 202 F.3rd 1360 (2 February 2000) ("*Delverde III*"), *rehg denied* (June 20, 2000). In *Delverde III*, the Federal Circuit held it was the intent of Congress, in enacting 19 U.S.C. § 1677(5)(F), that the DOC examine the particular facts and circumstances of a privatization sale, and determine whether the purchaser received (directly or indirectly) from the government both a financial contribution and a benefit. In June 2003, the DOC dropped the "same person" method, and adopted the above-described methodology.

Step One:

The DOC analyzed whether a post-privatization entity is the same legal person as the entity that received the original subsidy before privatization. The factors it checked included the continuity of general business operations, production facilities, and assets and liabilities, and retention of personnel. If these criteria led the DOC to conclude privatization did not create a new legal person, then it stopped its analysis of whether a "benefit" exists. It did not consider whether privatization occurred at arm's length and for fair market value. Rather, the DOC concluded automatically and irrebuttably the subsidy continues to exist for the post-privatization firm, precisely because it is the same person as before.

Step Two:

In contrast, suppose the continuity and retention criteria indicated the post-privatization entity was a new legal person, distinct from the entity that received the prior subsidy. Then, the DOC did not impose a CVD on goods produced after privatization on the basis of the pre-privatization subsidy. However, the DOC examined whether any new subsidy had been bestowed upon the new owners of the post-privatization entity as a result of the change in ownership. In particular, the DOC checked whether the sale was at arm's length and for fair market value. If it was not, then the DOC could find a new subsidy had been bestowed, and impose a CVD on that basis.

The "bottom line" was the DOC presumed conclusively that if an SOE and a post-privatized entity are the same legal person, then the benefit received by the SOE automatically continues to accrue to the newly privatized entity. Consequently, the DOC did not investigate the particularities of the case to determine whether a benefit does, in fact, carry through the privatization.

The gravamen of the complaint of the European Communities in *Certain Products* was the change in ownership methodology obviates the need for the DOC to establish the essential elements of a countervailable subsidy, namely, the existence of a financial contribution and a benefit from this contribution to the producers under investigation.

That is, framing its arguments under Articles 1:1(b), 10, 14, 19, and 21 of the *SCM Agreement*, the EC said of the revised change in ownership methodology:

In order to demonstrate that the two companies [an SOE and its privatized successor] are the same person, the DOC maintains that if a firm keeps the same factory, any of the same employees, any of the same customers, any of the same suppliers, this is sufficient reason to presume an automatic pass-through of subsidies.

[T]he DOC's approach is premised on a preposterous assertion: that subsidies somehow become glued to, live in and then automatically travel with assets wherever they may be sold and regardless of the amount paid for them.

Thus, under the DOC's approach, if an unsubsidized private company purchases a factory from a prior subsidized owner for 20 times the actual market value of the plant, the DOC would impose countervailing duties on the new owner.[7]

In sum, the EC argued the *British Steel* compelled the Appellate Body in *Certain Products* to find the same person methodology *per se* inconsistent with the *SCM Agreement*. The *Agreement*, as construed in *British Steel*, mandates a new determination of whether a benefit exists when a privatization results in a change of control.

The Appellate Body emphasized two key issues, and held as follows:

(1) *Extinction of Subsidy Benefits through a Privatization*

If a privatization is conducted at arm's length and for fair market value, then does that privatization *systematically* extinguish the benefit from a non-recurring financial contribution bestowed before privatization? Finding the Panel's "yes" answer too rigid, and based on too much faith in equity and debt markets, the Appellate Body overturned the Panel and responded "no."

(2) *Legality of Same Person Methodology*

Is the DOC change-in-ownership methodology, which effectively involves a same person test, consistent with the *SCM Agreement*? "No," responded the Appellate Body, like the Panel. The DOC's methodology, ruled the Appellate Body, transgressed Article 21:2-3 (covering Administrative and Sunset Reviews of outstanding CVD orders) and its interpretation of this provision in *British Steel*. Under the methodology, if the DOC concluded the pre- and post-privatization entity were the same legal person, then it automatically disregarded information submitted to it to support the contention that no benefit from a prior financial contribution continued to exist. And, the DOC automatically declined to determine whether a benefit continues to exist despite this information. Only if the DOC found a distinct legal person would it study the new information and determine whether a benefit exists—and, even in that circumstance, the DOC's inquiry would be limited to whether a new subsidy is provided to the owners of the privatized entity. Put succinctly, the methodology led inexorably to a pre-determined conclusion of continued accrual of a benefit from a prior financial contribution, if the DOC found the same person to exist before and after privatization. Because the methodology barred any further analysis whenever the DOC made this threshold finding, it was illegal under Article 21:2.

---

7. Joe Kirwin, *EU Will File WTO Challenge to Duties U.S. Imposed on Some EU Steel Imports*, 18 International Trade Reporter (BNA) 1194 (July 26, 2001) (*quoting* the Commission).

On balance, the U.S. prevailed on the first issue, but lost on the second issue, which was the key conceptual one.[8]

Consider what rationales support the Appellate Body holdings in *Certain Products*? Consider, too, what facts and holdings distinguish the *British Steel* and *Certain Products* cases? To what extent did the *British Steel* decision establish a precedent for the *Certain Products* case?

---

8. On a third issue, the legality of the American CVD statute, the Appellate Body held in favor of the U.S.

Part Three

Remedies against "Unfair" Trade (Continued): Causation in Antidumping and Countervailing Duty Cases

Chapter 18

Theories of Causation[1]

I. Why Causation Matters

In an AD case, it does not suffice to prove a dumping margin and injury or threat thereof exists. In a U.S. proceeding, a private petitioner also must prove material injury or threat to a domestic industry occurs "by reason of dumped" imports. Likewise, in a CVD investigation, a private petitioner must show more than the existence of an illegal subsidy and material injury or threat. To be successful, the injury or threat must occur "by reason of" the unlawful subsidy. Likewise, in WTO adjudication, a complainant must show the effect of dumping is material injury or threat, or an unlawful subsidy has one of three adverse effects—material injury or threat, nullification or impairment of benefits, or serious prejudice. A noun between prepositions ("by reason of"), and words that can be nouns or verbs ("effect"), are ambiguous synonyms for a time-honored and fundamental concept animating through every field of law: causation. In brief, causation is an indispensable element in any AD or CVD investigation.

What does "cause" mean in an AD or CVD case? The same question may be asked of remedies against fair foreign competition, such as a general safeguard action under GATT Article XIX and the WTO *Agreement on Safeguards*? To what extent must factors causing alleged injury (or threat) be identified and distinguished from one another? No less significant than the rules in Articles 3:1 and 3:4 of the WTO *Antidumping Agreement* on injury is Article 3:5, which concerns causation. Similarly, Article 15:5 of the *SCM Agreement* deals with causation.

Article 3:5 of the *Antidumping Agreement* requires proof dumped imports cause injury to a domestic industry, and of a causal relationship between dumping and injury, from an examination of all relevant evidence. It also calls for consideration of known factors other than dumping that, simultaneously with dumping, are injuring the domestic industry. Article 15:5 of the *SCM Agreement* is essentially a *verbatim* copy of Article 3:5.

Examples of possible causal factors, other than subject merchandise imports, are competition from non-dumped or non-subsidized merchandise, declines in demand

---

1. Documents Supplement References:
   (1) *Havana Charter* Article 34
   (2) GATT Articles VI, XVI
   (3) WTO *Antidumping Agreement* Article 3
   (4) WTO *SCM Agreement* Articles 1, 3, 5–6, 8, 15

for the domestically-produced like product, changes in consumption patterns, restrictive business practices, technological change, and poor productivity in the domestic industry. Any injury from these factors must not be attributed to injury caused by dumping or subsidization, *i.e.*, the causal effects of each independent variable operating on the domestic industry must be separated from the other.

The Article XIX general safeguard, and Article 4:2 of the *Safeguards Agreement*, also set out a causation standard. Is that standard the same as in the U.S. Escape Clause, Section 201 of the *Trade Act of 1974*, as amended? Why or why not? Are causation standards for safeguard relief the same as in AD and CVD law? Should they be, or should they be higher than the standards for an AD or CVD remedy? That is, should the causation standards for remedies against fair and unfair trade be the same? What about causation standards for product specific mechanisms, such as agricultural products?

II. Philosophical Perspectives: Aristotle, Hume, and Mill

Long before modern trade remedy law, philosophers explored a topic that would become central to that law—causation. What does it mean to say one event, X, "causes" another, Y? Under what circumstances is it correct to attribute causation, *i.e.*, when is it certain (if ever) that X "causes" Y? How are possible causal factors, such as X, identified in the first place? How is one possible causal factor, X, weighed against others to ascertain the relative importance of X and the other independent variables in "causing" Y? More recently, scholars of jurisprudence have addressed the problem of causation in law, albeit almost exclusively in domestic contexts such as Torts.

Modern trade lawyers know well the importance of causation to the outcome of an AD or CVD case, and likewise for a general safeguards case under GATT Article XIX and the WTO *Agreement on Safeguards*. Yet, trade remedy law is underdeveloped, even crude, in respect of its causation criteria. Might the profound explorations of philosophers provide assistance to trade lawyers—and specifically, legislators responsible for drafting the criteria, and judges charged with interpreting and enforcing the criteria? What nuggets might be mined from jurisprudence scholars?

At the risk of gross over-simplification, philosophical insights into causation from a few Ancient and Continental philosophers, and jurisprudential thinkers, are as follows.

- **Aristotle (384–322 B.C.) on Causation**

The first Ancient Greek philosopher to examine causation, Aristotle encapsulated into four words the entire inquiry: "on account of what?"[2] He responded by

---

2. ARISTOTLE, A NEW ARISTOTLE READER 98 (J.L. Ackrill ed., 1987). [Hereinafter, ARISTOTLE READER.]

delineating four types of causes, which he derived from the four common ways the Ancient Greek word "*aition*" was used:

Type 1: Material Cause—
      Substance of a Thing

In *Physics*, Aristotle wrote about:

> that out of which as a constituent a thing comes to be called a cause.[3]

By this he meant the ingredients that make up a thing, X, are the cause of that thing. They are the parts—the material—from which the thing comes into existence. Aristotle's examples were bronze, used to produce a statute, or silver, used to make a cup.

Material cause for Aristotle is what contemporary International Trade Lawyers would think about in ROO cases. That is because Aristotle equates "Material Cause" with "to be made of." The latter phrase lies at the heart of origination determinations.

Type 2: Formal Cause—
      What It Is To Be a Thing

Aristotle also wrote that:

> [a]ccording to another [meaning], the form or model is a cause; this is the account of what the being would be, and its genera—thus the cause of an octave is the ratio of two to one, and more generally number—and the parts which come into the account.[4]

In other words, "Formal Cause" is simply the form of a thing that gives the thing its essence, and that is recognized as doing so. To answer "what is it to be X?" is to identify the "formal cause" of X.

For instance, the round shape, red seams, white coating, and hard interior give a baseball its form, and thus are the formal cause of the baseball. Equating "Formal Cause" with recognized items that impart essence to a thing is redolent of the essential character test for classification in Customs Law. However, this verbal equation is confusing in modern English parlance. Semantically, "cause" and "what it is to be" are not comprehended as synonyms.

Type 3: Efficient Cause—
      That Which Produces a Thing

Material and Formal Cause are static, but for Aristotle, Efficient (as well as Final) Cause is dynamic. The first two kinds of causes explain X as it is, and what it is, but

---

3. ARISTOTLE, PHYSICS, THE FOUR CAUSES. Aristotle addresses causation in *Posterior Analytics* and *Metaphysics*, but in *Physics* he deals with the topic in the context of relationships among objects in the natural world. [Hereinafter, ARISTOTLE, FOUR CAUSES.]

4. ARISTOTLE, FOUR CAUSES.

not how X came to be X. "[W]hence comes the origin of change" is the Efficient Cause of a thing.[5] Aristotle wrote:

> Again, there is the primary source of the change or the staying unchanged.[6]

By this he meant the Efficient Cause of X is the thing or person that is responsible for X being X. If a change to X, or X staying put, results from the maker of X, then that maker is the Efficient Cause of X. The Efficient Cause is the reason for change or stability in X. Aristotle gave as an example (albeit a gender biased one) of efficient cause that "the father is a cause of the child."[7]

That example highlights the fact there may be two efficient causes (mother and father), or more (mother, father, and doctor), of a person (a child). Indeed, for Aristotle, "the man who has deliberated is a cause," which indicates the person(s) who thought about a new child (*e.g.*, grandparents or siblings) are an efficient cause.[8] Notably, to him, every physical substance—including a child—is a combination of matter (which, he said, the mother provides) and form (imparted by the father). Another illustration—one which ought to resonate with lawyers—Aristotle offered of Efficient Cause is an adviser is a cause of the action taken by the advised.

In common contemporary thinking and parlance, the idea of "cause" has been reduced to Efficient Cause. That is a result of the Scientific Revolution. Arguably, this reduction results in a poor, or at least inchoate, conception of causation, particularly because it neglects Aristotle's fourth meaning—Final Cause.

Type 4: Final Cause—
  Purpose of a Thing

The teleological meaning of "cause" for Aristotle is conveyed by the term "Final Cause." To identify "what is X for?," that is, what the purpose of X is, why does X exist?, is to delineate the Final Cause of X. As Aristotle puts it:

> [A] thing may be a cause as the end. . . .

>   . . .

> That is what something is for, as health might be what a walk is for. On account of what does he walk? We answer "To keep fit" and think that, in saying that, we have given the cause. And anything which, the change being effected by something else, comes to be on the way to the end, as slimness, purging, drugs, and surgical instruments come to be as means to health: all these are for the end, but differ in that the former are works and the latter are tools.[9]

As with Efficient Cause, Final Cause poses semantic difficulties for contemporary international trade lawyers. Effectively, Aristotle equates "Final Cause" with a

---

5. ARISTOTLE, FOUR CAUSES, Book II, Chapter 9.
6. ARISTOTLE, FOUR CAUSES.
7. ARISTOTLE, FOUR CAUSES.
8. ARISTOTLE, FOUR CAUSES.
9. ARISTOTLE READER, 98.

subordinating conjunction in English—"because." But, "because" also is used by them in a phrase like "injury to a domestic industry occurred because of subject merchandise."

Notably, Aristotle never claimed necessity to be an important element in causation. In contrast, Alexander of Aphrodisias (late second and early third centuries A.D.), urged that for a causal relationship, "[it] is necessary that the same effect will recur in the same circumstances, and it is not possible that it be otherwise."[10] "Necessary" is a word found in many international trade laws.

- **Hume (1711–1776) on Causation**

In *A Treatise of Human Nature*, Book I, Part III (1739–40) and *An Enquiry Concerning Human Understanding* (1748), the 18th century Scottish philosopher David Hume argued investigations of causation are unproductive, doubted (more so than Rene Descartes) the existence of causal relationships, and rejected the view that:

> whatever has a beginning must have a cause. . . .
>
>   . . .
>
> There is no object, which implies the existence of any other if we consider these objects in themselves, and never look beyond the idea which we form of them.[11]

That is because it is impossible to establish a necessary causal relationship between objects. Hume dissected the notion of causation into three elements: (1) continuity in space and time between cause and effect, (2) priority in time of cause relative to effect, and (3) the necessity of a link between a cause and effect.

In *An Enquiry Concerning Human Understanding*, Hume explained the first, contiguity in time, as:

> an object, followed by another, and where all the objects similar to the first are followed by objects similar to the second.[12]

The second element, he said, means "where if the first had not been, the second never had existed," which suggesting a temporal priority of a cause to its effect.[13] This element sometimes is called the counterfactual definition, or theory, of causation.[14] The first two elements—contiguity and priority—are indispensable features of the contemporary legal concept of proximate (or but-for) causation.

---

10. *Quoted in* Richard Sorabji, Necessity, Cause, and Blame: Perspectives on Aristotle's Theory 64–66 (1980).

11. *Quoted in* Bertrand Russell, The History of Western Philosophy 664–665 (1945). [Hereinafter, Russell.]

12. David Hume, An Enquiry Concerning Human Understanding 60 (Tom L. Beauchamp ed. 2000). [Hereinafter, Hume, Enquiry.]

13. Hume, Enquiry, 60.

14. *See* David Lewis, *Causation*, in Metaphysics: An Anthology 436, 436–443 (Jaegwon Kim & Ernest Sosa eds. 1999).

However, it is the third element on which Hume placed the greatest emphasis. To him, the third element is:

> an object, followed by another, and whose appearance always conveys the thought to that other.[15]

Said Hume, this element commonly is thought to be "causation." But, the relentless empiricist wrote:

> When we look about us towards external objects, and consider the operation of causes, we are never able, in a single instance, to discover any power or necessary connexion; any quality, which binds the effect to the cause, and renders the one an infallible consequence of the other.[16]

Thus, for example, if one billiard ball, X, strikes another, Y, and Y then moves, it is typically said that X "caused" the motion of Y. Hume disagreed, arguing the statement merely recites what we perceive, indeed what we habitually observe. In truth, staring at X and Y never will produce a sensory perception of a causal connection between them.

That is, for Hume, statements about causation are nothing more than assumptions about necessary connections between supposed causes and effects that spring from our expectations and habits. They are based on impressions, *i.e.*, on what physical senses—sight, sound, taste, and touch—perceive. However, it is impossible to have a sensory impression of a causal connection between events, because a sensory perception of necessity is impossible. Hume famously declares:

> We have no other notion of cause and effect, but that of certain objects, which have always conjoined together.[17]

There neither is nor can be such a thing as an impression of a causal connection. What we call causation is not *a priori* knowledge of links between events. Rather, it is *a posteriori* empirical experience of, *i.e.*, constantly witnessing, the conjunction of events.[18] We witness one event following another, and we thereby constantly associate ideas that one event follows another. But, we cannot perceive the critical

---

15. Hume, Enquiry, 60.

16. *Quoted in* Russell, 660.

17. *Quoted in* Russell, 665.

18. Immanuel Kant (1724–1804) objected to Hume's narrow empiricism, and his conclusion that causation is illusory. Kant argued in favor of the existence of causation by positing causation as an *a priori* category, *i.e.*, the idea of causation is innate to the human mind. Kant's proof was that we have an idea of causation even when it is not possible for us to observe a causal relationship. For example, causation must exist, because even if we do not watch individual articles of subject merchandise injuring a domestic industry, we know of the possibility of the relationship. Indeed, Kant argues that we cannot help but think in terms of, and know, causal relationships—again, because causation is an a priori cognitive category. Further, necessity is an element of this category. Kant wrote it must be the case that:
> in that which antecedes and event there be found the condition of a rule, according to which in this event follows always and necessarily.

Critique of Pure Reason 130 (1781) (J.M.D. Meiklejohn trans., Prometheus Books ed. 1990).

third element in an ostensible causal relationship—necessity, a necessary connection between cause and effect.

Another way to put the point is Hume views causation as correlation that is psychological in character. That conclusion is unduly pessimistic for international trade lawyers. Hume himself wrote:

> [H]ow must we be disappointed, when we learn, that this connexion, tie, or energy lies merely in ourselves, and is nothing but that determination of the mind, which is acquir'd by custom, and causes us to make a transition from an object to its usual attendant, and from the impression of one to the lively idea of the other? Such a discover not only cuts of all hope of ever attaining satisfaction, but even prevents our very wishes; since it appears that when we say we desire to know the ultimate and operating principle, as something which resides in the external object, we either contradict ourselves, or talk without a meaning.[19]

In brief, Hume's radical empiricist skepticism means a causal link is impossible to prove, and so, too, is proving the falsity of an ascribed causal relationship. Worse yet for trade lawyers, then, is the implication for Sunset Reviews of trade remedy orders. Hume's position means there is no proof conjoined events habitually experienced in the past will occur again. If there is no such thing as subject merchandise caused injury to a domestic industry, then there is no certainty that the effect or removing an AD or CVD order would likely be the re-occurrence of dumping or subsidization.

There has been no philosophically rigorous counter to Hume's demolition of *a priori* views of causation. Yet, the reality of a trade remedy case is it will not do to plead "there is no such thing as causation—Hume says so." But, Hume's conclusion is not pointless. It reminds trade lawyers that we tend to find cause where we want to find it. Thus, it pushes them to think carefully about how and when they use the "C" word, and about the empirical bases for attributing injury to imports of subject merchandise.

• Mill (1806–1873) on Causation

Less pessimistic about prospects for finding necessary causal relationships, and influenced by scientific views of causation, John Stuart Mill, a successor to David Hume, urged in his work, *System of Logic* (1843), that:

> . . . it is seldom if ever between a consequent and the single antecedent that [an] invariable sequence subsists. It is usually between a consequent and the sum of several antecedents, the concurrence of all of them being requisite to produce, that is to certain of being followed by the consequent.[20]

---

19. David Hume, A Treatise of Human Nature 266–267 (1739–1740) (Oxford University Press, 1978 ed.). [Hereinafter, Hume, Treatise.]

20. John Stuart Mill, System of Logic, Book III, Chapter V, Section 3 (1843) (Longmans, Green and Co. ed., 1952). [Hereinafter, Mill.]

A billiard ball, X, striking another, Y, is an example that rarely exists in nature. No one contends Y moved because of its own substance, or on its own volition. Other factors—such as X—were involved. Yet, in reality, causal relationships are far more complex than two balls. Accordingly, Mill famously defines cause not in the customary but slack way of one event happening immediately before another, but instead as the:

> sum total of all the conditions, positive and negative taken together; the whole of the contingencies of every description, which being realized, the consequent invariably follows.[21]

Rarely is a single factor accurately described as a "cause" of an event. If a factor truly is a "cause," then whenever it is manifest, the consequence invariably follows. Reality, observed Mill, is more complex: a consequence results when a set of necessary factors operate in conjunction. That set is properly said to be the "cause" of the effect. Consider whether it is Mill's view of the complexity of causes that comes closest, among philosophical perspectives, to causation criteria in modern trade remedy law. Observe, too, both Hume and Mill speak of cause in the Aristotelian sense of "Efficient Cause."

Further, there is a distinction between a "complexity" of causes, which are a set of joint conditions sufficient to bring about an event, and a "plurality" of causes.[22] The latter notion connotes that an event may result from one cause in one time or place, *i.e.*, in one spatio-temporal setting, but occur in another setting from a different cause. In other words, a "plurality" of causes exists whenever there are distinct situations in which different factors produce the same result.

III. Jurisprudential Perspectives: Hart and *Restatement*

- ## Hart (1907–1992) on Causation

One of the foremost legal philosophers of the 20th century, and one influenced both by Hume and post-modernism, was H.L.A. Hart (1907–1992) of Oxford University. With his colleague, Tony Honoré (1921–), Hart produced a classic in jurisprudence—*Causation and the Law* (1959). In it, they delineate three notions of causation that are:

> latent in ordinary thought from which the causal language of the lawyer . . . frequently draws its force and meaning.[23]

---

21. MILL, 238.
22. MILL, Book I, Chapter V, Section 3.
23. H.L.A. HART & TONY HONORÉ, CAUSATION AND THE LAW 2 (2nd ed. 1985). [Hereinafter, HART & HONORÉ.]

The first notion, contingency, is "usually human intervention, which initiates a series of physical changes, which exemplify general connections between types of events."[24] Here, manipulation of factors by a person brings about an intended change. The second notion is an occurrence "whereby one man by words or deeds provid[es] another with a reason for doing something."[25] Underlying this notion is one person inducing or provoking an event. The third notion is an event that violates a breach of a duty, such as the duty to act with reasonable care. The hallmark of this notion is the provision of an opportunity that may be exploited for good or ill.

None of these notions is satisfactory for legal purposes, because lawyers require:

singular statements that [identify] in complex situations certain particular events as causes, effects, or consequences of other particular events. . . .

[Moreover, the] chief concern [of lawyers] with causation is not discoverable connections between types of events, so not as to formulate laws of generalizations, but it is often to *apply* generalizations, which are already known or accepted as true . . . to particular concrete cases.[26]

To be sure, Hart appreciates that while lawyers speak of a factor as the cause of an occurrence, in truth it is never the case that when a:

single event of one kind occurs it is "invariably" followed by some occurrence of another kind.[27]

Accordingly, Hart defines a "cause" as an act that produces an effect if it:

is an intervention in the course of affairs which is *sufficient* to produce the harm without (1) the cooperation of the voluntary actions of others or (2) abnormal conjunctions of events.[28]

In effect, Hart posits cause as a factor that is sufficient to produce a result without an intervening event. That definition relates closely to the second element in Hume's scheme, and thus to the modern legal notion of proximate (or but-for) causation. Interestingly, Hart rejects Mills' concept of "plurality" of causes.[29] He also differentiate moral from legal responsibility.[30] To be held morally responsible for causing harm, one must have indeed caused the harm. Legal liability may be imposed even regardless of cause, as in cases of strict or vicarious liability.

Finally, and critically, in reviewing the above summary, consider whether and how causation criteria in trade remedy law might be put on a stronger, sharper foundation by importing into it the above philosophical and jurisprudential perspectives.

---

24. HART & HONORÉ.
25. HART & HONORÉ.
26. HART & HONORÉ, 10 (emphasis original).
27. HART & HONORÉ, 17.
28. HART & HONORÉ, 5 (emphasis original).
29. *See* HART & HONORÉ, 20.
30. *See* HART & HONORÉ, 10.

• *Restatement* (1965) **on Causation**

The *Restatement 2d of Torts* (1965) defines, at Section 431, "legal cause" as:

> The actor's negligent conduct is a legal cause of harm to another if (a) his conduct is a substantial factor in bringing about the harm, and (b) there is no rule of law relieving the actor from liability because of the manner in which his negligence has resulted in the harm.

"Substantial," as noted in Comment (a) to Section 431, requires that a:

> defendant's conduct ha[ve] such an effect in producing the harm as to lead reasonable men to regard it as a cause, using that word in the popular sense . . . . [In the popular sense] always lurks the idea of responsibility . . . .

This definition essentially equates "causation" with "substantial factor." Thus, it does not provide a basis for a more rigorous, philosophical grounding. Comment (a) to Section 431 essentially eschews any effort at such, distinguishing "substantial cause" from cause in a philosophical sense. The latter, as the Comment indicates:

> includes every one of the great number of events without which any happening would not have occurred.

In effect, the Comment equates philosophical cause with "but-for" causation. To be sure, Anglo-American tort law distinguishes between:

(1) "but-for" causation (also called "causation in fact," or the "*sine qua non*" formulation), which asks whether a harm would have occurred without an act, from

(2) "proximate" causation, which asks a legal policy question about justice and expedience, essentially inquiring into whether a specific cause in fact ought to be deemed a cause that gives rise to liability for the harm at issue.

The *Restatement* (in Section 9), as well as *Black's Law Dictionary*, refers to "proximate cause" as a cause that directly produces a result, and without which the result would not have occurred.

Might Anglo-American tort concepts of causation be of assistance in improving causation criteria in trade remedy law?

IV. Economic Methodologies: Correlation and Regression

Ancient, Continental, and legal philosophers have not crowded out economists in the exploration of causation. Typically in AD-CVD cases, causation is inferred from correlation. That is, for a particular period of investigation (POI), each side presents data on injury. Their presentations may take the form of graphs, charts (including histograms), diagrams, correlation coefficients, or other numerical measures. Petitioners try to show that (1) dumping or subsidization corresponds with

(2) injury or threat thereof, while respondents endeavor to demonstrate there is no connection between the two.

But, as the adage goes, correlation should not be confused with causation. Just because two events, like dumping an injury, or subsidization and injury, occur roughly contemporaneously does not mean the former caused the latter. To heed the adage, econometricians proffer multivariable regression analysis as a method to assess whether a causal relationship exists (*e.g.*, whether tariff reductions stimulate growth in GDP), and if so, measuring its quantitative impact (*e.g.*, how much of a tariff cut will produce how great an impact on GDP). Intuitively, the gist of regression analysis is to find the best possible equation for given data. Depicted on a graph, the equation should represent the closest possible fit to scatter points on the graph.

A generic (but simplified) formula in this analysis, where three causal factors are posited, is:

$$Y = a + b_1 X_1 + b_2 X_2 + b_3 X_3 + \epsilon$$

where:

Y = dependent variable hypothesized to be caused by the Independent variables

X_1, X_2, and X_3 = independent variables

a = a coefficient relating to the intercept of a regression line with the vertical (y) axis when the line is plotted on a graph

b_1 = a coefficient measuring the effect of X_1 on Y

b_2 = a coefficient measuring the effect of X_2 on Y

b_3 = a coefficient measuring the effect of X_3 on Y

ϵ = the error term, which captures the effect of all other factors on Y.

Thus, for example, Y could represent injury to a petitioning industry in a trade remedy case, X_1 could be subject merchandise imports, X_2 technological change, and X_3 interest rate costs. Values for the coefficients b_1, b_2, and b_3 would reflect the relative significant—*i.e.*, statistical causation—of X_1, X_2, and X_3, respectively, to Y. Of course, establishing a persuasive statistic to measure the independent and dependent variables, and gathering reliable data for each statistic is essential. Might these issues unduly influence the choice of a POI?

Econometricians perform a tests (such as the "t-test") to measure the statistical significance of each independent variable, utilize a statistic (called "R^2" or "R squared") to gauge the explanatory power of the entire regression model. They also check for problems endemic in the model, such as multi-collinearity, which occurs when there are causal relationships among the independent variables. That is, two or more of the variables designed to predict the behavior of the modeled outcome are correlated with one another. For instance, with injury measured by unemployment as a dependent variable, regressing it on bilateral trade deficits and exchange rates would lead to multi-collinearity, insofar as the independent variables (trade deficits and exchange rates) move with one another. The result of multi-collinearity is to increase standard errors in each of the coefficients.

Multivariate regression analysis is widely used not only by academics, but also by economists practicing in investment and commercial banks, government ministries, NGOs and think tanks, and IOs. However, multivariable regression analysis is not commonly used in the practice of trade remedy law—yet, at any rate. Trade remedy cases are expensive, and econometric analyses, with expert witnesses to boot, only drive up further those costs. Why incur them, if criteria for causation in AD, CVD, and safeguard law do not demand such sophisticated proof? In particular, if proof that injury to a domestic industry occurs during the POI when subject merchandise is dumped or subsidized, or when fairly traded imports surge, can be offered with arithmetic ratios, graphs, and charts, and such proof suffices, then what incentive exists to go further? As the criteria are presently, correlation tends to suffice as indicative of causation—even though the adage "correlation does not mean causation" is widely understood.

Finally, note the conflicting interests among developing countries and LDCs in the debate about the practical costs of upgrading causation criteria. Unless and until sophisticated econometric techniques are cheaply and widely available, then revising the criteria would inhibit their participation in AD, CVD, and safeguard cases. Yet, more rigorous causation standards might well make developed countries think twice before launching a trade remedy case against a poor country.

Chapter 19

Proving Causation: GATT-WTO Jurisprudence[1]

I. Limited GATT-WTO Guidance

It is illegal under GATT Article VI:1 and VI:6, and Articles 1, 3, 7, and 9 of the WTO *Antidumping Agreement*, to impose an AD duty without proof the subject merchandise causes material injury, threat of material injury, or material retardation of the establishment of an industry. That is also true with respect to a CVD. Illegal subsidization—that is, Yellow Light, or Prohibited, subsidization under Articles 5–6 of the WTO *SCM Agreement*—must be the cause of adverse effects (which may take the form of material injury, serious prejudice, or nullification or impairment of benefits).

Article 3:5 of the *Antidumping Agreement* deals with causation, essentially requiring an investigating authority to demonstrate a causal relationship between dumping on injury based on all relevant evidence. In its entirety, this provision states:

> It must be demonstrated that the dumped imports are, through the effects of dumping, as set forth in paragraphs 2 and 4, causing injury within the meaning of this Agreement. The demonstration of a causal relationship between the dumped imports and the injury to the domestic industry shall be based on an examination of all relevant evidence before the authorities. *The authorities shall also examine any known factors other than the dumped imports which at the same time are injuring the domestic industry, and the injuries caused by these other factors must not be attributed to the dumped imports.* Factors which may be relevant in this respect include, *inter alia,* the volume and prices of imports not sold at dumping prices, contraction in demand or changes in the patterns of consumption, trade restrictive practices of and competition between the foreign and domestic producers, developments in technology and the export performance and productivity of the domestic industry.[2]

---

1. Documents References:
   (1) *Havana (ITO) Charter* Article 34
   (2) GATT Articles VI, XVI
   (3) WTO *Antidumping Agreement* Article 3
   (4) WTO *SCM Agreement* Articles 1, 3, 5–6, 8, 15
2. Emphasis added.

Of critical importance are the third and fourth sentences of Article 3:5.

The third sentence instructs an investigating authority to "examine any *known factors* other than the dumped imports which at the same time are injuring the domestic industry."[3] This sentence also contains a non-attribution clause, whereby the authority is forbidden from attributing injuries caused by these other factors to the dumped imports. The "non-attribution" rubric derives from the mandate to avoid attributing causation of injury to dumped imports when, in reality, some other factor or factors are to blame.

The fourth and final sentence identifies potential causal factors other than dumping the authority may find relevant, such as changes in consumption patterns, competition between foreign and domestic producers, contraction in demand for the like product, export performance, productivity, restrictive trading practices, technology, and the volume and prices of non-dumped imports.

II. Five Step Causation Analysis and 2001 *Japan Hot Rolled Steel* Case

• **Facts**

In the 2001 *Japan Hot Rolled Steel* case, Japan appealed against a Panel ruling about causation.[4] Japan urged the Panel was wrong in saying the ITC had demonstrated, satisfactorily under Article 3:5 of the WTO *Antidumping Agreement*, a causal relationship between dumped imports and material injury to the American hot-rolled steel industry. The result of the Japanese appeal was mixed.

The Appellate Body reversed the Panel's finding the ITC had demonstrated the existence of a causal relationship between dumping and material injury. That reversal favored Japan. But, the Appellate Body also ruled the factual record was insufficient to allow for a complete analysis of the Japanese causation claim. That was a small victory for the U.S.

The Japanese appeal on causation focused on the language of Article 3:5 of the WTO *Antidumping Agreement*. The gravamen of the Japanese causation claim is suggested by the third known as the "non-attribution language."[5] First, said Japan, the ITC did not conduct an adequate examination of factors other than imports of hot-rolled steel that were allegedly dumped. Yet, these other factors also caused injury to domestic steel producers. Second, the ITC failed to ensure that injury

---

3. Emphasis added.

4. This discussion draws on *United States—Anti-Dumping Measures on Certain Hot-Rolled Steel Products from Japan*, WT/DS184/R, ¶¶ 2.1–2.9 (adopted as modified by the Appellate Body 23 August 2001) (hereinafter, *Japan Hot Rolled Steel* Panel Report); *United States—Anti-Dumping Measures on Certain Hot Rolled Steel Products from Japan*, ¶¶ 181–187 (adopted 23 August 2001) (hereinafter, *Japan Hot Rolled Steel* Appellate Body Report, WT/DS184/AB/R, ¶¶ 49(e), 181–187.

5. *See Japan Hot Rolled Steel* Appellate Body Report, ¶ 217.

caused by these other factors was not attributed to the dumped imports, *i.e.*, the ITC analysis confused damage caused by the other factors with damage supposedly caused by the imports.

What were these "other" factors? Japan listed four:

(1) An increase in the production capacity of mini-mills in the U.S.

(2) The effects of a strike at General Motors.

(3) A decline in demand for hot-rolled steel from the pipe and tube industry in the U.S.

(4) The effect of prices of non-dumped imports.

The Panel looked at these factors and the work of the ITC, and rejected the Japanese claim.

• **Panel Causation Holding**

In doing so, the Panel interpreted the non-attribution language of third sentence of Article 3:5. It said that the job of the investigating authority "is to examine and ensure that these other factors *do not break the causal link that appeared to exist between dumped imports and material injury on the basis of an examination of the volume and effects of dumped imports* under Articles 3.2 and 3.4 of the *Antidumping Agreement*."[6] In other words, Article 3:5 is an embellishment on Articles 3:2 and 3:4. The non-attribution language of Article 3:5 focuses on the chain of causation, from the volume and effects of the imports being dumped, to the injury to the petitioning industry, that would be established under Articles 3:2 and 3:4. Having established that chain, the non-attribution language demands a further inquiry: is there anything that disrupts the causal chain?

The Panel approach accorded with common sense, as any patient going to a medical doctor is aware. The task of a physician task is to examine an injury, and determine its cause. In that determination, the doctor must rule out all other possible causes, otherwise choice of the appropriate remedy to match the illness is impossible. But, exactly where did the Panel find support for its interpretation?

None other than *de facto* precedent—that of another Panel, and of the Appellate Body. The Panel cited a 1994 GATT Panel Report, *U.S. Atlantic Salmon Anti-Dumping Duties*,[7] plus a 2001 Appellate Body Report, *U.S. Wheat Gluten Safeguard*.[8] The jurisprudence developed in these Reports indicated it was not necessary for an investigating authority to demonstrate dumped imports, alone, caused injury.

---

6. *Hot Rolled Steel* Panel Report, ¶ 7.251, *quoted in Japan Hot Rolled Steel* Appellate Body Report, ¶ 217 (emphasis added).

7. *See Imposition of Anti-Dumping Duties on Imports of Fresh and Chilled Atlantic Salmon from Norway*, B.I.S.D. (41st Supp., vol. 1) 229 (1994) (adopted by the Committee on Antidumping Practices, 27 April 1994).

8. *See United States—Definitive Safeguard Measure on Imports of Wheat Gluten from the European Communities*, WT/DS166/AB/R (adopted 19 January 2001).

That is, there was no need to deduct the injury caused by other factors from the overall injury to the petitioning industry, and thereby obtain the extent of causation attributable solely to dumped imports. However, it is essential to avoid attributing an injury caused by another factor to the dumped imports. In brief, the Panel concluded the non-attribution language of Article 3:5 did not call for isolation of each of the other potential independent variables, nor for a finding that dumped imports alone were capable of causing the injury. Rather, the language mandated clarity of thought, *i.e.*, avoidance of confusion of every other variable with dumped imports.

- **Appellate Body Causation Holding**

The Japanese victory on its appeal of its causation claim was partial.[9] The Appellate Body held the factual record was insufficient to allow for a complete analysis of the Japanese causation claim. At the same time, the part of the appeal Japan did win was noteworthy. The Appellate Body overturned the legal interpretation by the Panel of Article 3:5 of the *Antidumping Agreement*, namely, that the ITC had demonstrated the existence of a causal relationship between dumping and material injury. Why?

As observed above, the Panel based its interpretation of the non-attribution language of Article 3:5 on the 1994 GATT Panel Report in *U.S. Atlantic Salmon Anti-Dumping Duties*, and on the 2001 Appellate Body Report in *Wheat Gluten*. Both are rather odd precedents to cite. The GATT Panel Report pre-dates the entry into force of the Uruguay Round *Antidumping Agreement*. Indeed, among the issues in that case were various provisions of the 1979 Tokyo Round *Antidumping Code*.[10] (To be sure, there are similarities in language between the texts.) As to the *Wheat Gluten* dispute, it concerned the Uruguay Round *Agreement on Safeguards*—it was not an AD case at all. Japan argued successfully to the Appellate Body that the Panel in *Hot-Rolled Steel* had erred in its interpretation of the non-attribution language.

Perhaps Japan noticed the oddity of the citations by the Panel, but it did not seem bothered by it. To the contrary, Japan said the error of the Panel lay in its interpretation of the *Wheat Gluten* case. It was, said Japan, necessary to separate and distinguish other causal factors, and evaluate their bearing on the health of the petitioning domestic industry. The Panel was wrong in reading *Wheat Gluten* to mean there was no need for isolation of causal factors through a deduction of other variables from the overall injury to ascertain the damage done by dumped imports. Thus, Japan itself cited the Appellate Body *Wheat Gluten* Report—and

---

9. This discussion draws on *Japan Hot Rolled Steel* Appellate Body Report, ¶¶ 219–236.

10. The dispute arose in 1991, when the Tokyo Round *Code* was in effect. *See United States—Atlantic Salmon Anti-Dumping Duties*, ¶¶ 1 (speaking of the "*Agreement on Implementation of the General Agreement on Tariffs and Trade*," and abbreviating it as the "*Agreement*") and 555 (referring to Articles 3:1, 3:2, and 3:3 of the *Agreement*). As the Appellate Body noted, the *Hot-Rolled Steel* Panel cited Paragraph 555 with approval. *See* Appellate Body Report, *Hot-Rolled Steel*, ¶ 218.

another safeguard decision of the Appellate Body, to boot, namely, in the 2001 *United States—Lamb Safeguard* case.[11]

Precisely correct, was the Appellate Body's response to Japan's argument. The Appellate Body held the Panel was wrong to conclude that the non-attribution language of Article 3:5 of the WTO *Antidumping Agreement* does not require an investigating authority to separate and distinguish the injurious effects of other known causal factors from the damage done by dumped imports:

> This provision [Article 3:5] requires investigating authorities, as part of their causation analysis, first to examine *all* "known factors," "other than dumped imports," which are causing injury to the domestic industry "at the same time" as dumped imports. Second, investigating authorities must ensure that injuries which are caused to the domestic industry by known factors, other than dumped imports, are not "*attributed* to the dumped imports." (Emphasis added [by Appellate Body].)

> The non-attribution language in Article 3:5 . . . applies solely in situations where dumped imports and other known factors are causing injury to the domestic industry *at the same time.* [Emphasis original.] In order that investigating authorities . . . are able to ensure that the injurious effects of the other known factors are not "attributed" to dumped imports, they must appropriately assess the injurious effects of those factors. Logically, such an assessment must involve separating and distinguishing the injurious effects of the other factors from the injurious effects of the dumped imports. If the injurious effects of the dumped imports are not appropriately separated and distinguished from the injurious effects of the other factors, the authorities will be unable to conclude that the injury they ascribe to dumped imports is actually caused by those imports, rather than by the other factors. Thus, in the absence of such separation and distinction of the different injurious effects, the investigating authorities would have no rational basis to conclude that the dumped imports are indeed causing the injury. . . . [12]

• **Five Step Causation Analysis**

The "bottom line" on causation, then, is a Five-Step analysis.[13] An investigating authority must:

(1) identify factors that could be causing injury to the petitioning industry,

(2) check to see these factors are operating simultaneously,

(3) examine all of these known factors to see if they indeed are having an injurious effect,

---

11. See *United States—Safeguard Measure on Imports of Fresh, Chilled or Frozen Lamb from New Zealand,* WT/DS177/AB/R and WT/DS178/AB/R (adopted 16 May 2001).

12. *Japan Hot Rolled Steel* Appellate Body Report, ¶¶ 222–23.

13. The Appellate Body, as quoted above, put it in terms of 2 steps. See *Japan Hot Rolled Steel* Appellate Body Report, ¶ 222.

(4) distinguish between two categories of known factors, namely, the injurious effects of dumped imports versus the injurious effects of all other known factors, and

(5) ensure that the damage done by other factors is not attributed to the dumped imports.

- **Use of Precedent**

The Appellate Body did not leave untouched the citation by the Panel to previous Reports. It made clear the Panel was wrong to follow the approach in the 1994 *United States—Atlantic Salmon Anti-Dumping Duties* case:

> In examining the meaning of the non-attribution language, the Panel considered that the panel report in *United States—Atlantic Salmon Anti-Dumping Duties* was "relevant and persuasive" and, in fact, the Panel based its interpretive approach, in part, on a passage from that panel report which included the following statement:
>
>> ... [the non-attribution language] did *not* mean that, in addition to examining the effects of the imports under Articles 3:1, 3:2 and 3:3, the USITC should somehow have *identified the extent of injury caused by these other factors* in order to *isolate* the injury caused by these factors from the injury caused by the imports from Norway. (Emphasis added [by Appellate Body].)
>
> It is clear to us that the interpretive approach adopted by the panel in *United States—Atlantic Salmon Anti-Dumping Duties* is at odds with the interpretive approach for Article 3:5 of the *Anti-Dumping Agreement* that we have just set forth. .... [I]n order to comply with the non-attribution language in that provision, investigating authorities must make an appropriate assessment of the injury caused to the domestic industry by the other known factors, and they must separate and distinguish the injurious effects of the dumped imports from the injurious effects of those other factors. This requires a satisfactory explanation of the nature and extent of the injurious effects of the other factors, as distinguished from the injurious effects of the dumped imports. However, the panel in *United States—Atlantic Salmon Anti-Dumping Duties*, expressly disavowed any need to "identify" the injury caused by the other factors. According to that panel, such separate identification of the injurious effects of the other causal factors is not required.
>
> By following the panel in *United States—Atlantic Salmon Anti-Dumping Duties*, the Panel, in effect, took the view that the USITC was not required to separate and distinguish the injurious effects of the other factors from the injurious effects of dumped imports, and that the nature and extent of the injurious effects of the other known factors need not be identified at all. However, in our view, this is precisely what the non-attribution language in Article 3:5 of the *Anti-Dumping Agreement* requires, in order to ensure that determinations regarding dumped imports are not based on

mere assumptions about the effects of those imports, as distinguished from the effects of the other factors.[14]

In effect, the Appellate Body said the non-attribution language of the later-in-time *Antidumping Agreement*, as it interpreted this language, over-ruled the GATT Panel Report.

Likewise, the Appellate Body took the Panel to task for misreading *U.S. Wheat Gluten Safeguard*, and not taken account of *U.S. Lamb Safeguard*. Interestingly, the Appellate Body did not fault the Panel for using these cases, even though they were safeguards matters. After all, there are "considerable similarities" in the non-attribution language of Article 3:5 of the WTO *Antidumping Agreement* and Article 4:2(b) of the *Agreement on Safeguards*.[15] Both demand injury caused to a domestic industry, at the same time, by factors other than imports not be confused with injury caused by imports.

Thus, the Appellate Body very nearly congratulated the Panel for its ability to think laterally in looking to *Wheat Gluten*, *Lamb Safeguard*, and the *Agreement on Safeguards* for guidance in interpreting the non-attribution language in the *Antidumping Agreement*.[16] The problem, said the Appellate Body, was the Panel rode roughshod over the message of *Wheat Gluten* and *Lamb Safeguard* with respect to non-attribution. The Appellate Body quoted the passages from its Reports that the Panel ought to have read with care. These passages were unambiguous: a separation or distinction among causal factors is required in the injury determination of a safeguards case.[17]

• **Did Appellate Body Go Far Enough?**

In coming to its conclusion, the Appellate Body spent several paragraphs in the *Japan Hot Rolled Steel* Report on how to conduct a causation analysis, and making clear that delineating among the injurious effects of known causal factors is required by the non-attribution language of Article 3:5 of the *Antidumping Agreement*. As discussed earlier, five separate steps are evident from the Appellate Body's analysis. Does this Five-Step Test mean a WTO Member must conduct its causation analysis according to "particular methods and approaches"? Absolutely not, stressed the Appellate Body. The non-attribution language is not so specific as to compel a particular evaluation methodology. Members are free to fill in the details for themselves.

---

14. *Japan Hot Rolled Steel* Appellate Body Report, ¶¶ 225–227 (emphasis in last paragraph added).

15. This provision states that "[w]hen factors other than increased imports are causing injury to the domestic industry at the same time, such injury shall not be attributed to increased imports." WTO *Agreement on Safeguards*, Article 4:2(b).

16. *See Japan Hot Rolled Steel* Appellate Body Report, ¶ 230 (last sentence).

17. *See Japan Hot Rolled Steel* Appellate Body Report, ¶¶ 231–232 (*quoting* the *Wheat Gluten* and *Lamb Safeguard* Reports, respectively).

Is the Appellate Body emphasis on this point believable? Arguably, the Appellate Body made the point in anticipation of criticism that it was infringing on the sovereignty of Members. On the one hand, it was doing its best to sketch out the obligations of Article 3:5 of the *Antidumping Agreement*. On the other hand, it was trying to fend off criticism that it was micro-managing injury investigations by reading more into the Article than exists.

Yet, the fact the Appellate Body clearly expects a separate identification of each known causal factor, and a distinct analysis thereof vis-à-vis dumped imports, suggests it is "judicially active." It will not tolerate a sloppy causation analysis in which the damage done to a petitioner by alternative independent variables are left fuzzy, and lumped together with dumped imports. Were that to happen, the AD remedy would become susceptible to protectionist abuse.

Protectionist abuse certainly was on the minds of the Japanese. In its May 2000 "White Paper," the Japanese METI warned that countries using dumping measures were hurting themselves. On balance, these countries were racking up economic losses of 0.03% to 0.06% of GDP each, owing to the higher import prices that, while helping to protect domestic industries, hurt consumers and unaffiliated industries.[18] Japan pointed out since 1997, steel products from not only Japan, but also 20 other countries had been the target of either an AD investigation in the U.S., or of AD duties imposed by the U.S.[19] The result was a "chilling effect" on international trade in steel.[20]

Japan was particularly victimized, with about 80% of its steel products subject to an AD duty.[21] Its producers, such as Nippon Steel, argued they had not intentionally boosted exports to the U.S. Rather, they were simply meeting demand from American steel consumers, particularly automakers.[22] (Of course, as any AD lawyer knows, intent does not matter in an AD case.) The U.S. shot back, accusing the Japanese of masterminding a conspiratorial attack against its AD laws.[23] The U.S. had one other shot, provided to it by financial market investors and analysts. Many

---

18. *See* Toshio Aritake, *Japanese Ministry's Annual Report Cites Abuse of Antidumping Measures*, 17 International Trade Reporter (BNA) 770 (18 May 2000). Interestingly, the White Paper also indicated Japan needs additional legal service providers to cope with disputes arising from economic de-regulation and trade liberalization. Japan has 17.0 lawyers per 100,000 people, and 2.3 judges per 100,000 people, in comparison with 352.5 and 11.6, respectively, in the U.S. *See id.*

19. *See* Daniel Pruzin, *Japan Calls U.S. Antidumping Practices "Abusive," Moves to Bring WTO Complaint*, 16 International Trade Reporter (BNA) 1783 (3 November 1999). [Hereinafter, *Japan Calls.*]

20. *Japan Calls.*

21. *See* Daniel Pruzin & Toshio Aritake, *Japan Seeks WTO Consultations with U.S. on Steel Dumping Duties*, 16 International Trade Reporter (BNA) 1915 (24 November 1999).

22. *See* International Trade Commission, Certain Hot-Rolled Steel Products from Japan, U.S. ITC Investigation No. 731-TA-807 (Final) (U.S. ITC Publication 3202, June 1999), Appendix 1 at 17.

23. *See* Gary G. Yerkey & Toshio Aritake, *U.S. Accuses Japan of Masterminding Attack on U.S. Antidumping Laws in WTO*, 16 International Trade Reporter (BNA) 1731 (27 October 1999)

of them charged Japanese steel makers had not been eliminating excess capacity or investing in new businesses quickly enough, and hence still were struggling with high costs.[24]

Paradoxically, then, it could be argued the Appellate Body did not go far enough in its activism. It did not say anything about the extent of causation of each of the various known factors. What if dumped imports are not the most important cause of injury, of what if there are equally important other causes? Moreover, is it permissible to lump together all of the other known factors, and weigh them against dumped imports? In brief, what remains fuzzy in the causation analysis under Article 3:5 of the *Antidumping Agreement* is whether the injurious effects of dumped imports must surpass a particular threshold (50%, for instance).

III. Non-Attribution Analysis, Collective versus Individual Effects, and 2003 *Brazil Iron Tube* Case

• **Facts**

As with the 2001 *Japan Hot-Rolled Steel* case, the 2003 *Brazil Iron Tube* case made important contributions to the evolving jurisprudence on causation in AD cases. In the latter dispute, Brazil raised intriguing arguments about causation, known factors, and attribution.[25] Specifically, Brazil asked whether the EC complied with Article 3:5 of the WTO *Antidumping Agreement* in assessing the causal relationship between dumped imports and injury, by

(1) Ruling the difference in the cost of production between a Brazilian exporter and the EC was not a known factor (aside from dumped imports that were injuring the EC industry),

(2) Not examining the collective impact of other known causal factors, and

(3) Not attributing injuries caused by those other known factors to dumped imports?

Brazil was unsuccessful in its challenge, as the Appellate Body reversed, holding in favor of the EC.

(comments of David L. Aaron, Undersecretary of Commerce for International Trade). The strategy may have worked, as clarification of certain aspects of AD law were put on the DDA.

24. *See* Alexandra Harney, *Japan to File Protest Over U.S. Dumping Claims*, FIN. TIMES, Nov. 18, 1999, 8.

25. This discussion draws on World Trade Organization, *Update of WTO Dispute Settlement Cases*, WT/DS/OV/16, 117–18 (17 October 2003), (www.wto.org); Appellate Body Report *European Communities—Anti-Dumping Duties on Malleable Cast Iron Tube or Pipe Fittings from Brazil*, WT/DS219/AB/R, ¶¶ 64(g), 167–95, 196(g) (adopted 18 August 2003) (complaint by Brazil) (hereinafter, *Cast Iron Tube* Appellate Body Report); Panel Report, *European Communities—Anti-Dumping Duties on Malleable Cast Iron Tube or Pipe Fittings from Brazil*, WT/DS219/R, ¶¶ 1.1–2.7 (adopted as modified by the Appellate Body 18 August 2003) (hereinafter, *Cast Iron Tube* Panel Report).

• **Appellate Body Causation Holding**

First, Brazil contested the finding of the EC that the relatively higher cost of production of the domestic industry in Europe was not a known factor other than dumped imports. Brazil argued the EC should have examined, as a known factor causing injury other than the dumped imports, the relative cost efficiency of the Brazilian exporter under investigation. Brazil gave evidence its exporter made the so-called "black heart" fittings at a lower cost of production than the like product made by European producers, which were "white heart fittings." In its causation analysis, the EC ought to have considered this cost of production difference, or comparative advantage, by engaging in a margins analysis. After all, the selling prices of the Brazilian and European products reflected the difference in cost efficiency, thus a significant reason for injury to the European industry was not due to the effects of dumping.

The problem with the first Brazilian challenge — from the viewpoint of the European Communities, Panel, and Appellate Body — was it neglected a key fact. Brazil had failed to mention the cost efficiency difference in the context of the EC causation analysis. True, Brazil mentioned it in the context of the dumping margin and injury determinations by European authorities, and true, Brazil thought mentioning it in those contexts would make cost efficiency a known factor when they did their causation analysis. But, under Article 3:5 of the *Antidumping Agreement*, an investigating authority can limit its causation examination only to those factors raised by the complainant and respondent in the context of the causality analysis, presumably because only those factors are known to it. In other words, raising a factor (such as cost efficiency) in one investigation phase does not render it a known factor in another phase.

The Appellate Body admitted the WTO *Antidumping Agreement* contained three ambiguities relevant to the case. First, the text does not expressly state how a causal factor other than dumped imports becomes "known," or should become "known," to an investigating authority. Second, the text fails to tell parties the manner in which they must raise a factor to make it "known." Third, the *Agreement* does not define the degree to which a factor must be unrelated to the dumped imports, nor does it state whether the factor must be extrinsic to the exporter and the dumped product, in order to qualify as a factor other than dumped imports. No matter, however, said the Appellate Body. It did not feel any need to resolve these uncertainties.

That was because the Brazilian challenge hinged on its factual pleading that its industry boasted relatively cheaper production costs. The EC rejected that pleading, finding the cost differential minimal, and the Panel affirmed the European finding. As a factual matter, the Appellate Body could not pursue it. However, it did endorse the legal interpretation of the EC and application of Article 3:5 — once European authorities determined the allegation of a cost differential lacked foundation, there was no such factor for it to analyze in the context of causation, and the EC was under no obligation to examine the effects of this differential when analyzing causation.

The second Brazilian second challenge on causation was about the non-attribution obligation in Article 3:5 of the *Antidumping Agreement*. The basic duty is a prohibition against attributing to dumped imports the injuries plaguing the domestic industry simultaneously caused by known factors other than dumped imports. The duty is premised on the undisputed rationale that only by separating and distinguishing the injurious effects on the domestic industry in the importing country of other factors from the effects of dumping is it possible to ascertain whether injury ascribed to dumped imports actually is caused by those imports. However, from the perspective of Brazil, the problem was not the obligation itself, but how the EC endeavored to meet it.

The EC analyzed causal factors other than dumped imports on an individual basis, but did not consider the collective effects of these factors. (In the case, those other factors were imports from third countries not subject to investigation, a decline in consumption in the EC, and substitution of products. The EC found the causal contribution to injury from two of these causal factors to be insignificant, and for one factor not sufficiently significant to break the causal link between dumped imports and injury.) Consequently, the EC was wrong to decide not to attribute to dumped imports the injuries caused by factors other than dumping, and it was wrong to conclude dumped imports caused material injury to its domestic industry.

More specifically, Brazil interpreted Article 3:5 of the *Antidumping Agreement* as calling for a Two-Step causation analysis. In Step One, an investigating authority must separate and distinguish the injurious effects of other causal factors individually from the effects of dumped imports. The EC had done that without fault, but not taken the second step. In Step Two, the authority must also separate and distinguish the collective effects of the other causal factors from the effects of dumped imports. To perform that task, the authority must evaluate the collective effect of the other factors on the alleged causal link between dumped imports and injury.

Why is Step Two needed in every AD investigation? Because, said Brazil, only by separating the collective effects of causal factors other than dumped imports from the effects of dumped imports will it be clear the other factors are not a sufficient cause to break the causal link between dumped imports and injury. If the EC had looked at the collective effects of other causal factors, then it would have realized those collective effects undermine the causal link between dumped imports and injury.

The Panel disagreed with this logic. It had confidence in the European causation methodology, saying that even though the European authorities analyzed each causal factor solely on an individual basis, that analysis ensured the they had not attributed improperly to dumped imports the effects of causal factors other than dumped imports. The European Communities, of course, defended its methodology on appeal, saying it was consistent with Article 3:5. It agreed with Brazil that Article 3:5 requires an investigating authority to separate and distinguish the injurious effects of various causal factors in order to ensure injuries caused by other factors are not attributed to dumped imports. But, it disagreed with Brazil on the necessity of a second step. The WTO *Antidumping Agreement* does not compel a particular methodology to fulfill the non-attribution obligation, and Brazil was trying to import one into the text of Article 3:5 without any textual basis for doing so.

The Appellate Body agreed with the European Communities. It held the non-attribution obligation in Article 3:5 does not require an investigating authority, when engaged in a causation analysis, to examine the effects of other causal factors collectively after it has examined their effects individually. The Appellate Body cited its 2001 *Japan Hot-Rolled Steel* Report, in which it explained the non-attribution obligation entailed separating and distinguishing the effects of other causal factors from the effects of dumped imports, so that all of these effects are not lumped together and become indistinguishable.

The Appellate Body also cited its *Hot-Rolled Steel* Report for the proposition the *Antidumping Agreement* does not prescribe any methodology by which an investigating authority must avoid attributing the injuries of other causal factors to dumped imports. In brief, as long as the authority fulfills the non-attribution obligation, it is free to choose any methodology to inquire into a causal link between dumped imports and injury.

Notwithstanding the precedent, the Appellate Body faulted the methodology proposed by Brazil. Step Two was not needed in every case, *i.e.*, it is not always necessary for an investigating authority to examine the collective effects of other causal factors on the domestic industry to be sure that injuries ascribed to dumped imports actually are caused by those imports rather than other factors. To be sure, some cases require a collective analysis. The Appellate Body cited approvingly the suggestion of the Panel that multiple insignificant factors could collectively constitute a significant cause of injury so as to sever the link between dumped imports and injury. However, the facts of a particular case dictate whether the second step advocated by Brazil is needed.

· **Knowns and Unknowns**

One aspect of the Appellate Body discussion of causation is particularly interesting for its future significance. The Appellate Body took issue with the Panel statement that an alleged causal factor could be known for purposes of the dumping and injury determinations, but not for the causation determination. Brazil thought this statement ludicrous. In contrast, the EC insisted on separate pleadings for each phase of the investigation (*i.e.*, Brazil should have mentioned the cost differential factor in the causation phase, rather than presuming the EC knew of it from the other phases).

The Appellate Body agreed with Brazil, stating:

a factor is either "known" to the investigating authority, or it is not "known"; it cannot be "known" in one stage of the investigation and unknown in a subsequent stage.[26]

Unfortunately, the Appellate Body declined to pursue a deeper epistemological analysis. Might different parts of the EC's AD investigating authority know different things? Is actual knowledge required, or constructive knowledge enough?

Worse yet, for loyal readers of WTO publications, the Appellate Body missed a wonderful opportunity at injecting humor into its Report. No less a figure than an American Secretary of Defense, Donald Rumsfeld, has shown considerable appreciation for epistemological difficulties, offering this insight (albeit in the context of firing real weapons, not trade remedies):

> The message is that there are known knowns—there are things that we know that we know. There are known unknowns—that is to say, there are things that we now know we don't know. But there are also unknown unknowns—there are things we do not know we don't know. And each year we discover a few more of those unknown unknowns.[27]

Apparently, at the time the Appellate Body drafted its Report, the insight of the controversial Defense Secretary was an unknown unknown. Or, was it a known unknown for some of the Appellate Body members? Whatever the answer, the insight now is a known known.

IV. Cross-Cumulation and 2014 *India Carbon Steel* Case

- **Cross-Cumulation of Subsidized Imports with Non-Subsidized Dumped Imports**[28]

The ITC, which of course is the U.S. agency responsible for determining whether subsidized or dumped imports causing or threaten to cause injury to domestic producers ("material injury" under U.S. law), traditionally assesses the impact of both (1) subsidized imports that are the subject of a CVD action and (2) non-subsidized imports that are subject to AD investigations in the common situation where simultaneous CVD and AD investigation petitions are filed with it and the DOC. This assessment is dubbed "cross-cumulation," and is subject to various procedural requirements. India challenged the ITC's cross-cumulation practices as being inconsistent with Articles 15:1, 15:2, 15:4 and 15:5 of the *SCM Agreement*.

---

26. Appellate Body Report, *Brazil Iron Tube*, ¶ 178.

27. *Quoted in* BBC News, www.bbc.co.uk/radio4/news/bh/rumsfeld.shtml.

28. *India Carbon Steel* Panel Report, ¶ 4.8–4.629; *India Carbon Steel* Appellate Body Report, ¶¶ 247–261, 261–265. This case is cited, and its facts summarized, in an earlier Chapter.

- **Panel Holding and Rationale**

The Panel accepted India's challenge, holding that under Article 15:3, the effects of imports that are not subject to a CVD investigation cannot be addressed cumulatively with those of imports that are subject to a CVD investigation. The U.S. argued that because Article 15:3 does not mention cross-cumulation of allegedly subsidized imports with dumped imports, or otherwise address the situation in which both CVD and AD investigations progress simultaneously, that Article does not regulate the topic. Put differently, just because Article 15:3 does not expressly authorize the use of cross-cumulation, does not mean that such a practice is prohibited under the *Agreement*.

The Panel rejected the American argument, and the U.S. filed a cross-appeal.

Article 15 of the *SCM Agreement* provides:

15.1 A determination of injury for purposes of Article VI of GATT 1994 shall be based on positive evidence and involve an objective examination of both *(a)* the volume of the *subsidized imports* and the effect of the *subsidized imports* on prices in the domestic market for like products and *(b)* the consequent impact of these imports on the domestic producers of such products.

15.2 With regard to the volume of the *subsidized imports*, the investigating authorities shall consider whether there has been a significant increase in subsidized imports, either in absolute terms or relative to production or consumption in the importing Member. With regard to the *effect of the subsidized imports on prices*, the investigating authorities shall consider whether there has been a significant price undercutting by the subsidized imports as compared with the price of a like product of the importing Member, or whether the effect of such imports is otherwise to depress prices to a significant degree or to prevent price increases, which otherwise would have occurred, to a significant degree. No one or several of these factors can necessarily give decisive guidance.

15.3 Where imports of a product from more than one country are simultaneously subject to countervailing duty investigations, the investigating authorities may cumulatively assess the effects of such imports only if they determine that *(a)* the amount of subsidization established in relation to the imports from each country is more than *de minimis* as defined in paragraph 9 of Article 11 [*i.e.*, less than 1% *ad valorem* for developed countries, 2% for developing countries, and 3% for LDCs, under Article 27:10(a)-11] and the volume of imports from each country is not negligible [which is undefined under Article 11:9 for developed countries, but which under Article 27:10(b) is less than 4% for developing countries and LDCs, unless their individual shares aggregate to more than 9% of total imports of the like product into the importing Member] and *(b)* a cumulative assessment of the effects of the imports is appropriate in light of the conditions of competition between the imported products and the conditions of competition between the imported products and the like domestic product.

15.4   The examination of the impact of the subsidized imports on the domestic industry shall include an evaluation of all relevant economic factors and indices having a bearing on the state of the industry, including actual and potential decline in output, sales, market share, profits, productivity, return on investments, or utilization of capacity; factors affecting domestic prices; actual and potential negative effects on cash flow, inventories, employment, wages, growth, ability to raise capital or investments and, in the case of agriculture, whether there has been an increased burden on government support programs. This list is not exhaustive, nor can one or several of these factors necessarily give decisive guidance.

15.5   It must be demonstrated that the *subsidized imports* are, through the effects of subsidies, causing injury within the meaning of this Agreement. The demonstration of a causal relationship between the subsidized imports and the injury to the domestic industry shall be based on an examination of all relevant evidence before the authorities. The authorities shall also examine any known factors other than the subsidized imports which at the same time are injuring the domestic industry, and the injuries caused by these other factors must not be attributed to the subsidized imports. Factors which may be relevant in this respect include, *inter alia,* the volumes and prices of non-subsidized imports of the product in question, contraction in demand or changes in the patterns of consumption, trade restrictive practices of and competition between the foreign and domestic producers, developments in technology and the export performance and productivity of the domestic industry.[29]

The Panel noted that under Article 15.3, the existence of imports simultaneously subject to CVD investigations from multiple countries is a pre-condition to cumulation under that Article. Article 15.3 does not address or regulate "cross-cumulation of the effects of subsidized imports with the effects of non-subsidized, dumped imports."

The Panel further noted that Articles 15:1, 15:2, 15.4, and 15:5 of the *SCM Agreement,* as well as GATT Article VI:6(a), each refers consistently to "subsidized imports," and that Article VI:6(a), which concerns both AD duties and CVDs, refers to "effects of the dumping or subsidization, as the case may be" when addressing injury, with no reference to the effects of the subsidy and dumping cumulatively. The Panel observed the Appellate Body Reports in *EC—Tube or Pipe Fittings* and *U.S.—Oil Country Tubular Goods Sunset Reviews,* cited by the United States in support of its position, "addressed the rationale for cumulation of the effects of dumped imports from several sources, but did not address the issue of cross-cumulation of the effects of dumped and subsidized imports."

---

29. Footnotes omitted.

In its analysis, the Panel considered "the main question to be whether the use of the term 'subsidized imports' in these provisions [Articles 15:1, 15:2, 15:4 and 15:5] limits the scope of the investigating authority's injury assessment to subsidized imports only." The Panel observed that under U.S. law,[30] the ITC in certain circumstances is required "to cumulate the effects of subsidized imports with the effects of dumped, non-subsidized imports." In the case at bar, the ITC cumulated the effects of subsidized imports from India with non-subsidized dumped imports from 6 other WTO Members that were subject only to parallel AD (but not CVD) investigations.

- **Significant Indian Appellate Victory**

The Appellate Body initially observed Article 15:3 refers to imports "simultaneously subject to countervailing duty investigations," permitting cumulation of such imports if the other conditions of Article 15.3 are met. It said "[t]he text is clear in stipulating that being subject to countervailing duty investigations is a prerequisite for the cumulative assessment of the effects of imports under Article 15:3." The Appellate Body suggested its finding in *EC—Bed Linen (Article 21.5—India)*, concerning zeroing in AD cases, was analogous to the *Carbon Steel* case of subsidized imports:

> It is clear from the text of Article 3:1 [of the WTO *Antidumping Agreement*] that investigating authorities must ensure that a 'determination of injury' is made on the basis of 'positive evidence' and an 'objective examination' of the volume and effect of imports that are dumped—and to the exclusion of the volume and effect of imports that are not dumped.

The Appellate Body concluded "Article 15:3 and Articles 15:1, 15:2, 15:4, and 15:5 of the *SCM Agreement* require that the injury analysis in the context of a countervailing duty determination be limited to consideration of the effects of subsidized imports." In other words, cumulation among subject merchandise in CVD cases was permissible, but cross-cumulation of subject merchandise in CVD and AD cases was illegal.

In further rebutting the American contentions, the Appellate Body questioned the U.S. reliance on *Tube or Pipe Fittings* and *Oil Country Tubular Goods*, saying those cases were not relevant. The Appellate Body pointed out the rationale of those cases "provides no basis for including non-subsidized imports within a cumulative assessment of the effects of subsidized imports from several countries in a countervailing duty investigation pursuant to Article 15 of the *SCM Agreement*." Moreover, although the U.S. argued "Article 15 must allow an investigating authority to take account of the effects that all unfairly traded imports are having on a domestic industry," the Appellate Body noted in rejecting that contention that "the phrase 'unfairly traded products' or similar language is not used in Article 15 of the *SCM Agreement*." So, there is no authority in Article 15 for an investigating authority to

---

30. 19 U.S.C. § 1677(7)(G).

"consider a single group of unfairly traded imports, rather than imports simultaneously subject to countervailing duty investigations."

This victory for India was significant. The Appellate Body found the Panel did not err in respect of its cross-cumulation holding. To be sure, it also found the Panel failed to comply with its duty under *DSU* Article 11 to make an objective assessment of the matter, when the Panel held the U.S. CVD statute was inconsistent "as such" with *SCM Agreement* Article 15. But, the Appellate Body went on to complete the analysis and found that the relevant provisions of the U.S. Code was inconsistent "as such" with Article 15. India had successfully challenged a key feature — cross-cumulation — of American trade remedy law.

Finally, the Appellate Body interpreted GATT Article VI:6(a), which provides:

> No contracting party shall levy any anti-dumping or countervailing duty on the importation of any product of the territory of another contracting party unless it determines that the effect of the dumping or subsidization, as the case may be, is such as to cause or threaten material injury to an established domestic industry, or is such as to retard materially the establishment of a domestic industry.

The U.S. relied on the Article VI:6(a) language "as the case may be" to justify its conclusion that the unfair trade practices covered in an injury determination by an administering authority could involve dumping, subsidization or both. The Appellate Body (supporting the Panel) disagreed. Rightly so, as the argument defied a common sense reading of Article VI:6(a). The Appellate Body said the disjunctive "or" in the phrase "dumping or subsidization" means the language "as the case may be" clarifies that injury may be caused either by dumping or subsidization (but not both). So, the Appellate Body upheld the Panel and rejected the U.S. cross-appeal.

Chapter 20

Proving Causation (Continued): American Jurisprudence[1]

I. "By Reason Of" and But-For Causation in American AD-CVD Law, and 2018 *Changhzhou Trina Solar Energy* Case

Causation jurisprudence in respect of AD and CVD determinations is more sophisticated in the U.S. than at the WTO level. That is true notwithstanding the statutory causation language is the generic, ambiguous phrase "by reason of" in 19 U.S.C. Sections 1671d(b) and 1673d(b). Or, perhaps, it is because of that ambiguity.

American judges have done what WTO Panels and the Appellate Body have failed to do: they have written crisp, clear, and brief opinions on the complex question of causation. Their considered judgments have elaborated on what "by reason of" means, thus yielding a body of common law to guide future petitioners and respondents in trade remedy cases. It means but-for causation.

So, consider the 2013 AD case of *Swiff-Train Co. v. United States*, which involved dumping of multi-layered wood flooring from China. The CIT remanded to the ITC for it to re-evaluate its final affirmative injury determination that American wood flooring countries were materially injured by reason of subject merchandise. Why? Because, said the CIT, the ITC failed to take account of the teaching of the U.S. Supreme Court in *Price Waterhouse v. Hopkins*:[2]

> Our appellate courts have explained that the "by reason of" language requires application of the "but-for" legal causation standard . . . .
>
> . . .
>
> [The ITC should] begin by assuming that [subject merchandise was] present [in the domestic market] at the time of [the POI], and then ask

---

   (1) *Havana (ITO) Charter* Article 34
   (2) GATT Articles VI, XVI
   (3) WTO *Antidumping Agreement* Article 3
   (4) WTO *SCM Agreement* Articles 1, 3, 5–6, 8, 15
2. *See* 490 U.S. 228, 240 (1989).

whether even if [subject merchandise] had been absent, [the performance of the domestic industry] would have transpired the same way.[3]

Such professional work of American judges contrasts with the monstrously long, endlessly repetitive WTO Panel and Appellate Body Reports. Through them, dedicated readers must trudge in a nearly vain search for a simple, workable causation test.

That is not to say the American decisions have been unproblematic. Every causation case, whether in the United States or at the WTO, produces more questions. But, the level of uncertainty, not to mention frustration, is far worse with the latter forum.

II. One or Two Steps and 1996
United States Steel Case

United States Steel Group v. United States,

United States Court of Appeals for the Federal Circuit,
96 F.3d 1352, 1355–1356, 1359–1362 (1996)

CLEVENGER, CIRCUIT JUDGE:

I.

On June 30, 1992, a group of United States steel companies [led by Bethlehem Steel Corporation] filed a petition with the International Trade Commission alleging that their industry had been harmed by subsidized and "Less Than Fair Value" (LTFV) imports of certain flat-rolled carbon steel products from numerous countries, and seeking the imposition of countervailing and antidumping duties against the subject imports. . . . After affirmative preliminary findings by the Department of Commerce . . . that the imports in question were indeed subsidized or being sold at LTFV, the Commission commenced an investigation to determine whether the imports had caused, or threatened to cause, a material injury to an industry in the United States. . . . In conducting its investigation, the Commission divided the broad category of flat-rolled carbon steel products into four "like products": (1) hot-rolled products; (2) cold-rolled products; (3) corrosion-resistant products; and (4) cut-to-length plate products . . . . The appeals in this case do not question the Commission's categorization of products, but instead concern only the Commission's determinations with respect to the hot-rolled and cold-rolled categories.

The Commission conducted its investigation over a three-year period, 1990–1992. During that period, the Commission collected large amounts of data concerning the

---

3. *See* No. 12-00010 (Slip Opinion 13-38, 20 March 2013).

subject imports including detailed information regarding the imports' value, prices, and volume of shipments. In addition, it collected extensive data on the production, capacity utilization, and inventory levels of foreign producers, and carefully examined the patterns of domestic consumption of the subject imports. On the basis of this data, the Commission made its determinations, the majority of which are not contested on this appeal. Of those that are, the Commission determined that most of the subject hot- and cold-rolled imports had not caused, and did not threaten to cause, material injury to a domestic industry. . . .

. . .

III.

. . .

C.

Bethlehem[] . . . questions the manner in which the Commission, and in this case, Commissioners Brunsdale and Crawford in particular, determine whether an industry in the United States is materially injured or threatened with material injury by reason of subsidized and/or LTFV imports. A review of the relevant statutes puts Bethlehem's argument in context.

> Countervailing and/or antidumping duties may not be imposed on merchandise found to be subsidized and/or dumped unless:
>
> . . . the Commission determines that—
>
> (A)   an industry in the United States—
>
>> (i)   is materially injured, or
>>
>> (ii)   is threatened with material injury
>
> . . .
>
> by reason of imports of that merchandise.

19 U.S.C. § 1671(a)(2) . . . (for subsidized merchandise); 19 U.S.C. § 1673(2) . . . (for LTFV merchandise). With respect to both subsidized and LTFV imports, "material injury" is defined as "harm which is not inconsequential, immaterial, or unimportant." 19 U.S.C. § 1677(7)(A) . . . .

The Commission makes its determinations by tallying the votes of the six individual commissioners, each of whom is obligated to determine whether particular imports cause or threaten to cause the requisite harm. [A sometimes overlooked fact that obviously weighs in favor of industries seeking protection is the following: in the event the ITC is equally divided, *i.e.*, a 3–3 vote, its injury determination (or any review thereof) is deemed affirmative. *See* 19 U.S.C. § 1677(11).] Congress has not left the commissioners at sea in the performance of their individual, and ultimately collective, duties. Instead, Congress has supplied the analytical tools, in the form of statutory tests, some of which must be applied and some of which may be applied before the Commission, acting through its commissioners, arrives at its measurement of the causal effects of particular imports. The statutory tests are many, and specific; in each case, the Commission:

(i) shall consider —

(I) the volume of imports of the merchandise which is the subject of the investigation,

(II) the effect of imports of that merchandise on prices in the United State for like products, and

(III) the impact of imports of such merchandise on domestic producers of like products, but only in the context of production operations within the United States; and

(ii) may consider such other economic factors as are relevant to the determination regarding whether there is material injury by reason of imports. . . .

19 U.S.C. § 1677(7)(B) . . . .

These three general tests are further refined explicitly in the statute. With regard to volume of imports, "the Commission shall consider whether the volume of imports of the merchandise, or any increase in that volume, either in absolute terms or relative to production of consumption in the United States, is significant." 19 U.S.C. § 1677(7)(c)(i) . . . . Concerning the effect of imports on price, the Commission must consider whether:

(I) there has been significant price under-selling by the imported merchandise as compared with the price of like products of the United States, and

(II) the effects of imports of such merchandise otherwise depresses prices to a significant degree or prevents price increases, which otherwise would have occurred, to a significant degree.

19 U.S.C. § 1677(7)(c)(ii) . . . .

When considering the impact of LTFV or subsidized imports on the state of the domestic industry, the specific commands made on the Commission by Congress are even more detailed:

In examining the impact required to be considered under subparagraph (B)(iii), the Commission shall evaluate all relevant economic factors which have a bearing on the state of the industry in the United States, including, but not limited to —

(I) actual and potential decline in output, sales, market share, profits, productivity, return on investments, and utilization of capacity,

(II) factors affecting domestic prices,

(III) actual and potential negative effects on cash flow, inventories, employment, wages, growth, ability to raise capital, and investment, and

(IV) actual and potential negative effects on the existing development and production efforts of the domestic industry, including efforts to develop a derivative or more advanced version of the like product.

The Commission shall evaluate all relevant economic factors described in this clause within the context of the business cycle and conditions of competition that are distinctive to the affected industry.

19 U.S.C. § 1677(7)(c)(iii) . . . . [As a result of the 1994 *Uruguay Round Agreements Act*, a fifth factor was added to this non-exclusive list: the magnitude of the dumping margin. *See* 19 U.S.C. § 1677(7)(c)(iii)(V).] Furthermore, . . . each commissioner is free to determine whether or not to exclude from the material injury analysis imports from countries deemed negligible. We note this additional factor simply to underscore the complicated . . . statutory tests that must or may be employed by each Commissioner in deciding whether the causal effects of particular imports support imposition of countervailing or antidumping duties.

Over the course of years, differing commissioners have employed differing methodologies to reach their conclusions on the extent to which LTFV and/or subsidized imports have harmed, or threatened to harm, domestic industries. . . . [T]he differing methodologies are described as the "one-step" and the "two-step" analyses. Under the one-step analysis, a Commissioner assesses in a unitary process both the current state of the domestic industry and whether that state is materially injured by reason of LTFV or subsidized imports. Under the two-step analysis, a commissioner first assesses the state of the relevant domestic industry. If the assessment produces a conclusion that the industry is materially injured, then the analysis proceeds to its second step, which is the separate inquiry asking whether the pertinent imports contribute in a non-*de minimis* way to such material injury. Over time, some Commissioners have opted for one of these methodologies, and others have preferred the second analytical tool. And in some instances, as with Commissioner Watson in this case, the commissioner simply recites the statutory language, without specifying which of the one- or two-step analyses, or some other analytical construct, has been used to assist the Commissioner in fulfilling the statutory requirements.

In this case, Commissioners Brunsdale and Crawford used the one-step analysis in reaching their determinations on material injury. According to Bethlehem, their use of the one-step analysis is forbidden by the relevant statutes, and the two-step method used by the other Commissioners in this case must be determined, by this Court, to be the only statutorily permitted tool of analysis for rendering material injury determinations. Bethlehem begins with the premise that the statutes require a determination of material injury whenever imports contribute in a non-*de minimis* way to further injury to a domestic industry. Since some Commissioners have characterized the effect of the two-step analysis in this manner, Bethlehem urges us to read the two-step analysis into the statute as the only permissible way to assess material injury. Bethlehem argues that the one-step method of analysis violates the statute because it necessarily requires a greater quantum of impact from imports on a domestic industry, in order to find material injury or threatened material injury, than would use of the two-step test. Bethlehem argues that the outcome of this case could change if we were to impose the two-step test on Commissioners Brunsdale and Crawford since it is possible that under the two-step test, they might assess the material injury aspect of the imports differently. Given the votes of other Commissioners in this case, additional votes of material injury could tip the scale in Bethlehem's favor.

Bethlehem advanced the same argument in the Court of International Trade, seeking to characterize the difference of modes of analysis of various commissioners as fundamentally different statutory interpretations. The Court of International Trade rejected that characterization, and instead held that the methods of analysis are simply that, and neither fails to comport with the statutory commands setting forth the manner in which the Commission is to dice a record to reach a material injury determination. Judge Restani, for the Court of International Trade, correctly noted that the two-step method has the virtue of some decision-making efficiencies, but that the statute by its terms does not mandate it as the only method of analysis. She also, rightly, noted that "[t]he statutory language fits very well with a one-step mode of analysis." . . . This is so, in part at least, because of the awkwardness of reading the statute to say that material injury *must* be determined in every case by asking, as Judge Restani put it, "if such imports were a non-*de minimis* contributing cause of the state of the 'materially injured industry.'" . . .

At bottom, Bethlehem seeks a ruling from this court that there should be a single methodology, applicable to each of the Commissioners, for determining whether a domestic industry is injured, or threatened with injury, by reason of subsidized and/or LTFV imports. The statute on its face compels no such uniform methodology, and we are not persuaded that we should create one, even were we so empowered.

Congress has crafted an intricate statute, and committed its enforcement to the Department of Commerce and the International Trade Commission. Congress has populated the Commission with six independent commissioners, each confirmed to office by the United States Senate. As Bethlehem candidly and commendably notes in its brief, commissioners are free to attach different weight to the various statutory tests which they are required to employ when evaluating the presence or threat of injury. Also, Bethlehem notes and does not challenge the indisputable proposition that each commissioner is free to attach different weight to factual information bearing on, and determinate of, the many statutory tests; and that commissioners may ultimately reach different factual conclusions on the same record. In the end, of course, the factual conclusions of each commissioner will drive the legal conclusion he or she reaches, namely, whether the requisite injury has been shown. The invitation to employ such diversity in methodologies is inherent in the statutes themselves, given the variety of the considerations to be undertaken and the lack of any Congressionally mandated procedure or methodology for assessment of the statutory tests.

This court has no independent authority to tell the Commission how to do its job. We can only direct the Commission to follow the dictates of its statutory mandate. So long as the Commission's analysis does not violate any statute and is not otherwise arbitrary and capricious, the Commission may perform its duties in the way it believes most suitable. Because we do not believe that the statute compels the commissioners to employ either the one-step or two-step approaches, we disagree with Bethlehem that Commissioners Brunsdale and Crawford employed a causation standard which was contrary to law, and therefore decline to reverse the Commission on this ground.

III. 2006 *Bratsk* Replacement-Benefit Test in American AD Law

Easily the significant and intriguing American judicial opinion on causation in the last few decades concerns the so-called "Replacement-Benefit Test" in the 2006 *Bratsk* case, issued by the Federal Circuit.[4]

- *Bratsk* **Facts**

On 7 March 2002, Globe Metallurgical Inc. and several union groups filed an AD petition with the ITC DOC.[5] Silicon metal is a commodity, so:

> it is interchangeable, regardless of its source. Therefore, price is the primary consideration for purchasers of silicon metal. The market for silicon metal consists of three segments: chemical, primary aluminum, and secondary aluminum. During the pertinent time period there were ten countries, other than the United States, which supplied silicon metal to the U.S. market: Argentina, Brazil, Canada, China, Korea, Norway, Russia, Saudi Arabia, South Africa, and Spain.[6]

The petitioners alleged Russian imports of silicon metal were being sold in the United States at LTFV, and that these LTFV sales had materially injured the domestic

---

4. *Bratsk Aluminum Smelter v. United States*, 444 F.3d 1369, 1372 (Fed. Cir. 2006). [Hereinafter, *Bratsk*.]

The convention in American legal citation is that if the American government is the appellant, the case name says "United States," but if it is the appellee, the acronym "U.S." is used. In keeping with the general convention of this treatise, "United States" is used throughout.

5. This discussion draws on John Foote, *Making Sense of Bratsk: Navigating the Federal Circuit's Creative New Approach to Causation in Antidumping Cases*, Paper for *Advanced International Trade Law*, University of Kansas School of (May 2008) (unpublished manuscript, on file with author); Memorandum from Devin S. Sikes to Raj Bhala, *Bratsk v. United States: A New Standard of Causation in Antidumping Cases?* (30 August 2007, on file with author). *See also* Devin S. Sikes, *The Need for New Causation Standards in Antidumping, Countervailing Duty & Safeguard Actions*, 7 MANCHESTER JOURNAL OF INTERNATIONAL ECONOMIC LAW 39–55 (2010) (critically analyzing and suggesting reforms to causation standards in American trade remedy law).

6. *Bratsk*, 444 F.3d 1369, 1372.

industry producing a like product, *i.e.*, American silicon metal producers. The subject merchandise was imported from Russia into the United States by five American companies: (1) Bratsk Aluminum Smelter, (2) Rual Trade Limited, (3) General Electric Silicones, (4) Saul Holding, and (5) Zao Kremny.[7] At the time of the case, Russia was not a Member of the WTO, and was treated by the DOC as a NME.

On 11 February 2003, the DOC rendered a final affirmative dumping margin determination, stating the subject merchandise was, or was likely to be, sold at LTFV, *i.e.*, dumped. On 24 March 2003, the ITC gave a final affirmative injury determination—and, concomitantly, causation analysis—that the domestic industry was materially injured by reason of the dumped imports. The ITC POI was three years, 1999, 2000, and 2001. Obviously, the American importers of subject merchandise, as well as the Russian producer-exporters of it, were not happy.

The ITC based its final injury determination by considering the standard 3 factors required by the American AD statute (19 U.S.C. Sections 1673d(b)) and 1677(7)(B) (i), (c), namely the (1) volume of subject merchandise imports, (2) effect on domestic prices of subject merchandise, and (3) impact of subject merchandise on domestic producers. The ITC found subject merchandise import volume was significant and increased during the POI. Domestic silicon metal producers lost market share during that POI, but the domestic industry was not in a position to satisfy more than a portion of American silicon demand.

As regards price effect, the ITC found that during the POI, subject merchandise "almost always undersold the domestic product . . . ." It also found that Russian silicon metal (the subject merchandise) was priced lower than non-subject imports. So, the ITC said price depression occurred:

> [I]in light of subject imports' increasing volumes and their significant underselling of, and high substitutability with, both domestic and non-subject silicon metal, we find significant price depression by the subject imports.[8]

Notably, in discussing price depression, the ITC also:

> recognized that non-subject imports [*i.e.*, imports of like merchandise not subject to the AD investigation] may have had an independent price depressive effect on domestic silicon metal prices. However, given the significant underselling by subject imports [*i.e.*, the merchandise from Russia under investigation], subject import volume surges during the period of investigation (POI), and the high degree of substitutability between subject

---

7. On 6 December 2004, 3 of the importers, Bratsk, Rual, and General Electric, filed a voluntary notice of dismissal on 6 December 2004, and thus were not parties to the appeal to the CIT. However, the 2 remaining importers, Sual Holding and Zao Kremny, continued the litigation, and the rubric from "Bratsk" attached to the case throughout.

8. *Quoted in Bratsk*, 444 F.3d 1369, 1372–1373.

imports and the domestic product, . . . the subject imports themselves . . .
significantly depressed domestic silicon metal prices . . . .[9]

As for the third variable, the impact of subject merchandise on American silicon
metal producers, the ITC easily found it was significantly adverse. The domestic
industry had lost market share, and it had had to close or convert to other uses some
of its silicon metal furnaces. To be sure, the ITC recognized the "domestic industry
lost [some of its] market share to non-subject imports, as well," but concluded:

> [R]egardless of the impact of non-subject imports on the domestic
> industry, . . . surges in subject import volume at prices that undersold and
> depressed domestic silicon metal prices to a significant degree during the
> POI had a material adverse impact on the domestic industry.[10]

Mention of non-subject imports by the ITC in its above-quoted causation passages
triggered litigation in the CIT, located in New York, and in the Federal Circuit,
located in Washington, D.C., known as *Bratsk Aluminum Smelter v. United States*
(*Bratsk*), culminating in a 2006 opinion from the Federal Circuit.[11] That opinion led
to more litigation, namely, *Mittal Steel Point Lisas Ltd. v. United States* (*Mittal Steel*),
a 2008 decision from the Federal Circuit.[12]

- **Novel Causation Argument?**

In the *Bratsk* case, the importers of Russian silicon metal, Saul and Zao, appealed
the decision of the ITC to the CIT. These Appellants argued the causation standard
set by the Federal Circuit in its 1997 decision, *Gerald Metals, Inc. v. United States*
(*Gerald Metals*) required:

> a specific determination as to whether the non-subject imports would sim-
> ply replace the subject imports, with the same impact on domestic prod-
> ucts, if the subject imports were excluded from the market.[13]

In other words, Saul and Zao said the ITC, in its causation analysis, should have
engaged in the following counter-factual inquiry:

> Suppose there were no subject merchandise imports. That would hap-
> pen if an AD order were imposed on subject merchandise. The AD duty
> on subject merchandise would impede the access of that merchandise into
> the American market, and maybe even knock it out of the market entirely.
> After all, the AD duty, on top of the normal most-favored nation (MFN)
> rate, will mean subject merchandise will be more expensive to domestic
> consumers than before.

---

9. *Quoted in Bratsk*, 444. F.3d 1369, 1373.

10. *Quoted in Bratsk*, 444. F.3d 1369, 1373.

11. *See Bratsk*, 444 F.3d 1369.

12. *See Mittal Steel Point Lisas Ltd. v. United States*, 542 F.3d 867, 30 International Trade
Reporter Decisions (ITRD) 1449–1458 (Fed. Cir. 2008). [Hereinafter, *Mittal Steel*.]

13. *See Gerald Metals, Inc. v. United States*, 132 F. 3d 716 (Fed. Cir. 1997).

But, the AD order is not the point. Whether an AD duty is effective or not, is not something we at the ITC are permitted by statute to consider.

What we are supposed to consider is this: if there were no subject merchandise, for whatever reason (such as it was sold at a non-dumped price, or it was not sold at all), would those buyers switch to other imports? That is, would merchandise from overseas that was not subject to an AD investigation (non-subject merchandise) simply replace the subject merchandise? If so, then would domestic producers of a like product be injured by the non-subject merchandise?

Suppose the answer to both questions in "yes." Then, we cannot say the subject merchandise caused the injury. We also might speculate an AD order would serve no purpose, but again, that is not the point. What is the point is the void created by the absence of dumped imports from the American market would have been filled by non-subject, and presumably non-dumped, imports.

In that scenario, the true cause of the woes of the domestic industry would not have been dumped subject merchandise, because even if it never existed in the first place, that industry would not have been able to compete with fairly priced foreign competition. So, it would be unjust to impose an AD order on subject merchandise, because it did not cause the injury. It would be like sending a man to prison for a crime he did not commit. Only if the answer to both questions is 'no' would it be true that the dumped merchandise caused injury, *i.e.*, would the man be guilty.

(The quotation is a hypothetical one constructed to state the argument in colloquial terms.) However, the ITC engaged in no such inquiry. Therein lay the problem.

In the Federal Circuit opinion in *Bratsk*, Judge Dyk stated: "[The ITC] dismissed our decision in *Gerald Metals* as being factually distinguishable."[14] That is, in its injury determination, the ITC never applied the 1997 *Gerald Metals* causation test, believing it to be inapposite. The CIT rejected the Appellant argument about causation, and remanded the case to the ITC on an unrelated issue. The ITC issued a remanded decision, which on 3 December 2004 the CIT affirmed in its entirety (hence including the ITC causation analysis).

Thus, at the trial court level, the causation claim, perhaps somewhat of a novel one, or perhaps one well-grounded on precedent, made by the Appellants was unsuccessful. Naturally, they appealed to the Federal Circuit.

- *Bratsk* Replacement-Benefit Test

Writing the *Bratsk* decision on behalf of the Federal Circuit, Judge Dyk pinpointed the issue: "the sole point of contention in this appeal is whether the Commission established that the injury to the domestic injury was 'by reason of' the

---

14. *Bratsk*, 444 F.3d 1369, 1373.

subject imports."[15] Squarely before the Court, then, was the question of causation: did Russian imports of silicon metal actually cause injury to American producers of that commodity, and what is the proper test for causation in the first place? But, given the facts of the case, that question really was about whether an additional causation inquiry—the one from *Gerald Metals*, namely, the Replacement-Benefit Test—was needed.

The Court succinctly summarized its jurisprudence on causation from the 1997 *Gerald Metals* case, plus the 2001 *Taiwan Semiconductor* and 2003 *Nippon Steel* cases (cited in the passage quoted below), namely:

> "An affirmative injury determination requires both (1) present material injury and (2) a finding that the material injury is '*by reason of*' the subject imports." *Gerald Metals, Inc.*, 132 F.3d at 719 (emphasis added [by Court]). We have previously explained that the "by reason of" requirement "mandates a showing of causal—not merely temporal—connection between the LTFV goods and the material injury." *Id.* at 720. We have not required the [International Trade] Commission to employ any particular methodology for determining whether this causation element has been met, and the "Commission need not isolate the injury caused by other factors from injury caused by unfair imports . . . ." *Taiwan Semiconductor Industry v. Int'l Trade Comm'n*, 266 F.3d 1339, 1345 (Fed. Cir. 2001) (quoting legislative history of the Uruguay Round Agreements Act); *see also Nippon Steel Corp. v. Int'l Trade Comm'n*, 345 F.3d 1381 (Fed. Cir. 2003) ("'Dumping' need not be the sole or principal cause of injury"). However, we have made clear that causation is not shown if the subject imports contributed only "minimally or tangentially to the material harm." *Gerald Metals*, 132 F. 3d at 722 . . . .[16]

In brief, the Federal Circuit took the position that the AD statute did not compel any uniform causation methodology, and consistently declined to create or impose one (which, in any event, would be the role of Congress).

But, the Federal Circuit then said in the silicon metals investigation, the ITC causation analysis was insufficiently detailed to comply with the test the Court set forth in *Gerald Metals*. So, the CIT erred in affirming the ITC injury determination and agreeing subject merchandise caused the injury. The key language of the *Bratsk* decision was this holding:

> [Under the causation standard of *Gerald Metals*,] [w]here commodity products are at issue and fairly traded, price competitive, non-subject imports are in the market, the [International Trade] Commission must explain *why the elimination of subject imports would benefit the domestic industry instead of resulting in the non-subject imports' replacement of the subject imports' market share without any beneficial impact on the domestic producers.*

---

15. *Bratsk*, 444 F.3d 1369, 1373.
16. *Bratsk*, 444 F. 3d. 1369, 1374 (emphasis original, footnote omitted).

. . .

. . . *Gerald Metals* did not, of course, establish a *per se* rule barring a finding of causation where the product is a commodity product and there are fairly traded imports priced below the domestic product. However, under *Gerald Metals*, the Commission is required to make a specific causation determination and in that connection to directly address [*sic*] *whether non-subject imports would have replaced the subject imports without any beneficial effect on domestic producers.*

. . .

In short, the Commission's summary finding of material injury is insufficiently detailed to comply with the requirements of *Gerald Metals*. We therefore vacate and remand the Court of International Trade's decision so that it may remand the case back to the Commission to specifically address [*sic*] *whether the non-subject imports would have replaced subject imports during the period of investigation.*

In ordering reconsideration by the Commission, *we do not suggest that the mere existence of fairly traded commodity imports at competitive prices precludes the Commission from finding material injury.* For example, it may well be that non-subject importers lack capacity to replace the subject imports or that the price of the non-subject imports is sufficiently above the subject imports such that the elimination of the subject imports would have benefited the domestic industry. *The point is that the Commission has to explain, in a meaningful way, why the non-subject imports would not replace the subject imports and continue to cause injury to the domestic industry.*[17]

In effect, the Federal Circuit called for exactly the counterfactual inquiry the Appellants sought. Under *Gerald Metals*, the ITC is required to make an additional specific causation determination that addresses directly whether non-subject imports would have replaced the subject imports without any beneficial effect on domestic producers. As indicated earlier, this inquiry sometimes is called the "Replacement-Benefit Test."

Of course, the *Bratsk* Court was careful to align its holding with its *Gerald Metals* precedent, so as not to appear that it was creating a new causation test. Only Congress had the power to legislate a new test under the AD statute.

- **Bratsk in Line with 1997 *Gerald Metals* and 2001 *Taiwan Semiconductor* Precedents**

So, in *Bratsk*, the Federal Circuit noted the *Gerald Metals* causation standard, *i.e.*, the Replacement-Benefit Test, is not limited to situations in which non-subject imports increase during the POI. Rather:

---

17. *Bratsk*, 444 F.3d 1369, 1374, 1375–1376, 1377 (emphasis added).

the obligation under *Gerald Metals* is triggered whenever the *antidumping investigation* is centered on a *commodity product*, and price competitive non-subject imports are a significant factor in the market.[18]

Yet, this language is not entirely expansive. Rather, it sets boundaries on the instances in which a causation inquiry about non-subject imports is necessary: only in an AD investigation, and only if the subject merchandise is a commodity product. Under *Bratsk*, that inquiry is unnecessary in a CVD investigation, or in an AD case in which subject merchandise is not a commodity product.

In *Gerald Metals*, the subject merchandise was Ukrainian imports of pure magnesium.[19] The DOC determined they were dumped. The ITC said they materially injured American magnesium producers. At play was non-subject merchandise, namely, fairly-traded imported magnesium from Russia. Yet, the ITC failed to consider whether the Russian imports would have replaced all or most of the subject imports, in the event an AD order were imposed on the Ukrainian merchandise.

In dissent, three ITC Commissioners said the presence of the non-subject imports undermined the causation determination of the Commission.[20] (Though there are 6 Commissioners, in the event of a 3–3 tie, a decision favors the petitioner, hence the final affirmative injury ITC determination.) The dissenting Commissioners said Russian non-subject magnesium was a perfect substitute for the Ukrainian magnesium subject to the AD investigation. Like the Ukrainian magnesium, Russian magnesium often undersold American magnesium.

In *Gerald Metals*, the CIT acknowledged the ITC did not examine the question of substitutability of non-subject imports for subject merchandise in the event an AD order were imposed. Nevertheless, the CIT affirmed the ITC determination. The Federal Circuit vacated the CIT decision, concluding:

> [T]he [International Trade] Commission must "'take[] into account contradictory evidence or evidence from which conflicting inferences could be drawn.'" [*Gerald Metals*,], 132 F.3d at 720 (*quoting Universal Camera Corp. v. NLRB, 340 U.S. 474, 487, 71 S.Ct. 456, 95 L.Ed. 456 (1951)). Given that the fairly-traded non-subject imports were substitutable for the Ukrainian subject imports and undersold the domestic product just as the subject imports had*, we held that the Commission must explain, in its analysis of the harm caused by the subject imports, *why domestic consumers would not have purchased the fairly traded non-subject imports. See id.* at 718, 720, 721–23.[21]

So, the Federal Circuit positioned its 2006 *Bratsk* opinion essentially as applying the precedent it set in 1997 in *Gerald Metals*.

---

18. *Bratsk*, 444 F.3d 1369, 1374 (emphasis added).
19. *Bratsk*, 444 F.3d 1369, 1374–1375.
20. *Bratsk*, 444 F.3d 1369, 1375 (emphasis added, footnote omitted).
21. *Bratsk*, 444 F.3d 1369, 1374–1375.

Further, in the 2001 *Taiwan Semiconductor* case, the Federal Circuit explained that while *Gerald Metals* was an AD decision before the *Uruguay Round Agreements Act* took effect on 1 January 1995 implementing the WTO treaties, neither the *Act* nor those treaties altered the causation standard. So, in *Taiwan Semiconductor*, the Federal Circuit again applied the *Gerald Metals* reasoning, this time to an AD investigation of static random access memory chips from Taiwan. They were sold at LTFV, but the ITC rendered a final negative determination, saying the volume of subject merchandise, and increases in that volume, were insufficient to prove that this merchandise materially contributed to any injury experienced by American SRAM producers:

> In particular, the [International Trade] Commission found that non-subject Korean imports of SRAMs were, like the subject imports, priced lower than the domestic product, and were at times priced lower than the subject imports as well. . . . [*Taiwan Semiconductor*, 266 F.3d 1339 (Fed. Cir. 2001)] at 1347. We affirmed the Commission's determination, noting that "substantial evidence supports the fact that the United States market share was impacted largely by non-subject imports," and that "in *Gerald Metals*, as in this [*Taiwan Semiconductor*] case, the record did not show that the subject imports caused the material injury in light of the dominant presence of non-subject imports in the marketplace." *Id.* at 1345–46, 1347.[22]

From the *Gerald Metals* precedent and its *Taiwan Semiconductor* progeny, the Federal Circuit in *Bratsk* inferred that an increase in the volume of subject merchandise, even at prices below the domestic like product, and even attended by a decline in the domestic share of the product market, is not enough to show causation of injury or threat thereof.

• *Bratsk* **Rationale**

Why did the *Bratsk* Court think the Replacement-Benefit Test was needed? Essentially, because the same conditions at play in *Gerald Metals* and *Taiwan Semiconductor* were at play in *Bratsk*. Silicon metal was interchangeable, regardless of where produced, as was magnesium in *Gerald Metals* and SRAMs in *Taiwan Semiconductor*. Non-subject imports were present in the American market, and a significant factor therein, in all three cases. Indeed, in *Bratsk*, as a percentage of total imports by volume, non-subject imports of silicon metal were high: they equaled 79.6%, 82.6%, and 73.0% in the 1999, 2000, and 2001 POI years. Generally, the non-subject silicon metal from Brazil, Canada, Saudi Arabia, and South Africa undersold American silicon metal during the POI, as did the subject merchandise from Russia:

> These circumstances suggest that the elimination of the subject imports from the domestic market might simply have increased the market share of the non-subject imports. *Gerald Metals thus requires the [International Trade] Commission to explain why — notwithstanding the presence and*

---

22. *Bratsk*, 444 F.3d 1369, 1375.

significance of the non-subject imports—it concluded that the subject imports caused material injury to the domestic industry. While there may be support for the Commission's ultimate determination of material injury in the record here, we find that the Commission did not sufficiently explain its decision in this regard.

. . .

. . . The Commission . . . attempted to support the link between subject imports and the domestic injury by pointing out that after subject imports were withdrawn from the market in 2002 following the Department of Commerce's preliminary [affirmative dumping margin] determination, silicon spot prices increased and prices for eleven domestic contracts increased during the fourth quarter of 2002. That spot prices may have increased after the Russian imports exited the market may be pertinent to the causation question, but that fact does not excuse the Commission's failure to address directly the causation issue in detail as required by *Gerald Metals.* The Commission did not explain how much the spot prices increased, the significance of that increase, or the significance of the eleven contracts for the domestic market.[23]

In sum, the ITC causation analysis was incomplete and sloppy.

Worse yet, it also was disrespectful. The *Bratsk* Court was particularly irritated with the ITC for its disrespect of *Gerald Metals,* deeming it to have no precedential value. The Federal Circuit rebuked the ITC for circumscribing *Gerald Metals* to unique facts distinguishable from those in *Bratsk,* namely, an increase in the volume of non-subject imports and a steady or declining volume of subject imports. The Court intoned:

The [International Trade Commission] is obligated to follow the holdings of our cases, not to limit those decisions to their particular facts. The holding of *Gerald Metals* is not limited to situations in which non-subject imports increased during the period of review.[24]

Simply put, the ITC could not write its own rules on causation and ignore the jurisprudence of the judiciary to which it was accountable.

- **What Triggers Replacement-Benefit Test?**

Manifestly, much turns on the definition of "commodity product." In *Bratsk,* the Federal Circuit defined a "commodity product" as one that is "generally interchangeable, regardless of its source."[25] In purchasing such products, "price is the primary consideration."[26] That definition could apply to a range of goods, from bot-

---

23. *Bratsk,* 444 F.3d 1369, 1376 (emphasis added).
24. *Bratsk,* 444 F.3d 1369, 1375.
25. *Bratsk,* 444 F.3d 1369, 1372.
26. *Bratsk,* 444 F.3d 1369, 1372.

tled water and pears to Bibles and hybrid cars. For many consumers of these items, price is the key determinant of their demand, and they do not focus on country of origin.

Or, just the opposite argument can be made under this definition: Evian does not taste like Fiji water; there is a difference between green bosch and red *d'anjou* pears; Catholic and Protestant Bibles do not contain exactly the same books (they differ on the *Apocrypha*); and the Toyota Prius arguably is the best established hybrid car. Perhaps these examples may be dismissed, as they are not "commodities" in the sense of "bulk commodities," so no concern need be given as to whether they are interchangeable. Yet, Taiwan Semiconductor involved SRAMs, which hardly are a commodity on the order of cocoa beans.

Aside from needing a "commodity product," much turns on 2 other factors:

(1) The presence of non-subject imports, and

(2) Their price vis-à-vis the price of a domestic like product.

Obviously, if there is no non-subject merchandise—*e.g.*, if, in *Bratsk*, there had been no silicon metal from countries other than Russia, if in *Taiwan Semiconductor*, there had been no SRAMs from other than Taiwan, and if in *Gerald Metals* there had been no magnesium from other than the Ukraine—then the Replacement-Benefit Test is inapplicable.

Even if there is non-subject merchandise—as in *Bratsk*, with silicon metals from Argentina, Brazil, Canada, China, Korea, Norway, Saudi Arabia, South Africa, and Spain, as in Taiwan Semiconductor, with SRAMs from Korea, and as in *Gerald Metals*, with magnesium from Russia—the Replacement-Benefit Test is inapplicable if that non-subject merchandise is sold at a price in the U.S. higher than the domestically produced like product. That is, only if the non-subject merchandise exists and is sold at a price below the domestic like product does it make sense to apply the Replacement-Benefit Test. That is because only in this scenario is it possible that the cause of materially injury (or threat thereof) to the domestic industry is from fairly-trade, lower-priced foreign competition, as distinct from dumped subject merchandise.

· **Dissent**

If the intention of the Federal Circuit was to restrict the Replacement-Benefit Test, *i.e.*, the special causation analysis about non-subject imports, to bulk commodities, then it did not say so. Moreover, are such commodities truly perfect substitutes? Is there no difference in product characteristics, consumer tastes and preferences, or end uses (to use the WTO Appellate Body test for "like products" from the 1996 *Japan Alcoholic Beverages* case) among these commodities? Perhaps a thought about something supposedly so generic as "crude oil" answers the question. Trying to delineate when a causation test does or does not apply based on the nature of subject merchandise not only complicates a case, but also leads to unsustainable distinctions.

Not surprisingly, these sorts of questions provoked a dissent in *Bratsk*, penned by Senior Judge Archer. He pointed out the pertinent passage in the 1997 *Gerald Metals* case never referenced the term "commodity products." That passage is:

> "We have considered the evidence on non-subject imports in this investigation and find, notwithstanding the presence of non-subject imports, that subject imports themselves caused material injury to the domestic industry and did not simply contribute to the injury in a 'tangential or minimal way.'" *Gerald Metals*, 132 F.3d at 722; *Taiwan Semiconductor Industry Assoc. v. United States*, 266 F.3d 1339, 1344 (Fed. Cir. 2001).[27]

Thus, in dissent, Judge Archer said the judgment of the CIT sustaining the ITC causation analysis should have been affirmed. He argued:

> Neither the statute [19 U.S.C. § 1673d(b)] nor *Gerald Metals* imposes the rigidity in findings or analysis that the majority seems to require. Indeed, the *Gerald Metals* opinion acknowledges the "unique circumstances" in that case. *Gerald Metals*, 132 F.3d at 722.[28]

Judge Archer endorsed the conclusion of the ITC, namely, that:

> the fact that non-subject imports may have contributed to the domestic industry's deterioration, along with subject imports, does not negate our [the ITC's] finding that subject imports themselves had a material adverse impact on the domestic industry.[29]

He did so because he felt there was ample evidence to support that finding:

> . . . the Commission performed the proper [causation] analysis and considered the statutorily enumerated [three] factors. *See* 19 U.S.C. § 1677(7)(B)(i) (2000). It concluded [on the first statutory injury factor, import volume of subject merchandise] that the volume and increase in volume of subject imports, both in absolute terms and relative to apparent domestic consumption and production in the United States, supported a finding of material injury determination. The Commission found that 1) the quantity of subject imports increased overall by 35.8% from 1999 to 2001 and by 38.6% from 2000–2001 (after showing a slight decrease from 1999 to 2000); 2) "the continued increase in subject import volume by 57.6 percent between the interim periods resulted in Russia being the largest single source of silicon metal imports in interim 2002": and 3) from 1999 to 2001 subject imports outpaces all other imports in gaining U.S. market share.
>
> . . .
>
> Given that "price is a key factor in purchasing decisions [to buy silicon metal]," the Commission [in respect of the second statutory injury factor,

---

27. *Quoted in Bratsk*, 444 F.3d 1369, 1379–1380 (dissenting opinion).
28. *Bratsk*, 444 F.3d 1369, 1379 (dissenting opinion).
29. *Quoted in Bratsk*, 444 F.3d 1369, 1379 (dissenting opinion).

price effects on the like domestic product] also concluded that underselling by subject imports supported a material injury determination, "finding that prices have been depressed to a significant degree by the subject imports." Although non-subject goods have at times also undersold the domestic product, the Commission found that purchaser price data "shows that imports from Russia have been priced at lower levels than non-subject imports." Specifically, the Commission noted that imports from Russia undersold South African chemical grade product in all eleven purchaser price comparisons and undersold Brazilian chemical grade product in ten of eleven purchaser price comparisons. . . .

[Hence,] "the subject imports themselves have significantly depressed domestic silicon metal prices in all three consumer segments (*i.e.*, chemical, primary and secondary aluminum customers)."

. . .

As part of its material injury determination [in respect of the third statutory factor, impact on domestic producers of a like product], the Commission specifically addressed the respondents' argument "that there was no causal nexus between subject imports and the injury suffered by the domestic industry because of the presence of interchangeable and readily available non-subject imports." The Commission found that "subject imports registered a 4.8 percentage point market share gain while non-subject imports lost 2.3 percentage points in market share from 2000 to 2001, the same year that the domestic industry suffered an operating loss for the first time during the . . . [POI] and idled, closed, or converted many of its silicon metal production facilities." Specifically, the Commission explained that Russian imports' share of total imports increased from 7.3% in the first quarter of 2001 to 26.2%, 31.4%, and 40.1%, respectively, in the remaining three quarters of 2001. Similarly, Russian imports' share of total imports was 31.5% in the first quarter 2002 and 36.9% in second quarter 2002, before declining to 11.6% in third quarter 2002, following the Commission's and Department of Commerce's preliminary determinations in this investigation. The Commission also observed that by quantity, non-subject import volume increased only by 25.8% from interim 2001 to interim 2002, whereas subject import volume increased by 57.6% during the same period.[30]

Additionally, as quoted above, Judge Archer dissented because he felt the ITC did examine the effect of both subject merchandise and interchangeable non-subject merchandise on the domestic industry.[31] That is, he viewed, contrary to the majority, that the ITC applied the *Gerald Metals* precedent.

---

30. *Bratsk*, 444 F.3d 1369, 1377–1379 (dissenting opinion) (footnote omitted).
31. *Bratsk*, 444 F.3d 1369, 1377–1378, 1380 (dissenting opinion).

In sum, did the majority stretch too far the meaning of *Gerald Metals*? Did it invent in *Bratsk* the Replacement-Benefit Test? Did it do so to admonish the ITC decision not to apply the *Gerald Metals* precedent, whatever it is? The Dissent certainly thought so.

• **Congressional Response**

Some Congressional politicians were concerned about the majority opinion in *Bratsk*. They feared the Federal Circuit had weakened U.S. AD law. Under *Bratsk*, in the causation analysis to support an affirmative material injury or threat determination involving a commodity product, the ITC needed to show fairly-priced non-subject imports would not replace subject merchandise, *i.e.*, put conversely, there would be no beneficial effect for domestic producers of a like product if subject merchandise were excluded from the American market (because non-subject imports would fill the void). This Replacement-Benefit test was an additional causation hurdle to imposing AD relief.

So, in 2008 a trade enforcement measure was introduced into the Senate to reverse the *Bratsk* decision.[32] It was not enacted, and the 2008 *Mittal Steel* decision clarified the *Bratsk* precedent.

IV. Clarifying *Bratsk* in 2008 *Mittal Steel* Case

• *Mittal Steel* **Background**

In the 2008 *Mittal Steel* case, the ITC rendered a final affirmative injury determination that LTFV subject merchandise caused material injury to domestic producers of a like product.[33] The dumped goods were steel wire rod from Trinidad and Tobago. The AD investigation began in August 2001, when American producers of steel wire rod filed petitions with the ITC and DOC. They alleged steel wire rod, not only from Trinidad and Tobago, but also 11 other countries, caused them material injury. The ITC agreed. It also found that LTFV imports from Trinidad and Tobago, in particular, alone caused material injury to the petitioners.

Mittal Steel Point Lisas Ltd. (Mittal Steel, formerly called Caribbean Ispat Ltd.) appealed this determination to the CIT. Mittal Steel argued the ITC wrongly interpreted an AD provision in the 1993 U.S. *Caribbean Basin Economic Recovery Act.*[34] That provision is codified at 19 U.S.C. Section 1677(7)(G)(ii)(III). At issue was whether the provision precludes cumulation of LTFV imports from non-*CBERA* countries with dumped imports from a *CBERA* country, such as Trinidad and Tobago. The CIT said it did. That is, the CIT backed the ITC, saying the ITC was

---

32. *See* Rossella Brevetti, *Ways and Means Trade Enforcement Measure Said to Be Under Discussion*, 25 International Trade Reporter (BNA) 710–711 (15 May 2008).

33. *See Mittal Steel*, 542 F.3d 867, 30 International Trade Reporter Decisions (ITRD) 1449, 1450.

34. *See* Public Law Number 98-67 (5 August 1983). This PTA has been amended on various occasions.

correct the *CBERA* provision bars the ITC from considering the effect of LTFV imports from non-*CBERA* countries when assessing whether subject merchandise from a *CBERA* country, such as Trinidad and Tobago, cause material injury to the U.S.

The Federal Circuit, with Judge Bryson writing for the Court (and no dissent), took a different view.[35] It said the CIT was wrong to conclude the ITC is prohibited from considering the effects of dumped imports from non-*CBERA* countries when studying the subject merchandise from Trinidad and Tobago. So, the Federal Circuit remanded the case for further proceeding. Significantly, it ordered the ITC to take into account its 2006 *Bratsk* decision:

> Based on the decision in *Bratsk*, we instructed the Commission "to make a specific causation determination and in that connection to directly address [*sic*] whether [other LTFV imports and/or fairly traded imports] would have replaced [Trinidad and Tobago's] imports without any beneficial effect on domestic producers. *Caribbean Ispat*, 450 F.3d at 1341 (*quoting Bratsk*, 444 F.3d at 1375).[36]

The Federal Circuit observed:

> In this case [*Mittal Steel*], as in *Bratsk*, the Commission's first final determination "did not specifically address whether Trinidad and Tobago's imports could or would be replaced by other imports so that the domestic industry would not benefit from the removal of Trinidad and Tobago's imports from the U.S. market." *Caribbean Ispat*, 450 F.3d at 1341.[37]

On remand, the ITC found that each of the three statutory material injury factors (specified in 19 U.S.C. Section 1677(7)(B)(i), namely, (1) volume of imports of subject merchandise, (2) price effects of subject merchandise on the domestic like product, and (3) impact of subject merchandise on domestic producers of the like product) supported a finding of material injury by reason of the dumped imports from Trinidad and Tobago.

As to the price effects factor, the ITC said injury to American steel wire rod producers could not be explained entirely by the presence in the U.S. of non-subject imports and non-Trinidadian subject merchandise. So, this factor, along with significant and increasing volume of Trinidadian subject merchandise, underselling by this merchandise resulting in significant price suppression, and declining domestic industry health in the POI of 1999 through 2001, led the ITC to believe material injury existed.

---

35. *See Caribbean Ispat Ltd. v. United States*, 450 F.3d 1336, 1341, 28 International Trade Reporter Decisions 1033 (Fed. Cir. 2006). [Hereinafter, *Caribbean Ispat*.] The CIT opinion in the case was *Caribbean Ispat Ltd. v. United States*, 366 F. Supp. 2d 1300, 27 International Trade Reporter Decisions 1551 (Ct. Int'l Trade 2005).

36. *Mittal Steel*, 542 F.3d 867, 30 International Trade Reporter Decisions (ITRD) 1449, 1451.

37. *Mittal Steel*, 542 F.3d 867, 30 International Trade Reporter Decisions (ITRD) 1449, 1455.

Also on remand, the ITC thought there was evidence in favor of a threat of material injury:

> With respect to the question whether the domestic industry was threatened with material injury in the foreseeable future, the [International Trade] Commission found that Mittal had the ability to increase its exports to the U.S.; that the subject imports from Trinidad and Tobago had undersold the prices for the domestic like product and were likely to continue to have a significant suppressing effect on domestic prices; and that the subject imports were likely to have a negative effect on the domestic industry's production and development efforts.[38]

Yet, on remand, the ITC rendered a negative material injury and threat finding. That was because of the *Bratsk* Replacement-Benefit Test, which the Federal Circuit instructed the ITC to apply.

- **ITC Remand Decision**

In its remand decision, the ITC made four points.[39] First, it understood the *Bratsk* Test to require treatment of all steel wire rod as a fungible commodity product. Second, it said there were non-Trinidadian imports in significant quantities in the American market. Third, it opined that the non-Trinidadian imports would have replaced the Trinidadian steel wire rod. Fourth, the ITC thought the absence or removal of the Trinidadian steel wire rod from the American market would have had no beneficial effect on American producers during the POI.

On the third point, the ITC said steel wire rod producers in countries other than Trinidad and Tobago had plenty of capacity, so that if they wanted to export a sufficient quantity of their product to replace fully Trinidadian steel wire rod, then they could do so. However, whether they actually would have exercised this ability was uncertain — the ITC said they could have done so, but did not say they would have done so. There was simply no evidence on which to render a decision on this point. So, by its own admission, the ITC simply presumed that the non-Trinidadian steel wire rod producers would have done so, *i.e.*, that non-subject imports would have replaced subject merchandise.

Why did the ITC make this presumption? The answer is:

> It [the ITC] applied that presumption based on its *perception* that this Court [the Federal Circuit] had required the [International Trade] Commission to make a negative determination unless evidence in the record supported the conclusion that "non-subject imports would not have replaced subject imports, or if they would have replaced them, [then they] would not have resulted in a benefit to the domestic industry." The Commission added that this Court *"appears to have created a presumption under*

---

38. *Mittal Steel*, 542 F.3d 867, 30 International Trade Reporter Decisions (ITRD) 1449, 1451.
39. *See Mittal Steel*, 542 F.3d 867, 30 International Trade Reporter Decisions (ITRD) 1449, 1451.

the Bratsk replacement/benefit test that if a foreign producer could 'replace' subject imports, it would."[40]

As to the fourth point, whether American steel wire rod producers would have benefited from the absence of Trinidadian subject merchandise, the ITC said "no." The ITC said there were considerable amounts of non-Trinidadian imports (*i.e.*, non-subject merchandise) sold in the U.S. at low prices or average unit values. These imports would have hurt American producers, so it was not possible to conclude that removing subject merchandise would have benefited those producers. In other words, said the ITC, subject merchandise did not materially injure the American steel wire rod manufacturers. The same was true in respect of threat of material injury.

The ITC made it plain it felt it was compelled to come to this conclusion because of the *Bratsk* Replacement-Benefit Test. The ITC put it bluntly that the evidence supported an affirmative injury determination, but the Court and its Test was forcing it to make a negative determination:

> The [International Trade] Commission stated that "we believe the Federal Circuit's decision in *Bratsk* and its remand order in this case compel us to reach a negative determination in this investigation, even though we believe an affirmative determination is consistent with the statute and supported by the factual record."[41]

There were two dissenting Commissioners, who said even applying the Bratsk Test, an affirmative determination was in order.

• **Appellate Arguments**

The American steel wire rod producers (the petitioners in the original AD investigation), Gerdau Ameristeel Corp. (Gerdau) and Keystone Consolidated Industries, In. (Keystone) appealed to the CIT the negative remand determination. But, the CIT affirmed the ITC decision. So, from the CIT, Gerdau and Keystone (collectively, the Appellants) sought a different result from the Federal Circuit.

The Appellants made 4 arguments.[42] First, they said the Replacement-Benefit Test was illegal. The Test had no basis in the AD statute, and thus the Federal Circuit had no power to create it in *Bratsk*. In effect, the Appellants wanted the Court to overturn the *Bratsk* precedent it had just set. Second, they said that the ITC was wrong to interpret Bratsk and the Federal Circuit remand order as mandating that all steel wire rod imports are interchangeable. Third, the Appellants contended that the ITC was wrong to apply a rebuttable presumption that subject merchandise

40. *See Mittal Steel*, 542 F.3d 867, 30 International Trade Reporter Decisions (ITRD) 1449, 1452 (emphasis added).

41. *Quoted in Mittal Steel*, 542 F.3d 867, 30 International Trade Reporter Decisions (ITRD) 1449, 1452.

42. *Mittal Steel*, 542 F.3d 867, 30 International Trade Reporter Decisions (ITRD) 1449, 1453–1454.

from Trinidad and Tobago would have been replaced by non-subject imports from countries with the production capacity to replace that merchandise. Fourth, Appellants said the ITC misapplied the Replacement-Benefit Test in its threat of material injury determination. Both Mittal Steel (the subject merchandise of which otherwise would have been hit with an AD order) and the ITC simply replied the ITC correctly followed the *Bratsk* Test and remand instructions.

- **Federal Circuit Holdings**

The Federal Circuit decision in *Mittal Steel* is overall an effort to clarify the *Bratsk* precedent and Replacement-Benefit Test. The Court did so in the context of the aforementioned arguments. So, the Court pointed out the ITC interpreted *Bratsk* and the remand instructions "too rigidly, in three respects."[43] That is, the Federal Circuit issued 3 key holdings, as follows, about the true meaning of *Bratsk* and correct application of the Replacement-Benefit Test.

First: Need to Make Finding about "Commodity Product"

First, the ITC was wrong to think it was barred from making a determination about one of the trigger factors, or prerequisites, for the Replacement-Benefit Test, namely, the existence of a "commodity product."[44] *Bratsk* does not compel the ITC to view all steel wire rod as interchangeable. Rather, whether subject merchandise is a commodity product is an issue the ITC should explicitly evaluate.

The Federal Circuit observed that in the remand proceedings, the ITC found there were no fewer than 11 major categories of steel wire rod, from low carbon wire rod (*e.g.*, industrial wire rod used for coat hangers and nails), to medium carbon wire rod, to high carbon wire rod. The Court said it had not, through its prior decision and remand order, made a factual finding that all steel wire rod on this continuum was fungible. All it had said was repeat the ITC view from the original investigation that there was a:

> high level of fungibility between subject imports from Trinidad and Tobago and the domestic product, and between subject imports from Trinidad and Tobago and imports from each of the other subject countries.[45]

Further, *Bratsk* did not automatically compel a conclusion to that effect.

To the contrary, it is the ITC — not an appellate court — that is the finder of facts in an AD investigation. So, it is up to the ITC to decide whether subject merchandise is fungible with the domestic like product and with non-subject imports.[46] Only if the decision of the ITC is clearly erroneous will the Court reverse it.

---

43. *Mittal Steel*, 542 F.3d 867, 30 International Trade Reporter Decisions (ITRD) 1449, 1454.

44. *See Mittal Steel*, 542 F.3d 867, 30 International Trade Reporter Decisions (ITRD) 1449, 1454–1455.

45. *Quoted in Mittal Steel*, 542 F.3d 867, 30 International Trade Reporter Decisions (ITRD) 1449, 1455.

46. *See Mittal Steel*, 542 F.3d 867, 30 International Trade Reporter Decisions (ITRD) 1449, 1455.

Second: Focus on Benefit from Hypothetical Removal of Subject Merchandise,
           Not on Benefit from AD Order

Second, the ITC was wrong to interpret *Bratsk* as calling for a decision whether an AD order would result in benefit to the domestic industry by eliminating subject merchandise from the American market. The Replacement-Benefit Test is not about whether an AD order would benefit the petitioning industry that makes a like domestic product. Rather, it is about whether the:

> hypothetical removal of the LTFV subject imports would have resulted in their replacement by non-subject or non-LTFV imports with no resulting benefit to the domestic industry.[47]

As the ITC itself observed, the AD (and CVD) statute does not permit the ITC to consider whether an AD (or CVD) order will be effective.

That is, the statute contemplates some orders will not give import relief to domestic producers. More fundamentally, the point of an AD order is not to remove subject merchandise from the U.S. market. Its purpose is to make level the competitive playing field, between subject merchandise and the like domestic product, by bumping up the subject merchandise price on account of it being sold at LTFV, *i.e.*, dumped.

So, the Federal Circuit made clear the ITC misread *Bratsk*:

> ... the [International Trade] Commission views *Bratsk* as holding that an antidumping order may be entered only if the Commission can determine that the order would be "effective" in the future by causing the elimination of the subject imports from the market, which imports would not then be replaced by non-subject imports.
>
> That characterization misses the point of *Bratsk*. The decision in *Bratsk* was not addressed to the potential effectiveness of any possible remedial order. Instead, it was directed to determining the cause of the injury already suffered by the domestic industry.[48]

The Federal Circuit continued by explaining that one "important" aspect—though "not necessarily dispositive"—of a causation inquiry is a but for test: "whether the subject imports are the 'but for' cause of the injury to the domestic industry."[49]

Quoting the 1989 United States Supreme Court decision in *Price Waterhouse v. Hopkins*, the Federal Circuit defined "but for" causation" as:

> But for causation is a hypothetical construct. In determining whether a particular factor was a but-for cause of a given event, we begin by assuming that that factor was present at the time of the event, and then ask whether

---

47. *Mittal Steel*, 542 F.3d 867, 30 International Trade Reporter Decisions (ITRD) 1449, 1454.
48. *Mittal Steel*, 542 F.3d 867, 30 International Trade Reporter Decisions (ITRD) 1449, 1455.
49. *Mittal Steel*, 542 F.3d 867, 30 International Trade Reporter Decisions (ITRD) 1449, 1455.

even if that factor had been absent, the event nevertheless would have transpired in the same way.[50]

So, in the context of *Bratsk*, and its parent, *Gerald Metals*, and in the *Mittal Steel* dispute, the but-for principle applies as follows: Would the conditions have been different for the domestic producers of a like product in the absence of dumping?[51] That is, would injury have occurred but for the presence of subject merchandise?

The Federal Circuit scolded the ITC for arguing that a but-for causation inquiry is at odds with its obligations under the AD statute. To the contrary, it is a proper part thereof. Indeed, the *Statement of Administrative Action* accompanying the 1994 *Uruguay Round Agreements Act* (the implementing legislation for all Uruguay Round accords, including the WTO *Antidumping Agreement*), reinforces the point.[52] It rightly explains the ITC must examine all relevant variables, including any known factors other than subject merchandise that could be the cause of injury to the domestic industry. That is because the ITC must "ensure that it is not attributing injury from other sources to the subject imports."[53] An attribution analysis is another way of describing but-for causation: to ask whether injury would have occurred without (but for) subject merchandise is to ask whether injury can be attributed to factors other than subject merchandise.

Indeed, the AD statute, 19 U.S.C. Section 1677(7)(B)(i), identifies 3 mandatory factors the ITC must consider. The mandatory factors are:

(I)   the volume of imports of the subject merchandise,

(II) the effect of imports of that merchandise on prices in the United States for domestic like products, and

(III) the impact of imports of such merchandise on domestic producers of domestic like products, but only in the context of production operations within the United States . . . .[54]

Critically, Section 1677(7)(B)(ii) says the ITC "may consider such other economic factors as are relevant to the determination regarding whether there is material injury by reason of imports."[55] To be sure, this language is permissive, *i.e.*, the ITC

---

50. *Mittal Steel*, 542 F.3d 867, 30 International Trade Reporter Decisions (ITRD) 1449, 1455–1456 (*quoting Price Waterhouse v. Hopkins*, 490 U.S. 228, 240 (1989)).

51. *See Mittal Steel*, 542 F.3d 867, 30 International Trade Reporter Decisions (ITRD) 1449, 1456.

52. *See Mittal Steel*, 542 F.3d 867, 30 International Trade Reporter Decisions (ITRD) 1449, 1456 (*citing* THE URUGUAY ROUND AGREEMENTS ACT: STATEMENT OF ADMINISTRATIVE ACTION, HOUSE OF REPRESENTATIVES DOCUMENT NUMBER 103-316, Vol. I, at 851–852 (27 September 1994)).

53. *Mittal Steel*, 542 F.3d 867, 30 International Trade Reporter Decisions (ITRD) 1449, 1456 (*quoting* THE URUGUAY ROUND AGREEMENTS ACT: STATEMENT OF ADMINISTRATIVE ACTION, HOUSE OF REPRESENTATIVES DOCUMENT NUMBER 103-316, Vol. I, at 851–852 (27 September 1994)).

54. *Quoted in Mittal Steel*, 542 F.3d 867, 30 International Trade Reporter Decisions (ITRD) 1449, 1451.

55. *Quoted in Mittal Steel*, 542 F.3d 867, 30 International Trade Reporter Decisions (ITRD) 1449, 1453.

has the discretion not to look at "other economic factors." But, contrary to the view of the ITC, its discretion is "not unbounded," *i.e.*, the permissive language does not mean the ITC can ignore relevant economic factors. To do so would be an abuse of discretion. Put directly, the ITC cannot ignore the presence of a significant volume of non-subject imports during the POI that were interchangeable with the subject merchandise.

So, the factor to study as a but-for cause of the given event, material injury to the domestic industry, is dumping by subject merchandise from Trinidad and Tobago. Suppose there had been no such dumping, meaning either the Trinidadian steel wire rod (1) had been sold at non-LTFV prices, or (2) had not been sold at all in the U.S. Would the American industry still have been hurt? If the answer is "yes," then the subject merchandise is not the but-for cause of that injury. There is some other cause, namely, competition from fairly priced, non-subject imports. As the Federal Circuit explained:

> . . . *Bratsk* (like *Gerald Metals*) directs that in cases involving commodity products in which non-LTFV imported goods are present in the market, the [International Trade] Commission must give consideration to the issue of "but for" causation by considering *whether the domestic industry would have been better off if the dumped goods had been absent from the market.* That inquiry is *not* concerned with whether an antidumping order would actually lead to the elimination of those goods from the market in the future or whether those goods would be replaced by goods from other sources. *Rather, the inquiry is a hypothetical one that sheds light on whether the injury to the domestic industry can reasonably be attributed to the subject imports.* The focus of the inquiry is on the cause of the injury in the past, *not* the prospect of effectiveness in the future.[56]

"All reasonable and logical enough," it might be remarked. However, to be fair to the ITC, the *Bratsk* decision—high quality as it was—did not exactly spell out this distinction, or speak of but-for causation.

In that regard, the Federal Circuit was empathetic, ending its opinion saying:

> In concluding that the [International Trade] Commission committed legal error in the remand proceedings in this case, we intend no criticism of the Commission's effort to comply with this Court's previous directions. Indeed, the error we have found flows largely from the Commission's effort to proceed with scrupulous attention to the terms of this Court's remand instructions. The problem may stem from a lack of sufficient clarity in our prior opinion [*Bratsk*], which we hope has been rectified in this one.[57]

---

56. *Mittal Steel*, 542 F.3d 867, 30 International Trade Reporter Decisions (ITRD) 1449, 1456 (emphasis added).

57. *Mittal Steel*, 542 F.3d 867, 30 International Trade Reporter Decisions (ITRD) 1449, 1458.

Adjudicators at the WTO might take note of the honesty and humility of the Federal Circuit judges here.

*Third: No Rebuttal Presumption that "Could Replace" Means "Would Replace"
or that "No Benefit" Would Have Followed*

Third, the ITC was wrong to think *Bratsk* created a rebuttal presumption that subject merchandise, if removed from the American market, would have been replaced by non-subject merchandise.[58] *Bratsk* did not create a presumption in favour of finding replacement, even if the trigger events (namely, existence of a commodity product and significant presence in the American market of price-competitive non-subject imports) exist. Rather, before and after *Bratsk*, it was and continues to be the responsibility of the ITC to determine whether a causal relationship exists between subject merchandise and injury to the domestic industry.[59]

So, there is no burden on the importer of subject merchandise to prove that subject merchandise did not cause injury to the domestic industry. That means the ITC cannot fulfill its obligation to address the causation question simply by saying the importer of subject merchandise failed to adduce evidence to negate causation.[60] Simply put, the respondent in an AD case does not have the burden of proving the negative.[61] Instead, the ITC must consider causation, and it has considerable discretion in how it does so. There is no particular analytical method it must follow, nor any presumption it must apply. What the ITC must do is "give full consideration to the causation issue and . . . provide a meaningful explanation of its conclusions."[62]

Likewise, the ITC was wrong to think that absent an affirmative finding that there would be no such replacement, the ITC must render a negative injury determination.[63] What was the ITC argument here? The ITC thought that, as a practical matter, in almost all AD investigations, neither it nor domestic producers (in effect, the petitioners seeking AD relief) would have data to rebut the presumption about replacement (that non-subject imports would have replaced subject merchandise). That was why, urged the ITC, the presumption amounted to a direction to render a negative determination. Only in the rare investigation would the ITC or domestic producers have substantial rebuttal evidence to the effect that (1) non-subject imports would not have replaced subject merchandise, or that (2) replacement of subject merchandise by non-subject merchandise would have benefitted the domestic producers (*i.e.*, not injured them).

---

58. *See Mittal Steel*, 542 F.3d 867, 30 International Trade Reporter Decisions (ITRD) 1449, 1456.

59. *See Mittal Steel*, 542 F.3d 867, 30 International Trade Reporter Decisions (ITRD) 1449, 1456–1457.

60. *See Mittal Steel*, 542 F.3d 867, 30 International Trade Reporter Decisions (ITRD) 1449, 1457.

61. *Bratsk* and *Mittal Steel* (*quoting Bratsk*) refer to the "petitioner" on this point, perhaps mistakenly. *See Mittal Steel*, 542 F.3d 867, 30 International Trade Reporter Decisions (ITRD) 1449, 1457.

62. *Mittal Steel*, 542 F.3d 867, 30 International Trade Reporter Decisions (ITRD) 1449, 1457.

63. *See Mittal Steel*, 542 F.3d 867, 30 International Trade Reporter Decisions (ITRD) 1449, 1456.

In the case, the ITC reasoned as follows: non-subject countries, and non-*CBERA* subject countries, had sufficient steel wire rod production capacity to replace fully subject merchandise from Trinidad and Tobago. Admittedly, there was no evidence they actually would have done so, but because of *Bratsk*, there was a presumption in favor of both replacement with no benefit to American producers of the like product. So, the ITC had to conclude "yes, the steel wire rod from countries not subject to the investigation, and steel wire rod from non-*CBERA* countries that was subject to the investigation, would have replaced the Trinidadian steel wire rod, and that replacement would not have benefited—it would have injured—the American steel wire rod companies."

This argument was unsuccessful. The reason why was best stated by the Court itself, which in doing so provided, in the most important passage of its opinion, an excellent summary of the *Bratsk-Mittal Steel* causation jurisprudence:

> What *Bratsk* held is that "where commodity products are at issue and fairly traded, price competitive, non-subject imports are in the market," the [International Trade] Commission would not fulfill its obligation to consider an important aspect of the problem if it failed to consider whether non-subject or non-LTFV imports would have replaced LTFV subject imports during the period of investigation without a continuing benefit to the domestic industry. [*Bratsk*,] 444 F.3d at 1369. Under those circumstances, *Bratsk* requires the Commission to consider whether replacement of the LTFV subject imports might have occurred during the period of investigation, and it requires the Commission to provide an explanation of its conclusion with respect to that factor. The Commission must further explain whether the record provides support for a finding that the domestic industry was materially injured "by reason of" the LTFV subject imports after it has considered the analysis described in *Gerald Metals* and *Bratsk* along with the statutorily mandated factors and any other relevant economic factors that the Commission elects to consider under Section 1677(7)(B)(ii). [*Bratsk*,] 444 F.3d at 1373 & n.3. *Bratsk* did not read into the antidumping statute a Procrustean formula for determining whether a domestic injury was "by reason of" subject imports. It simply required the Commission to consider the "but for" causation analysis in fulfilling its statutory duty to determine whether the subject imports were a substantial factor in the injury to the domestic industry, as opposed to a merely "incidental, tangential, or trivial" factor. *Nippon Steel Group v. Int'l Trade Comm'n*, 345 F.3d 1379, 1381 (Fed. Cir. 2003).[64]

---

64. *Mittal Steel*, 542 F.3d 867, 30 International Trade Reporter Decisions (ITRD) 1449, 1456.

Hence, the Federal Circuit vacated and remanded the decision of the CIT, instructing that Court to remand the case to the ITC for further consideration in light of the jurisprudence on the question of causation of material injury or threat thereof.[65]

V. Jurisprudence Summary in
2018 *Changhzhou Solar* Case

Changzhou Trina Solar Energy Co. v. U.S. International Trade Commission,

Federal Circuit Number 2016-1053 (22 January 2018)

Taranto, Circuit Judge:

Changzhou Trina Solar Energy Co., Ltd., and Yingli Green Energy Holding Company, Ltd., are Chinese producers of crystalline silicon photovoltaic cells, modules, laminates, and panels (CSPV products). Those products were imported into the United States and were the "subject imports" in the proceeding at issue here. Trina Solar (U.S.), Inc., and Yingli Green Energy Americas, Inc., imported the subject imports into the United States. The two producers and two importers—collectively, the Chinese Respondents—are appellants in this Court.

On October 19, 2011, appellee SolarWorld Americas, Inc., filed petitions seeking imposition on the subject imports of antidumping duties under 19 U.S.C. §§ 1673–1673h and countervailing duties under 19 U.S.C. §§ 1671–1671h. The U.S. Department of Commerce eventually agreed [in its 17 October 2012 final AD and CVD determinations] with SolarWorld that the subject imports were being sold in the United States at less than its fair value and were being unfairly subsidized by the Chinese government. The International Trade Commission . . . determined that "an industry in the United States is materially injured by reason of imports of crystalline silicon photovoltaic ('CSPV') cells and modules from China that [Commerce] has determined are subsidized and sold in the United States at less than fair value." *Crystalline Silicon Photo-voltaic Cells and Modules from China*, Inv. Nos. 701-TA-481 and 731-TA-1190), USITC Pub. 4360, at 415 (Nov. 2012) (Final) (*ITC Final Decision*); *Crystalline Silicon Photovoltaic Cells and Modules from China*, 77 Fed. Reg. 72, 884 (Dec. 6, 2012).

The Chinese Respondents appealed the Commission's determination. . . . [T]hey argued that the Commission had not properly found the required causal connection between the unfairly priced or subsidized imports and the weakened state of the domestic industry that it identified as "materially injured by reason of" the imports. The Court of International Trade rejected the challenge and

---

65. *See Mittal Steel*, 542 F.3d 867, 30 International Trade Reporter Decisions (ITRD) 1449, 1456.

sustained the Commission's determination. *Changzhou Trina Solar Energy Co., Ltd. v. U.S. Int'l Trade Comm'n*, 100 F. Supp. 3d 1314, 1331–32, 1349, . . . (Ct. Int'l Trade 2015).

. . . We review the Commission's determination using the same standard as the Court of International Trade: we ask whether it was "unsupported by substantial evidence on the record, or otherwise not in accordance with law." *Siemens Energy, Inc. v. United States*, 806 F.3d 1367, 1369 (Fed. Cir. 2015) (*quoting* 19 U.S.C. § 1516a(b) (1)(B)(i)). We affirm.

I

Congress has directed the federal government . . . to impose antidumping duties on "foreign merchandise . . . being, or . . . likely to be, sold in the United States at less than its fair value." 19 U.S.C. § 1673(1). Congress has likewise directed the government . . . to impose countervailing duties on "merchandise imported, or sold (or likely to be sold) for importation, into the United States" for which "the government of a country or any public entity within the territory of a country is providing, directly or indirectly, a countervailable subsidy with respect to the manufacture, production, or export" of that merchandise. *Id.* § 1671(a)(1). This case involves a requirement of both regimes.

Each regime divides the authority to make the required judgments between Commerce and the Commission. Commerce determines the existence of the unfair pricing or subsidies—for antidumping duties, "whether the subject merchandise is being, or is likely to be, sold in the United States at less than its fair value," *id.* § 1673d(a)(1); . . . for countervailing duties, "whether or not a countervailable subsidy is being provided with respect to the subject merchandise," *id.* § 1671d(a)(1); . . . , The Commission determines, for both kinds of duties, whether

> (A) an industry in the United States—(i) is materially injured, or (ii) is threatened with material injury, or (B) the establishment of an industry in the United States is materially retarded, by reason of imports, or sales (or the likelihood of sales) for importation, of the merchandise

for which Commerce has found unfair pricing or subsidies. *Id.* § 1673d(b)(1) (antidumping duty provision for final determination); *see* id. § 1671d(b)(1) (countervailing duty provision for final determination); . . . . For each of the antidumping and countervailing duty regimes, if both agencies answer their assigned questions affirmatively, Commerce issues the duty-imposing order. *See id.* §§ 1673d(c)(2), 1671d(c)(2); *Duferco Steel, Inc. v. United States*, 296 F.3d 1087, 1089 (Fed. Cir. 2002).

This case involves the Commission's determination that the domestic industry was . . . "materially injured . . . by reason of imports" of the Chinese Respondents' merchandise. . . . We have noted the two parts of such a finding: that there is "present material injury": and that "the material injury is 'by reason of' the subject imports." *Gerald Metals, Inc. v. United States*, 132 F.3d 716, 719 (Fed. Cir. 1997). Congress has further specified that, "[i]n making determinations" under the material-injury provisions for both antidumping and countervailing duties,

> the Commission, in each case—
>
> > (i) shall consider
> >
> > > (I) the volume of imports of the subject merchandise,
> > >
> > > (II) the effect of imports of that merchandise on prices in the United States for domestic like products, and
> > >
> > > (III) the impact of imports of such merchandise on domestic producers of domestic like products, but only in the context of production operations within the United States; and
> >
> > (ii) may consider such other economic factors as are relevant to the determination regarding whether there is material injury by reason of imports.
>
> 19 U.S.C. § 1677(7)(B). . . .

The language Congress used—injury "by reason of" specified conduct—is familiar in many legal contexts. Recently, the Supreme Court has repeatedly made explicit that, as a matter of settled ordinary legal meaning, the phrase requires, at a minimum, "but for" causation of the injury by the statutorily identified conduct. *See Burrage v. United States*, 134 S. Ct. 881, 889 . . . (2014) ("the phrase, 'by reason of,' requires at least a showing of 'but for' causation") (citation omitted); *Gross v. FBL Fin. Servs., Inc.*, 557 U.S. 167, 176 . . . (2009) (reasoning that adverse action "because of" age in the *Age Discrimination in Employment Act* means "by reason of" age, which has a settled meaning, so that "[t]o establish a disparate-treatment claim under the plain language of the *ADEA*[], a plaintiff must prove that age was the 'but-for' cause of the employer's adverse decision"); *Holmes v. Sec. Inv'r Prot. Corp.*, 503 U.S. 258, 265–68 . . . (1992) (reasoning that a statute permitting recovery for injuries suffered "by reason of" the defendant's violation "require[s] a showing that the defendant's violation . . . was," among other things, "a 'but for' cause of his injury"). . . .

. . .

Although Congress may use legal terms in unusual ways in particular statutes, "[i]t is a settled principle of interpretation that, absent other indication, Congress intends to incorporate the well-settled meaning of the common-law terms it uses." *Sekhar v. United States*, 570 U.S. 729 . . . (2013). . . . We see nothing that would justify finding that Congress was departing from the Court-recognized ordinary meaning when it directed the Commission to determine the existence of material injury "by reason of" unfairly priced or subsidized imports in 19 U.S.C. §§ 1673d(b)(1) and 1671d(b)(1). In particular, when Congress further prescribed a set of topics that the Commission "shall consider," it did not change the "by reason of" standard of §§ 1673d(b) and 1671d(b): it merely identified topics that the Commission must consider "[i]n making determinations" under those "by reason of" provisions. 19 U.S.C. § 1677(7)(B). And it confirmed the maintenance of the "by reason of" standard when it added that the Commission may consider "such other economic factors as are relevant to the determination regarding whether there is material injury by reason of imports." *Id.* § 1677(7)(B)(ii). We have been pointed to nothing in the statute that overrides the Supreme Court's rulings that "by reason of" requires, at the least, but-for causation. At oral argument before this court, counsel for the Commission properly agreed that but-for causation is required — though *how* the standard applies may vary with the facts. . . .

This conclusion is consistent with our precedents, especially when read in light of the Supreme Court's recent clarification of the default meaning of "by reason of." In *Mittal Steel Point Lisas Ltd. v. United States*, for example, this Court stressed the importance, though "not necessarily dispositive" character, of the inquiry into "whether the subject imports are the 'but for' cause of the injury to the domestic industry" — which "requires the finder of fact to ask whether conditions would have been different for the domestic industry in the absence of dumping." 542 F.3d 867, 876 (Fed. Cir. 2008). In support, the Court pointed to the explanation in the 1994 *Statement of Administrative Action* (deemed "authoritative" by 19 U.S.C. § 3512(d)) that the Commission must "'ensure that it is not attributing injury from other sources to the subject imports.'" *Mittal*, 542 F.3d at 877 (*quoting* H.R. Doc. No. 103-316, vol. 1, at 851–52 (1994), as reprinted in 1994 U.S.C.C.A.N. 4040, 4184–85). The Court summarized earlier cases that found Commission determinations lacking for insufficient analysis of "whether the domestic industry would have been better off if the dumped goods had been absent from the market." *Id.* at 876; *see* id. at 873–74, 877–79 (discussing *Bratsk Aluminium Smelter v. United States*, 444 F.3d 1369, 1373 (Fed. Cir. 2006), and *Gerald Metals*, 132 F.3d at 722). At the same time, the Court explained that this requirement "does not require the Commission to address the causation issue in any particular way." *Id.* at 878. Rather, the Court recognized "the Commission's broad discretion with respect to its choice of methodology." *Id.* at 873.

This Court's decision in *Swiff-Train Co. v. United States* is to the same effect. 793 F.3d 1355 (Fed. Cir. 2015). The Court there accepted the importance of a "proper but-for analysis," which the Court held the Commission had conducted when it "established cause-in-fact by identifying the injurious effect of subject imports on the domestic industry using the statutory factors, and then ensuring injury was not caused by factors other than subject imports." *Id.* at 1361. At the same time, the court reiterated propositions from earlier precedents — propositions that are consistent with a but-for causation requirement — that "the Commission need not isolate the injury caused by other factors from injury caused by unfair imports, nor demonstrate the subject imports are the 'principal' cause of injury." *Id.* at 1363. . . . More broadly, the Court reiterated that "this Court does not require use of any particular model or methodology," *id.* at 1361, including "an explicit counterfactual analysis," *id.* at 1362, to answer the prescribed causation question. . . . *See also id.* at 1362–63.

In short, the statutory language, Supreme Court precedent, our precedent, and precedent from other Circuits together support the conclusion that but-for causation is required under the "by reason of" standards of 19 U.S.C. §§ 1673d(b)(1) and 1671d(b)(1), while *how* the standard is best applied in particular circumstances may vary with the facts. The Commission may use a variety of methods of analysis for applying the standard to the myriad factual situations that may be presented. When facts such as the significant market presence of price-competitive non-subject imports are present, the Commission, to meet its obligation to "examine the relevant data and articulate a satisfactory explanation for its action," must engage in "additional" analysis, beyond what may suffice in the absence of such inquiry-complicating facts relevant to whether, considering other contributors, the subject imports account for material harm to the domestic industry. *Bratsk*, 444 F.3d at 1373, 1375. But the recognition that different facts call for different amounts of explanation in applying the statutory standard does not mean that the standard is different in different cases, any more than does the recognition of methodological discretion in applying the standard. The standard, requiring but-for causation, remains the same. . . . The substance of the Commission's analysis, not the specific formulation employed, determines whether the Commission has adequately answered the question of but-for causation on the particular facts in the matter before it.

II

. . . [T]he Chinese Respondents contend that the Commission did not adequately address the question of but-for causation. They argue . . . that the Commission failed to make findings, supported by substantial evidence, that the domestic industry would have been materially better off than it was during the period of investigation (POI) if the subject imports had not been introduced into the market. We reject that challenge. In substance, the Commission made that determination and had an adequate basis for doing so.

The Commission found "that there is a causal nexus between subject imports and the poor condition of the domestic industry and that the domestic industry is materially injured by reason of subject imports." *ITC Final Decision*. . . . It relied on findings it summarized as follows:

> [T]he picture emerges of a domestic industry (1) with a steadily declining market share despite phenomenal demand growth, (2) that has lost market share due primarily to the significant and increasing volume of subject imports from China, (3) that has faced significant underselling by subject imports from China and depressed and suppressed prices, (4) that consistently lost money throughout the POI despite the tremendous demand growth and significant cost reductions, (5) that by the end of the POI experienced declines even in many of the performance indicators that previously had shown some improvement, and (6) that reported recognizing asset write-offs and/or costs related to the closure of production facilities, revalued inventories, and/or asset impairments. *Id.*

Despite those findings, the Chinese Respondents argue that the Commission did not adequately address but-for causation because it insufficiently accounted for three facts about the marketplace in the POI—January 2009 to June 2012. One was the pressure CSPV sellers faced to lower their prices to meet the price at which utilities could buy natural gas for power generation—so-called "grid parity" [*i.e.*, solar power sellers match the cost levels of natural-gas-generated electricity provided to a grid during peak periods.] A second was the decline in government subsidies for solar-energy products, making it harder for sellers to offer low prices. The third was the increase in demand in the utility segment of the market, compared to other market segments.

The Chinese Respondents argue that, given the difficulties those facts posed for the domestic industry, the domestic industry would have been materially as badly off (in the POI) even had there been no unfairly priced and subsidized subject imports. More precisely, they argue that the Commission gave inadequate attention to whether the unfairly priced and subsidized subject imports were a but-for cause of any "material injury." Given the statutory definition of "material injury" as "harm which is not inconsequential, immaterial, or unimportant," 19 U.S.C. § 1677(7)(A), the question is whether the Commission found, with adequate reasons and substantial-evidence support, that the difference between the state of the domestic industry as it actually was in the POI and the state of the domestic industry as it would have been without the subject imports was more than inconsequential, immaterial, or unimportant.

We conclude that the Commission so found and had a sufficient basis for so finding. The Commission's summary, quoted above, rested on detailed findings about demand conditions and the business cycle in the domestic market, the roles of conventional and renewable sources of electricity, government incentives and regulations at federal, state, and local levels, domestic consumption trends, market segments, who was supplying the domestic market, what happened to prices and market shares during the POI, and the ways in which "the domestic industry's financial performance was very poor and deteriorating." *ITC Final Decision.* . . . The findings rested on various types of evidence, including the answers to questionnaires addressed to market participants such as purchasers.

The Commission found declining prices of the CSPV products and significant loss of market share to subject imports, despite increasing demand for the products. . . . And the Commission attributed a material portion of the adverse effects on the domestic industry to the subject imports. It found that "domestic producers lost sales and revenues due to competition from low-priced subject imports" and that "significant underselling of the domestic like product by subject imports from China . . . enabled subject importers to gain market share at the expense of the domestic industry." [*Id.*] And it characterized the "very poor and deteriorating" condition of the domestic industry as being "because of the significant volume and adverse price effects of subject imports." [*Id.*]

More specifically, the Commission addressed the three facts highlighted by the Chinese Respondents here, and it found that those facts did not account for the domestic industry's woes. Thus, the Commission recognized "there may have been additional factors exerting downward pricing pressure on CSPV products," but it found "that subject imports were a significant cause of the decline in prices of CSPV products during the POI." [*Id.*] It found that "the impetus toward grid parity fails to explain the significant underselling by subject imports demonstrated on this record." [*Id.*] It recognized the fluctuation of domestic government subsidies during the POI, but it found that, "during much of the POI, the overall mix of incentives was very favorable and stimulated demand substantially" and "a number of incentives remained available" even at the end of the POI. [*Id.*] It recognized that sales to utilities were "the fastest growing U.S. market segment," . . . but it found that "the domestic industry's declining market share was not limited to the utility segment" — "due to consistent and substantial underselling by subject imports, the domestic industry also lost market share in the residential and non-residential segments of the U.S. market, and non-subject imports also lost market share to increasing volumes of low-priced subject imports." [*Id.*]

The Commission determined:

> We find that the factors Respondents cite, all of which would have affected both the domestic like product and subject imports from China, *do not individually or collectively account for* the substantial margins of underselling by subject imports, the accelerating decline in prices in the U.S. market during the POI, the inability of the domestic industry to price its products at levels that would permit the recovery of its costs during a period of very significant demand growth, or the pace at which subject imports captured additional shares of this growing market at the domestic industry's expense throughout the POI. In sum, the significant and growing volume of low-priced subject imports from China competed directly with the domestic like product, was sold in the same channels of distribution to the same segments of the U.S. market, and undersold the domestic like product at significant margins, causing domestic producers to lose revenue and market share and leading to significant depression and suppression of the domestic industry's prices.

ITC Final Decision . . . (emphasis added). By determining that the facts highlighted by the Chinese Respondents did not account for (materially) all of the domestic industry's weakening during the POI, the Commission in substance made the required determination of but-for causation. And its explanation, relying on concrete evidence that we see no basis for deeming insufficient under the substantial-evidence test, was adequate to support the finding.

Part Four

Disciplines on Fishing Subsidies

Chapter 21

Issues and Consequences[1]

I. Why Fishing Subsidies Matter

Fishing subsidies are not extraneous to negotiations about trade remedies. Rather, they concern governmental support in a particular sector, and thus are squarely within the kind of measure subject to a classic trade remedy, namely, a CVD. Moreover, their link to poverty is obvious. Over two billion people depend on fish as a major source of protein and income.[2] Many poor people in developing countries and LDCs eke out a livelihood from scale-scale fishing. Muslim countries are no stranger to this phenomenon. Bangladesh, Malaysia, Indonesia, Somalia, and Yemen are among the examples. That also is true of non-Muslim countries with large Muslim coastal communities, including India, the Philippines, and Thailand. Such countries are not necessarily the most blameworthy, in terms of causing or exacerbating the over-fishing crisis.

Rather, it is developed countries that have considerable resources to subsidize large-scale commercial fishing fleets. The long-distance fishing fleets of the EU and China are not commercially viable, and survive only because of government subsidies for fuel, other operational expenses, and vessel construction and maintenance.[3] For example, this support allows foreign fleets to obtain more, bigger, and faster boats than they otherwise would have.

Even when developed countries seek to cut such subsidies, and provide alternative support to their fisherman to use environmentally sustainable catch methods, the fishermen do not always behave. In May 2011, for example, an undercover operation by the EU Fisheries Commission to crack down on illegal fishing discovered Italian fishermen use drift nets (which span several kilometres in length) to catch swordfish

---

1. Documents References:
   (1) *Havana (ITO) Charter* Preamble
   (2) GATT Preamble
   (3) *WTO SCM Agreement*

2. *See* Amy Tsui, *Members of Congress Ask USTR to Ensure WTO Talks Include End to Fishery Subsidies*, 28 International Trade Reporter (BNA) 1167 (14 July 2011) (*quoting* a letter dated 6 July 2011 to U.S. Trade Representative Ambassador Ron Kirk from 12 Senators and 30 Members of the House of Representatives).

3. *See* Amy Tsui, *Members of Congress Ask USTR to Ensure WTO Talks Include End to Fishery Subsidies*, 28 International Trade Reporter (BNA) 1167 (14 July 2011) (*quoting* a letter dated 6 July 2011 to USTR Ambassador Ron Kirk from 12 Senators and 30 Members of the House of Representatives).

and Atlantic bluefin tuna.[4] The tuna, which migrate to the Mediterranean Sea, along with dolphins, sharks, turtles, and whales, and some birds, are endangered species, all of which are ensnared in drift nets. Thus, the EU banned drift nets in 2002, and subsidized its fishermen to desist from their use. The Italian fishermen pocketed the subsidy, flouted the ban—and, Italian authorities, including the Coast Guard, did nothing. Consider, then, the impact on the countries of the Southern and Eastern Mediterranean—all of which, save for Israel, are Muslim. Their smaller-scale fishermen suffer from stock depletion caused by their European counterparts.

Nonetheless, from the American perspective, the link between disciplines on fish subsidies to promote sustainable development, on the one hand, and alleviating poverty and susceptibility to Islamist extremism, on the other hand, was lost. In the words of four former USTRs (William Brock, Carla Hills, Susan Schwab, and Clayton Yeutter) in an April 2011 letter to President Barack H. Obama, America viewed the matter as an opportunity to "set a historic precedent by showing that trade can directly benefit the environment *while promoting jobs, exports, and open markets*."[5] That is, at stake for the U.S. was an environmental measure that would not interfere with market access for American fish exports.

America focused on its commercial and recreational fisheries interests, which account for over two million jobs in the U.S.[6] For American policy in the Doha Round, the possibility subsidies by foreign governments might be at cross-purposes with America's counter-terrorism efforts was of marginal (if any) importance. Rather, they mattered because they undermined opportunities for American exporters in third countries, by putting American fisherman at a disadvantage.

For example, by cutting operating costs of foreign producers and exporters, they injured American coastal communities. Even environmental groups, such as Mission Blue, Oceana, and the WWF emphasized fishing subsidies "undermine[] U.S. trade opportunities in potential export markets" by "creating an uneven playing field and reducing the stocks on which U.S. fishers depend."[7] In truth, both rationales matter, or should.

---

4. *See* Guy Dinmore & Eleonora de Sabata, *Covert Mission Finds Sicily Skippers Still Use Drift Nets*, Financial Times, 21–22 May 2011, at 4. As a result, the European Court of Justice (ECJ) is likely to impose significant monetary penalties against Italy. *See id.*

For a discussion of some of the pertinent issues relating to fishing subsidies, see Seth Korman, Note, *International Management of a High Seas Fishery: Political and Property-Rights Solutions and the Atlantic Bluefin*, 51 Virginia Journal of International Law 697–748 (2011).

5. *Quoted in* Rossella Brevetti, *Allgeier Says Success of Fisheries Pact at WTO Would Help Sell Doha Package*, 28 International Trade Reporter (BNA) 768 (12 May 2011).

6. *See* Amy Tsui, *Members of Congress Ask USTR to Ensure WTO Talks Include End to Fishery Subsidies*, 28 International Trade Reporter (BNA) 1167 (14 July 2011) (*quoting* a letter dated 6 July 2011 to USTR Ambassador Ron Kirk from 12 Senators and 30 Members of the House of Representatives).

7. Rossella Brevetti, *Environmental Groups Ask Obama for Strong Fisheries Subsidy Pact in WTO*, 28 International Trade Reporter (BNA) 848 (26 May 2011) (paraphrasing an 11 May 2011 letter from these three environmental groups to President Barack H. Obama).

Unsurprisingly, by April 2011, the only points on which WTO Members agreed were incontrovertible facts:

(1) A global crisis of overcapacity and overfishing exists, with over 85% of the fisheries in the world being overexploited, fully exploited, depleted, or in need of recovery, and with 63% of fish stocks around the world requiring rebuilding.[8] (By December 2018, the crisis worsened: 93% of marine fisheries around the world were "fished at or beyond sustainable catch levels."[9]) In April 2011, the Chairman [of the Negotiating Group on Rules in the Doha Round] intoned:

> The longstanding blockage in these negotiations exists in spite of the strong consensus among delegations of all sizes and levels of development that the state of global fisheries resources is alarming and getting worse. Indeed all delegations, when referring to data, rely on the same statistics—those published by the FAO—the latest of which show that 85 per cent of world fish stocks are either fully- or over-exploited. All recognize that this is a crisis of exceptionally serious implications for all humankind, and particularly for the poor in many countries who are heavily dependent on fisheries as a source of nutrition and employment. Nor is there disagreement that developing as well as developed countries are major participants in global capture fishing, and that all countries face a common problem and share responsibility to contribute to finding solutions, although not necessarily on a uniform basis.[10]

(2) The crisis is due in part to the $30–34 billion annually (as of 2006) governments grant as fishing subsidies, including $20 billion (equivalent to 20–25% of revenues) to increase the capacity of fleets to fish for longer

---

8. *See* World Trade Organization, *Briefing Notes—Services*, www.wto.org; Amy Tsui, *Members of Congress Ask USTR to Ensure WTO Talks Include End to Fishery Subsidies*, 28 International Trade Reporter (BNA) 1167 (14 July 2011) (*quoting* a letter dated 6 July 2011 to USTR Ambassador Ron Kirk from 12 Senators and 30 Members of the House of Representatives); Jonathan Lynn, *Activists Say Fish Deal Hostage to WTO Deadlock*, Reuters, 29 October 2009 (hereinafter, *Activists Say*).

In a February 2014 report, *Fish to 2030: Prospects for Fisheries and Aquaculture*, the World Bank, FAO, and International Food Policy Research Institute (IFPRI) said that by 2030, 62% of fish consumption around the world will come from fish farms, with the fastest growing aquaculture output being Carp, catfish, and tilapia. *See* World Bank Report Number 83177-GLB, Agriculture and Environmental Services Discussion Paper 03, www.fao.org/docrep/019/i3640e/i3640e.pdf. Moreover, because of its rising middle class, 70% of global fish demand will come from Asia, with 38% of the total coming from China.

9. Bryce Baschuk, *WTO's Fishery Talks Remain Tangled After Years Adrift (1)*, 35 International Trade Reporter (BNA) (13 December 2018) (citing U.N. FAO data). [Hereinafter, *WTO's Fisheries Talks.*]

10. April 2011 Rules Document, *Negotiations on Fisheries Subsidies—Report by the Chairman*, TN/RL/W/254, Part I, ¶ 12 (21 April 2011), www.wto.org.

periods, more intensively, and at further distances.[11] As the Chairman put it: "most [Members] agree that subsidies play a major role in contributing to these problems [of overcapacity and overfishing], and that this is what is behind the negotiating mandate to strengthen disciplines on fisheries subsidies, including through a prohibition."[12]

(3) Overall, annual fishing subsidies (as of 2010) equal about 20% of the value of the world catch of fish.[13]

(4) Seven industrialized countries account for 90% of the subsidies—Canada, the EU, Japan, Korea, Russia, Taiwan, and U.S.[14]

(5) Fishing subsidies provided by the EU and Japan have helped contribute to a worldwide fishing fleet that is about 250% larger than needed to fish at sustainable levels.[15]

(6) Ominously, Brazil and China are increasing their subsidies nearly to the level of the industrialized countries. Over 50% of the large vessels that engage in unsustainable fishing are Chinese, and the Communist Party supports them with fuel subsidies.[16]

(7) The crisis has adverse economic and environmental effects.[17] It also impacts on nutrition and health, because over one billion people rely on fish as the key source of their protein.[18]

---

11. For instance, over 700 vessels with EU flags catch over one million tons of fish annually outside EU waters. They do so under "Foreign Partnership Agreements" (FPAs) with developing countries in the Caribbean, East Africa, West Africa, and the Pacific, and through accords with Iceland and Norway. *See* Daniel Pruzin, *Group Claims EU Subsidies to Fishery Sector Far Higher than EU's Official Figures Indicate*, 28 International Trade Reporter (BNA) 1491 (15 September 2011).

12. April 2011 Rules Document, *Negotiations on Fisheries Subsidies—Report by the Chairman*, TN/RL/W/254, Part I, ¶ 12 (21 April 2011), www.wto.org.

13. *See* Rossella Brevetti, *Environmental Groups Ask Obama for Strong Fisheries Subsidy Pact in WTO*, 28 International Trade Reporter (BNA) 848 (26 May 2011).

14. *See* Daniel Pruzin, *WTO Rules Chair Admits Little Progress on Sticking Points, Issues Fisheries Warning*, 26 International Trade Reporter (BNA) 1641 (3 December 2009).

15. *See* Amy Tsui, *USTR Hopes to Use Doha WTO Talks, TPP to Eliminate Fishing Subsidies, Support Oceans*, 27 International Trade Reporter (BNA) 1103 (22 July 2010).

EU fishing subsidies are understated, with the true figures being three times greater than those published by the European Commission (EC). The EC bases them on payments from the European Fisheries Fund (EEF), and thus excludes payments from individual EU states, with Spain, France, Denmark, and the United Kingdom being the top subsidizers (in 2009, respectively, $734, $362, $307, and $264). Most of the support from individual states is for fuel subsidies. Consequently, the EU fishing fleet is between two and three times larger in size than what is sustainable. *See* Daniel Pruzin, *Group Claims EU Subsidies to Fishery Sector Far Higher than EU's Official Figures Indicate*, 28 International Trade Reporter (BNA) 1491 (15 September 2011).

16. *See* Rossella Brevetti, *Allgeier Says Success of Fisheries Pact at WTO Would Help Sell Doha Package*, 28 International Trade Reporter (BNA) 768 (12 May 2011).

17. *See* December 2008 Draft Rules Text, Road Map, ¶ 2; *Activists Say*.

18. *See Activists Say*.

Despite widespread appreciation of these facts, the Members could not agree on a common strategy to deal with the crisis. Their disagreement persisted, as the April 2011 Rules Document indicated essentially no progress had been made from December 2008 through mid-2011.[19]

II. Three Way Split Over Eight Issues

In Doha Round negotiations over fishing subsidies, WTO Members were split three ways:

(1) First, Japan, Korea, and Taiwan were sceptical of a link between subsidies and over-fishing.

(2) Second, the so-called "Friends of Fish" on the other side—consisting of Argentina, Australia, Chile, Colombia, New Zealand, Norway, Iceland, Pakistan, Peru, and U.S.—sought stringent disciplines on fisheries subsidies.[20]

(3) Third, Brazil, China, India, Indonesia, and Mexico demanded exceptions, *i.e.*, S&D treatment that would allow flexibility to deviate from any such disciplines for poor countries.[21]

The desire of the second group for stringent disciplines clashed with the scepticism of the first group. And, the demands of the third group caused consternation among the second group, which feared exceptions for developing countries would undermine any new disciplines. Accordingly, Members disputed eight key areas, as follows.

• *First: Benchmarks?*

What metrics should be used to gauge the existence of overcapacity or overfishing objectively and precisely? This question seems straightforward. But:

> The National Fisheries Institute supports efforts for WTO countries to work together multilaterally to tackle the problem of fishing subsidies, said Gavin Gibbons, vice president of the NFI. But it is an "extraordinarily complex" problem because "one country's fishing subsidy is another country's

---

19. *See* Daniel Pruzin, *U.S. Criticizes WTO Chief Lamy's Assessment of Doha Impasse, Says NAMA Not Only Issue*, 28 International Trade Reporter (BNA) 724 (5 May 2011).

20. *See* World Trade Organization, *Briefing Notes—Rules*, www.wto.org. *See also See* Amy Tsui, *USTR Hopes to Use Doha WTO Talks, TPP to Eliminate Fishing Subsidies, Support Oceans*, 27 International Trade Reporter (BNA) 1103 (22 July 2010) (*quoting* Senator Ron Wyden (Democrat-Oregon), Chairman, Senate Finance Committee Subcommittee on International Trade, Customs, and Global Competitiveness, telling Mark Linscott, Assistant USTR for Environment and Natural Resources: "Let me just give you something to take back to Geneva—no fish subsidies agreement, you will have my opposition. Congress in my view is not going to accept it and all you have to do is look at this Committee to get an idea of how powerful this issue is.").

21. *See* Daniel Pruzin, *Officials at WTO Cite Mixed Results from Doha "Brainstorming" Sessions*, 27 International Trade Reporter (BNA) 1543 (14 October 2010).

infrastructure investment," he added. Countries may disagree, for example, on whether government support to build additional fishing vessels contributes to overcapacity, Gibbons said.[22]

In other words, the choice of measurement tool is related to the object to be measured. If some WTO Members agree that a certain object (*e.g.*, a fishing subsidy scheme) comes within the general ambit of what should be reduced, then they will pick a tool appropriate for measuring that object. Members opposing them, believing that object should not be subject to any reduction commitments (*e.g.*, because it relates to infrastructure development), will pick a different gauge.

- *Second: Judge?*

Should individual Members be permitted to self-judge overcapacity and overfishing?[23] Or, should some other party, group, or institution make those judgments?

- *Third: Fisheries Management?*

Should the core of a deal on fisheries subsidies be obligations about fisheries management, or a prohibition on subsidies? As the Chairman explained in April 2011:

91. From the outset of the negotiations, the issue of fisheries management has figured prominently in the debates. *Some delegations argue that if proper management is in place, subsidies cannot cause either overcapacity or overfishing. Others, however, consider that while fisheries management is important, it cannot on its own combat the pressure for overcapacity and overfishing brought to bear by subsidization.* In their view, the global crisis in fish stocks is ample evidence that fisheries management by itself is inadequate to control overcapacity and overfishing. In this regard, the example of the North Atlantic cod industry has been cited.

92. *These differences of view in turn are reflected in very different proposals as to the role that fisheries management should play in the disciplines. Delegations holding the former view consider that fisheries management should form the core of the new rules, and that the subsidy disciplines should play the auxiliary role of creating incentives for Members to adopt strong management systems.* Their proposals thus are to shorten the list of subsidies to be prohibited, and to make these prohibitions subject to certain management-related conditions (such as subsidizing the replacement of retired vessels with vessels of smaller capacity), and/or to put greater emphasis on adverse effects provisions, in which the existence and operation of the fisheries management system would play a pivotal role in determining whether subsidization had caused overcapacity and overfishing in a particular situation.

---

22. Bryce Baschuk, *Indonesia Seeks Exemptions in WTO Fisheries Debate*, International Trade Daily (BNA) (7 June 2017).

23. *See* December 2008 Draft Rules Text, Road Map, ¶ 6.

93. *Other delegations, however, maintain that the core of the disciplines must be a prohibition of certain subsidies, and that fisheries management should be a conditionality for making use of exceptions from the prohibition* (whether general exceptions or exceptions under special and differential treatment). They further consider that while having fisheries management in place can be a relevant factor in assessing whether non-prohibited subsidies have caused adverse effects to fish stocks, this by itself should not be sufficient for a successful rebuttal of a claim.[24]

In brief, Members could not agree on the basic paradigm for an agreement—whether it was about resource management or subsidy prohibition. This disagreement, of course, begged an important question: what are the key features of "fisheries management" to which all Members should adhere?[25]

• *Fourth: Prohibition?*

How should the scope of the fishing subsidy prohibition be delineated?[26] Should the subsidies ban apply to a comprehensive list, *i.e.*, a broad and strict prohibition, with coverage including a ban on support for:

(1) construction of new fishing vessels?

(2) repair and modification of existing vessels?

(3) operating costs of vessels and in- or near-port processing activities?

(4) fuel?

(5) port and other infrastructure facilities?

(6) incomes of fishermen?

(7) prices of fish products?

(8) destructive fishing practices?

(9) overfished fisheries?

(10) transfer of fishing or service vessels (from one to another country)?

(11) illegal, unreported, and unregulated (IUU) vessels (which accounted for $10–23 billion worth of fishing, as of June 2017,[27] and by December 2018, accounted for $23.5 billion, *i.e.*, "up to 20% of all wild marine fish caught"[28])?

---

24. April 2011 Rules Document, *Negotiations on Fisheries Subsidies—Report by the Chairman*, TN/RL/W/254, Part III.D.1 ¶¶ 91–93 (21 April 2011), www.wto.org (emphasis added). [Hereinafter, April 2011 Rules Document.]

25. *See* April 2011 Rules Document, Part III.D.1 ¶¶ 94–95 (emphasis added).

26. *See* April 2011 Rules Document, Part III.A.

27. *See* World Trade Organization, Sustainable Fishing, Climate Change among Issues Aired at Trade and Environment Committee, (27 June 2017), www.wto.org/english/news_e/news17_e/envir_20jun17_e.htm.

28. *WTO's Fisheries Talks* (*citing* Pew Charitable Trusts data).

(12) transfer of access rights (whereby one country that pays for fishing access rights in the waters of another country sells those rights to a third country)?[29]

Or, should a conditional approach to prohibition be used, allowing for certain fishing subsidies, such as artisanal (*i.e.*, small scale) fisheries, natural disaster relief, and *de minimis* support, and barring only subsidies most harmful to global fishing stocks?[30]

Related to these questions was how to draft a prohibition. Should a positive list of subsidies, akin to Article 1:1 of the WTO *SCM Agreement*, be created, with the scope of prohibited subsidies on the list "modulated by general exceptions"?[31] Or, would a negative list, identifying only particular types of subsidies as unlawful, be appropriate?

- *Fifth: Exemptions and S&D Treatment?*

For the benefit of poor countries, what specific types of fishing subsidy programs might be exempt from a prohibition on fishing subsidies, above and beyond the general exceptions to which any country could have recourse?[32] Accordingly, Members failed to agree on the possible exemptions for developing and least developed countries from any ban on fishing subsidies, as well as on technical assistance for such countries.[33]

As the Chairman stated in April 2011:

> virtually all of the proposals for special and differential treatment are based on permanent exceptions from various prohibitions, in various circumstances and subject to various conditions. That said, there are fundamentally different visions as to how S&DT [special and differential treatment] should be structured, what particular exceptions should be provided in which particular circumstances, and what conditions should apply to the different exceptions.[34]

Among the possible exemptions were subsidy programs:

(1) that contribute only minimally to overcapacity or overfishing,

(2) the effects of which could be controlled adequately by a fisheries management scheme,

---

29. *See* April 2011 Rules Document, Part III.A.3 ¶¶ 25–45.

30. *See* April 2011 Rules Document, Part III.A.2 ¶¶ 20–24; December 2008 Draft Rules Text, Road Map, ¶ 5; *See* Daniel Pruzin, *Officials at WTO Cite Mixed Results from Doha "Brainstorming" Sessions*, 27 International Trade Reporter (BNA) 1543 (14 October 2010).

31. April 2011 Rules Document, Part I, ¶ 10.

32. *See* April 2011 Rules Document, Part III.B.

33. *See* April 2011 Rules Document, Part III.B.7 (concerning technical assistance).

34. April 2011 Rules Document, Part III.B ¶ 46.

(3) that focus on small operations, *i.e.*, a "bottom tier" of activities that relate to artisanal (small-scale) or subsistence fishing, which would not contribute to overcapacity or overfishing,[35] or

(4) that are important to the economic development of a poor country.[36]

Members contested the parameters for exemptions, as well as the exemptions themselves. For example, how should "subsistence" fishing to be measured? How does it differ from "artisanal" activities? Would income and price support, funding for port infrastructure, and subsidies for the construction of small-decked and undecked vessels qualify for an exemption, because they matter to economic development?[37] In this respect, fuel subsidies, and support for other operating costs, were a "very divisive" topic.[38]

Should flexibilities for poor countries to derogate from any ban on fishing subsidies extend to support for activities on the high seas, that is, beyond the EEZ of those countries?[39] This question also provoked heated debate.

Developing countries argues that equity suggested "yes." Poor countries "are latecomers to high seas fisheries, and should be able to use whatever means they deem necessary in order to catch up to the developed world."[40] International law also suggested "yes," because "all countries have the right to a share of fisheries in international waters, but . . . the cost advantages of developed Members' fishing fleets are too great for . . . [developing countries] to overcome without subsidies."[41] Fairness, too, suggested "yes." Developed countries are responsible for over-fishing high seas stocks, but now seek to "impose a standstill on high seas fishing."[42] That standstill would hurt the vulnerable resources, *i.e.*, spawning and juvenile stocks, within the EEZs of developing countries. Nature, also, counseled for an affirmative answer: the distinction between EEZs and the high seas is artificial, because many stocks are highly migratory.[43]

Developed countries offered strong rebuttals. First, the high seas are "the most biologically and politically vulnerable" fishing areas, as there is no national jurisdiction and thus no mechanism to ensure the "internationally-shared fisheries resources" are "managed sustainably."[44] Second, any fishing activity outside of an EEZ is by definition "highly industrialized," not subsistence or artisanal, even if a

---

35. *See* April 2011 Rules Document, Part III.B.5 ¶¶ 58–67.
36. *See* December 2008 Draft Rules Text, Road Map, ¶ 5.
37. *See* April 2011 Rules Document, Part III.B.5 ¶¶ 68–72.
38. April 2011 Rules Document, Part III.B.5 ¶ 73.
39. *See* April 2011 Rules Document, Part III.B.6 (21 April 2011).
40. April 2011 Rules Document, Part III.B.6 ¶ 76.
41. April 2011 Rules Document, Part III.B.6 ¶ 76.
42. April 2011 Rules Document, Part III.B.6 ¶ 76.
43. April 2011 Rules Document, Part III.B.6 ¶ 77.
44. April 2011 Rules Document, Part III.B.6 ¶ 79 (21 April 2011). *See also id.*, ¶ 81 (on the problems of enforcing sustainable conditions for a S&D treatment exception that allows for a subsidy for fishing activities on the high seas).

poor country engages in such activity.[45] So, all countries should be subject to the same subsidy disciplines on high seas fishing. Third, a poor country can protect its spawning and juvenile stocks with a sound "national fisheries management" program.[46]

At the heart of the disagreement lay the fact poor countries demanded S&D treatment in connection with a problem for which they are partly to blame. The Chairman indicated as much in April 2011:

47. Among the considerations cited frequently in this context is the important role of developing countries in world marine capture production. According to FAO statistics, *six of the top ten fishing nations, and 11 of the top 15, are developing countries, and developing countries collectively account for about 70 per cent of global capture production. For many Members, given these facts S&DT cannot simply be a blanket carve-out from the disciplines for all developing Members, as in their view this would render the overall discipline ineffective.* A number of developing Members, while stressing that they do not seek a simple blanket carve-out, nevertheless consider the absolute figures to be *misleading* in that they mask the comparative efficiency and magnitude of countries' fishing activities, and thus their relative impacts on global fisheries resources. They argue instead that the use of catch *per capita*, or catch per fisher, as alternative measures, show that developing countries make less impact on global resources than do developed countries.

48. Some of the differences in the approaches advanced by different Members appear to relate to the *different rationales advanced for S&DT in the particular context of fisheries subsidies disciplines.* In this regard, objectives of S&DT that have been referred to in the discussions and proposals include: (1) *poverty alleviation, i.e.,* assistance for vulnerable, disadvantaged populations; (2) *development of the fisheries sector as a source of jobs, income and trade,* both to lift people out of poverty and to create new opportunities for economic development and linkages; (3) *building up domestic capacity* to exploit the fisheries resources within the national jurisdiction; (4) *enhanced policy flexibility* for Members with a small share of global fish catch, on the grounds that they have at most a negligible impact on global overcapacity and overfishing; (5) *extending domestic fishing activities beyond coastal areas,* both into the EEZ [Exclusive Economic Zone] and (in some cases) into the high seas, to relieve pressure on coastal fisheries resources, including spawning and juvenile populations; (6) *"catching up" to the developed world* in terms of vessels, technology, scale, and areas of operation; and (7) *exercising rights under international law* to exploit commercially valuable fish stocks in international waters, the products of which are traded

---

45. April 2011 Rules Document, Part III.B.6 ¶ 80.
46. April 2011 Rules Document, Part III.B.6 ¶ 80.

internationally. All proposals and discussions emphasize the need for the subsidies to be deployed and the subsidized activities to be conducted in a sustainable manner, although like the different approaches to the S&DT exceptions, the proposed approaches to the accompanying sustainability conditionalities vary greatly.[47]

In other words, there was considerable debate over the guilt of poor countries, and the theory underlying any S&D differential treatment they might get. Unsurprisingly, the Members could not agree on the practical matter of how to calibrate the nature, scale, and geographic scope of their activities that should be exempt from any disciplines.[48]

Also unresolved, then, were the precise fisheries management obligations a poor country would have to implement before having access to a S&D treatment exception that permitted it to subsidize its fisheries in some manner. Presumably, these obligations would require the country to implement "internationally-recognized best practices, including regular science-based stock assessments."[49] And, what transition rules would apply to developing and least developed countries, so that they might have more time to phase in their obligations?[50]

Finally, whether S&D treatment should be tailored for different categories of poor countries was in dispute. Members generally agreed LDCs ought to get the best of S&D treatment.[51] But, they worried that some developing, and even some developed, countries might behave unscrupulously and try to take advantage of the exemptions designed for LDCs.

Thus, "the U.S. and the EU reject[ed] the idea that large developing countries like China and India should receive special rights and more favorable trade terms that are generally allotted to small and economically disadvantaged nations."[52] Yet, Members could not agree on whether distinctions should be made among developing countries. Obviously, doing so along the lines of the draft agriculture and NAMA proposals (*e.g.*, with differentiations for NFIDCs, certain RAMs, and SVEs), or along new lines (*e.g.*, distinguishing developing countries with a small share of global wild fish capture) would risk making the fishing subsidy rules vastly more complex.[53]

- *Sixth: Notification?*

What scheme should be used for Members to notify one another of their fisheries subsidies, particularly if they sought to invoke a general or S&D treatment

47. April 2011 Rules Document, Part III.B ¶ 47.

48. *See* April 2011 Rules Document, Part I ¶ 10.

49. April 2011 Rules Document, Part I ¶ 10 (21 April 2011).

50. *See* April 2011 Rules Document, Part I ¶ 11 (21 April 2011).

51. *See* April 2011 Rules Document, Part III.B.2 ¶ 49.

52. Bryce Baschuk, *WTO Outlines Plan for Stalled Talks to End Fishing Subsidies*, 35 International Trade Reporter (BNA) 1026 (2 August 2018). [Hereinafter, *WTO Outlines.*]

53. *See* April 2011 Rules Document, Part III.B.3-4 ¶ 49.

exception?[54] How much advance notice must a Member provide?[55] To what forum should notice be given—the FAO, WTO, or some other entity?[56] What information would be sufficient to demonstrate that a Member qualified for an exception?[57]

Related to problems of notification were questions of what to do with information in a notification? Should there be a review of the practices of the notifying country, and if so, what kind of review should it be?[58] For example, if notification is to the FAO, then should it be empowered to render a judgment as to the soundness of the fisheries management system in a poor country, and the entitlement of that country to invoke an exception? Would this judgment be binding? Could it be used in a WTO adjudicatory proceeding? Should a non-notified subsidy be presumed rebuttably to be prohibited?[59]

- *Seventh: Remedy?*

To be meaningful, any discipline on fishing subsidies would have to have associated with it a remedy for breach.[60] Likewise, an unlawful subsidy would have to be attributed to the subsidizing government, not the flag of the vessel carrying subsidized fish (otherwise, it would be easy to circumvent the disciplines).[61] And, the rule of origin for fisheries product, used for customs and labeling purposes, would not affect this attribution. But, what should the legal criteria for the remedy be?

Should the "traffic light" scheme of the *SCM Agreement* be used, whereby certain subsidies are forbidden (Red Light) as long as they are specific, and are presumed irrebuttably to cause adverse effects, while other subsidies are actionable (Yellow Light) if they are both specific and cause adverse effects? What sort of "adverse effects" should be actionable—only those in relation to fish stocks, such as over-capacity and over-fishing, or any effect on trade?[62] What test should be used to establish a causal link between adverse effects and subsidization?[63] Is the mere absence of strong resource management enough to deem such a link exists, or must more be shown?

As to the remedy, should it be limited to a CVD, as per Article 7:9 of the *SCM Agreement*?[64] Or, should a WTO panel or the Appellate Body be empowered to fashion a different sort of remedy? Should the remedy be the same for all types of fish,

---

54. *See* April 2011 Rules Document, Part I ¶ 11, Part III.E ¶ 97.
55. *See* April 2011 Rules Document, Part III.E ¶¶ 99–100.
56. *See* April 2011 Rules Document, Part III.E ¶¶ 101–102.
57. *See* April 2011 Rules Document, Part I ¶ 11, Part III.E ¶ 104.
58. *See* April 2011 Rules Document, Part I ¶ 11, Part III.E ¶¶ 102–103.
59. *See* April 2011 Rules Document, Part I ¶ 11, Part III.E ¶ 98.
60. *See* April 2011 Rules Document, Part I ¶ 10, Part III.C ¶ 84.
61. *See* April 2011 Rules Document, Part I ¶ 1, Part III.C ¶¶ 84, 90.
62. *See* April 2011 Rules Document, Part I ¶ 1, Part III.C ¶ 87.
63. *See* April 2011 Rules Document, Part III.C ¶ 89.
64. *See* April 2011 Rules Document, Part III.C ¶ 89.

or should a distinction be made for highly migratory stocks?[65] Should the remedy cover only fish from the "same stock," or also a "directly competitive product"?[66]

- *Eighth: Enforcement?*

What methods should be used to monitor and survey any exempt fishing subsidy programs, to ensure the integrity of the prohibition is not undermined, and thus to help prevent overcapacity and overfishing?[67] For instance, should inspectors from the FAO review whether a poor country is implementing its fisheries management obligations?[68]

Thus, Chairman Valles simply put to the Members in his "Road Map" a long list of questions concerning fundamental issues to address.[69] They were back to square one.

III. 2001–2011 Doha Round Negotiations, But No Deal

These issues were under the negotiating mandate Members undertook three years before the Draft Text, in the December 2005 Hong Kong Ministerial Conference. And, following the Seventh Ministerial Conference in Geneva in November–December 2009, the Chairman readily admitted no progress had been made in the year since he issued his Text (*i.e.*, since December 2008).[70] Chairman Valles elaborated on that depressing conclusion in April 2010. Deciding to retire from his post as Chairman after 6 years, and return to Uruguay, he said the bottom-up approach embodied in the December 2008 Text had been fruitless, and—worse yet—Members had made no significant progress after 8 years of negotiations on bridging differences on AD or CVD rules.[71]

His successor, Ambassador Dennis Francis of Trinidad and Tobago, wrote in April 2011:

> 13. ... [W]hat then is the problem? Why have these negotiations been under-
> way for 10 years with little tangible progress in finding a solution? In my

---

65. *See* April 2011 Rules Document, Part III.C ¶ 88.

66. April 2011 Rules Document, Part III.C ¶ 88.

67. *See* December 2008 Draft Rules Text, Road Map ¶ 7.

68. *See* April 2011 Rules Document, Part I ¶ 10 (21 April 2011).

69. *See* December 2008 Draft Rules Text, Road Map ¶¶ 10–11 (concerning the prohibition of fishing subsidies), ¶¶ 12–13 (concerning general exemptions from the prohibition), ¶¶ 14–15 (concerning S&D treatment), ¶ 16 (concerning general disciplines on, and actionability of, fishing subsidies), ¶¶ 17–20 (concerning fisheries management), ¶¶ 21–22 (concerning transparency), ¶ 23 (concerning dispute settlement), ¶¶ 24–25 (concerning implementation), ¶¶ 26–27 (concerning transition rules).

70. *See* Daniel Pruzin, *WTO Rules Chair Admits Little Progress on Sticking Points, Issues Fisheries Warning*, 26 International Trade Reporter (BNA) 1641 (3 December 2009).

71. *See* Daniel Pruzin, *WTO Chair Cites Absence of Progress in Doha Antidumping, Subsidies Talks*, 27 International Trade Reporter (BNA) 659 (6 May 2010).

view, it seems that most (although not all) delegations, *rather than seeking to build convergence by indicating acceptance of the appropriate level of disciplines* (and of the policy changes that this would imply), to effectively address what is undeniably a common and rapidly worsening problem, appear to be focusing principally on *maintaining their own status quo by placing on "others" the main responsibility to implement solutions, while minimizing the impact of disciplines on their own activities*. Thus in spite of the nearly universal calls for disciplining subsidies in an effective way, many delegations in practice seem to *elevate the exceptions above the disciplines*. For some *developed* Members, a main reason given is that subsidies are necessary to *protect traditional ways of life, vulnerable coastal communities, and jobs in the fisheries sector*. For many *developing* Members, a main reason often cited is the need for policy space to subsidize in order to *harness fisheries as a basis for development, economic growth, and employment*. In the face of the sharp and continuing declines in the fisheries resources, however, *it is hard to see how such strategies can either protect communities and jobs or be a source of food security and stable growth over the long-term*.

14. . . . [A] unified, long-term strategic approach to cooperating to rationalize economic signals — including by giving priority to collectively reducing the level of capacity- and effort-enhancing subsidies — can actively promote and contribute to profitability of global fisheries, with the hugely advantageous additional benefits of economic and environmental sustainability. . . . [F]isheries are often compared to the *prisoner's dilemma*: non-cooperative pursuit of individual payoffs leads to overfishing, which in turn imposes economic loss (not to mention negative environmental effects) on all parties involved. In fact, it is widely-accepted that the economic benefits lost due to overfishing are significant — a World Bank Report gives an estimate of U.S. $50 billion annually, without counting the out-of-pocket additional costs of subsidies (estimated to be at least U.S. $ 16 billion annually). To put these figures in context, the value of the total global marine fish catch is around U.S. $ 90 billion. Like the prisoner's dilemma, however, fisheries are not a zero-sum game. Successful subsidy negotiations can help bring about a situation where profitability and economic and environmental stability are mutually reinforcing, contributing to sustainable wealth creation.

15. In order for the negotiations to make significant progress, I am of the view that negotiators will have to focus more on these incontrovertible realities no matter how inconvenient, and less on protecting their short-term defensive interests. Unless this happens, I do not hold great prospects for the fisheries subsidies negotiations.[72]

A more honest assessment was hard to come by.

---

72. April 2011 Rules Document, Part II ¶ 13 (emphasis added).

IV. Aiming for SDG Targets after 2013 December Bali Ministerial Conference

By their Ninth Ministerial Conference, from 3–6 December 2013 in Bali, Indonesia, WTO Members had made no progress on the aforementioned issues. The best they could muster was a joint pledge from the Friends of Fish Coalition — Argentina, Australia, Chile, Colombia, Costa Rica, Ecuador, Iceland, New Zealand, Norway, Pakistan, Peru, Philippines, and U.S.[73] In their statement, they pledged to refrain from expanding existing fishing subsidy programs or introducing new subsidies that might lead to over-fishing. They expressed regret no progress had been made on the topic in the Doha Round, and their pledge was not part of the Bali Package. Across the next two years, the state-of-play remained the same: stagnation.

In March 2016, the best the WTO could muster in the context of rules negotiations was that 28 its Members (out of over 160) expressed desire to forge trade rules to prevent overfishing.[74] Such rules would include bans on fishing in areas with limited stocks, disciplines on injurious fisheries subsidies (such as those that contribute to over-capacity, or support unreported, unregulated, or illegal operators), and mandates to enhance transparency. They were desperately needed: by then, about 30% of global fishing stocks were classified by the FAO as over-fished. Argentina, Australia, Canada, Colombia, Costa Rica, Fiji, Haiti, New Zealand, Pakistan, Paraguay, Peru, and U.S. were among the signatories to this "Group of 28" statement. But, with China conspicuously absent, a meaningful agreement, even a plurilateral one, was dubious. Obviously, the Statement failed to garner a consensus, despite it embodying Target 14:6 of the 169 Targets in the 17 U.N. SDGs, which are set out in Paragraph 54 of the United Nations Resolution (A/RES/70/1) of 25 September 2015, and which are to be achieved by 2030.[75]

That Target called for a complete elimination of subsidies that cause excess fishing capacity and over-fishing by 2020. By November 2016, the FAO called for subsidy cuts that would translate to positive affects for 30% of global fishing stocks, but with hardly three years before the Target date, the Members were nowhere near the Target.[76] That was despite a plurilateral effort the U.S. had led:

> In September [2016], the U.S. and 12 other WTO Members launched a plurilateral initiative to curb fishing subsidies and increase transparency over national programs that contribute to overfishing and overcapacity.

---

73. *See* Brian Flood, *U.S. Among "Friends of Fish" WTO Members Vowing to Limit Subsidies on Fisheries*, 30 International Trade Reporter (BNA) 1924 (12 December 2013).

74. *See* World Trade Organization, *WTO Members "Still Interested" in Securing Results in Rules Negotiations*, 22 March 2016, www.wto.org; Bryce Baschuk, *WTO Members Support Curbs on Fish Subsidies*, 33 International Trade Reporter (BNA) 450 (31 March 2016).

75. *See* https://sustainabledevelopment.un.org/?menu=1300. The formal title of the scheme is *Transforming Our World: The 2030 Agenda for Sustainable Development*.

76. *See* Bryce Baschuk, *New WTO Rules on Fishery Subsidies Could Emerge in 2017*, 33 International Trade Reporter (BNA) 1622 (17 November 2016). [Hereinafter, *New WTO Rules*.]

The members—which included most of the *Trans-Pacific Partnership's* [*TPP's*] 12 participants—said they want to eliminate subsidies that could result in overfishing in areas with limited fish stocks and prohibit subsidies for vessels used by illegal, unreported or unregulated operators.[77]

Any Member could participate in the plurilateral talks, which ran on a parallel track, and were complementary, to multilateral discussions. But, two of the world's largest catchers of fish, China and Japan, stayed out of the plurilateral, and India, with over 4,500 miles of coastline, and 14 million of its citizens dependent on fishing, said special and differential treatment for small fishing communities would be needed.[78]

Moreover, the November 2016 election of Donald J. Trump to the Presidency cast doubt on whether the Americans still would lead the initiative. In January 2017, participating Members hoped it would, and four of them offered proposals that suggested consensus on three topic areas, namely, the need for:

(1) Disciplines on subsidies that contribute to overcapacity and overfishing.

(2) Elimination of subsidies for IUU fishing.

(3) Special and differential treatment for developing countries and LDCs (including a "limit[ing] any proposed disciplines to large-scale industrial fishing operating outside national exclusive economic zones and sanction[ing] artisanal and small-scale fishing in territorial waters").[79]

These points emerged from four proposals offered by a diverse array of countries: the EU, LDC, ACP, and six Latin American members. With the change in the White House, the U.S. hesitated to make any definitive commitments, even though 90 percent of American seafood is imported, and about one-third of the imports caught in the wild are illegal.[80]

---

77. *New WTO Rules.*

78. *See New WTO Rules.*

79. Bryce Baschuk, *U.S. Could Sink WTO Deal to Curb Fishing Subsidies*, 34 International Trade Reporter (BNA) 152 (26 January 2017).

80. These statistics are based on a 2014 study in the journal, Marine Policy. *See* Rossella Brevetti, *Fish Importers Still on Hook as Court Backs Traceability Rule*, 34 International Trade Reporter (BNA) 1193 (7 September 2017).

Nevertheless, in August 2017, the U.S. Court of Appeals for the District of Columbia Circuit upheld a challenge to a regulation of the Department of Commerce concerning IUU fishing. *See Alfa International Seafood v. Ross*, D.D.C. Case Number 1:17-cv-00031 (28 August 2017) (Amit P. Mehta, Judge). The DOC rule, which applied to importers of seafood products such as blue crab, grouper, red snapper, and tuna, established the "Seafood Import Monitoring Program." The aim of the Program was to combat IUU fishing and fraud in the seafood industry, and thus protect not only seafood stocks, but also consumers and law-abiding fisherman. The Program required those importers to disclose specific information about their merchandise before it can enter the U.S. The mandatory disclosures covered:

(1) The area in which the seafood was captured or the aquaculture facility in which it was harvested.

Seeking to realize Target 14:6, Indonesia offered a new proposal to curb overfishing and cut excess capacity. Its June 2016 elaborated on earlier ideas about special and differential treatment for poor countries, and called for an exemption for such countries with small or artisanal fishing industries:

> The proposal is considered noteworthy because of Indonesia's status as the world's second-largest marine fishing nation, after China. Nearly 70 percent of the archipelagic nation's territory is covered by water, and Indonesians are heavily dependent on the oceans for their livelihoods, according to the proposal.[81]

Likewise, Norway proposed that Target 14:6 be addressed by "clear prohibitions 'of any kind' to vessels, owners, or operators" engaged in IUU:[82]

> The text of the proposal would require WTO members to ensure that if they grant fishing subsidies, they must ensure any beneficiaries are not listed as an IUU-vessel in a regional fisheries management organization, nor do they have a record of operating in waters "under the jurisdiction of any member without the permission of that member during the preceding five years."[83]

Regrettably, China muddied the waters, because it saw such proposals as applying to disputed territories and maritime jurisdictions.

---

    (2) The name of the entity (*e.g.,* company) to which the seafood product was landed or delivered.

    (3) The name and flag country of the vessel that harvested the seafood product.

In effect, the disclosures summed to a "traceability" requirement: enforcement authorities could secure the seafood chain against IUU if they understood each step and commercial party in the chain, and if they put the onus on those parties, especially fisherman, to fight IUU. Compliance with the disclosure requirements took effect on 1 January 2018 for so-called "priority species." *See* Rossella Brevetti, *Fish Importers Still on Hook as Court Backs Traceability Rule,* 34 International Trade Reporter (BNA) 1193 (7 September 2017).

    Of course, the National Fisheries Institute and food companies like the petitioner, Alfa International Seafood and Trident Seafoods Corporation, did not like the Program. They made two unsuccessful arguments against it. First, costs: they contended the record-keeping burden was expensive, costing about $53 million for American companies, and in turn causing higher consumer seafood prices and reduced consumer choice, to the extent the companies passed on compliance costs. But, in support of the Program was the fact both American consumers and fisherman are defrauded by illegally caught or mislabeled seafood. *See id.* Second, the petitioners argued there between the mandated disclosures and fighting IUU fishing and seafood fraud was insufficient, to which the Court replied there was "no shortage of literature" on the positive role that traceability recordkeeping has toward the policy goals. *See id.*

    81. Bryce Baschuk, *Indonesia Seeks Exemptions in WTO Fisheries Debate,* International Trade Daily (BNA), 7 June 2017.

    82. Bryce Baschuk, *Norway Asks WTO to Curb Subsidies for Illegal Fishing,* 34 International Trade Reporter (BNA) 958 (6 July 2017). [Hereinafter, *Norway Asks.*]

    83. *Norway Asks.*

Chapter 22

Post-2013 Bali Ministerial Conference Efforts[1]

I. China's Nine Dash Line Gets in Way

China's insistence on territorial sovereignty across the South China Sea, as it defined with its infamous Nine Dash Line, meant it refused to accept any proposal affecting that part of the Sea inside the Line. (Diagram 22-1 depicts the Line. Roughly half of world trade is transported in these waters.) In other words, as China intoned at an April 2017 Rules Negotiating Committee meeting, no waters covered by a territorial dispute could be covered by a fishing subsidies agreement. Apparently, notwithstanding the reality that fish swim where they like, Chinese sovereignty mattered most. And, China did not want the WTO to be the forum in which to discuss, much less adjudicate, its claim to the maritime territory within Nine Dash Line.

But, perhaps for cover, China initially linked its position on fishing subsidies to broader reforms across all trade remedies—a position from which, thankfully, China later backed off.[2] In June 2017, China to strengthen AD-CVD disciplines, focusing on transparency and due process so that respondents could effectively defend their rights, and administering authorities could make fair, impartial decisions, drawn largely from the April 2011 consolidated Draft Text on rules.[3] At a 14

---

1. Documents References:
   (1) *Havana (ITO) Charter* Preamble
   (2) GATT Preamble
   (3) *WTO SCM Agreement*

2. *See* Bryce Baschuk, *China Removes Key Hurdle to WTO Fisheries Negotiations*, 34 International Trade Reporter (BNA) 9 (20 July 2017) (noting that, though excluding tighter restrictions on anti-circumvention rules and Sunset Reviews, "China in June introduced a revised proposal to amend the WTO's *Antidumping Agreement (ADA)* and its *Agreement on Subsidies and Countervailing Measures (SCM)*. China proposed five goals: enhance transparency and strengthen due process; prevent antidumping measures from becoming 'permanent;' prevent antidumping measures from 'overreaching;' provide special consideration and treatment of small and medium-sized enterprises; and transplant similar provisions from the *ADA* [WTO *Antidumping Agreement*] and the *SCM* [Subsidies and Countervailing Measures] *Agreement*.").

3. China's proposal was World Trade Organization, Negotiating Group on Rules, *Follow-Up Paper on Enhancing Transparency and Strengthening Due Process in Anti-Dumping and Countervailing Proceedings—Communication from China*, TN/RL/GEN/190 (26 June 2017). *See* World Trade Organization, *China, EU Seek to Strengthen WTO Trade Remedy, Notification Disciplines*, (14 July 2017), www.wto.org/english/news_e/news17_e/rule_14jul17_e.htm. The April 2011 Draft Text

July 2014 meeting of the Negotiating Group on Rules, China "emphasized . . . that it was not linking negotiations on AD and CV disciplines with any other issue. China said it hoped this clarification would dispel the misgivings of some members and encourage them to engage further in the discussions."[4]

Diagram 22-1. Nine Dash Line[5]

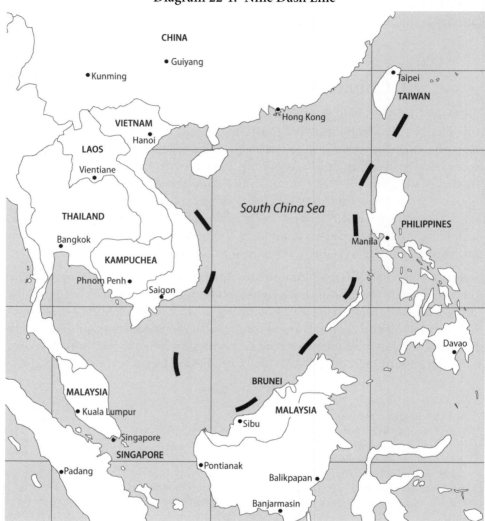

to which the Chinese referred was World Trade Organization, Negotiating Group on Rules, *Communication from the Chairman*, TN/RL/W/254 (21 April 2011).

4. World Trade Organization, *China, EU Seek to Strengthen WTO Trade Remedy, Notification Disciplines*, (14 July 2017), www.wto.org/english/news_e/news17_e/rule_14jul17_e.htm.

5. This map is adapted from www.phamhongphuoc.net/wp-content/uploads/2014/05/nine-dash-line-china.jpg.

Whether that de-linking applied to the Nine Dash Line seemed uncertain, but reaction to the Chinese proposal was "mixed," with some Members saying the Draft Text on which the proposal was based failed to embody any convergence of views across Members, or put colloquially, "we never left square one."[6]

The U.S., which does not provide significant subsidies to its fishing sector, but which hoped for a deal so that its fishermen would not have to compete against foreign subsidized industries, obviously opposed the Chinese Nine Dash Line, as did many other WTO Members. The apparent Chinese demand to link fishing subsidy reform to the Line seemed to sink prospects for a deal.[7] A pity indeed, given that in 2017 WTO Members has filed nearly one dozen distinct proposals to discipline fishing subsidies, the leitmotifs being "new trade disciplines in subsidies that contribute to overcapacity and overfishing;" "the elimination in subsidies for illegal, unreported, and unregulated fishing; and" "the need for special and differential treatment for developing countries and least developed countries."[8]

II. July 2017 Seven New Proposals

By July 2017, seven new specific textual proposals had been presented to the Negotiating Group on Rules.[9] They came from:

---

6. The EU tried with its own proposal, which also garnered a "mixed" response. The EU suggested:

> three options for improving subsidy reporting: asking the WTO Secretariat to circulate notifications of subsidy programs that have not been notified to the WTO but which other members have made the Secretariat aware of; establishing a "general rebuttable" presumption that would be written into the *SCM Agreement* under which non-notified subsidies would be presumed to be "actionable" and causing "serious prejudice" to the interests of other WTO Members; and establishing a presumption that subsidies are actionable only if another Member informs the WTO that the subsidies have not been notified, even after the Member granting the subsidy has been called on to do so beforehand.

World Trade Organization, *China, EU Seek to Strengthen WTO Trade Remedy, Notification Disciplines*, (14 July 2017), www.wto.org/english/news_e/news17_e/rule_14jul17_e.htm. "Some [Members] expressed reluctance with the idea of establishing a general rebuttable presumption which they said could alter existing rights and obligations of members under the *SCM Agreement*." *Id.* Contemporaneously, the EU proposal was World Trade Organization, Negotiating Group on Rules, *Improving Disciplines on Subsidies Negotiations — Communication from the European Union*, TN/RL/GEN/188 (30 May 2017). *See id.*

7. The OECD maintains a "Fishery Support Estimate (FSE) Database," which by year-end 2017 included data from no less than 31 countries, encompassing 50 percent of global fishing activities.

8. Bryce Baschuk, *China Removes Key Hurdle to WTO Fisheries Negotiations*, 34 International Trade Reporter (BNA) 9 (20 July 2017).

9. *See* World Trade Organization, *Fisheries Subsidies Talks Move Forward with Seven Proposals and Forthcoming Compilation* (18 July 2017), www.wto.org/english/news_e/news17_e/fish_20jul17_e.htm. [Hereinafter, *Fisheries Subsidies Talks.*]

(1) EU;[10]

(2) Indonesia;[11]

(3) Norway;[12]

(4) ACP;[13]

(5) LDC;[14]

(6) Joint submission by six Latin American countries (Argentina, Colombia, Costa Rica, Panama, Peru and Uruguay);[15]

(7) Joint submission by New Zealand, Iceland and Pakistan.[16]

All proposals embodied "prohibitions of subsidies that lead to overfishing and overcapacity."[17] However, there was no consensus on "the issue of the geographic scope or how different parts of the seas and oceans would be covered by the disciplines," though there appeared an "emerging clarity" that the prohibitions would be "restricted to subsidies to maritime fishing and will exclude subsidies granted for aquaculture and inland fishing."[18] No consensus existed on whether "certain

---

10. The proposal was World Trade Organization, Negotiating Group on Rules, *Advancing Toward a Multilateral Outcome on Fishing Subsidies in the WTO—European Union*, TN/RL/GEN181 (20 October 2016). *See* World Trade Organization, *Two New Proposals Discussed in Continuing Negotiations on Fisheries Subsidies* (14 June 2017), www.wto.org/english/news_e/news17_e/fish_14jun17_e.htm. [Hereinafter, *Two New Proposals*.]

11. Three Articles comprised this proposal:
> definitions and the suggested coverage of the agreement; prohibitions against subsidies for IUU fishing and certain types of subsidies which contribute to overcapacity and overfishing; and special and differential treatment for developing countries and LDCs, particularly with regard to artisanal and small-scale fishing, fishing within a Member's own exclusive economic zone (EEZ) and quotas in high seas, and technical assistance.

Two New Proposals Discussed. The proposal was World Trade Organization, Negotiating Group on Rules, *Proposal for Disciplines on Prohibitions and Special and Differential Treatment for Fisheries Subsidies—Communication from Indonesia*, TN/RL/GEN189 (6 June 2017). *See id.*

12. This proposal was World Trade Organization, *Negotiating Group on Rules, Discipline and Prohibition on Subsidies to IUU—Fishing—Communication from Norway*, TN/RL/GEN/19 (26 June 2017), www.wto.org.

13. This submission was a concept paper. *See Two New Proposals.*

14. This submission was a concept paper. *See Two New Proposals.*

15. Four Sections comprised this proposal:
> disciplines for subsidies for certain fishing activities, obligations for members to notify pertinent information to the WTO to enable surveillance of subsidies elimination, technical cooperation to help developing countries and . . . LDCs fulfil their commitments, and a provision for an annual review of the implementation progress.

Two New Proposals. The proposal was World Trade Organization, Negotiating Group on Rules, *Proposal for Disciplines on Fisheries Subsidies—Communication from Colombia, Costa Rica, Panama, Peru, and Uruguay*, TN/RL/GEN187 (29 May 2017). *See id.*

16. The proposal was World Trade Organization, Negotiating Group on Rules, *Proposed MC11 Fisheries Subsidies Disciplines: Implementing SDG Target 14:6—Communication from Iceland, New Zealand, and Pakistan*, TN/RL/GEN186 (27 April 2017). *See Two New Proposals.*

17. *Fisheries Subsidies Talks.*

18. *Fisheries Subsidies Talks.*

determinations by national, regional, and international fishery management authorities should have in WTO rules," and on special and differential treatment for developing and least developed countries.[19]

In July 2017, Ambassador Wayne McCook (Jamaica), the Chair of the Negotiating Group on Rules, circulated to WTO Members a "Compilation Matrix" that summarized the seven above-listed proposals.[20] The 39-page document was not a proposed text from the Chair, nor even an embodiment of an emerging consensus.[21]

It simply provide a "side-by-side presentation of the various proposals . . . [so as to] help Members as they prepare" for negotiations, perhaps with a view to reaching a deal at the 11th Ministerial Conference in Buenos Aires December. The U.S. added, in October 2017, it favored those negotiations focus on:

- prohibitions on subsidies provided for illegal, unreported, and unregulated (IUU) fishing, with no exceptions;
- a list of IUU fishing vessels and operators prepared by Regional Fishery Management Organizations;
- a prohibition on fisheries subsidies that negatively affect overfished stocks, with no exceptions;
- a standstill commitment for members to refrain from introducing new subsidies that contribute to overfishing or overcapacity; and
- a discussion of whether it is possible to calculate overcapacity in global fishing.[22]

However:

the U.S. called for negotiating parties to *abandon any sort of special and differential treatment for developing countries* and said any *new fisheries rules should apply to "territorial waters."*

Developing countries such as Indonesia and India have repeatedly called on members to provide certain exceptions for developing nations with artisanal and small-scale fishing operations.

In addition, China has sought a clear exception for any rules that apply to disputed territorial waters—an issue tied to Beijing's claim to modified reefs in the South China Sea, which are home to one of the busiest commercial shipping routes in the world.[23]

---

19. *Fisheries Subsidies Talks.*

20. *See* World Trade Organization, *Compilation of Seven Fisheries Subsidies Proposals Circulated to WTO Members* (28 July 2017), www.wto.org/english/news_e/news17_e/fish_28jul17_e.htm.

21. *See* World Trade Organization, Negotiating Group on Rules, *Fisheries Subsidies Compilation Matrix of Textual Proposals Received to Date*, TN/RL/W/273 (27 July 2017), www.wto.org/english /news_e/news17_e/fish_28jul17_e.htm.

22. Bryce Baschuk, *U.S. Flirts with New WTO Rules for Fishery Subsidies*, 34 International Trade Reporter (BNA) 1319 (5 October 2017). [Hereinafter, *U.S. Flirts.*]

23. *U.S. Flirts* (emphasis added).

With these (and other) disputes, unsurprisingly but starkly, the USTR, Ambassador Robert Lighthizer, declared (on 18 September, speaking in Washington, D.C.): "it's unlikely that the [11th] [WTO] Ministerial [Conference] in Buenos Aires is going to lead to negotiated outcomes."[24]

III. Sino-American Battles and December 2017 Buenos Aires Ministerial Conference

They kept trying in the months just preceding the Ministerial Conference. In October 2017, WTO Members compiled a new text that consolidated all seven fisheries subsidies proposals. The Chair, Ambassador McCook, said the text showed that Members had "achieved some convergence in their views about which subsidies contribute to illegal, unreported, and unregulated fishing, according to a participant at the meeting."[25] However, "[t]here was less movement . . . on issues related to capacity-building efforts, and the potential for special and differential treatment for developing and least developed countries."[26]

America and China remained key obstacles:

> The Trump administration previously rejected any special and differential treatment provisions for poor countries and said it would oppose any agreement that requires members to provide technical assistance and capacity building to poor countries.

> WTO negotiators also disagree about whether a fisheries deal should apply to a country's territorial waters—which is a point on which China is unwilling to concede.

> Instead, China has sought a clear exception for any rules that apply to disputed territorial waters—an issue tied to Beijing's claim to modified reefs in the South China Sea, which are home to one of the busiest commercial shipping routes in the world.[27]

Thus, "WTO Director-General Roberto Azevedo Oct. 16 said it's 'impossible to predict' what will happen with the fisheries negotiations." Yet, in November, both Members tried to remove some obstacles.

---

24. *Quoted in U.S. Flirts.*

25. Bryce Baschuk, *U.S. Skeptical WTO Can Forge Fisheries Deal in 2017,* 34 International Trade Reporter (BNA) 1385 (19 October 2017). [Hereinafter, *U.S. Skeptical.*] *See also* World Trade Organization, *WTO Fisheries Negotiations Take a Step Forward with Compilation Text and Chair's Assessment,* 12–13 October 2017, www.wto.org/english/news_e/news17_e/fish_17oct17_e.htm. [Hereinafter, *WTO Fisheries Negotiations.*]

26. *U.S. Skeptical.*

27. *U.S. Skeptical.*

Discussions proceeded in the Negotiating Group on Rules over the *Compilation Text*, which comprised seven previous proposals (those from New Zealand, Iceland and Pakistan; EU; Indonesia; ACP; a Latin American group composed of Argentina, Colombia, Costa Rica, Panama, Peru and Uruguay; LDCs; and Norway), and which had been circulated on 12 October.[28] On 1 November, China introduced a proposal that focused on subsidy disciplines on IUU fishing, as well as S&D treatment for developing countries and LDCs, and that contained "provisions for legal implications regarding territorial disputes and cooperation with certain organizations."[29]

In specific, first, the Chinese proposal (in Paragraph 1:1) contained an outright ban on fishing vessels, and then defined and outlawed (in Paragraph 1:2) IUU subsidies as follows:

1:2   For the purpose of this *Agreement* [referring to the final accord on fisheries subsidies], a fishery subsidy shall only be attributable to the Member granting it, regardless of the flag of the vessel.

1:3   For the purpose of this *Agreement*, IUU fishing activities shall be determined based on the following:

   1:3:1   IUU fishing activities shall be determined by the flag Member in accordance with its domestic laws and regulations, including through the form of listing. When the flag Member and the subsidizing Member are not the same, the fishing vessel concerned shall be notified to the subsidizing Member, and verified by the subsidizing Member through due procedure; or,

   1:3:2   IUU fishing activities shall be determined by the relevant Regional Fisheries Management Organizations (RFMOs) through listing and based on the following procedures:

      a.   The fishing vessel concerned shall be notified by the RFMO to the flag Member of the vessel concerned; and

      b.   The alleged IUU fishing activities shall be jointly investigated and verified by the flag Member with the relevant RFMO, based on positive evidence and due procedure, and in accordance with relevant international laws, agreements and rules of the RFMO.

1:4   A Member shall neither grant nor maintain a subsidy referred to in paragraph 1, until the IUU fishing activity concerned is punished and corrected in accordance with that Member's domestic laws and regulations, or the fishing vessel concerned is delisted by the relevant RFMO.

---

28. *See* World Trade Organization, *New Proposals Submitted for Draft Agreement on Fisheries Subsidies*, 3 November 2017, www.wto.org/english/news_e/news17_e/fish_03nov17_e.htm [hereinafter, *New Proposals Submitted*]; *WTO Fisheries Negotiations*.

29. *New Proposals Submitted*. The three-page Chinese proposal is World Trade Organization, *Prohibition of Subsidies to IUU Fishing—Proposal of China*, TN/RL/GEN/195 (1 November 2017), and is available through the *New Proposals* publication link.

On S&D treatment, the Chinese proposal (in Articles 2:1–2) called for a phase in period (defined as "X," *i.e.*, a yet to be determined number of years) for obligations for small scale, artisanal and/or subsistence fishing. Each WTO Member would have the sovereign policy space to define that type of fishing. However, the Chinese proposal also contained controversial provisions relating to the South China Sea dispute, namely:

3:1 Nothing in this *Agreement* shall be interpreted as having any legal implications regarding territoriality, sovereignty or maritime jurisdiction.

3:2 Any alleged IUU fishing activity involving disputes concerning territoriality, sovereignty or maritime jurisdiction shall be excluded from the scope of this *Agreement*, and shall not constitute IUU fishing under this *Agreement*.

The Chinese proposal for a "territorial carveout," which would preclude any WTO Member from challenging IIU fishing activity that is set within a controversy about territoriality, sovereignty, or maritime jurisdiction, was "aimed at ensuring that countries don't use the WTO as a forum to dispute Beijing's claim to modified reefs in the South China Sea, which are home to one of the busiest commercial shipping routes in the world."[30] Among many other Members, the U.S. "opposed China's territorial exemption request, because . . . it could provide WTO Members that subsidize fishing with a veto that undermines the Organization's effort to curb harmful fishery subsidies."[31] They could immunize themselves from suit by arguing their alleged IIU fishing occurs in disputed waters.

So, not surprisingly, two days earlier, America offered a rather different proposal from that by China. On 30 October, the U.S. called for provisions that (along with miscellaneous amendments to the *Compilation Text*) would increase transparency on fisheries subsidies, with a view to enhancing the compliance of Members as to notifications to the WTO on their subsidy schemes.[32] Setting aside the *Agreement on Agriculture*, the American proposal (in Paragraph 1(b)) targeted non-compliance with the transparency requirements in the following WTO agreements, *Decisions*, and *Understandings*:

Agreement on Implementation of Article VI of the GATT 1994 (Anti-Dumping)

Agreement on Subsidies and Countervailing Measures

Agreement on Safeguards

Understanding on the Interpretation of Article XVII of the GATT 1994 (State Trading)

---

30. *WTO Outlines.*

31. *WTO Outlines.*

32. The seven-page American proposal is World Trade Organization, *Procedures to Enhance Transparency and Strengthen Notification Requirements Under WTO Agreements — Communication from the United States*, JOB/GC/148, JOB/CTG/10 (30 October 2017), and is available through *New Proposals Submitted.*

Agreement on Implementation of Article VII of the GATT 1994 (Customs Valuation)

Agreement on Import Licensing Procedures

Agreement on Rules of Origin

Agreement on Preshipment Inspection

Decision on Notification Procedures for Quantitative Restrictions (G/L/59/Rev.1)

Agreement on Trade Related Investment Measures

Agreement on the Application of Sanitary and Phytosanitary Measures

Agreement on Technical Barriers to Trade

The American proposal mandated sanctions against any Member that fails to comply with the transparency rules in these agreements. This text was as follows:

6. For an agreement listed in paragraph 1(b), if a Member fails to provide the complete notification within one year of the deadline and the delinquent Member fails to cooperate with the Secretariat so that the Secretariat is unable to obtain enough information to provide a notification, the following administrative measures shall apply to the delinquent Member:

   (a) After one but less than two full years from a notification deadline, the following measures shall be applied to the delinquent Member at the beginning of the second year:

      (i) representatives of the delinquent Member *cannot be nominated to preside over WTO bodies*;

      (ii) *documentation will not be provided to delinquent Member* delegations in Geneva nor to the Member's capital;

      (iii) the *delinquent Member's access to the WTO Members' web site will be discontinued*;

      (iv) the Director-General will contact annually the Minister of the delinquent Member responsible for the WTO, or any other official at the appropriate level emphasizing the question of notifications;

      (v) the Secretariat will report annually to the Council on Trade in Goods on the status of the delinquent Member's notifications; and

      (vi) the delinquent Member will be subject to specific reporting at the General Council meetings.

   (b) After two but less than three full years following a notification deadline, the following measures shall be applied to the Member at the beginning of the third year, in addition to the measures in paragraph 6(a):

      (i) the Member will be *designated as an Inactive Member*;

      (ii) the Inactive Member will be *denied access to training or technical assistance* other than that necessary to meet their WTO Article XIV:2 obligations; and

(iii) when the Inactive Member takes the floor in the General Council it will be *identified as such*.

7. At the beginning of each year when measures will be applied, the Director-General will notify the Ministers of the Members responsible for the WTO of the administrative measures being applied with respect to the delinquent Member. Once the Member comes into compliance with its the measures will cease to apply.[33]

The American proposal was both novel and serious, in that it called for significant sanctions (as emphasized in Paragraphs 6–7 above) against non-transparent Members. The same sanctions would apply for a breach of the notification provisions of the *Agriculture Agreement*, but (as per Paragraphs 9–11 of the Proposal) with a different timetable.

On fishing subsidies in particular, pursuant to Article 25:3 of the *SCM Agreement*, the U.S. called (in Paragraph 12 of its proposal) on Members to provide these data:

(a) program name;

(b) legal authority for the program;

(c) name of recipient;

(d) vessel name and identification number;

(e) catch data by species in the fishery for which the subsidy is provided;

(f) status of the fish stocks in the fishery for which the subsidy is provided (overfished, fully fished, or underfished);

(g) fleet capacity in the fishery for which the subsidy is provided;

(h) conservation and management measures in place for the relevant fish stock; and

(i) total imports and exports per species.

America argued the "WTOs lack of transparency is 'problematic for traders and it undermines the proper functioning and operation of the WTO.'"[34]

Neither the Chinese nor American proposal engendered an immediate consensus, with Members calling for further study. Reactions were mixed, and a number of Members said that they needed to study the proposal further and consult with their capitals. Reaction was particularly negative against the American suggestion of penalties for failure to make timely disclosure, reactions were negative. Members observed that in 2017, the WTO Secretariat "reported that less than half of the WTO Members provided their 2015 subsidy notification, and a third of all WTO agriculture notifications are outstanding for the period between 1995 and 2015."[35]

---

33. Emphasis added.

34. Bryce Baschuk, *U.S. Transparency Proposal Panned by WTO Members*, 34 International Trade Reporter (BNA) 1507 (16 November 2017). [Hereinafter, *U.S. Transparency Proposal*.]

35. *U.S. Transparency Proposal*.

Though all WTO Members agreed that it's important to improve their compliance with WTO notification rules, Brazil, China, India, and 10 other WTO members said the U.S. proposal could have unintended consequences . . . .

. . .

India said the U.S. proposal should take account of the challenges and constraints of developing countries that are not able to provide timely notifications despite their willingness to do so.

Brazil and South Africa said the U.S.'s proposed punitive measures would harm those members who need greater assistance in meeting their notification requirements.

Rather than consider punitive actions, the U.S. should consider positive incentives to encourage members to improve their notification obligations, said the Norwegian delegation.[36]

Of course, positive incentives, especially if they required financial support, were not measures in which America was interested to sponsor.

IV. November 2017 Draft Texts

On 20 November 2017, the Chair of the Negotiating Group on Rules produced two draft texts. The first one proposed a ban on IUU fishing:

Article 3: Prohibited Subsidies

3:1   Subsidies [provided to] [granted to] a fishing [vessel, [regardless of the flag of the vessel involved,] or operator] engaged in IUU fishing,

[**ALT1:** including those]

[**ALT2:** [as] [while]]

[identified by,] determined by, or listed in an IUU fishing list[1] of:

a)   a Member in respect of vessels flying its flag [in accordance with its law] [in accordance with its domestic laws, regulations and administrative procedures]. [When the flag Member and the subsidizing Member are not the same, the fishing vessel concerned shall be notified to the subsidizing Member, and [the determination shall be] verified by the subsidizing Member [in accordance with its law.] [in accordance with its domestic laws, regulations and administrative procedures.]

b)   a subsidizing Member [in accordance with its domestic laws, regulations and administrative procedures].

---

36. *U.S. Transparency Proposal.*

c)   a Member in respect of foreign-flagged vessels found fishing in waters under its jurisdiction. In this case, a subsidizing Member shall, upon request by that Member [or on its own initiative,] [recognize] [take into account, as appropriate] this determination provided that the subsidizing Member promptly [verifies] [the determination] [determines], [in accordance with its law] [in accordance with its domestic laws, regulations and administrative procedures], [and] that the [relevant] international law and principles of non-discrimination, due process, [including a procedure for appeal or review,] and transparency were respected in making that determination.

ALT: a Member in respect of foreign-flagged vessels fishing in its waters, provided that the subsidizing Member promptly [verifies] [determines], [in accordance with its law] [in accordance with its domestic laws, regulations and administrative procedures], that the Member followed fair, transparent, and non-discriminatory procedures and acted in conformity with [international law] in making its determination [based on positive evidence].

d)   a Regional Fisheries Management Organization [or Arrangement] [including those organizations [or arrangements] of which Members are not Party], provided that the subsidizing Member promptly [investigates and] [verifies] [determines], [in accordance with its law] [in accordance with its domestic laws, regulations and administrative procedures], that the [vessel/operator] concerned has been listed [based on positive evidence] in accordance with the rules and procedures of that organization [or arrangement] [including a procedure for appeal or review] and in conformity with international law applicable to the subsidizing Member and those organizations [or arrangements] are in conformity with [FAO IPOA-IUU,] principles of non-discrimination, openness to all WTO Members, due process and transparency. [Provided, however, that in the case of fishing in waters under the national jurisdiction of a subsidizing Member, such determinations shall be made by the national authority of the subsidizing Member.][2]

[ALT: a Regional Fisheries Management Organization [or Arrangement] in accordance with the rules and procedures of that organization [or arrangement] and in conformity with international law.] [including verification mechanisms to enable Members that are not a party to those organizations [or arrangements] to engage in the listing process under the rules of procedure] [; and, if the subsidizing Member is not a party to a Regional Fisheries Management Organization [or Arrangement], provided that [it promptly verifies that] that organization [or arrangement] is in conformity with [FAO IPOA-IUU,] principles of non-discrimination, openness to all WTO Members, due process and transparency.]

e)   [the FAO [subject to its recognition by the SCM Committee.]]][37]

---

[1] For the purposes of paragraphs (a) and (b), each Member maintains the right to determine what constitutes such [identification,] determination, or listing of IUU fishing [based on paragraph 3 of IPOA-IUU].

[2] [For the purpose of this *Agreement*, Regional Fisheries Management Organizations shall be recognized by the FAO before XX-XX-201X, and incorporated as Annex 1 of this *Agreement.*]

[1] For the purposes of paragraphs (a) and (b), each Member maintains the right to determine what constitutes such [identification,] determination, or listing of IUU fishing [based on paragraph 3 of IPOA-IUU].

[2] [For the purpose of this *Agreement*, Regional Fisheries Management Organizations shall be recognized by the FAO before XX-XX-201X, and incorporated as Annex 1 of this *Agreement.*]

The second draft text proposed limits on fisheries subsidies:

Overfished Discipline (to replace 3:6–3:9)

3:6   Subsidies for fishing [and fishing related activities] [outside the territorial sea] [of] / [that negatively affect] [targeted] fish stocks that are in an overfished condition.

[The negative effect of such subsidies shall be determined] [by the subsidizing Member] based on the [best] scientific evidence [available to] [recognized by] [that Member.]]

[A fish stock is overfished if

[A it has not been assessed or has been assessed to be in an overfished condition.]

[B ALT1: it is recognized as such by the Member in whose [national jurisdiction] [EEZ] the fishing is taking place or by a Regional Fisheries Management Organization [or Arrangement] based on [best] scientific evidence available to [and recognized by] them.]

[B ALT2: the stock is at such a low level that mortality from fishing needs to be [restricted] to allow the stock to rebuild to a level that produces maximum sustainable yield or [alternative] reference points based on the [best] scientific evidence [available]. Fish stocks that are recognized as overfished by the national jurisdiction where the fishing is taking place or by a relevant fisheries management organization [or arrangement] shall also be considered overfished.]

---

37. World Trade Organization, Fisheries Subsidies, Working Documents on Prohibited Subsidies Relating to IUU Fishing and Overfished Stocks, Communication from the Chair, TN/RL/W/274, 20 November 2017, https://docs.wto.org/dol2fe/Pages/FE_Search/FE_S_S009-DP.aspx?language=E&CatalogueIdList=240285,240274,240284,240294,240287,240288,240273,240272,240286,240289&CurrentCatalogueIdIndex=5&FullTextHash=371857150&HasEnglishRecord=True&HasFrenchRecord=False&HasSpanishRecord=False. [Hereinafter, Working Documents.]

[**B ALT2** *bis*: the stock is at such a low level that mortality from fishing needs to be [restricted] to allow the stock to rebuild to a level that produces maximum sustainable yield or [alternative] reference points based on the [best] scientific evidence [available] and with no effective management plan in place. Fish stocks that are recognized as overfished by the national jurisdiction where the fishing is taking place or by a relevant fisheries management organization [or arrangement] shall be considered overfished.]

[**B ALT3**: the stock is at such a low level that mortality from fishing needs to be [restricted] to allow the stock to rebuild to a level that produces maximum sustainable yield or [alternative] reference points based on the [best] scientific evidence available [to the Member within its jurisdiction or to the relevant RFMO [or Arrangement]], [as recognized by the national jurisdiction where the fishing is taking place or by the relevant fisheries management organization [or arrangement.]]

[The determination by an RFMO [or Arrangement], shall be made after examination of the objections, if any, of the Member concerned].

In the cases of straddling and highly migratory fish stocks, shared among Members, the evaluation related to the fish stocks in the fishery for which the subsidy is provided shall be made pursuant cooperation of the Members involved.]

C ALT 1: [In the absence of sufficient data to make such a determination, the stock shall be presumed to be in an overfished condition.]

C ALT 2: [In the absence of scientific evidence to make such a determination due to a lack of capacity, this paragraph does not apply until the Member acquires the capacity to conduct stock assessments.]

3:7   [Subsidies [to vessels or operators fishing] [in connection with fishing and fishing related activities] in areas beyond national jurisdictions which are not aimed to fulfill a quota or a right established by a RFMO [or Arrangement].]

3:7   **ALT** [Subsidies [to vessels or operators fishing] [in connection with fishing and fishing related activities] in areas beyond national jurisdictions which are not aimed to fulfill a quota or a right established by a RFMO [or Arrangement] and which negatively affect targeted fish stocks that are in an overfished condition].

3:8   [Illustrative list of subsidies that do not negatively affect targeted fish stocks that are in an overfished condition:

     (a) subsidies that improve fishery management systems and [thus] promote sustainable fisheries including subsidies for research and development activities;

     (b) subsidies that improve hygiene, health, safety and working conditions for fishers;

    (c) subsidies aiming at improving the concerned Member's capacity to fight against IUU fishing;

    (d) subsidies for [permanent] cessation of fishing activities provided that the fishers concerned effectively cease all fishing activities within a reasonable timeframe after receiving the subsidy concerned.]

    (e) [subsidy programs of Members aimed to fulfill a quota or a right established by a RFMO][38]

The above quoted texts aimed to fill Target 14:6 of the United Nations SDGs. Interestingly, the U.S. changed its position, dropping a proposal "to set new restrictions on overfishing of freshwater habitats." Arguably, that change was orthogonal to the Target.

In any event, there was no consensus on either text. Members found plenty in the above-quoted texts about which to argue:

> Trade officials disagreed as to whether a WTO fisheries proposal should exclude fuel subsidies, which some Members said are the largest contributor of government fishery subsidies.
>
> The U.S. opposed India's proposed carve-out for all fuel subsidies in the accord, and India said Members should at least provide special and differential treatment to developing countries.
>
> The European Union pushed back against Russia's proposed language to prevent WTO Members from offering any kind of fuel subsidies or fuel schemes that benefit the fisheries sector.
>
>   . . .
>
> WTO Members continued to disagree about who, where, and how officials would determine the existence of illegal, unreported, and unregulated fishing, overfished stocks, overfishing, and overcapacity, according to a participant in the meetings.
>
> Separately, India offered language to exempt developing and least developed countries from any prohibition on unreported and unregulated fishing activities in their exclusive economic zones.
>
> India's proposal was opposed by Australia, Canada, the EU, New Zealand, and the U.S. Members also continue to disagree about how the proposal will treat disputed waters and territories.[39]

These disagreements, of course, were apparent from the heavily bracketed text quoted above.

---

38. Working Documents.

39. Bryce Baschuk, *Challenges Remain as WTO Negotiators Draft Fisheries Text*, 34 International Trade Reporter (BNA) 1545 (23 November 2017).

V. India to Blame?

Given that heavy bracketing, it was unsurprising that the WTO Members failed to achieve consensus on fishing subsidies at the December 2017 Buenos Aires Ministerial Conference. The EU best summed up the frustration:

> "Members cannot even agree to stop subsidizing illegal fishing," European Trade Commissioner Cecilia Malmstroem said on Twitter Dec. 13 [, 2017, the final day of the Ministerial Conference]. "Horrendous. The EU tried really hard, but destructive behaviour by several large countries made results impossible. How did we end up here?"[40]

One answer to that question was that India was to blame:

> Talks unravelled on Dec. 12 [2017] after India demanded special and differential treatment to help protect the 14 million Indian citizens that depend on the fisheries sector for their livelihood.
>
> "India blocked everything, even an agreement on the elimination of subsidies that drive illegal fishing. This is irresponsible," said Claire Nouvian, chief executive officer of the Bloom Association, an environmental advocacy organization.
>
> "It means the Indian government supports the ongoing destruction of the ocean and of artisanal fishers," Nouvian said . . . .[41]

Yet, casting blame on India was unfair. Why should the burden of proof be on a developing country with a large number of small-scale, subsistence fisherman for whom fishing is a matter of life-and-death.

By the end of the Buenos Aires Ministerial Conference, Members reached consensus on an anodyne statement:

> Members agreed to prohibit "certain forms of fisheries subsidies that contribute to overcapacity and overfishing, and eliminate subsidies that contribute to IUU fishing," according to a statement issued by the negotiating parties.
>
> Members also agreed to recognize that "appropriate and effective special and differential treatment for developing and least developed members should be an integral part of these negotiations," according to the statement.[42]

---

40. Bryce Baschuk, *Ban on Illegal Fishing Subsidies Eludes WTO Ministers in Argentina*, 34 International Trade Reporter (BNA) 1682 (21 December 2017). [Hereinafter, *Ban on Illegal Fishing.*]
    41. *Ban on Illegal Fishing.*
    42. *Ban on Illegal Fishing.*

VI. December 2017 Buenos Aires
WTO Ministerial *Decision*

At the 10–13 December 2017 WTO Ministerial Conference in Buenos Aires, Argentina, WTO Members failed to reach consensus on the aforementioned proposals, or indeed on any proposals, about fishing subsidies. They did nothing more than issue a statement about continuing their negotiations for another two years, with the hope of completing a deal in the biennium before the 2019 Ministerial Conference.[43] In their *Ministerial Decision on Fisheries Subsidies*, Members:

> agreed to continue to engage constructively in fisheries subsidies negotiations with a view to adopting an agreement by the next Ministerial Conference in 2019 on comprehensive and effective disciplines that prohibit certain forms of fisheries subsidies that contribute to overcapacity and overfishing, and eliminate subsidies that contribute to illegal, unreported and unregulated (IUU) fishing. Members also recognized that appropriate and effective special and differential treatment for developing country members and least developed country members should be an integral part of these negotiations.[44]

If the start of 2018 was any harbinger, they would fail again.[45] They could not agree whether to start up talks immediately, or take time to gather more data:

> The U.S. delegation urged WTO Members to begin the year by gathering information that could help them break through their disagreements, rather than delving immediately into textual negotiations.
>
> For instance, the WTO Secretariat could help move negotiations along by producing a list of fishing vessels and operators that are engaged in illegal, unreported, and unregulated fishing. . . .
>
> WTO Members also should submit their fishery subsidies notifications; share information on how they identify illegal, unreported, and unregulated fishing; and provide any requirements or offers for technical assistance. . . .
>
> The Chinese delegation agreed that Members should do their homework and compare international laws and domestic practices in order to work out practical proposals. . . .
>
> . . .

---

43. World Trade Organization, *Fisheries Subsidies—Ministerial Decision of 13 December 2017*, WT/MN(17)/64, WT/L/1031 (18 December 2017), www.wto.org/english/thewto_e/minist_e/mc11_e/mc11_e.htm.

44. World Trade Organization, *WTO Members Complete First Cluster of Meetings for Fisheries Subsidies Negotiations Since MC11*, 18 May 2018, www.wto.org/english/news_e/news18_e/fish_18may18_e.htm.

45. *See* Bruce Baschuk, *WTO Fisheries Talks Get Off to Slow Start in 2018*, 35 International Trade Reporter (BNA) 191 (8 February 2018).

Rather than delay negotiations, the European Union and several other members endorsed an immediate resumption of textual based discussions. . . .

The EU reminded delegates that at the conclusion of MC11 [*i.e.*, Ministerial Conference 11, the December 2017 Buenos Aires Ministerial Conference], Trade Ministers instructed them to build upon a pair of negotiating documents [quoted above] they'd produced in 2017.

The two documents remain heavily bracketed, however, because the negotiating parties continue to disagree about whether they should extend special and differential treatment to certain countries, among other issues. Brackets signal areas of disagreement.

Several WTO members supported the EU's view, including Canada, Ecuador, El Salvador, and Norway; members of the African, Caribbean, and Pacific Group of States; and the Latin American Group.[46]

And, amidst their disagreement, the Chairman of the Negotiating Group on Rules, and senior WTO negotiator on fisheries, Wayne McCook, quit.

VII. July 2018 Heavily Bracketed Draft Text

In May 2018, with a new Chairman of the Negotiating Group on Rules, Ambassador Roberto Zapata Barradas of Mexico, the WTO announced it had held the first substantive meetings on fishing subsidies since the 11th Ministerial Conference in December 2011 in Buenos Aires.[47] Among the topics Members discussed were subsidies for capital and operating costs of fishing, which increase or maintain the fishing capacity of Members and thereby contribute to over-capacity and over-fishing, and S&D treatment for developing countries and LDCs. They did not reach any deal, but they did publish a streamlined draft agreement that integrated ideas presented before, during, and after that Conference, with a view to engaging in text-based negotiations.

Following meetings in May–June 2018, WTO Members worked on, and published, a subsequent proposed agreement This July 2018 text is as follows.[48] Their

---

46. Bruce Baschuk, *WTO Fisheries Talks Get Off to Slow Start in 2018*, 35 International Trade Reporter (BNA) 191 (8 February 2018).

47. World Trade Organization, *WTO Members Complete First Cluster of Meetings for Fisheries Subsidies Negotiations Since MC11*, 18 May 2018, www.wto.org/english/news_e/news18_e/fish_18may18_e.htm.

48. The text is formally entitled, World Trade Organization, Negotiating Group on Rules, Fisheries Subsidies, Working Documents on: Definitions; Scope; Prohibited Subsidies Relating to IUU Fishing, Overfished Stocks, Overcapacity, Capacity-Enhancing Subsidies, and Overfishing; Notifications and Transparency; Special and Differential Treatment; Transitional Provisions; and Institutional Arrangements—Communication from the Chair, TN/RL/W/274/Rev.5, (26 July 2018). The text is at www.wto.org/english/news_e/news18_e/fish_26jul18_e.htm.

negotiations proceeded into 2019 on four areas: "our main topics: subsidies to illegal, unreported and unregulated (IUU) fishing; subsidies to fishing where stocks are overfished; subsidies contributing to fishing overcapacity and to overfishing; and cross-cutting issues which include special and differential treatment for developing and least-developed members, dispute settlement, institutional issues, and notification and transparency."[49] Note four key points about the text.

First, there are a large number of words and phrases in square brackets (*i.e.*, []). Those are the provisions on which Members—despite 17 years of negotiations since the launch of the Doha Round—had not agreed.[50] In particular, note:

> Nearly a fifth of the draft text contains bracketed provisions that propose an array of exemptions and extended time frames for developing countries to implement the terms of any fisheries agreement. For example, the text proposes exemptions that would still permit developing countries to subsidize certain fishery operations that contribute to overfishing as long as it takes place within their territorial waters.[51]

In other words, 20% of the bracketed text concerns S&D treatment. The U.S. and EU oppose it for large countries like China and India, whereas these countries insist on it, and on retaining their ability to self-designate as "developing."

Second, the disagreements were on vital topics, such as fishing fleet capacity, fuel subsidies, tax-removal schemes, and territorial delineations. In other words, the Members were nowhere near their goal of meeting the U.N. SDG 14:6—eliminating fishing subsidies that contribute to over-capacity, and over-fishing, by 2020. They also were vital in respect of S&D treatment: the U.S. and EU demanded that

---

49. World Trade Organization, *Members Kick Off 2019 with First Cluster of Fisheries Subsidies Meetings*, 18 January 2019, www.wto.org/english/news_e/news19_e/fish_15jan19_e.htm.

50. World Trade Organization, *Fisheries Subsidies—Working Documents on: Scope; Prohibited Subsidies Relating to IUU Fishing, Overfished Stocks, Overcapacity, Capacity-Enhancing Subsidies, and Overfishing; Notifications and Transparency; and Special and Differential Treatment, Communication from the Chair, Revision*, TN/RL/W/274/Rev.3, 18 May 2018. In fact, the Chair pointed out in a footnote that: "This Rev.3 is circulated exclusively to incorporate the new working document on scope. No changes have been made to the other texts as circulated in the Rev.2 version of this document." In other words, only on one topic (scope) had progress been made since 5 December 2017, before the Buenos Aires Ministerial Conference, when Rev. 2 was issued.

Negotiations in clusters around specific issues followed in the summer 2018, to no avail. *See, e.g.,* The World Trade Organization, *WTO Members Focus on Subsidies for Fishing in Overexploited Stocks at June Meetings*, 11 June 2018, www.wto.org/english/news_e/news18_e/fish_11jun18_e.htm (quoting the Chair of the Negotiating Group, Ambassador Roberto Zapata Barradas (Mexico): "The discussion brought back to light the many complex issues related to subsidies for fishing in overfished stocks, which will need to be resolved for us to make progress in our work"). The fact the talks were not text-based indicates how far apart Members were on those issues. Only when Members are closer to agreement on concepts and certain key details can they proceed to drafting and filling in a requisite text.

51. Bryce Baschuk, *WTO's Fishery Talks Remain Tangled After Years Adrift (1)*, 35 International Trade Reporter (BNA) (13 December 2018) (citing U.N. FAO data).

China and India, and all other developing countries, adhere to the same disciplines as they and all other developed countries.[52] China and India rejected what they saw as an effort to rewrite rules on qualification for developing country status in ways that would disregard the special needs of poor countries with large coastlines, even on seemingly simple matters such as collecting statistics to allow for better management of national fisheries programs so as to minimize IUU fishing. They needed the preferences associated with S&D treatment, such as exemptions from obligations, extended implementation periods, and technical assistance. (Interestingly, in September 2018, Taiwan declared it no longer would seek S&D treatment in new WTO agreements, including on fishing, e-commerce, services, or FDI facilitation, though it continued to regard itself as a developing country, because that would speed up the conclusion of new deals.[53]) Third, Sino-American tensions on national security matters explained some of the disagreements:

> China sought a ban on the ability of WTO Members to challenge illegal, unreported, and unregulated fishing activity "involving disputes concerning territoriality, sovereignty, or maritime jurisdiction."

> The Chinese request for a territorial carve-out is not new and is aimed at ensuring that countries don't use the WTO as a forum to dispute Beijing's claim to modified reefs in the South China Sea [*i.e.*, the Nine Dash Line], which are home to one of the busiest commercial shipping routes in the world.

> The U.S. delegation has consistently opposed China's territorial exemption because they say it could provide WTO Members that subsidize fishing with a veto that undermines the WTO's effort to curb harmful fishery subsidies, according to sources familiar with the matter.

> Separately, the U.S. singled out China for the size of its fishing fleet, which represents nearly a third of the global fishing capacity . . . .[54]

Fourth, perusing a bracketed text conveys a real sense of how trade negotiations are conducted, and proposed texts drafted, in practice. Put colloquially, they are not pretty processes.

---

52. *See* Bryce Baschuk, *WTO Fishery Talks Caught Up in U.S., China Special Treatment Spat*, 35 International Trade Reporter (BNA) 1210 (20 September 2018).

53. *See* Bryce Baschuk, *Taiwan Says it Won't Claim Special Rights in New WTO Talks*, 35 International Trade Reporter (BNA) 1210 (20 September 2018).

54. Bryce Baschuk, *Broad Gaps Remain in WTO Fisheries Negotiations*, 35 International Trade Reporter 686 (24 May 2018).

WTO, Negotiating Group on Rules,

Fisheries Subsidies — Working Document (Draft Negotiating Text), July 2018

Article 1: Definitions

For the purpose of this [instrument],

"[fishing] vessel" means any vessel, ship or other type of boat used for, equipped to be used for, or intended to be used for [commercial] fishing or fishing related activities [at sea] [and/or the definition for fishing vessel as applied in a Member's national laws];

"fishing" means [any activity, other than scientific research conducted by a scientific research vessel, that involves the catching, taking, or harvesting of [commercial living marine resources including] fish[, molluscs [and] crustaceans] [and aquatic plants]; or any attempt to do so; or any activity that can reasonably be expected to result in the catching, taking, or harvesting of fish [and any operations at sea in support of it].] [searching for, attracting, locating, catching, taking [or harvesting] [commercial living marine resources including] fish[, molluscs [and] crustaceans] [and aquatic plants] or any activity which can reasonably be expected to result in the attracting, locating, catching, taking [or harvesting of] fish [and shall be confined to wild marine [capture] [fishing]]];

["fishing [related] activities" means any operation in support of, or in preparation for, fishing, including the landing, packaging, processing [of fish at sea], transhipping or transporting of fish [that have not been previously landed at port], as well as the provisioning of personnel, fuel, gear and [other supplies] [at sea [except research activities]] [for the purpose of fishing];]

["operator" includes any person or enterprise involved in the operation, management or ownership of a [fishing] vessel;] ["operator" means any person or enterprise that owns or controls the operation or [management] of a [fishing] vessel];

"Illegal, unreported and unregulated fishing (IUU)" [has the same meaning as] [shall be interpreted in accordance with the definition set out in] paragraph 3 of the International Plan of Action to Prevent, Deter and Eliminate Illegal, Unreported and Unregulated Fishing of the UN Food and Agricultural Organization (FAO) [2001] [, as well as any modifications to, or replacements of, this instrument,] [shall be defined in accordance with Annex I of this instrument [and as implemented under national laws and regulations]. National and RFMO IUU lists, established in accordance with due process mechanisms, may be taken into account];

"overfished stock" [is where [the biomass of] a fish stock is at such a low level that mortality from fishing needs to be [restricted] [adjusted] to allow the stock to rebuild to a level that produces maximum sustainable yield or alternative reference points based on the [best] scientific evidence available] [to the Member within its jurisdiction or to the relevant RFMO [within its convention area] [by the RFMO in consultation with the Member]]. In the cases of straddling and highly migratory fish stocks, shared among Members, the evaluation related to the fish stocks in the fishery for which the subsidy is provided shall be made pursuant cooperation [and agreement] of the Members involved];

[As] [Fish stocks that are] [in an overfished condition are those] recognized as [such] overfished by the [national authorities of the Member] [national jurisdiction where the fishing is taking place] or by a relevant Regional Fisheries Management Organization [or Arrangement] [within its convention area] [and in consultation with the Member] [based on best scientific evidence available to them;] [shall also be considered overfished];]

["subsistence fishing" means fishing activities undertaken by an individual household for consumption by the members of that household and kin of the fishers as opposed to fishing activities undertaken for commercial purposes. Nevertheless, part of the fish caught can be sold or exchanged for other goods or services;]

["artisanal fisheries" shall be defined as those which operate within its territorial waters and mostly close to shore, use vessels which utilize primarily manual gear, and operated by individual fishermen or family members [for the purpose of subsistence or local trade];]

["small-scale fisheries" activities shall be defined as fishing activities which use vessels that are below [24 meters] in length [and/or [x] tonnage,] [provided the said limit is codified either in toto or in essence in the national laws or regulations of a Member at the time of adoption of this instrument]. [The size limitation refers to Harmonized definition in Conservation Management Measures (CMM) IOTC, concerning authorized fishing vessel, April 2016];]

["small-scale [and] artisanal] [fishers"] [fisheries"] ["[semi-industrial, commercial, or] subsistence fishing"] [should be interpreted and applied] [shall be defined] [in accordance with the [existing] laws and [/or] regulations] [of a Member at the time of adoption of this instrument]] [of the Member concerned] [and the international agreements] [to which the Members are party.] [entered into by the coastal State,] [taking into account the "Voluntary Guidelines for Securing Sustainable Small-Scale Fisheries in the Context of Food Security and Poverty Eradication" of the FAO (the SSF Guidelines)]

["large-scale industrial fishing" means fishing that is not semi-industrial, small-scale commercial, artisanal, or subsistence fishing [, in accordance with national laws and regulations];]

["inland fisheries" refers to fisheries carried out in freshwater or estuaries of a Member [as defined by the national laws and regulations] [and whose target species are those that spend all of their life-cycle therein] [or marine lagoons located inside the territory of a Member and/or connected to the points into sea];]

["aquaculture" means the farming of aquatic organisms, including fish, molluscs [and] crustaceans, [and aquatic plants] [as defined by the national laws and regulations] [provided that no capture fisheries are used to feed raised fish];]

["exclusive economic zone (EEZ)" [is] [shall be] defined [by principles] [according to principles] [found in Part V of the United Nations Convention on the Law of the Sea. Where any Member is not party to UNCLOS, similar principles on the exclusive economic zone adopted in domestic legislation may apply;]]

Article 2: Scope

2.1 [The instrument provides specific provisions regarding fisheries subsidies [and it is an integral part of the *Agreement on Subsidies and Countervailing Measures (SCM Agreement)*].]

2.2 This instrument applies [exclusively] to subsidies within the meaning of Article 1.1 of the *SCM Agreement* [that are specific within the meaning of Article 2 of that *Agreement*], to [vessels [, operators] [, fishing or fishing [related] activities] [at sea]] and shall be [confined][applicable] to subsidies to [wild marine [capture][fishing [or fishing [related] activities [at sea]][1][fisheries]. [Notwithstanding the scope of subsidies under Article 1.1 and Article 1.2 of the *SCM Agreement*, this instrument also covers other nature of subsidies or incentives benefiting fishing activities.]

---

[1] [For fishing related activities, if an operator owns more than one vessel, the provisions of this instrument will apply only to the vessel that has benefited from the subsidy.]

2.3 [For the purpose of this instrument, a subsidy shall be attributable to the Member granting it, regardless of the flag of the vessel involved [benefitting from the subsidy] [or the application of rules of origin to the fish involved.]]

2.4 This instrument shall not apply to:

- [subsidies for aquaculture],

- [fuel [subsidies] [de-taxation schemes]],

- [subsidies for inland fisheries],

- [subsidies for recreational fishing],

- Subsidies for [natural] disaster relief [,provided that the subsidies are directly related to the effects of that disaster, are limited to the affected geographic area, are time-limited, and in the case of reconstruction subsidies, only restore the affected area, the affected fishery,] [and/or the affected fleet to its pre-disaster state[2]],

---

[2] [This provision shall not apply to disciplines for IUU fishing.]

- [Subsidies for safety, research and development, and sustainability of stocks, [promoting sustainable fisheries] the acquisition and installation of equipment for vessel and crew safety, [including for their sanitary compliance] the adoption of techniques or technology aimed at reducing the environmental impact of wild marine capture (such as by catch reduction or turtle excluder devices) or for improving compliance with fisheries management regimes aimed at sustainable use and conservation (such as devices for vessel monitoring systems); and for increasing resilience or reducing vulnerability to climate change],

- [Subsidies for the installation of equipment for safety or for control and enforcement purposes, and equipment fitted for the purpose of reducing environmentally harmful emissions],

- [Subsidies directly resulting from agreements between WTO Members in which one party grants access to its exclusive economic zone to fishing vessels of another party].

2.5 [This instrument shall not [affect the claims][apply to matters] concerning disputed waters [or zones] of a Member] [[have] [be interpreted as having] legal implications regarding territoriality[, sovereignty] or delimitation of maritime jurisdictions.]] [Nothing in the reports of panels or the Appellate Body in dispute settlement proceedings involving the interpretation and application of the disciplines set out in Article 3 of this instrument shall have any legal or prejudicial implications regarding territoriality or delimitation of maritime jurisdiction of Members. The positions taken by Members in dispute settlement proceedings involving these provisions are without prejudice to the positions taken by them in proceedings in other fora regarding territoriality or delimitation of maritime jurisdiction. [Any alleged [unsubsidized] IUU fishing activity involving disputes concerning territoriality, sovereignty or maritime jurisdiction shall be excluded from the scope of this instrument and shall not constitute IUU fishing under this instrument.]]

2.6 [Any list of IUU fishing vessels, fish-stock assessment report or any technical report issued by a regional fisheries management organization shall only have effects for the purposes of the present instrument and its clauses and shall have no legal implications over territorial disputes or delimitation of maritime jurisdictions, or be interpreted as a change in the position of the parties involved in such disputes with regard to sovereignty or maritime jurisdiction, and cannot be invoked as recognition of such organizations on disputed areas.]

2.7 [Except as otherwise provided in this instrument, a Member does not thereby become bound by measures or decisions of, or recognize, any regional fisheries management organization of which it is not a Party.]

2.8 [Except for disciplines regarding IUU fishing, [and as otherwise provided in this instrument] in waters under national jurisdiction [in the EEZ] of a Member, disciplines of this instrument shall not be construed or applied in a manner that would prevent Members from applying measures to ensure small-scale [and] artisanal fishers [fishers which are not conducting large-scale industrial fishing] to access [or that would prevent small-scale [and] artisanal fishers from accessing] marine resources and markets, provided that their fisheries have a fisheries management[3] system, adapted as necessary to their particular situation, in the light of their respective capacities.]

---

[3] Fisheries management shall be defined and implemented in accordance to national legislation, taking into account the FAO Code of Conduct for Responsible Fisheries.

2.9 [Nothing in this instrument shall be construed or applied in a manner which will affect the rights of landlocked country Members under Public International Law.]

2.10 [Nothing in this instrument shall be construed or applied in a manner which will affect the rights of any Member when it is not part of some international treaties mentioned in this instrument.]

Article 3: Prohibited Subsidies

No Member shall grant or maintain any of the following subsidies within the meaning of Article 1.1 of the *SCM Agreement* [that are specific within the meaning of Article 2 of that *Agreement*] [to vessels, operators], [fishing or fishing activities]:

Illegal, Unreported and Unregulated (IUU) fishing

3.1 Subsidies [provided to] [granted to] a fishing [vessel, [regardless of the flag of the vessel involved,] or operator] engaged in IUU fishing,

[**ALT1**: including those]

[**ALT2**: [as] [while]]

[identified by,] determined by, or listed in an IUU fishing list[4] of:

(a) a Member in respect of vessels flying its flag [in accordance with its law] [in accordance with its domestic laws, regulations and administrative procedures]. [When the flag Member and the subsidizing Member are not the same, the fishing vessel concerned shall be notified to the subsidizing Member, and [the determination shall be] verified by the subsidizing Member [in accordance with its law.] [in accordance with its domestic laws, regulations and administrative procedures.]

(b) a subsidizing Member [in accordance with its domestic laws, regulations and administrative procedures].

(c) a Member in respect of foreign-flagged vessels found fishing in waters under its jurisdiction. In this case, a subsidizing Member shall, upon request by that Member [or on its own initiative,] [recognize] [take into account, as appropriate] this determination provided that the subsidizing Member promptly [verifies] [the determination] [determines], [in accordance with its law] [in accordance with its domestic laws, regulations and administrative procedures], [and] that the [relevant] international law and principles of non-discrimination, due process, [including a procedure for appeal or review,] and transparency were respected in making that determination.

ALT: a Member in respect of foreign-flagged vessels fishing in its waters, provided that the subsidizing Member promptly [verifies] [determines], [in accordance with its law] [in accordance with its domestic laws, regulations and administrative procedures], that the Member followed fair, transparent, and non-discriminatory procedures and acted in conformity with [international law] in making its determination [based on positive evidence].

(d) a Regional Fisheries Management Organization [or Arrangement] [including those organizations [or arrangements] of which Members are not Party], provided that the subsidizing Member promptly [investigates and] [verifies] [determines], [in accordance with its law] [in accordance with its domestic laws, regulations and administrative procedures], that the [vessel/operator] concerned has been listed [based on positive evidence] in accordance with the rules and procedures of that organization [or arrangement] [including a procedure for appeal or review] and in conformity with international law applicable to the subsidizing Member and those organizations [or arrangements] are in conformity with [FAO IPOA-IUU,] principles of non-discrimination, openness to all WTO Members, due process and transparency. [Provided, however, that in the case of fishing in waters under the national jurisdiction of a subsidizing Member, such determinations shall be made by the national authority of the subsidizing Member.][5]

[**ALT:** a Regional Fisheries Management Organization [or Arrangement] in accordance with the rules and procedures of that organization [or arrangement] and in conformity with international law.] [including verification mechanisms to enable Members that are not a party to those organizations [or arrangements] to engage in the listing process under the rules of procedure] [; and, if the subsidizing Member is not a party to a Regional Fisheries Management Organization [or Arrangement], provided that [it promptly verifies that] that organization [or arrangement] is in conformity with [FAO IPOA-IUU,] principles of non-discrimination, openness to all WTO Members, due process and transparency.]

(e) [the FAO [subject to its recognition by the SCM committee.]]]

---

[4] For the purposes of paragraphs (a) and (b), each Member maintains the right to determine what constitutes such [identification,] determination, or listing of IUU fishing [based on paragraph 3 of IPOA-IUU].

[5] [For the purpose of this *Agreement*, Regional Fisheries Management Organizations shall be recognized by the FAO before XX-XX-201X, and incorporated as Annex 1 of this *Agreement*.]

OVERFISHED DISCIPLINE (TO REPLACE 3.6–3.9)

3.6. Subsidies for fishing [and fishing related activities] [outside the territorial sea] [of] / [that negatively affect] [targeted] fish stocks that are in an overfished condition.

[The negative effect of such subsidies shall be determined] [by the subsidizing Member] based on the [best] scientific evidence [available to] [recognized by] [that Member.]

[This determination shall take into account the implementation of management measures designed to rebuild the concerned stocks, adapted as necessary to the particular situation of the fisheries in question.]

[A fish stock is overfished if

[**A** it has not been assessed or has been assessed to be in an overfished condition.]

[Members shall exercise due restraint when granting subsidies to vessels or operators that target unassessed stocks. Any Member can challenge a subsidy granted to vessels or operators that target unassessed stocks if it provides positive evidence that an unassessed stock is overfished.]

[**B ALT1**: it is recognized as such by the Member in whose [national jurisdiction] [EEZ] the fishing is taking place or by a Regional Fisheries Management Organization [or Arrangement] based on [best] scientific evidence available to [and recognized by] them.]

[**B ALT2**: the stock is at such a low level that mortality from fishing needs to be [restricted] to allow the stock to rebuild to a level that produces maximum sustainable yield or [alternative] reference points based on the [best] scientific evidence [available]. Fish stocks that are recognized as overfished by the national jurisdiction where the fishing is taking place or by a relevant fisheries management organization [or arrangement] shall also be considered overfished.]

[**B ALT2** *bis*: the stock is at such a low level that mortality from fishing needs to be [restricted] to allow the stock to rebuild to a level that produces maximum sustainable yield or [alternative] reference points based on the [best] scientific evidence [available] and with no effective management plan in place. Fish stocks that are recognized as overfished by the national jurisdiction where the fishing is taking place or by a relevant fisheries management organization [or arrangement] shall be considered overfished.]

[**B ALT3**: the stock is at such a low level that mortality from fishing needs to be [restricted] to allow the stock to rebuild to a level that produces maximum sustainable yield or [alternative] reference points based on the [best] scientific evidence available [to the Member within its jurisdiction or to the relevant RFMO [or Arrangement]], [as recognized by the national jurisdiction where the fishing is taking place or by the relevant fisheries management organization [or arrangement.]]

[The determination by an RFMO [or Arrangement], shall be made after examination of the objections, if any, of the Member concerned].

In the cases of straddling and highly migratory fish stocks, shared among Members, the evaluation related to the fish stocks in the fishery for which the subsidy is provided shall be made pursuant cooperation of the Members involved.]

3.X [Notwithstanding the provisions of Article 3.x, above, nothing in this [instrument] shall be construed to prohibit subsidies to fishing vessels, fishing or fishing activity in respect of fish stocks that are not overfished, provided that other fish stocks in an overfished condition situated in the same [geographical area/jurisdiction] are not targeted.]

C ALT 1 [In the absence of sufficient data to make such a determination, the stock shall be presumed to be in an overfished condition.]

C ALT 2 [In the absence of scientific evidence to make such a determination due to a lack of capacity, this paragraph does not apply until the Member acquires the capacity to conduct stock assessments.]

3.7. [Subsidies [to vessels or operators fishing] [in connection with fishing and fishing related activities] in areas beyond national jurisdictions which are not aimed to fulfill a quota or a right established by a RFMO [or Arrangement].]

3.7. ALT [Subsidies [to vessels or operators fishing] [in connection with fishing and fishing related activities] in areas beyond national jurisdictions which are not aimed to fulfill a quota or a right established by a RFMO [or Arrangement] and which negatively affect targeted fish stocks that are in an overfished condition].

3.8. [Illustrative list of subsidies that do not negatively affect targeted fish stocks that are in an overfished condition:

(a) subsidies that improve fishery management systems and [thus] promote sustainable fisheries including subsidies for research and development activities;

(b) subsidies that improve hygiene, health, safety and working conditions for fishers;

(c) subsidies aiming at improving the concerned Member's capacity to fight against IUU fishing;

(d) subsidies for [permanent] cessation of fishing activities provided that the fishers [or fishing vessels] concerned effectively cease all fishing activities within a reasonable timeframe after receiving the subsidy concerned.]

(e) [subsidy programs of Members aimed to fulfill a quota or a right established by a RFMO]

[Overcapacity] [Capacity enhancing subsidies][6] and Overfishing [to replace 3.10–3.15 of the room document]

[3.11 Subsidies:

i. [that increase [or allow to be maintained] the [marine fishing capacity] of [a fishing vessel] [or a fishing fleet of vessels][the total marine fishing capacity of the whole fishing fleet of vessels of a Member] [including fleet renewal programs];]

ii. [that support the acquisition of [machines and] equipment for fishing vessels [(including fishing gear and engine, fish-processing machinery, fish-finding technology, [refrigerators,] [or] machine for sorting or cleaning fish)] [or any other equipment on-board the fishing vessel] that increases [or maintains] the ability of [a fishing vessel][or a fishing fleet of vessels] to find fish;]

iii. [that support the [construction,] [acquisition] [modernization, renovation, modification, repair, upgrading] [renewal,] of [existing] fishing vessels;]

iv. [that support the importation or transfer of fishing vessels] [including through the creation of joint ventures with partners of those countries;]

v. [within the meaning of Art. 1:1 of the *SCM Agreement*, for provision or use of fuel or schemes which can reasonably be expected to result in the provision or use of fuel, which benefit the fisheries sector.]

vi. for [operational costs to fishing vessels and fishing related activities] [, including] license fees or similar charges, fuel, ice, bait, personnel, income support, price support, social charges, insurance, and at-sea support; or operating losses of such vessels or activities.

vii. [that enhance the capacity of large scale industrial fishing activities outside of the subsidizing Member's maritime jurisdiction.]

3.12 [Subsidies [to vessels or operators fishing] [in connection with fishing and fishing related activities] in areas beyond national jurisdictions which are not aimed to fulfill a quota or a right established by a RFMO] [and which negatively affect targeted fish stocks that are in an overfished condition].]

3.12 ALT [Subsidies [to vessels or operators fishing] [in connection with fishing or fishing related activities] in areas beyond the national jurisdiction of the subsidizing Member;] [and which negatively affect targeted fish stocks that are in an overfished condition.]

3.13 [Notwithstanding the provisions of Article 3.x, above, nothing in this [instrument] shall be construed to prohibit subsidies to fishing vessels, fishing or fishing activity in respect of fish stocks that are not overfished, provided that other fish stocks in an overfished condition situated in the same [geographical area/jurisdiction] are not targeted.]

---

[6] [Disciplines related to overcapacity shall be limited to areas beyond national jurisdiction and shall not cover subsidy programs of Members aimed to fulfill a quota or a right established by a RFMO.]

Article 6: Notification And [Transparency] [Surveillance]

6.1 Each Member shall provide the following information [as part of] [in addition to] its regular notifications [of fisheries subsidies] under Article 25.3 of the *SCM Agreement* [to the extent that a Member is providing subsidies prohibited under Article X of this instrument]:

(a) [program name, legal basis, and granting authority for the program;]

(b) [level and type] [amount and nature] of support provided;

(c) [type or kind of marine fishing activity that the program supports];

(d) [vessels and operators fishing in areas beyond national jurisdiction, for which the subsidy is granted];

(e) [name of the recipient and, where known, name and identification number of the fishing vessel];

(f) [catch data [by species] in the fishery for which the subsidy is provided];

(**g**) [status of the fish stocks in the fishery for which the subsidy is provided (*i.e.*, overfished, fully fished, or underfished)];

(**h**) [fleet capacity in the fishery for which the subsidy is provided];

(**i**) [conservation and management measures in place for the [relevant] fish stock [for which the subsidy is provided]] [as well as any relevant fishing capacity management plans]; and

(**j**) [total [imports and] exports [per species] [for which the subsidy is provided]].

[Each Member shall [endeavor to] provide the information set out in subparagraphs [(c)][(d)][(f)] through (j) [to the extent possible][where available] [where relevant, and to the extent practicable].]

6.2 [Each Member [shall][may] also provide, [to the extent possible,] information in relation to other subsidies that the Member provides to [[persons engaged in] fishing [or fishing-related activities]] [the fisheries sector] that are not covered by paragraph 6.1, in particular [aquaculture and] [fuel subsidies].]

6.2 ALT [Notwithstanding [Article 2.3] / [*chapeau* of Article 3] of this instrument, Members shall notify the information referred to in Article 6.1 with respect to non-specific subsidies for the provision or use of fuel or for schemes that can reasonably be expected to result in the provision or use of fuel, which benefit the fisheries sector.]

6.3 [Nothing in this notification provision requires the provision of confidential information, including confidential business [and/or scientific] information.]

6.4 [Each Member shall provide to the SCM Committee, within [one year] of the date of entry into force of this *Agreement*, a notification describing how it has implemented the prohibitions set out in Article XX. Each Member shall periodically update its notification in accordance with guidance to be established by the SCM Committee.]

6.5 [Each [subsidizing] Member shall notify the SCM Committee on an [annual basis] of any list of vessels [and operators] that it has [identified] [determined] as having engaged in IUU fishing.]

6.6 [In order to enable the effective surveillance of subsidies elimination established in Article 3.1.1 the SCM Committee shall, upon receipt, circulate communications from:

a. RFMOs[7] informing a determination finding that a vessel or operator has engaged in IUU fishing activities in waters covered by such organization, and;

b. Members informing a determination finding that a vessel of a third country flag state has engaged in IUU fishing activities within waters under the national jurisdiction of the Member making the determination.]

---

[7] [For the purpose of this *Agreement*, Regional Fisheries Management Organizations shall be recognized by the FAO before XX-XX-201X, and incorporated as Annex 1 of this *Agreement*.]

SPECIAL AND DIFFERENTIAL TREATMENT

TRANSITIONAL ARRANGEMENTS

[No Member shall be obliged to apply Article 3 of this *Agreement* before the expiry of a period of one year after entry into force of this *Agreement*. [The Parties may grant or maintain subsidies set out in [Article 1.1⁸] during a transitional period of [X] years following the entry into force of this *Agreement*, provided that the vessel benefitting from the subsidy does not target fish stocks that are in an overfished condition.⁹] [Existing subsidy programs which are inconsistent with Articles 1.2–1.4 shall be brought into conformity by 2020.]

[Developed Members shall not be obliged to apply Article 3 of this *Agreement* before the expiry of a period of [x] year[s] after entry into force of this *Agreement*.] [Developing countries are entitled to a [further] delay of [x] years, and LDCs are entitled to a [further] [x] years [a] delay of [x]years, after entry into force of this *Agreement*.] [In the case of LDCs having graduated from LDC status before the entry into force or during the transition period, these Members are entitled to utilize the remaining period of delay provided for LDCs.]

[A Member may grant or maintain subsidies set out in Article 3.11 during a transitional period of [X] years following the entry into force of this instrument, provided that the vessel benefitting from the subsidy does not target fish stocks that are in an overfished condition.]

---

⁸ [Capacity-enhancing subsidies].

⁹ As recognized as overfished by the national authorities of the Party or by the relevant Regional Fisheries Management Organization or Arrangement. In the absence of sufficient data to make such a determination, the stock shall be presumed to be in an overfished condition.

SPECIAL AND DIFFERENTIAL TREATMENT

LDCs

5.1 [Prohibitions other than those outlined in Articles 3.1, [3.5] and 3.6 above shall not apply to LDCs Members.]

Unreported and Unregulated Fishing

5.2 [With respect to Article 3.1, in order to establish measures against unreported and unregulated fishing, after the period stipulated in Article 7.1, developing countries [except for their] [not engaged in] large scale industrial distant-water fishing are entitled to apply [x] additional years [year] and LDCs [x] additional years of transition period, [except for illegal fishing] [to enable them to establish reporting mechanism and regulations through implementing Article 5.12]. [In the case of LDCs having graduated from LDC status before the entry into force or during the transition period, these Members are entitled to utilize the remaining period of delay provided for LDCs.]]

5.2 *bis* [Developing Members and LDCs declaring difficulties on small scale, artisanal and/or subsistence fishing shall have [X] years of transition period in implementing the disciplines related to unreported and unregulated aspects of such small scale, artisanal and/or subsistence fishing under Article 1.1.

For developing Members and LDCs making such declaration as set out in Article 2.1, if it receives the notification from a relevant flag Member or RFMO that its vessel is engaged in unreported or unregulated fishing, and if the unreported or unregulated fishing activity concerned has been determined in accordance with Article 1.3, the developing Member or LDC concerned shall endeavor to implement Article 1.1.]

5.2 *ter* [The prohibition under Art. 3.1 in respect of unreported and unregulated fishing shall not apply to developing countries including LDCs for fishing activities:

> **a.** In waters under the jurisdiction, including in the EEZ, of the subsidizing Member; and

> **b.** In areas beyond the EEZ of such Member, for a transitional period of [X] years from the date of entry into force of the *Agreement*.]

Overfished Stocks Prohibitions

[This prohibition shall not apply to fishing occurring within [their territorial waters] [the EEZ] of developing countries and LDCs. [In respect of fishing activities in high seas beyond the EEZ, such Members shall be entitled to a period of [X] years, after entry into force of this *Agreement*, to withdraw any subsidy for fish stocks that have been identified, based on positive evidence, as being in an overfished condition by an RFMO of which such developing country is a Member.]]

Overfishing and Overcapacity

5.3 [Nothing in Article [3.10], [3.12] and [3.13] shall prevent a developing country Member from maintaining or granting subsidies to the following activities conducted in accordance with the principle of protection and preservation of fisheries resources defined under Article 61 and 62 of the United Nations Conference on the Law of the Sea Treaty (UNCLOS):] [or where any Member is not party to UNCLOS, similar principles on protection and preservation of fisheries resources adopted in domestic legislation may apply:

[Notwithstanding the provisions of Articles [X] regarding overfishing, overcapacity, and capacity enhancing subsidies, developing countries and LDCs shall be allowed to provide subsidies for;] [Except for the prohibited subsidies related to IUU Fishing, developing and least developed countries' members shall be allowed to grant or maintain fisheries subsidies to their:]

- [subsistence fishing[10];]

- [artisanal fisheries[11] activities;]

- [Fishing activities related exclusively to artisanal and small scale fisheries[12] or the subsistence and livelihood of the fishermen and their families;]

- [small-scale fisheries activities[13];]

- [Fishing activities, which exclusively exploit fish stocks within the economic exclusive zone (EEZ)[14] of the Member granting the subsidy;] [fishing and fishing activity within their own EEZ[15];]

- [Fishing or fishing related activities provided that the purpose is to exploit underexploited resources in the member's own Economic Exclusive Zone; and

- Fishing or fishing related activities provided that the purpose is to exploit rights held by the member in high seas fishing quotas or any other rights established by a RFMO(s)/A(s)]

---

[10] The term "subsistence fishing" refers to fishing activities undertaken by an individual household for consumption by the members of that household and kin of the fishers as opposed to fishing activities undertaken for commercial purposes. Nevertheless, part of the fish caught can be sold or exchanged for other goods or services.

[11] For the purposes of this discipline, artisanal fisheries shall be defined as those which operate within its territorial waters and mostly close to shore, use vessels which utilize primarily manual gear, and operated by individual fishermen or family members for the purpose of subsistence or local trade.

[12] For the purpose of this *Agreement* "artisanal and small scale fisheries" shall be defined in accordance with national laws and regulations and the international agreements entered into by the coastal State, taking into account the "Voluntary Guidelines for Securing Sustainable Small-Scale Fisheries in the Context of Food Security and Poverty Eradication" of the FAO (The SSF Guidelines).

[13] For the purposes of this discipline, small-scale fisheries activities shall be defined as fishing activities which using vessels that are below [24 meters in length. The size limitation refers to Harmonized definition in Conservation Management Measures (CMM) IOTC, concerning authorized fishing vessel, April 2016.]]

[14] For the purpose of this *Agreements* "exclusive economic zone (EEZ)" shall be defined according to principles found in Part V of the United Nations Convention on the Law of the Sea. Where any Member is not party to UNCLOS, similar principles on the exclusive economic zone adopted in domestic legislation may apply.

[15] [Noting the rights, jurisdiction, and duties of coastal states among others, found under UNCLOS Part V.]

5.4 [Developing and least developed countries may grant or maintain subsidies referred to under Articles 3.11 and 3.13 if the following conditions are met:

- the vessel benefitting from the subsidy does not target fish stocks that are in an overfished condition; and

- the targeted stocks are managed on the basis of the best available science at the disposal of the concerned Member, consistent with the conservation and cooperation obligations under the relevant international law, as reflected in UNCLOS, conservation and management measures of competent RFMO(s)/A(s), and generally accepted standards for the conservation and management of fisheries resources; and

- the subsidizing Member has a management plan for the fleet segment it intends to subsidize.]

[The flexibility set out above shall be reviewed in view of the objectives set out in UN Sustainable Development Goal 14.4 and 14.6 at the end of the 10th year following the entry into force of this *Agreement*.]

5.5 [Fisheries subsidies which are not covered as subsidies to artisanal fisheries activities, shall be contingent on the following:

- the member has a fishery management plan in place that is effectively monitored and adequately enforced;
- the fisheries do not adversely affect resources governed by the fisheries management plan;
- the fishing activities will not adversely affect fishery resources of other members or the resources governed by relevant regional fisheries management organizations (RFMOs); and
- the member has control mechanism on fisheries subsidies to avoid overfishing and overcapacity.]

5.6 In order to bring any subsidy programs into conformity with the obligations provided in this provision, developing and least-developed country Members, that at [the time of entry into force/adoption] of this instrument, have not completed; or, need to update the information related to the status of the fish stocks in the fishery for which the subsidy is provided, shall be granted with a period of time of [X] and [Y] years, respectively, after entry into force, subject to comply with the transparency section provided below in paragraph 3.4.]

5.7 [Developing countries ranking among the world's [X] biggest in terms of marine capture production as determined by the FAO shall endeavour to refrain from making use of the flexibilities set out in Article 4.2.]

5.8 In the case of developing country Members, [paragraph 3.11] shall only apply to [their large scale industrial fishing and] fishing activity outside of their own EEZ.[16]

---

[16] [Noting the rights, jurisdiction, and duties of coastal states among others, found under UNCLOS Part V.]

5.9 Prohibitions for capacity enhancing/overcapacity subsidies shall not apply to small and vulnerable economies.[17]

---

[17] [For the purpose of this paragraph a small and vulnerable economy shall be defined as a Member whose share of global total of wild marine capture for years 2013 to 2015 is not more than XX percent.]

Technical Assistance and Capacity Building

5.10 [Upon request of a developing country or LDC Member] [and with reference to guidance provided by the *UN Fish Stocks Agreement*,] [Developed countries], [and developing countries in a position to do so] shall provide, [and relevant agencies are invited to provide,] targeted technical assistance and capacity building [assistance] [on mutually agreed terms and conditions] to developing countries, in particular LDCs and small, vulnerable economies (SVEs) to:

- address institutional and financial difficulties faced by LDCs and developing countries [with constraints to implement this *Agreement*] [countries in the implementation of this *Agreement*];

- establish reporting mechanisms and regulations to prevent unreported and unregulated fishing;
- to allow them to participate fully in any RFMO adjacent to their exclusive economic zone or archipelagic waters;
- to develop the capacity to initiate, implement, and enforce compliance with a fishery management plan in keeping with the FAO Code of Conduct on Responsible Fisheries and adequate to provide the showing required by Articles 5.8 and 5.9 of this instrument;
- conduct stock assessments;
- conduct monitoring, control and surveillance of fish stocks; and
- research and development]]

5.10 *Bis* [Developed country Members shall endeavor to provide targeted technical assistance and capacity building for conducting stock assessment to developing country and LDC Members.]

5.10 *Ter* [Technical and financial assistance and support for capacity building shall be provided to help developing and least-developed country Members acquire the necessary infrastructure and technical capacity for the conduct of effective stock assessments within their jurisdictions. The extent and the timing of implementation of Paragraph [XX (prohibition of subsidies in overfished stocks)] shall be related to the implementation capacities of developing and least-developed country Members. Where a developing or least-developed country Member continues to lack the necessary capacity, it will not be required to comply with the provisions of Paragraph [XX (prohibition of subsidies in overfished areas)] until effective implementation capacity has been acquired.]

5.11 [Members agree to implement an effective scheme of cooperation to help developing and least-developed country Members to acquire capacity building in the form of technical assistance in order to fulfill their commitments. This scheme could include bilateral and regional cooperation as well as technical assistance from relevant international organizations.

5.12 The provision of technical cooperation and capacity building under this instrument will be notified by providing Members and reviewed in the SCM Committee. The WTO shall cooperate with FAO and UNCTAD in the provision of technical assistance under this Article.

5.13 In order to bring any subsidy programs into conformity with the obligations provided in Article 3.6 developing and least-developed country Members, that at (the time of entry into force/adoption) of this instrument, have not completed; or, need to update the information related to the status of the fish stocks in the fishery for which the subsidy is provided, shall be granted with a period of time of [X] and [Y] years, respectively, after entry into force, subject to comply with Article 6.7]

5.14 [The operationalization of disciplines on fisheries subsidies should not impede the ability developing countries and LDCs to develop and diversify their fisheries sector.]

Transparency

Notification requirements shall not be burdensome on developing countries with capacity constraints, especially LDCs.]

[The notification requirements referred to under Article 4.1 shall not apply to LDC Members.]

Article 7 [Transitional Provisions]

[No Member shall extend the scope of [any such program] [a program inconsistent with this instrument], nor shall such a program be renewed upon its expiry].

Article 8 [Institutional Arrangements][18]

8.1 [The SCM Committee [shall] hold a [dedicated] [biennial] [review] [special session to evaluate the] of [Members'] [progress in the] [implementation of] [this instrument], [the agreed disciplines and make recommendations for their future improvements.], [the nature and extent of Members' subsidy programs, and the related fish stock status, production and trade]. [This review shall be supported by a WTO Secretariat report based on Members' notifications complemented by relevant information provided by Members to the Secretariat and information from other international organizations.]

8.2 [The Committee shall review the operation of this instrument after three years, and periodically thereafter.]

8.3 [The flexibility set out in Article 5.4 shall be reviewed in view of the objectives set out in UN Sustainable Development Goal 14 [target 4 and] target 6 at the end of the tenth year following the entry into force of this instrument.]

[8.4 The Committee shall encourage and facilitate ad hoc consultations or negotiations among Members on specific fisheries subsidies programs. The Committee shall develop a procedure to monitor the implementation of Article 3, in particular with the objective of achieving consistency among Members in applying the IUU prohibition.]

[8.5 The Committee shall maintain close contact with the relevant international organizations in the field of fisheries management, especially with the Food and Agriculture Organization of the United Nations (FAO), and relevant Regional Fisheries Management Organizations or Arrangements, with the objective of securing the best available scientific and technical advice for the administration of this Instrument [and in order to ensure that unnecessary duplication of effort is avoided].]

[8.6 In order to avoid unnecessary duplication, the Committee may decide to use the information generated by the procedures, particularly for notification, which are in operation in the relevant international organizations [in consultation with those Members having the information to be used].]

[**8.7** The Committee may invite experts from the relevant [national, regional and] international organizations [including research and academic institutions] to examine specific matters with respect to a particular guidelines, recommendations or decision. [The opinion of these experts is for reference only and not to be used as a legal document in a dispute settlement process.]]

[**8.8** For the purpose of this *Agreement*, the *Understanding on Rules and Procedures Governing the Settlement of Disputes* shall not apply to any measure or situation having relevance to any [issue of] [dispute or claim involving] territoriality, sovereignty or maritime jurisdiction [if so decided by the Dispute Settlement Body or by a Ministerial Conference by consensus].

8.8.1 Whenever any Member claims that there is a dispute under this agreement having any relevance to territoriality, sovereignty or maritime jurisdiction, the dispute proceeding concerned shall be automatically terminated immediately, [if so decided by the Dispute Settlement Body by consensus] [unless the DSB decides by consensus otherwise].

8.8.2 [If so decided by a Ministerial Conference by consensus,] Articles 8.8 and 8.8.1 shall be an integral part of the *Understanding on Rules and Procedures Governing the Settlement of Disputes*[.] [and] [T][t]his *Agreement* shall not enter into force unless Articles 8.8 and 8.8.1 are incorporated into Appendix 2 Special or Additional Rules and Procedures Contained in the Covered Agreements of the *Understanding on Rules and Procedures Governing the Settlement of Disputes.*

8.9 In order to [combat][address subsidies that contribute to] IUU fishing, the WTO is encouraged to increase its cooperation with the FAO and RFMOs [and other arrangements].]

[**8.10** WTO Members are encouraged to consider establishing [hotline] [open direct communication] and cooperation agreements to prevent and deal with IUU fishing based on the principles of the UNCLOS 1982.]

---

[18] [The "dispute/s" or "claim/s" involving territoriality, maritime jurisdiction, sovereignty and related issues over a specific fishing area referred to under Article 2 and Article 8 of this instrument refers to the outstanding disputes or claims between and among WTO Members filed in and within the jurisdiction of either of the following: (a) the International Tribunal for the Law of the sea; (b) the International Court of Justice; (c) and arbitral tribunal constituted in accordance with Annex VIII of UNCLOS; or (d) a special arbitral tribunal constituted in accordance with Annex VIII of UNCLOS.]

Part Five

Remedies against "Fair" Trade: Safeguards

Chapter 23

Rationales for Safeguards[1]

I. American Roots of and Influence on Safeguards

More than any other WTO Member, India loves the safeguard remedy of GATT Article XIX. From the founding of the WTO on 1 January 1995 though April 2014, it imposed 30 safeguard measures, exceeding its fellow Members. However, the origins of safeguards are not Indian.

Rather, the roots of the general safeguard, sometimes dubbed the "Escape Clause," lie in American trade law of the early 1940s. That is, the American remedy pre-dates Article XIX. Specifically, a 1943 accord between the U.S. and Mexico, a trade agreement negotiated pursuant to the *Reciprocal Trade Agreements Act of 1934* contained the first Escape Clause.[2] It said:

> If, *as a result of unforeseen developments and of the concession granted* on any article enumerated and described in the Schedules annexed to this Agreement, such article is being *imported in such increased quantities* and under such conditions as to *cause or threaten serious injury to domestic producers of like or similar articles*, the Government of either country shall be free to withdraw the concession, in whole or in part, or to modify it to the extent and for such time as may be necessary to prevent such injury.[3]

Escape Clauses like this one were the answer to complaints from Congress about the effects of liberalized trade. For instance, the "[l]egislative history of the 1945 congressional debate on the law that authorized the United States to join GATT is replete with congressional complaints of injury to domestic industry through concessions granted in trade treaties."[4] These roots of Article XIX still are vibrant.

---

1. Documents References:
   (1) *Havana (ITO) Charter* Article 40
   (2) GATT Articles XII, XVIII, XIX
   (3) WTO *Agreement on Safeguards*
   (4) WTO *Agreement on Agriculture*, Article 5
   (5) WTO *ATC Agreement*, Article 6:2
   (6) *NAFTA* Chapter 8
   (7) Relevant provisions in other FTAs

2. *See* Public Law Number 73-474, 48 Stat. 943 (1934), *codified in* scattered sections of title 19.

3. *Agreement Between the United States and Mexico Respecting Reciprocal Trade*, 23 December 1942, Art. XI, 57 Stat. 833, 845–46 (1943), E.A.S. No. 311 (emphasis added).

4. JOHN H. JACKSON, WORLD TRADE AND THE LAW OF GATT § 23.1 at 553 (1969). [Hereinafter, JACKSON 1969.]

The critical elements for Escape Clause relief in the language of Article XIX, and in America's statutory versions that have provided for this relief over the decades, are not all that different from the italicized language above.

In February 1947, President Harry S. Truman (1884–1972, President, 1945–1953) issued an Executive Order mandating the inclusion of an Escape Clause in every trade agreement negotiated by the U.S. under the authority of the *1934 Act*.[5] Accordingly, the ITC (or its predecessor, the Tariff Commission) has conducted Escape Clause investigations since 1948. President Truman's Order was issued when America and 21 other nations were in the thick of GATT and *ITO Charter* negotiations. Subsequent Executive Orders have amended the initial one, but the changes did not affect America's fundamental commitment to an Escape Clause. Indeed, in Section 7 of the *Trade Agreements Extension Act of 1951*, the Escape Clause became a permanent feature of American statutory law.[6]

Given American desires, it is hardly surprising drafters included the multilateral Escape Clause, Article XIX, in GATT. By the time of the 1946 London Preparatory Conference, the U.S. had 3 years of experience with an Escape Clause in its bilateral accord with Mexico. Since those negotiations, the American statutory embodiment of Article XIX, which is Section 201 of the *Trade Act of 1974* as amended,[7] has been amended by the *Trade Expansion Act of 1962*,[8] the *Trade Agreements Act of 1974*,[9] the *Trade and Tariff Act of 1984*,[10] the *Omnibus Trade and Competitiveness Act of 1988*,[11] and the *Uruguay Round Agreements Act of 1994*.[12]

"Section 201," or the "Escape Clause," is the generic term covering Sections 201–204, which are codified at 19 U.S.C. Sections 2251–2254. In a multilateral legal context, Section 201 derives legitimacy from this Article.

The U.S. was more than the principal force behind Article XIX in the GATT negotiations of the mid-1940s. It also advocated for the *Agreement on Safeguards* in the 1986–1994 Uruguay Round negotiations. As the Clinton Administration's *Statement of Administrative Action on the Agreement on Safeguards* indicates, America was concerned certain topics with which Section 201 dealt remained obscure in Article XIX.

---

5. *See* Executive Order No. 10004, 3 C.F.R. §§ 819–822 (9 October 1948) (revoking Executive Order No. 9832).

6. Public Law Number 82-50, 65 Stat. 72, 74 (1951).

7. *See Trade Act of 1974*, Public Law Number 93-618, § 201, 88 Stat. 1978, 2011-14 (3 January 1974), *codified at* 19 U.S.C. § 2251.

8. *See* Public Law Number 87-794, tit. II, § 201, 76 Stat. 872 (11October 1962).

9. *See* Public Law Number 96-39, tit. I, § 106(b)(3), 93 Stat. 144, 193 (26 July 1979).

10. *See* Public Law Number 98-573, tit. II, §§ 248-249, 98 Stat. 2948, 2998-99 (30 October 1984).

11. *See* Public Law Number 100-418, tit. I, § 1401, 102 Stat. 1107, 1225–41 (23 August 1988).

12. *See* Public Law Number 103-465, tit. III, §§ 301–304, 108 Stat. 4809, 4933–38 (8 December 1994).

Accordingly, in the Uruguay Round, American negotiators were successful in persuading their counterparts to incorporate some Section 201 concepts into the WTO *Agreement on Safeguards*. Examples of such concepts include:

(1) Criteria for determination of increased imports and injury or threat thereof.

(2) Procedures to ensure transparency.

(3) An eight-year cap on the duration of an Escape Clause measure.

(4) Expedited procedures for critical circumstances.

(5) The progressive liberalization of measures implemented under the Escape Clause (known as "degressivity").

(6) The right to re-impose safeguard restrictions at a later date.

As also indicated in the *Statement of Administrative Action*, the U.S. was concerned about two provisions in Article XIX:

(1) The requirement that an Escape Clause measure be applied on a non-discriminatory, MFN basis.

(2) The ability of countries whose exports are affected by Escape Clause measures to impose retaliatory measures against the country invoking the Clause, if they are not compensated by that country.

America argued these provisions discouraged use of the general safeguard remedy.

The first provision imposed on a large number of other contracting parties the costs of adjustment to fair foreign competition incurred by an industry in the contracting party invoking the Escape Clause. Thus, the first provision virtually ensured opposition from other contracting parties to an Escape Clause action. The second provision imposed the costs of retaliation or compensation on the contracting party invoking the Clause. Thus, the second provision was a clear disincentive to invoking the Clause.

The individual and combined effects of these provisions, urged the U.S., was contracting parties eschewed Article XIX. Instead, they addressed import surges through so-called gray area measures, *e.g.*, VERs. So, "the principal U.S. objective" in the Uruguay Round talks on safeguards "was to develop rules for the application of . . . Article XIX that would encourage WTO members to use rather than by-pass safeguards rules."[13]

The objective was largely achieved. The WTO *Agreement on Safeguards*, which entered into force on 1 January 1995, clarifies some obscurities of Article XIX,

---

13. *See Statement of Administrative Action for the Uruguay Round Agreement on Safeguards*, *in* Message from the President of the United States Transmitting the Uruguay Round Trade Agreements, Texts of Agreements Implementing Bill, Statement of Administrative Action and Required Supporting Statements, H.R. Doc. No. 316, vol. 1, 103rd Cong., 2d Sess. 956 (27 September 1994).

including rules on its application. Indeed, the second clause of the *Preamble* to the *Agreement* declares "the need to clarify and reinforce the disciplines of . . . Article XIX, . . . to re-establish multilateral control over safeguards and eliminate measures that escape such control." Further, Article 11:1(b) of the *Agreement* bans the use of VERs, OMAs, VRAs, or any other gray area measures:

> [B]ilateral VERs are considered *"grey area"* measures and are prohibited under WTO law. Although Article XIX of the GATT 1947 (the so-called *"Escape Clause"*) was the remedy provided for industries facing injurious import competition, it did not clearly specify the conditions under which *"safeguards measures"* may be imposed. As a consequence, VERs were commonly used by trading partners as a protectionist measure. The nature of the VERs was described in a 1984 GATT *Report*. In this *Report*, the Safeguard Committee pointed out that countries that accepted VERs did so because, *"they felt they had little choice and that the alternative was, or would have been, unilateral actions, countervailing actions, etc., involving greater harm to their exports in terms of both quantity and price."* Additionally, the *Report* concluded that the affected exporting countries did not seek a remedy under GATT dispute settlement procedures *"because these were considered cumbersome and time-consuming and there was fear that the industries involved could suffer serious, and perhaps irreparable, damage in the meantime."* The WTO Uruguay Round made reforms to the GATT and introduced the *Agreement on Safeguards*. The new rules on safeguards prohibit *"grey-area"* measures, and set a time limit (so-called *"Sunset Clause"*) on all safeguard actions. Article 11 of the *Agreement on Safeguards* states that *"a Member shall not seek, take or maintain any voluntary export restraints, orderly marketing arrangements or any other similar measures on the export or the import side. These include actions taken by a single Member as well as actions under agreements, arrangements and understandings entered into by two or more Members."* In 1984, the . . . [GATT] Director General stated that *"voluntary"* export restraints were contrary to the rules of the GATT and that they were *"only* 'outside the General Agreement' *in the sense that governments have not brought them formally to the GATT for examination."* As a consequence, VERs were completely phased out by the end of 1999, and the EU was the last WTO Member to phase out its voluntary restrictions on car imports from Japan.[14]

To be sure, neither GATT Article XIX nor the *Agreement* affects, nor could affect, reach private restraints of trade. That matter is left to the competition law and policy of each WTO Member.

---

14. FratiniVergano European Lawyers, *Entering the Second Phase to Avoid a Global "Trade War"? Trading Partners Negotiate Bilateral Exemptions or Request WTO Consultations Concerning U.S. Tariffs on Aluminium and Steel*, Trade Perspectives, issue 9, 4 May 2018 (emphasis original).

II. Evolution of Causation Standard in American Escape Clause

The various Congressional amendments through trade legislation in 1951, 1962, and 1974 were especially noteworthy with respect to the Escape Clause causation requirement:[15]

(1) Under President Truman's 1948 Executive Order, until the 1951 *Trade Agreements Act*, the verb "cause" was unmodified. A petitioner, that is, a domestic industry making a like or directly competitive product, had to show that serious injury to it was "caused" by imports.

(2) In the *1951 Act*, Congress relaxed the standard with the phrase "in whole or in part," *i.e.*, for the domestic industry to obtain relief, imports had to "cause in whole or in part" the injury.

(3) Subsequently, Congress thought the *1951 Act* language was too loose, so in the *1962 Trade Expansion Act*, it tightened it by deleting the *1951 Act* change, and inserting the adjective "major": imports had to be a "major" cause of injury. That implied imports had to be the single most important factor contributing to injury.

(4) The *1962 Act* causation test proved to be too difficult for petitioners to meet, so via the *1974 Trade Act*, Congress again relaxed the test, substituting "substantial" for "major." For imports to be a "substantial" cause implied there could be an equally important causal factor, but none more important than imports.

(5) Notably, for Trade Adjustment Assistance, Congress in the *1974 Act* left the "contributed importantly" test alone. That test is an easier one to satisfy, meaning Adjustment Assistance is (in theory) easier to obtain than Escape Clause relief.

(6) Also notably, for Section 406, the Market Disruption safeguard, in the *1974 Act* Congress eschewed either the higher "substantial cause" test of Section 201 or the lower "contributed importantly" requirement for Trade Adjustment Assistance. On the one hand, Congress sought to make Section 406 relief easier to get than Section 201 relief.[16] On the other hand, Congress wanted a Section 406 petitioner to prove a more direct causal relationship between increased imports and injury than a Trade Adjustment Assistance petitioner. So, Congress settled upon an intermediate standard: "significant" cause.

---

15. *See* Bruce E. Clubb, *United States Foreign Trade Law*, § 25.4.4 at 820–821 (Boston, Massachusetts: Little, Brown & Company, 1991) (emphasis added).

16. *See* SENATE REPORT NUMBER 1298, 93D CONGRESS, 2D SESSION 212 (1974), *reprinted in* 1974 UNITED STATES CODE CONGRESSIONAL & ADMINISTRATIVE NEWS 7186, 7344.

The importance of paying close attention to the applicable causation standard, and meeting or rebutting claims under it, cannot be over-emphasized. Trade remedy cases often are won or lost on causation.

III. Protectionism and Proliferation

Why include Article XIX in GATT, and why have a WTO *Agreement on Safeguards*? From a free trade perspective, it is readily apparent safeguards generally, and Article XIX in particular, is incongruous with the fundamental goal of GATT, namely, trade liberalization. They can be characterized, not unreasonably, as more than a derogation from the general spirit of GATT that healthy international competition, not interventionist government action, should dictate outcomes.

Worse yet, Article XIX is the most protectionist (though not necessarily the most protective) of all permissible trade remedies. A producer or foreign exporter targeted by an Escape Clause action has done nothing unfair. It is not alleged to have dumped. It is not alleged to have received a subsidy from its government subsidy. It is not alleged to have infringed on an IPR. Indeed, sometimes it is the failure to obtain relief under one of the unfair import competition laws that prompts an interested party to seek a safeguard remedy. For example, in September 1997, the U.S. Wheat Gluten Industry filed a Section 201 petition against the EU after its effort to seek relief under Section 301 of the *Trade Act of 1974*, as amended, failed.

In an Escape Clause action, all a foreign respondent has done is compete effectively in conformity with free market principles. More or less as a result of the operation of the economic law of comparative advantage, a domestic producer of a like or directly competitive product files a petition in which it claims actual or threatened harm from fair foreign competition. To bow to the petitioner's request is both to over-rule the market and provide a remedy where nothing unjust has occurred. Why, then, bow? That is, what purpose or purposes does safeguard relief serve?

Protectionism is not the only concern about the remedy. From a trade liberalizing perspective, proliferation is a problem, too. An FTA involving the U.S. without an Escape Clause is scarcely imaginable. An entire Chapter of *NAFTA* — Chapter 8 — is dedicated to creating and establishing parameters for the use of the remedy as among America, Canada, and Mexico. What safeguard provisions exist in other American FTAs? To what extent is *NAFTA* Chapter 8 a template for those provisions?

FTAs are not the only mechanism through which safeguards are proliferating. WTO texts themselves are a device. The Uruguay Round *Agreements on Agriculture*, in Article 5, and *ATC*, in Article 6:2, contain product-specific safeguards. That is, they contain trade remedies that may be used in specified sectors, against particular products. Accession agreements with WTO applicants also contain special safeguard mechanisms, which are product-specific and, by definition, country-specific.

The 11 January 2007 accession accord for Vietnam contains monitoring and remedial provisions in respect of T&A exports from that country. The December 2001 accession agreement for China has both a T&A safeguard, and a product-specific remedy for Chinese merchandise.

Proliferation can occur not only in the sense of creating novel safeguards, but also in terms of the use of extant and new remedies. In the latter respect, the legal criteria for use are critical. Like any weapon, the easier it is use, the more likely it will be used. There are two broad categories of criteria:

(1) Verbal formulas, which require proof of an import surge, injury or threat, causation, and (possibly) unforeseen circumstances associated with treaty obligations. Examples include GATT Article XIX and the WTO *Agreement on Safeguards*, and provisions in various FTAs.

(2) Arithmetic formulas, which involve application of a "Trigger Price" (*i.e.*, proving imports are sold below a threshold) or "Trigger Volume" (*i.e.*, proving imports are in quantities above a threshold). Examples include the WTO *Agreement on Agriculture*, and provisions in various FTAs.

Depending on the facts, a trigger formula may be easier to apply than a verbal formula. That is because trigger formulas do not require proof of injury or threat to a domestic producer of a like or competitive product, nor do they call for proof that surging imports caused injury or threat. As long as subject merchandise is imported at beneath a trigger price, or above a trigger volume, then the remedy may be imposed. Of course, if neither the price nor volume thresholds are breached, then a petitioner has the option of falling back on a verbal formula, and trying to exploit ambiguities in that formula to its benefit.

IV. Economic Arguments

Among the leading theoretical economic arguments for safeguard relief are that it helps restore competitiveness, and that it facilitates orderly contraction. In respect of the first argument, it is urged the Escape Clause will give a petitioning industry the protection it needs to get back on its feet, as it were. That is, measures undertaken pursuant to GATT Article XIX and the WTO *Agreement on Safeguards* give an industry hurt by free trade time to adjust to a liberalized trade environment:

> While GATT's primary goal is to establish a more open international trade environment, it recognizes the right of a government to part from free and open trade in certain circumstances. In particular, Article XIX allows a country to "escape" from negotiated tariff reductions, if the increased imports can be shown to "cause or threaten serious injury to domestic producers" of competitive products. In those cases, the country can unilaterally elect to reinstate the trade barrier that was in effect before

the concession. The provision was meant to give industries time to adjust to increased competition.[17]

By providing temporary protection, the relief gives an ailing industry time to generate profits, and reinvest these profits in factors of production so as to reduce its costs and thereby regain its competitive edge once protection is removed. That time may be critical for infant industries, which may have been exposed prematurely to free trade. In the long run, the international trade community, especially consumers in different countries, benefit because efficient competitors re-emerge.

This argument is not without its critics, even from the economically-minded. One scholar in the law and economics movement, Professor Sykes, states:

> First, it [the restoration of competitiveness argument] relies on the questionable assumption that governments can accurately identify and protect only those industries that can become "competitive" (or "competitive again" in the case of declining industries). The more probable outcome is that well-organized producer lobbies will secure protection irrespective of the impact such protection is likely to have on the "competitiveness" of their particular industry.
>
> Second, even if governments were competent to identify appropriate candidates for assistance and would properly exclude poor candidates, protection is not necessarily the best way to provide such assistance. Direct loans or subsidies to the troubled industry are in theory superior to protection, unless such measures entail sufficiently higher administrative costs. Loans or subsidies to cover periods of losses can be as effective as protection in enabling an industry to become "competitive," but they do not introduce the deadweight loss attributable to the protection-induced distortion of consumer prices.
>
> Finally, and most importantly, government intervention to restore "competitiveness" is simply unnecessary, at least in developed countries with substantial private capital markets. Private lenders will finance efforts to become "competitive" as long as the returns from such investments justify the apparent risk. Absent some distortion affecting the market rate of interest, therefore, economically worthwhile investments will be financed without government assistance. And, at any rate of interest, investment in industries that are unwilling or unable to borrow in the capital market diverts resources from other investments where the expected returns are greater.[18]

---

17. CONGRESSIONAL BUDGET OFFICE, HAS TRADE PROTECTION REVITALIZED DOMESTIC INDUSTRIES? 3 (November 1986).

18. Alan O. Sykes, *Protectionism as a "Safeguard": A Positive Analysis of the GATT "Escape Clause" with Normative Speculations*, 58 UNIVERSITY OF CHICAGO LAW REVIEW 255, 264 (1991). [Hereinafter, *Protectionism as "Safeguard."*]

To be sure, this criticism rests on a Neo-Classical economic perspective of Article XIX.

From that perspective, a deadweight loss is associated with virtually any tariff or non-tariff barrier, such as a quota. Either type of barrier causes the price of an imported good to rise. As a result, for two reasons, consumer surplus in an importing country erecting a barrier is likely to fall by more than the aggregate increase in producer surplus and — assuming a tariff is imposed — government revenue.

(1) An increase in the price of an imported good causes some consumers to cease consumption of that good. Because they exit the market, surplus associated with their consumption is lost.

(2) An increase in the price of an imported good induces an increase in domestic production of an article that is like or directly competitive with that good. Yet, this output is inefficient because the marginal cost to produce a unit is greater than the price of the import that the unit replaces. As a result, consumers pay a premium for the domestic like product.

Controversial assumptions afflict these ostensibly persuasive reasons. For example, it is a static view, neglecting implications of protection in the medium and long-term. It also is a view from the welfare of the importing country, not the exporting country, or the world economy. And, this perspective assumes safeguards are an economic issue, when in reality they may implicate non-economic concerns.

The second leading theoretical economic argument about the purpose of the safeguard remedy concerns orderly contraction. Surely the Escape Clause facilitates the orderly contraction of industries that cannot regain their competitive edge. Orderly contraction is a different form of adjustment than restoration of competitiveness. Thus, a single "adjustment" analysis is unrealistically broad. Relief prevents shock to factors of production, most notably labor. The protection from imports afforded by the relief slows the rate of contraction in an import-sensitive industry. Workers are not thrown from their jobs, and their wages are not slashed, without warning. Rather, they have time to find new work, or possibly retrain — *i.e.*, to adjust positively to a new global market context.

Stated differently, safeguard relief is a device to allocate costs of market adjustment. Trade liberalization is the consequence of tariff and non-tariff concessions. Products of certain industries are displaced by new, more competitive, imports. At least, mobile factors of a production in a domestic economy should shift to production of goods that can compete with imports in a liberalized trading regime. Yet, moving labor, human capital, and physical capital, and re-allocating or re-claiming land, takes time and money.

These costs have to be allocated in some way between or among countries, and between or among sectors within a country. In all instances, families and communities are at stake. For them, two questions must be addressed. First, should an importing country, exporting country, or both incur the costs of market adjustment? Second, how should these costs be allocated within a particular country?

On the first question, GATT Article XIX and the WTO *Agreement on Safeguards* allow an importing WTO Member to shift at least some market adjustment costs away from an injured domestic industry to an exporter or exporters in another Member. Regarding the second question, Article XIX allows an importing Member to shift at least some of the costs of market adjustment away from an injured domestic injury to domestic consumers (insofar as these consumers pay a higher price for imports, and a lower quantity of imports is made available to them).

Like the restoration of competitiveness argument, the orderly contraction argument is not without critics. Scholars enamored by law and economics urge delaying contraction is an economic vice. Delay means production factors are misallocated in an inefficient industry, one whose marginal cost of production for a unit of output exceeds unit price, for the period of delay. Instead, land, physical capital, labor, and human capital should be redeployed expeditiously to more efficient uses. Better to get pain over with quickly than drag it out. Of course, that prescription is easier to make than take.

V. Political Arguments

Two theoretical political arguments are offered for the safeguard remedy. First, inclusion of an Escape Clause in GATT was a significant reason why Congress agreed to American participation in GATT. That is because Congress appreciated Article XIX could serve as a political safety valve for protectionist pressures.

Suppose a politically powerful industry in complains of injury from a substantial increase in imports, and the increase is due to concessions granted in a trade-liberalizing accord. An Escape Clause allows the government of the importing country to alter unilaterally the accord to aid the affected industry. Absent this political safety valve, the pressures may be manifest in more (perhaps far more) protectionist ways than an Escape Clause petition. Any safeguard remedy affects only a single industry per case, and perhaps just a few firms in that industry. The more trade-restrictive alternative, but for the Clause, would be protectionist legislation. That legislation would affect an entire sector of an economy, and have reverberations throughout many other sectors.

The second justification draws on Public Choice Theory. Surely the Escape Clause encourages a country to enter into a greater number of tariff bindings than it otherwise would. As an American delegate to the original GATT negotiations stated:

> [an Escape Clause would] give more flexibility to the commitments undertaken.... Some provision of this kind seems necessary in order that countries will not find themselves in such a rigid position that they could not deal with situations of an emergency character. Therefore, the Article [establishing the Clause] would provide for a modification of commitments to meet such temporary situation [*sic*]. In order to safeguard the right given

and in order to prevent abuse of it, the Article would provide that before any action is taken under an exception, the member concerned would have to notify the organization and consult with them [*sic*], and with any other interested members.[19]

This view suggests Public Choice Theory helps explain the purpose of safeguards.

What is this Theory? Suffice it to say it is nothing more than the application of microeconomic tools to political behavior. As Professor Sykes explains, the Theory:

> suggests that policymaking under democratic government depends on the interplay of special interest forces in the political "marketplace." There is generally no reason to expect the democratic process systematically to yield "efficient," "equitable," or otherwise "correct" outcomes by any idealized criterion for measuring the success of policy. Rather, elected officials will pursue their self-interest. They will "supply" policy initiatives to interest groups that "demand" them, with the currency of the political marketplace in the form of votes or campaign contributions, for instance. Ultimately, well-organized groups — those most adept at lobbying and most capable of "paying" for policy initiatives — will have their interests vindicated, while diffuse, poorly organized interest groups may suffer.
>
> . . .
>
> Public choice [theory] predicts that elected officials will concern themselves far more with the impact of trade policy on producer interests than on consumer interests. Individual firms in import-competing or export-oriented industries often have much to gain from specific trade policy measures. And, especially in industries with a relatively small number of large firms, free-rider problems need not seriously impede efforts to influence policy, either because each firm has sufficient incentive to act individually or because interested firms can organize themselves to act collectively through a trade association or lobbying coalition. In contrast, the number of consumers is large and the amount at stake for each consumer on a given trade issue is modest. Consequently, the costs to each consumer of acting individually in an effort to influence the political process will usually exceed the potential gains. Thus, severe free-rider problems will often thwart the task of organizing consumers to act collectively to support liberal trade policies.[20]

Thus, the Theory predicts a politician will focus on concerns of producers adversely impacted by free trade, not of consumers benefited by trade liberalization.

---

19. United Nations Document EPCT/C.II/PV.7, at 3 (1946) *quoted in* JACKSON 1969, § 23.1 at 554–555.

20. *Protectionism as "Safeguard,"* 275–276.

In turn, the essential purpose of GATT Article XIX, the WTO *Agreement on Safeguards*, Section 201, and other safeguard provisions, is to authorize the focus on concerns of allegedly injured producers. As Professor Sykes further explains, it regulates the trade-off between:

> trade liberalization *ex ante* [*i.e.*, at the time a trade agreement takes effect] and opportunities to re-impose protection *ex post* [*i.e.*, after a trade agreement enters into force]. When self-interested political officials must decide whether to make trade concessions under conditions of uncertainty about their political consequences, the knowledge that those concessions are in fact "escapable" facilitates initial concessions and may reduce the social costs of protection over time. This defense of Article XIX, though conjectural, is nonetheless far more convincing than popular rhetoric about the importance of the escape clause for restoring competitiveness or facilitating an orderly contraction in declining industries, or the hypothesis that escape clause measures provide an *ex post* "safety valve" for protectionist pressures.[21]

In brief, Article XIX relieves a WTO Member of the fear commitments into which it enters are irrevocable.

Lifting this fear helps progressive trade liberalization. If political rewards are sufficient, and the cost of measured retaliation is accepted, then a WTO Member may renege on its commitments. By removing fear at the outset, a Member feels liberated to enter into major trade-expanding deals:

> Although the reduction of protectionist barriers is almost always in the public interest, elected officials or their subordinates may decline to pursue trade liberalization initiatives out of political self-interest, even if the political consequences of liberalization appear favorable at the time of the negotiations. The reason is that unanticipated changes in economic conditions may create circumstances in which the political rewards to an increase in protection (or the political costs of an irrevocable commitment to reduce protection) are great. Consequently, in the absence of an escape clause, trade negotiators may decline to make certain reciprocal concessions for fear of adverse political consequences in the future. But, with an escape clause in place the negotiators will agree on a greater number of reciprocal concessions, knowing that those concessions can be avoided later if political conditions dictate.[22]

In sum, the argument is safeguards ensure flexibility in reducing trade barriers. They boost chances of agreement by accommodating self-interests.

---

21. *Protectionism as "Safeguard,"* 259.
22. *Protectionism as "Safeguard,"* 278–279.

VI. Global Production and 1990
Certain Cameras Case

United States International Trade Commission,

Certain Cameras, Inv. No. TA-201-62,

U.S. ITC Pub 2315 (September 1990)

Additional Views of Acting Chairman Anne E. Brunsdale

I concur in the conclusion of my colleagues that increased imports are not a substantial cause of serious injury to the domestic industry producing certain cameras, and I join in their opinion. I present these additional views to elaborate on what I consider the most complex issue in this case—that is, how the Commission should consider the activities and products of U.S. firms that have assembly operations or parts manufacturing facilities abroad. In my view, this is a serious question, less for its bearing on this particular case, than for its likely importance in future cases. Increased globalization of industries is an inevitable consequence of changes in technology, especially in transportation and communications, and the growing integration of the world economy. Therefore, it is important that the Commission grapple with the issue to provide guidance for the future.

In this case, the Commission had to decide how to assess Kodak's domestic operations related to the production of 35mm and 110 cameras that were assembled or partially manufactured in Mexico and Brazil. Further, the Commission had to determine whether those Kodak cameras that are considered to be imports for customs purposes should also be considered imports for the purpose of this investigation. The main argument for using final assembly to determine the country of origin is that final assembly is the stage that transforms parts into the relevant "like or directly competitive article." If all parts are made in the U.S. but assembled abroad then, it is argued, the U.S. is simply a parts manufacturer and not a manufacturer of the like or directly competitive product. Since the court held in *United Shoe Workers of America, AFL-CIO v. Bedell,* a case involving the trade adjustment assistance laws, that parts are not to be considered as like or directly competitive with the finished article, it purportedly follows that final assembly is the critical factor.

I believe that such an argument is simplistic and that a distinction should be made between a mere manufacturer of component parts (as in *United Shoe*) and a manufacturer of the like product, such as Kodak, that has assembly operations abroad. The courts have made clear that firms in upstream industries do not have standing to file a case against imports of a downstream product. In this case, Kodak could not be considered part of the upstream "camera parts" industry, as distinct from the camera industry, because it does not sell parts on the open market and the foreign entities that assemble Kodak cameras abroad do not sell any other brands of cameras on the open market.

While it may make sense for final assembly to be the decisive factor in the determination of an import for customs purposes, it makes little sense for the Commission to adopt this standard without careful consideration of the consequences. Taken to their extreme, the problems with placing such importance on final assembly become obvious. A domestic screwdriver plant set up only to assemble imported parts would be able to seek relief from products that, except for assembly, are made in the United States. Using a customs standard, we would ignore the fact that the domestic content was substantially higher in the product assembled abroad. Therefore, granting relief to the so-called domestic industry would actually decrease productive activity in the United States. Perversely, the foreign country that supplied parts to the screwdriver plant would be the main beneficiary of such an action. This scenario demonstrates that a simplistic or arbitrary definition of imports or domestic production may prove to be detrimental to U.S. competitiveness in the long run. Therefore, the Commission should look further.

The import relief laws and their legislative history provide limited guidance in this area. While the Commission has addressed similar issues in the past, it has never dealt with this issue explicitly. In a previous 201 case involving motor vehicles, the Commission had to decide how to treat products that had over 50 percent U.S. value-added and were manufactured in Canada by wholly-owned subsidiaries of the U.S. firms. While the Commission decided that the products in that case were imports, certain Commissioners expressed the view that products exported for final assembly or minor finishing work should nonetheless be treated as domestic production. [*See Certain Motor Vehicles and Certain Chassis and Bodies Therefor*, Inv. No. TA-201-44, U.S.ITC Pub. 1110 (December 1980) at 15 (Views of Chairman Alberger), and at 101 (Views of Commissioner Stern).] In another 201 case the Commission had to decide if certain producers of motorcycles should be considered part of the domestic industry, despite the fact that their products contained a majority of foreign content. The Commission decided to include those producers in the domestic industry, with their production weighted by the domestic value-added. In explaining their decision, some Commissioners noted the significant productive resources those firms had in the United States. [*See Heavyweight Motorcycles, and Engines and Power Train Subassemblies Therefor*, Inv. No. 201-47, U.S.ITC Pub. 1342 (February 1983) at 9–10 (Views Chairman Eckes) and at 31 (Views of Commissioner Haggart).]

There are also a number of Title VII [*i.e.*, AD and CVD] cases where the Commission had to address similar issues. In a case involving radio pagers, it was decided that even though the pagers were assembled abroad and incorporated foreign parts, they should be considered as part of domestic production. [*See Certain Radio Paging and Alerting Receiving Devices from Japan*, Inv. No. 731-TA-102, U.S.ITC Pub. 1410 (August 1983) at 10 (Views of Chairman Eckes and Commissioner Haggart).] The significant percentage of domestic value-added of the products combined with the fact that domestic activities involved "considerable technical expertise and capital investment" was considered crucial to the determination.

In general, I believe that the Commission has taken a common sense approach and, on a case-by-case basis, has tried to interpret the import relief law at issue in this case in a manner consistent with its fundamental purpose—to provide the U.S. industry with the opportunity to compete in the international arena. Since domestic productive activity is the most important focus of the law, I favor an approach that considers the domestic industry to be all such domestic activity that adds value to the like product. I see no basis for giving greater weight to one kind of value-added activity over another. In addition, I would prefer not to exclude certain domestic productive activity because it contributed an insufficient percentage of domestic value-added to the ensuing final product. After all, there may be more domestic employment and investment generated from a product with a relatively low percentage of domestic value-added than from a product with a relatively high percentage of domestic value-added.

The difficulty with a strict value-added approach is that it cannot be used unless the data are presented in such a way as to allow consideration of all domestic value-added activities. In many cases, it would be impossible to allocate profits and employment in any reliable way. Without such data, Commissioners cannot carry out their statutory obligation to determine the impact of imports on the condition of the domestic industry in a rigorous way. When the data are not available to make a determination based strictly on domestic value-added, I would try to make distinctions for particular products. I would determine whether a good was domestic or imported, initially looking at its share of domestic content, both absolutely and in comparison to the industry average.

In this case, petitioner Keystone contends that the domestic industry should be defined to exclude the operations related to Kodak cameras that have value added in Mexico and Brazil. Kodak, on the other hand, suggests that all of its U.S. camera production activity should be included with the domestic industry, even if the camera is partially manufactured and/or assembled abroad. While I agree with Kodak in principle, the available data do not permit me to evaluate the domestic industry in the manner it suggested. A strict value-added approach in this case would not have allowed Commissioners to address the question of injury to the domestic industry producing conventional cameras. Therefore, I used an alternative approach whereby each product is considered domestic or imported based on its share of domestic content. There were five categories of products to evaluate for domestic content: Keystone cameras, Kodak's domestically produced cameras, Kodak's 110 cameras assembled in Mexico, Kodak's 35 mm cameras partially manufactured and assembled in Mexico, and Kodak's 35 mm cameras partially manufactured and assembled in Brazil.

Both Keystone and Kodak cameras that are assembled in the United States should be considered as domestic products based on their share of domestic content. [Both companies import foreign components for their cameras that are assembled in the U.S.] Kodak 110 cameras assembled in Mexico should also be considered as domestic products based on their share of U.S. value added, which is comparable to the domestic content of Keystone's cameras. The share of domestic content of Kodak 35 mm cameras partially manufactured in Brazil and Mexico was substantially lower than that of the other cameras. Petitioner states, however, that the Commission should be most concerned about final assembly—arguing that it is the true determinant of a domestic product. For the reasons stated above, I do not agree and therefore I find that there is no basis for excluding any Kodak 110 cameras from the domestic industry.

I do not believe that the percentage of domestic content in Kodak's 35 mm cameras partially manufactured in Brazil and Mexico is sufficient to consider them as domestic products. Lacking adequate data to isolate and assess the domestic activities attributable to these cameras, to the extent possible I excluded all domestic activities related to production of those cameras from the domestic industry. Including such activities would have only added support to my negative determination.

In view of the increasing globalization of industries, I expect that the Commission will be confronted with this issue many times in the future. The United States is currently pursuing policies that will open markets to foreign trade and investment. Thus, we can expect that U.S. companies will have increased opportunities to open plants and assembly operations in third countries and to benefit from those opportunities abroad, while foreign companies will benefit from increased opportunities in the United States and thereby will contribute to the U.S. economy. Because of increased competition, U.S. firms will be forced to look at alternatives that allow them to remain competitive in the long run. If U.S. firms are successful, this will result in increased employment and output in the United States.

Kodak is a case in point. Historically, Kodak has been a driving force in the domestic camera industry; even petitioner Keystone described itself as operating under Kodak's umbrella through various licensing agreements. Kodak undertakes R&D activity and the manufacturing of camera parts and sub-assemblies in the U.S. and has generated the bulk of employment in the camera industry, particularly if one considers the total wage bill. Kodak stated that some camera models would not be competitive unless a certain portion of their production was done abroad. By assembling those cameras abroad, Kodak has found a way to be competitive in the long run while maintaining significant domestic activity—the very purpose behind this import relief law. Excluding its activities from the domestic industry would undermine the very purpose of this law.

VII. Conventional Remedies, Yet Global Value-Added Chains

Can the argument of Commissioner Brunsdale in the 1990 *Certain Cameras* case be generalized to all trade remedies? Consider the facts articulated in April 2012 by WTO Director General Pascal Lamy (1947–):

In the past, goods were made in Mexico, or Mauritius, or Malaysia. Today, goods are made in the world. The expansion of global value chains means that most products are assembled with inputs from many countries. Products cross borders frequently during various stages of assembly. Trade in intermediate goods is the most dynamic sector of international trade, growing at a rate of 6 percent per year. And, this trade is taking place in high-technology sectors, which generate well-paying jobs. Twenty years ago, the import content of exports was 20 percent. Today, it is around 40 percent. More than half of global manufactured exports are components, which are inputs to other as yet unfinished goods. In Asia, the figure is more than 70 percent.

The thousands of companies involve in these global value chains realize that access to imported components at the cheapest prices is vital to retaining a competitive edge in tough global markets. In Minnesota, 58.5 percent of imported products are used by U.S. workers to manufacture goods in the United States.[23]

Do these facts suggest not only safeguards, but also AD and CVD remedies are outmoded? Like safeguards, these remedies long pre-date GATT, arising in an era in which national boundaries defined the production of many goods. The global value added chains indicate that world is disappearing.

Alternatively, even if a product is "Made in the World," is it important to distinguish remedies against unfair trade practices from safeguards, which aim at fair foreign competition? On the one hand, consider whether an AD or CVD duty justified on a good to which value was added in multiple countries, simply because dumping or certain types of subsidies are inherently unfair? On the other hand, safeguards are based in part on import surges, and more generally presume accurate data about bilateral trade balances. But, those balances ignore global value added chains, and ascribe all of the value of a product to its country of origin based on rules of origin. If trade is measured in value-added terms, then many gaping trade deficits shrink. For instance, the trade deficit of America with China (as of April 2012) falls by 40%.

One famous product shows why: the iPhone. Nominal trade data indicate a $1.9 billion surplus in favor of China this product in 2009. Yet, only 4% of the value of an iPhone is added in China. So, the true surplus is just $76 million. Critical and high-value components in the iPhone are imported into China from Japan, Germany, and Korea. If bilateral trade statistics reflected value added in each country, then the surplus position of China relative to the U.S. for the iPhone would be just $76 million. In contrast, the value-added based surplus positions of Japan, Germany, and Korea would be $685, $341, and $259 million, respectively.

---

23. "Trade Improves the Lives of People," Speech of Pascal Lamy, WTO Director General, to Minnesota Economic Club, Minneapolis, 17 April 2012, www.wto.org.

Another example is surprising: T&A merchandise. In February 2012, the Trans Pacific Partnership Apparel Coalition released an economic study, *Analyzing the Value for Apparel Designed in the United States and Manufactured Overseas*, concerning:

> where and how American workers contribute to the value and global production of apparel.

> The report, . . . found that on average, 70.3 percent of final retail price of studied apparel is created by workers in the United States. Specifically, the global value chain for apparel relies on a full range of highly-skilled and highly-compensated American workers in blue-collar and white-collar jobs that contribute to the design, development, production, importation, distribution and sale of apparel in the United States.[24]

To be sure, the Coalition sought lower tariffs on T&A imports, as its members were importers that turned the imports into finished products, from branded high fashion to innovative outdoor apparel. Still, its point is well taken: job creation in the U.S. is linked to these imports, so (as Kevin M. Burke, President and CEO, American Apparel & Footwear Association remarked), "When we get dressed each day, we wear U.S. jobs." Simply put, with a global value chain for the T&A industry, and with America at the higher end of that chain, lowering tariffs on T&A merchandise should not be seen as a zero sum game.

VIII. Are Those Chains New?

Consider whether there is yet another possibility, one which debunks the argument of Commissioner Brunsdale and questions the facts of Director General Lamy. In decades and centuries past, global value added chains existed. They had a different name: colonial linkages. For example, T&A manufactured in Manchester relied on cotton from India. It was Mahatma Gandhi (1869–1948) who protested non-violently. The Mahatma (which means "Great Soul") called on Indians to spin their own cloth (*khadi*, or *khaddar*, meaning homespun cloth) rather than rely on imported cloth and garments, and was pictured famously at his *charkha* (spinning wheel). The point Gandhi *Ji* (the suffix "*Ji*" shows respect) was making was that Indian self-rule (*swaraj*) and freedom from British domination depended on Indian self-sufficiency.

So, was it not always the case that many products were "Made in the World"? If so, then perhaps trade remedies are no more inapposite today than they were in

---

24. Press Release, Retail Industry Leaders Association, *Study Finds U.S. Workers Contribute Substantially to U.S. Apparel Imports*, 13 February 2013. The study is www.rila.org. I am grateful to David R. Jackson, International Licensing Analyst, Pacific Architects and Engineers, Washington, D.C., former Senior Director, Customs & Industry Compliance, Retail Industry Leaders Association (RILA), Washington, D.C., and University of Kansas J.D. Class of 2007, for these materials and his insights.

yesteryear. In the Colonial Era, peripheral countries depended on core countries to sell their raw materials and intermediate goods, and the core countries provided the highest value added in finishing the product. Following post–Second World War era independence movements, many of those peripheral countries still are poor, and still depend on market access to rich countries. But, many of them are better-positioned to produce finished goods. Conversely, as in the past, rich countries today seek to protect their higher-value added end of the global commodity chain. Tariff escalation (with lower tariffs on raw materials and intermediate goods, and higher tariffs on finished items), coupled with trade remedies, serves their interests.

Chapter 24

Legal Criteria for General Safeguards[1]

I. 2018 *Indonesia Iron* Case and Defining What Constitutes a "Safeguard"

In the 2018 *Indonesia Iron* case, excerpted below, both sides scored partial victories. The complainants, Taiwan and Vietnam, argued tariffs imposed by the respondent, Indonesia, constituted an illegal safeguard measure. Given the way in which the Appellate Body defined "safeguard," they lost. But, they prevailed on their claim that Indonesia's temporary trade restrictions violated the MFN rule.

WTO Appellate Body Report,

Indonesia — Safeguard on Certain Iron or Steel Products,

WT/DS490/AB/R, WT/DS496/AB/R (Issued 15 August 2018)

1. Introduction

1.1. Indonesia, the Separate Customs Territory of Taiwan, Penghu, Kinmen and Matsu (hereinafter Chinese Taipei), and Vietnam each appeal certain issues of law and legal interpretations developed in the Panel Report, *Indonesia — Safeguard on Certain Iron or Steel Products* (Panel Report). . . . [T]wo panels were established to consider complaints by, respectively, Chinese Taipei and Vietnam (the complainants) concerning a specific duty applied by Indonesia on imports of galvalume. [As the Appellate Body explained in footnote 6 of its *Report*: "Galvalume is defined under the specific duty as flat-rolled products of iron or non-alloy steel, of a width of 600 mm or more, clad, plated, or coated with aluminum-zinc alloys, containing by weight less than 0.6% of carbon, with a thickness not exceeding 0.7 mm, under

---

1. Documents References:
   (1) *Havana (ITO) Charter* Article 40
   (2) GATT Articles XII, XVIII, XIX
   (3) WTO *Agreement on Safeguards*
   (4) WTO *Agreement on Agriculture*, Article 5
   (5) WTO *ATC Agreement*, Article 6:2
   (6) *NAFTA* Chapter 8
   (7) Relevant provisions in other FTAs

harmonized system (HS) code 7210.61.11.00." Galvalume is used to make appliances and cars, and in the construction industry.] The specific duty was imposed following an investigation initiated and conducted under Indonesia's domestic safeguards legislation by Indonesia's competent authority (*Komite Pengamanan Perdagangan Indonesia*, or *KPPI*). The specific duty was adopted pursuant to Regulation No. 137.1/PMK.011/2014 (Regulation 137) of the Minister of Finance of the Republic of Indonesia, which entered into force on 22 July 2014. . . .

. . .

1.3. Before the Panel, Chinese Taipei and Vietnam raised several claims in relation to the specific duty applied by Indonesia on imports of galvalume. Specifically, the complainants claimed that Indonesia had acted inconsistently with: (i) Article XIX:1(a) of the General Agreement on Tariffs and Trade 1994 (GATT 1994) and Article 3.1 of the *Agreement on Safeguards* because *KPPI* failed to demonstrate the existence of "unforeseen developments," "the effect of the [GATT] obligations," and the "logical connection" between these two elements and the increase in imports that allegedly caused serious injury; (ii) Article XIX:1(a) of the GATT 1994 and Articles 2:1 and 3:1 of the *Agreement on Safeguards* . . . because *KPPI's* determination of increased imports was not based on an increase in imports that is "recent enough": (iii) Article XIX:1(a) of the GATT 1994 and Articles 2:1, 3:1, 4:2(a), and 4:2(c) of the *Agreement on Safeguards* because *KPPI* failed to provide a reasoned and adequate explanation of how the facts support the determination of threat of serious injury, including the evaluation of all relevant serious injury indicators; (iv) Article 4.1(b) of the *Agreement on Safeguards* (Vietnam only) because *KPPI's* finding of threat of serious injury is inconsistent with the definition of "threat of serious injury" under that provision; (v) Article XIX:1(a) of the GATT 1994 and Articles 2:1, 3:1, 4:2(b), and 4:2(c) of the *Agreement on Safeguards* because *KPPI* failed to establish a causal link and to conduct a proper non-attribution analysis in accordance with these provisions; and (vi) Articles 2:1, 3:1, 4:2(a), and 4:2(b) of the *Agreement on Safeguards* because *KPPI* failed to observe the required "parallelism" by applying the specific duty to a product that is different from the product that was the subject of its investigation, and failed to provide a reasoned and adequate explanation thereof.10 The complainants further alleged that Indonesia had acted inconsistently with: (i) Article 12:2 of the *Agreement on Safeguards* because Indonesia failed to provide "all pertinent information" in the notifications of the finding of threat of serious injury and the proposal to impose a safeguard measure to the Committee on Safeguards; and (ii) Article XIX:2 of the GATT 1994 and Article 12:3 of the *Agreement on Safeguards* because Indonesia failed to provide a reasonable opportunity to hold prior consultations.

1.4. The complainants additionally claimed that Indonesia acted inconsistently with Article I:1 of the GATT 1994 because it excluded the products originating in certain countries from the scope of application of the specific duty without according that exemption immediately and unconditionally to like products originating in the territory of other Members, including the complainants.

1.5. . . . [T]he Panel found that: (i) the specific duty applied by Indonesia on imports of galvalume does not constitute a safeguard measure within the meaning of Article 1 of the *Agreement on Safeguards*; and (ii) the application of the specific duty on imports of galvalume originating in all but 120 countries is inconsistent with Indonesia's obligation to accord most-favored nation (MFN) treatment under Article I:1 of the GATT 1994. Having concluded that the specific duty does not constitute a safeguard measure within the meaning of Article 1 of the *Agreement on Safeguards*, the Panel found that there was no legal basis to address the complainants' claims under the *Agreement on Safeguards* and the GATT 1994 with respect to the specific duty *as a safeguard measure*. Accordingly, the Panel dismissed the entirety of those claims.

1.6. In light of its finding that the application of the specific duty is inconsistent with Indonesia's obligations under Article I:1 of the GATT 1994, the Panel recommended, pursuant to Article 19:1 of the *DSU*, that Indonesia bring its measure into conformity with its obligations under the GATT 1994.

. . .

4. Issues Raised in this Appeal

4.1. The following issues are raised in this appeal:

. . .

   b.   with respect to the Panel's finding that the measure at issue is not a safeguard measure:

. . .

     ii.   whether the Panel erred in its interpretation and application of Article 1 of the *Agreement on Safeguards* and Article XIX of the GATT 1994 (raised by all participants);

. . .

5. Analysis of the Appellate Body

. . .

5.2 Whether the Panel erred in finding that Indonesia's specific duty on imports of galvalume is not a safeguard measure

5.15. Each participant in these proceedings appeals the Panel's finding that Indonesia's specific duty on imports of galvalume is not a safeguard measure within the meaning of Article 1 of the *Agreement on Safeguards*. They each allege that the Panel erred in its interpretation and application of Article 1 of the *Agreement on Safeguards* and Article XIX of the GATT 1994. . . .

. . .

5.2.1 The Panel's Findings

5.17. Before the Panel, both sides maintained, "albeit for somewhat different reasons," that Indonesia's specific duty on imports of galvalume constitutes a safeguard measure to which the disciplines of the *Agreement on Safeguards* apply. . . . Indonesia highlighted that the measure at issue had been adopted as a result of a safeguards investigation conducted by *KPPI* in accordance with Indonesia's domestic trade remedy regulations. The complainants, for their part, focused on the fact that the specific duty "suspends" Indonesia's MFN treatment obligation under Article I:1 of the GATT 1994.

. . .

5.19. The Panel noted that, under Article 1 of the *Agreement on Safeguards*, "safeguard measures . . . shall be understood to mean those measures provided for in Article XIX of GATT 1994." Turning to Article XIX:1(a) of the GATT 1994, the Panel expressed the view that the "measures provided for" under that provision are "measures that *suspend a GATT obligation* and/or *withdraw or modify a GATT concession*, in situations where, as a result of a Member's WTO commitments and developments that were 'unforeseen' at the time that it undertook those commitments, a product 'is being imported' into a Member's territory in 'such increased quantities and under such conditions as to cause or threaten serious injury to domestic producers of like or directly competitive products.'" [Emphasis original.] The Panel further observed that safeguard measures "must result in the suspension, withdrawal, or modification of a GATT obligation or concession for a particular purpose," namely, "they must operate '*to the extent and for such a time as may be necessary to prevent or remedy such injury*.'" [Emphasis original.] Thus, in the Panel's view, a safeguard measure can be deemed to exist only if the suspension or withdrawal relates to a GATT obligation or concession that a Member "finds it must be temporarily released from in order to pursue a course of action necessary to prevent or remedy serious injury." On this basis, the Panel held:

> [O]ne of the defining features of . . . safeguard measures . . . is the suspension, withdrawal, or modification of a GATT obligation or concession that *precludes a Member from imposing a measure to the extent necessary to prevent or remedy serious injury*, in a situation where all of the conditions for the imposition of a safeguard measure are satisfied. [Emphasis original.]

5.20. Applying this reasoning to the facts of this dispute, the Panel observed that Indonesia "has no binding tariff obligation with respect to galvalume in its WTO Schedule of Concessions" and is, therefore, "free to impose any amount of duty it deems appropriate" on that product, including the specific duty at issue in these proceedings. The Panel determined, therefore, that Indonesia's specific duty on imports of galvalume does not "suspend, withdraw, or modify Indonesia's obligations under Article II of the GATT 1994." Having made this finding, the Panel turned to assess whether the measure at issue suspends any other obligation incurred by Indonesia under the GATT 1994.

5.21. First, the Panel addressed Indonesia's argument that the measure at issue suspends "the GATT exception under Article XXIV of the GATT 1994." Indonesia maintained that the imposition of the specific duty on imports of galvalume from its regional trade agreement (RTA) partners suspends the tariff obligations incurred by Indonesia under the RTAs, which would have otherwise prevented it from countering the increased imports. The Panel disagreed with Indonesia, noting that Article XXIV of the GATT 1994 "is a *permissive* provision" that "does not impose any positive obligation . . . either to enter into [RTAs] or to provide a certain level of market access to its [RTA] partners through bound tariffs." According to the Panel, Indonesia's tariff commitments vis-à-vis its RTA partners are obligations assumed under the respective RTAs, not the *Marrakesh Agreement Establishing the World Trade Organization* (*WTO Agreement*). Therefore, the Panel concluded that there is "no basis" to assert that the specific duty suspends "the GATT exception under Article XXIV."

5.22. Second, the Panel addressed the contention that the imposition of the specific duty suspends Indonesia's MFN treatment obligation under Article I:1 of the GATT 1994. Indonesia observed that the special and differential (S&D) treatment disciplines set forth in Article 9:1 of the *Agreement on Safeguards* require it to exempt the 120 countries listed in Regulation 137 from the scope of application of the specific duty. According to Indonesia, this results in a "discriminatory" application of the measure that suspends the MFN treatment obligation under Article I:1 of the GATT 1994.

5.23. The Panel rejected Indonesia's argument. In the Panel's view, the exemption of certain developing country Members from the application of a safeguard measure under Article 9:1 is, by its own terms, "legally premised" on an importing Member's intention to apply a safeguard measure. Recalling its prior findings that the measure at issue does not suspend Indonesia's concessions under Article II or Article XXIV of the GATT 1994, the Panel considered that the legal premise for the application of Article 9:1 was not met and that, therefore, there is "no basis" for Indonesia's invocation of Article 9:1. Moreover, according to the Panel, Indonesia's exemption of the 120 countries listed in Regulation 137 from the scope of application of the specific duty is not "*necessary to remedy or prevent serious injury*," but rather has "the *sole* purpose" of providing the exempted countries with "continued access to the Indonesian galvalume market." [Emphasis original.] The Panel "fail[ed] to see how a course of action that *dilutes* the protective impact of a safeguard measure *in order to provide S&D* could result in the suspension of a Member's MFN obligations under Article I:1 for the purpose of Article XIX:1(a)," given that "the fundamental objective of Article XIX:1(a) is to allow Members to 'escape' their GATT obligations to the extent necessary to *prevent or remedy serious injury to a domestic industry*." [Emphasis original.] The Panel found further support in the General Interpretative Note to Annex 1A of the *WTO Agreement* (General Interpretative Note), which stipulates that "[i]n the event of conflict between a provision of the [GATT] 1994 and a provision of another agreement in Annex 1A to the [*WTO Agreement*], the provision of the other agreement shall prevail to the extent of the conflict." In the Panel's view, the effect of this rule is that the discriminatory application of a safeguard measure called for in Article 9:1 "is permissible *without having to suspend the operation of Article I:1*," because the former obligation "prevails *as a matter of law*" over the latter. [Emphasis original.]

5.24. Based on the foregoing, the Panel found that the measure at issue does not constitute a safeguard measure within the meaning of Article 1 of the *Agreement on Safeguards.*

. . .

5.2.3 Whether the Panel erred in its interpretation and application of Article 1 of the *Agreement on Safeguards* and Article XIX of the GATT 1994

. . .

5.2.3.2 Analysis of the Panel's interpretation and application of Article 1 of the *Agreement on Safeguards* and Article XIX of the GATT 1994

5.52. The claims and arguments raised by the participants on appeal require us to rule on the scope of measures subject to the disciplines of the *Agreement on Safeguards,* to the extent that this is required to resolve this dispute. . . . [W]e recall the rather unusual circumstances in which this question arose in the Panel proceedings. . . . [T]his is the first time in which claims of violation of the *Agreement on Safeguards* have been raised in a situation where: (i) the responding Member conducted an investigation with a view to complying with its obligations under the *Agreement on Safeguards* and imposed a duty in light of the outcome of that investigation, despite the fact that it was entitled to raise its applied MFN duty rate on imports of the subject product at any time and to any level, given that it has no tariff bindings on that product under Article II of the GATT 1994; and (ii) all parties have consistently argued that the duty at issue *is* a safeguard measure.

5.53. The Appellate Body has described safeguard measures as "extraordinary remedies" that "are imposed in the form of import restrictions" in "emergency situations," *i.e.*, "in the absence of any allegation of an unfair trade practice." [The Appellate Body cited its precedents in *Korea—Definitive Safeguard Measure on Imports of Certain Dairy Products*, WT/DS98/AB/R ¶ 86 (adopted 12 January 2000), *United States—Definitive Safeguard Measures on Imports of Circular Welded Carbon Quality Line Pipe from Korea*, WT/DS202/AB/R ¶ 80 (adopted 2 March 2002), and *United States—Definitive Safeguard Measures on Imports of Certain Steel Products*, WT/DS248/AB/R, WT/DS249/AB/R, WT/DS251/AB/R, WT/DS252/AB/R, WT/DS253/AB/R, WT/DS254/AB/R, WT/DS258/AB/R, WT/DS259/AB/R ¶ 347 (adopted 10 December 2003). The 2000 *Korea Dairy*, 2002 *Line Pipe*, and 2003 *Steel Safeguards* cases are discussed later in this Chapter.] As the Appellate Body has noted, the WTO disciplines on safeguards give WTO Members "the possibility, as trade is liberalized, of resorting to an effective remedy in an extraordinary emergency situation that . . . makes it necessary to protect a domestic industry temporarily." [The Appellate Body cited 2002 *Line Pipe*, ¶ 82.]

5.54. Article 1 of the *Agreement on Safeguards* specifies that the "safeguard measures" are "measures provided for in Article XIX of GATT 1994." Article XIX is entitled "Emergency Action on Imports of Particular Products." Paragraph 1(a) of Article XIX reads as follows:

If, as a result of unforeseen developments and of the effect of the obligations incurred by a Member under this Agreement, including tariff concessions, any product is being imported into the territory of that Member in such increased quantities and under such conditions as to cause or threaten serious injury to domestic producers in that territory of like or directly competitive products, the Member shall be free, in respect of such product, and to the extent and for such time as may be necessary to prevent or remedy such injury, *to suspend the obligation in whole or in part or to withdraw or modify the concession.* [Emphasis added.]

5.55. A plain reading of Article XIX:1(a) suggests that the "measures provided for" in that provision are measures that *suspend a GATT obligation* and/or *withdraw or modify a GATT concession*, in situations where a product "is being imported" into a Member's territory in "such increased quantities and under such conditions as to cause or threaten serious injury to domestic producers of like or directly competitive products." [Emphasis added.] In other words, the action contemplated under Article XIX:1(a) consists of the suspension, in whole or in part, of a GATT obligation or the withdrawal from or modification of a GATT concession. Absent such a suspension, withdrawal, or modification, we fail to see how a measure could be characterized as a safeguard measure.

5.56. Article XIX:1(a) further indicates that the measures provided for under that provision are those that suspend a GATT obligation or withdraw or modify a tariff concession "to prevent or remedy" serious injury to a Member's domestic industry caused or threatened by imports subject to a GATT obligation or tariff concession. The use of the word to" in this connection indicates that the suspension of a GATT obligation or the withdrawal or modification of a GATT concession must be designed to pursue a specific *objective*, namely preventing or remedying serious injury to the Member's domestic industry. Thus, for example, where a measure suspends a GATT obligation or withdraws or modifies a tariff concession, but that suspension, withdrawal, or modification does not have a demonstrable link to the objective of preventing or remedying injury, we do not consider that the measure in question could be characterized as one "provided for" under Article XIX.

5.57. That said, we note that Article XIX:1(a) does not expressly define the scope of measures that fall under the WTO safeguard disciplines. Rather, whether a particular measure constitutes a safeguard measure for purposes of WTO law can be determined only on a case-by-case basis. In carrying out this analysis, it is important to distinguish between the features that determine whether a measure can be properly characterized as a safeguard measure from the conditions that must be met in order for the measure to be consistent with the *Agreement on Safeguards* and the GATT 1994. Put differently, it would be improper to conflate factors pertaining to the legal characterization of a measure for purposes of determining the *applicability* of the WTO safeguard disciplines with the substantive conditions and procedural requirements that determine the WTO-*consistency* of a safeguard measure.

5.58. We further note that the text of Article XIX:1(a) does not expressly list the GATT obligations that may be suspended in order for a measure to qualify as a safeguard measure. While the Appellate Body has identified Articles II:1 and XI:1 of the GATT 1994 (addressing tariff concessions and the prohibition on quantitative restrictions, respectively) as typical examples of such obligations, it has not precluded the possibility that other GATT obligations may be relevant to this effect. [The Appellate Body cited its precedent in *Argentina—Safeguard Measures on Imports of Footwear*, WT/DS121/AB/R ¶ 95 (adopted 12 January 2000), which is discussed later in this Chapter.] We recall, however, our understanding that, in order for a measure to constitute a safeguard measure, the suspension of a GATT obligation or the withdrawal or modification of a tariff concession entailed by that measure must be designed to pursue the objective of preventing or remedying serious injury to the Member's domestic industry. This suggests that the range of GATT obligations that may relevantly be suspended for purposes of Article XIX is limited to obligations whose suspension has a demonstrable link to the prevention or remediation of serious injury.

5.59. To conclude our reading of Article XIX:1(a), we note that a Member's right to suspend a GATT obligation or to withdraw or modify a GATT concession is not unqualified. Rather, that Member may take such emergency action only "to the extent and for such time as may be *necessary*" to prevent or remedy serious injury. [Emphasis added.] Articles 5:1 and 7:1 of the *Agreement on Safeguards* equally specify, respectively, that safeguard measures shall be applied "only to the extent" and "only for such period of time" as may be "necessary to prevent or remedy serious injury and to facilitate adjustment." We do not consider these requirements to be relevant to the legal characterization of a measure as a safeguard measure for purposes of determining the *applicability* of the WTO safeguard disciplines. Instead, they relate to the WTO-*conformity* of a safeguard measure.

5.60. In light of the above, we consider that, in order to constitute one of the "measures provided for in Article XIX," a measure must present certain constituent features, absent which it could not be considered a safeguard measure. First, that measure must suspend, in whole or in part, a GATT obligation or withdraw or modify a GATT concession. Second, the suspension, withdrawal, or modification in question must be designed to prevent or remedy serious injury to the Member's domestic industry caused or threatened by increased imports of the subject product. In order to determine whether a measure presents such features, a panel is called upon to assess the design, structure, and expected operation of the measure as a whole. In making its independent and objective assessment, a panel must identify all the aspects of the measure that may have a bearing on its legal characterization, recognize which of those aspects are the most central to that measure, and, thereby, properly determine the disciplines to which the measure is subject. [Here the Appellate Body cited its precedent in *China—Measures Affecting Imports of Automobile Parts*, WT/DS339/AB/R, WT/DS340/AB/R, WT/DS342/AB/R, ¶ 171 (adopted 12 January 2009), which is discussed in a separate Chapter.] As part of its determination, a Panel should evaluate and give due consideration to all relevant factors, including the manner in which the measure is characterized under the domestic law of the Member concerned, the domestic procedures that led to the adoption of the measure, and any relevant notifications to the WTO Committee on Safeguards. However, no one such factor is, in and of itself, dispositive of the question of whether the measure constitutes a safeguard measure within the meaning of Article 1 of the *Agreement on Safeguards.*

[Here the Appellate Body cited its precedents in 2003 *Byrd Amendment*, ¶ 259, 2004 *Corrosion Resistant Steel Sunset Review*, fn. 87 at ¶ 87, 2004 *Softwood Lumber IV*, ¶ 56 2012 *Boeing*, ¶¶ 586, 593, and 2013 *Canada Renewable Energy*, ¶ 5.127, each of which is cited and discussed in separate Chapters.]

5.61. With these considerations in mind, we now turn to the Panel's reading of Article XIX:1(a). . . . [F]or the Panel, "one of the defining features" of safeguard measures "is the suspension, withdrawal, or modification of a GATT obligation or concession that precludes a Member from imposing a measure to the extent necessary to prevent or remedy serious injury, in a situation where all of the conditions for the imposition of a safeguard measure are satisfied." On appeal, all participants . . . take issue with the Panel's approach. . . . [T]hey express the view that the Panel conflated the constituent features of a safeguard measure with the conditions for the WTO-consistent application of a safeguard measure in light of the procedural and substantive requirements of the *Agreement on Safeguards.*

5.62. We, too, find the Panel's approach to be problematic. First, the Panel appears to have considered that, in order to qualify as a safeguard measure, a measure must operate "to the extent and for such a time as may be *necessary* to prevent or remedy . . . injury." [Emphasis original.] As discussed in Paragraph 5.59. above, the issue of whether a measure is applied to the extent and for such time as may be necessary to prevent or remedy serious injury is not relevant to determining whether that measure is a safeguard measure for purposes of the *applicability* of the *Agreement on Safeguards.* Instead, it relates to the separate question of whether a safeguard measure is in *conformity* with the procedural and substantive requirements of the *Agreement on Safeguards.* Second, the Panel seems to have suggested that in determining whether a measure is a safeguard measure, it is relevant to consider whether it was adopted in "*a situation where all of the conditions for the imposition of a safeguard measure are satisfied.*" [Emphasis added.] However, an assessment of whether the conditions for the imposition of a safeguard measure have been met is pertinent to the question of whether a WTO Member has applied a *safeguard* measure in a WTO-consistent manner. [Here the Appellate Body cited its precedents in 2002 *Line Pipe*, ¶ 84, and 2003 *Steel Safeguards*, ¶ 264.] Hence, we consider that the Panel conflated the constituent features of a safeguard measure with the conditions for the conformity of a safeguard measure with the *Agreement on Safeguards.*

5.63. We now turn to the Panel's application of Article 1 of the *Agreement on Safeguards* and Article XIX of the GATT 1994 to the measure at issue in these proceedings, which, to recall, relates to Indonesia's specific duty on imports of galvalume.

The Panel found that this measure does not constitute a safeguard measure on three grounds. First, it found that, since Indonesia has no tariff binding on galvalume in its WTO Schedule of Concessions, the measure at issue does not "suspend, withdraw, or modify Indonesia's obligations under Article II of the GATT 1994." Second, the Panel dismissed Indonesia's argument that the measure at issue suspends "the GATT exception under Article XXIV of the GATT 1994." In particular, the Panel observed that Indonesia's tariff commitments vis-à-vis its RTA partners are obligations assumed under the respective RTAs, not the *WTO Agreement*, such that there is "no basis" to assert that the measure at issue suspends "the GATT exception under Article XXIV." Third, the Panel rejected Indonesia's assertion that the exemption of 120 countries from the scope of application of the specific duty, which Indonesia considers to be mandated by Article 9:1, results in a discriminatory application of the measure at issue that suspends Indonesia's MFN treatment obligation under Article I:1 of the GATT 1994. . . . [T]he Panel considered that: (i) the application of Article 9:1 is "legally premised" on the qualification of a measure as a safeguard, which the Panel had already found not to be the case with the measure at issue; (ii) the exemption of 120 countries from the scope of application of the duty is not "necessary to remedy or prevent serious injury," thereby lacking a connection with the "the fundamental objective of Article XIX:1(a)": and (iii) the General Interpretative Note excludes the possibility that the application of Article 9:1, as the legally prevailing rule, suspends a Member's obligations under Article I:1. On appeal, the participants do not dispute the Panel's findings that the measure at issue does not entail a suspension, withdrawal, or modification of Indonesia's obligations under Articles II and XXIV. They do, however, take issue with the Panel's finding that the discriminatory application of the measure at issue by virtue of the disciplines of Article 9:1 cannot be deemed to suspend Indonesia's MFN treatment obligation under Article I:1.

5.64. . . . [i]n order to determine whether a measure constitutes a safeguard measure within the meaning of Article 1 of the *Agreement of Safeguards*, a Panel must objectively assess the design, structure, and expected operation of the measure as a whole, identify all the aspects of the measure that may have a bearing on its legal characterization, and recognize which aspects are the most central to the measure. [Here the Appellate Body cited its precedent in 2009 *China Auto Parts*, ¶ 171.] . . . [T]he Panel was required to ascertain whether the suspension, withdrawal, or modification of a GATT obligation or concession entailed by the measure at issue is designed to prevent or remedy serious injury.

5.65. . . . [B]oth Regulation 137 and the Final Disclosure Report expressly state that Indonesia's imposition of a specific duty on imports of galvalume seeks to counter a threat of serious injury caused by an alleged increase in imports of galvalume over the period of investigation. This element of the measure at issue may well be designed to pursue the specific objective of preventing or remedying serious injury to Indonesia's domestic industry. However, the imposition of the specific duty does not suspend any of Indonesia's GATT obligations, nor does it withdraw or modify any of Indonesia's GATT concessions. This is because, as the Panel rightly found and no participant has contested, Indonesia "has no binding tariff obligation with respect to galvalume in its WTO Schedule of Concessions" and is, therefore, "free to impose any amount of duty it deems appropriate" on that product.

5.66. Besides the imposition of the specific duty, the measure at issue provides for the exemption of the 120 countries listed in Regulation 137 from the scope of application of that duty. By its own terms, this exemption could be viewed as suspending Indonesia's MFN treatment obligation under Article I:1 of the GATT 1994. Indeed, the imposition of the duty on imports of galvalume from some, and not all, Members results in the discriminatory application of the measure at issue, as it departs from the obligation to "immediately and unconditionally" accord "any advantage, favor, privilege or immunity" to "like products" originating in all WTO Members. We note, however, that neither Regulation 137 nor the Final Disclosure Report indicates that the exemption is designed to pursue the specific objective of preventing or remedying serious injury. Before the Panel, Indonesia confirmed that the exemption is *neither intended nor designed* for that purpose. [Emphasis original.]

5.67. On appeal, Indonesia submits that "the sole purpose of the discriminatory application" of the specific duty "is to impose the . . . measure only to major exporting countries which contributed the most to the threat of serious injury suffered by Indonesian galvalume producers." According to Indonesia, the application of the measure to "all WTO Members regardless of [their] import share would not be necessary to remedy or prevent serious injury." Similarly, Vietnam submits that the selective application of the duty "reinforces" the requirement, under Article 5:1 of the *Agreement on Safeguards*, that safeguard measures not be applied beyond the extent necessary to prevent or remedy injury.

5.68. . . . [N]either Regulation 137 nor the Final Disclosure Report refers to the objective of targeting the major contributors to the threat of serious injury. Instead, those instruments expressly indicate that the exemption of 120 countries from the scope of application of the specific duty pursues the objective of complying with the disciplines of Article 9:1 of the *Agreement on Safeguards*. During the course of the Panel proceedings, Indonesia confirmed that the exemption is aimed at complying with the requirements of Article 9:1 Article 9:1 of the *Agreement on Safeguards* stipulates that safeguard measures "shall not be applied against a product originating in a developing country Member," provided that "its share of imports of the product concerned . . . does not exceed 3 per cent" and that "developing country Members with less than 3 per cent import share collectively account for not more than 9 per cent of total imports of the product concerned." The title of Article 9:1, "Developing Country Members," suggests that the purpose of this provision is to set forth S&D treatment requirements in favor of "developing countries whose individual exports are below a *de minimis* level." These disciplines set forth conditions for the WTO-*consistent* application of safeguard measures, and they do not speak to the question of whether a measure constitutes a safeguard measure for purposes of the *applicability* of the WTO safeguard disciplines. In fact, the design, structure, and expected operation of the measure at issue suggest to us that the central aspect of that measure, through which Indonesia seeks to prevent a threat of serious injury to its domestic industry, is the imposition of the specific duty. By contrast, the exemption of 120 countries from the scope of application of the specific duty has the result of allowing *more* imports of galvalume—albeit *de minimis*—into Indonesia's territory *for purposes of according S&D treatment*. Hence, in our view, it has not been demonstrated in the present case that the alleged suspension of Article I:1 entailed by the exemption is designed to prevent or remedy serious injury to Indonesia's domestic industry.

5.69. Even assuming that, as Indonesia and Vietnam now argue, the exemption of 120 countries from the scope of application of the specific duty seeks to "reinforce" the "necessity" requirement under Article 5:1 of the *Agreement on Safeguards* by targeting the major contributors to the threat of serious injury, this does not suffice to show that the alleged suspension of Article I:1 entailed by that exemption is designed to pursue the specific purpose of preventing or remedying serious injury. As discussed in Paragraph 5.59. above, the "necessity" requirement under Article 5:1 of the *Agreement on Safeguards* does not relate to the legal characterization of a measure for purposes of the *applicability* of the WTO safeguard disciplines, but rather pertains to a safeguard measure's *conformity* with those disciplines.

5.70. Having reviewed the design, structure, and expected operation of the measure at issue, coupled with all the relevant facts and arguments on record, we conclude that the measure does not present the constituent features of a safeguard measure for purposes of the applicability of the WTO safeguard disciplines. The imposition of the specific duty on galvalume may seek to prevent or remedy serious injury to Indonesia's industry, but it does not suspend any GATT obligation or withdraw or modify any GATT concession. While the exemption of 120 countries from the scope of application of the specific duty may arguably be seen as suspending Indonesia's MFN treatment obligation under Article I:1 of the GATT 1994, it has not been shown to be designed to prevent or remedy serious injury to Indonesia's domestic industry. Rather, that exemption appears to constitute an ancillary aspect of the measure, which is aimed at according S&D treatment to developing countries with *de minimis* shares in imports of galvalume as contemplated under Article 9:1 of the *Agreement on Safeguards*. The disciplines of Article 9:1 set out conditions for the WTO-*consistent* application of safeguard measures and do not speak to the question of whether a measure constitutes a safeguard measure for purposes of the *applicability* of the WTO safeguard disciplines. Hence, we find that the measure at issue, considered in light of those of its aspects most central to the question of legal characterization, does not constitute a measure "provided for in Article XIX of GATT 1994."

5.71. Based on the foregoing, and despite our reservations on certain aspects of the Panel's interpretation of Article XIX:1(a) of the GATT 1994, expressed in Paragraph 5.62. above, we uphold the Panel's overall conclusion . . . that the measure at issue does not constitute a safeguard measure within the meaning of Article 1 of the *Agreement on Safeguards*. Having upheld the Panel's conclusion, there is no legal basis for us to rule on the complainants' request for completion of the legal analysis with respect to their claims under Article XIX of the GATT 1994 and Articles 2.1, 3:1, 4:1, 4:2(a), 4:2(b), 4:2(c), 12:2, and 12:3 of the *Agreement on Safeguards*.

. . .

6. Findings and Conclusions

6.2.2 Whether the Panel erred in its interpretation and application of Article 1 of the *Agreement on Safeguards* and Article XIX of the GATT 1994

6.6. In order to constitute one of the "measures provided for in Article XIX," a measure must present certain constituent features, absent which it could not be considered a safeguard measure. First, that measure must suspend, in whole or in part, a GATT obligation or withdraw or modify a GATT concession. Second, the suspension, withdrawal, or modification in question must be designed to prevent or remedy serious injury to the Member's domestic industry caused or threatened by increased imports of the subject product. In order to determine whether a measure presents such features, a Panel is called upon to assess the design, structure, and expected operation of the measure as a whole. In making its independent and objective assessment, a panel must identify all the aspects of the measure that may have a bearing on its legal characterization, recognize which of those aspects are the most central to that measure, and, thereby, properly determine the disciplines to which the measure is subject. As part of its determination of whether a measure is a safeguard measure, a panel should evaluate and give due consideration, where relevant, to the manner in which the measure is characterized under the domestic law of the Member concerned, the domestic procedures that led to the adoption of the measure, and any relevant notifications to the WTO Committee on Safeguards. However, none of these is, in and of itself, dispositive of the question of whether the measure constitutes a safeguard measure within the meaning of Article 1 of the *Agreement on Safeguards*.

II. 1951 *Hatters' Fur* Case and Five Elements

While sometimes referred to as the "GATT Escape Clause," Article XIX also is dubbed the "general safeguard." The latter term distinguishes it from safeguards that may be invoked only in specific contexts: for BOP purposes (the GATT Articles XIX and XVIII BOP safeguards); in the agricultural sector (the Special Safeguard, or SSG, under Article 5 of the WTO *Agreement on Agriculture*); against imports from Communist countries (the Market Disruption Safeguard under Section 406 of the *Trade Act of 1974, as amended*); and country-specific safeguards (such as the China Safeguard under the WTO terms of accession for China and the Section 421 of the *1974 Act*).

Every safeguard, general or special, has unique features. But, the GATT Escape Clause, predicated on the earlier American Escape Clause, is the template from which the other safeguards at least start. The 1951 GATT Working Party Report in the *Hatters' Fur* case, the leading early GATT decision on Article XIX, summarizes the elements that must be proven to obtain general safeguard relief.

(a) there should be an abnormal development in the imports of the product in question in the sense that:

    (i) the product in question must be imported in increased quantities;

    (ii) the increased imports must be the result of unforeseen developments and of the effect of the tariff concession; and

    (iii) the imports must enter in such increased quantities and under such conditions as to cause or threaten serious injury to domestic producers of like or directly competitive products.

(b) The suspension of an obligation or the withdrawal or modification of a concession must be limited to the extent and the time necessary to prevent or remedy the injury caused or threatened.

(c) The contracting party taking action under Article XIX must give notice in writing to the CONTRACTING PARTIES before taking action. It must also give an opportunity to contracting parties substantially interested and to the CONTRACTING PARTIES to consult with it. As a rule consultation should take place before the action is taken, but in critical circumstances consultation may take place immediately after the measure is taken provisionally.[2]

In brief, careful parsing of Article XIX:1(a), and perusal of the *Hatters' Fur* Working Party Report, indicates there are five elements to an Escape Clause action:

(1) The result of unforeseen developments.

(2) The effect of GATT obligations.

(3) An increased level of imports (sometimes called a "surge").

(4) Causation.

(5) Serious injury or threat of serious injury.

Each element must be present, otherwise relief lawfully cannot be granted.

The WTO *Agreement on Safeguards* contains these elements, and Article 2:1 of the *Agreement* lays particular stress on the third and fourth element. Finally, as per *Hatters' Fur*, other provisions of Article XIX establish procedures to be followed before implementing an Escape Clause remedy, namely, notice and the opportunity for consultations. (As is common among other trade remedies, for safeguard relief there exists an exception to otherwise requisite procedures for critical circumstances.) Articles 3, 12, and 13 of the *Agreement* treat these (and other) procedures.

---

2. *See Report of the Intersessional Working Party on the Complaint of Czechoslovakia Concerning the Withdrawal by the United States of a Tariff Concession under the Terms of Article XIX of the General Agreement*, Geneva, November 1951 (GATT/CP/106, GATT/CP.6/SR.19, Sales No. GATT/1951–3), B.I.S.D., vol. 2 at 36 (1952) (adopted 27 September 1951).

III. "Like" or "Directly Competitive" Products

Note carefully the kind of product at issue—like or directly competitive. That is, imports of merchandise subject to an investigation (*i.e.*, subject merchandise) must be "like" or "directly competitive with" a product originating in the domestic economy of the importing country in which safeguard relief is contemplated. In an AD or CVD action, a "directly competitive" relationship is not close enough. Products must be "like." However, in a national treatment case under GATT Article III:2, second sentence, "substitutability" of products (as per Article III:1, and *Ad Article III, Paragraph 2*), suffices. Thus, the Escape Clause remedy contemplates a broader universe of targets than do the AD or CVD remedy, but less so than the national treatment obligation. Does this scheme make sense, particularly in view of the fact the Clause is directed at fairly trade foreign merchandise?

The meaning of "like or directly competitive" is the same in Section 201 as in the safeguard measure against Communist countries, Section 406 (discussed later). In turn, that phrase derives from GATT Article XIX:1(a). Under this jurisprudence, and based on evidence of legislative intent from Congress, a "like" product is one that is "*substantially identical*" to the imported merchandise under consideration.[3] That is, as the Senate Finance Committee Report accompanying the *1974 Act* explained, it is:

> substantially identical in *inherent* or intrinsic *characteristics* (*i.e.*, *materials from which made, appearance, quality, texture, etc.*).[4]

A "directly competitive" product" is one that is "*substantially equivalent for commercial purposes*" to the investigated import.[5] As the Senate Report said, it is:

> *not* substantially identical in . . . inherent or intrinsic characteristics, . . . [but *is*] *substantially equivalent for commercial purposes*, that is, . . . [is] *adapted to the same uses* and . . . *essentially interchangeable* therefor.[6]

Moreover:

> the term "like or directly competitive" as used in Sections 201 and 405(4) of the *Trade Expansion Act of 1962* has been the subject of recent court action. The Courts, in upholding the [International Trade Commission], concluded that *imported finished articles are not like or directly competitive with domestic component parts thereof*. (*United Shoe Workers of America, et al. v. Catherine Bedell, et al.*, 506 F.2d 174 (D.C. Cir. 1974)).[7]

So, are fresh mushrooms "like" or "directly competitive" with canned mushrooms?

---

3. Bruce E. Clubb, United States Foreign Trade Law, § 23.12.2 at 747 (Boston, Massachusetts: Little, Brown & Company, 1991) (emphasis added). [Hereinafter, Clubb.]

4. Senate Report Number 1298, 93d Congress, 2d Session, 120–121 (1974).

5. Clubb, § 23.12.2 at 747 (emphasis added).

6. Senate Report Number 1298, 93d Congress, 2d Session, 120–121 (1974).

7. Senate Report Number 1298, 93d Congress, 2d Session, 120–121 (1974) (emphasis added).

No, to the dismay of respondents in the August 1980 *Mushrooms* case.[8] The respondents, importers of foreign produced canned mushrooms, battled a Section 201 petition filed by beleaguered American canned mushroom producers seeking relief against canned imports. The respondents unsuccessfully argued fresh and canned mushrooms are "like" or "directly competitive." They knew domestic fresh mushroom producers were profitable, so if domestic fresh and canned mushrooms were considered together, then injury was less obviously concentrated on the canners, but rather diluted by the success of the fresh mushroom producers.

The International Trade Commission rejected the argument of the importers. It reasoned that only canned mushrooms have the same, or similar, appearances, qualities, or characteristics, and they bore intrinsic differences from fresh mushrooms. Fresh mushrooms differ from one another in quality, texture, and taste. Canned, but not fresh, mushrooms could be stored indefinitely, and cost less to prepare than fresh mushrooms. Canned mushrooms were less desirable in certain dishes, especially salads.

In sum, as Diagram 24-1 shows, "like products" constitute a true subset of "directly competitive products," but not *vice versa*.

**Diagram 24-1. Like versus Directly Competitive Products
(in Comparison with Foreign Imported Merchandise Subject to Investigation)**

Set of Directly Competitive Products

Not substantially identical in intrinsic characteristics, but substantially equivalent for commercial purposes, in that can be adapted to the same uses, essentially interchangeable

> *Subset of Like Products*
>
> Substantially identical inherent or intrinsic characteristics, such as materials from which made, appearance, quality, texture, etc.

IV. Limits on Safeguard Relief

Article XIX:1(a) of GATT, and Articles 2:1-2, 4:2, 5, 7–8, and 12:1 of the *Agreement on Safeguards*, lay out six important boundaries on the Escape Clause remedy, even if where all elements for its application are present:

---

8. *See Mushrooms*, Investigation Number TA-201-43, United States International Trade Commission Publication 1089 (August 1980).

(1) Scope

The scope of application of remedial measure is restricted to foreign merchandise that is "like" or "directly competitive" with a domestic product.

(2) Non-Discrimination

The remedy must be applied to subject merchandise irrespective of its source, *i.e.*, from all countries, on an MFN basis. This requirement easier to meet if relief is a tariff than a quota or TRQ (because of the problem of quota or TRQ allocation among countries).

(3) Parallelism

The scope of application of a safeguard remedy should be consistent with (*i.e.*, parallel to) the foreign merchandise examined during a safeguard investigation. After all, if an importing Member includes merchandise from all sources in its injury and causation determination, but excludes merchandise originating in certain countries (namely, partners in a FTA or CU) from remedial action, then application of the remedy is discriminatory. The problem, however, is some FTAs and CUs call for exactly this kind of exemption from a global safeguard remedy.

In the 2000 *Argentina Footwear Safeguard* case, the Appellate Body held Argentina could not rely on its status as a party to *MERCOSUR*, nor on GATT Article XXIV, as a defense for its safeguard remedy applied to footwear imports only from non-*MERCOSUR* countries. In the 2001 *Wheat Gluten* case (in which the U.S. exempted its *NAFTA* partner, Canada, from a safeguard), and 2002 *Line Pipe* case (in which the U.S. excluded both *NAFTA* partners, Canada and Mexico, from a safeguard), the Appellate Body affirmed imports included in an Escape Clause investigation must correspond to imports targeted for remedial action.

(4) Duration

The duration of remedial measure is limited to four years. The measure may be renewed once (for a total of eight years). There is no right to suspend a safeguard measure once it is imposed. If a domestic industry in the importing country applying the measure no longer requires the protection afforded by the measure, then that country should terminate the measure. To suspend the measure not only would be inconsistent with the *Safeguards Agreement*, but also would create legal uncertainty for exporters on whose products the safeguard had been imposed. They would wonder whether, and when, the country might re-impose the measure.

(5) Suspension of the Right to Retaliate

A WTO Member exporting merchandise targeted by a safeguard remedy has the right to receive substantially equivalent concessions from the importing Member, or to suspend such concessions with respect to that Member, unless that Member pays adequate compensation for the adverse effects of the remedy. But, that right is suspended for the first three years of a safeguard measure.

(6) Notification

A WTO Member must notify the Secretariat if the Member takes any one of three actions: (1) it initiates a safeguard investigation; (2) finds a domestic industry in the Member is seriously injured or threatened with serious injury because of increased imports, or (3) applies a safeguard measure. No delay in notification is permissible, *i.e.*, the notice must be "immediate."

These limits on safeguard relief provoke a number of questions.

First, does the four-year Sunset Rule provide support for the critique of the WTO dispute settlement mechanism that a *de facto* "Three Year Pass" exists? That is, can a WTO Member maintain a safeguard inconsistent with GATT-WTO standards for three years, not suffer retaliation, and not have to bother about an adverse Appellate Body decision?

Second, what is the proper relationship among GATT Article XXIV, Article 2:2 of the *Safeguards Agreement*, and Escape Clause remedies in FTAs and CUs? The Appellate Body has yet to offer a definitive ruling on the question. As a practical matter, how can a WTO Member that also is party to an FTA or CU stay within the bounds of parallelism? In the 2002 *Line Pipe* case, the Appellate Body suggested these possibilities:

(1) Complete exemption, wherein imports from FTA or CU parties are entirely exempt from a global safeguards investigation.

(2) Non-attribution, whereby imports from FTA or CU partners are included in a global investigation, but imports from non-FTA and non-CU sources are found to be the cause of injury or threat.

Are these scenarios practical to implement?

Third, do the above questions help explain why, as Professor Gantz puts it, the Appellate Body applies "very strict scrutiny" to safeguards relief?[9] What about critical circumstances, which are mentioned, but not defined precisely, in GATT Article XIX:2 and Article 6 of the *Safeguards Agreement*? Should the same limits apply on safeguard actions in those instances, and should they trigger strict scrutiny?

V. GATT-WTO Jurisprudence on Element 1: Unforeseen Circumstances, 1951 *Hatters' Fur* Case, Plus Four WTO Appellate Body Precedents

"Unforeseen developments" may be justified by analogy to the public international law principle of changed circumstances, specifically, the doctrine of *rebus sic*

---

9. Raj Bhala & David Gantz, *WTO Case Review 2002*, 20 Arizona Journal of International and Comparative Law 143, 179 (2003).

stantibus (*i.e.*, in these circumstances, or things staying as they are).[10] This doctrine holds that a treaty ceases to be obligatory upon a fundamental change of the circumstances on which it is based, where the effect of the change is to transform radically the extent of the obligations to be performed under the treaty.[11] Yet, the analogy, begs the central practical question: what are "unforeseen developments"?

• **1951 *Hatters' Fur* Case**

The enduring value of the 1951 GATT Working Party Report in *Hatters' Fur* (cited earlier) is partly its discussion of the meaning of "unforeseen developments." The dispute arose because in 1950 the U.S., pursuant to its Escape Clause, withdrew a concession on women's fur felt hats and hat bodies it had negotiated in the first Geneva Round of multilateral tariff negotiations in 1947. (The concession involved less than $2 million worth of imports.) The U.S. argued a change of women's hat styles resulted in increased imports, and this change was an "unforeseen development." The former Czechoslovakia challenged the U.S. action, claiming a change in hat styles did not satisfy the Article XIX:1(a) "unforeseen development" prerequisite.

A GATT Working Party was established to consider the Czech complaint. The Working Party, except for the U.S., agreed upon the following definition:

> [T]he term "unforeseen development" should be interpreted to mean developments occurring after the negotiation of the relevant tariff concession which it would not be *reasonable* to *expect* that the *negotiators of the country making the concession* could and should have foreseen at the time when the concession was negotiated.[12]

The *Hatters' Fur* definition of "unforeseen development" is a mixture of objective and subjective factors. The word "reasonable" intimates an objectively reasonable person could not have expected the negotiators of the country concerned to foresee the development. However, the fact "negotiators of the country making the concession" is spelled out suggests this objectively reasonable person must put herself in the position of the negotiators from the country concerned and see matters from their perspective, *i.e.*, understand their subjective position.

The Working Party, save for the U.S., agreed "that the fact that hat styles had changed did not constitute an 'unforeseen development' within the meaning of Article XIX."[13] This conclusion was inevitable. A different outcome would mean any contracting party could invoke the Escape Clause on the pretext imports of a product increased because of a change in style or fashion. Consumer tastes in the apparel industry change frequently and, therefore, always are foreseeable. So, the Working

---

10. *See* Kenneth W. Dam, The GATT 99, 106 (1970). [Hereinafter, Dam.]

11. *See* I Restatement of the Foreign Relations Law of the United States § 366 at 218 (1987).

12. *Quoted in* World Trade Organization, Guide to GATT Law and Practice—Analytical Index vol. 1 at 517 (6th ed. 1995) (emphasis added). [Hereinafter, GATT Analytical Index.]

13. *Quoted in* GATT Analytical Index, vol. 1 at 517.

Party's Report accepted the Czech argument "it is universally known that fashions are subject to constant changes."[14] U.S. negotiators should have anticipated a change in women's hat styles.

Nonetheless, the Working Party—except for Czechoslovakia—found the American Escape Clause action satisfied the "unforeseen developments" prerequisite. The specific facts of the case, "particularly the *degree to which the change in fashion affected the competitive situation*, could not reasonably be expected to have been foreseen by the United States authorities in 1947."[15] The application by the Working Party of its definition of "unforeseen developments" thus created a subtle, yet dispositive, distinction. A change in fashion always is foreseeable. Hence, such a change itself cannot satisfy the definition. But, the effect of a fashion change on market conditions is not necessarily foreseeable.

Overall, the inference to be drawn from the *Hatters' Fur* case may be, as Professor Dam puts it, that "the 'unforeseen developments' requirement envisages the presence of *very particular changed circumstances* and not merely of a general economic change."[16] After all, whenever tariff or non-tariff barriers are lowered, the possibility of injury or general economic change to the relevant domestic industry should be anticipated. Therefore, only "very particular changed circumstances" ought to satisfy the "unforeseen developments" prerequisite.

For almost half a century—from the 1951 *Hatters' Fur* case until the 2000 WTO action in *Argentina Footwear Safeguard* (cited below), there were few if any notable legal developments relating to the definition of "unforeseen developments." Indeed, the element almost was forgotten as an essentiality in the proper invocation of Article XIX. In the *Argentina* case, however, the Appellate Body made clear the element was as vital as ever. That and subsequent cases contribute—albeit modestly—to the jurisprudence on "unforeseen developments."

- **2000 *Argentina Footwear Safeguard* Case**[17]

The central issue on appeal concerned the language "as a result of unforeseen developments." The phrase exists in Article XIX:1(a), but not in the WTO *Agreement on Safeguards*. Did the Uruguay Round negotiators mean to extirpate this element from the Escape Clause by omitting it from the *Agreement*, *i.e.*, did the *Agreement* supersede GATT? "No," replied the Appellate Body.

The case arose out of an Argentine safeguard investigation in February 1997. Following the investigation, Argentina imposed provisional measures, in the form of minimum specific import duties, on certain footwear imports. Essentially,

---

14. *Quoted in* JOHN H. JACKSON, WORLD TRADE AND THE LAW OF GATT, § 23.3 at 561. [Hereinafter, JACKSON 1969.]

15. *Quoted in* GATT ANALYTICAL INDEX, vol. 1 at 517 (emphasis added).

16. DAM, 102 (1970) (emphasis added).

17. *See* Appellate Body Report, *Argentina—Safeguard Measures on Imports of Footwear*, WT/DS121/AB/R (adopted 12 January 2000).

Argentina computed for each product an average import price, and then multiplied that price by its bound MFN duty of 35%. The result was the specific minimum duty for the product. For each shipment of targeted merchandise, Argentina imposed the higher of the specific minimum duty or the *ad valorem* rate. In July 1997, Argentina's *Commission Nacional de Comercio Exterior* (*CNCE*) notified the WTO Committee on Safeguards of the *CNCE's* finding of serious injury to the Argentine footwear industry. In September 1997, *CNCE* imposed definitive Escape Clause relief, in the form of specific minimum duties, on imported footwear. (Argentina exempted its partners in *MERCOSUR*—Brazil, Paraguay, and Uruguay—from this relief. Pursuant to the *MERCOSUR* accord, the partners agreed not to impose safeguard relief against one another.) The EC challenged the safeguard, arguing Argentina failed to comply with the requirement in Article XIX:1(a) that relief not be granted without proof an increase in imports results from unforeseen developments.

The argument of the EC rested solely on the proposition GATT and the *Safeguards Agreement* are a single undertaking and constitute an integrated system of disciplines. The EC rejected alternative characterizations, namely, the two documents are in conflict, or the later-in-time *Agreement* supersedes the earlier-in-time GATT. All requirements of both documents had to be met before a WTO Member lawfully could impose a safeguard. One such requirement is "unforeseen developments," which the EC defined according to the ordinary meaning of the phrase, but in a circular fashion, as a sudden change in a course of action, event, or conditions that has not been foreseen. Argentina's rebuttal (with which the U.S., as a third party, agreed), was satisfaction of the elements in the *Agreement* necessarily meant satisfaction of Article XIX:1(a) of GATT. The documents conflicted, as the Uruguay Round negotiators left out the unforeseen developments element, but a *General Interpretative Note* to Annex 1A of the WTO *Multilateral Trade Agreements on Goods* called for giving priority to an MTA over GATT in the event of a conflict.

The WTO Panel, but not the Appellate Body, agreed with the Argentine position. Overturning the Panel's conclusion, the Appellate Body held "unforeseen developments" remains an essential element in an Escape Clause action. It based its holding on Article II of the *WTO Agreement*. This provision explains all of the accords in Annexes 1, 2, and 3 (and, therefore, includes GATT and the *Agreement on Safeguards*, which are in Annex 1A) are integral parts of the *WTO Agreement*, and all of them are binding on WTO Members. This "one treaty" view of the WTO texts calls for a harmonious interpretation of the equally mandatory provisions in the texts. Articles 1 and 11:1(a) of the *Agreement on Safeguards* reinforce this call, as does the Preamble to the *Agreement*, because they indicate not that the *Agreement* subsumes Article XIX of GATT, but rather that Article XIX remains in full force and effect. Put simply, the EC was right—all of the elements in Article XIX:1(a) and the *Agreement* must exist to support relief.

As for the meaning of "unforeseen developments," the Appellate Body unsurprisingly focused on the ordinary interpretation of these words, settling on the word "unexpected." The developments that lead to merchandise being imported in increased quantities so as to cause or threaten serious injury are "unforeseen" if they are "unexpected." Further, the increased imports are the "effect of obligations" incurred by a WTO Member (an element, like "unforeseen developments," which is set forth in Article XIX:1(a), but omitted from Article 2:1 of the *Agreement on Safeguards*) if the Member has incurred tariff concessions under GATT. In setting "unforeseen" and "unexpected" as synonyms, the Appellate Body expressly put its holding in the line of the 1951 *Hatters' Fur* Report. In that 1951 Report, the GATT Working Party defined an "unforeseen development" as one a contracting party could not reasonably have expected at the time it made a concession.

The Appellate Body did not rule on whether Argentina had satisfied the "unforeseen developments" element. That was because the Argentine safeguard violated Articles 2 and 4 of the *Safeguard Agreement*, and judicial economy rendered it unnecessary to go further.

- **2000 *Korea Dairy Safeguard* Case**[18]

The 2000 *Korea Dairy Safeguard* case stays in the *Hatters' Fur* tradition. As in the *Argentina Footwear Safeguard* case, in the *Korea Dairy Safeguard* case, at the Panel stage the ruling was the Uruguay Round negotiators effectively wrote the "unforeseen developments" element out of Escape Clause law. The Appellate Body reversed the Panel's ruling regarding "unforeseen circumstances."

But, the Appellate Body added nothing to its *Argentina Footwear Safeguard* holding, and tracked its reasoning from that case. Because the Panel said proof of "unforeseen circumstances" was unnecessary, the Appellate Body declined to rule on whether Korea's action embodied this element. To be sure, the *Korea Dairy Safeguard* Report stands equally ably for the propositions this element remains vital in an Escape Clause action, that Article XIX and the *Agreement* are part of an integrated treaty system and the elements of each document must be met, and that the term connotes unexpectedness.

- **2001 *Lamb Meat* Case**[19]

In 2001, the Appellate Body had another chance to amplify the definition of "unforeseen circumstances." The *Lamb Meat* case arose out of a safeguards investigation by the ITC in October 1998 of lamb meat imports. By a July 1999 Presidential Proclamation issued by President Bill Clinton, the U.S. imposed a TRQ on this product. The TRQ permitted imports at 9%, 6%, and 3% for in-quota shipments during the first three years of relief, respectively, and 40%, 32%, and 24% for above-quota shipments in those years, respectively. Argentina and New Zealand, the two major exporters of lamb meat to the U.S., successfully challenged the Section 201 action.

---

18. *See* Appellate Body Report, *Korea—Definitive Safeguard Measure on Imports of Certain Dairy Products*, WT/DS98/AB/R (adopted 12 January 2000).

19. *See* Appellate Body Report, *United States—Safeguard Measures on Imports of Fresh, Chilled or Frozen Lamb Meat from New Zealand and Australia*, WT/DS177/AB/R (complaint by Australia), WT/DS178/AB/R (adopted 16 May 2001).

In *Lamb Meat*, the U.S. offered a novel argument on "unforeseen developments." No specific finding about these developments, or explicit conclusion about them, is required. The ITC did not even consider "unforeseen developments" in its investigation. (The closest it came was a discussion of the change in the pattern of lamb meat imports, but it never explained whether or why this change was an "unforeseen development.") No worries, urged the U.S. All a competent authority need do is establish a factual basis for the existence of unforeseen developments.

Citing the 1951 GATT Working Party Report in *Hatters's Fur*, America said trade negotiators, when they make a tariff concession, normally do not foresee specific developments in a particular product market that lead to an import surge causing injury to a domestic industry. Essentially, the American argument stressed the reality of the mindset of trade negotiators, and the inherent inability to foresee injurious import surges long before they occur. The consequence of the argument was a minimal factual showing of market events should be enough to shift the burden of proof to the complainants — Australia and New Zealand — to prove the tariff negotiators did, in fact, have the requisite foresight. Australia and New Zealand saw through the argument. The ITC Report did not contain "reasoned conclusions" on "all pertinent issues of facts and law," as Article 3:1 of the *WTO Agreement on Safeguards* mandated. The argument was nothing more than an *ex post facto* attempt to extract necessary facts from this Report.

The Appellate Body did not respond with a holding that clarified "how" to demonstrate the existence of "unforeseen developments," and thus did not go beyond the earlier cases in defining this term. But, it did extend its jurisprudence by explaining "when" and "where" an analysis into unforeseen developments is required. As to "when," the Appellate Body held that a competent authority must render a finding before any Escape Clause relief is granted. That is because "unforeseen developments" is a prerequisite, not concomitant or consequence, of such relief. As to "where," this finding must be in the written decision of the competent authority.

The Appellate Body understood Section 201 does not require proof of "unforeseen developments." That omission, along with the fact the ITC completed its *Lamb Meat* investigation seven months before the Appellate Body circulated its Reports in *Argentina Footwear Safeguard* and *Korea Dairy Safeguard*, probably explained why the ITC did not deal with the topic. (The *Lamb Meat* safeguard took effect on 7 July 1999. The DSB adopted the other two Reports on 16 May 2001.) Still, the requirement existed Article XIX:1(a) of GATT, and in *Lamb Meat* the U.S. seemed to concede the requirement remains vital. That concession could be inferred, as the Appellate Body observed, from the change in America's argument from earlier cases. Unlike its position in *Argentina Footwear Safeguard* and *Korea Dairy Safeguard*, in *Lamb Meat* the U.S. did not contend the *Agreement on Safeguards* superseded Article XIX:1(a). Unfortunately for the American position, Appellate Body jurisprudence reaffirming the vitality of the requirement did not come in time for the ITC to adjust its methodology — *i.e.*, to start providing a reasoned, written conclusion.

The particular dispute ended on 31 August 2001, when the Administration of President George W. Bush agreed to implement the Appellate Body Report and remove the TRQs effective 15 November 2001. The American lamb meat industry thus got two and one-half years of protection. Yet, no answer to the basic question of the case emerged: does a change in product mix, as occurred in the lamb meat import market, qualify as an "unforeseen development"? The Appellate Body side-stepped this question, because it was not presented with an explicit ITC finding to this effect.

- **2003 *Steel Safeguard* Case**[20]

The *Steel Safeguard* case is "infamous" for a number of reasons, including the large number of issues at stake, the acrimony between the respondent and com-plainants, and the fact it arose in a presidential election cycle. The case began on 28 June 2001, when the ITC commenced an investigation, under Section 201, at the request of the American steel industry and unions. It concluded on 4 Decem-ber 2003, when President George W. Bush issued a Presidential Proclamation end-ing relief.

In respect of "unforeseen developments," the Appellate Body rejected the Ameri-can arguments. The U.S. argued the ITC investigative Report went far beyond the explanation the ITC had provided in the 2001 *Lamb Meat* case. America also emphasized the language of Article 3:1 of the *Agreement on Safeguards*, namely, that "[t]he competent authorities shall publish a report setting forth their findings and reasoned conclusions on all pertinent issues of fact and law." Because this language does not call for an explicit explanation of "unforeseen circumstances," surely it is possible for a competent authority to provide a "reasoned conclusion" without a "reasoned and adequate explanation."

The Appellate Body retorted it was impossible to have a reasoned conclusion, particularly one about an entire context, without reaching the conclusion in a con-nected, logical manner or expressing the conclusion in a logical form. If a compe-tent authority does not explain its finding, then a Panel—which is barred from conducting a *de novo* review of evidence, and from substituting its judgment for that of the authority—has no choice but to rule the authority failed to conduct a proper analysis.

The Appellate Body also rejected the American argument about aggregate analy-sis. Contrary to the Panel, the U.S. urged Article XIX:1(a) does not mandate a par-ticular kind of analysis about "unforeseen developments." Thus, it does not require showing imports of each product category subject to Escape Clause action increased because of such developments. Citing its decisions from 2000 in *Argentina Footwear*

---

20. *See* Appellate Body Report, *United States—Definitive Safeguard Measures on Imports of Certain Steel Products*, WT/DS248/AB/R, WT/DS249/AB/R, WT/DS251/AB/R, WT/DS252/AB/R, WT/DS253/AB/R, WT/DS254/AB/R, WT/DS258/AB/R, WT/DS259/AB/R (adopted 10 December 2003).

Safeguard and *Korea Dairy Safeguard*, the Appellate Body said there must be a logical connection between (1) unforeseen developments, and (2) a product subject to relief. In sum, the Appellate Body upheld the ruling of the Panel that an "unforeseen developments" analysis must occur on a product-by-product basis. The ITC talked about the overall effects of financial crises in the late 1990s in Russia and Asia, and of the strong American dollar, yet it did not connect the dots, as it were.

On balance, despite several Appellate Body rulings on "unforeseen circumstances." the multilateral trading system has not advanced much beyond the 1951 *Hatters' Fur* Report as to a definition of this term. The definition of "unforeseen circumstances" has stayed at "unexpected" ever since the *Hatters' Fur* case. Some kind of plausible unforeseen development must be identified, and some kind of nexus between them and an increase in subject imports must be shown. Yet, exactly how "unexpected" the development should be to qualify as "unforeseen," and exactly how the logical link to increased imports should be made, is not clear.

Two points, in fairness to the Appellate Body, ought to be made. First, it may be that a complete definition of "unforeseen circumstances" is impossible. The term never can connote anything but unexpectedness to be gauged in particular factual settings. Second, the Appellate Body ought not to be accused of changing the rules and applying a new regime retroactively. The "unforeseen developments" requirement is not new or different. Rather, it is as old as GATT itself.

VI. GATT-WTO Jurisprudence on Element 2: GATT Obligations

There is no GATT or WTO jurisprudence on the prerequisite to an Article XIX Escape Clause action that increased imports result from "the effect of the obligations incurred" under the GATT. Indeed, the *Agreement on Safeguards* does not contain this prerequisite. Notably, this element is not found in Section 201. To the extent it is an empty formalism with no real substantive effect in preparing an action, it seems inaccurate to call it a "prerequisite."

VII. GATT-WTO Jurisprudence on Element 3: Increased Imports and 2003 *Steel Safeguards* Case

An import surge may be measured in either of 2 ways. That point is not clear from the text of GATT Article XIX(a). But, Article 2:1 of the *Agreement on Safeguards* says as much:

(1) Absolute terms, meaning the volume of subject merchandise imports increases without regard to trends in domestic production or consumption of a like or directly competitive product.

(2) Relative terms, meaning the volume of imports rises when gauged against the volume of domestic production (though in absolute terms, that volume may be flat or in decline).

There is, however, little in the way of WTO jurisprudence on increased imports. The leading case is the 2003 *Steel Safeguards* action.

In that case, data indicated that during the 5½ year POI, imports of steel products into the U.S. did not increase in a steady trend. The POI was 1996–2000, plus the first 6 months of 2001 compared to the first six months of 2000. Most such imports increased in 1996–98, but shipments in some product categories fell in and after 1999, and declined precipitously in the first six months of 2001 relative to the first half of 2000.

The Panel disputed the conclusion of the ITC that imports in five product categories—certain cold flat-rolled steel, hot-rolled bar, stainless steel rod, stainless steel wire, and tin mill products, had "increased" in an absolute sense. In particular:

(1) CCFRS imports decreased significantly between 2000 and 2001 from 11.5 to 6.9 million short tons. The ITC noted this decrease, but focused on the fact CCFRS imports were higher at the end than the beginning of the relevant period. The Panel stressed the recent, sizeable decline.

(2) Hot-rolled bar imports decreased between 2000 and 2001 by 28.9%. The ITC acknowledged but failed to explain this decrease, instead emphasizing two other facts. First, the ITC characterized the increase in these imports from 1999 to 2000 as rapid and dramatic. The Panel observed it was a rise of only 11.9%. Second, imports of hot-rolled bar increased 52.5% between 1996 and 2000. The Panel pointed out the trend was not consistent, with altering periods of increase and decrease.

(3) Stainless steel rod imports increased from 1996–2000, and by 25% from 1999–2000. But, said the Panel, they declined by 31% in 2001 in comparison.

Thus, the Panel found violations of Article XIX:1(a) of GATT and Article 2:1 of the *Safeguards Agreement*.

On appeal, the U.S. argued the Panel misinterpreted Article XIX:1(a) and Article 2:1 (especially with respect to CCFRS, hot-rolled bar, and stainless steel rod). The Panel said these provisions require a showing of increased imports that is recent and sudden, and cited the 2000 Appellate Body decision in *Argentina Footwear Safeguard*, in which the Appellate Body opined an increase in imports "must have been recent enough, sudden enough, sharp enough, and significant enough . . . to cause or threaten to cause serious injury." The "increase" in CCFRS imports, concluded the Panel, was not "recent" (having occurred between 1996–1998), and the "increase" in imports of stainless steel rod (25% in 1999–2000) was followed by a disproportionate decrease (31% in 2001 versus 2000). The U.S. objected to the Panel's reading of Article XIX:1(a) of GATT, Article 2:1 of *Agreement*, and *Argentina Footwear Safeguard*. These sources called for a "recent, sudden, sharp, and significant" requirement. Yet, contended the U.S., all that is required is proof the level of imports has increased at the end of the POI in comparison with some unspecified earlier point in time.

Thus, connecting the beginning and endpoints of the POI, the U.S. highlighted statistics about imports of 4 major product categories of steel from 1998 to 2000:

(1) Carbon and alloy flat products increased 14.1%.

(2) Carbon alloy long products increased 64%.

(3) Carbon and alloy pipe and tube increased 72%.

(4) Stainless steel and alloy tool steel increased 87.6%.

Siding with the Panel, the EU countered the American formulation of how to measure "increased imports" would allow any simple increase to qualify. That formulation glossed over key trends within the POI. Starting in 1999, or the first 6 months of 2000, imports in many steel product categories declined, and for some categories the drop was marked.

The Appellate Body rejected the American formulation. It held the Panel had relied correctly on the *Argentina Footwear Safeguard* precedent. True, neither Article XIX:1(a) of GATT nor Article 2:1 of the *Agreement on Safeguards* contains the words "recent, sudden, sharp, or significant." But, the word "such" precedes the words "increased quantities." In addition, the context of an examination into import trends is set by Article 4:2(a) of the *Agreement*, which calls for an evaluation of "the rate and amount of the increase in imports of the product concerned in absolute and relative terms."

To be sure, the *Argentina Footwear Safeguard* decision does not establish an absolute legal standard. Moreover, the U.S. was correct in its position imports of investigated merchandise need not be increasing at the time of a final determination. Still, ruled the Appellate Body, the American formulation of drawing a line between two points in time is no standard at all. A nuanced analysis of trends is necessary. The American argument that a rise in CCFRS imports from 1996–98 was enough to qualify as an "increase" was not persuasive. That period of time simply was not recent enough, and the U.S. had not provided an explanation of how the 1996–1998 trend supported a finding of imports increasing in "such . . . quantities." Regarding hot-rolled bar imports, the Appellate Body said the Panel was right in faulting the ITC for not addressing the relevance of the decrease at the end of the POI. Similarly, the Appellate Body agreed with the Panel that the decrease in stainless steel rod imports at the end of the POI more than offset the earlier—and distant—increases.

Evidently, in proving an increase in imports emerges from the 2003 *Steel Safeguard* case, time is of the essence. Once imports have increased, either in absolute or relative terms, for a few years, then an Escape Clause action should be brought (if at all) immediately. Any delay in commencing the investigation creates opportunity for a new, downward trend in imports. Once the trend has reversed, it will stand out because it is the most recent phenomenon—and that may doom the case.

VIII. GATT-WTO Jurisprudence on Element 4: Causation and Three Appellate Body Precedents

Article 4:2(b) of the WTO *Agreement on Safeguards* states:

> When factors other than increased imports are causing injury to the domestic industry at the same time, such injury *shall not be attributed to* increased imports.[21]

That non-attribution should be a requirement before imposing a safeguard is obvious, but the Article 4:2(b) language sidesteps a crucial question about causation: how immediate, direct, and discreet must the "cause" be?

Conceptually, at one extreme, it could be necessary to prove that increased imports were the cause, because:

(1) there is a short time gap between increased imports and the injury,

(2) the increase leads directly to the injury, and

(3) no other factor contributes to the injury.

At the other extreme, it could be sufficient to prove simply that increased imports:

(1) precede the injury, even if the exact gap between the increase and injury is a few years,

(2) the increase is felt through intermediate factors, which in turn lead to injury, and

(3) additional factors beyond the increase contribute to the injury.

The first extreme obviously would cut down on the number of successful Escape Clause actions. The second extreme would encourage such actions. Between these two extremes there is a continuum of possibilities.

Article XIX does not pick a point on the continuum, nor are any useful insights provided in the 1951 GATT Working Party Report in *Hatters' Fur*, other than giving the WTO Member that invokes Article XIX "the benefit of any reasonable doubt."[22] Therefore, it is for domestic law to set forth a standard for causation. In Section 201, the U.S. does so with the adjective "substantial" in front of the noun "cause." WTO Appellate Body case law offers guidance.

• **2001 *Lamb Meat* Case**

In its 2001 *Lamb Meat* decision, the Appellate Body provides some guidance on the element of causation. Australia and New Zealand claimed the analysis by the

---

21. Emphasis added.

22. *Report of the Intersessional Working Party on the Complaint of Czechoslovakia Concerning the Withdrawal by the United States of a Tariff Concession under the Terms of Article XIX of the General Agreement*, Geneva, November 1951 (GATT/CP/106, GATT/CP.6/SR.19, Sales No. GATT/1951-3), B.I.S.D., vol. 2 at 36 (1952) (adopted 27 September 1951), *quoted in* GATT ANALYTICAL INDEX, vol. 1 at 518.

ITC, namely, that increased imports caused serious injury to the American lamb meat industry, was flawed. The ITC determined increased lamb meat imports alone were a necessary and sufficient cause of serious injury. The ITC isolated injury from other factors, thereby assuring it did not attribute injury from the other factors to the import surge. However, the complainants said the ITC failed to show it had not wrongly attributed to imports threat of serious injury caused by other factors. The sides differed over their view and application of the 2001 *Wheat Gluten Safeguard* case.[23]

Australia said in that case the Appellate Body clearly set out three conceptual steps for a causation analysis. First, injurious effects of imports must be distinguished from injurious effects of other factors. Second, injury caused by other factors must not be attributed to imports. Third, a genuine and substantial relationship of cause and effect must be demonstrated. The U.S. took the view that in *Wheat Gluten*, the Appellate Body reversed the Panel holding that imports have to be isolated from all other causes, and that imports have to be a *per se* cause of serious injury. In *Lamb Meat*, the Panel held the standard for causation means:

(1) Increased imports are necessary to cause or threaten injury.

(2) Increased imports also are sufficient to cause or threaten injury.

The injury caused by increased imports is serious enough to be a significant overall impairment in the state of the domestic industry. This three-pronged approach was the same the Panel took in *Wheat Gluten*. But, in *Wheat Gluten*, the Appellate Body rejected it. Not surprisingly, it did so in *Lamb Meat*, too. That is, in both cases the Appellate Body held this approach was too strict.

First, opined the *Lamb Meat* Appellate Body, a causal link can exist between increased imports and serious injury even if there are other factors that contribute simultaneously to the ill condition of a domestic industry. Second, what is crucial is the competent authority does not attribute erroneously serious injury to increased imports when, in fact, the injury results from other causal factors. Thus, held the Appellate Body, there are two conceptual steps in which the authority must engage:

(1) *Identification*

It must identify all causal factors contributing to serious injury.

(2) *Attribution*

It must separate out and distinguish injurious effects of the different factors.

In *Lamb Meat*, the Appellate Body found the ITC failed to take the second step. To be sure, the ITC did examine six factors, other than increased imports, alleged to contribute to the adverse condition of the American industry. Following Section 201, the ITC considered whether they were a more important cause than imports. In other words, the ITC performed a relative causal analysis. But, that kind of analysis

23. *See* Appellate Body Report, *United States—Definitive Safeguard Measures on Imports of Wheat Gluten from the European Communities*, WT/DS166/AB/R (adopted 19 January 2001).

fails to ensure serious injury caused by factors other than increased imports is not attributed to increased imports. Briefly put, a relative causation examination is not the same as a non-attribution analysis, thus the ITC investigation was inconsistent with Article 4:2 of the WTO *Agreement on Safeguards.*

The Appellate Body did not hold the ITC should have both separated out the injurious effects of imports from other factors, and attach relative weightings to each and every factor. How far must a competent authority go? Once it identifies the distinct factors, and walls off—though some credible statistical or other methodology—the effects of imports from other causes, then it is close to a full analysis. Is all that is left a quantitative measurement of the degree of causal contribution of each factor? If so, then should this final step also be mandatory, especially if the meaning of "cause" is to be taken seriously under Article XIX:1(a) and Article 4:2 of the *Safeguards Agreement?*

- **2002 *Line Pipe* Case**[24]

In the 2002 *Line Pipe* Case, the U.S. imposed Escape Clause relief on imports of line pipe on 18 February 2000 in the form of a TRQ for a period of three years and one day. Korea challenged the measure, though not the underlying American statute, Section 201. The U.S. set the in-quota threshold at 9,000 tons per year for imports from all sources, including Korea, and did not impose liability for a graduated tariff on shipments under this level. Notably, line pipe from America's *NAFTA* partners, Canada and Mexico, were excluded from the action pursuant to Article 802:1, which states that a global safeguard action will not be applied to a product from another *NAFTA* Party unless that product "contribute[s] importantly to the serious injury, or threat thereof, caused by the imports."

For above-quota shipments, the U.S. applied a graduate tariff of 19%, 15%, and 11%, respectively, in the three years of relief. (This relief, effected by Presidential Proclamation of President Bill Clinton, differed from the recommendation of the ITC—a not uncommon occurrence.) The case ultimately settled when the U.S. and Korea agreed to a modification of the TRQ. America provided Korea with a whopping country-specific in-quota threshold of 17,500 tons of line pipe per quarter.

The Escape Clause action followed a determination by the ITC that imported line pipe was a substantial cause of serious injury to a domestic industry. The ITC came to this conclusion after considering several factors, other than increased imports, alleged to cause injury or threat, and applying the Section 201 standard that increased imports be a cause that is important and not less than any other cause. The other factors included:

(1) Lower demand for line pipe because of less drilling for oil and gas (*i.e.,* less oil and gas production.

(2) Increased competition among American manufacturers of line pipe.

---

24. *See* Appellate Body Report, *United States—Definitive Safeguard Measures on Imports of Circular Welded Carbon Quality Line Pipe from Korea,* WT/DS202/AB/R (adopted 2 March 2002).

(3) A decline in export markets.

(4) A shift from the production of oil country tubular goods (OCTG) to the production of line pipe.

(5) A drop in the cost of raw materials.

Interestingly, three of the six ITC Commissioners agreed the imports were a substantial cause of serious injury to the American industry, two of them agreed they were a threat of serious injury, and one Commissioner voted against these findings. The ITC said the first causal factor did contribute to serious injury, increased imports were a more important cause.

The U.S. argued the ITC distinguished properly among the alternative alleged causal factors. Korea did not agree. The WTO Panel seized on this split among the Commissioners, holding it improper to base an Escape Clause action on either serious injury or threat of serious injury, which essentially was the wording of the ITC Report. The U.S., intoned the Panel, should pick one or the other, because they are mutually exclusive, and defend its choice as a basis. Applying Article 4:1(a)-(b) of the WTO *Agreement on Safeguards*, the Panel said it is logically inconsistent for serious injury and a clearly imminent threat of serious injury to exist at the same time. The Appellate Body disagreed, finding the language of the *Agreement* flexible enough to accommodate a determination of serious injury, threat, or both in combination.

Moreover, the Appellate Body was reluctant to tell the ITC, or the competent authority in any WTO Member, how to make decisions internally. In other words, the Appellate Body held it is not necessary to render a discrete either-or finding. Noting that, by definition, a threat finding allows for relief without a manifestation of serious injury, the Appellate Body cited the 1951 *Hatters' Fur* case to support its conclusion that a discrete determination of either threat or injury was necessary. After all, in *Hatters' Fur*, the GATT Working Party entertained a single analysis of serious injury or threat, but not a separate analysis of both.

Further, the Appellate Body interpreted and applied Article 4:2(b) of the WTO *Agreement on Safeguards* in a way resembling its discussion in the 2001 *Lamb Meat* case. Two conceptual steps are required for a proper causation analysis.

Step 1:

A causal link must be demonstrated, which presumes a distinction and separation among causal factors.

Step 2:

Injury caused by factors other than an import surge must not be attributed to the surge.

In *Line Pipe*, the Appellate Body pointed out Article 3:5 of the WTO *Antidumping Agreement* has language similar to the last sentence of Article 4:2(b) of the *Safeguards Agreement*. Citing the provisions, and its 2001 Report in *Japan Hot Rolled Steel*, the Appellate Body explained that in the injury phase of an antidumping investigation, it is necessary for the competent authority to identify known factors other than subject merchandise, and provide a satisfactory explanation of the nature and extent of these other factors as distinct from the injurious effects of the subject merchandise.

The problem with the ITC determination was its lack of an attribution analysis. The Appellate Body held the ITC failed to ensure it had not attributed to increased imports the injury caused by factors other than increased imports. In particular, as Korea pointed out, the ITC simply asserted it had not conflated causal factors. But, it did not give an explicit, reasoned, and adequate account of the nature and extent of the injurious effects of the decline in oil and gas drilling, as distinct from increased line pipe imports.

- **2003 *Steel Safeguard* Case**

In the *Steel Safeguard* case, the WTO Panel reviewing the ITC determination said that for seven steel products (certain cold flat rolled steel (CCFRS), cold-finished bar, fittings, flanges, and tool joints made of carbon and alloy (FFTJ), hot-rolled bar, stainless steel bar, and welded pipe), the ITC did not give a reasoned, adequate explanation for a causal link between increased imports and serious injury. The U.S. appealed, but for reasons of judicial economy, the Appellate Body declined to rule on the issue. At the request of the U.S. and several complainants and third-party participants, the Appellate Body (in its unadopted Report) gave guidance on the issue by referring to its earlier precedents, namely the 2001 *Wheat Gluten* Case, 2001 *Lamb Meat* Case, and 2002 *Line Pipe* Case.

The basic rule from these cases, suggested the Appellate Body in *Steel Safeguard*, is Articles 2:1, 3:1, and 4:2 of the *Agreement on Safeguards* oblige a competent authority to prove existence of a causal link between increased imports and serious injury (or threat) with objective evidence, and provide a reasoned and adequate explanation to support this demonstration. Without such proof and explanation, applying a remedy is unlawful. The Appellate Body went on to state the attribution analysis of the type done in an AD case, under Article 3:5 of the WTO *Antidumping Agreement*, is required in a safeguards case. That means an examination of the individual effects of other causal factors (*i.e.*, other than imports subject to investigation), but not necessarily of the collective effects of the other factors, on the domestic injury, plus assurance their effects are not erroneously attributed to the increased imports.

IX. GATT-WTO Jurisprudence on Element 5: Injury, 1951 *Hatters' Fur* Case, and WTO *Safeguards Agreement* Article 4:1–2

Unfortunately, the drafters of GATT did not define "serious" in Article XIX, just as they did not elaborate on the meaning of "material" in Articles VI and XVI. Presumably, "serious" is not "material," as treaty language cannot be read as superfluous. What, then, is "serious"?

The 1951 *Hatters' Fur* Working Party Report is of considerable assistance. The Working Party found evidence to support the American argument of a threat of serious injury to its industry. There was "a large and rapidly increasing volume of imports, while at the same time domestic production decreased or remained stationary." The Working Party rightly refused to characterize this evidence as conclusive.

> To sum up, the available data support the view that increased imports had caused or threatened some adverse effect to United States producers. Whether such a degree of adverse effect should be considered to amount to "serious injury" is another question, on which the data cannot be said to point convincingly in either direction, and *any view on which is essentially a matter of economic and social judgment involving a considerable subjective element.* In this connection it may be observed that *the Working Party naturally could not have the facilities available to the United States* authorities for examining interested parties and independent witnesses from the United States hat-making areas, and for forming judgments on the basis of such examination. Further, *it is perhaps inevitable that governments should on occasion lend greater weight to the difficulties or fears of their domestic producers than would any international body,* and that they may feel it necessary on social grounds, *e.g.,* because of lack of alternative employment in the localities concerned, to afford a higher degree of protection to individual industries which in terms of cost of production are not economic.[25]

The italicized text is remarkable for its candor and accuracy on three points.

First, appraising whether injury is "serious" is an art. Second, a multilateral dispute resolution body is in a less favorable position to make the appraisal than domestic authorities because of the constraints on investigative resources available to such a body. Third, domestic authorities may be expected in certain cases to be biased in favor of their ailing local industry and want to minimize or defer the social adjustment costs resulting from import competition.

Further clarification on the meaning of "serious" comes from Article 4:1-2 of the WTO *Agreement on Safeguards.* In brief, Article 4:1(a) defines "serious injury" in terms of a "significant overall impairment," which is intuitively obvious and somewhat circular. Defining "threat of serious injury" in terms of "clearly imminent" serious injury is only a slight improvement in precision. To be fair, however, perhaps these two definitions are about as helpful as can be expected. The key terms are inherently flexible to accommodate different facts and circumstances. Article 4:2(a), however, gives WTO Members specific guidance as to how to measure

---

25. *Quoted in* GATT ANALYTICAL INDEX, vol. 1 at 518. The formal title of the Report is *Report of the Intersessional Working Party on the Complaint of Czechoslovakia Concerning the Withdrawal by the United States of a Tariff Concession under the Terms of Article XIX of the General Agreement,* Geneva, November 1951 (GATT/CP/106, GATT/CP.6/SR.19, Sales No. GATT/1951-3), II B.I.S.D. at 36 (1952) (adopted 27 September 1951).

serious injury or threat thereof by identifying, in a non-exclusive manner, the key variables that ought to be considered.

In the abstract, the effect of most variables identified in Article 4:2(a) on the strength of an Escape Clause case is easy to predict. The greater the absolute or relative rate and amount of increase in imports, the greater the domestic market share taken by imports, and the more dramatic the decline in domestic sales, production, capacity utilization, profits, and employment, the stronger the argument that increased imports have caused serious injury or threat thereof. However, this generalization assumes all other factors are constant (*i.e.*, *ceteris paribus*).

Care is needed when analyzing the variables in Article 4:2(a) of the *Safeguards Agreement*. Consider hypothetical trends in productivity in the domestic industry:

(1) Suppose productivity as measured by output per person-hour falls. The drop might have little to do with increased imports, particularly if it results from a rise in the number of person-hours worked. This scenario might occur if the domestic industry hires more workers to meet increased demand, but not all of the workers are fully trained and integrated, and thus have not yet reached their maximum efficiency levels. It also might occur where the domestic industry is experiencing diminishing returns with respect to labor, and should invest in other factors of production like physical capital and technology.

(2) Alternatively, assume productivity tumbles because output declines. Did increased imports capture market share from domestic production, resulting in a decline in domestic factory orders, which in turn caused the drop in output? That is, are increased imports the culprit?

(3) Still another possibility is productivity rises because of downsizing in the domestic industry. The downsizing, which results in a fall of person-hours worked relative to output, may be caused by competition from increased imports.

In sum, analyzing the variables listed in Article 4:2(a) requires attention to how those variables are measured, what other factors bear on them, the extent to which they are correlated or even causally related to one another, and the POI. Generalizations about injury or threat variables should be regarded with some caution.

Chapter 25

America's Safeguard: Section 201 Escape Clause[1]

I. Terminology

America's general safeguard is Section 201 of the *Trade Act of 1974*, as amended, codified at 19 U.S.C. Section 2252 *et seq.* It is commonly referred to as the "Escape Clause." Thus, it is appropriate to use the term "safeguard" when referring to GATT Article XIX and the WTO *Agreement on Safeguards*, while reserving the term "Escape Clause" for Section 201. But, that distinction is by no means required, certainly not as a matter of law, and the terms "safeguard" and "Escape Clause" can be (and are) used interchangeably. Of course, "Section 201" uniquely and specifically references the U.S. remedy.

II. Section 201 Steps

The key players in an Escape Clause, or Section 201, action are the petitioner, importers and foreign manufacturers, ITC, and President. The ITC is responsible for investigating a case and rendering a determination as to whether a U.S. industry has been seriously injured or threatened with serious injury by imports. If it makes an affirmative determination, then it must recommend to the President the appropriate trade relief needed to alleviate the injury or threat. Whether remedial action is taken is for the President to decide in her sole discretion.

There are five basic steps in a Section 201 case. In most cases, the ITC is required to complete its work within six months.

---

1. Documents References:
   (1) *Havana (ITO) Charter* Article 40
   (2) GATT Articles XII, XVIII, XIX
   (3) WTO *Agreement on Safeguards*
   (4) WTO *Agreement on Agriculture*, Article 5
   (5) WTO *ATC Agreement*, Article 6:2
   (6) *NAFTA* Chapter 8
   (7) Relevant provisions in other FTAs

- **Step 1: Petition**

An entity which is "representative of an industry," such as a firm, certified or recognized union, group of workers, or trade association, may file a petition "for the purpose of facilitating positive adjustment to import competition."[2] The petition is filed with the ITC. "Positive adjustment" refers to (1) the ability of a U.S. industry to compete successfully with imports, or the orderly transfer of that industry's resources to other productive pursuits, and (2) the orderly transfer of dislocated workers in that industry to other productive pursuits.[3] The ITC must forward a copy of the petition to the USTR.[4] Within 120 days of filing the petition, the petitioner may submit to the ITC and USTR a plan for facilitating positive adjustment.[5]

Most petitions are filed by trade associations or companies, and unions often support a petition. However, a Section 201 case can be commenced in three other manners. First, the ITC may initiate the case on its own motion. Second, the executive branch—specifically, the President or the USTR—may request the ITC to commence a case. Third, the legislative branch may make this request in the form of a resolution from the House Ways and Means Committee or the Senate Finance Committee.[6]

The ITC's regulations specify the contents required for a petition. Generally, a petition must contain: (1) a description of the imported article concerned; (2) the names and addresses of the petitioners and the extent to which the petitioners are representative of a domestic industry (as measured by the percentage of domestic production of the like or directly competitive product accounted for by the petitioners); (3) import data; (4) domestic production data; (5) data showing injury; (6) a statement relating to the cause of injury; (7) a description of the relief sought; and (8) an explanation of the efforts that are or will be taken to compete with the imported article.

- **Step 2: ITC Investigation**

Upon receiving a petition or request, or adopting a motion, the ITC must commence promptly a Section 201 investigation. It must determine whether a particular article is being imported into the U.S. in "such increased quantities as to be a substantial cause of serious injury, or the threat thereof" to the domestic industry that produces a "like or directly competitive" product.[7] To obtain relief, there is no requirement a petitioner show a company exporting to the U.S. is engaged in unfair trade practices. To the contrary, Section 201 provides relief from *fair* foreign competition so that an American producer can improve its competitive position relative to foreign companies.

---

2. 19 U.S.C. § 2252(a)(1).
3. *See* 19 U.S.C. § 2251(b)(1).
4. *See* 19 U.S.C. § 2252(a)(3).
5. *See* 19 U.S.C. § 2252(a)(4).
6. *See* 19 U.S.C. § 2252(b)(1)(A).
7. 19 U.S.C. §§ 2251(a), 2252(b)(1)(A).

The underlying rationale for Section 201 is based upon the general concern that as the United States lowers tariff barriers to imports, or grants other trade concessions, domestic industries may, in effect, be caught off guard by the increasing import competition. Section 201 is referred to as the escape clause because it allows the United States to, in effect, escape from its obligations under GATT not to take restrictive actions against imports, absent evidence of unfair trading practices, such as dumping, by foreign manufacturers.[8]

Arguably, in one respect the substantive standards applied by the ITC are inconsistent with GATT Article XIX. This Article establishes a connection between trade liberalization and import protection. It provides that relief is appropriate if "the effect of the obligations incurred" by a Member (as well as "unforeseen developments") result in an increased volume of imports that causes injury. The *1974 Act* severed the connection between trade liberalization and import protection. Suppose there were a challenge in the WTO to the American statutory scheme. What would be the rebuttal? The U.S. could argue that injury can be inferred to result from trade concessions, because these concessions (in the form of tariff concessions) have touched the vast majority of articles.

The ITC must render a determination within 120 days of receiving a petition.[9] The ITC may extend this period to 150 days in an "extraordinarily complicated" case.[10] A shorter deadline—three months—is prescribed in cases of imports from Communist countries.[11] There are special rules for "critical circumstances" cases.[12] Critical circumstances exist if increased imports (either actual or relative to domestic production) are a substantial cause of serious injury, or the threat thereof, to a domestic industry producing an article that is like or directly competitive with the imported article, and a delay in taking action would cause damage to that industry "that would be difficult to repair."[13] There also are special rules regarding provisional relief for perishable products.[14] Such products include agricultural products with a short shelf life, growing season, or marketing period.[15]

The ITC must hold public hearings and afford interested parties and consumers the opportunity to be heard.[16] The statute requires the ITC to "take into account all economic factors which it considers relevant," and then provides a non-exhaustive list of such factors.[17] On serious injury, the ITC must consider "the significant idling

---

8. Thomas V. Vakerics et al., Antidumping, Countervailing Duty, and Other Trade Actions 14 (1987). [Hereinafter, Vakerics.] *See also id.*, 15, 271–272, 274–276.

9. *See* 19 U.S.C. § 2252(b)(2)(A).

10. 19 U.S.C. § 2252(b)(2)(B).

11. *See* 19 U.S.C. § 2436(a)(4).

12. 19 U.S.C. § 2252(d)(2)(A).

13. 19 U.S.C. § 2252(d)(2)(A).

14. *See* 19 U.S.C. § 2252(d)(1)(A).

15. *See* 19 U.S.C. § 2252(d)(5)(B).

16. *See* 19 U.S.C. § 2252(b)(3).

17. *See* 19 U.S.C. § 2252(c)(1).

of productive facilities in the domestic industry," "the inability of a significant number of firms to carry out domestic production operations at a reasonable level of profit," and "significant unemployment or underemployment within the domestic industry."[18]

As to threat of serious injury, the ITC must consider (under 19 U.S.C. Section 2252(c)(1)(B)):

(i) a decline in sales or market share, a higher and growing inventory (whether maintained by domestic producers, importers, wholesalers, or retailers), and a downward trend in production, profits, wages, productivity, or employment (or increasing underemployment) in the domestic industry,

(ii) the extent to which firms in the domestic industry are unable to generate adequate capital to finance the modernization of their domestic plants and equipment, or are unable to maintain existing levels of expenditures for research and development, [and]

(iii) the extent to which the United States market is the focal point for the diversion of exports of the article concerned by reason of restraints on exports of such article to, or on imports of such article into, third country markets . . . .

"Substantial cause" is defined as one that is "important and not less than any other cause."[19] Interestingly, a lower causation standard, "significant cause," is applied to imports from communist countries under Section 406.[20]

> Unlike antidumping or CVD cases in which the imports may be one of many causes of injury to a domestic industry, imports in a Section 201 action must be shown to be a substantial cause of serious injury, if relief is to be obtained. The injury requirement in a Section 201 action is, therefore, *more* stringent, in terms of causation, than is the injury requirement in an antidumping or CVD action.[21]

Under the *Trade Expansion Act of 1962*, as amended, the Escape Clause required a petitioner show that increased imports were a "major" cause of injury. In changing the word "major" to "substantial," the *1974 Act* liberalized the causation element. No adjective appears before the noun "cause" in GATT Article XIX or the WTO *Agreement on Safeguards*, essentially meaning the American causation standard is relatively more difficult to satisfy.

In two other respects, the *1974 Act* also made it easier for petitioners to obtain relief. First, it eliminated the link between trade concessions and increased imports. Second, it provided that a relative—not necessarily an absolute—increase in imports would suffice. The relative increase concept had been part of the original

---

18. *See* 19 U.S.C. § 2252(c)(1)(A).
19. 19 U.S.C. § 2252(b)(1)(B).
20. *See* 19 U.S.C. § 2436(e)(2)(A), (B)(ii).
21. Vakerics, 15 (emphasis added).

Escape Clause in the *Trade Agreements Extension Act of 1951*, but was removed in 1962 when the requirements for relief were tightened by the *1962 Act*. The trade-off for the relaxed requirements under the *1974 Act* was the specification import relief was temporary.

An important aspect of the causation analysis is that the ITC cannot "aggregate the causes of declining demand associated with a recession or economic downturn in the U.S. economy into a single cause of serious injury or threat of injury."[22] This proscription was added by the *1988 Act* after a famous case brought in 1980 by the United Auto Workers and Ford Motor Company.[23] In the *Certain Motor Vehicles* case, the ITC agreed with the petitioners that Japanese auto imports were a cause of the overall decline in consumption of American-made cars.

But, the ITC ruled a recession — brought about in part by the oil price increase of 1979, which caused a shift in market demand toward smaller cars — was a greater cause of serious injury to American car companies than increased imports. In reaching this decision, the ITC did not isolate each economic factor relevant to the matter of serious injury for the purpose of comparing them with the factor of increased imports. Rather, it aggregated negative economic factors in comparing them with increased imports. The 1988 amendment was motivated in part by a concern that such aggregation would make it virtually impossible for a domestic industry to obtain a favorable ITC determination during in times of recession.

To no one's surprise, the negative determination of the ITC in the automobile case led to political controversy. Numerous Congresspersons criticized the decision, and Chairman Charles A. Vanik (Democrat-Ohio) of the Trade Subcommittee of the House Ways and Means Committee called hearings to consider alternative trade action. Senator John C. Danforth (Republican-Missouri) introduced legislation, which was not enacted, that would have restricted Japanese car imports from 1981–1983 to 1.6 million units — an outright quota that plainly would have run afoul of GATT Article XI:1.[24]

President Ronald Reagan (1911–2004, President, 1981–1989) — an otherwise ardent free trader — accomplished via a different vehicle what Senator Danforth's bill would have achieved. In his 1980 Presidential campaign, Ronald Reagan promised relief for the auto industry from foreign competition. (Rich in Republican Party Convention delegate votes, and in Electoral College votes, Michigan and Ohio become particularly important states during election seasons!) After the election, the Reagan Administration negotiated a VRA with Japan to limit Japanese car exports to the U.S. The agreement limited Japanese car imports to the U.S. to roughly 1.68 million units annually 1981–1983. It was renewed in 1984 at the level of 1.85 million

---

22. 19 U.S.C. § 2252(c)(2)(A).

23. *See Report to the President on Certain Motor Vehicles and Certain Chassis and Bodies Therefor*, United States International Trade Commission Investigation Number TA-201-44 (3 December 1980), 45 Federal Register 85,194 (24 December 1980).

24. *See* S. 396, 97th Congress, 1st Session (1981); 127 CONGRESSIONAL RECORD 1786–1787 (1981).

units. In 1985, after record-setting profit and employment data for the American auto industry the previous year, the Reagan Administration decided not seek a fifth year of voluntary quotas. Some scholars argue this saga, coupled with the results of certain other cases from the mid- and late-1970s, discredited the Escape Clause, because politics undermined the impartial adjudicatory process of the ITC.

- **Step 3: ITC Recommendation**

If the ITC makes a negative determination, then the case is terminated. The President has no authority to invoke an escape-clause remedy in the event of a negative determination.

Suppose the ITC renders an affirmative determination that an article is being imported into the U.S. in such increased quantities as to be a substantial cause of serious injury or threat thereof to a domestic industry producing a like or directly competitive product. In this case the ITC must recommend to the President the remedy that would redress the injury and be most effective in helping the industry make a positive adjustment to import competition.[25] The relief is designed only as a temporary measure to help an afflicted domestic industry become more competitive with foreign imports.

The ITC may recommend the adjustment of tariffs, imposition of quotas or tariff-rate quotas, provision of trade adjustment assistance to workers or firms, or any combination thereof.[26] It also may recommend the President initiate international trade negotiations to address the underlying cause of the increase in the imports and alleviate the injury.[27] The ITC must a hold public hearing regarding its recommendation.[28] The ITC must provide the President with its report and recommendation within 180 days of the day the petition is filed.[29] The report must be made public.[30]

In addition, if the ITC recommends the provision of adjustment assistance, then the Secretaries of Labor and Commerce must be notified of this recommendation. The Secretary of Labor must give expedited consideration to a petition by workers in a domestic industry for certification of eligibility to apply for adjustment assistance. The Secretary of Commerce must give expedited consideration to a petition from a firm in a domestic industry for certification of eligibility to apply for adjustment assistance.[31]

---

25. *See* 19 U.S.C. §2252(e)(1).
26. *See* 19 U.S.C. §2252(e)(2).
27. *See* 19 U.S.C. §2252(e)(4)(A).
28. *See* 19 U.S.C. §2252(e)(5).
29. *See* 19 U.S.C. §2252(f)(1). A longer period (240 days) is permitted if the petition alleges critical circumstances exist.
30. *See* 19 U.S.C. §2252(f)(3).
31. *See* 19 U.S.C.§2252(g).

Unless the ITC finds "good cause" to reconsider its decision within a year, an Escape Clause proceeding regarding the same article cannot be brought for at least 1 year.[32]

In the 1979 *Sneaker Circus, Inc. v. Carter* case, the petitioner-plaintiffs were a retailer, wholesaler, and importer of non-rubber athletic footwear covered by 2 OMAs negotiated by the U.S. with Taiwan and Korea.[33] The OMAs established the number of pairs of such footwear that those countries would export to the U.S. The petitioners alleged the ITC, in making its good cause determination, failed to comply with Section 201. The ITC rendered an affirmative injury determination in September 1975. President Gerald R. Ford determined adjustment assistance, but not other import relief, was the most effective remedy. In September 1976, less than a year after the ITC submitted its report to President Ford, the Senate Finance Committee approved a resolution directing the ITC to institute a new footwear investigation. The resolution indicated that changed circumstances, such as an increase in imports and a rapid deteriorating in economic conditions in the domestic footwear industry, constitute good cause to commence a new investigation. The ITC agreed good cause existed. Ultimately, the Administration of President Jimmy Carter (1924, 1977–1981) negotiated the two OMAs.

The petitioners challenged the authority of the ITC to consider a good cause issue on the basis of a Senate Finance Committee resolution. They argued the ITC determination was invalid because the ITC can make a good cause determination only after the industry in question presents substantial new evidence. The *Sneaker Circus* court rejected this argument. Not only did it find that Section 201 is silent on the question of who may request a reinvestigation, but also that "there is nothing to indicate that the ITC could not make a good cause determination on its own motion without a request or petition for reinvestigation from some other entity or person."

• **Step 4: Presidential Action**

Within 60 days after the President receives an ITC report that contains an affirmative finding regarding serious injury, or threat thereof, to a domestic industry, the President must "take all appropriate and feasible action" to "facilitate efforts by the domestic industry to make a positive adjustment to import competition . . . ."[34] The President can request additional information from the ITC within 15 days of receiving the report, and it has 30 days to respond.[35] The President must act within

---

32. 19 U.S.C. § 2252(h).

33. *See* 457 F. Supp. 771 (E.D.N.Y. 1978), *aff'd without published opinion*, 614 F.2d 1290 (2d Cir. 1979).

34. 19 U.S.C. § 2253(a)(1)(A) and (4). If the President granted provisional relief under critical circumstances, then the time period is 50 days.

35. *See* 19 U.S.C. § 2253(a)(5).

30 days after receiving any supplemental report.[36] The action must "provide greater economic and social benefits than costs."[37] If the President follows the ITC recommendation, then the President must set forth a decision and reasons for it in a report to Congress. The report must be made on the date of the decision.[38]

In determining the appropriate relief, the President must consider not only the effectiveness of the relief in facilitating adjustment, but also the cost of the relief on consumers and the economy. The imposition of tariffs, quotas, or TRQs take effect within 15 days on which they are proclaimed unless the President also announces her intention to enter into international negotiations.[39] Then, the remedial measures take effect 90 days after the President's decision, and in effect the measures serve as a "bargaining chip."

The President may devise a remedy different from the one recommended by the ITC. Again, a report to Congress is required on the date the decision is made.[40] In *Sneaker Circus*, the petitioners argued that President Carter's remedy was not "commensurate with the injury found by the [International Trade] Commission." This language is found not in Section 201, but in a Report of the Senate Finance Committee concerning the *Trade Act of 1974*. However, the *Sneaker Circus* Court granted substantial deference to the President's negotiating authority. It found "the decision as to the countries with which OMAs should be negotiated is a purely political question," which is "precisely the type of question" that is not reviewable by the courts.

The President also is free to decline to proclaim any remedy, *i.e.*, to find no remedial action is warranted. If the President declines to follow the ITC recommendation (either because she recommends an alternative remedy or no remedy at all), then Congress could enact a bill implementing the recommendation. (Of course, Congress would need a two-thirds vote of each house to override the expected Presidential veto of the bill.) Upon the enactment of a joint resolution, the recommendation would take effect within 90 days of the date the President transmitted his report to Congress, and the President must proclaim such action.[41]

Unlike the AD or CVD remedies, but like unilateral retaliation under Section 301, the President has considerable discretion in an Escape Clause case. What are the arguments for and against this latitude, as opposed to automaticity, in different kinds of trade remedies?

---

36. *See* 19 U.S.C. § 2253(a)(4)(B). A different time period exists for a case of critical circumstances in which the President ordered provisional relief.
37. *See* 19 U.S.C. § 2253(a)(1)(A).
38. *See* 19 U.S.C. § 2253(b)(1).
39. *See* 19 U.S.C. § 2253(d)(1).
40. *See* 19 U.S.C. § 2253(b)(3).
41. *See* 19 U.S.C. § 2253(c), (d)(2).

- **Step 5: Monitoring, Modification, and Termination of Action**

The initial period during which a remedial action is in effect cannot exceed four years.[42] This period can be extended, though the total relief period cannot exceed eight years.[43] If a trade remedy is in effect for longer than three years, then the ITC must issue a report periodically to the President and Congress regarding the progress of workers and firms in the injured domestic industry at making a positive adjustment to import competition.[44] The President may reduce, modify, or terminate the action if she finds that the domestic industry "has not made adequate efforts to make a positive adjustment to import competition" or the remedial action is ineffective because of changed economic circumstances.[45] If an action is terminated, then the ITC must report to the President and Congress, and hold public hearings, on the effectiveness of that action at facilitating adjustment.[46] The report is due within 180 days of the termination of the action.[47]

III. January 2018 *Washers* and *Solar* Section 201 Cases

- **Nature of Relief Ordered**

In January 2018, President Donald J. Trump (1946–, President, 2017–) announced the U.S. would apply steep tariffs to imported large residential washing machines and solar power equipment, following October 2017 determinations by the ITC imports of these products were a substantial cause of serious injury to American manufacturers.[48] Not since 2003 had an American President invoked Section 201. In the *Washers* case, Mr. Trump declared a TRQ, namely:

   (1) In the first year of four-year relief, a 20% tariff on the 1st 1.2 million imported large residential washers, and a 50% tariff on units above the 1.2 million threshold.

---

42. *See* 19 U.S.C. §2253(e)(1)(A).

43. *See* 19 U.S.C. §2253(e)(1)(B)(ii).

44. *See* 19 U.S.C. §2254(a).

45. 19 U.S.C. §2254(b)(1)(A).

46. *See* 19 U.S.C. §2254(d)(1).

47. *See* 19 U.S.C. §2254(d)(3).

48. *See* Elaine Ramirez, *South Korea to Take Fight With U.S. Over Washers, Solar to WTO*, 35 International Trade Reporter (BNA) 123 (25 January 2018); Christopher Martin, Jim Efstathiou Jr., & Ari Natter, *Solar Around the World Exhales as Trump's Tariffs Lack Bite*, 35 International Trade Reporter (BNA) 129 (25 January 2018); Brian Flood, *U.S. Duties on Chinese Solar Products Survive Legal Appeal*, 35 International Trade Reporter (BNA) 130 (25 January 2018); *Trump Says No Trade War Despite Asia Outcry Over Tariffs*, BBC News, 23 January 2018, www.bbc.com/news/world-42786995 (hereinafter, *Trump Says*); Bloomberg News, *The Winners and Losers in Trump's Trade Crackdown*, Bloomberg, 23 January 2018, www.bloomberg.com/news/articles/2018-01-23/the-winners-and-losers-in-trump-s-trade-crackdown; Adam Haigh & Lilian Karunungan,

(2) In the third year, tariffs of 16% on imports up to 1.2 million units, and 40% thereafter.

In the *Solar* case, the President also opted for a TRQ:

(1) In each year of the four-year remedy, up to 2.5 GW of unassembled solar cells (which suffice for roughly 11.5 million panels) may be imported duty-free.[49]

(2) Above this threshold, in the first year, a 30% duty on imported solar cells and modules.

(3) A decline in this duty by five percentage points in years two and three each, to 15%, in year four.

The *Washers* remedy was more severe than that recommended by the ITC. The President ignored the ITC recommendation to exclude subject merchandise from Korea's LG Electronics, because they previously had been subject to AD duties. The *Solar* remedy was milder, as the ITC recommended a 35% duty.[50]

Here's What Trump's Tariffs on U.S. Imports Are Doing to Markets, BLOOMBERG, 23 January 2018, www.bloomberg.com/news/articles/2018-01-23/here-s-what-trump-s-tariffs-on-u-s-imports-are -doing-to-markets; Liam Denning, *Trump's Solar Tariffs: When the Levy Brakes*, BLOOMBERG, 22 January 2018, www.bloomberg.com/gadfly/articles/2018-01-23/trump-s-solar-tariffs-when-the -levy-brakes; Nick Turner, *Here's What Trump's Tariffs on U.S. Imports Are Doing to Markets*, BLOOMBERG, 22 January 2018; Nick Turner, *Whirlpool Says Its Adding Jobs After Trump Tariff Decision*, BLOOMBERG, 22 January 2018; www.bloomberg.com/news/articles/2018-01-22/whirlpool-says -it-s-adding-jobs-in-wake-of-trump-tariff-decision; David Lawder & Nichola Groom, *Trump Slaps Steep U.S. Tariffs on Imported Washers, Solar Panels*, REUTERS, 22 January 2018, www.reuters.com /article/us-usa-trade-tariffs/trump-slaps-steep-u-s-tariffs-on-imported-washers-solar-panels -idUSKBN1FB30B; Ju-Min Park & Stella Qiu, *Asia Protests at U.S. Solar, Washer Tariffs, Fears More to Come, Reuters*, 22 January 2018, www.reuters.com/article/us-usa-trade-tariffs-southkorea /asia-protests-at-u-s-solar-washer-tariffs-fears-more-to-come-idUSKBN1FC04B; Reuters Staff, *Mexico Criticizes U.S. Move on Imported Washers, Solar Panels*, REUTERS, 22 January 2018, www .reuters.com/article/us-usa-trade-tariffs-mexico/mexico-criticizes-u-s-move-on-imported -washers-solar-panels-idUSKBN1FC06F; Ayesha Rascoe & Nichola Groom, *Job Creator, or Job Killer? Trump Angers Solar Installers with Panel Tariff*, REUTERS, 22 January 2018, www.reuters .com/article/us-usa-trade-tariffs/job-creator-or-job-killer-trump-angers-solar-installers-with -panel-tariff-idUSKBN1FB30B; Henning Gloystein & Christoph Steitz, *U.S. Solar Panel Import Tariff to Hit European, Asian Manufacturers*, REUTERS, 22 January 2018, www.reuters.com/article /us-usa-trade-tariffs-solar/u-s-solar-panel-import-tariff-to-hit-european-asian-manufacturers -idUSKBN1FC0EZ.

49. A solar "cell" collects and absorbs sunlight. A solar "panel" gathers that energy from the cells, and then distributes it as power. Manufacturing the cells is one of the most difficult and costly steps in this chain. *See* Siri Bulusu, *India Exempts Some Solar Energy Firms With Contracts From Tariff*, 35 International Trade Reporter (BNA) 507 (12 April 2018). A solar "module" is a block of cells that, and when put together with other modules, make up a panel.

50. In February 2018, four Canadian solar producers and U.S. importers (Silfab Solar Inc., Heliene Inc., Canadian Solar (USA) Inc., and Canadian Solar Solutions Inc.) challenged the President's remedy in the CIT, alleging he exceeded his authority under the *Trade Act of 1974*, because he imposed a remedy when, in fact, the ITC never agreed on one. They also claimed he violated the 1993 *NAFTA Implementation Act*, which required that Canadian merchandise be exempt from a global safeguard, especially when a majority of the ITC finds (as it did with respect to solar

- **No *NAFTA* Exclusions**

Neither Section 201 action excluded Mexican merchandise, a possibility (excluding *NAFTA*-originating merchandise from a global safeguard action) the President could have invoked (under *NAFTA* Chapter 8). That meant $278 million worth of washing machines, and $1.127 billion worth of solar panels, made in Mexico were subject to the remedies. For example, Swedish-headquartered Electrolux AB makes washers in Mexico, and had relied on DFQF treatment under *NAFTA*. Mexico noted it was entitled to compensation (under *NAFTA* 802(6)). Canada was not, as the President followed the ITC recommendation to exclude Canadian (as well as Singaporean) panels, hence benefiting Canadian Solar, Inc. (and Singapore's REC). Here, there was an irony: Canadian Solar is Chinese-owned.

- **Winners**

These twin Section 201 actions were a mixed blessing. They were a boost to American washer and solar producers, but a setback to the renewable energy industry. Put differently, first, producers of subject merchandise outside America were losers, while manufacturers in the U.S., including foreign companies that had added, or were seeking to add, production capacity in the U.S., were winners. Second, the industry-wide effects depended on where a firm was situated in the chain of production and distribution, and on the significance of the Section 201 tariffs to their overall cost structure.

Whirlpool Corp. (which is headquartered in Benton Harbor, Michigan) was a petitioner in the *Washers* case, so it was a winner. In terms of market share, Whirlpool had a 43% share of the American washing machine market before the case. Easily, Whirlpool and General Electric (which boasted a Louisville, Kentucky, plant), dominated the American washing machine market. Ironically, a Chinese company, Qingdao Haier, Co., bought General Electric's home appliance division of GE in 2016, meaning China also was a beneficiary of President Trump's decision.

In the *Solar* case, the winning petitioners were Suniva and SolarWorld Americas. Ironically, Suniva, which was bankrupt, was majority-owned by a Chinese company, Shunfeng International Clean Energy Ltd., which is listed on the Hong

---

products) that Canadian products do not account for a substantial share of total U.S. imports, and do not contribute significantly to injury to the petitioning U.S. industry. The CIT declined to grant petitioners a TRO, saying they failed to show they were likely to prevail on the merits, because the President probably has the authority to issue Section 201 relief even if the Commissioners cannot agree on a remedy. The Court also said petitioners failed to prove a TRO would be in the public interest; rather, Section 201 authorizes the President to assess the pros and cons of a safeguard. The Federal Circuit rejected an appeal from the CIT ruling, denying a request that collection of the Section 201 tariffs be stayed until the merits of the case are decided. *See Silfab Solar, Inc. v. United States*, Federal Circuit Number 18-01718 (13 April 2018); *Silfab Solar, Inc. v. United States*, CIT Number 18-00023 (filed 7 February 2018), Slip Opinion 18-15 (5 March 2018); Brian Flood, *Solar Companies Lose Bid to Block Trump Tariffs*, 35 International Trade Reporter (BNA) 320 (8 March 2018); Brian Flood, *Canadian Solar Producers, U.S. Importers Challenge Trump Tariffs*, 35 International Trade Reporter (BNA) 236 (15 February 2018).

Kong Stock Exchange. A German parent, SolarWorld AG, controls SolarWorld. Former ITC Commissioner Brunsdale foresaw this irony in the 1990 *Certain Cameras* case, discussed in a separate Chapter. Eighty-three percent of solar installations in America use imported panels, most of which come from Asia: 36% from Malaysia, 21% from Korea, 9% each from Thailand and Vietnam, 8% from China (which is the world's largest producer of solar panels), and 17% from non-Asian sources. (In January–October 2016, 90% of solar module imports came from Asia.) Another Chinese beneficiary was Longi Green Energy Technology Co., which planned to increase solar cell and module production in the U.S. Still another beneficiary was First Solar, Inc., This Tempe, Arizona-based producer has offshore panel production. But, it uses technology in its panels that excludes them from the Section 201 order.

- **Losers**

The losers in the *Washers* case were the Korean respondents, Samsung Electronics Co. and LG Electronics. Combined, they had 25% of the market share in the U.S., shipping annually 2.5–3 million washers worth roughly $1 billion. They faced the choice of absorbing the Section 201 20% tariff, raising retail prices, or a combination thereof. LG choose the combination, raising the per unit washing machine price by 4%–8% (*i.e.*, $50).[51] Of course, merchandise made in the U.S. was immune, as obviously it was not made in the U.S. Anticipating the possibility of a Section 201 action against its imports, Samsung began producing washers in South Carolina before case, and hired over 600 workers there. Samsung planned for one million units from this factory (in 2018). Likewise, LG was constructing a factory in Tennessee, with production expected by 2019. Some American retailers also were losers in the outcome. For example, Sears sources its large, Kenmore-brand washers from LG's foreign factories, so they were subject to the remedial duties.

Losers in the *Solar* case included SunPower, which makes most of its solar panels in Mexico and Asia, Korea's Hawha Q Cells Co., Taiwan's Newo Solar Power Corp., and large Chinese producers of solar panels and/or components such as photovoltaic cells, particularly JinkoSolar Holding Co. (the world's largest producer, and China's biggest exporter, of solar panels), Trina Solar Ltd., and JA Solar Holdings Co.[52] All of them contemplated shifting production to the U.S. to avoid the

---

51. *See* David Lawder & Howard Schneider, *Trump's Next $100 Billion Tariff Dilemma: Hit Wal Mart or Apple Store*, Reuters, 20 April 2018, www.reuters.com/article/us-usa-trade -china-tariffs-analysis/trumps-next-100-billion-tariff-dilemma-hit-wal-mart-or-apple-store -idUSKBN1HR2YC.

52. Accordingly, in August 2018, China filed suit in the WTO against the U.S. safeguard action: "[t]he tariffs on imported photovoltaic goods and renewable energy subsidies hurt the legitimate rights and interests of China's renewable energy companies," they "give an unfair advantage to U.S. renewable energy industries," "and they have seriously distorted the international market for photovoltaic and related products, damaging China's trade interests." Stephanie Wong, *China Files WTO Complaint Over U.S. Renewable Energy Measures*, 35 International Trade Reporter (BNA) 1094 (16 August 2018). *See also United States — Safeguard Measure on Imports of Crystalline Silicon Photovoltaic Products, Request for Consultations by China*, WT/DS562/1 (16 August 2018), *United*

Section 201 remedies, and/or diversifying their export markets away from the U.S. to lessen their vulnerability to American protective measures. SunRun, Inc., an installer of solar energy systems, was another loser, as was any other American firm that relied on foreign panels or parts. But, foreseeing the remedies, these companies accelerated shipments to America in advance of the enforcement date. Solar panel imports from China were 11 times higher in the fourth quarter of 2017 than in the first three quarters of that year.[53] And, on top of the annual 2½ GW exemption, importers had stockpiled 5 GWs worth of solar equipment at American warehouses and ports, hence the effect of the remedies, in terms of supply constraints would not be felt for about six months after enforcement. Yet, in the long run, they and solar-power producing states like Arizona and North Carolina were losers.

Solar power was becoming cost-competitive in the U.S., with solar panel prices falling by 30% in 2016–2017. America is the world's fourth largest market (in terms of solar capacity, as of January 2018) for solar power equipment, after China, Japan, and Germany. Thanks in part to Chinese entry into this market, since 2010, the cost of solar modules had tumbled by 80%. That fall, however, said the winning petitioners, Suniva and SolarWorld, was due to a flood of cheap imports. China was the world's largest solar panel producer, and petitioners sought the maximum legal remedy of a 50% duty.

- **Jobs and Power**

Consider the specific job effects of Section 201 TRQs. In the American market, Whirlpool said it would add 500 jobs at its Clyde, Ohio factory, and invest in manufacturing innovation. But, how long would these jobs last against automation and artificial intelligence? As 2001 Nobel Prize Economics Prize winner Joseph Stiglitz (1943–) remarks:

> You can't build the world that we had in 1950, 1960—that's not going to come back. We are not going to reindustrialize. We can bring back some manufacturing, but it will be jobless manufacturing done by robots. So, what we have to do is find new industries, like installing solar panels. And what are we doing? We're making it more difficult to install solar panels.[54]

Was he right—would there be an increase in solar power investment thanks to the Section 201 protection? Yes and no.

On the one hand, the *Solar* remedy slowed the transition to renewable power, with an estimated 23,000 jobs lost in 2018 (thanks to a 20% drop in solar installations

States—*Certain Measures Related to Renewable Energy, Request for Consultations by China*, WT/DS563/1; World Trade Organization, *China Initiates Dispute Complaints Against U.S. Solar Cell Duties, Renewable Energy Measures*, 16 August 2018, www.wto.org/english/news_e/news18_e/ds562_563rfc_16aug18_e.htm.

53. *See* Christopher Martin, *China Flooded U.S. with Solar Panels Before Trump's Tariffs*, 35 International Trade Reporter (BNA) 238 (22 February 2018).

54. *Quoted in* Catherine Bosley, *Stiglitz Calls Trump's Tariffs "Bad for the Global Environment,"* 35 International Trade Reporter (BNA) 149 (25 January 2018).

from 11 to 9 gigawatts), and 10–15% fewer solar installations through 2023, thanks to the higher tariffs on cells and modules used as inputs into panels. In Maryland, for instance, 784 solar industry jobs were lost (as of May 2018).[55] Those tariffs meant a 3% rise in utility-scale, and 7% rise in residential-scale, solar power. U.S.-based cell and module producers lacked the production capacity to fill demand and offset these increases. They have no choice but to source from offshore. Indeed, the record of safeguard actions in destroying American jobs showed a negative cost-benefit analysis. The U.S. Chamber of Commerce, in May 2018 testimony in the context of a Section 301 action against China, explained that "President George W. Bush's tariffs on steel resulted in 200,000 job losses and $4 billion in lost wages in 2002, and President Barack Obama's duties on tires imported from China led to 2,500 job losses and cost U.S. consumers $1.1 billion in 2011."[56] (The Section 301 case, as well as the 2003 steel safeguard and 2011 Section 421 tires special safeguard, are discussed elsewhere.)

On the other hand, the 3%–7% figures were small. Panels make up 20–30% of the cost of a solar power facility. Other ingredients are inverters (needed to make the current useful), and "EPC" (engineering, procurement, and construction). And, only about 15% of the American workforce engaged in the solar industry are in manufacturing; most are in installation. So, the relatively low value of subject merchandise in solar projects meant higher tariffs on it would not have a big impact on project costs, and likewise the relatively low percentage of labor involved in these products would mean the protective remedy would not translate into many new jobs. In other words, claims of quashing investment in the U.S. were overblown. That said, foreign producers looked at possibilities to relocate production in America.

Alas, maybe helping renewables was not the point. The fossil fuel industry, such as coal producers, were winners. To the extent the *Solar* remedy translated into higher prices for consumers, conventional energy sources remained attractive. Note the irony, in terms of a utilitarian calculus: America's solar power industry employs (at the time of the Section 201 remedy) 260,000 workers—five times more than the coal industry. Of this amount, about 15% are engaged in manufacturing solar products, while solar installation and other parts of the industry account for the remainder.

• **Use of Section 201 as an AD-CVD Anti-Circumvention Device**

In addition to helping the fossil fuel industry, maybe using Section 201 as an anti-circumvention device was the point. After an array of AD-CVD cases against principally Chinese producer-exporters, the USTR said:

> China moved production elsewhere and evaded U.S. relief, while maintaining capacity. . . . Today, China dominates the global supply chain and, by its own admission, is looking to increase its capacity to account for 70 percent

---

55. *See* Rossella Brevetti, *Commerce Clearing Backlog of Requests for Tariff Exclusions*, 35 International Trade Reporter (BNA) 659 (17 May 2018).

56. Mark Niquette & Andrew Mayeda, *U.S. Business Groups Bash Trump Tariffs as China Talks Intensify*, 35 International Trade Reporter (BNA) 673 (17 May 2018).

of total planned global capacity expansions announced in the first half of 2017.[57]

Rather than play "cat-and-mouse" games with China, that is, addressing this behavior with AD-CVD scope determinations and circumvention orders, why not impose a global safeguard? If, indeed, combatting evasion was the point, then not exempting subject merchandise shipments from Mexico made sense.

Perhaps Narendra Modi, India's Prime Minister, had the last word. Speaking at the World Economic Forum in Davos:

> Forces of protectionism are raising their heads against globalisation. Their intention is not only to avoid globalisation themselves but they also want to reverse its natural flow . . . .[58]

There was a touch of irony in his remarks, in that India was planning a 70% remedial trade duty on Chinese solar panels.

IV. Delineating Domestic Industry amidst Global Value-Added Chains

As in a Section 406 Market Disruption Safeguard case concerning merchandise from a Communist country, in a Section 201 investigation, defining the scope of "like" or "directly competitive" products helps shape the answer to the follow-on question: which producers are part of the domestic industry? The obvious, and correct, answer is they constitute any firm (whether American or foreign) making the "like" or "directly" competitive product in the U.S.

Less obvious, however, is how to deal with intermediate products or imported components. First, should articles at different stages of the production process be considered as "directly competitive," and thus their producers lumped into a single domestic industry? Under both the *1962* and *1974 Acts*, the term "directly competitive" includes a good that is at an earlier or later stage of processing from the imported article, if "the imported article had an economic effect on domestic producers comparable to the effect that the importation of an article at the same stage of processing would have."[59]

---

57. *Quoted in* Brian Flood, *U.S. Duties on Chinese Solar Products Survive Legal Appeal*, 35 International Trade Reporter (BNA) 130 (25 January 2017).

58. *Quoted in Trump Says, supra.*

Note that the U.S. refused all requests (*e.g.*, from China, EU, Japan, and Korea) for compensation under the WTO *Safeguards Agreement*, and not surprisingly faced a *DSU* challenge from Korea. Korea alleged multiple violations to the *Agreement*, including the methodology the ITC used to determine injury to American producers of like products.

59. CLUBB, § 23.12.3 at 749, *citing* 19 U.S.C. § 2481(5).

Congress drafted this provision in the *1962 Act*, after the ITC rendered a negative determination against American cherry growers, which sought relief against imported processed cherries, on the ground the domestic unprocessed product was not "directly competitive" with the foreign processed one.[60] Following that negative determination and the *1962 Act* change in reaction to it, the ITC tended to respond "yes" to the above-framed question.[61] In the July 1984 *Unwrought Copper* case, the ITC defined the copper refining industry to include all four stages of copper production (mining, milling, smelting, and refining), because the industry was "like a pyramid," *i.e.*, all the factors of production were engaged in making a single article.[62] Likewise, in the August 1994 *Canned Tuna Fish* case, it held boats and fisherman, as well as processing facilities and workers, while two different productive groups, comprised a single industry.[63]

Second, should the fact a domestic producer of a "like" or "directly competitive" product uses one or more imported components disqualify it from being included in the domestic industry, and thus bar it from obtaining relief from imports? In a world of global supply chains, the question is relevant in many cases.

The question was called as early as the February 1983 *Motorcycles* case, in which Harley Davidson of Milwaukee, Wisconsin, successfully petitioned for Section 201 relief against foreign motorcycles and sub-assemblies.[64] ("Sub-assemblies" refers to parts made abroad and then imported into the U.S. for final assembly, testing, and packaging.) The importers were Honda, Kawasaki, Suzuki, and Yamaha, and the first two of these Japanese companies successfully argued they were part of the domestic industry for sub-assemblies: they fared relatively better than Harley-Davidson, so they sought to dilute its weak performance with their strong results, and thus impede an affirmative injury argument.

Significantly, the ITC looked at five different tests that could be used to determine whether a foreign firm (*e.g.*, the American subsidiary of Honda or Kawasaki) with operations in the U.S. is part of the "domestic industry":[65]

(1) Substantial Change Test

What changes does the firm make to the product before and after each stage of production in the U.S.?

(2) Value Added (Domestic Content) Test

---

60. CLUBB, § 23.12.2 fn. 7 at 749.

61. *See* CLUBB, § 23.12.2 at 749–750.

62. *Quoted in* CLUBB, § 23.12.2 at 750. *See Certain Canned Tuna Fish*, Investigation Number TA-201-52, United States International Trade Commission Publication 1549 (July 1984).

63. *See Certain Canned Tuna Fish*, Investigation Number TA-201-53, United States International Trade Commission Publication 1558 (August 1984).

64. *See Heavyweight Motorcycles, and Engines and Power Train Subassemblies Therefor*, Investigation Number TA-201-47, United States International Trade Commission Publication 1342 (February 1983).

65. *See* CLUBB, § 23.12.3 at 750–72 and fn. 15 at 751.

What is the percentage of American components and labor added in comparison with imported parts and foreign labor?

(3) Major Component Test

Is the essential element of the finished product is from overseas?

(4) Commitment to the U.S. Test

To what extent is the firm involved in the U.S., manifest through capital investments, domestic facilities, and employment?

(5) Degree of Control Test

To what degree does the firm have decision-making authority concerning production decisions in the U.S.?

The ITC rejected reliance on any single test, using all five of them. While the value added by Honda and Kawasaki in America to imported sub-assemblies was less than 50% of the finished motorcycle, the Commission found—using the other Tests—they were part of the domestic industry. Nevertheless, the ITC granted the Harley Davidson petition.

Part Six

Remedies against Non-Market Economies

Chapter 26

AD Cases against NMEs[1]

I. Problem of Computing Normal Value in NME

Suppose the home market of an exporter (or producer) of allegedly dumped merchandise is not a market economy. Such an economy is dubbed a "non-market economy." The term dates back to a 1935 bilateral trade agreement between the U.S. and former Soviet Union under which the Soviets were obligated to import $30 million worth of American products annually. Contemporary NME examples, says the DOC, include Armenia, Azerbaijan, Belarus, Georgia, Kyrgyzstan, Moldova, Tajikistan, Turkmenistan, Uzbekistan, and—most prominently—China and Vietnam. Query whether Iran, with the significant influence of the government, including the Revolutionary Guards, should be considered an NME if and when it joins the WTO.

In computing Normal Value for the dumping margin, price data from an NME are either unavailable or unreliable. By definition, in an NME, prices are set not by market forces of supply and demand, but by government fiat—or, at least, the government plays a major role in establishing prices. It would be unfair to compare Export Price or Constructed Export Price against a non-market price, because these Prices are market-driven values. The comparison would be "unfair" because of the distinct origin and nature of the prices in the importing and exporting countries. So, surrogate data, *i.e.*, information about prices from a third, or substitute, country, is used in lieu of data from the NME to calculate a dumping margin applicable to producer-exporters from the NME.

Importantly, even though GATT Article VI does not mention NMEs, its Interpretative Note, *Ad Article VI, Paragraph 1(2)*, anticipates they may raise problems in AD cases. Historically, this Note was inserted in 1955 "[t]o address imports from Czechoslovakia, then the only GATT member with a centrally planned economy."[2] The Note acknowledges that in the case of imports from a country in which (1) the state [*i.e.*, government] "has a complete or substantially complete monopoly of

---

1. Documents References:
   (1) *Havana (ITO) Charter* Article 34
   (2) GATT Article VI: and *Ad Article VI, Paragraph 1(2)*
   (3) WTO *Antidumping Agreement* Articles 1–2

2. K. William Watson, *Will Nonmarket Economy Methodology Go Quietly into the Night? U.S. Antidumping Policy Toward China After 2016*, CATO INSTITUTE POLICY ANALYSIS, Number 763, 28 October 2014, at 4, http://object.cato.org/sites/cato.org/files/pubs/pdf/pa763.pdf. [Hereinafter, *Nonmarket Economy Methodology*.]

its trade" and (2) "all domestic prices are fixed by the state," there may be "special difficulties . . . in determining price comparability for purposes of" calculating a dumping margin. In effect, the Note gives permission in an NME AD case to the relevant authority to disregard domestic prices and costs, and use as a surrogate prices and costs in a third country that possesses a market economy. Article 2:7 of the WTO *Antidumping Agreement* adds meekly that Article 2 of that *Agreement* (which concerns calculation of the dumping margin) "is without prejudice" to the GATT Note.

But, *Ad Article VI* does not establish criteria to determine whether a government has a "complete or substantially complete monopoly" on trade, or whether it "fixes all domestic prices." Likewise, this Note does not instruct WTO Members how to deal with those difficulties. Thus, from a free trade, or simply rule of law perspective, the Ad Article attracts criticism:

> The effect of this provision on NME antidumping is quite extreme. It seems to permit antidumping authorities to completely ignore international rules on how to determine normal value in antidumping investigations. Whether or not derogation from those disciplines was needed, the result was that NME methodology could be developed without any of the legal scrutiny given to regular antidumping techniques.

> It is unfortunate that the GATT contracting parties chose simply to exempt NME antidumping from existing rules rather than craft new rules.[3]

In any event, no other WTO text addresses these questions, which are detailed ones with potentially major ramifications on trade flows and patterns of products targeted in an NME AD investigation. Consequently, there is no harmonized set of rules on how to handle NME AD cases. Each Member is left to its own devices, within the broad parameters of GATT Article VI and the WTO *Antidumping Agreement*.

II. Four Key Issues

In practice, every WTO Member faces four issues arising from NMEs:

(1) *Definition*

How is an NME defined?

(2) *Proxy*

What proxy for Normal Value is used when subject merchandise originates in an NME?

(3) *Effects*

What are the practical consequences of NME treatment?

---

3. *Nonmarket Economy Methodology*, at 4.

(4) *Separate Rate*

> Can a respondent producer-exporter from an NME qualify for a separate AD duty rate?

The answer to the first issue sometimes comes during the accession process, and causes controversy thereafter. China is a case in point.

In its November 1999 bilateral agreement with the U.S., it acquiesced to NME treatment—allowing for the use of surrogate (also called "analog") data from third countries, like India—for 15 years following WTO accession, *i.e.*, until 11 December 2016. However, in November 2016, the U.S. announced that neither this agreement, as memorialized in Article 15(a)(ii) of the 11 December 2001 Chinese *Protocol of Accession*, nor WTO rules, mandated a change to (*i.e.*, dropped) application of NME rules to China.

Put differently, China's graduation to market economy status was not automatic as of that date, thanks to the rest of Article 15(a) (especially (a)(i)), and 15(d), which allow for NME treatment unless Chinese respondent producer-exporters can prove market economy conditions prevail in China. The U.S. said it would lose access to other trade remedy provisions that did not expire on that date if it made the change. So, the U.S. affirmed it would continue to use comparable market-based price and cost data whenever Chinese respondents could not adduce the requisite proof of market conditions in their country. Note the American announcement came six days before the Presidential election, in which allegedly unfair trade from China and consequent income and job losses were major issues. The EU did likewise, refusing to lift China's NME status.

A WTO case followed in December 2016. China filed suit against the U.S. and EU claiming the language of Article 15(a)(ii) of its *Accession Protocol* expired on 11 December 2016. The pertinent provisions of Article 15 say:

(a) In determining price comparability under Article VI of the GATT 1994 and the *Anti-Dumping Agreement*, the importing WTO Member shall use either Chinese prices or costs for the industry under investigation or a methodology that is not based on a strict comparison with domestic prices or costs in China based on the following rules:

> (i) If the *producers under investigation can clearly show that market economy conditions prevail in the industry* producing the like product with regard to the manufacture, production and sale of that product, the importing WTO Member shall use Chinese prices or costs for the industry under investigation in determining price comparability;

> (ii) The importing WTO Member may use a methodology that is not based on a strict comparison with domestic prices or costs in China *if the producers under investigation cannot clearly show that market economy conditions prevail in the industry* producing the like product with regard to manufacture, production and sale of that product.

. . .

(d) *Once China has established, under the national law of the importing WTO Member, that it is a market economy, the provisions of subparagraph (a) shall be terminated* provided that the importing Member's national law contains market economy criteria as of the date of accession. In any event, *the provisions of subparagraph (a)(ii) shall expire 15 years after the date of accession.* In addition, *should China establish, pursuant to the national law of the importing WTO Member, that market economy conditions prevail in a particular industry or sector, the non-market economy provisions of subparagraph (a) shall no longer apply to that industry* or sector.[4]

Manifestly, the text states other WTO Members may use AD methodologies "not based on a strict comparison with domestic prices or costs in China," only "if the producers under investigation cannot clearly show that market economy conditions prevail in the industry producing the like product." Article 15(d) states "the provisions of subparagraph (a)(ii) shall expire."

Yet, the *Protocol* seemed ambiguous. On the one hand, China pointed to the explicit expiration of Article 15(a)(ii), on 11 December 2016, contained in Article 15(d). China argued that only up until this date could other Members treat China as an NME, and only if Chinese respondent producer-exporters in case failed to prove market conditions prevailed. Once that date passed, respondents no longer had to prove market conditions prevailed.

On the other hand, the U.S. and EU pointed to the Article 15(a)(i), and the first and last sentences of Article 15(d). They said these provisions have no explicit expiry date (because Article 15(d) refers only to (a)(ii)). So, they and other Members could continue to use surrogate values in respect of Chinese producers, because China has failed to make reforms essential to showing its firms operated on market principles. That is, they interpreted these provisions to mean China is entitled to market economy treatment only if it can prove "market economy conditions prevail." With no expiry date, China will have to adduce this evidence beyond 11 December 2016, until it satisfies the first sentence of Article 15(d). Until China does so, and all of Article 15(a) expires, a Chinese respondent producer-exporter must prove market conditions prevail in its industry to get market economy treatment.

Might there be a third possibility, whereby China no longer automatically is treated as an NME (thanks to Article 15(a)(ii) and (d)), but nor does it automatically get market economy treatment (thanks to the alternative provisions). Rather, the decision by AD authorities in other Members is on a case-by-case basis, in which Chinese respondents have to prove their particular sector operates on market economy principles.

Vietnam is another illustration. Interestingly, so too are Russia, Turkey, and Ukraine. In 2002, the EU agreed to grant Russia market-economy status, in November 2005, it did so with respect to Turkey, and the next month it gave this status

---

4. Emphasis added.

to Ukraine. In its progress report for Turkey, it highlighted improvements in macroeconomic stabilization, public sector financial managements, banking regulation, and privatization. Yet, it admonished Turkey for not eliminating torture in jails, and called for further progress on acceptance of religious equality, freedom of expression, and rights of women and trade unions.

III. Issue 1: Definition of "NME"

Applying somewhat different NME criteria from the EU, the U.S. did not follow suit in respect of Russia or Ukraine. The DOC relies on six criteria to decide whether a country is an NME. So, the DOC does not simply designate a country as an "NME," but rather applies the criteria to the circumstances in that country to make a factual determination as to whether the country is an "NME." These factors, which Section 771(18)(A) of the *Omnibus Trade and Competitiveness Act of 1988* sets out, are:[5]

---

5. *See* 19 U.S.C. § 1677(18)(A).

There is a long history to the *1988 Act* criteria. *See Nonmarket Economy Methodology, supra*, at 4–6. Recall that recourse to a proxy for Normal Value requires a determination that sales of a foreign like product are not "in the ordinary course of trade." Sales by the respondent producer-exporter, or Constructed Value based on production costs, are the typical proxies. In 1962, the DOC decided all NME sales and costs were outside the "ordinary course," and that neither Third Country Price nor Constructed Value were feasible alternatives. None of the prices or costs of the respondent, whether derived from its home market or another country, could be used. So, the DOC looked to sales or costs of an entirely different producer-exporter, in an entirely different country, as a proxy. *See Fur Felt Hoods, Bodies, and Caps from Czechoslovakia*, 27 Federal Register 6099 (22 June 1962); *Jalousie-Louvre-Sized Sheet Glass from Czechoslovakia*, 27 Federal Register 8457 (15 August 1962). Between 1962–1968, the DOC acted via administrative fiat; not until 1968 did it publish AD regulations laying out what had become the use of Third Country Prices in NME cases. *See* Donald L. Cuneo & Charles B. Manuel Jr., *Roadblock to Trade: The State-Controlled Economy Issue in Antidumping Law Administration*, 5 FORDHAM INTERNATIONAL LAW JOURNAL number 2, 290–292 (1982). [Hereinafter, *Roadblock*.] Interestingly, in some instances the third country was the importing one, *i.e.*, the United States.

However, in 1975, in an infamously long case involving Polish golf carts, the DOC encountered a problem: the subject merchandise was made only in the producer-exporting country (Poland), and the importing country (America), so there was no third country from which to derive prices. Its solution was to use surrogate values for inputs and factors of production, and build up, or construct, a proxy for Normal Value. *See Electric Golf Cars from Poland*, 40 Federal Register 25497 (11 June 1975); *Roadblock, supra*, 292–295. That meant DOC could (and did) use input and factor prices from producer-exporters of merchandise in third countries that was not the same as the subject merchandise (albeit perhaps still close enough to be considered a "like" product), and it commonly did so. *See* Joseph P. Hornyak, *Treatment of Dumped Imports from Nonmarket Economy Countries*, 15 MARYLAND JOURNAL OF INTERNATIONAL LAW number 1, 27–29 (1991).

The collapse of the Berlin Wall on 9 November 1989 heralded the demise of Communism in Eastern Europe and the former Soviet Union. The economies of many such countries were or soon would be in transition from Communism to Capitalism, so the U.S. needed a cogent, systematic way to differentiate among them, and between them and truly NMEs. The 1988 *OTCA* laid out the path, codifying the above 6 criteria for NME status. Within these criteria, to accommodate

• **First Criterion: Currency**

Is the currency of the exporting country convertible into the currencies of other countries? The answer to this question arguably provides the most important evidence as to whether a country is driven by market forces. The fact the currency of that country is convertible links the economy of that country to world markets. The key is whether the currency is sufficiently convertible to integrate effectively the economy of the country with the world economy, and the prices in that country with world market prices.

In some cases, a country may have a currency that is internally, but not externally, convertible. Poland in the 1990s is an example. Internal convertibility meant Poland permitted individual Poles and Polish businesses to buy and sell its currency, the *złoty* (which means "golden") to facilitate import and export transactions. External non-convertibility meant it did not yet allow its currency to be traded freely on world markets. Still, coupled with the abolition of state-owned foreign trade monopolies and other market-oriented reforms, the DOC agreed to grant market economy status to Poland.

• **Second Criterion: Wages**

Are wages in the exporting country determined by free bargaining between labor and management? At least six variables help resolve this question: unemployment; freedom to strike; labor mobility; assistance in finding and being trained for jobs;

---

transition economies, DOC developed a so-called "Bubbles of Capitalism" approach, which it used in two 1991 cases, whereby "If an NME exporter could show that one or more of its factors of production was purchased from a supplier in a market economy or otherwise under market conditions, Commerce would use the exporter's own costs for that factor." *Nonmarket Economy Methodology*, 6 (*citing* Judith H. Bello, Alan F. Holmer & Jeremy O. Preiss, *Searching for 'Bubbles of Capitalism:' Application of the U.S. Antidumping and Countervailing Duty Laws to Reforming Nonmarket Economies*, 25 GEORGE WASHINGTON JOURNAL OF INTERNATIONAL LAW AND ECONOMICS 691–695 (1992)). In effect, "Bubbles of Capitalism" meant the use of traditional market-economy Constructive Value methodology, but within the setting of an NME.

In 1992, DOC dropped this approach, replacing it with the Market Oriented Industry, or MOI, Test. As per the "MOI" rubric, a respondent producer-exporter could try to prove its particular industry was "sufficiently free from government control." Specifically, DOC would not apply NME rules to the respondent, even if it haled from an NME, if the respondent proved there was (1) "virtually no government involvement in setting prices or amounts to be produced," (2) "typically private or collective ownership of firms in the industry," and (3) "market-determined prices for all significant inputs." *Id.*, 6 (*citing Chrome-Plated Lug Nuts from the People's Republic of China*, 57 Federal Register 15052 (24 April 1992); *Sulfanilic Acid from the People's Republic of China*, 57 Federal; Register 9409 (18 March 1992); *Import Administration Antidumping Manual*, Chapter 10, p. 32, http://enforcement.trade.gov/ admanual/index.html; Robert H. Lantz, *The Search for Consistency: Treatment of Nonmarket Economies in Transition under United States Antidumping and Countervailing Duty Laws*, 10 AMERICAN UNIVERSITY INTERNATIONAL LAW REVIEW number 3, 993–1059 (1995).

For early analyses of NME criteria, see, e.g., Jacob Viner, DUMPING: A PROBLEM IN INTERNATIONAL TRADE 239–257 (Chicago: University of Chicago Press, 1923); Peter Buck Feller, *The Antidumping Act and the Future of East-West Trade*, 66 MICHIGAN LAW REVIEW 117–119 (November 1967). For an overall argument the U.S. behaves lawlessly with respect to NME status and unfairly in applying MOI criteria, see *Nonmarket Economy Methodology*.

wage variations within a sector; and wage caps. Observe the latter indicates wage rates are imposed by the government, not negotiated between workers and management. Russia imposed such caps in the late 1990s.

- **Third Criterion: Investment**

Does the exporting country permit FDI in the country? Two variables matter here. First, to what extent is the entire economy of the country open to FDI (vis-à-vis only one or a few sectors open)? Second, does national treatment exist between foreign and like domestic producers?

- **Fourth Criterion: Ownership**

To what extent does the government of the exporting country own productive assets and enterprises in that country? Suppose a government owns the factors of production (land, labor, human capital, physical capital, and technology). Then, markets for those factors are likely to be distorted by non-commercial, political objectives of the government, and there are likely to be knock-on distortions in the markets of the goods and services those factors produce.

To be sure, state-owned or state-invested enterprises are observed in most if not all countries, particularly in certain strategic or sensitive sectors, or ones serving a particular need (*e.g.*, the rural poor). Thus, the DOC does not demand that there be no such government involvement in any sector. Rather, the DOC considers whether the level of government involvement in the country at issue is comparable to that observed in major market economy countries.

- **Fifth Criterion: Control**

To what extent does the government of the exporting country control decisions by enterprises to obtain and allocate resources, determine the nature and quantity of output, and set prices of resources and output? In brief, do domestic prices reflect market values? Private ownership reduces the probability of government control, but only if the government does more than transfer ownership to private individuals or businesses. The government liberates private managers from its interference and financial support.

Accordingly, the DOC examines the following variables to see if a government has given up control over allocation and pricing decisions: the government allows for inflation (versus takes stringent price stabilization measures), eliminates subsidies (versus continues support for enterprises), permits resource allocation based on efficiency (versus mandating resource flows from certain geographic regions of the country), and formally guarantees it will not interfere in decisions of firms about pricing.

- **Sixth Criterion: Other**

What other factors are appropriate to rendering a decision about NME status? This catch all category includes whether the country at issue has securities and anti-trust laws and regulators, and respects and enforces customs rules, trade remedies, and IPRs.

• **No Priority among Criteria**

The statute does not indicate any priority or weighting the DOC must give to these factors. Arguably, the factors most closely tied to what "Communism" entails—public ownership of the means of production—are the fourth and fifth, yet also arguably, all six are characteristic of central planning. Applying these criteria, in 2002, the DOC determined Russia—which acceded to the WTO on 22 August 2012—was an NME. Likewise, in 2006 the DOC applied them to China, deciding the facts justified continued treatment of China as an NME.

• **Indefinite Termination and No Appeal**

Significantly, once the DOC renders an NME designation, it stays in place until the DOC revokes it.[6] The DOC decision is final, not appealable, and not subject to

---

6. *See* 19 U.S.C. § 1677(18)(C)-(D); Joseph A. Laroski, Jr., *NMEs: A Love Story Nonmarket and Market Economy Status Under U.S. Antidumping Law*, 30 LAW AND POLICY IN INTERNATIONAL BUSINESS 369, 382 (1999).

DOC moved the following countries from NME to market economy status: "Poland (graduated in 1993), the Czech Republic (1998), Slovakia (1999), Hungary (2000), Latvia (2001), Kazakhstan (2002), Russia (2002), Romania (2002), Estonia (2003), Lithuania (2003), and Ukraine (2006)." *Nonmarket Economy Methodology*, fn. 17 at 14. As of August 2016, the following countries were considered NMEs: Armenia, Azerbaijan, Belarus, China, Georgia, Kyrgyzstan, Moldova, Russia, Tajikistan, Turkmenistan, Uzbekistan, and Vietnam. *Id.*, fn. 18 at 15. Interestingly, Armenia, Georgia, Kyrgyzstan, and Moldova are WTO Members, but unlike China, failed to negotiate in their Protocols of Accession any provisions on removal of that status. *See id.*, 5.

For additional articles on trade remedies and NMEs, see, e.g., James J. Nedumpara & Archana Subramanian, *China and the Non-Market Economy Treatment in Anti-Dumping Cases: Can the Surrogate Price Methodology Continue Post-2016?*, 4 JOURNAL OF INTERNATIONAL AND COMPARATIVE LAW issue 2, 253–278 (December 2017); Michael R. Andrusak, *A New Path for U.S. Designation of Nonmarket Economies*, University of Kansas School of Law Independent Study Research Paper (July 2012) (unpublished manuscript); David A. Gantz, *Polyethylene Retail Carrier Bags: Non-Market Economy Status and U.S. Unfair Trade Actions Against Vietnam*, 36 NORTH CAROLINA JOURNAL OF INTERNATIONAL LAW & COMMERCIAL REGULATION 85, 101 (2010); Christopher Blake McDaniel, *Sailing the Seas of Protectionism: The Simultaneous Application of Antidumping and Countervailing Duties to Nonmarket Economies—An Affront to Domestic and International Laws*, 38 GEORGIA JOURNAL OF INTERNATIONAL & COMPARATIVE LAW 741, 742 (2010); Dana Watts, Note, *Fair's Fair: Why Congress Should Amend U.S. Antidumping and Countervailing Duty Laws to Prevent "Double Remedies,"* 1 TRADE, LAW AND DEVELOPMENT number 1, 145–170 (spring 2009); Lawrence L. Herman, *The China Factor: Canada's Trade Remedy Response to China's Economic Challenge*, 33 CANADA—UNITED STATES LAW JOURNAL 25 (2008); Kimberley A. Tracey, *Non-Market Economy Methodology Under U.S. Antidumping Laws: A Protectionist Shield from Chinese Competition*, 15 WTR CURRENTS: INTERNATIONAL TRADE LAW JOURNAL 81, 88 (2006); Sungjoon Cho, *A Dual Catastrophe of Protectionism*, 25 NORTHWESTERN JOURNAL OF INTERNATIONAL LAW & BUSINESS 315, 330 (2005); Alexander Polouktov, *Non-Market Economy Issues in the WTO Anti-Dumping Law and Accession Negotiations: Revival of a Two-Tier Membership*, 36 JOURNAL OF WORLD TRADE 1, 11 (2002); Robert H. Lantz, *The Search for Consistency: Treatment of Nonmarket Economies in Transition Under United States Antidumping and Countervailing Duty Laws*, 10 AMERICAN UNIVERSITY JOURNAL OF INTERNATIONAL LAW & POLICY 993 (1995).

For government reports, see Congressional Research Service Report for Congress, *U.S. Trade Remedy Laws and Nonmarket Economies: A Legal Overview* (2012); United States Government Accountability Office, Report to Congressional Committees, *U.S.—China Trade: Eliminating*

judicial review. DOC will not alter an NME determination unless asked to do so by a respondent or foreign government in the context of an AD-CVD case.

- **Country versus Sector Approaches**

Embedded in the first question is another one: is it reasonable to label an entire economy of a country an NME? The American approach says "yes." Or, as a leading practitioner suggests, are the labels "market" and "non-market" too simplistic, and thus inaccurate, to capture the complexities of an economy?[7] The EU and some other WTO Members take this view. They do not designate an entire economy as "non-market." Their NME AD rules take an industry-by-industry approach, and allow for designation of a specific sector as "non-market." In determining whether an industry is governed by market economy principles, the EU applies five criteria to firms in an industry in question:[8]

(1) Decisions about prices, costs, and inputs are made based on market supply and demand signals.

(2) Accounting records are kept consistently with international standards and audited independently.

(3) Production costs, especially pertaining to asset depreciation, barter trade, and payment of debts, are not distorted.

(4) Bankruptcy and other commercial laws are applicable.

(5) Foreign currency conversions are made at a market rate.

Similarly, since June 2004, Canada has taken an industry-by-industry approach to the question of NME status. Until then, it followed the American economy-wide model.

But, the Canada Border Services Agency (CBSA) observed substantial progress in former Communist countries toward market liberalization, and thus reversed its policy of blanket characterizations and opted to examine individual sectors on a case-by-case basis. Notably, under Canada's *Special Import Measures Act* (*SIMA*), the burden of proof is on a petitioner to prove free market principles do not operate in the sector in question, *i.e.*, it is presumed that market conditions exist in the sector of the subject merchandise, unless Canadian producers of a like product prove otherwise.

Nonmarket Economy Methodology Would Lower Antidumping Duties for Some Chinese Companies (January 2006).

7. *See* GARY HORLICK, WTO AND NAFTA RULES AND DISPUTE RESOLUTION: SELECTED ESSAYS ON ANTIDUMPING, SUBSIDIES, AND OTHER MEASURES 287 (2003).

8. *See* Council Regulation (EC) Number 905/98 of 27 April 1998, *On Protection of Dumped Imports from Countries Not Members of the European Community*, OFFICIAL JOURNAL NUMBER L 128, 18–19, 30 April 1998, which amends Regulation (EC) Number 384/96 of 22 December 1995, *On Protection of Dumped Imports from Countries Not Members of the European Community*, OFFICIAL JOURNAL NUMBER L 56, 6 March 1996, 1–41.

IV. October 2017 DOC Legal Memo Confirming China's NME Status

Significantly, in October 2017, the DOC issued a 205-page legal memo confirming the status of China as an NME for AD-CVD purposes.[9]

United States Department of Commerce, International Trade Administration,

Memorandum on China's Status as a Non-Market Economy,

4–7, 26 October 2017

Executive Summary

The Department of Commerce ("Department") concludes that China is a non-market economy (NME) country because it does not operate sufficiently on market principles to permit the use of Chinese prices and costs for purposes of the Department's antidumping analysis. The basis for the Department's conclusion is that the state's role in the economy and its relationship with markets and the private sector results in fundamental distortions in China's economy.

At its core, the framework of China's economy is set by the Chinese government and the Chinese Communist Party (CCP), which exercise control directly and indirectly over the allocation of resources through instruments such as government ownership and control of key economic actors and government directives. The stated fundamental objective of the government and the CCP is to uphold the "socialist market economy" in which the Chinese government and the CCP direct and channel economic actors to meet the targets of state planning. The Chinese government does not seek economic outcomes that reflect predominantly market forces outside of a larger institutional framework of government and CCP control. In China's economic framework, state planning through industrial policies conveys instructions regarding sector-specific economic objectives, particularly for those sectors deemed strategic and fundamental.

The Chinese government and the CCP's legal and actual ownership and control over key economic actors and institutions pervades China's economy, including the largest financial institutions and leading enterprises in manufacturing, energy, and infrastructure. China's authorities use this control selectively to affect the interaction of supply and demand and accordingly distort the incentives of market actors. This ability to affect these market forces is apparent in crucial facets of the economy, from the formation of exchange rates and input prices to the movement of labor, the use of land, the allocation of domestic and foreign investment, and market entry

---

9. The Memorandum is A-570-053 Investigation, Public Document E&C VI: MJH/TB, from Leah Wils-Owens, Office of Policy, Enforcement & Compliance, for Gary Taverman, Deputy Assistant Secretary, for Antidumping and Countervailing Duty Operations, https://enforcement.trade .gov/download/prc-nme-status/prc-nme-review-final-103017.pdf.

and exit. Because of the significant distortions arising from China's institutional structure and the control the government and the CCP exercise through that structure, the Department finds that China remains a NME country for purposes of the U.S. antidumping law.

The Department's overall conclusion is based upon its analysis of six factors established in U.S. law. In determining whether a country is an NME under Section 771(18)(A) of the *Tariff Act of 1930*, Section 771(18)(B) requires that the Department take into account (1) the extent to which the currency of the foreign country is convertible into the currency of other countries; (2) the extent to which wage rates in the foreign country are determined by free bargaining between labor and management; (3) the extent to which joint ventures or other investments by firms of other foreign countries are permitted in the foreign country; (4) the extent of government ownership or control of the means of production; (5) the extent of government control over the allocation of resources and over the price and output decisions of enterprises; and (6) such other factors as the administering authority considers appropriate.

Under Factor 1, with respect to currency convertibility, the Department observes that the *renminbi* (*RMB*) is convertible into foreign currencies for trade purposes, the Chinese government has made market-oriented modifications to its capital account and exchange rate system, and has taken steps to develop its foreign exchange (FOREX) market. However, the Chinese government still maintains significant restrictions on capital account transactions and intervenes considerably in onshore and offshore FOREX markets. The Chinese government also maintains approval requirements for all major capital account transactions; does not disclose the weights attached to price quotes that are used to calculate the central parity rate for the *RMB*; and intervenes to limit the extent of price divergence between the onshore and offshore FOREX markets.

Under Factor 2, the Department observes variability in wages across regions, sectors, and enterprises in China. However, the Department continues to find significant institutional constraints on the extent to which wage rates are determined through free bargaining between labor and management. The Chinese government prohibits the formation of independent trade unions to represent labor, and workers do not have the legal right to strike, which is an important lever in collective action and negotiation with management over wages. Labor unions are under the control and direction of the All-China Federation of Trade Unions (ACFTU), a government-affiliated and CCP organ. Certain legal remedies exist for an individual to challenge labor contract and wage-related violations in particular cases; however, significant institutional barriers exist that limit their effectiveness. In addition, government restrictions on labor mobility imposed by the *hukou* (household registration) system continue to inhibit and guide labor flows, causing distortions on the supply side of the labor market.

Under Factor 3, the Department finds that the Chinese government's foreign investment regime is particularly restrictive relative to that of other major economies. Despite some government efforts to streamline procedures, China continues to impose significant barriers to foreign investment, including equity limits and local partner requirements, opaque approval and regulatory procedures, and technology transfer and localization requirements. It is the Chinese government's foreign investment regime, not the market primarily, that channels foreign investment to sectors and technologies the Chinese government determines to support, while limiting foreign investment in those sectors that the Chinese government finds strategically important to maintain under its control alone.

Under Factor 4, the Department finds that the Chinese government continues to exert significant ownership and control over the means of production, as demonstrated by (1) the role and prevalence of state-invested enterprises (SIEs)[1] throughout the enterprise sector and (2) the system of land ownership and land-use rights. [Footnote 1 to this sentence explains: "This determination uses the term 'state-invested enterprise' or 'SIE' when referring to an enterprise in which the Government of China has any ownership stake. Though the term generally has the same meaning as 'state-owned enterprise' or 'SOE,' the definition of 'SOE' sometimes varies depending on the context in which it is used, and the Department has adopted the term 'SIE' to avoid confusion. This determination will use the term 'SOE' when citing others' use of that term. The Department used the same approach in its *Memorandum on Public Bodies, Section 129 Proceeding: United States — Countervailing Duty Measures on Certain Products from the People's Republic of China* (WTO/DS437), October 15, 2015."]

The prevalence of SIEs in China's economy is significant, and their relative "economic weight" is substantial in comparison with other major economies. The size of the SIE sector may also understate the actual extent of government ownership and control. The Chinese government allocates resources to SIEs in what it deems strategically important sectors, such that SIEs are not strictly disciplined by market principles of supply and demand. At the same time, however, the government requires that SIEs undertake large-scale investments to help stabilize China's macro-economy. The government also intervenes extensively in the enterprise sector to shield SIEs from the consequences of economic failure, facilitates mergers and acquisitions to achieve government, not enterprise, objectives, and enables the rise of large enterprise groups under government ownership and control. An important channel for government influence over firm decision-making is the CCP's ability to appoint key personnel in enterprises and participate in corporate decision-making through Party Committees in those enterprises.

The Chinese government exercises significant control over land, another key means of production analyzed under Factor 4. All land in China is property of the state, as either collectively-owned rural land or state-owned urban land. Because the government controls rural land acquisition and monopolizes the distribution of urban land-use rights, the government remains the final arbiter of who uses the land and for what purpose. Government decisions in distributing land-use rights are informed, on one hand, by incentives to generate revenue for local governments, and on the other, by national policies that allocate construction quotas and restrict the use of arable land for non-farming purposes. Land-use rights holders, in turn, face limits with respect to the tenure and the scope of use. Rural land-use rights holders face the additional challenges of incomplete documentation and inadequate compensation for the loss of use rights. The result of these dynamics is an inefficient land market in which rural and urban land are segmented and large swathes of land are misallocated either to small farm plots or to underutilized urban infrastructure.

Under Factor 5, the Department finds that the Chinese government plays a significant role in resource allocations. State planning remains an important feature of the Chinese government's industrial policies, as evidenced by formal mechanisms of plan formulation, tasking, and review, and the scope and specificity of sectoral-level plans. Various institutions participate in plan formulation and execution, including central agencies with legislative and regulatory authority, thousands of local government authorities, various organs of the CCP, and the enterprise sector. The Chinese government employs numerous mechanisms to implement industrial policy objectives, including, *inter alia*, investment approvals, access standards, guidance catalogues, financial supports, and quantitative restrictions. Science and technology development, industrial restructuring and upgrading, and the geographic distribution of industry are three areas that demonstrate the extent to which the government uses industrial policies to influence economic outcomes.

The Chinese government exerts a high degree of control over prices it deems essential or strategic. Its ability to set and guide factor input prices, in particular, results in distorted costs and prices throughout the economy. In the electricity sector, for example, the government owns the largest grid operators, formally sets prices, and employs "differential pricing" as a policy tool to achieve capacity shedding and other industrial policy objectives.

The financial sector plays a pivotal role in misallocating resources in China's economy. The government retains ownership and control over the largest commercial banks, while the majority of bank and interbank loans, as well as corporate bond transactions, occur between state-owned and -controlled parties. Credit continues to be allocated to SIEs in spite of high levels of corporate debt, giving rise to soft budget constraints and implicit government guarantees that undermine the market-determined pricing of risk. The emerging "shadow banking" sector, in turn, serves largely as a means for state-owned and -controlled parties to lend and borrow capital through opaque institutions and channels outside the formal banking sector. These fundamental distortions permeate throughout China's financial sector.

Under Factor 6, the Department finds China's legal system continues to function as an instrument by which the Chinese government and the CCP can secure discrete economic outcomes, channel broader economic policy, and pursue industrial policy goals. Key legal institutions, such as the courts, are structured to respond to their direction, whether broad or case-specific. Individuals and firms are constrained in their ability to have meaningful independent input into administrative rulemaking or to challenge administrative decisions. As a general matter, to the extent that individuals and firms seek to act independently of government or CCP direction, the legal system does not provide the venue for them to achieve these objectives on a systemic or consistent basis. In addition, firms continue to face challenges in obtaining impartial outcomes, either because of corruption or local protectionism.

After assessing the six factors, the Department finds that the Chinese government continues to maintain and exercise broad discretion to allocate resources with the goal of achieving specific economic outcomes. China's institutional structure and the control the Chinese government and the CCP exercise through that structure result in fundamental economic distortions, such that non-market conditions prevail in the operation of China's economy. These non-market conditions are built upon deeply entrenched institutional and governance features of China's Party-state, and on a legal mandate to "maintain a leading role for the state sector." Accordingly, China is an NME country. It does not operate sufficiently on market principles to permit the use of Chinese prices and costs for purposes of the Department's antidumping analysis.

[China's MOFCOM responded to the DOC Memo with a 3 November 2017 Press Release, calling on the U.S. to "rectify the wrongdoings as soon as possible," and amending the *DSU* complaint against America that it initially lodged in 2016.[10]]

V. Issue 2: Proxy for Normal Value

- **Criteria for Selection of Third (Surrogate) Country and 2014 *Ad Hoc Shrimp* Case**

On the second issue, the proxy used for Normal Value in an NME AD case is a third, or "surrogate," country. Theoretically, recourse to a third country in this instance is the same as when the home market of the exporter is not an NME, but the sales in that market are non-existent, insufficient, or below cost of production (COP). The underlying problem in both cases is home market sales do not afford an adequate basis for comparison with Export Price or Constructed Export Price. Thus, in an NME case, a third country is used.

Specifically, to calculate Normal Value, an administering authority like the DOC takes the factors of production (FOPs) employed in making subject merchandise, such as energy and other utilities, labor, land, human capital, physical capital, raw materials, other representative capital costs, and technology. But, the DOC values them at prices in a market economy country. That market economy is that third country, and the relevant NME AD statute is 19 U.S.C. Section 1677b(c):

   (1) In general. If—

        (A) the subject merchandise is exported from a nonmarket economy country, and

---

10. *Quoted in* Bryce Baschuk, *China Reboots WTO Consultations Over Non-Market Economy Row,* 34 International Trade Reporter (BNA) 1477 (9 November 2017).

(B) the administering authority finds that available information does not permit the normal value of the subject merchandise to be determined under subsection (a),

the administering authority shall determine the normal value of the subject merchandise on the basis of the value of the factors of production utilized in producing the merchandise and to which shall be added an amount for general expenses and profit plus the cost of containers, coverings, and other expenses. Except as provided in paragraph (2), the valuation of the factors of production shall be based on the *best available information* regarding the values of such factors *in a market economy country or countries considered to be appropriate by the administering authority.*

(2) Exception. If the administering authority finds that the available information is *inadequate* for purposes of determining the normal value of subject merchandise under paragraph (1), the administering authority shall determine the normal value on the basis of the price at which merchandise that is—

(A) comparable to the subject merchandise, and

(B) produced *in one or more market economy countries that are at a level of economic development comparable to that of the nonmarket economy country,*

is sold in other countries, including the United States.

(3) Factors of production. For purposes of paragraph (1), the factors of production utilized in producing merchandise include, but are not limited to—

(A) hours of labor required,

(B) quantities of raw materials employed,

(C) amounts of energy and other utilities consumed, and

(D) representative capital cost, including depreciation.

(4) Valuation of factors of production. The administering authority, in valuing factors of production under paragraph (1), shall utilize, to the extent possible, the prices or costs of factors of production *in one or more market economy countries* that are—

(A) at a *level of economic development comparable to that of the nonmarket economy country,* and

(B) *significant producers of comparable merchandise.*

(5) Discretion to disregard certain price or cost values. In valuing the factors of production under paragraph (1) for the subject merchandise, the administering authority may disregard price or cost values without further investigation if the administering authority has determined that broadly available export subsidies existed or particular instances of subsidization occurred

with respect to those price or cost values or if those price or cost values were subject to an antidumping order.[11]

As the italicized language indicates, the statute raises as many questions as it answers, but in brief it directs DOC to value FOPs based on the best available information as to what the values of each pertinent FOP would be in a market economy—that is, in a surrogate country. The DOC tacks on amounts for general expenses, profits, and packing.

There is similarity, conceptually, between this calculation and the calculation of Constructed Value. "Constructed Value" refers to a full account of the COP, plus an amount for profit. Both are "bottom up" calculations, except that all data in the Constructed Value computation are from the home market of the exporter.

How does the DOC choose among multiple possible surrogates for the actual country of the respondent producer-exporter, and obtain these prices from that surrogate? That is, how does it pick the right third country from which to derive data for Normal Value as a proxy for Normal Value in the NME? The authority considers two key factors:

(1) *Production*

What country is a "significant producer" of goods comparable to the subject merchandise?

(2) *Development*

What country is at a "comparable level of economic development" with the NME for which it would serve as a surrogate?

Both criteria leave the authority with plenty of manoeuvring room.

For instance, in the 2014 case of *Ad Hoc Shrimp Trade Action Committee v. United States*, the CIT upheld a decision of the DOC in an Administrative Review to choose Bangladesh instead of the Philippines as the surrogate market economy for Vietnam.[12] U.S. shrimp producers pointed out that differentials in Gross National

---

11. Emphasis added.

12. *See Ad Hoc Shrimp Trade Action Committee v. United States*, CIT Number 12-00314 (Slip Opinion 14–59); Brian Flood, *Trade Court Upholds Dumping Margins For Vietnamese Warmwater Shrimp*, 31 International Trade Reporter 1028 (BNA) (5 June 2014). *See also Vinh Hoan Corporation v. Catfish Farmers of America, et al.* Federal Circuit Number 2015-1344 (12 April 2016) (a case involving an AD duty rate of $0.06 per kilogram on subject merchandise, frozen fish fillets from Vietnam, in which the respondents argued the DOC unfairly inflated the duty rate because of its use of Philippine surrogate data from the World Trade Atlas for byproducts (broken fillets and fish skin and waste) and Bangladeshi surrogate data for overhead expenses; the Supreme Court denied *writ of certiorari*, Number 16-00092, 31 October 2016). In effect, the Courts deferred to DOC expertise.

For another AD NME case in which the CIT upheld the decision of DOC to use Bangladeshi data to value inputs used to make frozen fish fillets, see *Catfish Farmers of America v. United States*, Number 12-00087 (Slip Opinion 15-29, 30 March 2016). The subject merchandise was Vietnamese fillets. The Catfish Farmers of America (a domestic trade group) unsuccessfully argued the Bangladeshi data were unreliable because they included dead or sluggish fish, whereas Vietnamese

Income (GNI) between the Philippines and Vietnam were less than those between Bangladesh and Vietnam, and inferred the DOC should have selected the Philippines as the surrogate. They lost against the DOC argument that Bangladeshi FOP data were of superior quality, being product specific and covering the POR, whereas the Philippine statistics did not include shrimp sizes the respondent sold in the U.S.

As for Bangladeshi labor rates, they were lower than those in the Philippines, hence U.S. shrimp producers did not like the DOC using them: lower Bangladeshi

---

producers used only whole, live fish. The CIT deferred to DOC on the choice of surrogate data source, and consequently AD duties were zero on fillets from Vinh Hoan Corporation, and $0.19 per kilogram (up from $0.03 per kilo) on other Vietnamese producer-exporters. *See* Brian Flood, *Court Sustains Revised Fish Fillet Duties*, 33 International Trade Reporter (BNA) 494 (7 April 2016).

For still another AD NME case in which the CIT approved the DOC's discretion, see *Vulcan Threaded Products Inc. v. United States*, Number 16-00268, Slip Opinion 18-45 (18 April 2018). At issue, as the CIT nicely put it, was:

> What are the limits of agency discretion when evaluating which information to use from an imperfect swirl of economic data? More specifically, did the Department of Commerce . . . choose the "best available information" in this case to calculate what it effectively cost to produce steel threaded rod in China in order to determine whether Chinese manufacturers are "dumping" their products in the United States at below market prices?
>
> . . .
>
> Although Commerce is required to value FOPs using the "best available information," Commerce has discretion to determine what constitutes the best available information. *Id*. at 1293 [*citing Jiaxing Bro. Fastener Co. v. United States*, 822 F.3d 1289 (Fed. Cir. 2016)]. In evaluating the reliability and completeness of the data, Commerce's practice is to "use investigation or review period-wide price averages, prices specific to the input in question, prices that are net of taxes and import duties, prices that are contemporaneous with the period of investigation or review, and publicly available data." Import Admin., U.S. Dep't Commerce, Non–Market Economy Surrogate Country Selection Process, Policy Bulletin 04.1 (2004), https://enforcement.trade.gov/policy/bull04-1.html. This evaluation is a context-specific, industry-specific, and fact-intensive inquiry; as such, "Commerce is required to base surrogate country selection on the facts presented in each case, and not on grounds of perceived tradition. Each administrative review is a separate exercise of Commerce's authority that allows for different conclusions based on different facts in the record." *Jiaxing*, 822 F.3d at 1299. . . .

Threaded steel wire rods from China was the subject merchandise, on which the DOC imposed AD duties ranging from zero to 11.07%. (Such rods are used in construction, specifically, as electrical conduit support, fire protection sprinkler systems, HVAC ductwork, and plumbing pipes. The Chinese producer-exporters included Jiaxing Brother Fastener Co., Ltd., IFI & Morgan Ltd., RMB Fasteners Ltd., and Zhejiang New Oriental Fasteners Co., and RMB Fasteners Ltd.) The domestic petitioner, Vulcan Threaded Products, Inc. of Pelham, Alabama, produced like products, and said those rates were too low, because DOC improperly used surrogate data from Bulgaria to compute Normal Value. Vulcan said DOC should have selected Thailand, not Bulgaria, as the surrogate market economy. Not so, said the CIT. The DOC:

> selected the Bulgarian data, in part, because they were more specific with regard to diameter for steel wire rod. Specifically, the Bulgarian . . . HTS had a separate breakout for wire rod between 14 and 32mm, whereas the Thai HTS only covered the lower range of steel wire rod diameters.

The CIT rejected Vulcan's argument "that the 'paucity' of imports of steel wire rod with diameters of 14mm and greater to Bulgaria invalidates Commerce's rationale for selecting the Bulgarian data," as well as Vulcan's argument that the Thai data were superior to the Bulgarian data because

labor costs meant a lower proxy for Normal Value, a lower dumping margin, and thus a lower AD duty against shrimp imports from Vietnam. The CIT found the Bangladeshi rates were not aberrational, so it was reasonable to rely on them rather than Philippine figures or data from multiple countries.

What metrics define "significant" production? Must the goods be "like," or does mere comparability suffice? What indicators of development define a third country as comparable to the NME—economic variables like *per capita* GDP, or quality of life factors such as education enrollment and doctors per 100,000, or all of the above? Perhaps most importantly, do the answers to such questions change from NME to NME, or over time with respect to a particular NME?

- **Example of 2014 *Jinan Yipin* Corporation Case**

The 2014 CIT case of *Jinan Yipin Corp., Ltd. v. United States* illustrates the basic principles articulated above.[13] Did the DOC used the correct surrogate data to value FOPs in its remand determination of AD duty rates for the subject merchandise, Chinese fresh garlic? The CIT answered "yes," upholding the DOC determination, with the result the three Chinese investigated companies—Jinan Yipin Corp.,

---

"Bulgarian data include steel wire rod with a carbon content of less than 0.25 percent whereas the Thai data only includes steel wire rod with a carbon content of 0.23 percent or less." The CIT held the DOC's use of Bulgarian surrogate data was supported by substantial evidence, and thus reasonable. *See also* Brian Flood, *Duties on Chinese Steel Rod Won't Be Raised, Court Rules*, 35 International Trade Reporter (BNA) 577 (26 April 2018) (discussing this case).

And, yet another AD NME case in which the CIT had to evaluate whether the DOC's selection of surrogate data from one country over another is *Fine Furniture (Shanghai) Ltd. v. United States* (Number 16-00145, 26 November 2018). The subject merchandise was multi-layered hardwood flooring from China entered into the U.S. between December 2013 and November 2014. The CIT upheld the 17.37% AD duty rate DOC computed on the basis of surrogate data from Romania, against claims by the Chinese respondent producer-exporter, Fine Furniture (Shanghai) Ltd. that DOC should have used data from Thailand. The CIT held there was substantial evidence to support the DOC findings that, with respect to the inputs the respondent used to make the subject merchandise: (1) Romanian labor data were more industry-specific than Thai labor data, and also were contemporaneous with the POR, whereas Thai data were non-contemporaneous; (2) Romanian single-tariff electricity data, and Romanian raw materials (lumber, glue, and veneers), were more specific to the subject merchandise produced in China than Thai electricity and raw materials data. The CIT also noted approvingly the equal weighting DOC gives to specificity and contemporaneity. *See also* Brian Flood, *Chinese Flooring Exporters Lose Challenge to U.S. Duties*, 35 International Trade Reporter (BNA) (29 November 2018) (summarizing this case).

13. *See* Number 06-00189 (Slip Opinion 14-34, 28 March 2014); Brian Flood, *Court Upholds Remand Results In Chinese Garlic Dumping Case*, 31 International Trade Reporter (BNA) 634 (3 April 2014).

The U.S. has imposed AD duties on fresh Chinese garlic since 1994. For another CIT case involving a dispute about how DOC computed surrogate labor costs (*i.e.*, the surrogate wage rate) connected with raw garlic production, see *Shenzhen Xinboda Indust. Co. v. United States*, Number 11-00267 (30 January 2019); Brian Flood, *Chinese Garlic Exporter Escapes Duties*, Bloomberg Law International Trade News (31 January 2019). After a periodic review of fresh garlic entries from November 2008-October 2009, DOC computed rates as high as $4.71 per kg. Shenzhen Xinboda objected to the rate DOC assigned its merchandise, $0.06 per kg. The CIT upheld a second remand decision the DOC made under protest to slash the AD duty rate to zero.

Linshu Dading Private Agricultural Products Co., and Sunny Import and Export Co.—retained the revised AD duty rates the DOC calculated on remand, which were *de minimis* or zero.

American producers of garlic—Christopher Ranch LLC, The Garlic Co., Valley Garlic and Vessey and Co, and the Fresh Garlic Producers Association—obviously hoped for a higher AD duty rate to be imposed on the Chinese imports. The CIT upheld the FOP surrogate values the DOC used for labor, cardboard packing cartons, and plastic jars and lids. But, what about the garlic itself?

The American producers argued the DOC was wrong to use surrogate FOP data from India, specifically, the Indian Agricultural Marketing Information Network (Agmarknet). Initially, the DOC used data for a single type of garlic, namely, large bulb, grown in five Indian States under sunlight. The American producers said the DOC failed to prove large-bulb sunlit grown garlic was similar to the subject merchandise, and in an earlier decision, the CIT agreed, remanding the case to the DOC. Then, the CIT said the Indian data included post-harvest garlic, meaning that the data reflected a final product, not an intermediate input like some of the subject merchandise.

On remand, the DOC used Agmarknet data for an average of six types of garlic grown in the five Indian states. Again the American producers complained, saying only three of the Indian garlic categories were comparable to the subject merchandise, which was large-bulb garlic, so the DOC should have excluded the three garlic bulb types with a diameter of less than 50 centimeters. This time, the CIT sided with the DOC. True, "in principle" the American producers were correct, but "perfect data is [*sic*] virtually non-existent in the real world." To do what the producers wanted—filtering the Indian data further—would distort the dumping margin calculation. Indeed, their argument was self-interested: the three categories of Indian garlic they sought to exclude from the surrogate Normal Value computation were the cheapest ones, so with their exclusion, the dumping margin would be widened, and the AD duty higher.

- **Problem of Computing Labor Costs, 2010 *Dorbest*, 2011 *Shandong*, and *Camau Frozen Seafood* Cases**

Computing labor costs in NME cases has provoked controversy. In establishing Normal Value in an NME AD case, the DOC must estimate them using a surrogate. That is because in an NME, market forces of supply and demand do not set wage rates. Rather, they are set or influenced by the government. Until June 2011, the DOC used a multivariable regression model to estimate the world-wide relationship between *per capita* GDP and hourly manufacturing wages. Estimating the parameters of this model meant the DOC looked at data from several surrogate market economies.

Specifically, the DOC used multi-country averaging of data from market economies, plugging these data into its regression model, to yield a surrogate for the cost of labor in an NME. The DOC thought this approach desirable, because it minimized variation in wages across countries. The DOC pointed out there is a considerable variability in wage rates across countries that are comparable economically. So, relying on wage rate data from a single country might distort the surrogate for NME labor costs and, in turn, distort the computation of Normal Value.

However, in *Dorbest Ltd. v. United States*, 604 F.3d 1363, 1372 (Fed. Cir. 2010), the Federal Circuit invalidated the regulation under which the DOC computed labor costs (19 C.F.R. Section 351.408(c)(3)). The DOC was compelled to come up with a better manner to account for all direct and indirect labor costs in an NME than obtaining data from multiple countries and plugging those numbers into a regression model. The DOC resorted to the manner in which it computes a proxy for the other (non-labor) factors of a production in an NME, namely, obtain industry-specific data from one surrogate market economy. Thus, in response to *Dorbest*, the DOC relies on a single surrogate for wages.

The April 2011 CIT decision in *Shandong Rongxin Import & Export Co. Ltd.*, in which the CIT held invalid the reliance by the DOC solely on exports to define "significant producer," reinforced the June 2011 change in methodology the DOC uses for estimating labor costs.[14] For the DOC to comply with *Dorbest* and *Shandong* would have required the DOC to base an average wage calculation on a data from such a small pool of countries that the DOC could not achieve the goal of minimizing variability in wages across countries. The DOC realized it might as well pick a primary surrogate market economy and use data from it for all factors of production. The ILO publishes these data in Chapter 6A of its *Yearbook of Labor Statistics*. The Chapter 6A data cover all costs related to labor: wages, benefits, housing, training, and other items. (In contrast, Chapter 5B data encompass only direct compensation and bonuses.)

So, under its new—as of June 2011—labor valuation methodology, the DOC decided to allow use of a single surrogate country from which to extract data as a proxy for labor costs in an NME. Yet, the single-country surrogate approach engendered controversy. In the July 2013 case of *Camau Frozen Seafood Processing Imp. Exp. Corp. v. United States*, the CIT considered an NME AD case involving frozen warm water shrimp from Vietnam.[15] In a review of an AD order against this subject merchandise, the DOC valued Vietnamese labor using one data set: from the Bangladesh Bureau of Statistics (BBS). However, data from the Philippines were available, published in the ILO *Yearbook of Labor Statistics*, and Philippine wage rates were considerably higher than Bangladeshi ones.

The CIT appreciated the losing argument of the DOC: averaging would not eliminate completely the wide distortion, because Bangladeshi and Philippine wage levels were so disparate, and were collected at different levels of aggregation. But, held the CIT, the DOC failed to justify its choice of one data set over another. Ironically,

---

14. *See* CIT Number 09-00316 (Slip Opinion 11-45 (21 April 2011).
15. *See* CIT Number 11-00399 (Slip Opinion 13-95 (31 July 2013).

in an earlier Administrative Review of the same order, the DOC had used Philippine data from the ILO *Yearbook*. It seemed the DOC choose expedience over accuracy: in this Review, there were no Bangladeshi data published in the ILO *Yearbook*, so the DOC turned to the BBS. In other words, the DOC failed to show the Bangladeshi wage rates were the best available information to use as a surrogate value for Vietnamese labor costs.

- **Problem of Input Valuation and August 2013 85% Rule**

Also provoking controversy is the valuation of inputs in an NME AD proceeding. To calculate Normal Value in an NME case, the DOC must value the factors of production of the NME respondent producer-exporter. It does so using surrogate values from a market economy that is (1) at a comparable level of economic development as the NME in question, and (2) a significant producer of the input in question.[16]

At issue is what happens when a respondent producer-exporter buys inputs during the POI or POR from a market economy supplier, and pays for the inputs with the currency of that market economy (or other hard currency). Is the price paid by the respondent the best available information to value the input purchased, and thus include in Normal Value? On the one hand, the input comes from a market economy supplier. On the other hand, market economy purchases of the input might not account for a meaningful amount, or substantially all, of the purchases of that input.

The long-standing practice of the DOC, under 19 C.F.R. Section 351.408(c)(1), was to take the weighted-average price the NME respondent pays to the market economy supplier as the value for each input in question. However, suppose some part of an input comes from a market economy supplier, and some other part is sourced from a supplier in the NME. Or, suppose the respondent gets the input from multiple sources: some market economy suppliers, and some NME suppliers. Then, the DOC uses the weighted-average market economy purchase price paid for the input by the respondent to the market economy supplier as the price for the entire input (in effect, disregarding the price associated with the portion of the input from the NME supplier). But, the DOC does so only if the volume of the market economy input as a share of total purchases by the respondent of inputs from all sources is "meaningful."

In 2006, the DOC defined "meaningful" via a rebuttable presumption: market economy input prices represent the best available information to value the entirety of an input if the total volume of the input the respondent purchases from all market economy suppliers exceeds 33% of the total quantity of the input it purchased from all sources (market economy and NME suppliers). If this threshold is not met, then the DOC uses as the value of the input the weighted average of the maker

---

16. Of course, the DOC does not accept as a surrogate a market economy input purchase price if (1) that input itself may have been dumped, (2) is from a country it suspects provides general export subsidies, (3) does not reflect *bona fide* sales, or (4) is otherwise not acceptable in a dumping margin calculation.

economy purchase price and an appropriate surrogate value based on the relative amounts of the input purchased in the NME and imported from other countries.

In July 2012, the DOC issued a proposed new threshold: re-defining "meaningful" as "substantially all," and equating the latter with 85%. Moreover, it is not enough for an input to be purchased through a market economy supplier. The input must actually be produced in a market economy country. The DOC issued the rule in final form in August, with effect for all NME cases on or after 1 September 2013.[17] The rule affects any entity producing merchandise in an NME exported to the U.S. that is the target of an AD investigation or order. Typically, American companies are not among such entities.

So, under the August 2012 "85% Input Rule," "substantially all" of an input, defined as 85% of the input, must be purchased by the NME respondent producer-exporter from 1 or more market economy suppliers if the DOC is to use the purchase price paid for the input as the value for the input and, in turn, to include that value in the pertinent factor of production. Otherwise, the DOC selects a surrogate value, one of its own choosing from a different market economy supplier. The DOC justified the change by saying if only 33% of the purchases by an NME respondent are from market economy suppliers, then that quantity is too small to be sufficiently representative of the input prices the respondent would pay to buy all of the input from market economy suppliers.

Practically speaking, the DOC uses the weighted-average purchase price paid to a market economy supplier to value an input bought from both market and NME sources only if 85% or more of the input purchases come from market economy suppliers (whether in one or multiple market economies). Mathematically:

$$85\% = \frac{\text{Volume of Input Purchased from Foreign Market Economy Suppliers}}{\text{Total Purchases of the Input from all Sources, both NME suppliers and Foreign Market Suppliers}}$$

As under the 33% threshold, if the 85% threshold is not met, then the DOC uses a weighted average of market purchase prices and surrogate values for NME purchase prices. In brief, only if 85% of the total purchased volume of an input into subject merchandise is obtained from a market economy supplier will the DOC accept the purchase price paid by the respondent to the supplier as the accurate value of the input.[18]

---

17. *See* 78 Federal Register 46,799 (2 August 2013).

18. *See* Court Number 12-00039 (2 February 2015); Brian Flood, *Trade Court Affirms Dumping Rate On Chinese Tapered Roller Bearings*, 32 International Trade Reporter (BNA) 350 (12 February 2015). The 2013 *Peer Bearing* case, concerning Constructed Export Price, is discussed in a separate Chapter.

As in many instances of shifts in American trade policy, concern about China, and to a lesser degree, Vietnam, explains the increased threshold. The DOC said 85% would provide greater accuracy in the calculation of a proxy for Normal Value in NME AD cases. The DOC was worried NME input prices were unreliable because of cost or supply distortions. Possibly, some NME input suppliers in countries like China and Vietnam artificially lowered the price of the inputs they sold to respondents. With lower input prices, a respondent could claim lower costs of production, and thus lower figures for the proxy for Normal Value, and in turn, lessen or eliminate a dumping margin and consequent AD duty.

To be sure, the higher threshold increases the chance of a higher dumping margin. That is because the DOC is less likely to rely on the costs incurred by an NME respondent producer-exporter in the NME or that respondent's own market economy suppliers, and more likely to use surrogate values from a market economy. Those values are higher than the respondent's costs, leading to a higher figure for Normal Value, and thus a wider dumping margin.

- **Application of 33% Rule and 2015 *Peer Bearing* Case**

The 2015 CIT case of *Changshan Peer Bearing Co., Ltd. v. United States* both illustrates the 33% rule and intimates some flexibility, if not uncertainty, about it. In an Administrative Review, the DOC assigned Changshan, a Chinese producer of tapered roller bearings, a 14.98% AD duty based on valuing an important input into the roller bearings—so called "bearing quality alloy steel bar"—using surrogate import data from India. The average unit value for the Indian data was much higher than that for purchases Changshan made from market economy suppliers. But, Changshan made those purchases in the latter part of the POR. The Indian surrogate data covered the time before the Swedish conglomerate AB SKF bought Changshan. Changshan argued the DOC should have used prices for steel bar charged by market suppliers, after the Swedish company acquired it. Using Indian data artificially inflated the dumping margin, because it boosted the proxy for Normal Value (*i.e.*, Constructed Value with surrogate data from a Third Country) against which the DOC compared subject merchandise sale prices in the U.S.

The DOC defended its use of Indian surrogate data, invoking the 33% rule: Changshan's market economy purchases of steel bar failed to comprise at least 33% of its total purchases of that input during the POR. The CIT rejected the 33% rule without more explanation, saying that this rule, which really was a practice the DOC concocted, "is not, by itself, sufficient to accomplish a comparison of the two data sources for the purpose of determining the most suitable surrogate value for the steel bar input." Fortunately for the DOC (after the CIT remanded the case to it in January 2014), it provided additional reasoning: the market economy purchases were not the BIA, because they (1) came only from the period after Changshan was acquired by the Swedish firm, *i.e.*, they covered only post-, not pre-acquisition production, (2) were not publicly available, (3) were not broad-based market averages, and (4) were not from a country that was economically comparable to China.

The last reason was puzzling: if the DOC was treating China as an NME, then how could it expect the input purchases to be from a country economically akin to China, and still call them market economy ones? Nevertheless, the CIT deferred to the discretion of the DOC, saying its explanation of the use of Indian surrogate data was adequate, and affirmed the 14.98% rate.

• **Surrogate Data for Packing and 2013 *Taian Ziyang* Case**

Surrogate data may be used even for items like packing. In the 2013 case of *Taian Ziyang Food Co. Ltd. v. United States*, the CIT upheld the determination of the DOC in a ninth Administrative Review of an AD order against fresh garlic from China.[19] At issue in the case was whether the DOC was correct to use price quotas from India on the value of cardboard packing cartons and plastic jars and lids use to ship fresh garlic.

One source, favored by domestic American producers, was Indian import statistics from the *World Trade Atlas*. (Use of such statistics would boost the surrogate for Normal Value, exacerbate the dumping margin, and thus lead to a higher AD duty on their Chinese competitors.) The other source, used by the DOC, was price quotes from India submitted by the Chinese that were subject to the AD order. Both sources were distorted in that they included freight charges, and the price quotes for the plastic jars and lids were not contemporaneous with the period of the Administrative Review.

Nevertheless, the CIT agreed with the DOC: the price quotes from India were more accurate surrogate data than figures about India from the *Atlas*, because they were more specific to the subject merchandise, Chinese fresh garlic.

• **Surrogate Data for International Freight Expenses and 2017 *American Tubular Products* Case**

Surrogate data also may be used for international freight expenses. In the 2017 case of *American Tubular Products, LLC v. United States*, the Federal Circuit upheld a dumping margin of 137.62% against oil country tubular goods (OCTG), which are seamless rolled steel products that have a drill pipe, casing, and tube, made in China by Jiangsu Chengde Steel Tube Share and imported into America by American Tubular Products.[20] Jiangsu said it paid international freight expenses to market economy carriers, and that the prices were at market economy rates. Not true, said the DOC, and the Court agreed.

In fact, Jiangsu paid freight charges to a freight forwarder in China, which then paid the agents located in China of Korean carriers. So, Jiangsu could not overcome the presumption that government action—the first two transactions, from Chengdu to the freight forwarder, and from the forwarder to the agents—distorted the prices it paid for freight.

---

19. *See* Number 05-00399 (Slip Opinion 13-80, 24 June 2013).

20. *See* Number 2016-11272/13/17 (13 February 2017); Rossella Brevetti, *Appeals Court Backs Steep Dumping Rate on Steel Tubing*, 34 International Trade Reporter (BNA) 283 (16 February 2017).

- **Reliability of Surrogate Data and 2013 *Blue Mushroom* Case**

As per the holding of the CIT in the 2013 case of *Blue Field (Sichuan) Foods Industrial Company v. United States*, surrogate data must be reliable and non-distortive.[21] Mushrooms were the subject merchandise imported by Blue Field. Its American competitor, Monterey Mushrooms, Inc., was successful in obtaining an AD order against the imports. After the 11th Administrative Review, the AD duty rate was 2.17%. But, in the 12th Administrative Review, the DOC assigned a whopping 308.33% rate. The difference was attributable to use by the DOC of mushroom price data from Colombia. Those data included rice straw and cow manure, which are inputs into mushrooms.

Blue Field successfully argued the surrogate values for these inputs were aberrationally high. For rice straw, prices in India, Indonesia, and the U.S. varied from $10 to $90.08 per metric ton. The Colombian data the DOC used was $1,350.00 per metric ton, a surrogate value double the price of rice in Colombia. The CIT declared that nonsense. Rice straw, which is a low-cost by-product of rice grain cultivation, should be cheaper than the primary good, rice. As for cow manure, alternative proposed prices from the Philippines Blue Field were cheaper than those from Colombia. The DOC hypocritically rejected the Philippine data, saying it included chicken and swine manure. Yet, the Colombian surrogate contained mixed fertilizer. Not surprisingly, the CIT reminded the DOC its determinations must be based on substantial evidence, and remanded the case to the agency to re-compute the dumping margin.

- **Choice between Imperfect Surrogate Data Sets and 2014 *Lifestyle* Case**

In some NME AD cases, the DOC is faced with a devil's choice, namely, picking the better of two imperfect data sets from which to derive surrogate data. So, the DOC is not, and cannot be, held to a standard of perfection. The DOC is expected to provide a "reasonable" explanation as to why it opts for one data set over another.[22]

---

21. *See* Number 12-00320 (Slip Opinion 13-142, 14 November 2013); Brian Flood, Court Faults *Commerce on Surrogate Values For Chinese Mushroom Dumping Calculations*, 30 International Trade Reporter (BNA) 1885 (5 December 2013).

22. *Jiaxing Brother Fastener Co. v. United States*, CIT, Number 12-00384 (Slip Opinion 14-115, 25 September 2014); Brian Flood, *Court Sustains Antidumping Duty Rate For Chinese Steel Threaded Rod Imports*, 31 International Trade Reporter (BNA) 1760 (2 October 2014).

In this dispute, the DOC selected surrogate data from Thailand over that from the Philippines to value overhead, general, and administrative expenses, and profit ratios, for steel threaded rod (as distinct from steel wire garment hangers) from two Chinese producer-exporters, Jiaxing Brother Fastener Company, Ltd. and RMB Fasteners, Ltd. They preferred the Philippine data, arguing there were more financial statements to support those data, and that only one Thai surrogate company made articles akin to the subject merchandise. The DOC admitted the shortcomings in the Thai data, but successfully pointed to virtues outweighing them: the carbon content of the steel in the Thai data was closer to that of the subject merchandise than the Philippine data, and nearly all of the manufacturing costs and Normal Value of the subject merchandise consisted of steel inputs. Finding the DOC explanation reasonable, the CIT sustained the 19.68 AD duty on subject merchandise.

In *Lifestyle Enterprises, Inc. v. United States*, the Federal Circuit sided with the DOC and Chinese respondent, Guangdong Yihua Timber Industry Company, overturning a ruling by the CIT.[23] The subject merchandise was wooden bedroom furniture, and the Philippines was the surrogate country. In its preliminary Administrative Review findings, the DOC computed a 40.74% dumping margin using Philippines National Statistics Office data. These data were on imports of several types of wood into the Philippines based on dollars-per-volume. Gunagdong Yihua challenged the preliminary results. The DOC recalculated the margin at 29.89% using weight-based data on Philippine wood imports published in the *World Trade Atlas* on a price-per-weight basis.

The CIT said the DOC failed to justify its choice between two imperfect data sets. The CIT said weight-based data understated the surrogate value of the wood input Guangdong Yihua used in its furniture. Those data did not reflect the fact Gunagdong Yihua would have to pay a higher price per kilogram for the low-moisture, kiln-dried wood it used. Thus, said the CIT, weight-based data artificially deflated Normal Value of subject merchandise. The CIT told the DOC to switch back to volume-based data, which it did under protest, resulting in a higher 40.74% dumping margin.

The Federal Circuit over-ruled the CIT. The Federal Circuit said the DOC adequately explained why weight-based data were preferable to volume-based Philippine import data. The volume-based data preferred by the CIT were unreliable, because importers reported weight and value, but not always volume. The Statistics Office had to plug missing volume information with a conversion factor that was the same for all types of imported wood. That factor was based on a presumptive wood density, which in reality was far higher than the density of the wood the respondent used in its furniture. The Federal Circuit said the CIT erred in asserting its judgment as to the best data over that of the DOC, and reinstated the original margin. On remand, the DOC recomputed an AD margin of 21.53%, using weight-based data, and the CIT upheld the new margin.[24]

- **Surrogate Data versus Market Economy Purchases and 2014 *Hartford Fire* Case**

Suppose a respondent in an NME AD case claims its purchases of inputs were from market economy suppliers. Must the DOC use only market economy purchases to value those inputs, or may the DOC look to surrogate data from a third country? The 2014 case of *Hartford Fire Insurance Company v. United States* raised this issue, and the Federal Circuit ruled the DOC has the discretion to use surrogate

---

23. *See Lifestyle Enterprises, Inc. v. United States*, Federal Circuit Number 2013-1323 (2 June 2014); Brian Flood, *Federal Circuit Returns Furniture Case To Commerce, Faulting Trade Court Ruling*, 31 International Trade Reporter (BNA) 1023 (5 June 2014).

24. *See Lifestyle Enterprises, Inc. v. United States*, CIT Number 09-00378 (Slip Opinion 14-125, 28 October 2014); Brian Flood, *Court Affirms Antidumping Duty Rate For Chinese Furniture Manufacturer*, 31 International Trade Reporter (BNA) 1963 (6 November 2014).

data.[25] The subject merchandise was wooden bedroom furniture from China, on which AD duties had been imposed since 2005. Representing domestic producers of like products were the American Furniture Manufacturers Committee for Legal Trade and the Vaughan-Bassett Furniture Company, Inc. (collectively, AFMC). Dalian Huafeng Furniture Group Co. Ltd. was the producer-exporter of subject merchandise, and the importer of this merchandise was Home Meridian International, Inc. (collectively, Huafeng).

Huafeng was a mandatory respondent. It gave the DOC data on its purchases of wood that it used to make furniture. Those input purchases, said Huafeng, were from market economy suppliers. When these market price data were used to compute the dumping margin, the result was 11.79%. The DOC rejected these data, opting for 2009 import data from the Philippines. That is, the DOC used surrogate values to gauge the price of the wood inputs Huafeng used. Unsurprisingly, the result was a higher Normal Value than with the data Huafeng presented, and so a higher dumping margin—41.75%.

For two reasons, the DOC disregarded the market economy purchases. First, the surrogate data were contemporaneous with the POR of the Administrative Review, 1 January to 31 December 2009. The market data Huafeng submitted were from 2008, not 2009. Second, Huafeng could not prove 100% of the wood inputs it used to make subject merchandise came from market suppliers at market economy prices. So, said the DOC, the Philippine surrogate data were the "best available information" under 19 U.S.C. Section 1677b(c)(1)(B).

In coming to this conclusion, the DOC interpreted its own regulation, which stated it "*normally* will use the price [of an input, *e.g.*, of wood] paid [by the respondent, *e.g.*, Huafeng] to the market supplier."[26] "Normally" does not mean "invariably," The DOC has discretion not to use market economy data, if it believes other data are the best information available. The Federal Circuit agreed, thus overruling a CIT decision in favor of Huafeng and the 11.79% margin, and reinstating the 41.75% margin. In sum, there is no mandate that the DOC use only market economy purchase price data for inputs when valuing those inputs; it can use surrogate data, instead.

- **Embedded Product Classification Issue and 2018 *Jinko Solar* Case**

In some NME AD cases, not only the choice of surrogate country, but also the product classification, may be at issue, in respect of establishing an appropriate surrogate for Normal Value. That is, the embedded in the choice of a third country is

---

25. *See* Number 2013-1585 (1 December 2014); Rossella Brevetti, *Appeals Court Backs Commerce Remand Results in Valuing Inputs for Furniture*, 31 International Trade Reporter (BNA) 2096 (4 December 2014).

26. 19 C.F.R. § 351.408(c)(1) (emphasis added). The DOC also pointed to its rules, *Antidumping Methodologies: Market Economy Inputs, Expected Non-Market Economy Wages, Duty Drawback; and Request for Comments*, 71 Federal Register 61,716 (19 October 2006).

a question of product classification of what would be in a non-NME AD case the identification of foreign like product for which Normal Value is measured.

For example, in *Jinko Solar Co. Ltd. v. United States*, the CIT reviewed AD margins for Changzhou Trina Solar Energy Co. Ltd. and Renesola Jiangsu Ltd. of 78.42% and 26.71%, respectively, on scrapped solar cells (*i.e.*, solar cells that are broken during the manufacturing process and sold as scrap for recycling or reprocessing) from China.[27] SolarWorld Americas Inc., a domestic producer, objected to the use by the DOC of South African import data to value the scrapped cells, namely, its use of the value of used batteries imported into South Africa, a market economy, as a proxy for the value of scrap cells from China, an NME. The DOC relied on HTS Sub-Heading 8548.10, "Waste and scrap of primary cells, primary batteries and electric storage batteries; spent primary cells, spent primary and electric storage batteries."

SolarWorld said the better proxy for Normal Value was to value the cells using the value of polysilicon, because polysilicon is the principal raw material that is recovered from scrapped cells. SolarWorld pointed to import data from Thailand under HTS Sub-Heading 2804.69, which covers imports of polysilicon of less than 99.99% purity. To be sure, this Sub-Heading does not reference scrap metals; it concerns only silicon. But, Sub-Heading 8548.19 has nothing to do with photovoltaic cells, whereas 2804.69 is specific to the primary raw material of which the scrap by-product of a solar cell consists.

To be sure, neither of the two Sub-Headings exactly covered scrapped solar cells. The DOC simply analogized those cells to batteries based on nature, composition, and function. Both crapped solar cells and batteries are engineered products comprised of similar components, and both are used to generate electricity. And, the DOC said Sub-Heading 8548.10 covers scrap materials, whereas 2804.69 does not.

The CIT disagreed, saying the word "scrap" in Sub-Heading 8548.10, and the ability of a product to generate electricity, do not approximate the value of a scrapped solar cell as closely as does the main component of that cell, polysilicon. After re-calculating the AD margins using Sub-Heading 2804.69, the DOC determined they remained unchanged. Still, domestic solar producers found the case a useful precedent for future NME AD actions they might launch.

VI. Constructed Value, Surrogate Input Values, and 2015 *TPEA*

When in June 2015 via the *TPEA* Congress extended the *GSP* and *AGOA*, reauthorized TAA, and granted the President TPA, it also amended AD and CVD law in anticipation that China would no longer be treated as an NME after 11

---

27. *See* Slip Opinion 18-61, Number 15-00080 (25 May 2018); Rossella Brevetti, *Trade Court Backs High Duty Rates in Solar Ruling*, 35 International Trade Reporter (BNA) 725 (31 May 2018).

December 2016, as per its 11 December 2001 WTO accession commitments, specifically Article 15(a)(ii) of its *Accession Protocol*. The thrust of those amendments was to give the DOC broader discretion in interpreting AD-CVD rules than it might otherwise have under Federal Circuit and CIT jurisprudence—and, therefore, allow it to put high remedial duties on Chinese merchandise despite its transition to market economy status.[28] In this respect, two such amendments were particularly important.

First, Section 504 of the *TPEA* allowed DOC to use Constructed Value whenever it finds a "particular market situation" exists in the home market of a respondent producer-exporter and a third country market that prevents DOC from computing Normal Value or Third Country Price, respectively. "Particular market situation" is undefined in the pertinent provision of the *Tariff Act of 1930*, Section 773, and the *TPEA* did not insert a definition. (Article 2:2 of the WTO *Antidumping Agreement* uses the same phrase, "particular market situation . . . in the domestic market of the exporting country," also without definition.) To the contrary, the *TPEA* amended the Section to make it easier for DOC to declare a "particular market situation" exists, reject Normal Value based on the producer-exporter's home market, reject Third Country Price as a proxy using data from a third market (such as the largest non-U.S. market of the producer-exporter), and proceed to Constructed Value as a proxy for Normal Value. The amended Section states:

> For purposes of [Calculating Constructed Value], if a *particular market situation* exists such that the *cost of materials and fabrication* or other processing of any kind *does not accurately reflect the cost of production* in the *ordinary course of trade*, the [DOC] may use *another* calculation methodology under this Sub-Title, or *any other* calculation methodology.[29]

Petitioners may argue that notwithstanding China's graduation to a market economy, a "particular market situation" exists in China, and Chinese input and manufacturing costs do not reliably reflect the ordinary course of trade in China. In effect, the argument is that considerable state interference affecting prices remains, so DOC ought to use Constructed Value. Note the same argument could be made not only to any former NME, but also to any market economy, regardless of whether it once was classified as an NME. Note also the phrase is inherently ambiguous,

---

28. *See* Eric Emerson & Henry Cao, *Impact of the Amendments to U.S. Antidumping and Countervailing Duty Law in the Trade Preferences Extension Act of 2015*, 32 International Trade Reporter 1518 (BNA) (27 August 2015). [Hereinafter, *Impact.*]

29. Emphasis added.

Relatedly, DOC proposed new regulations in 2016 indicating its preference to compute dumping margins from Constructed Value based on data from the home market of the exporter, instead of Third Country Price, for two reasons: it was easier to collect input data in that market; and there would be no need to engage in a "like" product analysis (whereas with Third Country Pricing, DOC must determine that sales in that good sold in that country are like that of the subject merchandise).

hence it can cause uncertainty for importers that seek to know in advance their liability (if any) for AD duties.

The DOC used the Section 504 "particular market situation" provision for the first time in April 2017, when it raised AD duties on OCTG (*i.e.*, casing, drill, and pipe equipment used in the oil and gas industries) from Korea.[30] In the original investigation, DOC computed AD rates of 9.89% and 15.75%, but in an Administrative Review covering July 2014-August 2015, DOC recalculated the margins at 2.76% and 24.9%, based on "market distortions" in Korean, specifically, the price of electricity and hot-rolled steel coil, both of which are inputs into the subject merchandise. So, the DOC disregarded production costs in Korea as outside the ordinary course of trade, and thus not accurately reflecting those costs. Though Korea was the first target, indubitably Congress enacted Section 504 with China in mind. If and when the U.S. dropped NME treatment of China, then it could fall back on this Section to use surrogate data based on a finding of a "particular market situation in China." That also is true with respect to Vietnam, which under its 2007 WTO *Accession Protocol* argues it is entitled to market economy treatment in 2018.

The second key *TPEA* amendment concerned selection of surrogate values.[31] The change provides:

> In valuing the factors of production . . . , the [DOC] *may disregard price or cost without further investigation* if the [DOC] has determined that *broadly available export subsidies* existed or particular instances of subsidization occurred with respect to those price or cost values, or if those price or cost values were subject to an antidumping order.[32]

---

30. *See* U.S. Department of Commerce, Press Release, Department of Commerce Finds Dumping of Oil Country Tubular Goods from the Republic of Korea in Groundbreaking Ruling (11 April 2017), www.commerce.gov/news/press-releases/2017/04/department-commerce-finds -dumping-oil-country-tubular-goods-republic.

31. *See Impact.*

32. Emphasis added.

Note that under pre- and post-*TPEA* rules, DOC sometimes is called upon to decide whether an item into subject merchandise should be treated as a direct input or an overhead expense. The context may be COP for Normal Value based on surrogate data from a third country. Or, it may be computation of Constructed Value. In either context, the proxy for Normal Value is higher if an input is included in the proxy as a direct input than if it is viewed as an overhead (or other indirect) expense. The outcome of disputes turns on highly intensive facts.

For example, in and NME AD case, *U.S. Magnesium LLC v. United States*, Number 2015-1864 (6 October 2016), the Federal Circuit reviewed a DOC decision to treat retorts, which are steel alloy tubes used to purify magnesium, as overhead expenses. The subject merchandise was pure magnesium exported from China's Tianjin Magnesium International Co., which is used in aluminum alloys for automotive parts and beverage cans, and to remove sulfur from iron and steel. DOC used Constructed Value as a proxy for Normal Value, and imposed a 51.6% AD duty on the magnesium. The American producer, Salt Lake City-based U.S. Magnesium, said the duty should be higher, because retorts are a direct input.

The relevant statutory provision was 19 U.S.C. § 1677b(f)(1)(A), concerning special rules for calculating COP or Constructed Value:

This change gave DOC a relatively free hand to (1) reject purportedly subsidized surrogate inputs used in subject merchandise of a respondent producer-exporter, regardless of proof that the input producers actually received subsidies, (2) pick inputs from a different surrogate country, and (3) thereby exacerbate the dumping margin.

To understand this technical but significant amendment, recall that when DOC computes Normal Value for a respondent producer-exporter from an NME, DOC may use costs (*e.g.*, of materials) from surrogate countries that have market economies, to avoid the price distortions associated with state controls in the NME. The outcome, in theory, is a market-based COP for the respondent, which then forms part of Normal Value. Thus, for example, instead of relying on input data from China, the DOC would use the cost of those inputs during the same POI in India or Thailand. As an exception, if the Chinese respondent purchases a sufficiently large amount of that input (*e.g.*, wood for furniture) from a market economy country (*e.g.*, Indonesia), then DOC uses the actual purchase price the respondent paid as the input value (*e.g.*, the cost of Indonesia wood).

Suppose a candidate surrogate country provides "broadly available export subsidies." India, Indonesia, and Korea are examples. Then, the price of inputs from that subsidizing country would be lower, precisely because of the subsidy. Not surprisingly, then, DOC disregards these subsidized, low-value inputs, and chooses instead surrogates from another market economy. Those alternative surrogate are almost sure to be higher in value than the ones from the candidate, resulting in a higher proxy for Normal Value, and, in turn, a wider dumping margin.

Likewise, if the respondent producer-exporter itself bought inputs from the candidate, then DOC would disregard the prices of those inputs, and use an alternative

---

> Costs shall normally be calculated based on records of the exporter or producer of the merchandise, if such records are kept in accordance with the generally accepted accounting principles of the exporting country . . . and reasonably reflect the costs associated with the production and sale of the merchandise.

In applying the statute, normally DOC distinguishes direct inputs from overhead expenses using a four-factor test:

> "1) whether the input is physically incorporated into the final product; 2) the input's contribution to the production process and finished product; 3) the relative cost of the input; and, 4) the way the cost of the input is typically treated in the industry." *Certain Steel Nails from the People's Republic of China*, 78 Fed. Reg. 16651, 78 ITADOC 16651, Issues & Decision Memorandum, at Comment 4 (Dep't of Commerce Mar. 5, 2013).

But, depending on the facts, DOC relies on a case-by-case approach, as in *U.S. Magnesium*. For 2 reasons, DOC treated the retorts as an overhead expense: they were (1) not physically incorporated into the finished merchandise, and (2) replaced infrequently (about 60 days after use, because of the high heat and pressure of the "Pidgeon process" to make magnesium metal).

A Majority of the Court agreed DOC was not locked into a strict four-factor test, and had reasonably evaluated the totality of the circumstances. The Dissent countered retorts are direct inputs because they are: (1) consumed during the production process; (2) a significant unit cost of production; and (3) treated by the magnesium production industry as direct inputs. The Dissent also said DOC acted inconsistently with its prior decisions in which it treated catalysts and electrodes as direct inputs, though they were not physically incorporated into a final good.

surrogate. To continue the above example, the DOC would ignore wood prices from China, and from Indonesia as a possible surrogate for Chinese wood input costs, with respect to a Chinese respondent producer-exporter of furniture, if DOC judged Indonesia to provide broadly available subsidies. DOC might pick wood prices from Canada, instead. The Canadian prices likely would be higher than the Chinese or Indonesian ones, hence the dumping margin would be larger, because the proxy for Normal Value incorporates the Canadian prices.

According to pre-*TPEA* Federal Circuit and CIT precedents, the DOC could not reject surrogate values from countries providing broadly available export subsidies, unless the DOC offered a good reason for doing so. It was not obligated to engage in a formal investigation as to whether a candidate surrogate country actually sponsored such subsidies. But, according to the 2003 CIT decision in *China National Machine Imports & Exports Corporation v. United States*, which the Federal Circuit affirmed in 2004, it was "essential" for the DOC to give "substantial, specific evidence, and an adequate elucidation for its determinations."[33] Likewise, in the 2005 case of *Fuyao Glass Industry Group v United States*, the CIT ruled DOC could not reject surrogate data unless DOC proved (1) during the POI, export subsidies existed in the candidate country, (2) the respondent was part of the industry that received the subsidy, and (3) it would have been normal for the respondent to receive the subsidy.[34]

VII. Issue 3: Practical Effects

The DOC criteria for an NME provoke the third question, about practical effects. The answer many respondents give is hard-bitten, perhaps cynical. They suggest in NME AD cases, an administering authority essentially is free to "make up the numbers."

What this comment means is it is easy to inflate Normal Value by choice of a third country, and thereby increase the likelihood of a final affirmative dumping margin determination. If the proxy for the NME is a high-cost country, such as Japan, then Normal Value is likely to be high, especially in comparison with low-cost places such as Indonesia.

VIII. Issue 4: Separate Rate Analysis and 2013 *Yangzhou Gifts* and *Advanced Tech* Cases, and 2017 *Changzhou Hawd Flooring* Case

• Six Standard Factors

The fourth question concerns a rebuttable presumption the DOC employs, namely, that the export activities of all respondent producer-exporters in an NME

---

33. 293 F. Supp. 2d 1334 (CIT 2003), *aff'd* 104 Fed. Appx. 183 (Fed. Cir. 2004).
34. 29 CIT 109 (2005); *Impact*.

are subject to the control of the government and, therefore, should be assessed a single AD duty rate. The DOC presumes all NME respondents that are state-controlled enterprises are part of a single entity that the government of the NME controls. The DOC assigns those respondents a single country-wide AD rate. It is for a respondent to rebut this assumption and thereby qualify for an individual rate, which typically is lower than the country-wide one.

So, a state-controlled respondent contending it is not dumping, or it is dumping margin is less than that of others, must prove it is sufficiently independent from the NME government to qualify for a separate rate. To meet this burden, the respondent must prove its independence from the government as both a *de jure* and *de facto* matter. In this "separate rate analysis," the DOC considers the following standard factors:

(1) *Pricing*

Are export prices set or subject to the approval of the government?

(2) *Authority*

Is the respondent authorized to negotiate and sign contracts, especially export sales contracts?

(3) *Management*

Is the respondent autonomous from the government in picking its managers?

(4) *Ownership*

Are any owners of the respondent also government officials?

(5) *Profits*

Does the respondent retain proceeds from its export sales?

(6) *Scope*

Is the respondent affiliated with any company that produces or sells merchandise in the home market, U.S., or a third country that is subject merchandise, *i.e.*, a good covered by the scope of the AD investigation?

These factors emphasize direct control by an NME government over the export behavior of a respondent. Should the DOC also examine indirect influence, whereby the role of the government in the NME affects decisions by the respondent? After all, have the methods of ownership and control used by governments become more sophisticated and subtle?

For any exporter from an NME that does not qualify for a separate rate, the DOC applies an NME-wide rate. Thus, in an NME case, an importer of subject merchandise enters that merchandise at:

(1) A company-specific rate, *i.e.*, the cash deposit rate the DOC establishes for the particular producer-exporter of the merchandise,

(2) A separate rate, *i.e.*, the cash deposit rate the DOC establishes following a separate rate analysis under the above criteria, or

(3) An NME-wide rate, which is akin to an All Others Rate (AOR) in an AD case not involving an NME.[35]

As in any AD case, in a case with an NME, entries of subject merchandise are suspended from liquidation, upon a preliminary affirmative dumping margin determination, until the DOC orders CBP to liquidate those entries, following an Administrative Review.

A producer-exporter of subject merchandise not specifically reviewed in an Administrative Review is a "non-reviewed exporter." Its merchandise ultimately is liquidated at the cash deposit rate applicable at the time this merchandise enters the U.S. In certain cases, this rate may be the same as the cash deposit rate for a reviewed exporter, *i.e.*, a producer-exporter that undergoes an Administrative Review.

However, the DOC may find in the course of that Review the cash deposit rate is incorrect, either too low or too high. When it does, the DOC does not recalculate the duty rate for the non-reviewed exporter. Rather, it applies the NME-wide rate. This practice creates an incentive for producer-exporters and importers of subject merchandise to participate in both original AD investigations and Administrative Reviews, and to apply for a separate cash deposit rate in either or both stages. Why? Because the NME-wide rate is nearly certain to be higher than a separate rate.

---

35. Technically, an "AOR" and "country-wide rate" are distinct concepts. An AOR equals the weighted average dumping margins or countervailable subsidy rates established for exporters and producers individually investigated, excluding any zero and *de minimis* dumping margins or countervailable subsidy rates. An AOR applies to all respondents not individually investigated. A single country-wide subsidy rate, which is applicable to all respondent producer-exporters, is used if the DOC limits its investigation (*e.g.*, in a CVD case, under 19 U.S.C. Section 1677f-1(e)(2)(B)). It is based on industry-wide data concerning pricing or use of countervailable subsidies.

Is a country-wide rate established on the basis of data from exporters or producers, assuming the facts of a case entail a distinction? The answer is exporters, and is the teaching of *Michaels Stores, Inc. v. United States*, Number 12-00146 (Slip Opinion, 21 August 2013). In this dispute, the CIT held the pertinent regulation whereby the DOC sets a country-wide AD rate for imports from a NME calls for use of rates based on exporters, not individual rates assigned to producers.

Pencils imported from China by Michaels Stores were the subject merchandise. In liquidation instructions associated with two Administrative Review periods, the DOC ordered CBP to impose cash deposit rates on the basis of the (1) individual AD rate for an exporter, if the DOC had calculated such a rate for that exporter, or (2) China-wide rate, if the DOC had not assigned an individual rate to that exporter. Michaels Stores bought the pencils from five non-producer exporters in China, not from the three Chinese manufacturers. The DOC assigned a country-wide AD rate to the exporters, as none of them had requested an Administrative Review. However, Michaels posted cash deposits at the individual AD rates the DOC had assigned to the producers. They were lower than the country-wide rate. CBP assessed supplemental AD duties on Michaels, to make up the difference, and the DOC agreed, arguing cash deposit rates should be assigned on the basis of the identity of the exporter, not the identity of the producer.

CBP and the DOC were correct, said the CIT. Why? First, an exporter's AD rate is preferable to a producer's rate. Typically, an exporter is the party that sets prices and knows which merchandise is shipped to the U.S. Second, even if a separate rate is calculated for a producer, the producer likely will use a state-owned exporter to ship goods to the U.S. Doing so allows that producer to dump goods, yet benefit from a lower AD rate.

• **Simple Average Methodology and *Yangzhou Gifts* Case**

Application by the DOC of a separate analysis was tested in a 2013 case, *Yangzhou Bestpak Gifts & Crafts Co. Ltd. v. United States*.[36] Overturning the CIT, the Federal Circuit decided in favor of a Chinese producer-exporter of narrow woven ribbons. The DOC used a separate analysis for the respondent Yangzhou Gifts, resulting in a 123.83% AD duty. In doing so, the DOC applied a reasonable simple average methodology in an unreasonable way, so the Federal Circuit vacated and remanded the CIT decision that had favored the DOC.

In *Yangzhou Gifts*, the DOC chose two exporters, Ningbo Jintian Import & Export Company Ltd., and Yama Ribbons & Bows Company Ltd., for separate rate status. Yama got a *de minimis* dumping margin. Because Jintian refused to cooperate in investigation, the DOC used AFA, and assigned to it the China-wide rate of 247.65%.[37] Twelve additional Chinese exporters, including Yangzhou, sought a separate rate analysis. In this analysis, the DOC computed the separate rate by the simple average of the (1) Yama *de minimis* rate and (2) Jintian and China-wide AFA rate. The result was 123.83%.

To be sure, nothing in the U.S. AD statutes addresses whether the DOC can compute separate rates by taking a simple average of *de minimis* and adverse facts available rates. The DOC may use "any reasonable method," a lenient standard indeed, under Section 735(c)(5)(B) of the *Tariff Act of 1930*, as amended (codified at 19 U.S.C. Section 1673d(c)(5)(B)), with the comparable provision on a country-wide subsidy rate in Section 1671d(c)(5)(B). But, said the Court, application of a simple average and AFA China-wide rate in the case at bar was unreasonable. The evidentiary record was insubstantial to show a simple average reflected economic reality.

The DOC defended its method by explaining it relied on Average Unit Values, defined as the ratio of the total value of sales a Chinese respondent producer-exporter made to its total quantity of sales. Surely an AUV gives a rough estimate of the pricing practices of the respondent. The logic is that the higher the AUV, the higher the Export (or Constructed Export) Price, and thus the less the dumping margin. Further, Yama had a high AUV, Jintian a low AUV, and Yangzhou an AUV in between the two extremes. A simple average of the Yama and Jintian AUVs equalled a rate that was close to the AUV of Yangzhou. Therefore, the DOC asserted, the average AUV reasonably reflected the potential dumping margin of Yangzhou.

Not so, held the Court. The use of AUV estimates untethered to actual dumping margins of the respondents was unreasonable. Indeed, the only detailed information DOC obtained and considered came from a single investigated respondent,

---

36. *See* Number 2012-1312 (20 May 2013).

37. A high country-wide rate based on AFA is not unusual. *See, e.g., Mark David v. United States*, CIT Number 14-132 (Slip Opinion 14-132, 18 November 2014) (sustaining the 216.01% China-wide rate based on AFA in an Administrative Review for subject merchandise, wooden bedroom furniture, produced and exported by Shanghai Maoji Import and Export Company to Mark David USA in High Point, N.C.).

Yama, hence that was the only well-substantiated, reasonably calculated dumping margin. To move from that computation to a country-wide separate rate was to leap.

- **Proof of Control and 2013 *Advanced Tech* Case**

In *Advanced Technology & Materials Co., Ltd. v. United States*, the CIT agreed with a remand decision by the DOC that a Chinese exporter failed to show it was free of Chinese government control.[38] That exporter, Beijing-located ATM, shipped diamond saw blades to America. It argued it should not have to pay the whopping 164% country-wide AD rate, but rather a lower separate rate.

For sound reasons, the DOC presumed Advanced Tech and its affiliates constituted a single entity controlled by the Chinese government. First, throughout the POI, the majority shareholder of Advanced Tech and its affiliates was the Central Iron and Steel Research Institute. A Chinese government agency owned and controlled this Institute. Second, the Institute put four of its senior officers on the Board of Directors of Advanced Tech, and nominated the other five directors.

Advanced Tech argued the DOC failed to prove the Chinese government agency actively controlled it and its affiliates through the Institute. That was a losing argument, because it inverted the burden of proof: the respondent must rebut the presumption of government control; the DOC need not prove the respondent is free of that control.

Advanced Tech had a better argument, namely, that in its CVD investigation, the DOC said prices were set by market forces in more than 90% of products traded in China. Surely that finding indicated the government did not control Advanced Tech or its affiliates. Unfortunately for Advanced Tech, this argument was outside the scope of the remand decision of the DOC, and separately the Federal Circuit agreed with the presumption of state control in the Chinese context.[39]

---

38. *See* Number 09-00511 (Slip Opinion 13-129, 11 October 2013); Brian Flood, *Trade Court: Diamond Sawblade Exporter Subject to China-Wide Antidumping Rate*, 30 International Trade Reporter (BNA) 1592 (17 October 2013).

For a separate but related case, see *Diamond Sawblades Manufacturers Coalition v. United States*, CIT, Number 13-00241 (Slip Opinion Number 14-112, 23 September 2014); Brian Flood, *Court Returns Chinese Diamond Sawblades Dumping Review to Commerce Department*, 31 International Trade Reporter (BNA) 1761 (2 October 2014) (permitting the DOC to reconsider the eligibility for a separate rate analysis in an AD Administrative Review of certain affiliates of ATM, in light of the *Advanced Tech* holding).

39. In separate proceedings, the CIT upheld a revised AD duty rate of 82.12% the DOC assigned to diamond saw blades exported by a group of affiliated Chinese firms. As explained above, the DOC followed the presumption in NME cases that all state-controlled firms are part of a single entity (in effect, the government), and hence must be assigned the same country-wide AD rate. A particular firm may rebut the presumption of state control, and thereby get a separate rate, but it must show it is *de jure* and *de facto* independent of that control. One firm, ATM, and its affiliate, Cliff International Ltd., originally qualified for a separate and far lower rate—0.15%. But, on reconsideration, the DOC found the Central Iron and Steel Research Institute was the major shareholder of ATM, and the Institute was owned and controlled by the Chinese government, namely, China's State-Owned Assets Supervision and Administration Commissions of the State Council.

- **Representativeness, "Other Reasonable Methods" and
  2017 *Changzhou Hawd Flooring* Case**

In *Changzhou Hawd Flooring Co. v. United States*, the subject merchandise was multi-layered wood flooring.[40] The plaintiff producer-exporters were separate rate respondents. There were too many companies for the DOC to investigate individually, so it did not do so for 74 of them. (The DOC had sent its AD questionnaire to 190 companies, of which 90 filed timely responses.) The DOC computed a single country-wide duty rate of 25.62% for China, based on NME rules. The DOC departed from its expected practice of computing the separate rate dumping margin as the simple average of rates it assigned to individual companies. This practice presumes the individually-investigated companies are representative of the industry in question. In this case, however, the AD rate for the three mandatory respondents the DOC investigated individually was *de minimis*. So, the DOC turned to "other reasonable methods."

The country-wide rate for China was not *de minimis*, so the DOC presumed the separate rate would (or should) not be, either. But, the DOC never calculated a specific separate rate. It simply ordered non-*de minimis* separate rate duty rates. The Federal Circuit (per judge Taranto) explained:

> In investigations involving exporters from market economies, 19 U.S.C. § 1673d(c)(5) establishes the method for determining the rate for entities that are not individually investigated, the so-called all-others rate [AOR]. Commerce has relied on that statutory provision in determining the separate rate for exporters and producers from nonmarket economies that demonstrate their independence from the government but that are not individually investigated. *See Albemarle*, 821 F.3d at 1348 [*Albemarle Corp. & Subsidiaries v. United States*, 821 F.3d 1345 (Fed. Cir. 2016)].

So, on remand, the DOC assigned ATM the China-wide rate of 82.12%. *See Diamond Sawblades Manufacturers' Coalition v. United States*, Number 13-0078 (Slip Opinion 15-105, 23 September 2015); Brian Flood, *Court Upholds Higher Duties on Chinese Sawblades*, 32 International Trade Reporter (BNA) 1696 (1 October 2015).

That is, DOC imposed a China-wide AD duty rate on ATM of 82.12% for subject merchandise entries in 2009–2010, and 82.05% for entries in 2010–2011, even though ATM cooperated with DOC. ATM challenged the first Administrative Review, covering 2010–2011. Agreeing with DOC and upholding the CIT ruling, the Federal Circuit said DOC may presumed a producer-exporter in a NME is controlled by the government, and thus is not entitled to an individualized rate, unless that firm proves it is *de jure* and *de facto* independent from the government. *See Diamond Sawblades Mfrs. Coal. v. United States*, Number 2016-1254, 2016-1255 (7 August 2017); *Diamond Sawblades Mfrs. Coal. v. United States*, Number 2016-1253 (7 August 2017); Brian Flood, *Chinese Sawblade Makers Lose Pair of Dumping Appeals*, 34 International Trade Reporter (BNA) 1108 (10 August 2017). The Federal Circuit also said the CIT erroneously rejected the claim a different producer-exporter, Weihai Xiangguang Mechanical Industrial Co., engaged in targeted dumping.

40. *See* Number 2015-1904 (15 February 2017); Brian Flood, *Chinese Flooring Companies Win Duty Appeal*, 34 International Trade Reporter (BNA) (23 February 2017).

The statute says that where the "estimated weighted average dumping margins established for all exporters and producers individually investigated are zero or *de minimis* margins, or are determined entirely under [19 U.S.C. § 1677e]," Commerce "may use any reasonable method to establish the estimated all-others rate for exporters and producers not individually investigated, including averaging the estimated weighted average dumping margins determined for the exporters and producers individually investigated." 19 U.S.C. § 1673d(c)(5)(B). But the *Statement of Administrative Action* accompanying the *Uruguay Round Agreements Act*—which Congress has deemed "authoritative," 19 U.S.C. § 3512(d)—states that the "expected method" is to "weight-average the zero and *de minimis* margins and margins determined pursuant to the facts available, provided that volume data is available." . . . If Commerce reasonably concludes that "this method is not feasible" or would result "in an average that would not be reasonably reflective of potential dumping margins for non-investigated exporters or producers," it "may use other reasonable methods."

Albemarle explains that Congress thus expressed a preference for the expected method, . . . a preference reflecting how Commerce selects mandatory respondents . . . . Here, Commerce chose the exporters whose quantity-and-value questionnaires indicated that they were the largest exporters by volume, as expressly authorized by 19 U.S.C. § 1677f-1(c)(2) (2010). *Albemarle* explains: "The very fact that the statute contemplates using data from the largest volume exporters suggests an assumption that those data can be viewed as representative of all exporters." 821 F.3d at 1353. "The statute assumes that, absent [evidence that the largest exporters are not representative], reviewing only a limited number of exporters will enable Commerce to reasonably approximate the margins of all known exporters." *Id.* "[T]he representativeness of the investigated exporters is the essential characteristic that justifies an 'all others' rate based on a weighted average for such respondents." *Id.* (quoting *Nat'l Knitwear & Sportswear Ass'n v. United States*, 779 F. Supp. 1364, 1373–74, . . . (Ct. Int'l Trade 1991)). And, recognizing that the presumption of representativeness may be overcome, *Albemarle* holds that, in order to depart from the expected method, "Commerce must find based on substantial evidence that there is a reasonable basis for concluding that the separate respondents' dumping is different." *Id.*

Pointing to *Albermarle's* observation that the mandatory respondents in that case accounted for "a majority of the market," id. at 1353, Commerce argues that *Albemarle's* requirement of a showing of unrepresentativeness for departing from the expected method does not apply where the mandatory respondents do not account for "a majority of the market." . . . [DOC Brief.] But that argument takes too narrow a view of *Albemarle*. The court did not rely for its statutory analysis on the observation that the particular respondents accounted for a "majority of the market." It relied on the statutory standards for selecting mandatory respondents under § 1677f-1(c)(2), which, the court held, make the mandatory respondents representative unless evidence shows otherwise. . . . The statutory standards—involving either a statistical sample, 19 U.S.C. § 1677f-1(c)(2)(A), or the largest exporters by volume, *id.* § 1677f-1(c)(2)(B)—are not tied to a "majority" share of a "market," of the imports at issue, or any other class or collection.

Thus, the mandatory respondents in this matter are assumed to be representative. Under *Albemarle*, Commerce could not deviate from the expected method unless it found, based on substantial evidence, that the separate rate firms' dumping is different from that of the mandatory respondents. But it has not done so.

In sum, the Court ruled the DOC failed to justify its departure from the expected norm of calculating the separate rate the simple average of the rates of the individually investigated companies. Why would a low AD rate computed in this manner not reflect the dumping behavior of the separate rate companies? That was the question the DOC needed to answer before turning to another "reasonable method."

IX. January 2011 American Policy Change on Dumping Margin Adjustments for Export Taxes in NME AD Cases

In August 2010, the DOC announced a Trade Law Enforcement Initiative to capture more closely how producer-exporters in NMEs function. As part of this Initiative, in January 2011, the DOC declared it was reversing its longstanding practice that it cannot apply Section 772(c)(2)(B) of the *Tariff Act of 1930*, as amended, in an NME AD proceeding.[41] This Section directs the DOC to make an adjustment in the Dumping Margin calculation to Export Price or Constructed Export Price by "the amount" of any export tax, duty, or other charge imposed by the exporting country on the subject merchandise, if that tax, duty, or charge is included in the Export Price or Constructed Export Price. The adjustment is a deduction from that Price. The logic behind this adjustment is an NME government would not impose an export tax on a foreign like product sold in its country (the home market), so if that tax is included in the price of subject merchandise sold in the U.S., then that price is artificially inflated by the amount of the tax, and the dumping margin is artificially lowered by the tax.

The DOC based its prior practice against deducting export taxes, duties, or charges from Export Price and Constructed Export Price on the following rationale: government intervention in a NME is pervasive, so it is impossible for the DOC to make an accurate evaluation of "the amount" of tax paid by a NME respondent to

---

41. *See* 19 U.S.C. § 1677a(c)(2)(B).

an NME government. However, the DOC decided that by January 2011, China and Vietnam, and possibly other NMEs, had evolved sufficiently away from Soviet-era command economies that it could determine "the amount" of tax an NME levied on exports of subject merchandise during the POI or POR of an AD case.

This decision followed its March 2007 pronouncement that it could determine whether an NME had bestowed a measureable benefit (via a subsidy, which could take the form of a tax measure) on a producer-exporter respondent. Thus, under the new practice, the DOC deducted from Export Price or Constructed Export Price any export tax, duty, or other charge placed on subject merchandise from an NME by the government of that NME. In effect, the DOC ceased to differentiate NME from non-NME producer-exporter respondents with respect to the application of the export tax deduction.

Given the Dumping Margin formula, any subtraction from Export Price or Constructed Export Price lowers that Price, and thus enlarges the Dumping Margin. So, the DOC policy shift provided greater protection to domestic producers of products that were like those of subject merchandise. Many U.S. producers felt competitive pressures from their NME counterparts. But, by inflating the dumping margin and thereby the amount of AD duties, it raised costs to domestic consumers of subject merchandise, including businesses that use the merchandise as an input in their production process.

Chapter 27

CVD Cases against NMEs[1]

I. 1986 *Georgetown Steel* Case

One crucial similarity between the 2000 *British Steel* and 2003 *Certain Products* cases (discussed in a separate Chapter) was that neither involved an NME, nor even an economy in transition from Communism or Socialism to Capitalism. They involved SOEs from market economies. Similarly, in the 2004 *Canada Wheat Board* case (also discussed in a separate Chapter) in which the U.S. prevailed on claims involving commercial considerations under GATT Article XVII:1 and national treatment under Article III:4, the country at issue—Canada—was a market economy.[2] All such cases concerned the carry through, or not, of the benefits of pre-privatization subsidies.

In 1984, the question of NME status first arose in the context of CVD investigations. The exporting countries at issue were Soviet bloc countries, such as the former Czechoslovakia and East Germany, along with the U.S.S.R. itself. Domestic industries in the U.S. argued CVD law could not be used in an NME context, because it is impossible in that context to measure the benefit of a subsidy to a firm receiving the subsidy. The firm is an SOE, indeed a hallmark of an NME is state-ownership of all productive enterprises. Thus, a subsidy is a financial contribution from one arm of a socialist or communist government to another arm of the same government. There is little, if any, transparency in the arrangement.

In the landmark 1986 case of *Georgetown Steel Corporation v. United States*, the Federal Circuit essentially stated it could not see why the application of CVD law to an NME would be unreasonable.[3] This case arose in 1983 when Georgetown Steel sought relief from the DOC in the form of CVDs on NME imports. The DOC took the position that CVDs do not apply to NMEs. The CIT overruled the DOC, saying they did. But, on appeal to the Federal Circuit, the DOC prevailed, as the Court reinstated the original decision of the DOC.

---

1. Documents References:
   (1) *Havana (ITO) Charter* Articles 25–29
   (2) GATT Articles VI, XVI–XVII
   (3) WTO *SCM Agreement*
  2. *See Canada—Measures Relating to Exports of Wheat and Treatment of Imported Grain*, WT/DS276/AB/R (adopted 27 September 2004).
  3. *See* 801 F.2d 1308–1318 (Fed. Cir. 1986).

Nevertheless, *Georgetown Steel* case widely understood to mean CVDs either could not, or should not, be applied in the NME context. Until March 2007, DOC policy reflected that interpretation. The DOC declined to extend the CVD statute to NMEs.

II. March 2007 American Policy Reversal

On 30 March 2007, the DOC announced via a memorandum a dramatic reversal of long-standing policy. No longer would it abstain from applying CVD law to NMEs, as it had for 21 years. Any country—NME or not—was within the scope of the anti-subsidy remedy. The policy of not applying CVD law against NME had two rationales. First, actors in an NME respond to government directives, not subsidies. Second, it is too difficult to calculate accurately the level of subsidization in an NME.

What prompted the policy change? China. As David Spooner, Assistant Secretary of Commerce for Import Administration, said, perhaps it was that:

> [t]he China of 2007 is not the Soviet bloc of the mid-1980s, when we formulated our non-market anti-subsidy laws. It would be a divorce from reality if we said there was an absence of market forces in the Chinese economy.[4]

In other words, China now was a hybrid economy. It had advanced sufficiently beyond a Soviet-style command economy by enacting major new reforms, and sustaining them. To be sure, 55% of the GDP of China is generated by SOEs (as of 2007).[5] But, those SOEs responded to market forces, and, of course, the other 45% of Chinese GDP came from private entities. In consequence, the DOC now could identify and compute the value of a transfer of a specific financial contribution from the Chinese government to an enterprise or firm, and calculate the benefit to that recipient. The DOC self-imposed a uniform cut-off of 11 December 2001, the date of WTO approval of the terms of accession of China, as the date from which it would gauge subsidies.

Skepticism is in order. Never mind that the Sino-Soviet split occurred in the late 1950s, *i.e.*, set aside the point China and the former Soviet Union embarked on different economic paths long ago, so reference to the Soviets is inapposite. Is the real reason for the policy reversal a combination of (1) U.S. legal defeats in *British Steel* and *Certain Products*, (2) U.S. concern about new WTO Members, such as China and Vietnam, which are NMEs, as well as NMEs in the queue to join the WTO, and

---

4. *Quoted in* Kathleen E. McLaughlin, *U.S. Countervailing Duties Against China Could Lead to Further Action, Spooner Says*, 24 International Trade Reporter (BNA) 590 (26 April 2007). *See also Rep. English Says NME-CVD Bill Could Reach House Floor in April*, 24 International Trade Reporter 554–555 (BNA) (19 April 2007).

5. *See* Len Bracken, *Fisher Says Countervailing Duty Measure Backs Approach of Georgetown Steel Memo*, 29 International Trade Reporter (BNA) 359 (8 March 2012).

(3) pressure from Congress, manifest in proposed bills to allow the DOC to apply CVD law to NMEs?

The third factor raises the question of authority. *Georgetown Steel* purportedly stood for the proposition the DOC lacks authority to apply CVD laws against NMEs. The CIT, however, thought otherwise, as the Federal Circuit reversed it in that case. Evidently, the CIT never changed its view. In *Government of the People's Republic of China v. United States*, the CIT held there was no statutory bar to using CVD law against NMEs—effectively the same position it had in *Georgetown Steel*.[6]

To implement the policy shift, the DOC decided to rely on benchmarks from third countries as a way of measuring subsidies in an NME. (The obvious analogy is with the use of Third Country Price in a dumping margin calculation involving an NME.) Might that reliance be illegal under Article 14 of the WTO *SCM Agreement*? If a Third Country subsidy benchmark is used as a proxy in a case involving China, might that use violate China's terms of accession to the WTO?

III. Double Counting Problem

In 2006, one month after an important NME AD investigation involving lined paper from China, a seminal case emerged concerning the application of CVD law to an NME—China. The American petitioners asked the DOC to remove the status of China as an NME, and thereby apply CVD law to Chinese exports. The DOC applied its NME analysis, and agreed that for CVD purposes, China is not an NME. Hence, CVD law could be applied to China. The DOC relied on the following key findings:

(1) The Chinese government does not set 90% of the wages or prices in China.

(2) The Chinese currency, the *yuan* (*renminbi*) is freely convertible.

(3) The private sector in China is flourishing.

(4) The Chinese government allows some flexibility in credit and resource allocation.

(5) Overall, the Chinese economy no longer looks like that of the former Soviet Union, which was the kind of paradigm in which the Georgetown Steel decision was reached.

In turn, the DOC treated China as market economy, and applied CVD law, in five major cases in 2006–2008, involving products such as coated free sheet paper, pipes, and pneumatic off-road tires. Overall, between March 2007, when the DOC announced the reversal of its long-standing policy not to apply the CVD remedy to NMEs, and September 2009, when the CIT issued its first landmark *GPX Tire* decision, there were 19 cases filed against China that involved parallel CVD and NME

---

6. *See* 24 ITR 496 (5 April 2007).

AD investigations. By August 2010, when it issued its second *GPX Tire* decision, there were 25 such cases.

Obviously, the different outcomes in the AD and CVD context raise theoretical and practical questions. As a theoretical matter, why is it justified to treat China (or any other country) as an NME for one trade remedy (AD), but not in the other trade remedy (CVD)? Are the criteria used different, and if so, should they be? Moreover, is it appropriate to characterize an entire economy that is in transition, such as China, as either "market" or "NME"? Or, does it make more sense to identify on a sector-by-sector or industry-by-industry basis "market" versus "non-market" status, as occurs under Canadian trade remedy law?

As a practical matter, it is difficult—if not impossible—to defend the asymmetric treatment of a factor of production or input in the AD and CVD contexts. That is, the asymmetry between treating China as an NME for AD purposes, and applying CVD law to China, thereby treating it as a market economy, is not logical. The problem of asymmetric treatment in parallel CVD-NME AD investigations is sometimes called "double counting," which reflects what happens because of the treatment.[7] In turn, "double counting" results in a "double remedy" (though the terms are typically used interchangeably), namely, "the simultaneous imposition of [a] countervailing duty . . . and [an] anti-dumping duty . . . on the same product."[8] The problem "arise[s] when the same situation [*i.e.*, in the same AD-CVD investigation of the same subject merchandise] of subsidization is offset, fully or partially, twice: first, under the antidumping . . . proceedings, due to the specific NME methodology applied to calculate a Normal Value . . . [of a foreign like product], and for the second time, in the course of an anti-subsidy investigation."[9]

In specific, the "first count" occurs as follows, in an AD investigation: an input price is not useable because the country of the respondent is an NME, such as China. A proxy is used, namely, the price of the input in India, as a basis for calculating Constructed Value in China. The result typically is a higher figure for Constructed Value, because the price of the input in India is higher than the price of the comparable input in China. In other words, in the NME AD investigation, the DOC cannot base Normal Value on price data from the NME—because the country of the respondent is an NME. The DOC must use a proxy for Normal Value, the alternative being Constructed Value (or, conceivably, Third Country Price). In computing Constructed Value, the DOC identifies the FOPs and inputs used by the respondent producer in the NME. But, the DOC values those factors and inputs using figures

---

7. For a discussion double counting, see, e.g., James P. Durling & Thomas J. Prusa, *The Problem of "Double Remedies" in International Trade Disputes and the Economics of Pass-Through*, 21 TULANE JOURNAL OF INTERNATIONAL AND COMPARATIVE LAW number 2, 513–544 (2013).

8. Katarzyna Kaszubska, *Double Remedy: Beyond the Non-Market Economy Status, in* NON-MARKET ECONOMIES IN THE GLOBAL TRADING SYSTEM 131–153, 131 (J.S. Nedumpara & W. Zhou eds., 2018). [Hereinafter, Kaszubska.]

9. Kaszubska, 131.

from a market economy. In theory, the DOC selects a market economy at a comparable level of development to the NME in question, and also is a significant producer of comparable merchandise to that under investigation. In practice, as the example suggests, it is debatable whether China and India are comparable.

The "second count" then happens in a CVD investigation of the same subject merchandise as the NME AD case: the in-country (*i.e.*, in China) input price in the CVD investigation is not usable under Article 14(d) of the WTO *SCM Agreement*. The DOC, therefore, uses the price of the input in India. Consequently, the cost of production of the subject merchandise is elevated, because of the Indian input price (again, it is higher than that of the comparable input in China). With a higher cost of production, the subsidization rate ultimately computed by the DOC also is higher. In turn, the CVD is increased. In brief, the double-counting problem is one of cumulatively counting a higher input price in both an AD and CVD investigation, and building that higher price into the AD duty and CVD.

As just suggested, the incongruity is evident in the context of factors of production and inputs used in subject merchandise. To give a fuller illustration, consider the following hypothetical simultaneous investigation of subject merchandise for alleged dumping and illegal subsidization. Assume the DOC treats the exporting country — China — as a NME for AD, but not CVD, purposes. In practice, for the AD investigation, the DOC values an input into the subject merchandise using the price from the Indian market. That also is true for the values of the factors of production, like wage rates. In other words, the DOC uses Indian prices as a proxy for unreliable Chinese prices. In the CVD investigation, the DOC also uses the value of inputs and factors from India.

Thus, the DOC asks the Chinese respondent producer-exporter what factors and inputs it uses in the manufacturing of the subject merchandise. Focusing just on the input, suppose the producer-exporter says it uses input X, which in China is valued (in U.S. dollar terms) at $100. The DOC explains that because China is a NME for AD purposes, it does not trust the $100 value of input X, and will not take that figure into the computation of Constructed Value. The DOC thus turns to India, and values input X according to Indian pricing, which by assumption is $200. Constructed Value then includes the higher $200 figure for input X, and when compared with Export Price (or Constructed Export Price), the dumping margin is elevated (*ceteris paribus*, *i.e.*, assuming all other variables are constant).

Turning to the CVD investigation, the DOC does not treat China as an NME, but rather as a market economy. Therefore, in applying CVD law to China, the DOC must figure out the cost of production of the subject merchandise, and the degree to which that cost is subsidized by the government of China. The DOC asks the respondent producer-exporter what factors and inputs it employs to make the subject merchandise. The answer again (focusing on the inputs) is that input X is used, and the value of that input according to Chinese pricing is $100. However, the DOC values input X at $200, the Indian price, not the Chinese price. That is, the DOC uses in the CVD investigation the input value from the parallel NME AD investigation. Worse yet, the DOC essentially treats the $200 price for input X as a subsidized price—subsidized by the Chinese government. That is because the DOC computes a subsidization rate for the subject merchandise based on the third-country (Indian) input price.

Therein is the asymmetry: for AD purposes, the inputs and factor values are elevated simply because they are Indian instead of Chinese figures. The result is an exacerbated dumping margin. For CVD purposes, the DOC says the subject merchandise is subsidized, but its determination is based on valuations from the Indian—not Chinese—market. The asymmetry is perverse, because the AD methodology used by the DOC is that for NMEs, but the CVD methodology it uses is that for market economies. After all, until March 2007, the DOC said it could not apply CVDs to NMEs because subsidies are too difficult to calculate in those countries, and treated China as an NME for subsidy purposes—and, there are no special CVD rules for NMEs. Again, the DOC treats China as an NME for AD purposes, but as a market economy for CVD purposes. In doing so, the DOC does not adjust its AD or CVD methodologies to avoid double counting.

Moreover, with the asymmetry, the subsidization rate is elevated because the DOC uses Indian prices. It is not logical, consistent, or fair to assert simultaneously that subject merchandise is dumped using Indian prices, and also say it is subsidized, using Indian prices. India has nothing to do with conferring a subsidy to the respondent producer-exporter. The subsidy, if it exists, is paid by an organ of the Chinese government. Using Indian factor and input prices as a justification for finding the input is subsidized by the Chinese government makes little sense.

IV. September 2009, August 2010, October 2010, December 2011, and October 2013 *GPX Tire* Decisions

What is the defense the DOC offered of the above methodology in a case involving a simultaneous CVD/NME AD investigation? Briefly put: American trade remedy law does not instruct the DOC that it cannot engage in these practices. That defense failed spectacularly in September 2009, in a key case before the CIT, *GPX International Tire Corp. v. (GPX I)*.[10] In *GPX I*, the CIT ordered the DOC to make a choice:

(1) Either cease imposing the CVD law against China, or

(2) Change the NME methodology in AD cases to reflect the application of CVD duties to China and thereby correct the problem of double-counting.

---

10. *See* Ct. Int'l Trade, Consol. Court No. 08-00285 (Slip. Op. 09-103, 18 September 2009); Rossella Brevetti, *CIT Rejects Commerce Interpretation in GPX Case, Orders End of CVDs on Tires*, 27 International Trade Reporter (BNA) 1208 (12 August 2010); Rossella Brevetti, *CIT Ruling Rejects Commerce's Interpretation in China AD/CVD Case*, International Trade Reporter (BNA) 1268 (24 September 2009).

To be sure, the CIT decision was not the last word on the matter. The CIT remanded the case to the DOC. The CIT ruling was the first on the merits of the March 2007 DOC decision to apply the CVD law to China, and of the DOC's defense of double counting.

The petitioners in the underlying parallel CVD and NME AD investigations that gave rise to the *GPX I* decision were the Titan Tire Corp. of Des Moines, Iowa, and the United Steel, Paper and Forestry, Rubber, Manufacturing, Energy, Allied Industrial and Union of Pittsburgh, Pennsylvania. In the CIT case, the petitioners were joined by Bridgestone Americas, Inc., and Bridgestone Americas Tire Operations, LLC. The respondents in the underlying investigations, and plaintiffs in the CIT proceedings, were GPX International Tire Corp., Hebei Starbright Tire Co. Ltd. (a wholly owned subsidiary of GPX), and Tianjin United Tire & Rubber International Co. Ltd. In the underlying investigations, the DOC rendered final affirmative determinations, resulting in the application of CVDs and NME AD duties to the subject merchandise—pneumatic off-the-road tires (OTR) from China. GPX was the importer of the subject merchandise from Hebei and Tianjin.

Before the CIT, the plaintiffs raised two key issues and arguments:

(1) The CVD statute could not be applied to an NME, *i.e.*, the DOC was wrong to apply that statute to China. The DOC misread the statute, and misinterpreted the applicable precedent, namely, the 1986 *Georgetown Steel* case, which precludes application of the statute to NMEs.

(2) Applying to China both the CVD statute, and the AD law using the NME methodology, resulted in double-counting. Chinese respondents were punished twice for the same allegedly unfair trade practice.

Essentially, the CIT ruled in favor of the DOC on the first, but not the second, issue.

On the first issue, the CIT held that the statutory language did not bar the DOC from applying the CVD law to imports from China. The CIT concluded the *Georgetown Steel* case was ambiguous as to whether the DOC could or could not apply the CVD remedy to NMEs—the *Georgetown Steel* court did not forbid imposition of CVDs on imports from an NME. But, the CIT said there was no need for it to resolve this ambiguity. Rather, the CIT cited *National Cable & Telecommunications Association v. Brand X Internet Services.*[11] In that case, the Supreme Court held that before a court engages in judicial construction of a statute in a manner that may trump the interpretation of that statute by the relevant agency, the court must conclude that the statute unambiguously requires construction by the court.

Thus, the CIT looked to the relevant CVD statute—19 U.S.C. Sections 1671 and 1677(5)—to see what they said about imposing CVDs against NME imports. Drawing in part on legislative history, the CIT held the statutory language does not deprive the DOC of the authority to impose CVDs on NME imports. In other

---

11. *See* 545 U.S. 967 (2005).

words, the DOC indeed can apply the CVD law to a NME like China. But, the CIT reminded the DOC it has the discretion not to impose CVDs when it applies the NME AD methodology. The CIT warned it is not clear how — or even whether — the CVD and NME AD statutes work together in a parallel investigation. These statutes give no guidance as to how the DOC is to account for instances when they overlap in a parallel CVD — NME AD investigation.

On the second issue, the CIT held that the interpretation of the DOC of the NME AD statute, in relation to the CVD statute, was unreasonable. It was both unlawful and unfair for the DOC to impose CVDs on China under the normal market economy methodology, while simultaneously imposing AD duties based on the NME methodology. The CIT said if the DOC wanted to apply the CVD remedy to China, against which the DOC also uses the NME AD methodology, then the DOC had to take corrective action. Otherwise, this kind of parallel investigation, and imposition of a parallel remedy, was wrong.

Specifically, the DOC had to avoid double-counting of market-economy CVDs and NME AD duties. That is, the DOC had to adopt additional policies and procedures in its NME AD and CVD methodologies to account for the imposition of CVDs to products from and NME country. In its NME AD investigation, the DOC did not compare the Export Price of the subject merchandise with the Normal Value of the foreign like product in China. Had it done so, then both sides of the Dumping Margin formula would be equally affected by any subsidy, as both the price of the merchandise sold in the U.S. and in China potentially would be affected by the subsidy — in all probability, both would be lower on account of the subsidy.

Instead, the DOC used a proxy for Normal Value, namely Constructed Value, for which it relied on data from a third country, such as India. Those data were unaffected by any Chinese subsidy, because the Chinese government obviously did not confer financial contributions to firms and enterprising operating in the third country. Thus, in the NME AD investigation, the DOC compared an Export Price that is potentially affected by the Chinese subsidy against Constructed Value that is not affected by a subsidy. The result likely was a widened dumping margin, because Export Price was reduced by the subsidy, but not Constructed Value. Then, in the parallel CVD investigation, the DOC computed a subsidization rate, and based a CVD on it.

Herein was the double-counting, said the CIT. First, the NME AD methodology incorporated the effect of the subsidy on Export Price, without any adjustment to the proxy for Normal Value, Constructed Value. The result was a dilated dumping margin. Second, the subsidization rate reflected the subsidy, too. The DOC did not make any adjustment to this rate when computing the value of the subsidy. (As the earlier hypothetical illustration suggests, the DOC may even base the rate on unsubsidized input prices from a third country, which are sure to be higher than subsidized prices in China.)

Note that double-counting is even worse to the extent the DOC uses in Constructed Value input prices, as well as factor prices, from India. The result is a double penalty against China—once in the AD duty, and once in the CVD—for the same breach, namely, a subsidy. The CIT challenged the DOC to consider whether it could impose all the remedy necessary through an NME AD duty, because that duty alone most likely accounts for the measurable competitive advantage respondents get from a subsidy. If the DOC persisted in entertaining parallel investigations, then, again, it needed to take steps to eschew double-counting.

Another way to characterize the CIT holding in *GPX I* on the second issue is as follows: the DOC could not change its anti-subsidy policy and apply CVDs to China on the ground that China is now a hybrid economy, without also refining its CVD rules, NME AD rules, or both to account for the fact China really is a hybrid economy. Failure to fine-tune the rules suggested the DOC was doing little else than sticking China with as many trade remedies as could be piled on at once. That result was blatantly protectionist.

In August 2010, the CIT issued its decision reviewing the first remand determination rendered by the DOC—*GPX International Tire Corp. v. United States* (*GPX II*).[12] The CIT held it is unlawful to levy a CVD while simultaneously imposing an AD duty computed using the NME methodology without making an adjustment to avoid the double-counting of duties. Without an appropriate adjustment, applying both the CVD and AD remedies, and using the NME methodology in connection with AD duties, yields a double-counting of duties and thereby punishes twice the respondent firms for the same unfair trade practice. Ruling in favor of the plaintiffs, GPX, Hebei, and Tianjin, the CIT said the DOC failed to comply with the September 2009 remand decision in which the CIT ordered the DOC to devise an adjustment to avoid double-counting duties. Thus, the CIT remanded again.

Following the CIT remand decision in *GPX II*, the DOC said in its second remand determination it had only three choices:

(1) Not apply the CVD law,

(2) Treat China as a market economy and apply the AD law (along with the CVD law), or

(3) Continue to impose a CVD, but offset the CVD against the AD duty cash deposit rate for each respondent, *i.e.*, deduct from this rate the amount of the CVD.

As to the first option, the DOC said the CVD statute (19 U.S.C. § 1671) required it to apply CVD law if a country furnishes a countervailable subsidy.

In its August 2010 decision, the CIT rejected the DOC's interpretation of the CVD statute as misguided. The CIT read the second option as tantamount to an

---

12. *See* Ct. Int'l Trade, Consol. Court No. 08-00285 (Slip. Op. 10-84, 4 August 2010).

admission by the DOC it could not figure out an adjustment to avoid duty double-counting. Consequently, the DOC selected the third option, thinking it the least confusing. But, the CIT said this option was inconsistent with the relevant trade remedy statutes. Why?

The offset of the AD duty cash deposit rate by a CVD renders a concurrent CVD and AD investigation unnecessary. The same remedial price adjustment could be obtained simply by conducting a standard NME AD investigation. That is, the off-set makes the CVD investigation pointless, because the combination of the CVD subsidization margin and NME AD cash deposit rate always equals the unaltered NME AD margin from a standard NME AD investigation. In turn, running two parallel investigations is unreasonable, because it imposes expenses on all parties. Put simply, as the CIT did, concurrent imposition of CVDs and AD duties under the NME methodology created a "high potential" for, and might "very well" result in, double-counting. Thus, in *GPX II*, the CIT ordered the DOC to forego imposition of CVD law on the subject merchandise.

In its second remand determination, issued in September 2010, the DOC responded with a respectful protest. It disagreed with the CIT that concurrent imposition of CVDs on Chinese goods and application of the NME AD methodology on those goods created a high potential for, and could result in, double counting of duties. The DOC also objected to the conclusion of the CIT that the DOC is not statutorily required to apply CVD law under 19 U.S.C. Section 1671, and that the CVD and AD statute require coordination of concurrent duties. Yet, the DOC responded by complying with the CIT order, excluding the requisite Chinese respondents (Hebei and Tianjin) from its CVD order. Concomitantly, the importer of the subject merchandise (GPX) requested the CIT to order the DOC to cease collection of the CVD cash deposit rate. Given the plaintiffs made no showing of irreparable harm, and the risk to the DOC if the duty obligation were unsecured, in October 2010, the CIT refused this request, pending an expected appeal. That refusal came in *GPX International Tire Corp. v. United States* (*GPX III*).[13]

Taken together, the decisions in *GPX I*, *II*, and *III* stood for the proposition that the DOC cannot impose CVD law on exports from NMEs. Unsurprisingly, American manufacturers of competing tires, along with the DOC, appealed to the Federal Circuit. They argued that the DOC has the authority to impose CVDs on NMEs, along with AD duties. They premised their argument on the plain meaning of the CVD statutory language, which says a CVD "shall be imposed" if the prerequisites are met, and does not distinguish between market economies and NMEs. They lost. The Federal Circuit upheld the decision of the CIT, albeit on different grounds.[14]

---

13. *See* Ct. Int'l. Trade, Consol. Court No. 08-00285 (Slip Op. 10-112, 1 October 2010).
14. *See* Rossella Brevetti, *Federal Circuit Says CVD Law Inapplicable to NME Countries*, 28 International Trade Reporter (BNA) 2040 (22 December 2011).

In particular, on 19 December 2011, the Federal Circuit handed down a dramatic decision in *GPX International Tire Corp. v. United States*.[15] It held the CVD statute bars the DOC from imposing the CVD remedy on any NME, *i.e.*, the DOC is not authorized to apply CVDs to NMEs. The decision essentially turned back the clock to 1983, when the DOC adopted the policy, which it maintained until March 2007, that CVD law does not apply to a NME, and which the Federal Circuit upheld in the 1986 *Georgetown Steel* case. The Appeals Court examined the amendments and re-enactment of CVD law by Congress in the *Omnibus Trade and Competitiveness Act of 1988* and the *Uruguay Round Agreements Act of 1994*, and invoked the rationale of legislative ratification. Through these legislative enactments, Congress ratified the original 1983 DOC policy against applying CVD law to NMEs, and the 1986 *Georgetown Steel* decision. That is, Congress agreed with, and adopted the position taken at the time by, the DOC that government payments to enterprises in a NME cannot be characterized as "subsidies." The March 2007 reversal by the DOC of its policy thus was contrary to the intent of Congress manifest in the *1988* and *1994* Acts.

Moreover, said the Court, the CVD statute is not as clear on its face as the DOC would have it. The statute says that if:

> the administering authority determines that the government of a country ... is providing, directly or indirectly, a countervailable subsidy [and if mate-rial injury occurs by reason of that subsidy], then there shall be imposed upon such merchandise a countervailing duty, in addition to any other duty imposed, equal to the amount of the net countervailable subsidy.

This language begs the question whether a government payment in a NME country is a "countervailable subsidy." If the DOC sought to implement a new policy, such as that in its March 2007 memorandum, then the appropriate way to do so was through a statutory change approved by Congress.

Within days of the Federal Circuit ruling, that is exactly what the Administration of President Barack H. Obama (1961–, President, 2009–2017) sought. On 18 January 2012, the USTR and Secretary of Commerce sent a joint letter to the Senate Finance and House Ways and Means Committees declaring urgent legislation to over-ride the decision. The Administration sought to amend AD NME and CVD law to clarify CVD law can be applied to NMEs, and that both trade remedies can be imposed simultaneously on the same subject merchandise. Otherwise, said the President, America would suffer substantial adverse economic effects from injuri-ous, subsidized imports, including from the 24 CVD orders against subject mer-chandise from NMEs the Federal Circuit ordered the DOC to revoke effective 2 February 2012. That merchandise included aluminum, chemicals, paper, steel, and tires, and in the actions underlying the orders, the petitioning American industries

---

15. *See* 666 F.3d. 732 (Fed. Cir. 2011) (33 ITRD 1545).

covered over 80 SMEs, and Fortune 500 companies, in 38 states. Perhaps many would be hurt, a politically unwise consequence in a Presidential election year.

Using expedited procedures, Congress moved quickly.[16] On 5 March 2012, the Senate passed by unanimous consent legislation (S. 2153) overturning the 19 December 2011 *GPX* decision. The next day, the House of Representatives did so (H.R. 4105) by a 370–39 vote. Shortly thereafter, on 13 March, President Obama signed the legislation, Public Law 112-99. The identical bills added a sub-section to the *Tariff Act of 1930*, as amended (Section 701(f)), making clear that the CVD provisions of the *1930 Act* apply to NMEs.[17] Overriding the Federal Circuit decision, the new law had two key features:

(1) Section 1(a) granted DOC the authority to impose CVDs on subsidized imports from any NME, meaning not only China, but also Vietnam and several other countries, by clarifying the intent of Congress that it believes the DOC can render reliable calculations as to subsidies provided in NMEs.

However, the DOC is not required to impose CVDs on subsidized imports from NMEs, if the DOC cannot identify and calculate government subsidies in that NME "because the economy of that country is essentially comprised of a single entity."

(2) Section 2(a) responded not only to the adverse decision of the Federal Circuit in *GPX*, but also of the WTO Appellate Body in the *AD-CVD* case (discussed below).

This Section pertains to cases in which the DOC determines a countervailable subsidy increases the weighted average dumping margin, and is designed to prevent double counting of remedies. The DOC is required to make an adjustment to a dumping remedy when a double remedy exists, namely, the DOC must reduce AD duties in a NME case if it imposes CVDs simultaneously on the same subject merchandise, if a respondent producer-exporter can prove that because of a countervailed domestic subsidy and use of NME surrogate value methodology, the price of its exports to the U.S. increased. The operative statutory language is:

> [If the DOC decides a] countervailable subsidy has been demonstrated to have reduced the average price of imports of the class or kind of merchandise [*i.e.*, subject merchandise] during the relevant [period, then the DOC must reduce the AD duty by the amount

---

16. *See* Rossella Brevetti, *President Signs Legislation Restoring Subsidy Remedy for Nonmarket Economies*, 29 International Trade Reporter (BNA) 400 (15 March 2012); Rossella Brevetti, *Congress OKs Bill Restoring Subsidy Remedy Against China; Legislation Goes to President*, 29 International Trade Reporter (BNA) 352 (8 March 2012); Len Bracken, *Fisher Says Countervailing Duty Measure Backs Approach of Georgetown Steel Memo*, 29 International Trade Reporter (BNA) 359 (8 March 2012).

17. *See* 19 U.S.C. § 1677f-1(f).

of the increase in the weighted average dumping margin the DOC estimates].[18]

As the CIT said in its November 2014 *Wheatland Tube* decision, whether the evidentiary burden of proof is on a respondent to establish it is entitled to a double remedy offset is unclear.[19] That is because of the vague passive present perfect tense in the clause "has been demonstrated." The tense is vague, and does not identify which actor — petitioner or respondent — has the burden. So, the DOC has discretion to allocate the burden of proof of the statutory criteria for a double remedy offset.

In any event, this showing means the CVD remedy worked by compelling an increase in prices of subject merchandise. Once made, the DOC must decide whether it can reasonably estimate the extent to which the dumping margin increased (thanks to the un-countervailed subsidy that allowed for lower import prices, *i.e.*, for a lower Export or Constructed Export Price and/or surrogate value methodology that created a high Third Country Price as a proxy for Normal Value). If the DOC can compute this estimate, then it must make an appropriate adjustment by reducing the dumping margin by the amount by which the subsidy exacerbated this margin.

In its May 2015 *Wheatland Tube* decision, the CIT upheld the DOC practice of estimating and applying an offset to AD duties whenever double counting occurred.[20] Specifically, the DOC sought direct evidence of the effect of subsidies on costs, namely, industry-specific data from respondents. Those data concerned how a countervailable government subsidy affects the costs of the respondent, and in turn its pricing, and thereby the DOC's computation of an AD duty. With this "apples-to-apples" comparison of costs and prices, the DOC could see if it risked imposing a double remedy if it imposed both a CVD and an AD duty on the same subject merchandise.

In effect, the new law restored the *status quo ante* that existed before the *GPX* decision.

Supporters of the March 2012 amendment to the *1930 Act* hailed it as an important step to help tens of thousands of American workers across nearly 40 states. For instance, between 2002 and 2009, China provided roughly $33 billion in subsidies to its paper industry. By 2009, China replaced the U.S. as the largest producer of paper and paper products. Workers in paper mills in Maine were made redundant. Yet, when the DOC applied simultaneous AD and CVD duties to coated paper imports from China, one Maine mill hired 100 employees. As another illustration,

---

18. 19 U.S.C. § 1677f-1(f)(1)(B).

19. *See Wheatland Tube Co. v. United States*, Number 12-00298 (Slip Opinion 14-137, 26 November 2014); Rossella Brevetti, *Court Sends Double Remedies Adjustment On Pipes from China Back to Commerce*, 31 International Trade Reporter (BNA) 2100 (4 December 2014).

20. *See Wheatland Tube Co. v. United States*, Number 12-00298 (Slip Opinion 15-44, 7 May 2015); Brian Flood, *Commerce Won't Adjust AD Duties on Steel Welded Pipes from China*, International Trade Daily (BNA), 11 May 2015.

supporters touted economic studies showing direct export subsidies from China account for 7.3% of the price advantage enjoyed by Chinese over American goods. (The undervaluation of the Chinese *yuan* accounted for an additional 25–40% price advantage.) Supporters also counseled the *GPX* decision was wrongheaded, because it used the doctrine of legislative ratification to freeze one interpretation by the DOC of the *1930 Act*, and thereby robbed the DOC of the flexibility it needs to alter its interpretation as circumstances warrant.

In October 2013, two other dimensions of the *GPX* dispute were the subjects of fourth CIT decision, *GPX International Tire Corporation v. United States* (*GPX IV*): did the Chinese government subsidize GPX when GPX bought Hebei, and did it subsidize Tianjin in forgiving the debt of Tianjin? The DOC thought so, and the CIT agreed.[21]

First, Hebei was not a fully privatized entity when, in 2006, GPX acquired it. Thus, the DOC was right not to presume the transaction was at arm's length for fair market value. Indeed, there was evidence to the contrary: GPX bought Hebei subject to a worker retention agreement, meaning GPX had to promise job security to existing workers, even at the expense of profits.

Second, the Bank of China (a state owned financial institution) never treated its loans to Tianjin as ordinary commercial debt. Rather, it transferred the debt obligations of Tianjin to a government-owned management company. (Later, they were transferred to an American investment firm.) The history of those loans showed no regular payments, inexplicable waivers of interest, no serious efforts to minimize the loss to the Bank of China, and repeated renegotiations. Hence, the DOC was correct to conclude the Bank of China forgave unpaid debt obligations of Tianjin.

V. Constitutional Retroactivity and March 2013 *GPX* and March 2013 *Guangdong Wireking* Decisions

Notably, under Section 1(b) of the March 2012 amendment to the *1930 Act*, the new law applied retroactively to all DOC CVD proceedings initiated on or after 20 November 2006, and thus covered 24 investigations (23 of them involving Chinese goods), and 1 involving Vietnamese goods. Because the law applied retroactively, critics charged the new law violated three provisions of the U.S. Constitution: the Article I, Section 9 prohibition on *ex post facto* law (as the law allows for retroactive CVDs with no adjustment for double counting); the 5th Amendment Equal Protection Clause (as the law created a particular class of parties to which both AD and CVD duties could be imposed retroactively); and the 5th Amendment guarantee of due process (as retroactive application had an adverse impact on importers but

---

21. *See* No. 08-00285 (30 October 2013); Brian Flood, *Court Upholds Countervailing Duties On Chinese Pneumatic Tire Exporters*, 30 International Trade Reporter (BNA) 1727 (7 November 2013).

served no legitimate legislative purpose furthered by a rational means). Indeed, in May 2012, GPX International Tire Corporation raised these claims against the government before the Federal Circuit. Also among the critics was China, which said the law violated WTO rules.

In a January 2013 ruling, the CIT upheld the Constitutionality of the March 2012 amendment authorizing the DOC to impose CVDs on NMEs.[22] In that action, the CIT remanded the case to DOC to reconsider its CVD ruling. The issues in the January 2013 case, which was on remand from the Federal Circuit, were the constitutionality of the new law allowing the DOC to impose CVDs on NMEs, and the particular final affirmative CVD determination by the DOC for pneumatic off-the-road tires. These issues were unsurprising, as the underlying investigation was one of the first in which the DOC abandoned its policy that it could not apply CVDs to merchandise from NMEs.

GPX claimed the statute was unconstitutional, because if violated the due process and equal protection provisions of the 5th Amendment, and the *Ex Post Facto* Clause of the Constitution. GPX pointed out the statute did not make any adjustment for double counting in AD-CVD proceedings between 20 November 2006 and 13 March 2012. It only did so for investigations launched after the latter date. The CIT rejected both contentions. Applying Rational Basis Scrutiny, the CIT said the law was rationally related to legitimate government interests and, therefore, not a 5th Amendment violation. Moreover, GPX failed to show the new law upended a vested right with which that law interfered. And, the law, if it was a retrospective change (not just a mere clarification of existing law), was remedial, not penal, in nature. To be sure, the CIT agreed certain DOC findings were not consistent with the law, or supported by substantial evidence, hence the remand. For example, the DOC said Starbright received countervailable subsidies in 2006, when Starbright acquired Hebei Tire. The DOC used its change of ownership methodology to reach this conclusion, because it said Hebei Tire was not wholly private after the sale. But there was evidence that the transaction was an arms-length.

In a March 2013 decision, the CIT again upheld the constitutionality of the retroactive application of the March 2012 amendment.[23] The CIT said a CVD is non-criminal and remedial in nature, and imposed in relation to harm caused by a subsidy. In contrast, the *Ex Post Facto* Clause bars retroactive application of criminal laws. The Court also rejected the claim of the plaintiff, Guangdong Wireking, and plaintiff-intervenor, the Chinese Ministry of Commerce Bureau of Fair Trade for Imports and Exports, that the new law violated due process guarantees by imposing retroactively a CVD. Importers of subject merchandise had no vested right in duty assessments that excluded CVDs. The CIT added that the need to protect domestic

---

22. *See GPX International Tire Corp. v. United States*, (Ct. Int'l Trade, No. 08-00285, 7 January 2013).

23. *See Guangdong Wireking Housewares & Hardware Co., Ltd. v. United States*, No. 09-00422 (Slip Opinion 13-31, 12 March 2013).

industry from unlawful foreign subsidies is a rational basis for retroactive application of CVDs under Section 1(b) of the March 2012 amendment to the *1930 Act*.

Finally, the CIT upheld the underlying DOC subsidy determination. That determination included a finding that suppliers of wire rod to Guangdong Wireking were "authorities" under 19 U.S.C. Section 1677(5), *i.e.*, they were governmental or public entities providing a financial contribution and thereby a benefit. Looking past form to substance, corporate ownership and control realities allowed the Chinese government to pass benefits through private and quasi-private channels.[24]

In March 2013, the Federal Circuit affirmed the CIT rulings in the *GPX* case.[25] Retroactive application from 20 November 2006 of CVD laws to NME imports, pursuant to Section 1(b) of the March 2012 statute amending the *1930 Act*, by which Congress changed retroactively the Federal Circuit December 2011 decision in *GPX*, was permissible under the *Ex Post Facto* Clause. The Court's rationale was this *Clause* is violated only if a punishment is imposed backwards in time for an act that was not

---

24. In January 2014, a WTO Panel rejected a Chinese complaint that the March 2012 American legislation violated transparency obligations under GATT Article X. The Panel held China failed to prove its allegations that America violated Article X:1-3 by failing to publish the legislation promptly, and in a manner that allows foreign governments and traders to become familiar with it, by enforcing it retroactively, and by administering it in a way that was not impartial. *See* Daniel Pruzin, *WTO Panel Rejects China's Complaint Against U.S. Countervailing Duties Law*, 31 International Trade Reporter (BNA) 8 (2 January 2014).

25. *See Guangdong Wireking Housewares & Hardware Co. v. United States*, Federal Circuit, No. 13-1404 (18 March 2014); Rossella Brevetti, *Appeals Court Says 2012 CVD Law Did Not Violate Ex Post Facto Clause*, 31 International Trade Reporter (BNA) 536 (20 March 2014).

In a March 2015 decision, *GPX International Tire Corp. v. United States*, the Federal Circuit considered an appeal from a group of tire companies against the CIT ruling that upheld the legality of the DOC calculations of CVD duties against Chinese tire imports. *See* Number 14-01188 (consolidated with Number 14-01248 (13 March 2015). Their appeal was on Constitutional grounds, under the Due Process Clause of the 5th Amendment, specifically the *Ex Post Facto* Clause.

The Federal Circuit affirmed the CIT decision, agreeing the 2012 law that authorized the DOC to apply retroactively to 2006 CVDs to NMEs back to 2006 did not violate the Due Process Clause of the Constitution. The Federal Circuit provided four rationales:

(1) The controversial legislation was not "wholly new" law; instead, it "simply extended Commerce's ability to impose CVD to a new group of importers";

(2) The DOC applied the new law to resolve uncertainty over whether CVD law could be applied to NMEs.

(3) Chinese producer-exporters of China had known since at least 2006 of the change in CVD NME policy, because the DOC published a "Notice of Opportunity to Comment" on whether economic conditions in China justified application of CVD law to an NME.

(4) The law was remedial, that is, directed to providing relief to domestic tire producers via CVDs, rather than punitive.

See CROWELL MORING, THIS MONTH IN INTERNATIONAL TRADE—MARCH 2015, *Federal Circuit Affirms Application of U.S. Anti-Subsidy Law to Non-Market Economies Constitutional* (7 April 2015), www.crowell.com/NewsEvents/All/This-Month-in-International-Trade-March-2015-ITB05.

This affirmance was the second time the Federal Circuit ruled as such, thus heralding an end to litigation on the issue (assuming no Supreme Court decision to the contrary). Had the Federal Circuit ruled otherwise, CVD orders issued between 20 November 2006, and 13 March 2012, would have been terminated.

punishable at the time it was committed, or if a punishment is increased for an act committed before that increase. But, the Congressional amendment was not punitive in nature; rather, it was remedial. In reaching this conclusion, the Court explained:

> Wireking's mistake lies in its attempt to parse the antidumping law into discrete parts and apply the *ex post facto* analysis to each detached portion. Even if the 2012 law could be considered separately from the overall antidumping and countervailing duty law, treating aspects of the 2012 legislation in isolation is not consistent with Supreme Court authority.

In brief, the amendment was part of a corpus of AD-CVD law, which is about trade remedies.

VI. Double Counting and March 2011 *U.S. AD-CVD* Case

Ironically, the *GPX* controversy was set within the broader context of a March 2011 WTO Appellate Body ruling in favor of China and against the U.S. In the U.S. — AD-CVD case, the Appellate Body held double counting of AD and CVD duties — that is, the offsetting of the same unlawful subsidization twice, once by the imposition of AD duties using the NME methodology, and secondly by the concurrent imposition of CVDs — violates Article 19:3 of the *SCM Agreement*.[26] This provision states CVDs must be levied "in the appropriate amounts in each case."

The Appellate Body explained that when an administrative agency calculates a dumping margin, it does so based on a low price (Export or Constructed Export Price). That low price is made possible because of a subsidy. Hence, if an AD duty is imposed based on the low price, and also a CVD is imposed to offset the subsidy, there is double counting. That double remedy was inappropriate. The third key point of the new law was designed to ensure the U.S. complied with the Appellate Body ruling.

In a second WTO ruling, a Panel held in March 2014 that China was correct in its argument the U.S. failed to investigate, and thus failed to avoid application of, double remedies in respect of AD and CVD duties, in 25 previous investigations launched between 20 November 2006 and 13 March 2012. That merchandise, valued at $7.2 billion annually, was citric acid and citrate salts, coated and thermal paper, kitchen shelves, off road tires, oil country tubular goods, photovoltaic cells, steel and drill pipe, steel wire and grating, wind towers, and woven sacks.[27] This WTO case concerned retroactive application of CVDs against Chinese subject merchandise.

---

26. *See United States — Definitive Anti-Dumping and Countervailing Duties on Certain Products from China*, WT/DS379/AB/R (adopted 25 March 2011).

27. *See* Daniel Pruzin, *WTO Panel Issues Mixed Ruling in Case By China Against U.S. Countervailing Duties*, 31 International Trade Reporter (BNA) 616 (3 April 2014).

Essentially, the Panel applied the precedent of the March 2011 Appellate Body ruling, saying America failed to present any "cogent reasons" for the Panel to depart from this ruling. Accordingly, the U.S. should go back and review so-called "Section 129 proceedings" for each of the 25 CVD orders to see if double counting occurred.

The Chinese victory was not absolute. China lost its transparency arguments against the U.S., namely, that Section 1(b) of the 2012 *GPX* legislation, Public Law 112-99, which re-established the authority of the DOC to impose CVDs on NMEs retroactive to all investigations initiated on or after 20 November 2006, was illegal under GATT Article X:2, which states that no measure of general application:

> effecting an advance in a rate of duty or other charge on imports or impos-ing a new or more burdensome requirement, restriction or prohibition on imports shall be enforced before such measure has been officially published.

China argued the U.S. (1) did not publish this legislation promptly in a way to allow traders to become acquainted with it, (2) enforced the legislation before publish-ing it, and (3) did not administer CVD rules in a uniform, impartial, or reasonable manner.

The Panel said technically, the U.S. "enforced" Section 1(b), because it gave the DOC authority to engage in CVD investigations on Chinese merchandise before 13 March 2012 (when the legislation was enacted). But, two of the three Panelists said America did not breach Article X:2, because (in the words of that provision) Section 1(b) did not "effect[] an advance in a rate of or other charge on imports or impos[e] a new or more burdensome requirement . . . ." That is because Sec-tion 1(b) did not lead to any change in the CVD rates already being imposed on Chinese merchandise, nor did it put any "new requirement" on Chinese imports, and thus did not impose any "new burden" on them.

One dissenting Panelist sided with China. The Dissent thought Section 1(b) did affect an "advance in duties" before official publication of the law in 2012, by boost-ing CVDs in respect of AD-CVD cases on or after 20 November 2006, which could be and were in fact applied.

VII. Market Benchmarks, Government-Related Entities, and 2015 *China CVD* Case

• Facts[28]

The general problem of establishing a benchmark to gauge the extent (if any) of a financial contribution and benefit therefrom under Article 1 of the *SCM Agreement*

---

28. Appellate Body Report, *United States — Countervailing Duty Measures on Certain Products from China*, WT/DS437/AB/R (adopted 16 January 2015). [Hereinafter, *China CVD* Appellate Body Report.] The Panel Report is *United States — Countervailing Duty Measures on Certain Prod-ucts from China*, WT/DS437/R (adopted as modified by the Appellate Body, 16 January 2015). The facts are covered in *China CVD* Appellate Body, ¶¶ 1.1–1.6.

exists with respect to NMEs. The 2015 *China CVD* dispute is an example. In that case, the DOC imposed CVDs following 17 original investigations between 2007 and 2012. The subject merchandise consisted of 17 products from China, including aluminum extrusions, citric acid, drill pipe, kitchen shelving, lawn groomers, line pipe, magnesia bricks, oil country tubular goods, pressure pipe, print graphics, seamless pipe, steel cylinders, steel sinks, solar panels, thermal paper, wind towers, and wire strand.

- **Panel Results**

At the Panel stage, China was successful in many of its claims, most importantly that the DOC violated Article 1:1(a)(1) of the *SCM Agreement* with its "rebuttable presumption." That presumption was that a majority SOE is rebuttably presumed to be a "public body" under this Article. Yet, China was unsuccessful in its claims that calculation of a benefit analysis, and the related market benchmarks the DOC used, were inconsistent with Articles 1:1(b) and 14(d) of the. So, China appealed those claims.[29]

- **Did U.S. Violate *SCM Agreement* Articles 1:1(b) and 14(d)?**[30]

The key Chinese appeal concerned whether the DOC was justified when it rejected the use of in-country private prices of goods in China as benchmarks for calculating the benefit conferred to the companies under investigation. The DOC rejected the use of in-country (*i.e.*, domestic Chinese) prices, because it found those prices were distorted in China due to the role SOEs played in providing the goods in question. China argued that in all of the 17 original investigations, the DOC incorrectly equated SOEs with public bodies. The Panel disagreed with China, finding instead that "only in a few cases" did the DOC refer to the SOEs as public bodies.[31]

On appeal, China argued the legal standard for determining what constitutes "government," and thus what is a "public body," under Article 1:1(a)(1)(iii) of the *SCM Agreement*, should also apply to the definition of "government" under Article

---

29. Also in its appeal, China made three claims with respect to Article 2:1 of the *SCM Agreement*. First, China appealed the sequence of the Specificity Analysis under Article 2:1 of the *SCM Agreement* used by the U.S. DOC. The Appellate Body agreed it is not necessary to proceed in order of the paragraphs of the provisions when conducting a Specificity Analysis. Second, as regards Article 2:1 of the *Agreement*, the Appellate Body accepted the Chinese position that it was not possible that an unwritten, or hidden, subsidy scheme existed (*i.e.*, a *de facto* subsidy scheme), but also said there was not enough evidence to complete an analysis. Third, also under Article 2:1, the Appellate Body said China was correct that the Panel failed to identify properly a "granting authority," as distinct from the jurisdiction of the granting authority, but again the Appellate Body was unable to complete the analysis. Additionally, on appeal, China claimed the Panel erred when it found China had not established that the DOC acted inconsistently with America's obligations under Article 12:7 of the *SCM Agreement* by not relying on facts on the record in 42 "adverse" facts available (AFA) determinations when it conducted the 17 CVD investigations. The Appellate Body sided with China, but chose not to complete the legal analysis, because it would be of little value for the dispute at hand and would also raise due process concerns.

30. *See China CVD* Appellate Body Report, ¶¶ 4.29–4.107.

31. *China CVD* Appellate Body Report, ¶ 4.33 (*quoting China CVD* Panel Report, ¶ 7.180).

14(d) of that *Agreement*. Citing the 2005 *Softwood Lumber IV* case,[32] China contended that the "government" that provides the financial contribution in question must be the same "government" whose predominant role in the market may distort private prices (thus allowing for use of out-of-country prices in the benchmark analysis under Article 14(d)). If the "government" that provides the disputed subsidy is not the same as the entity allegedly involved in the market, then in-country prices must be accepted as a basis for the benchmark.

The U.S. countered that China's argument was premised on an incorrect interpretations of Article 14(d) and the Appellate Body decision in *Softwood Lumber IV*, when considered in context and in conjunction with the 2011 Appellate Body decision in *U.S. AD-CVD*.[33] In its view, the "financial contribution" and "benefit" elements of a subsidy are, by definition, different. So, they require distinct inquiries into the nature of the relevant government intervention in the marketplace. One government entity could provide a subsidy, while a different SOE was involved in buying and selling goods in the domestic market, and rejection of in-country prices as a benchmark would be justified, simply because of the activities of the SOE.

The Appellate Body sided with China, insofar as it agreed there is a single legal standard that defines the term "government" under the *SCM Agreement*. The Appellate Body might have done better to leave matters at this juncture, on the logic that the same term used in the same text should be defined the same way, unless the text indicated otherwise. However, the Appellate Body muddied the waters.

To the Appellate Body, the relevant term under Article 14(d) of the *SCM Agreement* was not "government." Instead, it said an analysis under Article 14(d) asks, in part, whether the goods in question were provided by private or "government-related entities." The Appellate Body invented this term—"government-related entities"—and defined it in a footnote as:

> all government bodies, whether national or regional, public bodies, and any other government-owned entities for which there has not been a "public body" determination.[34]

Citing its own textual interpretation of Article 14(d) from *Softwood Lumber IV*, the Appellate Body recognized use of the term "government" in the first sentence of the provision, but stated the remainder of the provision supports use of the term "government-related entities." Why? Because that remainder focuses on prevailing

---

32. *See* Appellate Body Report, *United States—Final Countervailing Duty Determination with respect to Certain Softwood Lumber from Canada*, WT/DS257/AB/R (adopted 20 December 2005). This case is discussed in a separate Chapter.

33. *See* Appellate Body Report, *United States—Countervailing and Anti-dumping Measures on Certain Products from China*, WT/DS449/AB/R (adopted 22 July 2014). This case is discussed in a separate Chapter.

34. *China CVD* Appellate Body Report, fn. 509 at ¶ 4.43.

market conditions. The Appellate Body interpretation then proceeded to rely heavily on its own analyses in the 2014 *India Carbon Steel* and 2011 *Airbus* cases.[35]

The essential point, then, is that based on previous jurisprudence, in-country prices are preferred as a benchmark. But, the most important factor for any benchmark used is that the prices are market-determined. Government predominance in, or control of, a pertinent market are just some of numerous factual evidence that may be available, and should be considered, on case-by-case basis.

Ultimately, the Appellate Body sided with China. The Panel failed to examine properly each of the challenged determinations in light of the legal standard applicable under Article 14(d) of the *SCM Agreement*. That is to say, the Panel failed to conduct a case-by-case analysis of whether the DOC properly checked that the relevant prices in China were (1) market determined or (2) distorted by governmental intervention. The Appellate Body completed the legal analysis, finding that the rejection of in-country prices in China by the DOC was inconsistent with U.S. obligations under Articles 1:1(b) and 14(d) with respect to the CVD investigations on line pipe, oil country tubular goods, pressure pipe, and solar panels.

- **New Legal Ground?**

Did the 2015 *China CVD* case break new legal ground? On the one hand, the Appellate Body reinforced previous jurisprudence, indicating that use of alternative benchmarks under Article 14(d) must be based on a finding that in-country prices are not market-determined. On the other hand, when interpreting Article 14(d), and explaining this point, the Appellate Body chose to create and define a new term: "government-related entities." Might that new term affect future disputes and the application of Article 14(d)? Are there now three types of entities — "government," "public body," and "government-related" — for purposes of a market benchmark analysis.

---

35. These cases are cited and discussed in separate Chapters.

Chapter 28

Market Disruption[1]

I. Evolution of Trade with Communist Countries and Section 406

- **Overview**

Section 406 of the *Trade Act of 1974*, as amended by the *Omnibus Trade and Competitiveness Act of 1988 (OTCA)*, creates a safeguard-like remedy for merchandise from Communist countries.[2] The remedy is redolent of Escape Clause relief (the general safeguard) under Section 201 of the *1974 Act*, in that there is no allegation that the targeted imports are unfairly traded. They are not necessarily dumped, benefiting from an unlawful subsidy, or infringing on a valid U.S. IPR. Rather, they are increasing at an alarming rate, causing disruption to the American market.

But, there are four key differences between Sections 201 and 406. For Section 406: the standard for proving (1) injury and (2) causation is lower, and (3) the procedure for obtaining relief is faster, than under Section 201, and (4) the investigation focuses on, and any remedy targets, merchandise from a single country (as opposed to all imports, regardless of origin, of a specific product).

- **Section 5 of *1951 Act***

Section 406 was enacted at the height of the Cold War and the Nixon-Kissinger policy of *Détente* toward the former Soviet Union and its allies. Following its signing of GATT on 30 October 1947, the America applied the MFN rule to all other contracting parties as a matter of obligation under GATT Article I:1. As a matter of practice, from 1948 to 1951, it did so to the U.S.S.R. and its Eastern Bloc allies,

---

1. Documents Supplement References:
   (1) *Havana (ITO) Charter* Article 40
   (2) GATT Article XIX
   (3) WTO *Agreement on Safeguards*
This discussion draws on: William H. Lash III, U.S. International Trade Regulation: A Primer Chapter 6 (Problems of Imports from Non-Market Economies) (Washington, D.C., The AEI Press, 1998) (hereinafter, Lash); Bruce E. Clubb, United States Foreign Trade Law, Volume I, Chapters 8 (The Cold War: The Development of Export Controls and Special Treatment for Communist Bloc Countries), 25 (Market Disruption) (Boston, Massachusetts: Little, Brown & Company, 1991) (hereinafter, Clubb); Barry E. Cohen, *Sections 201 and 406 of the Trade Act of 1974, And Their Relationship to Competition Law and Policy*, 56 Antitrust Law Journal 467–486 (1987). Statutory and legislative history quotes below are from Clubb.
   2. *See* 19 U.S.C. § 2436.

none of which save for the former Czechoslovakia was a contracting party. But, as relations between the non-Communist West and Eastern Bloc, the First and Second Worlds, deteriorated into a Cold War, Congress ordered the President to remove MFN treatment from all countries "dominated by international communism." It did so in via Section 5 of the *Trade Agreements Extension Act of 1951*, which said:[3]

> As soon as practicable, the President shall take such action as is necessary to suspend, withdraw, or prevent the application of any reduction in any rate of duty, or binding of any existing customs or excise treatment, or other concession contained in any trade agreement entered into under authority of Section 350 of the *Tariff Act of 1930*, as amended and extended, to imports from the Union of Soviet Socialist Republics and to imports from any nation or area dominated or controlled by the foreign government or foreign organization controlling the world Communist movement.[4]

Consequently, in 1951, President Harry S. Truman (1884–1972, President, 1945–1953) terminated MFN treatment for Albania, Bulgaria, China (People's Republic), Estonia, East Germany (plus the Soviet Sector of Berlin), Indochina (specifically, the areas of Cambodia, Laos, and Vietnam under Communist control), Kuril Islands, Latvia, Lithuania, Mongolia (Outer), North Korea, Romania, Southern Sakhalin, and Tannu Tuva.[5] In 1952, he did so with respect to Hungary, Poland, and Tibet. With respect to Czechoslovakia, the U.S. obtained a waiver from the GATT contracting parties to allow it to suspend its obligations, which they granted effective 2 November 1951 at the 6th Session of GATT negotiations.

• **Special Cases of Yugoslavia, Poland, and Cuba**

The former Yugoslavia, Poland, and Cuba were special cases. From mid-1952 until 1959, no Communist country except for the former Yugoslavia received MFN treatment from the U.S. Yugoslavia was a special case because at the time of the *1951 Trade Agreements Extension Act*, the Soviet Union and its allies subjected it to an economic blockade. Hence, America did not regard it as dominated by the Soviet Union or communism. In 1959, at the 1959 GATT Session, Yugoslavia and Poland stated their interest in becoming contracting parties, though each acknowledged their economic systems precluded them from full participation in GATT. In addition to the U.S., the contracting parties accorded Yugoslavia GATT treatment on a reciprocal basis, *i.e.*, to the degree it gave such treatment to the contracting parties.

In 1959, GATT granted Poland received a provisional, limited contracting party status whereby any contracting party could enter into a trade agreement with Poland, and obliging Poland to disclose information about its trade laws. The U.S. did sign such a deal, but it did not call for MFN treatment. On 16 November 1960, weeks before finishing his second term, President Dwight D. Eisenhower (1890–1969,

---

3. *See* Public Law Number 82-50, 65 Stat. 72, 73, 19 U.S.C. § 1362.
4. Emphasis added.
5. *See* Clubb, Volume I, §§ 8.2.1–8.2.2 and fns. 3–4.

President, 1953–1961) certified under the *1951 Act* that Poland was not dominated by the Soviet Union or world communism, and thereby accorded it MFN treatment. In 1982, President Ronald Reagan withdrew it, following the crackdown by Communist authorities on Solidarity, but restored it in 1987 with a shift in policies there.[6]

As for Cuba, it was not Communist until the 1959 Revolution. When its leader, Fidel Castro (1926–2016, in office, 1959–2011), took power, President Eisenhower proclaimed an import embargo under the 1917 *Trading with the Enemy Act*. President John F. Kennedy (1917–1963, President, 1961–1963) signed the *Tariff Classification Act of 1962*, Section 401(a) of which made clear that Cuba qualified as a country dominated by Communism and, therefore, must be denied MFN treatment.

- **Section 231 of *1962 Act* and Three-Pronged Kennedy Cold War Strategy**

Congress was unhappy with the granting of MFN treatment in these three special cases. Thus, it inserted Section 231 into the *Trade Expansion Act of 1962*, which states:

> The President shall, as soon as practicable, suspend, withdraw, or prevent the application of the reduction, elimination, or continuance of any existing duty or other import restriction, or the continuance of any duty-free or excise treatment, proclaimed in carrying out any trade agreement under this title or under Section 350 of the *Tariff Act of 1930*, to products, *whether imported directly or indirectly, of any country or area dominated or controlled by Communism.*[7]

The italicized language broadened the scope of MFN withdrawal from that under Section 5 of the *1951 Act*: Congress did not want Yugoslavia, Poland, or Cuba to get MFN treatment. Yet, Congress quickly amended this language via Section 402(b) of the *Foreign Assistance Act of 1963*:

> The President may extend the benefits of trade agreement concessions made by the United States to products, whether imported directly or indirectly, of a country or area . . . which, at the time of enactment of this subsection, was receiving trade concessions, when he determines that such treatment would be *important to the national interest* and would *promote the independence of such country or area from domination or control by international communism*, and reports this determination and the reasons therefor to Congress.[8]

This amendment reflected the policy the three-pronged Cold War strategy of the Kennedy Administration: Development, Engagement, and Defense.

Development referred to helping poor countries build their economies, societies, and governmental institutions, so they would be less vulnerable to Communism.

---

6. Poland was exempt from MFN denial under the *1974 Act*, discussed below, and thus had unconditional MFN treatment. When President Reagan suspended this treatment, he did so under the authority of Section 125 of the *1974 Act*.

7. Emphasis added.

8. Emphasis added.

Engagement entailed working with local populations in their home countries through programs like the Peace Corps and Alliance for Progress. Defense meant relying on more than mutually assured destruction (MAD) through nuclear weaponry to offset Soviet and Chinese power. It meant flexible responses to and deterrence of Communist insurgencies, using Special Operations Forces. Trade relations factored into the Development strategy, hence the *1962 Act* gave the President the authority to give MFN treatment to a country if doing so would help wean it off or keep it free from Communism—a result surely in the American national interest.

President Kennedy used this authority to certify Yugoslavia and Poland, hence their MFN treatment continued uninterrupted. Of course, neither he nor his immediate successor, Lyndon B. Johnson (1908–1973, President, 1963–1969), did so with respect to the Soviet Union or Mainland China. Those countries were dominated by, and indeed directed, the world Communist movement. It would have been laughable to think MFN treatment from the U.S. would encourage them to become independent of Communism.

- **Ongoing Problem: Promote Trade with, or Penalize, Foreign Country?**

Over time, some Eastern Bloc countries became full GATT contracting parties. Yugoslavia did so in 1969, following its agreement to decentralize its foreign trade operations and establish a permanent customs tariff. Romania joined in 1971, and Hungary in 1973. Yet, the problem of trading with Communist countries bespoke a general one with which America grapples today: to what extent should trade be fostered or eschewed with a country that is neither friendly with nor hostile to the U.S.?

The problem is manifest, for example, in countries whose governments are populated with officials rather sympathetic to Islamist extremism, or perhaps even to Israel, given some of its policies in the Occupied Territories that are at variance with American preferences. On the one hand, encouraging trade could create a moral hazard problem, as the foreign governments feel they can behave with impunity. On the other hand, ostracizing them may drive them further away from the U.S.

- *Détente* **and** *1974 Act*

Détente entailed peaceful co-existence with the Soviet orbit and Communist China. The strategy was concocted by President Richard M. Nixon (1913–1994, President, 1969–1974) and his Secretary of State, Henry M. Kissinger (1923–). Hence, trade relations between the non-Communist west and Communist Bloc, the First and Second Worlds, could grow. In 1972, the Nixon Administration signed a trade agreement with the Soviet Union calling for MFN treatment on a limited number of products. But, such trade could grow only under tight restrictions, and in any event the deal with the U.S.S.R. needed Congressional approval.

That approval came through Title IV of the *Trade Act of 1974*, which repealed Section 231 of the *1962 Act*.[9] It was commonly referred to as the *Jackson-Vanik Amend-*

---

9. *See* Public Law Number 93-618, § 402(a), 88 Stat. 1978, 2056-2057.

ment, though technically that rubric covers just Section 402 of Title IV. Section 401 of this enabling legislation authorized the President to accord the U.S.S.R. and PRC MFN treatment, as well as other Communist countries, but subject to 2 conditions:

(1) They meet specific human rights criteria, particularly free, unrestricted emigration of religious minorities, such as Soviet and Eastern European Jews (Section 402).

(2) They conclude a bilateral trade accord with the U.S. that establishes reciprocal non-discriminatory treatment (under Section 405).

Over time, American Presidents used this authority to grant MFN treatment to Communist countries, for example, in 1975 to Romania (which not only was the first such country, but also the only one the U.S. declared eligible for the GSP program), in 1978 to Hungary, and in 1990 to the PRC.

Congress repealed the *Jackson-Vanik Amendment* in 2012, when it granted PNTR to Russia in connection with its 22 August 2012 accession to the WTO. With the end of the Cold War and the collapse of both Soviet- and Chinese-dominated Communism, the *Amendment* had served its purpose. But, Section 406 of the *1974 Act* remained.

• **Why Section 406?**

The American concern about increasing trade from Communist countries was their merchandise might cause disruption to product markets in America. Recall that in a Communist economic system, all factors of production (land, labor, physical capital, human capital, and technology) are owned collectively. There is no public-private distinction; all is public. From a Capitalist economic perspective, that means subsidies are pervasive in a Communist country. The price of inputs, intermediate goods, and finished products are not based on the market forces of supply and demand. Rather, they are set by central planners, using sophisticated input-models with hundreds of equations and Linear Algebra techniques for solutions. In turn, central planners can focus factors of production in particular sectors, promoting exports of certain merchandise, and thereby gaining a dominant position in the American market.

Accordingly, the U.S. was concerned its private sector producers would face competition from subsidized merchandise from Communist countries. Worse yet, if those countries overproduced, which they were wont to do for certain goods, then they might export that surplus to the U.S. The result could be dumping. But, the application of traditional AD and CVD remedies could prove difficult. Ascertaining Normal Value would be impossible in Communist country, as would be measuring a net subsidization rate: there were no reliable market-based benchmarks in the country to use. The Senate Finance Committee Report accompanying the *1974 Act* articulated these points, with a striking example from Canada:

> The Committee recognizes that a communist country, through control
> of the distribution process and the price at which articles are sold,

disrupt the domestic markets of its trading partners and thereby injure pro-
ducers in those countries. In particular, *exports from communist countries*
could be directed so as to flood domestic markets within a shorter time period
than could occur under free market conditions. In this regard, the Committee has taken into account the problems which East-West trade poses for
certain sectors of the American economy. For example, the U.S. watch and
clock industry is in a particularly vulnerable position, because of Eastern
European countries' capacity for penetrating markets with underpriced
clocks and watches. When Canada provided most favored nation status to
communist-bloc countries in the 1960's, low-priced East European clock
imports increased dramatically, to the point where sales of such imports
surpassed those of domestic Canadian producers. In the face of such
imports, traditional unfair remedies, such as under the *Antidumping Act*,
have proved inappropriate or ineffective, because of the difficulty of their
application to products from State-controlled economies.[10]

Simply put, American producers of an article that is like or directly competitive
with a product from a Communist country might be flooded with imports of that
product, given that producers in that country operate outside the constraints of
market supply and demand, and oblivious to market price signals.

Exacerbating these concerns was another. Under the DOC interpretation of the
1986 *Georgetown Steel* case, to which it adhered until March 2007, the U.S. eschewed
imposition of CVDs on NMEs. Even if the traditional remedies against unfair practices could work, their deployment might be too slow to cope with sudden rapid
influx of substantial imports from a Communist country. This kind of surge could
occur because of the control of pricing and distribution exerted by a Communist
government.

Therefore, Congress designed Section 406 as a necessary protective defense alternative to the traditional remedies against unfair trade practices. Congress explicitly
modeled Section 406 after the general Section 201 Escape Clause. But, it crafted
the Section 406 criteria to be easier for a petitioner to satisfy and get relief than
Section 201.

Section 406 also reflected the political economy theory of safeguards: to coax
Cold Warrior politicians into liberalizing trade with the Soviet bloc, Section 406
assured them there was an "out." Consequently, Section 406 is rather a hybrid remedy, combining features of those against unfair and fair foreign trade behavior. Put
differently, Section 406 is an example of the dynamic tension in American trade
policy between building trade relations with actual or potential adversaries and
ostracizing them.

---

10. SENATE REPORT NUMBER 1298, 93D CONGRESS, 2D SESSION 212 (1974), *reprinted in* 1974
UNITED STATES CODE CONGRESSIONAL AND ADMINISTRATIVE NEWS 7186, 7342–7343 (emphasis
added). [Hereinafter, SENATE REPORT 1298.]

Section 406 is quite a large "out." It applies to any Communist country, regardless of whether the U.S. grants MFN treatment to merchandise from that country. Of course, that begs the question what countries count as "Communist," particularly after the November 1989 fall of the Berlin Wall. The statute uses a circular definition: a "Communist" country is any one dominated or controlled by communism. Aside from the circularity, what constitutes "domination or control" may, in some instances, be debatable. North Korea undoubtedly would qualify, as likely would Cuba: neither yet boasts multiparty elections whereby the Communist Party rulers are in danger of losing their positions. But, these countries already are subject to American trade sanctions, so Section 406 would be relevant only if and when the U.S. lifted them. For the same reason, China and Vietnam also ought to qualify.

II. Section 406 Market Disruption Safeguard

• **Concept of "Market Disruption"**

Section 406(a) requires the ITC to investigate whether merchandise originating from a Communist country causes "market disruption" to a domestically produced article.[11] The imported good must be "like or directly competitive" with the domestic article. There is no requirement that the domestic producer be an entirely American one; what matters is that production is in the U.S. Hypothetically, Garmin, whose international headquarters are in Kansas, but which is a Taiwanese company, could obtain relief from market disruption caused by merchandise from a Communist country.

Manifestly, the key legal criterion is "market disruption"—when does it occur? The answer (in Section 406(e)(2)(A)) is it exists whenever imports of an article originating in a Communist country that is "like or directly competitive" with a product made by a "domestic industry" in the U.S. increase "rapidly," so as to be a "significant" cause of "material" injury, or threat thereof, to that domestic industry.[12] Thus, "market disruption" does not mean havoc to the entire American economy. Rather, it is defined in terms of a specific domestic industry. So, the job of the ITC is to investigate wither subject merchandise from a Communist country has "increased rapidly" so as to be a "significant cause" of "material" injury or threat thereof to a producer in the U.S. of a "like or directly competitive" product.

Note "significant cause" is a lower threshold than the Section 201 "substantial" causation test. And, "material" injury is a lower threshold than the Section 201 "serious" injury requirement. As for a "rapid" increase in imports, that happens if they have grown, either actual or relative to domestic production of a like or directly competitive product in the importing country, "significantly" during a recent period of time. There is no specific quantitative benchmark, such as a 25% increase

---

11. *See* at 19 U.S.C. § 2436(a).
12. *See* 19 U.S.C. § 2436(e)(2)(A).

in value or volume during a recent one year period. So, there is room for argument in characterizing import data as "significant" and, therefore, "rapid" — or not.

Note also a Section 406 investigation can be launched, and a follow-on remedy imposed, on a country-by-country basis. This feature is redolent of Section 301 and Special 301 investigations, but contrasts with AD, CVD, safeguard, and Section 337 actions. For example (as discussed below), in 1978 the American Clothespin and Veneer Products Association sought Section 406 relief claiming market disruption from clothespin imports from China, Poland, and Romania. The involvement of three different exporting countries necessitated three concurrent ITC investigations. In contrast, had the Association sought AD or CVD relief, then a single investigation of clothespins from all three sources would have sufficed.

- **Communism and ROO**

Section 406 has a rule of origin in Section 406: the merchandise alleged to cause market disruption must be from a "Communist" country. In the 1982 *Chinese Canned Mushrooms* case, American canned mushroom producers sought Section 406 relief (in addition to already existing Escape Clause relief) against the like product from the Chinese Mainland.[13] Imports also increased from Hong Kong and Macao, which at the time were colonies of Britain and Portugal, respectively. The ITC explained they had to be excluded from the investigation, and any relief that might be provided (none was in the end) could be imposed only on canned mushrooms from the Mainland.

What, then, is a "Communist" country? The statutory definition is tautological: a "Communist" country is "any country dominated or controlled by communism."[14] Is "Communism" a time-bound concept, referring to the bygone Cold War era? In turn, have "Communist" countries diminished in number following the collapse of the Berlin Wall in November 1989, suggesting Section 406 is increasingly anachronistic? Unchained to any particular country of origin, is the Escape Clause the better remedy?[15]

Or, is "Communist" an epithet flexible enough to accommodate countries in which there is a substantial degree of public ownership and control of the means of production? If so, then might the remedy have enduring deployment capabilities? Either way, are there lessons from the Section 406 criteria and jurisprudence for other remedies?

- *1988 OTCA* **Easing**

Despite the lower legal thresholds for obtaining Section 406 relative to Section 201 relief, Congress was dismayed that hardly any Section 406 investigations led to a

---

13. *See Canned Mushrooms from the People's Republic of China*, Investigation Number TA-406-9, United States International Trade Commission Publication 1293 (September 1982); Lᴀsʜ 81.

14. 19 U.S.C. § 2436(e)(1).

15. Consider that as of 1998, there were roughly 50 Section 201 cases, 10 times the number of Section 406 cases. *See* Lᴀsʜ, 81. Both remedies, in their principal form used today, date from the same legislation, the *Trade Act of 1974* as amended (though each has roots long before 1974).

remedy. In truth, that was because there were few such cases, as trade between the U.S. and Communist Bloc was modest in the 1970s and 1980s. Nevertheless, in the *1988 OTCA*, Congress further eased the burden on petitioners.[16]

First, the *1988 Act* explained:

> Imports of an article shall be considered to be increasing *rapidly* if there has been a *significant* increase in such imports (either actual or relative to domestic production) during a *recent period* of time.[17]

Why make this change? There were only 11 Section 406 petitions filed between 1974 and 1988, when Congress enacted changes to Section 406 under the *OTCA*. In 4 of those 11 investigations, the ITC decided that imports of merchandise from a Communist country were not "increasing rapidly." So, Congress not only made the change, but also made clear it did not want the Commission to take a narrow view of what "increasing rapidly" means, and thereby knock out petitions.[18] Still, equating "rapid" with "significant," and referring to a "recent period," hardly constituted a precise definition of "increasing rapidly." Congress in the *1988 Act* left open the question of quantitative benchmarks: how much, and over what period, is "significant"?

Second, the *1988 Act* said "significant cause" means "a cause which contributes significantly to the material injury of the domestic industry, but need not be equal to or greater than any other cause." While the first clause was tautological, the second means imports need not be the greatest cause, or even equal to any other cause. Again put in circular terms, what matters, said the House Conference Report accompanying the *Act*, is whether there is a "direct and significant causal link" between rapidly increased imports, on the one hand, and material injury or threat thereof, on the other hand.[19]

Though no quantitative assessment is needed, by way of example, suppose rapidly increasing imports are just 25% of the reason for the injury. Other factors count for a higher percentage, such as technological change being 40% and declining consumer demand being 35%. The imports still could be deemed "important."

Third, the *1988 Act* addressed the question: to what factors must the ITC look in ascertaining whether "market disruption" is occurring? Section mandates that it looks at:

(1) Volume of imports.

(2) Effect of imports on prices for like or directly competitive articles.

(3) Impact of imports on domestic production of like or directly competitive articles.

---

16. *See* Public Law Number 100-418, § 1411, 102 Stat. 1107, 1242.

17. 19 U.S.C. § 2436(e)(2).

18. *See* Clubb, Volume I, § 25.4.3 (*citing* House of Representatives Conference Report Number 576, 100th Congress, 2d Session 690 (1988)).

19. House Conference Report Number 576, 100th Congress, 2d Session 690 (1988).

(4) Evidence of disruptive pricing practices.

(5) Efforts to manage trade patterns in an unfair manner.

These factors are not exclusive, *i.e.*, the ITC may look at other evidence. No one factor necessarily is dispositive.

Arguably, the *1988 Act* amendments to Section 406 had little practical effect. Between 1974, when Congress created the Section 406 remedy, and 1998, there were only 4 investigations in which the ITC rendered an affirmative determination of market disruption. Of those instances, the President granted relief just once, the 1987 *Chinese Tungsten* case.[20] (This and other cases are discussed below.)

- **Element 1: "Like or Directly Competitive" Product**

The meaning of "like or directly competitive" is the same in Section 406 as in Section 201. In turn, that phrase derives from GATT Article XIX:1(a). Under this jurisprudence, and based on evidence of legislative intent from Congress, a "like" product is one that is *"substantially identical"* to the imported merchandise under consideration.[21] A "directly competitive" product" is one that is *"substantially equivalent for commercial purposes"* to the investigated import.[22]

- **Element 2: "Domestic Industry"**

As in a Section 201 case, in a Section 406 investigation, defining the scope of "like" or "directly competitive" products helps shape the answer to the follow-on question: which producers are part of the domestic industry? The obvious, and correct, answer is they constitute any firm (whether American or foreign) making the "like" or "directly" competitive product in the U.S. Also as in a Section 201 case, the possibility of intermediate products and imported components exists, complicating the delineation of the domestic industry. By statute (namely, Section 406(a)(2)), the same factors apply in a Section 406 as in a Section 201 investigation.[23]

- **Element 3: "Rapid" Increase**

Imports of merchandise subject to a Section 406 investigation must increase "rapidly." The measurement of this increase may be in absolute terms, or relative to output from the domestic industry producing a like or directly competitive product:

> Assume that the domestic market for a product is 1 million units. Assume that subject imports rise from 100,000 units to 150,000 when the domestic market is contracting to 800,000 units. This might constitute a rapid increase under Section 406. The [International Trade] Commission interprets *rapidly increasing* to mean *"abnormal* increases in imports."[24]

---

20. *See Ammonium Paratungstate and Tungstic Acid from the People's Republic of China*, Investigation Number TA-406-11, United States International Trade Publication 1982, at 14 (June 1987).

21. Clubb, §23.12.2 at 747 (emphasis added).

22. Clubb, §23.12.2 at 747 (emphasis added).

23. *See* 19 U.S.C. §2436(a)(2).

24. Lash, 72 (emphasis on "abnormal" added; other emphases original).

Data on volume or value are acceptable, though an interesting question would arise if and when volume data show one trend, but value data a different one. That could occur for reasons of price or currency fluctuations, and might undermine a case for relief, because those fluctuations could suggest that they, not imports from a Communist country, caused or threatened injury to the domestic industry.

The aforementioned points lead to two practical questions.

(1) Is it necessary to consider rises in imports from a Communist country in relation to imports from all other countries?

In one scenario, Communist country imports could be rising, but so also could imports from other foreign sources. In another scenario, imports from the Communist country could be up, but imports from the other overseas sources down.

The first scenario would suggest imports from the Communist country are not necessarily the cause of the woes of the petitioning American industry. Both, or just one, of those phenomena could be relevant independent variables, and if so, it ought to be necessary to ensure injury or threat caused by non-Communist imports is not wrongly attributed to Communist imports. Otherwise, the foundation for granting relief would be unjust: producer-exporters not entirely to blame, or not to blame at all, would be hit with protectionist measures.

The second scenario would suggest imports from the Communist country are replacing imports from other countries. In turn, the overall level of foreign competition facing the American industry is essentially unchanged. If Section 406 relief were granted in this scenario, then the beneficiaries would be not only American producers, but also non-Communist producer-exporters. Yet, the latter bunch is not the intended beneficiary of Section 406(a), at least not according to its legislative history.[25] Relief, if any, is supposed to be against merchandise from a Communist country. Hence, in the 1982 *Chinese Canned Mushrooms* case, the International Trade Commission rejected the proposition put by the importer of canned mushrooms from the PRC that both total imports and imports from the Communist country in question must be rising.[26]

Thus, all that is necessary to show is a rapid increase in imports from that particular country. That is, Section 406 does not require total imports to be rising rapidly, only imports from the Communist country in question.

(2) Over what period of time must imports be increasing?

This question is crucial to distinguishing a reasonable increase in imports from a Communist country, which would not cause market disruption in

---

25. *See* CLUBB, § 25.4.3 at 813–814.
26. *See Canned Mushrooms from the People's Republic of China*, Investigation Number TA-406-9, United States International Trade Commission Publication 1293 (September 1982).

the U.S., and which could lead to those imports gaining a "respectable market share" in the U.S., from a striking surge that would cause market disruption and give those imports a position they would not have under usual, fair conditions.[27] In other words, whether imports are increasing rapidly is inherently a temporal issue. Further, this issue is redolent of the issue of defining the POI in an AD or CVD case.

Section 406 does not answer the question "over what period of time?" at all. Its legislative history in the *1974 Trade Act* does, albeit imprecisely. The Senate Finance Committee Report explains the increase:

> must have occurred during a *recent period of time* as determined by the [International Trade] Commission taking into account any *historical trade levels* which may have existed.[28]

The idea is data on imports from the Communist country in question should not be stale, and whether imports are in line with, or markedly different from, general trends, matters. The imprecision is in the failure to define endpoints: when should the POI start and finish? The *1988 Act* amendments did not define these endpoints.

So, the ITC had to answer the question, and did so in 3 cases: 1984 *Soviet Ferrosilicon*, 1982 *Chinese Canned Mushrooms*, and 1982 *Chinese Ceramics*. In each case, the ITC defined the endpoints as 3 years.[29] That is, it studied import trends over the most recent 3 year period for which reliable data were available. Put differently, Section 406 is concerned about "abnormal" increases (though "abnormal" is not defined in the statute or its legislative history), and three years is about the right POI to judge whether the increases are, indeed, abnormal.

But, must the POI in a Section 406 case always be three years? No. The Joint Conference Committee Report accompanying the *1988 Act* identifies two different scenarios: a one-year POI, and a POI of two-to-three years:

> In applying the term "rapidly," the ITC should examine whether imports have *recently surged over historical levels*. In conducting this inquiry, the ITC should *balance the amount of the increase and the period of time involved*. Thus, if the ITC finds that the increase is *concentrated in a single year*, it should look for a *relatively sharp increase*. If . . . the increase has occurred

---

27. *See* Senate Report 1298, *reprinted in* 1974 United States Code Congressional and Administrative News 7186, 7344.

28. Senate Report 1298, *reprinted in* 1974 United States Code Congressional and Administrative News 7186, 7344.

29. *See Ferrosilicon from the U.S.S.R.*, Investigation Number TA-406-10, United States International Trade Commission Publication 1484 at 8–9 (February 1984); *Canned Mushrooms from the People's Republic of China*, Investigation Number TA-406-9, United States International Trade Commission Publication 1293 at 10–11 (September 1982); *Ceramic Kitchenware and Tableware from the People's Republic of China*, Investigation Number TA-406-8, United States International Trade Commission Publication 1279 at 9–11 (August 1982).

over a *2–3 year period*, the longer period will provide a *more stable basis for comparison* and *may show a steady trend toward higher import levels that meets the "rapidly increasing" requirement*. Thus, in the latter situation, the *increase need not be as sharp or as dramatic as that required over a shorter period*. If imports have fluctuated up and down, the fact that imports are on a rapid upswing can satisfy the "rapidly increasing" requirement, even though imports have not reached levels attained in a previous period.[30]

From this legislative history, four inferences can be drawn.

First, there are not quantitative benchmarks that cover all cases. "Rapidly increasing" means a recent "import surge," but what qualifies as a surge, and how near in time, or over what period of time, the surge must be depends on the case. On these points, the ITC has discretion. Second, the shorter the definition of the POI, the more pronounced the import surge should be, and conversely, the longer that definition, the less pronounced the surge should be, to grant relief. Logically, it almost always is easy to partition a long span of time into shorter intervals, and define as the POI one interval in which imports jump. Doing so can be a bias in favor of the petitioner. So, if the ITC is to entertain a short POI, then the import spike had better be dramatic. Third, a longer POI is preferable to a shorter one, because it avoids time splicing and bias—a "more stable basis for comparison," as the Joint Committee put it. Fourth, the increase need not be monotonic. There can be ups and downs in import trends during the POI.

- **Element 4: "Material" Injury or Threat**

As is true for all International Trade Law remedies, Section 406 presumes "no harm, no foul." Unless a domestic industry making a product that is like or directly competitive with imported merchandise can prove that merchandise caused, or threatened to cause, it with material injury, then no Section 406 relief is available. As the 1982 *East German Wax* case explained, proof of either material injury or threat is enough, because—rather obviously—the statute uses the disjunctive "or."[31] That begs the question of what is "material" injury or threat thereof?

Neither Section 406, nor its big brother Section 201, defines the term. That is, the *Trade Act of 1974* contains no definition of the term. Indeed, the adjective modifying "injury" in the two safeguard statutes are different: relief from imports from a Communist country under Section 406 requires proof of "material" injury (or threat); whereas relief from imports from a non-Communist country under the Section 201 Escape Clause demands proof of "serious" injury (or threat). Which is the higher burden on the petitioner, and why is there a difference between them?

---

30. House of Representatives Conference Report Number 576, 100th Congress, 2d Session 690 (1988) (emphasis added).

31. *See Unrefined Montan Wax from East Germany*, Investigation Number TA-406-7, United States International Trade Publication 1214, at 12 (January 1982).

"Serious" injury is a higher threshold than "material" injury. That is clear from the Senate Finance Committee Report accompanying Section 406.[32] In writing the *1974 Act*, Congress could have picked either standard for either remedy, and could have harmonized the standard between the two remedies. Instead, Congress opted to use the standard in GATT Article XIX of "serious" injury for Section 201, so that the American Escape Clause would mirror the multilateral general safeguard. But, it chose to borrow from the GATT Article VI:1 AD provision the lower standard of "material," and put it into the Section 406 remedy. The obvious question, but one unanswered in either Section 406 or the legislative history to the *1974 Act*, is whether "material" injury has the same meaning for purposes of Section 406 as it does for AD law.

With no definition of "materiality" in Section 406, the ITC had to decide what factors to consider when evaluating whether a domestic industry is injured or threatened with injury by imports from a Communist country. Following passage of the *1974 Act*, until its amendment by the *1988 Act*, the ITC looked at the same variables in a Section 406 case as it did in a Section 201 case. In the latter context, the ITC must look at (*inter alia*) (1) "significant idling of productive facilities in the domestic industry," (2) inability of a significant number of firms to produce domestically at a "reasonable level of profit," and (3) "significant unemployment or underemployment" in the domestic industry.[33]

The 1982 *Chinese Canned Mushrooms* case is an example of the ITC transferring over to Section 406 the Escape Clause injury variables.[34] Before that case, the American canned mushroom industry received relief under Section 201. So, imports of the like product were falling, yet the industry sought additional relief, this time under Section 406. The ITC was split 2–2, so it did not grant relief.[35] Two Commissioners observed during the period in which Chinese imports increased most dramatically, the profitability of American producers grew. Moreover, fluctuations in domestic industry employment levels easily could be attributed to changes in the productivity of workers, as opposed to Chinese imports. Note the ITC used the Section 201 variables in Section 406 cases such as *Chinese Canned Mushrooms*, even though nothing in Section 406 directed it to do so, and even though Congress in the *1974 Act* (in Section 406(a)(2)) applied certain provisions of Section 201 to Section 406 context, but not the injury factors.

With the *1988 Act* amendments to Section 406, Congress gave the ITC a list of four variables (set out earlier) to examine.[36] Summarized, the ITC looks at the (1)

---

32. *See* SENATE REPORT 1298, *reprinted in* 1974 UNITED STATES CODE CONGRESSIONAL AND ADMINISTRATIVE NEWS 7186, 7343–7344.

33. 19 U.S.C. § 2252(c)(1)(A).

34. *See Canned Mushrooms from the People's Republic of China*, Investigation Number TA-406-9, United States International Trade Commission Publication 1293 (September 1982).

35. *See* LASH 81 (also observing under Section 406, a tie vote results in a negative determination; however that rule is not set out in the statute, 19 U.S.C. § 2436).

36. *See* 19 U.S.C. § 2436(e)(2)(C).

volume, (2) price effects, and (3) impact of Communist country merchandise, and (4) for evidence of efforts at disruptive pricing or managing trade patterns in an unfair manner. Interestingly, only the fourth factor is innovative. The ITC had applied the previous variables before the amendment.[37]

Regarding threat of material injury, it is important to appreciate that rapidly increasing imports are not of themselves a sufficient basis to conclude a domestic industry is in peril of market disruption caused by imports from a Communist country. That much is clear from the 1983 *Soviet Ferrosilicon* case.[38] In the case, production of ferrosilicon, and employment in that industry, in the U.S. tumbled around 40% between 1982 and 1983. Soviet imports rose from the second half of 1983 from zero to 3.8% of American production. Data also showed rising Soviet market share in the U.S., lost sales to Soviet imports, and price underselling vis-à-vis American producers. The ITC agreed with the USTR, which initiated a Section 406 petition, that (1) those imports increased rapidly, and (2) the domestic industry suffered material injury.

But, the ITC said (1) was not a significant cause of (2), nor was (1) a significant cause of threat of (2). Rather, other market conditions were significant causes. In a key insight, the ITC said threat of material injury occurs only if:

> injury, although not yet existing, is *clearly imminent if import trends continued unabated*.[39]

The dissent (by renowned Commissioner and International Trade scholar Alfred E. Eckes, Jr. (1942–)) said the facts bespoke a "classic case of market disruption."[40] The dissent argued the majority ignored the national security purpose of Section 406: to prevent the U.S. from dependence on Communist merchandise for strategic items. That ferrosilicon was a vital agricultural raw material product, with "far reaching implications for national defense and this country's industrial base," should not be doubted.[41]

- **Element 5: "Significant" Cause**

Section 406 relief requires proof imports from a Communist country are a "significant" cause of material injury or threat thereof. The Senate Finance Committee defined "significant" in its Report accompanying the 1974 *Trade Act* to be a standard less rigorous than the Section 201 "substantial" causation test, but more rigorous, in the sense of requiring a more direct causal link, than the "contribute importantly" Trade Adjustment Assistance test. This intermediate standard means, said the ITC in the 1979 *Soviet Ammonia* case, and in the 1987 *Chinese Tungsten*

---

37. *See* CLUBB, §25.4.4 at 820.

38. *See Ferrosilicon from the U.S.S.R.*, Investigation Number TA-406-10, United States International Trade Commission Publication 1484 (February 1984).

39. *Quoted in* LASH, 80 (emphasis added).

40. *Quoted in* LASH, 80.

41. *Quoted in* LASH, 80.

Case, that rapidly increasing imports must be directly related to injury in a causal manner, but they need not be the only cause, or a cause that is equal to or exceeds all other causes.[42] Rather, the imports simply need to be an important cause, but, again, "important" does not mean "unique" cause, nor does it mean "equal to or greater than" some other cause.

• **Procedures**

As intimated, the entirety of a Section 406 case falls within the ambit of the ITC. Such a case is launched with the ITC in one of four manners:[43]

(1) *Sua sponte, i.e.,* on the motion of the ITC itself.

(2) At the request of the Executive Branch of the U.S. government, specifically, the President or USTR.

(3) Upon a resolution from the Legislative Branch, namely, a resolution from either the Senate Finance Committee or House Ways and Means Committee (*i.e.,* either of the two Congressional Committees responsible for international trade matters).

(4) A petition from a private sector entity, which could be a firm, union, group of workers, or trade association, associated with an industry in the U.S., *i.e.,* a domestic producer of a product that is "like or directly competitive" with the allegedly offending foreign merchandise.

As to the fourth method, the entity must be representative of the industry producing a like domestic product.

But, unlike the 25% and 50% Standing Tests in AD-CVD law, there is no quantitative benchmark for representativeness in Section 406. As with Section 201, Section 406 simply requires that the complainant be "an entity, including a trade association, firm, certified or recognized union, or group of workers, *which is representative of an industry.*"[44] With both remedies, it is unclear what "representative" means. Does it mean "typical" of the firms or workers in the industry, or could an entity act as an agent for them, and be considered "representative"?[45] Perhaps a clue comes from the requirement that the petitioner is asked by the ITC via a questionnaire to disclose (*inter alia*) the percentage of the industry the petitioning

---

42. *See Ammonium Paratungstate and Tungstic Acid from the People's Republic of China*, Investigation Number TA-406-11, United States International Trade Publication 1982, at 14 (June 1987); *Anhydrous Ammonia from the U.S.S.R.*, Investigation Number TA-406-5, United States International Trade Commission Publication 1006 at 27 (October 1979).

43. *See* 19 U.S.C. § 2436(a)(1). Presidential initiation is rare, but occurred in the second of two *Soviet Ammonia* cases. *See Anhydrous Ammonia from the U.S.S.R.*, Investigation Number TA-406-6, United States International Trade Commission Publication 1051 (April 1980). *See* CLUBB, § 25.6.1 at 824.

44. *See* 19 U.S.C. § 2436(a)(1) (emphasis added), which incorporates by reference the same standing requirement contained in § 2252(a)(1) for the Section 201 Escape Clause.

45. *See* CLUBB, § 25.6.2 at 824.

producers represent, the names of unrepresented producers, plus data on domestic production.

Once it a Section 406 petition is filed, the ITC has an outer time limit of three months to complete its investigation and issue a final report to the President, including remedy recommendations and any dissenting views.[46] In the investigation, the ITC sends questionnaires to and has *ex parte* meetings with the petitioner and respondent, conducts on-site visits, and holds a public hearing.

If the ITC renders an affirmative determination that market disruption exists, then it must make a remedy recommendation to the President. The President has final decision as to whether to provide a remedy, and if so, which one. Thus, unlike AD-CVD cases, but like Section 201 cases, there is Presidential discretion in Section 406 cases. So, every Section 201 or 406 case requires the White House to expend political capital, either in favor of (1) relief and, therefore, in favor of the protected domestic industry, but against importing companies and other domestic consumers, or (2) free trade and, therefore, in favor of importers and consumers, but against domestic producers.

A Section 406 remedy could be imposing tariffs or quantitative restrictions (such as quotas or auctioning import licenses) on the imported merchandise, or imposing or tightening TRQs on that merchandise, or some combination thereof. (Tightening a TRQ could take the form of a lower in-quota volume threshold, or a higher in-quota tariff.) The goal must be to rectify existing and prevent further market disruption to the afflicted domestic industry. Relief also could take the form of an OMA negotiated with the target Communist country, or otherwise entering into international negotiations. The remedy could be a combination of the aforementioned measures. Any remedy is temporary, specifically, it can last for up to five years, and can be renewed only once for up to three years.

Thus, the remedy possibilities under Section 406 are the same as those under Section 201, with the exception of an OMA with a WTO Member.[47] OMAs, also called VERs or VRAs, generally are forbidden under Article 11:1(b) of the WTO *Agreement on Safeguards*. (Only if they were negotiated between private parties would they skirt this prohibition, but then they might run afoul of a domestic antitrust law.)

Upon receipt of the ITC recommendation, the President has 60 days to advise Congress what, if any, remedy he will provide. Within 15 days of his decision to authorize relief, the President must issue a Proclamation granting it—with one exception. He may take 60 days from the date of the determination to negotiate an OMA. President Ronald Reagan used this form of relief in the 1987 *Chinese Tungsten* case. Suppose the President orders a remedy, and duly notifies Congress of it,

---

46. *See* 19 U.S.C. § 2436(a)(4); CLUBB, § 25.5 at 822–823.
47. *See* 19 U.S.C. § 2253(a)(3).

but it is different from that recommended by the ITC. By joint resolution, Congress may disapprove of the decision of the President, in which case the ITC recommendation takes effect within 90 days of the notification. Of course, the President could veto the resolution, subject to a Congressional override of that veto. Here again, the scenario under Section 406 is the same as that under Section 201.[48]

Section 406 also creates the possibility of emergency relief, before an ITC determination. Section 406(c) empowers the President to grant temporary, expedited relief against imports from a Communist country if he has reasonable grounds to believe market disruption is occurring. Should he grant this relief, he must ask the ITC to conduct a Section 406(a) investigation, and must terminate it on the day of a negative ITC determination. If the ITC determination if affirmative, then the President must terminate it as well, and possibly supplant it with a new remedy tailored around the ITC findings.

Finally, as under Section 201, Presidential determinations under Section 406 generally are not subject to judicial review. No Section 406 case ever has been appealed to the CIT. The Political Question Doctrine tends to block such review, hence courts may review — if at all — Section 406 cases with respect to procedural due process questions.[49]

- **GATT-WTO Consistency?**

Is Section 406 consistent with GATT-WTO law? The issue did not arise for most of the post–Second World War era, because Section 406 targeted Communist countries, which were not GATT contracting parties, nor WTO Members. The targets would have had no standing under GATT Article XXIII or the WTO *DSU* to sue the U.S. The question also did not arise with respect to China. That is because (as explained below), following its 11 December 2001 WTO accession, the Section 421 country-specific safeguard applied to China for 12 years, until 31 December 2013.

But, what about Russia, Tajikistan, or other former Soviet bloc countries that have acceded to the WTO? Suppose they are targeted with a Section 406 remedy. Could they claim under the *DSU* that this remedy violates GATT-WTO law?

On the one hand, Section 406 is not unlike the conventional safeguard in GATT Article XIX and the WTO *Agreement on Safeguards*. The legal criteria for applying it are similar to the general safeguard. But, on the other hand, it does not pre-date GATT, and thus is not grandfathered under GATT-WTO law, nor is there an express permission in that law for additional safeguards not provided in that law. Consequently, it may be the safest use of Section 406 is against Communist countries not yet in the WTO. As there are ever fewer of them, the remedy may be a weapon of diminishing value.

---

48. *See* 19 U.S.C. § 2253(c).

49. *See Maple Leaf Fish Co. v. United States*, 762 F.2d 86, 89–90 (Fed. Cir. 1985) and *Sneaker Circus, Inc. v. Carter*, 566 F.2d 396, 399–400 (2d Cir. 1977), both of which are Section 201 appeals involving limited review on procedural matters.

III. 1987 Section 406 *Chinese Tungsten* Case

- **Facts, Holding, and Rationale**[50]

Thus far, the 1987 *Chinese Tungsten* case is the only Section 406 investigation resulting in both an affirmative ITC determination on market disruption and relief granted by the President.[51] China received MFN treatment from the U.S. in 1980. As to a "rapid increase" in imports, in 1983, Chinese exports of tungsten products (which were intermediate goods to make tungsten powders) accounted for 3% of the American market, and by 1986, 17%.

As to "material injury" to American producers, these imports underpriced domestic production, which declined. In the U.S., between 1982 and 1986, the tungsten industry endured a cycle of bust, boom, and bust, as measured by trends in consumption and capacity utilization, but overall had operating losses, and employment fell by 31%.

As for "significant causation," the ITC based its affirmative market disruption finding on price undercutting. While the decline in American demand contributed to the material injury of the domestic industry, Chinese imports were a significant cause. They increased as measured both by market share and volume. These gains were due to aggressive pricing below prices charged by domestic producers: Chinese tungsten prices fell by 71% more than those of American tungsten.

An interesting business statistic provided a basis for the causation finding. For the domestic industry, the ITC looked at the ratio of:

$$\frac{\text{Cost of Goods Sold (\textit{i.e.}, COGS)}}{\text{Net Sales (which depends in part on sale prices)}}$$

For the years after 1984, this ratio consistently rose, meaning that costs increased but sales fell. The rise in this ratio occurred even though raw materials used to produce tungsten products fell. Why? Because of the relatively more dramatic decline in sales by American tungsten producers, a decline that occurred because of price depression caused by Chinese imports. In brief, even though the input costs faced by domestic producers fell, they could not raise or even maintain prices of their finished product, because of price undercutting by Chinese exporters.

- **Relief**

The ITC recommended imposition of quotas on Chinese tungsten for five years, such that those imports would be capped at 7.5% of domestic consumption. The ITC based its quota calculation on average imports between 1982 and 1984, which essentially were a baseline against which to gauge the abnormal increase in Chinese

---

50. This discussion draws on: WILLIAM H. LASH III, U.S. INTERNATIONAL TRADE REGULATION: A PRIMER 75–76 (Washington, D.C., The AEI Press, 1998).

51. *See Ammonium Paratungstate and Tungstic Acid from the People's Republic of China*, Investigation Number TA-406-11, United States International Trade Publication 1982, at 14 (June 1987).

tungsten imports, and thus a reasonable *status quo ante* to which to return. Interestingly, one Commissioner favored a stricter quota (set on the basis of 1984 imports), while two others favored a more generous one (17.2% of domestic consumption). The ITC also considered, but rejected, tariff relief. It feared Chinese exporters might absorb any increased tariff, thus undermining or defeating the purpose of that relief.

President Ronald Reagan (1911–2004, President, 1981–1989) accepted the determination of the ITC. He ordered relief via an OMA, under which China voluntarily agreed to limit its tungsten exports for five years at the average level of the 1982–1984 period.

IV. Affirmative Market Disruption Determinations Thrice, But No Relief [52]

In three of the four Section 406 investigations in which the ITC rendered an affirmative determination, the President declined to provide remedy. What were these cases, why did the ITC find in favor of market disruption, and why did the President reject relief?

• **1979–1980 *Soviet Ammonia* Case**

The 1979–1980 *Soviet Ammonia* case originated in a 1973 countertrade (barter) agreement between the Occidental Petroleum Corporation and Soviet Union.[53] Under the deal, associated with the Nixon-Kissinger policy of *détente*, the U.S Export-Import Bank financed via loans the construction of ammonia plants in the Soviet Union. Occidental contributed technology to build the plants, and in exchange got an exclusive 20-year right to buy ammonia from the plants and sell it in the U.S. The ammonia was for use in agricultural fertilizer.

Between 1978 and 1979, the share of the American market (measured by domestic consumption) of Soviet ammonia imported under this deal rose from 2 to 6%, and by 1981 was forecast to hit 12%. Consequently, American producers of ammonia—competitors of Occidental—claimed market disruption, and filed a Section 406 petition. They said they were threatened with injury from unstable natural gas prices, and evidence for that threat included increases in Soviet production capacity over the previous five years in excess of projected Soviet and world market demand, and a decline in operating profit, which turned into a loss in 1978–1979. They also pointed to the disadvantage at which they were placed by forward price contracts Occidental had with the Soviets: those contracts locked in ammonia prices for Occidental, while American competitors had to pay spot market prices, which rose because of increasing raw materials costs.

---

52. This discussion draws on LASH, 72–75, 76–80.

53. *See Anhydrous Ammonia from the U.S.S.R.*, Investigation Number TA-406-5, United States International Trade Commission Publication 1006 (October 1979).

The ITC reached an affirmative determination, and in doing so pointed out the link to national security: ammonia used in fertilizer was critical to maintaining agricultural production efficiency, on which both the American and the economy of the free world depended. Yet, President Jimmy Carter (1924–, President, 1977–1981) declined relief. Why?

President Carter said it was not in the national interest to impose trade barriers on Soviet ammonia imports. On the one hand, he had solid justifications, provided by in the dissenting opinion of two Commissioners. The dissent said Soviet ammonia imports were not the cause of material injury, because a close examination of the industry suffered between 1975 and 1978 revealed three facts:

(1) A decline in demand and a rise in energy input costs were the causes of material injury;

(2) Material injury to the domestic industry existed in 1975, before the increase in Soviet ammonia imports;

(3) Forecasts about the effects of Occidental forward pricing contracts were unreliable given the fluctuations in ammonia prices generally

(4) Soviet imports did not increase "rapidly," but rather steadily gained market share in the U.S.

(5) Imports generally had increased, so even if Soviet ammonia were removed from the American market, ammonia from third countries likely would fill the void.

Moreover, the dissent argued that by 1979, the domestic industry was on the verge of recovery. That was because between 1975 and 1979:

(1) The principal consequence of the decline in demand and higher energy input costs was closure of old, inefficient ammonia plants;

(2) The industry made large capital expenditures, investing in new plants with modern technology.

Thus, once demand picked up and energy prices stabilized, the domestic industry was well positioned with lean, efficient production facilities.

On the other hand, in December 1979, just two months after the ITC determination, the Soviets invaded Afghanistan in a Cold War effort to ensure that country remained in its orbit. The Soviets would occupy Afghanistan until forced to withdraw in February 1989. President Carter reacted not only with an American boycott of the Summer 1980 Olympic Games in Moscow (which the Soviets repaid with their own boycott of the 1984 Los Angeles Summer Olympics), but also by setting temporary quotas on Soviet ammonia, and by self-initiating a second Section 406 investigation of Soviet ammonia. Certainly, he hoped the ITC again would render an affirmative determination of market disruption. It did not.[54] Economic history

---

54. *See Anhydrous Ammonia from the U.S.S.R.*, Investigation Number TA-406-6, United States International Trade Commission Publication 1051 (April 1980).

proved the dissent from the first case correct: the domestic industry experienced a boom, with a reversal in the decline in profitability, and a 12% increase in capacity utilization.

- **1978 *Chinese, Polish, and Romanian Clothespins* Cases**

The Clothespin and Veneer Products Association, representing domestic producers, petitioned for three concurrent Section 406 cases against China, Poland, and Romania.[55] The Association argued imports flooded the American market between 1975 and 1977, resulting in material injury evidenced between 1973 and 1978 by a (1) 17% drop in domestic capacity utilization, and (2) decline in average industry profit margin from 8.3% to 0.7%. The investigation against Poland and Romania collapsed, as data showed imports from them at best grew moderately, but the case against China continued. Chinese clothespins occupied 20% of the American market in 1978, up from zero in just four years.

The ITC agreed to recommend relief against Chinese clothespins, in the form of a quota. Chinese clothespins caused market disruption, because they (1) displaced sales from American competitors, and (2) underpriced American clothespins, resulting in price depression in the U.S. As in the *Soviet Ammonia* case, President Carter declined to put up protective barriers. He reasoned Chinese imports comprised just 27% of all clothespin imports into America, and if they were subject to a quota, like merchandise from third countries would replace them to meet U.S. demand. Indeed, Taiwanese imports were a greater threat to U.S. producers than Chinese imports: the share of total clothespin imports into the U.S. accounted for by Taiwan surged from 47% to 88% between 1976 and 1979.

That figure—27%—led President Carter to suggest the more appropriate remedy than Section 406 would be Section 201. That was because the Escape Clause empowered him to impose relief against clothespins from all sources. So, in 1979, following an affirmative Section 201 determination by the ITC, President Carter granted safeguard relief in the form of a tariff.

- **1994 *Chinese Honey* Case**

In the 1994 *Chinese Honey* case, the ITC rendered its third positive Section 406 finding, but President Bill Clinton (1946–, President, 1993–2001) declined to provide relief.[56] Chinese honey imports into the U.S. surged from 1989 to 1992 by a whopping 141%. American honey production was uneven. But, based on

---

55. *See Clothespins, Report to the President*, 46 Federal Register 62,338 (1981); *Clothespins from the People's Republic of China, the Polish People's Republic, and the Socialist Republic of Romania*, Investigations Numbers TA-406-2, TA 406-3, and TA-406-4, United States International Trade Commission Publication (1981).

56. *See Honey from China*, Investigation Number TA-406-13, United States International Trade Commission Publication 2715 (January 1994). This discussion draws on: William H. Lash III, U.S. International Trade Regulation: A Primer 72–75 (Washington, D.C., The AEI Press, 1998).

unemployment data, American beekeepers were not material injured, and though their net income fell by 14%, the net income of American honey packers increased by 8%.

The ITC found Chinese imports posed a threat of material injury to the American honey industry, based on increased inventories since 1992, overall declining profitability, a loss of 13% of the domestic market share, and financial difficulties in seeking to repair or enhance equipment. The facts Chinese and American honey were close substitutes, and domestic producers could do little else other than sell at home, exacerbated the threat.

So, the majority of the six-member ITC called for a remedy, but even they were not of the same mind. Three of them (Chairman Newquist and Commissioners Rohr and Nuzum) recommended a TRQ for three years whereby an in quota duty of 25% would be imposed on Chinese honey imports up to 12.5 million pounds, and shipments above this volume threshold would face an over-quota duty of 50%. One Commissioner (Vice Chairman Watson) suggested a less stringent TRQ: 15% on the first 60 million pounds, and 25% thereafter. Manifestly, the difference between the two TRQs lay in the severity of the perceived threat: the lower the volume threshold and higher the tariff, the greater the sense of danger. The fifth Commissioner (Crawford) called for a flat 10% tariff on all Chinese honey, saying any TRQ would impose administrative burdens on American authorities, and put allocative costs on Chinese authorities (as they would have to pick which exporters would ship under versus over the TRQ threshold).

Perhaps the most interesting opinion was the dissent (from Commissioner Brunsdale). It argued there was no market disruption, as domestic production had increased by almost 25% between 1989 and 1992, when honey imports rose dramatically. The Dissent also said not all honey is alike: darker Chinese honey is higher in moisture content, tastes sour owing to fermentation, and sometimes has chemical additives (including sweeteners), in contrast to lighter, sweeter domestic honey. So, Chinese honey is used by American companies for industrial purposes, while domestic honey is sold on the retail market. The reason for greater Chinese imports was an increase in industrial demand, whereas the competition domestic honey faces, in terms of a substitute product, is from Argentina and Canada.

The Dissent predicted that removing Chinese honey from the American market via a Section 406 remedy would create a void that Mexican honey would fill, as it was the most likely substitute for industrial use, *i.e.*, American producers would not be much affected. And, the Dissent observed the financial health of the American beekeeping industry historically hinged on farm subsidies, which had dropped from 50% to 13% of the average income of a beekeeper between 1988 and 1992. The real threat, then, was from a further decline in government support.

Given the differences of opinion as to the right remedy, and the insightful Dissent, President Clinton decided relief was not in the "national economic interest of the United States."[57] First, like the Dissent, he cited the probability of increased imports from other countries, should Chinese products face a TRQ or higher tariffs. Second, he said the costs to American honey users outweighed the benefits to domestic beekeepers. Finally, he was chary of adopting a protectionist measure orthogonal to his overall policy of free trade.

These points are fair enough, but think about the first one: does it, and should it, matter that Section 406 relief against one country might lead to replacement of imports from that country by exporters from another country, with no benefit to American producers? Does this reason, which is akin to that offered by the Dissent in the first *Soviet Ammonia* case, sound like the 2006 *Bratsk* Replacement-Benefit Test (discussed in a separate Chapter) used for commodities in AD cases?

V. Section 421 Country-Specific Market Disruption Safeguard Against China

• **Established and Emerging Powers**

What happens when an established power and an emerging power meet? In International Trade Law, one answer is a country-specific or product-specific safeguard. Concerned about a surge in imports from the rising power, the established power adds to its existing trade arsenal another weapon: a safeguard remedy against products from the emerging power. That is precisely what happened between America and China when the former negotiated in November 1999 with the latter over accession of the latter to the WTO. Section 421 implements that specific safeguard.

To be sure, U.S. businesses cannot compete against Chinese SOEs that do not operate on commercial principles, or with behind-the-Great Wall protections like indigenous technology policies. Section 421 does not entirely address these non-transparent problems. That is, Section 421 focuses on import competition faced by domestic producers of a like product, but not competition faced by American exporters in China. The commercial terms of China's WTO accession were supposed to have resolved problems American exporters face in China. Section 421 concerns problems producers in the U.S. face thanks to Chinese import competition.

The U.S. got the safeguard into the accession agreement because it could. The established power was the indispensable nation for producer-exporters in the emerging power. The latter had little choice but to accept the special remedy, knowing the remedy had an inherent Sunset Date, and perhaps thankful that at least no other country could have pushed it to accept that remedy.

---

57. William J. Clinton, *Message to the Congress Reporting on Trade with China*, *in* PUBLIC PAPERS OF THE PRESIDENTS OF THE UNITED STATES: WILLIAM J. CLINTON, 1994, vol. 1, 747 (Washington, D.C.: Government Printing Office, 1995).

• **Legal Criteria**

Market disruption is a safeguard remedy exogenous to the GATT-WTO system. Within that system, not every safeguard relief measure arises under GATT Article XIX. That much is evident from the Uruguay Round agreements, such as the *Agreement on Agriculture*, which (in Article 5) establishes a Special Safeguard (SSG) for farm products, and from the now-elapsed WTO *ATC*, which (in Article 6) created a transitional safeguard mechanism. It also is evident from the tortuous, unsuccessful Doha Round negotiations over a Special Safeguard Mechanism (SSM). Yet another example of Escape Clause-like relief that is not related to Article XIX is a Country-Specific Safeguard, which famously was negotiated in the context of the accession of the People's Republic of China to the WTO. That accession was agreed on 11 December 2001, and the special remedy associated with China is (logically enough) sometimes called the "China-Specific Safeguard," or more generally, a "Country-Specific Safeguard."

Section 421, or to be technically accurate, Sections 421–423, of the *Trade Act of 1974* as amended, is the new version of Section 406 that addresses market disruption caused by import surges specifically from the People's Republic of China. As part of its accession negotiations, specifically, the 15 November 1999 *United States-China Bilateral Trade Agreement (BTA)*, China agreed to be subject to a Country-Specific Safeguard. This safeguard was multilateralized, *i.e.*, made available to all WTO Members, by virtue of the *Protocol on the Accession of the People's Republic of China to the WTO (Accession Protocol)* to the WTO.

Why did China agree to a remedy specifically targeting Middle Kingdom merchandise? It had no choice. When China negotiated for WTO accession, it did so amidst a world-wide climate of fear its manufacturing would lead to import surges in many countries. The WTO Members felt GATT Article XIX was not enough to protect them against fair Chinese competition. So, to the "belt" of this Article they added the "suspenders" of the Country-Specific Safeguard.

Section 421 implements this Safeguard in U.S. trade law. The China-specific safeguard takes the place of Section 406, which ceased to apply to China following its WTO accession. Section 421 was passed on 10 October 2000, in connection with Section 103 of Public Law 106-286, which granted China PNTR, *i.e.*, MFN treatment. By virtue of the GATT Article I:1 MFN obligation, the U.S. was obliged to provide that treatment (or otherwise invoke the Non-Application Rule of Article XXXV of GATT and Article XIII of the *WTO Agreement*). Notably, Section 421 had a sunset date of 12 years from the accession of China to the WTO, *i.e.*, 11 December 2013.[58]

The legal criteria for Section 421 relief are identical to those of Section 406. So, to launch the anti-Chinese import surge remedy, a domestic industry or workers can petition for relief against products of Chinese origin. Alternatively, the ITC can self-initiate a petition, or one can come from the President, or the Senate Finance or

---

58. *See* Section 423 of the *1974 Act*, codified at 19 U.S.C. § 2451b(c).

House Ways and Means Committee can pass a motion. The ITC is responsible for the investigation and recommendations.

To get protection, petitioners must show subject merchandise is being imported into the U.S. in such increased quantities as to cause or threaten to cause "market disruption" to producers of a "like or directly competitive product."[59] In turn, again like Section 406, "market disruption" is defined to occur where Chinese-origin imports:

> are increasing rapidly, either absolutely or relatively, so as to be a significant cause of material injury or threat of material injury to the domestic industry.[60]

"Significance" means:

> a cause which contributes significantly to the material injury of the domestic industry, but need not be equal to or greater than another cause.[61]

Manifestly, these criteria match those of Section 406.

As in a Section 406 case, in a Section 421 investigation the Commission regards as evidence of "market disruption" (1) the volume of subject merchandise imports, (2) the effect of subject merchandise on prices of like or directly competitive American products (*i.e.*, price suppression or depression), and (3) the effect of subject merchandise on the domestic industry making such products.[62] No single factor is dispositive as to whether market disruption exists.

• **Procedures**

As for the procedures to seek relief, they are nearly the same as those under Section 406, including the holding of a public hearing and a tight timetable, with minor exceptions to meet the *BTA*.[63] And, as under Section 406, the entire span from petition to proclamation is 150 days. The ITC has 60 days from receipt of a Section 421 petition to reach a determination.[64] Within 20 days after that determination, it must issue its written report to the President and USTR, including recommendations as to an appropriate remedy. Interestingly, unlike AD/CVD injury and Section 406 determinations, a tie vote among the Commissioners is deemed neither affirmative nor negative; rather, the President can pick which side is the

---

59. *See* Section 421(a) of the *1974 Act*, codified at 19 U.S.C. § 2451(a).
60. *See* Section 421(c)(1) of the *1974 Act*, codified at 19 U.S.C. § 2451(c)(1).
61. *See* Section 421(c)(2) of the *1974 Act*, codified at 19 U.S.C. § 2451(c)(2).
62. *See* Section 421(d) of the *1974 Act*, codified at 19 U.S.C. § 2451(d).
63. *See* Section 421(e)-(m) of the *1974 Act*, codified at 19 U.S.C. § 2451(e)-(m).
64. The deadlines are slightly different, and the possibility of provisional relief exists, where a petitioner alleges critical circumstances, in which case the ITC makes a preliminary determination on critical circumstances, and a preliminary determination on market disruption. *See* Section 421(e)-(i) of the *1974 Act*, codified at 19 U.S.C. § 2451(e)-(i). Provisional relief is possibly only of "delay in taking action . . . would cause damage to the relevant domestic industry which would be difficult to repair." Id, Section 421(i)(1), 19 U.S.C. § 2451(i)(1).

ITC decision.[65] The USTR then weighs in on remedial action within 55 days of getting the ITC report.[66]

Notably, if the ITC recommends relief, then the President first must request consultations with the Chinese to rectify the market disruption, which must begin within five days of the ITC determination. Only if consultations fail after 60 days must the President decide, within 25 days after the end of this consultation period, whether to grant relief.[67] Suppose China and the U.S. reach an agreement through consultations, but the President later finds the bilateral deal is not correcting market disruption or preventing a threat thereof. Then, the President must start consultations with China again, or launch a new Section 421 case. Suppose China does not adhere to its commitment under an agreement? Then, the President must order prompt relief.

- **Relief**

Relief, if any, is granted by the President, but only for such time as the President finds necessary to remedy actual market disruption, or prevent the threat of it from manifesting.[68] The presumption favors relief. That presumption is overcome only if the President finds relief would have a net adverse impact on the American economy (*i.e.*, the benefits of protection exceed the costs), or if in an "extraordinary case," relief would cause "serious harm to the national security" of the U.S.[69]

The empirical record shows how easily the presumption is overcome. Relief was granted only once in the six cases in which the ITC rendered an affirmative determination, the *China Tires* case. In four straight instances, President George W. Bush declined to provide Section 421 relief, overcoming the presumption on either or both grounds.

- **Innovative Section 422 Trade Diversion Remedy**

Astutely, when America negotiated its bilateral WTO accession agreement with China, it anticipated third countries might impose safeguard relief against Chinese merchandise, and China then might divert the targeted merchandise to the American market. So, in the 1999 *BTA*, the U.S. included a remedy against Chinese goods diverted to the American market by virtue of a third country safeguard. Section 422 of the *1974 Act* implements this remedy. The criteria are that a third-country

---

65. *See* Section 421(e) of the *1974 Act*, codified at 19 U.S.C. § 2451(e).

66. *See* Section 421(h)(2) of the *1974 Act*, codified at 19 U.S.C. § 2451(h)(2).

67. The 150 day span is computed as follows: 60 days for an ITC determination, plus 20 days for an ITC report, plus 55 days for the USTR to make a remedy recommendation, plus 15 days for the President to act on the USTR recommendation concerning the ITC report. The 60 days for consultations with China are included in the overall 150 day period, and are launched within five days of the ITC determination.

68. *See* Section 421(a), (j)-(k) of the *1974 Act*, codified at 19 U.S.C. § 2451(a), (j)-(k). The President also has the authority to modify, reduce, terminate, or extend relief. *See id.*, Section 421(n), 19 U.S.C. § 2451(n).

69. Section 421(k)(1)-(2) of the *1974 Act*, codified at 19 U.S.C. § 2451(k(1)-(2).

safeguard action against Chinese merchandise "has caused, or threatens to cause, a significant diversion of trade into the domestic market of the United States."[70]

CBP monitors third country actions and provides its results to the ITC, which — upon a petition from an entity that is representative of an industry, such as a firm, trade association, union, or group of workers — then renders a determination on trade diversion under these criteria.[71] If that determination is affirmative, then the President must consult with China and/or the third country.[72] If consultations fail to address the trade diversion, then the President must determine whether relief is appropriate.[73] As with Section 406 and 421 actions, the total time from petition to relief for a Section 422 action is 150 days.

VI. 2011 Section 421 *China Tires* Case

• **Facts**

The tires investigation, targeting tires for passenger and light truck vehicles from China, was not the first Section 421 action brought against China. In four of six previous instances, the ITC adjudicated such cases and recommended relief.[74] But, President George W. Bush (1946–, President, 2001–2009) declined to provide such relief. In the fifth Section 421 case, President Barack H. Obama (1961–, President, 2009–2017) agreed to follow the ITC recommendation in favor of relief. In so doing, he catalyzed a dispute that ultimately landed with the WTO Appellate Body.[75] His invocation of Section 421, in 2009, was the first (and perhaps only) use of the China-Specific Safeguard against China in the world.

On 20 April 2009, the ITC received an initial complaint regarding the subject merchandise, tires, from the United Steel, Paper and Forestry, Rubber, Manufacturing, Energy, Allied Industrial and Service Workers International Union (USW). The resulting safeguard measure against the tires entered into force on 26 September 2009.

---

70. *See* Section 422(b)(1) of the *1974 Act*, codified at 19 U.S.C. § 2451a(b)(1).

71. *See* Section 422(a) of the *1974 Act*, codified at 19 U.S.C. § 2451a(a). The universe of potential petitioners is the same in a Section 422 as in a Section 201 Escape Clause action, indeed, the former provision cites to the latter one. *See* Section 422(b)(1) of the *1974 Act*, codified at 19 U.S.C. § 2451a(b)(1), and Section 202(a)(1) of the *1974 Act*, codified at 19 U.S.C. § 2252(a)(1).

72. *See* Section 422(d)-(g) of the *1974 Act*, codified at 19 U.S.C. § 2451a(d)-(g).

73. *See* Section 422(h)-(j) of the *1974 Act*, codified at 19 U.S.C. § 2451a(h)-(j).

74. *See* Amy Tsui, *Progress Still Possible in U.S. — China Trade; Trade Enforcement Center Adds to Tensions*, 29 International Trade Reporter (BNA) 618 (19 April 2012).

75. *See* Appellate Body Report, *United States — Measures Affecting Imports of Certain Passenger Vehicle and Light Truck Tires from China*, WT/DS399/AB/R (adopted 5 October 2011); WTO Panel Report, *United States — Measures Affecting Imports of Certain Passenger Vehicle and Light Truck Tires from China*, WT/DS399/R (adopted as modified by the Appellate Body, 5 October 2011). [Hereinafter, *China Tires* Appellate Body Report and *China Tires* Panel Report, respectively.]

The POI was from 2004 to 2008. The ITC divided the relevant tire market into two separate markets: the replacement market; and the original equipment manufacturer (OEM) market. The replacement market "consists of customers buying tires to use as replacement tires for cars *already* on the road" and "accounts for about 80% of the total U.S. market."[76] The ITC further divided the replacement market into three Tiers. Those Tiers were based on brand and price. Tier 1 consisted of premium brands. Tier 2 had "secondary, associate, or foreign producer brands." Tier 3 "includes private label, mass market, lesser-known brands, and non-branded tires."

As for the OEM market, it "consists of tires produced for sale to manufacturers of *new* passenger vehicle and light trucks," and "represents about 20% of the total U.S. market." The ITC did not further sub-divide the OEM market into distinct categories.

Following an affirmative determination and recommendation for relief from the ITC, President Obama approved Section 421 relief. The remedy consisted of an additional tariff rate applied to subject merchandise for three years. The additional tariff rate for the first year was 35% *ad valorem*. The tariff rate fell to 30% in the second year, and dropped again to 25% in the third year.

- **Two Appellate Issues: "Increasing Rapidly" and "Significant Cause"**

Before the Panel, China lost every allegation it raised. Unfortunately for China, it also lost every issue it raised on appeal. China appealed two broad decisions by the Panel.

First, China claimed the Panel erred in determining the ITC properly found the subject merchandise was "rapidly increasing" within the meaning of Paragraph 16:4 of the 2001 *Accession Protocol* of China to the WTO. Second, China argued the Panel erred in holding the ITC properly found the subject merchandise to be "a significant cause" of material injury to the American domestic tire industry within the meaning of the *Protocol*. Both criteria, of course, are incorporated into Section 421.

- **What Does Imports "Increasing Rapidly" Mean?**

Paragraphs 16:1 and 16:4 of the *Accession Protocol* were relevant to the standard for (*i.e.*, definition of the phrase) "increasing rapidly." Paragraph 16:1 states:

> In cases where products of Chinese origin are being imported into the territory of any WTO Member in *such increased quantities or under such conditions as to cause or threaten to cause market disruption to the domestic producers of like or directly competitive products*, the WTO Member so affected may request consultations with China with a view to seeking a mutually satisfactory solution, including whether the affected WTO Member should pursue application of a measure under the *Agreement on*

---

76. *China Tires* Appellate Body Report, ¶ 203 fn 448 (emphasis added). *See id.*, for the subsequent 3 quotes, with emphasis in the third quote.

Safeguards. Any such request shall be notified immediately to the Committee on Safeguards.[77]

Manifestly, this language tracks that of (but is not *verbatim* with) GATT Article XIX. Paragraph 16:4 of the *Protocol* says:

> Market disruption shall exist whenever imports of an article, like or directly competitive with an article produced by the domestic industry, are *increasing rapidly*, either absolutely or relatively, so as to be a significant cause of material injury, or threat of material injury to the domestic industry. In determining if market disruption exists, the affected WTO Member shall consider objective factors, including the volume of imports, the effect of imports on prices for like or directly competitive articles, and the effect of such imports on the domestic industry producing like or directly competitive products.[78]

China put up two arguments as to why the standard in the *Protocol* is higher for import increases than analogous standards in safeguard provisions in other GATT-WTO texts.

First, as to a textual interpretation, China contended the word "'increasing' requires investigating authorities to focus on the most recent past."[79] China also said the adverb "'rapidly' implies a focus on the rates of increase in imports."[80] China fixed on the present tense form of the phrase "increasing rapidly." China claimed the use of the present tense distinguished the *Protocol* from other WTO texts, which use the past tense.

The U.S. countered successfully that an investigating authority (such as the ITC) may exercise discretion when establishing a POI, and also that the rate of increase in imports of subject merchandise is irrelevant. The authority may "select any period, provided that it allows for an assessment of import increases during a 'recent period.'"[81] The rate of increase in imports does not matter, because the adverb "'rapidly' does not embody a 'comparative or relative concept.'"[82] As for textual and contextual comparisons between the China-Specific Safeguard in the *Protocol* and GATT-WTO safeguards, the U.S. dismissed them. There are too many differences between the *Protocol* and other agreements to warrant the kind of comparison attempted by the Chinese.

Second, China recalled the 2000 *Argentina Footwear* case, where the Appellate Body commented on the "extraordinary" nature of safeguards under the WTO

---

77. *WTO Protocol on the Accession of the People's Republic of China*, WT/L/432, ¶ 16:1 (23 November 2001) (emphasis added). [Hereinafter, *Protocol*.]
78. *Protocol*, ¶ 16:4 (emphasis added).
79. *See China Tires* Appellate Body Report, ¶ 127.
80. *See China Tires* Appellate Body Report, ¶ 127.
81. *China Tires* Appellate Body Report, ¶ 129.
82. *China Tires* Appellate Body Report, ¶ 129.

Agreement on Safeguards.[83] According to China, the *Protocol* shares this same "extraordinary" nature with that *Agreement*, because the *Protocol* similarly establishes disciplines on "fair trade."[84] But, said China, the *Protocol* is even more trade distorting than traditional general safeguard relief under GATT Article XIX and the *Safeguards Agreement*: a Country-Specific Safeguard, which is not applied on an MFN, but instead exclusively against Chinese merchandise, disfigures import and export patterns to a greater degree than the general safeguard, which must be applied on that basis. Thus, China said, "this 'extra-extraordinary' nature of measures under the *Protocol* must be taken into account" when defining what "increasing imports" means.[85]

The U.S. disputed the Chinese claim the *Protocol* embodies a higher import increase standard than GATT or other WTO agreements. The Chinese read too much into the expression "extraordinary remedy" as used by the Appellate Body in the *Argentina Footwear* case. Instead, America asserted:

> The Appellate Body's conclusion that a safeguard measure is an "extraordinary remedy" stems from the express reference to "emergency actions" and "unforeseen developments" in the text of Article XIX of the GATT 1994, and neither of these terms are [*sic*] present in the text of Section 16 of the *Protocol*.[86]

To buttress their point, the Americans observed the injury determination standard is lower in the *Protocol* than the WTO *Agreement on Safeguards*. That legal fact further undermined the Chinese argument for a heightened standard under the *Protocol*.

- **Holding on Imports "Increasing Rapidly"**

Following the 1969 *Vienna Convention on the Law of Treaties*, the Appellate Body examined the ordinary meaning and context of the phrases "increasing rapidly" and "absolutely or relatively" in Paragraph 16:4 of the *Protocol*, and the phrases "are being imported" "in such increased quantities" in Paragraph 16:1. The Appellate Body examined, as it customarily does, the *Oxford English Dictionary* (*OED*), along with the overall purpose of Paragraph 16. IT also relied on its own precedent. Regarding the phrase "are being imported," the Appellate Body pointed to similar language in the *Argentina Footwear* case. There, it determined the analogous phrase "is being imported" implied the increase was "sudden and recent."[87] The Appellate

---

83. *China Tires* Appellate Body Report, ¶ 128 (*quoting* WTO Appellate Body Report, *Argentina—Safeguard Measures on Imports of Footwear*, WT/DS121/AB/R ¶¶ 94–95 (adopted 12 January 2000)).

84. *China Tires* Appellate Body Report, ¶ 128 (*quoting* 2000 *Argentina Footwear* Appellate Body Report, ¶¶ 94–95).

85. *China Tires* Appellate Body Report, ¶ 128.

86. *China Tires* Appellate Body Report, ¶ 130.

87. *China Tires* Appellate Body Report, ¶ 137 (*quoting* 2000 *Argentina Footwear* Appellate Body Report, ¶ 130).

Body extended that meaning to the phrase "are being imported" in the *Protocol*, finding:

> In sum, imports from China will be "increasing rapidly" under Paragraph 16:4 of the *Protocol* when they are *increasing at great speed or swiftly, either in relative or absolute terms*. Such import increases must be occurring over a *short and recent period of time*, and must be of a *sufficient absolute or relative magnitude so as to be a significant cause of material injury to the domestic industry*.[88]

The highlighted language is how the Appellate Body defined whether imports are "increasing rapidly." In effect, it created a three-part test: (1) great speed or swiftness; (2) short and recent period; and (3) sufficiency to be a significant cause of material injury.

• **Application of "Increasing Rapidly" Standard**

Did the ITC fail to prove subject merchandise was "increasing rapidly"? China said "yes," offering three arguments based on the fact:

> the rate of increase in subject imports in the last year of . . . the period of investigation indicated that subject imports were not "increasing rapidly" within the meaning of Paragraph 16:4.[89]

First, China claimed the ITC should have focused more on the most recent part of the POI, and less on earlier parts of that period.

The U.S. retorted investigating authorities have discretion to establish the POI, as long as it shows imports increased in a "recent period." The U.S. also asserted the ITC:

> expressly reasoned that the two largest "year-to-year increases" with respect to the ratio of the "subject imports to U.S. production" and "market share of the Chinese imports" occurred "at the end of the period in 2007 and 2008."[90]

The Appellate Body agreed. The Chinese claim that tense "are increasing" requires investigators to "focus exclusively on import increases that occurred during the *most* recent past" was incorrect.[91]

Relying partly on *Argentina Footwear*, the Appellate Body said although the POI must be recent enough to "provide a reasonable indication of current trends in imports," the analysis does not need to be "limited to import data relating to the very end of the period of investigation."[92] The Appellate Body said investigators

---

88. *China Tires* Appellate Body Report, ¶ 140 (emphasis added).
89. *China Tires* Appellate Body Report, ¶ 141.
90. *China Tires* ¶ 145.
91. *China Tires* ¶ 146.
92. *China Tires* ¶ 147 (citing 2001 *Argentina Footwear* Appellate Body Report).

need to compare the earlier and later periods within the POI to determine whether subject merchandise is "being imported . . . in such increased quantities" as the *Protocol* requires.[93]

Second, China urged ITC was required to "focus . . . on the rates of increase in subject imports."[94] China argued "'rapidly' is a relative concept, which conveys the idea that something is increasing more quickly than something else."[95] The U.S. responded the Panel correctly found this adverb means "swiftly" or "quickly," as opposed to "more swiftly" or "more quickly."[96]

Agreeing with the U.S., the Panel accepted the finding of the ITC that imports increased rapidly. China was unsatisfied with this finding, because the rate of increase declined in the last year of the POI. The U.S. responded the ITC "did examine the rates of increase in subject imports in the final years of the period of investigation" and "emphasized that the 'two largest year to year increases' in these metrics occurred in 2007 and 2008."[97]

The Appellate Body upheld the Panel:

> [A] decline in the *rates* of increase in imports towards the end of the period of investigation does not detract from the USITC's conclusion that imports from China were "increasing rapidly," particularly when import increases at the end of the period of investigation remained significant both in relative and in absolute terms.[98]

This statement reflects long-standing safeguards jurisprudence that it is appropriate to examine rates in increase of subject merchandise in absolute terms, and/or terms relative to production of the like domestic product. Just because the rate of increase in either absolute or relative terms decelerates does not automatically detract from the force of the argument for imposing a trade remedy.

Third, China contended the ITC should have compared rates of increase in subject imports from the most recent year to earlier years during the POI. Surely the phrase "increasing rapidly" suggests "imports must be increasing more rapidly than some other benchmark."[99] Furthermore, the ITC did not sufficiently explain why imports were found to be "'increasing rapidly' when the rate of increase in subject imports in 2008 was lower than the rates of increase in the previous years."[100] According to China, the lower ending rate does not indicate a "rapid" increase, as the *Protocol* requires.

---

93. *China Tires* ¶ 148.
94. *China Tires* Appellate Body Report, ¶ 154.
95. *China Tires* Appellate Body Report, ¶ 154.
96. *China Tires* Appellate Body Report, ¶ 156.
97. *China Tires* Appellate Body Report, ¶ 157.
98. *China Tires* Appellate Body Report, ¶ 162.
99. *China Tires* Appellate Body Report, ¶ 163.
100. *China Tires* Appellate Body Report, ¶ 164.

The U.S. said again "'rapid' does not require an 'accelerating rate of increase' over the [POI]."[101] America stressed the subject import volumes were reasonably determined to be increasing rapidly, not only in absolute terms, but also in relative terms.

The Appellate Body completely dismissed the Chinese allegations. The ITC demonstrated sufficiently the quantity of subject imports rose in the 2006–2007 and 2007–2008 periods within the POI, and that the market share of subject merchandise increased in every part of the POI.

Thus, after hearing the separate arguments by China, the Appellate Body upheld the finding by the Panel that the ITC properly assessed "whether imports from China met the specific threshold under Paragraph 16:4 of the . . . *Protocol* of 'increasing rapidly.' "[102] The bottom line teaching is that an investigating authority has considerable discretion to examine trends in importation of subject merchandise within a POI, *i.e.*, it is not confined to rendering an affirmative determination about increasing imports only where data show steady or accelerating rates. Put differently, the authority can draw inferences by compare and contrast different portions within a POI, including the starting and ending portions.

- **What Does "Significant Cause" Mean?**

As to the second appellate issue, did the ITC properly find "rapidly increasing imports form China were 'a significant cause' of material injury to the domestic industry under Paragraph 16:4 of *China's Accession Protocol*"?[103] Conceptually, China made the same argument on this issue as on the first one, namely, its *Protocol* set a higher standard for imposition of a trade remedy than the analogous GATT-WTO trade remedy agreements. That is, the *Protocol* contains an enhanced standard of causation, because the *Protocol*, unlike other WTO texts, modifies "cause" with the adjective "significant." And, as before, China argued the purpose of the *Protocol* reinforces the heightened standard, because of the "extra-extraordinary" nature of the *Protocol*.

The U.S. responded the ordinary standard in trade remedy litigation under GATT-WTO texts, as interpreted by the Appellate Body, is "genuine and substantial" causation. The adjective "significant" does not increase the typical standard. Furthermore, the purpose of the *Protocol* does not support a heightened standard. The U.S. contrasted the *Protocol* with the title and language of GATT Article XIX: "measures under the *Protocol* are not 'emergency actions' resulting from 'unforeseen developments.'"[104] To the contrary, the *Protocol* explicitly sets out a lower injury threshold than does GATT. The key inference the U.S. drew from comparing the *Protocol* and GATT was not too draw too strong an inference: there were important distinctions in their language and purpose.

---

101. *China Tires* Appellate Body Report, ¶ 165.
102. *China Tires* Appellate Body Report, ¶ 170.
103. *China Tires* Appellate Body Report, ¶ 171.
104. *China Tires* Appellate Body Report, ¶ 174.

• **Holding on Standard for "Significant Cause"**

Again finding in favor of the U.S., the Appellate Body began by addressing the legal standard of causation. It looked at the ordinary meaning of and context surrounding "significant cause," predictably pointing to the *OED* and precedent. According to the 2001 *United States Wheat Gluten* case, the word "cause":

> denot[es] a relationship between, at least, two elements, whereby the first element has, in some way, "brought about," "produced" or "induced" the existence of the second element.[105]

As for "significant," it:

> describes the causal relationship or nexus that must be found to exist between rapidly increasing imports and material injury to the domestic industry, which must be such that rapidly increasing imports make an *"important" or "notable"* contribution in bringing about material injury to the domestic injury. Such assessment must be carried out on the basis of the objective factors listed in the second sentence of Paragraph 16:4.[106]

Here again, the Appellate Body consumed paragraphs and pages to define a key term ("significant") in a manner both obvious and nearly tautological ("important" or "notable"). For the reader well-versed in Appellate Body reports, the pattern was familiar: practicing law and adjudicating cases using synonyms from a treasured dictionary, rather than providing deep insights or brilliant tests.

In any event, the Appellate Body dismissed the claim by China that the use of "significant" creates a higher causation standard than other WTO accords. The Appellate Body also noted the purpose of Paragraph 16 of the *Protocol*:

> is to afford temporary relief to domestic industries that are exposed to market disruption as a result of a rapid increase in Chinese imports of like or directly competitive products, subject to the conditions and requirements provided therein.[107]

So, the purpose of the *Protocol* did not bolster the Chinese argument. Moreover, the *Protocol* has a lower injury threshold than the other WTO agreements, as the U.S. argued. The Appellate Body concluded:

> Paragraph 16:4 of the *Protocol* sets forth a distinct causation standard whereby rapidly increasing imports must be "a *significant* cause" of material injury to the domestic industry. This causation standard requires that

---

105. *China Tires* Appellate Body Report, ¶ 176 (*quoting* WTO Appellate Body Report, *United States—Definitive Safeguard Measures on Imports of Wheat Gluten from the European Communities*, WT/DS166/AB/R, ¶ 67 (adopted 19 January 2001), in turn *quoting The New Shorter Oxford English Dictionary*, 4th ed., L. Brown (ed.) (Clarendon Press, 1993), vol. 1, 1958).

106. *China Tires* Appellate Body Report, ¶ 180 (emphasis added).

107. *China Tires* Appellate Body Report, ¶ 184.

rapidly increasing imports from China make an *important contribution* in bringing about material injury to the domestic industry.[108]

The Appellate Body also noted a finding of causation must be determined according to the "objective criteria" according to the second sentence of Paragraph 16:4.

- **"Significant Causation," Conditions of Competition, Correlation, and Non-Attribution**

The Appellate Body considered the "significant cause" standard in light of 3 further Chinese contentions: conceptually, (1) conditions of competition matter, (2) correlation between subject merchandise volumes and injury variables is important, and (3) a non-attribution analysis is necessary.

First, China claimed the ITC was required to look at the:

> *degree of competitive* overlap between imported and domestic products, and . . . identify a coincidence both in the "year-by-year changes" and in the "degree of magnitude" between subject imports and injury factors.[109]

The U.S. disagreed, re-emphasizing the *Protocol* does not contain a heightened causation standard. The U.S. argued there is no "specific methodology" to determine causation, nor a requirement of "correspondence between the magnitude of changes in subject imports and the magnitude of changes in the performance indicators of the domestic industry."[110]

Agreeing with the U.S., the Appellate Body determined Paragraph 16:4 allows for discretion by investigating authorities to determine a specific methodology to determine "significant causation." It reviews those methodologies on a case by case basis, which the Appellate Body noted is in accordance with its 2011 *Airbus* decision.

Second, the Appellate Body said conditions of competition and "correlation between movements in imports and injury factors are merely 'analytical tools.'"[111] Neither is "dispositive" to the determination of causation.[112] Regarding correlation between movements in (1) import volumes and (2) injury factors, the 2000 *Argentina Footwear* case again was helpful. There, the Appellate Body found even if no correlation exists between those 2 variables, subject merchandise still could be the cause of injury, if there is "a *very* compelling analysis of why causation still is present."[113] Of course, that statement stretches the bounds of statistical possibility: while correlation does not equate with causation, query whether causation is possible when variables are uncorrelated.

---

108. *China Tires* Appellate Body Report, ¶ 185 (emphasis added).
109. *China Tires* Appellate Body Report, ¶ 186 (original emphasis and underlining).
110. *China Tires* Appellate Body Report, ¶ 187.
111. *China Tires* Appellate Body Report, ¶ 192.
112. *China Tires* Appellate Body Report, ¶ 192.
113. *China Tires* Appellate Body Report, ¶¶ 193–194 (adopted 5 October 2011); 2000 *Argentina Footwear* Appellate Body Report, ¶ 144 (original emphasis).

Third, in its non-attribution claim, China said there is "an inherent requirement to consider other possible causes of injury" when determining causation.[114] The heightened standard in the *Protocol* meant investigating authorities must look at the separate effects of subject imports and other possible causes of injury. The U.S. did not gainsay the need for a non-attribution analysis. An authority must consider the effects of other possible causal factors. But, that authority has discretion as to how to assess their effects.

The Appellate Body looked at its 2008 compliance decision *Cotton* case, as had the Panel and the U.S. Following its 2005 *Cotton* decision, the Appellate Body said even in the absence of explicit language, there must be some analysis of the "injurious effects" of factors other than the subject merchandise to show the subject merchandise meets the causation standard under Paragraph 16:4 of the *Protocol*.[115] Whether the effects of other factors are properly analyzed is a case-by-case determination.

What is interesting about this Appellate Body statement is its context. It would be considered commonplace for trade remedies based directly on provisions in GATT or a Uruguay Round text. But, here the Appellate Body is saying non-attribution analyses are relevant to remedies specially created in terms of accession.

In sum, the teaching on causation from the *China Tires* case is modest: "significant cause" is defined in a somewhat circular way to mean "important" or "notable" contribution in leading to the material injury of a domestic industry, and to confirm this contribution, a non-attribution analysis is necessary.

• **Application of "Significant Cause" Standard and Conditions of Competition**

As to application of the "significant cause" standard, China followed through on its conceptual arguments, and gave three reasons why the ITC improperly determined subject merchandise was "a 'significant cause' of material injury to the domestic industry."[116] The ITC justification for saying Chinese tire imports significantly caused injury to American producers was weak because: (1) direct competition between Chinese and American tires was minimal, (2) increases in subject merchandise were insufficiently correlated with injury variables, and (3) injury could be attributed to variables other than subject merchandise. China lost all three arguments.

China asserted the competitive conditions in the domestic tire market showed "'attenuated' competition between subject imports and domestic tires."[117] According to China, the ITC failed to analyze properly the conditions of competition in the (1) replacement market, (2) OEM market, and (3) overall market (meaning the

---

114. *China Tires* Appellate Body Report, ¶ 196.
115. *China Tires* Appellate Body Report, ¶ 201; *see also* WTO Appellate Body Report, *United States — Subsidies on Upland Cotton — Recourse to Article 21.5 of the DSU by Brazil*, WT/DS267/AB/RW (adopted 20 June 2008).
116. *China Tires* Appellate Body Report, ¶ 171.
117. *China Tires* Appellate Body Report, ¶ 171.

OEM and replacement market combined). A nuanced understanding of the three types of tire markets, and of distinctions within one of those markets (three sub-product markets within the replacement market), showed subject merchandise did not compete directly, at least not to any major degree, with American tires. Consequently, Chinese imports could not have been the "significant cause" of the woes of the American tire producers.

In the replacement market, China claimed the ITC did not fully analyze evidence that the majority of domestic tire production occurred in Tier 1, where the domestic industry faced extremely limited competition from Chinese tire producers. Instead, subject merchandise was prevalent in the second and third Tiers. Conditions of competition, even in Tiers 2 and 3, were not a reasonable basis on which to find its tires were "a significant cause" of material injury to the domestic industry.

The U.S. said "significant quantities" of domestic and Chinese tires competed in Tiers 2 and 3 in the last POI, which sufficiently showed competition between the subject merchandise and domestic tires. The Appellate Body agreed. Indeed, the lack of completely distinct Tiers "suggests a greater degree of competitive overlap across these Tiers than otherwise would have existed had such Tiers been clearly delineated."[118] Moreover, there were sufficient market share data in the second and third Tiers to justify the ITC conclusion that competition existed between subject merchandise and domestic tires in the American replacement market.

As to conditions of competition in the OEM market, China said American producers focused more on this than the replacement market. So, the Panel "should have assessed whether competition in [the OEM] market was significant," as opposed to focusing on trends in imports of Chinese tires.[119] According to China, competition from Chinese tire producers in the OEM market was, in fact, insignificant. The OEM market share for subject merchandise was no more than 5% during the POI. The lack of competition in both the OEM and Tier 1 replacement market pointed to a "'highly attenuated' degree of competition between Chinese imports and domestic tires in the U.S. market."[120] Regrettably, said China, neither the Panel nor the ITC gave a reasonable explanation about causation in light of this dearth of competition.

The U.S. rebuttal was successful: the presence of Chinese tires in the OEM market was growing, and, in turn, there was significant competition in the entire market. According to the U.S., the OEM market share for subject imports grew during the POI, while the OEM market share for domestic tires decreased. The U.S. also noted "a volume of 2.3 million tires from China, representing a 5% market share in 2008, could not be considered 'negligible.'"[121]

---

118. *China Tires* Appellate Body Report, ¶ 208.
119. *China Tires* Appellate Body Report, ¶ 216.
120. *China Tires* Appellate Body Report, ¶ 203.
121. *China Tires* Appellate Body Report, ¶ 217.

The Panel rejected the assertion by China that the volume of subject merchandise was "negligible."[122] It ruled the volume of domestic tire shipments decreased by 46% over the 2004–2008 POI. Conversely, the volume of subject tire shipments increased by a whopping 1,785% during the same period.

The Appellate Body upheld yet criticized the Panel for relying primarily on an "end-point comparison of relative volumes and market share" in finding an increasing degree of competition between the domestic tires and subject merchandise in the OEM market.[123] It did so because of its own precedents. In 2000 *Argentina Footwear*, 2003 *Steel Safeguards*, and 2011 *Airbus*, the Appellate Body "expressed reservations" over such end-point comparisons.[124] Ultimately, the Appellate Body recognized the Panel, while relying too heavily on the end-point comparison, did do a minimal amount more by looking beyond the OEM market to the overall market. It would have preferred a detailed assessment of the ITC analysis of the OEM market. But, it agreed the OEM market is less important than the replacement market for Chinese and American producers.

As to the overall market, China also cast doubt on the finding of the ITC concerning causation, given that "approximately 60% of U.S. production went into Tier 1 of the replacement market and the OEM market, where Chinese imports held only a 2–3% combined market share."[125] But, the U.S. responded the ITC properly found:

> there was "significant competition" between Chinese and domestic tires in Tiers 2 and 3 of the U.S. replacement market, [so] that Chinese imports in different segments could impact prices and volumes of domestic tires in other segments because there were "no clear dividing lines" between the tiers of the replacement market, and that subject imports were taking a "growing though smaller" share of the OEM market.[126]

For reasons redolent of those it offered about the replacement and OEM markets, the Appellate Body rejected the Chinese contentions with respect to the overall market.

The Appellate Body said the overall effect of the "significant presence" of subject merchandise in Tiers 2 and 3 of the replacement market, and the increasing presence of subject merchandise in Tier 1 of the replacement market and the OEM market, was enough to side with the U.S. And, the degree of competition in the

---

122. *China Tires* Appellate Body Report, ¶ 218.

123. *See China Tires* Appellate Body Report, ¶ 219.

124. *See China Tires* Appellate Body Report, ¶ 220; Appellate Body Report, *Argentina—Safeguard Measures on Imports of Footwear*, WT/DS121/AB/R (adopted 12 January 2000); Appellate Body Report, *United States—Definitive Safeguard Measures on Imports of Certain Steel Products*, WT/DS248/AB/R, WT/DS249/AB/R, WT/DS251/AB/R, WT/DS252/AB/R, WT/DS253/AB/R, WT/DS254/AB/R, WT/DS258/AB/R, WT/DS259/AB/R (adopted 10 December 2003); Appellate Body Report, *European Communities and Certain Member States—Measures Affecting Trade in Large Civil Aircraft*, WT/DS316/AB/R, (adopted 1 June 2011).

125. Appellate Body Report, *United States—Measures Affecting Imports of Certain Passenger Vehicle and Light Truck Tires from China*, WT/DS399/AB/R, ¶ 221 (adopted 5 October 2011).

126. *China Tires* Appellate Body Report, ¶ 222.

replacement market "was sufficient to establish that competition in the overall U.S. market was significant."[127] Thus, the Appellate Body confirmed the ITC "did not err in its assessment of the conditions of competition in the overall U.S. market."[128]

- **Application of "Significant Cause" Standard and Correlation between Increases in Subject Merchandise and Injury**

China said the ITC improperly relied on "an 'overall coincidence' between import increases and declines in injury factors" when determining causation.[129] The Panel should have required "a more specific degree of correlation," said China. Instead, the Panel neglected to explain fully an apparent "disconnect in the trends between 2007 and 2008."[130] China also argued the Panel failed to:

> take into account the effects of "attenuated competition" on underselling, and failed to address adequately the fact that non-subject imports also undersold domestic tires.[131]

China asserted the ratio of the cost of goods sold to sales (COGS/sales) in 2007 showed domestic tire producers did not "suffer[] a 'cost price squeeze' in the POI."[132]

The U.S. responded the *Protocol* "did not require a strict correlation in the degrees of changes in subject imports and injury factors."[133] Several "injury indicators"— such as production, net sales, and hours worked—dropped each year during the POI. Other variables, including operating margins, productivity, and operating income, fell during three of the four years during the POI. So, despite improvement of some factors in 2007, the Panel correctly found an overall correlation. The U.S. also asserted "an improvement in the COGS/sales ratio in 2007 does not suggest an absence of correlation."[134]

Ruling against China, the Appellate Body looked at the alleged "trend disconnect" between 2007 and 2008. The Chinese argument was based on an implicit assumption the *Protocol* mandated a "stricter degree of correlation" than other WTO agreements. That assumption was false. Recalling its 2000 *Argentina Footwear* Report, the Appellate Body emphasized:

> the analysis of correlation focuses on "the *relationship* between *movements* in imports (volume and market share) and the *movements* in injury factors."[135]

---

127. *China Tires* Appellate Body Report, ¶ 224.
128. *China Tires* Appellate Body Report, ¶ 226.
129. *China Tires* Appellate Body Report, ¶ 171.
130. *China Tires* Appellate Body Report, ¶ 228.
131. *China Tires* Appellate Body Report, ¶ 229.
132. *China Tires* Appellate Body Report, ¶ 242.
133. *China Tires* Appellate Body Report, ¶ 230.
134. *China Tires* Appellate Body Report, ¶ 231 (adopted 5 October 2011).
135. *China Tires* Appellate Body Report, ¶ 237 (adopted 5 October 2011) (*quoting* WTO Appellate Body Report, *Argentina—Safeguard Measures on Imports of Footwear*, WT/DS121/AB/R, ¶ 144 (adopted 12 January 2000) (emphasis original)).

The Appellate Body also intoned this case stood for another, related proposition: while correlation can suggest "a causal link," it is not dispositive.[136]

The Appellate Body said determining correlation between increases in subject merchandise and decreases in injury factors is "not an exact science."[137] So, a correlation analysis should attempt to show "a *temporal* coincidence between an upward trend in *subject imports* and a downward trend in the performance indicators of the domestic industry."[138] There is no requirement these trends move in "strict simultaneity."[139]

That is, given that increases in subject merchandise imports may be affected differently, even uniquely, by different injury factors, it does not make sense to require strict correlation between those imports and the injury factors. China insisted on a lock-step march, with subject merchandise imports rising and injury factors worsening. A flexible, case-by-case approach is preferable (though of course it cannot be too malleable, either), and a "trend disconnect" is not fatal to the claim of the complainant in a Product-Specific Safeguard action. Consequently, the Appellate Body also was unconvinced by the data and correlations China offered to support its argument.

Second, the Appellate Body looked at correlation between import increases, domestic prices and profitability, specifically the improvement in the COGS/sales ratio in 2007. It said the COGS/sales ratio in 2007 "does not *per se* undermine the finding of the ITC that subject imports negatively affected domestic prices."[140] And, because there is no strict correlation requirement, the increased ratio in three out of the four years of the POI is sufficient to call the ITC assessment reasonable.

Certainly, the Appellate Body noted, one injury factor of many is not necessarily determinative of overall injury. What matters is that assessment by an investigating authority is reasonable and follows the causation standard (whereby a "significant cause" is an "important" or "notable" contribution to the material injury of a domestic injury). Here, the U.S. was correct: "reliance on an overall coincidence between an upward movement in subject imports and a downward movement in injury factors reasonably support[ed]" the ITC causation determination.[141]

• **Application of "Significant Cause" Standard and Non-Attribution**

As for the non-attribution analysis that forms an indispensable part of an inquiry into causation, China claimed the ITC did not properly address causes of injury other than that attributed to the subject merchandise. The Panel had relied on the 2005 Appellate Body Report in *Cotton* to determine a non-attribution

---

136. *China Tires* Appellate Body Report, ¶ 237.
137. *China Tires* Appellate Body Report, ¶ 238.
138. *China Tires* Appellate Body Report, ¶ 239.
139. *China Tires* Appellate Body Report, ¶ 239.
140. *China Tires* Appellate Body Report, ¶ 245.
141. *China Tires* Appellate Body Report, ¶ 249.

analysis was required, even though there is no express mandate for one in the *Proto-col*. The Appellate Body agreed with the Panel. That agreement was tantamount to an impressive bit of interstitial lawmaking: the Appellate Body applied a causation standard established for other trade remedies to the Country-Specific Safeguard in the *Protocol*.

According to the Appellate Body, "some form of non-attribution analysis is *inherent* in the establishment of a causal link between rapidly increasing imports from China and material injury to the domestic injury."[142] The Appellate Body declared:

> this determination [of causation] can only be made if an investigating authority properly ensures that effects of other known causes are not such as to suggest that subject imports are in fact only a "remote" or "minimal" cause, rather than a "significant" cause of material injury to the domestic industry."[143]

The Appellate Body noted whether an assessment of other factors is properly conducted is established on a case-by-case basis. Therefore, some cases necessarily require a comprehensive analysis, while other cases call for less thoroughness.

China attributed the injury suffered by the American tire industry to three factors other than Chinese tire imports. The first factor was the business strategy of the American industry. China argued the domestic industry voluntarily shifted production from lower value tires manufactured in foreign countries to higher value tires manufactured in the U.S. According to China, this production shift created "a supply gap in the U.S. market that was filled by imports from both China and other sources."[144]

However, the ITC determined this shift was involuntary, and was a reaction to the increase in subject merchandise from China. The ITC based its finding on relevant news articles, and evidence related to plant closings by large American tire manufacturers. The Appellate Body examined the record, and said the Panel analysis was adequate. The Panel did not err "in its review of the USITC's analysis of the U.S. domestic industry's business strategy and the reasons for the three U.S. plant closures."[145]

China said the second causal factor the Panel failed to "evaluate seriously" was decline in American consumer demand for tires.[146] Chinese data showed a decrease in demand throughout the POI, followed by a sharper decline in 2008 due to economic recession. The U.S. countered the demand fluctuated, but even during periods of sagging demand, the market share of Chinese producers increased.

---

142. *China Tires* Appellate Body Report, ¶ 252 (emphasis original).
143. *China Tires* Appellate Body Report, ¶ 252.
144. *China Tires* Appellate Body Report, ¶ 252.
145. *China Tires* Appellate Body Report, ¶ 284.
146. *China Tires* Appellate Body Report, ¶¶ 259, 285.

Conversely, the market share of American producers decreased at a rate consistent with the decline in demand. So, decreased domestic demand did not explain the injury to the domestic industry.

The Appellate Body examined the record and determined the Panel "carefully examined the correlation between trends in subject imports and changes in demand over the full period of investigation."[147] The Appellate Body also emphasized the "bulk" of the decrease in demand occurred during the recession in 2008, which both the Panel and the ITC took care to analyze separately.[148] The Appellate Body determined the Panel was right to uphold the ITC determination that "subject imports had injurious effects independent of any injury caused by changes in demand."[149]

China asserted the third causal factor was non-subject imports from foreign countries other than China. China claimed non-subject imports had greater market share than subject merchandise. China also said non-subject imports were lower priced than American tires. (Notably, China did not say whether non-subject tires were priced lower than subject tires.) The Panel noticed that the market share of non-subject tires declined during the POI (as did the market share of American tires). It drew the obvious inference: that decline in market share was associated with the rise in market share of Chinese tires. As for under-pricing by non-subject merchandise, the Panel said those goods had a higher unit value than did subject merchandise. The Panel did not explain this point well, but seems to have thought the per tire value of non-subject tires was greater than that of Chinese tires, therefore, a comparison of tire prices was simplistic.

Overall, the Panel said the Chinese points about market share and pricing of non-subject merchandise were unpersuasive. Their impact on injuring the American tire industry was much less than the effects of subject merchandise on that industry. The Appellate Body agreed, and determined the Panel did not err in finding the ITC assessment reasonable.

Finally, China claimed the Panel erred in finding:

> China "failed to establish that in the context of the present case, the USITC should have provided a cumulative assessment of the effects of the other causes of injury."[150]

This appellate argument was largely the same as what China put to the Panel. Moreover, this argument was founded on an improper understanding of the causation standard set forth in Paragraph 16:4 of the *Protocol*.

---

147. *China Tires* Appellate Body Report, ¶ 290.
148. *China Tires* Appellate Body Report, ¶ 294.
149. *China Tires* Appellate Body Report, ¶ 298.
150. *China Tires* Appellate Body Report, ¶ 309 (*quoting* the Panel Report).

The Appellate Body said the Panel analysis was sufficient, thereby agreeing the ITC properly attributed injury to Chinese tires. So, the Appellate Body agreed the ITC:

> properly established that rapidly increasing imports from China were "a significant cause" of material injury to the US domestic industry within the meaning of Paragraph 16:4 of the *Protocol*.[151]

With this conclusion, the second of the Two Steps was complete. Imports of subject merchandise had increased rapidly during the POI (Step 1), and that increase caused injury to the domestic producer of a like or directly competitive product (Step 2).

- **Extending Trade Remedy Jurisprudence to Protocol-Based Remedies**

In the *China Tires* case, the Appellate Body held:

(1) "Increasing rapidly" means subject merchandise rises in an absolute or relative sense, with great speed or swiftness, in a short and recent period, and with sufficiency to be a significant cause of material injury

(2) "Significant cause" means an "important" or "notable" contribution in leading to the material injury of the allegedly afflicted domestic industry, as confirmed by a non-attribution analysis that covers a range of objective factors to ensure causation by them is not wrongly attributed to causation by subject merchandise.

In reaching these holdings, the Appellate Body interpreted language peculiar to the *Accession Protocol* of China. It might have been tempted to issue idiosyncratic rulings, *i.e.*, definitions of key terms specific to that *Protocol*.

To some extent, it did. The holdings do spring from the Product-Specific Safeguard. But, the larger message of the *China Tires* case is the extent to which the Appellate Body tried to square its holdings with those in trade remedy disputes arising out of standard GATT-WTO texts. In effect, the Appellate Body appears to extend as much of its jurisprudence from those texts to the new Safeguard.

That is clear from its repeated citation to itself in the 2000 *Argentina Footwear* and 2005 *Cotton* cases, and its rejection of Chinese arguments that the language of the *Protocol* mandates a higher standard for imposition of the Safeguard than the standard in those other texts. (Note *de facto stare decisis* lurks in the *Tires* case, as the Appellate Body (and Panel) rationalizes its opinions not just on safeguard provisions specific to the *Accession Protocol*, but also on precedent regarding other WTO agreements. That harmonizes key legal terminology and concepts throughout all the WTO agreements.) Put colloquially, the Appellate Body seemed to say "that while the China-Specific Safeguard is a distinct remedy, in practice it really is not that different from other safeguards."

---

151. *China Tires* Appellate Body Report, ¶ 115.

Why might the Appellate Body essentially equalize, or nearly so, a safeguard carved out in an accession protocol with existing comparable remedies? After all, is it not one of the last powerful bastions of free trade? Should it not make it harder, not easier, to impose protectionist measures?

One answer is it spins the proverbial seamless web of the law. Why have multiple disjointed remedies with radically different legal triggers, where a broadly consistent set suffices? Another answer is the Appellate Body feared emasculating a trade remedy the U.S. and other major trading powers deliberately created for use against China. Consider the counter-factual: the Appellate Body agrees with the Chinese arguments the Product-Specific Safeguard has higher standards for imposition than other GATT-WTO remedies. That finding would infuriate China's trading partners, which negotiated an extra, if rather redundant, remedy for political and economic cover with domestic constituents. It would vitiate those political and economic purposes of the remedy, because the higher trigger standards would make the remedy nearly impossible to use.

- **Irony**

If a key reason for the American safeguard against Chinese tires was to protect American jobs, then query whether the remedy was worth the cost. An April 2017 joint report by economists at the IMF, World Bank, and WTO pointed out:

> **Just as lower tariffs can benefit vast segments of a country's population, the imposition of tariffs can be costly and have third-order effects on downstream industries.** This was evident in the case of the U.S. imposition of additional tariffs on Chinese tires imports in 2009, which cost at least $900,000 for each job saved on an estimated annual basis — about 22 times the average wage of those workers — and was associated with three times as many job *losses* in other sectors . . . .[152]

In other words, trade remedies inflict significant costs on consumers and third parties.

---

152. INTERNATIONAL MONETARY FUND, THE WORLD BANK, WORLD TRADE ORGANIZATION, MAKING TRADE AND ENGINE OF GROWTH FOR ALL: THE CASE FOR TRADE AND FOR POLICIES TO FACILITATE ADJUSTMENT, 21 (April 2017) (emphasis original), www.wto.org/english/news_e /news17_e/wto_imf_report_07042017.pdf.

Part Seven

Unilateral Remedies

Chapter 29

Rationales for Unilateral Retaliation[1]

I. Civil Disobedience

Professor Robert Hudec (1935–2003) considers whether America's Section 301 of the *Trade Act of 1974*, as amended (codified at 19 U.S.C Section 2411 *et seq.*) represents a legitimate form of civil disobedience directed at achieving change given that multilateral dispute resolution in the international trading system is a cumbersome — if not unresponsive — process:

> The obligation not to retaliate without GATT authority presumes that GATT will be able to rule on the disputed legal claim, and, later, on the request to retaliate. If GATT is, in fact, unable to rule, the complainant may be free to resort to "self-help" in some circumstances.[2]

Put differently, Section 301 is a "disagreeable necessity, a 'lesser evil' chosen to prevent a more damaging outcome."[3] That outcome is the failure of the multilateral trading system because of ineffectual dispute resolution mechanisms.

However, does the same logic apply to FTAs? Moreover, is the premise of justifying Section 301 with Civil Disobedience false? The approach assumes multilateral dispute resolution mechanisms are ineffectual. That is a harsh judgment against the *DSU*. For all its actual or purported flaws — a certain lack of transparency, being over-burdened with cases, lacking private party representation, and confusion over how to deal with alleged non-compliance, to name a few — it is hard to say the system is utterly broken. Justice can be, and has been, obtained by many WTO Members in many cases, and few would advocate scrapping the *DSU* in favor of a retreat to Walden Pond *à propos* the Transcendentalist Henry David Thoreau (1817–1862).

---

1. Documents References:
   (1) *Havana (ITO) Charter* Articles 41, 47, 66, 92–97
   (2) GATT Article XXIII
   (3) WTO *DSU* Articles 21–23
2. Robert E. Hudec, *Thinking About the New Section 301: Beyond Good and Evil, in* Aggressive Unilateralism: America's 301 Trade Policy and the World Trading System 113, 121 (Jagdish Bhagwati & Hugh T. Patrick, eds., 1990). [Hereinafter, Hudec, *Thinking About the New Section 301.*]
3. Hudec, *Thinking About the New Section 301*, 131.

II. Game Theory

• What Is Game Theory?

Economists have long used game-theoretic models to analyze Section 301 negotiations. This approach has been adopted by legal scholars who adhere to a law and economics perspective on international trade law. Professor Alan Sykes uses Non-Cooperative Game Theory to support his argument that the mandatory retaliation provision of Section 301 is a "sensible strategic response to the problem of 'cheating'" under an international trade agreement.[4] A non-cooperative game is one in which the players cannot assume promises always will be kept. So, parties to international trade agreements cannot assume their commitments are binding. Why? Because there is no external authority to compel the parties to honor their commitments.

Game Theory posits a trade agreement between the U.S. and Japan that resembles the well-known Prisoner's Dilemma model. The U.S. promises to reduce the tariff on Japanese widgets to zero in exchange for a Japanese promise to accord duty-free treatment to American gadgets. Each country can choose to comply with the agreement, or cheat on the other country.

> Presumably, the elimination of the tariff on Japanese widgets . . . imposes a political cost on U.S. officials. If tariff reductions are politically advantageous, they will be undertaken unilaterally and trading partners will not need to offer concessions in return. Likewise, the elimination of the tariff on U.S. gadgets no doubt imposes a political cost on Japanese officials. The trade agreement is possible despite these political costs because concessions abroad yield political benefits to officials in each country—exporters gain and "reward" the political officials who are responsible for obtaining the concession. It is also reasonable to suppose that if one country cheats, officials in the other country forfeit most or all of the political gains from obtaining the concession—exporters will not reward officials who obtain concessions on paper that do not materialize in practice. It follows that officials in each country would prefer an environment in which the tariff abroad remained at zero, but the tariff at home was raised ("compliance" by the other country, "cheating" at home). They would then avoid the political costs associated with the concession at home, yet reap the political benefits associated with the concession abroad.

> Thus the "payoff structure" for this trade agreement game has the following properties: In each country, officials are better off if both trading nations comply with the agreement than if they both cheat. If only one nation cheats and the other complies, officials in the cheating nation are

---

4. Alan O. Sykes, *"Mandatory" Retaliation for Breach of Trade Agreements: Some Thoughts on the Strategic Design of Section 301*, 8 BOSTON UNIVERSITY INTERNATIONAL LAW JOURNAL 301, 303 (1990). [Hereinafter, *"Mandatory" Retaliation.*]

better off yet, but officials in the complying nation are worse off than if they also cheated.

Figure I illustrates this payoff structure. The numbers are arbitrary, except that they obey the above inequalities.

Figure I

Japanese Strategy

		Comply	Cheat
U.S.	Comply	(10, 10)	(0, 15)
Strategy	Cheat	(15, 0)	(5, 5)

For each possible combination of strategies, Figure I provides an ordered pair representing the payoff to officials in each country. The payoff to U.S. officials is the first number, and the payoff to Japanese officials the second. Thus, for example, if Japan cheats and the U.S. complies, U.S. officials receive a payoff of zero and Japanese officials receive a payoff of 15.[5]

On the basis of the payoff structure, in a single-play game — *i.e.*, where the U.S. and Japan must decide once on a course of action that cannot be modified subsequently in response to the course adopted by the other country — each country will cheat.

The numbers in the payoff structure indicate American officials are better off cheating regardless of whether Japan complies or cheats (because 15 > 10 and 5 > 0, respectively). Conversely, Japanese officials are better off cheating regardless of the American course of action (because if the U.S. complies, Japan obtains 15 by cheating but only 10 by complying, and if the U.S. cheats, Japan gets 5 by cheating and zero by complying). As a result, each country will earn the same payoff (5, 5). No doubt each side would be better off if both countries complied with the agreement, "[b]ut that outcome is untenable because the initial promise to comply is not binding, and because in a single play game neither side can punish the other for cheating in a future period."[6]

• **Repeat Players**

What if the game is played repeatedly? After all, a model based on the single play game is not realistic. The U.S. and Japan have a long history of trade relations that includes many moves and countermoves. Their relations are more akin to a chess match that never ends than a single play game. In a multiple-play game, it can be argued "sustained compliance is by no means assured."[7] The U.S. and Japan would announce that if the other party cheats during one period, then it will cheat in the

---

5. *"Mandatory" Retaliation*, 306.

6. *"Mandatory" Retaliation*, 307.

7. *"Mandatory" Retaliation*, 307.

subsequent period. The threat of subsequent retaliatory cheating, however, may not deter cheating in the previous period. In a two-period game:

> [i]n the second period, each player confronts the payoff matrix in Figure I, with no opportunity to punish the other player in the future for cheating (the game will be over). Hence, cheating becomes the dominant strategy for each player in the second period. And, each player can figure this out in the first period—for example, Japan knows that the United States will cheat in the second period regardless of which strategy Japan chooses in the first period. The United States threat to punish cheating is thus an empty one, and would have no deterrent effect on Japan in the first period. Cheating becomes the dominant strategy for Japan in the first period just as in the single-play game. This reasoning also applies to the United States, and so both countries would cheat in both periods.
>
> Precisely the same logic applies to a game that is repeated four times, five times, and n times, as long as each player knows the number of repetitions. Acting "rationally," both players anticipate that they will each cheat in the last period, and so they have no reason not to cheat in the next to last period, no reason not to cheat in the next to next to last period, and so forth.[8]

Even in an infinite horizon game—one that has no end—the threat to cheat may be one that is potentially credible for an indefinite time. To motivate compliance, a country could employ a "tit-for-tat" strategy, behaving in the current period as the other country did in the previous period. Alternatively, a country may employ a "grim" strategy in which it complies until it discovers the other country is cheating, and thereafter cheats forever. Still another alternative would be a "massive retaliation" strategy whereby a country declares that cheating of the other country abrogates the entire agreement.

In a Game Theory context, mandatory retaliation under Section 301(a) serves as a credible device to sanction and, therefore, deter cheating on a commitment in a trade agreement. Yet, the utility of Section 301 is limited in two respects. First, suppose the U.S. retaliates unilaterally in a case where cheating is not blatant, or where the alleged cheater has a legitimate defense (such as under GATT Article XI, XII, XVI, XX, or XXI). (In respect of Article XXI, note the WTO Panel Report, Russia – Measures Concerning Traffic in Transit, WT/DS/512/R, issued 5 April 2019, where the Panel asserted jurisdiction over this defense, and defined "emergency" as war or heightened tensions that could lead to war.) Then, the U.S. risks both infamy and counter-retaliation. In turn, its trading partners may be disinclined to negotiate trade deals with the U.S.

Second, the mandatory retaliation provision requires a tit-for-tat, or measured, response. The USTR cannot employ grim and massive retaliation strategies, and this fact undermines the credibility of any retaliatory threat under Section 301. In game theoretic terms, retaliation is credible only if it wipes out the gain that accrues

---

8. *"Mandatory" Retaliation*, 307–308.

to a cheater from cheating. Otherwise, a cheater will continue to cheat and accept the retaliation. Instead of ruling out *a priori* two strategies, the game theoretic approach suggests that the amount of retaliation should be linked to the amount of the cheater's gain.

There are concerns about a Game-Theoretic analysis of mandatory retaliation under Section 301:

(1) Is it realistic to assume that parties to international trade agreements do not view their commitments as binding?

(2) Is it reasonable to conceptualize international trade agreements as a payoff structure involving two players?

(3) Are the predictions of the payoff structure subject to manipulation?

(4) What happens if the time horizons of the negotiating parties differ?

(5) Should the payoff structure be dynamic?

(6) Would preservation of reputation be an incentive to comply?

III. Utilitarianism

• **Does Unilateral Retaliation "Work"?**

There is little debate as to whether Section 301 is efficacious from an empirical standpoint. Reflecting a consensus of scholarly opinion, Professor Taylor rightly points out the statute is not a panacea for America's trade problems.[9] The U.S. used Section 301 between 1985–1995 to (1) pursue GATT violations, (2) set the Uruguay Round agenda, and (3) mitigate a persistent trade deficit with Japan. She concludes the practical effects, in these 3 categories of use, were limited, and potentially conflicted with GATT.

Still, no one contends Section 301 is ineffectual. The consensus is it works — sometimes, in some cases. The open issues are exactly how effective unilateral retaliation is, and why. Most empirical studies conclude retaliation or threats thereof "work," by which some of them mean an agreement was reached, while others mean a trade liberalization result was obtained, *i.e.*, the target foreign country removed or changed its disputed act, policy, or practice. Indirect direct evidence that Section 301 works comes from the average length of time it took to complete Section 301 cases during the 1975–1997 period: 15 months.[10] That average is faster than the textbook 12–18 months for a *DSU* adjudication, plus the additional standard 15-month RPT. It suggests the mere threat of unilateral retaliation may be a faster way for America to persuade a foreign government to change its behavior than plodding through the multilateral process.

---

9. *See* C. O'Neal Taylor, *The Limits of Economic Power: Section 301 and the World Trade Organization Dispute Settlement System*, 30 Vanderbilt Journal of Transnational Law 209 (1997).

10. *See* Randy Woods, *Trump's Retro China Trade Tool Has One Huge Advantage Over WTO*, 34 International Trade Reporter (BNA) 1217 (14 September 2017).

• 1994 Bayard-Elliott Study

Possibly the most careful, comprehensive empirical study of unilateral trade retaliation is *Reciprocity and Retaliation in U.S. Trade Policy* (1994), by Thomas O. Bayard and Kimberly Ann Elliott. They analyze 72 cases brought under Section 301, Special 301, and Super 301 between 1975 and June 1994 in which the outcomes were reasonably clear. They define a "successful" outcome as "one in which U.S. negotiating objectives—that is, improved market access for U.S. exporters of goods and services, reduced export subsidies by the European Union and others, and improved protection for intellectual property rights . . . —were at least partially achieved."[11]

Bayard and Elliott conclude unilateral retaliation is reasonably effective as an American trade policy weapon. In spite of frequent, bitter denunciations of Section 301, exercise of the statute seems to have had a net liberalizing effect on world trade. Specifically, in 35 of the 72 cases—about half of the time—the U.S. achieved its negotiating objectives. Interestingly, the success rate has varied over time. Generally, the rate was higher in the mid-1980s, prior to the passage of the *Omnibus Trade and Competitiveness Act of 1988* and Super 301.

What factors contributed to a successful outcome? On the basis of multi-variable regression analysis, Bayard and Elliott find:

> a successful outcome is more likely the more dependent the target country is on the U.S. market, the larger the U.S. bilateral deficit with the target is, and the more transparent the targeted trade barrier is. There is some evidence that success is less likely if the target has a record of counter-retaliating against US exports in trade disputes [as, for example, the EU, Canada, and China have done], but the result is not statistically significant. Surprisingly, neither public nor explicit threats . . . appear to affect outcomes in Section 301 cases.
>
>   . . .
>
> Unexpectedly, GATT procedures do not appear to add much leverage: the success rate for cases in which a GATT panel ruled against a target's policies (54 percent) was not significantly different from that for cases in which there was no GATT ruling or GATT rules were not applicable (47 percent). But, there is still evidence of some deference to GATT rules in these cases. In every case where a GATT panel found a violation or evidence of nullification or impairment, changes in the offending policy were made. In almost half, however, the target country replaced the illegal trade barrier with another type of barrier or disagreed with the U.S. interpretation of what had been agreed.
>
>   . . .

---

11. THOMAS O. BAYARD & KIMBERLY ANN ELLIOTT, RECIPROCITY AND RETALIATION IN U.S. TRADE POLICY 59 (1994). [Hereinafter, BAYARD & ELLIOTT.]

There is also a stronger positive correlation between GATT dispute settlement procedures and success if the European Community is excluded. Cases with GATT rulings, other than those involving the Community, were successful 71 percent of the time (vs. 54 percent overall). Cases involving GATT rulings against the European Community ultimately were judged to be failures on five of eight occasions. Each time the Community changed the offending practice, but it exploited ambiguities in GATT or the bilateral agreements to continue to protect its agricultural producers and processors.[12]

In other words, three variables are critical in predicting the success of an action.

First, Section 301 is an effective tool if the target foreign government is vulnerable because the U.S. is a key destination for its country's exports. In the 35 of 72 successful Section 301 cases, the ratio of the target country's exports to the U.S. as a percentage of the target's GNP, which is a measure of its export dependence on the U.S., was 7.5%. In the 37 of 72 failed cases, the average target country's export dependence was 4.3% of its GNP. Obviously, as the share of a target country's GNP accounted for by exports to the U.S. rises, the stakes rise, and American retaliation can inflict serious damage. The practical message for all of America's trading partners is to diversify their export markets, because over-reliance on the American market is dangerous.

Second, the absolute size of the bilateral trade balance between the U.S. and the target foreign country is significant. In successful cases, the average bilateral deficit of the U.S. was $15 billion, while in failed cases it was $2 billion. Why is this variable important? One argument could be the U.S. is more likely to "bargain hard" and take retaliatory action if it faces a greater imbalance, thus a target foreign government perceives threats of retaliation as credible and is more likely to modify its behavior.

Third, the more transparent the act, policy, or practice in question, the more likely that a Section 301 action will be successful. This result seems based on the common sense notion that if the USTR can "see it," then it is easier for the USTR to urge its elimination or modification.

A 4th variable that can influence the outcome of a Section 301 case is whether there are interest groups in the target foreign country that support the U.S. position. For example, do Japanese consumer groups lobby their government to liberalize its import regime with respect to American agricultural goods? Does India seek to replace traditional socialist planning and import substitution policies with market-oriented, trade liberalization policies? Of course, whether a strong reform-oriented constituency exists depends on the degree of political freedom and participation in the target country.

The overall empirical record on Section 301, suggesting the practical utility of this weapon, is philosophically troubling. The probability of success of unilateral

---

12. BAYARD & ELLIOTT, 86, 90.

retaliation, under the right conditions, elides features unique to each case. Trade disputes are aggregating and assessed into a "win-loss" record—an approach some observers take to participation in *DSU* cases. Empirical studies are motivated by the question "did we win or not?," not by concerns of equity.

Surely procedural and substantive due process ought to matter. First, were results obtained in a fair manner? Ends cannot justify means. Results obtained through unequal bargaining power are inherently unfair. Asymmetry arises when a target foreign country does not have the ability to strike the U.S. as hard as the U.S. can hit the target. That difference in vulnerability—when there is no market in the target country particularly valuable to American exporters—arises especially when the target is a poor country.

Second, were the results obtained by unilateral retaliation just? Ideally, a target country should abandon or change its behavior because it is the right course of action. "Right" not in terms of U.S. economic aims, but because it is an appropriate balance among those aims, the target's legitimate concerns, and interest of the international community in trade liberalization. Or, "right" simply in a moral sense. Perhaps when there is a multilateral consensus on "unreasonable" or "discriminatory" measures, it be possible to ensure the outcome in Section 301 investigations (especially under Section 301(b), given the notably ambiguous terms in that statute) is just.

Chapter 30

Section 301[1]

I. Section 301, Super 301, and Special 301

Section 301 of the *Trade Act of 1974*, as amended, is the most potent and controversial weapon in the American trade remedy arsenal. It is not the only such weapon. "Super 301" and "Special 301" also exist. What are they? How are they different from "Section 301"? The term "Section 301" commonly is used to include Sections 301–309 of the *1974 Act*.[2] (Super 301 follows, and Special 301 precedes, these provisions.[3])

Section 301 authorizes the President to enforce U.S. rights under trade agreements and take action against unfair foreign trade practices. In contrast to AD, CVD, Section 201, and Section 337 cases, where the focus of attention typically is on the behavior of foreign private parties, a Section 301 case pertains to the acts, policies, or practices of a foreign sovereign government. Since the 1974 inception of Section 301, the USTR has undertaken roughly 120 Section 301 investigations. The most common target is the EU. Japan, Korea, and Taiwan are the second, third, and fourth most common targets, respectively. The single biggest target is China, thanks to a March 2018 Section 301 action that catalyzed a Sino-American Trade War (discussed in a separate Chapter).

The unilateral nature of Section 301, coupled with the types of retaliatory measures it authorizes, renders it susceptible to the criticism it is inconsistent with GATT and the *DSU*. Yet, as the USTR itself states, it remains the "principal" statute for addressing allegedly unfair foreign trade practices that affect American exports of goods and services. To appreciate arguments about the GATT consistency of Section 301, it is necessary to understand its history and operation. Super and Special 301 are unilateral weapons, too. The latter focuses on IPRs. What is the emphasis of the former?

---

1. Documents References:
   (1) *Havana (ITO) Charter* Articles 41, 47, 66, 92–97
   (2) GATT Article XXIII
   (3) WTO *DSU* Articles 21–23
2. *See* 19 U.S.C. §§ 2411–2419.
3. Super 301 is codified at 19 U.S.C. § 2420. Special 301 is codified at 19 U.S.C. § 2242.

II. Historical Antecedents of Section 301

For over two centuries, the President has had the authority to retaliate against discriminatory foreign trade practices that burden U.S. commerce. To be sure, Article I, Section 8, Clause 3 of the U.S. Constitution—the Commerce Clause—gives Congress the power to regulate foreign trade. However, Congress imparts that power to the Executive branch. Of course, Congress does so subject to the delegation doctrine, which in brief and simplistic terms means Congress must not abdicate its Constitutional duty by giving the President unbounded authority, but rather set parameters on the President's conduct of foreign trade. (Recall from a separate Chapter the key delegation doctrine cases arising in the context of international trade, and how jurisprudence in this area has evolved.)

For instance, Congress empowered by statute President George Washington (1732–1799, President, 1789–1797) to lay embargoes and other restrictions on imports and exports if he determined foreign countries discriminating against the U.S. A century later, in the 1892 case of *Field v. Clark*, the Supreme Court upheld an 1890 statute empowering the President to impose retaliatory tariffs on imports from a foreign country if that country imposes duties on American goods that the President deems reciprocally unequal and unreasonable.[4] The case involved the Constitutionality of Congress' delegation of power to the President. The Court's ruling remains good law, and probably bars a Court from ruling that Congress acted unconstitutionally in delegating power to the President under Section 301.

In the *Tariff Act of 1930*, the President was given potent authority to impose tariffs on goods from foreign countries that discriminated against American products.[5] The *Reciprocal Trade Agreements Act of 1934* contained a provision akin to Section 301 authorizing the President to negotiate with, or impose retaliatory duties against, a country whose import restrictions unduly restricted U.S. exports.[6]

More recent origins of Section 301 lie in Section 252 of the *Trade Expansion Act of 1962*, which, in turn, reflected Congressional concern during the Kennedy era over the enforcement of American trade rights in a dramatically changing international economy. Professor Robert Hudec (1935–2003), explains:

> The United States Congress has generally regarded itself as the final (and only true) protector of reciprocity in foreign trade commitments. The Congress harbors a lingering suspicion that the Executive Branch can be persuaded on occasion to sacrifice United States economic interests for the sake of friendly political relations. This suspicion surfaces regularly in congressional appraisal of major GATT tariff negotiations. Each new grant

---

4. 143 U.S. 649 (1892).

5. *See Tariff Act of 1930*, ch. 497, title III, § 303, 46 Stat. 590, 687, codified as amended at 19 U.S.C. § 1303, repealed by the *Uruguay Round Agreements Act of 1994*, Public Law Number 103-465, title II, § 261(a), 8 December 1994, 108 Stat. 4908.

6. *See Act of 1934*, ch. 474, § 1, 48 Stat. 943, 943–44, codified as amended at 19 U.S.C. § 1351.

of negotiating authority has typically been preceded by a Congressional tongue-lashing over the one-sided results of the previous negotiations.

By the 1960's, this chorus had grown to include a second theme—the charge that other GATT members had not been living up to their general legal obligations, and worse, that the eager-to-please Executive Branch had been unwilling to assert United States legal rights against the violators. The criticism led to the enactment of Section 252 of the *Trade Expansion Act of 1962*. The section directed the President to seek the removal of illegal restrictions, forbade the President from using tariff concessions to pay for their removal, and authorized retaliation in the event they were not removed. Section 252(c) also authorized retaliation in the case of legal but "unreasonable" restrictions, but in this case the statute instructed the President to have "due regard for the international obligations of the United States."

. . .

Congressional criticism re-emerged after the 1967 Kennedy Round agreement. This time it included an attack on the GATT itself. GATT obligations seemed not to cover some of the new trade practices devised by the EEC; other GATT provisions appeared outdated by more recent wisdom. In addition, there seemed to be a growing reluctance within GATT to enforce those obligations which were clear.

Moral outrage and self-righteousness aside, the criticism had some basis in fact. The economic world of the 1960's had come to include new powers such as Japan, the EEC, and a surprisingly well-organized coalition of developing countries, each with demands not fully anticipated by the 1947 GATT blueprint. The GATT (and particularly the United States) had adjusted to these new demands by deferring, and ultimately shelving, legal objections to some of the new trade practices that had emerged. Instead, the GATT increasingly turned to "pragmatic" solutions that would adjust the competing interests. Viewed from the perspective of the Congress, of course, all these accommodations were violations gone unpunished.

. . .

Section 301 is a revised and strengthened version of the old section 252. In scope, it covers not only import restrictions, but also other discriminatory acts or policies, export subsidies, and export embargoes. The new section authorizes a greater quantity of retaliation than section 252. Finally, it seems to give the President substantially greater freedom to ignore international obligations when using his retaliatory authority.[7]

---

7. Robert E. Hudec, *Retaliation Against "Unreasonable" Foreign Trade Practices: The New Section 301 and GATT Nullification and Impairment*, 59 Minnesota Law Review 461 515 (1975). For a case involving the Section 252 of the *1962 Act*, see *United States v. Star Industries, Inc.*, 462 F.2d 557 (C.C.P.A. 1972), *cert. denied* 409 U.S. 1076 (1972).

Since it enacted Section 301 in 1974, Congress has remained steadfast in its support for the statute. Indeed, it strengthened the statute through Section 1303 of the *Omnibus Trade and Competitiveness Act of 1988*. Section 1303 added Section 182 to the *1974 Act*—the Special 301 provision. Further, the *1988 Act* amended Section 301 to mandate retaliation in certain cases. Finally, that *Act* buttressed Section 301 by adding Super 301. Congress insisted on the threat of unilateral sanctions under Super 301 as a *quid pro quo* for extending fast-track trade negotiation authority of President Ronald Reagan. That authority was critical to complete both the Uruguay Round and *NAFTA*.

III. How Section 301 Operates

WTO Panel Report,

United States — Sections 301–310 of the Trade Act of 1974,
WT/DS152/R (Adopted 27 January 2000) (Not Appealed)

II. Factual Aspects

. . .

C. Procedures

2.12. Sections 301–310 of the *Trade Act of 1974* [19 U.S.C. §§ 2411–2420] provide a means by which U.S. citizens may petition the United States government to investigate and act against potential violations of international trade agreements. [*See* 19 U.S.C. § 2412(a)(2).] These provisions also authorize the USTR to initiate such investigations at her own initiative. [*See* 19 U.S.C. § 2412(b).] The USTR is a cabinet level official serving at the pleasure of the President, and her office is located within the Executive Office of the President. [*See* 19 U.S.C. § 2171(a), (b)(1).] The USTR operates under the direction of the President and advises and assists the President in various Presidential functions. [*See* 19 U.S.C. § 2171(c)(1).]

2.13. According to Section 302 [19 U.S.C. § 2412], investigations may be initiated either upon citizen petition or at the initiative of the USTR. After a petition is filed, the USTR decides within 45 days whether or not to initiate an investigation. If the investigation is initiated, the USTR must, according to Section 303, request consultations with the country concerned, normally on the date of initiation but in any case not later than 90 days thereafter. [*See* 19 U.S.C. § 2413(a)(1).]

2.14. Section 303(a)(2) [19 U.S.C. § 2413(a)(2)] provides that, if the investigation involves a trade agreement and a mutually acceptable resolution is not reached "before the earlier of A) the close of the consultation period, if any, specified in the trade agreement, or B) the 150th day after the day on which consultation commenced," the USTR must request proceedings under the formal dispute settlement procedures of the trade agreement.

2.15. Section 304(a) [19 U.S.C. § 2414(a)] provides that on or before the earlier of "(i) the date that is 30 days after the date on which the dispute settlement procedure is concluded, or (ii) the date that is 18 months after the date on which the investigation is initiated," "[o]n the basis of the investigation initiated under Section 302 and the consultations (and the proceedings, if applicable) under Section 303, the Trade Representative shall . . . determine whether" U.S. rights are being denied. If the determination is affirmative, USTR shall at the same time determine what action it will take under Section 301.

2.16. If the DSB adopts rulings favorable to the United States on a measure investigated under Section 301, and the WTO Member concerned agrees to implement that ruling within the reasonable period foreseen in Article 21 of the *DSU*, the USTR can determine that the rights of the United States are being denied but that "satisfactory measures" are being taken that justify the termination of the Section 301 investigation.

2.17. Section 306(a) [19 U.S.C. 2416(a)] requires the USTR to "monitor" the implementation of measures undertaken by, or agreements entered into with, a foreign government to provide a satisfactory resolution of a matter subject to dispute settlement to enforce the rights of the United States under a trade agreement.

2.18. Section 306(b) [19 U.S.C. § 2416(b)] provides:

   "(1) **In general.** — If, on the basis of the monitoring carried out under subsection (a), the Trade Representative considers that a foreign country is not satisfactorily implementing a measure or agreement referred to in subsection (a), the Trade Representative shall determine what further action the Trade Representative shall take under section 301(a). For purposes of section 301, any such determination shall be treated as a determination made under section 304(a)(1).

   (2) **WTO dispute settlement recommendations.** — If the measure or agreement referred to in subsection (a) concerns the implementation of a recommendation made pursuant to dispute settlement proceedings under the World Trade Organization, and the Trade Representative considers that the foreign country has failed to implement it, the Trade Representative shall make the determination in paragraph (1) no later than 30 days after the expiration of the reasonable period of time provided for such implementation under paragraph 21 of the *Understanding on Rules and Procedures Governing the Settlement of Disputes* . . . ."

2.19. Section 305(a)(1) [19 U.S.C. § 2415(a)(1)] provides that, "Except as provided in paragraph (2), the Trade Representative shall implement the action the Trade Representative determines under Section 304(a)(1)(B), subject to the specific direction, if any, of the President regarding such action" "by no later than . . . 30 days after the date on which such determination is made."

2.20. According to Section 305(a)(2)(A) [19 U.S.C. § 2415(a)(2)(A)], however, "the [USTR] may delay, by not more than 180 days, the implementation" of any action under Section 301 in response to a request by the petitioner or the industry that would benefit from the Section 301 action or if the USTR determines "that substantial progress is being made, or that a delay is necessary or desirable to obtain United States rights or satisfactory solution with respect to the acts, policies, or practices that are the subject of the action."

IV. What Section 301 Says

- Substantive Criteria and Definitions

TRADE ACT OF 1974, AS AMENDED, 19 U.S.C. SECTIONS 2411–2420

§ 2411. Actions by United States Trade Representative

(a) Mandatory action.

   (1) If the United States Trade Representative determines under section 2414(a)(1) of this title that—

      (A) the rights of the United States under any trade agreement are being denied; or

      (B) an act, policy, or practice of a foreign country—

         (i) violates, or is inconsistent with, the provisions of, or otherwise denies benefits to the United States under, any trade agreement, or

         (ii) is unjustifiable and burdens or restricts United States commerce;

   the Trade Representative shall take action authorized in subsection (c), subject to the specific direction, if any, of the President regarding any such action, and shall take all other appropriate and feasible action within the power of the President that the President may direct the Trade Representative to take under this subsection, to enforce such rights or to obtain the elimination of such act, policy, or practice. Actions may be taken that are within the power of the President with respect to trade in any goods or services, or with respect to any other area of pertinent relations with the foreign country.

   (2) The Trade Representative is not required to take action under paragraph (1) in any case in which—

      (A) the Dispute Settlement Body (as defined in section 3531(5) of this title has adopted a report, or a ruling issued under the formal dispute settlement proceeding provided under any other trade agreement finds, that—

         (i) the rights of the United States under a trade agreement are not being denied, or

         (ii) the act, policy, or practice—

(I) is not a violation of, or inconsistent with, the rights of the United States, or

(II) does not deny, nullify, or impair benefits to the United States under any trade agreement; or

(B) the Trade Representative finds that —

(i) the foreign country is taking satisfactory measures to grant the rights of the United States under a trade agreement,

(ii) the foreign country has —

(I) agreed to eliminate or phase out the act, policy, or practice, or

(II) agreed to an imminent solution to the burden or restriction on United States commerce that is satisfactory to the Trade Representative,

(iii) it is impossible for the foreign country to achieve the results described in clause (i) or (ii), as appropriate, but the foreign country agrees to provide to the United States compensatory trade benefits that are satisfactory to the Trade Representative,

(iv) in extraordinary cases, where the taking of action under this subsection would have an adverse impact on the United States economy substantially out of proportion to the benefits of such action, taking into account the impact of not taking such action on the credibility of the provisions of this subchapter, or

(v) the taking of action under this subsection would cause serious harm to the national security of the United States.

(3) Any action taken under paragraph (1) to eliminate an act, policy, or practice shall be devised so as to affect goods or services of the foreign country in an amount that is equivalent in value to the burden or restriction being imposed by that country on United States commerce.

(b) Discretionary action.

If the Trade Representative determines under section 2414(a)(1) of this title that —

(1) an act, policy, or practice of a foreign country is unreasonable or discriminatory and burdens or restricts United States commerce, and

(2) action by the United States is appropriate, the Trade Representative shall take all appropriate and feasible action authorized under subsection (c) of this section, subject to the specific direction, if any, of the President regarding any such action, and all other appropriate and feasible action within the power of the President that the President may direct the Trade Representative to take under this subsection, to obtain the elimination of that act, policy, or practice. Actions may be taken that are within the power of the

President with respect to trade in any goods or services, or with respect to any other area of pertinent relations with the foreign country.

(c) **Scope of authority.**

(1) For purposes of carrying out the provisions of subsection (a) or (b), the Trade Representative is authorized to —

(A) suspend, withdraw, or prevent the application of, benefits of trade agreement concessions to carry out a trade agreement with the foreign country referred to in such subsection;

(B) impose duties or other import restrictions on the goods of, and, notwithstanding any other provision of law, fees or restrictions on the services of, such foreign country for such time as the Trade Representative determines appropriate;

(C) in a case in which the act, policy, or practice also fails to meet the eligibility criteria for receiving duty-free treatment under subsections (b) and (c) of section 2462 of this title [19], subsections (b) and (c) of section 2702 of this title, or subsections (c) and (d) of section 3202 of this title, withdraw, limit, or suspend such treatment under such provisions, notwithstanding the provisions of subsection (a)(3) of this section; or

(D) enter into binding agreements with such foreign country that commit such foreign country to —

(i) eliminate, or phase out, the act, policy, or practice that is the subject of the action to be taken under subsection (a) or (b) of this section,

(ii) eliminate any burden or restriction on United States commerce resulting from such act, policy, or practice, or

(iii) provide the United States with compensatory trade benefits that —

(I) are satisfactory to the Trade Representative, and

(II) meet the requirements of paragraph (4).

(2) (A) Notwithstanding any other provision of law governing any service sector access authorization, and in addition to the authority conferred in paragraph (1), the Trade Representative may, for purposes of carrying out the provisions of subsection (a) or (b) of this section —

(i) restrict, in the manner and to the extent the Trade Representative determines appropriate, the terms and conditions of any such authorization, or

(ii) deny the issuance of any such authorization.

(B) Actions described in subparagraph (A) may only be taken under this section with respect to service sector access authorizations granted, or applications therefor pending, on or after the date on which—

   (i) a petition is filed under section 2412(a) of this title, or

   (ii) a determination to initiate an investigation is made by the Trade Representative under section 2412(b) of this title.

(C) Before the Trade Representative takes any action under this section involving the imposition of fees or other restrictions on the services of a foreign country, the Trade Representative shall, if the services involved are subject to regulation by any agency of the Federal Government or of any State, consult, as appropriate, with the head of the agency concerned.

(3) The actions the Trade Representative is authorized to take under subsection (a) or (b) may be taken against any goods or economic sector—

(A) on a nondiscriminatory basis or solely against the foreign country described in such subsection, and

(B) without regard to whether or not such goods or economic sector were involved in the act, policy, or practice that is the subject of such action.

(4) Any trade agreement described in paragraph (1)(C)(iii) shall provide compensatory trade benefits that benefit the economic sector which includes the domestic industry that would benefit from the elimination of the act, policy, or practice that is the subject of the action to be taken under subsection (a) or (b) of this section, or benefit the economic sector as closely related as possible to such economic sector, unless—

(A) the provision of such trade benefits is not feasible, or

(B) trade benefits that benefit any other economic sector would be more satisfactory than such trade benefits.

(5) If the Trade Representative determines that actions to be taken under subsection (a) or (b) of this section are to be in the form of import restrictions, the Trade Representative shall—

(A) give preference to the imposition of duties over the imposition of other import restrictions, and

(B) if an import restriction other than a duty is imposed, consider substituting, on an incremental basis, an equivalent duty for such other import restriction.

(6) Any action taken by the Trade Representative under this section with respect to export targeting shall, to the extent possible, reflect the full benefit level of the export targeting to the beneficiary over the period during which the action taken has an effect.

(d) Definitions and special rules.

For purposes of this chapter [19 U.S.C. §§ 2411 *et seq.*] —

(1) The term "commerce" includes, but is not limited to —

    (A) services (including transfers of information) associated with international trade, whether or not such services are related to specific goods, and

    (B) foreign direct investment by United States persons with implications for trade in goods or services.

(2) An act, policy, or practice of a foreign country that burdens or restricts United States commerce may include the provision, directly or indirectly, by that foreign country of subsidies for the construction of vessels used in the commercial transportation by water of goods between foreign countries and the United States.

(3) (A) An act, policy, or practice is unreasonable if the act, policy, or practice, while not necessarily in violation of, or inconsistent with, the international legal rights of the United States, is otherwise unfair and inequitable.

    (B) Acts, policies, and practices that are unreasonable include, but are not limited to, any act, policy, or practice, or any combination of acts, policies, or practices, which —

        (i) denies fair and equitable —

            (I) opportunities for the establishment of an enterprise,

            (II) provision of adequate and effective protection of intellectual property rights notwithstanding the fact that the foreign country may be in compliance with the specific obligations of the *Agreement on Trade-Related Aspects of Intellectual Property Rights* referred to in section 3511 (d) of this title [19],

            (III) nondiscriminatory market access opportunities for United States persons that rely upon intellectual property protection, or

            (IV) market opportunities, including the toleration by a foreign government of systematic anti-competitive activities by enterprises or among enterprises in the foreign country that have the effect of restricting, on a basis that is inconsistent with commercial considerations, access of United States goods or services to a foreign market,

        (ii) constitutes export targeting, or

        (iii) constitutes a persistent pattern of conduct that —

            (I) denies workers the right of association,

            (II) denies workers the right to organize and bargain collectively,

(III) permits any form of forced or compulsory labor,

(IV) fails to provide a minimum age for the employment of children, or

(V) fails to provide standards for minimum wages, hours of work, and occupational safety and health of workers.

(C) (i) Acts, policies, and practices of a foreign country described in subparagraph (B)(iii) shall not be treated as being unreasonable if the Trade Representative determines that—

(I) the foreign country has taken, or is taking, actions that demonstrate a significant and tangible overall advancement in providing throughout the foreign country (including any designated zone within the foreign country) the rights and other standards described in the subclauses of subparagraph (B)(iii), or

(II) such acts, policies, and practices are not inconsistent with the level of economic development of the foreign country.

(ii) The Trade Representative shall publish in the Federal Register any determination made under clause (i), together with a description of the facts on which such determination is based.

(D) For purposes of determining whether any act, policy, or practice is unreasonable, reciprocal opportunities in the United States for foreign nationals and firms shall be taken into account, to the extent appropriate.

(E) The term "export targeting" means any government plan or scheme consisting of a combination of coordinated actions (whether carried out severally or jointly) that are bestowed on a specific enterprise, industry, or group thereof, the effect of which is to assist the enterprise, industry, or group to become more competitive in the export of a class or kind of merchandise.

(F) (i) For the purposes of subparagraph (B)(i)(II), adequate and effective protection of intellectual property rights includes adequate and effective means under the laws of the foreign country for persons who are not citizens or nationals of such country to secure, exercise, and enforce rights and enjoy commercial benefits relating to patents, trademarks, copyrights and related rights, mask works, trade secrets, and plant breeder's rights.

(ii) For purposes of subparagraph (B)(i)(IV), the denial of fair and equitable nondiscriminatory market access opportunities includes restrictions on market access related to the use, exploitation, or enjoyment of commercial benefits derived from exercising intellectual property rights in protected works or fixations or products embodying protected works.

(4) (A) An act, policy, or practice is unjustifiable if the act, policy, or practice is in violation of, or inconsistent with, the international legal rights of the United States.

(B) Acts, policies, and practices that are unjustifiable include, but are not limited to, any act, policy, or practice described in subparagraph (A) which denies national or most-favored-nation treatment or the right of establishment or protection of intellectual property rights.

(5) Acts, policies, and practices that are discriminatory include, when appropriate, any act, policy, and practice which denies national or most-favored-nation treatment to United States goods, services, or investment.

(6) The term "service sector access authorization" means any license, permit, order, or other authorization, issued under the authority of Federal law, that permits a foreign supplier of services access to the United States market in a service sector concerned.

(7) The term "foreign country" includes any foreign instrumentality. Any possession or territory of a foreign country that is administered separately for customs purposes shall be treated as a separate foreign country.

(8) The term "Trade Representative" means the United States Trade Representative.

(9) The term "interested persons," only for purposes of sections 2412(a)(4)(B), 2414(b)(1)(A), 2416(c)(2), and 2417(a)(2) of this title [19], includes, but is not limited to, domestic firms and workers, representatives of consumer interests, United States product exporters, and any industrial user of any goods or services that may be affected by actions taken under subsection (a) or (b) of this section.

- **Monstrous Wording but Strategic Ambiguity**

Among candidates for the worst worded American trade statute, Section 301 is at the top of the list. The trigger events for mandatory retaliation are not entirely clear. That is partly because there are tautologies and overlaps among key terms. It seems the USTR can take unilateral action against almost any kind of foreign act, policy, or practice, anytime. If a petitioner has the domestic political lobbying clout with the USTR, and if the geopolitical and economic timing for a case is good, then the USTR certainly has room for manoeuvre in the statute.

Arguably, the linguistic monstrosity of Section 301 is a weapon in itself. Foreign governments never can be certain whether America will, or will not, bring a case. The statutory language is ambiguous, and the USTR can use that ambiguity strategically. Consider a military analogy: under the 1979 *Taiwan Relations Act*, exactly how will the U.S. respond if the PRC were to use or threaten force against

Taiwan?[8] The answer is uncertain. That uncertainty is a strategic ambiguity favoring the U.S. Like foreign trading governments, the PRC is kept guessing—and, the U.S. hopes, errs on the side of caution.

V. Is Section 301 GATT-WTO Consistent?

• **Rebuttals to Attacks against Section 301**

European governments (among others) are fond of attacking the U.S. for its unilateral threats or acts in international affairs. Section 301 is one illustration, albeit a less publicly renowned one than military actions, such as the Iraq invasion launched in March 2003. Their attack is somewhat hypocritical. Some of them appear to have Section 301-type laws of their own.

There also is a lack of understanding to the attack. Because the Foreign Commerce Clause of the U.S. Constitution (Article I, Section 8, Clause 3) gives Congress, not the President, the power to regulate foreign trade, any action the President takes must be under authority delegated by Congress. Section 301 is one such delegation. So, for example, Section 301 authorizes the President to take retaliatory action, as allowed by the WTO *DSU* in a case in which America prevails as a complainant, if the losing respondent fails to comply or pay compensation. It would be inefficient for Congress to re-delegate this authority on each occasion in which the President needed it following a win at the WTO.

Finally, there is a lack of practical sense in the attack against Section 301. The subject matter jurisdiction of the GATT-WTO legal regime, broad as it is, is not without limits. Does it cover currency manipulation? Maybe, maybe not. Does it cover labor rules? No, other than prison labor in GATT Article XX(e). What about competition policy? Definitely not. So, the USTR needs authority against "acts, policies, or practices" of foreign governments not covered by GATT or other WTO agreements.

To be sure, some existing or proposed FTAs cover more topics than GATT-WTO rules, *i.e.*, "second-generation" regional deals are "deeper" than multilateral accords. But, by definition, FTAs are limited to a subset of foreign governments. So, while Section 301 maybe less relevant in the context of FTAs with broad subject matter coverage, it remains useful for non-FTA parties. And, even in the FTA context, the President may need the authority Section 301 provides to engage in trade retaliation, once the U.S. exhausts the relevant FTA dispute settlement process.

• **2000 *Section 301* Case**

Despite these points, the EU launched an attack under the WTO DSU against Section 301. Reputedly, the attack was in response to the American victories in the

---

8. *See* Public Law Number 96-8, 93 Stat. 14, 22 U.S.C. §§ 3301–3316.

1997 Bananas and 1998 *Beef Hormones* case (discussed in a separate Chapter), and reputedly dubbed "Sir Leon's revenge" (after the then EU Trade Commissioner, Sir Leon Brittan (1939–2015)).

WTO Panel Report,

United States — Sections 301–310 of the Trade Act of 1974,
WT/DS152/R (Adopted 27 January 2000) (Not Appealed)[9]

- **Issues**

On 25 November 1998, the EU filed a complaint against the U.S. stating the American Section 301 legislation, specifically Sections 304–306, ran afoul of *DSU* Article 23:2(a). The EU challenged Section 304 on the basis it requires the USTR to act unilaterally in deciding a violation has occurred by a given date. Under *DSU* Article 23:2(a), Members that wish to redress a violation of obligations, nullifications, or impairment of benefits must not make a determination to the effect that a violation has occurred. It is for the "WTO through the *DSU* process — not for an individual WTO Member — to determine that a WTO inconsistency has occurred (Article 23:2(a))."[10]

The U.S. counted that Section 304 "merely sets out in the statutory language itself that the USTR has the power and right to [make a determination of inconsistency]."[11] So, at issue was whether that discretion is itself a violation. If so, then could that violation be remedied by a *Statement of Administrative Action*, submitted by the President, to and approved by Congress, explaining that any Section 301 determination be based on Panel or Appellate Body findings adopted by the DSB.

- **Findings**

The Panel found Sections 304(a)(2)(A), 305(a), and 306(b) of the *Trade Act of 1974*, as amended, were not inconsistent with Article 23:2(a) or (c) of the *DSU* or with any GATT 1994 provisions cited. But, the Panel Report made a technical *de facto* versus *de jure* distinction, basing its finds on U.S. undertakings articulated in the Statement of Administrative Action approved by the U.S. Congress and confirmed in statements by the US to the Panel. The Panel's distinction was based on the following theory:

> "Conformity can be ensured in different ways in different legal systems. It is the end result that counts, not the manner in which it is achieved. Only by understanding and respecting the specificities of each Member's legal system, can a correct evaluation of conformity be established."[12]

---

9. Hereinafter, *Section 301* Panel Report.
10. *Section 301* Panel Report, ¶ 7.38.
11. *Section 301* Panel Report, ¶ 7.50.
12. *Section 301* Panel Report, ¶ 7.24.

- *De Jure* Inconsistency Based on Statutory Discretion

The Panel found the "statutory language of Section 304 creates a *prima facie* violation of Article 23.2(a)."[13] The language of Section 304 "does not mandate the USTR to make a decision of inconsistency in violation of Article 23 in each and every specific dispute," however it reserves the right to the USTR to breach Article 23:2(a) through an *ad hoc*, specific action in a given dispute.[14]

In a lengthy but important footnote, the Panel laid out 4 elements that would constitute a breach of *DSU* Article 23:2(a). A WTO Member violates Article 23:2(a) if:

(1) A Member takes an action "in such cases," where the Member seeks redress against a violation by another Member of that other Member's obligations, or against a transgression committed by that other Member which amounts to non-violation nullification or impairment;

(2) The Member's act is a "determination," an action with a high degree of firmness or immutability, and thus essentially is a final decision;

(3) Member's determination is one to the effect a violation has occurred, or its benefits have been nullified or impaired; and

(4) Member makes the determination *before* DSB findings in the case have been adopted.[15]

If the USTR were to exercise its power under Section 304 to make a determination of inconsistency, before exhaustion of *DSU* procedures, then the U.S. would meet these four elements and, therefore, violate Article 23:2(a). However, the Americans argued the legislation does not mandate the USTR take an action in such cases. It merely provides the USTR with discretion to redress a violation of obligations, nullifications, or impairment of benefit.

The parties submitted their arguments on whether only mandatory or also discretionary national laws are prohibited. The Panel refused to make a bright line rule. Instead, the Panel left it to the precise interpretation of Article 23. In its view, a Panel must interpret a disputed provision in good faith, as required by the 1969 *Vienna Convention on the Law of Treaties*, specifically, Article 31:1, which states: "A treaty shall be interpreted in good faith in accordance with the ordinary meaning to be given to the terms of the treaty in their context and in the light of its object and purpose."

The Panel found Article 23:1 means: "Members are obligated generally to (a) have recourse to and (b) abide by *DSU* rules and procedures. These rules and procedures include most specifically in Article 23.2(a) a prohibition on making a unilateral

---

13. *Section 301* Panel Report, ¶ 7.99.
14. *Section 301* Panel Report, ¶ 7.50.
15. *Section 301* Panel Report, fn. 657 at ¶ 7.50.

determination of inconsistency prior to exhaustion of *DSU* proceedings."[16] The discretion reserved to the USTR under Section 304 created a violation. "In each and every case when a determination is made whilst *DSU* proceedings are not yet exhausted, Members locked in a dispute with the U.S. will be subject to a mandatory determination by the USTR under a statute which explicitly puts them in that very danger which Article 23 was intended to remove."[17]

The Panel further elaborated with an analogy of two farmers with adjacent land and a history of trespassing. In the past, the farmers exerted self-help remedies by threat of force and force itself. Exploitation of land near their mutual boundary suffered, because of the potential danger. The farmers reached an agreement to resort always and exclusively to the police and courts, and never use force. After the agreement took effect, one farmer erected a large sign on the mutual boundary stating: "No Trespassing. Trespassers may be shot on sight." The sign did not say that trespassers "will" be shot. One could argue the sign did not violate the agreement. But, the farmers promised always and exclusively to make seek redress through the police and courts. Like the farmer, the U.S. agreed not to retaliate, and instead use the *DSU* to handle any trade disputes. However, the U.S. passed Section 301 permitting it to use its discretion to retaliate.

The language of Section 304 statutorily reserves the right for USTR to use its discretion to unilaterally make a determination. The USTR's discretion to make such determinations effectively removed the guarantee that Article 23 is intended to give not only to Members, but also indirectly also to individuals and the market place. So, the Panel held, "the USTR's discretion under Section 304 does not . . . ensure the consistency of Section 304."[18] Therefore, Section 304 precludes, at least *prima facie*, compliance with Article 23:2(a).

- *De Facto* **Consistency Based on Non-Statutory Elements of Section 304**

Vitally, the Panel did not stop with this ruling. It continued by stating: "[a]lthough [the Panel] found . . . that the statutory language of Section 304 creates a *prima facie* violation of Article 23:2(a), this does not, in and of itself, establish a U.S. violation."[19] The legislation was created for use by the USTR to apply to all of America's trade relationships, not just those with WTO Members. The Panel acknowledged U.S. officials had broad discretion in setting out different standards of application of Section 304, including whether or not the context was a WTO dispute.

"[T]he U.S. Administration has carved out WTO covered situations from the general application of the [1974] *Trade Act* [*i.e.*, Section 301]. It did this in a most authoritative way, *inter alia*, through a *Statement of Administrative Action* ("*SAA*")

---

16. *Section 301* Panel Report, ¶ 7.59.
17. *Section 301* Panel Report, ¶ 7.61.
18. *Section 301* Panel Report, ¶ 7.96.
19. *Section 301* Panel Report, ¶ 7.99.

submitted by the President to, and approved by, Congress."[20] One of these under-takings was to "base any Section 301 determination that there has been a violation or denial of U.S. rights . . . on the panel or Appellate Body findings adopted by the DSB."[21] This limitation of discretion effectively would preclude a determination of inconsistency prior to exhaustion of *DSU* proceedings. Therefore, the *SAA* and U.S. statements before the Panel effectively removed any serious threat Section 301 pre-sented. They "also remove[d] the *prima facie* inconsistency and fulfil[led] the guar-antees incumbent on the U.S. under Article 23."[22] In the analogy of the farmer, the SAA and U.S. statements to the Panel were similar to the farmer adding to bottom of the original sign: "In case of trespass by neighbors . . . immediate recourse to the police and the courts of law will be made." As in the case, with this addition the agreement has been respected.

So, Section 304 creates a *prima facie* violation of *DSU* Article 23:2(a). The viola-tion may be remedied by "any lawful means by which the U.S. Administration could curtail the discretionary element," *i.e.*, any means the U.S. could use to restore the guarantees embodied in Article 23 to its WTO partners.[23] The Panel found the *SAA* and statements made by the U.S. to it provided such a remedy. The *prima facie* vio-lation of the Section 304 statutory language was under this alternative methodol-ogy. Therefore, the Panel found that while *de jure* inconsistent with U.S. obligations under Article 23:2, Section 304 was *de facto* consistent with them.

VI. Jurisprudential Contrast between 1998 *India Patent Protection* and 2000 *Section 301* Case

Background:

Recall in the 1998 *India Patent Protection* case (discussed in a separate Chapter) that in 1996, the U.S. requested consultations with India concerning the alleged absence of India's "Mailbox Rule," under which patent applications for pharmaceu-tical and agricultural chemical products could be filed, and the lack of a mechanism to grant exclusive market rights for those products.[24] The U.S. claimed violations of *TRIPS Agreement* Articles 27, 65, and 70.

The Panel, as upheld by the Appellate Body, found India's filing system based on "administrative practice" for pharmaceutical and agricultural chemical prod-ucts did not meet the requirements of *TRIPs* Article 70.8. The filing system did not provide the "means" which applications for patents for such inventions could be

---

20. *Section 301* Panel Report, ¶ 7.109.

21. *Section 301* Panel Report, ¶ 7.109.

22. *Section 301* Panel Report, ¶ 7.131.

23. *Section 301* Panel Report, ¶ 7.134.

24. *See* Appellate Body Report, *India — Patent Protection for Pharmaceutical and Agricultural Chemical Products*, WT/DS50/AB/R (adopted 16 January 1998).

securely filed as required by *TRIPs* Article 70:9(a). In theory, a patent application filed under the administrative instructions could be rejected by an Indian court under contradictory mandatory provisions of Section 5 of India's *Patent Act of 1970*. Additionally, the Appellate Body agreed with the Panel that India did not have a mechanism in place to granting exclusive marketing rights for the products covered by Article 70:8(a), thus violating Article 70:9.

Discrepancy between Cases:

In the 2000 *Section 301* case, the Panel found the *de jure* language of Section 301 was in clear violation of America's WTO obligations. The Panel conducted a thorough analysis of those obligations under *DSU* Article 23:2. The Panel found identified 4 elements that make up an Article 23:2(a) breach, all of which the Section 301 legislation meet. Therefore, the statutory language undoubtedly violated Article 23.2. However, the Panel further assessed the reality of the situation, *i.e.*, how the U.S. applies Section 301. If found that any lawful means by which the U.S. Administration could curtail the discretionary element would remedy the situation. The *SAA* and assurances U.S. gave to the panel were a remedy to the violation. Thus, as *de facto* practice, the Panel said Section 301 was consistent with WTO obligations.

India was not as lucky as the U.S. Under the same logic, India did not have law on its books consistent with WTO obligations. The law in place (*Patent Act of 1970*) required the Indian courts to act contradictory to India's obligations under *TRIPs* Articles 70:8 and 70:9. So, India violated those Articles. But, India's "administrative practice" provided a remedy to its WTO obligations, creating a Mailbox Rule and a mechanism for granting exclusive marketing rights, meeting both obligations. Therefore, the Panel and Appellate Body ought to have considered Indian administrative practice, just as the Panel considered U.S. administrative practice in the *Section 301* case, with the rationale:

> "Conformity can be ensured in different ways in different legal systems. It is the end result that counts, not the manner in which it is achieved. Only by understanding and respecting the specificities of each Member's legal system, can a correct evaluation of conformity be established."[25]

(To be sure, the *India Patent Protection* case was chronologically first.) But, that is not what happened.

The *India Patent Protection* Panel relied heavily on the formalistic manner in which WTO obligations are implemented, not the substantive end result. The end result in India was a Mailbox Rule and mechanism to granting exclusive marketing rights, correcting any violation of WTO obligations. If the Panel used the same rationale in the as in the *Section 301* case, then any lawful means by which India could ensure enforcement of the administrative practice would remedy the

---

25. *Section 301* Panel Report, ¶ 7.24.

situation. Yet, the Panel did not provide the same overly accommodating alternative to India as the U.S. got.

Each Member failed *prima facie* to meet its WTO obligations. India failed because it implemented them through administrative practice, and not legislation. The U.S. failed because it had legislation allowing it to make a decision to retaliate prior to the *DSU* making a determination. However, the Panel found the U.S. corrected its over-allocation of discretion by implementing a *SAA*. An *SAA* is not law, yet the Panel treated it as a *de jure* instrument, thus finding the U.S. does not violate its obligations. If WTO adjudicators had applied consistent reasoning, then India's administrative practice should remedy the *prima facie* WTO violation (or *vice versa*—America's should not have).

Could this discrepancy be due to an unequal amount of trust the judges of Geneva place in America vis-à-vis India? The U.S. *SAA* and statements to one Panel, while not law, removed any threat to WTO Members and gave an effective remedy to the *prima facie* violation of Section 301. However, for another Panel, Indian administrative practice, which creates a Mailbox Rule and mechanism for exclusive marketing rights, did not alleviate the apprehension of Members and violated WTO obligations. There jurisprudential discrepancy in the treatment of the respondents, America and India, should be obvious. The question is why in similar situations different outcomes occurred?

Chapter 31

Section 301 and Sino-American Trade War[1]

I. March 2018 Section 301 Action Announced

Following a Section 301 investigation the USTR launched in August 2017 and its issuance of a 215-page *Report*, President Donald J. Trump (1946–, President, 2017–) announced in March 2018 tariffs valued against up to 1,300 different Chinese products.[2] They included aerospace, electronics, footwear, home items, ICT goods,

---

1. Documents References:
   (1) *Havana (ITO) Charter* Articles 41, 47, 66, 92–97
   (2) GATT Article XXIII
   (3) WTO *DSU* Articles 21–23

2. *See* United States Trade Representative, *Findings of the Investigation into China's Acts, Policies, and Practices Related to Technology Transfer, Intellectual Property, and Innovation Under Section 301 of the Trade Act of 1974* (22 March 2018), https://ustr.gov/sites/default/files/Section%20 301%20FINAL.PDF [hereinafter, *Section 301 China Investigation Findings*]; United States Trade Representative, Section 301 Fact Sheet (undated), https://ustr.gov/sites/default/files/USTR%20 301%20Fact%20Sheet.pdf [hereinafter, *China Section 301 Fact Sheet*]; Presidential Memorandum on the Actions by the United States Related to the Section 301 Investigation (22 March 2018), www .whitehouse.gov/presidential-actions/presidential-memorandum-actions-united-states-related -section-301-investigation/, [hereinafter, *Trump China Section 301 Memo*]; Crowell Moring, *International Trade—USTR: China Discriminates Against U.S. Firms Related to Tech Transfer, IP, and Trade Secrets* (24 March 2018), www.crowell.com/NewsEvents/AlertsNewsletters/all/USTR-China -Discriminates-Against-US-Firms-Related-to-Tech-Transfer-IP-and-Trade-Secrets [hereinafter, *USTR: China Discriminates*]; *China Pledges Action on Tech Transfer as Trump Plans Tariffs (3)*, 35 International Trade Reporter (BNA) 398 (22 March 2018); *Trump Set to Announce China Sanctions After IP Probe*, BBC News, 21 March 2018, www.bbc.com/news/business-43494001; Lesley Wroughton & Roberta Rampton, *Trump Moves Toward China Tariffs in Warning Shot on Technology Transfer*, REUTERS, 22 March 2018; Lesley Wroughton & Roberta Rampton, *Trump Moves Toward China Tariffs in Warning Shot on Technology Transfer*, REUTERS, 22 March 2018; Andrew Mayeda, Jennifer Jacobs & Saleha Mohsin, *Trump's Plan to Impose Stiff Tariffs on China Rattles Investors*, BLOOMBERG, 21 March 2018 [hereinafter, *Trump's Plan*]; Andrew Mayeda, Jennifer Jacobs & Saleha Mohsin, *Trump to Announce $50 Billion in China Tariffs, Sources Say*, BLOOMBERG, 21 March 2018, www .bloomberg.com/news/articles/2018-03-21/u-s-planning-action-against-china-over-ip-in-very -near-future [hereinafter, *Trump to Announce*]; Steve Matthews, Alan Bjerga & Andrew Mayeda, *Here Are U.S. Targets Most Vulnerable to China Trade Retaliation*, BLOOMBERG, 21 March 2018, www .bloomberg.com/news/articles/2018-03-22/here-are-u-s-targets-most-vulnerable-to-china-trade -retaliation [hereinafter, *"Here Are U.S. Targets"*]; David Chance & Steve Holland, *Trump Set for China Tariff Announcement on Thursday, Trade War Fears Grow*, REUTERS, 21 March 2018, www .reuters.com/article/us-usa-trade/trump-set-for-china-tariff-announcement-on-thursday-trade

machinery, and T&A. The Section 301 investigation targeted acts, policies, and practices of the Chinese government that infringed on U.S. IP rights. Mr. Trump was not the first American President to spotlight Chinese IP practices; every President since Bill Clinton (1946, President, 1993–2001) had done so. But, Mr. Trump was the first to take serious remedial action, after what officials in his Administration contended was a long string of broken promises by the CCP to reform its IP enforcement scheme, coupled with appeasement by his predecessors.

The Trump Administration remedy was four-pronged. First, it imposed 25% tariffs, valued at $50–$60 billion, which equalled the estimated economic damage from IP theft by China. These tariffs, of course, were on top of the on top of the applied MFN duties, and on top of any AD/CVDs.

Second, it said it would consider restrictions on Chinese FDI. The President gave the Treasury Department 60 days to determine the most effective ways to restrict Chinese FDI in American companies with strategic technology.

Third, perhaps mindful of the 2000 *Section 301* Panel Report (discussed earlier), the Administration launched a WTO case against China. The core claim was under the National Treatment rule in Article 3 of the *TRIPs Agreement*, namely, against China's "discriminatory technology licensing practices":[3]

> China appears to be breaking WTO rules by denying foreign patent holders, including U.S. companies, basic patent rights to stop a Chinese entity from using the technology after a licensing contract ends. China also appears to be breaking WTO rules by imposing mandatory adverse contract terms that discriminate against and are less favorable for imported foreign technology.

> These Chinese policies hurt innovators in the United States and worldwide by interfering with the ability of foreign technology holders to set market-based terms in licensing and other technology-related contracts.[4]

In its WTO claim, the Administration cited four Chinese measures that violate this Article:[5] *Foreign Trade Law*; *Regulations on the Administration of the Import and*

-war-fears-grow-idUSKBN1GX20V; David Chance & Steve Holland, *UPDATE 4—Trump Set for China Tariff Announcement on Thursday, Trade War Fears Grow*, CNBC, 21 March 2018, www .cnbc.com/2018/03/21/reuters-america-update-4-trump-set-for-china-tariff-announcement-on -thursday-trade-war-fears-grow.html.

Notably, some prominent companies, such as Nike and Louis Vitton, praised China's efforts to combat IP piracy, at least with respect to protecting trademarks of famous branded goods by (for example) cracking down on counterfeiting and smuggling rings. *See Nike and LVMH Praise China's Efforts to Combat Piracy (Correct)*, 35 International Trade Reporter (BNA) 1477 (15 November 2018). China pointed out that: "It's unrealistic to expect any country to root out counterfeiting and IP infringement completely," and thus "One shouldn't rashly impose unilateral sanctions and disrupt multilateral rules because of a few problems with IP protection." *Id.* (*quoting* Wang Hejun, Chief, Trade Remedy and Investigation Bureau, MOFCOM).

3. *USTR: China Discriminates.*

4. *Trump China Section 301 Memo.*

5. United States Trade Representative, Following President Trump's Section 301 Decisions, USTR Launches New WTO Challenge Against China (March 2018), https://ustr.gov/about-us

Export of Technologies; *Regulations for the Implementation of the Law on Chinese-Foreign Equity Joint Ventures*; and *Contract Law*.

The claim focused on matters the U.S. felt were within WTO jurisdiction. Thus, the U.S. excluded from its WTO pleading three of the four conclusions from the USTR *Investigation Report* (discussed below): (1) "forced technology transfer practices via joint venture requirements and foreign ownership restrictions," (2) "investment and acquisition of U.S. companies that require the transfer of U.S. technologies and intellectual property," and (3) "support for cyber theft of sensitive commercial information and trade secrets," were not part of the claim. Again, perhaps mindful of that Panel Report, the USTR emphasized it "made no findings in the Section 301 investigation that the licensing measures at issue are inconsistent with China's *TRIPs Agreement* obligations," but "[r]ather, as for any WTO dispute, the matter will be resolved by the parties or findings may be sought through WTO dispute settlement . . . ."[6]

Fourth, the Administration suspended any remedial action for 60 days. (Technically, there was a 30-day comment period to determine what Chinese imports should be subject to retaliate, plus a 30-day consultation period once the USTR published America's retaliation list.) During this time, American businesses and consumers could lobby for their interests in respect of higher import duties on Chinese merchandise, while China could negotiate a settlement to avert what it said, in respect of the action, was a declaration of a trade war.[7]

What Section 301 investigation findings prompted these hefty measures, which risked starting a trade war, given China's pledge to retaliate against an array of

---

/policy-offices/press-office/press-releases/2018/march/following-president-trump%E2%80%99s -section. Supporting America's demands for enhanced IP protection in China, the EU also launched *DSU* claim against China (and supplemented its defenses against Chinese takeovers of strategic European businesses, including companies in the EU infrastructure, media, and technology sectors). EU Trade Commission Cecilia Malmstroem intoned:

> "Technological innovation and know-how is the bedrock of our knowledge-based economy," Malmstroem said. "It's what keeps our companies competitive in the global market. We cannot let any country force our companies to surrender this hard-earned knowledge at its border."

Quoted in Jonathan Stearns, *EU Takes China to the WTO Over Technology-Transfer Practices (2)*, 35 International Trade Reporter (BNA) 760 (7 June 2018). So, the EU "target[ed] rules in China on the import and export of technologies and on Chinese-foreign equity joint ventures, including measures the EU said "discriminate against non-Chinese companies and treat them worse than domestic ones." *Id.*

6. *Quoted in* Bryce Baschuk, *China, U.S. Trade Barbs Over Who Is Threatening Trade System (1)*, 35 International Trade Reporter (BNA) 424 (29 March 2018). [Hereinafter, *China, U.S. Trade Barbs.*]

7. Executive Deputy Director of the China Center for International Economic Exchanges (a government-linked think tank), and Former Vice Minister of Commerce, Wei Jianguo, said:

> If Trump really signs the order [which, of course, he did], that is a declaration of trade war with China. . . . China is not afraid, nor will it dodge a trade war.

Quoted in Andrew Mayeda & Toluse Olorunnipa, *Trump's China Tariffs Fuel Trade War Fears, Driving Down Stocks*, Bloomberg, 22 March 2018; *Trump's Plan.*

American products? In the language of the statue, the USTR found that Chinese government "acts, policies, and practices" with respect to IP, trade secrets (*e.g.*, algorithms and formulae), technology transfer, and innovation were "unjustifiable" and "discriminated" against U.S. businesses, "violated" pertinent "international agreements," and "unfairly" "burdened or restricted" U.S. commerce. In particular, the USTR drew four key conclusions in its *Investigation Findings*:

"Following a thorough analysis of available evidence, USTR, with the assistance of the interagency Section 301 committee, prepared findings showing that the acts, policies, and practices of the Chinese government related to technology transfer, intellectual property, and innovation are unreasonable or discriminatory and burden or restrict U.S. commerce."

- "China uses joint venture requirements, foreign investment restrictions, and administrative review and licensing processes to force or pressure technology transfers from American companies." That is, China compels American firms to reveal and/or transfer their technology to Chinese entities by mandating as a condition of market access a JV with, and technology transfer to, a Chinese partner.

- "China uses discriminatory licensing processes to transfer technologies from U.S. companies to Chinese companies." China limits the FDI activities of American firms by restricting the terms of technology licenses.

- "China directs and facilitates investments and acquisitions which generate large-scale technology transfer." The CCP essentially orders its companies to invest in American firms with the aim of obtaining technology the CCP decides is strategic for Chinese industries.

- "China conducts and supports cyber intrusions into U.S. computer networks to gain access to valuable business information"[8] Arguably, this conclusion was the most ominous one: the Chinese government directs, or itself conducts, cyberattacks on the computer networks of American companies to steal their trade secrets.

Simply put, the USTR found compelling evidence that China engaged in government-led, market distorting measures that purloined U.S. IP to gain unfairly an advantage in manufacturing and AI.

So, as USTR Ambassador Robert Lighthizer (1947–) said:

"Our view is that we have a very serious problem of losing our intellectual property, which is really the biggest single advantage of the American economy. We are losing that to China" in a way that doesn't reflect economic fundamentals.[9]

---

8. *China Section 301 Fact Sheet*, 1–2.
9. *Quoted in Trump to Announce.*

The cost of that loss—counterfeit goods, pirated software, and stolen trade secrets—was as much as $600 billion, almost double the $375 billion bilateral trade deficit America ran with China (in 2017). And, CCP behavior posed a threat to national security: China could use the IP it wrongfully obtained for military purposes. The President's top trade advisor, Peter Navarro, added poignantly:

> Trump's actions represent a "seismic shift from an era dating back to Nixon and Kissinger, where we had as a government viewed China in terms of economic engagement." "That process has failed."

> "The problem is that with the Chinese in this case, talk is not cheap. It has been very expensive for America" . . . . "Finally, the President decided that we needed to move forward."[10]

American firms understood. John Frisbee, President of the U.S.-China Business Council stated that China "has been promising market-opening measures and protection of intellectual property for some time, but what the U.S. business community is waiting for is action."[11]

Despite it being adversely affected by systematic Chinese IP misappropriation, giants in the American business community—including Amazon, Google, Facebook, Gap, Levi's, Microsoft, Target, and Wal-Mart—opposed the Section 301 action.[12] Corporate America, along with consumers, feared retaliation by China. China's retaliation list included a 25% tariff on pork, plus cotton, sorghum (*i.e.*, milo), soybeans, and some ICT items.[13] And, "'Boeing orders will be replaced by Airbus,' the Communist Party newspaper said in an editorial."[14] The CCP concocted its retaliation list mindful of U.S. State that delivered Electoral College votes to Mr. Trump in the 2016 general election.

China's retaliation options extended far beyond goods. In educational services, China could steer scholarship funding to its students headed for Australia, Canada, and New Zealand—not America. In finance, China could devalue the *yuan* relative

---

10. *Quoted in Trump's China Tariffs.*

11. *Quoted in China Renews Pledges to Open Economy, Protect IP Rights*, Reuters, 24 March 2018, www.reuters.com/article/us-china-forum-economy/china-renews-pledges-to-open-economy-protect-ip-rights-idUSKBN1H1033. [Hereinafter, *China Renews Pledges.*]

12. *See* Letter to President Donald J. Trump, from Abercrombie & Fitch *et al.*, 19 March 2019, https://fonteva-customer-media.s3.amazonaws.com/00D61000000dOrPEAU/psDunXQF_RILA%20301%20Letter.pdf; Letter to President Donald J. Trump, from Information Technology Industry Council, 18 March 2018, www.itic.org/dotAsset/883ba45b-a06a-4b2a-b6ab-5c84c8a4a865.pdf; Leticia Miranda, *Target, Levi's, And Gap Warn That Trump's Trade War Will Hike Up Prices*, BuzzFeed News, 22 March 2018, www.buzzfeed.com/leticiamiranda/target-levis-and-gap-warn-that-trumps-trade-war-will-hike?utm_term=.nhd4yJ7Q5A#.dkRgK7DmER [hereinafter, *Target, Levi's, And Gap*].

13. *See* Valerie Volcovici, *Mnuchin: Trump not afraid of a trade war with China—Fox News*, Reuters, 25 March 2018, www.reuters.com/article/us-usa-trade-china-tariff/mnuchin-trump-not-afraid-of-a-trade-war-with-china-fox-news-idUSKBN1H10UA.

14. *Quoted in Here Are U.S. Targets.*

to the dollar, making its exports more price-competitive in dollar terms (but rendering it susceptible to a currency manipulation charge). Also, in finance, China could sell billions of dollars' worth of its U.S. Treasury security holdings, which would push up yields, thereby raising borrowing costs for the U.S. government. China was the largest holder of Treasuries, accounting for about 10% of outstanding Treasuries. (As of 26 November 2018, total U.S. Treasury debt was valued at $15.97 trillion.[15] China's holdings were worth $1.15 trillion and $1.19 trillion, as of 30 September 2018 and 30 September 2017, respectively.) Of course, as China was aware, liquidating Treasuries rapidly and in large volumes would diminish the value of China's portfolio, as prices (which move inversely with yields) would fall (with the outward shift in the supply curve of the securities), and could destabilize other financial markets with contagion effects world-wide.[16]

Corporate America's opposition, however, showed its Janus-face: 43% of overall exports from China are from MNCs, and overall foreign (including many American) companies accounted for 59% of exports from China subject to the U.S. tariffs, *i.e.*, many of Corporate America's products would be adversely affected by the tariffs, and American companies would be denied equity infusions from Chinese investors.[17] Levi's is a case in point:

> Levi Strauss & Co., which co-signed the letter to Trump [referenced above], has been aggressively cracking down on Chinese counterfeiters of its brand since the early aughts. In 2012, it sued and won a case against a Chinese company that used one of its trademarked stitches. It's also fighting a suit in a Beijing court against two Chinese companies that allegedly sold copies of their product without authorization . . . .

> Though Levi's tenaciously battles Chinese counterfeiters, it doesn't support Trump's tariffs as a way to protect US intellectual property. . . . [Levi's said] its success as an "inclusive" brand has only been possible through "a free and fair trade system."[18]

"Unilateral tariff impositions risk retaliation and destabilizing the global economy, in which case American brands, workers, and consumers will ultimately suffer . . . ." Moreover:

---

15. *See* David Brunnstrom, David Lawder & Matt Spetalnick, *Exclusive: China Envoy Warns of Dire Consequences if U.S. Hardliners Hold Sway*, REUTERS, 27 November 2018, www.reuters.com /article/us-usa-trade-china-exclusive/exclusive-china-envoy-warns-of-dire-consequences-if-u-s -hardliners-hold-sway-idUSKCN1NW2AQ. [Hereinafter, *China Envoy Warns.*]

16. Reducing the rate of purchases also could be a self-inflicted wound (as the demand curve for Treasuries would shift in, thanks to less Chinese buying), and unsettle financial markets. Hence, China's Ambassador to the U.S., Cui Tiankai, said "This [selling Treasuries, or slowing the purchases of them] is very dangerous, this is like playing with fire." *Quoted in China Envoy Warns.*

17. *See* David Lawder & Elias Glenn, *Trump says U.S. Tariffs on Chinese Goods Could Exceed $500 Billion*, Reuters, 4 July 2018, www.reuters.com/article/us-usa-trade-china/china-warns-u-s-is -opening-fire-on-the-world-with-tariff-threats-idUSKBN1JV063.

18. *Quoted in Target, Levi's And Gap.*

while the share of exports produced by Chinese companies has grown from 42 percent in 2005 to the current 57 percent, it remains heavily skewed toward lower-end manufacturing. Chinese companies now produce more than half the country's furniture exports, for instance—nearly double the share in 2006. In many cases, foreign companies have moved out of these sectors, relocating factories outside the mainland in search of cheaper labor costs.[19]

In other words, the Section 301 remedy could harm the very American companies they are designed to help.

Apple is another case in point of the bind in which Corporate America found itself. Tim Cook's remark in Beijing at the China Development Forum, just two days after Mr. Trump signed the Section 301 order—that the business community "has always supported the idea that open markets foster new ideas and allow entrepreneurship to thrive," and that "[t]he strongest companies and economies are those that are open—those that thrive on diversity of people and ideas" was simultaneously anodyne and self-serving.[20] The company of which he is CEO sources many parts, and assembles, iPhones and other devices on the Mainland, and profits from the low applied MFN tariffs China receives in its major markets, like America. Corporate America's stance was redolent of an insight attributed to Lenin: when it comes time to hang Capitalism, the Capitalists will compete to sell the hangman the rope.

That said, IP was not the only motivation for the Section 301 action. The Trump Administration hoped it would help reduce the bilateral trade deficit by at least $100 billion.[21] Commerce Secretary Wilbur Ross linked the two motivations: the deficit was "inspired by evil practices."[22] So, the Administration wanted China to cut its auto tariffs, buy more American semiconductors, and grant greater access to U.S. banks.[23] But, with respect to a significant cut in the deficit, the Administration was sure to be disappointed, as long-term macroeconomic factors, especially savings and investment rates, determine trade deficits, and there is little any one trade remedy can do to alter those factors. And, the $506 billion China exported to America contributed 2.5% to Chinese GDP, and the $50 billion in exports America contemplated

19. *See* David Hoffman & Erik Lundh, *A Pyrrhic Victory for Trade Hawks*, Bloomberg, 31 May 2018, www.bloomberg.com/view/articles/2018-05-31/trump-s-china-tariffs-will-hurt-u-s-companies-more.

20. *Quoted in China Renews Pledges*.

21. *See Trump Gamble for Quick Trade Deal with China Seen as Long Shot*, 35 International Trade Reporter (BNA) 615 (3May 2018); Ben Blanchard & Brenda Goh, *China Blames U.S. for Staggering Trade Surplus as Tariffs Loom*, Reuters, 21 March 2018.

22. *Quoted in* Andrew Mayeda, *U.S. Downplays Prospects of Breakthrough in China Meetings*, 35 International Trade Reporter (BNA) 613 (3 May 2018).

23. *See* William Selway & Ben Brody, *Mnuchin "Hopeful" Truce Can Be Reached With China on Trade*, Bloomberg, 26 March 2018, www.bloomberg.com/news/articles/2018-03-25/mnuchin-cautiously-hopeful-china-trade-deal-can-be-reached. [Hereinafter, *Mnuchin "Hopeful."*]

targeting contributed just 0.25% to its GDP.[24] So, it would take a full-blown change in the status quo, say through a trade war, to shrink significantly the deficit.

However, in another respect, the Administration hoped the Section 301 action would change Chinese government behavior. China realized its bilateral surplus position rendered it vulnerable to American tariffs, and countries in that position are more likely to change their behavior in response to a Section 301 action than those that do not rely heavily on the American market. To the extent the President targeted merchandise that competes with domestic (American) made products, but which is made in China and uses supply chains in Asia, China was indeed vulnerable Examples included certain electronics, IT, and telecom goods, furniture, shoes, toys, T&A — all of which were made with little or no involvement by American firms. Indeed, China pledged it would open its economy yet further to trade and investment, especially in manufacturing, by slashing tariffs and taxes. Yet, those moves would help the CCP boost employment, which would help keep it in power. And, its promise to treat foreign firms on par with Chinese ones, and protect IP rights, was nothing more than a rehash of what it was obliged to do under the national treatment rules of GATT and the *TRIPs Agreement*.[25]

II. Trade War?

Would the Section 301 case catalyze a Sino-American Trade War? There is no official definition of "trade war." But, it is generally understood to connote cycles of tit-for tat retaliation between two or more countries, in the form of tariffs and/or non-tariff barriers, with each cycle possible escalating the severity of those barriers (for example, in terms of their size and/or the scope of products they cover), and with the further possibilities of third countries putting up their own barriers to defend against trade diversion, even dumping, of products imported by and/or exported from the combatant countries, and of collateral damage in the form of consumers and producer across the world injured, though they were innocent in that their behavior had little if anything to do with the causes of the underlying dispute.

In the Section 301 Sino-American context, each side expressed confidence in its own abilities. Bravado common in military conflicts carries over to trade battles:

- From the Chinese Ministry of Commerce:

  "China doesn't hope to be in a trade war, but is not afraid of engaging in one."[26]

---

24. Ryan Woo & Adam Jourdon, *China Urges U.S. Away from "Brink" as Trump Picks Trade Weapons*, Reuters, 22 March 2018, www.reuters.com/article/us-usa-trade-china/china-urges-u-s-away-from-brink-as-trump-picks-trade-weapons-idUSKBN1GY3E1 (*citing* research by Mark Williams, Chief Asia Economist, Capital Economics). [Hereinafter, *China Urges.*]

25. *See China Renews Pledges* (discussing the promises of Executive Vice Premier Han Zheng made at the March 2018 China Development Forum in Beijing, following the Section 301 action).

26. *Quoted in China Urges.*

- From the American Treasury Secretary:

  "We're not afraid of a trade war, but that's not our objective. In a negotiation you have to be prepared to take action."[27]

During a floor debate in March 2018 at the WTO, China attacked the U.S. for putting the WTO "under siege" with its "purely unilateral" tariffs and "unscrupulous unilateral" action.[28] America said China's attack was the real threat:

  The WTO system is not threatened—as China claims—where a Member takes steps to address harmful, trade-distorting policies not directly covered by WTO rules . . . .

  To the contrary, what does threaten the WTO is where a Member, such as China, asserts that the mere existence of the WTO prevents any action by any member to address unfair, trade-distorting policies . . . .

      . . .

  If the WTO is seen instead as protecting those Members that choose to adopt policies that can be shown to undermine the fairness and balance of the international trading system, then the WTO and the international trading system will lose all credibility and support among our citizens.[29]

Each side thus prepared for war.

As America sharpened its Section 301 target list, China looked to add to the $3 billion retaliation list, which had American fruit, nuts, and wine on it, and which it had drawn up in response to the March 2018 Section 232 national security action that hit its steel and aluminum exports. Possible additions included computer chips and cross-sectoral retaliation against American service providers, such as financial and tourism suppliers.

In early April, the USTR published in the *Federal Register* a 58-page retaliation list, and 11 hours later, China published its counter-retaliation list.[30] Thereafter, China

---

27. *Quoted in Mnuchin "Hopeful."*

28. *Quoted in China, U.S. Trade Barbs.*

29. *Quoted in China, U.S. Trade Barbs.*

30. Office of the United States Trade Representative, *Notice of Determination and Request for Public Comment Concerning Proposed Determination of Action Pursuant to Section 301: China's Acts, Policies, and Practices Related to Technology Transfer, Intellectual Property, and Innovation*, , 83 Federal Register number 67, 14906-14954 (6 April 2018); Office of the United States Trade Representative, Docket Number USTR-2018-0005, *Notice of Determination and Request for Public Comment Concerning Proposed Determination of Action Pursuant to Section 301: China's Acts, Policies, and Practices Related to Technology Transfer, Intellectual Property, and Innovation*, (3 April 2018), https:// ustr.gov/sites/default/files/files/Press/Releases/301FRN.pdf; *Wall Street Recovers From Trade Fears*, BBC News, 4 April 2018, www.bbc.com/news/business-43632315 [hereinafter, *Wall Street Recovers*]; Bloomberg News, Bloomberg, *Trump's Scattergun Tariff List Sends China Companies Scrambling*, 4 April 2018, www.bloomberg.com/news/articles/2018-04-04/stocks-to-watch-after-trump-announces-proposed-china-tariffs [hereinafter, *Trump's Scattergun*]; Andrew Mayeda, *U.S. Leaves Door Open to China Talks Amid Trade-War Fears*, BloombergQuint, 3 April 2018, www

also wasted no time suing the U.S. at the WTO, filing the claim on 4 April 2018, alleging America's Section 301 25% *ad valorem* tariffs, imposed only on Chinese merchandise, would breach the GATT Article I:1 MFN and Article II:1 tariff binding rules, and *DSU* Article 23 procedures.[31] (Perhaps mindful of the 2000 *Section 301* Panel precedent, China did not appear to try an "as such" challenge to Section 301.)

Neither side started firing "live rounds" at that point, as they had about 60 days to pull back from the brink of a trade war. China replied it "strongly condemns and firmly opposes" the proposed American tariffs, deriding them as "unilateralistic and protectionist."[32] President Trump tweeted:

> We are not in a trade war with China, that war was lost many years ago by the foolish, or incompetent, people who represented the U.S. Now we have a Trade Deficit of $500 Billion a year, with Intellectual Property Theft of another $300 Billion. We cannot let this continue![33]

That tweet was ironic, as the President had boasted one month earlier — in the context of the Section 232 steel and aluminum cases (discussed in a separate Chapter) that "trade wars are good, and easy to win."[34] That boast seemed motivated by a sense China was uniquely vulnerable because of its bilateral deficit — crudely put, China needed the U.S. more than the U.S. needed China. But, that boast neglected China's 19th and early 20th century history of humiliation at the hands of Western imperial powers: *kowtowing* to a new 21st century emperor would be unacceptable. It also neglected the fact that in some particular product categories, the U.S. enjoyed

---

.bloombergquint.com/technology/2018/04/03/u-s-china-tariff-list-takes-aim-at-technologies -beijing-covets?utm_campaign=website&utm_source=sendgrid&utm_medium=newsletter [hereinafter, *U.S. Leaves Door Open*]; Andrew Mayeda, *U.S. Leaves Door Open to China Talks Amid Trade War Fears*, BLOOMBERG, 3 April 2018, www.bloomberg.com/politics/articles/2018-04-03/u-s -china-tariff-list-takes-aim-at-technologies-beijing-covets [hereinafter, *U.S. Leaves Door Open to China Talks*]; David Lawder, *U.S. Escalates China Trade Showdown with Tariffs on $50 Billion in Imports*, REUTERS, 3 April 2018, www.reuters.com/article/us-usa-china-trade/u-s-escalates-china -trade-showdown-with-tariffs-on-50-billion-in-imports-idUSKCN1HA2Q9 [hereinafter, *U.S. Escalates*].

Initially, the Section 301 action provoked submission of over 3,000 comments to the USTR; by 6 September, the USTR received approximately 6,100 comments. *See* Office of the United States Trade Representative, Notice of Determination and Request for Public Comment Concerning Proposed Determination of Action Pursuant to Section 301, USTR-2018-0005, 6 April 2018, www .regulations.gov/docket?D=USTR-2018-0005; Steve Holland & David Lawder, *Trump Ups Ante on China, Threatens Duties on Nearly All Its Imports*, REUTERS, 9 September 2018; Mark Niquette & Andrew Mayeda, *U.S. Business Groups Bash Trump Tariffs as China Talks Intensify*, 35 International Trade Reporter (BNA) 673 (17 May 2018).

31. *See* World Trade Organization, *United States — Tariff Measures on Certain Goods from China, Request for Consultations*, WT/DS543/1, G/L/1219 (5 April 2018), www.wto.org/english /news_e/news18_e/ds543rfc_05apr18_e.htm.

32. *Quoted in Wall Street Recovers.*

33. *Quoted in Wall Street Recovers.*

34. *Quoted in Trump Doubles Down, "Trade Wars are Good, and Easy to Win,"* CNBC, 2 March 2018, https://www.cnbc.com/2018/03/02/trump-trade-wars-are-good-and-easy-to-win.html.

a trade surplus, hence Chinese counter-retaliation against Section 301 tariffs would erode or erase that surplus.

The boast also seemed odd to reconcile with other public pronouncements. On 4 April, Mr. Trump tweeted: "That [trade] war [with China] was lost many years ago by the foolish, or incompetent, people who represented the U.S."[35] Then, on 6 April, he said in a radio interview: "We've already lost the trade war. We don't have a trade war, we've lost the trade war."

Whatever the coherence, or lack thereof, in these utterances, the theory of the American Section 301 retaliation list was to maximize the damage to China's economy, while minimizing the pain felt by American consumers. China thus would have an incentive to respond constructively to America's long-standing concerns about Chinese IP acts, policies, and practices. And, it would be easier—though not easy—for American consumers of Chinese products to support the Section 301 action. As one USTR official explained:

> USTR developed the tariff targets using a computer algorithm designed to choose products that would inflict maximum pain on Chinese exporters, but limit the damage to U.S. consumers.
>
> A USTR official said the product list got an initial scrub by removing products identified as likely to cause disruptions to the U.S. economy and those that needed to be excluded for legal reasons.
>
> "The remaining products were ranked according to the likely impact on U.S. consumers, based on available trade data involving alternative country sources for each product," the official, who spoke on condition of anonymity. . . . [36]

The American list contained 1,333 products, identified at the 8-digit HTSUS level, spanning 223 different HTSUS Headings, embracing items as diverse as backhoes, biscuit ovens, and false teeth.[37] The United States said it would put a 25% tariff (on top of applied MFN rate, plus any AD-CVD or safeguard duties), which translated into $50 billion in annual trade.

III. *"Made in China 2025"* Industrial Policy

The American list took aim at 10 economic sectors the CCP picked for its *"Made in China 2025"* Major Technical Roadmap; in these sectors, the CCP wanted China

---

35. *Quoted in* Michael Martina & Steve Holland, *Trump Threatens More China, Beijing Ready to Hit Back*, REUTERS, 6 April 2018, www.reuters.com/article/us-usa-trade-china/trump-threatens-more-china-tariffs-beijing-ready-to-hit-back-idUSKCN1HD0NW. [Hereinafter, *Trump Threatens More.*]

36. *Quoted in U.S. Trade Escalates.*

37. *See* Mark Niquette, *As CEOs Fight China Tariffs, Trump Hears Pleas to Add More (1)*, 35 International Trade Reporter (BNA) 590 (26 April 2018). [Hereinafter, *As CEOs Fight.*]

to become an "advanced manufacturing power" within a decade.[38] "*Made in China 2025*"—also called the "*Green Book*," after the color of the cover of its original October 2015 publication by the National Manufacturing Strategy Advisory Committee, and updated in January 2018 (without the green cover)—was an eye-popping 296-page economic nationalist strategy, combining mercantilist schemes with Communist planning.

Overall, the CCP targets were:

Industry: Domestic Market Share 2025 (%)

Agricultural machinery	95
New-energy vehicles	90
Mobile communication equipment	80
Industrial robots 70	

Industry: Global Market Share 2025 (%)

Integrated circuits	56
General purpose aeroplanes	40[39]

The CCP asserted such targets were non-binding, unofficial, and applied equally to Chinese and foreign firms operating in China.[40] That assertion appeared to be undermined by the November 2018 disclosure in *People's Daily* (the CCP's official newspaper) that "Jack Ma, the head of e-commerce giant Alibaba Group Holding Ltd and China's best-known capitalist, is a Communist Party member, . . . debunking a public assumption the billionaire was politically unattached."[41] It seemed there was no clear line between China's public and private sector, hence industrial policy was not a suggestion by the former to the latter.

The level of granularity of the targets suggested the *Green Book* was full-scale industrial policy to which Chinese firms paid close attention in practice. For each

---

38. *U.S. Leaves Door Open to China Talks*. In 2017, the CCP announced a separate strategy for AI. *See id. See also As Trump Mulls Tariffs, China's Industrial Ambitions Loom Large*, 35 International Trade Reporter (BNA) 1144 (6 September 2018) (summarizing the *Green Book*). [Hereinafter, *As Trump Mulls Tariffs*.]

39. *As Trump Mulls Tariffs*.

40. The CCP also urged the U.S. not to take the *Green Book* too seriously, nor to behave hypocritically. After all:

> China is not alone in supporting its industries. Industrial policy was central to Japan's rapid growth in the 1970s and 1980s and the *Made in China 2025* plan itself draws heavily from Germany's "Industry 4.0 Plan" adopted in 2013. In the U.S., breakthroughs in semiconductors, nuclear power, imaging technology and others were all aided by industrial policy,

As Trump Mulls.

41. *Alibaba's Jack Ma is a Communist Party Member, China State Paper Reveals*, REUTERS, 26 November 2018, www.reuters.com/article/us-alibaba-jack-ma/alibabas-jack-ma-is-a-communist-party-member-china-state-paper-reveals-idUSKCN1NW073.

sector, the CCP identified specific numerical targets to reach by 2025, often with interim targets by 2020. Those sectors and targets were:[42]

(1) Advanced IT (including AI and robotics)

By 2020, at least half of the industrial robots used in China should be made by Chinese firms, with two or three "domestic champions; and by 2025, that figure should be 70%, and local robotics systems should be "perfected" so as to globally competitive.

By 2025, at least 40% of the chips used in Chinese-produced smartphones should be made in China.

By 2025, at least 60% of the industrial censors used in advanced manufacturing should be sourced from Chinese firms.

And, by 2025, there should be no gap in quality between Chinese versus foreign computers and cloud systems.

(2) Advanced basic materials (including essential strategic materials)

By 2025, Chinese producers of advanced basic materials used in sectors such as construction and T&A should hold 90% of the domestic market. Chinese producers of rare earths, special alloys, and other strategic materials should hold 85% of the home market.

(3) Advanced rail equipment

Chinese railway train producers already dominate their home market, so by 2020, at least 30% of their sales should be overseas, and by 2025, at least 40%.

(4) Agricultural machinery

By 2020, domestic firms should produce 90% of the equipment used by Chinese farmers, and 95% by 2025; with respect to high-tech machines (*e.g.*, tractors), the figures should be 30% by 2020 and 60% by 2025.

(5) Aircraft (including aerospace)

By 2020, the revenues earned by Chinese airlines should be at least 100 billion *yuan* ($15.90 billion), and 200 billion *yuan* by 2025.

By 2025, Chinese aircraft manufacturers should hold a home market share of 10 percent, and the domestically created CJ-1000A should be past the commercial prototype stage and ready for sale.

---

42. *See U.S. Escalates*; *Factbox: Made in China 2025: Beijing's Big Ambitions from Robots to Chips*, REUTERS, 20 April 2018. [Hereinafter, *Factbox*.] *See also* The State Council, The People's Republic of China, *Made in China 2025*, http://english.gov.cn/2016special/madeinchina2025/ (posting announcements and articles concerning the strategy); Central Committee of the Communist Party of China, The 13th Five-Year Plan for Economic and Social Development of the People's Republic of China (2016–2020), http://en.ndrc.gov.cn/newsrelease/201612/P020161207645765233498.pdf (containing 80 Chapters on topics ranging from innovation and the cyber-economy to socialist cultural and ethical progress, and socialist democracy and the rule of law).

By 2025, 80% of civil space industry equipment should be sourced from Chinese manufacturers.

(6) Electric power equipment

By 2025, Chinese companies should dominate the local market for smart, connected vehicle technology.

(7) Marine engineering

By 2025, China should be a world leader in manufacturing out-at-sea engineering equipment, and hold an 80% share of the market in critical systems used in this equipment.

(8) New energy vehicles

By 2025, led by two domestic champions making new energy vehicles, Chinese companies should hold 80% of the domestic market for EVs and plug-in hybrid vehicles.

(9) Pharmaceuticals

By 2025, Chinese drug companies should meet international standards and have developed between five and 10 medicines approved by the FDA and/or EU regulators. Chinese medical equipment producers should have 70% of the domestic market share in middle- and high-end devices used at county-level hospitals.

(10) Shipbuilding

By 2025, China should be a world leader in manufacturing high-technology ships, and hold an 80% share of the market in critical systems used in these ships.

The CCP put roughly $300 billion worth of subsidies behind its scheme.[43] Simply put, there was no market capitalism here. Rather, the CCP was importing back to China a hallmark of Communism—broad, deep, ambitious, state-funded central planning—in a container of Middle Kingdom nationalism. Obviously, the more protected the Chinese market remained from foreign import competition, the easier it would be for the CCP to reach its targets—and, in turn, bolster its legitimacy at the apex of a one-party state.

Not surprisingly, the USTR characterized "*Made in China 2025*" as industrial policy that "aims to replace advanced technology imports with domestic products and build a dominant position in future industries." "To be clear," as Bloomberg's

---

43. *See* David J. Lynch & Emily Rauhala, *U.S. and China Announce New Tariffs in Escalation of Trade War*, The Washington Post, 15 June 2018, www.washingtonpost.com/business/economy /trump-imposes-import-taxes-on-chinese-goods-and-warns-of-additional-tariffs/2018/06/15 /da909ecc-7092-11e8-bf86-a2351b5ece99_story.html?utm_term=.b74416630d23&wpisrc=al _news__alert-world-alert-national&wpmk=1. [Hereinafter, *U.S. and China Announce.*]

Editorial Board put it, "China isn't wrong to harbor such ambitions."[44] Moreover, its pursuit of them was not a zero-sum game:

> [S]o far as the basic economics goes, its success needn't disadvantage the U.S. or any other country. The U.S. didn't get rich in the last century at Europe's expense: Its innovations raised living standards everywhere. That's what trade and commerce do. In a well-functioning global system, successful economies prosper together.[45]

The problem was the means by which the CCP pursued its ends, namely, IP theft and misappropriation:

> China isn't playing by the rules. It wants access to other countries' markets and technologies but is slow to grant access to its own. And its technological push has often relied on questionable or outright illegal methods—from rampant cyber-theft of commercial and military secrets, to subtler violations of the spirit if not always the letter of the country's obligations as a member of the World Trade Organization.

> The 200-page report produced by the U.S. Trade Representative's Office as part of its investigation of Chinese intellectual-property theft is a litany of such complaints. Companies report (mostly anonymously, for fear of retaliation) various forms of pressure to make them share technology with their Chinese joint-venture partners. Permits are withheld, and approvals delayed. Demands are made through private channels, with no paper trail to prove a breach of China's WTO commitments. Foreign companies that give way may find themselves competed out of the market once their former partners have mastered the technology for themselves.

> China also uses internal and semi-official documents to set demanding self-sufficiency targets—which do not comport well with WTO undertakings. In sectors such as telecommunications and aviation, companies are directed to source 70 percent of their core components domestically by 2025. The government supports its tech companies with tax rebates, cheap financing and direct capital injections, often without reporting the money as subsidies, as generally required by the WTO. Such aid can make up more than 10 percent of operating revenue at some robot and machine-tool makers.[46]

Thus, America felt it had little choice but to blunt Chinese ambitions—*i.e.*, development of a comparative advantage through dubious IP behavior.

---

44. The Editors, *Dealing with China's High Tech Ambitions*, Bloomberg, 24 April 2018, www .bloomberg.com/view/articles/2018-04-25/how-the-u-s-should-handle-china-s-high-tech -ambitions. [Hereinafter, *Dealing with China's High Tech Ambitions*.]

45. *Dealing with China's High Tech Ambitions*.

46. *Dealing with China's High Tech Ambitions*.

IV. American Retaliation and Chinese Counter-Retaliation Lists

Taking its cue from the 11 sectors in which China sought dominance, the USTR identified its top 10 categories for targeting under Section 301. In descending order of the number of products the USTR listed with HTS numbers at the 6-digit level, they were:[47]

(1) Industrial Machinery (including nuclear technology, plus industrial robots and machine parts): 537 items

(2) Electrical Machinery (including TV and sound recorders, plus bakery ovens, dishwashers, flat panel TV screens, and sewing machines): 241 items

(3) Optical Equipment (including medical and surgical devices, plus light-emitting diodes and malaria diagnostic kits): 164 items

(4) Iron and steel: 152 items

(5) Vehicles (excluding railway and tramway, but including electric vehicles, gasoline vehicles with engines less than three liters, and SUVs): 48 items

(6) Pharmaceutical products (including antibiotics): 47 items

(7) Organic chemicals: 38 items

(8) Aluminum-based items: 27 items

(9) Railway vehicles and equipment: 17 items

(10) Aircraft and spacecraft (including communication satellite parts, plus aircraft turbo propellers and rocket launchers): 16 items

To offset the overall effect of adverse price rises for American consumers, not included on the list were computers, consoles, mobile phones, toys, shoes, T&A items, video games. And, with respect to over 20 products on the list—such as artillery weapons, communication satellites, and large aircraft—America did not import them (in 2017) from China. Notably, this list was a proposed one. The USTR gave 60 days for comment, hence exporters, importers, and consumers of Chinese products could examine the items and suggest changes.

In mirror image, the theory of the Chinese Section 301 counter-retaliation list was to maximize damage to America's economy, and undermine support for the Section 301 action against American consumers. The Chinese list also targeted politically significant products, *i.e.,* ones from States that supported candidate Trump in the 2016 Presidential election: agricultural and industrial interests across the Heartland thus were in the Chinese sites. The Chinese list contained 106 products on which the CCP said it would impose a 25% tariff, representing $50 billion in annual trade—matching the American figures, for as MOFCOM intoned, it

---

47. *See U.S. Leaves Door Open to China Talks Amid Trade-War Fears.*

sought a "measure of equal intensity and scale against U.S. goods."[48] The Chinese list included:

- Agricultural and Natural Resource Products:

  Corn, cotton, frozen beef, lobsters, orange juice, propane, sorghum, soybeans, tobacco and tobacco products (cigarettes and cigars), wheat, and whisky.[49]

- Industrial Products:

  Aircraft, electric vehicles, lubricants, SUVs, and trucks.

But, in contrast to American administrative procedures, there was no transparent notice-and-comment period. The CCP simply dictated the list, with any debate about inclusions or exclusions behind closed doors.

- **Pros and Cons of the Section 301 Case**

Because of global supply chains with Chinese links, several sectors of the U.S. economy opposed the Section 301 tariffs. For example:

  Americana Development and the Champion Safe Co. of Provo, Utah, said in comments to the Office of U.S. Trade Representative that their cost for steel has risen by about 25 percent. That creates an unfair price advantage

---

48. *Quoted in U.S. Escalates.*

49. The effects of the 25% Chinese counter-retaliatory tariff (effective 6 July 2018) on the lobster industry in Maine, coupled with Canada's FTA with the EU (*CETA*, signed on 30 October 2016, and effective 21 September 2017, discussed in a separate Chapter), was dramatic:

  The blow is significant for Maine, the country's top producer and exporter. The state's lobstermen had found a lucrative market in China, where consumer demand has grown exponentially in recent years. In 2017, U.S. exports of live lobsters to China were worth $128.5 million, up from a third of that in 2015. Maine's dealers have responded by scrambling to find other markets . . . [especially in Asia,] including Singapore and Taiwan. . . .

  . . .

  One problem for American lobstermen is their Canadian rivals. Thanks to a trade agreement Prime Minister Justin Trudeau struck with the EU, Canadian crustaceans now land in Europe duty-free. U.S. lobsters, meanwhile, face an 8 percent tariff with no sign of imminent relief. . . .

  As a result, dealers in Maine have begun investigating whether to open bonded warehouses so they can sell Canadian lobsters to clients in Europe and China, bypassing tariffs. Others have already begun shifting operations across the border to Canada to take advantage of the tariff advantage there. "This guy [Trump] has handed Canada the lobster industry—a $1.5 billion industry," [Mark] Barlow [owner of Island Seafood, a Maine-based company that, until the Sino-American Trade War, exported to China one out of every five love lobsters it trapped] says. "He's just handed it to Trudeau: 'Here you go, boys.'"

  Across the border, Canadians have started to complain about trans-shipping. . . . "Lobster from Maine is coming into Canada and being exported to China," says Geoff Irvine, Executive Director of the Lobster Council of Canada. "Everybody knows what's happening. . . . Anything that isn't Canadian lobster should not be sold as Canadian lobster."

Shawn Donnan, *Lobsters Get Caught in Trade War as Tariffs Bring Pain to Maine*, 35 International Trade Reporter (BNA) 1485 (15 November 2018).

for Chinese companies that sell finished steel wheels and safes to the U.S., and so far have escaped the lengthy tariff list, the companies said.

Without tariffs on Chinese steel wheels and wheel assemblies, Americana — one of the last U.S. companies making steel wheels for RVs — will have no choice but to reduce production and staffing, Pizzola said.

Ray Crosby, president of Champion Safe, said that if the playing field isn't leveled, his firm may shutter its production facility in Utah, which employs about 100 people, and join other U.S. safe makers that now manufacture in China. "We've seen our industry disappear over to China," Crosby said.[50]

Likewise, American retailers were fearful of a Section 301 trade war. Neither shoes nor T&A were on the Chinese retaliation list. But, cotton was, *i.e.*, American exports of cotton to China faced a 25% tariff. Cotton shirts made in China and destined for the shelves of American stores would be more expensive, dampening retail demand.

Interestingly, China faced the problem of running out of products against which to retaliate, because of the lesser range of products it imports from the United States than it exports to the United States.[51] China thus considered alternatives, such as

---

50. *Quoted in As CEOs Fight.* Note, too, some American firms took advantage of the Section 301 case to argue for product inclusions that would benefit their economic interests:

> Other companies argue for tariffs on their Chinese competition because it would help their business and achieve Trump's goal of boosting U.S. manufacturing and employment.
>
> Kason Industries of Newnan, Ga., makes panel fasteners and hinges for walk-in coolers and freezers. It's asking for tariffs on certain Chinese hinges and parts that contain steel as a large part of their value, said Burl Finkelstein, Kason's Vice President of Operations. Finkelstein said because Chinese companies are government subsidized, they're able to sell a finished product for less than his cost to purchase steel. A tariff on fabricated products would help equalize the cost of making products in the U.S. he said.
>
> "It's much easier to go overseas," Finkelstein said. "We're not taking the easy way out."
>
> . . .
>
> Radionic Industries Inc. is a 78-year-old Chicago company that's the last in the U.S. to make fluorescent lighting ballasts, according to President and Chief Executive Officer Jeffrey Winton. He's asking for a tariff of as much as 50 percent on magnetic ballasts imported from China, even while saying that history shows protectionist actions don't work.
>
> "A significant tariff increase on these products would clearly increase our production and sales volume, and bring about the hiring of more American workers," Winton said.

Quoted in id. Did such arguments reflect little else than rent-seeking behavior? Would acquiescing to them effect change in Chinese IP practices?

51. *See China is Studying Yuan Devaluation as a Tool in Trade Spat*, Bloomberg, 9 April 2018, www.bloomberg.com/news/articles/2018-04-09/china-is-said-to-study-yuan-devaluation-as-a -tool-in-trade-spat [hereinafter, *China is Studying*]; Chris Anstey, *China's Running Out of U.S. Imports to Target*, Reuters, 6 April 2018, www.bloomberg.com/news/articles/2018-04-06/china-s -running-out-of-u-s-imports-to-target. Between the inauguration of Donald Trump as President and his declaration of a Section 301 action, the *yuan* had gained 9% in value against the dollar, and on 9 April 2018 was at its strongest level (6.3186 *yuan*/dollar in onshore trading) since August 2015. *See China is Studying.*

funding fewer students to study in America (shifting them to other educational destinations, like Australia, Canada, New Zealand, and the U.K.), and limiting travel packages for Chinese tourists to America (sending them to third countries).

Another option was gradually devaluing the *yuan* relative to the dollar. That would offset the effects of a 25% tariff on its exports to America, but it also would increase the financial stress on Chinese companies, many of which were heavily indebted, to service their dollar-denominated offshore loans. It also would undermine China's arguments that it is not an NME for AD-CVD purposes (as a freely floating currency is one criterion for market economy treatment), and give credence to the argument it is a currency manipulator. Selling a portion of its vast holdings of U.S. Treasury securities was still another an option, though that would push down bond prices and push up yields. The former effect would hurt the value of its portfolio, while the other could increase its own borrowing costs.

Indubitably, then, each side had its vulnerabilities. For example, on one side, American businesses eagerly use China as a manufacturing and export platform, profiting both from relatively lower Chinese wages, and MFN treatment extended to China by all WTO Members following China's 11 December 2001 accession. Indeed:

> Most of the companies that will suffer from the first rounds of [Section 232 steel and aluminum] tariffs [imposed by the U.S.] are not actually Chinese firms, according to research from Syracuse University Economics Professor Mary Lovely.
>
> Using Chinese export data, she and researcher Yang Liang found that 87 percent of electronics-related products targeted were from non-Chinese multinationals and foreign-invested joint ventures.[52]

Small wonder why, then, the U.S. Chamber of Commerce lobbied against the Section 301 (and Section 232) trade remedies.[53] Its argument focused on the damage to exports, State-by-State, caused by Chinese counter-retaliation against American merchandise:

> For example, nearly $4 billion worth of exports from Texas could be targeted by retaliatory tariffs, the Chamber said, including $321 million in meat the state sends to Mexico each year and $494 million in grain sorghum it exports to China.[54]

---

52. David Lawder & Howard Schneider, *Surprises Lurk in Trump's Tariff List, from Thermostats to Vaping Devices*, Reuters, 25 June 2018, www.reuters.com/article/us-usa-trade-china-consumer-analysis/surprises-lurk-in-trumps-china-tariff-list-from-thermostats-to-vaping-devices-idUSKBN1JL30W. [Hereinafter, *Surprises Lurk*.]

53. *See* Ginger Gibson, *Top U.S. Business Group Assails Trump's Handling of Trade Dispute*, Reuters, 2 July 2018, www.reuters.com/article/us-usa-trade-chamber-exclusive/exclusive-largest-u-s-business-group-attacks-trump-on-tariffs-idUSKBN1JS0VL. [Hereinafter, *Top U.S. Business Group*.]

54. *Top U.S. Business Group.*

All true, but what the Chamber did not say is that the interests of its members that produce in and export from China would be hurt by the U.S. trade remedies. As for China's vulnerability, one example was that 58% of all of aviation imports into China originate in the U.S. (as of 2016).[55] Imposing tariffs on them, absent a reliable substitute source, was not an option.

On the other side, roughly 18.2% of all Chinese exports go to America (as of 2016).[56] China had no interest in losing big chunks of the American market on account of Section 301 tariffs. For decades, American consumers had been vital to China's export-led growth. And, China over-relied on semiconductor chips made by U.S. companies, particularly Intel Corp. and Qualcomm, Inc.[57] The second largest telecom producer, Zhongxing Telecommunications Corp. (ZTE), based in Shenzhen, was an infamous example: Qualcomm chips were in 50%–60% of ZTE's phones.[58] ZTE illegally shipped telecom network equipment, which incorporated American parts, to Iran in violation of U.S. export controls, and lied to American authorities about it. So, in April 2018, the Trump Administration decided to (1) impose a seven-year import ban on American firms selling products to ZTE, (2) revoke for seven years ZTE's privilege to export goods from the U.S., and (3) re-impose $300 million fine on ZTE. These moves underscored ZTE's dependence on Qualcomm chips. (In June, ZTE settled the charges, agreeing to pay a $1 billion fine, replace its management board, and hire a compliance team approved by U.S. authorities.[59] The U.S. suspended the moratorium on ZTE purchases of U.S. goods for 10 years, but reserved the right to re-impose it should ZTE misbehave.[60])

Stunningly, in May 2018, the Trump Administration climbed down, ordering DOC not to follow through, with Mr. Trump tweeting "too many jobs in China lost."[61] Why this "America First" President was concerned about at-risk ZTE employees in China was unclear. One speculation was the climb down was a bargaining chip with China, to win concessions in the Section 301 case. Yet, the CCP remained resolute in its *Made in China 2025* target that at least 40% of the chips

---

55. *See* U.S. Department of Commerce, China Country Commercial Guide, Export.gov, *China—Aviation* (25 July 2017), www.export.gov/article?id=China-Aviation.

56. *See Wall Street Recovers.*

57. *See* Elias Glenn & Cate Cadell, *Exclusive: China Looks to Speed Up Chip Plans as U.S. Trade Tensions Boil—Sources*, REUTERS, 19 April 2018, www.reuters.com/article/us-usa-trade -china-chips-exclusive/exclusive-china-looks-to-speed-up-chip-plans-as-u-s-trade-tensions-boil -sources-idUSKBN1HQ1QP.

58. *See* Department of Commerce, *In the Matter of: Zhongxing Telecommunications Equipment Corporation*, 83 Federal Register 17644 (23 April 2018).

59. *See China's Telco Giant ZTE Sees Shares Collapse 39%*, BBC NEWS, 13 June 2018, www.bbc .com/news/business-44463976.

60. *ZTE Vows to Shake Things Up After Securing a U.S. Reprieve*, 35 International Trade Reporter (BNA) 797 (14 June 2018).

61. David Meyer, *"Too Many Jobs in China Lost:" Why On Earth Is "America First" Trump Vowing to Save China's ZTE?*, FORBES, 14 May 2018, http://fortune.com/2018/05/14/china-iran-zte -donald-trump/.

used in Chinese-made smartphones should be sourced from Chinese "domestic champions." Toward this end, the CCP set up a multi-billion-dollar National Integrated Circuitry Investment Fund. And, the irony, if not hypocrisy, of the climb down to help a company that violated American sanctions against Iran, coupled with a contemporaneous withdrawal of the U.S. from the *JCPOA* and re-imposition of sanctions against Iran, was stunning.

To illustrate the adage "no one wins in a trade war," some vulnerabilities cut both ways. For instance:

> Though the tariffs target Chinese drug makers, those on the losing side may be American pharmaceutical companies that make generics such as Mylan NV. The 25 percent tariff would be placed on raw ingredients for drugs such as insulin used by diabetics, the anti-allergic-reaction drug epinephrine, as well as vaccines, blood products and antidepressants, according to the list.
>
> For brand-name drugs, raw ingredients used by manufacturers are typically a tiny fraction of the cost of a product. They can be more important for generic medications that are essentially low-cost commodity products.[62]

As another illustration, "China is the world's largest soybean importer and biggest buyer of U.S. soybeans in trade worth about $14 billion last year."[63] About 60% of America's soybean exports go to China, which accounts for 30% of Chinese soybean imports, with an additional 50% of those imports originating in Brazil (which is the world's largest soybean exporter).[64] Thus, imposing tariffs on American soybeans would hurt not only American farmers, but also Chinese farmers who use soybeans in livestock feed—particularly pigs (pork is China's "most popular meat"), chickens, and even fish—and Chinese consumers who rely on soybeans for protein in their diet, and for their cooking oil.[65] It also would adversely affect China's biodiesel

---

62. *Trump's Scattergun.*

63. *U.S. Leaves Door Open.*

64. *See* Lucien O. Chauvin, *U.S. Least Protectionist Country, Says Commerce Secretary Ross,* 35 International Trade Reporter (BNA) 553 (19 April 2018) [hereinafter, *U.S. Least Protectionist*]; *Trump Threatens Further $100 Billion In Tariffs Against China,* BBC News, 6 April 2018, www.bbc .com/news/business-43664243 [hereinafter, *Trump Threatens Further*].

65. *See* He Huifeng, *China Says U.S. Farmers May Never Regain Market Share Lost in Trade War,* South China Morning Post (Hong Kong) and Politico, 11 August 2018, www.politico.com /story/2018/08/11/farmers-china-soy-bean-market-share-734773?cid=apn [hereinafter, *China Says U.S. Farmers*]; *Trump Threatens Further*; Tatian Freitas, *China Food Giant Said to Expand in Brazil Amid U.S. Tensions,* 35 International Trade Reporter (BNA) 668 (17 May 2018) (reporting that "China's food giant Cofco International is positioning itself to increase soybean purchases from Brazil as trade tensions escalate between the U.S. and the Asian nation," and "Cofco has strengthened its team that buys, stores, and sells farmer crops, known as origination, in the South American country, recently hiring as many as 12 people to work directly with farmers in Mato Grosso, Goias, Parana, and Rio Grande do Sul states," and that Cofco sought "to improve logistics for shipping from Brazil" by "consolidating port operations at two neighboring terminals it currently uses in Santos Port, the largest in Latin America," and by "seeking the renewal of its port

industry. China could look to soybean imports from Argentina, Brazil, and India, but thanks to higher transportation costs and/or lower economies of scale *vis-à-vis* American farmers, they were not necessarily price competitive alternatives. And, Brazil already exported about 90% of its soybean harvest to China, so without expanding output, it could not meet increased short-term Chinese demand.[66] Sorghum imports were a similar story: China needed them for hog and poultry feed, and as an ingredient in *baiju* (a Chinese liqueur).[67]

Nevertheless, in late April and early May 2018, China stopped buying American soybeans, shifting to Brazilian and Canadian sources, and in September 2018, China (specifically, its official *China Daily* publication) took out a four-page section in *the Des Moines Register* (Iowa's largest newspaper), called "The Fruit of a President's Folly."[68] (America's Ambassador to China, former Iowa Governor Terry Branstad (1946–), hit back in the same newspaper:

---

concessions that are expected to expire in coming years, allowing for investment to increase export capacity").

66. *See U.S. Least Protectionist.*

The history of Brazil's emergence as a principal producer-exporter of soybeans dates to 1973, when President Richard M. Nixon (1913–1994, President, 1969–1974) embargoed exports of the crop to Japan, amidst trade conflict with that country:

> In 1973, the U.S. dominated global soybean production, with output more than five times higher than No. 2 China. At that point, Brazil didn't even make it into the top 10. Nixon's embargo, though, sent shock waves through Japan, a top importer that relied on the U.S. for more than 88 percent of its supplies.
>
> In response, Japan invested heavily in Brazil's soybean industry, helping accelerate growth in the key Cerrado agricultural region. . . .
>
> While Brazil's growers now [November 2018] produce about 4 percent fewer soybeans than American farmers, the Latin American country was able to overtake the U.S. as the world's top exporter in the 2012–2013 season.
>
> Brazil is once again in a position to gain. With the U.S.-China trade war ongoing, Latin America's biggest economy is set to ship out 77 million metric tons of soybeans this season. . . .

Isis Almeida, *Trump Trade War Fallout Could Haunt U.S. Soy Farmers for Years*, 35 International Trade Reporter (BNA) 1525 (22 November 2018).

67. *See* Karl Plume & P.J. Huffstutter, *Exclusive: U.S. Sorghum Armada U-Turns at Sea After China Tariffs*, REUTERS, 19 April 2018, www.reuters.com/article/us-usa-trade-china-sorghum -exclusive/exclusive-u-s-sorghum-armada-u-turns-at-sea-after-china-tariffs-idUSKBN1HR03Z.

68. *See* Alfred Cang, Megan Durisin & Mario Parker, *Soybean Data Confirm China Is Cancelling U.S. Shipments*, 35 International Trade Reporter (BNA) 640 (10 May 2018); Mario Parker, *China Shunning U.S. Soybeans on Trade Tensions, Bunge CEO Says*, BLOOMBERG, 2 May 2018, www .bloomberg.com/amp/news/articles/2018-05-02/china-has-stopped-buying-u-s-soybean-supplies -bunge-ceo-says.

Note, however, that the EU increased purchases of American soybeans. By September 2018, the EU was America's best customer for the commodity, with U.S. soybeans comprising 52% of all EU soybean supplies. The EU did so not entirely to bailout American farmers; it hoped to avoid Section 232 tariffs on its autos and auto parts, which the Trump Administration threatened (discussed in a separate Chapter). *See* Richard Bravo, *EU Buys More U.S. Soybeans as Trade War Hits American Farmland*, 35 International Trade Reporter (BNA) 1227 (27 September 2018).

On Sept. 23, the *China Daily*—a newspaper the Chinese Communist Party uses to circulate propaganda to foreign audiences—took out a paid advertisement in the *Des Moines Register* criticizing U.S. actions on trade.

In disseminating its propaganda, China's government is availing itself of America's cherished tradition of free speech and a free press by placing a paid advertisement in the *Des Moines Register*. In contrast, at the newsstand down the street here in Beijing, you will find limited dissenting voices and will not see any true reflection of the disparate opinions that the Chinese people may have on China's troubling economic trajectory, given that media is under the firm thumb of the Chinese Communist Party. Even in the case of this op-ed, one of China's most prominent newspapers dodged the offer to publish.

. . .

. . . [T]he Chinese, guided by their *Made in China 2025* industrial plan, are now engaged in a sustained campaign to acquire our technologies and intellectual property through practices ranging from forced technology transfer and the evasion of export controls to outright theft through cyber-enabled means and traditional spycraft. Many Iowans remember the case in which a Chinese agent attempted to literally steal the seed corn from our fields.

. . .

For over a decade, the United States has attempted to negotiate with China in a cooperative and constructive manner. After careful study and analysis, the United States concluded that a stronger response to China's unfair trade practices was needed.

The administration implemented tariffs to obtain elimination of China's unfair policies and begin to level the playing field between American companies and their Chinese competitors. Unfortunately, China has responded to such action by taking further steps to harm American workers, farmers and businesses through retaliatory actions—and is now doubling down on that bullying by running propaganda ads in our own free press.[69]

By September, China was importing apples from Poland, kiwis from Italy, and navel oranges from Egypt—rather than from America.[70]

American farmers searched for new markets.[71] For example, Midwestern soybean farmers courted buyers from Sri Lanka. Yet, it would take 11,000 markets the size

---

69. Terry Branstad, *Responding to China's Ad in the Des Moines Register, Trump's Ambassador Calls Out China*, Des Moines Register, 30 September 2018, www.desmoinesregister.com/story /opinion/2018/09/30/trump-administration-china-compete-level-playing-field/1452878002/.

70. *See* Livia Yap & Dan Murtaugh, *Trump Trade Wind Blow Egypt Oranges to Shanghai Fruit Shops (1)*, 35 International Trade Reporter (BNA) 1226 (20 September 2018).

71. P.J. Huffstutter & Karl Plume, *U.S. Farmers Scramble to Contain Trade-War Damage, Find New Markets*, Reuters, 14 November 2018, www.reuters.com/article/us-usa-trade

of Sri Lanka to make up for the lost Chinese market. Similarly, USDA-organized export promotion trips to El Salvador, Guatemala, and Honduras, even though successful, could not match the commercial meaningfulness of China: the November 2018 commitment of these three Central American nations to buy $49 million worth of U.S. farm goods ranging from feed grains to wine across the following year was just 0.035% of America's 2017 agricultural commodity exports.

Some battles in the trade war were invisible. In May, China ceased issuing PSI certificates for American scrap metals (*e.g.*, scrap aluminum and copper), meaning it would not certify them as free from SPS threats, and thus were banned from entry into China.[72] China also intensified its scrutiny of an array of U.S. merchandise, including fruit, lumber, and pork. China claimed its inspections were in accord with the scientific principles referenced in the *SPS Agreement*.[73] Allegedly, there were pests in some American apples and wooden logs. Likewise, China applied scrupulously its TBT measures, subjecting Ford and premium Lincoln cars to supplementary technical checks.

V. Initial Negotiations Fail

Still, the two sides continued to hurl threats at each other in short order. On 6 April, President Trump directed the USTR to identify Chinese merchandise on which an additional $100 billion worth of tariffs could be imposed. MOFCOM immediately replied:

> The result of this behavior is to smash your own foot with a stone. . . . If the United States announces an additional $100 billion list of tariffs, China has already fully prepared, and will not hesitate to immediately make a fierce counter strike.[74]

-troubleshooters-insight/u-s-farmers-scramble-to-contain-trade-war-damage-find-new-markets -idUSKCN1NJ1LS.

Amidst the search by U.S. soybean farmers for new markets, one of many unintended consequences of the Sino-American Trade War emerged: higher crop storage costs suffered by farmers, but higher profits for owners, such as Andersons, Archer Daniels Midland Co. and Bunge Ltd., of crop storage facilities (grain elevators). Farmers had three options: (1) self-storage (e.g., by moving animals and implements out of their barns and putting their excess soybeans in the barns); (2) letting their crops rot in their fields; or (3) paying higher storage fees to grain elevator operators (*e.g.*, 40% more, or 3–6 cents per bushel, in central Illinois). *See* Mark Weinraub & P.J. Huffstutter, *Harvesting in a Trade War: U.S. Crops Rot as Storage Costs Soar*, REUTERS, 21 November 2018, www.reuters.com/article/us-usa-trade-china-grains/harvesting-in-a-trade-war-u-s-crops-rot-as -storage-costs-soar-idUSKCN1NQ0GA.

72. *China to Suspend Checks on U.S. Scrap Metal Shipments, Halting Imports*, REUTERS, 4 May 2018, www.reuters.com/article/us-china-waste-united-states/china-to-suspend-checks-on-u-s-scrap -metal-shipments-halting-imports-idUSKBN1I50JF. The suspension initially was for one month.

73. *China Is Said to Increase Scrutiny of U.S. Farm Product Imports*, 35 International Trade Reporter (BNA) 666 (17 May 2018).

74. *Trump Threatens More* (*quoting* Gao Feng, Spokesman, Ministry of Commerce).

The President acknowledged Americans might incur a "little pain" in the short term, that "we may take a hit," but opined: "you know what, ultimately we're going to be much stronger for it."[75]

Empirically, that "hit" was estimated at a cumulative Sino-American reduction in real GDP growth of 1%, and a drop in real global GDP growth (for 2019) from 3% to 2.5%. Under the scenario of $50 billion worth of Section 301 tariffs, 134,000 jobs in the U.S. would be lost, including over 67,000 in agriculture.[76] Ironically, of the total, 77,500 would be in States candidate Trump won in the 2016 Presidential election.

Negotiations to resolve the dispute did not start off well.[77] China accused the Trump Administration of suffering "anxiety disorder," while the Administration saw China as protecting itself behind a "Great Wall of Denial."[78] On 10 April 2018, President Xi Jinping (1953–, President, 2013–) delivered a major address to the Boao Forum For Asia that was conciliatory and even statesmanlike in style, but offered no new major substantive concessions. He suggested China could cut its bilateral trade surplus by $50 by importing more agricultural products, LNG, luxury goods, and semiconductors from the U.S. He indicated China would open its market further to banking and insurance services, e-commerce, and FDI. But, exactly when and how these goals would be realized was unclear. Would foreign investors be allowed a 100% equity stake in a local insurance company? Would China finally comply with the 2012 WTO Panel decision in a case it lost against the U.S. concerning Modes I and III delivery of electronic payment services and China's market access and national treatment obligations under *GATS* Articles XVI and XVII, respectively, and allow foreign credit card companies like MasterCard and Visa to process payments?[79]

---

75. *Quoted in Trump Threatens More.*

76. *See* Mark Niquette, *Trump's China Tariffs Risk Costing U.S. Jobs, New Study Shows*, 35 International Trade Reporter (BNA) 614 (3 May 2018) (discussing a study by Trade Partnership Worldwide LLC commissioned by the Consumer Technology Association and National Retail Federation, both of which opposed the Section 301 action).

77. *See* Keith Zhai, *China Talks Stalled on Trump's Demands Over High-Tech Industries*, BLOOMBERG, 10 April 2018, www.bloomberg.com/news/articles/2018-04-10/u-s-china-talks-said-to-have -stalled-over-high-tech-industry; David Fickling & Anjani Trivedi, *Xi's Warmed Up Trade Leftovers Aren't So Unpalatable*, BLOOMBERG QUINT (India), 10 April 2010, www.bloombergquint .com/opinion/2018/04/10/xi-s-warmed-up-trade-leftovers-aren-t-so-unpalatable [hereinafter, *Xi's Warmed Up*]; Kevin Yao & Elias Glenn, *China's Xi Renews Pledges to Open Economy, Cut Tariffs This Year, As U.S. Trade Row Deepens*, REUTERS, 9 April 2018, www.reuters.com/article/us-usa -trade-china/chinas-xi-renews-pledges-to-open-economy-cut-tariffs-this-year-as-u-s-trade-row -deepens-idUSKBN1HH084 [hereinafter, *China's Xi*].

78. Kevin Yao & Lindsay Dunsmuir, *China Blames U.S for Trade Frictions, but Trump Voices Optimism*, REUTERS, 9 April 2018, www.reuters.com/article/us-usa-trade-china/china-blames-u-s -for-trade-frictions-but-trump-voices-optimism-idUSKBN1HG0WB.

79. The case is WTO Panel Report, *China—Certain Measures Affecting Electronic Payment Services*, WT/DS413/R (adopted 31 August 2012, not appealed). In it, the Panel held as follows:

Likewise, his offer to cut auto tariffs below 25% (to 10%–15%) was ambiguous — would that be to bound, or applied, MFN duties?[80] And, its value to American producers was dubious:

> China imports just over 1 million cars into its 20 million-a-year-plus auto market. Of that amount, most are German-branded luxury SUVs.... General Motors Co., Ford Motor Co. and Fiat Chrysler Automobiles NV exported around 50,000 to 60,000 cars from the U.S. to China last year [2017] worth around $2 billion, versus the more than 150,000 luxury SUVs that BMW AG and Daimler AG sent from their U.S. factories.
>
> . . .
>
> It's simply cheaper to build cars in China than in North America, *so the only major beneficiaries of lower import tariffs are likely to be makers of prestige vehicles whose volumes aren't large enough to justify a local plant* — think Toyota Motor Corp.'s Lexus, Honda Motor Co.'s Acura and Hyundai Motor Co.'s new Genesis marque.
>
> GM's Cadillac is already turning out fancy cars from a Shanghai joint-venture factory, with sales up 51 percent last year. Along with its Chinese partners, GM is expected to produce 15 new or refreshed models in China

---

(1) On market access:
China maintains CUP [China UnionPay] as a monopoly supplier for the clearing of certain types of *RMB*-denominated payment card transactions. The specific transactions in respect of which the Panel determined that CUP is a sole supplier involve *RMB* payment cards issued in China and used in Hong Kong, China or Macao, China, or *RMB* payment cards issued in Hong Kong, China or Macao, China and used in China. [*GATS*] Article XVI:2(a) requires Members not to limit the number of service suppliers where market access commitments have been undertaken. The Panel found that China acted inconsistently with its Mode 3 market access commitment under Article XVI:2(a) . . . by granting CUP a monopoly for the clearing of these types of *RMB* payment card transactions.
World Trade Organization, Dispute Settlement, DS413, *China — Certain Measures Affecting Electronic Payment Services*, www.wto.org/english/tratop_e/dispu_e/cases_e/ds413_e .htm. [Hereinafter, *Summary.*]

(2) On national treatment:
China maintains a requirement that all payment cards issued in China must bear the "Yin Lian"/"UnionPay" logo and be interoperable with that network, a requirement that all terminal equipment in China must be capable of accepting "Yin Lian"/"UnionPay" logo cards, and finally, a requirement that acquiring institutions post the "Yin Lian"/"UnionPay" logo and be capable of accepting all payment cards bearing the "Yin Lian"/"UnionPay" logo. The Panel found each of these requirements to be inconsistent with China's Mode 1 and Mode 3 national treatment obligations under Article XVII of the *GATS*. It found, through these requirements, that China modifies the conditions of competition in favor of CUP and therefore fails to provide national treatment to EPS suppliers of other Members, contrary to China's commitments.
Id.

80. *See China Is Said to Mull Cutting Car Import Duty by About Half,* 35 International Trade Reporter (BNA) 611 (3 May 2018).

this year. Ford, meanwhile, has pushed ahead with its luxury Lincoln brand, as it rehashes its business in the nation.[81]

Moreover, "Chinese officials have been promising since at least 2013 to ease restrictions on foreign joint ventures in the auto industry, which would allow foreign firms to take a majority stake,"[82] and they included such plans in an official planning document in 2017. They chafed under two severe restrictions: they could not set up a wholly-owned factory, and their equity participation in a JV had been capped since 1994 at 50%. Thus, "Tesla's Chief Executive Elon Musk . . . railed against an unequal playing field in China," because he "wants to retain full ownership over a manufacturing facility" he sought to build there.

Facing the Section 301 action, China said it would phase out foreign ownership caps: for full EVs and plug-in hybrids in 2018; for commercial vehicles in 2020; and for cars generally by 2022.[83] But, that pledge was self-serving:

> The real beneficiary of China's proposals is China. The goal is to marshal foreign companies, foreign capital and foreign technology to help China defeat foreign competitors in the global economy.
>
> A classic example is the recently announced deregulation in the automobile sector. Beijing promised to eliminate a requirement that overseas carmakers form joint ventures with Chinese partners to manufacture cars locally. For electric vehicles, that restriction could be dropped as early as this year. Some international firms will benefit by being able to set up wholly owned operations, most of all Tesla Inc.
>
> But that's not the real purpose of the change. Electric vehicles are a targeted industry in China, marked for special support in the nation's *Made in China 2025* industrial program. The Chinese want to dominate the production of electric vehicles, and this "reform" is a necessary step to get there.
>
> . . . [As] Bill Russo, founder of Shanghai consultancy Automobility, explain[ed]: The reform "eliminates the only reason that may block global EV manufacturers and suppliers from investing in China capacity, making China the odds-on winner in the global race to electric transportation."

---

81. *Xi's Warmed Up* (emphasis added). China considered a cut in its 25% auto tariff to 10%–15%. But, with a 25% counter-retaliatory levy on American cars, the beneficiary of that cut would be EU and Japanese luxury brands, like BMW and Toyota. *See China Weighs Cutting Car Import Duty by About Half*, Bloomberg, 25 April 2018, www.bloomberg.com/news/articles/2018-04-26 /china-is-said-to-mull-cutting-car-import-duty-by-about-half.

82. *China's Xi*.

83. *China Opens Car Market After U.S. Tensions*, BBC News, 17 April 2018, www.bbc.com /news/business-43800233.

It's notable that the joint-venture rule for regular cars will be lifted far more slowly. Unlike new energy vehicles, old-fashioned combustion engine cars aren't a priority.[84]

And, President Xi stood resolutely behind CCP industrial policy, namely, the *Made in China 2025* program and the need to bolster high-tech sectors through subsidies and IP acquisition—including EVs of the sort that interested Tesla. Moreover, analysts feared that "[f]oreign countries may already be in a box," because the culture of entry and distribution in China through a JV structure was so entrenched it was not in the interests of foreign companies to alter.[85]

Doubts also circled China's pledge to remove restriction on foreign investment banks. They no longer would have to operate through a JV with a local brokerage firm, which they found frustrating thanks to dubious quality and conflicts of interest with such firms.[86] The likes of Citigroup, Goldman Sachs, and J.P. Morgan Chase could set up wholly-owned Chinese subsidiaries that offered full financial services. But, to offer new products like securities lending, they would need a license, and the Chinese government would grant such licenses based on its prudential regulations. As for China's promise to remove equity caps on fund managers and life insurers, it first declared that intention in November 2017, well before the Section 301 action.

In brief, President Xi's declarations were nothing much new, and seemed to herald little more than "China is opening sectors where they already have a distinct advantage, or a stranglehold over the sector."[87] That was the practice the CCP fol-

---

84. Michael Schuman, *In Trade Talks, China Is Too Clever by Half*, BLOOMBERG, 29 April 2018, www.bloomberg.com/view/articles/2018-04-30/in-trade-talks-china-is-too-clever-by-half.

85. Norihiko Shirouzu & Adam Jourdan, *China to Open Auto Market as Trade Tensions Simmer*, REUTERS, 17 April 2018, www.reuters.com/article/us-china-autos-regulation/china-to-open-auto-market-as-trade-tensions-simmer-idUSKBN1HO0YA (*quoting* James Chao, Chief, Asia-Pacific, IHS Markit Ltd.).

86. *See* Cathy Chan, *Wall Street Finds China Door Remains Ajar After Trade Spat*, 35 International Trade Reporter (BNA) 558 (19 April 2018).

87. *China's Xi* (*quoting* Jonas Short, Head, Everbright Sun Hung Kai, Beijing). China essentially admitted as much, but cast the declarations in nationalistic CCP rhetoric:

    "I can tell you clearly that China's announcement of major opening-up measures has nothing to do with the current China-U.S. economic and trade conflicts," Foreign Ministry spokesman Geng Shuang told a regular news briefing April 11 in Beijing. "China's opening up is free from outside interference and the outside world cannot interfere with it."

    During a long-planned address to mark the 40th anniversary of China's economic opening, [President] Xi reaffirmed or expanded several proposals to increase imports, lower foreign-ownership limits on manufacturing and boost the protection of intellectual property. The policies, which China has been rolling out for months as part of its own economic development plans, also address issues central to U.S. trade complaints.

    . . .

    "People who understand the operations of the Chinese government should all understand that the introduction of so many major initiatives requires repeated consideration, thoughtful and careful planning," Geng said . . . "And it is impossible to make decisions in a short period of time."

lowed ever since it drew up its foreign investment regime in 1995: the list of industries in which foreigners could invest would be "tweaked as soon as domestic companies reach the scale and sophistication to effectively compete with offshore rivals."[88] And, his offer to accelerate negotiations to join the *GPA* was laughable: China pledged in 2001, as part of its WTO accession package, to become a party to the *GPA*.[89]

VI. Surprising May 2018 Truce

The two sides tried direct talks. After their initial round of meetings in Beijing in May 2018, China said the Americans needed to be "rational and pragmatic."[90] Among the demands the Chinese found irrational and unpragmatic were that China must (1) cut its annual trade surplus by $200 billion by year-end 2020, (2) eliminate all subsidies in the *Made in China 2025* program, and (3) not counter-retaliate against the American Section 301 tariffs. China said its trade surplus could be reduced only gradually, not via "unilateral, ill-thought-through trade actions," and added:

> Making China a scapegoat for the ills of the U.S. economy may appease some uninformed voters, but it would hardly reduce the trade deficit. China will further open up its economy so the international community can benefit from its large and fast-developing market. But China will do so on its own conditions, not to suit the agenda of other countries.[91]

After further direct talks, the two sides surprised the world trading community: they called a truce in their trade war.

The text of the truce was a *Joint Communiqué* that said:

> At the direction of President Donald J. Trump and President Xi Jinping, on May 17 and 18, 2018, the United States and China engaged in constructive consultations regarding trade in Washington, D.C. The United States delegation included Secretary of the Treasury Steven T. Mnuchin, Secretary of Commerce Wilbur L. Ross, and United States Trade Representative Robert E. Lighthizer. The Chinese delegation was led by State Council Vice Premier Liu He, Special Envoy of President Xi.

Quoted in Keith Zhai, *China Says Xi's Reform Pledges Unrelated to U.S. Trade Tensions*, 35 International Trade Reporter (BNA) 548 (19 April 2019).

88. *Xi's Warmed Up.*

89. *See* Bryce Baschuk, *China Pushing Bid to Join WTO Procurement Pact, Xi Says*, 35 International Trade Reporter (BNA) 488 (12 April 2018).

90. *China Softens Tone on Trade After U.S. Leaves Empty Handed*, 35 International Trade Reporter (BNA) 625 (10 May 2018). [Hereinafter, *China Softens Tone*.]

91. *China Softens Tone.*

There was a consensus on taking effective measures to *substantially reduce the United States trade deficit in goods with China*. To meet the growing consumption needs of the Chinese people and the need for high-quality economic development, China will *significantly increase purchases of United States goods and services*. This will help support growth and employment in the United States.

Both sides agreed on *meaningful increases in United States agriculture and energy exports*. The United States will send a team to China to work out the details.

The delegations also discussed expanding trade in manufactured goods and services. There was consensus on the need to create favorable conditions to increase trade in these areas.

Both sides attach paramount importance to intellectual property protections, and agreed to *strengthen cooperation*. China will *advance relevant amendments to its laws and regulations* in this area, including the Patent Law.

Both sides agreed to encourage two-way investment and to strive to create a *fair, level playing field* for competition.

Both sides agreed to continue to engage at high levels on these issues and to seek to resolve their economic and trade concerns in a proactive manner.[92]

Accordingly, the U.S. agreed not to impose its Section 301 25% tariffs, nor any sanctions on ZTE, and China said it would avoid imposing counter-retaliatory measures.[93]

President Trump said China "fold[ed]," and tweeted: "China has agreed to buy massive amounts of ADDITIONAL Farm/Agricultural Products—would be one of the best things to happen to our farmers in many years!"[94] Yet, the terse *Joint Communiqué* imposed no obligations on China. The fundamental purpose of the Section 301 case—to rectify China's IP misappropriation—was addressed with nothing more than a vague promise to accelerate appropriate changes in Chinese law. That was a refrain China had been singing since its 11 December 2001 accession.

---

92. The White House, *Joint Statement of the United States and China Regarding Trade Consultations*, 19 May 2018, www.whitehouse.gov/briefings-statements/joint-statement-united-states-china-regarding-trade-consultations/.

93. China dropped its AD-CVD investigation on U.S. sorghum, but said it did so under its "Public Interest" Test, *i.e.*, imposing 178.6% remedial duties on that merchandise, as it had preliminarily in April 2018, would be averse to Chinese public interest, particularly the downstream breeding industry, pork producers, and retail consumers. *See China Scraps Probe into near $1 Billion U.S. Sorghum Imports (2)*, 35 International Trade Reporter (BNA) 696 (24 May 2018); *China Will "Significantly" Boost U.S. Purchases. By How Much Is The Question*, Bloomberg, 19 May 2018, www.bloomberg.com/news/articles/2018-05-19/china-to-significantly-boost-buying-of-u-s-goods-white-house.

94. *Quoted in* Ben Blanchard, Michael Martina & Susan Heavey, *Trade War Fears Ebb as U.S., China Agree to Continue Talks*, Reuters, 21 May 2018, www.reuters.com/article/us-usa-trade-china/china-praises-positive-steps-in-u-s-trade-row-says-didnt-give-in-idUSKCN1IM06R. [Hereinafter, *Trade War Fears*.]

Likewise, the secondary goal of cutting the bilateral trade deficit by $100 or $200 billion was not addressed with an unequivocal numerical target (let alone one in the $100–$200 billion range), nor with a time frame; rather, just another vague pledge to buy more American stuff.

To be sure, in May 2018, China's State Council Tariff Commission announced it would:

> cut tariffs on nearly 1,450 imported consumer goods ranging from food and beverages to home appliances starting July 1 . . . .
>
> The tariff reductions come roughly a week after Beijing said it would cut import duties on imported passenger cars from 25 percent to 15 percent. They also come just days after President Donald Trump said he's moving ahead with plans to impose tariffs on $50 billion worth of Chinese imports and curb investment in sensitive technology.
>
> Most-favored-nation tariff rates will apply to the 1,449 items included in the list . . . .
>
> Clothing, shoes, sportswear, washing machines, refrigerators, makeup, and healthcare goods will all benefit from the reduced tariffs . . . .
>
> For example, average tariffs on clothing, shoes, sports, and fitness goods will be cut from 15.9 percent to 7.1 percent, while average tariffs on household appliances will weigh in at 8 percent, down from 20.5 percent.
>
> As for cosmetics and some health-care products, average import duties will be cut from 8.4 percent to 2.9 percent . . . .[95]

China said the cuts would help meet domestic consumer demand. However, even if China instituted a measure — a legally enforceable promise — to buy more American imports, that measure might be challengeable by third countries as illegal under the GATT Article I:1 MFN rule, as China would be preferring U.S. merchandise over that from all other Members. And, if the promise was voluntary, then not even the CCP necessarily could ensure its enforcement by non-SOE Chinese companies, especially if American goods were higher cost and/or lower quality than local or other foreign items. Not a word was said about subsidies from the CCP and its *Made in China 2025* industrial policy.

Small wonder why the former Chairman of the American Chamber of Commerce in China, James Zimmerman, a Beijing-based lawyer, opined:

> the Trump Administration's move to walk back its threatened trade actions was premature, and a "lost opportunity" for American companies, workers and consumers.

---

95. Linly Lin, *China Publishes Full List of 1,449 Items Subject to Tariff Cuts* , 35 International Trade Reporter (BNA) 765 (7 June 2018).

"The Chinese are in a state of quiet glee knowing that Trump's trade team backed off on sanctions without getting any real and meaningful concessions out of Beijing"[96] . . . .

What might explain the truce, despite the lack of any "hard law" obligations incumbent on China to make genuine structural changes?

One possibility was the Trump Administration realized there was no way to close the deficit in the amount, and with the speed, it wanted:

> Economists at Morgan Stanley estimated exports of U.S. agricultural products, primarily beef, and energy, mostly liquified natural gas, could add between $60 billion and $90 billion to sales to China over a period of years. That is far less than the $200 billion reduction in China's trade surplus that President Donald Trump had demanded at the start of talks.[97]

Another possibility was the Administration wanted Chinese support for its overtures to North Korea, in the hopes China would pressure North Korea to abandon its nuclear weapons. Either explanation, however, suggested a lack of foresight, *i.e.*, both the economic and military points were well known before the Administration launched the Section 301 case. And, calling the truce suggested to China that America was (to quote Chairman Mao's memorable metaphor) a "paper tiger." Even when the U.S. might have strong case, concerning IP theft and the *Made in China 2025* subsidies, America folded quickly.

VII. Truce Ends, June 2018 White House *Report on China's Economic Aggression*

- **Bilateral Talks Fail**

The truce lasted hardly one month. Direct bilateral talks failed, with the U.S. unimpressed by a Chinese pledge to buy roughly $70 billion more of American products. That pledge hardly addressed the core issues of the Section 301 case — IP misappropriation, industrial policy, and the trade deficit. So, following the receipt of over 3,154 public comments, on 29 May 2018, the U.S. announced it would publish on 15 June a final list of $50 billion worth of Chinese imports against which

---

96. *Quoted in Trade War Fears.* Senator Charles Schumer (Democrat-New York) expressed the same sentiment, namely, that none of the fundamental trade tensions had been resolved. The Senator "thought it would be a mistake for Trump to settle for 'a promise to buy goods' with so many larger issues on the table, saying: "If President Xi is going . . . to fail to take strong actions on intellectual property, cyber theft, and American companies having free access to sell goods in China . . . we will have lost . . . ." *Quoted in* Lindsay Dunsmuir, *U.S., China Putting Trade War on Hold, Treasury's Mnuchin Says*, REUTERS, 20 May 2018, www.reuters.com/article/us-usa-trade-mnuchin/u-s-china-putting-trade-war-on-hold-treasurys-mnuchin-says-idUSKCN1IL0JG.

97. *Trade War Fears.*

it would impose 25% Section 301 tariffs, with implementation shortly thereafter.[98] The U.S. made clear the target list would be merchandise "containing industrially significant technology, including those related to the '*Made in China 2025*'
program."[99] The U.S. also announced that on 30 June, it would publish new restrictions on Chinese FDI, again with implementation shortly thereafter. And, it would
pursue at the WTO its *TRIPs Agreement* claims against China.

Notably, the U.S. called on China not only to rectify its IP practices, and correct
the bilateral trade imbalance, but also indicated it wanted "tariffs and taxes between
the two countries be reciprocal in nature and value."[100] The President occasionally
had decried the difference between America's applied MFN car tariff of 2.5% and
China's of 25%. That difference, of course, reflected decades of post-Second World
War MTNs in which the U.S. had participated prior to the Chinese WTO accession,
and China's December 2001 *Accession Protocol*. Following the early GATT rounds,
MTN tariff concessions were made on the basis of reciprocity, but not on a product-
by-product approach. Rather, they reflected an overall balance of concessions—for
example, a cut of X% on product A against a cut of Y% on product B, evaluated
across thousands of products. Did the U.S. request for tariff reciprocity signal a mis-
understanding of the MTN negotiating process? Or, was the request a negotiating
strategy to secure enhanced access for American cars in the Chinese market?

China was both "surprised and unsurprised."[101] It thought the *Joint Communiqué* bode well, and said the Trump Administration announcement "obviously [was]
contrary to the consensus reached between the two sides in Washington not long
ago." Chinese Foreign Ministry Spokeswoman Hua Chunying pointed out, "Every
flip-flop in international relations simply depletes a country's credibility," and a
China *Global Times* editorial said, "The world faces an extremely mercurial White
House administration," adding "The Chinese government has the ability and wisdom to handle such situations."[102] That "ability and wisdom" translated to a threat

---

98. *See* The White House, *Statement on Steps to Protect Domestic Technology and Intellectual Property from China's Discriminatory and Burdensome Trade Practices*, 29 May 2018, www
.whitehouse.gov/briefings-statements/statement-steps-protect-domestic-technology-intellectual
-property-chinas-discriminatory-burdensome-trade-practices/. [Hereinafter, *Statement on Steps*.]
The comments, as well as transcripts of the public hearings, are posted at Office of the United
States Trade Representative, *Notice of Determination and Request for Public Comment Concerning
Proposed Determination of Action Pursuant to Section 301*, USTR-2018-0005, www.regulations.gov
/docket?D=USTR-2018-0005.

99. *Statement on Steps*, ¶ 3.

100. *Statement on Steps*.

101. *Quoted in Trump's China Tariffs Could Be Imposed in June*, BBC News, 29 May 2018, http://
www.bbc.com/news/business-44294131.

102. *Quoted in China Slams Trump's "Flip-Flop" on Tariffs as Trade Spat Worsens*, 35 International Trade Reporter (BNA) 764 (7 June 2018).

of "'resolute and forceful' measures to protect its interests if Washington insists upon acting in an 'arbitrary and reckless manner.'"[103]

- **June 2018 White House** *Report*

The Trump Administration fired back with a scathing 35-page testament to China's misdeeds, excerpted below.

White House Office of Trade and Manufacturing,

*How China's Economic Aggression Threatens the Technologies
and Intellectual Property of the United States and World,*
1–2, 6, 12–14, 16, 20 (June 2018)[104]

I. China's Strategies of Economic Aggression

The Chinese government is implementing a comprehensive, long-term industrial strategy to ensure its global dominance. . . . Beijing's ultimate goal is for domestic companies to replace foreign companies as designers and manufacturers of key technology and products first at home, then abroad.

U.S.-China Economic and Security Review Commission

The People's Republic of China (China) has experienced rapid economic growth to become the world's second largest economy while modernizing its industrial base and moving up the global value chain. However, much of this growth has been achieved in significant part through aggressive acts, policies, and practices that fall outside of global norms and rules (collectively, "economic aggression"). Given the size of China's economy and the extent of its market-distorting policies, China's economic aggression now threatens not only the U.S. economy but also the global economy as a whole.

In some respects, China has been transparent about its aggressive acts, policies, and practices. They are revealed in Chinese government documents, through behaviors of Chinese State actors, and from reports produced by business organizations, think tanks, and government agencies. Four categories of such economic aggression which are <u>outside</u> the scope of this *Report* include:

(1) ***Protect China's Home Market from Imports and Competition:***

This category features high tariffs, non-tariff barriers, and other regulatory hurdles.

---

103. *Quoted in* Michael Martina & Ben Blanchard, *China Vows to Protect its Interests From "Reckless" U.S. Trade Threats*, Reuters, 29 May 2018, www.reuters.com/article/us-usa-trade-china /china-vows-to-protect-its-interests-from-reckless-u-s-trade-threats-idUSKCN1IU1GQ.

104. Footnotes omitted; emphases original; minor formatting changes. The *Report*, released on 20 June, contained 163 footnotes, and to some degree was a synopsis of findings from sources around the world. Though it offered no policy recommendations, doubtless its purpose was to marshal support for the Section 301 action.

(2) *Expand China's Share of Global Markets:*

Industrial policy tools include financial support to boost exports and the consolidation of State-Owned Enterprises into "national champions" that can compete with foreign companies in both the domestic and global markets. Chinese enterprises also benefit from preferential policies that lead to subsidized overcapacity in China's domestic market, which then depresses world prices and pushes foreign rivals out of the global market.

(3) *Secure and Control Core Natural Resources Globally:*

China uses a predatory "debt trap" model of economic development and finance that proffers substantial financing to developing countries in exchange for an encumbrance on their natural resources and access to markets. These resources range from bauxite, copper, and nickel to rarer commodities such as beryllium, titanium, and rare earth minerals. This predatory model has been particularly effective in countries characterized by weak rule of law and authoritarian regimes.

(4) *Dominate Traditional Manufacturing Industries:*

China has already achieved a leading position in many traditional manufacturing industries. It has done so in part through preferential loans and below-market utility rates as well as lax and weakly enforced environmental and health and safety standards. As the European Chamber of Commerce has documented: "For a generation, China has been the factory of the world." By 2015, China already accounted for 28 percent of global auto production, 41 percent of global ship production, more than 50 percent of global refrigerator production, more than 60 percent of global production of color TV sets, and more than 80 percent of global production of air conditioners and computers.

In addition, China pursues two categories of economic aggression that are <u>the focus of this *Report*</u>. These include:

(5) *Acquire Key Technologies and Intellectual Property From Other Countries, Including the United States*

(6) *Capture the Emerging High-Technology Industries That Will Drive Future Economic Growth and Many Advancements in the Defense Industry*

This *Report* will document the major acts, policies, and practices of Chinese industrial policy used to implement these two strategies. Through such implementation, the Chinese State seeks to access the crown jewels of American technology and intellectual property. . . .

II. How China Seeks to Acquire Technologies and Intellectual Property and Capture Industries of the Future

Chinese industrial policy seeks to "introduce, digest, absorb, and re-innovate" technologies and . . . IP from around the world. This policy is carried out through:

(A) State-sponsored IP theft through physical theft, cyber-enabled espionage and theft, evasion of U.S. export control laws, . . . counterfeiting and piracy [, and reverse engineering];

. . .

(B) coercive and intrusive regulatory gambits to force technology transfer from foreign companies, typically in exchange for limited access to the Chinese market;

. . .

[China uses 15 specific instruments of coercion:]

(1) foreign ownership restrictions such as forced joint ventures and partnerships that explicitly or tacitly require or facilitate technology transfers; (2) adverse administrative approvals and licensing processes; (3) discriminatory patent and other IP rights restrictions; (4) security reviews; (5) secure and controllable technology standards; (6) data localization; (7) burdensome and intrusive testing; (8) discriminatory catalogues and lists; (9) government procurement restrictions; (10) imposition of indigenous technology standards that deviate significantly from international norms and that may provide backdoor Chinese access to source codes; (11) forced research and development ("R&D localization"); (12) antimonopoly laws; (13) Expert Review Panels; (14) Chinese Communist Party Committees that influence corporate governance; and (15) placement of Chinese employees at foreign joint ventures"

(C) economic coercion through export restraints on critical raw materials and monopsony purchasing power;

. . .

[That is:]

China has a commanding share of a wide range of critical raw materials essential to the global supply chain and production of high-technology and high value-added products. For example, China is the world's dominant producer of rare earths, tungsten, and molybdenum [as well as cobalt, which is used in batteries for EVs, and super-alloys for jet engines and spacecraft, for which China accounts for about 80% of global output, and lithium]. China has used export restraints, including export quotas and export duties, to restrict access to critical raw materials. [More specifically, "China produced more than 80 percent of the world's rare-earth metals and compounds in 2017," according to U.S. Geological Survey data, and China "has about 37 percent of global reserves and supplied 78 percent of U.S. imports."[105]]

---

105. *Trump Tariff List Targets High-Tech Minerals That U.S. Needs*, 35 International Trade Reporter (BNA) 978 (19 July 2018).

China's State-Owned Enterprises have significant monopsony purchasing power in select markets, *e.g.,* aviation. China seeks to use its significant purchasing power in select markets to extract concessions from foreign sellers. Concessions may include increased localized production and the forced transfer of foreign technology. Exercising this monopsony power can strengthen the Chinese manufacturing base and supply chain, particularly in the high-technology space.

(D)   methods of information harvesting that include open source collection; placement of non-traditional information collectors at U.S. universities, national laboratories, and other centers of innovation; and talent recruitment of business, finance, science, and technology experts;

. . .

[Notably, with respect to placement:]

More than 300,000 Chinese nationals annually attend U.S. universities or find employment at U.S. national laboratories, innovation centers, incubators, and think tanks, and Chinese nationals now account for approximately one third of foreign university and college students in the United States and about 25 percent of graduate students specializing in science, technology, engineering, or math (STEM).

(E)   State-backed, technology-seeking Chinese investment.

. . .

[In particular:]

The Chinese government has institutionalized the industrial policy of inducing investment in "encouraged" high-technology sectors using the financial resources and regulatory instruments of the State. China's government has a multi-billion dollar set of State-backed funds that contribute to technology investment and uses an array of State actors to implement its strategies of acquiring foreign technologies and intellectual property.

From 2006 to 2014, much of China's outbound . . . FDI focused on the acquisition of core natural resources. However, since 2015, China has increasingly directed capital to acquire high-technology areas of the U.S. economy in particular.

In policy documents such as *Made in China 2025*, China has articulated the target list of technology sectors it seeks to dominate. Much of recent Chinese investment behavior appears consistent with this target list.

For example, since 2012, *CB Insights* has catalogued more than 600 high-technology investments in the United States worth close to $20 billion conducted by China-based investors, with artificial intelligence, augmented and virtual reality, and robotics receiving particular focus. China's biggest sovereign wealth fund, the China Investment Corporation, has used a significant fraction of the $800 billion of assets under management for a venture fund focusing on Silicon Valley.

. . .

III. Conclusion

. . .

Given the size of China's economy, the demonstrable extent of its market-distorting policies, and China's stated intent to dominate the industries of the future, China's acts, policies, and practices of economic aggression now targeting the technologies and IP of the world threaten not only the U.S. economy but also the global innovation system as a whole.

• **Section 301 and National Security**

Is there a legal problem in using Section 301 to defend national security?[106] The statutory criteria concern "unreasonable" or "discriminatory" foreign government measures that "burden" or "restrict" U.S. commerce. Pliable as these words are, is it unreasonable and discriminatory to torque them into a national security case? Is Section 232, which explicitly speaks of "national security," the correct statute to use? Or, is the U.S. left with no choice but to use Section 301 in instances when foreign government behavior does not involve imports? (Recall that Section 232 speaks of imports impairing national security, and thus might be difficult to deploy against Chinese IP misappropriation.)

These questions should be considered not only on their own merits, but also in light of the potential costs and benefits from any Section 301 action can impose on America. U.S. jobs may be lost, for example, positions contingent on exports to China, or dependent on imports from China. U.S. prices may rise, for instance, because of higher raw materials, intermediate goods, and finished products imported from China. But, manufacturing capacity may, in the long run, increase in the U.S. to supply the domestic market by "knocking out" foreign transactions on which U.S. businesses and consumers previously had relied. And, the action might work—it might bring about meaningful change in the alleged offending foreign government act, policy, or practice.

VIII. More Retaliation and Counter-Retaliation

• **Four Waves**

On 15 June 2018, the Section 301 battle front in a broad Sino-American Trade War opened in earnest. President Donald J. Trump triggered a 25% tariff (on top

---

106. *See* John Harney & Jonathan Stearns, *Trump Faults China's Economic Policy as Threat to U.S. Security*, BLOOMBERG, 20 June 2018, www.bloomberg.com/news/articles/2018-06-20/trump-faults-china-s-economic-policy-as-threat-to-u-s-security.

of the applicable MFN rate, and any AD-CVD remedy) on $50 billion worth of Chinese imports.[107] In the language of Section 301, the U.S. argued certain Chinese "acts" (specifically, laws), "policies," and "practices" were "unreasonable" or "discriminatory" and harmed U.S. IPRs and technology. In the language of the President, the Section 301 action was justified as "essential to preventing further unfair transfers of American technology and intellectual property to China, which will protect American jobs."[108]

Free-trade oriented Republicans in Congress, and politicians from farm states fearing Chinese counter-retaliation, disagreed with the use of tariffs to solve these issues. Democrats offered strong support for the President. For instance, Senator Charles Schumer (New York), intoned: "China is our real trade enemy, and their theft of intellectual property and their refusal to let our companies compete fairly threatens millions of future American jobs."[109]

Specifically, the key features of the American Section 301 action were as follows:

(1) The U.S. trimmed its April list of 1,333 potential targets, focusing on Chinese imports that were strategically important to China for its *Made in 2025* industrial policy, that is, "goods from China that contain industrially significant technologies," including "goods related to China's *Made in China 2025* strategic plan to dominate the emerging high-technology industries that will drive future economic growth for China, but hurt economic growth for the United States and many other countries."[110]

---

107. *See* The White House, *Statement by the President Regarding Trade with China*, 15 June 2018, www.whitehouse.gov/briefings-statements/statement-president-regarding-trade-china/ [hereinafter, *15 June 2018 Presidential Statement*]; Office of the United States Trade Representative, *USTR Issues Tariffs on Chinese Products in Response to Unfair Trade Practices*, 15 June 2018, https://ustr .gov/about-us/policy-offices/press-office/press-releases/2018/june/ustr-issues-tariffs-chinese -products; Office of the United States Trade Representative, Docket Number USTR-2018-0018, *Notice of Action and Request for Public Comment Concerning Proposed Determination of Action Pursuant to Section 301: China's Acts, Policies, and Practices Related to Technology Transfer, Intellectual Property, and Innovation*, https://ustr.gov/sites/default/files/enforcement/301Investigations /301FRN.pdf, 83 Federal Register number 119, 28710-28756 (20 June 2018); David Lawder & Ben Blanchard, *Trump Sets $50 Billion in China Tariffs with Beijing Ready to Strike Back*, REUTERS, 15 June 2018, www.reuters.com/article/us-usa-trade-china-ministry/trump-sets-50-billion-in-china -tariffs-with-beijing-ready-to-strike-back-idUSKBN1JB0KC [hereinafter, *Trump Sets $50 Billion*]; *Trump Puts 25% Tariff on Chinese Goods*, BBC NEWS, 15 June 2018, www.bbc.com/news/business -44498484 [hereinafter, *Trump Puts 25% Tariff*].

108. *Quoted in Trump Puts 25% Tariff.*

109. *Quoted in Trump Puts 25% Tariff.*

110. *15 June 2018 Presidential Statement.* Likewise, USTR Ambassador Robert Lighthizer explained that the list "focuses on products from industrial sectors that contribute to or benefit from the '*Made in China 2025*' industrial policy, which include industries such as aerospace, information and communications technology, robotics, industrial machinery, new materials and automobiles." *Quoted in* Vicki Needham & Max Greenwood, *Trump Announces Tariffs on $50 Billion in Chinese Goods*, THE HILL, 15 June 2018, http://thehill.com/homenews/administration/392421 -trump-announces-tariffs-on-50-billion-in-chinese-goods?userid=5271.

(2) The new list contained 1,102 HTSUS product categories, at the 8-digit classification level, dropped 515 items, and included 285 new items such as semiconductor industry products. The new list sought to minimize damage to American consumers by, for example, deleting goods that had been on the draft list, such as aluminum and steel pipe, catheters and needles, golf carts, monitors, pharmaceutical goods (under the 4-digit HTSUS categories of 3002–3004), smart cards, TVs, syringes, and weapons. (Cell phones also were not subject to retaliation, nor did they appear on the Wave Three list, but they fell under Wave Four, discussed below.) That said, the list was not entirely free of blows to consumers:

> . . . [O]f the 1,102 products targeted by the United States Trade Representative office, initially just 1 percent that will have a 25 percent tariff slapped on them in stages from July 6 are "consumer goods."

> . . . [M]ost of the targeted products are classified as either "capital goods" or "intermediate items."

> The idea is to force companies to shift their supply chains away from China or boost efficiencies to make up any cost differences. But ultimately, that would still hurt U.S. consumers. . . .

> "From our perspective, it kind of doesn't matter where in the supply chain you impose the tariff, because it's ultimately going to be a tax on Americans," said Josh Kallmer, senior vice president for global policy at the Information Technology Industries Council, which represents major tech firms.

> . . .

> The industry classifications throw up some perhaps unexpected groupings, indicating what economists say is the arbitrary impact of tariffs.

> For instance, the Nest thermostat, assembled in China and sold in the United States by Alphabet Inc's . . . Google for around $250, is classified in the "capital goods category" of imports and will be subject to the tariffs.

Note the U.S. excluded from Section 301 tariffs goods made in Hong Kong or Macau (which are separate customs territories from the Mainland). *See* U.S. Customs and Border Protection, Section 301 Frequently Asked Questions, www.cbp.gov/print/214575. The tariffs apply based on the country of origin, not the country of export, hence ROOs to decide whether merchandise is "Made in China" were critical to the implementation of the Section 301 action. For example, CBP explained in the FAQ that the tariffs are imposed on a "set," under GRI 3(b), if the item in the set that imparts to the set its "essential character" is Made in China. Likewise, in some instances (as on 2 November 2018, in two New York rulings, NY N301371 and NY N301202) CBP applied a "substantial transformation" test to determine if merchandise is "made in China."

Imports of Chinese-made vaping devices to the tune of $300 million a year will be hit, as will $16 million of electronics effects units, used by rock bands to distort guitar sounds.

. . . [B]oth of these fall into a $1.1 billion U.S. category of miscellaneous electrical equipment proposed for a second, $16 billion round of tariffs.[111]

In other words, product classifications can be over-inclusive, causing *bona fide* consumer items to be hit with tariffs. And, regardless of the precision or lack thereof of the classifications, the long run impact of imposing a tariff at any stage in a cross-border supply chain is adverse to the consumer, insofar as that tariff is incorporated into the cost of finished merchandise and thereby passed on to retail customers.

(3) The U.S. divided the 1,102 targets into two categories: an initial group of 818 product groups, representing $34 billion in annual trade;[112] and a second group of 284 proposed items amounting to $16 billion worth of Chinese goods.[113] (Following public comments, the U.S. excluded five products from the second group, trimming that total to 279 items.[114])

(4) Tariffs in the first group took effect on 6 July. Goods in this group included agricultural machinery, aircraft, aircraft tires, certain consumer electronics items (*e.g.*, battery packs, capacitors, disk drives, Internet-connected LED lights and disk drives), certain printed circuit assemblies, commercial dishwashers, control panels, electric motors, hydraulic and pneumatic engines, lasers, marine items, motor vehicles, ships, switches, and turbines.

(5) Tariffs in the second group took effect on 23 August. Goods in the second group included control panels, e-cigarettes, e-scooters, engines and motors, locomotives, machines, motorcycles, plastics, plastic sheets and tubes, speedometers, and vaporizers. However, the U.S. kept China guessing as to what items in the second group it would hit, and when, not only

---

111. *Surprises Lurk.* See also Selina Wang, *The Trade War Is Already Hurting American Gadget Makers*, 35 International Trade Reporter (BNA) 108 (26 July 2018 (discussing the Section 301 lists). [Hereinafter, *The Trade War.*]

112. The USTR published these 818 items as "List 1," https://ustr.gov/sites/default/files /enforcement/301Investigations/List%201.pdf. Note that a new 8-digit Sub-Heading in Chapter 99 was created for this purpose (9903.88.01).

113. The USTR published these 284 items as "List 2," https://ustr.gov/sites/default/files /enforcement/301Investigations/List%202.pdf;

114. *See* Office of the United States Trade Representative, *USTR Finalizes Second Tranche of Tariffs on Chinese Products in Response to China's Unfair Trade Practices*, 7 August 2018, https:// ustr.gov/about-us/policy-offices/press-office/press-releases/2018/august/ustr-finalizes-second -tranche. The items dropped from the list included alginic acid (HTS 3913.10.00), certain containers (8609.00.00), and floating docks (8905.90.10). The itemized list of the 279 items, presented at the 8-digit HTS level, is entitled "Second Tranche," available at https://ustr.gov/sites/default/files /enforcement/301Investigations/Final%20Second%20Tranche.pdf.

to allow for public comment, but also perhaps as a strategy to leverage pressure on China to settle the dispute.

(6) The 1,102 targets fell into six sectors, and Chinese exports to the U.S. (as of 2017) were valued at $46.2 billion: Aircraft and vehicles (worth $2.7 billion); base metals ($1.7 billion); chemicals ($0.7 billion); electrical equipment, machinery, and mechanical appliances ($34.2 billion); miscellaneous ($6.8 billion); and plastics and rubber ($0.05 billion).

(7) The U.S. said importers could apply for product exclusions.[115] For example, a company reliant on a certain Chinese product subject to retaliation could ask that the item not be subject to the 25% retaliation.

---

115. *See* Office of the United States Trade Representative, Docket Number USTR-2018-0025, Procedures to Consider Requests for Exclusion of Particular Products from the Determination of Action Pursuant to Section 301: China's Acts, Policies, and Practices Related to Technology Transfer, Intellectual Property, and Innovation, 9 July 2018, https://ustr.gov/sites/default/files /enforcement/301Investigations/FRN%20exclusion%20process.pdf; Office of the United States Trade Representative, Procedures To Consider Requests for Exclusion of Particular Products From the Determination of Action Pursuant to Section 301: China's Acts, Policies, and Practices Related to Technology Transfer, Intellectual Property, and Innovation, 83 Federal Register number 133, 32181-32184 (11 July 2018); United States Trade Representative, USTR Releases Product Exclusion Process for Chinese Products Subject to Section 301 Tariffs, 9 July 2018, https://ustr.gov/about-us /policy-offices/press-office/press-releases/2018/july/ustr-releases-product-exclusion.

The Section 301 action provoked thousands of requests for product exclusions, that is, requests to be left off a list of products against which the U.S. sought retaliation, and/or for product exemptions, that is, requests to be exempted from Section 301 tariffs once a list was finalized. (The term "exclusion" typically was used to cover both processes.) As of 12 October 2018, the USTR reported it had received over 2,700 such requests with respect to the Wave One tariffs, denied 543 of them. With the large and growing backlog, a bipartisan group of almost 170 members of Congress called on the USTR to develop a streamlined process for Waves One and Two lists, and declare a process for the Wave Three list. *See* Mark Niquette, *U.S. Lawmakers Urge Exclusion Process for Latest Trump Tariffs*, 35 International Trade Reporter (BNA) 1351 (18 October 2018). By 8 November 2018, the USTR had reviewed 9,928 product exclusion requests with respect to the Wave One tariffs, denied 816 of them, and granted none. By 7 December, the USTR had granted none of the 11,675 requests, and denied nearly 1,500 of them. *See* Rossella Brevetti & Jasmine Ye Han, *Corporate America Goes 0-for-1,500 in Bid to Ease China Tariffs (2)*, 35 International Trade Reporter (BNA) 1611 (13 December 2018).

One high-profile exclusion request came from GM, which sought to exclude its Envision SUV from the list of merchandise subject to the 25% tariff. This model, which sells in the U.S. for $35,000, is assembled only in China, and accounts for 19% of GM's U.S. sales (in 2017, when it sold 41,000 Envisions in the U.S., and 200,000 in China). The tariff would make it unaffordable for many American car shoppers. *See* Paul Lienert & David Shepardson, *GM Seeks to Exclude China-Made Buick SUV From Tariff, Reuters,* 2 August 2018, www.reuters.com/article/us-usa-trade-gm /gm-seeks-to-exclude-china-made-buick-suv-from-tariff-idUSKBN1KN313. Tesla made a similar argument for the electronic brain it manufactures in China and installs in its EVs in its California facility. *See* David Shephardson, *Tesla Urges Tariff Exemption for Chinese-Made Car Computer "Brain,"* REUTERS, 4 January 2019, www.reuters.com/article/us-autos-tariffs-tesla/tesla-urges -tariff-exemption-for-chinese-made-car-computer-brain-idUSKCN1OZ00C. These computers were hit by a 25% Section 301 tariff, which drove up the costs, and undermined the profitability of, Tesla's new Model 3 luxury sedan. Tesla said no alternative manufacturer could make the brain with the necessary technical specifications, at least not without a delay of 18 months.

Exclusion requests were due on 9 October 2018, which gave companies three months, as the USTR published its procedure for applying for exclusions on 9 July. Exclusions for a product would last for one year, and (unlike the Section 232 steel and aluminum exclusions, which were product-by-product and importer-by-importer) would cover all importers of that product. That is, a particular exclusion applies to all imports of the product, regardless of whether the importer of the shipment of that product filed the request for the exclusion. While this difference allowed importers to free ride on the successful application of any one of them, it also reduced the enormous burden the DOC had put upon itself in

---

Finally, on 28 December 2018, the USTR granted a few requests—31 in total—to the Section 301 tariffs, specifically to the Wave One duties that had been in effect since 6 July on 818 8-digit HTSUS Sub-Heading categories. The relief from the 25% applied retroactively to 6 July, and prospectively for one year from the date of the Federal Register notice (*i.e.*, to 28 December 2019), to the following product categories:

(1) The USTR gave complete exemptions to seven product categories at the 10-digit HTSUS level, namely, 8412.21.0075, 8418.69.0120, 8480.71.8045, 8482.10.5044, 8482.10.5048, 8482.10.5052, and 8525.60.1010. The affected merchandise was certain hydraulic engines, drinking water coolers, injection molds for plastics, ball bearings, and citizens band (CB) radios.

(2) The USTR gave exclusions to 24 types of products based on new, unique product-specific descriptions. The types included products certain outboard engines, belt conveyors, parts of papermaking machines, radiation therapy systems, and thermostats

See Office of the United States Trade Representative, *Notice of Product Exclusions: China's Acts, Policies, and Practices Related to Technology Transfer, Intellectual Property, and Innovation*, 83 Federal Register 67463-67468 (28 December 2018), www.govinfo.gov/content/pkg/FR-2018-12-28/pdf/2018-28277.pdf.

Notwithstanding the aforementioned exclusions the USTR granted to the 25% Wave One tariffs, the USTR made clear it would not grant any exclusions to the Wave Three duties of 10% on $200 billion worth of Chinese imports, unless Sino-American negotiations to end the Trade War failed, and the President ordered an increase in those duties to 25%. The announcement came via an 11 January 2019 letter from the USTR to an 18 October 2018 letter inquiry from 11 Democratic Senators. *See* Letter from Robert E. Lighthizer, The United States Trade Representative, to The Honorable Tim Kaine, United States Senate, 11 January 2019, www.crowell.com/files/20190111-Lighthizer-Letter-to-Sen-Tim-Kaine.pdf, and Letter from Senator Tim Kaine et al., to The Honorable Robert Lighthizer, United States Trade Representative, 18 October 2018, www.kaine.senate.gov/imo/media/doc/Kaine%20Tariff%20Decision%20Letter%2010.18.18.pdf.

Note that a request to exclude a product from a retaliation list is done based on the product description itself. If that request is denied, and a product is listed, then a request for an exemption is done on the basis of the HTSUS code, typically at the 8- or 10-digit level. That is partly because CBP imposes tariffs based on such codes, so its doing so ideally should be a mechanical process. In contrast, the decision about leaving a product off a retaliation list does not involve tariff imposition, and (to some degree) is a policy choice about products to be covered, or not, by the retaliation. Note, too, a single HTS code, even at the 8- or 10-digit level, can include multiple products. Note, also, that unlike steel and aluminum goods subject to the Section 232 action brought by the Trump Administration, products subject to the Section 301 tariffs were eligible for duty drawback when those products are exported. Finally, note that reclassification of a product (*i.e.*, switching HTS Sub-Headings), either to exclude it from a list or exempt it from retaliation, can raise suspicions at CBP of duty evasion, and render the importer liable to civil and criminal penalties.

processing exclusions in the Section 232 cases, and on CBP in administering them.

The USTR mandated that exclusion requests had to identify the product by its 10-digit HTSUS classification (not by actual or principal use, name of producer-exporter or importer, trade name, or ultimate purchaser), with a separate request for each product exclusion sought. The USTR also signalled it would decide on the applications based on whether the (a) product is available only from China, or from the U.S. or third countries, and whether substitutes may be found in the U.S. or third countries, (b) strategically important or related to the *Made in China 2025* industrial policy, and (c) a 25% tariff would impose severe economic harm to the applicant or other U.S. interests.

Under these criteria, exclusion grants proved hard to obtain. (Similar criteria applied to a request for an exemption from the tariffs, if a product was subject to retaliation.) If interests in the U.S., such as domestic producers of a like or directly competitive product, opposed the request, then the probability of a grant dimmed. In any event, an approved exclusion request was for one year, not permanent.

(8) The U.S. pledged an additional $100 billion worth of tariffs on Chinese goods, and even threatened to hit as much as $500 billion worth of Chinese merchandise, if China did not change its offending IP practices, and/ or "if China engages in retaliatory measures, such as imposing new tariffs on United States goods, services, or agricultural products; raising non-tariff barriers or taking punitive actions against American exporters or American companies operating in China."[116]

(9) The President himself re-issued the threat on 20 July, saying he was "ready to go" with tariffs on all $500 billion worth of Chinese imports into the U.S., adding: "I'm not doing this for politics. I'm doing this to do the right thing for our country." "We are being taken advantage of and I don't like it."[117]

Six days later, the President's Ambassador to the WTO, the Deputy USTR, Dennis Shea, told WTO Members castigated China as "the most protectionist, mercantilist economy in the world," and said "China's size magnifies the harm caused by its state-led, mercantilist approach to trade and investment, and this harm is growing every day and can no longer be

---

116. *Trump Sets $50 Billion* (*quoting* President Trump).

117. *Quoted in* Terrence Dopp, *Trump Says He's Ready to Impose Tariffs on All China Goods*, 35 International Trade Reporter (BNA) 109 (26 July 2018). *See also Trump Ready to Tax "All" Chinese Imports*, BBC News, 20 July 2018, www.bbc.co.uk/news/business-44898629 (*quoting* the President: "I'm ready to go to 500.").

tolerated."[118] The same day, 26 July, the USTR, Ambassador Robert Lighthizer, had a candid interchange in his Senate testimony. The USTR was asked by Senator Brian Schatz (Democrat-Hawaii):

> How do we have leverage in a situation where they [China] have unending patience and we have almost none? You don't pick stupid fights.[119]

Ambassador Lighthizer replied:

> If your conclusion is that China taking over all of our technology and the future of our children is a stupid fight, then you're right, we should capitulate. My view is that's how we got where we are.[120]

(10) All items subject to the 25% tariffs imported into an FTZ had to classified as PF status, except for items qualifying for domestic status (in effect, U.S.-origin good).

(11) The U.S. promised Chinese FDI restrictions, tougher export controls, and designation of certain Chinese persons as SDNs, which it announced on 30 June.[121] Specifically, CFIUS, the inter-agency panel led by the Department of the Treasury that advises the President on whether to block acquisitions of a U.S. business by a foreign entity, was modernized and strengthened under new legislation, the *Foreign Investment Risk Review Modernization Act*. Congress passed *FIRRMA* on 1 August 2018, as part of the *National Defense Authorization Act* for 2019, and on 13 August the President signed the *NDAA*.

(12) *FIRRMA* vastly broadened the scope of transactions CFIUS may review—its subject matter jurisdiction—with the key term, "covered transactions." No longer was CFIUS limited to reviewing one type of transaction, namely: (i) any merger, acquisition, or takeover that could result in control of a U.S. business. With *FIRRMA*, CFIUS could review four additional ones types of FDI: (ii) real estate transactions, *i.e.*, purchase or leases of

---

118. *Quoted in* Bryce Baschuk, *China Rails Against U.S. Trade Attacks as New Tariffs Loom (2)*, 35 International Trade Reporter (BNA) 1037 (2 August 2018).

119. *Quoted in* Andrew Mayeda, Jenny Leonard & Mark Niquette, *U.S. Downplays Hopes for China Deal Amid EU, NAFTA Progress*, 35 International Trade Reporter (BNA) 1048 (2 August 2018). [Hereinafter, *U.S. Downplays*.]

120. *Quoted in U.S. Downplays*.

121. *See* David Lawder & Doina Chiacu, *Trump to Use U.S. Security Review Panel to Curb China Tech Investments*, Reuters, 27 June 2018, www.reuters.com/article/us-usa-trade-china/trump -administration-to-use-review-panel-to-curb-china-tech-investments-idUSKBN1JN1K0.

The Trump Administration rejected a stronger approach, namely, outright restrictions on Chinese FDI under broad statutory sanctions authority such as the *IEEPA*, in part because companies are familiar with CFIUS review, whereas invoking the *IEEPA* might have deterred inbound FDI. *See id.*; David Lawder, *Trump Officials Send Mixed Signals on China Investment Curbs, Markets Sink*, Reuters, 25 June 2018, Reuters, www.reuters.com/article/us-usa-trade-china/trump-officials -send-mixed-signals-on-china-investment-curbs-markets-sink-idUSKBN1JL33J.

land near any U.S. military installation or sensitive location, or of any air, land, or sea port); (iii) non-controlling investments, *i.e.*, any investment in "critical infrastructure," "critical technology," which includes "emerging and foundational technologies," or "sensitive personal data" of U.S. citizens, even if the investment does not result in a foreigner holding a controlling interest in the target asset; (iv) any change in the rights a foreign investor has in a U.S. business that could result in control of that business, or in a non-controlling investment covered under category (iii); and (v) any transaction intended to evade or circumvent a CFIUS review.[122]

The third category is particularly noteworthy. Under it, CFIUS may check a proposed Chinese acquisition of a U.S. company with sensitive (that is, industrially significant) technology or infrastructure. Likewise, CFIUS may consider whether a potential deal would give a Chinese acquirer access to material non-public information, or personal data of Americans. And, under category (iii), CFIUS may review a deal involving any firm in which Chinese interests have a 25% or more interest, and advise the President to block the Chinese acquirer from buying such a company, and from transferring a minority interest in such companies to a Chinese entity.[123]

To be sure, *FIRRMA* does not mention "China" or "Chinese," and thus covers all FDI sources, but given the pervasive Congressional concern about the *Made in China 2025* industrial policy, along with reports about

---

122. *FIRRMA* also included complementary procedural changes to facilitate CFIUS review of potential FDI transactions. For example, it established expedited notification, whereby a party may submit a short *Declaration* form of five or less pages, and obtain a response from CFIUS within 30 days. The legislation also gave CFIUS more time to conduct its study, extending the initial review period from 30 to 45 days, leaving the investigation phase at 45 days, but allowing CFIUS in "extraordinary circumstances" to extend that phase for another 15 days. Obviously, the longer CFIUS takes to review a transaction, the greater the uncertainty, and thus the greater the disincentive, for a foreign acquirer to "stay in the deal." And, any challenge to a CFIUS decisions must be made to the U.S. Court of Appeals for the District of Columbia Circuit. *See* Venable LLP, Lindsay B. Meyer, Ashley W. Craig, Alexander W. Koff, Jeffrey G. Weiss, Neha Dhindsa & Devin A. Sefton, International Trade Alert, *Significant Expansive Changes to CFIUS and Export Controls Approved by Congress*, 2 August 2018, www.venable.com/significant-expansive-changes-to-cfius-and-export-controls-approved-by-congress-08-02-2018/.

Not surprisingly, the broadened scope of the term "covered transactions" meant that CFIUS review encompassed many of the same sectors the CCP promoted in its Made in China 2025 industrial policy, including aerospace, biopharmaceuticals and high-performance medical equipment, electricity equipment, ICT, new materials, ocean engineering and high-tech ships. *See* Crowell & Moring, Robert Holleyman, Alan Gourley, Addie Cliffe, Evan Yu, & Jing Jing Zhang, THIS MONTH IN INTERNATIONAL TRADE—OCTOBER 2018, *Treasury CFIUS Pilot Program Overlaps with Made in China 2025 Sectors*, 8 November 2018, www.crowell.com/NewsEvents/AlertsNewsletters/all/Treasury-CFIUS-Pilot-Program-Overlaps-with-Made-in-China-2025-Sectors.

123. *See* Kevin Yao & Ben Blanchard, *China to Pursue More Trade with France, EU Raises "Difficult Issues,"* REUTERS, 24 June 2018, www.reuters.com/article/us-china-eu/china-eu-agree-to-fight-protectionism-but-eu-repeats-complaints-idUSKBN1JL0B8.

the CCP's pervasive security apparatus, the legislative intent is clear enough.[124]

(13) As to "emerging and foundational technologies," the *Export Controls Act of 2018*, a different part of the *NDAA*, added this term (as it did not previously exist in the USML or CCL). The *ECA* charged DOC (working collaboratively with other agencies) to identify what technologies are "emerging and foundational" and "essential to the national security of the United States." DOC establishes controls for the export of such technology, applying criteria such as the potential end use and end users of that technology, and export destination of the technology. Shipment of such technology without a license to any country subject to an embargo is illegal. Because China is subject to an arms embargo, shipment would require a license. In effect, the *ECA* obliges DOC to identify early-stage technology that implicate American national security, and thereby needs to be protected from falling into unwanted hands that might develop it and use it to threaten the U.S. The DOC's work on defining such technology, and enforcing export controls on it, complements reviews by CFIUS under category (iii) through its delineations of protected technology.

Predictably, China counter-retaliated against the sweeping American action.

China struck back with its own 25% tariff (also on top of its applied MFN rates, and any AD-CVD remedies, and also effective 6 July). That, of course, increased the prospect the U.S. would escalate the battle with further tariffs on more imports (which it did, as discussed below). MOFCOM accused the Trump Administration of being "fickle," "provoking a trade war," and "not only damaging bilateral interests, but also undermining the world trade order."[125]

---

124. *See U.S. Pushes Back on Foreign Takeover Deals*, BBC News, 14 August 2018, www.bbc.co .uk/news/business-45177254; Cate Cadell, *From Laboratory in Far West, China's Surveillance States Spreads Widely*, Reuters, 14 August 2018, www.reuters.com/article/us-china-monitoring-insight /from-laboratory-in-far-west-chinas-surveillance-state-spreads-quietly-idUSKBN1KZ0R3.

125. *Quoted in Trump Announces Tariffs*. Chinese State media lambasted the Trump Administration for behaving like a "gang of hoodlums." *See* Michael Martina & David Lawder, *China Blames U.S. for "Largest Scale Trade War" as Tariffs Kick In*, Reuters, 5 July 2018, www.reuters.com /article/us-usa-trade-china/china-state-media-slams-trumps-gang-of-hoodlums-as-tariffs-loom -idUSKBN1JW07L.

Serious as the matter was, the initial round of retaliation imposed by the U.S. affected just 0.1% of global GDP, and 0.6% of global trade. *See China and Russia Hit Back at Trump Tariffs*, BBC News, 6 July 2018, www.bbc.com/news/business-44742714. Yet, the prospect not only of escalation by both sides, but also by third countries, loomed. Indeed, following the U.S. levies, Russia imposed additional duties of 25%-40% on "a range of products imported from the U.S. that can be replaced by locally made equivalents," including fiber optics, mining tools, oil and gas industry items, and road building equipment. *Id.* Of course, Russia was not a target of the Section 301 case, but it took the opportunity of that case to boost protections in association with the Section 232 steel and aluminum cases, in which its merchandise was affected. *See* Olga Tanas, *Russia Slaps Import Duties on Some U.S. Goods in Tariffs Fight*, 35 International Trade Reporter 915 (12 July 2018).

China selected 659 categories of U.S. exports. These exports were drawn from a list China had previously compiled in June 2018, and thus covered a range of American agricultural items, cars, and marine products (including roughly 300 parts used to make boats). These goods fell into eight sectors, and the value of American exports (as of 2017) to China of the products summed to $49.8 billion: aircraft and vehicles ($27.6 billion); animals and animal products ($0.03 billion); chemicals ($2.1 billion); food (such as fruit, meat, nuts, and soybeans), beverages, and tobacco ($0.3 billion); mineral fuels ($1.7 billion); plastics and rubber ($3.5 billion); T&A ($1 billion); and vegetables ($13.7 billion). Cotton, too, was included.[126] Though MOFCOM said its measures were of the "same scale and the same strength" as America's, China's response appeared to be asymmetric—hitting about $50 billion of U.S. goods as against the first category of $34 billion the U.S. targeted.[127] China applied its counter-retaliation on 545 of the categories on 6 July, to coincide with America's levies.[128] With respect to 128 categories, China added to the counter-retaliatory duties it already was imposing (*e.g.*, 15% on fruits and nuts, and 25% on pork) in response to America's Section 232 steel and aluminum tariffs (discussed in a separate Chapter). For such items, the levies were stiff indeed (*e.g.*, a cumulative tariff of 71% on American pork).[129]

---

126. *See China Says U.S. Farmers.*

127. *Quoted in U.S. and China Announce.*

128. *See* Doina Chiacu, Edward Taylor & Yawen Chen, *German Carmakers Join American Farmers on Front Line of U.S.-China Trade War*, REUTERS, 20 June 2018, www.reuters.com/article /us-usa-trade-china/washingtons-capricious-trade-actions-will-hurt-u-s-workers-china-warns -idUSKBN1JH072. [Hereinafter, *German Carmakers*.]

129. There are some American agricultural exports for which just one or a handful of countries is the only market, for cultural and culinary reasons. Certain pork products and China is an example:

> Before the U.S.-China trade war, American pig processors exported nine out of every 10 pigs' feet and heads they shipped overseas to China and Hong Kong—for prices higher than they would fetch anywhere else.
>
> . . .
>
> Those parts and others that most Americans won't eat—hearts, tongues, stomachs, entrails—have a special place in Chinese culinary culture and, consequently, in the profit margins of U.S. pork exporters.
>
> . . .
>
> Exporting pig offal to China has been a money-maker because consumers there enjoy its strong flavor. Stewed pigs' feet with white beans, for instance, is a famous dish from Sichuan province, one of the country's culinary capitals.
>
> At least one product exported to China has almost zero value anywhere else: hind pigs' feet. Rear feet are nearly impossible to sell elsewhere because they have holes in them from where hogs are hung upside down in packing houses, which turns off consumers in other countries. . . .
>
> . . .
>
> China will likely have little trouble finding supplies to replace U.S. pig offal. . . .
>
> An expansion of its domestic hog industry had already made buyers less dependent on American pork before the trade tensions.
>
> Chinese buyers could also import more from Europe. . . .
>
> . . .

Of the remaining 114 product groupings, which included asphalt, autos, bicycles, chemicals, coal, fish meal, medical equipment, paper and paper waste, propane, refined fuel and petroleum products (including aviation fuel, diesel, gasoline, and lubricating oil, but not crude oil) scrap metal (*e.g.,* copper scrap), steel, wood waste, China did not initially identify a date for implementing its counter-retaliation. Subsequently, it matched the U.S. date. So, for example, on U.S. auto imports, China slapped a 25% counter-retaliatory duty on top of its MFN rate of 15%, resulting in an overall levy of 40% on American car imports.[130] American companies, facing competition from European and Japanese exporters in China—which is the world's largest car market—could not easily pass on the 25% duty to Chinese consumers, and were compelled to raise their prices.

Effective 23 August 2018, China expanded this figure—from 114 to 333 product groupings, and imposed them on that date, to coincide with Wave Two of America's tariffs.[131] The value of trade remained the same, $16 billion, notwithstanding the increase in the number of products against which the Chinese counter-retaliated, but obviously the breadth of the counter-attack widened. Chinese tariffs covered 90% of American agricultural imports into China—about 517 different items in the first and second counter-retaliatory Waves of 6 July and 23 August.[132] The U.S. was (in 2017) the source for 19% of all of its farm imports. China bet that it could find alternative sources to plug this 19% gap, and thus at least partly shield its consumers from import-driven inflation, while pressuring American farmers into lobbying the Trump Administration to back down.

The average value of U.S. offal exports to China was about 76 cents per pound in 2017. . . .
If packers do not sell them elsewhere for human consumption, the by-products will be rendered in the United States for about 18 cents per pound [as pet food]—a decrease equating to a loss of $1.55 per hog for the volume exported to China . . . .

Tom Polansek, *Trade War Puts the Hoof into U.S. Pig Part Exports to China*, Reuters, 17 July 2018, www.reuters.com/article/us-usa-trade-china-pork/trade-war-puts-the-hoof-into-u-s-pig-part-exports-to-china-idUSKBN1K71EA.

130. *Trump Says China Agreed to Reduce Tariffs on U.S. Car Imports*, BBC News, 3 December 2018, www.bbc.com/news/business-46422320. [Hereinafter, *Trump Says China*.]

131. *See* Ryan Woo & David Lawder, *China to Slap Additional Tariffs on $16 Billion of U.S. Goods*, Reuters, 8 August 2018, www.reuters.com/article/us-usa-trade-china-tariffs/china-to-slap-additional-tariffs-on-16-billion-worth-of-u-s-goods-idUSKBN1KT1IW; *China to Hit U.S. with Tariffs on U.S. Imports Worth $16 Bn.*, BBC News, 8 August 2018, www.bbc.co.uk/news/business-45113866. Among the items noted on the expanded list against which China retaliated were busses. *See* Michael Martina & David Lawder, *U.S.-China Talks on Trade War Resume as New Tariffs Kick In*, Reuters, 22 August 2018, www.reuters.com/article/us-usa-trade-china/u-s-china-escalate-trade-war-impose-more-tariffs-idUSKCN1L809K. Thus, for example, China ceased buying crude oil from the U.S. in August; China had been buying it since September 2016, following America's decision in December 2015 to lift its ban on crude oil exports. *See* Sheela Tobben, *China Slams Brakes on U.S. Crude Oil Imports Amid Trade Tensions*, 35 International Trade Reporter (BNA) 1322 (11 October 2018) (also reporting "American oil producers, particularly those who operate in the key Permian Basin of West Texas and New Mexico, risk feeling the pain from the ongoing tensions as they increasingly look to foreign shores to market their supplies, as local demand becomes saturated.").

132. *See China Says U.S. Farmers.*

Note the similarities and distinctions in the American and Chinese sectors. There was same-sectoral retaliation in aircraft and vehicles, chemicals, and plastics and rubber. But cross-sectoral retaliation in machinery and equipment (by the U.S.) and agricultural goods (by China). What economic and political factors might explain these patterns?

• **Wave Three Difference**

Did China underestimate the resolve of the U.S. to promote not just "free," but also "fair," trade, even if that meant striking hard at Chinese merchandise in ways that would inflict some short-term damage to the U.S. economy? Arguably, yes, because America saw itself as the victim. "Rather than altering those [unfair] practices," said President Trump, China "is now threatening United States companies, workers, and farmers *who have done nothing wrong.*"[133] Indeed, the U.S. saw Chinese behavior as nothing short of predatory. At the Detroit Economic Club, Secretary of State Mike Pompeo intoned:

> Chinese leaders over these past few weeks [May–June 2018] have been claiming openness and globalization, but *it's a joke.* Let's be clear. *It's the most predatory economic government that operates against the rest of the world today.* This is a problem that's long overdue in being tackled.[134]

Thus, as Secretary of Commerce Wilbur Ross intoned, "We have to create a situation where it's more painful for them to continue their bad practices than it is to reform."[135]

To be sure, China declared cuts to tariffs on 1,449 consumer imports (effective 1 July), and it eased FDI restrictions (effective 28 July) in the agriculture, aircraft manufacturing, automotive, banking, heavy industry, insurance, power grid, and shipbuilding sectors via a new version of its "Negative List" (by which China's National Development and Reform Commission identifies limits on, and prohibitions to, FDI — the Commission trimmed the list from 63 in June 2017 to 48 in June 2018).[136] But, such pronouncements simply did not matter. Many of these moves were previously announced and/or long-anticipated. And, some of them were phased in over three to five years (*e.g.*, removing ownership limits in the auto and insurance sectors), while others were subject to caveats (*e.g.*, allowing FDI in breeding new crops excluded corn and wheat).

---

133. *Quoted in Trump Tariffs: U.S. Escalates Trade Threats to China*, BBC News, 19 June 2018, www.bbc.com/news/business-44529149.

134. *Quoted in* Nick Wadhams & Sarah Gardner, *Pompeo Calls China's Appeals for More Trade Openness a "Joke,"* Bloomberg, 18 June 2018, www.bloomberg.com/politics/articles/2018-06-18 /pompeo-calls-china-s-appeals-for-more-trade-openness-a-joke. [Hereinafter, *Pompeo Calls.*]

135. *Quoted in* Andrew Mayeda, *Ross Signals More Tariff Pain Ahead in China Trade Battle*, 35 International Trade Reporter (BNA) 1077 (9 August 2018).

136. *See* Se Young Lee & Yawen Chen, *China Further Eases Foreign Investment Curbs*, Reuters, 28 June 2018, www.reuters.com/article/us-china-economy-foreign-investment/china-unveils -further-rollbacks-in-foreign-investment-curbs-idUSKBN1JO23M; *German Carmakers.*

Rather, the "problem" was "long overdue," and went beyond market access. That was a thinly veiled criticism of previous U.S. Presidents, from Bill Clinton through Barack H. Obama, who had failed to perceive the seriousness of the "joke." The Secretary of State called Chinese IP misappropriation "an unprecedented level of larceny," and asked rhetorically:

> If you look around, there have been those who have criticized some of the tariffs. But just ask yourself, would China have allowed America to do to it what China has done to America?[137]

That "joke" would sap America's long-term economic strength, and thereby undermine its national security. So, responding to Chinese counter-retaliation (chronicled above), President Donald J. Trump vowed more Section 301 levies, of 10% on an additional $200 billion worth of Chinese goods, if China persisted in its counter-retaliation and "refuses to change its practices."[138]

That meant a total of $450–$500 billion worth of Chinese exports would be hit with American Section 301 tariffs—nearly equal to the value of all of Chinese exports to the U.S. (in 2017, which was $505 billion). The U.S. was poised to impose all four Waves of Section 301 tariffs, in terms of the value of targeted Chinese imports: (1) the initial $34 billion (effective 6 July 2018); (2) another $16 billion (effective 23 August); (3) another $200 billion (on or after 6 September); and (4) a final $200 billion.[139]

In August 2018, China recorded a record monthly bilateral trade surplus with America, due to a rush of shipments to avoid the onset of Wave Three tariffs, and to strong import demand associated with strong U.S. growth.[140] President Trump responded on 7 September by boosting the Wave Four retaliation figure, to $267 billion, saying they were "ready to go on short notice if I want."[141] When Apple, Inc., complained that Wave Four tariffs would affect all of its products (*e.g.*, iPhones and MacBooks), he tweeted:

> Apple prices may increase because of the massive Tariffs we may be impos-
> ing on China—but there is an easy solution where there would be ZERO

---

137. *Quoted in Pompeo Calls.*

138. *Trump Tariffs* (*quoting* Mr. Trump); David Lawder & Michael Martina, *White House Piles Pressure on China after Trump Tariff Threat*, REUTERS, 18 June 2018, www.reuters.com/article/us -usa-trade-china-trump/trump-threatens-to-hit-china-with-new-tariffs-on-200-billion-in-goods -idUSKBN1JE2ZQ.

139. Correspondingly, the specific identification of Chinese merchandise targets in each Wave were known as Lists 1, 2, 3, and 4.

140. *See* Elias Glenn & Lusha Zhang, *China's Record Trade Surplus with U.S. Adds Fuel to Trade War Fire*, REUTERS, 8 September 2018, www.reuters.com/article/us-china-economy-trade/chinas -record-trade-surplus-with-u-s-adds-fuel-to-trade-war-fire-idUSKCN1LO068.

141. *Quoted in* Stephen Nellis, *Apple Says U.S. Tariffs Would Hit a "Wide Range" of Products*, REUTERS, 7 September 2018, www.reuters.com/article/us-apple-tariffs/apple-says-u-s-tariffs-on -china-would-hit-wide-range-of-products-idUSKCN1LN2JY.

tax, and indeed a tax incentive. Make your products in the United States instead of China. Start building new plants now.[142]

Of course, this solution was not the only one. Section 301 tariffs applied only to merchandise "Made in China" under the pertinent ROO for that merchandise. Companies had two other options. They could continue to manufacture in China, yet reconfigure their operations so as to flunk the ROO, for example, by not substantially transforming inputs in China, or by not adding sufficient value in China. Or, they could close operations in China, and shift them to a third country in the Asia-Pacific region, such as India, Indonesia, Malaysia, Philippines, Thailand.

Nonetheless, the four Waves obviously were not idle threats. With the first Wave in place, and the second Wave looming, the President elaborated on the Wave Three threat, announcing it on 10 July 2018. His USTR published a list of $200 billion worth of additional Chinese imports on which America would impose 10% duties on or after 30 August.[143] The 195-page product list contained 6,031 items, at the HTSUS level, spanning the entirety of the HTSUS, such as agricultural products (*e.g.*, rice) and minerals, chemicals, gasses, iron, metals, steel, and valves, thus including consumer goods, or inputs into them, such as air conditioners, baseball caps and gloves, batteries, beauty products, bedsheets, bicycles, building materials, carpets, cat and dog food, chemicals and tires, cloud data and internet items (*e.g.*, computer servers, modems, routers, and networking and switching gear) coal, ceramics, computer equipment (including parts for machines used to make semiconductors), electronics (including cameras, recording devices, and TV components) fans, food items (including fruit, soy sauce, tilapia fish, and vegetables), forks and knives, furniture, doors, golf bags, hammers, handbags and luggage, hardware devices and parts (*e.g.*, cables, chargers, glass, power adapters, semiconductors, surge protectors, and wires), hats, leather, lighting products, microscopes, motors, paper and other wood products, photocopiers, plastics, printed circuit assemblies and boards, rain jackets,

---

142. *Quoted in Trump Tells Apple to Make Products in U.S. to Avoid China Tariffs*, REUTERS, 8 September 2018, www.reuters.com/article/us-usa-trade-china-apple/trump-tells-apple-to-make -products-in-u-s-to-avoid-china-tariffs-idUSKCN1LO0SX.

By no means was Apple alone in its concern. Virtually every consumer product would be subject to the 25% Wave Four tariffs, including athletic apparel, eyewear (*e.g.*, goggles and sunglasses), footwear (e.g., running, tennis, and soccer shoes, and rubber boots), fridges, freezers, gloves and mittens, hearing aids, legwear (e.g., pantyhose and socks) scarves, shawls, shirts (e.g., tank tops and T-shirts), shoes, sweaters, underwear (e.g., bras, girdles, corsets, garters, girdles, and suspenders), watches, Thus, manufacturers and retailers across the American economy, from Footlocker to Lululemon Athletica, Macy's to Walmart, Samsonite to Target Corp., warned of the damage to consumer interests (and, thus, to their own) of Wave Four tariffs. *See* Angus Whitley, Bruce Einhorn & Daniela Wei, *Trump's Next Trade War Shot Could Hit Americans From Head to Toe*, 35 International Trade Reporter (BNA) 1187 (13 September 2018).

143. *See* Natalie Sherman, *U.S. Fires Next Shot in China Trade War*, BBC NEWS, 10 July 2018, www.bbc.com/news/business-44788817; *U.S. to Slap Tariffs on Extra $200 Billion Worth of Chinese Imports*, REUTERS, 10 July 2018, www.reuters.com/article/us-usa-trade-china-tariffs/u-s-to-slap -tariffs-on-extra-200-billion-of-chinese-imports-idUSKBN1K0336 [hereinafter, *U.S. to Slap*]; *The Trade War Is Already Hurting*.

sewing machines, skis, stoves, T&A, tires, toilet paper, vacuum cleaners, wool, and yarn.[144] Put differently, on top of the additional $34 billion worth of products subject to 25% tariffs, the additional $200 worth of products would mean nearly half of all merchandise imported from China would be subject to Section 301 tariffs.[145]

Soon after announcing the third Wave of retaliation against $200 billion worth of Chinese merchandise, the President upped the pressure on China, saying the retaliatory tariff rate in that Wave (like Wave One) would be 25%, not 10%.[146] The USTR, Ambassador Lighthizer, explained that "[t]he increase in the possible rate of the additional duty is intended to provide the administration with additional options to encourage China to change its harmful policies and behavior and adopt policies that will lead to fairer markets and prosperity for all of our citizens."[147] Obviously, a higher tariff (*e.g.*, 25%) would pose a greater the market access impediment to Chinese merchandise, and increase the probability of firms shifting their supply chains out of China to the U.S. or third countries. Conversely, a lower tariff (*e.g.*, 10%) would be less expensive for the CCP to offset through subsidies to adversely affected firms. China avowed that "U.S. pressure and blackmail won't

---

144. *See* Office of the United States Trade Representative, Docket Number USTR-2018-0026, *Request for Comments Concerning Proposed Modification of Action Pursuant to Section 301: China's Acts, Policies, and Practices Related to Technology Transfer, Intellectual Property, and Innovation*, https://ustr.gov/sites/default/files/301/2018-0026%20China%20FRN%207-10-2018_0.pdf.

Identifying Chinese products subject to retaliation based on HTS product categories, even at the 8-digit level, raises the problem of over-inclusiveness with respect to certain such categories. For example, HTS code 85.17.62.00, "Machines for the reception, conversion and transmission or regeneration of voice, images or other data, including switching and routing apparatus," covers both "consumer-use modems and routers and the commercial network equipment used by data centers and broadband internet providers." David Lawder, *Home Modems, Routers, Hit by U.S. China Tariffs, as "Smart Tech" Goods Escape*, REUTERS, 24 September 2018, www.reuters.com /article/us-usa-trade-china-tech/home-modems-routers-hit-by-u-s-china-tariffs-as-smart-tech -goods-escape-idUSKCN1M40E1. This "catch-all category saw $23 billion in U.S. imports from China and $47.6 billion from the world last year [2017]," and is "the largest component of U.S. President Donald Trump's latest [Wave Three] tariffs targeting Chinese goods." *Id.* Of course, the problem of under-inclusiveness occurs, too, where one 8-digit HTS category does not capture all the merchandise intended to be targeted. Both problems result from the use of HTS categories for a purpose they were not primarily constructed, namely, unilateral trade remedy retaliation and counter-retaliation.

145. *See* David J. Lynch & Danielle Paquette, *Trump Makes Good on Threat to Target an Additional $200 Billion in Chinese Imports with Tariffs*, THE CHICAGO TRIBUNE, 10 July 2018, www .chicagotribune.com/business/ct-trump-china-trade-war-20180710-story.html.

146. *See* Se Young Le & Christian Shepherd, *China Plans Tariffs on $60 Billion of U.S. goods in Latest Trade Salvo*, REUTERS, 3 August 2018, www.reuters.com/article/us-usa-trade-china-commerce /china-plans-tariffs-on-60-billion-of-u-s-goods-in-latest-trade-salvo-idUSKBN1KO1M2. [Hereinafter, *China Plans Tariffs.*]

147. *Quoted in* David Lawder & Ben Blanchard, *Trump Administration Adds to China Trade Pressure with Higher Tariff Plan*, REUTERS, 1 August 2018, www.reuters.com/article/us-usa -trade-china/trump-administration-adds-to-china-trade-pressure-with-higher-tariff-plan -idUSKBN1KM63U. [Hereinafter, *Trump Administration Adds.*]

have an effect," and vowed (further) counter-retaliation (discussed below) so as to "resolutely protect our legitimate rights."[148]

Plainly, the Administration was fed up with a lack of engagement by the CCP on the underlying merits of the dispute. The USTR, Ambassador Robert Lighthizer, remarked:

> For over a year, the Trump administration has patiently urged China to stop its unfair practices, open its market, and engage in true market competition.
>
> Rather than address our legitimate concerns, China has begun to retaliate against U.S. products. . . . There is no justification for such action.[149]

He called Chinese practices "an existential threat to America's most critical comparative advantage and the future of our economy."[150] The U.S. Chamber of Commerce replied:

> Tariffs are taxes, plain and simple. Imposing taxes on another $200 billion worth of products will raise the costs of every day goods for American families, farmers, ranchers, workers, and job creators. It will also result in retaliatory tariffs, further hurting American workers.[151]

This reply was predictable, of course, because many of the targeted items were ones its members produced and exported from China, which meant either the members would be forced to absorb the tariffs, attempt to pass them onto American consumers — or reorient their global supply chains away from China. It was echoed by the European Union Chamber of Commerce in China. But, it and indeed the American Chamber understood and agreed (as the EU Chamber put it) that "the root cause of the U.S. China trade war is 'China's incomplete market opening.'"[152]

China's MOFCOM said it was "shocked," and its Foreign Ministry accused the U.S. of "typical bullying," characterized the Section 301 action as "a fight between unilateralism and multilateralism, protectionism and free trade, might and rules," and proclaimed that "China stands in line with the international community on the correct side of history to together protect the rules of the multilateral trade order."[153]

---

148. *Trump Administration Adds* (*quoting* Chinese Foreign Ministry spokesman Geng Shuang, Spokesman, Ministry of Foreign Affairs, China).

149. *Quoted in U.S. to Slap.*

150. Office of the United States Trade Representative, Statement by U.S. Trade Representative Robert Lighthizer on Section 301 Action, 10 July 2018, https://ustr.gov/about-us/policy-offices/press-office/press-releases/2018/july/statement-us-trade-representative, *also quoted in Trump Makes Good.*

151. *Quoted in U.S. to Slap.*

152. *Quoted in China Accuses U.S. of Trade Bullying as New Tariffs Imposed*, BBC News, 24 September 2018, www.bbc.com/news/business-45622075. The EU Report is *European Business in China Position Paper 2018/2019* (18 September 2018), http://www.europeanchamber.com.cn/en/publications-position-paper.

153. *Quoted in* Tony Munroe & Eric Beech, *China Says Will Hit Back After U.S. Proposes Fresh Tariffs on $200 Billion in Goods*, Reuters, 11 July 2018, www.reuters.com/article/us-usa

The U.S., said China, was putting a "knife to its neck."[154] China published (on 24 September 2018) saying that while it was "only natural" the two countries would have trade disputes, because of their different economic systems and developmental stages (discussed below), an extensive White Paper (36,000 Mandarin characters), America "has brazenly preached unilateralism, protectionism and economic hegemony, making false accusations against many countries and regions, particularly China, intimidating other countries through economic measures such as imposing tariffs, and attempting to impose its own interests on China through extreme pressure."[155]

Yet, China was limited in an in-kind response: it imported only about $135 billion worth of American merchandise, hence it would run out of goods against which to counter-retaliate before getting to the $200 billion figure. To be sure, the CCP said it would hit U.S. imports, plus amended the suit it had lodged in April 2018 at the WTO against America.[156] The U.S. was unmoved by the WTO lawsuits. Summarized, it told China:

-trade-china/china-says-will-hit-back-after-u-s-proposes-fresh-tariffs-on-200-billion-in-goods -idUSKBN1K1074.

154. Yawen Chen & Ben Blanchard, *China Says U.S. Putting "Knife To Its Neck," Hard To Proceed On Trade*, REUTERS, 24 September 2018, www.reuters.com/article/us-usa-trade-china-talks/china -says-u-s-putting-knife-to-its-neck-hard-to-proceed-on-trade-idUSKCN1M509S.

155. Jasmine Wang, *China Releases White Paper on China-U.S. Trade Friction: Xinhua*, 35 International Trade Reporter (BNA) 1252 (27 September 2018) (*quoting* China's official state news agency, Xinhua).

The text, translated into English, is 71 pages. *See* Information Office of the State Council of the People's Republic of China, *The Facts and China's Position on China — U.S. Trade Friction* (September 2018), www.xinhuanet.com/english/2018-09/24/c_137490176.htm. China argued (*inter alia*) that it imposes no legal requirement for technology transfer with respect to FDI or JVs, and that its technological progress has occurred because of its opening to the global economy, and the hard work of its citizens. *See U.S. Tariffs Won't Force China to Back Down, Trade Minister Says*, 35 International Trade Reporter (BNA) 1322 (11 October 2018).

156. *See* World Trade Organization, *United States — Tariff Measures on Certain Goods from China, Request for Consultations by China, Addendum*, WT/DS543/1/Add.1, G/L/1219/Add.1 (6 July 2018), https://docs.wto.org/dol2fe/Pages/FE_Search/FE_S_S009-DP.aspx?language=E&Cat alogueIdList=246636,244911,244601,244313&CurrentCatalogueIdIndex=0&FullTextHash=&Has EnglishRecord=True&HasFrenchRecord=True&HasSpanishRecord=True; Bryce Baschuk, *China Updates WTO Challenge to $34 Billion in U.S. Tariffs (1)*, 35 International Trade Reporter (BNA) 912 (12 July 2018). The original complaint is World Trade Organization, *United States — Tariff Measures on Certain Goods from China, Request for Consultations*, WT/DS543/1, G/L/1219 (5 April 2018), www.wto.org/english/news_e/news18_e/ds543rfc_05apr18_e.htm. The gist of the violation nullification or impairment complaint remained that the U.S. Section 301 actions allegedly (1) violated the GATT Article I:1 MFN principle by failing to accord Chinese products "treatment no less favorable than that provided for" in America's WTO Schedule of Concessions, and (2) violated *DSU* provisions requiring the U.S. to seek recourse to the DSB before imposing retaliatory tariffs against China. America's rebuttals included the argument that many of Chinese acts, policies, and practices that motivated the Section 301 action were not dealt with by any GATT-WTO covered agreement (including the *TRIPs Agreement*).

China initiated another *DSU* claim following Wave Two, that is, following U.S. imposition of 25% Section 301 tariffs on $16 billion worth of Chinese merchandise. This complaint argued

"We're not going to care about the WTO as you fuel overcapacity, wreck industries and steal IP (intellectual property). We're not going to sit on our hands."[157]

From the American perspective, China was looking to a venue, the WTO, to resolve controversies that simply were not within the subject matter jurisdiction of *DSU* Panels or the Appellate Body. *Made in China 2025* industrial policy and its nefarious consequences were not directly addressed by the Uruguay Round GATT-WTO agreements. And, the U.S. believed China—because of its dependence on the American markets for exports, manifest in its huge bilateral trade surplus on which the CCP partly relied to keep Chinese citizens employed and thereby avoid mass social unrest that could challenge Party rule—might fit the pattern (discussed in a separate Chapter) of countries against which Section 301 was likely to be successful, in terms of compelling a change in behavior (though China was, of course, far larger than any other Section 301 target).

The difference in Sino-American ability to retaliate with tariffs showed up on 3 August 2018, when China announced its list of American imports against which it was counter-retaliating in Wave Three: President Trump had targeted $200 billion worth of merchandise for 25% tariffs, but China countered with 5%–25% tariffs on $60 billion worth of merchandise.[158] In other words, China had matched Waves One and Two, dollar-for-dollar, and tariff rate-for-tariff rate, but not Wave Three.

---

the U.S. violated the GATT Article I:1 MFN rule, and the Article II:1(a)-(b) tariff binding rule. *See* World Trade Organization, *United States—Tariff Measures on Certain Goods From China II, Request for Consultations*, WT/DS565/1, G/L/1260 (27 August 2018), www.wto.org/english/news _e/news18_e/ds565rfc_27aug18_e.htm. With the failure of consultations, China asked for a Panel to adjudicate its complaint. *See* Bryce Baschuk, *China to Ask WTO to Determine Legality of U.S. Tariffs*, 35 International Trade Reporter (BNA) 1613 (13 December 2018).

The U.S. fired back at China with a complaint alleging China violated the national treatment rule in *TRIPs Agreement* Article 3 (along with Article 28), failing to afford foreign IPR holders treatment no less favorable than China provides to domestic IPR holders. The factual predicate the U.S. alleged was:

> China denies foreign patent holders the ability to enforce their patent rights against a Chinese joint-venture party after a technology transfer contract ends. China also imposes mandatory adverse contract terms that discriminate against and are less favorable for imported foreign technology. Therefore, China deprives foreign intellectual property rights holders of the ability to protect their intellectual property rights in China as well as freely negotiate market-based terms in licensing and other technology-related contracts.

USTR Press Release, https://ustr.gov/sites/default/files/files/Press/Releases/US%20Cons%20Req% 20China%20-%20Final.pdf, referenced in Bryce Baschuk, *WTO to Grant Dispute Inquiry into Chinese IP Policies Nov. 21*, 35 International Trade Reporter (BNA) 1464 (15 November 2018); Bryce Baschuk, *U.S. Takes Aim at China in WTO, Escalating Stakes of Trade War*, 35 International Trade Reporter (BNA) 1366 (25 October 2018).

157. *See* Michael Martina & David Lawder, *Much Detail, Little Progress, in U.S.-China Talks, Sources Say*, REUTERS, 25 August 2018, https://www.reuters.com/article/us-usa-trade-china-talks /much-detail-little-progress-in-u-s-china-talks-sources-say-idUSKCN1LA050.

158. *See China Says U.S. Farmers*; *China Plans Tariffs*.

With this Wave, China announced or proposed counter-retaliatory tariffs on $110 billion worth of American goods ($50 billion in Waves One and Two, $34 and $16 billion each, and $60 in Wave Three), but surely knew it imported only $130 billion from America (in 2017). Still, the 5,207 types of goods China targeted—20% of which were chemicals, and 387 of which were farm goods—included an array of merchandise, including auto windscreens, candy, commodity plastics, foods containing chocolate, helicopters, iron ore, roasted coffee, semiconductors, steel, small- and medium-sized aircraft, sugar, vegetables, and vegetable oil. Condoms, too, were on the list. China hit back with an *ad hominem* attack on the President, saying "he was starring in his own 'street fighter-style deceitful drama of extortion and intimidation.'"[159]

Wave Three tariffs kicked in on 24 September 2018.[160] The President adjusted them from his original announcement in two respects. First, following public comments, he agreed to trim the product retaliation list marginally, by 297 items—still worth about $200 billion.[161] Thus, instead of retaliating against 6,031 HTS 8-digit product categories, the U.S. hit 5,745 categories (including 1,363 chemical and plastic products). Among the 297 excluded items were 140 chemical inputs (used in agriculture, such as herbicides, in manufactured goods, such as phosphorus and vinyl chloride, both used to make plastic pipes, and in textiles), certain consumer electronics (*e.g.*, Bluetooth devices and smartwatches, like the Apple watch), and certain health and safety products (*e.g.*, bicycle helmets, child car seats, playpens, and high chairs). Baseball caps stayed on the list, affecting 89% of the caps sold in America, as that was the percentage that came from China (as of 2017).[162] However, almost certainly, they would appear on the Wave Four list.

---

159. Engen Tham, *Chinese Newspaper Mocks Trumps Claim of Winning Trade War as "Wishful Thinking*," Reuters, 6 August 2018, www.reuters.com/article/us-usa-trade-china/chinese-state-newspaper-says-trumps-claims-of-winning-trade-war-are-wishful-thinking-idUSKBN1KS02G (quoting the overseas edition of the CCP newspaper, *People's Daily*).

160. *See* The White House, Statement from the President, 17 September 2018, www.whitehouse.gov/briefings-statements/statement-from-the-president-4/ [hereinafter, 17 September 2018 Statement]; Office of the United States Trade Representative, *USTR Finalizes Tariffs on $200 Billion of Chinese Imports in Response to China's Unfair Trade Practices*, 17 September 2018, https://ustr.gov/about-us/policy-offices/press-office/press-releases/2018/september/ustr-finalizes-tariffs-200. The White House made the announcement on 17 September 2017, after the New York Stock Exchange closed, though financial markets world-wide already had priced in the Wave Three tariffs.

161. *See* Office of the United States Trade Representative, *Tariff List—September 17, 2018*, https://ustr.gov/sites/default/files/enforcement/301Investigations/Tariff%20List_09.17.18.pdf. Part 1 of this Wave Three List contained 5,745 items, while Part 2 identified items excluded from the *List*, thereby limiting the scope of Chinese products subject to counter-retaliation. In contrast to the Waves One and Two announcements, no mechanism was provided for exempting products from the Wave Three tariffs

162. *See* Shawn Donnan, *Trump's China Tariffs Hit Another American Icon: Baseball Caps*, 35 International Trade Reporter (BNA) 1383 (25 October 2018). Interestingly, "New Era Cap, which is the official supplier of headwear to Major League Baseball, said . . . all caps worn by Major League players on the field during games are manufactured in the U.S." *Id.*

Second, the President set the Wave Three tariff rate at 10%, not 25%, temporarily, from 24 September until 31 December 2018. On 1 January 2019, the rate would rise to 25%. The lag time in moving from 10% to 25% gave American producer-exporters in China time to shift their supply chains back to the U.S., or to third countries. It also gave American consumers time to adjust their purchase decisions, with a view to the Christmas shopping season. Both groups would suffer less by not having the full 25% rate thrust on them immediately. Moreover, in view of Wave Three of Chinese counter-retaliation against certain U.S. items, American producer-exporters in China that imported inputs from the U.S. subject to the Chinese tariffs had to factor in higher input costs (thanks to the Chinese tariffs), plus higher U.S. retail prices (thanks to the U.S. tariffs). For example, consider an American company making candles in China that imported wax from the U.S. The Chinese imposed a counter-retaliatory tariff of 25% on the wax, in response to a Wave Three U.S. tariff on the finished merchandise, *i.e.*, the candle. That company thus suffered at both ends of the commercial chain (especially if it could not pass on the full tariff amounts to retail consumers owing to a competitive market for candles) — but less so with a 10% tariff during the fall 2018.

The President repeated both the reason for taking the Section 301 action, and the frustration the U.S. felt in dealing with China:

> China is engaged in numerous unfair policies and practices relating to United States technology and intellectual property — such as forcing United States companies to transfer technology to Chinese counterparts. These practices plainly constitute a grave threat to the long-term health and prosperity of the United States economy.
>
> . . .
>
> For months, we have urged China to change these unfair practices, and give fair and reciprocal treatment to American companies. We have been very clear about the type of changes that need to be made, and we have given China every opportunity to treat us more fairly. But, so far, China has been unwilling to change its practices.[163]

Hence, the President threatened to move immediately to Wave Four:

> . . . if China takes retaliatory action against our farmers or other industries, we will immediately pursue phase three, which is tariffs on approximately $267 billion of additional imports.[164]

Countering America's Wave Three tariffs, of course, is exactly what China did.

In less than 24 hours after President Trump authorized the Wave Three tariffs, China announced it would hit back at 5,207 products, valued at $60 billion, of

---

163. *17 September 2018 Statement.*
164. *17 September 2017 Statement.*

American imports effective the same date as the U.S. action, 24 September 2018.[165] China said the U.S. action had injected "new uncertainty" into Sino-American trade negotiations, again accused America of "trade bullyism," and "intimidating other countries through economic measures," and asserted:[166]

> China has always emphasized that the only correct way to resolve the China-U.S. trade issue is via talks and consultations held on an equal, sincere and mutually respectful basis. But at this time, everything the United States does not give the impression of sincerity or goodwill.[167]

China returned to its Party line in November 2018, saying it would not be "bullied and oppressed by imperialist powers," but rather "blaze its own trail," and—in a thinly veiled rebuke of Mr. Trump and his supporters—asserted: "Such rapid changes [as China's economic rise] have split some countries and societies [*i.e.*, the U.S.]," and "[t]he polarization of right-leaning populism has manifested itself in political demands, which has led to unilateral policies against globalization and seriously affected the international political ecosystem."[168] President Xi Jinping pointedly denounced "the practices of law of the jungle and winner take all," which he said "are a dead end," as well as "beggar-thy-neighbor" trade policies.[169]

Nevertheless, China fell short of offering dramatic new proposals to resolve the Sino-American Trade War; indeed, how it could modify *Made in China 2025* while retaining a socialist market economy with the CCP at the helm was unclear. The OECD observed China ranked a lowly 59th out of 62 countries surveyed for openness to FDI, thanks to its market access restrictions and regulatory barriers.[170] They were among what U.S. Commerce Secretary Wilbur Ross called the "evil practices of China."[171] And, as for bullying, the Commerce Secretary intoned:

---

165. *China Hits Back at Trump with Tariffs on $60bn of U.S. Goods*, BBC News, 18 September 2018, www.bbc.co.uk/news/business-45555749.

166. *China Accuses*; Se Young Lee & Ming Zhang, *China Says U.S. Trying to Force it to Submit on Trade as New Tariffs Kick In*, Reuters, 23 September 2018, www.reuters.com/article/us-usa-trade-china/china-says-u-s-trying-to-bully-it-into-submission-as-fresh-tariffs-kick-in-idUSKCN1M404F (both *quoting* Xinhua, China's official state news agency).

167. Yawen Chen & David Lawder, *China Says Trump Forces Its Hand, Will Retaliate Against New U.S. Tariffs*, Reuters, 17 September 2018, www.reuters.com/article/us-usa-trade-china-tariffs/china-says-trump-forces-its-hand-will-retaliate-against-new-u-s-tariffs-idUSKCN1LX2M3 (*quoting* Geng Shuang, Spokesman, Chinese Ministry of Commerce).

168. David Tweed, Enda Curran & Alfred Cang, *China's Trade Olive Branch Can't Dispel Fears of Clash with U.S.*, 35 International Trade Reporter (BNA) 1428 (8 November 2018) (*quoting* Wang Qishan, Vice President, at a Bloomberg's New Economy Forum in Singapore on 6 November 2018).

169. *Quoted in Xi's Swipes at Trump Show China Standing Its Ground in Trade War*, 35 International Trade Reporter (BNA) 147 (8 November 2018) (speaking at the 5 November 2018 Shanghai Trade Fair). [Hereinafter, *Xi's Swipes*.]

170. *See Xi's Swipes*.

171. *Quoted in* Devin Leonard & Jenny Leonard, *Wilbur "Killer" Ross Isn't Worried About the Trade Wars*, 35 International Trade Reporter (BNA) 1443 (8 November 2018). [Hereinafter, *Wilbur "Killer" Ross*.]

They were afraid. It's just like a bully in the schoolyard. A bully's a bully if all the other kids say, "Oh, my God, that's the bully. We have to give in to whatever the bully wants." Bullies are only bullies if the other kids are willing to let them be bullies. Let two little kids gang up on the bully, beat him up a bit, and, you know what? That's the end of the bully.[172]

The "they" and "all the other kids" were the EU and other countries that were emboldened by America's courage to stand up to China, the real bully.

Notwithstanding the competing bullying narratives, the Chinese adjusted their Wave Three counter-retaliatory tariff rates slightly, trimming them from 5%, 10%, 15%, and 20% to just 5% and 10%. For instance, it imposed a 5% on 1,600 products, such as computers, small aircraft, and textiles, and a 10% tariff on over 3,500 items, including chemicals, meat, wheat, and wine. LNG, too, was on the Chinese 10% duty list, highlighting the point that China targeted exports from States that supported candidate Trump in the 2016 Presidential election.[173] As a result of the three Waves, America had imposed tariffs on $250 billion worth of Chinese merchandise, and the Chinese had done so on roughly $130 billion worth of merchandise. Therein lay the difference: the U.S. had hit about half of its imports from China, whereas China had hit back at essentially all of its imports from the U.S.

China's counterretaliation at lower levels may have been calculated for reasons similar to those of the U.S. The CCP may have wanted to spare Chinese consumers the shock of immediate, higher-level tariffs, and give Chinese producers time to adjust to a possible phasing in of elevated tariffs. Chinese GDP growth had been slowing in recent periods, and though the Party said it had stimulatory fiscal and monetary policy tools available, it might not have wanted to dampen aggregate demand with high tariffs that would discourage both consumption and investment.

The restraint (if it be called that) both countries showed in not rocketing retaliatory and counter-retaliatory tariffs to the highest threatened levels gave them the opportunity to find a negotiated settlement and end the Sino-American Trade War. Whether they would do so was uncertain. After all, in announcing Wave Three, President Trump had threatened to impose Wave Four tariffs on the final $267 billion of Chinese imports if China did what it did, namely, counter-retaliated against Wave Three. Thus, the two sides, and indeed the world, braced for Wave Four.[174]

---

172. *Quoted in Wilbur "Killer" Ross.*

173. At least one Chinese purchaser of U.S.-origin LNG swapped out that cargo for LNG from a third country, so as to avoid the 10% Chinese counter-retaliatory tariff. *See* Stephen Stapczynski, *Chinese LNG Buyer Is Said to Dodge U.S. Tariff in Cargo Swap*, 35 International Trade Reporter (BNA) 1323 (11 October 2018) (reporting: "The cargo swapped by the Chinese buyer is for November [2018] delivery and originated from Cheniere's Sabine Pass project in Louisiana, . . . [and] the transaction was completed at the end of September"). Notwithstanding the legality (or lack thereof) of the swap under Chinese law, the move was evidence of growing Chinese efforts to eschew U.S. LNG.

174. *See Trump Says He Expects to Raise China Tariffs: Wall Street Journal*, REUTERS, 26 November 2018, www.reuters.com/article/us-usa-trade-china/trump-says-he-expects-to-raise-china

- **Energy Trade and Iran Sanctions**

LNG and other energy-related items on China's list were particularly noteworthy. They suggested China had no intention of complying with the re-imposition of American sanctions against Iran, (which occurred on 6 August and 6 November, as discussed in a separate Chapter) following America's withdrawal from the *Iran Nuclear Deal*. China could spite America by buying oil and NG from Iran, in defiance of the sanctions, along with other suppliers (*e.g.*, Australia, Russia, and Qatar), plus impose levies on any supplies it imported from the U.S., in defiance of the Section 301 action.[175] Among the injured U.S. companies would be Houston-based Cheniere Energy.

In February 2018, the month before the Trump Administration launched the Section 301 action, Cheniere "signed the first-ever long-term deal between a U.S. LNG exporter and a Chinese state-owned energy company," and which viewed the Chinese market as reason for "building more port terminals to ship gas abroad."[176] Offshore terminal construction to serve the Chinese market was on hold as long as the Sino-American Trade War raged. Likewise, Alaskan energy interests, such as the Alaska Gasline Development Corp., were a casualty: "China had been expected to buy about 75 percent of its future LNG through a yet-to-be-built Alaskan pipeline [the $43 billion Alaska LNG Project designed to match Chinese LNG demand with Alaskan North Slope supply for 100 years], so any tariffs that result from trade disputes could cause problems."[177]

- **China's Non-Tariff Options**

Notwithstanding the limits to which China could counter-retaliate against American imports, the CCP had other options. China could resort to NTBs — qualitative measures — in goods, services, and FDI: it could hold up customs clearance, SPS, and TBT inspections on goods (including spot checks and unplanned visits), defer approvals on licenses for service market access (*e.g.*, bank branching, issuance of credit cards, and electronic funds transfers) and new or expansions of existing investments, and for mergers, delay IP (especially patent) grants, and step up prosecutions of American companies for alleged antitrust, labor, or environmental

---

-tariffs-wall-street-journal-idUSKCN1NV2MV (reporting in the run-up to the 30 November 2018 G-20 Summit in Buenos Aires, the President threatened an increasing Wave Three tariffs of 10% to 25%, and imposition of Wave Four tariffs, if his Chinese counterpart, Xi Jinping, did not strike a deal to end the Sino-American Trade War).

175. *See* Susan Heavey & Yawen Chen, *China to Penalize $60 Billion of U.S. Imports in Tit-for-Tat Move*, Reuters, 18 September 2018, www.reuters.com/article/us-usa-trade-china-response/china-to-penalize-60-billion-of-u-s-imports-in-tit-for-tat-move-idUSKCN1LY22V; Adam Allington, *Gas Tariffs Could Jeopardize Companies' Links to China (1)*, 35 International Trade Reporter (BNA) 1074 (9 August 2018). [Hereinafter, *Gas Tariffs*.]

176. *Gas Tariffs*.

177. *Gas Tariffs*.

violations.[178] China also could support consumer boycotts of American products, and divert students (through scholarship funding) away from U.S. educational institutions to competitors in Australia, Canada, England, and New Zealand, and encourage tourists to holiday elsewhere. (China said its tourists are worth $115 billion to the U.S. economy.[179]) And, China could restrict exports of certain items, claiming it needs to ensure they are in sufficient supply for domestic needs. So, for instance, an American producer-exporter operating in China that sources an input domestically (*i.e.*, from Chinese suppliers) could be barred from exporting the finished merchandise it manufactures, based on the Chinese government contention that the input should be available in the merchandise to Chinese consumers.

Most ominously, China could unsettle international financial markets. First, it could engineer a devaluation of the *yuan* relative to the dollar. Second, China could sell off large amounts of U.S. Treasury securities. However, neither move would be costless to China. Devaluation would render China vulnerable to charges of currency manipulation, and (by making imports even more expensive, on top of the 25% counter-retaliatory tariffs) lead to import-driven inflation. Liquidating Treasuries would undermine the value of its portfolio of those instruments, and leave China flush with cash in search of low-risk non-U.S. investments.

- **Chinese Doubts**

In any event, China itself expressed doubt about the wisdom of taking on the U.S. in a protracted Section 301 battle—or, at least certain observers within China did:[180]

> . . . [P]rominent academics have begun to question if China's slowing, trade-dependent economy can withstand a sustained attack from [President] Trump, which has already started to weigh on stock prices. The sentiments are being expressed in carefully worded essays circulated on China's heavily censored internet and . . . repeated in the halls of government offices, too.
>
> The essays have raised concerns that the ruling Communist Party underestimated the depth of anti-China sentiment in Washington and risked a premature showdown with the world's sole superpower. Such views push the bounds of acceptable public debate in a nation where dissent can lead to censure or even jail time, and are particularly bold given [Chinese leader] Xi [Jinping] has amassed unrivalled control while leading China to a more assertive role on the world stage.
>
> "It seems like Chinese officials were mentally unprepared for the approaching trade friction or trade war," Gao Shanwen, Chief Economist for Beijing-based

---

178. *See* Dave Sebastian, *China Could Turn to Non-Tariff Barriers in Trade Spat with U.S.*, 35 International Trade Reporter (BNA) 886 (5 July 2018).

179. *See China Says.*

180. *See China Begins to Question Whether It's Ready for a Trade War*, Bloomberg, 25 June 2018, www.bloomberg.com/politics/articles/2018-06-25/as-trade-war-looms-china-wonders-whether-it-s-up-for-the-fight. [Hereinafter, *China Begins.*]

Essence Securities Co., whose biggest shareholders include large state-owned enterprises, wrote in one widely circulated commentary. "Anti-China views are becoming the consensus among the U.S. public and its ruling party."

. . .

The essays have been noticed by key officials. Gao's piece was circulated last week among bureaucrats at the Commerce Ministry, which has been on the front lines of the trade dispute. . . .

Other officials expressed scepticism about the senior leadership's strategy. . . . One Finance Ministry official said the country had made a "major misjudgment" of the U.S.'s commitment to a long-term confrontation with China.

. . .

Xi has a lot at stake personally. He cast aside former leader Deng Xiaoping's maxim to "hide" China's strength and "bide" its time, and last year [2017] outlined a vision to complete China's rise as a global power by 2050. That included building a "world-class" military and boosting clout through his Belt-and-Road Initiative to finance infrastructure from Asia to Europe and beyond. Presidential term limits were also removed, allowing him to rule indefinitely.

Yu Zhi, an Economics Professor from Shanghai University of Finance and Economics, questioned the wisdom of a more assertive foreign policy in a recent article published in Singapore's *Lianhe Zaobao* newspaper. . . .

"Has China completed the task of 'getting rich'? Has China completed the primary stage of socialism as Deng Xiaoping described? Can you begin to compete directly with the United States and other Western countries?" Yu wrote. "China should rethink its general strategic direction."

. . .

The dispute threatens Xi's attempt to guide China into an era of slower growth without a recession that could loosen the Communist Party's 69-year grip on power.[181]

There were economic reasons to doubt an adversarial approach, namely, self-inflicted damage. By December 2018, it was estimated the Chinese and American economies each lost about $2.9 billion annually because of their respective tariffs on corn, sorghum, soybeans, and wheat.[182]

---

181. *China Begins.*

182. *See* Michael Hirtzer & Tom Polansek, *Trade Wars Cost U.S., China Billions of Dollars Each in 2018*, REUTERS, 28 December 2018, www.reuters.com/article/us-usa-trade-china/trade-wars-cost-u-s-china-billions-of-dollars-each-in-2018-idUSKCN1OR1JH (reporting on empirical research by Professor Wally Tyner, Department of Agricultural Economics, Purdue University). Part of the cost to China was caused by its shift away from American, and toward Brazilian, soybeans. Chinese

Still, power lay at the core of the dispute. Since the reforms Deng catalyzed in 1978, the CCP had nursed the Chinese public on the proposition that it would shepherd the economy for the benefit of the people, and allow them to pursue wealth, but the people had to accept its authoritarian, one-Party rule. So, the CCP proceeded with counter-retaliatory measures, suggesting the Party worried any climb down would be a loss of face on the global stage, which would catalyze a political revolution against it at home.

- **History Matters**

In embracing counter-retaliation, the Party recalled the painful history of pre-Communist China, when the country kowtowed to foreign imperial powers.[183] During China's last dynasty, the *Qing* Dynasty (1636–1912), Chinese tea became popular with European consumers, and China ran a trade surplus. The British East India Company shipped tea from China to England, and paid for it with opium grown by the British in India (essentially by auctioning Indian-grown opium for silver to independent traders, who then shipped the opium to China). Opium consumption in China rose, and China's trade surplus was erased. The *Qing* Dynasty Emperor refused to legalize and tax opium, and in 1839 banned trade in the narcotic. The *Qing* Imperial Commissioner, Lin Zexu, seized 20,283 chests (2.66 million pounds) of opium (destroying it in June 1839 at Humen, a town in Guangdong, on the banks of the Pearl River—an episode loosely akin to the Boston Tea Party). China blockaded trade in Canton (the port city in Guangdong province through which much opium trade occurred). The British reacted with gunboat diplomacy, sending in the Royal Navy to defeat the China in the First Opium War (1839–1842). China was forced to sign the 1842 *Treaty of Nanking*—one of several unequal treaties, as China calls them—whereby China ceded Hong Kong Island to the British Empire, opened five ports to British traders, indemnified the British, and granted the British rights of extraterritoriality in China. (In the Second Opium War, 1856–1860, the British inflicted another defeat on the *Qing* Dynasty, and social chaos in China ensued.) Less than a century later, from 1931–1945, China suffered again from foreign dominance, this time at the hands of non-western imperialists, namely, the Japanese.

---

demand pushed up the price of Brazilian soy futures to record premium levels over American soy futures on the Chicago Board of Trade (CBOT).

183. *See* John King Fairbank & Merle Goldman, *China: A New History* Chapters 9–10, 16 (2nd ed., 2006); John King Fairbank, *The Great Chinese Revolution: 1800–1985* Chapters 5–7, 14 (1986); John King Fairbank, *Trade and Diplomacy on the China Coast: The Opening of the Treaty Ports, 1842–1854* (1964) Alpha History, *Foreign Imperialism in China* (2018, https://alphahistory.com /chineserevolution/foreign-imperialism-in-china/; Columbia University, *Key Points in Developments in East Asia—Japan in China,* 1937–1945, (2009), http://afe.easia.columbia.edu/main_pop /kpct/kp_japanchina.htm; Indiana University Northwest, *Japanese Imperialism*, www.iun.edu /~hisdcl/G369_2002/japanese_imperialism.htm (undated); David Fickling, *China's Trade-War Tack is Steeped in History*, Bloomberg, 18 September 2018, www.bloombergquint.com/global-economics /2018/09/18/china-s-trade-war-tack-is-steeped-in-history#gs.nw_wO8M.

Mindful of the suffering inflicted by hegemonic powers on China in the 19th and 20th centuries, the CCP was loathe to *kowtow* to the U.S. in the 21st century. The Party had little interest in a compromise in the Section 301 Sino-American Trade War that would be redolent of the weakness China had once showed.

IX. Third Country, Business, and WTO Considerations, and Development Economics

- **EU Support?**

By no means did the EU support the use of Section 301, that is, the invocation of tariffs, as a way to address the underlying claims made by the Trump Administration against China. But, the EU did support those claims.[184] That was unsurprising. As seriously as America takes IP protection and enforcement, the EU does so even more seriously. The EU, for example, champions the moral rights of authors in its copyright laws, and protects geographic indications on a range of exquisite food and beverage items. The alignment of interests extends to topics like overcapacity in the steel and aluminum industries, orderly privatizations of SOEs, and appropriate levels of euro-*yuan* exchange rates. So, on 3 July 2018 in Brussels, in advance of a 16–17 July Sino-European Summit in Beijing. China tried to persuade the EU to side with it in the Section 301 action. The EU not only said no, but also affirmed its agreement with the American claims.

By September 2018, while still not viewing tariffs as the means that would resolve the issues America had raised in its Section 301 action against China, the EU openly sided with the United States. So, too, did Japan. With the U.S., the EU and Japan issued a *Joint Statement*. The document did not mention China by name, but it did not need to.

Joint Statement on Trilateral Meeting of the Trade Ministers of the United States, Japan, and the European Union (25 September 2018)[185]

Statement on Concerns with Non-Market-Oriented Policies and Practices of Third Countries

The Ministers reiterated their concern with and confirmed their shared objective to address non-market-oriented policies and practices of third countries that lead to

---

184. *See* Robin Emmott & Noah Barkin, *Exclusive, China Presses Europe for Anti-U.S. Alliance on Trade*, REUTERS, 3 July 2018, www.reuters.com/article/us-usa-trade-china-eu-exclusive /exclusive-china-presses-europe-for-anti-u-s-alliance-on-trade-idUSKBN1JT1KT.

185. https://ustr.gov/about-us/policy-offices/press-office/press-releases/2018/september/joint -statement-trilateral (Mr. Hiroshige Seko, Minister of Economy, Trade and Industry of Japan, Ambassador Robert E. Lighthizer, United States Trade Representative, and Mrs. Cecilia Malmström, European Commissioner for Trade).

severe overcapacity, create unfair competitive conditions for their workers and businesses, hinder the development and use of innovative technologies, and undermine the proper functioning of international trade, including where existing rules are not effective.

The Ministers recalled that market-oriented conditions are fundamental to a fair, mutually advantageous global trading system and that their citizens and businesses operate under market-oriented conditions. They discussed actions being taken and possible measures that could be undertaken in the near future.

Accordingly, they directed their staff to further their discussion on various elements or indications that signal that non-market oriented policies and practices exist for businesses and industries, to enhance information sharing on non-market-oriented policies and practices of third countries, to engage with other trading partners on identifying means to maintain market-oriented conditions, and to deepen discussions on enforcement and rule-making as tools to address these problems.

Statement on Industrial Subsidies and State-Owned Enterprises

The Ministers reviewed and confirmed progress regarding possible new rules on industrial subsidies and State-Owned Enterprises so as to promote a more level playing field for their workers and businesses. The Ministers highlighted the importance of securing a level playing field given the challenges posed by third parties developing State Owned Enterprises into national champions and setting them loose in global markets—resulting in distortions that negatively affect farmers, industrial producers, and workers in the Ministers' home countries. The Ministers recognized the progress of their work, and the continued need to deepen their shared understanding, on the basis for strengthening rules on industrial subsidies and State Owned Enterprises, including how to develop effective rules to address market-distorting behavior of state enterprises and confront particularly harmful subsidy practices such as: state-owned bank lending incompatible with a company's creditworthiness, including due to implicit government guarantees; government or government-controlled investment fund equity investment on non-commercial terms; non-commercial debt-to-equity swaps; preferential input pricing, including dual pricing; subsidies to an ailing enterprise without a credible restructuring plan; and subsidies leading to or maintaining overcapacity.

The trilateral partners continue exploring how to increase the costs of transparency and notification failures and how to strengthen the ability to obtain information on subsidies.

The Ministers also confirmed their commitment to continue working together to maintain the effectiveness of existing WTO disciplines.

On that basis, they agreed to intensify discussions among themselves and expressed their intention to advance their respective internal steps before the end of 2018 with the aim of initiating a negotiation on more effective subsidy rules soon thereafter. The Ministers emphasized the need to ensure the participation of key trading partners in these future negotiations.

Statement on Concerns with Forced Technology Transfer Policies and Practices of Third Countries

The Ministers recalled their shared view that no country should require or pressure technology transfer from foreign companies to domestic companies, including, for example, through the use of joint venture requirements, foreign equity limitations, administrative review and licensing processes, or other means. The Ministers found such practices to be deplorable.

The Ministers again condemned government actions that support the unauthorized intrusion into, and theft from, the computer networks of foreign companies to access their sensitive commercial information and trade secrets and use that information for commercial gain. Recalling that forced technology transfer policies and practices create unfair competitive conditions for their workers and businesses, hinder the development and use of innovative technologies, and undermine the proper functioning of international trade, the Ministers will reach out to and build consensus with other like-minded partners. The Ministers also agreed to deepen their investigation and analysis of the full range of harmful technology transfer policies and practices and their effects.

The Ministers affirmed their commitment to effective means to stop harmful forced technology transfer policies and practices, and to this end, deepen discussions on enforcement and rule-making as tools to address these problems.

. . .

- **November 2018 USTR Section 301 China Case *Report Update***

In the aftermath of this *Joint Statement*, China presented the U.S. with written responses to the concerns underlying America's Section 301 Action.[186] In November 2018, The Chinese listed 142 topics, and slotted them into three categories: "issues the Chinese are willing to negotiate for further action, issues they are already working on, and issues they consider off limits." The U.S. was unimpressed. With respect to the first category, China already had pledged market access concessions or trade reforms. It was offering America nothing new, and its commitment to rehashed pledges was dubious. For instance, China previously promised to ease restrictions that impeded U.S. entities from owning Chinese companies, but had failed to follow through. Worse yet, the third category was replete with America's most serious concerns. Declaring those topics non-negotiable showed China's failure to appreciate the U.S. position on them and/or to be intransigent.

That failure, of course, unacceptable to the U.S. In November 2018, the USTR issued an *Report Update* on the Section 301 case. The *Report Update* not only summarizes the Sino-American Trade War to date, but also intimates why the War had

---

186. *See* Jeff Mason & Steve Holland, *Exclusive: China Offer Unlikely to Spur Major Trade Breakthrough—Senior U.S. Official*, REUTERS, 15 November 2018, www.reuters.com/article/us-usa-trade-china-exclusive/exclusive-china-offer-unlikely-to-spur-major-trade-breakthrough-senior-u-s-official-idUSKCN1NK2UA.

not ended: each side perceived the behavior of the other as an existential threat to the other. To America, China jeopardized American national security by undermining the IPRs and manufacturing base that are foundations for that security, thanks to Chinese IP misappropriation, strategic sector targeting, and illegal subsidies. To China, America threatened the basis of CCP power and legitimacy, namely, continued economic growth that relied on IP and industrial policy. To the Trump Administration, the CCP avoided honest engagement on the substantive causes of the War, and poured the old wine of "*Made in 2025*" into new bottles labelled "*Catalogue*" and "*Roadmap.*" To the CCP, the Trump Administration sought to contain China's rise through coercion and ignored its efforts at reform.

Office of the United States Trade Representative,

Update Concerning China's Acts, Policies and Practices Related to Technology Transfer, Intellectual Property, and Innovation,
3–9 (20 November 2018)[187]

I. Overview

A. Background

On August 14, 2017, the President instructed the U.S. Trade Representative to determine under Section 301 of the *Trade Act of 1974* whether to investigate China's laws, policies, practices, or actions that may be unreasonable or discriminatory and that may be harming American intellectual property rights, innovation, or technology development. On August 18, 2017, the . . . USTR initiated a Section 301 investigation of China's acts, policies, and practices related to technology transfer, intellectual property, and innovation. On the date of initiation, USTR requested consultations with the Government of China concerning the issues under investigation. Instead of accepting the request, China's Ministry of Commerce expressed "strong dissatisfaction" with the United States and decried the investigation as "irresponsible" and "not objective."

On March 22, 2018, USTR issued the *Findings of the Investigation into China's Acts, Policies, and Practices Related to Technology Transfer, Intellectual Property, and Innovation under Section 301 of the Trade Act of 1974* (the "*Section 301 Report*"). Based on this *Report*, USTR determined the following Chinese actions are unreasonable or discriminatory and burden or restrict U.S. commerce:

1. China uses foreign ownership restrictions, such as . . . JV requirements and foreign equity limitations, and various administrative review and licensing processes, to require or pressure technology transfer from U.S. companies.

2. China's regime of technology regulations forces U.S. companies seeking to license technologies to Chinese entities to do so on non-market-based terms that favor Chinese recipients.

---

187. https://ustr.gov/sites/default/files/enforcement/301Investigations/301%20Report%20Update.pdf

3. China directs and unfairly facilitates the systematic investment in, and acquisition of, U.S. companies and assets by Chinese companies to obtain cutting-edge technologies and intellectual property and generate the transfer of technology to Chinese companies.

4. China conducts and supports unauthorized intrusions into, and theft from, the computer networks of U.S. companies to access their sensitive commercial information and trade secrets.

After USTR issued the *Section 301 Report*, the United States continued to engage China to resolve the unfair trade acts, policies, and practices included in the investigation. A cabinet-level U.S. delegation traveled to Beijing on May 4, 2018, to discuss a range of bilateral economic issues, including China's policies addressed in the *Section 301 Report*. This high-level engagement continued on May 17, 2018, when senior administration officials hosted a trade delegation from China in Washington, D.C. Another high-level U.S. delegation met with its Chinese counterparts in Beijing on June 2 and 3, 2018 for additional discussions on trade and other issues.10 Each of these meetings gave China an opportunity to address U.S. concerns—but China failed to do so adequately.

The United States has also worked closely with the . . . EU and Japan, who share many of the concerns expressed by the United States regarding China's acts, policies, and practices related to technology transfer, intellectual property, and innovation.

- At the conclusion of trilateral meetings held in May 2018, the trade ministers of the United States, Japan, and the EU (the "Ministers") "confirmed their shared view that no country should require or pressure technology transfer from foreign companies to domestic companies, including, for example, through the use of JV requirements, foreign equity limitations, administrative review and licensing processes, or other means."

- At the conclusion of trilateral meetings held in September 2018, the Ministers "further recalled their shared view that no country should require or pressure technology transfer from foreign companies to domestic companies, including, for example, through the use of JV requirements, foreign equity limitations, administrative review and licensing processes, or other means. The Ministers found such practices to be deplorable." The Ministers also "affirmed their commitment to effective means to stop harmful forced technology transfer policies and practices, and to this end, deepen discussions on enforcement and rule-making as tools to address these problems."

Despite repeated U.S. engagement efforts and international admonishments of its trade technology transfer policies, China did not respond constructively and failed to take any substantive actions to address U.S. concerns.

As a result of China's ongoing failure to respond constructively to U.S. concerns, USTR imposed tariffs on July 6, 2018 and August 23, 2018 on approximately $50 billion of Chinese imports as part of the U.S. response to China's unfair trade practices related to the forced transfer of American technology and intellectual property. The United States also requested dispute settlement consultations with China in the . . . WTO on March 23, 2018 concerning certain measures pertaining to the licensing of intellectual property rights, and the United States is now pursuing dispute settlement before the WTO on those issues.

China, however, made clear—both in public statements and in government-to-government communications—that it would not change its policies in response to the initial Section 301 action. Indeed, China largely denied there were problems with respect to its policies involving technology transfer and intellectual property. The Information Office of China's State Council issued a 71-page *"White Paper"* in September 2018 that dismissed the Section 301 investigation's findings and denounced U.S. actions as "trade bullyism." Furthermore, China responded to the U.S. action by attempting to cause further harm to the U.S. economy, by increasing duties on certain U.S. exports to China.

These actions demonstrated that USTR's initial tariff action was no longer appropriate to obtain the elimination of China's unfair trade acts, policies, and practices. In addition, the burden or restriction on United States commerce of these acts, policies, and practices continues to increase, including following the one-year investigation period. Accordingly, under direction of the President, USTR imposed additional tariffs on approximately $200 billion of imports from China on September 24, 2018.

USTR has undertaken this *Update* as part of its ongoing monitoring and enforcement effort. In preparing this *Update*, USTR has relied upon publicly available material, and has consulted with other government agencies. . . . China fundamentally has not altered its acts, policies, and practices related to technology transfer, intellectual property, and innovation, and indeed appears to have taken further unreasonable actions in recent months.

- . . . China continues its policy and practice of conducting and supporting cyber-enabled theft and intrusions into the commercial networks of U.S. companies and those of other countries [*e.g.*, Australia, Canada, EU, Japan, and Korea], as well as other means by which China attempts illegally to obtain information. This conduct provides the Chinese government with unauthorized access to intellectual property, including trade secrets, or confidential business information, as well as technical data, negotiating positions, and sensitive and proprietary internal business communications. [Indeed, "cyber-enabled theft against the United States has increased in frequency and sophistication since the issuance of the USTR's initial findings in March," and "Chinese state actors have improved their methods of infiltration and concealment by using tools that leave few, if any, unique traces, making attribution more difficult."[188]]

---

188. Venable LLP, Lindsay Meyer, Ashley Craig, Jeff Weiss, Liz Lowe & Wes Sudduth, International Trade Alert, *USTR Issues Updated Section 301 Report on China*, 28 November 2018, www

- Despite the relaxation of some foreign ownership restrictions and certain other incremental changes in 2018, the Chinese government has persisted in using foreign investment restrictions to require or pressure the transfer of technology from U.S. companies to Chinese entities. Numerous foreign companies and other trading partners share U.S. concerns regarding China's technology transfer regime. [Moreover, the sectors in which China removed or relaxed foreign ownership restrictions were ones in which "China already has an internal reason for inviting more foreign participation or where market conditions already favor Chinese companies."[189]]

- [With respect to] China's discriminatory licensing restrictions . . . , the United States has requested consultations and is pursuing dispute settlement under the WTO in *China — Certain Measures Concerning the Protection of Intellectual Property Rights* (WT/DS542). China continues to maintain these discriminatory licensing restrictions. [Specifically, "China maintains policies that interfere with the ability of foreign technology holders to set market-based terms in licensing and other technology-related contracts, and deny foreign patent holders basic patent rights to stop a Chinese entity from using technology after a licensing contract ends."]

- Despite an apparent aggregate decline in Chinese outbound investment in the United States in 2018, the Chinese government continues to direct and unfairly facilitate the systematic investment in, and acquisition of, U.S. companies and assets by Chinese entities, to obtain cutting-edge technologies and intellectual property and generate large-scale technology transfer in industries deemed important by state industrial plans [*i.e.*, the Made in China 2025 industrial policy]. Chinese outbound investment is increasingly focused on venture capital (VC) investment in U.S. technology centers such as Silicon Valley, with Chinese VC investment reaching record levels in 2018. [As a result, and as discussed earlier, "stricter reforms . . . [for] oversight by . . . CFIUS by means of the *Foreign Risk Review Modernization Act of 2018 (FIRRMA)* were recently adopted to address these very concerns."]

B. China's Technology Policies Persist

As detailed in the introduction to the *Section 301 Report*, official publications of the Chinese government and the Chinese Communist Party (CCP) set out China's

---

.venable.com/ustr-issues-updated-section-301-report-on-china-11-28-2018/. [Hereinafter, *USTR Issues.*]

189. *USTR Issues*. Those sectors included education, insurance, medical care, and telecommunications, but China's timetable was unclear (with Chinese Vice Premier Liu He saying the liberalizations would occur "as fast and as early as possible"), and some of the pledges resembled earlier ones (even dating as far back as China's December 2001 WTO accession commitments, for example, with respect to 51% foreign equity ownership in local Chinese insurance companies). *Quoted in* Xiaoqing Pi, *China Vows to Open Its Markets Ahead of Trump-Xi Talks at G-20*, 35 International Trade Reporter (BNA) 1535 (29 November 2018).

ambitious technology-related industrial policies. These policies are driven in large part by China's goals of dominating its domestic market and becoming a global leader in a wide range of technologies, especially advanced technologies. The most prominent industrial policy is "*Made in China 2025,*" initiated in 2015. Industrial sectors that contribute to or benefit from the "Made in China 2025" industrial policy include aerospace, information and communications technology, robotics, industrial machinery, new materials, and automobiles.

In the period following the publication of the *Section 301 Report*, China has deliberately downplayed the importance of and reduced official media attention on the *Made in China 2025* policy. In late June, China's Internet Propaganda Ministry reportedly circulated a *Propaganda Oral Notice* directing media outlets to "not make further use of '*Made in China 2025,*' or there will be consequences." Also in late June, the Hong Kong paper *South China Morning Post* asked Wang Xinzhe, Chief Economist at China's Ministry of Industry and Information Technology (MIIT), whether the Chinese government "would withhold or adjust" the *Made in China 2025* policy. In his response, Mr. Wang made no mention at all of the policy, stating only that "the ministry was following guidelines" set during the CCP's 2017 National Congress regarding "upgrading the manufacturing industry."

In addition, the May 2018 project guide for China's Industrial Transformation and Upgrading Fund—a government fund that provides financing to technology-related programs in sectors linked to *Made in China 2025*—no longer references the industrial policy by name, even though it still targets the same high-technology industries. (*Made in China 2025* featured prominently in the Fund's administrative measure, issued in December 2016, and its 2017 project guide published in August 2017.)

Despite this transparent attempt to deemphasize *Made in China 2025* in public, China continues to implement this industrial policy on a large scale. In February 2018, the National Strategic Advisory Committee on Building a Powerful Manufacturing Nation published the *Made in China 2025 Key Area Technology and Innovation Greenbook — Technology Roadmap (2017)* ("*2017 Roadmap*"), which updates and replaces the 2015 *Made in China 2025 Key Area Technology Roadmap* ("*2015 Roadmap*") discussed in the *Section 301 Report*. The updated document again sets explicit market share and other targets to be filled by Chinese producers References in a litany of national and subnational normative documents, such as 13th five-year sectoral plans (2016–2020), as well as their implementing measures, confirm the continuing importance of *Made in China 2025* and China's persistent pursuit of its goals.

China also appears to have reinvigorated the "Strategic Emerging Industries" policy, a high-technology industrial policy started in 2010. . . . China issued a draft for comment in September 2018 of the latest version of the *Strategic Emerging Industry Development Key Product and Service Catalogue* ("*SEI Catalogue*"). As shown in Table 1, sectors covered in the catalogue illustrate a high degree of overlap with *Made in China 2025*.

Table 1. Comparison of the Sectors Targeted by the 2018 *SEI Catalogue* and the *Made in China 2025* 2017 Roadmap

Topic	SEI Catalogue	2017 Roadmap
New Generation Information Technology Industry	Chapter 1	Chapter 1
High End Equipment Manufacturing Industry	Chapter 2	Chapter 2
New Materials Industry	Chapter 3	Chapter 9
Biotech Industry	Chapter 4	Chapter 10
New Energy Vehicle Industry	Chapter 5	Chapter 6
New Energy Industry	Chapter 6	Chapter 7
Creative Data Industry	Chapter 8	Chapter 1

In March 2018, a new agreement was signed by the National Development and Reform Commission (NDRC) and the Export-Import Bank of China to provide financial products worth CNY 800 billion ($122 billion) to companies in Strategic Emerging Industries. China has also enhanced fiscal supports specific to Strategic Emerging Industries for fiscal-year 2018.

. . .

China quickly dismissed the *Report Update*, calling all the accusations "groundless."[190] And, compelling as the *Report Update* seemed to be, not all prominent American economists were convinced. Former Federal Reserve Chairman Alan Greenspan (1926–, Chair, 1987–2006) said this:

> President Donald Trump's tariff policies [are] "insane" and . . . "why we're doing it probably is very deep in the psyche of somebody."

> . . .

> President Donald Trump's tariff policies "insane" and said "why we're doing it probably is very deep in the psyche of somebody."

> "It's an excise tax, and people think of tariffs other than what it is," he added. "It's a tax, and everybody engaged in warfare of this type, it would mean that you're withdrawing credit or purchasing power from a whole series of countries."

> Greenspan said the notion that China would outrace the U.S. in all economic respects "is a mistake," pointing to their lower gross domestic product *per capita*.[191]

---

190. *China Says U.S. Accusations of Unfair Trade Practices "Groundless,"* REUTERS, 22 November 2018, www.reuters.com/article/us-usa-trade-china/china-says-u-s-accusations-of-unfair-trade-practices-groundless-idUSKCN1NR0JK (*quoting* MOFCOM spokesman Gao Feng, who said: "The U.S side made new groundless accusations against the Chinese side, and China finds it totally unacceptable").

191. *Quoted in* Ivan Levingston, *Greenspan Calls Trump Tariff Policies "Insane," Both Sides Lose,* 35 International Trade Reporter (BNA) 1525 (22 November 2018).

Was the Chairman Greenspan correct economically, but naïve politically?

- **December 2018 Temporary Ceasefire**

At the December 2018 G-20 Summit in Buenos Aires, Argentina, President Donald J. Trump met with his Chinese counterpart, President Xi Jinping. Discussing the Sino-American Trade War over a formal dinner, the two leaders agreed on the following points:[192]

(1) The U.S. would defer raising the Wave Three tariff rate on $200 billion worth of Chinese imports from 10% to 25% from 30 December 2018 for an additional 90 days, but would proceed with that increase if no deal were reached at the end of the extended negotiating period. The deadline was midnight Eastern Time on 1 March 2019.[193]

Whether that deadline was realistic was dubious, not merely because of the reduced number of negotiating days owing to the Christmas, New Year, and Chinese New Year holidays, and the fact no face-to-face meetings were scheduled until January 2019.[194] Expectations and limitations were at issue. Though the USTR demanded no specific negotiating outcomes by 1 March 2019, it expected "structural changes by China on forced technology transfer, intellectual property protection, non-tariff barriers, cyber intrusions and theft, services and agriculture."[195] From the CCP perspective, however, the *Made in China 2025* was a red line the Trump Administration could not cross, insofar as the power of the Party was based on its achieving the targets in that industrial policy, which, in turn, required continued support for SOEs and the practices of which America complained.

(2) China would classify Fentanyl as a controlled substance, with the White House declaring "President Xi, in a wonderful humanitarian gesture, has agreed to designate Fentanyl as a Controlled Substance, meaning that

---

192. The White House, *Statement from the Press Secretary Regarding the President's Working Dinner with China*, 1 December 2018, www.whitehouse.gov/briefings-statements/statement-press-secretary-regarding-presidents-working-dinner-china/ [hereinafter, *China Dinner Statement*]; *Trump Says China*; *U.S.-China Trade War: Deal Agreed to Suspend New Trade Tariffs*, BBC News, 2 December 2018, www.bbc.com/news/world-latin-america-46413196; Quint Forgey & Doug Palmer, *Trump Announces Chinese Rollback of Auto Tariffs*, Politico, 2 December 2018, www.politico.com/story/2018/12/02/trump-china-auto-tariffs-1037422?cid=apn; Roberta Rampton & Michael Martina, *U.S., China, Agree on Trade War Ceasefire After Trump, Xi Summit*, Reuters, 1 December 2018, www.reuters.com/article/us-g20-argentina/u-s-china-agree-trade-war-ceasefire-after-trump-xi-summit-idUSKCN1O031C [hereinafter, *U.S., China Agree*].

193. *See U.S. Sets New March 2 Date for China Tariff Increases Amid Talks*, Reuters, 14 December 2018, www.reuters.com/article/us-usa-trade-china-tariffs/u-s-sets-new-march-2-date-for-china-tariff-increases-amid-talks-idUSKBN1OD2QL?utm_source=applenews. [Hereinafter, *U.S. Sets.*]

194. *See* Demetri Sevastopulo & James Politi, *China Moves to Cut U.S. Car Tariffs in First Sign of Trade War Détente*, Financial Times, 12 December 2018. [Hereinafter, *China Moves.*]

195. *U.S. Sets.*

people selling Fentanyl to the United States will be subject to China's maximum penalty under the law."

(3) China would impose no new counter-measures against American products, and instead would endeavor to import more U.S. merchandise, such as soybeans, in an effort to reduce its bilateral trade surplus. According to the U.S., China pledged to "purchase a not yet agreed upon, but very substantial, amount of agricultural, energy, industrial, and other products from the United States to reduce the trade imbalance between our two countries."[196]

China said it was "willing to increase imports in accordance with the needs of its domestic market and the people's needs, including marketable products from the United States, to gradually ease the imbalance in two-way trade."[197] By mid-December 2018, China resumed purchases of American soybeans.[198]

(4) China would lower its tariffs on U.S. autos from 40% back to 15%, though the timetable for it doing so was uncertain, and China did not confirm this point at the Buenos Aires dinner.

China clarified the timetable, announcing on 10 December that it would reduce tariffs on 144 types of U.S.-origin autos imports by 25 percentage points.[199] China also would suspend its 5% counter-retaliatory tariff on 67 auto parts. The reduction would be for three months, starting 1 January 2019 (which suggested an extra month beyond the 1 March deadline the USTR set). The U.S. continued with its 27.5% tariff on Chinese cars and car parts, *i.e.*, with the 25% Section 301 tariff it imposed in July 2018, on top of the 2.5% MFN tariff.

(5) The two sides would immediately intensify their talks to resolve outstanding issues, namely, said the U.S. "on structural changes with respect to forced technology transfer, intellectual property protection, non-tariff barriers, cyber intrusions and cyber theft."[200] China said "[t]he two sides agreed to mutually open their markets, and as China advances a new round of reforms, the United States' legitimate concerns can be progressively resolved."[201]

Note that in Buenos Aires, the agreement on these points was uncertain. Neither side produced a written record of the 2 ½-hour dinner, much less an agreement with specific, verifiable points. Rather, these points were cobbled together from press

---

196. *China Dinner Statement.*

197. *U.S., China Agree* (*quoting* Chinese State Councilor Wang Yi).

198. *U.S. Sets*; *UPDATE 5—China to Halt Added Tariffs on U.S.-Made Cars in Easing of Trade Tensions*, REUTERS, 14 December 2018, www.reuters.com/article/china-usa-auto/update-5-china -to-halt-added-tariffs-on-u-s-made-cars-in-easing-of-trade-tensions-idUSL3N1YJ3NA [hereinafter, *China to Halt*].

199. *See China Moves*; *China to Halt*.

200. *China Dinner Statement.*

201. *U.S., China Agree* (*quoting* Chinese State Councilor Wang Yi).

statements and tweets, and some were unconfirmed. Only weeks after the dinner did the aforementioned clarifications emerge, and then only episodically.

The Buenos Aires "agreement" was unimpressive. Point (1) meant the U.S. was postponing implementation of the increase from 10% to 25% of Wave Three tariffs for 90 days, from 31 December 2018 to 1 March 2019. Judging from the CCP's response to the November 2018 USTR Section 301 *Report Update*, there was no indication the CCP was ready to engage on the key, long-held American substantive concerns. Point (2) was welcome, but this public health matter was about America's opioid crisis and had little to do with the Trade War. Point (3) also was welcome, but temporarily boosting imports of American products was unlikely to resolve the large bilateral imbalance, the causes of which lay in low American structural savings and investment levels. Point (4) was commercially unimportant, insofar as American cars do not sell well in China for reasons other than tariffs. China exported just 53,300 vehicles to the U.S. (in 2017), and imported only 280,208 cars from American-made vehicles—just 10% of its total car imports.[202] American cars are large, gas-guzzling, and environmentally unfriendly. Chinese consumers who seek them as a status symbol can afford a tariff of 15% or 40%. As for point (5), again, American expectations versus CCP limitations meant reaching a deal would be difficult, perhaps even more so with President Trump describing tweeting on 4 December that he is a "Tariff Man," and that there would be a "REAL DEAL with China, or no deal at all."[203]

Arguably, China got the better of the Buenos Aires agreement. China gave up nothing, and judged not all American concerns to be "legitimate." Any additional tariffs China would have slapped on American merchandise would be to counter America's increase from 10% to 25% of Wave Three tariffs. But, China gained 90 additional days before the U.S. planned to implement that increase.

· **Negotiations to End the Trade War**

Across December 2018 and January 2019, the U.S. and China considered ways to end their Trade War. With respect to the bilateral trade imbalance, China said it would cut tariffs on certain products (*e.g.*, on cars, from 40% to 15%). The U.S. read these statements to be warmed-over versions of past promises.

China also offered to increase imports of American goods (*e.g.*, corn, soybeans, and wheat), with a view to eliminating its bilateral trade surplus in six years (*i.e.*, by 2024).[204] Here, too, there was nothing new, or as the BBC put it: "These are not

---

202. *See China to Halt*; Bloomberg News, *China Is Said to Move on U.S. Car Tariff Cut Trump Tweeted About*, 35 International Trade Reporter (BNA) 1611 (13 December 2018).

203. Tim Rostan, *Trump Says He's "Tariff Man," and Twitter Decides it's a Super Hero Name*, Market Watch, 4 December 2018, www.marketwatch.com/story/trump-says-hes-tariff-man-and-twitter-decides-its-a-superhero-name-2018-12-04.

204. *See* David Lawder, *Explainer: How U.S.-China Talks Differ from Any Other Trade Deal*, Reuters, 18 January 2019, www.reuters.com/article/us-usa-trade-china-explainer/explainer-how-u-s-china-talks-differ-from-any-other-trade-deal-idUSKCN1PC2L0 [hereinafter, *Explainer*]; *China is Said to Offer Path to End U.S. Trade Imbalance (3)*, Bloomberg Law International Trade News (18 January 2019), https://news.bloomberglaw.com/international-trade/china-is-said-to-offer-path-to-end-us-trade-imbalance-3-2.

concessions, but steps that are in line with reform and opening up already planned by President Xi."[205] Moreover, the U.S. countered the offer was contingent on Chinese domestic demand for American agricultural and industrial products. The U.S. pointed out if China simply switched purchase sources (for example, buying more soybeans from the U.S. and fewer from Brazil), then it might create or exacerbate one bilateral imbalance (with Brazil) by eliminating or reducing another one (with America) mitigate one, with no net improvement in the global structural imbalances for which it was largely to blame. And, some of the items China sought to purchase were high-tech goods that raised national security concerns, *i.e.*, these items would advance China's strategic goals at America's expense.

As for IP protection, China noted two points. First, it argued:

> The advances in China in the past 70 years are not a godsend, nor a gift from others. Rather, they are made by the Chinese people through vision, hard work, courage, reform and innovation.[206]

In effect, China contended it did not steal its way to success. That was a contention at which American public and private sector officials has long scoffed.

Second, China created a specialized court to enforce IPRs.[207] China had relied on IP courts in Beijing, Shanghai, and Guangzhou, which handled both trials and appeals. As of 1 January 2019, the Supreme People's Court said a new body, functioning as an appeals court, would handle seven types of IP cases: computer software; invention, design, and plant patents; integrated circuit layout design; IP-related monopolies; technical secrets. The Vice President of the Supreme Court served as its Chief Judge. The U.S. pointed out no judicial body in China was independent of the CCP. Indeed, the announcement in China's official news agency proclaimed the new body was a "'major decision and arrangement' by Chinese Communist Party (CCP) authorities."[208] In the words of Tang Jingyuan, a U.S.-based commentator:

> In China, the CCP reigns supreme, and all courts are led by it. In other words, courts rule on cases based on the needs and discretion of the Party.
>
> Once an issue touches upon the Party's sensitive interests, like the "*Made in China 2025*" effort or companies like Huawei, the court will be obstructed in arriving at a verdict. The Party wouldn't allow the court to let a Chinese company lose a lawsuit . . . .[209]

---

205. *China Hails "Important Progress" in U.S. Trade Talks*, BBC News, 1 February 2019, www.bbc.com/news/business-47081689.

206. Shawn Donnan, *China's Wang Uses Davos Speech to Offer Rebuttal of Trump*, Bloomberg Law International Trade News, 23 January 2019, https://news.bloomberglaw.com/international-trade/chinas-wang-uses-davos-speech-to-offer-rebuttal-of-trump-1 (*quoting* Wang Qishan, Vice President, China). [Hereinafter, *China's Wang*.]

207. *See* Nicole Hao, *Chinese Regime Establishes Supreme Court Body to Resolve Intellectual Property Disputes*, The Epoch Times, 3 January 2019, www.theepochtimes.com/chinese-regime-establishes-supreme-court-body-to-resolve-intellectual-property-disputes_2756391.html. [Hereinafter, *Chinese Regime*.]

208. *Quoted in Chinese Regime*.

209. *Quoted in Chinese Regime*.

Hence, the U.S. doubted the IP court would assure foreign investors they had an impartial forum in which to adjudicate disputes about forced technology transfer (that is, *de jure* or *de facto* requirements they hand over technology to local JV partners to gain access to the Chinese market) and theft (including cyber-theft) of trade secrets, and through which to obtain even-handed enforcement of judgments. Moreover, China required more enforcement resources to protect IPRs, plus criminal penalties (*e.g.*, imprisonment) to punish serious IP infringements.

Most importantly, regarding the *Made in China 2025* industrial policy, China defended it:

> "*Made-in-China 2025* is a *natural result* of China's development of its manufacturing industry," Xiao Yaqing, chairman of the State-owned Assets Supervision and Administration Commission, said [at the January 2018 World Economic Forum in Davos, Switzerland.] "Our industrial development is *needed by China* and will be a *contribution to the world*. We've seen the gap and *we must have our own industrial capability*."[210]

And, viewing the Trade War as part of China's movement away from 19th century isolationism and imperialism, China intoned "we reject the practices of the strong bullying the weak and self-claimed supremacy," and argued globalization was an "inevitable trend of history" that helped transform China from "a weak and impoverished agrarian country" to a country producing higher-value added merchandise. At bottom, the Chinese argument was two-pronged: industrial policy is "essential for us and both good and unavoidable for you."[211] Nothing in that argument moved the USTR, which continued to seek commercially meaningful structural changes, including SOE reforms to ensure they operate on market terms, removing state-support for producer-exporters, eliminating equity caps that limit FDI in a Chinese venture, and providing genuine national treatment to foreign investors under China's *Foreign Investment Law* (which, by its rubric, retained a "foreign"-versus-"Chinese" distinction).[212]

With respect to all outstanding controversies—market access, IP, and industrial policy—the USTR made clear that even if China came up with acceptable ideas,

---

210. *China Regulator Defends Made-in-China 2025, Hopes for Trade Deal*, Bloomberg Law International Trade News, 23 January 2019, https://news.bloomberglaw.com/international-trade/china-regulator-defends-made-in-china-2025-hopes-for-trade-deal-1.

211. *China's Wang* (*quoting* Wang Qishan, Vice President, China).

212. In March 2019, China's National People's Congress (NPC) voted 2,929 in favor, 8 against, and 8 abstentions, for a new *Foreign Investment Law* that took effect on 1 January 2020. See *China Foreign Investment Law: Bill Aims to Ease Global Concerns*, Bbc News, 15 March 2019, www.bbc.com/news/business-47578883. While the new Law "aim[ed] to create a more level playing field between domestic and foreign businesses," the American Chamber of Commerce in China "said some provisions were 'still quite general and do not address a number of the persistent concerns of foreign companies or foreign-invested enterprises in China.'" Id. In other words, the new Law was long on intentions and short on commitments.

the USTR would hold China accountable.[213] China would need to agree to a regular review of its trade reforms. The USTR wanted a mechanism specific to China whereby America could assess whether China implemented its reforms. If China failed to do so, then the U.S. reserved the right to reimpose the Section 301 tariffs. Thus, the USTR refused to take tariffs "off the table" in exchange for promises of change. But for China, periodic compliance checks by the U.S. could prove humiliating—a loss of face. Manifestly, the USTR sought to import into a potential peace agreement with China the concepts and practices of verification and enforcement that are commonplace in an arms control treaty, or associated with an export control or trade sanctions measure, but which in GATT-WTO accords are handled under the *DSU*, and in FTAs are dealt with through adjudication (such as panels) or arbitration (including ISDS).[214]

- **Multinational Business Planning: Intel Case Study**

The Sino-American Trade War, triggered by the Section 301 action, posed challenges for many of America's household name MNCs that rely on cross-border supply chains to make and ship global products. Intel Corp., the largest semiconductor producer in the world, was a case in point.[215] On the second U.S. retaliation list, computer memory and processor chips were included. Intel sourced many of its chips from China. Intel had no choice but to plan to shift production among various overseas and domestic facilities:

> Intel could shift its production strategies to avoid much of the blow [from Section 301 tariffs on chips]. Intel produces raw chips at six so-called wafer fabs, with three in the United States, one in Ireland, one in Israel and one in China. From there, chips go to so-called assembly and test facilities.
>
> After that, they are sold to Intel's customers, large computer brands or contract manufacturers who work on their behalf. Most of those entities are legally based in China because that is where most electronics are built, and that explains why Intel booked $14.8 billion in China revenue in 2017.
>
> But it is Intel's $12.5 billion revenue from the United States that is at risk. If Intel makes a chip at its U.S. plants in Oregon, Arizona or New Mexico, then sends it to China for low-level assembly work and then brings it back so it can be put into a device manufactured in the United States, the chip would get hit by the tariff.[216]

The task for Intel and many other MNCs was tariff minimization: they had to consider re-organizing its global supply chains to shield itself from the Section 301

---

213. *See* Michael Martina & Chris Prentice, *Exclusive: U.S. Demands Regular Review of China Trade Reform*, Reuters, 18 January 2019, www.reuters.com/article/us-usa-china-trade-exclusive /exclusive-u-s-demands-regular-review-of-china-trade-reform-idUSKCN1PC2AG.

214. *See Explainer.*

215. *See* Stephen Nellis, *Intel Has Paths Around Trump's China tariffs, Analysts Say*, Reuters, 18 June 2018, www.reuters.com/article/us-intel-trade/intel-has-paths-around-trumps-china-tariffs -analysts-say-idUSKBN1JF07O. [Hereinafter, *Intel Has Paths.*]

216. *Intel Has Paths.*

action. Essential to this task was differentiating which products were, and were not, subject to the tariffs:

> ... Intel also has assembly and test centers in Costa Rica, Malaysia and Vietnam. Chips from non-Chinese wafer fabs sold to American companies that pass through those facilities likely would not be hit.
>
> ...
>
> Intel does have a factory in Dalian, China where it makes flash memory chips. The kind of flash memory chips Intel makes are not targeted by the tariff list. But the risks of a broader escalation of a trade war could hurt Intel's efforts to expand into new areas.
>
> ...
>
> The assembly and test work that many chipmakers carry out in China makes up only about 10 percent of the value of a chip, with the design and manufacturing making up the bulk of a chip's value.[217]

Note the technical and strategic dimensions of differentiating targeted from non-targeted products. Technically, it is a customs classification matter at the 4-, 6-, or 8-digit HTSUS level. Strategically, the question involves a prognostication as to whether the Section 301 battle signals a wider, long-term Sino-American trade war, and if so, how Intel should respond.

Note also the irony of the Intel case study. The reason America launched the Section 301 battle was alleged Chinese IP misappropriation. Intel is at the forefront of ICT companies at risk from that misappropriation, hence in theory it is a beneficiary of a U.S. victory in the battle. But, in practice, Intel has to avoid being a casualty of friendly fire.

· **WTO in Crisis**

Truce or no truce, the Sino-American trade war could not but adversely affect the multilateral trading system, specifically the institution of the WTO. At a May 2018 WTO General Council meeting, the two countries hurled invectives at each other. Chinese WTO Ambassador Zhang Xiangchen, called America's attacked America's Section 301 and Section 232 actions as "dangerous and devasting," and with respect to the appointment of new Appellate Body judges, said that "[b]y taking the selection process as a hostage, the U.S. is abusing the decision-making mechanism of consensus."[218] Ambassador Zhang added:

> Any one of these, if left untreated, will fatally undermine the functioning of the WTO. But the reality is that the WTO is currently confronted with "three hard blows."[219]

---

217. *Intel Has Paths.*

218. *Quoted in* Tom Miles, *U.S. and China Each Say the Other is Wrecking the WTO System,* REUTERS, 8 May 2018, www.reuters.com/article/us-usa-trade-wto/u-s-and-china-each-say-the-other-is-wrecking-the-wto-idUSKBN1I91TM. [Hereinafter, *U.S. and China.*]

219. *Quoted in U.S. and China.*

That point missed the mark. So, too, did the Chinese Ambassador's statements that, "In fact, many U.S. companies have made great profits by establishing joint ventures in China, with profits earned in China exceeding their profits earned in the U.S. home market," and that China had a "'legitimate right' as a WTO Member to make reservations on market access and those reservations have "no connection with forced technology transfers."[220]

These points were red herrings. The Deputy USTR, and U.S. WTO Ambassador, Dennis Shea, fired a sharp counter-attack aimed at the true target—China's IP misappropriation in pursuit of its industrial policy:

> Mr. Chairman [of the WTO General Council], we have now entered the realm of Alice in Wonderland. White is black. Up is down.
>
> It is amazing to watch a country that is the world's most protectionist, mercantilist economy [*i.e.*, China] position itself as the self-proclaimed defender of free trade and the global trading system. The WTO must avoid falling down this rabbit hole into a fantasy world, lest it lose all credibility.
>
> If the WTO wishes to remain relevant, it must—with urgency—confront the havoc created by China's state capitalism.[221]

Ambassador Shea cited seven ways in which China "consistently . . . undermine[s] the global system of open and fair trade:" (1) market access barriers; (2) forced technology transfer; (3) IP theft; (4) indigenous innovation policies and the *Made in China 2025* scheme; (5) discriminatory TBTs; (6) government subsidies that create chronic industrial overcapacity (especially in the aluminum and steel sectors); and (7) FDI restrictions.[222] Thus, it was "perplexing" for China to claim it was a "victim."[223] Later, he elaborated:

> Shea specifically criticized China's use of foreign ownership restrictions to require U.S. companies to partner with Chinese companies as an *"unwritten"* condition of operating in the Chinese marketplace.
>
> "These requirements preclude foreign companies from entering the market on their own terms, and lay the foundation for China to coerce the transfer of technology". . . .
>
> This is a "lose-lose choice for foreign companies" . . . . "They must either transfer their technology to the new China-based joint venture, or they must cede access to one of the world's fastest-growing markets, thus harming both their short-term growth and their long-term competitiveness."

---

220. *Quoted in* Bryce Baschuk, *U.S., China Spar Over Forced Tech Transfer Practices at WTO*, 35 International Trade Reporter (BNA) 720 (31 May 2018) (reporting on Sino-American arguments at a 28 May 2018 WTO meeting). [Hereinafter, *U.S., China Spar.*]

221. *Quoted in U.S. and China.*

222. Bryce Baschuk, *Chinese Trade Policies Risk WTO Credibility, U.S. Envoy Says*, 35 International Trade Reporter 626 (10 May 2018). [Hereinafter, *Chinese Trade Policies.*]

223. *Quoted in Chinese Trade Policies.*

Shea also criticized China's use of administrative licensing and approval processes to "coerce technology transfer in exchange for the numerous approvals needed to establish and operate a business in China."

"At each stage of the approval process, vaguely worded provisions provide government officials with significant discretion to impose technology transfer requirements or otherwise pursue China's industrial policy objectives". . . .

"The policies create the legal conditions for Chinese economic actors to effectively coerce foreign companies to transfer technology to Chinese firms on non-market terms". . . . "If left unchecked, the commercial effect of these policies will erode all of our economies and our long-term competitiveness."[224]

"Fundamentally," said Ambassador Shea, "China has made the decision to engage in a systematic, state-directed, and non-market pursuit of other Members' cutting-edge technology in service of China's industrial policy."

Mr. Shea also ascribed blame to the Appellate Body for "steadily worsening rupture of trust," thanks to their adventurous interpretations that lead to new rules to which negotiators never agreed, and failure to adhere to the 90-day time limit for appeals. He argued: "Something has gone terribly wrong in this system when those charged with adjudicating the rules [*i.e.*, the Appellate Body] are so consistently disregarding those very rules. . . ." Mr. Zhang said that without the WTO dispute settlement system, "[u]ltimately, we will not be able to effectively control the unilateralism and protectionism," Mr. Shea said it was "perplexing" for China to claim it was a "victim" of American trade remedies.[225]

WTO spokesman Keith Rockwell summarized the debate, indicating that "many [Members] express[ed] concern that the U.S. actions could make the system dysfunctional, and [were] prepared to discuss its views, while rejecting any linkage between judicial appointments and reforming the WTO."[226] Overall, the debate "was extraordinary in its intensity," and "[i]t was unusual to see these two very prominent members laying it all on the line in terms of what they think." But, he added optimistically, "[t]his was a discussion that we had to have."

- **Differential Developmental Economic Stages**

Amidst the WTO debate, 41 developing and WTO Members—excluding China and the U.S.—bemoaned the "divergent positions on trade and development."[227]

---

224. *Quoted in U.S. China Spar* (emphasis added).
225. *Quoted in Chinese Trade Policies.*
226. *Quoted in U.S. and China.*
227. Communication from Argentina, Australia, Bangladesh, Benin, Brazil, Canada, Chile, Colombia, Costa Rica, Côte d'Ivoire, Dominican Republic, El Salvador, Guatemala, Hong Kong China, Iceland, Kazakhstan, Kenya, Republic of Korea, Lao People's Democratic Republic, Liechtenstein, Malaysia, Mali, Mexico, Republic of Moldova, Myanmar, New Zealand, Nigeria, Norway, Pakistan, Panama, Paraguay, Peru, Qatar, Singapore, Switzerland, Thailand, the former Yugoslav

Consider, then, the extent to which Sino-American negotiations hampered by the different stages of economic growth of the two sides? Joseph Stiglitz (1943–), winner of the 2001 Nobel Economics Prize, explained:

> The U.S. refuses to recognize that China is a developing country. Different countries are at different stages of development. It is fundamental to the establishment of the WTO. . . . You would never have had developing countries sign onto the WTO if you didn't recognize their right to development. It is a fundamental right and they [China] are not going to give up that right. We [the U.S.] see China as a big country and refuse to recognize their right to development.[228]

Stiglitz thus all but endorsed "*Made in China 2025*," and defended China's technology transfer schemes:

> Of course, they have a strategy to grow. What responsible developing country doesn't have a strategy? Every developing economist says the important part of development is that the state plays a role bringing it up. It would be derelict if the government didn't push this.
>
> . . .
>
> China's view of the forced taking of IP is: "We told the firms we want joint ventures and part of joint ventures is helping us develop and part of that is transferring IP and technology. Those are the terms that we made clear. No one had to come in. You came in. It was not a violation of WTO rules for us. Maybe you should have tried to negotiate that at the WTO, but you failed."[229]

Recall the Rostow Stages of Growth Model and Professor Douglas Irwin's three-phased division of American trade history. Apply these theories to the economic historical phase of each country. Was China—not yet a mature, consumption-driven, middle income country—akin to the U.S. in America's decades between the end of the Civil War (1965) and birth of GATT (1947), when restrictive trade policies to bolster industrialization triumphed over reciprocal trade liberalization that came through the GATT rounds?

Likewise, consider the differences in their stages of political development and consequent approaches to human rights. President Xi included in his speech an admonition that "arrogance had become obsolete and would be repudiated:"[230]

Republic of Macedonia, Turkey, Ukraine, Uruguay, and Viet Nam, delivered on 7 May 2018, ¶ 4, www.wto.org/english/news_e/news18_e/gc_07may18_e.pdf.

228. *Quoted in* Enda Curran, *Stiglitz Says True U.S.-China Trade Accord "Almost Impossible,"* BLOOMBERG, 18 April 2018, www.bloomberg.com/news/articles/2018-04-19/stiglitz-says-true-u-s-china-trade-accord-almost-impossible. [Hereinafter, *Stiglitz Says.*]

229. *Quoted in Stiglitz Says.* In other words, China's position was "it has no technology transfer requirements enshrined in its laws and any such transfers are a result of legitimate transactions." Jeff Mason, *Exclusive: China Shifts Position on Tech Transfers, Trade Talks Progress – U.S. Officials,* REUTERS, 27 March 2019, www.reuters.com/article/us-usa-china-trade-exclusive/exclusive-china-shifts-position-on-tech-transfers-trade-talks-progress-u-s-officials-idUSKCN1R905P

230. *China's Xi (quoting* President Xi).

> Human society is facing a major choice to open or close, to go forward or backward. In today's world, the trend of peace and cooperation is moving forward, and the Cold War mentality and zero-sum-game thinking are outdated.[231]

That warning dripped with irony: how "open" was China to discussing trade linkages, namely, the 3Ts—Taiwan, Tiananmen, and Tibet? China ordered airlines to stop calling Taiwan a "country." That, said the White House, was "Orwellian nonsense."[232] Nonetheless, the USTR, Ambassador Robert Lighthizer, insisted:

> It is not my objective to change the Chinese system. It seems to work for them. . . . But I have to be in a position where the United States can deal with it, where the United States isn't the victim of it and that's where our role is.[233]

How far was it possible to "deal with" that Communist system, given the *Made in China 2025* policy, and more fundamentally, given the values of that system?

Conversely, consider the extent to which the two countries might have shared interests? For example, WIPO reported that China (as of 2017) was the second largest filer of patents, behind the U.S. and ahead of Japan.[234] That would suggest a common cause against patent infringement.

X. Open Society War?

- **Not a "Cold War" or "Thucydides Trap," but an "Open Society War"**

Regardless of whether, how, and when the U.S. and China resolve their commercial differences, the Sino-American Trade War is best understood as a battle in a broad, deep conflict—an Open Society War. None other than the thoughtful investor, George Soros (1930–), and his intellectual mentor, the renowned philosopher, Karl Popper (1902–1994), suggest this characterization. Popper wrote *The Open Society and Its Enemies* (1945) while at the University of Canterbury, New Zealand, and joined (in 1946) the London School of Economics, where Soros was his student (from 1947–54). At the January 2019 World Economic Forum in Davos, Switzerland, it was Soros who delivered the most important speech.[235] Applying Popper's

---

231. *Quoted in China's Xi Vows More Openness Amid Trump Trade Dispute*, 35 International Trade Reporter (BNA) 487 (12 April 2018).

232. *China Softens Tone.*

233. *Quoted in* David Lawder, *Trump Trade Chief Wants to Open China, Not Change its Economic System*, REUTERS, 1 May 2018, www.reuters.com/article/us-usa-trade-china/ustr-lighthizer-says-wants-to-open-china-not-change-its-economic-system-idUSKBN1I246K.

234. *See* Daniel Moss, *China's Strengths in a Trade War are also its Weaknesses*, BLOOMBERG QUINT (India), 9 April 2018, www.bloombergquint.com/opinion/2018/04/09/china-s-strengths-in-a-trade-war-are-also-its-weaknesses.

235. *See* George Soros, Remarks Delivered at the World Economic Forum, 24 January 2019, www.georgesoros.com/2019/01/24/remarks-delivered-at-the-world-economic-forum-2/. [Hereinafter, January 2019 Soros Speech.]

concept of an "open society," Soros castigated the closed nature of Chinese governance, singling out President Xi Jinping (1953–, President, 2013–) and the abuse of large, data-rich information technology to spin a "web of totalitarian control the likes of which not even George Orwell could have imagined."[236]

To be sure, there are at least two other characterizations of the Sino-American Trade War: "Cold War" and "Thucydides Trap."[237] Both are flawed. Throughout the Soviet-American Cold War, the two superpowers had very little trade and FDI relations, and there was no nexus of supply chains dependent on them. Their fighting was "hot," through proxies across Third World countries. Today's American and Chinese economies are intertwined. Indeed, theirs is the most important bilateral economic relationship in the world on which many other countries depend. And, while the two powers flex their military muscles across the Nine Dash Line (discussed in a separate Chapter) and the Formosa Straits, they have (thus far) avoided widespread agency-based conflicts.

Calling the Trade War a "Thucydides Trap" mistakenly casts the U.S. as in decline. America's global economic and military reach remain unparalleled. Its conscious, bipartisan link of trade and national security policies shows it understands the sources of its power. America post-9/11 is not at all like Britain post-Second World War, nor is America "fearful" of a rising China in the sense that democratic Ancient Athens was of oligarchic Sparta in the Peloponnesian War (431–404 B.C.). For all its self-inflicted wounds and undignified political leaders, America remains the beacon of hope because of its long-term commitment to freedom — to an open society. As politically incorrect as it is to say, few millennials would migrate to China over America if offered a choice free of job, family, or language constraints.

The Soros-Popper formulation is that underlying the Sino-American trade fight is a conflict over openness in all aspects of human endeavor. To see why that is correct, that what is happening is an "Open Society War," consider two questions:

First: In practice, do the four specific areas of dispute in the Section 301 case suggest the Chinese economy is "open"?

Second: In theory, does governance in China bear the three hallmarks of an "open" society?

The case for a negative answer to both questions is strong.

---

236. January 2019 Soros Speech. Mr. Soros is not alone in commenting that China has become less open under the leadership of President Xi than his predecessors, contrary to the expectations of the West throughout the 1990s and early 2000s. *See* NICHOLAS R. LARDY, THE STATE STRIKES BACK: THE END OF ECONOMIC REFORM IN CHINA? (Washington, D.C.: Peterson Institute for International Economics, January 2019); Arvind Subramanian & Josh Felman, *The Coming China Shock*, PROJECT SYNDICATE, 5 February 2019, www.project-syndicate.org/commentary/coming-china-shock -end-of-exceptionalism-by-arvind-subramanian-and-josh-felman-2019-02.

237. For these respective characterizations, see, e.g., Robert D. Kaplan, *A New Cold War Has Begun*, FOREIGN POLICY, 7 January 2019, https://foreignpolicy.com/2019/01/07/a-new-cold-war-has -begun/; GRAHAM ALLISON, DESTINED FOR WAR: CAN AMERICA AND CHINA ESCAPE THUCYDIDES'S TRAP? (New York, N.Y.: Houghton Mifflin Harcourt, 2017).

- **Four Trade Controversies and Openness of Chinese Economy**

As to the first question, the core controversies raised by *Made in China 2025* pertain to market access, subsidies, SOE reform, and IPR protection. Market access is *ipso facto* about openness. Explicit industrial policy-based market share targets impede, even annul, market-based outcomes. China's pledge (in January 2019 talks with the USTR) to boost purchases of soybeans only reinforce the reality of state control: SOEs are the buyers, the soybeans are for state reserves, and thus these purchases are immune from the 25% counter-retaliatory tariff the CCP imposes in the Trade War.[238] The pledge to close its trade surplus with America by 2024 neglects the truth (that economists tire of recounting) that differential savings and investment rates cause bilateral trade imbalances. The pledge also neglects the fact that Chinese tariff and non-tariff barriers, including JV expectations (if not outright requirements), plus the CCP's grip on the *yuan* (discussed in a separate Chapter), have embedded in the psyche of American producer-exporters the sense that the Chinese market is difficult to "crack" open.

Subsidies are about whether central or sub-central government support to an enterprise or industry is lawful under the WTO *Agriculture* and *SCM Agreements*. They also are about transparency. Finding out exactly what officials in Beijing and provincial capitals are or are not giving to Chinese firms mystifies American competitors seeking a level playing field against those firms in the Chinese and third-country markets. That is why the USTR repeatedly and pointedly bemoans the tardy, incomplete nature of Chinese notifications to the WTO.

SOEs raise the problem of whether they operate on commercial terms when they compete with private companies. They also require definition: what criteria identify whether a particular entity is state owned or otherwise acts as a governmental body? Sunshine illuminates both issues: opening the books and records of SOEs (while protecting confidential business information) shows how whether they behave in response to arm's length supply and demand pricing; and seeing their ownership and control structure, and their authority and influence patterns, shows whether they are "public" or "private." But, it is overcast in China, as the uproar over Huawei's relationship to the CCP suggests.[239]

---

238. *See* Karl Plume, *Exclusive: China Buys U.S. Soybeans A Day After Trade Talks — Traders*, Reuters, 1 February 2019, www.reuters.com/article/us-usa-trade-china-soybeans/exclusive-china -buys-u-s-soybeans-a-day-after-trade-talks-traders-idUSKCN1PQ5CK.

239. *See* Sheridan Prasso, *China's Digital Silk Road is Looking More Like An Iron Curtain*, Bloomberg, 9 January 2019, www.bloomberg.com/news/features/2019-01-10/china-s-digital-silk-road-is -looking-more-like-an-iron-curtain (reporting "China is exporting to at least 18 countries sophisticated surveillance systems capable of identifying threats to public order and has made it easier to repress free speech in 36 others, according to an October [2018] report published by Washington watchdog Freedom House"). The Freedom House study is Adrian Shahbaz, *Freedom on the Net — The Rise of Digital Authoritarianism*, Freedom House, https://freedomhouse.org/report/freedom -net/freedom-net-2018/rise-digital-authoritarianism.

Respecting IPRs is about openness, too. An IPR is granted only after competition among entrepreneurial inventors as diverse as the young Steve Jobs (1955–2011) to established PhRMA companies. The IPR is a reward for the winner, and an incentive for the next round of competitors. Forcible technology transfers, whether through JV contracts or state-sponsored cyberattacks, disrupts this process and its outcomes. IP misappropriation awards monopoly patent, trademark, and copyright privileges not on the basis of merit, but rather insider dealing, and incentivizes unscrupulous, rent-seeking behavior under the guise of industrial policy. Here, again, Huawei is a case in point: is its technology a result and/or enabler of espionage?

• **Chinese Governance and Three Hallmarks of Open Society**

To address the second question, recall what Popper taught Soros and the world in *The Open Society and Its Enemies* and apply that teaching to China. Horrified by events in the 1930s, Popper was rare among scholars to critique and condemn both fascism and communism, and traced the origins of both to Plato, Hegel, and Marx. Popper's reading of these "false prophets" has been criticized: maybe Popper took Plato too seriously at his word, or maybe Popper read too much mysticism into Hegel. But, "got them wrong," Popper did not, and besides, whose exegesis of any difficult philosophical text is immune from questioning? Moreover, Popper's *tour de force* is a defense of liberal democracy that endures, and to which Soros dedicates his eleemosynary Open Society Foundations. For them, an "open" society bears three hallmarks.

First, it is a democracy. Democracy need not take a particular form, but the irreducible requirement is the government can be removed without bloodshed, at least at periodic intervals. *"All that counts is whether the government can be removed without bloodshed,"* he says.[240] Popper never advocated violence, except as a last resort in two limited cases: against a tyranny that made non-violent reform impossible, but then only to establish democracy; or to save democracy from attack by an existential threat, as happened across Europe in the 1930s.

The CCP shows no sign of openness to multi-party elections or other peaceful forms of transitions of power, as occurs in Taiwan. To the contrary, changes to China's Constitution instilled in October 2017 at the 19th National Congress of the CCP, under the rubric of "Xi Jinping Thought on Socialism with Chinese Characteristics in a New Era," cement CCP control over all aspects of life. Five months after conferring the honor of mention in the Constitution on Mr. Xi, an honor conferred only on Mao Zedong (1893–1976) and Deng Xiaoping (1904–1997), the National People's Congress abolished Presidential term limits, thus projecting his position and "Thought" indefinitely. Mr. Xi is no Maoist, but he is no fan of Deng's openness, either, as Steve Tsang, Director of the China Institute at the University of London School of Oriental and African Studies explains: "Xi sees no place for political

---

240. *Quoted in* HERBERT KEUTH, THE PHILOSOPHY OF KARL POPPER 242 (Cambridge, England: Cambridge University Press, 2015) (emphasis original). [Hereinafter, KEUTH.]

experimentation or liberal values in China, and regards democratization, civil society, and universal human rights as anathema."[241] Just ask Uyghur Muslims detained in what human rights organizations decry as a network of camps about the likelihood of "democracy" in Popper's sense of the term. Or ask long-suffering Tibetan Buddhists. The U.S. *Reciprocal Access to Tibet Act* (H.R. 1872), which both the House and Senate passed unanimously, and President Trump signed on 19 December 2018, is about openness.[242] *RATA* calls for American diplomats, journalists, and tourists to have the same, equal access to the Tibet Autonomous Region as their Chinese counterparts have across America.

Second, "critical rationalism" prevails in an open society. Popper means criticism is tolerated, and errors are corrected. "[O]ne of the best senses of 'reason' and 'reasonableness,'" he declares, is "openness to criticism."[243] The CCP rightly criticizes internal corruption. Yet, the Party errs insofar as prosecutions of wayward cadres are persecutions of dissident colleagues. From the Great Firewall to the 2010 WTO Appellate Body Report in the *Audio Visual Products* case, censorial CCP limits on tolerance abound. Note the importance of a liberal arts education, especially in the humanities, to foster "critical rationalism."

The reason critical rationalism is absent is the presence of what Popper calls "crude monism." A closed society fails to differentiate man-made rules from natural law. Distinctions of right-versus-wrong conduct that rulers impose, and those distinctions embedded in the human heart from an extrinsic, higher source, are indistinguishable. With the CCP as the source and summit of law, China seems "crudely monistic." This feature is the one on which Soros most focuses, declaring at Davos:

> I use "open society" as shorthand for a society in which the rule of law prevails as opposed to rule by a single individual and where the role of the state is to protect human rights and individual freedom. In my personal view, an open society should pay special attention to those who suffer from discrimination or social exclusion and those who can't defend themselves.[244]

Experience backs his view: he's a survivor of Nazi-occupied Hungary.

Finally, an open society is free of "historicism." Popper knew Marx to be a determinist, meaning Marx believed history moves according to inexorable laws. For Marx, the law is materialism that drives class struggle between the bourgeoise and proletariat. The struggle is resolved, the exploitative drudgery capital imposes on labor ends, when class tensions burst into a revolution that reconfigures production. Historicism is a tenet of CCP ideology, proven correct by the 1949 Communist Revolution. Since then, history advances through utopian social engineering: from

---

241. Steve Tsang, *What is Xi Jinping Thought?*, PROJECT SYNDICATE, 5 February 2019, www.project-syndicate.org/commentary/china-xi-jinping-thought-reform-by-steve-tsang-2019-02.

242. *See* www.congress.gov/bill/115th-congress/house-bill/1872.

243. *Quoted in* KEUTH, 240.

244. January 2019 Soros Speech.

the 1966–76 Cultural Revolution and population control to obedience to Confucian values and adherence to industrial policy, the CCP constructs a stable, harmonious society. The edifice is not economically egalitarian in outcome, but it is one in which citizens believe (falsely or not) they might get rich.

Popper's open society and its friends like Soros reject historicism. Deterministic laws exclude the possibility of rational political intervention, of choice, and thus of decision-making accountability. Moreover, Popper warned that Marx's "attempt to make heaven on earth invariably produces hell."[245] So, Popper favors the piecemeal social engineering typical in an open society. Change should occur incrementally to avoid excesses and allow for reversal if it is misguided.

- **Odd Bedfellows**

No case is airtight. Reasonable minds can differ as to the "openness" of China's economy and society. History will be the ultimate judge in the Open Society War. But already, the Section 301 case has made bedfellows of adversaries: Messrs. Soros and Trump. The President accused the Financier of funding protests against his Supreme Court pick, Brett Kavanaugh.[246] The Financier called the President a "narcissist" who "considers himself all-powerful" and "is willing to destroy the world."[247] Yet, America would betray its core liberal democratic principles if it did not insist on openness in trade relations with China, and would jeopardize its economic strength—and thus its national security—if it failed to obtain from China substantive, structural, and verifiable reform. That is an historical choice in favor of an open society of which Popper's student would be proud.

- **Towards an End to the War?**

As the deadline of midnight on 1 March 2019 for elevating Wave Three tariffs from 10% to 25% approached, America and China negotiated tirelessly to end the Trade, or Open Society, War that had started with the 22 March 2018 USTR *Section 301 Report*, and led to Wave One tariffs, effective 6 July, 25% on $34 billion worth of Chinese imports, Wave Two Tariffs effective 23 August, of 25% on $16 billion, and Wave Three tariffs effective 24 September of 10% on $200 billion, initially scheduled to increase to 25% on 1 January 2019, postponed to 2 March). The two sides outlined six MOUs, as follows:[248]

---

245. *Quoted in* Keuth, 240.

246. *See* https://twitter.com/realDonaldTrump/status/1048196883464818688.

247. *Quoted in Trump is "Willing to Destroy the World:" George Soros*, New York Post, 9 June 2018, https://nypost.com/2018/06/09/trump-is-willing-to-destroy-the-world-george-soros/.

248. *See* Kevin Yao & Dominque Patton, *China Pledges to Expand Financial Market Opening as U.S. Trade Delegation Arrives*, Reuters, 27 March 2019, www.reuters.com/article/us-china-boao/china-pledges-to-sharply-expand-financial-market-opening-as-trade-talks-loom-idUSKCN1R9076; Jeff Mason, *Exclusive: U.S., China Sketch Outlines of Deal to End Trade War – Sources*, Reuters, 20 February 2019, www.reuters.com/article/us-usa-trade-china-deal-exclusive/exclusive-u-s-china-sketch-outlines-of-deal-to-end-trade-war-sources-idUSKCN1QA07U; *Factbox: U.S., China Drafting Memorandums for Possible Trade Deal*, Reuters, 20 February 2019, www.reuters.com/article/us-usa-trade-china-deal-factbox/factbox-u-s-china-drafting-memorandums-for-possible-trade-deal-idUSKCN1QA07W [hereinafter, *Factbox*].

(1) Agriculture

Under this MOU, China would liberalize market access to American exports of beef, grains, poultry, and other farm products, plus cut tariffs on ethanol and distiller dried grains (an ethanol by-product).[249] The MOU also would require China to speed up approval of GM seeds (so that American farmers hesitant to plant those seeds without knowing whether the resulting crops will be eligible for entry into China can do so).

(2) Currency

This MOU would prevent China from devaluating the *yuan*, as the U.S. said it did in 2018 after America initially imposed the Section 301 tariffs to offset the effects of those tariffs. Rather, China would have to maintain stability in the *yuan*-dollar exchange rate.

(3) Forced Technology Transfer and Cyber Theft

This MOU would oblige China to ensure foreign companies are not pressured to transfer their technology "through joint venture requirements, unfair business licensing and product approval practices, or other forms of coercion."[250] It also would require China to prosecute hackers, and any support for cybertheft of trade secrets.

(4) IPRs

This MOU would call on China to strengthen its IP licensing laws to ensure that licensed IP is not stolen, and to step up criminal prosecutions of copyright violations.

---

249. Ethanol is a case study of how markets improvise to cope with government interventions. *See* Chris Prentice & A. Ananthalakshmi, *Long, Strange Trip: How U.S. Ethanol Reaches China Tariff-Free*, REUTERS, 7 February 2019, www.reuters.com/article/us-usa-trade-ethanol-insight/long-strange-trip-how-u-s-ethanol-reaches-china-tariff-free-idUSKCN1PW0BR. Absent the counter-retaliatory tariffs China imposed on American merchandise, U.S.-origin ethanol would be shipped from ports such as Texas City and Beaumont, Texas, move through the Panama Canal, and be discharged at a Chinese port, such as Zhoushan. However, on 23 and 27 June 2018, after loading 25,000 and 10,000 tons, respectively, at those two Texas ports, and proceeding through the Canal, a cargo of ethanol arrived on 13–15 August near Singapore, and a ship-to-ship transfer occurred (from the *High Seas* tanker ship to the *QUDS* tanker ship), with the cargo moving to the port of Kuantan, in Malaysia. At that port, an additional 12,074 tons of Asian-origin ethanol was loaded, after which the cargo sailed to Zhoshan, where it arrived on 26–30 August. All of the cargo was unloaded, free of the up to 70% counter-retaliatory duty that China otherwise would have levied had the ethanol been shipped directly from America. In not imposing the duty, China followed rules to which China had agreed with ASEAN, namely, that U.S. ethanol blended with at least 40% Asian-made fuel essentially was considered as non-U.S. origin, and thus free of duty. The circuitous route and blending of ethanol, though inefficient and distortive of market-based trade flows (*e.g.*, Malaysia had not exported ethanol for at least three years before the Section 301 case), was lawful (and, apparently, replicated on at one other occasion). Of course, this creativity helped American ethanol producers cope with their status as collateral damage in the Sino-American dispute, but undermined the protective effect for Unipec (a Chinese state-owned company under the parent, Sinopec) of China's counter-retaliation. *See id.*

250. *Factbox.*

(5) NTBs

The *Made in China 2025* industrial subsidies would be dealt with by this MOU, as would be business licensing procedures, product standard reviews, and other measures that unfairly advantage Chinese over American firms and merchandise. The obligations incumbent on China would address the billions of dollars of anticipated Chinese investments in its strategic high-technology sectors (*e.g.*, aerospace, AI, EVs, pharmaceuticals, robotics, and semiconductors) in which China seeks a dominant position, so that China does not create excess capacity, and over-produce, as occurred in the aluminum and steel sectors.

(6) Services

Via this MOU, China would open further its financial services markets to foreign suppliers, especially credit card companies (*e.g.*, MasterCard and Visa) so they can compete with Chinese monopolies (namely, China UnionPay Ltd.) with respect to bank- and non-bank card payments, and credit rating companies. China also would ensure its regulations that allow foreign insurance companies to take controlling stakes in local JVs are transparent and applied in a non-discriminatory manner, expand the scope of permissible foreign bank activities, and allow foreign cloud computing services greater freedom.

The gist of each MOU was to lay out specific Chinese commitments, coupled with specific metrics by which the U.S. could verify whether China fulfilled those commitments, and an enforcement mechanism to ensure China did so that included periodic reviews of Chinese progress. Ultimately, the U.S. reserved the right to reimpose any Section 301 tariffs that it withdrew, if China did not undertake the structural reforms the MOUs identified.

Additionally, the U.S. and China drafted a list of 10 American exports (agricultural commodities, energy, industrial products, and high-tech goods such as semiconductors) that China would buy to help shrink its bilateral trade surplus. And, at the insistence of President Trump, both sides agreed they would not call their arrangements "MOUs."[251] The President thought MOUs were not binding, and

---

251. *Trump's Trade Chief Lectures His Boss and Gets Earful in Return*, BLOOMBERG LAW INTERNATIONAL TRADE NEWS, 22 February 2019, https://news.bloomberglaw.com/international-trade/trumps-trade-chief-lectures-his-boss-and-gets-earful-in-return. The Oval Office exchange between the President and USTR, in the presence of China's top chief negotiator, Liu He, was comical:

Trump told gathered reporters that the memorandums would "be very short term. I don't like MOUs because they don't mean anything. To me, they don't mean anything."

Lighthizer then jumped in to defend the strategy, with Trump looking on. "An MOU is a binding agreement between two people," he said. "It's detailed. It covers everything in great detail. It's a legal term. It's a contract."

But the president, unswayed, fired back at Lighthizer. "By the way I disagree," Trump said. The top Chinese negotiator, Vice Premier Liu He, laughed out loud.

"The real question is, Bob," Trump said, "how long will it take to put that into a final binding contract?"

Quoted in id.

thus demanded they call them "trade agreements." That rubric, however, raised the prospect Congress might seek to review and vote on the package of deals.

Citing "substantial progress" in the negotiations, but not specifying the nature of that "progress" or explaining why it was "substantial," on 24 February 2018 the President decided to extend the deadline of midnight, 1 March, for increasing the Wave Three tariffs from 10% to 25%.[252] For how long, he did not say, and the USTR announcement in the Federal Register indicated the suspension was indefinite. But, Congress stated that if no MOUs/agreement was reached by 17 March, then the USTR must delineate a process for importers of Chinese products to pursue product exclusion requests.[253]

Already, some U.S. companies were re-orienting their production out of China to avoid entirely Section 301 tariffs. For example, Kent, the bicycle manufacturer, moved its production of bike frames from China to Cambodia, which not only had relatively lower labor costs, but also qualified for GSP treatment based on a 35% value added ROO (discussed in a separate Chapter).[254] Specialized Bicycle Components had done so already, leaving China for Cambodia, Taiwan, and Vietnam as of December 2018. As a CPTPP Party, Vietnam was especially attractive.

Such moves were smart. Companies did not necessarily need to onshore production from China to the U.S., nor did they have to cease using all Chinese parts. Rather, they needed to blend the best arrangement of production location, sourcing options, and potential preferential trading arrangements, and adjust accordingly. Bicycle production in the U.S. had plummeted from 15 million in the 1970s to 500,000 in 2019, though still, 94% of finished bikes, and 60% of components (e.g.,

---

252. Quoted in Carlos Barria, *Trump Announces Delay of Tariffs on Chinese Goods Due to "Substantial Progress" in Talks to End U.S.-China Trade War*, Business Insider, 26 February 2019, https://www.businessinsider.com/trump-china-tariff-increase-delayed-past-march-1-deadline-2019-2.

253. *See* Office of the United States Trade Representative, Notice of Modification of Section 301 Action: China's Acts, Policies, and Practices Related to Technology Transfer, Intellectual Property, and Innovation, 28 February 2019, https://ustr.gov/sites/default/files/enforcement/301Investigations/301_Notice_2-28-2019.pdf.

Congress did so on 15 February 2019, mandating that regardless of whether or when the Wave Three rate increases from 10% to 25%, the USTR must lay out an exclusion process for this Wave of tariffs, in a joint House-Senate statement accompanying a budget bill. The statement said:

> It is concerning that there is no exclusion process for goods subject to tariffs in round 3 of the Section 301 proceeding, as was done in the first two rounds. USTR shall establish an exclusion process for tariffs imposed on goods subject to Section 301 tariffs in round 3. This process should be initiated no later than 30 day after enactment of this Act, following the same procedures as those in rounds 1 and 2, allowing stakeholders to request that particular products classified within a tariff subheading subject to new round 3 tariffs be excluded from the Section 301 tariffs.

Explanatory Statement Submitted by Mrs. Lowey, Chairwoman of the House Committee on Appropriations, Regarding H.J. Resolution 31, *Consolidated Appropriations Act 2019*, at 38, https://docs.house.gov/billsthisweek/20190211/116hrpt9-JointExplanatoryStatement-u1.pdf.

254. *See* Rajesh Kumar Singh, *How U.S. Bike Companies Are Steering Around Trump's China Tariffs*, Reuters, 26 February 2019, www.reuters.com/article/us-usa-trade-bicyles-insight/how-u-s-bike-companies-are-steering-around-trumps-china-tariffs-idUSKCN1QF0G1. [*Hereinafter, How U.S. Bike Companies.*]

handlebars, seats, tires, and tubes), sold in the U.S. were made in China.[255] The lack of deep-water port capacity and inability to accommodate large container vessels still kept China in the bike race vis-à-vis Cambodia, Vietnam, and other South East Asian countries. And, significantly, even when bike companies shifted from China to a South East Asian country, they moved robots out of Chinese facilities for work such as welding, and put them in their new factories. So, the job-creation impact in such countries was limited—as it would be (or would have been) in the U.S. (*a fortiori*, given the higher labor costs).

As businesses made adjustments to their global supply chains, political leaders and trade negotiators on both sides searched for the kind of substantial progress that America could accept, and China could give, to end the War.[256] The USTR, Ambassador Robert Lighthizer, put it quite rightly in his February 2019 Congressional testimony that America "is not foolish enough" abandon the threat of Section 301 tariffs following any single trade negotiation with China, because "[t]he reality is this [structural changes in China] is a challenge that will go on for a long, long time," and China presented the "most severe challenge" ever faced by American trade policymakers.[257] His admonition proved correct, because in March 2019 it was clear China "had yet to offer 'meaningful concessions,'" such as on e-commerce topics.[258] China's offer on digital trade was inadequate, and it refused to concede three key points: (1) cessation of discrimination against providers of foreign cloud computing; (2) reduction of restrictions on transfers of overseas data; and (3) relaxation of data localization rules that mandated companies store data in China. In April 2019, the situation changed. Frequent, intensive talks between the two sides yielded substantial progress on the six key areas noted above, and on an enforcement mechanism (possibly including offices in each country). A deal appeared at hand.

---

255. *How U.S. Bike Companies.*

256. For examples of Chinese and non-Chinese companies shifting operations from China to Mexico, and exporting from Mexico to the U.S., see *Matthew Townsend & Eric Martin, U.S. and China Got Into A Trade War And Mexico Won*, BLOOMBERG, 27 March 2019, www.bloomberg.com/news/articles/2019-03-27/who-is-winning-trump-s-trade-war-with-china-so-far-it-s-mexico. This consequence is unintended, insofar as a hoped-for result of the Section 301 action is to onshore production and jobs in America

257. *Quoted in* David Lawder, *U.S. Trade Chief Sees Long-term China Challenges, Continued Tariff Threat*, REUTERS, 27 February 2019, www.reuters.com/article/us-usa-trade-china-house/u-s-trade-chief-sees-long-term-china-challenges-continued-tariff-threat-idUSKCN1QG250. *See also* Opening Statement of USTR Robert Lighthizer to the House Ways and Means Committee, 27 February 2019, https://ustr.gov/about-us/policy-offices/press-office/press-releases/2019/february/opening-statement-ustr-robert (describing, with respect to China, the "large and growing trade deficit and their unfair trade practices—including technology transfer issues, failure to protect intellectual property, large subsidies, cyber theft of commercial secrets and other problems—as major threats to our economy," and indeed, an "existential problem."

258. *See China Refuses to Concede on U.S. Demands to Ease Curbs on Tech Firms: FT*, REUTERS, 24 March 2019, www.reuters.com/article/us-usa-trade-china-tech/china-refuses-to-concede-on-u-s-demands-to-ease-curbs-on-tech-firms-ft-idUSKCN1R506Q (*quoting a Financial Times report*).

Part Eight

Currency Manipulation

Chapter 32

GATT Article XV and IMF Article IV[1]

I. GATT Article XV:1–3 Cooperation and Consultation

- **Historical Context**

In yesteryear, Article XV was a candidate for the title of "most obscure provision in GATT." Because of alleged currency manipulation by China (and even allegedly by Japan and Korea), it is has become a hotly debated provision.[2]

The Article, entitled "Exchange Arrangements," contains nine Paragraphs. Each one presumes familiarity with terms and concepts from international finance, as each deals with matters at the intersection of finance and trade. Further, all of them were drafted in a long-past era of fixed exchange rates. Thus, Article XV hardly is easy reading. Yet, at the time of drafting, the terms and concepts Article XV embodies were widely understood, particularly among politicians—including American congressmen—who demanded disciplines against the manipulation of exchange rates. Examples of manipulation at the time—actual or feared—included devaluing an exchange rate (to make exports less expensive and imports more expensive), maintaining multiple exchange rates (to make imports more expensive), and requiring a license to exchange local into foreign currency to pay for imports (and thereby discourage importation).[3] So, it is important to put Article XV in its historical context, specifically, the concerns of policy makers at the time. They did not want to see trade liberalization undermined by devious exchange rate policies.

---

1. Documents References:
   (1) *Havana (ITO) Charter* Articles 41, 47, 66, 92–97
   (2) GATT Article XV
   (3) WTO *SCM Agreement* Articles 1–6, Annex

2. As to the specific but world-wide dispute over alleged manipulation by China of its currency, the literature is large and growing. *See, e.g.,* Simon Evenett, ed., THE U.S.—CHINA CURRENCY DISPUTE: NEW INSIGHTS FROM ECONOMICS, POLITICS, AND LAW (London, England: Centre for Economic Policy Research (CEPR)/VoxEU.org Publication, 2010) (especially Section 5, pages 109–154, "Does the Crisis-Era *Renminbi* Regime Violate WTO Rules? Is the Threat of WTO Litigation Credible?").

3. *See* JOHN H. JACKSON, WORLD TRADE AND THE LAW OF GATT § 18.1 at 479–80 (1969). [Hereinafter, JACKSON 1969.]

• **Organization**

One approach to Article XV is to organize its 9 Paragraphs according to what kind of country they address. Some Paragraphs (particularly, Article XV:1–3) address contracting parties (WTO Members) that are also members of the IMF.[4] Other Paragraphs (namely, Article XV:6–8) address contracting parties (Members) that are not IMF members. Still other Paragraphs (notably, Article XV:4–5 and 9) address contracting parties (Members), regardless of their status in the IMF. These Paragraphs are of general application and, in practice, of greatest interest.

• **Member Cooperation**

As regards the first five Paragraphs, the first three deal with cooperation between the contracting parties (Members) and IMF. Article XV:1–3 provides:

1. The CONTRACTING PARTIES shall seek co-operation with the International Monetary Fund to the end that the CONTRACTING PARTIES and the Fund may pursue a coordinated policy with regard to exchange questions within the jurisdiction of the Fund and questions of quantitative restrictions and other trade measures within the jurisdiction of the CONTRACTING PARTIES.

2. In all cases in which the CONTRACTING PARTIES are called upon to consider or deal with problems concerning monetary reserves, balances of payments or foreign exchange arrangements, they shall consult fully with the International Monetary Fund. In such consultations, the CONTRACTING PARTIES shall accept all findings of statistical and other facts presented by the Fund relating to foreign exchange, monetary reserves and balances of payments, and shall accept the determination of the Fund as to whether action by a contracting party in exchange matters is in accordance with the Articles of Agreement of the International Monetary Fund, or with the terms of a special exchange agreement between that contracting party and the CONTRACTING PARTIES. The CONTRACTING PARTIES, in reaching their final decision in cases involving the criteria set forth in paragraph 2(a) of Article XII or in paragraph 9 of Article XVIII, shall accept the determination of the Fund as to what constitutes a serious decline in the contracting party's monetary reserves, a very low level of its monetary reserves or a reasonable rate of increase in its monetary reserves, and as to the financial aspects of other matters covered in consultation in such cases.

---

4. For discussions of the relationship between GATT and the IMF, *see, e.g.,* ORIN KIRSHNER ED., THE BRETTON WOODS—GATT SYSTEM: RETROSPECT AND PROSPECT AFTER FIFTY YEARS (1996); PETER B. KENEN ED., MANAGING THE WORLD ECONOMY: FIFTY YEARS AFTER BRETTON WOODS (1994); D.E. Siegel, *Legal Aspects of the IMF/WTO Relationship: The Fund's Articles of Agreement and the WTO Agreements,* 96 AMERICAN JOURNAL OF INTERNATIONAL LAW 561 (2002).

For explanations of the Bretton Woods System, *see, e.g.,* KENNETH W. DAM, THE RULES OF THE GLOBAL GAME (2001); KENNETH W. DAM, THE RULES OF THE GAME (1984); HAROLD JAMES, INTERNATIONAL MONETARY COOPERATION SINCE BRETTON WOODS (1996).

3. The CONTRACTING PARTIES shall seek agreement with the Fund regarding procedures for consultation under paragraph 2 of this Article.[5]

The assumption of the above-quoted Paragraphs, namely, that a contracting party (Member) also is a member of the IMF, is a safe one. Membership in the Fund and WTO has expanded vastly since the 1940s, and most countries belong to both IOs. The exceptional cases tend to involve participation in the IMF, but not WTO.

II. GATT Article XV:6–9 and Non-IMF Members

GATT drafters allowed for the peculiar instance of a country being a contracting party, but not an IMF member. They addressed Paragraphs 6 through 8 of Article XV to this scenario:

6. Any contracting party which is not a member of the Fund shall, within a time to be determined by the CONTRACTING PARTIES after consultation with the Fund, become a member of the Fund, or, failing that, enter into a special exchange agreement with the CONTRACTING PARTIES. A contracting party which ceases to be a member of the Fund shall forthwith enter into a special exchange agreement with the CONTRACTING PARTIES. Any special exchange agreement entered into by a contracting party under this paragraph shall thereupon become part of its obligations under this Agreement.

7. (a) A special exchange agreement between a contracting party and the CONTRACTING PARTIES under paragraph 6 of this Article shall provide to the satisfaction of the CONTRACTING PARTIES that the objectives of this Agreement will not be frustrated as a result of action in exchange matters by the contracting party in question.

   (b) The terms of any such agreement shall not impose obligations on the contracting party in exchange matters generally more restrictive than those imposed by the *Articles of Agreement of the International Monetary Fund* on members of the Fund.

8. A contracting party which is not a member of the Fund shall furnish such information within the general scope of section 5 of Article VIII of the *Articles of Agreement of the International Monetary Fund* as the CONTRACTING PARTIES may require in order to carry out their functions under this Agreement.[6]

In either instance—whether a country is a member of both IOs, or of just the WTO—a question may arise as to exchange controls.

---

5. *See also* JACKSON 1969, § 26.6 at 693–696 (recounting the early history of the relationship between GATT and the IMF).

6. *See also* JACKSON 1969, § 18.3 at 486–491 (discussing special exchange agreements between contracting parties that were not IMF members, which as of 1969 were only seven countries—Barbados, Cuba, Czechoslovakia, Malta, Poland, Rhodesia, and Switzerland).

Suppose a country implements exchange restrictions. What rules take precedence in the event of a conflict: GATT, or the *Articles of Agreement of the International Monetary Fund* (IMF *Articles*) (or, for a non-IMF member, special arrangements of that non-member with the IMF)? The drafters put the answer in Paragraph 9, which states:

> *Nothing in this Agreement* shall preclude:
>
> (a) the use by a contracting party of exchange controls or exchange restrictions in accordance with the Articles of Agreement of the International Monetary Fund or with that contracting party's special exchange agreement with the CONTRACTING PARTIES, or
>
> (b) the use by a contracting party of restrictions or controls on imports or exports, the sole effect of which, additional to the effects permitted under Articles XI, XII, XIII and XIV, is to make effective such exchange controls or exchange restrictions.[7]

In other words, under Article XV:9(a), exchange controls designed and implemented in a manner consistent with the IMF *Articles* (or special bilateral arrangements with the IMF) are deemed lawful under GATT. Article XV:9(b) supplements this point by authorizing trade restrictions in furtherance of exchange controls, as long as they comport with Articles XI through XIV of GATT.

Just how large is the safe harbor in Article XV:9? In particular, could a contracting party (Member) implement an exchange measure that frustrates the intent of GATT, and thus violates Article XV:4, but take refuge in this harbor? The *chapeau* suggests — by use of the words "Nothing in this Agreement" — that satisfaction of the conditions in either Sub-Paragraph result in a complete immunity from suit under any Article of GATT, including Article XV:4. That argument might have been made by Greece in a 1952 dispute, *Special Import Taxes Instituted by Greece*. But, this GATT Panel case ended without the need for adjudication under Article XV.

III. GATT Article XV:4–5 and Frustration

· **Central Importance of Paragraphs 4–5**

In Article XV, the real action, as it were, is in Paragraph 4 and 5. These Paragraphs are of general application, *i.e.*, they address each contracting party (WTO Member), whether or not it belongs to the IMF. Article XV:4–5 state:

> 4. Contracting parties shall not, by exchange action, *frustrate* the intent of the provisions of this Agreement, nor, by trade action, the intent of the provisions of the Articles of Agreement of the International Monetary Fund.

---

7. Emphasis added.

5. If the CONTRACTING PARTIES consider, at any time, that exchange restrictions on payments and transfers in connection with imports are being applied by a contracting party in a manner *inconsistent with the exceptions provided for in this Agreement for quantitative restrictions*, they shall report thereon to the Fund.[8]

Article XV:5 obligates a WTO Member to report to the IMF an allegation against another Member that the other Member maintains exchange controls inconsistent with GATT.

But, Paragraph 5 does not confer subject matter jurisdiction on the IMF to adjudicate the claim. If one Member complains another Member's exchange control regime violates Article XI:1 or XIII, then the WTO will handle the complaint. What value, then, is there on tattling to the IMF? At least, reporting the matter to the IMF creates pressure, in addition to the WTO complaint, on the Member with the regime.

• **What Does "Frustrate" Mean?**

Paragraph 4 contains the word "frustrate." It modifies the "intent" of both GATT and the IMF *Articles*. Therefore, the substantive obligation in Article XV:4 is not to frustrate the intent of either agreement. Immediately, the obligation poses three problems.

First, what is the "intent" of GATT and the *Articles*, and how is it to be discerned reliably? Second, does "intent" relate to the "letter" and "spirit" of GATT and the IMF Articles, and if so, how? Would a contracting party (WTO Member) breach the substantive obligation if it followed the "letter" of GATT or the IMF *Articles*, but not the "spirit" of them? Third, does the obligation concerning the intent of the IMF *Articles* apply to a country that is not an IMF Member, and if so, how? Nothing in the rest of GATT answers these questions, and there is essentially no jurisprudence on Article XV that sheds light on them.

The word "frustrate," however, poses the most pressing problem. Evidently, the drafters of GATT did not want a contracting party to design or implement exchange controls that undermine trade liberalization commitments under GATT. But, what did they mean by this critical term? "Frustration" is the legal standard the established to determine whether that occurs. This standard has a long history in

---

8. Emphasis added. *See also* JACKSON 1969, § 18.4 at 489–495 (observing provisions in GATT, in addition to Article XV:4, contain commitments relating to exchange restrictions, most notably: Article I:1 (embracing within the scope of the MFN obligation any customs duty or charge imposed on international payments for imports and exports); II:3 (barring alteration of the method of converting currencies so as to impair the value of a concession); II:6 (permitting adjustments to specific duties and charges following a devaluation of more than 20%); V:2–3 (concerning subsidization, which as explained in an Interpretative Note, *Ad Article VI, Paragraphs 2 and 3 item 2*, may be caused by multiple currency rates); VII:4 (restricting discretion to design customs valuation rules that depend on exchange rates); and, VIII:4 (applying the disciplines on customs fees and formalities to the use of exchange controls)).

contract law, of course, but not in multilateral trade law. Logically, the Public International Law understanding of the term is relevant. That is because the substantive legal obligation in Article XV:4 is not to frustrate a treaty, namely, GATT.

Fortunately, the delegate from New Zealand to the 1946 London Preparatory Conference asked about the meaning of the word "frustrate." The result was insertion of an Interpretative Note.[9] *Ad Article XV, Paragraph 4.* It helps define this vital term:

> The word "frustrate" is intended to indicate, for example, that infringements of the *letter* of any Article of this Agreement by exchange action shall *not* be regarded as a violation of that Article *if*, in practice, there is no appreciable departure from the *intent* of the Article. Thus, a contracting party which, as part of its exchange control operated in accordance with the *Articles of Agreement* of the International Monetary Fund, requires payment to be received for its exports in its own currency or in the currency of one or more members of the International Monetary Fund will not thereby be deemed to contravene Article XI or Article XIII. Another example would be that of a contracting party which specifies on an import license the country from which the goods may be imported, for the purpose not of introducing any additional element of discrimination in its import licensing system but of enforcing permissible exchange controls.[10]

The Note sets compliance with the intent of the IMF *Articles* as the benchmark for behavior that does not frustrate GATT.

· **Three Problems with IMF Benchmark**

Yet, applying this benchmark is problematical for three reasons. First, discerning the intent of the drafters of the IMF *Articles* at the 1944 Bretton Woods Conference is required. Second, it is necessary to delineate the "letter" from "spirit" of the Articles. Third, in the modern world of flexible exchange rates, the relevance of the IMF *Articles* is diminished. That is, there are situations involving the exchange rate of the currencies of 2 WTO Members, in which one Member complains the FX policy of the other Member frustrates the intent of GATT, but no provision in the IMF *Articles* is implicated.

· **1952 *Greek Import Taxes* GATT Panel Report**

The only case dealing with Article XV:4 is the 1952 GATT Panel Report in *Special Import Taxes Instituted by Greece*.[11] France complained about a special tax Greece levied on certain imported merchandise, alleging the tax violated the national treatment obligation of Article III:2. Greece eliminated the tax, but on 31 December 1951 substituted it with a new "contribution." The purpose of the contribution was to offset the depreciation of the Greek *drachma*, which had fallen substantially

---

9. *See* John H. Jackson, World Trade and the Law of GATT § 18.2 at 482.
10. Emphasis added.
11. *See* B.I.S.D. (1st Supp.) 48–51 (1953) (adopted 3 November 1952).

against foreign currencies. The contribution was a tax on foreign currency used to pay for imported merchandise. The Bank of Greece collected the contribution at the time a Greek importer paid for merchandise from overseas (*e.g.*, when a bank credit opened for the payment). The amount of the contribution varied—25%, 50%, 100%, or 150% of the c.i.f. value of imports—depending on how useful and necessary the merchandise was judged by the Greek Government.[12] Did this scheme pose a question under Article XV:4?

The GATT Panel could not agree on the proper characterization of the contribution.[13] Was it an "internal tax" in violation of Article III:2? France applied this characterization, because like domestic products did not suffer from the contribution. If it was not an "internal tax," then was it a "charge" under Article II? The U.K. accepted this characterization, and thus urged the scheme violated the bound commitments in the Greek Schedule of Concessions. Greece resisted these characterizations, and urged the contribution was nothing more than a tax on foreign exchange allocated to pay for imports. Under this characterization, the relevant GATT provision was Article XV:4, and the question was whether the contribution "frustrated" the intent of GATT.

The GATT Panel never resolved this issue.[14] It deferred consideration of the point until Greece provided more information about the contribution scheme. Conceivably, Greece might have argued Article XV:9 is a general defense against exchange controls and restrictions—even exchange measures that frustrate the intent of GATT.[15] That is, Greece might have used Paragraph 9(a) as a shield from a GATT suit, saying its contribution scheme conforms with the IMF *Articles*. Pursuant to Article XV:2, that argument would have required a determination from the IMF that the scheme did satisfy the *Articles*. This interesting possibility never materialized. In 1953, Greece devalued the *drachma* by 50%, repealed the scheme, and the case effectively ended.

A final point about Paragraph 4 of Article XV worth considering is its relationship to Paragraph 9 of that Article. During the 1948 Havana Conference, the negotiators appeared hesitant to clarify this relationship. Language at the start of Paragraph 9 stating "Subject to paragraph 4 of this Article" was deleted.[16] The deletion put Article XV:9 in conformity with its corresponding provision in the *ITO Charter*, Article 24:8, and this amendment to Article XV:9 took effect on 14 December 1948 (when a Protocol Amending Part II and Article XXVI entered into force). However,

---

12. *See* Jackson 1969, § 18.2 at 484.

13. *See* B.I.S.D. (1st Supp.) ¶¶ 1–2, 5, 7–9 at 48–50 (1953) (adopted 3 November 1952).

14. *See* B.I.S.D. (1st Supp.) ¶ 12 at 51 (1953) (adopted 3 November 1952).

15. *See* Jackson 1969, § 18.2 at 484–485.

16. *See* World Trade Organization, Guide to GATT Law and Practice—Analytical Index, vol. 1 at 441 (Geneva, Switzerland: World Trade Organization, 6th ed. 1995). [Hereinafter, GATT Analytical Index.] Your Textbook author is indebted to his former student at the University of Kansas School of Law, Conor Warde, Esq., for this insight.

the advantage of the language was it ensured that in the event of a conflict between Paragraphs 4 and 9, the earlier Paragraph would control.

In practice, then, if the IMF approved (or at least did not criticize) an exchange rate measure, then that measure would be immune from suit under GATT. With the exclusion of the language, it is not clear whether Paragraph 4 or 9 controls in a conflict. Conversely, there is an advantage following from the deletion. There is plenty of room for the WTO and IMF to cooperate on exchange matters.

IV. Chinese Currency Policy

- **Criticisms of Chinese Currency Policy**

With increasing stridence and exasperation since the early 1990s, many in the private and public sectors of WTO Members have called for China to be labeled a "currency manipulator." The calls have been nothing short of demands from the U.S., EU, and Brazil especially given the ever-expanding trade deficits of those countries with China, and their concerns about recovering manufacturing jobs and incomes since the 2008 global economic slump. The topic figured prominently in the 2012 American Presidential Election, with one candidate (Governor Mitt Romney (Republican)) pledging repeatedly to dub China a "currency manipulator" on the first day he took office.[17]

The common denominator of all criticisms about the behavior of the *yuan* is the CCP intentionally undervalues its currency. Why? Because the CCP allegedly seeks to render Chinese exports to the U.S. (or the EU, Brazil, or other WTO Members) cheaper (when denominated in dollar terms, which American consumers would pay), while at the same time increasing the price of American exports to China (when those dollar-denominated exports are translated back to *yuan*, which Chinese consumers would pay). The end result, critics say, of the undervalued exchange rate is an unfair advantage, or un-level competitive playing field, favoring China against American manufacturers in particular. Many of the critics say this advantage is tantamount to an export subsidy.

- **Facts about Chinese Currency Policy**

To evaluate these criticisms and consider any legal ramifications that might follow from them, it is necessary to understand what the Chinese FX rate regime was and is. There has been not one regime, but several, as the currency policy of the ruling CCP has evolved. The seminal developments were:

---

17. *Quoted in* Aaron Lorenzo, *Romney's Focus on China Exchange Rate, Tariff Threat Seen by Some as Misdirected*, 29 International Trade Reporter (BNA) 1692 (25 October 2012). [Hereinafter, *Romney's Focus.*]

(1) In 1986, the CCP established a dual FX rate regime.[18] Under it, exporters sold sell their export earnings denominated in foreign currencies in a regulated market. A separate, distinct internal Chinese market for foreign exchange existed. But, the exchange rate in the first market was more favorable to exporters than the one they otherwise would face in the second one, *i.e.*, they could obtain more *yuan* per U.S. dollar (or other unit of hard currency).

(2) In 1994, the CCP eliminated the dual-rate regime, and replaced it with a market-based managed floating exchange rate system. On a daily basis, the PBC simply determined and announced an exchange rate for *yuan* against foreign currencies, which was applicable to all interested parties.

(3) In 1995, the CCP changed its currency policy, pegging the *yuan* in a *de facto* sense to the U.S. dollar. That peg lasted for a decade, surviving the 1997–1999 Asian Economic Crisis.

(4) In July 2005, the CCP replaced the long-standing *de facto* peg with a crawling peg, meaning the *yuan* floated against the dollar within a 0.3% (up or down) band. Shortly thereafter, the CCP widened the band to 0.5% (up or down).

(5) But, also in July 2005, and within a week of establishing the band, the CCP changed its policy again. It replaced the crawling peg against the dollar with a managed float system whereby the PBOC set the value of the *yuan* against a basket of hard currencies, including the dollar, *yen*, and *euro*. This valuation translated into an exchange rate of 8.28 *yuan* to the dollar.

To be specific, the CCP employs 2 main methods to control the *RMB* exchange rate. First, it deploys domestic and international measures to increase the *RMB* supply by issuing *RMB*, and concurrently to decrease the supply of foreign exchange by purchasing hard currencies. By accumulating a large amount of foreign reserves, the CCP counters pressure on the *RMB* to appreciate.[19] Second, the CCP imposes strict capital controls. These controls ensure the adjustment of *RMB* supply effectively maintains a specified level of *RMB* exchange.[20]

Via these strict controls, China has maintained a relatively stable exchange rate, with a slight appreciation trend since 2006.

---

18. This recounting of the evolution of Chinese currency policy draws from Bryan Mercurio & Celine Sze Ning Leung, *Is China a "Currency Manipulator"?: The Legitimacy of China's Exchange Regime Under the Current International Legal Framework*, 43 THE INTERNATIONAL LAWYER 1257, 1261–1262 (2009). [Hereinafter, Mercurio & Leung.]

19. Mercurio & Leung, 1262.

20. Mercurio & Leung, 1262 (*citing* Paul V. Sharobeem, *Biting the Hand that Feeds Us: A Critical Analysis of U.S. Policy Trends Concerning Chinese Currency Manipulation*, 19 FLORIDA JOURNAL OF INTERNATIONAL LAW 697, 698 (2007)).

(6) Since 2006, the appreciation trend has continued. In January 2015, the FX rate was 6.23 *yuan* per dollar. In other words, across 10 years since the 8.28 *yuan* per dollar peg, the CCP has let China's currency rise against the dollar by 25%, an annual average appreciation of 2.5%.

In sum, China modified its currency regime several times, beginning with its change in 1986 when the government introduced a dual-exchange rate regime under which exporters sold their earnings in a regulated market separate from the inner China market (thus allowing those exporters to receive more *RMB* for a unit of foreign exchange than the inner market).[21] In 2005, China moved to a crawling peg, before finally settling on a managed float system. Under this system, the Chinese government determines the *RMB* exchange rate in view of exchange rates of a basket of currencies consisting of the dollar, *yen*, *euro*, and a few other currencies.

As indicated, since July 2005, the CCP has retained a managed float system. But, under significant pressure from many of its foreign trading partners, the CCP gradually permitted the *yuan* to appreciate against that basket. For example, in 2006, the CCP permitted a 3.1% appreciation of the *yuan* against the dollar. In 2007, it permitted an additional 5.8%. In 2008, it allowed another 7.2% appreciation. Overall, said the CRS from July 2005 to April 2009, the appreciation summed to 18.7%.[22]

- **Example of Undervaluation, Commodity Price Inflation, and Revaluation**

To illustrate the FX principles associated with the debate about Chinese currency policy, a hypothetical example is useful. The illustration combines the ideas of currency undervaluation and revaluation with a phenomenon observed in the 2008–2012 period, namely, rises in world commodity prices. It shows how Chinese currency revaluation would offset a rise in those prices.

Suppose soybean initially sells for U.S. $500 per metric ton. (Soybeans typically are priced in units of metric tons, though for futures and other financial contracts they are priced in bushels.) Because of commodity price inflation (driven by supply and demand factors, financial market speculation, and so forth), soybean prices rise by 10% to $550 per metric ton. (This assumption is realistic, as soybean prices trended upward since 2008.[23]) Assume China imports soybean from abroad. (This assumption also is realistic. Indeed, exports of soybeans from the U.S. and Brazil to China "are . . . [as of December 2012] the largest agricultural trade relationships in the world."[24])

---

21. *See* Mercurio & Leung, 1261 (*citing* Barry Naughton, *The Chinese Economy: Transitions and Growth* 383 (2007).

22. *See* Mercurio & Leung, 1261–1262 (*citing* Wayne M. Morrison & Marc Labonte, *China's Currency: A Summary of the Economic Issues*, CONGRESSIONAL RESEARCH SERVICE REPORT, RS21625 (13 April 2009), www.fas.org).

23. For a long-term price chart of soybean, 2000 through 2011, see *Soybean Price Chart*, www.mongabay.com/images/commodities/charts/soybean.html.

24. Robin Harding, *Concern Over Resource Nationalism*, FINANCIAL TIMES, 10 December 2012, at 2.

Suppose also the *yuan*/dollar exchange rate is *RMB* 6.50 per dollar. But, the CCP agrees to a revaluation of 10%, meaning a change in *RMB* 0.65 per dollar. The revalued rate, therefore, is *RMB* 5.85 per dollar. Observe this change is a "revaluation," not an "appreciation," because it is an official act of the Chinese government. It represents a strengthening of the *RMB* relative to the dollar. Thus, it is a "revaluation," not a "devaluation," because it takes fewer *yuan* to obtain one dollar. Under the former rate of *RMB* 6.50 per dollar, each *RMB* was worth only 15 American cents. With the stronger rate of *RMB* 5.85 per dollar, each *RMB* is worth 17 cents.[25] (The initial exchange rate is close to the December 2012 actual rate. But, the extent of revaluation, at least in the short term, is not realistic.)

Consider the before-and-after effects of the revaluation. At the old exchange rate of *RMB* 6.50 per dollar, the price of soybean, with the 10% inflation rise, translated from $550 would have been *RMB* 3,570 per metric ton. That calculation is:

$$\frac{RMB\ 6.50}{\$1} = \frac{RMB\ x}{\$550} \quad \text{solving for x, x} = 3{,}570.00$$

With the strengthening of the *RMB* to 5.85 per dollar, the soybean price per metric ton is *RMB* 3,210.75:

$$\frac{RMB\ 5.85}{\$1} = \frac{RMB\ x}{\$550} \quad \text{solving for x, x} = 3{,}217.50$$

Thus, Chinese consumers will spend 3,217.50 *yuan*, instead of 3,570 *yuan*.

In effect, even though soybean has become more expensive on world commodity markets, through the operation of the exchange rate—the increased value of the *yuan* relative to the dollar—Chinese consumers can purchase the same amount of soybean (a metric ton) at a cheaper price. Simply put, the revaluation of their currency by 10% offsets the 10% inflation in the price of soybean.

Suppose there had there been no commodity price inflation, or that prices fell back by 10%. With the soybean price at $500, Chinese consumers could purchase a metric ton for just 2,295 *yuan*:

$$\frac{RMB\ 5.85}{\$1} = \frac{RMB\ x}{\$500} \quad \text{solving for x, x} = 2925.00$$

---

25. That is clear from the simple ratios:

$$\frac{RMB\ 6.50}{\$1} = \frac{RMB\ 1}{\$0.15}$$

and

$$\frac{RMB\ 5.85}{\$1} = \frac{RMB\ 1}{\$0.17}$$

These effects are precisely what American exporters seek: *RMB* revaluation so that American products remain price competitive, even in the event of inflation. Their hope — like that of non-Chinese producer-exporters around the world — is Chinese consumers will buy more of their goods, as their currency strengthens in relative terms. Conversely, with no revaluation, Chinese consumers face the brunt of commodity price inflation.

To be sure, from the perspective of Chinese producer-exporters, currency revaluation renders their wares relatively less competitive on international markets. Translating dollars into *yuan* to purchase Chinese goods, with a weaker *yuan* (and, conversely, a stronger dollar), makes those goods appealing to foreign buyers. That appeal is alleged to be a subsidy, because the weaker currency is by operation not of FX market forces, but official CCP action, namely, not permitting an appropriate revaluation.

• **Undervalued by How Much?**

Economists quarrel over the exact amounts, with some alleging less and others more, and thus dispute the degree of *yuan* undervaluation relative to the dollar. By one account, the *yuan* appreciated against the dollar by 30% between 2006 and 2012.[26] Moreover, despite the slow appreciation of the *yuan*, between 2000 and 2012, American exports to China increased by 542%, whereas to the rest of the world they grew 80%. In 2007, the size of the external trade surplus enjoyed by China reached its zenith at 10% of Chinese GDP. By 2012, that figure had tumbled to 2%.

So, by how much was the *yuan* undervalued relative to the dollar? Economists did not agree on the answer. The extent of their estimates of undervaluation ranges from 15% to 60%, depending on the calculation method of some economists such that no consensus has emerged. Reasons for the variances in numbers include adoption of different economic functions and methodologies used to calculate the values such that no estimation method has been able to conclude authoritatively the *RMB* is misaligned.[27]

Notably, some critics formulate an argument against China based on comparing *yuan* appreciation against the dollar relative to third-country currencies. Some argue the lower appreciation of the *RMB* against the U.S. dollar, in comparison to other currencies that have appreciated more substantially in the same time frame, is an effective depreciation of the *RMB*, hence the *RMB* remains undervalued.

Notwithstanding disputes over the extent of undervaluation, many foreign trading partners of China found appreciation of the *yuan* far too gradual. So, in 2010, G-20 countries called on China to allow faster appreciation. The G-20 exhortation met with modest success. China had a fixed rate on 1 July 2005 of 8.28 *RMB*/$1. On 8 August 2012 the rate was 6.36 *RMB*/$1. On 4 October 2012, it was 6.25 *RMB*/$1.

---

26. *See Romney's Focus* (discussing remarks by Nicholas Lardy, Senior Fellow, Peterson Institute for International Economics).

27. *See* Mercurio & Leung, 1266.

• **Other Countries Guilty?**

The topic of FC rate misalignment issue is neither new nor limited to China. It is a reoccurring issue in international economic relations implicating many countries. Examples come from the oil-boom years of 2003–July 2008 and currencies of the UAE, Kuwait, Saudi Arabia, Bahrain, and Venezuela, all of which depreciated by about 20% against the U.S. dollar.[28] Examples also include FTA negotiations, such as *TPP*.

V. Currency Manipulation under IMF *Article* IV(1)(iii)

The oft-repeated allegation the Chinese *yuan* (also called the *renminbi*, which means "people's money," or *RMB*) is undervalued relative to the U.S. dollar and other currencies leads ineluctably to a legal question: are Chinese exchange rate policies consistent with international law? In particular, what claims, if any, might a WTO Member take against China, and how persuasive might these claims be? The U.S. has not labeled China a "currency manipulator" since July 1994. The IMF has never declared China to have its exchange rate misaligned (*i.e.*, to have deviated from a long-run equilibrium). No action has been brought to the WTO pursuant to the *DSU*. So, the question calls for legal prognostication. Several scholars have responded with their forecasts.

All scholars focus on two potential sources of law: GATT-WTO rules, and related relevant provisions of the *IMF Articles*. No scholar advances an argument against China that a consensus of scholars would agree is a "slam dunk."

Of course, when approached to revalue the *RMB*, much less threatened with legal action, China repeats its traditional position: currency regulation is an inherently sovereign act and a domestic measure within the domestic jurisdiction of a state.[29] On the one hand, there exist economists who pour scorn on this argument. Professor Mussa argues that because an exchange rate is the value of one currency against another, it is logically impossible for two countries to maintain conflicting exchange rates with respect to the currency of the other, and therefore nonsense to suggest each country has a sovereign right to determine its exchange rate.[30]

On the other hand, there exist legal scholars who defend the Chinese position. Professors Mercurio and Leung argues the mere fact the right of one person conflicts with the right of another person does not necessarily deprive both persons of

---

28. Mercurio & Leung, fn. 10 at 1260 (*citing* Arvind Subramanian & Aaditya Mattoo, *Currency Undervaluation and Sovereign Wealth Funds: A New Role for the World Trade Organization* 2 (Center for Global Development, Working Paper Number 142 (2008))).

29. *See* Mercurio & Leung, 1268.

30. *See* Mercurio & Leung, 1269 (*citing* Michael Mussa, *IMF Surveillance Over China's Exchange Rate Policy*, 8 (Peterson Institute for International Economics, 19 October 2007)).

their respective rights.[31] Specifically, Professors Mercurio and Leung conclude that while China has clearly manipulated its currency, the measures are not inconsistent with the IMF *Articles* or the WTO agreements.[32]

Suppose China is right, *i.e.*, it is exerting its inherent sovereign right to determine its currency and, therefore, is not in violation of any international law. Is China "off the hook"? The answer is "not necessarily." Some scholars point to the fact China is a signatory to a number of international agreements. Those accords bind (*i.e.*, impose constraints on) the ability of their signatories with respect to exchange rate policy, and thus generate some degree of legal accountability of one signatory to another. The key such texts are the GATT-WTO agreements and IMF *Articles*. Therefore, it is to these texts that the U.S. or any other country looking to bring a claim against China would base an argument to hold China legally accountable.

The various arguments raised by scholars are discussed below. The arguments are organized according to the basis for a potential legal claim. First, arguments drawing on the IMF *Articles* are reviewed. Thereafter, arguments on GATT Article XV are evaluated. Finally, arguments using the WTO *SCM Agreement* are treated. Later, claims based on U.S. law are discussed.

In discussing all such arguments, it is useful to keep in mind that none guarantees a "win" for the U.S. or other potential complainants against China. Thus, the varying arguments can be seen not only from a litigation posture, but also from a negotiation stance. They may well be a platform to advance practical discussions with China may be launched in order to find an amicable solution for both countries involved as well as providing some clarity to specific provisions of the agreements.

• Potential Claim Based on IMF *Article* IV(1)(iii)

When considering a potential claim against China regarding exchange rate policies, scholars tend to look first to the IMF *Articles* for guidance. The initial purpose of the IMF was to prevent competitive devaluations that were common in the Great Depression era. As a result, the IMF *Articles* obliged countries that were members of the Fund to maintain a system of fixed exchange rates based upon gold, until 1971 where President Richard M. Nixon (1913–1994, President, 1969–1974) announced the U.S. would allow the market to determine the comparative value of its currency.[33]

Thereafter, countries that were IMF members were authorized to adopt any exchange arrangement, as long as it was not pegged to gold. Many states choose to freely float their currency or pegged their currency to the U.S. dollar. China took a different (albeit not unique) course. It elected to peg loosely its currency to a basket of currencies.

---

31. Mercurio & Leung, 1269.
32. *See* Mercurio & Leung, 1257.
33. *See* Mercurio & Leung, 1270.

In reviewing the Chinese currency regime within the IMF framework, Article IV is of utmost importance. That is because it addresses exchange arrangements. Article IV(1) says countries that are Fund members must adhere to the following obligations:

(i) Endeavour to direct its economic and financial policies toward the objective of fostering orderly economic growth with reasonable price stability, with due regard to its circumstances;

(ii) Seek to promote stability by fostering orderly underlying economic and financial conditions and a monetary system that does not tend to produce erratic disruptions;

(iii) *Avoid manipulating exchange rates or the international monetary system in order to prevent effective balance of payments adjustment or to gain an unfair competitive advantage over other members*; and

(iv) Follow exchange rate policies compatible with the undertakings under this Section.[34]

Of particular interest to potential claimants against China is Article IV(1)(iii).

This provision states plainly that a country should avoid manipulating exchange rates or the international monetary system. It might be assumed this provision is the basis for a surefire claim against China. However, many interpretive issues arise from the pertinent language.

- **Examples of Interpretative Difficulties under IMF *Article* IV(1)(iii)**

An example of interpretative difficulties associated with IMF Article IV(1)(iii) is whether the list in that provision is exhaustive. That is, would manipulating exchange rates for reasons other than to prevent effective BOP adjustment or to gain an unfair competitive advantage over other IMF members not be in conflict with the provision (assuming those purposes are consistent with their Article IV obligations)?

Another instance of interpretative difficulty is evident from evaluating Chinese compliance with Article IV(1)(iii). The following questions must be addressed: (1) does China "manipulate" its exchange rate or the international monetary system, and (2) if so, does it manipulate in order to prevent "effective balance of payments adjustment" or to gain an "unfair competitive advantage" over other countries that are IMF members?

The latter example leads to yet another set of interpretative issues. The terms "manipulate" and "unfair competitive advantage" are vague. Neither is defined in the IMF *Articles*. So, the terms provide leeway for interpretive dispute as to whether to read the terms narrowly or broadly. Depending on the characterization of the facts and legal approach to defining these terms, China might have "manipulated" its currency.

---

34. Emphasis added.

- ### June 2007 IMF Executive Board *Decision* on Surveillance

To provide some clarification of these terms, in June 2007 the IMF Executive Board adopted a new *Decision on Bilateral Surveillance over Members Policies* to assist in the interpretation of "manipulation," "unfair advantage," and "fundamental misalignment."[35] This *Decision* defined "manipulation" as policies targeted at, and actually affecting, the level of an exchange rate. Additionally, manipulation may cause the exchange rate to move or may prevent such movement.

Applying the June 2007 *Decision*, a country holding membership in the IMF will be considered to be manipulating exchange rates in order to gain an unfair advantage over other members only if the Fund determines both that:

(1) That country is engaged in these policies for the purpose of securing fundamental exchange rate misalignment in the form of an undervalued exchange rate, and

(2) The purpose of securing such misalignment is to increase net exports.

The *Decision* further explains that when the underlying current account of the country in question is not in equilibrium (which may be due to exchange rate policies, but also could be due to unsustainable domestic policies or to market imperfections), the exchange rate is "fundamentally misaligned."

Therefore, applying both Article IV(1)(iii) and the *Decision*, to make a claim China has breached its obligation under that Article, a claimant must show China manipulated exchange rates through policies that were targeted and actually affected the level of the exchange rate. Moreover, the claimant must show China did so to prevent effective balance of payments adjustment, or to gain an unfair advantage for the purpose of securing fundamental exchange rate misalignment in the form of an undervalued exchange rate and to increase net exports. Manifestly, successful showing on these points is difficult, all the more so because (at least by custom), a member of the IMF is given the benefit of any reasonable doubt regarding the purpose of its policies.

- ### Unfair Advantage?

Demonstrating China gained an "unfair advantage" would be hard to quantify. Professors Bryan Mercurio and Celine Sze Ning Leung examined the bilateral trade deficit of the U.S. with China as an example of the difficulty proving China obtained an "unfair advantage." More than half of Chinese exports are produced by foreign owned enterprises (*e.g.*, American MNCs using China as an export base). Thus, any advantage gained by China through cheaper exports is shared with foreign enterprises.[36]

---

35. *IMF Executive Board Adopts New Decision on Bilateral Surveillance Over Members' Policies*, INTERNATIONAL MONETARY FUND (21 June 2007), www.imf.org/external/np/sec/pn/2007/pn0769 .htm.

36. *See* Mercurio & Leung, 1281.

Consider as a realistic illustration the business model employed by Apple, Inc. Although much of the technical and creative aspects of their goods are a product of American labor, the company uses manufacturing companies in China to produce parts of its final products. Therefore, to argue an "unfair advantage" has been conferred to China alone seems asymmetric, *i.e.*, to deny the reality the American and Chinese economies benefit from the success of Apple. Additionally, Professors Mercurio and Leung characterize China as an export-oriented economy that is "a mere production platform," because China relies on the importation of inputs from other East Asian countries.

Taking account of the high standard to meet the "unfair advantage" test of Article IV(1)(iii), the majority of legal scholars conclude pursuing action under this provision is unlikely to be successful. Likewise, demonstrating China has manipulated its exchange rate with the intention to achieve an unfair advantage is difficult. That is because of the political sensitivity associated with proving official Chinese intent.

- **Motivation of Increasing Net Exports?**

Professors Robert W. Staiger and Alan O. Sykes argue it is difficult to prove the purpose of Chinese exchange rate policies.[37] When Chinese officials are confronted about these policies, surely they will deny they manipulate the *RMB*-dollar exchange rate to increase net exports, and will provide alternative salubrious motivations.[38] They may have an ally in the UNCTAD, and among certain academic economists.

UNCTAD has defended Chinese currency policies by suggesting that rapid appreciation would be a threat to the stability of China and the Far East region. Similarly, Professor McKinnon indicates Chinese policies have created an anchor for its monetary policy that has, in turn, controlled inflation within the Chinese economy and created a favorable environment for steady economic growth.[39] Alternative reasons for Chinese policies, coupled with the fact China would be entitled to the "benefit of any reasonable doubt," leaves the potential for success based on Article IV(1)(iii) dubious, or at least nearly impossible to prove, regardless of the merits.[40]

In respect of motivation, some commentators argue Chinese exchange-rate policy is in compliance with Article IV as whole. They state China satisfies its obligations to promote orderly economic growth and stability by fostering orderly economic and financial conditions, and minimizing disruptions in its monetary system. Under this view, the Chinese regime could be characterized as important in stabilizing not only its economy, but also the economy of its region, and indeed the global economy. By imposing capital and currency controls internally, it enables the economy to grow steadily and stably, thereby supporting economic growth

---

37. *See* R. Staiger & A. O Sykes, *"Currency Manipulation" and World Trade*, 9 WORLD TRADE REVIEW 583, 591 (2010). [Hereinafter, *"Currency Manipulation."*]
38. *See "Currency Manipulation,"* 591.
39. *See "Currency Manipulation,"* 591.
40. *See "Currency Manipulation,"* 591.

and avoiding inflation.[41] Conversely, if China were to dramatically alter its current exchange regime, then it would disrupt the financial and economic stability of those economies that use exports from China, and those that provide inputs to China's manufacturing.

A final point about motivation is worth mentioning. Recall the new language of Article IV (quoted earlier), which took effect in 1978, states that countries should seek in their foreign exchange and monetary policies to promote orderly economic growth and financial stability, and should "avoid manipulation of exchange rates or the international monetary system *to prevent effective balance of payments adjustment or to gain unfair competitive advantage over other members.*"[42] Some IMF member countries have claimed they are not in violation of Article IV. They assert they are not seeking to gain competitive advantage (although this may be the result of their actions). To date, the IMF never has publically challenged a statement by a member country of its objective concerning its currency policies.[43]

- **Problem of Enforcement**

Bringing a claim under the IMF might not be the best option for the U.S., considering the lack of strong enforcement power of the IMF. Professor Claus Zimmerman points out the rights and obligations established by the IMF exist only between every IMF member country, on the one hand, and the IMF as an institution, on the other hand. These rights and obligations do not horizontally between members (as they do under GATT-WTO agreements). The obligation not to manipulate exchange rates under Article IV(1)(iii) runs between countries that are members of the IMF and the IMF itself, not between or among those countries. So, violations of the IMF *Articles* do not give rise to legal claims by individual IMF members against each other.[44]

Putting that important legal point aside, the IMF is ill-equipped to pressure China to change its conduct.[45] The IMF lacks both an effective enforcement mechanism and a credible penalty for violations. Unlike the WTO *DSU*, which allows for the possibility of retaliation against a non-compliant WTO Member, the IMF is granted power only to oversee compliance of each member country with its obligations.

Specifically, IMF Article IV(3) says the Fund "shall oversee the international monetary system in order to ensure its effective operation, and shall oversee the compliance of each member with its obligations under Article IV(1)." Oversight in

---

41. *See* Mercurio & Leung, 1282.

42. Emphasis added.

43. *See* John E. Sanford, *Currency Manipulation: The IMF and WTO*, Congressional Research Service (28 January 2011), www.fas.org/sgp/crs/misc/RS22658.pdf. [Hereinafter, Congressional Research Service.]

44. *See* Claus D. Zimmerman, *Exchange Rate Misalignment and International Law*, 105 American Journal of International Law 423, 433 (2011). [Hereinafter, *Exchange Rate Misalignment.*]

45. *See* "Currency Manipulation," 592.

the form of bilateral surveillance involves assessment of the policies of each IMF member country by the IMF staff, followed by consultations between the staff and the monetary authorities of that country. The assessment and advice of the IMF are intended to assist the country in making policy choices, and enable other IMF member countries to discuss these policy choices with that country.

The conception of this consultation process is far from that of an adversarial dispute process.[46] Rather, the objective of the process are persuasion (where necessary) and consensus. The IMF is unlikely to punish a member country. Instead, the IMF likely would give that country notice of its assessment, and grant the country reasonable time to rectify domestic policies prior to a formal finding of a breach of an IMF obligation. Significantly, no IMF consultation ever has concluded that a member country was out of compliance with its obligations regarding exchange rate policies, or any other matter.[47]

How, then, does the IMF "punish" a member country, if matters rise to a level requiring a sanction of some kind? The IMF curtails access of that country to resources of the Fund, suspends its voting rights, or expels it from the Fund (which it has never done). These possible sanctions work as powerful threats against small economies, but they provide little economic leverage (although some reputational) against large economies like China, the U.S., and Japan.[48]

In sum, the IMF can exercise surveillance and provide recommendations to a country through the required Article IV consultations on their monetary policy. But, the IMF cannot compel a country to change its exchange rate. The IMF is nothing more, or less, than a forum for discourse and consultations. In that forum, the IMF or any member country can urge a particular member country to alter its exchange rate policies. But, the authority to make the changes is purely a sovereign matter.

- **IMF Depends on China**

Manifestly, the IMF lacks adequate leverage power against China to try to curtail its conduct. The coercive device often used against other countries is the threat a member country may be cut off from IMF borrowings if it does not pursue the appropriate policies. That leverage is lacking against China, because it has no need to borrow from the IMF due to its extensive FX reserves.

Put bluntly, China has no need to play by the rules of the IMF. The absence of credible sanctions leaves much doubt as to the IMF's effectiveness. In fact, the reverse is true: the IMF may well need to play by Chinese rules. That is because China is an important member that can, and does, contribute capital to the IMF.

---

46. *See "Currency Manipulation,"* 592.

47. *See "Currency Manipulation,"* 593 (*citing* Michael Mussa, *"IMF Surveillance over China's Exchange Rate Policy,"* 19 October 2007 (mimeo)).

48. *See Exchange Rate Misalignment,* 433.

In June 2012, China pledged to commit $43 billion to boost the coffers of the IMF.[49] The Chinese contribution was (ironically) conditional, at least implicitly. The Chinese based their funding to the IMF on the assumption governance reform would occur within the IMF to give emerging economies, particularly the BRICS group (Brazil, Russia, India, China, and South Africa), greater power and voting rights within the Fund.[50] At a time when western countries that typically accounted for a large portion of IMF funding were decreasing their contributions, surely the IMF would not admonish publically its newest, largest donor.

VI. Currency Manipulation under GATT Article XV

Action in the WTO likely is the preferred method to address currency manipulation, given the concerns noted earlier, particularly the lack of an enforcement mechanism under IMF auspices. The WTO *DSU*, by contrast, boasts a credible regime requiring compliance, but failing that, payment of compensation by the losing WTO Member in a case, or failing that, retaliation against that Member. To date, the WTO has not addressed currency manipulation. So, if a WTO Member were to bring a case before a Panel under GATT Article XV, it would be the first under the *DSU*. Thus, analysis of the topic calls for legal prognostication.

GATT Article XV is rightly referenced as a potential legal basis for a currency manipulation claim. It is the provision that most directly addresses FX rates. Generally, Article XV requires cooperation between the WTO and IMF to "pursue a coordinated policy with regards to exchange questions that are within the jurisdiction of the Fund." Article XV:2 specifically calls on the WTO to "consult fully" with the IMF in all cases the WTO concerning foreign exchange. The WTO is to do so in order to establish whether the exchange measures at issue are consistent with the IMF *Articles*.

GATT Article XV:4 states "contracting parties [*i.e.*, WTO Members] shall not, by exchange action, frustrate the intent of the provisions of this Agreement [*i.e.*, GATT], nor by trade action, the intent of the provisions of the *Articles of Agreement of the International Monetary Fund*." The *Ad Article* to Article XV:4 provides clarification. This Interpretative Note signals the word "frustrate" means infringements of the letter of any GATT Article by an FX rate measure of a WTO Member shall not be regarded as a violation of the Article in question, in practice, the measure does not depart appreciably from the intent of that Article.

Essentially, a Member can commit a technical breach of a GATT provision, as long as that breach does not undermine the intent of that provision. Therefore, to

49. *See* Ian Talley, Aaron Back & Shen Hong, *Countries Give Figures on Pledges to Boost IMF Account*, Wall Street Journal (19 June 2012), http://online.wsj.com/article/SB100014240527023 03379204577476081207610576.html. [Hereinafter, *Countries Give Figures*.]

50. *See Countries Give Figures*.

assess a claim of currency manipulation against China under Article XV:4, two fundamental questions must be resolved. First, is the exchange rate policy of China an "exchange action"? Second, if so, then does that "exchange action" frustrate the intent of GATT?

- **Frustration?**

Scholarly opinion conflicts over whether it is possible to satisfy this two-pronged standard of GATT Article XV:4. That is not surprising. The *Ad Article* provides an example as to what would not frustrate the intent of GATT.[51] But, nothing in the Article, its Interpretative Note, or any other provision of GATT provides guidance as to what type of exchange practices would frustrate the intent.

The lack of a clear expression as to what action would "frustrate the intent," plus the fact an Article XV:4 claim is rather novel, has left legal scholars wondering how best to interpret the phrase. For example, in Contract Law, a contract can be "frustrated" by the occurrence of events or circumstances that render performance of the contract *"virtually impossible."*[52] In contrast, applying the definition of "frustrate" in *Black's Law Dictionary* with respect to the intent of GATT would mean merely *"hindering the intent's attainment,"* which is a much is a much lower bar to satisfy.[53] Possibly, then, the lack of clarity in how to interpret "frustrate" weakens the possibility of succeeding under Article XV. Of course, such situations are precisely when adjudication may be useful to provide the needed clarification.

- **Intent of GATT?**

Defining "frustration" is not the end of the matter. Determining the intent of GATT to assess whether an action "frustrates the intent" requires additional interpretation. What is the purpose, or intent, of GATT? Some scholars characterize that intent as liberalizing trade through reducing and removing trade barriers. Under this interpretation, Chinese FX rate policies frustrate the intent of Article XV:4. Those policies — namely, an undervalued *yuan* relative to other currencies — hinder the natural flow of trade by increasing exports from China, and boosting the price of imports.

In contrast, if the historical context during the drafting of GATT is considered, then it can be argued Chinese monetary policies resemble the then-prevalent practice by several countries of deliberately maintaining an undervalued currency. As a result, perhaps the drafters included Article XV to prevent similar actions from undermining trade liberalization.[54]

Professors Mercurio and Leung suggest the belief the intent of GATT was solely to liberalize trade is incomplete. They argue the *Preamble* of the GATT must be considered to discern the full intent of the document. The *Preamble* states:

---

51. *See "Currency Manipulation,"* 607 fn. 49.
52. Mercurio & Leung, 1287 (emphasis added).
53. Mercurio & Leung, 1287 (emphasis added).
54. *See* Mercurio & Leung, 1289.

Recognizing that their relations in the field of trade and economic endeavor should be conducted with a view of raising standards of living, ensuring full employment, and a large and steadily growing volume of real income and effective demand, developing the full use of the resources of the world and expanding the production and exchange of goods . . . Being desirous of contributing to these objectives by entering into reciprocal and mutually advantageous arrangements directed to the substantial reduction of tariffs and other barriers to trade and to the elimination of discriminatory treatment in international commerce . . . .[55]

These Professors read the *Preamble* to mean contracting parties agreed to conduct trade and economic relations to achieve the goals of "raising standards of living, ensuring full employment and a large and steadily growing volume of real income and effective demand, developing the full use of the resources of the world, and expanding the production and exchange of goods."[56]

Trade liberalization by cutting and eliminating tariffs and NTBs is just one possible method to achieve the goals the *Preamble* articulates. Thus, Professors Mercurio and Leung argue the possibility that while Chinese exchange policies undermine trade liberalization, they only "undermine[] a means to achieve the intent of the GATT, but not the intent itself."[57] In sum, depending on how the intent of GATT is characterized, a decision as to whether an action frustrates that intent can fall in favor of either China (as respondent in WTO litigation) or the U.S. (and other complainants).

- **WTO-IMF Relationship?**

Another issue is the relationship between the WTO and IMF under GATT Article XV. Some scholars note a deferential tone towards the IMF that runs throughout the Article. For example, Article XV:1 requires WTO Members to:

seek cooperation with the International Monetary Fund to the end that the Contracting Parties and the Fund may pursue a coordinate policy with regard to exchange questions within the jurisdiction of the Fund.

Similarly, Article XV:2 requires Members to consult fully with the IMF, and accept all findings and determinations of the Fund in exchange matters.

The connection between the WTO and IMF runs directly from WTO Members to the Fund. After all, Article XV:2 says:

2. In all cases in which the CONTRACTING PARTIES are called upon to consider or deal with problems concerning monetary reserves, balances of payments or foreign exchange arrangements, they shall consult fully with the

---

55. Mercurio & Leung, 1289 (2009) (*quoting* General Agreement on Tariffs and Trade, Preamble, 30 October 1947, 61 Stat A-11, 55 U.N.T.S. 194).

56. Mercurio & Leung, 1289 (*citing* General Agreement on Tariffs and Trade, Preamble, 30 October 1947, 61 Stat. A-11, 55 U.N.T.S. 194).

57. Mercurio & Leung, 1290.

International Monetary Fund. In such consultations, the CONTRACTING PARTIES shall accept all findings of statistical and other facts presented by the Fund relating to foreign exchange, monetary reserves and balances of payments, and shall accept the determination of the Fund as to whether action by a contracting party in exchange matters is in accordance with the *Articles of Agreement of the International Monetary Fund*, or with the terms of a special exchange agreement between that contracting party and the CONTRACTING PARTIES. The CONTRACTING PARTIES, in reaching their final decision in cases involving the criteria set forth in paragraph 2(a) of Article XII or in paragraph 9 of Article XVIII, shall accept the determination of the Fund as to what constitutes a serious decline in the contracting party's monetary reserves, a very low level of its monetary reserves or a reasonable rate of increase in its monetary reserves, and as to the financial aspects of other matters covered in consultation in such cases.

From this provision, the role of the WTO Secretariat is not entirely clear, but presumably is (at least) one of support and facilitation.

Regardless, from Article XV:2, that is, based on the need for a WTO Member to consult with the IMF, some scholars infer it would not be possible for an "exchange action" to frustrate the intent of GATT if that action is not a violation of the IMF *Articles of Agreement*.[58] For example, Professors Sykes and Staiger believe it to be unlikely that a WTO panel or the Appellate Body would conclude that certain economic policies, similar to those of China, would frustrate the intent of GATT absent an IMF determination of currency manipulation.[59] Put differently, such scholars argue Article XV:2 creates a sequential process: any adverse WTO judgment against China must piggyback on a prior adverse judgment by the IMF.

Suppose, to the contrary, a WTO Panel were to consider a claim FX rate policies frustrate the intent of GATT without violating the IMF *Articles*. A problem arises in accumulating evidence of the frustration. Professors Mercurio and Leung argue that even if Chinese exchange arrangement is found to be inconsistent with its IMF *Agreement* Article IV obligations, GATT Article XV:9(a) offers China a potential immunity.[60]

GATT Article XV:9 states:

9. Nothing in this Agreement [*i.e.*, GATT] shall preclude:

(a) the use by a contracting party of exchange controls or exchange restrictions in accordance with the *Articles of Agreement of the International Monetary Fund* or with that contracting party's special exchange agreement with the CONTRACTING PARTIES, or

---

58. *See "Currency Manipulation,"* 608.
59. *See "Currency Manipulation,"* 608.
60. Mercurio & Leung, 1292.

(b) the use by a contracting party of restrictions or controls on imports or exports, the sole effect of which, additional to the effects permitted under Articles XI, XII, XIII and XIV, is to make effective such exchange controls or exchange restrictions.

The exception in Article XV: 9(a) can be interpreted to mean that as long as the exchange restrictions of a WTO Member do not violate the IMF *Articles*, then there can be no violation under GATT. Therefore, arguably, a formal finding by the IMF is a prerequisite for concluding an exchange rate policy is in breach GATT. Another way to put the point is that Article XV: 9(a) suggests in the event of a conflict between GATT and the IMF *Articles* as regards currency policy, the latter should prevail over the former.

Additional complexity arises because the exception is introduced by the words "nothing in this agreement." Professor Zimmerman asks "whether the exception under the Article applies to potential violations under other multilateral agreements on trade in goods in Annex 1A that are silent on whether any of the exceptions set forth in GATT apply to the rights and obligations under that specific agreement?"[61]

Ripple effects that might occur should the WTO rule on such a case are another policy concern. Typically, macroeconomic policies undertaken by countries to influence trade have never been challenged nor condemned under GATT-WTO dispute settlement procedures.[62] Suppose that adjudicatory system were to produce a ruling that certain macroeconomic policies affecting trade are, or are not, illegal. Might that ruling open a Pandora's Box, creating political strife among WTO Members?

Given the factual and legal complexities of the matter, Professors Sykes and Staiger predict a WTO Panel would not conclude with confidence that the trade effects from alleged currency manipulation are sufficient to "frustrate[] the intent." Suppose they are right. Then, critics of China and other alleged currency manipulators would themselves be frustrated with the WTO dispute settlement system. Suppose they are wrong. Then, respondents like China would be frustrated. Regardless of whether their prediction is right or wrong, many Members (especially actual or prospective respondents in currency manipulation cases) would perceive the WTO Panels and Appellate Body have arrogated to themselves a subject matter jurisdiction they do not, under GATT-WTO texts, rightfully possess.

· **2012 Brazil Proposal**

Indeed, one of the few issues upon which some WTO Members have been able to agree is that the WTO should not be the principle forum to address trade and exchange rate controversies. In 2012, Brazil called for action by WTO Members to discuss the inadequacies of the current framework in relation to FX rate misalignment. Brazil proposed a WTO Working Group clarify matters of exchange misalignment by performing assessments on the following concepts: determining (1)

---

61. *Exchange Rate Misalignment*, 466.
62. *"Currency Manipulation,"* 608.

when currency misalignment exists and what might trigger the use of remedies; (2) the time frame and scope of application of trade remedies; (3) how the remedies should be applied; and (4) whether prior investigation is necessary to begin applying remedies.[63]

The Brazilian calls for action at the WTO were met by skepticism from the U.S. and EU, in particular. American officials believed further analysis was a good idea. But, they stressed the "International Monetary Fund was the proper forum for discussions on exchange rate issues."[64] Their statement seemed an indication the U.S. was chary of pursuing action at the WTO against China.

Unsurprisingly, China bluntly rejected the Brazilian proposal for discussions at the WTO. Specifically, the Deputy Permanent Representative of China to the WTO, Zhu Hong, argued the WTO "is not the right forum to discuss the exchange rate issue."[65] Ambassador Zhu asserted that:

> using trade measures, be it the increase of tariff rates or the imposition of trade remedies, would not do any good to resolve the exchange rate issue, rather it would pose serious challenges to basic WTO rules.[66]

Zhu suggested the quantitative easing monetary policy pursued by the U.S. Federal Reserve in the aftermath of the September 2008 global financial crisis is the cause of the high volatility of currencies suffered by many countries.[67] So, the Chinese Ambassador agreed with the American approach that currency misalignment is an issue best left within the confines of the IMF. He declared: "the right path to resolve this issue is by enhancing the responsibility of and promoting coordination among the international reserve currency issuers."[68]

WTO Director General Pascal Lamy weighed in on behalf of China. He cautioned Members against mixing currency conflicts, typically within the jurisdiction of the IMF, with trade actions before the WTO. Lamy suggested WTO policies would be unable to find a solution to macroeconomic issues like exchange rate management. Lamy asserted: "trade cannot become the scapegoat for the pitfalls and drawbacks of the international monetary system, or current non-system."[69] This claim was both ironic and pusillanimous: in many public statements, particularly in respect of trying to resurrect Doha Round negotiations, the Director General energetically

---

63. Daniel Pruzin, *Brazil Calls for WTO Talks on Remedies to Address Currency "Misalignments,"* BLOOMBERG BNA INTERNATIONAL TRADE DAILY (6 November 2012), www.bna.com/news/.

64. Daniel Pruzin, *China Rejects Brazil's Call for WTO Trade Remedies to Counter Currency Misalignments,* BLOOMBERG BNA INTERNATIONAL TRADE DAILY (27 November 2012), www.bna .com/news/. [Hereinafter, *China Rejects.*]

65. *China Rejects.*

66. *China Rejects.*

67. *China Rejects.*

68. *China Rejects.*

69. Daniel Pruzin, *Chinese Official Calls for Cease-Fire in Spat Over Global Currency on Seminar's Sidelines,* BLOOMBERG BNA INTERNATIONAL TRADE DAILY (28 MARCH 2012), www.bna.com /news/.

stated, perhaps even overstated, the significance of the WTO and international trade to the global economy.

Yet, when given an opportunity to take on an issue of genuinely global importance, namely, the rate of exchange of the *yuan* against the dollar and other currencies, the Director General balked.

In sum, the translation and interpretation of the impacts of currency misalignment into an equivalent set of trade policy actions is fraught with complexity. Ultimately, it can be judged only after a variety of subtle conceptual and empirical questions are answered. Not only are the qualitative effects of significant currency devaluation (*i.e.*, of the *yuan* against the dollar) unclear, but also the task of quantifying those effects is a daunting one. Any real trade effects on the currency practices of China may depend on (for example) which prices are most flexible and have done adjusted the most, and how well foreign exchange traders anticipate Chinese exchange rate movements.[70] As a practical matter, argue Professors Staiger and Sykes, uncertainty about such variables make it difficult to conclude that Chinese currency policies "frustrate the intent" of GATT-WTO commitments.[71]

---

70. *See "Currency Manipulation,"* 605.
71. *See "Currency Manipulation,"* 606.

Chapter 33

Alternative Strategies[1]

I. Currency Manipulation under WTO *SCM Agreement*

- **Currency Undervaluation as Red Light Subsidy?**

Most analysts agree an undervalued currency lowers the cost of production (COP) of a firm relative to world prices, which then helps boost exports from that firm. It is less clear, however, whether the intentional undervaluation by a country of its currency to achieve that goal would be considered an export subsidy under the WTO's current definition of the term.[2]

Article 1 of the WTO *SCM Agreement* says a subsidy shall be deemed to exist if there is a financial contribution by a government or any public body within the territory of a Member, and "if a benefit is thereby conferred." "Financial contribution" covers the direct transfer of funds, foregone government revenue such as tax credits, government purchased goods or services other than general infrastructure, government payments to a funding mechanism, or government entrustment or direction of a private body to act on its behalf. Article 2 creates a Specificity Test. A subsidy must be "specific" in terms of enterprise or industry (or group thereof); if it is generally available, then it is not unlawful under the *Agreement*.

Further, the *SCM Agreement* creates a Traffic Light System, identifying as Red Light subsidies the most pernicious support, in the sense of two categories of subsidies that distort the pattern of trade more than any other: export subsidies and import substitution subsidies. (Article 3 concerns Red Light subsidies.) Precisely because they are the most trade distorting of subsidies, export and import substitution subsidies are deemed irrebuttably to cause adverse effects (namely, injury, price depression or suppression, or nullification or impairment of benefits). There is no need to show a Red Light subsidy is specific. It is deemed so. The obvious question is whether an undervalued exchange rate is a Red Light export subsidy, *i.e.*, support that is contingent in law (*de jure*) or in fact (*de facto*) on export performance.

---

1. Documents References:
   (1) *Havana (ITO) Charter* Articles 41, 47, 66, 92–97
   (2) GATT Article XV
   (3) WTO *SCM Agreement* Articles 1–6, Annex
2. *See* CONGRESSIONAL RESEARCH SERVICE at 3.

- **Two Key Issues**

Some scholars argue the U.S. should treat currency manipulation as an illegal subsidy. To make this claim, the U.S. would need to address successfully two issues: (1) prove currency undervaluation is a financial contribution made by the Chinese government; and (2) demonstrate currency undervaluation conferred a benefit on Chinese producer-exporters that is contingent on their export performance. Note there is no need to satisfy the Specificity Test if the subsidy is a Red Light one. That is clear from Article 2:3 of the *SCM Agreement*. Thus, the suggestion by Professor Zimmerman to the contrary (that there is a third issue, proving specificity) is misleading.[3]

- **Issue 1: Financial Contribution?**

The Sub-paragraphs of Article 1:1(a)(1) of the *SCM Agreement* outline situations in which a financial contribution can exist, not only through a direct transfer of funds, but also where a government does not collect the revenue to which it is entitled. Some scholars viewed the list of categories in Article 1 provides to be exhaustive. Under this reading, maintaining an undervalued exchange rate policy might not constitute a financial contribution as outlined in the Article, because it is not explicitly referenced or clearly implied in the Sub-paragraphs.

One counter-argument is a country with an undervalued real FX rate will exchange all export earnings at the undervalued rate. Thus, it will overpay producers exporting from its territory.[4] The overpayment could be categorized as either a direct governmental transfer of funds to exporters, or as governmental revenue forgone. Professor Zimmerman believes this argument to be unpersuasive, because the overpayment of exporters would not specifically involve a direct transfer of funds from the government. In fact, the transfer of funds would be from the banking sector to exporters. This belief naively ignores the involvement of the Chinese government in the banking sector, *i.e.*, there are state-owned commercial banks (SOCBs) that likely would make the necessary transfers to exporters. Even if private banks made such transfers, they would be acting under the watchful eye of the CCP.

---

3. As a technical matter, the discussion of the Traffic Light System, in some sources is neither complete nor accurate. For example, Professor Zimmerman writes:

> A plain reading of the specificity requirements in *ASCM* Article 2 reveals that the subsidization that allegedly arises from maintaining an undervalued real exchange rate would satisfy the "specificity" requirement only if one could successfully argue that it constituted a prohibited subsidy taking the form of an export subsidy — that is a subsidy that is "contingent, in law or in fact, whether solely or as one of several other conditions, upon export performance" (ASCM Article 3.1 (a) in combination with Article 2.3).

Exchange Rate Misalignment, 447. This contorted sentence is imprecise. If currency undervaluation is a Yellow Light (Prohibited) Subsidy under Articles 5–6, then to be actionable, a complainant must show that undervaluation meets the Specificity Test. There is no one way a complainant might prove this point. If currency undervaluation is a Red Light subsidy, then the question of specificity simply does not arise, because of Article 2:3.

4. *See Exchange Rate Misalignment*, 448.

Professor Zimmerman rejects the argument for a second reason. He rightly points out that under the WTO *SCM Agreement*, a financial contribution is not the same as a benefit. To argue the concept of financial contribution is about the effects, rather than the nature, of a government action "would essentially write it out of the *Agreement* leaving the concepts of benefits and specificity as the sole determinants of subsidies."[5] However, this point misses the mark: it does not defeat the argument, but rather highlights what a claimant must prove to be successful. Well-standing WTO Appellate Body jurisprudence under the *SCM Agreement* makes clear success requires proof of a benefit to recipients, as distinct from proof of a financial contribution.

An alternative argument for the existence of a "financial contribution" is the suggestion the government (*e.g.*, China) may forego revenue as result of exchange intervention. A 2007 CVD petition filed against China by the U.S. was argued on similar terms.[6] The petitioners alleged that when China lowers the value of the *RMB*, it makes imports more expensive, and thus China foregoes tariff revenue when imports are elastically demanded.

• **Issue 2: Benefit Conferred?**

If a country can determine a financial contribution was made, then the issue then turns to determining whether a benefit was conferred. Recognizing a benefit exists is a completely different matter from quantifying the benefit. Scholars suggest major measurement problems exist. Since exchange of exports earnings occurs at an undervalued rate, exporters obtain more units of domestic currency per unit of foreign currency earned than if the exchange rate were valued according to underlying economic fundamentals.[7] Professor Zimmerman suggests looking to the 1999 WTO *Canada Aircraft* case for clarification.[8]

The Appellate Body in *Canada Aircraft* interpreted a "benefit" in its ordinary sense of encompassing some form of advantage.[9] Applying this precedent to alleged Chinese currency manipulation, a WTO adjudicator would need to decide whether the financial contribution (from currency undervaluation) places the recipient (Chinese producer exporters) in a more advantageous position than would have been true but for the financial contribution.[10]

So, to determine whether exporters are "better off" with the undervaluation, it is necessary to show how an undervalued FX rate affects overall export sales and earnings of exporters. A complainant needs to demonstrate the undervalued exchange

---

5. *See Exchange Rate Misalignment*, 448.

6. *See "Currency Manipulation,"* 610 (*citing Inside US Trade*, 28 September 2007, at 22) Although the International Trade Administration eventually imposed countervailing duties in the case, it did not base the duties on any purported currency manipulation.

7. *See Exchange Rate Misalignment*, 450.

8. *See* WTO Appellate Body Report, *Canada—Measures Affecting the Export of Civilian Aircraft*, WT/DS70/AB/R (adopted 20 August 1999). [Hereinafter, *Canada Aircraft*.]

9. *See Canada Aircraft*, ¶ 149.

10. *See Exchange Rate Misalignment*, 450 and fn. 125.

rate gave foreign producers (in the country of the undervalued currency) a competitive advantage that allowed them to export more than they otherwise would have been able to. Then, the complainant needs to adduce evidence that increases in export volumes resulted in increased profits for the exporter. An exporter benefits from currency undervaluation only if it produces more output, which raise its exports, and in turn the increased exports lead to increased profits.

Evidently, each link in this chain of logic requires empirical data. The argument could falter in the attempt to prove increased exports resulted in increased profits. A respondent (*e.g.*, China) could claim a multitude of reasons as to why an exporter saw an increase in profits. While currency undervaluation may be one reason for an increase, it is not the only possible contributing factor.

- **Issue 3: Specificity?**

Professor Zimmerman indicates there is a third hurdle for America or other complainant to bring a WTO claim against China for FX undervaluation concerns the Specificity Test. That is not so, at least not if currency manipulation is a Red Light export subsidy. In that instance, specificity is deemed irrebuttably to exist by virtue of Article 2:3 of the *SCM Agreement*. Only if the claim is that currency undervaluation is a Yellow Light subsidy must specificity be proved.

Specificity can be satisfied in terms of enterprise or industry specificity, regional specificity, or in situations in which subsidies target export goods, or goods using domestic inputs.[11] Professor Zimmerman believes a claimant is likely to falter because of the common argument often proposed by defenders of Chinese policies: an FX rate policy cannot be specific, as it is not limited to any particular sector of the Chinese economy. While exporters may be the ones that benefit most from an undervalued exchange rate, the specificity standard cannot be met. That is because the subsidy arising from maintenance of an undervalued real FX rate is broadly available across the entire Chinese economy. Granting of this subsidy is never conditioned, either in law or in fact, upon actual or anticipated exportation.

Scholars are split on the issue: the same argument in favor of specificity could be an argument against it. Professors Staiger and Sykes contend undervalued currencies tend to favor exporting firms. That export stimulus resulting from an undervalued exchange rate might be deemed "specific."[12] But, it is equally likely import-competing firms are favored, too, when there are real effects of devaluation. Their logic is domestic producers in the country of the undervalued currency face competition from higher-priced imports, They are higher priced, because of the undervalued currency. Hence, domestic producers benefit from the undervaluation in selling domestically, just as exporters benefit in exporting abroad. Given this diffusion of benefits, undervaluation is not specific. So, they say, the argument for specificity is not obvious.[13]

---

11. *See Exchange Rate Misalignment*, 477.
12. "Currency Manipulation," 609 (*citing Inside US Trade*, 23 October 2009, p. 18).
13. *See* "Currency Manipulation," 609 (*citing Inside US Trade*, 23 October 2009, p. 18).

This ambiguity can be cleared up: depending on the facts, currency undervaluation may be a *de facto* specific Yellow Light subsidy. The domestic producers benefiting from undervaluation may be confined to a few, or even one, industry. Then, adding them to the universe of beneficiaries populated by exporters is not expanding that universe much at all. The subsidy remains *de facto* specific, under Article 2:1(c) of the *SCM Agreement*, as only certain enterprises benefit in practice from it, or account for disproportionate use of the subsidy. Indeed, some of the domestic producers may be in the same sector as some of the exporters (*e.g.*, T&A, steel, or cars).

That is, if, in fact, a subsidy is limited to a few industries, then it still may pass muster under Article 2:1(c) of the *Agreement*. Critics of Chinese exchange rate and monetary policies argue those policies satisfy the requirement, as they are contingent on anticipated export performance. It is only after an exporter is paid in U.S. dollars that proceeds of the sale are converted into *RMB* at the undervalued rate of exchange.[14]

Still, satisfying the Specificity Test is not easy. As evidence of the difficulty, Professors Staiger and Sykes point to the fact the DOC declined to initiate a CVD investigation of Chinese currency practices.[15] The reasoning for the denial was petitioners failed to allege sufficiently the receipt of excess *yuan* was contingent on exports or export performance. Petitioners were unable to show receipt of the excess *RMB* was independent of the type of transaction or commercial activity for which the dollars are converted, of the particular company or individuals converting the dollars.[16] Whether the DOC would take the same approach under its newer, more welcoming, approach to CVD cases against NMEs is unclear.

As for *de jure* export contingency, Professors Mercurio and Leung argue it does not occur in the Chinese regime. That is because the legislative framework of China does not mandate the benefit be contingent upon the exportation of goods. Further, they argue the exchange rate policy promotes economic stability, and any conditionality upon export performance may merely be incidental rather than intentional.[17]

II. Currency Manipulation under American Trade Law

• *1988 Act*

Designation of China as a "currency manipulator" by the U.S. would be a major (albeit largely symbolic) move. In 1988 Congress enacted the *Exchange Rates and International Economic Policy Coordination Act*, part of the *Omnibus Trade and*

---

14. Mercurio & Leung, 1297.
15. *See "Currency Manipulation,"* 609 (*citing Inside US Trade*, 23 October 2009, at 18).
16. *"Currency Manipulation,"* 609 (*citing Inside US Trade*, 23 October 2009, p. 18).
17. Mercurio & Leung, 1298.

Competitiveness Act of 1988 (*OTCA*). That enactment calls for official identification of countries that manipulate their currencies. The essence of "manipulation" is a foreign government pursues an exchange rate policy that undermines free markets by intentionally driving down the value of its currency relative to another currency to obtain an advantage in trade (namely, increasing exports and dampening imports) over the country of that other currency.

Following designation of China as a currency manipulator, the U.S. would be required to engage in dialogue with China regarding an adjustment of the *RMB*. Some observers urge this designation, of China in particular, under the theory of "name and shame." However, others say a designation would have no practical effect. The CCP is hardly bothered by public branding followed by talking, but may well be annoyed and thus disinclined to listen.

In any event, the requirement to talk to a country that is designated a "currency manipulator" is in 22 U.S.C. Section 5304(b). The Secretary of the Treasury is to:

> analyze on an annual basis the exchange rate policies of foreign countries . . .
> and consider whether countries manipulate the rate of exchange . . . for
> purposes of preventing effective balance of payments adjustments or gain-
> ing unfair competitive advantage in international trade.

If the Secretary finds countries with material global Current Account surpluses and significant bilateral trade surpluses with the U.S. engage in manipulation, then he is to:

> take action to initiate negotiations with such foreign countries on an expe-
> dited basis . . . for the purpose of ensuring that such countries regularly
> and promptly adjust the rate of exchange between their currencies and the
> United States dollar to permit effective balance of payments adjustments
> and to eliminate the unfair advantage.[18]

Furthermore, 22 U.S.C. Section 5305 requires a yearly written report, every 15 October, on international economic policy, including FX rate policy, from the Treasury Department, with regular updates every six months.

In brief, the Treasury Department is supposed to publish biannual reports. Often, it delays issuance of such reports. Under the Administration of President Barack H. Obama, it frequently did so.[19] The Administration argued postponements allowed for more time to engage in constructive diplomacy with China on revaluing the *yuan*.

Notably, nothing in the *OTCA* gives the Treasury Department the power to raise tariffs, or impose NTBs, in the event it designates a country a currency manipulator. (Considerable misinformation about the actual trade remedy was bantered

---

18. 22 U.S.C. 5304(b).

19. *See Romney's Focus* (discussing remarks by Nicholas Lardy, Senior Fellow, Peterson Institute for International Economics).

about during the 2012 Presidential campaign.) The Department has no unilateral remedy; its only recourse is to talk with the other country in an expeditious manner to try to eliminate the unfair advantage enjoyed by that country because of its manipulation. (Likewise, the USTR is not empowered to take unilateral action, *e.g.*, under Section 301 of the *Trade Act of 1974*, as amended.) Thus, Treasury Secretary Timothy Geithner pointed out branding a country a currency manipulator carries with it no effective trade sanction.[20] Indeed, as a legal matter, authority to alter applied tariff rates rests with the DOC, and ultimately the President acting under delegated authority from Congress.

Not since July 1995 has the Treasury Department designated a country a currency manipulator. It cited China five times as a currency manipulator between May 1992 and July 1994 over issues such as its dual exchange rate system, periods of currency devaluation, restrictions on imports, and lack of access to FX by importers. (For most of that time, it operated with two exchange rates, but it unified the dual rate in January 1994 as part of reforms to embrace a "socialist market economy."[21])

In each case, the Treasury entered into negotiations with China, per the *OTCA* requirement. As reported by the GAO, the negotiations resulted in China making "substantial reforms to their foreign exchange regimes."[22] Its currency appreciated and trade balances declined significantly.

China has not been the only recipient of the "currency manipulator" designation. As indicated, the Treasury Department was first required to make semi-annual reports on economic and FX rate policies under the *OTCA*. Since 1988, Treasury has dubbed three countries "currency manipulators," Taiwan, Korea, and China, citing Taiwan in 1988 and again in 1992, and Korea in 1988. For Taiwan, each citation lasted for at least two six-month reporting periods, while the citation for China lasted for five periods, ending in 1994.[23]

• **September 2004 Section 301 Petitions against China**

Consider, the Sino-American dispute shortly after China acceded to the WTO on 1 December 2001. Were it not for decisions in 2004 by the USTR against bringing a case about China pegging its currency, the WTO Appellate Body might well have opined on the meaning of this word. Between 1994 and July 2005, China pegged its currency (the *yuan*, or *renminbi*) to the U.S. dollar at the rate of 8.28 *yuan* to the dollar.[24] On 30 September 2004, 22 members of the House of Representatives

---

20. *See Romney's Focus*, (discussing remarks by Treasury Secretary Timothy Geithner).

21. Jason Lange, *U.S. Says China Not Seeking Trade Edge with Weak Yuan*, Reuters (25 May 2012), www.reuters.com/article/2012/05/25/us-usa-china-currency-idUSBRE84O0Q820120525.

22. United States General Accountability Office, *Treasury Assessments Have Not Found Currency Manipulation, But Concerns About Exchange Rates Continue*, GAO-05-351 (April 2005) at 14, www.gao.gov/cgi-bin/getrpt?GAO-05-351. [Hereinafter, 2005 GAO Report.]

23. *See* 2005 GAO Report, 13.

24. The precise peg was 8.277 *yuan* per dollar. *See* Jonathan Anderson, *How I Learned to Stop Worrying and Forget the Yuan*, 168 Far Eastern Economic Review 37, 38 (December 2004).

and eight members of the Senate—the so-called "Congressional China Currency Action Coalition"—filed a petition with the USTR under Section 301 of *the Trade Act of 1974*, as amended, alleging China intentionally undervalued the *yuan*/dollar rate.[25] (All but one of the signatories was a Democrat, and the filing occurred in the midst of a general election.)

The Congressional Coalition petition resembled a filing on 9 September 2004 by a group of industrial trade associations and labor unions. But, the earlier petition sought an across-the-board levy on Chinese products. Within days, the USTR rejected the private sector filing, calling the relief sought "reckless" and saying it "would put up walls around America."[26] In contrast, the Coalition did not seek an across-the-board tariff against all Chinese products. Rather, it called upon the USTR to pressure China to revalue the *yuan*, and file a WTO case if China refused, but it did not demand specific relief.

In its petition, the Congressional Coalition alleged China undervalued the *yuan* against the dollar by between 15% and 40%. There were two results. First, the undervalued *yuan* thwarted American exports to China (by making the American exports more expensive, in *yuan* terms, to Chinese consumers). Second, the undervalued *yuan* boosted Chinese exports to the U.S. (by making Chinese exports, in dollar terms, cheaper to American consumers).

Among the claims in the petition was one under Article 3:1(a) of the WTO *SCM Agreement*. The essence of this claim was the undervalued *yuan* is an illegal export subsidy. A key premise of the petition was the bilateral trade imbalance between the U.S. and China was both large and mattered. As the Chief Asian Economist for UBS Warburg put it, China still was: "a relatively small player on the global scene, and its neighbors are much more important in determining the fate of the United States economy."[27]

The Coalition conveniently ignored the fact the Chinese Current Account surplus ($40 billion in 2004) was a small fraction (1/15 in 2004) of the American imbalance. Likewise, it neglected the fact the combined surplus of Japan, Korea, and Taiwan was far larger ($230 billion, and $275 billion if Malaysia and Singapore are included) than that of China. Other Asian countries accounted for more of America's trade deficit than China.

---

25. *See* Christopher S. Rugaber, *Thirty Members of Congress Seek Trade Case on China's Currency Peg*, 21 International Trade Reporter (BNA) 1640, 1641 (7 October 2004).

26. *Quoted in* Christopher S. Rugaber, *Thirty Members of Congress Seek Trade Case on China's Currency Peg*, 21 International Trade Reporter (BNA) 1640, 1641 (7 October 2004). The Congressional Coalition petition was the third on the topic. The first petition, in April 2004, was filed by a coalition of American manufacturers and labor unions. The USTR rejected this petition before it was officially filed. The second petition (described above) was filed in early September. *See* Christopher S. Rugaber, *China's President Hu Thanks Bush for Rejecting § 301 Currency Petitions*, 21 International Trade Reporter (BNA) 1925 (25 November 2004).

27. Jonathan Anderson, *How I Learned to Stop Worrying and Forget the Yuan*, 168 Far Eastern Economic Review 37, 41 (December 2004). The statistics quoted above are from this source.

In response, the Administration of President George W. Bush (1946–, President, 2001–2009) continued to urge China to move as rapidly as possible to a flexible, market-based FX rate. From time to time, various Chinese officials indicated China indeed was moving toward a floating rate, but declined to offer a timetable.[28] In the end, the USTR did not to commence a Section 301 investigation. Hence, the case never matured into a full-blown WTO dispute. Not surprisingly, at the November 2004 annual meeting of the APEC forum, China's President, Hu Jintao, thanked President Bush for rejecting the petition.[29]

While WTO adjudication might have yielded an important jurisprudential contribution on Article XV:4, there were a number of reasons why—from an American perspective—this particular case would have been the wrong one to bring. First, studies by the U.S. Treasury Department showed China had not manipulated its currency for the benefit of trade. Second, while China had a bilateral trade surplus with America, it had an overall trade balance. Large deficit in China's trade with other Asian countries offset the surplus with the U.S. Third, the *yuan*-dollar exchange rate was not necessarily the underlying cause of the bilateral surplus with America. China had a domestic savings rate of 45%–50%, while America's rate was 1.5%. Current Account deficits are partly attributable to low savings rates.

From an economic standpoint, even if the U.S. pursued a case against China in the WTO, and even if, contrary to the argument of some economists, the *yuan* exchange regime actually had a substantial impact on trade patterns, the case might not have been one to win.[30] The low *yuan*/dollar rate benefitted important sectors of the American economy. Consumers enjoyed cheaper Chinese products. American importers, distributors, and retailers of those products correspondingly reap rewards. American portfolio investors in China obtain healthy returns on financial instruments of Chinese export companies. Foreign direct investors from the U.S. (the shareholders of which included many Americans) can use China as a competitive export platform.

- **Monetary Policy or Currency Manipulation?**

The U.S. Senate in October 2011 for the first time passed a bill that would have required the administration to slap penalties on Chinese imports if Beijing failed to adopt market-based exchange rates. The *Currency Exchange Rate Oversight Reform Act* would "treat[] currency manipulation as a foreign subsidy, triggering American

---

28. *See, e.g.*, Christopher S. Rugaber, *Chinese Official Refuses to Provide Timetable for Moving to Flexible Currency*, 21 International Trade Reporter (BNA) 1684, 1685 (14 October 2004) (*quoting* Li Ruogu, Deputy Governor, People's Bank of China: "We have already said, time and again, we are moving toward a more market-based . . . flexible exchange rate. How long will it take? I don't know. I've said many times, because China has an 8,000-year history, a decade is only a short period.").

29. *See* Christopher S. Rugaber, *China's President Hu Thanks Bush for Rejecting § 301 Currency Petitions*, 21 International Trade Reporter (BNA) 1925 (25 November 2004).

30. The argument the *yuan*/dollar rate did not matter is made forcefully by Jonathan Anderson, *How I Learned to Stop Worrying and Forget the Yuan*, 168 FAR EASTERN ECONOMIC REVIEW 37–42 (December 2004).

tariffs on Chinese goods."[31] The bill passed the Senate with a 63–35 vote.[32] However, the House took no action and the legislation died. All subsequent efforts—and there have been many—at similar legislation have failed.[33]

A key reason for this lack of success is writing statutory language that does not return to haunt the U.S. It is vital to distinguish (1) legitimate monetary policy from (2) currency manipulation. Central banks such as the Federal Reserve affect the supply of U.S. dollars using three classic techniques:

(1) open market operations (OMOs), whereby the Federal Reserve Bank of New York works through primary dealers in U.S. Treasury securities to buy or sell those securities (thus increasing or decreasing the quantity of dollars available, respectively, as the dealers pay for or receive dollars for the Treasuries);

(2) altering the discount rate, that is, the interest rate Federal Reserve Banks charge to commercial banks for obtaining funds from the Fed's discount window (with a lower rate allowing banks to borrow more cheaply, and in turn lend more cheaply to the private sector, thus increasing the money supply).

(3) changing the reserve requirement, which is the fraction of deposits commercial banks must keep in their accounts at their local Federal Reserve bank (whereby lowering the reserve ratio means banks have more funds to lend to the private sector, and thus the supply of dollars increases).

Central banks in other countries use similar techniques.

None of these methodologies constitutes currency manipulation. Rather, "manipulation" would be direct intervention in FX markets—buying or selling dollars against a foreign currency—with a view to gaining an advantage in trade through a depreciated FX rate (thanks to buying dollars and selling the other currency), which would stimulate exports, or an appreciated rate (thanks to the reverse), which would stimulate imports. (The latter scenario is less likely.) In turn, proving "manipulation" would be difficult. A central bank might intervene in FX markets quietly and indirectly, for legitimate reasons. An obvious one is not wanting powerful hedge funds

31. Michael Bowman, *China Currency Bill Passes US Senate*, VOICE OF AMERICA (10 October 2011), www.voanews.com/content/china-currency-bill-passes-us-senate-131558133/168091.html.

32. *See* S.1619: *Currency Exchange Rate Oversight Reform Act of 2011*, GOVTRACK.US, www.govtrack.us/congress/bills/112/s1619.

33. *See generally* Rebecca M. Nelson, United States Congressional Research Service, *Current Debates Over Exchange Rates: Overview and Issues for Congress*, 7-5700, R43242 (26 September 2013), www.fas.org/sgp/crs/misc/R43242.pdf (discussing the consequences of the U.S. enacting currency regulations against foreign countries based on "manipulation," including the problems of defining "manipulation" in an inflexible manner, and the possibility unilateral American legislation might provoke other countries to retaliate against the U.S.); Stephanie Cohen, *CRS Highlights Potential "Consequences" If U.S. Pursues Exchange Rate Regulations*, 30 International Trade Reporter (BNA) 1509 (3 October 2013) (discussing the CRS Report).

to take positions against it, as when George Soros' (1930–) fund "broke" the Bank of England by short-selling pound sterling (worth $10 billion) in September 1992, costing the Bank £ 3.4 billion in an unsuccessful defense of its currency, and forcing England to exit the Exchange Rate Mechanism and devalue the pound.

At the same time, monetary policy does affect FX rates, insofar as those rates are determined by the supply and demand of one currency against another. Expansionary monetary policy (euphemistically, "quantitative easing") thus can lead to a depreciated exchange rate of the currency in which the money supply has expanded relative to a foreign currency. The crux of the legislative problem thus is clear: on the one hand, a provision may be under-inclusive, failing to catch bona fide instances of manipulation; on the other hand, it may be over-inclusive, encompassing monetary easing.

- **Theory of Name and Shame**

The concept of labeling China a currency manipulator to spur action by China was discussed frequently by Presidential, Senatorial, and Congressional candidates during the 2012 American general election. Blaming China and labeling the country as a currency manipulator was a popular selling point for Americans who lost their manufacturing jobs. Critics countered the proposal to name and shame China was political bluster unlikely to change Chinese policy.

Yet, some scholars suggest such an action might create the opposite of the desired effect. Nicholas Lardy, Senior Fellow at the Peterson Institute for International Economics, warned China could retaliate against unilateral tariffs or trigger a trade war.[34] Lardy argued the negative global implications would actually hinder the American economy considering China is the third largest buyer of exports from the U.S., behind only Canada and Mexico. Lardy suggested American officials should "declare victory on Chinese currency," which he said appreciated 30% in a recent 6 year period (roughly 2007–2012).[35] Derek Scissors, Senior Research Fellow at the Heritage Foundation, urges the "*RMB's* value is far from the most important issue in the U.S.-China economic relations."[36] There are issues of greater importance, like IP protection, competition with SOEs and private Chinese companies, and investment restrictions.[37]

In considering these pro-China arguments, one question ought not to go unasked. Currency revaluation by China would hurt exporters from that country, but who are those exporters? Many of them are U.S. MNCs that use China as a manufacturing base and export platform. Many, too, are Japanese and Taiwanese companies using China for the same purpose. Simply put, are these arguments veiled plutocratic corporate apologies?

---

34. *See Romney's* (discussing remarks by Secretary of the Treasury Secretary Timothy Geithner).
35. *Romney's Focus* (discussing remarks by Treasury Secretary Timothy Geithner).
36. *Romney's Focus* (discussing remarks by Treasury Timothy Geithner).
37. *See Romney's Focus* (discussing remarks by Treasury Secretary Timothy Geithner).

Some scholars champion alternative approaches to addressing currency misalignment. Dr. C. Fred Bergsten of the Peterson Institute for International Economics contends the U.S. employ a new strategy of "countervailing currency intervention" (CCI) in which America would offset Chinese purchases of American dollars by purchasing Chinese *RMB* should the Chinese refuse to revalue their currency.[38] He points to the fact America has bought foreign currencies on past occasions, as recently as the *euro* in 2000 and Japanese *yen* in 1998, to stabilize currencies.[39] Although those interventions were at the request of other countries, which believed their currencies had become too weak, purchasing the *RMB* would involve the same market techniques. The objective would be to push a specific FX rate towards equilibrium levels to rectify the misalignment that was distorting global trade. The obvious flaw with CCI is that if it is not coordinated with the central banks of other countries, then it risks becoming a series of competitive devaluations akin to the Beggar-Thy-Neighbor Policies that exacerbated the Great Depression of the 1920s and early 1930s.

Dr. Bergsten further suggests Congress should adopt legislation to permit the U.S. to treat currencies that are substantially and deliberately undervalued as constituting export subsidies for purposes of calculating and applying CVDs.[40] That is, some scholars advocate imposing CVDs directly against China, in lieu of filing a WTO complaint. The idea assumes Chinese policies are characterized properly as export subsidies justifying CVDs. Arguably, applying CVDs unilaterally is preferred to a WTO case. Unilateral action (which would surely trigger a Chinese complaint) could continue for roughly three years before incurring any adverse decision from the WTO Appellate Body against those CVDs. (Cynically, the U.S. could take advantage of the "Three Year Pass Rule" in WTO dispute settlement.) During that period, the CVDs might pressure China to relax its currency practices on at least a transitory basis.

This strategy has its own challenges. There are the (previously discussed) legal hurdles of proving the existence of a "financial contribution" and "benefit," and possibly needing to satisfy the Specificity Test. Further, proof of material injury or threat thereof, by reason of export subsidization in the form of currency undervaluation, is necessary. Demonstrating material injury likely is a costly proceeding, as authorities need to analyze the injury question for every "industry" in which CVDs are contemplated. It is unclear how many industries might bear the expenses and uncertainties of pursuing a CVD remedy, much less how many could succeed.[41] Technically, the answer would come only through industry polling when the 25% and 50% tests for standing are checked.

---

38. *See* Dr. C. Fred Bergsten, *The Need for A Robust Response to Chinese Currency Manipulation— Policy Options for the Obama Administration Including Countervailing Currency Intervention*, 10 The Journal of International Business and Law 269, 270 (2011). [Hereinafter, *The Need.*]

39. *See The Need*, 278.

40. *See The Need*, 278.

41. *"Currency Manipulation,"* 614.

In the grand scheme, a unilateral CVD might do little to benefit an import-competing industry. The remedial duties would apply only to imports from a subsidizing nation, such as China. Thus, those duties on Chinese products would not help the American import-competing industry if it faces a highly elastic supply of imports from other countries. That is, third countries could commence or increase low-priced, and presumably unsubsidized, shipments of merchandise into the U.S., seeing that Chinese producer-exporters are competitively disadvantaged in the American market because of the CVDs. The domestic producers would then have "beaten" their Chinese competitors with the CVDs, only to have induced new competition from third countries.

- **American Political Pressure**

Amidst the scholarly debate, frustration over FX manipulation grew in the U.S. and across the world. Senator Orrin Hatch (Republican-Utah) demanded Treasury Secretary Geithner outline the position of the Obama Administration on Chinese currency manipulation before a round of *TPP* negotiations began in December 2012:

> Given the large and growing trade deficit with China, it is simply unacceptable for the Administration of President Barack H. Obama to continually shirk responsibility to articulate, in a timely manner, a clear and coherent policy regarding currency misalignment and manipulation.[42]

Senator Hatch previously offered an amendment to the *Currency Exchange Rate Oversight Reform Act* (S.1619). This amendment set a new negotiating objective for ongoing and future trade negotiations: any deal must have a prohibition on the Parties fundamentally misaligning their currencies, and commit them to collaborate to mitigate the adverse trade and economic effects of currency misalignment by non-Parties.[43]

When *TPP* negotiations concluded in October 2015, the 12 Parties agreed on a skeletal framework to address alleged FX misalignment. Finance Ministers from the Parties could convene, study the matter in dispute, and make recommendations, but they had no enforceable mechanism to use. That framework was the first in any U.S. FTA to address directly currency manipulation. Nevertheless, in January 2017, the U.S. withdrew from *TPP*. The framework remains in the *CPTPP*.

- **2015 *TFTEA***

Until the 2015 *TFTEA*, American trade legislation never included a remedy against currency manipulation. The *TFTEA* stopped short of authorizing DOC to levy punitive tariffs or CVDs on originating in countries engaged in currency manipulation. But, the statute (specifically, Section 701, 19 U.S.C. § 4421) included

---

42. Press Release, *Hatch Calls on Obama Administration to Outline Position on China Currency Manipulation*, UNITED STATES SENATE COMMITTEE ON FINANCE (18 October 2012), www.finance.senate.gov/newsroom/ranking/release/?id=2fc3a886-e940-475c-91ee-48861fa338b0. [Hereinafter, Press Release.]

43. Press Release.

four directions to the Executive branch. First, the Department of the Treasury must study the FX policies of any major American trading partner that meets the following three criteria, and ask whether that country:

(1) a bilateral trade surplus over $20 billion,

(2) a current account surplus of over 3% of its GDP, and

(3) persistently engages in one-sided intervention in FX markets, specifically, devaluing its currency by purchasing foreign assets equal or exceeding 2% of its GDP?

Notably, though the Chinese currency (from January–October 2018) depreciated by 5.6% against the U.S. dollar, the Treasury Department (in 2018) again declined to dub China a "currency manipulator," finding China flunked the first high-trade surplus criterion, but not the second or third criteria.[44]

Second, within 180 days of its enactment, and every 180 days thereafter, the Treasury Department must submit to Congress a report on all trading partners engaged in currency manipulation. The Department also keeps a "watch list" of countries at risk of gaming their currencies against the dollar. Whether the Department considers a country whose currency is misaligned through (1) outright manipulation versus (2) unintentional action to be a distinction without a difference is unclear.

Third, the President must "enhance engagement" with foreign countries the Treasury Department determines practice "persistent one-sided intervention in the foreign exchange market." If the country does not alter its FX behavior, then disciplinary action may follow. That is the fourth direction. The President must bar firms from those countries from government procurement contracts, whether for goods or services. Moreover, OPIC (*i.e.*, the IDFC) is forbidden from financing new projects in which those firms were involved.

III. Multilateral Bargaining

A common theme amongst legal scholars discussing currency manipulation is a belief in the multilateral approach, that is, multiple countries coming together and negotiating at a large forum, such as the G-20. They believe the U.S., or any other country looking to address the FX rate policies of China, should not act on its own. Bilateral discussion with China or unilateral action is risky and ineffective if their goal is to compel China to allow its currency to appreciate. Unilateral action surely would draw the ire of China, causing China to refuse to allow further loosening of its monetary policy. Even worse, such action might catalyze a trade war, with deleterious consequences for the global economy.

---

44. *See* David Lawder, *U.S.-China Trade Talks Must Cover Currency, U.S. Treasury Chief Says*, REUTERS, 12 October 2018, www.reuters.com/article/us-imf-worldbank-mnuchin/u-s-china-trade-talks-must-cover-currency-u-s-treasury-chief-says-idUSKCN1MM0VQ.

Less enthusiastic internationalists look askance at the multilateral approach. They see the IMF and WTO as incapable of addressing currency manipulation. Because of the structure of each IO and their somewhat overlapping mandates, the intricacies of currency manipulation test the limitations of both bodies. While some IMF *Articles* directly address currency exchange matters, the IMF itself lacks the enforcement power found within the WTO dispute settlement process. Yet, as for that process, Professor Charles Archie is dubious:

> because the majority of WTO actions are based on individual articles of the WTO agreements, which closely regulate specific trade actions in specific markets. Currency manipulation has not been defined by the WTO nor has a judicial body interpreted it to be a sanctionable act.[45]

Additionally, some scholars point to the length of the proceedings as conflicting with the ability to provide adequate remedies for a time-sensitive issue.[46] The consultation periods required under either IMF rules of the *DSU* hinder a swift, just remedy and justice for an aggrieved country.

Multilateral bargaining approach is appealing in that it entails a forum for nations to participate in negotiations and discussions within diplomatic channels. Negotiations in this type of forum allow for greater flexibility in interactions amongst officials and offer access for all interested parties. Multilateral bargaining also is less antagonistic than unilateral action and offers parties more in developing consensus on global agenda items and helping to persuade other parties to conform to global policies.[47]

Speaking at a two-day seminar at the WTO in March 2012, Li Ruogu, President of the Export-Import Bank of China, gave further credence to the multilateral approach. Mr. Li asserted the issue of exchange rates was better suited for discussion amongst the G-20, or a similar forum, as the WTO mandate is to liberalize trade barriers and promote free trade among countries, not discuss currency exchanges.[48] That assertion neglects the provisions of GATT, like Article XV, in which exchange rates are mentioned. Moreover, it falsely presumes topics are separable, when manifestly they are integrally linked.

Proponents of multilateral bargaining often point to past success in relations with China. For example, in 2004, the U.S. and four other WTO Members, confronted China over its VAT designed to benefit domestic semiconductors.[49] Instead

---

45. Charles V. Archie, *China Cannot Have Its Cake and Eat it Too: Coercing the PRC to Reform Its Currency Exchange Policy to Conform to Its WTO Obligations*, N.C. Journal of International Law & Commerce Regulation Vol. XXXVII 248, 294 (2011). [Hereinafter, *China Cannot.*]

46. *China Cannot*, 288.

47. *See China Cannot*, 297.

48. Daniel Pruzin, *Chinese Official Calls for Cease-Fire in Spat Over Global Currency on Seminar's Sidelines*, Bloomberg Bna International Trade Daily (28 March 2012), www.bna.com/news/.

49. *See China Cannot*, 299.

of pursuing the issue through the WTO, America worked with China through the Joint Commission on Commerce and Trade to settle the dispute.[50]

Another success cited is the 2010 G-20 meeting in Paris. Delegates coaxed China into discussing currency exchange rates, and China eventually agreed to support the inclusion of FX and monetary policies in the list of factors for monitoring global economic distress and the causes of imbalances.[51] Thus, goes the argument, influence from other G-20 nations is more likely to be effective in persuading China to alter its monetary policies than bilateral talks or unilateral sanctions. The onus will be on the CCP to risk ostracism from the global community if it does not act.[52]

Professor Archie reasons the U.S. should follow the multilateral approach as

> any other method risks disenchanting other nations through unilateral actions; provides impetus for further Chinese non-compliance; aggravates an already frayed relationship with China; escalates a trade dispute into a currency war; or causes general discord amongst global leaders.[53]

The more each nation can do to perpetuate an atmosphere of cooperation, the greater each nation can realize the benefits of a more cohesive global economy.

IV. GATT Article II:6(a) Argument by Brazil

Many overseas countries criticize the political posturing of the U.S. against China as hypocritical. American economic policies are said to distort FX rates, too. Critics point to the increase in printed money, as well as Federal Reserve quantitative easing (QE), as *de facto* intervention by the U.S. in exchange rate markets.[54] Such intervention in the currency markets weakens the dollar, thus boosting U.S. exports, and thereby weakens the American case against China. It gives China a convenient excuse not to cooperate fully in any global or bilateral currency exchange discussions, let alone any binding commitments to reform.[55]

Brazil, in particular, has criticized the QE policies pursued by the Federal Reserve as a deliberate devaluation of the dollar for economic and trade gains. Brazil took aim at "massive monetary expansion" by the Federal Reserve, as well as at the unprecedented bailout of banks during the financial crisis, alleging both led to an

---

50. *See China Cannot*, 299.

51. *See China Cannot*, 302 (*citing generally* Liz Alderman, *As G20 Leaders Set Deal, Geithner Criticizes China*, New York Times, at A10 (20 February 2011)).

52. *See China Cannot*, 298.

53. *China Cannot*, 304.

54. *See* Charles Riley, *China's Currency Becomes Election Issue*, CNN Money (21 October 2012), http://money.cnn.com/2012/10/21/news/economy/china-currency-manipulation/index.html.

55. *See China Cannot*, 285.

artificial appreciation of the Brazilian *real*, and a flood of imported goods at artificially low prices.[56]

Thus, facing volatile fluctuations of the Brazilian *real* and drops in the Brazilian balance of trade in industrial goods, the Brazilian President, Dilma Rousseff (1947–), denounced the actions as a global "currency war" based on "expansionary monetary policy" which distorted the competition.[57] As purported evidence of the distortion, the largest Brazilian textile producer pointed to the Brazilian balance of trade in industrial goods fluctuating from a $5.1 billion surplus in 2006 to a $92.5 billion deficit in 2011. The CEO of the company declared "most of these imports come from countries with depreciated currencies."[58] Brazil was particularly critical of U.S. monetary policy as it vocalized the need to address currency misalignment.

To address the situation, Brazil led the charge to initiate discussions on possible trade remedy measures at the WTO that could be used by Members to assess the negative impact on trade from exchange rate misalignment. The Brazilian Ambassador to the WTO, Roberto Carvalho de Azevêdo (1957–), declared "(e)xisting provisions and mechanisms are inadequate given the degree and type of volatility that afflicts currencies in the 21st century,"[59] a direct shot at the ineffectiveness of the IMF. Further, Brazil stated, "the WTO is systematically ill-equipped to cope with the challenges posed by the macro- and micro-economic trade effects caused by exchange rate asymmetries." Ambassador Azevêdo noted that "pretending that we don't have a serious and pressing issue before us is not an option." He suggested Members not look at whether currency misalignment was the result of manipulation or market fundamentals, but instead look at it "from an objective perspective" as to whether there has been a misalignment. If so, then "a country is automatically entitled to make an adjustment."[60]

Indeed, Brazil has been a leader in urging talks on possible solutions to currency misalignment. In 2011, Brazil submitted two petitions to the WTO Working Group on Trade, Debt, and Finance seeking to investigation the connection between international trade and exchange rates.[61] The first proposal for a work program note fiscal

---

56. Daniel Pruzin, *Brazil Calls for WTO Talks on Remedies to Address Currency 'Misalignments'*, BLOOMBERG BNA INTERNATIONAL TRADE DAILY (6 November 2012), www.bna.com/news/. [Hereinafter, *Brazil Calls*.]

57. Daniel Pruzin, *Chinese Official Calls for Cease-Fire in Spat Over Global Currency on Seminar's Sidelines*, BLOOMBERG BNA INTERNATIONAL TRADE DAILY (28 MARCH 2012), www.bna.com/news/. [Hereinafter, *Chinese Official*.]

58. *Chinese Official.*

59. *Brazil Calls.*

60. *Brazil Calls.*

61. WTO Working Group on Trade, Debt, and Finance, *"The Relationship between Exchange Rates and International Trade: Submission by Brazil"* (13 April 2011) WT/WGTDF/W/53; WTO Working Group on Trade, Debt, and Finance, *"The Relationship between Exchange Rates and International Trade: Submission by Brazil"* (20 September 2011) WT/WGTDF/W/56. [Hereinafter, Brazil Submissions.]

and monetary policies during the global financial crisis "caused relative exchange rates among major trading partners to fluctuate frequently, with potentially differ-ent long-term impacts on their respective trade balances."[62]

The second Brazilian submission asked for an examination of the:

> available tools and remedies in the existing multilateral system, if any, to compensate for or otherwise redress those currency fluctuations that may impair commitments undertaken by Members in successive rounds of negotiation. In addition, addressing that issue may help prevent the over-stretching of multilateral While many countries have resigned themselves to inaction due to unclear GATT and IMF provisions that seemingly directly address the issue of currency manipulation, Brazil in particular has pro-posed several different GATT based arguments for possible action to coun-teract the actions of other countries' monetary policies.[63]

Although the submissions by Brazil have yet to bear any fruit in terms of *bona fide* action, it has not stopped the country or other legal scholars from postulating more creative GATT arguments beyond the often cited GATT Article XV:4.

Brazil offered a creative legal argument: apply GATT Article II:6(a), referencing the Schedules of Concessions of WTO Members, as a method to allow Members to adjust their tariffs in response to exchange rate policies.[64] Article II:6(a) provides that specific duties, charges, and margins of preference may be adjusted to take into account a sharp change in the par value of a currency. To make such adjustments, *"contracting parties [i.e., WTO Members] must concur"* that:[65]

> such adjustments will not impair the value of the concessions provided for in the appropriate schedules.[66]

Presumably under this scenario, a Member would adjust its tariffs to correspond with the depreciated currency to bring value closer to its actual value.

What obstacle would a complainant face in arguing a claim under GATT Article II:6(a)? One hurdle would be gathering consensus amongst WTO Members on the adjustments. The respondent purportedly undervaluing its currency likely would argue against the adjustments as undermining the value of concessions in Tariff Schedules. Whether the concept of reverse consensus would apply in this situation, as in WTO DSB decision making, is worthy of consideration. Using the reverse con-sensus rule would vastly facilitate reaching consensus for the adjustments. But, the

---

62. Brazil Submissions.

63. An Hertogen, *The Forgotten GATT Articles on Exchange Rates*, page 20 (citing WTO Work-ing Group on Trade, Debt, and Finance, *The Relationship between Exchange Rates and International Trade: Submission by Brazil,'* (20 September 2011) WT/WGTDF/W/56.20 September 2011 (n 130) [9]). [Hereinafter, *The Forgotten GATT Articles.*]

64. *Chinese Official.*

65. Emphasis added.

66. GATT Article II:6(a).

next question that would need to be addressed would concern the length of time the adjustments are to be applied, as well as addressing the scope and breadth of the adjustment.

Notably, however, in June 2013, following his designation as WTO Director General, Ambassador Azevêdo had a change of heart. He said the IO, the helm of which he was about to take, should not deal with FX distortions.[67] The WTO lacked both the "competence" and "jurisdiction" to deal with the topic, and argued: "The WTO is strictly foreign trade. The exchange question is much wider."[68] Manifestly, that distinction was false: there is no clear boundary between trade and foreign exchange. The incoming Director General also reversed himself on his September 2011 characterization that an "exchange war" was underway, fueled by Federal Reserve quantitative easing. In June 2013, he said: "exchange rates fluctuate within certain limits set by each government. If this is an exchange war, I don't know."[69]

China and the U.S. backed the Director General. These WTO Members did not consider the WTO the right forum for discussing currency misalignments, no matter how profoundly they affected trade. Their reasoning, however, was rather different: China said the topic would "pose serious challenges to basic WTO rules," while the U.S. preferred to discuss the matter in the IMF.[70] The Chinese rationale could have been rebutted with the simple point: "of course, that is precisely the point," while the American rationale could have been met by accommodating the Fund into talks with the WTO. Nevertheless, in October 2013, in the run up to the December 2013 Bali Ministerial Conference, the WTO decided not to discuss FX rates.

If there was an excuse for these bald faced reversals by Mr. Azevêdo, then it was concern about the future of the WTO. Ambassador Azevêdo admitted his biggest challenge as Director General was to re-establish the "relevancy" of the WTO, because, as he said, "the WTO was worn down and today few people follow closely what it does."[71] True enough, but surely he might enhance its relevancy by taking on the hard issue of currency manipulation?

V. Hertogen GATT Article XII:3(a) Argument

After studying the two submissions made by Brazil to the WTO Working Group on Trade, Debt, and Finance, Professor An Hertogen of the University of Auckland, New Zealand, put forth another creative argument. She considered a possible claim under GATT Article XII:3(a), a provision scholars, and even Brazil, ignored. Article

---

67. *See* Ed Taylor, *WTO's Azevêdo Says Organization Should Stay Out of Exchange Rate Debate*, 30 International Trade Reporter (BNA) 966 (27 June 2013). [Hereinafter, *WTO's Azevedo.*]

68. *Quoted in WTO's Azevedo.*

69. *WTO's Azevedo.*

70. Daniel Pruzin, *WTO Members Agree to Shelve Talks on Trade, Exchange Rates*, 30 International Trade Reporter (BNA) 1581 (17 October 2013). [Hereinafter, *WTO Members.*]

71. *WTO's Azevedo.*

XII:3(a) references allowing trade restrictions to safeguard the BOP. But, Professor Hertogen contends the scope of the Article may be read as "exceeding the case of restrictions to safeguard the balance of payments."[72]

Explicitly, Article XII:3(a) provides:

> Contracting Parties undertake, in carrying out their domestic policies, to pay due regard to the need for maintaining or restoring equilibrium in their balance of payments on a sound and lasting basis and to the desirability of avoiding an uneconomic employment of productive resources. They recognize that to achieve these ends, it is desirable so far as possible to adopt measures, which expand rather than contract international trade.[73]

Professor Hertogen asserts a plain reading of the provision emphasizing "domestic policies" as a broad term suggests the Article is meant to apply "more broadly to all domestic policies that can affect equilibrium on the balance of payments, including those regarding the exchange rate valuation."[74] As further evidence, the reference to the "desirability of avoiding an uneconomic employment of productive resources" intimates an endeavor to avoid specific consequences of domestic policies, not solely limited to a balance of payments.[75]

Following this logic, a complainant would argue Chinese exchange rate policies violate Article XII:3(a) by creating a trade imbalance among trading partners. That is, China maintained an undervalued currency in order to stimulate exports, resulting in increasing prices of imports and lower demand for imported products of Members. However the growing demand for Chinese exports should have caused exchange rate appreciation as demand for the currency increase. The complainant would point to the reality that Chinese currency has not appreciated at nearly a pace commensurate with the explosive growth of its exports. Therefore, the monetary policies of China run afoul the requirement of Article XII:3(a) to "pay due regard" to maintaining equilibrium. Additionally, policies that avoid currency appreciation could be considered "an uneconomic employment of productive resources."

Pursuing action under Article XII:3(a) means crossing an empirical barrier. Similar to Article XV:4 (discussed earlier), a complainant pursuing action under Article XII:3(a) would face the difficulty of being able to portray accurately the relationship between the exchange rate policies and trade. Taking into account how often countries, like the U.S., use China as a manufacturing base in which goods of various development stages are traded internationally prior to reaching their end user, it would be difficult to pinpoint the impact of exchange rate misalignment on trade.

Pursuing an Article XII:3(a) claim for currency manipulation also means crossing a legal barrier. That barrier is the uncertainty as to whether "to pay due regard"

---

72. *The Forgotten GATT Articles*, at 10.
73. GATT Article XII:3(a).
74. *The Forgotten GATT Articles*, at 10.
75. *The Forgotten GATT Articles*, at 11.

implies a binding obligation. Professor Hertogen sees no reason why the undertaking should not be viewed as binding, even though other scholars view the provision as "more exhortative than mandatory."[76] She acknowledges the requirement as "only an obligation of conduct rather than an obligation of result."[77] Specifically, the Article does not explicitly require a WTO Member to adopt domestic policies ensuring BOP equilibrium.

Instead, as long as a Member can demonstrate that due regard as to the potential effects was given when enacting the policies, it could be argued they meet the obligation to "pay due regard." So, to transform Article XII:3(a) into an effective provision, Professor Hertogen suggests WTO Members be willing to hold each other accountable when their domestic monetary or foreign exchange rate policies threaten BOP equilibrium, or lead to inefficient allocation or unemployment of productive resources.[78]

VI. Drop Case and Hope for Unilateral Chinese Action

A common theme in many scholarly articles is pursuit of currency misalignment claims against China is highly risky. Aggressive unilateral action by the U.S. against China might spark a trade war or cause further instability to the financial markets. Another common theme is the prospect for speedy, resolute change in Chinese FX rate policy via foreign legal pressure is grim. Still, on various grounds, several scholars argue the U.S. should pursue the matter. For instance, bringing a claim would draw attention to the matter of currency misalignment. Additionally, an Appellate Body ruling is necessary to shed light on the vagueness of terms persistent throughout the IMF *Articles* and WTO agreements. Further, such a claim would highlight the need to reform the WTO itself to handle cases in which pertinent treaty language is all but impotent.[79]

Some scholars argue a rise of 20% is necessary to reflect the real value of the *yuan* against the U.S. dollar.[80] If China were to allow that to occur, then it would drastically decrease the value of the foreign reserves of any country maintaining dollars.

---

76. *The Forgotten GATT Articles*, at 12 (*citing* Raj Bhala, *Modern GATT Law: A Treatise on the General Agreement on Tariffs and Trade* 1011 (London: England, Sweet & Maxwell, 1st ed., 2005)).

77. *The Forgotten GATT Articles*, at 12 (noting in the *India Quantitative Restrictions* case, India argued before the WTO Panel that the obligation to "pay due regard" in Article XVIII:11, a parallel provision on the BOP exception for developing countries, is not mandatory or enforceable). *See* Panel Report, *India — Quantitative Restrictions on Imports of Agricultural, Textile and Industrial Products*, WT/DS90/R, ¶ 3.229 (adopted as modified by the Appellate Body, 6 April 1999). However, the Panel and the Appellate Body did not analyze this argument.).

78. *The Forgotten GATT Articles*, at 12.

79. *See The Need*, 277.

80. *The Need*, 280.

China holds an extensive foreign reserve surplus of dollars. With the aim of keeping its currency more or less fixed to the dollar, China purchased large quantities of U.S. Treasury securities as the country ran large trade surpluses. As a result, the majority of its FX reserves are denominated in dollars. Any fall in value of the dollar would result in a large capital loss for China.[81]

So, if China it were to allow the *RMB* to appreciate rapidly against the dollar, then the Chinese would lose billions, as the value of their dollar reserves would weaken. However, perhaps allowing that to occur might be in the best long-term interests of China. It would decrease Chinese dependence on American currency reserves, provide greater flexibility in transitioning its economy from an export-driven economy to a domestic consumer based economy, and perhaps ultimately allow the country to achieve its status as a global reserve currency.

Arguably, the Mainland Chinese government has been laying out the groundwork for the expansion of the use of the *reminbi* throughout Asia and beyond.[82] China began trade-settlement programs for cross-border trade to be settled in *RMB* instead of dollars in multiple cities. China announced in early 2012, in an agreement between the British government and Hong Kong Monetary Authority (HKMA), a planned offshore *yuan* hub in London.[83] Chinese state planners will be able to make the *RMB* into a world reserve currency only if they loosen capital controls and float their currency, *i.e.*, allow the RMB to appreciate against the dollar.[84]

Professor Terry Chang urges that appreciation of the *RMB* is crucial for China to transform from an export-driven to a consumption-driven economy.[85] He says the view of critics concerning global financial instability and decreases in Chinese exports are true, but only in the short term. Revaluing the *yuan* is in step with the long-range goals of Beijing to transition gradually into a domestic consumption and financial investment-driven economy. Further, an appreciated *yuan* may help Chinese consumers, as they can benefit from the increased purchasing power of the *yuan* they hold.

Chinese Capital Account liberalization also would unlock Chinese domestic savings for investment offshore, and allow Chinese banks to become more competitive internationally. Those banks could service both foreign and domestic customers in

---

81. Terry E. Chang, *Slow Avalanche: Internationalizing the Renminbi and Liberalizing China's Capital Account*, 25 Columbia Journal of Asian Law, number 1, 63, 79 fn. 97 (2012) (*citing* Paul Krugman, *China's Dollar Trap*, N.Y. Times (2 April 2009), at A29, www.nytimes.com/2009/04/03/opinion/03krugman.html). [Hereinafter, *Slow Avalanche*.]

82. *See Slow Avalanche*, 77.

83. *See* Slow Avalanche, 77 (*citing* William Kemble-Diaz, *UK Government Jumps on the Bandwagon as Yuan Market Blooms*, Wall St. J. (20 January 2012), www.wsj.com/articles/luxembourg-covets-offshore-trade-in-chinas-yuan-1406489042.

84. *See Slow Avalanche*, 66 (*citing* Joe Leahy, *Redback Vies for Share of Latam Trade*, Beyond Brics (7 June 2011), http://blogs.ft.com/beyond-brics/2011/06/07/redback-vies-for-share-of-latam-trade/).

85. *See Slow Avalanche*, 88.

Chinese currency.[86] And, *RMB* internationalization be an assertion of political and economic power within Asian and around the world. A study by Arvind Subramanian and Martin Kessler of the Peterson Institute for International Economics suggests the influence of the dollar is waning in the emerging world, particularly East Asia, as more countries follow a *yuan* standard.[87] *RMB* internationalization would lessen even more Chinese dependence on the fate of the dollar.[88]

VII. Not Just Sino-American Issue

Some scholars suggest the question of currency manipulation "made a lot of sense in 2000 or 2004 or 2008 but it doesn't make much sense in 2012."[89] They add that China is not the worst currency manipulator in the world. Arguably, Singapore, Switzerland, Taiwan, and Japan rank higher.[90]

Moreover, in the 2012 IMF Article IV consultation with China, the IMF observed the real effective FX rate of the *yuan* appreciated by "some 30 percent since the 2005 exchange rate reform, and by 8 percent over the past year (ending in April 2012)."[91] While the IMF noted the *RMB* was undervalued moderately, it was keen to stress the improvements the country had been making in allowing its currency to appreciate. The IMF recommended China allow the Real Effective Exchange Rate to continue to appreciate by reducing interventionist actions and making it two-sided over the medium term.[92]

In response to IMF assessments at the conclusion of the 2012 consultation for China, Mr. Tao Zhang, IMF Executive Director for China, contested the findings.

---

86. *See Slow Avalanche*, 97.

87. *The Rise of the Yuan: Turning from Green to Red*, THE ECONOMIST (20 October 2012), www.economist.com/news/finance-and-economics/21564880-yuan-displacing-dollar-key-currency.

88. *See Slow Avalanche*, 97.

89. Ezra Klein, *Five Facts You Need to Know About China's Currency Manipulation*, WASHINGTON POST BLOG (22 October 2012), www.washingtonpost.com/blogs/wonkblog/wp/2012/10/22/five-facts-you-need-to-know-about-chinas-currency-manipulation/. [Hereinafter, *Five Facts*.]

90. *See Five Facts* (referencing list from Joe Gagnon, an economist at the Peterson Institution for International Economics).

91. *See* IMF Country Report No. 12/195, *People's Republic of China 2012 Article IV Consultation*, INTERNATIONAL MONETARY FUND (July 2012) at 21, www.imf.org/external/pubs/ft/scr/2012/cr12195.pdf.

92. The REER is:
   is the weighted average of a country's currency in relation to an index or basket of other major currencies, adjusted for the effects of inflation. The weights are determined by comparing the relative trade balance of a country's currency against each country within the index. This exchange rate is used to determine an individual country's currency value relative to the other major currencies in the index, such as the U.S. dollar, Japanese *yen* and the *euro*.
INVESTOPEDIA, *Real Effective Exchange Rate (REER)*, www.investopedia.com/terms/r/reer.asp#ixzz5NKoTq9Eb.

He argued the assessment by IMF staff that the *RMB* was moderately undervalued against a broad basket of currencies was not consistent with reality.[93] Specifically, Mr. Zhang argued "the sharp decline in the current account surplus and the recent two-way movements in the *renminbi* suggested that the currency is roughly in equilibrium."[94] Other indicators such as forward rates in the onshore and offshore FX markets, pointed to a close to equilibrium exchange rate. Mr. Zhang touted the fact Chinese authorities widened the trading band of the *renminbi* against the dollar in April 2012. This move further increased the two-way flexibility of the *renminbi* exchange rate, facilitating the move of the exchange rate toward its equilibrium. Further, Mr. Zhang voiced a commitment to allow market forces to play a larger role in determining movements in the *renminbi*, and to continue reform in the Chinese exchange rate regime in this direction. That apparently occurred. In 2015, the IMF declared the *yuan* no longer was "undervalued" (arguably implying it once was), and across 2006–2016, the BIS reported China's REER appreciated 36%.

Still, the often defensive, argumentative, or hostile reaction of many CCP officials raises broad questions:[95] Does China base its foreign economic policy (of which currency policy is a species) too much on pride, and not enough on collaboration? Is it the case that when the rest of the world asks of China, the ruling oligarchy too easily rejects the request? Is China neurotically focused on avoiding the impression it *kowtows* to America, permitting the U.S. to set its exchange rate policy?

These uncomfortable queries are not just for Sino-American relations. China might not have embraced calls by Brazil for action at the WTO level. But, China has few if any natural allies, some obvious enemies, and many skeptics. If more countries experience adverse effects of Chinese FX policies on their domestic currency, the size of the latter camps could grow, which would not be in the long-term interests of China.

---

93. *See Statement by Mr. Tao Zhang, IMF Executive Director, at the Conclusion of the 2012 Article IV Consultation with People's Republic of China*, INTERNATIONAL MONETARY FUND (July 2012) at 4, www.imf.org/external/pubs/ft/scr/2012/cr12195.pdf. [Hereinafter, *Statement.*]

94. *See Statement.*

95. *See Five Facts.*

Index

References are to Chapter and Sections.